Object-Oriented
Software
Construction
SECOND EDITION

Bertrand Meyer

ISE Inc.
Santa Barbara (California)

Prentice Hall PTR
Upper Saddle River, New Jersey 07458
http://www.prenhall.com

Library of Congress Cataloging-in-Publication Data

Meyer, Bertrand
    Object-oriented software construction / Bertrand Meyer -- 2nd ed.
      p. cm.
    Includes bibliographical references and index.
    ISBN 0-13-629155-4
    1. Object-oriented programming (Computer science) 2. Computer
software--Development. I. Title.
QA76.64.M493   1997
005.1'17--dc21   97-2407
                          CIP

Editorial/production supervision: *Eileen Clark*
Cover design director: *Jerry Votta*
Cover design: *Talar Agasyon*
Manufacturing manager: *Alexis Heydt*
Acquisitions editor: *Russ Hall*
Editorial Assistant: *Maureen Diana*
Marketing Manager: *Miles Williams*

Published by Prentice Hall PTR
Prentice-Hall, Inc.
A Simon & Schuster Company
Upper Saddle River, New Jersey 07458

The publisher offers discounts on this book when ordered in bulk quantities.
For more information, contact:
        Corporate Sales Department
        Prentice Hall PTR
        One Lake Street
        Upper Saddle River, NJ 07458
        Phone: 800-382-3419 Fax: 201-536-7141
        E-mail: corpsales@prenhall.com

Printed in the United States of America
10 9 8 7 6 5 4 3 2

ISBN 0-13-629155-4

Prentice-Hall International (UK) Limited, *London*
Prentice-Hall of Australia Pty. Limited, *Sydney*
Prentice-Hall Canada Inc., *Toronto*
Prentice-Hall Hispanoamericana, S.A., *Mexico*
Prentice-Hall of India Private Limited, *New Delhi*
Prentice-Hall of Japan, Inc., *Tokyo*
Simon & Schuster Asia Pte. Ltd., *Singapore*
Editora Prentice-Hall do Brasil, Ltda., *Rio de Janeiro*

SHORT TABLE OF CONTENTS

(The full table of contents starts on page xvii.)

Author's address:

Bertrand Meyer
Interactive Software Engineering Inc. (ISE)
270 Storke Road, Suite 7
Santa Barbara, CA 93117
USA
805-685-1006, fax 805-685-6869
<meyer@tools.com>, http://www.tools.com

Preface

*B*orn in the ice-blue waters of the festooned Norwegian coast; amplified (by an aberration of world currents, for which marine geographers have yet to find a suitable explanation) along the much grayer range of the Californian Pacific; viewed by some as a typhoon, by some as a tsunami, and by some as a storm in a teacup — a tidal wave is hitting the shores of the computing world.

"Object-oriented" is the latest *in* term, complementing and in many cases replacing "structured" as the high-tech version of "good". As is inevitable in such a case, the term is used by different people with different meanings; just as inevitable is the well-known three-step sequence of reactions that meets the introduction of a new methodological principle: (1) "it's trivial"; (2) "it cannot work"; (3) "that's how I did it all along anyway". (The order may vary.)

Let us have this clear right away, lest the reader think the author takes a half-hearted approach to his topic: I do not see the object-oriented method as a mere fad; I think it is not trivial (although I shall strive to make it as limpid as I can); I know it works; and I believe it is not only different from but even, to a certain extent, incompatible with the techniques that most people still use today — including some of the principles taught in many software engineering textbooks. I further believe that object technology holds the potential for fundamental changes in the software industry, and that it is here to stay. Finally, I hope that as the reader progresses through these pages, he will share some of my excitement about this promising avenue to software analysis, design and implementation.

"Avenue to software analysis, design and implementation". To present the object-oriented method, this books resolutely takes the viewpoint of software engineering — of the methods, tools and techniques for developing quality software in production environments. This is not the only possible perspective, as there has also been interest in applying object-oriented principles to such areas as exploratory programming and artificial intelligence. Although the presentation does not exclude these applications, they are not its main emphasis. Our principal goal in this discussion is to study how practicing software developers, in industrial as well as academic environments, can use object technology to improve (in some cases dramatically) the quality of the software they produce.

Structure, reliability, epistemology and classification

Object technology is at its core the combination of four ideas: a structuring method, a reliability discipline, an epistemological principle and a classification technique.

The *structuring method* applies to software decomposition and reuse. Software systems perform certain actions on objects of certain types; to obtain flexible and reusable systems, it is better to base their structure on the object types than on the actions. The resulting concept is a remarkably powerful and versatile mechanism called the **class**, which in object-oriented software construction serves as the basis for both the modular structure and the type system.

The *reliability discipline* is a radical approach to the problem of building software that does what it is supposed to do. The idea is to treat any system as a collection of components which collaborate the way successful businesses do: by adhering to **contracts** defining explicitly the obligations and benefits incumbent on each party.

The *epistemological principle* addresses the question of how we should describe the classes. In object technology, the objects described by a class are only defined by what we can do with them: operations (also known as *features*) and formal properties of these operations (the contracts). This idea is formally expressed by the theory of **abstract data types**, covered in detail in a chapter of this book. It has far-reaching implications, some going beyond software, and explains why we must not stop at the naïve concept of "object" borrowed from the ordinary meaning of that word. The tradition of information systems modeling usually assumes an "external reality" that predates any program using it; for the object-oriented developer, such a notion is meaningless, as the reality does not exist independently of what you want to do with it. (More precisely whether it exists or not is an irrelevant question, as we only know what we can use, and what we know of something is defined entirely by how we can use it.)

Abstract data types are discussed in chapter 6, which also addresses some of the related epistemological issues.

The *classification technique* follows from the observation that systematic intellectual work in general and scientific reasoning in particular require devising taxonomies for the domains being studied. Software is no exception, and the object-oriented method relies heavily on a classification discipline known as **inheritance**.

Simple but powerful

The four concepts of class, contract, abstract data type and inheritance immediately raise a number of questions. How do we find and describe classes? How should our programs manipulate classes and the corresponding objects (the *instances* of these classes)? What are the possible relations between classes? How can we capitalize on the commonalities that may exist between various classes? How do these ideas relate to such key software engineering concerns as extendibility, ease of use and efficiency?

Answers to these questions rely on a small but powerful array of techniques for producing reusable, extendible and reliable software: polymorphism and dynamic binding; a new view of types and type checking; genericity, constrained and unconstrained; information hiding; assertions; safe exception handling; automatic garbage collection. Efficient implementation techniques have been developed which permit applying these ideas successfully to both small and large projects under the tight constraints of commercial software development. Object-oriented techniques have also had a considerable impact on user interfaces and development environments, making it possible to produce much better interactive systems than was possible before. All these important ideas will be studied in detail, so as to equip the reader with tools that are immediately applicable to a wide range of problems.

Organization of the text

In the pages that follow we will review the methods and techniques of object-oriented software construction. The presentation has been divided into six parts.

Chapters 1 to 2.   Part A is an introduction and overview. It starts by exploring the fundamental issue of software quality and continues with a brief survey of the method's main technical characteristics. This part is almost a little book by itself, providing a first view of the object-oriented approach for hurried readers.

Chapters 3 to 6.   Part B is not hurried. Entitled "The road to object orientation", it takes the time to describe the methodological concerns that lead to the central O-O concepts. Its focus is on modularity: what it takes to devise satisfactory structures for "in-the-large" system construction. It ends with a presentation of abstract data types, the mathematical basis for object technology. The mathematics involved is elementary, and less mathematically inclined readers may content themselves with the basic ideas, but the presentation provides the theoretical background that you will need for a full understanding of O-O principles and issues.

Chapters 7 to 18.   Part C is the technical core of the book. It presents, one by one, the central technical components of the method: classes; objects and the associated run-time model; memory management issues; genericity and typing; design by contract, assertions, exceptions; inheritance, the associated concepts of polymorphism and dynamic binding, and their many exciting applications.

Chapters 19 to 29.   Part D discusses methodology, with special emphasis on analysis and design. Through several in-depth case studies, it presents some fundamental *design patterns*, and covers such central questions as how to find the classes, how to use inheritance properly, and how to design reusable libraries. It starts with a meta-level discussion of the intellectual requirements on methodologists and other advice-givers; it concludes with a review of the software process (the lifecycle model) for O-O development and a discussion of how best to teach the method in both industry and universities.

Chapters 30 to 32.   Part E explores advanced topics: concurrency, distribution, client-server development and the Internet; persistence, schema evolution and object-oriented databases; the design of interactive systems with modern ("GUI") graphical interfaces.

Part F is a review of how the ideas can be implemented, or in some cases emulated, *Chapters 33 to 35.* in various languages and environments. This includes in particular a discussion of major object-oriented languages, focusing on Simula, Smalltalk, Objective-C, C++, Ada 95 and Java, and an assessment of how to obtain some of the benefits of object orientation in such non-O-O languages as Fortran, Cobol, Pascal, C and Ada.

Part G (*doing it right*) describes an environment which goes beyond these solutions *Chapter 36.* and provides an integrated set of tools to support the ideas of the book.

As complementary reference material, an appendix shows some important reusable *Appendix A.* library classes discussed in the text, providing a model for the design of reusable software.

A Book-Wide Web

It can be amusing to see authors taking pains to describe recommended paths through their books, sometimes with the help of sophisticated traversal charts — as if readers ever paid any attention, and were not smart enough to map their own course. An author is permitted, however, to say in what spirit he has scheduled the different chapters, and what path he had in mind for what Umberto Eco calls the Model Reader — not to be confused with the real reader, also known as "you", made of flesh, blood and tastes.

The answer here is the simplest possible one. This book tells a story, and assumes that the Model Reader will follow that story from beginning to end, being however invited to avoid the more specialized sections marked as "skippable on first reading" and, if not mathematically inclined, to ignore a few mathematical developments also labeled explicitly. The real reader, of course, may want to discover in advance some of the plot's later developments, or to confine his attention to just a few subplots; every chapter has for that reason been made as self-contained as possible, so that you should be able to intake the material at the exact dosage which suits you best.

Because the story presents a coherent view of software development, its successive topics are tightly intertwined. The margin notes offer a subtext of cross references, a Book-Wide Web linking the various sections back and forth. My advice to the Model Reader is to ignore them on first reading, except as a reassurance that questions which at some stage are left partially open will be fully closed later on. The real reader, who may not want any advice, might use the cross references as unofficial guides when he feels like cheating on the prearranged order of topics.

Both the Model Reader and the real reader should find the cross references mostly useful in subsequent readings, to make sure that they have mastered a certain object-oriented concept in depth, and understood its connections with the method's other components. Like the hyperlinks of a WWW document, the cross references should make it possible to follow such associations quickly and effectively.

The CD-ROM that accompanies this book and contains all of its text provides a *See "About the* convenient way to follow cross references: just click on them. All the cross references *accompanying CD-* have been preserved. *ROM", page xiv.*

The notation

In software perhaps even more than elsewhere, thought and language are closely connected. As we progress through these pages, we will carefully develop a notation for expressing object-oriented concepts at all levels: modeling, analysis, design, implementation, maintenance.

Here and everywhere else in this book, the pronoun "we" does not mean "the author": as in ordinary language, "we" means you and I — the reader and the author. In other words I would like you to expect that, as we develop the notation, you will be involved in the process.

This assumption is not really true, of course, since the notation existed before you started reading these pages. But it is not completely preposterous either, because I hope that as we explore the object-oriented method and carefully examine its implications the supporting notation will dawn on you with a kind of inevitability, so that you will indeed feel that you helped design it.

This explains why although the notation has been around for more than ten years and is in fact supported by several commercial implementations, including one from my company (ISE), I have downplayed it as a language. (Its name does appear in one place in the text, and several times in the bibliography.) This book is about the object-oriented method for reusing, analyzing, designing, implementing and maintaining software; the language is an important and I hope natural consequence of that method, not an aim in itself.

In addition, the language is straightforward and includes very little else than direct support for the method. First-year students using it have commented that it was "no language at all" — meaning that the notation is in one-to-one correspondence with the method: to learn one is to learn the other, and there is scant extra linguistic decoration on top of the concepts. The notation indeed shows few of the peculiarities (often stemming from historical circumstances, machine constraints or the requirement to be compatible with older formalisms) that characterize most of today's programming languages. Of course you may disagree with the choice of keywords (why *do* rather than *begin* or perhaps *faire*?), or would like to add semicolon terminators after each instruction. (The syntax has been designed so as to make semicolons optional.) But these are side issues. What counts is the simplicity of the notation and how directly it maps to the concepts. If you understand object technology, you almost know it already.

Most software books take the language for granted, whether it is a programming language or a notation for analysis or design. Here the approach is different; involving the reader in the design means that one must not only explain the language but also justify it and discuss the alternatives. Most of the chapters of part C include a "discussion" section explaining the issues encountered during the design of the notation, and how they were resolved. I often wished, when reading descriptions of well-known languages, that the designers had told me not only what solutions they chose, but why they chose them, and what alternatives they rejected. The candid discussions included in this book should, I hope, provide you with insights not only about language design but also about software construction, as the two tasks are so strikingly similar.

Analysis, design and implementation

It is always risky to use a notation that externally looks like a programming language, as this may suggest that it only covers the implementation phase. This impression, however wrong, is hard to correct, so frequently have managers and developers been told that a gap of metaphysical proportions exists between the ether of analysis-design and the underworld of implementation.

Well-understood object technology reduces the gap considerably by emphasizing the essential unity of software development over the inevitable differences between levels of abstraction. This *seamless* approach to software construction is one of the important contributions of the method and is reflected by the language of this book, which is meant for analysis and design as well as for implementation.

"SEAMLESSNESS AND REVERSIBIL-ITY", 28.6, page 930.

Unfortunately some of the recent evolution of the field goes against these principles, through two equally regrettable phenomena:

- Object-oriented implementation languages which are unfit for analysis, for design and in general for high-level reasoning.

- Object-oriented analysis or design methods which do not cover implementation (and are advertized as "language-independent" as if this were a badge of honor rather than an admission of failure).

Such approaches threaten to cancel much of the potential benefit of the approach. In contrast, both the method and the notation developed in this book are meant to be applicable throughout the software construction process. A number of chapters cover high-level design issues; one is devoted to analysis; others explore implementation techniques and the method's implications on performance.

The environment

Software construction relies on a basic tetralogy: method, language, tools, libraries. The method is at the center of this book; the language question has just been mentioned. Once in a while we will need to see what support they may require from tools and libraries. For obvious reasons of convenience, such discussions will occasionally refer to ISE's object-oriented environment, with its set of tools and associated libraries.

The environment is used only as an example of what can be done to make the concepts practically usable by software developers. Be sure to note that there are many other object-oriented environments available, both for the notation of this book and for other O-O analysis, design and implementation methods and notations; and that the descriptions given refer to the state of the environment at the time of writing, subject, as anything else in our industry, to change quickly — for the better. Other environments, O-O and non O-O, are also cited throughout the text.

The last chapter, 36, summarizes the environment.

Acknowledgments (quasi-absence thereof)

The first edition of this book contained an already long list of thanks. For a while I kept writing down the names of people who contributed comments or suggestions, and then at some stage I lost track. The roster of colleagues from whom I have had help or borrowed ideas has now grown so long that it would run over many pages, and would inevitably omit some important people. Better then offend everyone a little than offend a few very much.

A few notes in the margin or in chapter-end bibliographic sections give credit for some specific ideas, often unpublished.

So these acknowledgments will for the most part remain collective, which does not make my gratitude less deep. My colleagues at ISE and SOL have for years been a daily source of invaluable help. The users of our tools have generously provided us with their advice. The readers of the first edition provided thousands of suggestions for improvement. In the preparation of this new edition (I should really say of this new book) I have sent hundreds of e-mail messages asking for help of many different kinds: the clarification of a fine point, a bibliographical reference, a permission to quote, the details of an attribution, the origin of an idea, the specifics of a notation, the official address of a Web page; the answers have invariably been positive. As draft chapters were becoming ready they were circulated through various means, prompting many constructive comments (and here I must cite by name the referees commissioned by Prentice Hall, Paul Dubois, James McKim and Richard Wiener, who provided invaluable advice and corrections). In the past few years I have given countless seminars, lectures and courses about the topics of this book, and in every case I learned something from the audience. I enjoyed the wit of fellow panelists at conferences and benefited from their wisdom. Short sabbaticals at the University of Technology, Sydney and the Università degli Studi di Milano provided me with a influx of new ideas — and in the first case with three hundred first-year students on whom to validate some of my ideas about how software engineering should be taught.

The large bibliography shows clearly enough how the ideas and realizations of others have contributed to this book. Among the most important conscious influences are the Algol line of languages, with its emphasis on syntactic and semantic elegance; the seminal work on structured programming, in the serious (Dijkstra-Hoare-Parnas-Wirth-Mills-Gries) sense of the term, and systematic program construction; formal specification techniques, in particular the inexhaustible lessons of Jean-Raymond Abrial's original (late nineteen-seventies) version of the Z specification language, his more recent design of B, and Cliff Jones's work on VDM; the languages of the modular generation (in particular Ichbiah's Ada, Liskov's CLU, Shaw's Alphard, Bert's LPG and Wirth's Modula); and Simula 67, which introduced most of the concepts many years ago and had most of them right, bringing to mind Tony Hoare's comment about Algol 60: that it was such an improvement over most of its successors.

Foreword to the second edition

$\mathcal{M}$any events have happened in the object-oriented world since the first edition of *OOSC* (as the book came to be known) was published in 1988. The explosion of interest alluded to in the Preface to the first edition, reproduced in the preceding pages in a slightly expanded form, was nothing then as compared to what we have seen since. Many journals and conferences now cover object technology; Prentice Hall has an entire book series devoted to the subject; breakthroughs have occurred in such areas as user interfaces, concurrency and databases; entire new topics have emerged, such as O-O analysis and formal specification; distributed computing, once a specialized topic, is becoming relevant to more and more developments, thanks in part to the growth of the Internet; and the Web is affecting everyone's daily work.

This is not the only exciting news. It is gratifying to see how much progress is occurring in the software field — thanks in part to the incomplete but undeniable spread of object technology. Too many books and articles on software engineering still start with the obligatory lament about the "software crisis" and the pitiful state of our industry as compared to *true* engineering disciplines (which, as we all know, never mess things up). There is no reason for such doom. Oh, we still have a long, long way to go, as anyone who uses software products knows all too well. But given the challenges that we face we have no reason to be ashamed of ourselves as a profession; and we are getting better all the time. It is the ambition of this book, as it was of its predecessor, to help in this process.

This second edition is not an update but the result of a thorough reworking. Not a paragraph of the original version has been left untouched. (Hardly a single line, actually.) Countless new topics have been added, including a whole chapter on concurrency, distribution, client-server computing and Internet programming; another on persistence and databases; one on user interfaces; one on the software lifecycle; many design patterns and implementation techniques; an in-depth exploration of a methodological issue on which little is available in the literature, how to use inheritance well and avoid misusing it; discussions of many other topics of object-oriented methodology; an extensive presentation of the theory of abstract data types — the mathematical basis for our subject, indispensable to a complete understanding of object technology yet seldom covered in detail by textbooks and tutorials; a presentation of O-O analysis; hundreds of new bibliographic and Web site references; the description of a complete object-oriented development environment (also included on the accompanying CD-ROM for the reader's enjoyment) and of the underlying concepts; and scores of new ideas, principles, caveats, explanations, figures, examples, comparisons, citations, classes, routines.

The reactions to *OOSC*-1 have been so rewarding that I know readers have high expectations. I hope they will find *OOSC*-2 challenging, useful, and up to their standards.

Santa Barbara   B.M.
                                                                                  January 1997

About the accompanying CD-ROM

The CD-ROM that comes with this book contains the **entire hyperlinked text** in Adobe Acrobat format. It also includes Adobe's Acrobat Reader software, enabling you to read that format; the versions provided cover major industry platforms. If you do not already have Acrobat Reader on your computer, you can install it by following the instructions. The author and the publisher make no representations as to any property of Acrobat and associated tools; the Acrobat Reader is simply provided as a service to readers of this book, and any Acrobat questions should be directed to Adobe. You may also check with Adobe about any versions of the Reader that may have appeared after the book.

To get started with the CD-ROM, open the Acrobat file *README.pdf* in the OOSC_2 directory, which will direct you to the table of contents and the index. You can only open that file under Acrobat Reader; if the Reader has not been installed on your computer, examine instead the plain-text version in the file *readme.txt* in the top-level directory. The instructions also appear at the end of this book.

The presence of an electronic version will be particularly useful to readers who want to take advantage of the thousands of cross-references present in this book (see "A Book-Wide Web", page viii). Although for a first sequential reading you will probably prefer to follow the paper version, having the electronic form available on a computer next to the book alllows you to follow a link once in a while without having to turn pages back and forth. The electronic form is particularly convenient for a later reading during which you may wish to explore links more systematically.

All links (cross-references) appear in blue in the Acrobat form, as illustrated twice above (but not visible in the printed version). To follow a link, just click on the blue part. If the reference is to another chapter, the chapter will appear in a new window. The Acrobat Reader command to come back to the previous position is normally Control-minus-sign (that is, type – while holding down the CONTROL key). Consult the on-line Acrobat Reader documentation for other useful navigational commands.

Bibliographical references also appear as links, such as [Knuth 1968], in the Acrobat form, so that you can click on any of them to see the corresponding entry in the bibliography of appendix E.

The CD-ROM also contains:

- Library components providing extensive material for Appendix A.
- A chapter from the manual for a graphical application builder, providing mathematical complements to the material of chapter 32.

In addition, the CD-ROM includes a time-limited version of an advanced **object-oriented development environment** for Windows 95 or Windows NT, as described in chapter 36, providing an excellent hands-on opportunity to try out the ideas developed throughout the book. The "Readme" file directs you to the installation instructions and system requirements.

Acknowledgments: The preparation of the hyperlinked text was made possible by the help of several people at Adobe Inc., in particular Sandra Knox, Sarah Rosenbaum and the FrameMaker Customer Support Group. Special thanks are due — for the printed book as well as the CD — to Russ Hall and Eileen Clark of Prentice Hall.

On the bibliography, Internet sources and exercises

This book relies on earlier contributions by many authors. To facilitate reading, the discussion of sources appears in most cases not in the course of the discussion, but in the "Bibliographical notes" sections at chapter end. Make sure you read these sections, so as to understand the origin of many ideas and results and find out where to learn more.

The bibliography starts on page 1203. References are of the form [*Name* 19xx], where *Name* is the name of the first author, and refer to the bibliography in appendix E. This convention is for readability only and is not intended to underrate the role of authors other than the first. The letter M in lieu of a *Name* denotes publications by the author of this book, listed separately in the second part of the bibliography.

Aside from the bibliography proper, some references appear in the margin, next to the paragraphs which cite them. The reason for this separate treatment is to make the bibliography usable by itself, as a collection of important references on object technology and related topics. Appearance as a margin reference rather than in the bibliography does not imply any unfavorable judgment of value; the division is simply a pragmatic assessment of what belongs in a core list of object-oriented references.

***

Although electronic references will undoubtedly be considered a matter of course a few years from now, this must be one of the first technical books (other than books devoted to Internet-related topics) to make extensive use of references to World-Wide-Web pages, Usenet newsgroups and other Internet resources.

Electronic addresses are notoriously volatile. I have tried to obtain from the authors of the quoted sources some reassurance that the addresses given would remain valid for several years. Neither they nor I, of course, can provide an absolute guarantee. In case of difficulty, note that on the Net more things move than disappear: keyword-based search tools can help.

***

Most chapters include exercises of various degrees of difficulty. I have refrained from providing solutions, although many exercises do contain fairly precise hints. Some readers may regret the absence of full solutions; I hope, however, that they will appreciate the three reasons that led to this decision: the fear of spoiling the reader's enjoyment; the realization that many exercises are design problems, for which there is more than one good answer; and the desire to provide a source of ready-made problems to instructors using this book as a text.

***

For brevity and simplicity, the text follows the imperfect but long-established tradition of using words such as "he" and "his", in reference to unspecified persons, as shortcuts for "he or she" and "his or her", with no intended connotation of gender.

A modest soul is shocked by objects of such kind

And all the nasty thoughts that they bring to one's mind.

Molière, *Tartuffe*, Act III.

Contents

PART H: APPENDICES

Part A:

The issues

Part A will define the goals of our search by taking a close look at the notion of software quality, and, for readers who do not fear a spoiler, provide a capsule preview of the highlights of object technology.

1

Software quality

$\mathcal{E}$ngineering seeks quality; software engineering is the production of quality software. This book introduces a set of techniques which hold the potential for remarkable improvements in the quality of software products.

Before studying these techniques, we must clarify their goals. Software quality is best described as a combination of several factors. This chapter analyzes some of these factors, shows where improvements are most sorely needed, and points to the directions where we shall be looking for solutions in the rest of our journey.

1.1 EXTERNAL AND INTERNAL FACTORS

We all want our software systems to be fast, reliable, easy to use, readable, modular, structured and so on. But these adjectives describe two different sorts of qualities.

On one side, we are considering such qualities as speed or ease of use, whose presence or absence in a software product may be detected by its users. These properties may be called **external** quality factors.

> Under "users" we should include not only the people who actually interact with the final products, like an airline agent using a flight reservation system, but also those who purchase the software or contract out its development, like an airline executive in charge of acquiring or commissioning flight reservation systems. So a property such as the ease with which the software may be adapted to changes of specifications — defined later in this discussion as *extendibility* — falls into the category of external factors even though it may not be of immediate interest to such "end users" as the reservations agent.

Other qualities applicable to a software product, such as being modular, or readable, are **internal** factors, perceptible only to computer professionals who have access to the actual software text.

In the end, only external factors matter. If I use a Web browser or live near a computer-controlled nuclear plant, little do I care whether the source program is readable or modular if graphics take ages to load, or if a wrong input blows up the plant. But the key to achieving these external factors is in the internal ones: for the users to enjoy the visible qualities, the designers and implementers must have applied internal techniques that will ensure the hidden qualities.

The following chapters present of a set of modern techniques for obtaining internal quality. We should not, however, lose track of the global picture; the internal techniques are not an end in themselves, but a means to reach external software qualities. So we must start by looking at external factors. The rest of this chapter examines them.

1.2 A REVIEW OF EXTERNAL FACTORS

Here are the most important external quality factors, whose pursuit is the central task of object-oriented software construction.

Correctness

> **Definition: correctness**
>
> Correctness is the ability of software products to perform their exact tasks, as defined by their specification.

Correctness is the prime quality. If a system does not do what it is supposed to do, everything else about it — whether it is fast, has a nice user interface... — matters little.

But this is easier said than done. Even the first step to correctness is already difficult: we must be able to specify the system requirements in a precise form, by itself quite a challenging task.

Methods for ensuring correctness will usually be **conditional**. A serious software system, even a small one by today's standards, touches on so many areas that it would be impossible to guarantee its correctness by dealing with all components and properties on a single level. Instead, a layered approach is necessary, each layer relying on lower ones:

Application system
Compiler
Operating System
Hardware

Layers in software development

In the conditional approach to correctness, we only worry about guaranteeing that each layer is correct *on the assumption* that the lower levels are correct. This is the only realistic technique, as it achieves separation of concerns and lets us concentrate at each stage on a limited set of problems. You cannot usefully check that a program in a high-level language X is correct unless you are able to assume that the compiler on hand implements X correctly. This does not necessarily mean that you trust the compiler blindly, simply that you separate the two components of the problem: compiler correctness, and correctness of your program relative to the language's semantics.

In the method described in this book, even more layers intervene: software development will rely on libraries of reusable components, which may be used in many different applications.

Layers in a development process that includes reuse

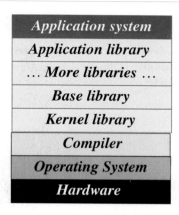

The conditional approach will also apply here: we should ensure that the libraries are correct and, separately, that the application is correct assuming the libraries are.

Many practitioners, when presented with the issue of software correctness, think about testing and debugging. We can be more ambitious: in later chapters we will explore a number of techniques, in particular typing and assertions, meant to help build software that is correct from the start — rather than debugging it into correctness. Debugging and testing remain indispensable, of course, as a means of double-checking the result.

It is possible to go further and take a completely formal approach to software construction. This book falls short of such a goal, as suggested by the somewhat timid terms "check", "guarantee" and "ensure" used above in preference to the word "prove". Yet many of the techniques described in later chapters come directly from the work on mathematical techniques for formal program specification and verification, and go a long way towards ensuring the correctness ideal.

Robustness

> ### Definition: robustness
>
> Robustness is the ability of software systems to react appropriately to abnormal conditions.

Robustness complements correctness. Correctness addresses the behavior of a system in cases covered by its specification; robustness characterizes what happens outside of that specification.

Robustness versus correctness

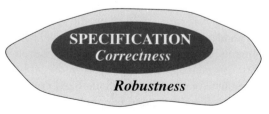

As reflected by the wording of its definition, robustness is by nature a more fuzzy notion than correctness. Since we are concerned here with cases not covered by the specification, it is not possible to say, as with correctness, that the system should "perform its tasks" in such a case; were these tasks known, the abnormal case would become part of the specification and we would be back in the province of correctness.

This definition of "abnormal case" will be useful again when we study exception handling. It implies that the notions of normal and abnormal case are always relative to a certain specification; an abnormal case is simply a case that is not covered by the specification. If you widen the specification, cases that used to be abnormal become normal — even if they correspond to events such as erroneous user input that you would prefer not to happen. "Normal" in this sense does not mean "desirable", but simply "planned for in the design of the software". Although it may seem paradoxical at first that erroneous input should be called a normal case, any other approach would have to rely on subjective criteria, and so would be useless.

On exception handling see chapter 12.

There will always be cases that the specification does not explicitly address. The role of the robustness requirement is to make sure that if such cases do arise, the system does not cause catastrophic events; it should produce appropriate error messages, terminate its execution cleanly, or enter a so-called "graceful degradation" mode.

Extendibility

> ### Definition: extendibility
> Extendibility is the ease of adapting software products to changes of specification.

Software is supposed to be *soft*, and indeed is in principle; nothing can be easier than to change a program if you have access to its source code. Just use your favorite text editor.

The problem of extendibility is one of scale. For small programs change is usually not a difficult issue; but as software grows bigger, it becomes harder and harder to adapt. A large software system often looks to its maintainers as a giant house of cards in which pulling out any one element might cause the whole edifice to collapse.

We need extendibility because at the basis of all software lies some human phenomenon and hence fickleness. The obvious case of business software ("Management Information Systems"), where passage of a law or a company's acquisition may suddenly invalidate the assumptions on which a system rested, is not special; even in scientific computation, where we may expect the laws of physics to stay in place from one month to the next, our way of understanding and modeling physical systems will change.

Traditional approaches to software engineering did not take enough account of change, relying instead on an ideal view of the software lifecycle where an initial analysis stage freezes the requirements, the rest of the process being devoted to designing and building a solution. This is understandable: the first task in the progress of the discipline was to develop sound techniques for stating and solving fixed problems, before we could worry about what to do if the problem changes while someone is busy solving it. But now with the basic software engineering techniques in place it has become essential to recognize and address this central issue. Change is pervasive in software development: change of requirements, of our understanding of the requirements, of algorithms, of data representation, of implementation techniques. Support for change is a basic goal of object technology and a running theme through this book.

Although many of the techniques that improve extendibility may be introduced on small examples or in introductory courses, their relevance only becomes clear for larger projects. Two principles are essential for improving extendibility:

- *Design simplicity*: a simple architecture will always be easier to adapt to changes than a complex one.

- *Decentralization*: the more autonomous the modules, the higher the likelihood that a simple change will affect just one module, or a small number of modules, rather than triggering off a chain reaction of changes over the whole system.

The object-oriented method is, before anything else, a system architecture method which helps designers produce systems whose structure remains both simple (even for large systems) and decentralized. Simplicity and decentralization will be recurring themes in the discussions leading to object-oriented principles in the following chapters.

Reusability

> ### Definition: reusability
>
> Reusability is the ability of software elements to serve for the construction of many different applications.

The need for reusability comes from the observation that software systems often follow similar patterns; it should be possible to exploit this commonality and avoid reinventing solutions to problems that have been encountered before. By capturing such a pattern, a reusable software element will be applicable to many different developments.

Reusability has an influence on all other aspects of software quality, for solving the reusability problem essentially means that less software must be written, and hence that more effort may be devoted (for the same total cost) to improving the other factors, such as correctness and robustness.

Here again is an issue that the traditional view of the software lifecycle had not properly recognized, and for the same historical reason: you must find ways to solve one problem before you worry about applying the solution to other problems. But with the growth of software and its attempts to become a true industry the need for reusability has become a pressing concern.

Chapter 4.   Reusability will play a central role in the discussions of the following chapters, one of which is in fact devoted entirely to an in-depth examination of this quality factor, its concrete benefits, and the issues it raises.

Compatibility

Definition: compatibility
Compatibility is the ease of combining software elements with others.

Compatibility is important because we do not develop software elements in a vacuum: they need to interact with each other. But they too often have trouble interacting because they make conflicting assumptions about the rest of the world. An example is the wide variety of incompatible file formats supported by many operating systems. A program can directly use another's result as input only if the file formats are compatible.

Lack of compatibility can yield disaster. Here is an extreme case:

DALLAS — Last week, AMR, the parent company of American Airlines, Inc., said it fell on its sword trying to develop a state-of-the-art, industry-wide system that could also handle car and hotel reservations.

AMR cut off development of its new Confirm reservation system only weeks after it was supposed to start taking care of transactions for partners Budget Rent-A-Car, Hilton Hotels Corp. and Marriott Corp. Suspension of the $125 million, 4-year-old project translated into a $165 million pre-tax charge against AMR's earnings and fractured the company's reputation as a pacesetter in travel technology. […]

As far back as January, the leaders of Confirm discovered that the labors of more than 200 programmers, systems analysts and engineers had apparently been for naught. The main pieces of the massive project — requiring 47,000 pages to describe — had been developed separately, by different methods. When put together, they did not work with each other. When the developers attempted to plug the parts together, they could not. Different "modules" could not pull the information needed from the other side of the bridge.

AMR Information Services fired eight senior project members, including the team leader. […] In late June, Budget and Hilton said they were dropping out.

San Jose (Calif.) Mercury News, July 20, 1992. Quoted in the "comp. risks" Usenet newsgroup, 13.67, July 1992. Slightly abridged.

The key to compatibility lies in homogeneity of design, and in agreeing on standardized conventions for inter-program communication. Approaches include:

- Standardized file formats, as in the Unix system, where every text file is simply a sequence of characters.

- Standardized data structures, as in Lisp systems, where all data, and programs as well, are represented by binary trees (called lists in Lisp).

- Standardized user interfaces, as on various versions of Windows, OS/2 and MacOS, where all tools rely on a single paradigm for communication with the user, based on standard components such as windows, icons, menus etc.

More general solutions are obtained by defining standardized access protocols to all important entities manipulated by the software. This is the idea behind abstract data types and the object-oriented approach, as well as so-called *middleware* protocols such as CORBA and Microsoft's OLE-COM (ActiveX).

On abstract data types see chapter 6.

Efficiency

> ### Definition: efficiency
>
> Efficiency is the ability of a software system to place as few demands as possible on hardware resources, such as processor time, space occupied in internal and external memories, bandwidth used in communication devices.

Almost synonymous with efficiency is the word "performance". The software community shows two typical attitudes towards efficiency:

- Some developers have an obsession with performance issues, leading them to devote a lot of efforts to presumed optimizations.

- But a general tendency also exists to downplay efficiency concerns, as evidenced by such industry lore as "make it right before you make it fast" and "next year's computer model is going to be 50% faster anyway".

It is not uncommon to see the same person displaying these two attitudes at different times, as in a software case of split personality (Dr. Abstract and Mr. Microsecond).

Where is the truth? Clearly, developers have often shown an exaggerated concern for micro-optimization. As already noted, efficiency does not matter much if the software is not correct (suggesting a new dictum, "*do not worry how fast it is unless it is also right*", close to the previous one but not quite the same). More generally, the concern for efficiency must be balanced with other goals such as extendibility and reusability; extreme optimizations may make the software so specialized as to be unfit for change and reuse. Furthermore, the ever growing power of computer hardware does allow us to have a more relaxed attitude about gaining the last byte or microsecond.

All this, however, does not diminish the importance of efficiency. No one likes to wait for the responses of an interactive system, or to have to purchase more memory to run a program. So offhand attitudes to performance include much posturing; if the final system is so slow or bulky as to impede usage, those who used to declare that "speed is not that important" will not be the last to complain.

This issue reflects what I believe to be a major characteristic of software engineering, not likely to move away soon: software construction is difficult precisely because it requires taking into account many different requirements, some of which, such as correctness, are abstract and conceptual, whereas others, such as efficiency, are concrete and bound to the properties of computer hardware.

For some scientists, software development is a branch of mathematics; for some engineers, it is a branch of applied technology. In reality, it is both. The software developer must reconcile the abstract concepts with their concrete implementations, the mathematics of correct computation with the time and space constraints deriving from physical laws and from limitations of current hardware technology. This need to please the angels as well as the beasts may be the central challenge of software engineering.

The constant improvement in computer power, impressive as it is, is not an excuse for overlooking efficiency, for at least three reasons:

- Someone who purchases a bigger and faster computer wants to see some actual benefit from the extra power — to handle new problems, process previous problems faster, or process bigger versions of the previous problems in the same amount of time. Using the new computer to process the previous problems in the same amount of time will not do!

- One of the most visible effects of advances in computer power is actually to *increase* the lead of good algorithms over bad ones. Assume that a new machine is twice as fast as the previous one. Let n be the size of the problem to solve, and N the maximum n that can be handled by a certain algorithm in a given time. Then if the algorithm is in O (n), that is to say, runs in a time proportional to n, the new machine will enable you to handle problem sizes of about $2 * N$ for large N. For an algorithm in O (n^2) the new machine will only yield a 41% increase of N. An algorithm in O (2^n), similar to certain combinatorial, exhaustive-search algorithms, would just add one to N — not much of an improvement for your money.

- In some cases efficiency may affect correctness. A specification may state that the computer response to a certain event must occur no later than a specified time; for example, an in-flight computer must be prepared to detect and process a message from the throttle sensor fast enough to take corrective action. This connection between efficiency and correctness is not restricted to applications commonly thought of as "real time"; few people are interested in a weather forecasting model that takes twenty-four hours to predict the next day's weather.

  Another example, although perhaps less critical, has been of frequent annoyance to me: a window management system that I used for a while was sometimes too slow to detect that the mouse cursor had moved from a window to another, so that characters typed at the keyboard, meant for a certain window, would occasionally end up in another.

  In this case a performance limitation causes a violation of the specification, that is to say of correctness, which even in seemingly innocuous everyday applications can cause nasty consequences: think of what can happen if the two windows are used to send electronic mail messages to two different correspondents. For less than this marriages have been broken, even wars started.

Because this book is focused on the concepts of object-oriented software engineering, not on implementation issues, only a few sections deal explicitly with the associated performance costs. But the concern for efficiency will be there throughout. Whenever the discussion presents an object-oriented solution to some problem, it will make sure that the solution is not just elegant but also efficient; whenever it introduces some new O-O mechanism, be it garbage collection (and other approaches to memory management for object-oriented computation), dynamic binding, genericity or repeated inheritance, it will do so based on the knowledge that the mechanism may be implemented at a reasonable cost in time and in space; and whenever appropriate it will mention the performance consequences of the techniques studied.

Efficiency is only one of the factors of quality; we should not (like some in the profession) let it rule our engineering lives. But it is a factor, and must be taken into consideration, whether in the construction of a software system or in the design of a programming language. If you dismiss performance, performance will dismiss you.

Portability

> ### Definition: portability
>
> Portability is the ease of transferring software products to various hardware and software environments.

Portability addresses variations not just of the physical hardware but more generally of the **hardware-software machine**, the one that we really program, which includes the operating system, the window system if applicable, and other fundamental tools. In the rest of this book the word "platform" will be used to denote a type of hardware-software machine; an example of platform is "Intel X86 with Windows NT" (known as "Wintel").

Many of the existing platform incompatibilities are unjustified, and to a naïve observer the only explanation sometimes seems to be a conspiracy to victimize humanity in general and programmers in particular. Whatever its causes, however, this diversity makes portability a major concern for both developers and users of software.

Ease of use

> ### Definition: ease of use
>
> Ease of use is the ease with which people of various backgrounds and qualifications can learn to use software products and apply them to solve problems. It also covers the ease of installation, operation and monitoring.

The definition insists on the various levels of expertise of potential users. This requirement poses one of the major challenges to software designers preoccupied with ease of use: how to provide detailed guidance and explanations to novice users, without bothering expert users who just want to get right down to business.

As with many of the other qualities discussed in this chapter, one of the keys to ease of use is structural simplicity. A well-designed system, built according to a clear, well thought-out structure, will tend to be easier to learn and use than a messy one. The condition is not sufficient, of course (what is simple and clear to the designer may be difficult and obscure to users, especially if explained in designer's rather than user's terms), but it helps considerably.

This is one of the areas where the object-oriented method is particularly productive; many O-O techniques, which appear at first to address design and implementation, also yield powerful new interface ideas that help the end users. Later chapters will introduce several examples.

Software designers preoccupied with ease of use will also be well-advised to consider with some mistrust the precept most frequently quoted in the user interface literature, from an early article by Hansen: **know the user**. The argument is that a good designer must make an effort to understand the system's intended user community. This view ignores one of the features of successful systems: they always outgrow their initial audience. (Two old and famous examples are Fortran, conceived as a tool to solve the problem of the small community of engineers and scientists programming the IBM 704, and Unix, meant for internal use at Bell Laboratories.) A system designed for a specific group will rely on assumptions that simply do not hold for a larger audience.

See Wilfred J. Hansen, "User Engineering Principles for Interactive Systems", Proceedings of FJCC 39, AFIPS Press, Montvale (NJ), 1971, pp 523-532.

Good user interface designers follow a more prudent policy. They make as limited assumptions about their users as they can. When you design an interactive system, you may expect that users are members of the human race and that they can read, move a mouse, click a button, and type (slowly); not much more. If the software addresses a specialized application area, you may perhaps assume that your users are familiar with its basic concepts. But even that is risky. To reverse-paraphrase Hansen's advice:

User Interface Design principle

Do not pretend you know the user; you don't.

Functionality

Definition: functionality

Functionality is the extent of possibilities provided by a system.

One of the most difficult problems facing a project leader is to know how much functionality is enough. The pressure for more facilities, known in industry parlance as *featurism* (often "*creeping featurism*"), is constantly there. Its consequences are bad for internal projects, where the pressure comes from users within the same company, and worse for commercial products, as the most prominent part of a journalist's comparative review is often the table listing side by side the features offered by competing products.

Featurism is actually the combination of two problems, one more difficult than the other. The easier problem is the loss of consistency that may result from the addition of new features, affecting its ease of use. Users are indeed known to complain that all the "bells and whistles" of a product's new version make it horrendously complex. Such comments should be taken with a grain of salt, however, since the new features do not come out of nowhere: most of the time they have been requested by users — *other* users. What to me looks like a superfluous trinket may be an indispensable facility to you.

The solution here is to work again and again on the consistency of the overall product, trying to make everything fit into a general mold. A good software product is based on a small number of powerful ideas; even if it has many specialized features, they should all be explainable as consequences of these basic concepts. The "grand plan" must be visible, and everything should have its place in it.

The more difficult problem is to avoid being so focused on features as to forget the other qualities. Projects commonly make such a mistake, a situation vividly pictured by Roger Osmond in the form of two possible paths to a project's completion:

Osmond's curves; after **[Osmond 1995]**

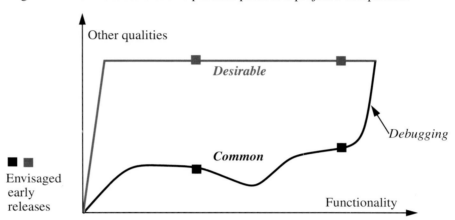

The bottom curve (black) is all too common: in the hectic race to add more features, the development loses track of the overall quality. The final phase, intended to get things right at last, can be long and stressful. If, under users' or competitors' pressure, you are forced to release the product early — at stages marked by black squares in the figure — the outcome may be damaging to your reputation.

What Osmond suggests (the color curve) is, aided by the quality-enhancing techniques of O-O development, to maintain the quality level constant throughout the project for all aspects but functionality. You just do not compromise on reliability, extendibility and the like: you refuse to proceed with new features until you are happy with the features you have.

This method is tougher to enforce on a day-to-day basis because of the pressures mentioned, but yields a more effective software process and often a better product in the end. Even if the final result is the same, as assumed in the figure, it should be reached sooner (although the figure does not show time). Following the suggested path also means that the decision to release an early version — at one of the points marked by colored squares in the figure — becomes, if not easier, at least simpler: it will be based on your assessment of whether what you have so far covers a large enough share of the full feature set to attract prospective customers rather than drive them away. The question "is it good enough?" (as in "will it not crash?") should not be a factor.

As any reader who has led a software project will know, it is easier to approve such advice than to apply it. But every project should strive to follow the approach represented by the better one of the two Osmond curves. It goes well with the *cluster model* introduced in a later chapter as the general scheme for disciplined object-oriented development.

Timeliness

> ### Definition: timeliness
>
> Timeliness is the ability of a software system to be released when or before its users want it.

Timeliness is one of the great frustrations of our industry. A great software product that appears too late might miss its target altogether. This is true in other industries too, but few evolve as quickly as software.

Timeliness is still, for large projects, an uncommon phenomenon. When Microsoft announced that the latest release of its principal operating system, several years in the making, would be delivered one month early, the event was newsworthy enough to make (at the top of an article recalling the lengthy delays that affected earlier projects) the front-page headline of *ComputerWorld*.

"NT 4.0 Beats Clock", Computer-World, vol. 30, no. 30, 22 July 1996.

Other qualities

Other qualities beside the ones discussed so far affect users of software systems and the people who purchase these systems or commission their development. In particular:

- **Verifiability** is the ease of preparing acceptance procedures, especially test data, and procedures for detecting failures and tracing them to errors during the validation and operation phases.
- **Integrity** is the ability of software systems to protect their various components (programs, data) against unauthorized access and modification.
- **Repairability** is the ability to facilitate the repair of defects.
- **Economy**, the companion of timeliness, is the ability of a system to be completed on or below its assigned budget.

About documentation

In a list of software quality factors, one might expect to find the presence of good documentation as one of the requirements. But this is not a separate quality factor; instead, the need for documentation is a consequence of the other quality factors seen above. We may distinguish between three kinds of documentation:

- The need for *external* documentation, which enables users to understand the power of a system and use it conveniently, is a consequence of the definition of ease of use.
- The need for *internal* documentation, which enables software developers to understand the structure and implementation of a system, is a consequence of the extendibility requirement.
- The need for *module interface* documentation, enabling software developers to understand the functions provided by a module without having to understand its implementation, is a consequence of the reusability requirement. It also follows from extendibility, as module interface documentation makes it possible to determine whether a certain change need affect a certain module.

Rather than treating documentation as a product separate from the software proper, it is preferable to make the software as self-documenting as possible. This applies to all three kinds of documentation:

- By including on-line "help" facilities and adhering to clear and consistent user interface conventions, you alleviate the task of the authors of user manuals and other forms of external documentation.

- A good implementation language will remove much of the need for internal documentation if it favors clarity and structure. This will be one of the major requirements on the object-oriented notation developed throughout this book.

- The notation will support information hiding and other techniques (such as assertions) for separating the interface of modules from their implementation. It is then possible to use tools to produce module interface documentation automatically from module texts. This too is one of the topics studied in detail in later chapters.

All these techniques lessen the role of traditional documentation, although of course we cannot expect them to remove it completely.

Tradeoffs

In this review of external software quality factors, we have encountered requirements that may conflict with one another.

How can one get *integrity* without introducing protections of various kinds, which will inevitably hamper *ease of use*? *Economy* often seems to fight with *functionality*. Optimal *efficiency* would require perfect adaptation to a particular hardware and software environment, which is the opposite of *portability*, and perfect adaptation to a specification, where *reusability* pushes towards solving problems more general than the one initially given. *Timeliness* pressures might tempt us to use "Rapid Application Development" techniques whose results may not enjoy much *extendibility*.

Although it is in many cases possible to find a solution that reconciles apparently conflicting factors, you will sometimes need to make tradeoffs. Too often, developers make these tradeoffs implicitly, without taking the time to examine the issues involved and the various choices available; efficiency tends to be the dominating factor in such silent decisions. A true software engineering approach implies an effort to state the criteria clearly and make the choices consciously.

Necessary as tradeoffs between quality factors may be, one factor stands out from the rest: correctness. There is never any justification for compromising correctness for the sake of other concerns such as efficiency. If the software does not perform its function, the rest is useless.

Key concerns

All the qualities discussed above are important. But in the current state of the software industry, four stand out:

- *Correctness* and *robustness*: it is still too difficult to produce software without defects (bugs), and too hard to correct the defects once they are there. Techniques for improving correctness and robustness are of the same general flavors: more systematic approaches to software construction; more formal specifications; built-in checks throughout the software construction process (not just after-the-fact testing and debugging); better language mechanisms such as static typing, assertions, automatic memory management and disciplined exception handling, enabling developers to state correctness and robustness requirements, and enabling tools to detect inconsistencies before they lead to defects. Because of this closeness of correctness and robustness issues, it is convenient to use a more general term, **reliability**, to cover both factors.

- *Extendibility* and *reusability*: software should be easier to change; the software elements we produce should be more generally applicable, and there should exist a larger inventory of general-purpose components that we can reuse when developing a new system. Here again, similar ideas are useful for improving both qualities: any idea that helps produce more decentralized architectures, in which the components are self-contained and only communicate through restricted and clearly defined channels, will help. The term **modularity** will cover reusability and extendibility.

As studied in detail in subsequent chapters, the object-oriented method can significantly improve these four quality factors — which is why it is so attractive. It also has significant contributions to make on other aspects, in particular:

- *Compatibility*: the method promotes a common design style and standardized module and system interfaces, which help produce systems that will work together.

- *Portability*: with its emphasis on abstraction and information hiding, object technology encourages designers to distinguish between specification and implementation properties, facilitating porting efforts. The techniques of polymorphism and dynamic binding will even make it possible to write systems that automatically adapt to various components of the hardware-software machine, for example different window systems or different database management systems.

- *Ease of use*: the contribution of O-O tools to modern interactive systems and especially their user interfaces is well known, to the point that it sometimes obscures other aspects (ad copy writers are not the only people who call "object-oriented" any system that uses icons, windows and mouse-driven input).

- *Efficiency*: as noted above, although the extra power or object-oriented techniques at first appears to carry a price, relying on professional-quality reusable components can often yield considerable performance improvements.

- *Timeliness, economy* and *functionality*: O-O techniques enable those who master them to produce software faster and at less cost; they facilitate addition of functions, and may even of themselves suggest new functions to add.

In spite of all these advances, we should keep in mind that the object-oriented method is not a panacea, and that many of the habitual issues of software engineering remain. Helping to address a problem is not the same as solving the problem.

1.3 ABOUT SOFTWARE MAINTENANCE

The list of factors did not include a frequently quoted quality: maintainability. To understand why, we must take a closer look at the underlying notion, maintenance.

Maintenance is what happens after a software product has been delivered. Discussions of software methodology tend to focus on the development phase; so do introductory programming courses. But it is widely estimated that 70% of the cost of software is devoted to maintenance. No study of software quality can be satisfactory if it neglects this aspect.

What does "maintenance" mean for software? A minute's reflection shows this term to be a misnomer: a software product does not wear out from repeated usage, and thus need not be "maintained" the way a car or a TV set does. In fact, the word is used by software people to describe some noble and some not so noble activities. The noble part is modification: as the specifications of computer systems change, reflecting changes in the external world, so must the systems themselves. The less noble part is late debugging: removing errors that should never have been there in the first place.

Breakdown of maintenance costs. Source: **[Lientz 1980]**

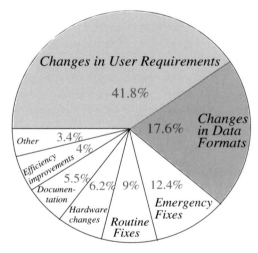

The above chart, drawn from a milestone study by Lientz and Swanson, sheds some light on what the catch-all term of maintenance really covers. The study surveyed 487 installations developing software of all kinds; although it is a bit old, more recent publications confirm the same general results. It shows the percentage of maintenance costs going into each of a number of maintenance activities identified by the authors.

More than two-fifths of the cost is devoted to user-requested extensions and modifications. This is what was called above the noble part of maintenance, which is also the inevitable part. The unanswered question is how much of the overall effort the industry could spare if it built its software from the start with more concern for extendibility. We may legitimately expect object technology to help.

The second item in decreasing order of percentage cost is particularly interesting: effect of changes in data formats. When the physical structure of files and other data items change, programs must be adapted. For example, when the US Postal Service, a few years ago, introduced the "5+4" postal code for large companies (using nine digits instead of five), numerous programs that dealt with addresses and "knew" that a postal code was exactly five digits long had to be rewritten, an effort which press accounts estimated in the hundreds of millions of dollars.

For another example, see "How long is a middle initial?", page 125.

> Many readers will have received the beautiful brochures for a set of conferences — not a single event, but a sequence of sessions in many cities — devoted to the "millennium problem": how to go about upgrading the myriads of date-sensitive programs whose authors never for a moment thought that a date could exist beyond the twentieth century. The zip code adaptation effort pales in comparison. Jorge Luis Borges would have liked the idea: since presumably few people care about what will happen on 1 January 3000, this must be the tiniest topic to which a conference series, or for that matter a conference, has been or will ever be devoted in the history of humanity: *a single decimal digit.*

The issue is not that some part of the program knows the physical structure of data: this is inevitable since the data must eventually be accessed for internal handling. But with traditional design techniques this knowledge is spread out over too many parts of the system, causing unjustifiably large program changes if some of the physical structure changes — as it inevitably will. In other words, if postal codes go from five to nine digits, or dates require one more digit, it is reasonable to expect that a program manipulating the codes or the dates will need to be adapted; what is not acceptable is to have the knowledge of the exact length of the data plastered all across the program, so that changing that length will cause program changes of a magnitude out of proportion with the conceptual size of the specification change.

The theory of abstract data types will provide the key to this problem, by allowing programs to access data by external properties rather than physical implementation.

Chapter 6 covers abstract data types in detail.

Another significant item in the distribution of activities is the low percentage (5.5%) of documentation costs. Remember that these are costs of tasks done at maintenance time. The observation here — at least the speculation, in the absence of more specific data — is that a project will either take care of its documentation as part of development or not do it at all. We will learn to use a design style in which much of the documentation is actually embedded in the software, with special tools available to extract it.

The next items in Lientz and Swanson's list are also interesting, if less directly relevant to the topics of this book. Emergency bug fixes (done in haste when a user reports that the program is not producing the expected results or behaves in some catastrophic way) cost more than routine, scheduled corrections. This is not only because they must be performed under heavy pressure, but also because they disrupt the orderly process of delivering new releases, and may introduce new errors. The last two activities account for small percentages:

- One is efficiency improvements; this seems to suggest that once a system works, project managers and programmers are often reluctant to disrupt it in the hope of performance improvements, and prefer to leave good enough alone. (When considering the "first make it right, then make it fast" precept, many projects are probably happy enough to stop at the first of these steps.)

- Also accounting for a small percentage is "transfer to new environments". A possible interpretation (again a conjecture in the absence of more detailed data) is that there are two kinds of program with respect to portability, with little in-between: some programs are designed with portability in mind, and cost relatively little to port; others are so closely tied to their original platform, and would be so difficult to port, that developers do not even try.

1.4 KEY CONCEPTS INTRODUCED IN THIS CHAPTER

- The purpose of software engineering is to find ways of building quality software.

- Rather than a single factor, quality in software is best viewed as a tradeoff between a set of different goals.

- External factors, perceptible to users and clients, should be distinguished from internal factors, perceptible to designers and implementors.

- What matters is the external factors, but they can only be achieved through the internal factors.

- A list of basic external quality factors was presented. Those for which current software is most badly in need of better methods, and which the object-oriented method directly addresses, are the safety-related factors correctness and robustness, together known as reliability, and the factors requiring more decentralized software architectures: reusability and extendibility, together known as modularity.

- Software maintenance, which consumes a large portion of software costs, is penalized by the difficulty of implementing changes in software products, and by the over-dependence of programs on the physical structure of the data they manipulate.

1.5 BIBLIOGRAPHICAL NOTES

Several authors have proposed definitions of software quality. Among the first articles on subject, two in particular remain valuable today: [Hoare 1972], a guest editorial, and [Boehm 1978], the result of one of the first systematic studies, by a group at TRW.

The distinction between external and internal factors was introduced in a 1977 General Electric study commissioned by the US Air Force [McCall 1977]. McCall uses the terms "factors" and "criteria" for what this chapter has called external factors and internal factors. Many (although not all) of the factors introduced in this chapter correspond to some of McCall's; one of his factors, maintainability, was dropped, because, as explained, it is adequately covered by extendibility and verifiability. McCall's study discusses not only external factors but also a number of internal factors ("criteria"), as well as *metrics*, or quantitative techniques for assessing satisfaction of the internal factors. With object technology, however, many of that study's internal factors and metrics, too closely linked with older software practices, are obsolete. Carrying over this part of McCall's work to the techniques developed in this book would be a useful project; see the bibliography and exercises to chapter 3.

The argument about the relative effect of machine improvements depending on the complexity of the algorithms is derived from [Aho 1974].

On ease of use, a standard reference is [Shneiderman 1987], expanding on [Shneiderman 1980], which was devoted to the broader topic of software psychology. The Web page of Shneiderman's lab at *http://www.cs.umd.edu/projects/hcil/* contains many bibliographic references on these topics.

The Osmond curves come from a tutorial given by Roger Osmond at TOOLS USA [Osmond 1995]. Note that the form given in this chapter does not show time, enabling a more direct view of the tradeoff between functionality and other qualities in the two alternative curves, but not reflecting the black curve's potential for delaying a project. Osmond's original curves are plotted against time rather than functionality.

The chart of maintenance costs is derived from a study by Lientz and Swanson, based on a maintenance questionnaire sent to 487 organizations [Lientz 1980]. See also [Boehm 1979]. Although some of their input data may be considered too specialized and by now obsolete (the study was based on batch-type MIS applications of an average size of 23,000 instructions, large then but not by today's standards), the results generally seem still applicable. The Software Management Association performs a yearly survey of maintenance; see [Dekleva 1992] for a report about one of these surveys.

The expressions *programming-in-the-large* and *programming-in-the-small* were introduced by [DeRemer 1976].

For a general discussion of software engineering issues, see the textbook by Ghezzi, Jazayeri and Mandrioli [Ghezzi 1991]. A text on programming languages by some of the same authors, [Ghezzi 1997], provides complementary background for some of the issues discussed in the present book.

2

Criteria of object orientation

*I*n the previous chapter we explored the goals of the object-oriented method. As a preparation for parts B and C, in which we will discover the technical details of the method, it is useful to take a quick but wide glance at the key aspects of object-oriented development. Such is the aim of this chapter.

One of the benefits will be to obtain a concise memento of what makes a system object-oriented. This expression has nowadays become so indiscriminately used that we need a list of precise properties under which we can assess any method, language or tool that its proponents claim to be O-O.

This chapter limits its explanations to a bare minimum, so if this is your first reading you cannot expect to understand in detail all the criteria listed; explaining them is the task of the rest of the book. Consider this discussion a preview — not the real movie, just a trailer.

Warning:
SPOILER!

Actually a warning is in order because unlike any good trailer this chapter is also what film buffs call a *spoiler* — it gives away some of the plot early. As such it breaks the step-by-step progression of this book, especially part B, which patiently builds the case for object technology by looking at issue after issue before deducing and justifying the solutions. If you like the idea of reading a broad overview before getting into more depth, this chapter is for you. But if you prefer *not* to spoil the pleasure of seeing the problems unfold and of discovering the solutions one by one, then you should simply skip it. You will not need to have read it to understand subsequent chapters.

2.1 ON THE CRITERIA

Let us first examine the choice of criteria for assessing objectness.

How dogmatic do we need to be?

The list presented below includes all the facilities which I believe to be essential for the production of quality software using the object-oriented method. It is ambitious and may appear uncompromising or even dogmatic. What conclusion does this imply for an environment which satisfies some but not all of these conditions? Should one just reject such a half-hearted O-O environment as totally inadequate?

Only you, the reader, can answer this question relative to your own context. Several reasons suggest that some compromises may be necessary:

- "Object-oriented" is not a boolean condition: environment A, although not 100% O-O, may be "more" O-O than environment B; so if external constraints limit your choice to A and B you will have to pick A as the least bad object-oriented choice.

- Not everyone will need all of the properties all the time.

- Object orientation may be just one of the factors guiding your search for a software solution, so you may have to balance the criteria given here with other considerations.

All this does not change the obvious: to make informed choices, even if practical constraints impose less-than-perfect solutions, you need to know the complete picture, as provided by the list below.

Categories

The set of criteria which follows has been divided into three parts:

- *Method and language*: these two almost indistinguishable aspects cover the thought processes and the notations used to analyze and produce software. Be sure to note that (especially in object technology) the term "language" covers not just the programming language in a strict sense, but also the notations, textual or graphical, used for analysis and design.

- *Implementation and environment*: the criteria in this category describe the basic properties of the tools which allow developers to apply object-oriented ideas.

- *Libraries*: object technology relies on the reuse of software components. Criteria in this category cover both the availability of basic libraries and the mechanisms needed to use libraries and produce new ones.

This division is convenient but not absolute, as some criteria straddle two or three of the categories. For example the criterion labeled "memory management" has been classified under method and language because a language can support or prevent automatic garbage collection, but it also belongs to the implementation and environment category; the "assertion" criterion similarly includes a requirement for supporting tools.

2.2 METHOD AND LANGUAGE

The first set of criteria covers the method and the supporting notation.

Seamlessness

The object-oriented approach is ambitious: it encompasses the entire software lifecycle. When examining object-oriented solutions, you should check that the method and language, as well as the supporting tools, apply to analysis and design as well as implementation and maintenance. The language, in particular, should be a vehicle for thought which will help you through all stages of your work.

The result is a seamless development process, where the generality of the concepts and notations helps reduce the magnitude of the transitions between successive steps in the lifecycle.

These requirements exclude two cases, still frequently encountered but equally unsatisfactory:

- The use of object-oriented concepts for analysis and design only, with a method and notation that cannot be used to write executable software.

- The use of an object-oriented programming language which is not suitable for analysis and design.

In summary:

> An object-oriented language and environment, together with the supporting method, should apply to the entire lifecycle, in a way that minimizes the gaps between successive activities.

Classes

The object-oriented method is based on the notion of class. Informally, a class is a software element describing an abstract data type and its partial or total implementation. An abstract data type is a set of objects defined by the list of operations, or *features*, applicable to these objects, and the properties of these operations.

> The method and the language should have the notion of class as their central concept.

Assertions

The features of an abstract data type have formally specified properties, which should be reflected in the corresponding classes. Assertions — routine preconditions, routine postconditions and class invariants — play this role. They describe the effect of features on objects, independently of how the features have been implemented.

Assertions have three major applications: they help produce reliable software; they provide systematic documentation; and they are a central tool for testing and debugging object-oriented software.

> The language should make it possible to equip a class and its features with assertions (preconditions, postconditions and invariants), relying on tools to produce documentation out of these assertions and, optionally, monitor them at run time.

In the society of software modules, with classes serving as the cities and instructions (the actual executable code) serving as the executive branch of government, assertions provide the legislative branch. We shall see below who takes care of the judicial system.

Classes as modules

Object orientation is primarily an architectural technique: its major effect is on the modular structure of software systems.

The key role here is again played by classes. A class describes not just a type of objects but also a modular unit. In a pure object-oriented approach:

> Classes should be the only modules.

In particular, there is no notion of main program, and subprograms do not exist as independent modular units. (They may only appear as part of classes.) There is also no need for the "packages" of languages such as Ada, although we may find it convenient for management purposes to group classes into administrative units, called *clusters*.

Classes as types

The notion of class is powerful enough to avoid the need for any other typing mechanism:

> Every type should be based on a class.

Even basic types such as *INTEGER* and *REAL* can be derived from classes; normally such classes will be built-in rather than defined anew by each developer.

Feature-based computation

In object-oriented computation, there is only one basic computational mechanism: given a certain object, which (because of the previous rule) is always an instance of some class, call a feature of that class on that object. For example, to display a certain window on a screen, you call the feature *display* on an object representing the window — an instance of class *WINDOW*. Features may also have arguments: to increase the salary of an employee e by n dollars, effective at date d, you call the feature *raise* on e, with n and d as arguments.

Just as we treat basic types as predefined classes, we may view basic operations (such as addition of numbers) as special, predefined cases of feature call, a very general mechanism for describing computations:

> Feature call should be the primary computational mechanism.

A class which contains a call to a feature of a class C is said to be a **client** of C. Feature call is also known as **message passing**; in this terminology, a call such as the above will be described as passing to e the message "raise your pay", with arguments d and n.

Information hiding

When writing a class, you will sometimes have to include a feature which the class needs for internal purposes only: a feature that is part of the implementation of the class, but not of its interface. Others features of the class — possibly available to clients — may call the feature for their own needs; but it should not be possible for a client to call it directly.

The mechanism which makes certain features unfit for clients' calls is called information hiding. As explained in a later chapter, it is essential to the smooth evolution of software systems.

In practice, it is not enough for the information hiding mechanism to support exported features (available to all clients) and secret features (available to no client); class designers must also have the ability to export a feature selectively to a set of designated clients.

> It should be possible for the author of a class to specify that a feature is available to all clients, to no client, or to specified clients.

An immediate consequence of this rule is that communication between classes should be strictly limited. In particular, a good object-oriented language should not offer any notion of global variable; classes will exchange information exclusively through feature calls, and through the inheritance mechanism.

Exception handling

Abnormal events may occur during the execution of a software system. In object-oriented computation, they often correspond to calls that cannot be executed properly, as a result of a hardware malfunction, of an unexpected impossibility (such as numerical overflow in an addition), or of a bug in the software.

To produce reliable software, it is necessary to have the ability to recover from such situations. This is the purpose of an exception mechanism.

> The language should provide a mechanism to recover from unexpected abnormal situations.

In the society of software systems, as you may have guessed, the exception mechanism is the third branch of government, the judicial system (and the supporting police force).

Static typing

When the execution of a software system causes the call of a certain feature on a certain object, how do we know that this object will be able to handle the call? (In message terminology: how do we know that the object can process the message?)

To provide such a guarantee of correct execution, the language must be typed. This means that it enforces a few compatibility rules; in particular:

- Every entity (that is to say, every name used in the software text to refer to run-time objects) is explicitly declared as being of a certain type, derived from a class.

- Every feature call on a certain entity uses a feature from the corresponding class (and the feature is available, in the sense of information hiding, to the caller's class).

- Assignment and argument passing are subject to **conformance rules**, based on inheritance, which require the source's type to be compatible with the target's type.

In a language that imposes such a policy, it is possible to write a **static type checker** which will accept or reject software systems, guaranteeing that the systems it accepts will not cause any "feature not available on object" error at run time.

> A well-defined type system should, by enforcing a number of type declaration and compatibility rules, guarantee the run-time type safety of the systems it accepts.

Genericity

For typing to be practical, it must be possible to define type-parameterized classes, known as generic. A generic class *LIST* [*G*] will describe lists of elements of an arbitrary type represented by *G*, the "formal generic parameter"; you may then declare specific lists through such derivations as *LIST* [*INTEGER*] and *LIST* [*WINDOW*], using types *INTEGER* and *WINDOW* as "actual generic parameters". All derivations share the same class text.

> It should be possible to write classes with formal generic parameters representing arbitrary types.

This form of type parameterization is called **unconstrained** genericity. A companion facility mentioned below, constrained genericity, involves inheritance.

Single inheritance

Software development involves a large number of classes; many are variants of others. To control the resulting potential complexity, we need a classification mechanism, known as inheritance. A class will be an heir of another if it incorporates the other's features in addition to its own. (A *descendant* is a direct or indirect heir; the reverse notion is *ancestor*.)

> It should be possible to define a class as inheriting from another.

Inheritance is one of the central concepts of the object-oriented methods and has profound consequences on the software development process.

Multiple inheritance

We will often encounter the need to combine several abstractions. For example a class might model the notion of "infant", which we may view both as a "person", with the associated features, and, more prosaically, as a "tax-deductible item", which earns some deduction at tax time. Inheritance is justified in both cases. *Multiple* inheritance is the guarantee that a class may inherit not just from one other but from as many as is conceptually justified.

Multiple inheritance raises a few technical problems, in particular the resolution of *name clashes* (cases in which different features, inherited from different classes, have the same name). Any notation offering multiple inheritance must provide an adequate solution to these problems.

> It should be possible for a class to inherit from as many others as necessary, with an adequate mechanism for disambiguating name clashes.

The solution developed in this book is based on *renaming* the conflicting features in the heir class.

Repeated inheritance

Multiple inheritance raises the possibility of *repeated* inheritance, the case in which a class inherits from another through two or more paths, as shown.

Repeated inheritance

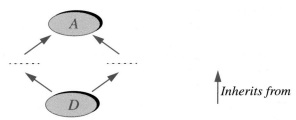

Inherits from

In such a case the language must provide precise rules defining what happens to features inherited repeatedly from the common ancestor, A in the figure. As the discussion of repeated inheritance will show, it may be desirable for a feature of A to yield just one feature of D in some cases (*sharing*), but in others it should yield two (*replication*). Developers must have the flexibility to prescribe either policy separately for each feature.

> Precise rules should govern the fate of features under repeated inheritance, allowing developers to choose, separately for each repeatedly inherited feature, between sharing and replication.

Constrained genericity

The combination of genericity and inheritance brings about an important technique, constrained genericity, through which you can specify a class with a generic parameter that represents not an arbitrary type as with the earlier (unconstrained) form of genericity, but a type that is a descendant of a given class.

A generic class *SORTABLE_LIST*, describing lists with a *sort* feature that will reorder them sequentially according to a certain order relation, needs a generic parameter representing the list elements' type. That type is not arbitrary: it must support an order relation. To state that any actual generic parameter must be a descendant of the library class *COMPARABLE*, describing objects equipped with an order relation, use constrained genericity to declare the class as *SORTABLE_LIST [G –> COMPARABLE]*.

> The genericity mechanism should support the constrained form of genericity.

Redefinition

When a class is an heir of another, it may need to change the implementation or other properties of some of the inherited features. A class *SESSION* describing user sessions in an operating system may have a feature *terminate* to take care of cleanup operations at the end of a session; an heir might be *REMOTE_SESSION*, handling sessions started from a different computer on a network. If the termination of a remote session requires supplementary actions (such as notifying the remote computer), class *REMOTE_SESSION* will redefine feature *terminate*

Redefinition may affect the implementation of a feature, its signature (type of arguments and result), and its specification.

> It should be possible to redefine the specification, signature and implementation of an inherited feature.

Polymorphism

With inheritance brought into the picture, the static typing requirement listed earlier would be too restrictive if it were taken to mean that every entity declared of type *C* may only refer to objects whose type is exactly *C*. This would mean for example that an entity of type *C* (in a navigation control system) could not be used to refer to an object of type *MERCHANT_SHIP* or *SPORTS_BOAT*, both assumed to be classes inheriting from *BOAT*.

> As noted earlier, an "entity" is a name to which various values may become attached at run time. This is a generalization of the traditional notion of variable.

Polymorphism is the ability for an entity to become attached to objects of various possible types. In a statically typed environment, polymorphism will not be arbitrary, but controlled by inheritance; for example, we should not allow our *BOAT* entity to become attached to an object representing an object of type *BUOY*, a class which does not inherit from *BOAT*

> It should be possible to attach entities (names in the software texts representing run-time objects) to run-time objects of various possible types, under the control of the inheritance-based type system.

Dynamic binding

The combination of the last two mechanisms mentioned, redefinition and polymorphism, immediately suggests the next one. Assume a call whose target is a polymorphic entity, for example a call to the feature *turn* on an entity declared of type *BOAT*. The various descendants of *BOAT* may have redefined the feature in various ways. Clearly, there must be an automatic mechanism to guarantee that the version of *turn* will always be the one deduced from the actual object's type, regardless of how the entity has been declared. This property is called dynamic binding.

> Calling a feature on an entity should always trigger the feature corresponding to the type of the attached run-time object, which is not necessarily the same in different executions of the call.

Dynamic binding has a major influence on the structure of object-oriented applications, as it enables developers to write simple calls (meaning, for example, "call feature *turn* on entity *my_boat*") to denote what is actually several possible calls depending on the corresponding run-time situations. This avoids the need for many of the repeated tests ("Is this a merchant ship? Is this a sports boat?") which plague software written with more conventional approaches.

Run-time type interrogation

Object-oriented software developers soon develop a healthy hatred for any style of computation based on explicit choices between various types for an object. Polymorphism and dynamic binding provide a much preferable alternative. In some cases, however, an object comes from the outside, so that the software author has no way to predict its type with certainty. This occurs in particular if the object is retrieved from external storage, received from a network transmission or passed by some other system.

The software then needs a mechanism to access the object in a safe way, without violating the constraints of static typing. Such a mechanism should be designed with care, so as not to cancel the benefits of polymorphism and dynamic binding.

The **assignment attempt** operation described in this book satisfies these requirements. An assignment attempt is a conditional operation: it tries to attach an object to an entity; if in a given execution the object's type conforms to the type declared for the entity, the effect is that of a normal assignment; otherwise the entity gets a special "void" value. So you can handle objects whose type you do not know for sure, without violating the safety of the type system.

> It should be possible to determine at run time whether the type of an object conforms to a statically given type.

Deferred features and classes

In some cases for which dynamic binding provides an elegant solution, obviating the need for explicit tests, there is no initial version of a feature to be redefined. For example class *BOAT* may be too general to provide a default implementation of *turn*. Yet we want to be able to call feature *turn* to an entity declared of type *BOAT* if we have ensured that at run time it will actually be attached to objects of such fully defined types as *MERCHANT_SHIP* and *SPORTS_BOAT*.

In such cases *BOAT* may be declared as a deferred class (one which is not fully implemented), and with a deferred feature *turn*. Deferred features and classes may still possess assertions describing their abstract properties, but their implementation is postponed to descendant classes. A non-deferred class is said to be *effective*.

> It should be possible to write a class or a feature as deferred, that is to say specified but not fully implemented.

Deferred classes (also called abstract classes) are particularly important for object-oriented analysis and high-level design, as they make it possible to capture the essential aspects of a system while leaving details to a later stage.

Memory management and garbage collection

The last point on our list of method and language criteria may at first appear to belong more properly to the next category — implementation and environment. In fact it belongs to both. But the crucial requirements apply to the language; the rest is a matter of good engineering.

Object-oriented systems, even more than traditional programs (except in the Lisp world), tend to create many objects with sometimes complex interdependencies. A policy leaving developers in charge of managing the associated memory, especially when it comes to reclaiming the space occupied by objects that are no longer needed, would harm both the efficiency of the development process, as it would complicate the software and occupy a considerable part of the developers' time, and the safety of the resulting systems, as it raises the risk of improper recycling of memory areas. In a good object-oriented environment memory management will be automatic, under the control of the *garbage collector*, a component of the runtime system.

The reason this is a language issue as much as an implementation requirement is that a language that has not been explicitly designed for automatic memory management will often render it impossible. This is the case with languages where a pointer to an object of a certain type may disguise itself (through conversions known as "casts") as a pointer of another type or even as an integer, making it impossible to write a safe garbage collector.

> The language should make safe automatic memory management possible, and the implementation should provide an automatic memory manager taking care of garbage collection.

2.3 IMPLEMENTATION AND ENVIRONMENT

We come now to the essential features of a development environment supporting object-oriented software construction.

Automatic update

Software development is an incremental process. Developers do not commonly write thousands of lines at a time; they proceed by addition and modification, starting most of the time from a system that is already of substantial size.

When performing such an update, it is essential to have the guarantee that the resulting system will be consistent. For example, if you change a feature f of class C, you must be certain that every descendant of C which does not redefine f will be updated to have the new version of f, and that every call to f in a client of C or of a descendant of C will trigger the new version.

Conventional approaches to this problem are manual, forcing the developers to record all dependencies, and track their changes, using special mechanisms known as "make files" and "include files". This is unacceptable in modern software development, especially in the object-oriented world where the dependencies between classes, resulting from the client and inheritance relations, are often complex but may be deduced from a systematic examination of the software text.

> System updating after a change should be automatic, the analysis of inter-class dependencies being performed by tools, not manually by developers.

It is possible to meet this requirement in a compiled environment (where the compiler will work together with a tool for dependency analysis), in an interpreted environment, or in one combining both of these language implementation techniques.

Fast update

In practice, the mechanism for updating the system after some changes should not only be automatic, it should also be fast. More precisely, it should be proportional to the size of the changed parts, not to the size of the system as a whole. Without this property, the method and environment may be applicable to small systems, but not to large ones.

> The time to process a set of changes to a system, enabling execution of the updated version, should be a function of the size of the changed components, independent of the size of the system as a whole.

Here too both interpreted and compiled environments may meet the criterion, although in the latter case the compiler must be incremental. Along with an incremental compiler, the environment may of course include a global optimizing compiler working on an entire system, as long as that compiler only needs to be used for delivering a final product; development will rely on the incremental compiler.

Persistence

Many applications, perhaps most, will need to conserve objects from one session to the next. The environment should provide a mechanism to do this in a simple way.

An object will often contain references to other objects; since the same may be true of these objects, this means that every object may have a large number of *dependent* objects, with a possibly complex dependency graph (which may involve cycles). It would usually make no sense to store or retrieve the object without all its direct and indirect dependents. A persistence mechanism which can automatically store an object's dependents along with the object is said to support **persistence closure**.

> A persistent storage mechanism supporting persistence closure should be available to store an object and all its dependents into external devices, and to retrieve them in the same or another session.

For some applications, mere persistence support is not sufficient; such applications will need full **database support**. The notion of object-oriented database is covered in a later chapter, which also explores other persistent issues such as *schema evolution*, the ability to retrieve objects safely even if the corresponding classes have changed.

Documentation

Developers of classes and systems must provide management, customers and other developers with clear, high-level descriptions of the software they produce. They need tools to assist them in this effort; as much as possible of the documentation should be produced automatically from the software texts. Assertions, as already noted, help make such software-extracted documents precise and informative.

> Automatic tools should be available to produce documentation about classes and systems.

Browsing

When looking at a class, you will often need to obtain information about other classes; in particular, the features used in a class may have been introduced not in the class itself but in its various ancestors. This puts on the environment the burden of providing developers with tools to examine a class text, find its dependencies on other classes, and switch rapidly from one class text to another.

This task is called browsing. Typical facilities offered by good browsing tools include: find the clients, suppliers, descendants, ancestors of a class; find all the redefinitions of a feature; find the original declaration of a redefined feature.

S is a "supplier" of C if C is a client of S. "Client" was defined on page 24.

> Interactive browsing facilities should enable software developers to follow up quickly and conveniently the dependencies between classes and features.

2.4 LIBRARIES

One of the characteristic aspects of developing software the object-oriented way is the ability to rely on libraries. An object-oriented environment should provide good libraries, and mechanisms to write more.

Basic libraries

The fundamental data structures of computing science — sets, lists, trees, stacks… — and the associated algorithms — sorting, searching, traversing, pattern matching — are ubiquitous in software development. In conventional approaches, each developer implements and re-implements them independently all the time; this is not only wasteful of efforts but detrimental to software quality, as it is unlikely that an individual developer who implements a data structure not as a goal in itself but merely as a component of some application will attain the optimum in reliability and efficiency.

An object-oriented development environment must provide reusable classes addressing these common needs of software systems.

> Reusable classes should be available to cover the most frequently needed data structures and algorithms.

Graphics and user interfaces

Many modern software systems are interactive, interacting with their users through graphics and other pleasant interface techniques. This is one of the areas where the object-oriented model has proved most impressive and helpful. Developers should be able to rely on graphical libraries to build interactive applications quickly and effectively.

> Reusable classes should be available for developing applications which provide their users with pleasant graphical user interface.

Library evolution mechanisms

Developing high-quality libraries is a long and arduous task. It is impossible to guarantee that the design of library will be perfect the first time around. An important problem, then, is to enable library developers to update and modify their designs without wreaking havoc in existing systems that depend on the library. This important criterion belongs to the library category, but also to the method and language category.

> Mechanisms should be available to facilitate library evolution with minimal disruption of client software.

Library indexing mechanisms

Another problem raised by libraries is the need for mechanisms to identify the classes addressing a certain need. This criterion affects all three categories: libraries, language (as there must be a way to enter indexing information within the text of each class) and tools (to process queries for classes satisfying certain conditions).

> Library classes should be equipped with indexing information allowing property-based retrieval.

2.5 FOR MORE SNEAK PREVIEW

Although to understand the concepts in depth it is preferable to read this book sequentially, readers who would like to complement the preceding theoretical overview with an advance glimpse of the method at work on a practical example can at this point read chapter 20, a case study of a practical design problem, on which it compares an O-O solution with one employing more traditional techniques.

That case study is mostly self-contained, so that you will understand the essentials without having read the intermediate chapters. (But if you do go ahead for this quick peek, you must promise to come back to the rest of the sequential presentation, starting with chapter 3, as soon as you are done.)

2.6 BIBLIOGRAPHICAL NOTES AND OBJECT RESOURCES

This introduction to the criteria of object orientation is a good opportunity to list a selection of books that offer quality introductions to object technology in general.

[Waldén 1995] discusses the most important issues of object technology, focusing on analysis and design, on which it is probably the best reference.

[Page-Jones 1995] provides an excellent overview of the method.

[Cox 1990] (whose first edition was published in 1986) is based on a somewhat different view of object technology and was instrumental in bringing O-O concepts to a much larger audience than before.

[Henderson-Sellers 1991] (a second edition is announced) provides a short overview of O-O ideas. Meant for people who are asked by their company to "go out and find out what that object stuff is about", it includes ready-to-be-photocopied transparency masters, precious on such occasions. Another overview is [Eliëns 1995].

The *Dictionary of Object Technology* [Firesmith 1995] provides a comprehensive reference on many aspects of the method.

All these books are to various degrees intended for technically-minded people. There is also a need to educate managers. [M 1995] grew out of a chapter originally planned for the present book, which became a full-fledged discussion of object technology for executives. It starts with a short technical presentation couched in business terms and continues with an analysis of management issues (lifecycle, project management, reuse policies). Another management-oriented book, [Goldberg 1995], provides a complementary perspective on many important topics. [Baudoin 1996] stresses lifecycle issues and the importance of standards.

Coming back to technical presentations, three influential books on object-oriented languages, written by the designers of these languages, contain general methodological discussions that make them of interest to readers who do not use the languages or might even be critical of them. (The history of programming languages and books about them shows that designers are not always the best to write about their own creations, but in these cases they were.) The books are:

- *Simula BEGIN* [Birtwistle 1973]. (Here two other authors joined the language designers Nygaard and Dahl.)

- *Smalltalk-80*: *The Language and its Implementation* [Goldberg 1983].

- *The C++ Programming Language*, *second edition* [Stroustrup 1991].

Chapter 29 discusses teaching the technology.

More recently, some introductory programming textbooks have started to use object-oriented ideas right from the start, as there is no reason to let "ontogeny repeat phylogeny", that is to say, take the poor students through the history of the hesitations and mistakes through which their predecessors arrived at the right ideas. The first such text (to my knowledge) was [Rist 1995]. Another good book covering similar needs is [Wiener 1996]. At the next level — textbooks for a second course on programming, discussing data structures and algorithms based on the notation of this book — you will find [Gore 1996] and [Wiener 1997]; [Jézéquel 1996] presents the principles of object-oriented software engineering.

The Usenet newsgroup *comp.object*, archived on several sites around the Web, is the natural medium of discussion for many issues of object technology. As with all such forums, be prepared for a mixture of the good, the bad and the ugly. The Object Technology department of *Computer* (IEEE), which I have edited since it started in 1995, has frequent invited columns by leading experts.

Magazines devoted to Object Technology include:

- The *Journal of Object-Oriented Programming* (the first journal in the field, emphasizing technical discussions but for a large audience), *Object Magazine* (of a more general scope, with some articles for managers), *Objekt Spektrum* (German), *Object Currents* (on-line), all described at *http://www.sigs.com*.

- *Theory and Practice of Object Systems*, an archival journal.

- *L'OBJET* (French), described at *http://www.tools.com/lobjet*.

The major international O-O conferences are OOPSLA (yearly, USA or Canada, see *http://www.acm.org*); *Object Expo* (variable frequency and locations, described at *http://www.sigs.com*); and TOOLS (Technology of Object-Oriented Languages and Systems), organized by ISE with three sessions a year (USA, Europe, Pacific), whose home page at *http://www.tools.com* also serves as a general resource on object technology and the topics of this book.

Part B:

The road to object orientation

See the comments on this text on page 43.

The second [precept I devised for myself] was to divide each of the difficulties which I would examine into as many parcels as it would be possible and required to solve it better.

The third was to drive my thoughts in due order, beginning with these objects most simple and easiest to know, and climbing little by little, so to speak by degrees, up to the knowledge of the most composite ones; and assuming some order even between those which do not naturally precede one another.

René Descartes, *Discourse on the Method* (1637)

Part B will examine the software engineering requirements that lead us, almost inexorably, to object technology.

3

Modularity

$\mathcal{F}$rom the goals of extendibility and reusability, two of the principal quality factors introduced in chapter 1, follows the need for flexible system architectures, made of autonomous software components. This is why chapter 1 also introduced the term *modularity* to cover the combination of these two quality factors.

Modular programming was once taken to mean the construction of programs as assemblies of small pieces, usually subroutines. But such a technique cannot bring real extendibility and reusability benefits unless we have a better way of guaranteeing that the resulting pieces — the **modules** — are self-contained and organized in stable architectures. Any comprehensive definition of modularity must ensure these properties.

A software construction method is modular, then, if it helps designers produce software systems made of autonomous elements connected by a coherent, simple structure. The purpose of this chapter is to refine this informal definition by exploring what precise properties such a method must possess to deserve the "modular" label. The focus will be on design methods, but the ideas also apply to earlier stages of system construction (analysis, specification) and must of course be maintained at the implementation and maintenance stages.

As it turns out, a single definition of modularity would be insufficient; as with software quality, we must look at modularity from more than one viewpoint. This chapter introduces a set of complementary properties: five *criteria*, five *rules* and five *principles* of modularity which, taken collectively, cover the most important requirements on a modular design method.

For the practicing software developer, the principles and the rules are just as important as the criteria. The difference is simply one of causality: the criteria are mutually independent — and it is indeed possible for a method to satisfy one of them while violating some of the others — whereas the rules follow from the criteria and the principles follow from the rules.

You might expect this chapter to begin with a precise description of what a module looks like. This is not the case, and for a good reason: our goal for the exploration of modularity issues, in this chapter and the next two, is precisely to analyze the properties which a satisfactory module structure must satisfy; so the form of modules will be a conclusion of the discussion, not a premise. Until we reach that conclusion the word "module" will denote the basic unit of decomposition of our systems, whatever it actually is. If you are familiar with non-object-oriented methods you will probably think of the subroutines present in most programming and design languages, or perhaps of packages as present in Ada and (under a different name) in Modula. The discussion will lead in a later chapter to the O-O form of module — the class — which supersedes these ideas. If you have encountered classes and O-O techniques before, you should still read this chapter to understand the requirements that classes address, a prerequisite if you want to use them well.

3.1 FIVE CRITERIA

A design method worthy of being called "modular" should satisfy five fundamental requirements, explored in the next few sections:

- Decomposability.

- Composability.

- Understandability.

- Continuity.

- Protection.

Modular decomposability

> A software construction method satisfies Modular Decomposability if it helps in the task of decomposing a software problem into a small number of less complex subproblems, connected by a simple structure, and independent enough to allow further work to proceed separately on each of them

The process will often be self-repeating since each subproblem may still be complex enough to require further decomposition.

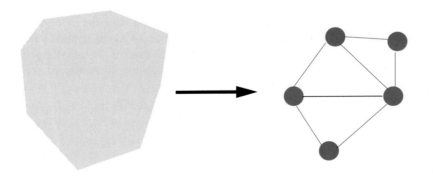

Decomposabil-ity

A corollary of the decomposability requirement is *division of labor*: once you have decomposed a system into subsystems you should be able to distribute work on these subsystems among different people or groups. This is a difficult goal since it limits the dependencies that may exist between the subsystems:

- You must keep such dependencies to the bare minimum; otherwise the development of each subsystem would be limited by the pace of the work on the other subsystems.

- The dependencies must be known: if you fail to list all the relations between subsystems, you may at the end of the project get a set of software elements that appear to work individually but cannot be put together to produce a complete system satisfying the overall requirements of the original problem.

As discussed below, top-down design is not as well suited to other modularity criteria.

The most obvious *example* of a method meant to satisfy the decomposability criterion is **top-down design**. This method directs designers to start with a most abstract description of the system's function, and then to refine this view through successive steps, decomposing each subsystem at each step into a small number of simpler subsystems, until all the remaining elements are of a sufficiently low level of abstraction to allow direct implementation. The process may be modeled as a tree.

A top-down hierarchy

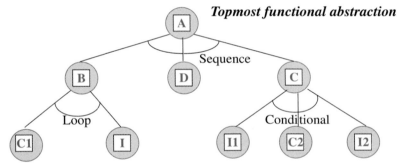

The term "temporal cohesion" comes from the method known as structured design; see the bibliographical notes.

A typical *counter-example* is any method encouraging you to include, in each software system that you produce, a global initialization module. Many modules in a system will need some kind of initialization — actions such as the opening of certain files or the initialization of certain variables, which the module must execute before it performs its first directly useful tasks. It may seem a good idea to concentrate all such actions, for all modules of the system, in a module that initializes everything for everybody. Such a module will exhibit good "temporal cohesion" in that all its actions are executed at the same stage of the system's execution. But to obtain this temporal cohesion the method would endanger the autonomy of modules: you will have to grant the initialization module authorization to access many separate data structures, belonging to the various modules of the system and requiring specific initialization actions. This means that the author of the initialization module will constantly have to peek into the internal data structures of the other modules, and interact with their authors. This is incompatible with the decomposability criterion.

> In the object-oriented method, every module will be responsible for the initialization of its own data structures.

Modular composability

A method satisfies Modular Composability if it favors the production of software elements which may then be freely combined with each other to produce new systems, possibly in an environment quite different from the one in which they were initially developed.

Where decomposability was concerned with the derivation of subsystems from overall systems, composability addresses the reverse process: extracting existing software elements from the context for which they were originally designed, so as to use them again in different contexts.

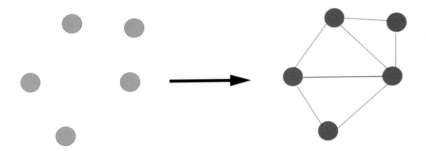

Composability

A modular design method should facilitate this process by yielding software elements that will be sufficiently autonomous — sufficiently independent from the immediate goal that led to their existence — as to make the extraction possible.

Composability is directly connected with the goal of reusability: the aim is to find ways to design software elements performing well-defined tasks and usable in widely different contexts. This criterion reflects an old dream: transforming the software design process into a construction box activity, so that we would build programs by combining standard prefabricated elements.

- *Example 1: subprogram libraries.* Subprogram libraries are designed as sets of composable elements. One of the areas where they have been successful is numerical computation, which commonly relies on carefully designed subroutine libraries to solve problems of linear algebra, finite elements, differential equations etc.

- *Example 2: Unix Shell conventions.* Basic Unix commands operate on an input viewed as a sequential character stream, and produce an output with the same standard structure. This makes them potentially composable through the | operator of the command language ("shell"): $A \mid B$ represents a program which will take A's input, have A process it, send the output to B as input, and have it processed by B. This systematic convention favors the composability of software tools.

- *Counter-example: preprocessors.* A popular way to extend the facilities of programming languages, and sometimes to correct some of their deficiencies, is to use "preprocessors" that accept an extended syntax as input and map it into the standard form of the language. Typical preprocessors for Fortran and C support graphical primitives, extended control structures or database operations. Usually, however, such extensions are not compatible; then you cannot combine two of the preprocessors, leading to such dilemmas as whether to use graphics or databases.

The figure illustrating top-down design was on page 41.

Composability is independent of decomposability. In fact, these criteria are often at odds. Top-down design, for example, which we saw as a technique favoring decomposability, tends to produce modules that are *not* easy to combine with modules coming from other sources. This is because the method suggests developing each module to fulfill a specific requirement, corresponding to a subproblem obtained at some point in the refinement process. Such modules tend to be closely linked to the immediate context that led to their development, and unfit for adaptation to other contexts. The method provides neither hints towards making modules more general than immediately required, nor any incentives to do so; it helps neither avoid nor even just detect commonalities or redundancies between modules obtained in different parts of the hierarchy.

That composability and decomposability are both part of the requirements for a modular method reflects the inevitable mix of top-down and bottom-up reasoning — a complementarity that René Descartes had already noted almost four centuries ago, as shown by the contrasting two paragraphs of the *Discourse* extract at the beginning of part B.

Modular understandability

> A method favors Modular Understandability if it helps produce software in which a human reader can understand each module without having to know the others, or, at worst, by having to examine only a few of the others.

See "ABOUT SOFTWARE MAIN-TENANCE", 1.3, page 17.

The importance of this criterion follows from its influence on the maintenance process. Most maintenance activities, whether of the noble or not-so-noble category, involve having to dig into existing software elements. A method can hardly be called modular if a reader of the software is unable to understand its elements separately.

Understandability

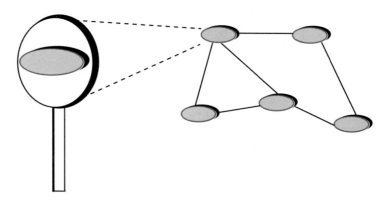

This criterion, like the others, applies to the modules of a system description at any level: analysis, design, implementation.

- *Counter-example*: *sequential dependencies*. Assume some modules have been so designed that they will only function correctly if activated in a certain prescribed order; for example, B can only work properly if you execute it after A and before C, perhaps because they are meant for use in "piped" form as in the Unix notation encountered earlier:

$$A \mid B \mid C$$

  Then it is probably hard to understand B without understanding A and C too.

In later chapters, the modular understandability criterion will help us address two important questions: how to document reusable components; and how to index reusable components so that software developers can retrieve them conveniently through queries. The criterion suggests that information about a component, useful for documentation or for retrieval, should whenever possible appear in the text of the component itself; tools for documentation, indexing or retrieval can then process the component to extract the needed pieces of information. Having the information included *in* each component is preferable to storing it elsewhere, for example in a database of information *about* components.

See also, later in this chapter, "Self-Documentation", page 54.

Modular continuity

> A method satisfies Modular Continuity if, in the software architectures that it yields, a small change in a problem specification will trigger a change of just one module, or a small number of modules.

This criterion is directly connected to the general goal of extendibility. As emphasized in an earlier chapter, change is an integral part of the software construction process. The requirements will almost inevitably change as the project progresses. Continuity means that small changes should affect individual modules in the structure of the system, rather than the structure itself.

See "Extendibility", page 6.

The term "continuity" is drawn from an analogy with the notion of a continuous function in mathematical analysis. A mathematical function is continuous if (informally) a small change in the argument will yield a proportionally small change in the result. Here the function considered is the software construction method, which you can view as a mechanism for obtaining systems from specifications:

software_construction_method: *Specification* → *System*

Continuity

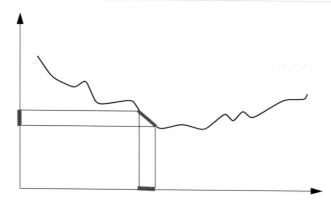

       This mathematical term only provides an analogy, since we lack formal notions of size for software. More precisely, it would be possible to define a generally acceptable measure of what constitutes a "small" or "large" change to a program; but doing the same for the specifications is more of a challenge. If we make no pretense of full rigor, however, the concepts should be intuitively clear and correspond to an essential requirement on any modular method.

This will be one of our principles of style: Symbolic Constant Principle, page 884.

- *Example 1: symbolic constants.* A sound style rule bars the instructions of a program from using any numerical or textual constant directly; instead, they rely on symbolic names, and the actual values only appear in a constant definition (**constant** in Pascal or Ada, preprocessor macros in C, *PARAMETER* in Fortran 77, constant attributes in the notation of this book). If the value changes, the only thing to update is the constant definition. This small but important rule is a wise precaution for continuity since constants, in spite of their name, are remarkably prone to change.

See "Uniform Access", page 55.

- *Example 2: the Uniform Access principle.* Another rule states that a single notation should be available to obtain the features of an object, whether they are represented as data fields or computed on demand. This property is sufficiently important to warrant a separate discussion later in this chapter.

- *Counter-example 1: using physical representations.* A method in which program designs are patterned after the physical implementation of data will yield designs that are very sensitive to slight changes in the environment.

- *Counter-example 2: static arrays.* Languages such as Fortran or standard Pascal, which do not allow the declaration of arrays whose bounds will only be known at run time, make program evolution much harder.

Modular protection

> A method satisfies Modular Protection if it yields architectures in which the effect of an abnormal condition occurring at run time in a module will remain confined to that module, or at worst will only propagate to a few neighboring modules.

The underlying issue, that of failures and errors, is central to software engineering. The errors considered here are run-time errors, resulting from hardware failures, erroneous input or exhaustion of needed resources (for example memory storage). The criterion does not address the avoidance or correction of errors, but the aspect that is directly relevant to modularity: their propagation.

The question of how to handle abnormal cases is discussed in detail in chapter 12.

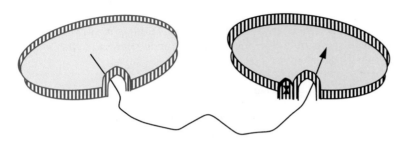

Protection violation

- *Example*: *validating input at the source*. A method requiring that you make every module that inputs data also responsible for checking their validity is good for modular protection.

More on this topic in "Assertions are not an input checking mechanism", page 345

- *Counter-example*: *undisciplined exceptions*. Languages such as PL/I, CLU, Ada, C++ and Java support the notion of exception. An exception is a special signal that may be "raised" by a certain instruction and "handled" in another, possibly remote part of the system. When the exception is raised, control is transferred to the handler. (Details of the mechanism vary between languages; Ada or CLU are more disciplined in this respect than PL/I.) Such facilities make it possible to decouple the algorithms for normal cases from the processing of erroneous cases. But they must be used carefully to avoid hindering modular protection. The chapter on exceptions will investigate how to design a disciplined exception mechanism satisfying the criterion.

On exception handling, see chapter 12.

3.2 FIVE RULES

From the preceding criteria, five rules follow which we must observe to ensure modularity:

- Direct Mapping.

- Few Interfaces.

- Small interfaces (weak coupling).

- Explicit Interfaces.

- Information Hiding.

The first rule addresses the connection between a software system and the external systems with which it is connected; the next four all address a common issue — how modules will communicate. Obtaining good modular architectures requires that communication occur in a controlled and disciplined way.

Direct Mapping

Any software system attempts to address the needs of some problem domain. If you have a good model for describing that domain, you will find it desirable to keep a clear correspondence (mapping) between the structure of the solution, as provided by the software, and the structure of the problem, as described by the model. Hence the first rule:

> The modular structure devised in the process of building a software system should remain compatible with any modular structure devised in the process of modeling the problem domain.

This advice follows in particular from two of the modularity criteria:

- Continuity: keeping a trace of the problem's modular structure in the solution's structure will make it easier to assess and limit the impact of changes.

- Decomposability: if some work has already been done to analyze the modular structure of the problem domain, it may provide a good starting point for the modular decomposition of the software.

Few Interfaces

The Few Interfaces rule restricts the overall number of communication channels between modules in a software architecture:

> Every module should communicate with as few others as possible.

Communication may occur between modules in a variety of ways. Modules may call each other (if they are procedures), share data structures etc. The Few Interfaces rule limits the number of such connections.

Types of module interconnection structures

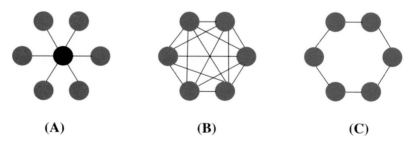

(A)   **(B)**   **(C)**

More precisely, if a system is composed of n modules, then the number of intermodule connections should remain much closer to the minimum, $n-1$, shown as **(A)** in the figure, than to the maximum, $n\,(n-1)\,/2$, shown as **(B)**.

This rule follows in particular from the criteria of continuity and protection: if there are too many relations between modules, then the effect of a change or of an error may propagate to a large number of modules. It is also connected to composability (if you want a module to be usable by itself in a new environment, then it should not depend on too many others), understandability and decomposability.

Case **(A)** on the last figure shows a way to reach the minimum number of links, $n-1$, through an extremely centralized structure: one master module; everybody else talks to it and to it only. But there are also much more "egalitarian" structures, such as **(C)** which has almost the same number of links. In this scheme, every module just talks to its two immediate neighbors, but there is no central authority. Such a style of design is a little surprising at first since it does not conform to the traditional model of functional, top-down design. But it can yield robust, extendible architectures; this is the kind of structure that object-oriented techniques, properly applied, will tend to yield.

Small Interfaces

The Small Interfaces or "Weak Coupling" rule relates to the size of intermodule connections rather than to their number:

> If two modules communicate, they should exchange as little information as possible

An electrical engineer would say that the channels of communication between modules must be of limited bandwidth:

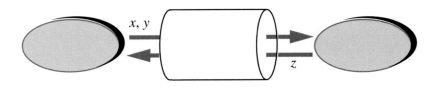

Communication bandwidth between modules

The Small Interfaces requirement follows in particular from the criteria of continuity and protection.

An extreme *counter-example* is a Fortran practice which some readers will recognize: the "garbage common block". A common block in Fortran is a directive of the form

COMMON /common_name/ variable$_1$,… variable$_n$

indicating that the variables listed are accessible not just to the enclosing module but also to any other module which includes a *COMMON* directive with the same *common_name*. It is not infrequent to see Fortran systems whose every module includes an identical gigantic *COMMON* directive, listing all significant variables and arrays so that every module may directly use every piece of data.

The problem, of course, is that every module may also misuse the common data, and hence that modules are tightly coupled to each other; the problems of modular continuity (propagation of changes) and protection (propagation of errors) are particularly nasty. This time-honored technique has nevertheless remained a favorite, no doubt accounting for many a late-night debugging session.

Developers using languages with nested structures can suffer from similar troubles. With block structure as introduced by Algol and retained in a more restricted form by Pascal, it is possible to include blocks, delimited by **begin** … **end** pairs, within other blocks. In addition every block may introduce its own variables, which are only meaningful within the syntactic scope of the block. For example:

The Body *of a block is a sequence of instructions. The syntax used here is compatible with the notation used in subsequent chapters, so it is not exactly Algol's. "--" introduces a comment.*

local-- Beginning of block B1
    x, y: *INTEGER*
do

    … Instructions of B1 …

    local -- Beginning of block B2
        z: *BOOLEAN*
    do
        … Instructions of B2 …
    end --- of block B2

    local -- Beginning of block B3
        y, z: *INTEGER*
    do
        … Instructions of *B3* …
    end -- of block B3

    … Instructions of B1 (continued) …

end -- of block B1

Variable x is accessible to all instructions throughout this extract, whereas the two variables called z (one *BOOLEAN*, the other *INTEGER*) have scopes limited to B2 and B3 respectively. Like x, variable y is declared at the level of B1, but its scope does not include B3, where another variable of the same name (and also of type *INTEGER*) locally takes precedence over the outermost y. In Pascal this form of block structure exists only for blocks associated with routines (procedures and functions).

With block structure, the equivalent of the Fortran garbage common block is the practice of declaring all variables at the topmost level. (The equivalent in C-based languages is to introduce all variables as external.)

On clusters see chapter 28. The O-O alternative to nesting is studied in "The architectural role of selective exports", page 209.

Block structure, although an ingenious idea, introduces many opportunities to violate the Small Interfaces rule. For that reason we will refrain from using it in the object-oriented notation devised later in this book, especially since the experience of Simula, an object-oriented Algol derivative supporting block structure, shows that the ability to nest classes is redundant with some of the facilities provided by inheritance. The architecture of object-oriented software will involve three levels: a system is a set of clusters; a cluster is a set of classes; a class is a set of features (attributes and routines). Clusters, an organizational tool rather than a linguistic construct, can be nested to allow a project leader to structure a large system in as many levels as necessary; but classes as well as features have a flat structure, since nesting at either of those levels would cause unnecessary complication.

Explicit Interfaces

With the fourth rule, we go one step further in enforcing a totalitarian regime upon the society of modules: not only do we demand that any conversation be limited to few participants and consist of just a few words; we also require that such conversations must be held in public and loudly!

> Whenever two modules A and B communicate, this must be obvious from the text of A or B or both.

Behind this rule stand the criteria of decomposability and composability (if you need to decompose a module into several submodules or compose it with other modules, any outside connection should be clearly visible), continuity (it should be easy to find out what elements a potential change may affect) and understandability (how can you understand A by itself if B can influence its behavior in some devious way?).

One of the problems in applying the Explicit Interfaces rule is that there is more to intermodule coupling than procedure call; data sharing, in particular, is a source of indirect coupling:

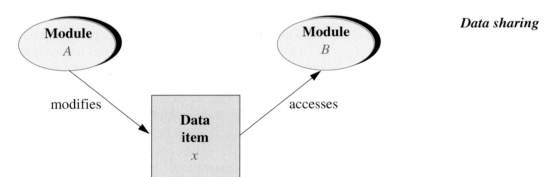

Data sharing

Assume that module A modifies and module B uses the same data item x. Then A and B are in fact strongly coupled through x even though there may be no apparent connection, such as a procedure call, between them.

Information Hiding

The rule of Information Hiding may be stated as follows:

> The designer of every module must select a subset of the module's properties as the official information about the module, to be made available to authors of client modules.

Application of this rule assumes that every module is known to the rest of the world (that is to say, to designers of other modules) through some official description, or **public** properties.

Of course, the whole text of the module itself (program text, design text) could serve as the description: it provides a correct view of the module since it *is* the module! The Information Hiding rule states that this should not in general be the case: the description should only include *some* of the module's properties. The rest should remain non-public, or **secret**. Instead of public and secret properties, one may also talk of exported and private properties. The public properties of a module are also known as the **interface** of the module (not to be confused with the user interface of a software system).

The fundamental reason behind the rule of Information Hiding is the continuity criterion. Assume a module changes, but the changes apply only to its secret elements, leaving the public ones untouched; then other modules who use it, called its *clients*, will not be affected. The smaller the public part, the higher the chances that changes to the module will indeed be in the secret part.

We may picture a module supporting Information Hiding as an iceberg; only the tip — the interface — is visible to the clients.

A module under Information Hiding

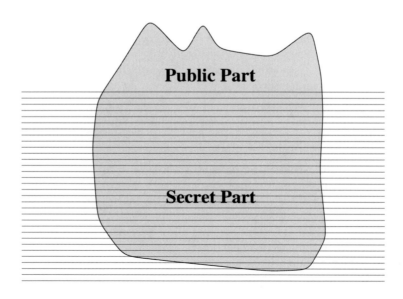

Public Part

Secret Part

As a typical example, consider a procedure for retrieving the attributes associated with a key in a certain table, such as a personnel file or the symbol table of a compiler. The procedure will internally be very different depending on how the table is stored (sequential array or file, hash table, binary or B-Tree etc.). Information hiding implies that uses of this procedure should be independent of the particular implementation chosen. That way client modules will not suffer from any change in implementation.

Information hiding emphasizes separation of function from implementation. Besides continuity, this rule is also related to the criteria of decomposability, composability and understandability. You cannot develop the modules of a system separately, combine various existing modules, or understand individual modules, unless you know precisely what each of them may and may not expect from the others.

Which properties of a module should be public, and which ones secret? As a general guideline, the public part should include the specification of the module's functionality; anything that relates to the implementation of that functionality should be kept secret, so as to preserve other modules from later reversals of implementation decisions.

This first answer is still fairly vague, however, as it does not tell us what is the specification and what is the implementation; in fact, one might be tempted to reverse the definition by stating that the specification consists of whatever public properties the module has, and the implementation of its secrets! The object-oriented approach will give us a much more precise guideline thanks to the theory of abstract data types.

See chapter 6, in particular "Abstract data types and information hiding", page 144.

To understand information hiding and apply the rule properly, it is important to avoid a common misunderstanding. In spite of its name, information hiding does not imply *protection* in the sense of security restrictions — physically prohibiting authors of client modules from accessing the internal text of a supplier module. Client authors may well be permitted to read all the details they want: preventing them from doing so may be reasonable in some circumstances, but it is a project management decision which does not necessarily follow from the information hiding rule. As a technical requirement, information hiding means that client modules (whether or not their authors are permitted to read the secret properties of suppliers) should only rely on the suppliers' public properties. More precisely, it should be impossible to write client modules whose correct functioning depends on secret information.

> In a completely formal approach to software construction, this definition would be stated as follows. To prove the correctness of a module, you will need to assume some properties about its suppliers. Information hiding means that such proofs are only permitted to rely on public properties of the suppliers, never on their secret properties.

See the comments on conditional correctness on page 4.

Consider again the example of a module providing a table searching mechanism. Some client module, which might belong to a spreadsheet program, uses a table, and relies on the table module to look for a certain element in the table. Assume further that the algorithm uses a binary search tree implementation, but that this property is secret — not part of the interface. Then you may or may not allow the author of the table searching module to tell the author of the spreadsheet program what implementation he has used for tables. This is a project management decision, or perhaps (for commercially released software) a marketing decision; in either case it is irrelevant to the question of information hiding. Information hiding means something else: that *even if the author of the spreadsheet program knows* that the implementation uses a binary search tree, he should be unable to write a client module which will only function correctly with this implementation — and would not work any more if the table implementation was changed to something else, such as hash coding.

One of the reasons for the misunderstanding mentioned above is the very term "information hiding", which tends to suggest physical protection. "Encapsulation", sometimes used as a synonym for information hiding, is probably preferable in this respect, although this discussion will retain the more common term.

By default "Ada" always means the most widespread form of the language (83), not the more recent Ada 95. Chapter 33 presents both versions.

As a summary of this discussion: the key to information hiding is not management or marketing policies as to who may or may not access the source text of a module, but strict **language rules** to define what access rights a module has on properties of its suppliers. As explained in the next chapter, "encapsulation languages" such as Ada and Modula-2 made the first steps in the right direction. Object technology will bring a more complete solution.

3.3 FIVE PRINCIPLES

From the preceding rules, and indirectly from the criteria, five principles of software construction follow:

- The Linguistic Modular Units principle.
- The Self-Documentation principle.
- The Uniform Access principle.
- The Open-Closed principle.
- The Single Choice principle.

Linguistic Modular Units

The Linguistic Modular Units principle expresses that the formalism used to describe software at various levels (specifications, designs, implementations) must support the view of modularity retained:

> **Linguistic Modular Units principle**
>
> Modules must correspond to syntactic units in the language used.

The language mentioned may be a programming language, a design language, a specification language etc. In the case of programming languages, modules should be separately compilable.

What this principle excludes at any level — analysis, design, implementation — is combining a method that suggests a certain module concept and a language that does not offer the corresponding modular construct, forcing software developers to perform manual translation or restructuring. It is indeed not uncommon to see companies hoping to apply certain methodological concepts (such as modules in the Ada sense, or object-oriented principles) but then implement the result in a programming language such as Pascal or C which does not support them. Such an approach defeats several of the modularity criteria:

- Continuity: if module boundaries in the final text do not correspond to the logical decomposition of the specification or design, it will be difficult or impossible to maintain consistency between the various levels when the system evolves. A change of the specification may be considered small if it affects only a small number of specification modules; to ensure continuity, there must be a direct correspondence between specification, design and implementation modules.

- Direct Mapping: to maintain a clear correspondence between the structure of the model and the structure of the solution, you must have a clear syntactical identification of the conceptual units on both sides, reflecting the division suggested by your development method.

- Decomposability: to divide system development into separate tasks, you need to make sure that every task results in a well-delimited syntactic unit; at the implementation stage, these units must be separately compilable.

- Composability: how could we combine anything other than modules with unambiguous syntactic boundaries?

- Protection: you can only hope to control the scope of errors if modules are syntactically delimited.

Self-Documentation

Like the rule of Information Hiding, the Self-Documentation principle governs how we should document modules:

Self-Documentation principle

The designer of a module should strive to make all information about the module part of the module itself.

What this precludes is the common situation in which information about the module is kept in separate project documents.

> The documentation under review here is **internal** documentation about components of the software, not **user** documentation about the resulting product, which may require separate products, whether paper, CD-ROM or Web pages — although, as noted in the discussion of software quality, one may see in the modern trend towards providing more and more on-line help a consequence of the same general idea.

"About documen-tation", page 14.

The most obvious justification for the Self-Documentation principle is the criterion of modular understandability. Perhaps more important, however, is the role of this principle in helping to meet the continuity criterion. If the software and its documentation are treated as separate entities, it is difficult to guarantee that they will remain compatible — "in sync" — when things start changing. Keeping everything at the same place, although not a guarantee, is a good way to help maintain this compatibility.

Innocuous as this principle may seem at first, it goes against much of what the software engineering literature has usually suggested as good software development practices. The dominant view is that software developers, to deserve the title of software engineers, need to do what other engineers are supposed to: produce a kilogram of paper for every gram of actual deliverable. The encouragement to keep a record of the software construction process is good advice — but not the implication that software and its documentation are different products.

Such an approach ignores the specific property of software, which again and again comes back in this discussion: its changeability. If you treat the two products as separate, you risk finding yourself quickly in a situation where the documentation says one thing and the software does something else. If there is any worse situation than having no documentation, it must be having wrong documentation.

> A major advance of the past few years has been the appearance of *quality standards* for software, such as ISO certification, the "2167" standard and its successors from the US Department of Defense, and the Capability Maturity Model of the Software Engineering Institute. Perhaps because they often sprang out of models from other disciplines, they tend to specify a heavy paper trail. Several of these standards could have a stronger effect on software quality (beyond providing a mechanism for managers to cover their bases in case of later trouble) by enforcing the Self-Documentation principle.

"Using assertions for documentation: the short form of a class", page 389. See also chapter 23 and its last two exercises.

This book will draw on the Self-Documentation principle to define a method for documenting classes — the modules of object-oriented software construction — that includes the documentation of every module in the module itself. Not that the module *is* its documentation: there is usually too much detail in the software text to make it suitable as documentation (this was the argument for information hiding). Instead, the module should *contain* its documentation.

In this approach software becomes a single product that supports multiple **views**. One view, suitable for compilation and execution, is the full source code. Another is the abstract interface documentation of each module, enabling software developers to write client modules without having to learn the module's own internals, in accordance with the rule of Information Hiding. Other views are possible.

We will need to remember this rule when we examine the question of how to document the classes of object-oriented software construction.

Uniform Access

Also known as the Uniform Reference principle.

Although it may at first appear just to address a notational issue, the Uniform Access principle is in fact a design rule which influences many aspects of object-oriented design and the supporting notation. It follows from the Continuity criterion; you may also view it as a special case of Information Hiding.

Let x be a name used to access a certain data item (what will later be called an object) and f the name of a feature applicable to x. (A feature is an operation; this terminology will also be defined more precisely.) For example, x might be a variable representing a bank account, and f the feature that yields an account's current balance. Uniform Access addresses the question of how to express the result of applying f to x, using a notation that does not make any premature commitment as to how f is implemented.

In most design and programming languages, the expression denoting the application of f to x depends on what implementation the original software developer has chosen for feature f: is the value stored along with x, or must it be computed whenever requested? Both techniques are possible in the example of accounts and their balances:

A1 • You may represent the balance as one of the fields of the record describing each account, as shown in the figure. With this technique, every operation that changes the balance must take care of updating the *balance* field.

A2 • Or you may define a function which computes the balance using other fields of the record, for example fields representing the lists of withdrawals and deposits. With this technique the balance of an account is not stored (there is no *balance* field) but computed on demand.

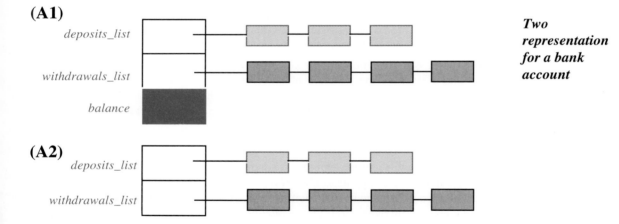

(A1)

deposits_list

withdrawals_list

balance

(A2)

deposits_list

withdrawals_list

Two representation for a bank account

A common notation, in languages such as Pascal, Ada, C, C++ and Java, uses $x \cdot f$ in case A1 and $f(x)$ in case A2.

Choosing between representations A1 and A2 is a space-time tradeoff: one economizes on computation, the other on storage. The resolution of this tradeoff in favor of one of the solutions is typical of representation decisions that developers often reverse at least once during a project's lifetime. So for continuity's sake it is desirable to have a feature access notation that does not distinguish between the two cases; then if you are in charge of x's implementation and change your mind at some stage, it will not be necessary to change the modules that use f. This is an example of the Uniform Access principle.

In its general form the principle may be expressed as:

> ## Uniform Access principle
>
> All services offered by a module should be available through a uniform notation, which does not betray whether they are implemented through storage or through computation.

Few languages satisfy this principle. An older one that did was Algol W, where both the function call and the access to a field were written $a\ (x)$. Object-oriented languages should satisfy Uniform Access, as did the first of them, Simula 67, whose notation is $x.f$ in both cases. The notation developed in part C will retain this convention.

The Open-Closed principle

Another requirement that any modular decomposition technique must satisfy is the Open-Closed principle:

> ## Open-Closed principle
>
> Modules should be both open and closed.

The contradiction between the two terms is only apparent as they correspond to goals of a different nature:

- A module is said to be open if it is still available for extension. For example, it should be possible to expand its set of operations or add fields to its data structures.

- A module is said to be closed if it is available for use by other modules. This assumes that the module has been given a well-defined, stable description (its interface in the sense of information hiding). At the implementation level, closure for a module also implies that you may compile it, perhaps store it in a library, and make it available for others (its *clients*) to use. In the case of a design or specification module, closing a module simply means having it approved by management, adding it to the project's official repository of accepted software items (often called the project *baseline*), and publishing its interface for the benefit of other module authors.

The need for modules to be closed, and the need for them to remain open, arise for different reasons. Openness is a natural concern for software developers, as they know that it is almost impossible to foresee all the elements — data, operations — that a module will need in its lifetime; so they will wish to retain as much flexibility as possible for future changes and extensions. But it is just as necessary to close modules, especially from a project manager's viewpoint: in a system comprising many modules, most will depend on some others; a user interface module may depend on a parsing module (for parsing command texts) and on a graphics module, the parsing module itself may depend on a lexical analysis module, and so on. If we never closed a module until we were sure it includes all the needed features, no multi-module software would ever reach completion: every developer would always be waiting for the completion of someone else's job.

With traditional techniques, the two goals are incompatible. Either you keep a module open, and others cannot use it yet; or you close it, and any change or extension can trigger a painful chain reaction of changes in many other modules, which relied on the original module directly or indirectly.

The two figures below illustrate a typical situation where the needs for open and closed modules are hard to reconcile. In the first figure, module A is used by client modules B, C, D, which may themselves have their own clients (E, F, ...).

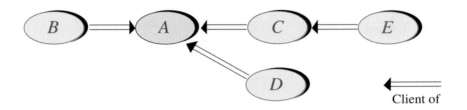

A module and its clients

Later on, however, the situation is disrupted by the arrival of new clients — B' and others — which need an extended or adapted version of A, which we may call A':

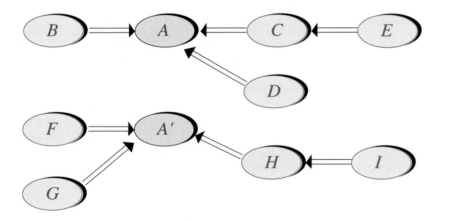

Old and new clients

With non-O-O methods, there seem to be only two solutions, equally unsatisfactory:

N1 • You may adapt module A so that it will offer the extended or modified functionality (A') required by the new clients.

N2 • You may also decide to leave A as it is, make a copy, change the module's name to A' in the copy, and perform all the necessary adaptations on the new module. With this technique A' retains no further connection to A.

The potential for disaster with solution N1 is obvious. A may have been around for a long time and have many clients such as B, C and D. The adaptations needed to satisfy the new clients' requirements may invalidate the assumptions on the basis of which the old ones used A; if so the change to A may start a dramatic series of changes in clients, clients of clients and so on. For the project manager, this is a nightmare come true: suddenly, entire parts of the software that were supposed to have been finished and sealed off ages ago get reopened, triggering a new cycle of development, testing, debugging and documentation. If many a software project manager has the impression of living the Sisyphus syndrome — the impression of being sentenced forever to carry a rock to the top of the hill, only to see it roll back down each time — it is for a large part because of the problems caused by this need to reopen previously closed modules.

On the surface, solution N2 seems better: it avoids the Sisyphus syndrome since it does not require modifying any existing software (anything in the top half of the last figure). But in fact this solution may be even more catastrophic since it only postpones the day of reckoning. If you extrapolate its effects to many modules, many modification requests and a long period, the consequences are appalling: an explosion of variants of the original modules, many of them very similar to each other although never quite identical.

In many organizations, this abundance of modules, not matched by abundance of available functionality (many of the apparent variants being in fact quasi-clones), creates a huge *configuration management* problem, which people attempt to address through the use of complex tools. Useful as these tools may be, they offer a cure in an area where the first concern should be prevention. Better avoid redundancy than manage it.

Exercise E3.6, page 66, asks you to discuss how much need will remain for configuration management in an O-O context.

Configuration management will remain useful, of course, if only to find the modules which must be reopened after a change, and to avoid unneeded module recompilations.

But how can we have modules that are both open and closed? How can we keep A and everything in the top part of the figure unchanged, while providing A' to the bottom clients, and avoiding duplication of software? The object-oriented method will offer a particularly elegant contribution thanks to inheritance.

The detailed study of inheritance appears in later chapters, but here is a preview of the basic idea. To get us out of the *change or redo* dilemma, inheritance will allow us to define a new module A' in terms of an existing module A by stating the differences only. We will write A' as

class A' **inherit**

    A **redefine** f, g, ... **end**

feature

    f **is** ...

    g **is** ...

    ...

    u **is** ...

    ...

end

where the **feature** clause contains both the definition of the new features specific to A', such as u, and the redefinition of those features (such as f, g, ...) whose form in A' is different from the one they had in A.

The pictorial representation for inheritance will use an arrow from the heir (the new class, here A') to the parent (here A):

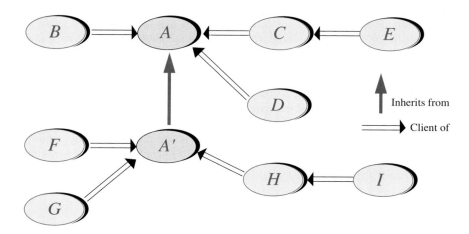

Adapting a module to new clients

Thanks to inheritance, O-O developers can adopt a much more incremental approach to software development than used to be possible with earlier methods.

One way to describe the open-closed principle and the consequent object-oriented techniques is to think of them as a *organized hacking*. "Hacking" is understood here as a slipshod approach to building and modifying code (not in the more recent sense of breaking into computer networks, which, organized or not, no one should condone). The hacker may seem bad but often his heart is pure. He sees a useful piece of software, which is *almost* able to address the needs of the moment, more general than the software's original purpose. Spurred by a laudable desire not to redo what can be reused, our hacker starts modifying the original to add provisions for new cases. The impulse is good but the effect is often to pollute the software with many clauses of the form **if** *that_special_case* **then**..., so that after a few rounds of hacking, perhaps by a few different hackers, the software starts resembling a chunk of Swiss cheese that has been left outside for too long in August (if the tastelessness of this metaphor may be forgiven on the grounds that it does its best to convey the presence in such software of both holes and growth).

The organized form of hacking will enable us to cater to the variants without affecting the consistency of the original version.

A word of caution: nothing in this discussion suggests *dis*organized hacking. In particular:

- If you have control over the original software and can rewrite it so that it will address the needs of several kinds of client at no extra complication, you should do so.

- Neither the Open-Closed principle nor redefinition in inheritance is a way to address design flaws, let alone bugs. *If there is something wrong with a module, you should fix it* — not leave the original as it is and try to correct the problem in a derived module. (The only potential exception to this rule is the case of flawed software which you are not at liberty to modify.) The Open-Closed principle and associated techniques are intended for the adaptation of healthy modules: modules that, although they may not suffice for some new uses, meet their own well-defined requirements, to the satisfaction of their own clients.

Single Choice

The last of the five modularity principles may be viewed as a consequence of both the Open-Closed and Information Hiding rules.

Before examining the Single Choice principle in its full generality, let us look at a typical example. Assume you are building a system to manage a library (in the non-software sense of the term: a collection of books and other publications, not software modules). The system will manipulate data structures representing publications. You may have declared the corresponding type as follows in Pascal-Ada syntax:

> **type** *PUBLICATION* =
>   **record**
>   *author, title*: *STRING*;
>   *publication_year*: *INTEGER*
>   **case** *pubtype*: (*book, journal, conference_proceedings*) **of**
>   *book*: (*publisher*: *STRING*);
>   *journal*: (*volume, issue*: *STRING*);
>   *proceedings*: (*editor, place*: *STRING*)   -- Conference proceedings
>   **end**

This particular form uses the Pascal-Ada notion of "record type with variants" to describe sets of data structures with some fields (here *author, title, publication_year*) common to all instances, and others specific to individual variants.

> The use of a particular syntax is not crucial here; Algol 68 and C provide an equivalent mechanism through the notion of union type. A union type is a type *T* defined as the union of pre-existing types *A*, *B*, …: a value of type *T* is either a value of type *A*, or a value of type *B*, … Record types with variants have the advantage of clearly associating a tag, here *book, journal, conference_proceedings*, with each variant.

Let *A* be the module that contains the above declaration or its equivalent using another mechanism. As long as *A* is considered open, you may add fields or introduce new variants. To enable *A* to have clients, however, you must close the module; this means that you implicitly consider that you have listed all the relevant fields and variants. Let *B* be a typical client of *A*. *B* will manipulate publications through a variable such as

> *p*: *PUBLICATION*

and, to do just about anything useful with p, will need to discriminate explicitly between the various cases, as in:

    case p **of**

        book: ... Instructions which may access the field $p.publisher$ ...

        journal: ... Instructions which may access fields $p.volume, p.issue$ ...

        proceedings: ... Instructions which may access fields $p.editor, p.place$ ...

    end

The **case** instruction of Pascal and Ada comes in handy here; it is of course on purpose that its syntax mirrors the form of the declaration of a record type with variants. Fortran and C will emulate the effect through multi-target goto instructions (**switch** in C). In these and other languages a multi-branch conditional instruction (**if** ... **then** ... **elseif** ... **elseif** ... **else** ... **end**) will also do the job.

Aside from syntactic variants, the principal observation is that to perform such a discrimination every client must know the exact list of variants of the notion of publication supported by A. The consequence is easy to foresee. Sooner or later, you will realize the need for a new variant, such as technical reports of companies and universities. Then you will have to extend the definition of type *PUBLICATION* in module A to support the new case. Fair enough: you have modified the conceptual notion of publication, so you should update the corresponding type declaration. This change is logical and inevitable. Far harder to justify, however, is the other consequence: any client of A, such as B, will also require updating if it used a structure such as the above, relying on an explicit list of cases for p. This may, as we have seen, be the case for most clients.

What we observe here is a disastrous situation for software change and evolution: a simple and natural addition may cause a chain reaction of changes across many client modules.

The issue will arise whenever a certain notion admits a number of variants. Here the notion was "publication" and its initial variants were book, journal article, conference proceedings; other typical examples include:

- In a graphics system: the notion of figure, with such variants as polygon, circle, ellipse, segment and other basic figure types.

- In a text editor: the notion of user command, with such variants as line insertion, line deletion, character deletion, global replacement of a word by another.

- In a compiler for a programming language, the notion of language construct, with such variants as instruction, expression, procedure.

In any such case, we must accept the possibility that the list of variants, although fixed and known at some point of the software's evolution, may later be changed by the addition or removal of variants. To support our long-term, software engineering view of the software construction process, we must find a way to **protect** the software's structure against the effects of such changes. Hence the Single Choice principle:

Single Choice principle
Whenever a software system must support a set of alternatives, one and only one module in the system should know their exhaustive list.

By requiring that knowledge of the list of choices be confined to just one module, we prepare the scene for later changes: if variants are added, we will only have to update the module which has the information — the point of single choice. All others, in particular its clients, will be able to continue their business as usual.

See "DYNAMIC BINDING", 14.4, page 480.

Once again, as the publications example shows, traditional methods do not provide a solution; once again, object technology will show the way, here thanks to two techniques connected with inheritance: polymorphism and dynamic binding. No sneak preview in this case, however; these techniques must be understood in the context of the full method.

The Single Choice principle prompts a few more comments:

- The number of modules that know the list of choices should be, according to the principle, exactly one. The modularity goals suggest that we want *at most one* module to have this knowledge; but then it is also clear that *at least one* module must possess it. You cannot write an editor unless at least one component of the system has the list of all supported commands, or a graphics system unless at least one component has the list of all supported figure types, or a Pascal compiler unless at least one component "knows" the list of Pascal constructs.

- Like many of the other rules and principles studied in this chapter, the principle is about **distribution of knowledge** in a software system. This question is indeed crucial to the search for extendible, reusable software. To obtain solid, durable system architectures you must take stringent steps to limit the amount of information available to each module. By analogy with the methods employed by certain human organizations, we may call this a **need-to-know** policy: barring every module from accessing any information that is not strictly required for its proper functioning.

See the second figure on page 58.

- You may view the Single Choice principle as a direct consequence of the Open-Closed principle. Consider the publications example in light of the figure that illustrated the need for open-closed modules: A is the module which includes the original declaration of type $PUBLICATION$; the clients $B, C, \ldots$ are the modules that relied on the initial list of variants; A' is the updated version of A offering an extra variant (technical reports).

- You may also understand the principle as a strong form of Information Hiding. The designer of supplier modules such as A and A' seeks to hide information (regarding the precise list of variants available for a certain notion) from the clients.

3.4 KEY CONCEPTS INTRODUCED IN THIS CHAPTER

- The choice of a proper module structure is the key to achieving the aims of reusability and extendibility.

- Modules serve for both software decomposition (the top-down view) and software composition (bottom-up).

- Modular concepts apply to specification and design as well as implementation.

- A comprehensive definition of modularity must combine several perspectives; the various requirements may sometimes appear at odds with each other, as with decomposability (which encourages top-down methods) and composability (which favors a bottom-up approach).

- Controlling the amount and form of communication between modules is a fundamental step in producing a good modular architecture.

- The long-term integrity of modular system structures requires information hiding, which enforces a rigorous separation of interface and implementation.

- Uniform access frees clients from internal representation choices in their suppliers.

- A closed module is one that may be used, through its interface, by client modules.

- An open module is one that is still subject to extension.

- Effective project management requires support for modules that are both open and closed. But traditional approaches to design and programming do not permit this.

- The principle of Single Choice directs us to limit the dissemination of exhaustive knowledge about variants of a certain notion.

3.5 BIBLIOGRAPHICAL NOTES

The design method known as "structured design" [Yourdon 1979] emphasized the importance of modular structures. It was based on an analysis of module "cohesion" and "coupling". But the view of modules implicit in structured design was influenced by the traditional notion of subroutine, which limits the scope of the discussion.

The principle of uniform access comes originally (under the name "uniform reference") from [Geschke 1975].

The discussion of uniform access cited the Algol W language, a successor to Algol 60 and forerunner to Pascal (but offering some interesting mechanisms not retained in Pascal), designed by Wirth and Hoare and described in [Hoare 1966].

Information hiding was introduced in two milestone articles by David Parnas [Parnas 1972] [Parnas 1972a].

Configuration management tools that will recompile the modules affected by modifications in other modules, based on an explicit list of module dependencies, are based on the ideas of the Make tool, originally for Unix [Feldman 1979]. Recent tools — there are many on the market — have added considerable functionality to the basic ideas.

Some of the exercises below ask you to develop metrics to evaluate quantitatively the various informal measures of modularity developed in this chapter. For some results in O-O metrics, see the work of Christine Mingins [Mingins 1993] [Mingins 1995] and Brian Henderson-Sellers [Henderson-Sellers 1996a].

EXERCISES

E3.1 Modularity in programming languages

Examine the modular structures of any programming language which you know well and assess how they support the criteria and principles developed in this chapter.

E3.2 The Open-Closed principle (for Lisp programmers)

Many Lisp implementations associate functions with function names at run time rather than statically. Does this feature make Lisp more supportive of the Open-Closed principle than more static languages?

E3.3 Limits to information hiding

Can you think of circumstances where information hiding should *not* be applied to relations between modules?

E3.4 Metrics for modularity (term project)

The criteria, rules and principles of modularity of this chapter were all introduced through qualitative definitions. Some of them, however, may be amenable to quantitative analysis. The possible candidates include:

- Modular continuity.
- Few Interfaces.
- Small Interfaces.
- Explicit Interfaces.
- Information Hiding.
- Single Choice.

Explore the possibility of developing modularity metrics to evaluate how modular a software architecture is according to some of these viewpoints. The metrics should be size-independent: increasing the size of a system without changing its modular structure should not change its complexity measures. (See also the next exercise.)

E3.5 Modularity of existing systems

Apply the modularity criteria, rules and principles of this chapter to evaluate a system to which you have access. If you have answered the previous exercise, apply any proposed modularity metric.

Can you draw any correlations between the results of this analysis (qualitative, quantitative or both) and assessments of structural complexity for the systems under study, based either on informal analysis or, if available, on actual measurements of debugging and maintenance costs?

E3.6 Configuration management and inheritance

(This exercise assumes knowledge of inheritance techniques described in the rest of this book. It is not applicable if you have read this chapter as part of a first, sequential reading of the book.)

The discussion of the open-closed principle indicated that in non-object-oriented approaches the absence of inheritance places undue burden on configuration management tools, since the desire to avoid reopening closed modules may lead to the creation of too many module variants. Discuss what role remains for configuration management in an object-oriented environment where inheritance *is* present, and more generally how the use of object technology affects the problem of configuration management.

If you are familiar with specific configuration management tools, discuss how they interact with inheritance and other principles of O-O development.

4

Approaches to reusability

" Follow the lead of hardware design! It is not right that every new development should start from scratch. There should be catalogs of software modules, as there are catalogs of VLSI devices: when we build a new system, we should be ordering components from these catalogs and combining them, rather than reinventing the wheel every time. We would write less software, and perhaps do a better job at that which we do get to write. Wouldn't then some of the problems that everybody complains about — the high costs, the overruns, the lack of reliability — just go away? Why is it not so?"

You have probably heard remarks of this kind; perhaps you have uttered them yourself. As early as 1968, at the now famous NATO conference on software engineering, Doug McIlroy was advocating "*mass-produced software components*". Reusability, as a dream, is not new.

It would be absurd to deny that some reuse occurs in software development. In fact one of the most impressive developments in the industry since the first edition of this book was published in 1988 has been the gradual emergence of reusable components, often modest individually but regularly gaining ground; they range from small modules meant to work with Microsoft's Visual Basic (VBX) and OLE 2 (OCX, now ActiveX) to full libraries, also known as "frameworks", for object-oriented environments.

Another exciting development is the growth of the Internet: the advent of a wired society has eased or in some cases removed some of the logistic obstacles to reuse which, only a few years ago, might have appeared almost insurmountable.

But this is only a beginning. We are far from McIlroy's vision of turning software development into a component-based industry. The techniques of object-oriented software construction make it possible for the first time to envision a state of the discipline, in the not too distant future, in which this vision will have become the reality, for the greatest benefit not just of software developers but, more importantly, of those who need their products — quickly, and at a high level of quality.

In this chapter we will explore some of the issues that must be addressed for reusability to succeed on such a large scale. The resulting concepts will guide the discussion of object-oriented techniques throughout the rest of this book.

4.1 THE GOALS OF REUSABILITY

We should first understand why it is so important to improve software reusability. No need here for "motherhood and apple pie" arguments: as we will see, the most commonly touted benefits are not necessarily the most significant; by going beyond the obvious we can make sure that our quest for reuse will pursue the right targets, avoid mirages, and yield the highest return on our investment.

Expected benefits

From more reusable software you may expect improvements on the following fronts:

- **Timeliness** (in the sense defined in the discussion of software quality factors: speed of bringing projects to completion and products to market). By relying on existing components we have *less* software to develop and hence can build it faster.

- **Decreased maintenance effort**. If someone else is responsible for the software, that someone is also responsible for its future evolutions. This avoids the *competent developer's paradox*: the more you work, the more work you create for yourself as users of your products start asking you for new functionalities, ports to new platforms etc. (Other than relying on someone else to do the job, or retiring, the only solution to the competent software developer's paradox is to become an *in*competent developer so that no one is interested in your products any more — not a solution promoted by this book.)

- **Reliability**. By relying on components from a reputed source, you have the guarantee, or at least the expectation, that their authors will have applied all the required care, including extensive testing and other validation techniques; not to mention the expectation, in most cases, that many other application developers will have had the opportunity to try these components before you, and to come across any remaining bugs. The assumption here is not necessarily that the component developers are any smarter than you are; simply that the components they build — be they graphics modules, database interfaces, sorting algorithms ... — are *their* official assignment, whereas for you they might just be a necessary but secondary chore for the attainment of *your* official goal of building an application system in your own area of development.

- **Efficiency**. The same factors that favor reusability incite the component developers to use the best possible algorithms and data structures known in their field of specialization, whereas in a large application project you can hardly expect to have an expert on board for *every* field touched on by the development. (Most people, when they think of the connection between reusability and efficiency, tend to see the reverse effect: the loss of fine-tuned optimizations that results from using general solutions. But this is a narrow view of efficiency: in a large project, you cannot realistically perform such optimizations on every piece of the development. You can, however, aim at the best possible solutions in your group's areas of excellence, and for the rest rely on someone else's expertise.)

This section is based on the more extensive discussion of management aspects of reuse in the book "Object Success" [M 1995].

- **Consistency**. There is no good library without a strict emphasis on regular, coherent design. If you start using such a library — in particular some of the best current object-oriented libraries — its style will start to influence, through a natural process of osmosis, the style of the software that you develop. This is a great boost to the quality of the software produced by an application group.

- **Investment**. Making software reusable is a way to preserve the know-how and inventions of the best developers; to turn a fragile resource into a permanent asset.

Many people, when they accept reusability as desirable, think only of the first argument on this list, improving productivity. But it is not necessarily the most important contribution of a reuse-based software process. The reliability benefit, for example, is just as significant. It is extremely difficult to build guaranteeably reusable software if every new development must independently validate every single piece of a possibly huge construction. By relying on components produced, in each area, by the best experts around, we can at last hope to build systems that we trust, because instead of redoing what thousands have done before us — and, most likely, running again into the mistakes that they made — we will concentrate on enforcing the reliability of our truly new contributions.

This argument does not just apply to reliability. The comment on efficiency was based on the same reasoning. In this respect we can see reusability as standing apart from the other quality factors studied in chapter 1: by enhancing it you have the potential of enhancing **almost all** of the other qualities. The reason is economic: if, instead of being developed for just one project, a software element has the potential of serving again and again for many projects, it becomes economically attractive to submit it to the best possible quality-enhancing techniques — such as formal verification, usually too demanding to be cost-effective for most projects but the most mission-critical ones, or extensive optimization, which in ordinary circumstances can often be dismissed as undue perfectionism. For reusable components, the reasoning changes dramatically; improve just one element, and thousands of developments may benefit.

This reasoning is of course not completely new; it is in part the transposition to software of ideas that have fundamentally affected other disciplines when they turned from individual craftsmanship to mass-production industry. A VLSI chip is more expensive to build than a run-of-the-mill special-purpose circuit, but if well done it will show up in countless systems and benefit their quality because of all the design work that went into it once and for all.

Reuse consumers, reuse producers

If you examined carefully the preceding list of arguments for reusability, you may have noted that it involves benefits of two kinds. The first four are benefits you will derive from basing your application developments on existing reusable components; the last one, from making your *own* software reusable. The next-to-last (consistency) is a little of both.

This distinction reflects the two aspects of reusability: the **consumer view**, enjoyed by application developers who can rely on components; and the **producer view**, available to groups that build reusability into their own developments.

In discussing reusability and reusability policies you should always make sure which one of these two views you have in mind. In particular, if your organization is new to reuse, remember that it is essentially impossible to start as a reuse producer. One often meets managers who think they can make development reusable overnight, and decree that no development shall henceforth be specific. (Often the injunction is to start developing "business objects" capturing the company's application expertise, and ignore general-purpose components — algorithms, data structures, graphics, windowing and the like — since they are considered too "low-level" to yield the real benefits of reuse.) This is absurd: developing reusable components is a challenging discipline; the only known way to learn is to start by using, studying and imitating good existing components. Such an approach will yield immediate benefits as your developments will take advantage of these components, and it will start you, should you persist in your decision to become a producer too, on the right learning path.

> ### Reuse Path principle
>
> Be a reuse consumer before you try to be a reuse producer.

Here too "Object Success" explores the policy issues further.

4.2 WHAT SHOULD WE REUSE?

Convincing ourselves that Reusability Is Good was the easy part (although we needed to clarify *what* is really good about it). Now for the real challenge: how in the world are we going to get it?

The first question to ask is what exactly we should expect to reuse among the various levels that have been proposed and applied: reuse of personnel, of specifications, of designs, of "patterns", of source code, of specified components, of abstracted modules.

Reuse of personnel

The most common source of reusability is the developers themselves. This form of reuse is widely practiced in the industry: by transferring software engineers from project to project, companies avoid losing know-how and ensure that previous experience benefits new developments.

This non-technical approach to reusability is obviously limited in scope, if only because of the high turnover in the software profession.

Reuse of designs and specifications

Occasionally you will encounter the argument that we should be reusing designs rather than actual software. The idea is that an organization should accumulate a repository of blueprints describing accepted design structures for the most common applications it develops. For example, a company that produces aircraft guidance systems will have a set of model designs summarizing its experience in this area; such documents describe module templates rather than actual modules.

This approach is essentially a more organized version of the previous one — reuse of know-how and experience. As the discussion of documentation has already suggested, the very notion of a design as an independent software product, having its own life separate from that of the corresponding implementation, seems dubious, since it is hard to guarantee that the design and the implementation will remain compatible throughout the evolution of a software system. So if you only reuse the design you run the risk of reusing incorrect or obsolete elements.

These comments are also applicable to a related form of reuse: reuse of specifications.

To a certain extent, one can view the progress of reusability in recent years, aided by progress in the spread of object technology and aiding it in return, as resulting in part from the downfall of the old idea, long popular in software engineering circles, that the only reuse worthy of interest is reuse of design and specification. A narrow form of that idea was the most effective obstacle to progress, since it meant that all attempts to build actual components could be dismissed as only addressing trivial needs and not touching the truly difficult aspects. It used to be the dominant view; then a combination of theoretical arguments (the arguments of object technology) and practical achievements (the appearance of successful reusable components) essentially managed to defeat it.

"Defeat" is perhaps too strong a term because, as often happens in such disputes, the result takes a little from both sides. The idea of reusing designs becomes much more interesting with an approach (such as the view of object technology developed in this book) which removes much of the gap between design and implementation. Then the difference between a module and a design for a module is one of degree, not of nature: a module design is simply a module of which some parts are not fully implemented; and a fully implemented module can also serve, thanks to abstraction tools, as a module design. With this approach the distinction between reusing modules (as discussed below) and reusing designs tends to fade away.

Design patterns

In the mid-nineteen-nineties the idea of *design patterns* started to attract considerable attention in object-oriented circles. Design patterns are architectural ideas applicable across a broad range of application domains; each pattern makes it possible to build a solution to a certain design issue.

Chapter 21 discusses the undoing pattern.

Here is a typical example, discussed in detail in a later chapter. The *issue*: how to provide an interactive system with a mechanism enabling its users to undo a previously executed command if they decide it was not appropriate, and to reexecute an undone command if they change their mind again. The *pattern*: use a class *COMMAND* with a precise structure (which we will study) and an associated "history list". We will encounter many other design patterns.

[Gamma 1995]; *see also* [Pree 1994].

One of the reasons for the success of the design pattern idea is that it was more than an idea: the book that introduced the concept, and others that have followed, came with a catalog of directly applicable patterns which readers could learn and apply.

Design patterns have already made an important contribution to the development of object technology, and as new ones continue to be published they will help developers to benefit from the experience of their elders and peers. How can the general idea contribute to reuse? Design patterns should not encourage a throwback to the *"all that counts is design reuse"* attitude mentioned earlier. A pattern that is *only* a book pattern, however elegant and general, is a pedagogical tool, not a reuse tool; after all, computing science students have for three decades been learning from their textbooks about relational query optimization, Gouraud shading, AVL trees, Hoare's Quicksort and Dijkstra's shortest path algorithm without anyone claiming that these techniques were breakthroughs in reusability. In a sense, the patterns developed in the past few years are only incremental additions to the software professional's bag of standard tricks. In this view the new contribution is the patterns themselves, not the idea of pattern.

As most people who have looked carefully at the pattern work have recognized, such a view is too limited. There seems to be in the very notion of pattern a truly new contribution, even if it has not been fully understood yet. To go beyond their mere pedagogical value, patterns must go further. A successful pattern cannot just be a book description: it must be a **software component**, or a set of components. This goal may seem remote at first because many of the patterns are so general and abstract as to seem impossible to capture in actual software modules; but here the object-oriented method provides a radical contribution. Unlike earlier approaches, it will enable us to build reusable modules that still have replaceable, not completely frozen elements: modules that serve as general schemes (*patterns* is indeed the appropriate word) and can be adapted to various specific situations. This is the notion of *behavior class* (a more picturesque term is *programs with holes*); it is based on O-O techniques that we will study in later chapters, in particular the notion of deferred class. Combine this with the idea of groups of components intended to work together — often known as *frameworks* or more simply as *libraries* — and you get a remarkable way of reconciling reusability with adaptability. These techniques hold, for the pattern movement, the promise of exerting, beyond the new-bag-of-important-tricks effect, an in-depth influence on reusability practices.

See *"Programs with holes"*, page 505.

Reusability through the source code

Personnel, design and specification forms of reuse, useful as they may be, ignore a key goal of reusability. If we are to come up with the software equivalent of the reusable parts of older engineering disciplines, what we need to reuse is the actual stuff of which our products are made: executable software. None of the targets of reuse seen so far — people, designs, specifications — can qualify as the off-the-shelf components ready to be included in a new software product under development.

If what we need to reuse is software, in what form should we reuse it? The most natural answer is to use the software in its original form: source text. This approach has worked very well in some cases. Much of the Unix culture, for example, originally spread in universities and laboratories thanks to the on-line availability of the source code, enabling users to study, imitate and extend the system. This is also true of the Lisp world.

The economic and psychological impediments to source code dissemination limit the effect that this form of reuse can have in more traditional industrial environments. But a more serious limitation comes from two technical obstacles:

See also *"Formats for reusable component distribution"*, page 79 below.

- Identifying reusable software with reusable source removes information hiding. Yet no large-scale reuse is possible without a systematic effort to protect reusers from having to know the myriad details of reused elements.

- Developers of software distributed in source form may be tempted to violate modularity rules. Some parts may depend on others in a non-obvious way, violating the careful limitations which the discussion of modularity in the previous chapter imposed on inter-module communication. This often makes it difficult to reuse some elements of a complex system without having to reuse everything else.

A satisfactory form of reuse must remove these obstacles by supporting abstraction and providing a finer grain of reuse.

Reuse of abstracted modules

All the preceding approaches, although of limited applicability, highlight important aspects of the reusability problem:

- Personnel reusability is necessary if not sufficient. The best reusable components are useless without well-trained developers, who have acquired sufficient experience to recognize a situation in which existing components may provide help.

- Design reusability emphasizes the need for reusable components to be of sufficiently high conceptual level and generality — not just ready-made solutions to special problems. The classes which we will encounter in object technology may be viewed as design modules as well as implementation modules.

- Source code reusability serves as a reminder that software is in the end defined by program texts. A successful reusability policy must produce reusable program elements.

The discussion of source code reusability also helps narrow down our search for the proper units of reuse. A basic reusable component should be a software element. (From there we can of course go to *collections* of software elements.) That element should be a *module* of reasonable size, satisfying the modularity requirements of the previous chapter; in particular, its relations to other software, if any, should be severely limited to facilitate independent reuse. The information describing the module's capabilities, and serving as primary documentation for reusers or prospective reusers, should be *abstract*: rather than describing all the details of the module (as with source code), it should, in accordance with the principle of Information Hiding, highlight the properties relevant to clients.

The term **abstracted module** will serve as a name for such units of reuse, consisting of directly usable software, available to the outside world through a description which contains only a subset of each unit's properties.

The rest of part B of this book is devoted to devising the precise form of such abstracted modules; part C will then explore their properties.

More on distribution formats below.

The emphasis on abstraction, and the rejection of source code as the vehicle for reuse, do not necessarily prohibit *distributing* modules in source form. The contradiction is only apparent: what is at stake in the present discussion is not how we will deliver modules to their reusers, but what they will use as the primary source of information about them. It may be acceptable for a module to be distributed in source form but reused on the basis of an abstract interface description.

4.3 REPETITION IN SOFTWARE DEVELOPMENT

To progress in our search for the ideal abstracted module, we should take a closer look at the nature of software construction, to understand what in software is most subject to reuse.

Anyone who observes software development cannot but be impressed by its repetitive nature. Over and again, programmers weave a number of basic patterns: sorting, searching, reading, writing, comparing, traversing, allocating, synchronizing… Experienced developers know this feeling of *déjà vu*, so characteristic of their trade.

A good way to assess this situation (assuming you develop software, or direct people who do) is to answer the following question:

> *How many times over the past six months did you, or people working for you, write some program fragment for table searching?*

Table searching is defined here as the problem of finding out whether a certain element x appears in a table t of similar elements. The problem has many variants, depending on the element types, the data structure representation for t, the choice of searching algorithm.

Chances are you or your colleagues will indeed have tackled this problem one or more times. But what is truly remarkable is that — if you are like others in the profession — the program fragment handling the search operation will have been written at the lowest reasonable level of abstraction: by writing code in some programming language, rather than calling existing routines.

To an observer from outside our field, however, table searching would seem an obvious target for widely available reusable components. It is one of the most researched areas of computing science, the subject of hundreds of articles, and many books starting with volume 3 of Knuth's famous treatise. The undergraduate curriculum of all computing science departments covers the most important algorithms and data structures. Certainly not a mysterious topic. In addition:

See bibliographic references on page 99.

- It is hardly possible, as noted, to write a useful software system which does not include one or (usually) several cases of table searching. The investment needed to produce reusable modules is not hard to justify.

- As will be seen in more detail below, most searching algorithms follow a common pattern, providing what would seem to be an ideal basis for a reusable solution.

4.4 NON-TECHNICAL OBSTACLES

Why then is reuse not more common?

Most of the serious impediments to reuse are technical; removing them will be the subject of the following sections of this chapter (and of much of the rest of this book). But of course there are also some organizational, economical and political obstacles.

The NIH syndrome

An often quoted psychological obstacle to reuse is the famous Not Invented Here ("NIH") syndrome. Software developers, it is said, are individualists, who prefer to redo everything by themselves rather than rely on someone else's work.

This contention (commonly heard in managerial circles) is not borne out by experience. Software developers do not like useless work more than anyone else. When a good, well-publicized and easily accessible reusable solution is available, it gets reused.

Consider the typical case of lexical and syntactic analysis. Using parser generators such as the Lex-Yacc combination, it is much easier to produce a parser for a command language or a simple programming language than if you must program it from scratch. The result is clear: where such tools are available, competent software developers routinely reuse them. Writing your own tailor-made parser still makes sense in some cases, since the tools mentioned have their limitations. But the developers' reaction is usually to go by default to one of these tools; it is when you want to use a solution not based on the reusable mechanisms that you have to argue for it. This may in fact cause a new syndrome, the **reverse** of NIH, which we may call HIN (Habit Inhibiting Novelty): a useful but limited reusable solution, so entrenched that it narrows the developers' outlook and stifles innovation, becomes counter-productive. Try to convince some Unix developers to use a parser generator other than Yacc, and you may encounter HIN first-hand.

Something which may externally look like NIH does exist, but often it is simply the developers' understandably cautious reaction to new and unknown components. They may fear that bugs or other problems will be more difficult to correct than with a solution over which they have full control. Often such fears are justified by unfortunate earlier attempts at reusing components, especially if they followed from a management mandate to reuse at all costs, not accompanied by proper quality checks. If the new components are of good quality and provide a real service, fears will soon disappear.

What this means for the producer of reusable components is that quality is even more important here than for more ordinary forms of software. If the cost of a non-reusable, one-of-a-kind solution is N, the cost R of a solution relying on reusable components is never zero: there is a learning cost, at least the first time; developers may have to bend their software to accommodate the components; and they must write some interfacing software, however small, to call them. So even if the reusability savings

$$r = \frac{R}{N}$$

and other benefits of reuse are potentially great, you must also convince the candidate reusers that the reusable solution's quality is good enough to justify relinquishing control.

See [M 1995].

This explains why it is a mistake to target a company's reusability policy to the potential reusers (the *consumers*, that is to say the application developers). Instead you should put the heat on the *producers*, including people in charge of acquiring external components, to ensure the quality and usefulness of their offering. Preaching reuse to application developers, as some companies do by way of reusability policy, is futile: because application developers are ultimately judged by how effectively they produce their applications, they should and will reuse not because you tell them to but because you have done a good enough job with the reusable components (developed or acquired) that it will be *profitable* for their applications to rely on these components.

The economics of procurement

A potential obstacle to reuse comes from the procurement policy of many large corporations and government organizations, which tends to impede reusability efforts by focusing on short-term costs. US regulations, for example, make it hard for a government agency to pay a contractor for work that was not explicitly commissioned (normally as part of a Request For Proposals). Such rules come from a legitimate concern to protect taxpayers or shareholders, but can also discourage software builders from applying the crucial effort of *generalization* to transform good software into reusable components.

"GENERALIZA-TION", 28.5, page 928

On closer examination this obstacle does not look so insurmountable. As the concern for reusability spreads, there is nothing to prevent the commissioning agency from including in the RFP itself the requirement that the solution must be general-purpose and reusable, and the description of how candidate solutions will be evaluated against these criteria. Then the software developers can devote the proper attention to the generalization task and be paid for it.

Software companies and their strategies

Even if customers play their part in removing obstacles to reuse, a potential problem remains on the side of the contractors themselves. For a software company, there is a constant temptation to provide solutions that are purposely *not* reusable, for fear of not getting the next job from the customer — because if the result of the current job is too widely applicable the customer may not need a next job!

I once heard a remarkably candid exposé of this view after giving a talk on reuse and object technology. A high-level executive from a major software house came to tell me that, although intellectually he admired the ideas, he would never implement them in his own company, because that would be killing the goose that laid the golden egg: more than 90% of the company's business derived from renting manpower — providing analysts and programmers on assignment to customers — and the management's objective was to bring the figure to 100%. With such an outlook on software engineering, one is not likely to greet with enthusiasm the prospect of widely available libraries of reusable components.

The comment was notable for its frankness, but it triggered the obvious retort: if it is at all possible to build reusable components to replace some of the expensive services of a software house's consultants, sooner or later someone will build them. At that time a company that has refused to take this route, and is left with nothing to sell but its consultants' services, may feel sorry for having kept its head buried in the sand.

It is hard not to think here of the many engineering disciplines that used to be heavily labor-intensive but became industrialized, that is to say tool-based — with painful economic consequences for companies and countries that did not understand early enough what was happening. To a certain extent, object technology is bringing a similar change to the software trade. The choice between people and tools need not, however, be an exclusive one. The engineering part of software engineering is not identical to that of mass-production industries; humans will likely continue to play the key role in the software construction process. The aim of reuse is not to replace humans by tools (which is often, in spite of all claims, what has happened in other disciplines) but to change the distribution of what we entrust to humans and to tools. So the news is not all bad for a software company that has made its name through its consultants. In particular:

- In many cases developers using sophisticated reusable components may still benefit from the help of experts, who can advise them on how best to use the components. This leaves a meaningful role for software houses and their consultants.

- As will be discussed below, reusability is inseparable from extendibility: good reusable components will still be open for adaptation to specific cases. Consultants from a company that developed a library are in an ideal position to perform such tuning for individual customers. So selling components and selling services are not necessarily exclusive activities; a components business can serve as a basis for a service business.

- More generally, a good reusable library can play a strategic role in the policy of a successful software company, even if the company sells specific solutions rather than the library itself, and uses the library for internal purposes only. If the library covers the most common needs and provides an extendible basis for the more advanced cases, it can enable the company to gain a competitive edge in certain application areas by developing tailored solutions to customers' needs, faster and at lower cost than competitors who cannot rely on such a ready-made basis.

Accessing components

Another argument used to justify skepticism about reuse is the difficulty of the component management task: progress in the production of reusable software, it is said, would result in developers being swamped by so many components as to make their life worse than if the components were not available.

Cast in a more positive style, this comment should be understood as a warning to developers of reusable software that the best reusable components in the world are useless if nobody knows they exist, or if it takes too much time and effort to obtain them. The practical success of reusability techniques requires the development of adequate databases of components, which interested developers may search by appropriate keywords to find out quickly whether some existing component satisfies a particular need. Network services must also be available, allowing electronic ordering and immediate downloading of selected components.

These goals do raise technical and organizational problems. But we must keep things in proportion. Indexing, retrieving and delivering reusable components are engineering issues, to which we can apply known tools, in particular database technology; there is no reason why software components should be more difficult to manage than customer records, flight information or library books.

Reusability discussions used to delve forever into the grave question "how in the world are we going to make the components available to developers?". After the advances in networking of the past few years, such debates no longer appear so momentous. With the World-Wide Web, in particular, have appeared powerful search tools (AltaVista, Yahoo…) which have made it far easier to locate useful information, either on the Internet or on a company's Intranet. Even more advanced solutions (produced, one may expect, with the help of object technology) will undoubtedly follow. All this makes it increasingly clear that the really hard part of progress in reusability lies not in organizing reusable components, but in building the wretched things in the first place.

A note about component indexing

On the matter of indexing and retrieving components, a question presents itself, at the borderline between technical and organizational issues: how should we associate indexing information, such as keywords, with software components?

The Self-Documentation principle suggests that, as much as possible, information about a module — indexing information as well as other forms of module documentation — should appear in the module itself rather than externally. This leads to an important requirement on the notation that will be developed in part C of this book to write software components, called classes. Regardless of the exact form of these classes, we must equip ourselves with a mechanism to attach indexing information to each component.

"Self-Documenta-tion", page 54.

The syntax is straightforward. At the beginning of a module text, you will be invited to write an **indexing clause** of the form

indexing
      index_word1: *value, value, value…*
      index_word2: *value, value, value…*
      …
      … Normal module definition (see part C) …

More details in "In-dexing clauses", page 890.

Each *index_word* is an identifier; each *value* is a constant (integer, real etc.), an identifier, or some other basic lexical element.

There is no particular constraint on index words and values, but an industry, a standards group, an organization or a project may wish to define their own conventions. Indexing and retrieval tools can then extract this information to help software developers find components satisfying certain criteria.

As we saw in the discussion of Self-Documentation, storing such information in the module itself — rather than in an outside document or database — decreases the likelihood of including wrong information, and in particular of forgetting to update the information when updating the module (or conversely). Indexing clauses, modest as they may seem, play a major role in helping developers keep their software organized and register its properties so that others can find out about it.

Formats for reusable component distribution

Another question straddling the technical-organizational line is the form under which we should distribute reusable components: source or binary? This is a touchy issue, so we will limit ourselves to examining a few of the arguments on both sides.

"Using assertions for documentation: the short form of a class", page 389.

For a professional, for-profit software developer, it often seems desirable to provide buyers of reusable components with an interface description (the *short form* discussed in a later chapter) and the binary code for their platform of choice, but not the source form. This protects the developer's investment and trade secrets.

Binary is indeed the preferred form of distribution for commercial application programs, operating systems and other tools, including compilers, interpreters and development environments for object-oriented languages. In spite of recurring attacks on the very idea, emanating in particular from an advocacy group called the League for Programming Freedom, this mode of commercial software distribution is unlikely to recede much in the near future. But the present discussion is not about ordinary tools or application programs: it is about libraries of reusable software components. In that case one can also find some arguments in favor of source distribution.

For the component producer, an advantage of source distribution is that it eases porting efforts. You stay away from the tedious and unrewarding task of adapting software to the many incompatible platforms that exist in today's computer world, relying instead on the developers of object-oriented compilers and environments to do the job for you. (For the *consumer* this is of course a counter-argument, as installation from source will require more work and may cause unforeseen errors.)

Some compilers for object-oriented languages may let you retain some of the portability benefit without committing to full source availability: if the compiler uses C as intermediate generated code, as is often the case today, you can usually substitute portable C code for binary code. It is then not difficult to devise a tool that obscures the C form, making it almost as difficult to reverse-engineer as a binary form.

T. B. Steel: "A First Version of UNCOL", Joint Computer Conf., vol. 19, Winter 1961, pages 371-378.

Also note that at various stages in the history of software, dating back to UNCOL (UNiversal COmputing Language) in the late fifties, people have been defining low-level instruction formats that could be interpreted on any platform, and hence could provide a portable target for compilers. The ACE consortium of hardware and software companies was formed in 1988 for that purpose. Together with the Java language has come the notion of Java bytecode, for which interpreters are being developed on a number of platforms. But for the component producer such efforts at first represent more work, not less: until you have the double guarantee that the new format is available on every platform of interest *and* that it executes target code as fast as platform-specific solutions, you cannot forsake the old technology, and must simply add the new target code format to those you already support. So a solution that is advertised as an end-all to all portability problems actually creates, in the short term, more portability problems.

ISE's compilers use both C generation and bytecode generation.

Perhaps more significant, as an argument for source code distribution, is the observation that attempts to protect invention and trade secrets by removing the source form of the implementation may be of limited benefit anyway. Much of the hard work in the construction of a good reusable library lies not in the implementation but in the design of the components' interfaces; and that is the part that you are bound to release anyway. This is particularly clear in the world of data structures and algorithms, where most of the necessary techniques are available in the computing science literature. To design a successful library, you must embed these techniques in modules whose interface will make them useful to the developers of many different applications. This interface design is part of what you must release to the world.

Also note that, in the case of object-oriented modules, there are two forms of component reuse: as a client or, as studied in later chapters, through inheritance. The second form combines reuse with adaptation. Interface descriptions (short forms) are sufficient for client reuse, but not always for inheritance reuse.

Finally, the educational side: distributing the source of library modules is a good way to provide models of the producer's best engineering, useful to encourage consumers to develop their own software in a consistent style. We saw earlier that the resulting standardization is one of the benefits of reusability. Some of it will remain even if client developers only have access to the interfaces; but nothing beats having the full text.

The chapter on teaching object technology develops this point in "Apprenticeship", page 944.

Be sure to note that even if source is available it should not serve as the primary documentation tool: for that role, we continue to use the module interface.

This discussion has touched on some delicate economic issues, which condition in part the advent of an industry of software components and, more generally, the progress of the software field. How do we provide developers with a fair reward for their efforts and an acceptable degree of protection for their inventions, without hampering the legitimate interests of users? Here are two opposite views:

- At one end of the spectrum you will find the positions of the League for Programming Freedom: all software should be free and available in source form.

See the bibliographical notes.

- At the other end you have the idea of *superdistribution*, advocated by Brad Cox in several articles and a book. Superdistribution would allow users to duplicate software freely, charging them not for the purchase but instead for each use. Imagine a little counter attached to each software component, which rings up a few pennies every time you make use of the component, and sends you a bill at the end of the month. This seems to preclude distribution in source form, since it would be too easy to remove the counting instructions. Although JEIDA, a Japanese consortium of electronics companies, is said to be working on hardware and software mechanisms to support the concept, and although Cox has recently been emphasizing enforcement mechanisms built on regulations (like copyright) rather than technological devices, superdistribution still raises many technical, logistic, economic and psychological questions.

An assessment

Any comprehensive approach to reusability must, along with the technical aspects, deal with the organizational and economical issues: making reusability part of the software development culture, finding the right cost structure and the right format for component distribution, providing the appropriate tools for indexing and retrieving components. Not surprisingly, these issues have been the focus of some of the main reusability initiatives from governments and large corporations\, such as the STARS program of the US Department of Defense (*Software Technology for Adaptable, Reliable Systems*) and the "software factories" installed by some large Japanese companies.

Important as these questions are in the long term, they should not detract our attention from the main roadblocks, which are still technical. Success in reuse requires the right modular structures and the construction of quality libraries containing the tens of thousands of components that the industry needs.

The rest of this chapter concentrates on the first of these questions; it examines why common notions of module are not appropriate for large-scale reusability, and defines the requirements that a better solution — developed in the following chapters — must satisfy.

4.5 THE TECHNICAL PROBLEM

What should a reusable module look like?

Change and constancy

Software development, it was mentioned above, involves much repetition. To understand the technical difficulties of reusability we must understand the nature of that repetition.

Such an analysis reveals that although programmers do tend to do the same kinds of things time and time again, these are not *exactly* the same things. If they were, the solution would be easy, at least on paper; but in practice so many details may change as to defeat any simple-minded attempt at capturing the commonality.

> A telling analogy is provided by the works of the Norwegian painter Edvard Munch, the majority of which may be seen in the museum dedicated to him in Oslo, the birthplace of Simula. Munch was obsessed with a small number of profound, essential themes: love, anguish, jealousy, dance, death… He drew and painted them endlessly, using the same pattern each time, but continually changing the technical medium, the colors, the emphasis, the size, the light, the mood.

Such is the software engineer's plight: time and again composing a new variation that elaborates on the same basic themes.

Take the example mentioned at the beginning of this chapter: table searching. True, the general form of a table searching algorithm is going to look similar each time: start at some position in the table t; then begin exploring the table from that position, each time checking whether the element found at the current position is the one being sought, and, if not, moving to another position. The process terminates when it has either found the element or probed all the candidate positions unsuccessfully. Such a general pattern is applicable to many possible cases of data representation and algorithms for table searching, including arrays (sorted or not), linked lists (sorted or not), sequential files, binary trees, B-trees and hash tables of various kinds.

It is not difficult to turn this informal description into an incompletely refined routine:

```
has (t: TABLE, x: ELEMENT): BOOLEAN is
            -- Is there an occurrence of x in t?
    local
        pos: POSITION
    do
        from
            pos := INITIAL_POSITION (x, t)
        until
            EXHAUSTED (pos, t) or else FOUND (pos, x, t)
        loop
            pos := NEXT (pos, x, t)
        end
        Result := not EXHAUSTED (pos, t)
    end
```

(A few clarifications on the notation: **from** … **until** … **loop** … **end** describes a loop, initialized in the **from** clause, executing the **loop** clause zero or more times, and terminating as soon as the condition in the **until** clause is satisfied. *Result* denotes the value to be returned by the function. If you are not familiar with the **or else** operator, just accept it as if it were a boolean **or**.)

or else is explained in "Non-strict boolean operators", page 454.

Although the above text describes (through its lower-case elements) a general pattern of algorithmic behavior, it is not a directly executable routine since it contains (in upper case) some incompletely refined parts, corresponding to aspects of the table searching problem that depend on the implementation chosen: the type of table elements (*ELEMENT*), what position to examine first (*INITIAL_POSITION*), how to go from a candidate position to the next (*NEXT*), how to test for the presence of an element at a certain position (*FOUND*), how to determine that all interesting positions have been examined (*EXHAUSTED*).

Rather than a routine, then, the above text is a routine pattern, which you can only turn into an actual routine by supplying refinements for the upper-case parts.

The reuse-redo dilemma

All this variation highlights the problems raised by any attempt to come up with general-purpose modules in a given application area: how can we take advantage of the common pattern while accommodating the need for so much variation? This is not just an implementation problem: it is almost as hard to *specify* the module so that client modules can rely on it without knowing its implementation.

These observations point to the central problem of software reusability, which dooms simplistic approaches. Because of the versatility of software — its very softness — candidate reusable modules will not suffice if they are inflexible.

A frozen module forces you into the **reuse or redo** dilemma: reuse the module exactly as it is, or redo the job completely. This is often too limiting. In a typical situation, you discover a module that may provide you with a solution for some part of your current job, but not necessarily the exact solution. Your specific needs may require some adaptation of the module's original behavior. So what you will want to do in such a case is to reuse *and* redo: reuse some, redo some — or, you hope, reuse a lot and redo a little. Without this ability to combine reuse and adaptation, reusability techniques cannot provide a solution that satisfies the realities of practical software development.

So it is not by accident that almost every discussion of reusability in this book also considers extendibility (leading to the definition of the term "modularity", which covers both notions and provided the topic of the previous chapter). Whenever you start looking for answers to one of these quality requirements, you quickly encounter the other.

"The Open-Closed principle", page 57. This duality between reuse and adaptation was also present in the earlier discussion of the Open-Closed principle, which pointed out that a successful software component must be usable as it stands (closed) while still adaptable (open).

The search for the right notion of module, which occupies the rest of this chapter and the next few, may be characterized as a constant attempt to reconcile reusability and extendibility, closure and openness, constancy and change, satisfying today's needs and trying to guess what tomorrow holds in store.

4.6 FIVE REQUIREMENTS ON MODULE STRUCTURES

How do we find module structures that will yield directly reusable components while preserving the possibility of adaptation?

The table searching issue and the *has* routine pattern obtained for it on the previous page illustrate the stringent requirements that any solution will have to meet. We can use this example to analyze what it takes to go from a relatively vague recognition of commonality between software variants to an actual set of reusable modules. Such a study will reveal five general issues:

- Type Variation.

- Routine Grouping.

- Implementation Variation.

- Representation Independence.

- Factoring Out Common Behaviors.

Type Variation

The *has* routine pattern assumes a table containing objects of a type *ELEMENT*. A particular refinement might use a specific type, such as *INTEGER* or *BANK_ACCOUNT*, to apply the pattern to a table of integers or bank accounts.

But this is not satisfactory. A reusable searching module should be applicable to many different types of element, without requiring reusers to perform manual changes to the software text. In other words, we need a facility for describing type-parameterized modules, also known more concisely as **generic** modules. Genericity (the ability for modules to be generic) will turn out to be an important part of the object-oriented method; an overview of the idea appears later in this chapter.

"Genericity", page 96.

Routine Grouping

Even if it had been completely refined and parameterized by types, the *has* routine pattern would not be quite satisfactory as a reusable component. How you search a table depends on how it was created, how elements are inserted, how they are deleted. So a searching routine is not enough by itself as a unit or reuse. A self-sufficient reusable module would need to include a set of routines, one for each of the operations cited — creation, insertion, deletion, searching.

This idea forms the basis for a form of module, the "package", found in what may be called the encapsulation languages: Ada, Modula-2 and relatives. More on this below.

Implementation Variation

The *has* pattern is very general; there is in practice, as we have seen, a wide variety of applicable data structures and algorithms. Such variety indeed that we cannot expect a single module to take care of all possibilities; it would be enormous. We will need a family of modules to cover all the different implementations.

A general technique for producing and using reusable modules will have to support this notion of module family.

Representation Independence

A general form of reusable module should enable clients to specify an operation without knowing how it is implemented. This requirement is called Representation Independence.

Assume that a client module *C* from a certain application system — an asset management program, a compiler, a geographical information system... — needs to determine whether a certain element *x* appears in a certain table *t* (of investments, of language keywords, of cities). Representation independence means here the ability for *C* to obtain this information through a call such as

$present := has (t, x)$

without knowing what kind of table t is at the time of the call. C's author should only need to know that t is a table of elements of a certain type, and that x denotes an object of that type. Whether t is a binary search tree, a hash table or a linked list is irrelevant for him; he should be able to limit his concerns to asset management, compilation or geography. Selecting the appropriate search algorithm based on t's implementation is the business of the table management module, and of no one else.

This requirement does not preclude letting clients choose a specific implementation when they create a data structure. But only one client will have to make this initial choice; after that, none of the clients that perform searches on t should ever have to ask what exact kind of table it is. In particular, the client C containing the above call may have received t from one of its own clients (as an argument to a routine call); then for C the name t is just an abstract handle on a data structure whose details it may not be able to access.

"Information Hiding", page 51.

You may view Representation Independence as an extension of the rule of Information Hiding, essential for smooth development of large systems: implementation decisions will often change, and clients should be protected. But Representation Independence goes further. Taken to its full consequences, it means protecting a module's clients against changes not only during the *project lifecycle* but also *during execution —* a much smaller time frame! In the example, we want *has* to adapt itself automatically to the run-time form of table t, even if that form has changed since the last call.

"Single Choice", page 61.

Satisfying Representation Independence will also help us towards a related principle encountered in the discussion of modularity: Single Choice, which directed us to stay away from multi-branch control structures that discriminate among many variants, as in

if "t is an array managed by open hashing" **then**
    "Apply open hashing search algorithm"
elseif "t is a binary search tree" **then**
    "Apply binary search tree traversal"
elseif
    (etc.)
end

"DYNAMIC BIND-ING", 14.4, page 480.

It would be equally unpleasant to have such a decision structure in the module itself (we cannot reasonably expect a table management module to know about all present and future variants) as to replicate it in every client. The solution is to hide the multi-branch choice completely from software developers, and have it performed automatically by the underlying run-time system. This will be the role of **dynamic binding**, a key component of the object-oriented approach, to be studied in the discussion of inheritance.

Factoring Out Common Behaviors

If Representation Independence reflects the client's view of reusability — the ability to ignore internal implementation details and variants –, the last requirement, Factoring Out Common Behaviors, reflects the view of the supplier and, more generally, the view of developers of reusable classes. Their goal will be to take advantage of any commonality that may exist within a family or sub-family of implementations.

The variety of implementations available in certain problem areas will usually demand, as noted, a solution based on a family of modules. Often the family is so large that it is natural to look for sub-families. In the table searching case a first attempt at classification might yield three broad sub-families:

- Tables managed by some form of hash-coding scheme.
- Tables organized as trees of some kind.
- Tables managed sequentially.

Each of these categories covers many variants, but it is usually possible to find significant commonality between these variants. Consider for example the family of sequential implementations — those in which items are kept and searched in the order of their original insertion.

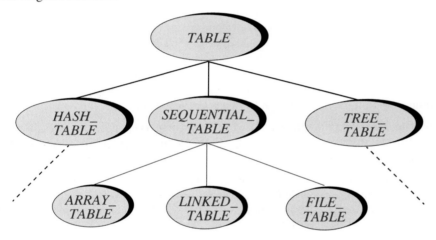

Some possible table implementations

Possible representations for a sequential table include an array, a linked list and a file. But regardless of these differences, clients should be able, for any sequentially managed table, to examine the elements in sequence by moving a (fictitious) **cursor** indicating the position of the currently examined element. In this approach we may rewrite the searching routine for sequential tables as:

"ACTIVE DATA STRUCTURES", 23.4, page 774, will explore details of the cursor technique.

```
has (t: SEQUENTIAL_TABLE; x: ELEMENT): BOOLEAN is
        -- Is there an occurrence of x in t?
    do
        from start until
                after or else found (x)
        loop
                forth
        end
        Result := not after
    end
```

This form relies on four routines which any sequential table implementation will be able to provide:

- *start*, a command to move the cursor to the first element if any.

- *forth*, a command to advance the cursor by one position. (Support for *forth* is of course one of the prime characteristics of a sequential table implementation.)

- *after*, a boolean-valued query to determine if the cursor has moved past the last element; this will be true after a *start* if the table was empty.

- *found* (*x*), a boolean-valued query to determine if the element at cursor position has value *x*.

Sequential structure with cursor

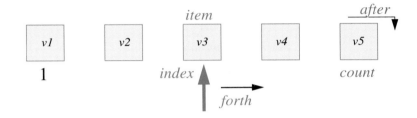

The general routine pattern was on page 82.

At first sight, the routine text for *has* at the bottom of the preceding page resembles the general routine pattern used at the beginning of this discussion, which covered searching in any table (not just sequential). But the new form is not a routine pattern any more; it is a true routine, expressed in a directly executable notation (the notation used to illustrate object-oriented concepts in part C of this book). Given appropriate implementations for the four operations *start*, *forth*, *after* and *found* which it calls, you can compile and execute the latest form of *has*.

For each possible sequential table representation you will need a representation for the cursor. Three example representations are by an array, a linked list and a file.

The first uses an array of *capacity* items, the table occupying positions 1 to *count*. Then you may represent the cursor simply as an integer *index* ranging from 1 to *count* + *1*. (The last value is needed to represent a cursor that has moved "*after*" the last item.)

Array representation of sequential table with cursor

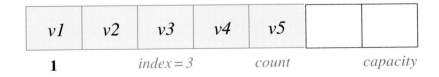

The second representation uses a linked list, where the first cell is accessible through a reference *first_cell* and each cell is linked to the next one through a reference *right*. Then you may represent the cursor as a reference *cursor*.

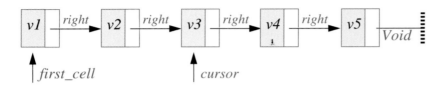

*Linked list
representation
of sequential
table with
cursor*

The third representation uses a sequential file, in which the cursor simply represents the current reading position.

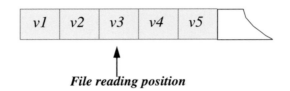

File reading position

*Sequential file
representation
of a sequential
table with
cursor*

The implementation of the four low-level operations *start*, *forth*, *after* and *found* will be different for each variant. The following table gives the implementation in each case. (The notation $t @ i$ denotes the i-th element of array t, which would be written $t[i]$ in Pascal or C; *Void* denotes a void reference; the Pascal notation $f\uparrow$, for a file f, denotes the element at the current file reading position.)

*In this table index is
abbreviated as i
and cursor as c.*

	start	*forth*	*after*	*found (x)*
Array	$i := 1$	$i := i + 1$	$i > count$	$t @ i = x$
Linked list	$c := first\_cell$	$c := c.right$	$c = Void$	$c.item = x$
File	rewind	read	end_of_file	$f\uparrow = x$

The challenge of reusability here is to avoid unneeded duplication of software by taking advantage of the commonality between variants. If identical or near-identical fragments appear in different modules, it will be difficult to guarantee their integrity and to ensure that changes or corrections get propagated to all the needed places; once again, configuration management problems may follow.

All sequential table variants share the *has* function, differing only by their implementation of the four lower-level operations. A satisfactory solution to the reusability problem must include the text of *has* in only one place, somehow associated with the general notion of sequential table independently of any choice of representation. To describe a new variant, you should not have to worry about *has* any more; all you will need to do is to provide the appropriae versions of *start*, *forth*, *after* and *found*.

4.7 TRADITIONAL MODULAR STRUCTURES

Together with the modularity requirements of the previous chapter, the five requirements of Type Variation, Routine Grouping, Implementation Variation, Representation Independence and Factoring Out Common Behaviors define what we may expect from our reusable components — abstracted modules.

Let us study the pre-O-O solutions to understand why they are not sufficient — but also what we should learn and keep from them in the object-oriented world.

Routines

The classical approach to reusability is to build libraries of routines. Here the term *routine* denotes a software unit that other units may call to execute a certain algorithm, using certain inputs, producing certain outputs and possibly modifying some other data elements. A calling unit will pass its inputs (and sometimes outputs and modified elements) in the form of *actual arguments*. A routine may also return output in the form of a *result*; in this case it is known as a *function*.

> The terms *subroutine*, *subprogram* and *procedure* are also used instead of *routine*. The first two will not appear in this book except in the discussion of specific languages (the Ada literature talks about subprograms, and the Fortran literature about subroutines.) "Procedure" will be used in the sense of a routine which does not return a result, so that we have two disjoint categories of routine: procedures and functions. (In discussions of the C language the term "function" itself is sometimes used for the general notion of routine, but here it will always denote a routine that returns a result.)

Routine libraries have been successful in several application domains, in particular numerical computation, where excellent libraries have created some of the earliest success stories of reusability. Decomposition of systems into routines is also what one obtains through the method of top-down, functional decomposition. The routine library approach indeed seems to work well when you can identify a (possibly large) set of individual problems, subject to the following limitations:

R1 • Each problem admits a simple specification. More precisely, it is possible to characterize every problem instance by a small set of input and output arguments.

R2 • The problems are clearly distinct from each other, as the routine approach does not allow putting to good use any significant commonality that might exist — except by reusing some of the design.

R3 • No complex data structures are involved: you would have to distribute them among the routines using them, losing the conceptual autonomy of each module.

The table searching problem provides a good example of the limitations of subroutines. We saw earlier that a searching routine by itself does not have enough context to serve as a stand-alone reusable module. Even if we dismissed this objection, however, we would be faced with two equally unpleasant solutions:

• A single searching routine, which would try to cover so many different cases that it would require a long argument list and would be very complex internally.

- A large number of searching routines, each covering a specific case and differing from some others by only a few details in violation of the Factoring Out Common Behaviors requirement; candidate reusers could easily lose their way in such a maze.

More generally, routines are not flexible enough to satisfy the needs of reuse. We have seen the intimate connection between reusability and extendibility. A reusable module should be open to adaptation, but with a routine the only means of adaptation is to pass different arguments. This makes you a prisoner of the Reuse or Redo dilemma: either you like the routine as it is, or you write your own.

Packages

In the nineteen-seventies, with the progress of ideas on information hiding and data abstraction, a need emerged for a form of module more advanced than the routine. The result may be found in several design and programming languages of the period; the best known are CLU, Modula-2 and Ada. They all offer a similar form of module, known in Ada as the package. (CLU calls its variant the cluster, and Modula the module. This discussion will retain the Ada term.)

This approach is studied in detail, through the Ada notion of package, in chapter 33. Note again that by default "Ada" means Ada 83. (Ada 95 retains packages with a few additions.)

Packages are units of software decomposition with the following properties:

P1 • In accordance with the Linguistic Modular Units principle, "package" is a construct of the language, so that every package has a name and a clear syntactic scope.

P2 • Each package definition contains a number of declarations of related elements, such as routines and variables, hereafter called the **features** of the package.

P3 • Every package can specify precise access rights governing the use of its features by other packages. In other words, the package mechanism supports information hiding.

P4 • In a compilable language (one that can be used for implementation, not just specification and design) it is possible to compile packages separately.

Thanks to P3, packages deserve to be seen as abstracted modules. Their major contribution is P2, answering the Routine Grouping requirement. A package may contain any number of related operations, such as table creation, insertion, searching and deletion. It is indeed not hard to see how a package solution would work for our example problem. Here — in a notation adapted from the one used in the rest of this book for object-oriented software — is the sketch of a package *INTEGER_TABLE_HANDLING* describing a particular implementation of tables of integers, through binary trees:

> **package** *INTEGER_TABLE_HANDLING* **feature**
>
> > **type** *INTBINTREE* **is**
> >
> > > **record**
> > >
> > > > -- Description of representation of a binary tree, for example:
> > > >
> > > > *info*: *INTEGER*
> > > >
> > > > *left*, *right*: *INTBINTREE*
> > >
> > > **end**

new: *INTBINTREE* **is**
    -- Return a new *INTBINTREE*, properly initialized.
do ... **end**

has (*t*: *INTBINTREE*; *x*: *INTEGER*): *BOOLEAN* **is**
    -- Does *x* appear in *t*?
do ... Implementation of searching operation ... **end**

put (*t*: *INTBINTREE*; *x*: *INTEGER*) **is**
    -- Insert *x* into *t*.
do ... **end**

remove (*t*: *INTBINTREE*; *x*: *INTEGER*) **is**
    -- Remove *x* from *t*.
do ... **end**

end -- package *INTEGER_TABLE_HANDLING*

This package includes the declaration of a type (*INTBINTREE*), and a number of routines representing operations on objects of that type. In this case there is no need for variable declarations in the package (although the routines may have local variables).

Client packages will now be able to manipulate tables by using the various features of *INTEGER_TABLE_HANDLING*. This assumes a syntactic convention allowing a client to use feature *f* from package *P*; let us borrow the CLU notation: *P$f*. Typical extracts from a client of *INTEGER_TABLE_HANDLING* may be of the form:

    -- Auxiliary declarations:
x: *INTEGER*; *b*: *BOOLEAN*

    -- Declaration of *t* using a type defined in *INTEGER_TABLE_HANDLING*:
t: *INTEGER_TABLE_HANDLING$INTBINTREE*

    -- Initialize *t* as a new table, created by function *new* of the package:
t := *INTEGER_TABLE_HANDLING$new*

    -- Insert value of *x* into table, using procedure *put* from the package:
INTEGER_TABLE_HANDLING$put (*t*, *x*)

    -- Assign *True* or *False* to *b*, depending on whether or not *x* appears in *t*
    -- for the search, use function *has* from the package:
b := *INTEGER_TABLE_HANDLING$has* (*t*, *x*)

Note the need to invent two related names: one for the module, here *INTEGER_TABLE_HANDLING*, and one for its main data type, here *INTBINTREE*. One of the key steps towards object orientation will be to merge the two notions. But let us not anticipate.

A less important problem is the tediousness of having to write the package name (here *INTEGER_TABLE_HANDLING*) repeatedly. Languages supporting packages solve this problem by providing various syntactic shortcuts, such as the following Ada-like form:

    with *INTEGER_TABLE_HANDLING* **then**
        ... Here *has* means *INTEGER_TABLE_HANDLING$has*, etc. ...
    end

Another obvious limitation of packages of the above form is their failure to deal with the Type Variation issue: the module as given is only useful for tables of integers. We will shortly see, however, how to correct this deficiency by making packages generic.

The package mechanism provides information hiding by limiting clients' rights on features. The client shown on the preceding page was able to declare one of its own variables using the type *INTBINTREE* from its supplier, and to call routines declared in that supplier; but it has access neither to the internals of the type declaration (the **record** structure defining the implementation of tables) nor to the routine bodies (their **do** clauses). In addition, you can hide some features of the package (variables, types, routines) from clients, making them usable only within the text of the package.

"Supplier" is the inverse of "client". Here the supplier is INTEGER_TABLE_ HANDLING.

> Languages supporting the package notion differ somewhat in the details of their information hiding mechanism. In Ada, for example, the internal properties of a type such as *INTBINTREE* will be accessible to clients unless you declare the type as **private**.

Often, to enforce information hiding, encapsulation languages will invite you to declare a package in two parts, interface and implementation, relegating such secret elements as the details of a type declaration or the body of a routine to the implementation part. Such a policy, however, results in extra work for the authors of supplier modules, forcing them to duplicate feature header declarations. With a better understanding of Information Hiding we do not need any of this. More in later chapters.

See "Using assertions for documentation: the short form of a class", page 389 and "Showing the interface", page 804.

Packages: an assessment

Compared to routines, the package mechanism brings a significant improvement to the modularization of software systems into abstracted modules. The possibility of gathering a number of features under one roof is useful for both supplier and client authors:

- The author of a supplier module can keep in one place and compile together all the software elements relating to a given concept. This facilitates debugging and change. In contrast, with separate subroutines there is always a risk of forgetting to update some of the routines when you make a design or implementation change; you might for example update *new*, *put* and *has* but forget *remove*.

- For client authors, it is obviously easier to find and use a set of related facilities if they are all in one place.

The advantage of packages over routines is particularly clear in cases such as our table example, where a package groups all the operations applying to a certain data structure.

But packages still do not provide a full solution to the issues of reusability. As noted, they address the Routine Grouping requirement; but they leave the others unanswered. In particular they offer no provision for factoring out commonality. You will have noted that *INTEGER_TABLE_HANDLING*, as sketched, relies on one specific choice of implementation, binary search trees. True, clients do not need to be concerned with this choice, thanks to information hiding. But a library of reusable components will need to provide modules for many different implementations. The resulting situation is easy to foresee: a typical package library will offer dozens of similar but never identical modules in a given area such as table management, with no way to take advantage of the commonality. To provide reusability to the clients, this technique sacrifices reusability on the suppliers' side.

Even on the clients' side, the situation is not completely satisfactory. Every use of a table by a client requires a declaration such as the above:

t: *INTEGER_TABLE_HANDLING$INTBINTREE*

forcing the client to choose a specific implementation. This defeats the Representation Independence requirement: client authors will have to know more about implementations of supplier notions than is conceptually necessary.

4.8 OVERLOADING AND GENERICITY

Two techniques, overloading and genericity, offer candidate solutions in the effort to bring more flexibility to the mechanisms just described. Let us study what they can contribute.

Syntactic overloading

Overloading is the ability to attach more than one meaning to a name appearing in a program.

The most common source of overloading is for variable names: in almost all languages, different variables may have the same name if they belong to different modules (or, in the Algol style of languages, different blocks within a module).

More relevant to this discussion is **routine overloading**, also known as operator overloading, which allows several routines to share the same name. This possibility is almost always available for arithmetic operators (hence the second name): the same notation, $a + b$, denotes various forms of addition depending on the types of a and b (integer, single-precision real, double-precision real). But most languages do not treat an operation such as "+" as a routine, and reserve it for predefined basic types — integer, real and the like. Starting with Algol 68, which allowed overloading the basic operators, several languages have extended the overloading facility beyond language built-ins to user-defined operations and ordinary routines.

In Ada, for example, a package may contain several routines with the same name, as long as the signatures of these routines are different, where the signature of a routine is defined here by the number and types of its arguments. (The general notion of signature also includes the type of the results, if any, but Ada resolves overloading on the basis of the arguments only.) For example, a package could contain several square functions:

The notation, compatible with the one in the rest of this book, is Ada-like rather than exact Ada. The REAL type is called FLOAT in Ada; semicolons have been removed.

square (*x*: *INTEGER*): *INTEGER* **is do** … **end**
square (*x*: *REAL*): *REAL* **is do** … **end**
square (*x*: *DOUBLE*): *DOUBLE* **is do** … **end**
square (*x*: *COMPLEX*): *COMPLEX* **is do** … **end**

Then, in a particular call of the form *square* (*y*), the type of *y* will determine which version of the routine you mean.

A package could similarly declare a number of search functions, all of the form

has (*t*: "SOME_TABLE_TYPE"; *x*: *ELEMENT*) **is do** ... **end**

supporting various table implementations and differing by the actual type used in lieu of "SOME_TABLE_TYPE". The type of the first actual argument, in any client's call to *has*, suffices to determine which routine is intended.

These observations suggest a general characterization of routine overloading, which will be useful when we later want to contrast this facility with genericity:

<table>
<tr><td>

Role of overloading

Routine overloading is a facility for clients. It makes it possible to write the same client text when using different implementations of a certain concept.

</td></tr>
</table>

See the correspond-ing definition of ge-nericity on page 97.

What does routine overloading really bring to our quest for reusability? Not much. It is a syntactic facility, relieving developers from having to invent different names for various implementations of an operation and, in essence, placing that burden on the compiler. But this does not solve any of the key issues of reusability. In particular, overloading does nothing to address Representation Independence. When you write the call

has (*t*, *x*)

you must have declared *t* and so (even if information hiding protects you from worrying about the details of each variant of the search algorithm) you must know exactly what kind of table *t* is! The only contribution of overloading is that you can use the same name in all cases. Without overloading each implementation would require a different name, as in

has_binary_tree (*t*, *x*)
has_hash (*t*, *x*)
has_linked (*t*, *x*)

Is the possibility of avoiding different names a benefit after all? Perhaps not. A basic rule of software construction, object-oriented or not, is the **principle of non-deception**: differences in semantics should be reflected by differences in the text of the software. This is essential to improve the understandability of software and minimize the risk of errors. If the *has* routines are different, giving them the same name may mislead a reader of the software into believing that they are the same. Better force a little more wordiness on the client (as with the above specific names) and remove any danger of confusion.

The further one looks into this style of overloading, the more limited it appears. The criterion used to disambiguate calls — the signature of argument lists — has no particular merit. It works in the above examples, where the various overloads of *square* and *has* are all of different signatures, but it is not difficult to think of many cases where the signatures would be the same. One of the simplest examples for overloading would seem to be, in a graphics system, a set of functions used to create new points, for example under the form

p1 := *new_point* (*u*, *v*)

More on syntactic overloading in "Multiple creation and overloading", page 239 and "O-O development and overloading", page 564.

There are two basic ways to specify a new point: through its cartesian coordinates x and y (the projections on the horizontal axis), and through its polar coordinates ρ and θ (the distance to the origin, and the angle with the horizontal axis). But if we overload function *new_point* we are in trouble, since both versions will have the signature

new_point (p, q: REAL): POINT

This example and many similar ones show that type signature, the criterion for disambiguating overloaded versions, is irrelevant. But no better one has been proposed.

The recent Java language regrettably includes the form of syntactic overloading just described, in particular to provide alternative ways to create objects.

Semantic overloading (a preview)

"DYNAMIC BINDING", 14.4, page 480.

The form of routine overloading described so far may be called **syntactic overloading**. The object-oriented method will bring a much more interesting technique, dynamic binding, which addresses the goal of Representation Independence. Dynamic binding may be called **semantic overloading**. With this technique, you will be able to write the equivalent of *has* (t, x), under a suitably adapted syntax, as a request to the machine that executes your software. The full meaning of the request is something like this:

How remarkably concise software languages are in comparison!

Dear Hardware-Software Machine:

Please look at what t is; I know that it must be a table, but not what table implementation its original creator chose — and to be honest about it I'd much rather remain in the dark. After all, my job is not table management but investment banking [or compiling, or computer-aided-design etc.]. The chief table manager here is someone else. So find out for yourself about it and, once you have the answer, look up the proper algorithm for has for that particular kind of table. Then apply that algorithm to determine whether x appears in t, and tell me the result. I am eagerly waiting for your answer.

I regret to inform you that, beyond the information that t is a table of some kind and x a potential element, you will not get any more help from me.

With my sincerest wishes,

Your friendly application developer.

Unlike syntactic overloading, such semantic overloading is a direct answer to the Representation Independence requirement. It still raises the specter of violating the principle of non-deception; the answer will be to use **assertions** to characterize the common semantics of a routine that has many different variants (for example, the common properties which characterize *has* under all possible table implementations).

Because semantic overloading, to work properly, requires the full baggage of object orientation, in particular inheritance, it is understandable that non-O-O languages such as Ada offer syntactic overloading as a partial substitute in spite of the problems mentioned above. In an object-oriented language, however, providing syntactic overloading on top of dynamic binding can be confusing, as is illustrated by the case of C++ and Java which both allow a class to introduce several routines with the same name, leaving it to the compiler and the human reader to disambiguate calls.

Genericity

Genericity is a mechanism for defining parameterized module patterns, whose parameters represent types.

This facility is a direct answer to the Type Variation issue. It avoids the need for many modules such as

INTEGER_TABLE_HANDLING

ELECTRON_TABLE_HANDLING

ACCOUNT_TABLE_HANDLING

by enabling you instead to write a single module pattern of the form

TABLE_HANDLING [*G*]

where G is a name meant to represent an arbitrary type and known as a **formal generic parameter**. (We may later encounter the need for two or more generic parameters, but for the present discussion we may limit ourselves to one.)

Such a parameterized module pattern is known as a **generic module**, although it is not really a module, only a blueprint for many possible modules. To obtain one of these actual modules, you must provide a type, known as an **actual generic parameter**, to replace G; the resulting (non-generic) modules are written for example

TABLE_HANDLING [*INTEGER*]

TABLE_HANDLING [*ELECTRON*]

TABLE_HANDLING [*ACCOUNT*]

using types *INTEGER*, *ELECTRON* and *ACCOUNT* respectively as actual generic parameters. This process of obtaining an actual module from a generic module (that is to say, from a module pattern) by providing a type as actual generic parameter will be known as **generic derivation**; the module itself will be said to be generically derived.

> Two small points of terminology. First, generic derivation is sometimes called generic instantiation, a generically derived module then being called a generic instance. This terminology can cause confusion in an O-O context, since "instance" also denotes the run-time creation of objects (*instances*) from the corresponding types. So for genericity we will stick to the "derivation" terminology.
>
> Another possible source of confusion is "parameter". A routine may have formal arguments, representing values which the routine's clients will provide in each call. The literature commonly uses the term parameter (formal, actual) as a synonym for argument (formal, actual). There is nothing wrong in principle with either term, but if we have both routines and genericity we need a clear convention to avoid any misunderstanding. The convention will be to use "argument" for routines only, and "parameter" (usually in the form "generic parameter" for further clarification) for generic modules only.

Internally, the declaration of the generic module *TABLE_HANDLING* will resemble that of *INTEGER_TABLE_HANDLING* above, except that it uses *G* instead of *INTEGER* wherever it refers to the type of table elements. For example:

To be compared with INTEGER_ TABLE_HAN- DLING, page 90.

package *TABLE_HANDLING* [*G*] **feature**
    type *BINARY_TREE* **is**
      record
        info: *G*
        left, right: *BINARY_TREE*
      end
    has (*t*: *BINARY_TREE*; *x*: *G*): *BOOLEAN*
      -- Does *x* appear in *t*?
    do … end
    put (*t*: *BINARY_TREE*; *x*: *G*) **is**
      -- Insert *x* into *t*.
    do … end
  (Etc.)
end -- package *TABLE_HANDLING*

Chapter 10 discuss- es O-O genericity.

It is somewhat disturbing to see the type being declared as *BINARY_TREE*, and tempting to make it generic as well (something like *BINARY_TREE* [*G*]). There is no obvious way to achieve this in a package approach. Object technology, however, will merge the notions of module and type, so the temptation will be automatically fulfilled. We will see this when we study how to integrate genericity into the object-oriented world.

It is interesting to define genericity in direct contrast with the definition given earlier for overloading:

See the correspond- ing definition of overloading on page 94.

> ### Role of genericity
> Genericity is a facility for the authors of supplier modules. It makes it possible to write the same supplier text when using the same implementation of a certain concept, applied to different kinds of object.

What help does genericity bring us towards realizing the goals of this chapter? Unlike syntactic overloading, genericity has a real contribution to make since as noted above it solves one of the main issues, Type Variation. The presentation of object technology in part C of this book will indeed devote a significant role to genericity.

Basic modularity techniques: an assessment

We have obtained two main results. One is the idea of providing a single syntactic home, such as the package construct, for a set of routines that all manipulate similar objects. The other is genericity, which yields a more flexible form of module.

All this, however, only covers two of the reusability issues, Routine Grouping and Type Variation, and provides little help for the other three — Implementation Variation, Representation Independence and Factoring Out Common Behaviors. Genericity, in particular, does not suffice as a solution to the Factoring issue, since making a module generic defines two levels only: generic module patterns, parameterized and hence open to variation, but not directly usable; and individual generic derivations, usable directly but closed to further variation. This does not allow us to capture the fine differences that may exist between competing representations of a given general concept.

On Representation Independence, we have made almost no progress. None of the techniques seen so far — except for the short glimpse that we had of semantic overloading — will allow a client to use various implementations of a general notion without knowing which implementation each case will select.

To answer these concerns, we will have to turn to the full power of object-oriented concepts.

4.9 KEY CONCEPTS INTRODUCED IN THIS CHAPTER

- Software development is a highly repetitive activity, involving frequent use of common patterns. But there is considerable variation in how these patterns are used and combined, defeating simplistic attempts to work from off-the-shelf components.

- Putting reusability into practice raises economical, psychological and organizational problems; the last category involves in particular building mechanisms to index, store and retrieve large numbers of reusable components. Even more important, however, are the underlying technical problems: commonly accepted notions of module are not adequate to support serious reusability.

- The major difficulty of reuse is the need to combine reuse with adaptation. The "reuse or redo" dilemma is not acceptable: a good solution must make it possible to retain some aspects of a reused module and adapt others.

- Simple approaches, such as reuse of personnel, reuse of designs, source code reuse, and subroutine libraries, have experienced some degree of success in specific contexts, but all fall short of providing the full potential benefits of reusability.

- The appropriate unit of reuse is some form of abstracted module, providing an encapsulation of a certain functionality through a well-defined interface.

- Packages provide a better encapsulation technique than routines, as they gather a data structure and the associated operations.

- Two techniques extend the flexibility of packages: routine overloading, or the reuse of the same name for more than one operation; genericity, or the availability of modules parameterized by types.

- Routine overloading is a syntactic facility which does not solve the important issues of reuse, and harms the readability of software texts.

- Genericity helps, but only deals with the issue of type variation.

- What we need: techniques for capturing commonalities within groups of related data structure implementations; and techniques for isolating clients from having to know the choice of supplier variants.

4.10 BIBLIOGRAPHICAL NOTES

The first published discussion of reusability in software appears to have been McIlroy's 1968 *Mass-Produced Software Components*, mentioned at the beginning of this chapter. His paper [McIlroy 1976] was presented in 1968 at the first conference on software engineering, convened by the NATO Science Affairs Committee. (1976 is the date of the proceedings, [Buxton 1976], whose publication was delayed by several years.) McIlroy advocated the development of an industry of software components. Here is an extract:

> *Software production today appears in the scale of industrialization somewhere below the more backward construction industries. I think its proper place is considerably higher, and would like to investigate the prospects for mass-production techniques in software...*

> *When we undertake to write a compiler, we begin by saying "What table mechanism shall we build?". Not "What mechanism shall we use?"...*

> *My thesis is that the software industry is weakly founded [in part because of] the absence of a software components subindustry... Such a components industry could be immensely successful.*

One of the important points argued in the paper was the necessity of module families, discussed above as one of the requirements on any comprehensive solution to reuse.

> *The most important characteristic of a software components industry is that it will offer families of [modules] for a given job.*

Rather than the word "module", McIlroy's text used "routine"; in light of this chapter's discussion, this is — with the hindsight of thirty years of further software engineering development — too restrictive.

A special issue of the IEEE *Transactions on Software Engineering* edited by Biggerstaff and Perlis [Biggerstaff 1984] was influential in bringing reusability to the attention of the software engineering community; see in particular, from that issue, [Jones 1984], [Horowitz 1984], [Curry 1984], [Standish 1984] and [Goguen 1984]. The same editors included all these articles (except the first mentioned) in an expanded two-volume collection [Biggerstaff 1989]. Another collection of articles on reuse is [Tracz 1988]. More recently Tracz collected a number of his *IEEE Computer* columns into a useful book [Tracz 1995] emphasizing the management aspects.

One approach to reuse, based on concepts from artificial intelligence, is embodied in the MIT Programmer's Apprentice project; see [Waters 1984] and [Rich 1989], reproduced in the first and second Biggerstaff-Perlis collections respectively. Rather than actual reusable modules, this system uses patterns (called *clichés* and *plans*) representing common program design strategies.

Ada is covered in chapter 33; see its "BIBLIOGRAPHICAL NOTES", 33.9, page 1097.

Three "encapsulation languages" were cited in the discussion of packages: Ada, Modula-2 and CLU. Ada is discussed in a later chapter, whose bibliography section gives references to Modula-2, CLU, as well as Mesa and Alphard, two other encapsulation languages of the "modular generation" of the seventies and early eighties. The equivalent of a package in Alphard was called a form.

An influential project of the nineteen-eighties, the US Department of Defense's STARS, emphasized reusability with a special concern for the organizational aspects of the problem, and using Ada as the language for software components. A number of contributions on this approach may be found in the proceedings of the 1985 STARS DoD-Industry conference [NSIA 1985].

The two best-known books on "design patterns" are [Gamma 1995] and [Pree 1994].

[Weiser 1987] is a plea for the distribution of software in source form. That article, however, downplays the need for abstraction; as pointed out in this chapter, it is possible to keep the source form available if needed but use a higher-level form as the default documentation for the users of a module. For different reasons, Richard Stallman, the creator of the League for Programming Freedom, has been arguing that the source form should always be available; see [Stallman 1992].

[Cox 1992] describes the idea of superdistribution.

A form of overloading was present in Algol 68 [van Wijngaarden 1975]; Ada (which extended it to routines), C++ and Java, all discussed in later chapters, make extensive use of the mechanism.

Genericity appears in Ada and CLU and in an early version of the Z specification language [Abrial 1980]; in that version the Z syntax is close to the one used for genericity in this book. The LPG language [Bert 1983] was explicitly designed to explore genericity. (The initials stand for Language for Programming Generically.)

The work cited at the beginning of this chapter as the basic reference on table searching is [Knuth 1973]. Among the many algorithms and data structures textbooks which cover the question, see [Aho 1974], [Aho 1983] or [M 1978].

Two books by the author of the present one explore further the question of reusability. *Reusable Software* [M 1994a], entirely devoted to the topic, provides design and implementation principles for building quality libraries, and the complete specification of a set of fundamental libraries. *Object Success* [M 1995] discusses management aspects, especially the areas in which a company interested in reuse should exert its efforts, and areas in which efforts will probably be wasted (such as preaching reuse to application developers, or rewarding reuse). See also a short article on the topic, [M 1996].

5

Towards object technology

*E*xtendibility, reusability and reliability, our principal goals, require a set of conditions defined in the preceding chapters. To achieve these conditions, we need a systematic method for decomposing systems into modules.

This chapter presents the basic elements of such a method, based on a simple but far-reaching idea: build every module on the basis of some object type. It explains the idea, develops the rationale for it, and explores some of the immediate consequences.

A word of warning. Given today's apparent prominence of object technology, some readers might think that the battle has been won and that no further rationale is necessary. This would be a mistake: we need to understand the basis for the method, if only to avoid common misuses and pitfalls. It is in fact frequent to see the word "object-oriented" (like "structured" in an earlier era) used as mere veneer over the most conventional techniques. Only by carefully building the case for object technology can we learn to detect improper uses of the buzzword, and stay away from common mistakes reviewed later in this chapter.

5.1 THE INGREDIENTS OF COMPUTATION

The crucial question in our search for proper software architectures is *modularization*: what criteria should we use to find the modules of our software?

To obtain the proper answer we must first examine the contending candidates.

The basic triangle

Three forces are at play when we use software to perform some computations:

The three forces of computation

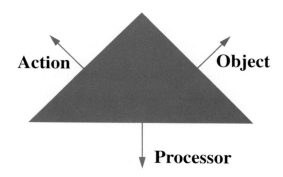

To execute a software system is to use certain *processors* to apply certain *actions* to certain *objects*.

The processors are the computation devices, physical or virtual, that execute instructions. A processor can be an actual processing unit (the CPU of a computer), a process on a conventional operating system, or a "thread" if the OS is multi-threaded.

The actions are the operations making up the computation. The exact form of the actions that we consider will depend on the level of granularity of our analysis: at the hardware level, actions are machine language operations; at the level of the hardware-software machine, they are instructions of the programming language; at the level of a software system, we can treat each major step of a complex algorithm as a single action.

The objects are the data structures to which the actions apply. Some of these objects, the data structures built by a computation for its own purposes, are internal and exist only while the computation proceeds; others (contained in the files, databases and other persistent repositories) are external and may outlive individual computations.

Processors will become important when we discuss **concurrent** forms of computation, in which several sub-computations can proceed in parallel; then we will need to consider two or more processors, physical or virtual. But that is the topic of a later chapter; for the moment we can limit our attention to non-concurrent, or *sequential* computations, relying on a single processor which will remain implicit.

Concurrency is the topic of chapter 30.

This leaves us with actions and objects. The duality between actions and objects — what a system does *vs.* what it does it to — is a pervasive theme in software engineering.

A note of terminology. Synonyms are available to denote each of the two aspects: the word *data* will be used here as a synonym for *objects*; for *action* the discussion will often follow common practice and talk about the *functions* of a system.

The term "function" is not without disadvantages, since software discussions also use it in at least two other meanings: the mathematical sense, and the programming sense of subprogram returning a result. But we can use it without ambiguity in the phrase *the functions of a system*, which is what we need here.

The reason for using this word rather than "action" is the mere grammatical convenience of having an associated adjective, used in the phrase *functional decomposition*. "Action" has no comparable derivation. Another term whose meaning is equivalent to that of "action" for the purpose of this discussion is *operation*.

Any discussion of software issues must account for both the object and function aspects; so must the design of any software system. But there is one question for which we must choose — the question of this chapter: what is the appropriate criterion for finding the modules of a system? Here we must decide whether modules will be built as units of functional decomposition, or around major types of objects.

From the answer will follow the difference between the object-oriented approach and other methods. Traditional approaches build each module around some unit of functional decomposition — a certain piece of the action. The object-oriented method, instead, builds each module around some type of objects.

This book, predictably, develops the latter approach. But we should not just embrace O-O decomposition because the title of the book so implies, or because it is the "in" thing to do. The next few sections will carefully examine the arguments that justify using object types as the basis for modularization — starting with an exploration of the merits and limitations of traditional, non-O-O methods. Then we will try to get a clearer understanding of what the word "object" really means for software development, although the full answer, requiring a little theoretical detour, will only emerge in the next chapter.

We will also have to wait until the next chapter for the final settlement of the formidable and ancient fight that provides the theme for the rest of the present discussion: the War of the Objects and the Functions. As we prepare ourselves for a campaign of slander against the functions as a basis for system decomposition, and of corresponding praise for the objects, we must not forget the observation made above: in the end, our solution to the software structuring problem must provide space for both functions and objects — although not necessarily on an equal basis. To discover this new world order, we will need to define the respective roles of its first-class and second-class citizens.

5.2 FUNCTIONAL DECOMPOSITION

We should first examine the merits and limitations of the traditional approach: using functions as a basis for the architecture of software systems. This will not only lead us to appreciate why we need something else — object technology — but also help us avoid, when we do move into the object world, certain methodological pitfalls such as premature operation ordering, which have been known to fool even experienced O-O developers.

Continuity

*"Modular continu-
ity", page 44.*
A key element in answering the question "should we structure systems around functions or around data?" is the problem of extendibility, and more precisely the goal called *continuity* in our earlier discussions. As you will recall, a design method satisfies this criterion if it yields stable architectures, keeping the amount of design change commensurate with the size of the specification change.

Continuity is a crucial concern if we consider the real lifecycle of software systems, including not just the production of an acceptable initial version, but a system's long-term evolution. Most systems undergo numerous changes after their first delivery. Any model of software development that only considers the period leading to that delivery and ignores the subsequent era of change and revision is as remote from real life as those novels which end when the hero marries the heroine — the time which, as everyone knows, marks the beginning of the really interesting part.

To evaluate the quality of an architecture (and of the method that produced it), we should not just consider how easy it was to obtain this architecture initially: it is just as important to ascertain how well the architecture will weather change.

*Top-down design
was sketched in
"Modular decom-
posability", page 40.*
The traditional answer to the question of modularization has been top-down functional decomposition, briefly introduced in an earlier chapter. How well does top-down design respond to the requirements of modularity?

Top-down development

> *There was a most ingenious architect who had contrived a new method*
> *for building houses, by beginning at the roof, and working downwards*
> *to the foundation, which he justified to me by the like practice of those*
> *two prudent insects, the bee and the spider.*
>
> Jonathan Swift: *Gulliver's Travels*, Part III, *A*
> *Voyage to Laputa, etc.*, Chapter 5.

The top-down approach builds a system by stepwise refinement, starting with a definition of its abstract function. You start the process by expressing a topmost statement of this function, such as

[C0]

"Translate a C program to machine code"

or:

[P0]

"Process a user command"

and continue with a sequence of refinement steps. Each step must decrease the level of abstraction of the elements obtained; it decomposes every operation into a combination of one or more simpler operations. For example, the next step in the first example (the C compiler) could produce the decomposition

[C1]

"Read program and produce sequence of tokens"
"Parse sequence of tokens into abstract syntax tree"
"Decorate tree with semantic information"
"Generate code from decorated tree"

or, using an alternative structure (and making the simplifying assumption that a C program is a sequence of function definitions):

[C'1]

from

"Initialize data structures"

until

"All function definitions processed"

loop

"Read in next function definition"
"Generate partial code"

end

"Fill in cross references"

In either case, the developer must at each step examine the remaining incompletely expanded elements (such as "Read program ..." and "All function definitions processed") and expand them, using the same refinement process, until everything is at a level of abstraction low enough to allow direct implementation.

We may picture the process of top-down refinement as the development of a tree. Nodes represent elements of the decomposition; branches show the relation "*B* is part of the refinement of *A*".

Top-down design: tree structure

(This figure first appeared on page 41.)

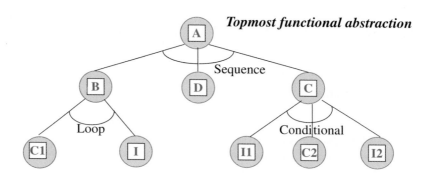

The top-down approach has a number of advantages. It is a logical, well-organized thought discipline; it can be taught effectively; it encourages orderly development of systems; it helps the designer find a way through the apparent complexity that systems often present at the initial stages of their design.

The top-down approach can indeed be useful for developing individual algorithms. But it also suffers from limitations that make it questionable as a tool for the design of entire systems:

- The very idea of characterizing a system by just one function is subject to doubt.

- By using as a basis for modular decomposition the properties that tend to change the most, the method fails to account for the evolutionary nature of software systems.

Not just one function

In the evolution of a system, what may originally have been perceived as the system's main function may become less important over time.

Consider a typical payroll system. When stating his initial requirement, the customer may have envisioned just what the name suggests: a system to produce paychecks from the appropriate data. His view of the system, implicit or explicit, may have been a more ambitious version of this:

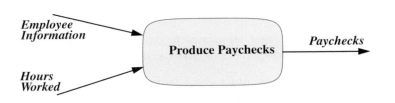

The system takes some inputs (such as record of hours worked and employee information) and produces some outputs (paychecks and so on). This is a simple enough functional specification, in the strict sense of the word functional: it defines the program as a mechanism to perform one function — pay the employees. The top-down functional method is meant precisely for such well-defined problems, where the task is to perform a single function — the "top" of the system to be built.

Assume, however, that the development of our payroll program is a success: the program does the requisite job. Most likely, the development will not stop there. Good systems have the detestable habit of giving their users plenty of ideas about all the other things they could do. As the system's developer, you may initially have been told that all you had to do was to generate paychecks and a few auxiliary outputs. But now the requests for extensions start landing on your desk: Could the program gather some statistics on the side? I did tell you that next quarter we are going to start paying some employees monthly and others biweekly, did I not? And, by the way, I need a summary every month for management, and one every quarter for the shareholders. The accountants want their own output for tax preparation purposes. Also, you are keeping all this salary information, right? It would be really nifty to let Personnel access it interactively. I cannot imagine why that would be a difficult functionality to add.

This phenomenon of having to add unanticipated functions to successful systems occurs in all application areas. A nuclear code that initially just applied some algorithm to produce tables of numbers from batch input will be extended to handle graphical input and output or to maintain a database of previous results. A compiler that just translated valid source into object code will after a while double up as a syntax verifier, a static analyzer, a pretty-printer, even a programming environment.

This change process is often incremental. The new requirements evolve from the initial ones in a continuous way. The new system is still, in many respects, "the same system" as the old one: still a payroll system, a nuclear code, a compiler. But the original "main function", which may have seemed so important at first, often becomes just one of many functions; sometimes, it just vanishes, having outlived its usefulness.

If analysis and design have used a decomposition method based on the function, the system structure will follow from the designers' original understanding of the system's main function. As the system evolves, the designers may feel sorry (or its maintainers, if different people, may feel angry) about that original assessment. Each addition of a new function, however incremental it seems to the customer, risks invalidating the entire structure.

It is crucial to find, as a criterion for decomposition, properties less volatile than the system's main function.

Finding the top

Top-down methods assume that every system is characterized, at the most abstract level, by its main function. Although it is indeed easy to specify textbook examples of algorithmic problems — the Tower of Hanoi, the Eight Queens and the like — through their functional "tops", a more useful description of practical software systems considers each of them as offering a number of services. Defining such a system by a single function is usually possible, but yields a rather artificial view.

Take an operating system. It is best understood as a system that provides certain services: allocating CPU time, managing memory, handling input and output devices, decoding and carrying out users' commands. The modules of a well-structured OS will tend to organize themselves around these groups of functions. But this is not the architecture that you will get from top-down functional decomposition; the method forces you, as the designer, to answer the artificial question "what is the topmost function?", and then to use the successive refinements of the answer as a basis for the structure. If hard pressed you could probably come up with an initial answer of the form

"Process all user requests"

which you could then refine into something like

from

boot

until

halted **or** *crashed*

loop

"Read in a user's request and put it into input queue"

"Get a request *r* from input queue"

"Process *r*"

"Put result into output queue"

"Get a result *o* from output queue"

"Output *o* to its recipient"

end

Refinements can go on. From such premises, however, it is unlikely that anyone can ever develop a reasonably structured operating system.

Even systems which may at first seem to belong to the "one input, one abstract function, one output" category reveal, on closer examination, a more diverse picture. Consider the earlier example of a compiler. Reduced to its bare essentials, or to the view of older textbooks, a compiler is the implementation of one input-to-output function: transforming source text in some programming language into machine code for a certain platform. But that is not a sufficient view of a modern compiler. Among its many services, a compiler will perform error detection, program formating, some configuration management, logging, report generation.

Another example is a typesetting program, taking input in some text processing format — TₑX, Microsoft Word, FrameMaker … — and generating output in HTML, Postscript or Adobe Acrobat format. Again we may view it at first as just an input-to-output filter. But most likely it will perform a number of other services as well, so it seems more interesting, when we are trying to characterize the system in the most general way, to consider the various types of data it manipulates: documents, chapters, sections, paragraphs, lines, words, characters, fonts, running heads, titles, figures and others.

The seemingly obvious starting point of top-down design — the view that each new development fulfills a request for a specific function — is subject to doubt:

> **Real systems have no top.**

Functions and evolution

Not only is the main function often not the best criterion to characterize a system initially: it may also, as the system evolves, be among the first properties to change, forcing the top-down designer into frequent redesign and defeating our attempts to satisfy the continuity requirement.

Consider the example of a program that has two versions, a "batch" one which handles every session as a single big run over the problem, and an interactive one in which a session is a sequence of transactions, with a much finer grain of user-system communication. This is typical of large scientific programs, which often have a "let it run a big chunk of computation for the whole night" version and a "let me try out a few things and see the results at once then continue with something else" version.

The top-down refinement of the batch version might begin as

[B0] -- Top-level abstraction

       "Solve a complete instance of the problem"

[B1] -- First refinement

    "Read input values"

    "Compute results"

    "Output results"

and so on. The top-down development of the interactive version, for its part, could proceed in the following style:

[I1]

> "Process one transaction"

[I2]

> **if** "New information provided by the user" **then**
> > "Input information"
> > "Store it"
> **elseif** "Request for information previously given" **then**
> > "Retrieve requested information"
> > "Output it"
> **elseif** "Request for result" **then**
> > **if** "Necessary information available" **then**
> > > "Retrieve requested result"
> > > "Output it"
> > **else**
> > > "Ask for confirmation of the request"
> > > **if** Yes **then**
> > > > "Obtain required information"
> > > > "Compute requested result"
> > > > "Output result"
> > > **end**
> > **end**
> **else**
> > (Etc.)

Started this way, the development will yield an entirely different result. The top-down approach fails to account for the property that the final programs are but two different versions of the same software system — whether they are developed concurrently or one has evolved from the other.

This example brings to light two of the most unpleasant consequences of the top-down approach: its focus on the external interface (implying here an early choice between batch and interactive) and its premature binding of temporal relations (the order in which actions will be executed).

Interfaces and software design

System architecture should be based on substance, not form. But top-down development tends to use the most superficial aspect of the system — its external interface — as a basis for its structure.

The focus on external interfaces is inevitable in a method that asks "What will the system do for the end user?" as the key question: the answer will tend to emphasize the most external aspects.

The user interface is only one of the components of a system. Often, it is also among the most volatile, if only because of the difficulty of getting it right the first time; initial versions may be of the mark, requiring experimentation and user feedback to obtain a satisfactory solution. A healthy design method will try to separate the interface from the rest of the system, using more stable properties as the basis for system structuring.

It is in fact often possible to build the interface separately from the rest of the system, using one of the many tools available nowadays to produce elegant and user-friendly interfaces, often based on object-oriented techniques. The user interface then becomes almost irrelevant to the overall system design.

Chapter 32 dis- cusses techniques and tools for user interfaces.

Premature ordering

The preceding examples illustrate another drawback of top-down functional decomposition: premature emphasis on temporal constraints. Each refinement expands a piece of the abstract structure into a more detailed *control* architecture, specifying the order in which various functions (various pieces of the action) will be executed. Such ordering constraints become essential properties of the system architecture; but they too are subject to change.

Recall the two alternative candidate structures for the first refinement of a compiler:

[C1]

> "Read program and produce sequence of tokens"
> "Parse sequence of tokens into abstract syntax tree"
> "Decorate tree with semantic information"
> "Generate code from decorated tree"

[C'1]

> **from**
> > "Initialize data structures"
> **until**
> > "All function definitions processed"
> **loop**
> > "Read in next function definition"
> > "Generate partial code"
> **end**
>
> "Fill in cross references"

As in the preceding example we start with two completely different architectures. Each is defined by a control structure (a sequence of instructions in the first case, a loop followed by an instruction in the second), implying strict ordering constraints between the elements of the structure. But freezing such ordering relations at the earliest stages of design is not reasonable. Issues such as the number of passes in a compiler and the sequencing of various activities (lexical analysis, parsing, semantic processing, optimization) have many possible solutions, which the designers must devise by considering space-time tradeoffs and other criteria which they do not necessarily master at the beginning of a project. They can perform fruitful design and implementation work on the components long before freezing their temporal ordering, and will want to retain this sequencing freedom for as long as possible. Top-down functional design does not provide such flexibility: you must specify the order of executing operations before you have had a chance to understand properly what these operations will do.

See the bibliogra-
phical notes for
references on the
methods cited.

Some design methods that attempt to correct some of the deficiencies of functional top-down design also suffer from this premature binding of temporal relationships. This is the case, among others, with the dataflow-directed method known as structured analysis and with Merise (a method popular in some European countries).

Object-oriented development, for its part, stays away from premature ordering. The designer studies the various operations applicable to a certain kind of data, and specifies the effect of each, but defers for as long as possible specifying the operations' order of execution. This may be called the **shopping list** approach: list needed operations — all the operations that you may need; ignore their ordering constraints until as late as possible in the software construction process. The result is much more extendible architectures.

Ordering and O-O development

The observations on the risks of premature ordering deserve a little more amplification because even object-oriented designers are not immune. The shopping list approach is one of the least understood parts of the method and it is not infrequent to see O-O projects fall into the old trap, with damaging effects on quality. This can result in particular from misuse of the *use case* idea, which we will encounter in the study of O-O methodology.

Chapter 11 pre-
sents assertions.

The problem is that the order of operations may seem so obvious a property of a system that it will weasel itself into the earliest stages of its design, with dire consequences if it later turns out to be not so final after all. The alternative technique (under the "shopping list" approach), perhaps less natural at first but much more flexible, uses logical rather than temporal constraints. It relies on the assertion concept developed later in this book; we can get the basic idea now through a simple non-software example.

Consider the problem of buying a house, reduced (as a gross first approximation) to three operations: finding a house that suits you; getting a loan; signing the contract. With a method focusing on ordering we will describe the design as a simple sequence of steps:

[H]

> *find_house*
> *get_loan*
> *sign_contract*

In the shopping list approach of O-O development we will initially refuse to attach too much importance to this ordering property. But of course constraints exist between the operations: you cannot sign a contract unless (let us just avoid saying *until* for the time being!) you have a desired house and a loan. We can express these constraints in logical rather than temporal form:

[H'1]

> *find_property*
> > **ensure**
> > > *property_found*
>
> *get_loan*
> > **ensure**
> > > *loan_approved*
>
> *sign_contract*
> > **require**
> > > *property_found* **and** *loan_approved*

The notation will only be introduced formally in chapter 11, but it should be clear enough here: **require** states a precondition, a logical property that an operation requires for its execution; and **ensure** states a postcondition, a logical property that will follow from an operation's execution. We have expressed that each of the first two operations achieves a certain property, and that the last operation requires both of these properties.

Why is the logical form of stating the constraints, H'1, better than the temporal form, H1? The answer is clear: H'1 expresses the minimum requirements, avoiding the overspecification of H1. And indeed H1 is too strong, as it rules out the scheme in which you get the loan first and then worry about the property — not at all absurd for a particular buyer whose main problem is financing. Another buyer might prefer the reverse order; we should support both schemes as long as they observe the logical constraint.

Now imagine that we turn this example into a realistic model of the process with the many tasks involved — title search, termite inspection, pre-qualifying for the loan, finding a real estate agent, selling your previous house if applicable, inviting your friends to the house-warming party... It may be possible to express the ordering constraints, but the result will be complicated and probably fragile (you may have to reconsider everything if you later include another task). The logical constraint approach scales up much more smoothly; each operation simply states what it needs and what it guarantees, all in terms of abstract properties.

Exercise E6.7, page 162 (in the next chapter).

These observations are particularly important for the would-be object designer, who may still be influenced by functional ideas, and might be tempted to rely on early identification of system usage scenarios ("use cases") as a basis for analysis. This is incompatible with object-oriented principles, and often leads to top-down functional decomposition of the purest form — even when the team members are convinced that they are using an object-oriented method.

We will examine, in our study of O-O methodological principles, what role can be found for use cases in object-oriented software construction.

"Use cases", page 738.

Reusability

After this short advance incursion into the fringes of object territory, let us resume our analysis of the top-down method, considering it this time in relation to one of our principal goals, reusability.

Working top-down means that you develop software elements in response to particular subspecifications encountered in the tree-like development of a system. At a given point of the development, corresponding to the refinement of a certain node, you will detect the need for a specific function — such as analyzing an input command line — and write down its specification, which you or someone else will then implement.

The context of a module in top-down design

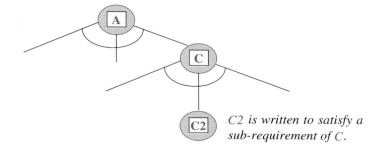

C2 is written to satisfy a sub-requirement of C.

The figure, which shows part of a top-down refinement tree, illustrates this property: *C2* is written to satisfy some sub-requirement of *C*; but the characteristics of *C2* are entirely determined by its immediate context — the needs of *C*. For example, *C* could be a module in charge of analyzing some user input, and *C2* could be the module in charge of analyzing one line (part of a longer input).

This approach is good at ensuring that the design will meet the initial specification, but it does not promote reusability. Modules are developed in response to specific subproblems, and tend to be no more general than implied by their immediate context. Here if *C* is meant for input texts of a specific kind, it is unlikely that *C2*, which analyzes one line of those texts, will be applicable to any other kind of input.

One can in principle include the concern for extendibility and generality in a top-down design process, and encourage developers to write modules that transcend the immediate needs which led to their development. But nothing in the method encourages generalization, and in practice it tends to produce modules with narrow specifications.

The very notion of top-down design suggests the reverse of reusability. Designing for reusability means building components that are as general as possible, then combining them into systems. This is a bottom-up process, at the opposite of the top-down idea of starting with the definition of "the problem" and deriving a solution through successive refinements.

On the project and product culture see [M 1995].

This discussion makes top-down design appear as a byproduct of what we can call the *project culture* in software engineering: the view that the unit of discourse is the individual project, independently of earlier and later projects. The reality is less simple: project *n* in a company is usually a variation on project *n* – *1*, and a preview of project *n* + *1*. By focusing on just one project, top-down design ignores this property of practical software construction,

Production and description

One of the reasons for the original attraction of top-down ideas is that a top-down style may be convenient to explain a design once it is in place. But what is good to document an existing design is not necessarily the best way to produce designs. This point was eloquently argued by Michael Jackson in *System Development*:

> *Top-down is a reasonable way of describing things which are already fully understood... But top-down is not a reasonable way of developing, designing, or discovering anything. There is a close parallel with mathematics. A mathematical textbook describes a branch of mathematics in a logical order: each theorem stated and proved is used in the proofs of subsequent theorems. But the theorems were not developed or discovered in this way, or in this order...*

Quotation from [Jackson 1983], pages 370-371.

> *When the developer of a system, or of a program, already has a clear idea of the completed result in his mind, he can use top-down to describe on paper what is in his head. This is why people can believe that they are performing top-down design or development, and doing so successfully: they confuse the method of description with the method of development... When the top-down phase begins, the problem is already solved, and only details remain to be solved.*

Top-down design: an assessment

This discussion of top-down functional design shows the method to be poorly adapted to the development of significant systems. It remains a useful paradigm for small programs and individual algorithms; it is certainly a helpful technique to *describe* well-understood algorithms, especially in programming courses. But it does not scale up to large practical software. By developing a system top-down you trade short-term convenience for long-term inflexibility; you unduly privilege one function over the others; you may be led to devoting your attention to interface characteristics at the expense of more fundamental properties; you lose sight of the data aspect; and you risk sacrificing reusability.

5.3 OBJECT-BASED DECOMPOSITION

The case for using objects (or more precisely, as seen below, object types) as the key to system modularization is based on the quality aims defined in chapter 1, in particular extendibility, reusability and compatibility.

The plea for using objects will be fairly short, since the case has already been made at least in part: many of the arguments against top-down, function-based design reappear naturally as evidence in favor of bottom-up, object-based design.

This evidence should not, however, lead us to dismiss the functions entirely. As noted at the beginning of this chapter, no approach to software construction can be complete unless it accounts for both the function and object parts. So we will need to retain a clear role for functions in the object-oriented method, even if they must submit to the objects in the resulting system architectures. The notion of abstract data type will provide us with a definition of objects which reserves a proper place for the functions.

Extendibility

If the functions of a system, as discussed above, tend to change often over the system's life, can we find a more stable characterization of its essential properties, so as to guide our choice of modules and meet the goal of continuity?

The types of objects manipulated by the system are more promising candidates. Whatever happens to the payroll processing system used earlier as an example, it likely will still manipulate objects representing employees, salary scales, company regulations, hours worked, pay checks. Whatever happens to a compiler or other language processing tool, it likely will still manipulate source texts, token sequences, parse trees, abstract syntax trees, target code. Whatever happens to a finite element system, it likely will still manipulate matrices, finite elements and grids.

This argument is based on pragmatic observation, not on a proof that object types are more stable than functions. But experience seems to support it overwhelmingly.

The argument only holds if we take a high-level enough view of objects. If we understood objects in terms of their physical representations, we would not be much better off than with functions — as a matter of fact probably worse, since a top-down functional decomposition at least encourages abstraction. So the question of finding a suitably abstract description of objects is crucial; it will occupy all of the next chapter.

Reusability

The discussion of reusability pointed out that a routine (a unit of functional decomposition) was usually not sufficient as a unit of reusability.

See "Factoring Out Common Behaviors", page 85.

The presentation used a typical example: table searching. Starting with a seemingly natural candidate for reuse, a searching routine, it noted that we cannot easily reuse such a routine separately from the other operations that apply to a table, such as creation, insertion and deletion; hence the idea that a satisfactory reusable module for such a problem should be a collection of such operations. But if we try to understand the conceptual thread that unites all these operations, we find the type of objects to which they apply — tables.

Such examples suggest that object types, fully equipped with the associated operations, will provide stable units of reuse.

Compatibility

Another software quality factor, compatibility, was defined as the ease with which software products (for this discussion, modules) can be combined with each other.

It is difficult to combine actions if the data structures they access are not designed for that purpose. Why not instead try to combine entire data structures?

5.4 OBJECT-ORIENTED SOFTWARE CONSTRUCTION

We have by now accumulated enough background to consider a tentative definition of object-oriented software construction. This will only be a first attempt; a more concrete definition will follow from the discussion of abstract data types in the next chapter.

See page 147 for the final definition.

Object-oriented software construction (definition 1)

Object-oriented software construction is the software development method which bases the architecture of any software system on modules deduced from the types of objects it manipulates (rather than the function or functions that the system is intended to ensure).

An informal characterization of this approach may serve as a motto for the object-oriented designer:

OBJECT MOTTO

Ask not first what the system does:

Ask what it does it to!

To get a working implementation, you will of course, sooner or later, have to find out what it does. Hence the word *first*. Better later than sooner, says object-oriented wisdom. In this approach, the choice of main function is one of the very last steps to be taken in the process of system construction.

The developers will stay away, as long as possible, from the need to describe and implement the topmost function of the system. Instead, they will analyze the types of objects of the system. System design will progress through the successive improvements of their understanding of these object classes. It is a bottom-up process of building robust and extendible solutions to parts of the problem, and combining them into more and more powerful assemblies — until the final assembly which yields a solution of the original problem but, everyone hopes, is not the *only* possible one: the same components, assembled differently and probably combined with others, should be general enough to yield as a byproduct, if you have applied the method well and enjoyed your share of good luck, solutions to future problems as well.

For many software people this change in viewpoint is as much of a shock as may have been for others, in an earlier time, the idea of the earth orbiting around the sun rather than the reverse. It is also contrary to much of the established software engineering wisdom, which tends to present system construction as the fulfillment of a system's function as expressed in a narrow, binding requirements document. Yet this simple idea — look at the data first, forget the immediate purpose of the system — may hold the key to reusability and extendibility.

5.5 ISSUES

The above definition provides a starting point to discuss the object-oriented method. But besides providing components of the answer it also raises many new questions, such as:

- How to find the relevant object types.

- How to describe the object types.

- How to describe the relations and commonalities between object types.

- How to use object types to structure software.

The rest of this book will address these issues. Let us preview a few answers.

Finding the object types

See chapter 22.

The question "how shall we find the objects?" can seem formidable at first. A later chapter will examine it in some detail (in its more accurate version, which deals with object *types* rather than individual objects) but it is useful here to dispel some of the possible fears. The question does not necessarily occupy much of the time of experienced O-O developers, thanks in part to the availability of three sources of answers:

- Many objects are there just for the picking. They directly model objects of the physical reality to which the software applies. One of the particular strengths of object technology is indeed its power as a modeling tool, using software object types (classes) to model physical object types, and the method's inter-object-type relations (client, inheritance) to model the relations that exist between physical object types, such as aggregation and specialization. It does not take a treatise on object-oriented analysis to convince a software developer that a call monitoring system, in a telecommunications application, will have a class *CALL* and a class *LINE*, or that a document processing system will have a class *DOCUMENT*, a class *PARAGRAPH* and a class *FONT*.

- A source of object types is reuse: classes previously developed by others. This technique, although not always prominent in the O-O analysis literature, is often among the most useful in practice. We should resist the impulse to invent something if the problem has already been solved satisfactorily by others.

- Finally, experience and imitation also play a role. As you become familiar with successful object-oriented designs and design patterns (such as some of those described in this book and the rest of the O-O literature), even those which are not directly reusable in your particular application, you will be able to gain inspiration from these earlier efforts.

We will be in a much better position to understand these object-finding techniques and others once we have gained a better technical insight into the software notion of object — not to be confused with the everyday meaning of the word.

Describing types and objects

A question of more immediate concern, assuming we know how to obtain the proper object types to serve as a basis for modularizing our systems, is how to describe these types and their objects.

Two criteria must guide us in answering this question:

• The need to provide representation-independent descriptions, for fear of losing (as noted) the principal benefit of top-down functional design: abstraction.

• The need to re-insert the functions, giving them their proper place in software architectures whose decomposition is primarily based on the analysis of object types since (as also noted) we must in the end accommodate both aspects of the object-function duality.

The next chapter develops an object description technique achieving these goals.

Describing the relations and structuring software

Another question is what kind of relation we should permit between object types; since the modules will be based on object types, the answer also determines the structuring techniques that will be available to make up software systems from components.

In the purest form of object technology, only two relations exist: client and inheritance. They correspond to different kinds of possible dependency between two object types A and B:

• B is a client of A if every object of type B may contain information about one or more objects of type A.

• B is an heir of A if B denotes a specialized version of A.

Some widely used approaches to analysis, in particular information modeling approaches such as entity-relationship modeling, have introduced rich sets of relations to describe the many possible connections that may exist between the element of a system. To people used to such approaches, having to do with just two kinds of relation often seems restrictive at first. But this impression is not necessarily justified:

• The client relation is broad enough to cover many different forms of dependency. Examples include what is often called aggregation (the presence in every object of type B of a subobject of type A), reference dependency, and generic dependency.

• The inheritance relation covers specialization in its many different forms.

• Many properties of dependencies will be expressed in a more general form through other techniques. For example, to describe a 1-to-n dependency (every object of type B is connected to at least one and at most n objects of type A) we will express that B is a client of A, and include a **class invariant** specifying the exact nature of the client relation. The class invariant, being expressed in the language of logic, covers many more cases than the finite set of primitive relations offered by entity-relationship modeling or similar approaches.

5.6 KEY CONCEPTS INTRODUCED IN THIS CHAPTER

- Computation involves three kinds of ingredient: processors (or threads of control), actions (or functions), and data (or objects).

- A system's architecture may be obtained from the functions or from the object types.

- A description based on object types tends to provide better stability over time and better reusability than one based on an analysis of the system's functions.

- It is usually artificial to view a system as consisting of just one function. A realistic system usually has more than one "top" and is better described as providing a set of services.

- It is preferable not to pay too much attention to ordering constraints during the early stages of system analysis and design. Many temporal constraints can be described more abstractly as logical constraints.

- Top-down functional design is not appropriate for the long-term view of software systems, which involves change and reuse.

- Object-oriented software construction bases the structure of systems on the types of objects they manipulate.

- In object-oriented design, the primary design issue is not what the system does, but what types of objects it does it to. The design process defers to the last steps the decision as to what is the topmost function, if any, of the system.

- To satisfy the requirements of extendibility and reusability, object-oriented software construction needs to deduce the architecture from sufficiently abstract descriptions of objects.

- Two kinds of relation may exist between object types: client and inheritance.

5.7 BIBLIOGRAPHICAL NOTES

The case for object-based decomposition is made, using various arguments, in [Cox 1990] (original 1986), [Goldberg 1981], [Goldberg 1985], [Page-Jones 1995] and [M 1978], [M 1979], [M 1983], [M 1987], [M 1988].

The top-down method has been advocated in many books and articles. [Wirth 1971] developed the notion of stepwise refinement.

Of other methods whose rationales start with some of the same arguments that have led this discussion to object-oriented concepts, the closest is probably Jackson's JSD [Jackson 1983], a higher-level extension of JSP [Jackson 1975]. See also Warnier's data-directed design method [Orr 1977]. For a look at the methods that object technology is meant to replace, see books on: Constantine's and Yourdon's structured design [Yourdon 1979]; structured analysis [DeMarco 1978], [Page-Jones 1980], [McMenamin 1984], [Yourdon 1989]; Merise [Tardieu 1984], [Tabourier 1986].

Entity-relationship modeling was introduced by [Chen 1976].

6

Abstract data types

*This opened my mind, I started to grasp what it means to use the tool known as algebra. I'll be damned if anyone had ever told me before: over and again Mr. Dupuy [the mathematics teacher] was making pompous sentences on the subject, but not once would he say this simple word: it is a **division of labor**, which like any division of labor produces miracles, and allows the mind to concentrate all of its forces on just one side of objects, on just one of their qualities.*

What a difference it would have made for us if Mr. Dupuy had told us: This cheese is soft or it is hard; it is white, it is blue; it is old, it is young; it is yours, it is mine, it is light or it is heavy. Of so many qualities let us consider only the weight. Whatever that weight may be, let us call it A. Now, without thinking of the weight any more, let us apply to A everything that we know of quantities.

Such a simple thing; yet no one was saying it to us in that faraway province…

Stendhal, *The Life of Henry Brulard*, 1836.

For abstraction consists only in separating the perceptible qualities of bodies, either from other qualities, or from the bodies to which they apply. Errors arise when this separation is poorly done or wrongly applied: poorly done in philosophical questions, and wrongly applied in physical and mathematical questions. An almost sure way to err in philosophy is to fail to simplify enough the objects under study; and an infallible way to obtain defective results in physics and mathematics is to view the objects as less composite than they are.

Denis Diderot, *A Letter on the Blind for the Benefit of Those Who Can See*, 1749.

*L*etting objects play the lead role in our software architectures requires that we describe them adequately. This chapter shows how.

You are perhaps impatient to dive into the depths of object technology and explore the details of multiple inheritance, dynamic binding and other joys; then you may at first look at this chapter as an undue delay since it is mostly devoted to the study of some mathematical concepts (although all the mathematics involved is elementary).

But in the same way that even the most gifted musician will benefit from learning a little music theory, knowing about abstract data types will help you understand and enjoy the practice of object-oriented analysis, design and programming, however attractive the concepts might already appear without the help of the theory. Since abstract data types establish the theoretical basis for the entire method, the consequences of the ideas introduced in this chapter will be felt throughout the rest of this book.

There is more. As we will see at chapter end, these consequences actually extend beyond the study of software proper, yielding a few principles of intellectual investigation which one may perhaps apply to other disciplines.

6.1 CRITERIA

To obtain proper descriptions of objects, we need a method satisfying three conditions:

- The descriptions should be precise and unambiguous.

- They should be complete — or at least as complete as we want them in each case (we may decide to leave some details out).

- They should not be **overspecifying**.

The last point is what makes the answer non-trivial. It is after all easy to be precise, unambiguous and complete if we "spill the beans" by giving out all the details of the objects' representation. But this is usually *too much* information for the authors of software elements that need to access the objects.

This observation is close to the comments that led to the notion of information hiding. The concern there was that by providing a module's source code (or, more generally, implementation-related elements) as the primary source of information for the authors of software elements that rely on that module, we may drown them in a flood of details, prevent them from concentrating on their own job, and hamper prospects of smooth evolution. Here the danger is the same if we let modules use a certain data structure on the basis of information that pertains to the structure's representation rather than to its essential properties.

"Information Hiding", page 51.

6.2 IMPLEMENTATION VARIATIONS

To understand better why the need for abstract data descriptions is so crucial, let us explore further the potential consequences of using physical representation as the basis for describing objects.

A well-known and convenient example is the description of stack objects. A stack object serves to pile up and retrieve other objects in a last-in, first-out ("LIFO") manner, the latest inserted element being the first one to be retrieved. The stack is a ubiquitous structure in computing science and in many software systems; the typical compiler or interpreter, for example, is peppered with stacks of many kinds.

> Stacks, it must be said, are also ubiquitous in didactic presentations of abstract data types, so much so that Edsger Dijkstra is said to have once quipped that "abstract data types are a remarkable theory, whose purpose is to describe stacks". Fair enough. But the notion of abstract data type applies to so many more advanced cases in the rest of this book that I do not feel ashamed of starting with this staple example. It is the simplest I know which includes about every important idea about abstract data types.

Stack representations

Several possible physical representations exist for stacks:

Three possible representations for a stack

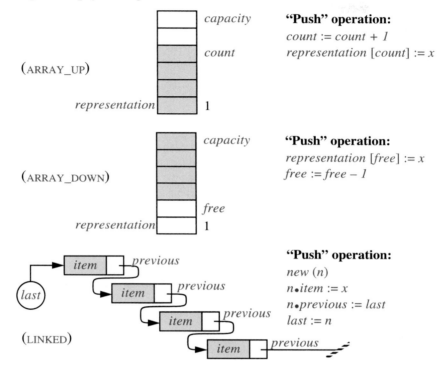

"**Push**" **operation:**
$count := count + 1$
$representation\ [count] := x$

"**Push**" **operation:**
$representation\ [free] := x$
$free := free - 1$

"**Push**" **operation:**
$new\ (n)$
$n \bullet item := x$
$n \bullet previous := last$
$last := n$

The figure illustrates three of the most common representations. Each has been given a name for ease of reference:

- ARRAY_UP: represent a stack through an array *representation* and an integer *count* whose value ranges from 0 (for an empty stack) to *capacity*, the size of the array *representation*; stack elements are stored in the array at indices 1 up to *count*.

- ARRAY_DOWN: like ARRAY_UP, but with elements stored from the end of the array rather than from the beginning. Here the integer is called *free* (it is the index of the highest free array position, or 0 if all positions are occupied) and ranges from *capacity* for an empty stack down to 0. The stack elements are stored in the array at indices *capacity* down to *free + 1*.

- LINKED: a linked representation which stores each stack element in a cell with two fields: *item* representing the element, and *previous* containing a pointer to the cell containing the previously pushed element. The representation also needs *last*, a pointer to the cell representing the top.

Next to each representation, the figure shows a program extract (in Pascal-like notation) giving the corresponding implementation for a basic stack operation: pushing an element x onto the top.

For the array representations, ARRAY_UP and ARRAY_DOWN, the instructions increase or decrease the top indicator (*count* or *free*) and assign x to the corresponding array element. Since these representations support stacks of at most *capacity* elements, robust implementations should include guards of the respective forms

if *count* < *capacity* **then** …
if *free* > *0* **then** …

which the figure omits for simplicity.

For LINKED, the linked representation, pushing an element requires four operations: create a new cell n (done here with Pascal's *new* procedure, which allocates space for a new object); assign x to the new cell's *item* field; chain the new cell to the earlier stack top by assigning to its *previous* field the current value of *last*; and update *last* so that it will now be attached to the newly created cell.

Although these are the most frequently used stack representations, many others exist. For example if you need **two** stacks of elements of the same type, and have only limited space available, you may rely on a single array with two integer top markers, *count* as in ARRAY_UP and *free* as in ARRAY_DOWN; one of the stacks will grow up and the other will grow down. The representation is full if and only if *count* = *free*.

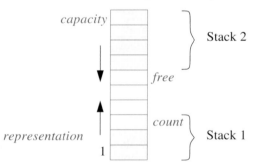

Head-to-head representation for two stacks

The advantage, of course, is to lessen the risk of running out of space: with two arrays of capacity n representing stacks under ARRAY_UP or ARRAY_DOWN, you exhaust the available space whenever *either* stack reaches n elements; with a single array of size $2n$ holding two head-to-head stacks, you run out when the *combined* size reaches $2n$, a less likely occurrence if the two stacks grow independently. (For any variable values p and q, $max\,(p + q) \leq max\,(p) + max\,(q)$.)

Each of these and other possible representations is useful in some cases. Choosing one of them as "the" definition of stacks would be a typical case of overspecification. Why should we consider ARRAY_UP, for example, more representative than LINKED? The most visible properties of ARRAY_UP — the array, the integer *count*, the upper bound — are irrelevant to an understanding of the underlying structure.

The danger of overspecification

Why is it so bad to use a particular representation as specification?

"ABOUT SOFT-WARE MAINTE-NANCE", 1.3, page 17.

The results of the Lientz and Swanson maintenance study, which you may recall, give a hint. More than 17% of software costs was found to come from the need to take into account changes of data formats. As was noted in the discussion, too many programs are closely tied to the physical structure of the data they manipulate. A method relying on the physical representation of data structures to guide analysis and design would not be likely to yield flexible software.

So if we are to use objects or object types as the basis of our system architectures, we should find a better description criterion than the physical representation.

How long is a middle initial?

Lest stacks make us forget that, beyond the examples favored by computer scientists, data structures are ultimately connected with real-life objects, here is an amusing example, taken from a posting on the Risks forum (*comp.risks* Usenet newsgroup) of the dangers of a view of data that is too closely dependent on concrete properties:

Risks forum, 10.74, 3 Jan. 1993. Posting by Darrell D.E. Long: ``Dehumanization by old Cobol programs''. *Abbreviated.*

See exercise E6.5, page 161.

My dear mother blessed (or perhaps cursed) all of her children with two middle initials, in my case "D" and "E". This has caused me a good deal of trouble.

It seems that TRW sells certain parts of your credit information, such as your name and a demographic profile. I recently got a new credit card from Gottchalks and found to my chagrin that my name had been truncated to "Darrell D. Long". I went to the credit manager and was assured that things would be fixed. Well, two things happened: I got a new credit card, this time as "Darrell E. Long", and TRW now has an annotation in my file to the effect "File variation: middle initial is E". Soon after this I start getting mail for "Darrell E. Long" (along with the usual "Darrell Long" and "Darrell D. Long" and the occasional "Darrell D. E. Long").

I called up the credit bureau and it seems that the programmer who coded up the TRW database decided that all good Americans are entitled to only one middle initial. As the woman on the phone patiently told me "They only allocated enough megabytes (sic) in the system for one middle initial, and it would probably be awfully hard to change".

Aside from the typical example of technobabble justification ("megabytes"), the lesson here is the need to avoid tying software to the exact physical properties of data. TRW's system seems similar to those programs, mentioned in an earlier discussion, which "knew" that postal codes consist of exactly five digits.

See page 18.

The author of the message reproduced above was mainly concerned about junk mail, an unpleasant but not life-threatening event; the archives of the Risks forum are full of computer-originated name confusions with more serious consequences. The "millenium problem", mentioned in the discussion of software maintenance, is another example of the dangers of accessing data based on physical representation, this one with hundreds of millions of dollars' worth of consequences.

6.3 TOWARDS AN ABSTRACT VIEW OF OBJECTS

How do we retain completeness, precision and non-ambiguity without paying the price of overspecification?

Using the operations

In the stack example, what unites the various representations in spite of all their differences is that they describe a "container" structure (a structure used to contain other objects), where certain operations are applicable and enjoy certain properties. By focusing not on a particular choice of representation but on these operations and properties, we may be able to obtain an abstract yet useful characterization of the notion of stack.

The operations typically available on a stack are the following:

- A command to push an element on top of a stack. Let us call that operation *put*.

- A command to remove the stack's top element, if the stack is not empty. Let us call it *remove*.

- A query to find out what the top element is, if the stack is not empty. Let us call it *item*.

- A query to determine whether the stack is empty. (This will enable clients to determine beforehand if they can use *remove* and *item*.)

In addition we may need a creator operation giving us a stack, initially empty. Let us call it *make*.

> Two points may have caught your attention and will deserve more explanation later in this chapter. First, the operation names may seem surprising; for the moment, just think of *put* as meaning *push*, *remove* as meaning *pop*, and *item* as meaning *top*. Details shortly (on the facing page, actually). Second, the operations have been divided into three categories: creators, which yield objects; queries, which return information about objects; and commands, which can modify objects. This classification will also require some more comments.

In a traditional view of data structures, we would consider that the notion of stack is given by some data declaration corresponding to one of the above representations, for example (representation ARRAY_UP, Pascal-like syntax):

count: *INTEGER*

representation: **array** [*1 .. capacity*] **of** *STACK_ELEMENT_TYPE*

where *capacity*, a constant integer, is the maximum number of elements on the stack. Then *put*, *remove*, *item*, *empty* and *make* would be routines (subprograms) that work on the object structures defined by these declarations.

The key step towards data abstraction is to reverse the viewpoint: forget for the moment about the representation; take the operations themselves as defining the data structure. In other words, a stack **is** any structure to which clients may apply the operations listed above.

A laissez-faire policy for the society of modules

The method just outlined for describing data structures shows a rather selfish approach to the world of data structures: like an economist of the most passionate supply-side, invisible-hand, let-the-free-market-decide school, we are interested in individual agents not so much for what they *are* internally as for what they *have* to offer to each other. The world of objects (and hence of software architecture) will be a world of interacting agents, communicating on the basis of precisely defined protocols.

The economic analogy will indeed accompany us throughout this presentation; the agents — the software modules — are called *suppliers* and *clients*; the protocols will be called *contracts*, and much of object-oriented design is indeed *Design by Contract*, the title of a later chapter.

See "BEYOND SOFTWARE", 6.6, page 147.

As always with analogies, we should not get too carried away: this work is not a textbook on economics, and contains no hint of its author's views in that field. It will suffice for the moment to note the remarkable analogies of the abstract data type approach to some theories of how human agents should work together. Later in this chapter we will again explore what abstract data types can tell us beyond their original area of application.

Name consistency

For the moment, let us get back to more immediate concerns, and make sure you are comfortable with the above example specification in all its details. If you have encountered stacks before, the operation names chosen for the discussion of stacks may have surprised or even shocked you. Any self-respecting computer scientist will know stack operations under other names:

Common stack operation name	Name used here
push	*put*
pop	*remove*
top	*item*
new	*make*

Why use anything else than the traditional terminology? The reason is a desire to take a high-level view of data structures — especially "containers", those data structures used to keep objects.

Stacks are just one brand of container; more precisely, they belong to a category of containers which we may call **dispensers**. A dispenser provides its clients with a mechanism for storing (*put*), retrieving (*item*) and removing (*remove*) objects, but without giving them any control over the choice of object to be stored, retrieved or removed. For example, the LIFO policy of stacks implies that you may only retrieve or remove the element that was stored last. Another brand of dispenser is the queue, which has a first-in, first-out (FIFO) policy: you store at one end, retrieve and remove at the other; the element that you retrieve or remove is the oldest one stored but not yet removed. An example of a container which is **not** a dispenser is an array, where you choose, through integer indices, the positions where you store and retrieve objects.

Because the similarities between various kinds of container (dispensers, arrays and others) are more important than the differences between their individual storage, retrieval and removal properties, this book constantly adheres to a standardized terminology which downplays the differences between data structure variants and instead emphasizes the commonality. So the basic operation to retrieve an element will always be called *item*, the basic operation to remove an element will always be called *remove* and so on.

These naming issues may appear superficial at first — "cosmetic", as programmers sometimes say. But do not forget that one of our eventual aims is to provide the basis for powerful, professional libraries of reusable software components. Such libraries will contain tens of thousands of available operations. Without a systematic and clear nomenclature, both the developers and the users of these libraries would quickly be swamped in a flood of specific and incompatible names, providing a strong (and unjustifiable) obstacle to large-scale reuse.

Naming, then, is *not* cosmetic. Good reusable software is software that provides the right functionality and provides it under the right names.

The names used here for stack operations are part of a systematic set of naming conventions used throughout this book. A later chapter will introduce them in more detail.

Chapter 26, in particular "CHOOSING THE RIGHT NAMES", 26.2, page 879.

How not to handle abstractions

In software engineering as in other scientific and technical disciplines, a seminal idea may seem obvious once you have been exposed to it, even though it may have taken a long time to emerge. The bad ideas and the complicated ones (they are often the same) often appear first; it takes time for the simple and the elegant to take over.

This observation is true of abstract data types. Although good software developers have always (as a result of education or mere instinct) made good use of abstraction, many of the systems in existence today were designed without much consideration of this goal.

I once did a little involuntary experiment which provided a good illustration of this state of affairs. While setting up the project part of a course which I was teaching, I decided to provide students with a sort of anonymous marketplace, where they could place mock "for sale" announcements of software modules, without saying who was the source of the advertisement. (The idea, which may or may not have been a good one, was to favor a selection process based only on a precise specification of the modules' advertized facilities.) The mail facility of a famous operating system commonly favored by universities seemed to provide the right base mechanism (why write a new mail system just for a course project?); but naturally that mail facility shows the sender's name when it delivers a message to its recipients. I had access to the source of the corresponding code — a huge C program — and decided, perhaps foolishly, to take that code, remove all references to the sender's name in delivered messages, and recompile.

Aided by a teaching assistant, I thus embarked on a task which seemed obvious enough although not commonly taught in software engineering courses: systematic program *de*construction. Sure enough, we quickly found the first place where the program accessed the sender's name, and we removed the corresponding code. This, we naïvely thought, would have done the job, so we recompiled and sent a test mail message; but the sender's name was still there! Thus began a long and surreal process: time and again, believing we had finally found the last reference to the sender's name, we would remove it, recompile, and mail a test message, only to find the name duly recorded once again in its habitual field. Like the Hydra in its famous fight, the mailer kept growing a new head every time we thought we had cut the last neck.

Finally, repeating for the modern era the earlier feat of Hercules, we slew the beast for good; by then we had removed more than twenty code extracts which all accessed, in some way or other, information about the message sender.

Writing MAIL_ MESSAGE is the topic of exercise E6.4, page 161.

Although the previous sections have only got us barely started on our road to abstract data types, it should be clear by now that any program written in accordance with even the most elementary concepts of data abstraction would treat *MAIL_MESSAGE* as a carefully defined abstract notion, supporting a query operation, perhaps called *sender*, which returns information about the message sender. Any portion of the mail program that needs this information would obtain it solely through the *sender* query. Had the mail program been designed according to this seemingly obvious principle, it would have been sufficient, for the purpose of my little exercise, to modify the code of the *sender* query. Most likely, the software would also then have provided an associated command operation *set_sender* to update sender information, making the job even easier.

What is the real moral of that little story (besides lowering the reader's guard in preparation for the surprise mathematical offensive of the next section)? After all, the mail program in question is successful, at least judging by its widespread use. But it typifies the current quality standard in the industry. Until we move significantly beyond that standard, the phrase "software engineering" will remain a case of wishful thinking.

Oh yes, one more note. Some time after my brief encounter with the mail program, I read that certain network hackers had intruded into the computer systems of highly guarded government laboratories, using a security hole of that very mail program — a hole which was familiar, so the press reported, to all those in the know. I was not in the know; but, when I learned the news, I was not surprised.

6.4 FORMALIZING THE SPECIFICATION

The glimpse of data abstraction presented so far is too informal to be of durable use. Consider again our staple example: a stack, as we now understand it, is defined in terms of the applicable operations; but then we need to define these operations!

Informal descriptions as above (*put* pushes an element "on top of" the stack, *remove* pops the element "last pushed" and so on) do not suffice. We need to know precisely how these operations can be used by clients, and what they will do for them.

An abstract data type specification will provide this information. It consists of four paragraphs, explained in the next sections:

- TYPES.

- FUNCTIONS.

- AXIOMS.

- PRECONDITIONS.

These paragraphs will rely on a simple mathematical notation for specifying the properties of an abstract data type (ADT for short).

> The notation — a mathematical formalism, not to be confused with the software notation of the rest of this book even though for consistency it uses a similar syntactic style — has no name and is not a programming language; it could serve as the starting point for a formal *specification* language, but we shall not pursue this avenue here, being content enough to use self-explanatory conventions for the unambiguous specification of abstract data types.

Specifying types

The TYPES paragraph indicates the types being specified. In general, it may be convenient to specify several ADTs together, although our example has only one, *STACK*.

By the way, what is a type? The answer to this question will combine all the ideas developed in the rest of this chapter; a type is a collection of objects characterized by functions, axioms and preconditions. If for the moment you just view a type as a set of objects, in the mathematical sense of the word "set" — type *STACK* as the set of all possible stacks, type *INTEGER* as the set of all possible integer values and so on — you are not guilty of any terrible misunderstanding. As you read this discussion you will be able to refine this view. In the meantime the discussion will not be too fussy about using "set" for "type" and conversely.

On one point, however, you should make sure to avoid any confusion: an abstract data type such as *STACK* is not an object (one particular stack) but a collection of objects (the set of all stacks). Remember what our real goal is: finding a good basis for the modules of our software systems. As was noted in the previous chapter, basing a module on one particular object — one stack, one airplane, one bank account — would not make sense. O-O design will enable us to build modules covering the properties of all stacks, all airplanes, all bank accounts — or at least of some stacks, airplanes or accounts.

An object belonging to the set of objects described by an ADT specification is called an **instance** of the ADT. For example, a specific stack which satisfies the properties of the *STACK* abstract data type will be an instance of *STACK*. The notion of instance will carry over to object-oriented design and programming, where it will play an important role in explaining the run-time behavior of programs.

The TYPES paragraph simply lists the types introduced in the specification. Here:

> **TYPES**
>
> • *STACK* [*G*]

Our specification is about a single abstract data type *STACK*, describing stacks of objects of an arbitrary type *G*.

Genericity

See "Genericity", page 96.

In *STACK* [*G*], *G* denotes an arbitrary, unspecified type. *G* is called a **formal generic parameter** of the abstract data type *STACK*, and *STACK* itself is said to be a generic ADT. The mechanism permitting such parameterized specifications is known as genericity; we already encountered a similar concept in our review of package constructs.

It is possible to write ADT specifications without genericity, but at the price of unjustified repetition. Why have separate specifications for the types "stack of bank accounts", "stack of integers" and so on? These specifications would be identical except where they explicitly refer to the type of the stack elements — bank accounts or integers. Writing them, and then performing the type substitutions manually, would be tedious. Reusability is desirable for specifications too — not just programs! Thanks to genericity, we can make the type parameterization explicit by choosing some arbitrary name, here *G*, to represent the variable type of stack elements.

As a result, an ADT such as *STACK* is not quite a type, but rather a type pattern; to obtain a directly usable stack type, you must obtain some element type, for example *ACCOUNT*, and provide it as **actual generic parameter** corresponding to the formal parameter *G*. So although *STACK* is by itself just a type pattern, the notation

STACK [*ACCOUNT*]

is a fully defined type. Such a type, obtained by providing actual generic parameters to a generic type, is said to be **generically derived**.

The notions just seen are applicable recursively: every type should, at least in principle, have an ADT specification, so you may view *ACCOUNT* as being itself an abstract data type; also, a type that you use as actual generic parameter to *STACK* (to produce a generically derived type) may itself be generically derived, so it is perfectly all right to use

STACK [*STACK* [*ACCOUNT*]]

specifying a certain abstract data type: the instances of that type are stacks, whose elements are themselves stacks; the elements of these latter stacks are bank accounts.

As this example shows, the preceding definition of "instance" needs some qualification. Strictly speaking, a particular stack is an instance not of *STACK* (which, as noted, is a type pattern rather than a type) but of some type generically derived from *STACK*, for example *STACK* [*ACCOUNT*]. It is convenient, however, to continue talking about instances of *STACK* and similar type patterns, with the understanding that this actually means instances of their generic derivations.

Similarly, it is not quite accurate to talk about *STACK* being an ADT: the correct term is "ADT pattern". For simplicity, this discussion will continue omitting the word "pattern" when there is no risk of confusion.

The distinction will carry over to object-oriented design and programming, but there we will need to keep two separate terms:

•The basic notion will be the **class**; a class may have generic parameters.

•Describing actual data requires **types**. A non-generic class is also a type, but a generic class is only a type pattern. To obtain an actual type from a generic class, we will need to provide actual generic parameters, exactly as we derive the ADT *STACK [ACCOUNT]* from the ADT pattern *STACK*.

Later chapters will explore the notion of genericity as applied to classes, and how to combine it with the inheritance mechanism.

Chapter 10 and appendix B.

Listing the functions

After the TYPES paragraph comes the FUNCTIONS paragraph, which lists the operations applicable to instances of the ADT. As announced, these operations will be the prime component of the type definition — describing its instances not by what they are but by what they have to offer.

Below is the FUNCTIONS paragraph for the *STACK* abstract data type. If you are a software developer, you will find the style familiar: the lines of such a paragraph evoke the **declarations** found in typed programming languages such as Pascal or Ada. The line for *new* resembles a variable declaration; the others resemble routine headers.

FUNCTIONS

- *put*: $STACK [G] \times G \to STACK [G]$
- *remove*: $STACK [G] \nrightarrow STACK [G]$
- *item*: $STACK [G] \nrightarrow G$
- *empty*: $STACK [G] \to BOOLEAN$
- *new*: $STACK [G]$

Each line introduces a mathematical function modeling one of the operations on stacks. For example function *put* represents the operation that pushes an element onto the top of a stack.

Why functions? Most software people will not naturally think of an operation such as *put* as a function. When the execution of a software system applies a *put* operation to a stack, it will usually modify that stack by adding an element to it. As a result, in the above informal classification of commands, *put* was a "command" — an operation which may modify objects. (The other two categories of operations were creators and queries).

See also "The imperative and the applicative", page 351.

An ADT specification, however, is a mathematical model, and must rely on well-understood mathematical techniques. In mathematics the notion of command, or more generally of changing something, does not exist as such; computing the square root of the number 2 does not modify the value of that number. A mathematical expression simply defines certain mathematical objects in terms of certain other mathematical objects: unlike the execution of software on a computer, it never changes any mathematical object.

Yet we need a mathematical concept to model computer operations, and here the notion of function yields the closest approximation. A function is a mechanism for obtaining a certain result, belonging to a certain target set, from any possible input belonging to a certain source set. For example, if **R** denotes the set of real numbers, the function definition

$square\_plus\_one$: $\mathbf{R} \rightarrow \mathbf{R}$
$square\_plus\_one$ $(x) = x^2 + 1$ \qquad (for any x in $\mathbf{R}$)

introduces a function $square\_plus\_one$ having **R** as both source and target sets, and yielding as result, for any input, the square of the input plus one.

The specification of abstract data types uses exactly the same notion. Operation put, for example, is specified as

put: $STACK\ [G] \times G \rightarrow STACK\ [G]$

which means that put will take two arguments, a $STACK$ of instances of G and an instance of G, and yield as a result a new $STACK\ [G]$. (More formally, the source set of function put is the set $STACK\ [G] \times G$, known as the **cartesian product** of $STACK\ [G]$ and G; this is the set of pairs $<s, x>$ whose first element s is in $STACK\ [G]$ and whose second element x is in G.) Here is an informal illustration:

Applying the put **function**

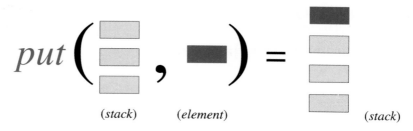

(*stack*) \qquad (*element*) \qquad\qquad (*stack*)

With abstract data types, we only have functions in the mathematical sense of the term; they will produce neither side effects nor in fact changes of any kind. This is the condition that we must observe to enjoy the benefits of mathematical reasoning.

When we leave the ethereal realm of specification for the rough-and-tumble of software design and implementation, we will need to reintroduce the notion of change; because of the performance overhead, few people would accept a software execution environment where every "push" operation on a stack begins by duplicating the stack. Later we will examine the details of the transition from the change-free world of ADTs to the change-full world of software development. For the moment, since we are studying how best to specify types, the mathematical view is the appropriate one.

The role of the operations modeled by each of the functions in the specification of *STACK* is clear from the previous discussion:

- Function *put* yields a new stack with one extra element pushed on top. The figure on the preceding page illustrates *put* (*s*, *x*) for a stack *s* and an element *x*.

- Function *remove* yields a new stack with the top element, if any, popped; like *put*, this function should yield a command (an object-changing operation, typically implemented as a procedure) at design and implementation time. We will see below how to take into account the case of an empty stack, which has no top to be popped.

- Function *item* yields the top element, if any.

- Function *empty* indicates whether a stack is empty; its result is a boolean value (true or false); the ADT *BOOLEAN* is assumed to have been defined separately.

- Function *new* yields an empty stack.

The FUNCTIONS paragraph does not fully define these functions; it only introduces their **signatures** — the list of their argument and result types. The signature of *put* is

$$STACK \ [G] \times G \rightarrow STACK \ [G]$$

indicating that *put* accepts as arguments pairs of the form $<s, x>$ where *s* is an instance of *STACK* [*G*] and *x* is an instance of *G*, and yields as a result an instance of *STACK* [*G*]. In principle the target set of a function (the type that appears to the right of the arrow in signature, here *STACK* [*G*]) may itself be a cartesian product; this can be used to describe operations that return two or more results. For simplicity, however, this book will only use single-result functions.

The signature of functions *remove* and *item* includes a crossed arrow $\nrightarrow$ instead of the standard arrow used by *put* and *empty*. This notation expresses that the functions are not applicable to all members of the source set; it will be explained in detail below.

The declaration for function *new* appears as just

$$new: STACK$$

with no arrow in the signature. This is in fact an abbreviation for

$$new: \rightarrow STACK$$

introducing a function with no arguments. There is no need for arguments since *new* must always return the same result, an empty stack. So we just remove the arrow for simplicity. The result of applying the function (that is to say, the empty stack) will also be written *new*, an abbreviation for *new* ( ), meaning the result of applying *new* to an empty argument list.

Function categories

The operations on a type were classified informally at the beginning of this chapter into creators, queries and commands. With an ADT specification for a new type *T*, such as *STACK* [*G*] in the example, we can define the corresponding classification in a more rigorous way. The classification simply examines where *T* appears, relative to the arrow, in the signature of each function:

- A function such as *new* for which *T* appears only to the right of the arrow is a **creator function**. It models an operation which produces instances of *T* from instances of other types — or, as in the case of a constant creator function such as *new*, from no argument at all. (Remember that the signature of *new* is considered to contain an implicit arrow.)

- A function such as *item* and *empty* for which *T* appears only on the left of the arrow is a **query function**. It models an operation which yields properties of instances of *T*, expressed in terms of instances of other types (*BOOLEAN* and the generic parameter *G* in the examples).

- A function such as *put* or *remove* for which *T* appears on both sides of the arrow is a **command function**. It models an operation which yields new instances of *T* from existing instances of *T* (and possibly instances of other types).

An alternative terminology calls the three categories "constructor", "accessor" and "modifier". The terms retained here are more directly related to the interpretation of ADT functions as models of operations on software objects, and will carry over to class features, the software counterparts of our mathematical functions.

The AXIOMS paragraph

We have seen how to describe a data type such as *STACK* through the list of functions applicable to its instances. The functions are known only through their signatures.

To indicate that we have a stack, and not some other data structure, the ADT specification as given so far is not enough. Any "dispenser" structure, such as a first-in-first-out queue, will also satisfy it. The choice of names for the operations makes this particularly clear: we do not even have stack-specific names such as *push*, *pop* or *top* to fool ourselves into believing that we have defined stacks and only stacks.

This is not surprising, of course, since the FUNCTIONS paragraph declared the functions (in the same way that a program unit may declare a variable) but did not fully define them. In a mathematical definition such as the earlier example

$$square\_plus\_one: \mathbf{R} \rightarrow \mathbf{R}$$

$$square\_plus\_one\ (x) = x^2 + 1 \qquad \text{(for any } x \text{ in } \mathbf{R}\text{)}$$

the first line plays the role of the signature declaration, but there is also a second line which defines the function's value. How do we achieve the same for the functions of an ADT?

Here we should not use an explicit definition in the style of the second line of *square_plus_one*'s definition, because it would force us to choose a representation — and this whole discussion is intended to protect us from representation choices.

Just to make sure we understand what an explicit definition would look like, let us write one for the stack representation ARRAY_UP as sketched above. In mathematical terms, choosing ARRAY_UP means that we consider any instance of *STACK* as a pair *<count, representation>*, where *representation* is the array and *count* is the number of pushed elements. Then an explicit definition of *put* is (for any instance *x* of *G*):

$$put (<count, representation>, x) = <count + 1, representation [count+1: x]>$$

where the notation $a [n: v]$ denotes the array obtained from a by changing the value of the element at index n so that it is now v, and keeping all other elements, if any, as they are.

This definition of function put is just a mathematical version of the implementation of the put operation sketched in Pascal notation, next to representation ARRAY_UP, in the picture of possible stack representations at the beginning of this chapter.

Figure page 123.

But this is not what we want; "Free us from the yoke of representations!", the motto of the Object Liberation Front and its military branch (the ADT brigade), is also ours.

The political branch specializes in class-action suits.

Because any explicit definition would force us to select a representation, we must turn to **implicit** definitions. We will refrain from giving the values of the functions of an ADT specification; instead we will state properties of these values — all the properties that matter, but those properties only.

The AXIOMS paragraph states these properties. For *STACK* it will be:

AXIOMS

For any x: G, s: *STACK* [G],

A1 • $item (put (s, x)) = x$

A2 • $remove (put (s, x)) = s$

A3 • $empty (new)$

A4 • **not** $empty (put (s, x))$

The first two axioms express the basic LIFO (last-in, first-out) property of stacks. To understand them, assume we have a stack s and an instance x, and define s' to be $put (s, x)$, that is to say the result of pushing x onto s. Adapting an earlier figure:

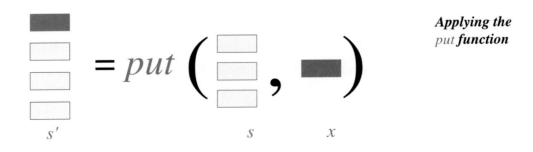

$$s' \qquad\qquad s \qquad x$$

*Applying the put **function***

Here axiom A1 tells us that the top of s' is x, the last element that we pushed; and axiom A2 tells us that if we remove the top element from s', we get back the stack s that we had before pushing x. These two axioms provide a concise description of the fundamental property of stacks in pure mathematical terms, without any recourse to imperative reasoning or representation properties.

Axioms A3 and A4 tell us when a stack is empty and when it is not: a stack resulting from the creator function *new* is empty; any stack resulting from pushing an element on an existing stack (empty or not) is non-empty.

These axioms, like the others, are predicates (in the sense of logic), expressing that a certain property is always true for every possible value of s and x. Some people prefer to read A3 and A4 in the equivalent form

> For any x: G, s: *STACK* $[G]$
>
> A3' • *empty* (*new*) = **true**
> A4' • *empty* (*put* (s, x)) = **false**

under which you may also view them, informally at least, as defining function *empty* by induction on the size of stacks.

Two or three things we know about stacks

ADT specifications are **implicit**. We have encountered two forms of implicitness:

- The ADT method defines a set of objects implicitly, through the applicable functions. This was described above as defining objects by what they have, not what they are. More precisely, the definition never implies that the operations listed are the only ones; when it comes to a representation, you will often add other operations.

- The functions themselves are also defined implicitly: instead of explicit definitions (such as was used for *square_plus_one*, and for the early attempt to define *put* by reference to a mathematical representation), we use axioms describing the functions' properties. Here too there is no claim of exhaustiveness: when you eventually implement the functions, they will certainly acquire more properties.

This implicitness is a key aspect of abstract data types and, by implication, of their future counterparts in object-oriented software construction — classes. When we define an abstract data type or a class, we always talk *about* the type or class: we simply list the properties we know, and take these as the definition. Never do we imply that these are the only applicable properties.

Implicitness implies openness: it should always be possible to add new properties to an ADT or a class. The basic mechanism for performing such extensions without damaging existing uses of the original form is inheritance.

"More on implicitness", page 149.
The consequences of this implicit approach are far-reaching. The "supplementary topics" section at the end of this chapter will include more comments about implicitness.

Partial functions

The specification of any realistic example, even one as basic as stacks, is bound to encounter the problems of undefined operations: some operations are not applicable to every possible element of their source sets. Here this is the case with *remove* and *item*: you cannot pop an element from an empty stack; and an empty stack has no top.

The solution used in the preceding specification is to describe these functions as partial. A function from a source set X to a target set Y is partial if it is not defined for all members of X. A function which is not partial is **total**. A simple example of partial function in standard mathematics is *inv*, the inverse function on real numbers, whose value for any appropriate real number x is

$$inv\ (x) = \frac{1}{x}$$

Because *inv* is not defined for $x = 0$, we may specify it as a partial function on **R**, the set of all real numbers:

inv: $\mathbf{R} \nrightarrow \mathbf{R}$

To indicate that a function may be partial, the notation uses the crossed arrow $\nrightarrow$; the normal arrow $\rightarrow$ will be reserved for functions which are guaranteed to be total.

The **domain** of a partial function in $X \nrightarrow Y$ is the subset of X containing those elements for which the function yields a value. Here the domain of *inv* is $\mathbf{R} - \{0\}$, the set of real numbers other than zero.

The specification of the *STACK* ADT applied these ideas to stacks by declaring *put* and *item* as partial functions in the FUNCTIONS paragraph, as indicated by the crossed arrow in their signatures. This raises a new problem, discussed in the next section: how to specify the domains of these functions.

In some cases it may be desirable to describe *put* as a partial function too; this is necessary to model implementations such as ARRAY_UP and ARRAY_DOWN, which only support a finite number of consecutive *put* operations on any given stack. It is indeed a good exercise to adapt the specification of *STACK* so that it will describe bounded stacks with a finite capacity, whereas the above form does not include any such capacity restriction. This is a new use for partial functions: to reflect implementation constraints. In contrast, the need to declare *item* and *remove* as partial functions reflected an abstract property of the underlying operations, applicable to all representations.

Exercise E6.9, page 162.

Preconditions

Partial functions are an inescapable fact of software development life, merely reflecting the observation that not every operation is applicable to every object. But they are also a potential source of errors: if f is a partial function from X to Y, we are not sure any more that the expression $f\ (e)$ makes sense even if the value of e is in X: we must be able to guarantee that the value belongs to the domain of f.

For this to be possible, any ADT specification which includes partial functions must specify the domain of each of them. This is the role of the PRECONDITIONS paragraph.

For *STACK*, the paragraph will appear as:

> ## PRECONDITIONS
> - *remove* (*s*: *STACK* [*G*]) **require not** *empty* (*s*)
> - *item* (*s*: *STACK* [*G*]) **require not** *empty* (*s*)

where, for each function, the **require** clause indicates what conditions the function's arguments must satisfy to belong to the function's domain.

The boolean expression which defines the domain is called the **precondition** of the corresponding partial function. Here the precondition of both *remove* and *item* expresses that the stack argument must be non-empty. Before the **require** clause comes the name of the function with dummy names for arguments (*s* for the stack argument in the example), so that the precondition can refer to them.

Mathematically, the precondition of a function f is the **characteristic function** of the domain of f. The characteristic function of a subset A of a set X is the total function $ch: X \rightarrow BOOLEAN$ such that $ch(x)$ is true if x belongs to A, false otherwise.

The complete specification

The PRECONDITIONS paragraph concludes this simple specification of the *STACK* abstract data type. For ease of reference it is useful to piece together the various components of the specification, seen separately above. Here is the full specification:

> ## ADT specification of stacks
>
> ## TYPES
> - *STACK* [*G*]
>
> ## FUNCTIONS
> - *put*: *STACK* [*G*] × *G* → *STACK* [*G*]
> - *remove*: *STACK* [*G*] ↠ *STACK* [*G*]
> - *item*: *STACK* [*G*] ↠ *G*
> - *empty*: *STACK* [*G*] → *BOOLEAN*
> - *new*: *STACK* [*G*]
>
> ## AXIOMS
> For any x: G, s: *STACK* [*G*]
>
> A1 • *item* (*put* (*s*, *x*)) = *x*
>
> A2 • *remove* (*put* (*s*, *x*)) = *s*
>
> A3 • *empty* (*new*)
>
> A4 • **not** *empty* (*put* (*s*, *x*))
>
> ## PRECONDITIONS
> - *remove* (*s*: *STACK* [*G*]) **require not** *empty* (*s*)
> - *item* (*s*: *STACK* [*G*]) **require not** *empty* (*s*)

Nothing but the truth

The power of abstract data type specifications comes from their ability to capture the essential properties of data structures without overspecifying. The stack specification collected on the preceding page expresses all there is to know about the notion of stack in general, excluding anything that only applies to some particular representations of stacks. All the truth about stacks; yet nothing but the truth.

This provides a general model of computation with data structures. We may describe complex sequences of operations by mathematical expressions enjoying the usual properties of algebra; and we may view the process of carrying out the computation (executing the program) as a case of algebraic simplification.

In elementary mathematics we have been taught to take an expression such as

$$cos^2 (a - b) + sin^2 (a + b - 2 \times b)$$

and apply the rules of algebra and trigonometry to simplify it. A rule of algebra tells us that we may simplify $a + b - 2 \times b$ into $a - b$ for any a and b; and a rule of trigonometry tells us that we can simplify $cos^2 (x) + sin^2 (x)$ into 1 for any x. Such rules may be combined; for example the combination of the two preceding rules allow us to simplify the above expression into just 1.

In a similar way, the functions defined in an abstract data type specification allow us to construct possibly complex expressions; and the axioms of the ADT allow us to simplify such expressions to yield a simpler result. A complex stack expression is the mathematical equivalent of a program; the simplification process is the mathematical equivalent of a computation, that is to say, of executing such a program.

Here is an example. With the specification of the *STACK* abstract data type as given above, we can write the expression

> *item (remove (put (remove (put (put (*
> *remove (put (put (put (new, x1), x2), x3)),*
> *item (remove (put (put (new, x4), x5)))), x6)), x7)))*

Let us call this expression *stackexp* for future reference. It is perhaps easier to understand *stackexp* if we define it in terms of a sequence of auxiliary expressions:

s1 = new
s2 = put (put (put (s1, x1), x2), x3)
s3 = remove (s2)
s4 = new
s5 = put (put (s4, x4), x5)
s6 = remove (s5)
y1 = item (s6)
s7 = put (s3, y1)
s8 = put (s7, x6)
s9 = remove (s8)

$s10 = put\ (s9,\ x7)$

$s11 = remove\ (s10)$

$stackexp = item\ (s11)$

Whichever variant of the definition you choose, it is not hard to follow the computation of which *stackexp* is a mathematical model: create a new stack; push elements $x1$, $x2$, $x3$, in this order, on top of it; remove the last pushed element ($x3$), calling $s3$ the resulting stack; create another empty stack; and so on. Or you can think of it graphically:

Stack manipulations

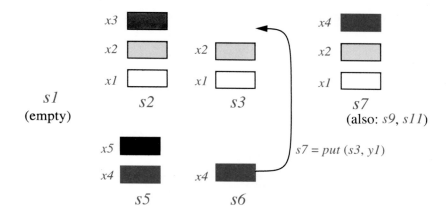

- You can easily find the value of such an ADT expression by drawing figures such as the above. (Here you would find $x4$.) But the theory enables you to obtain this result formally, without any need for pictures: just apply the axioms repeatedly to simplify the expression until you cannot simplify any further. For example:

  - Applying A2 to simplify $s3$, that is to say *remove (put (put (put (s1, x1), x2), x3))*, yields *put (put (s1, x1), x2)*. (With A2, any consecutive *remove-put* pair cancels out.)

  - The same axiom indicates that $s6$ is *put (s4, x4)*; then we can use axiom A1 to deduce that $y1$, that is to say *item (put (s4, x4))*, is in fact $x4$, showing that (as illustrated by the arrow on the above figure) $s7$ is obtained by pushing $x4$ on top of $s3$.

And so on. A sequence of such simplifications, carried out as simply and mechanically as the simplifications of elementary arithmetic, yields the value of the expression *stackexp*, which (as you are invited to check for yourself by performing the simplification process rigorously) is indeed $x4$.

This example gives a glimpse of one of the main theoretical roles of abstract data types: providing a formal model for the notion of program and program execution. This model is purely mathematical: it has none of the imperative notions of program state, variables whose values may change in time, or execution sequencing. It relies on the standard expression evaluation techniques of ordinary mathematics.

6.5 FROM ABSTRACT DATA TYPES TO CLASSES

We have the starting point of an elegant mathematical theory for modeling data structures and in fact, as we just saw, programs in general. But our subject is software architecture, not mathematics or even theoretical computing science! Have we strayed from our path?

Not by much. In the search for a good modular structure based on object types, abstract data types provide a high-level description mechanism, free of implementation concerns. They will lead us to the fundamental structures of object technology.

Classes

ADTs will serve as the direct basis for the modules that we need in the search begun in chapter *3*. More precisely, an object-oriented system will be built (at the level of analysis, design or implementation) as a collection of interacting ADTs, partially or totally implemented. The basic notion here is **class**:

Definition: class

A class is an abstract data type equipped with a possibly partial implementation.

So to obtain a class we must provide an ADT and decide on an implementation. The ADT is a mathematical concept; the implementation is its computer-oriented version. The definition, however, states that the implementation may be partial; the following terminology separates this case from that of a fully implemented class:

Definition: deferred, effective class

A class which is fully implemented is said to be **effective**. A class which is implemented only partially, or not at all, is said to be **deferred**. Any class is either deferred or effective.

To obtain an effective class, you must provide all the implementation details. For a deferred class, you may choose a certain style of implementation but leave some aspects of the implementation open. In the most extreme case of "partial" implementation you may refrain from making any implementation decision at all; the resulting class will be fully deferred, and equivalent to an ADT.

How to produce an effective class

Consider first the case of effective classes. What does it take to implement an ADT? Three kinds of element will make up the resulting effective class:

E1 • An ADT specification (a set of functions with the associated axioms and preconditions, describing the functions' properties).

E2 • A choice of representation.

E3 • A mapping from the functions (*E1*) to the representation (*E2*) in the form of a set of mechanisms, or **features**, each implementing one of the functions in terms of the representation, so as to satisfy the axioms and preconditions. Many of these features will be routines (subprograms) in the usual sense, although some may also appear as data fields, or "attributes", as explained in the next chapters.

For example, if the ADT is *STACK*, we may choose as representation (step *E2*) the solution called ARRAY_UP above, which implements any stack by a pair

<representation, count>

where *representation* is an array and *count* an integer. For the function implementations (*E3*) we will have features corresponding to *put*, *remove*, *item*, *empty* and *new*, which achieve the corresponding effects; for example we may implement *put* by a routine of the form

> *put* (*x*: *G*) **is**
>   -- Push *x* onto stack.
>   -- (No check for possible stack overflow.)
>   **do**
>   *count* := *count* + *1*
>   *representation* [*count*] := *x*
>   **end**

The combination of elements obtained under *E1*, *E2* and *E3* will yield a class, the modular structure of object technology.

The role of deferred classes

For an effective class, all of the implementation information (*E2*, *E3* above) must be present. If any of it is missing, the class is deferred.

The more deferred a class, the closer it is to an ADT, gussied up in the kind of syntactic dress that will help seduce software developers rather than mathematicians. Deferred classes are particularly useful for analysis and for design:

- In object-oriented analysis, no implementation details are needed or desired: the method uses classes only for their descriptive power.

- In object-oriented design, many aspects of the implementation will be left out; instead, a design should concentrate on high-level architectural properties of the system — what functionalities each module provides, not how it provides them.

- As you move your design gradually closer to a full implementation, you will add more and more implementation properties until you get effective classes.

But the role of deferred classes does not stop there, and even in a fully implemented system you will often find many of them. Some of that role follows from their previous applications: if you started from deferred classes to obtain effective ones, you may be well inspired to keep the former as ancestors (in the sense of inheritance) to the latter, to serve as a living memory of the analysis and design process.

Too often, in software produced with non-object-oriented approaches, the final form of a system contains no record of the considerable effort that led to it. For someone who is asked to perform maintenance — extensions, ports, debugging — on the system, trying to understand it without that record is as difficult as it would be, for a geologist, to understand a landscape without having access to the sedimentary layers. Keeping the deferred classes in the final system is one of the best ways to maintain the needed record.

Deferred classes also have purely implementation-related uses. They serve to classify groups of related types of objects, provide some of the most important high-level reusable modules, capture common behaviors among a set of variants, and play a key role (in connection with polymorphism and dynamic binding) in guaranteeing that the software architecture remains decentralized and extendible.

The next few chapters, which introduce the basic object-oriented techniques, will at first concentrate on effective classes. But keep in mind the notion of deferred class, whose importance will grow as we penetrate the full power of the object-oriented method.

Abstract data types and information hiding

A particularly interesting consequence of the object-oriented policy of basing all modules on ADT implementations (classes) is that it provides a clear answer to a question that was left pending in the discussion of information hiding: how do we select the public and private features of a module — the visible and invisible parts of the iceberg?

See the mention of vagueness in the middle of page 52.

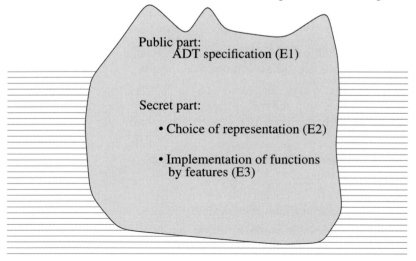

Public part:
      ADT specification (E1)

Secret part:

• Choice of representation (E2)

• Implementation of functions
  by features (E3)

The ADT view of a module under information hiding

If the module is a class coming from an ADT as outlined above, the answer is clear: of the three parts involved in the transition, *E1*, the ADT specification, is public; *E2* and *E3*, the choice of representation and the implementation of the ADT functions in terms of this representation, should be secret. (As we start building classes we will encounter a fourth part, also secret: auxiliary features needed only for the internal purposes of these routines.)

So the use of abstract data types as the source of our modules gives us a practical, unambiguous guideline for applying information hiding in our designs.

Introducing a more imperative view

The transition from abstract data types to classes involves an important stylistic difference: the introduction of change and imperative reasoning.

As you will remember, the specification of abstract data types is change-free, or, to use a term from theoretical computing science, *applicative*. All features of an ADT are modeled as mathematical functions; this applies to creators, queries and commands. For example the push operation on stacks is modeled by the command function

$$put: STACK\ [G] \times G \rightarrow STACK\ [G]$$

specifying an operation that returns a new stack, rather than changing an existing stack.

Classes, which are closer to the world of design and implementation, abandon this applicative-only view and reintroduce commands as operations that may change objects.

For example, *put* will appear as a routine which takes an argument of type G (the formal generic parameter), and modifies a stack by pushing a new element on top — instead of producing a new stack.

This change of style reflects the imperative style that prevails in software construction. (The word "operational" is also used as synonym for "imperative".) It will require the corresponding change in the axioms of ADTs. Axioms A1 and A4 of stacks, which appeared above as

A1 • *item* (*put* (*s*, *x*)) = *x*
A4 • **not** *empty* (*put* (*s*, *x*))

will yield, in the imperative form, a clause known as a **routine postcondition**, introduced by the keyword ensure in *put* (*x*: *G*) **is**

>   -- Push *x* on top of stack

require

>   … The precondition, if any …

do

>   … The appropriate implementation, if known …

ensure

>   *item* = *x*
>
>   **not** *empty*

end

Here the postcondition expresses that on return from a call to routine *put*, the value of *item* will be *x* (the element pushed) and the value of *empty* will be false.

Other axioms of the ADT specification will yield a clause known as the **class invariant**. Postconditions, class invariants and other non-applicative avatars of an ADT's preconditions and axioms will be studied as part of the discussion of assertions and Design by Contract.

"THE ADT CON-NECTION", 11.10, page 373.

Back to square one?

If you followed carefully, starting with the chapter on modularity, the line of reasoning that led to abstract data types and then classes, you may be a little puzzled here. We started with the goal of obtaining the best possible modular structures; various arguments led to the suggestion that objects, or more precisely object types, would provide a better basis than their traditional competitors — functions. This raised the next question: how to describe these object types. But when the answer came, in the form of abstract data types (and their practical substitutes, classes), it meant that we must base the description of data on… the applicable functions! Have we then come full circle?

No. Object types, as represented by ADTs and classes, remain the undisputed basis for modularization.

It is not surprising that both the object and function aspects should appear in the final system architecture: as noted in the previous chapter, no description of software issues can be complete if it misses one of these two components. What fundamentally distinguishes object-oriented methods from older approaches is the distribution of roles: object types are the undisputed winners when it comes to selecting the criteria for building modules. Functions remain their servants.

In object-oriented decomposition, no function ever exists just by itself: every function is attached to some object type. This carries over to the design and implementation levels: no feature ever exists just by itself; every feature is attached to some class.

Object-oriented software construction

The study of abstract data types has given us the answer to the question asked at the beginning of this chapter: how to describe the object types that will serve as the backbone of our software architecture.

See page 116 for the original definition.
We already had a definition of object-oriented software construction: remaining at a high level of generality, it presented the method as "basing the architecture of any software system on modules deduced from the types of objects it manipulates". Keeping that first definition as the framework, we can now complement it with a more technical one:

> ### Object-oriented software construction (definition 2)
>
> Object-oriented software construction is the building of software systems as structured collections of possibly partial abstract data type implementations.

This will be our working definition. Its various components are all important:

• The basis is the notion of *abstract data type*.

• For our software we need not the ADTs themselves, a mathematical notion, but ADT *implementations*, a software notion.

• These implementations, however, need not be complete; the *"possibly partial"* qualification covers deferred classes — including the extreme case of a fully deferred class, where none of the features is implemented.

• A system is a *collection* of classes, with no one particularly in charge — no top or main program.

• The collection is *structured* thanks to two inter-class relations: client and inheritance.

6.6 BEYOND SOFTWARE

As we are completing our study of abstract data types it is worth taking a moment to reflect on the significance of this notion outside of its immediate intended application area.

What the ADT approach tells us is that a successful intellectual investigation should renounce as futile any attempt at knowing things from the inside, and concentrate instead on their usable properties. Do not tell me what you are; tell me what you have — what I can get out of you. If we need a name for this epistemological discipline, we should call it the *principle of selfishness*.

If I am thirsty, an orange is something I can squeeze; if I am a painter, it is color which might inspire my palette; if I am a farmer, it is produce that I can sell at the market; if I am an architect, it is slices that tell me how to design my new opera house, overlooking the harbor; but if I am none of these, and have no other use for the orange, then I should not talk about it, as the concept of orange does not for me even exist.

The principle of selfishness — you are but what you have — is an extreme form of an idea that has played a central role in the development of science: abstraction, or the importance of separating concerns. The two quotations at the beginning of this chapter, each in its own remarkable way, express the importance of this idea. Their authors, Diderot and Stendhal, were writers rather than scientists, although both obviously had a good understanding of the scientific method (Diderot was the living fire behind the Great Encyclopedia, and Stendhal prepared for admission into the École Polytechnique, although in the end he decided that he could do better things with his life). It is striking to see how both quotations are applicable to the use of abstraction in software development.

Yet there is more than abstraction to the principle of selfishness: the idea, almost shocking at first, that a property is not worth talking about unless it is useful in some direct way to the talker.

This suggests a more general observation as to the intellectual value of our field.

Over the years many articles and talks have claimed to examine how software engineers could benefit from studying philosophy, general systems theory, "cognitive science", psychology. But to a practicing software developer the results are disappointing. If we exclude from the discussion the generally applicable laws of rational investigation, which enlightened minds have known for centuries (at least since Descartes) and which of course apply to software science as to anything else, it sometimes seems that experts in the disciplines mentioned may have more to learn from experts in software than the reverse.

Software builders have tackled — with various degrees of success — some of the most challenging intellectual endeavors ever undertaken. Few engineering projects, for example, match in complexity the multi-million line software projects commonly being launched nowadays. Through its more ambitious efforts the software community has gained precious insights on such issues and concepts as size, complexity, structure, abstraction, taxonomy, concurrency, recursive reasoning, the difference between description and prescription, language, change and invariants. All this is so recent and so tentative that the profession itself has not fully realized the epistemological implications of its own work.

Eventually someone will come and explain what lessons the experience of software construction holds for the intellectual world at large. No doubt abstract data types will figure prominently in the list.

6.7 SUPPLEMENTARY TOPICS

The view of abstract data types presented so far will suffice for the uses of ADTs in the rest of this book. (To complement it, doing the exercises will help you sharpen your understanding of the concept.)

If, as I hope, you have been conquered by the elegance, simplicity and power of ADTs, you may want to explore a few more of their properties, even though the discussion of object-oriented methods will not use them directly. These supplementary topics, which may be skipped on first reading, are presented in the next few pages:

- Implicitness and its relationship to the software construction process.
- The difference between specification and design.
- The differences between classes and records.
- Potential alternatives to the use of partial functions.
- Deciding whether a specification is complete or not.

The bibliographical references to this chapter point to more advanced literature on abstract data types.

More on implicitness

The implicit nature of abstract data types and classes, discussed above, reflects an important problem of software construction.

One may legitimately ask what difference there is between a simplified ADT specification, using the function declarations

$x: POINT \rightarrow REAL$
$y: POINT \rightarrow REAL$

and the record type declaration which we may express in a traditional programming language such as Pascal under the form

type
    $POINT =$
        record
            x, y: **real**
        end

At first sight, the two definitions appear equivalent: both state that any instance of type $POINT$ has two associated values x and y, of type $REAL$. But there is a crucial if subtle difference:

- The Pascal form is closed and explicit: it indicates that a $POINT$ object is made of the two given fields, and no other.
- The ADT function declarations carry no such connotation. They indicate that one may query a point about its x and its y, but do not preclude other queries — such as a point's mass and velocity in a kinematics application.

From a simplified mathematical perspective, you may consider that the above Pascal declaration is a definition of the mathematical set $POINT$ as a cartesian product:

$POINT \triangleq REAL \times REAL$

where $\triangleq$ means "is defined as": this defines $POINT$ fully. In contrast, the ADT specification does not explicitly define $POINT$ through a mathematical model such as the cartesian product; it just characterizes $POINT$ implicitly by listing two of the queries applicable to objects of this type.

If at some stage you think you are done with the specification of a certain notion, you may want to move it from the implicit world to the explicit world by identifying it with the cartesian product of the applicable simple queries; for example you will identify points with $<x, y>$ pairs. We may view this identification process as the very definition of the transition from analysis and specification to design and implementation.

Specification versus design

The last observation helps clarify a central issue in the study of software: the difference between the initial activities of software development — specification, also called analysis — and later stages such as design and implementation.

The software engineering literature usually defines this as the difference between "defining the problem" and "building a solution". Although correct in principle, this definition is not always directly useful in practice, and it is sometimes hard to determine where specification stops and design begins. Even in the research community, people routinely criticize each other on the theme "you advertize notation x as a specification language, but what it really expresses is designs". The supreme insult is to accuse the notation of catering to *implementation*; more on this in a later chapter.

See "The clouds and the precipice", page 905.

The above definition yields a more precise criterion: to cross the Rubicon between specification and design is to move from the implicit to the explicit; in other words:

> ### Definition: transition from analysis (specification) to design
>
> To go from specification to design is to identify each abstraction with the cartesian product of its simple queries.

The subsequent transition — from design to implementation — is simply the move from one explicit form to another: the design form is more abstract and closer to mathematical concepts, the implementation form is more concrete and computer-oriented, but they are both explicit. This transition is less dramatic than the preceding one; indeed, it will become increasingly clear in the pages that follow that object technology all but removes the distinction between design and implementation. With good object-oriented notations, what our computers directly execute (with the help of our compilers) is what to the non-O-O world would often appear as designs.

Classes versus records

Another remarkable property of object technology, also a result of the focus on implicit definition, is that you can keep your descriptions implicit for a much longer period than with any other approach. The following chapters will introduce a notation enabling us to define a class under the form

```
class POINT feature
    x, y: REAL
end
```

This looks suspiciously close to the above Pascal record type definition. But in spite of appearances the class definition is different: it is implicit! The implicitness comes from inheritance; the author of the class or (even more interestingly) someone else may at any time define a new class such as

> **class** *MOVING_POINT* **inherit**
>   *POINT*
> **feature**
>   *mass*: *REAL*
>   *velocity*: *VECTOR* [*REAL*]
> **end**

which extends the original class in ways totally unplanned for by the initial design. Then a variable (or entity, to use the terminology introduced later) of type *POINT*, declared as

> *p1*: *POINT*

may become attached to objects which are not just of type *POINT* but also of any descendant type such as *MOVING_POINT*. This occurs in particular through "polymorphic assignments" of the form

> *p1* := *mp1*

where *mp1* is of type *MOVING_POINT*.

These possibilities illustrate the implicitness and openness of the class definition: the corresponding entities represent not just points in the narrow sense of direct instances of class *POINT* as initially defined, but, more generally, instances of any eventual class that describes a concept derived from the original.

See "The Open-Closed principle", page 57.

The ability to define software elements (classes) that are directly usable while remaining implicit (through inheritance) is one of the major innovations of object technology, directly answering the Open-Closed requirement. Its full implications will unfold progressively in the following chapters.

Not surprisingly for such a revolutionary concept, the realm of new possibilities that it opens still scares many people, and in fact many object-oriented languages restrict the openness in some way. Later chapters will mention examples.

Alternatives to partial functions

Among the techniques of this chapter that may have caused you to raise your eyebrows is its use of partial functions. The problem that it addresses is inescapable: any specification needs to deal with operations that are not always defined; for example, it is impossible to pop an empty stack. But is the use of partial functions the best solution?

It is certainly not the only possible one. Another technique that comes to mind, and is indeed used by some of the ADT literature, is to make the function total but introduce special error values to denote the results of operations applied to impossible cases.

For every type T, this method introduces a special "error" value; let us write it ω_T. Then for any function f of signature

> f: … Input types … $\rightarrow T$

it specifies that any application of f to an object for which the corresponding computer operation may not be executed will produce the value ω_T.

Although usable, this method leads to mathematical and practical unpleasantness. The problem is that the special values are rather bizarre animals, which may unduly disturb the lives of innocent mathematical creatures.

Assume for example that we consider stacks of integers — instances of the generic derivation *STACK [INTEGER]*, where *INTEGER* is the ADT whose instances are integers. Although we do not need to write the specification of *INTEGER* completely for this discussion, it is clear that the functions defining this ADT should model the basic operations (addition, subtraction, "less than" and the like) defined on the mathematical set of integers. The axioms of the ADT should be consistent with ordinary properties of integers; typical among these properties is that, for any integer n:

[Z1]

$$n + 1 \neq n$$

Now let n be the result of requesting the top of an empty stack, that is to say, the value of *item (new)*, where *new* is an empty stack of integers. With the "special error element" approach, n must be the special value $\omega_{INTEGER}$. What then is the value of the expression $n + 1$? If the only values at our disposal are normal integers and $\omega_{INTEGER}$, then we ought to choose $\omega_{INTEGER}$ as the answer:

$$\omega_{INTEGER} + 1 = \omega_{INTEGER}$$

This is the only acceptable choice: any other value for $\omega_{INTEGER} + 1$, that is to say, any "normal" integer q, would mean in practical terms that after we attempt to access the top of an empty stack, and get an error value as a result, we can miraculously remove any trace of the error, simply by adding one to the result! This might have passed when all it took to erase the memory of a crime was a pilgrimage to Santiago de Compostela and the purchase of a few indulgences; modern mores and computers are not so lenient.

But choosing $\omega_{INTEGER}$ as the value of $n + 1$ when n is $\omega_{INTEGER}$ violates the above Z1 property. More generally, $\omega_{INTEGER} + p$ will be $\omega_{INTEGER}$ for any p. This means we must develop a new axiom system for the updated abstract data type (*INTEGER* enriched with an error element), to specify that every integer operation yields $\omega_{INTEGER}$ whenever any one of its arguments is $\omega_{INTEGER}$. Similar changes will be needed for every type.

The resulting complication seems unjustifiable. We cannot change the specification of integers just for the purpose of modeling a specific data structure such as the stack.

With partial functions, the situation is simpler. You must of course verify, for every expression involving partial functions, that the arguments satisfy the corresponding preconditions. This amounts to performing a sanity check — reassuring yourself that the result of the computation will be meaningful. Having completed this check, you may apply the axioms without further ado. You need not change any existing axiom systems.

Is my specification complete?

Another question may have crossed your mind as you were reading the above example of abstract data type specification: is there is any way to be sure that such a specification describes all the relevant properties of the objects it is intended to cover? Students who are asked to write their first specifications (for example when doing the exercises at the end of this chapter) often come back with the same question: when do I know that I have specified enough and that I can stop?

In more general terms: does a method exist to find out whether an ADT specification is complete?

If the question is asked in this simple form, the answer is a plain no. This is true of formal specifications in general: to say that a specification is complete is to claim that it covers all the needed properties; but this is only meaningful with respect to some document listing these properties and used as a reference. Then we face one of two equally disappointing situations:

- If the reference document is informal (a natural-language "requirements document" for a project, or perhaps just the text of an exercise), this lack of formality precludes any attempt to check systematically that the specification meets all the requirements described in that document.

- If the reference document is itself formal, and we are able to check the completeness of our specification against it, this merely pushes the problem further: how do we ascertain the completeness of the reference document itself?

In its trivial form, then, the completeness question is uninteresting. But there is a more useful notion of completeness, derived from the meaning of this word in mathematical logic. For a mathematician, a theory is complete if its axioms and rules of inference are powerful enough to prove the truth or falsity of any formula that can be expressed in the language of the theory. This meaning of completeness, although more limited, is intellectually satisfying, since it indicates that whenever the theory lets us express a property it also enables us to determine whether the property holds.

How do we transpose this idea to an ADT specification? Here the "language of the theory" is the set of all the **well-formed expressions**, those expressions which we may build using the ADT's functions, applied to arguments of the appropriate types. For example, using the specification of *STACK* and assuming a valid expression x of type G, the following expressions are well-formed:

> *new*
> *put* (*new*, *x*)
> *item* (*new*)   -- If this seems strange, see comments on the next page.
> *empty* (*put* (*new*, *x*))
> *stackexp*   -- The complex expression defined on page 140.

The expressions *put* (*x*) and *put* (*x*, *new*), however, are not well-formed, since they do not abide by the rules: *put* always requires two arguments, the first of type *STACK* [*G*] and the second of type *G*; so *put* (*x*) is missing an argument, and *put* (*x*, *new*) has the wrong argument types.

The third example in the preceding box, *item* (*new*), does not describe a meaningful computation since *new* does not satisfy the precondition of *item*. Such an expression, although well-formed, is not **correct**. Here is the precise definition of this notion:

> ### Definition: correct ADT expression
>
> Let $f(x_1, \ldots, x_n)$ be a well-formed expression involving one or more functions on a certain ADT. This expression is correct if and only if all the x_i are (recursively) correct, and their values satisfy the precondition of f, if any.

Do not confuse "correct" with "well-formed". Well-formedness is a structural property, indicating whether all the functions in an expression have the right number and types of arguments; correctness, which is only defined for a well-formed expression, indicates whether the expression defines a meaningful computation. As we have seen, the expression *put* (*x*) is not well-formed (and so it is pointless to ask whether it is correct), whereas the expression *item* (*new*) is well-formed but not correct.

An expression well-formed but not correct, such as *item* (*new*), is similar to a program that compiles (because it is built according to the proper syntax and satisfies all typing constraints of the programming language) but will crash at run time by performing an impossible operation such as division by zero or popping an empty stack.

Of particular interest for completeness, among well-formed expressions, are **query expressions**, those whose outermost function is a query. Examples are:

The "queries" in our example, returning a result of type other than STACK, are item and empty. See "Function categories", page 134.

> *empty* (*put* (*put* (*new*, *x1*), *x2*))
> *item* (*put* (*put* (*new*, *x1*), *x2*))
> *stackexp*   -- See page 140

A query expression denotes a value which (if defined) belongs not to the ADT under definition, but to another, previously defined type. So the first query expression above has a value of type *BOOLEAN*; the second and third have values of type *G*, the formal generic parameter — for example *INTEGER* if we use the generic derivation *STACK* [*INTEGER*].

Query expressions represent external observations that we may make about the results of a certain computation involving instances of the new ADT. If the ADT specification is useful, it should always enable us to find out whether such results are defined and, if so, what they are. The stack specification appears to satisfy this property, at least for the three example expressions above, since it enables us to determine that the three expressions are defined and, by applying the axioms, to determine their values:

> *empty* (*put* (*put* (*new*, *x1*), *x2*)) = *False*
> *item* (*put* (*put* (*new*, *x1*), *x2*)) = *x2*
> *stackexp* = *x4*

Transposed to the case of arbitrary ADT specifications, these observations suggest a pragmatic notion of completeness, known as *sufficient* completeness, which expresses that the specification contains axioms powerful enough to enable us to find the result of any query expression, in the form of a simple value.

Here is the precise definition of sufficient completeness. (Non-mathematically inclined readers should skip the rest of this section.)

Definition: sufficient completeness

An ADT specification for a type T is sufficiently complete if and only if the axioms of the theory make it possible to solve the following problems for any well-formed expression e:

S1 • Determine whether e is correct.

S2 • If e is a query expression and has been shown to be correct under *S1*, express e's value under a form not involving any value of type T.

In *S2*, expression e is of the form $f(x_1, ..., x_n)$ where f is a query function, such as *empty* and *item* for stacks. *S1* tells us that e has a value, but this is not enough; in this case we also want to know what the value is, expressed only in terms of values of other types (in the *STACK* example, values of types *BOOLEAN* and G). If the axioms are strong enough to answer this question in all possible cases, then the specification is sufficiently complete.

Sufficient completeness is a useful practical guideline to check that no important property has been left out of a specification, answering the question raised above: when do I know I can stop looking for new properties to describe in the specification? It is good practice to apply this check, at least informally, to any ADT specification that you write — starting with your answers to the exercises of this chapter. Often, a formal proof of sufficient correctness is possible; the proof given below for the *STACK* specification defines a model which can be followed in many cases.

As you may have noted, *S2* is optimistic in talking about "the" value of e: what if the axioms yield two or more? This would make the specification useless. To avoid such a situation we need a further condition, known from mathematical logic as consistency:

Definition: ADT consistency

An ADT specification is consistent if and only if, for any well-formed query expression e, the axioms make it possible to infer at most one value for e.

The two properties are complementary. For any query expression we want to be able to deduce exactly one value: at least one (sufficient completeness), but no more than one (consistency).

Proving sufficient completeness

(This section and the rest of this chapter are supplementary material and its results are not needed in the rest of the book.)

Non-mathematically inclined readers may skip to "KEY CONCEPTS INTRODUCED IN THIS CHAPTER", 6.8, page 159

The sufficient completeness of an abstract data type specification is, in general, an undecidable problem. In other words, no general proof method exists which, given an arbitrary ADT specification, would tell us in finite time whether or not the specification is sufficiently complete. Consistency, too, is undecidable in the general case.

It is often possible, however, to prove the sufficient completeness and the consistency of a particular specification. To satisfy the curiosity of mathematically inclined readers, it is interesting to prove, as a conclusion to this chapter, that the specification of *STACK* is indeed sufficiently complete. The proof of consistency will be left as an exercise.

Proving the sufficient completeness of the stack specification means devising a valid rule addressing problems *S1* and *S2* above; in other words the rule must enable us, for an arbitrary stack expression *e*:

S1 • To determine whether *e* is correct.

S2 • If *e* is correct under *S1* and its outermost function is *item* or *empty* (one of the two query functions), to express its value in terms of *BOOLEAN* and *G* values only, without any reference to values of type *STACK* [*G*] or to the functions of *STACK*'s specification.

It is convenient for a start to consider only well-formed expressions which do not involve any of the two query functions *item* and *empty* — so that we only have to deal with expressions built out of the functions *new*, *put* and *remove*. This means that only problem *S1* (determining whether an expression is defined) is relevant at this stage. Query functions and *S2* will be brought in later.

The following property, which we must prove, yields a rule addressing *S1*:

Weight Consistency rule

A well-formed stack expression *e*, involving neither *item* nor *empty*, is correct if and only if its weight is non-negative, and any subexpression of *e* is (recursively) correct.

Here the "weight" of an expression represents the number of elements in the corresponding stack; it is also the difference between the number of nested occurrences of *put* and *remove*. Here is the precise definition of this notion:

> ## Definition: weight
>
> The weight of a well-formed stack expression not involving *item* or *empty* is defined inductively as follows:
>
> W1 • The weight of the expression *new* is 0.
>
> W2 • The weight of the expression *put* (*s*, *x*) is *ws* + *1*, where *ws* is the weight of *s*.
>
> W3 • The weight of the expression *remove* (*s*) is *ws* — *1*, where *ws* is the weight of *s*.

Informally, the Weight Consistency rule tells us that a stack expression is correct if and only if the expression and every one of its subexpressions, direct or indirect, has at least as many *put* operations (pushing an element on top) as it has *remove* operations (removing the top element); if we view the expression as representing a stack computation, this means that we never try to pop more than we have pushed. Remember that at this stage we are only concentrating on *put* and *remove*, ignoring the queries *item* and *empty*.

This intuitively seems right but of course we must prove that the Weight Consistency rule indeed holds. It will be convenient to introduce a companion rule and prove the two rules simultaneously:

> ## Zero Weight rule
>
> Let *e* be a well-formed and correct stack expression not involving *item* or *empty*. Then *empty* (*e*) is true if and only if *e* has weight 0.

The proof uses induction on the nesting level (maximum number of nested parentheses pairs) of the expression. Here again, for ease of reference, are the earlier axioms applying to function *empty*:

> ## STACK AXIOMS
>
> For any *x*: *G*, *s*: *STACK* [*G*]
>
> A3 • *empty* (*new*)
>
> A4 • **not** *empty* (*put* (*s*, *x*))

An expression *e* with nesting level 0 (no parentheses) may only be of the form *new*; so its weight is 0, and it is correct since *new* has no precondition. Axiom A3 indicates that *empty* (*e*) is true. This takes care of the base step for both the Weight Consistency rule and the Zero Weight rule.

For the induction step, assume that the two rules are applicable to all expressions of nesting level *n* or smaller. We must prove that they apply to an arbitrary expression *e* of nesting level *n* + *1*. Since for the time being we have excluded the query functions from our expressions, one of the following two forms must apply to *e*:

E1 • $e = put\ (s, x)$

E2 • $e = remove\ (s)$

where x is of type G, and s has nesting level n. Let ws be the weight of s.

In case *E1*, since *put* is a total function, e is correct if and only if s is correct, that is to say (by the induction hypothesis) if and only if s and all its subexpressions have non-negative weights. This is the same as saying that e and all its subexpressions have non-negative weights, and so proves that the Weight Consistency rule holds in this case. In addition, e has the positive weight $ws + 1$, and (by axiom A4) is not empty, proving that the Zero Weight rule also holds.

In case *E2*, expression e is correct if and only if both of the following conditions hold:

EB1 • s and all its subexpressions are correct.

EB2 • **not** *empty* (s) (this is the precondition of *remove*).

Because of the induction hypothesis, condition *EB2* means that ws, the weight of s, is positive, or, equivalently, that $ws - 1$, the weight of e, is non-negative. So e satisfies the Weight Consistency rule. To prove that it also satisfies the Zero Weight rule, we must prove that e is empty if and only if its weight is zero. Since the weight of s is positive, s must contain at least one occurrence of *put*, which also appears in e. Consider the outermost occurrence of *put* in e; this occurrence is enclosed in a *remove* (since e has a *remove* at the outermost level). This means that a subexpression of e, or e itself, is of the form

   remove (put (stack_expression, g_expression))

which axiom A2 indicates may be reduced to just *stack_expression*. Performing this replacement reduces the weight of e by 2; the resulting expression, which has the same value as e, satisfies the Zero Weight rule by the induction hypothesis. This proves the induction hypothesis for case *E2*.

The proof has shown in passing that in any well-formed and correct expression which does not involve the query functions *item* and *empty* we may "remove every *remove*", that is to say, obtain a canonical form that involves only *put* and *new*, by applying axiom A2 wherever possible. For example, the expression

   put (remove (remove (put (put (remove (put (put (new, x1), x2)), x3), x4))), x5)

has the same value as the canonical form

   put (put (new, x1), x5)

For the record, let us give this mechanism a name and a definition:

Canonical Reduction rule

Any well-formed and correct stack expression involving neither *item* nor *empty* has an equivalent "canonical" form that does not involve *remove* (that is to say, may fsonly involve *new* and *put*). The canonical form is obtained by applying the stack axiom A2 as many times as possible.

This takes care of the proof of sufficient completeness but only for expressions that do not involve any of the query functions, and consequently for property *S1* only (checking the correctness of an expression). To finish the proof, we must now take into account expressions that involve the query functions, and deal with problem *S2* (finding the values of these query expressions). This means we need a rule to determine the correctness and value of any well-formed expression of the form $f(s)$, where s is a well-formed expression and f is either *empty* or *item*.

The rule and the proof of its validity use induction on the nesting level, as defined above. Let n be the nesting level of s. If n is 0, s can only be *new* since all the other functions require arguments, and so would have at least one parenthesis pair. Then the situation is clear for both of the query functions:

- *empty* (*new*) is correct and has value true (axiom A3).
- *item* (*new*) is incorrect since the precondition of *item* is **not** *empty* (*s*).

For the induction step, assume that s has a nesting depth n of one or more. If any subexpression u of s has *item* or *empty* as its outermost function, then u has a depth of at most $n - 1$, so the induction hypothesis indicates that we can determine whether u is correct and, if it is, obtain the value of u by applying the axioms. By performing all such possible subexpression replacements, we obtain for s a form which involves no stack function other than *put*, *remove* and *new*.

Next we may apply the idea of canonical form introduced above to get rid of all occurrences of *remove*, so that the resulting form of s may only involve *put* and *new*. The case in which s is just *new* has already been dealt with; it remains the case for which s is of the form *put* (s', x). Then for the two expressions under consideration:

- *empty* (*s*) is correct, and axiom A3 indicates that the value of this expression is **false**.
- *item* (*s*) is correct, since the precondition of *item* is precisely **not** *empty* (*s*); axiom A1 indicates that the value of this expression is x.

This concludes the proof of sufficient completeness since we have now proved the validity of a set of rules — the Weight Consistency rule and the Canonical Reduction rule — enabling us to ascertain whether an arbitrary stack expression is correct and, for a correct query expression, to determine its value in terms of *BOOLEAN* and *G* values only.

6.8 KEY CONCEPTS INTRODUCED IN THIS CHAPTER

- The theory of abstract data types (ADT) reconciles the need for precision and completeness in specifications with the desire to avoid overspecification.
- An abstract data type specification is a formal, mathematical description rather than a software text. It is *applicative*, that is to say change-free.
- An abstract data type may be generic and is defined by functions, axioms and preconditions. The axioms and preconditions express the semantics of a type and are essential to a full, unambiguous description.
- To describe operations which are not always defined, partial functions provide a convenient mathematical model. Every partial function has a precondition, stating the condition under which it will yield a result for any particular candidate argument.
- An object-oriented system is a collection of classes. Every class is based on an abstract data type and provides a partial or full implementation for that ADT.

- A class is effective if it is fully implemented, deferred otherwise.

- Classes should be designed to be as general and reusable as possible; the process of combining them into systems is often bottom-up.

- Abstract data types are implicit rather than explicit descriptions. This implicitness, which also means openness, carries over to the entire object-oriented method.

- No formal definition exists for the intuitively clear concept of an abstract data type specification being "complete". A rigorously defined notion, *sufficient completeness*, usually provides the answer. Although no method is possible to ascertain the sufficient completeness of an arbitrary specification, proofs are often possible for specific cases; the proof given in this chapter for the stack specification may serve as a guide for other examples.

6.9 BIBLIOGRAPHICAL NOTES

A few articles published in the early nineteen-seventies made the discovery of abstract data types possible. Notable among these are Hoare's paper on the "proof of correctness of data representations" [Hoare 1972a], which introduced the concept of abstraction function, and Parnas's work on information hiding mentioned in the bibliographical notes to chapter *3*.

Abstract data types, of course, go beyond information hiding, although many elementary presentations of the concept stop there. ADTs proper were introduced by Liskov and Zilles [Liskov 1974]; more algebraic presentations were given in [M 1976] and [Guttag 1977]. The so-called ADJ group (Goguen, Thatcher, Wagner) explored the algebraic basis of abstract data types, using category theory. See in particular their influential article [Goguen 1978], published as a chapter in a collective book.

Several specification languages have been based on abstract data types. Two resulting from the work of the ADJ group are CLEAR [Burstall 1977] [Burstall 1981] and OBJ-2 [Futatsugi 1985]. See also Larch by Guttag, Horning and Wing [Guttag 1985]. ADT ideas have influenced formal specification languages such as Z in its successive incarnations [Abrial 1980] [Abrial 1980a] [Spivey 1988] [Spivey 1992] and VDM [Jones 1986]. The notion of abstraction function plays a central role in VDM. Recent extensions to Z have established a closer link to object-oriented ideas; see in particular Object Z [Duke 1991] and further references in chapter *11*.

The phrase "separation of concerns" is central in the work of Dijkstra; see in particular his "Discipline of Programming" [Dijkstra 1976].

The notion of sufficient completeness was first published by Guttag and Horning (based on Guttag's 1975 thesis) in [Guttag 1978].

The idea that going from specification to design means switching from the implicit to the explicit by identifying an ADT with the cartesian product of its simple queries was suggested in [M 1982] as part of a theory for describing data structures at three separate levels (physical, structural, implicit).

EXERCISES

E6.1 Points

Write a specification describing the abstract data type *POINT*, modeling points in plane geometry. The specification should cover the following aspects: cartesian and polar coordinates; rotation; translation; distance of a point to the center; distance to another point.

E6.2 Boxers

Members of the Association Dijonnaise des Tapeventres, a boxing league, regularly compete in games to ascertain their comparative strength. A game involves two boxers; it either results in a winner and a loser or is declared a tie. If not a tie, the outcome of a game is used to update the ranking of players in the league: the winner is declared better than the loser and than any boxer *b* such that the loser was previously better than *b*. Other comparative rankings are left unchanged.

Specify this problem as a set of abstract data types: *ADT_LEAGUE*, *BOXER*, *GAME*. (**Hint**: do not introduce the notion of "ranking" explicitly, but model it by a function *better* expressing whether a player is better than another in the league.)

E6.3 Bank accounts

Write an ADT specification for a "bank account" type with operations such as "deposit", "withdraw", "current balance", "holder", "change holder".

How would you add functions representing the opening and closing of an account? (**Hint**: these are actually functions on another ADT.)

E6.4 Messages

Consider an electronic mail system with which you are familiar. In light of this chapter's discussion, define *MAIL_MESSAGE* as an abstract data type. Be sure to include not just query functions but also commands and creators.

E6.5 Names

See "How long is a middle initial?", page 125.

Devise a *NAME* abstract data type taking into account the different components of a person's name.

E6.6 Text

Consider the notion of text, as handled by a text editor. Specify this notion as an abstract data type. (This statement of the exercise leaves much freedom to the specifier; make sure to include an informal description of the properties of text that you have chosen to model in the ADT.)

E6.7 Buying a house

Write an abstract data type specification for the problem of buying a house, sketched in the preceding chapter. Pay particular attention to the definition of logical constraints, expressed as preconditions and axioms in the ADT specification.

"Ordering and O-O development", *page 111.*

E6.8 More stack operations

Modify the ADT specification of stacks to account for operations *count* (returning the number of elements on a stack), *change_top* (replacing the top of the stack by a given element) and *wipe_out* (remove all elements). Make sure to include new axioms and preconditions as needed.

E6.9 Bounded stacks

Adapt the specification of the stack ADT presented in this chapter so that it will describe stacks of bounded capacity. (Hint: introduce the capacity as an explicit query function; make *put* partial.)

E6.10 Queues

Describe queues (first-in, first-out) as an abstract data type, in the style used for *STACK*. Examine closely the similarities and differences. (**Hint**: the axioms for *item* and *remove* must distinguish, to deal with *put* (s, x), the cases in which s is empty and non-empty.)

E6.11 Dispensers

(This exercise assumes that you have answered the previous one.)

Specify a general ADT *DISPENSER* covering both stack and queue structures.

Discuss a mechanism for expressing more specialized ADT specifications such as those of stacks and queues by reference to more general specifications, such as the specification of dispensers. (**Hint**: look at the inheritance mechanism studied in later chapters.)

E6.12 Booleans

Define *BOOLEAN* as an abstract data type in a way that supports its use in the ADT definitions of this chapter. You may assume that equality and inequality operations ($=$ and $\neq$) are automatically defined on every ADT.

E6.13 Sufficient completeness

(This exercise assumes that you have answered one or more of the preceding ones.) Examine an ADT specification written in response to one of the preceding exercises, and try to prove that it is sufficiently complete. If it is not sufficiently complete, explain why, and show how to correct or extend the specification to satisfy sufficient completeness.

E6.14 Consistency

Prove that the specification of stacks given in this chapter is consistent.

Part C:

Object-oriented techniques

See the comments on this text on pages 168 and 169.

"But", I said, "when you discovered the marks on the snow and on the branches, you did not yet know [the horse] Brownie. In a certain way these marks were telling us about all horses, or at least about all horses of that kind. Should we not say then that the book of nature talks to us only in terms of essences, as taught by some very distinguished theologians?"

"Not at all, my Dear Adso", replied the master. […] "The imprint in that place and at that time of day told me that at least one among all possible horses had passed there. So that I found myself half-way between the study of the concept of horse and the knowledge of one individual horse. And in any case what I knew of the universal horse was given to me by the mark, which was singular. You could say that at that time I was held prisoner between the singularity of that mark and my ignorance, which took the very hazy form of a universal idea. If you see something afar, and do not understand what it is, you will satisfy yourself by defining it as a large body. Once you have come closer you will define it as being an animal, even if you do not yet know whether it is a horse or an ass. And finally, when it is closer, you will be able to say that it is a horse even if you do not know yet whether it is Brownie or Fanny. And only when you are at the right distance will you see that it is Brownie (in other words that horse and not another, however you decide to call it). And that will be the full knowledge, the intuition of the singular." […]

"Thus the ideas, which I had used before to imagine a horse which I had not seen yet, were pure signs, as were pure signs of the horse idea the imprint on the snow: and we use signs, and signs of signs, only when we lack the things."

Umberto Eco, *The Name of the Rose*, Day One, Terce.

Part C

Object-Oriented Techniques

Part C will cover in detail the set of concepts and techniques that form the basis of object technology.

7

The static structure: classes

$\mathcal{E}$xamining the software engineering background of our discussion, you have seen the reasons for demanding a better approach to modular design: reusability and extendibility. You have realized the limitations of traditional approaches: centralized architectures limiting flexibility. You have discovered the theory behind the object-oriented approach: abstract data types. You have heard enough about the problems. On to the solution!

This chapter and the others in part C introduce the fundamental techniques of object-oriented analysis, design and programming. As we go along, we will develop the necessary notation.

Our first task is to examine the basic building blocks: classes.

7.1 OBJECTS ARE NOT THE SUBJECT

What is the central concept of object technology?

Think twice before you answer "object". Objects are useful, but they are not new. Ever since Cobol has had structures; ever since Pascal has had records; ever since the first C programmer wrote the first C structure definition, humanity has had objects.

Objects are studied in detail in the next chapter. Objects remain important to describe the execution of an O-O system. But the basic notion, from which everything in object technology derives, is **class**, previewed in the preceding chapter. Here again is the definition:

> ### Definition: class
>
> A class is an abstract data type equipped with a possibly partial implementation.

Abstract data types are a mathematical notion, suitable for the specification stage (also called analysis). Because it introduces implementations, partial or total, the notion of class establishes the necessary link with software construction — design and implementation. Remember that a class is said to be effective if the implementation is total, deferred otherwise.

Like an ADT, a class is a type: it describes a set of possible data structures, called the *instances* of the class. Abstract data types too have instances; the difference is that an instance of an ADT is a purely mathematical element (a member of some mathematical set), whereas an instance of a class is a data structure that may be represented in the memory of a computer and manipulated by a software system.

For example if we have defined a class *STACK* by taking the ADT specification of the previous chapter and adding adequate representation information, the instances of that class will be data structures representing individual stacks. Another example, developed in the rest of this chapter, is a class *POINT* modeling the notion of point in a two-dimensional space, under some appropriate representation; an instance of that class is a data structure representing a point. Under one of the representations studied below, the cartesian representation, each instance of *POINT* is a record with two fields representing the horizontal and vertical coordinates, x and y, of a point.

The definition of "class" yields as a byproduct a definition of "object". An object is simply an instance of some class. For example an instance of class *STACK* — a data structure representing a particular stack — is an object; so is an instance of class *POINT*, representing a particular point in two-dimensional space.

The software texts that serve to produce systems are classes. Objects are a run-time notion only: they are created and manipulated by the software during its execution.

The present chapter is devoted to the basic mechanisms for writing software elements and combining them into systems; as a consequence, its focus is on classes. In the next chapter, we will explore the run-time structures generated by an object-oriented system; this will require us to study some implementation issues and to take a closer look at the nature of objects.

7.2 AVOIDING THE STANDARD CONFUSION

A class is a model, and an object is an instance of such a model. This property is so obvious that it would normally deserve no comments beyond the preceding definitions; but is has been the victim of so much confusion in the more careless segment of the literature that we must take some time to clarify the obvious. (If you feel that you are immune to such a danger, and have avoided exposure to sloppy object-oriented teaching, you may wish to skip this section altogether as it essentially belabors the obvious.)

The next section, for readers who do not like the belaboring of the obvious, is "THE ROLE OF CLASSES", 7.3, page 169.

What would you think of this?

> *Among the countries in Europe we may identify the Italian. The Italian has a mountain chain running through him North-South and he likes good cooking, often using olive oil. His climate is of the Mediterranean type, and he speaks a beautifully musical language.*

See e.g. Oliver Sacks, ``The Man Who Mistook His Wife for a Hat and Other Clinical Tales", Harper Perennials, 1991.
If someone in a sober state talked or wrote to you in this fashion, you might suspect a new neurological disease, the inability to distinguish between categories (such as the Italian nation) and individuals members of these categories (such as individual Italians), reason enough to give to the ambulance driver the address of Dr. Sacks's New York clinic.

Yet in the object-oriented software literature similar confusions are common. Consider the following extract from a popular book on O-O analysis, which uses the example of an interactive system to discuss how to identify abstractions:

[Coad 1990], 3.3.3, page 67.

> *[W]e might identify a "User" Object in a problem space where the system does not need to keep any information about the user. In this case, the system does not need the usual identification number, name, access privilege, and the like. However, the system does need to monitor the user, responding to requests and providing timely information. And so, because of required Services on behalf of the real world thing (in this case, User), we need to add a corresponding Object to the model of the problem space.*

In the same breath this text uses the word *objects*, *user* and *thing* in two meanings belonging to entirely different levels of abstraction:

Exercise E7.1, page 216, asks you to clarify each use of "Object" in this text.

- A typical user of the interactive system under discussion.

- The *concept* of user in general.

Although this is probably a slip of terminology (a peccadillo which few people can claim never to have committed) rather than a true confusion on the authors' part, it is unfortunately representative of how some of the literature deals with the model-instance distinction. If you start the study of a new method with this kind of elementary mix-up, real or apparent, you are not likely to obtain a rational approach to software construction.

The mold and the instance

Take this book — the copy which you are currently reading. Consider it as an object in the common sense of the term. It has its own individual features: the copy may be brand new, or already thumbed by previous readers; perhaps you wrote your name on the first page; or it belongs to a library and has a local identification code impressed on its spine.

The basic properties of the book, however, such as its title, publisher, author and contents, are determined by a general description which applies to every individual copy: the book is entitled *Object-Oriented Software Construction*, it is published by Prentice Hall, it talks about the object-oriented method, and so on. This set of properties defines not an object but a class of objects (also called, in this case, the **type** of these objects; for the time being the notions of type and class may be considered synonymous).

Call the class *OOSC*. It defines a certain mold. Objects built from this mold, such as your copy of the book, are called ***instances*** of the class. Another example of mold would be the plaster cast that a sculptor makes to obtain an inverted version of the design for a set of identical statues; any statue derived from the cast is an instance of the mold.

In the quotation from *The Name of the Rose* which opens part C, the Master is explaining   *Page 163.*
how he was able to determine, from traces of the snow, that Brownie, the Abbot's horse,
earlier walked here. Brownie is an instance of the class of all horses. The sign on the snow,
although imprinted by one particular instance, includes only enough information to
determine the class (horse), not its identity (Brownie). Since the class, like the sign,
identifies all horses rather than a particular horse, the extract calls it a sign too.

Exactly the same concepts apply to software objects. What you will write in your
software systems is the description of classes, such as a class *LINKED_STACK* describing
properties of stacks in a certain representation. Any particular execution of your system
may use the classes to create objects (data structures); each such object is derived from a
class, and is called an **instance** of that class. For example the execution may create a linked
stack object, derived from the description given in class *LINKED_STACK*; such an object
is an instance of class *LINKED_STACK*.

The class is a software text. It is static; in other words, it exists independently of any
execution. In contrast, an object derived from that class is a dynamically created data
structure, existing only in the memory of a computer during the execution of a system.

This, of course, is in line with the earlier discussion of abstract data types: when
specifying *STACK* as an ADT, we did not describe any particular stack, but the general
notion of stack, a mold from which one can derive individual instances ad libitum.

The statements "*x* is an instance of *T*" and "*x* is an object of type *T*" will be
considered synonymous for this discussion.

With the introduction of inheritance we will need to distinguish between the *direct*   See "Instances",
instances of a class (built from the exact pattern defined by the class) and its *instances* in   page 475.
the more general sense (direct instances of the class or any of its specializations).

Metaclasses

Why would so many books and articles confuse two so clearly different notions as class
and object? One reason — although not an excuse — is the appeal of the word "object", a
simple term from everyday language. But it is misleading. As we already saw in the
discussion of seamlessness, although some of the objects (class instances) which O-O
systems manipulate are the computer representations of objects in the usual sense of the
term, such as documents, bank accounts or airplanes, many others have no existence
outside of the software; they include in particular the objects introduced for design and
implementation purposes — instances of classes such as *STATE* or *LINKED_LIST*.

Another possible source of confusion between objects and classes is that in some
cases we may need to treat classes themselves as objects. This need arises only in special
contexts, and is mainly relevant to developers of object-oriented development
environments. For example a compiler or interpreter for an O-O language will manipulate
data structures representing classes written in that language. The same would hold of other
tools such as a browser (a tool used to locate classes and find out about their properties)
or a configuration management system. If you produce such tools, you will create objects
that represent classes.

Pursuing an analogy used earlier, we may compare this situation to that of a Prentice Hall employee who is in charge of preparing the catalog of software engineering titles. For the catalog writer, OOSC, the concept behind this book, is an object — an instance of a class "catalog entry". In contrast, for the reader of the book, that concept is a class, of which the reader's particular copy is an instance.

Some object-oriented languages, notably Smalltalk, have introduced a notion of **metaclass** to handle this kind of situation. A metaclass is a class whose instances are themselves classes — what the *Name of the Rose* extract called "signs of signs".

We will avoid metaclasses in this presentation, however, since they bring more problems than benefits. In particular, the addition of metaclasses makes it difficult to have static type checking, a required condition of the production of reliable software. The main applications of metaclasses are better obtained through other mechanisms anyway:

*"Universal classes",
page 580.*

- You can use metaclasses to make a set of features available to many or all classes. We will achieve the same result by arranging the inheritance structure so that all classes are descendants of a general-purpose, customizable class *ANY*, containing the declarations of universal features.

*See "The creation
instruction", page
232.*

- A few operations may be viewed as characterizing a class rather than its instances, justifying their inclusion as features of a metaclass. But these operations are few and known; the most obvious one is object creation — sufficiently important to deserve a special language construct, the creation instruction. (Other such operations, such as object duplication, will be covered by features of class *ANY*.)

- There remains the use of metaclasses to obtain information about a class, such as a browser may need: name of the class, list of features, list of parents, list of suppliers etc. But we do not need metaclasses for that. It will suffice to devise a library class, *E_CLASS*, so that each instance of *E_CLASS* represents a class and its properties. When we create such an instance, we pass to the creation instruction an argument representing a certain class *C*; then by applying the various features of *E_CLASS* to that instance, we can learn all about *C*.

In practice, then, we can do without a separate concept of metaclass. But even in a method, language or environment that would support this notion, the presence of metaclasses is no excuse for confusing molds and their instances — classes and objects.

7.3 THE ROLE OF CLASSES

Having taken the time to remove an absurd but common and damaging confusion, we may now come back to the central properties of classes, and in particular study why they are so important to object technology.

To understand the object-oriented approach, it is essential to realize that classes play two roles which pre-O-O approaches had always treated as separate: module and type.

Modules and types

Programming languages and other notations used in software development (design languages, specification languages, graphical notations for analysis) always include both some module facility and some type system.

A module is a unit of software decomposition. Various forms of module, such as *See chapter 3.* routines and packages, were studied in an earlier chapter. Regardless of the exact choice of module structure, we may call the notion of module a **syntactic** concept, since the decomposition into modules only affects the form of software texts, not what the software can do; it is indeed possible in principle to write any Ada program as a single package, or any Pascal program as a single main program. Such an approach is not recommended, of course, and any competent software developer will use the module facilities of the language at hand to decompose his software into manageable pieces. But if we take an existing program, for example in Pascal, we can always merge all the modules into a single one, and still get a working system with equivalent semantics. (The presence of recursive routines makes the conversion process less trivial, but does not fundamentally affect this discussion.) So the practice of decomposing into modules is dictated by sound engineering and project management principles rather than intrinsic necessity.

Types, at first sight, are a quite different concept. A type is the static description of certain dynamic objects: the various data elements that will be processed during the execution of a software system. The set of types usually includes predefined types such as *INTEGER* and *CHARACTER* as well as developer-defined types: record types (also known as structure types), pointer types, set types (as in Pascal), array types and others. The notion of type is a **semantic** concept, since every type directly influences the execution of a software system by defining the form of the objects that the system will create and manipulate at run time.

The class as module and type

In non-O-O approaches, the module and type concepts remain distinct. The most remarkable property of the notion of class is that it subsumes these two concepts, merging them into a single linguistic construct. A class is a module, or unit of software decomposition; but it is also a type (or, in cases involving genericity, a type pattern).

Much of the power of the object-oriented method derives from this identification. Inheritance, in particular, can only be understood fully if we look at it as providing both module extension and type specialization.

What is not clear yet is *how* it is possible in practice to unify two concepts which appear at first so distant. The discussion and examples in the rest of this chapter will answer this question.

7.4 A UNIFORM TYPE SYSTEM

An important aspect of the O-O approach as we will develop it is the simplicity and uniformity of the type system, deriving from a fundamental property:

> ## Object rule
>
> Every object is an instance of some class.

The Object rule will apply not just to composite, developer-defined objects (such as data structures with several fields) but also to basic objects such as integers, real numbers, boolean values and characters, which will all be considered to be instances of predefined library classes (*INTEGER, REAL, DOUBLE, BOOLEAN, CHARACTER*).

This zeal to make every possible value, however simple, an instance of some class may at first appear exaggerated or even extravagant. After all, mathematicians and engineers have used integers and reals successfully for a long time, without knowing they were manipulating class instances. But insisting on uniformity pays off for several reasons:

- It is always desirable to have a simple and uniform framework rather than many special cases. Here the type system will be entirely based on the notion of class.

The mathematical axioms defining integers are known as Peano's axioms.

- Describing basic types as ADTs and hence as classes is simple and natural. It is not hard, for example, to see how to define the class *INTEGER* with features covering arithmetic operations such as "+", comparison operations such as "<=", and the associated properties, derived from the corresponding mathematical axioms.

- By defining the basic types as classes, we allow them to take part in all the O-O games, especially inheritance and genericity. If we did not treat the basic types as classes, we would have to introduce severe limitations and many special cases.

   As an example of inheritance, classes *INTEGER*, *REAL* and *DOUBLE* will be heirs to more general classes: *NUMERIC*, introducing the basic arithmetic operations such as "+", "–" and "∗", and *COMPARABLE*, introducing comparison operations such as "<". As an example of genericity, we can define a generic class *MATRIX* whose generic parameter represents the type of matrix elements, so that instances of *MATRIX [INTEGER]* represent matrices of integers, instances of *MATRIX [REAL]* represent matrices of reals and so on. As an example of combining genericity with inheritance, the preceding definitions also allow us to use the type *MATRIX [NUMERIC]*, whose instances represent matrices containing objects of type *INTEGER* as well as objects of type *REAL* and objects of any new type *T* defined by a software developer so as to inherit from *NUMERIC*.

With a good implementation, we do not need to fear any negative consequence from the decision to define all types from classes. Nothing prevents a compiler from having special knowledge about the basic classes; the code it generates for operations on values of types such as *INTEGER* and *BOOLEAN* can then be just as efficient as if these were built-in types in the language.

Reaching the goal of a fully consistent and uniform type system requires the combination of several important O-O techniques, to be seen only later: expanded classes, to ensure proper representation of simple values; infix and prefix operators, to enable usual arithmetic syntax (such as $a < b$ or $-a$ rather than the more cumbersome $a \cdot less\_than\ (b)$ or $a \cdot negated$); constrained genericity, needed to define classes which may be adapted to various types with specific operations, for example a class *MATRIX* that can represent matrices of integers as well as matrices of elements of other numeric types.

7.5 A SIMPLE CLASS

Let us now see what classes look like by studying a simple but typical example, which shows some of the fundamental properties applicable to almost all classes.

The features

The example is the notion of point, as it could appear in a two-dimensional graphics system.

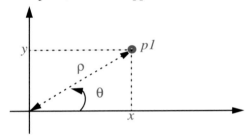

A point and its coordinates

To characterize type *POINT* as an abstract data type, we would need the four query functions x, y, ρ, θ. (The names of the last two will be spelled out as *rho* and *theta* in software texts.) Function x gives the abscissa of a point (horizontal coordinate), y its ordinate (vertical coordinate), ρ its distance to the origin, θ the angle to the horizontal axis. The values of x and y for a point are called its cartesian coordinates, those of ρ and θ its polar coordinates. Another useful query function is *distance*, which will yield the distance between two points.

Then the ADT specification would list commands such as *translate* (to move a point by a given horizontal and vertical displacement), *rotate* (to rotate the point by a certain angle, around the origin) and *scale* (to bring the point closer to or further from the origin by a certain factor).

The name translate *refers to the "translation" operation of geometry.*

It is not difficult to write the full ADT specification including these functions and some of the associated axioms. For example, two of the function signatures will be

x: *POINT* $\rightarrow$ *REAL*
translate: *POINT* $\times$ *REAL* $\times$ *REAL* $\rightarrow$ *POINT*

and one of the axioms will be (for any point p and any reals a, b):

$x\ (translate\ (p1, a, b)) = x\ (p1) + a$

expressing that translating a point by $<a, b>$ increases its abscissa by a.

*Exercise E7.2, page
216.*
You may wish to complete this ADT specification by yourself. The rest of this discussion will assume that you have understood the ADT, whether or not you have written it formally in full, so that we can focus on its implementation — the class.

Attributes and routines

Any abstract data type such as *POINT* is characterized by a set of functions, describing the operations applicable to instances of the ADT. In classes (ADT implementations), functions will yield features — the operations applicable to instances of the class.

*"Function catego-
ries", page 134.*
We have seen that ADT functions are of three kinds: queries, commands and creators. For features, we need a complementary classification, based on how each feature is implemented: by space or by time.

The example of point coordinates shows the difference clearly. Two common representations are available for points: cartesian and polar. If we choose cartesian representation, each instance of the class will contain two fields representing the x and y of the corresponding point:

*Representing a
point in
cartesian
coordinates*

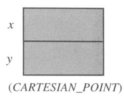

(*CARTESIAN_POINT*)

If *p1* is the point shown, getting its x or its y simply requires looking up the corresponding field in this structure. Getting ρ or θ, however, requires a computation: for ρ we must compute $\sqrt{x^2 + y^2}$, and for θ we must compute *arctg* (y/x) with non-zero x.

If we use polar representation, the situation is reversed: ρ and θ are now accessible by simple field lookup, x and y require small computations (of $\rho\ cos\ \theta$ and $\rho\ sin\ \theta$).

*Representing a
point in polar
coordinates*

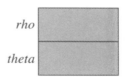

(*POLAR_POINT*)

This example shows the need for two kinds of feature:

- Some features will be represented by space, that is to say by associating a certain piece of information with every instance of the class. They will be called **attributes**. For points, x and y are attributes in cartesian representation; *rho* and *theta* are attributes in polar representation.

- Some features will be represented by time, that is to say by defining a certain computation (an algorithm) applicable to all instances of the class. They will be called **routines**. For points, *rho* and *theta* are routines in cartesian representation; *x* and *y* are routines in polar representation.

A further distinction affects routines (the second of these categories). Some routines will return a result; they are called **functions**. Here *x* and *y* in polar representation, as well as *rho* and *theta* in cartesian representation, are functions since they return a result, of type *REAL*. Routines which do not return a result correspond to the commands of an ADT specification and are called **procedures**. For example the class *POINT* will include procedures *translate*, *rotate* and *scale*.

Be sure not to confuse the use of "function" to denote result-returning routines in classes with the earlier use of this word to denote the mathematical specifications of operations in abstract data types. This conflict is unfortunate, but follows from well-established usage of the word in both the mathematics and software fields.

The following tree helps visualize this classification of features:

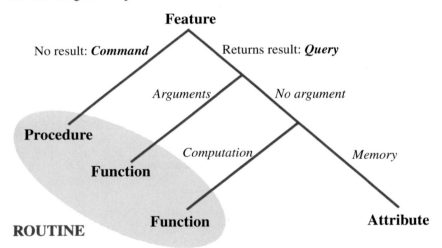

Feature classification, by role

This is an external classification, in which the principal question is how a feature will look to its clients (its users).

We can also take a more internal view, using as primary criterion how each feature is implemented in the class, and leading to a different classification:

Feature classification, by implementation

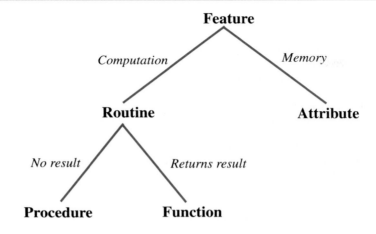

Uniform access

One aspect of the preceding classifications may at first appear disturbing and has perhaps caught your attention. In many cases, we should be able to manipulate objects, for example a point *p1*, without having to worry about whether the internal representation of *p1* is cartesian, polar or other. Is it appropriate, then, to distinguish explicitly between attributes and functions?

The answer depends on whose view we consider: the supplier's view (as seen by the author of the class itself, here *POINT*) or the client's view (as seen by the author of a class that uses *POINT*). For the supplier, the distinction between attributes and functions is meaningful and necessary, since in some cases you will want to implement a feature by storage and in others by computation, and the decision must be reflected somewhere. What would be wrong, however, would be to force the **clients** to be aware of the difference. If I am accessing *p1*, I want to be able to find out its x or its ρ without having to know how such queries are implemented.

See "Uniform Access", page 55.
The Uniform Access principle, introduced in the discussion of modularity, answers this concern. The principle states that a client should be able to access a property of an object using a single notation, whether the property is implemented by memory or by computation (space or time, attribute or routine). We shall follow this important principle in devising a notation for feature call below: the expression denoting the value of the x feature for *p1* will always be

   $p1.x$

whether its effect is to access a field of an object or to execute a routine.

> As you will have noted, the uncertainty can only exist for queries without arguments, which may be implemented as functions or as attributes. A command must be a procedure; a query with arguments must be a function, since attributes cannot have arguments.

The Uniform Access principle is essential to guarantee the autonomy of the components of a system. It preserves the class designer's freedom to experiment with various implementation techniques without disturbing the clients.

> Pascal, C and Ada violate the principle by providing a different notation for a function call and for an attribute access. For such non-object-oriented languages this is understandable (although we have seen that Algol W, a 1966 predecessor to Pascal, satisfied uniform access). More recent languages such as C++ and Java also do not enforce the principle. Departing from Uniform Access may cause any internal representation change (such as the switch from polar to cartesian or some other representation) to cause upheaval in many client classes. This is a primary source of instability in software development.

The Uniform Access principle also yields a requirement on documentation techniques. If we are to apply the principle consistently, we must ensure that it is not possible to determine, from the official documentation on a class, whether a query without arguments is a function or an attribute. This will be one of the properties of the standard mechanism for documenting a class, known as the short form.

"Using assertions for documentation: the short form of a class", page 389.

The class

Here is a version of the class text for *POINT*. (Any occurrence of consecutive dashes -- introduces a comment, which extends to the end of the line; comments are explanations intended for the reader of the class text and do not affect the semantics of the class.)

> **indexing**
>
> > *description*: "*Two-dimensional points*"
>
> **class** *POINT* **feature**
>
> > *x, y*: *REAL*
> > > -- Abscissa and ordinate
> >
> > *rho*: *REAL* **is**
> > > -- Distance to origin (0, 0)
> > > **do**
> > > > *Result* := *sqrt* (*x* ^ 2 + *y* ^ 2)
> > > **end**
> >
> > *theta*: *REAL* **is**
> > > -- Angle to horizontal axis
> > > **do**
> > > > …Left to reader (exercise E7.3, page 216) °
> > > **end**

> *distance* (*p*: *POINT*): *REAL* **is**
>   -- Distance to *p*
>   **do**
> $Result := sqrt ((x - p_\bullet x) \wedge 2 + (y - p_\bullet y) \wedge 2)$
>   **end**
>
> *translate* (*a*, *b*: *REAL*) **is**
>   -- Move by *a* horizontally, *b* vertically.
>   **do**
> $x := x + a$
> $y := y + b$
>   **end**
>
> *scale* (*factor*: *REAL*) **is**
>   -- Scale by *factor*.
>   **do**
> $x := factor * x$
> $y := factor * y$
>   **end**
>
> *rotate* (*p: POINT; angle*: *REAL*) **is**
>   -- Rotate around *p* by *angle*.
>   **do**
>   …Left to reader (exercise E7.3, page 216) …
>   **end**

end

The next few sections explain in detail the non-obvious aspects of this class text.

The class mainly consists of a clause listing the various features and introduced by the keyword **feature**. There is also an **indexing** clause giving general *description* information, useful to readers of the class but with no effect on its execution semantics. Later on we will learn three optional clauses: **inherit** for inheritance, **creation** for non-default creation and **invariant** for introducing class invariants; we will also see how to include two or more **feature** clauses in one class.

7.6 BASIC CONVENTIONS

Class *POINT* shows a number of techniques which will be used throughout later examples. Let us first look at the basic conventions.

Recognizing feature kinds

Features *x* and *y* are just declared as being of type *REAL*, with no associated algorithm; so they can only be attributes. All other features have a clause of the form

    is
        do
            … Instructions…
        end

which defines an algorithm; this indicates the feature is a routine. Routines *rho*, *theta* and *distance* are declared as returning a result, of type *REAL* in all cases, as indicated by declarations of the form

        rho: *REAL* **is** …

This defines them as functions. The other two, *translate* and *scale*, do not return a result (since they do not have a result declaration of the form :*T* for some type *T*), and so they are procedures.

Since *x* and *y* are attributes, while *rho* and *theta* are functions, the representation chosen in this particular class for points is cartesian.

Routine bodies and header comments

The body of a routine (the **do** clause) is a sequence of instructions. You can use semicolons, in the Algol-Pascal tradition, to separate successive instructions and declarations, but the semicolons are optional. We will omit them for simplicity between elements on separate lines, but will always include them to delimit instructions or declarations appearing on the same line.

For details see "The War of the Semicolons", page 897.

All the instructions in the routines of class *POINT* are assignments; for assignment, the notation uses the := symbol (again borrowed from the Algol-Pascal conventions). This symbol should of course not be confused with the equality symbol =, used, as in mathematics, as a comparison operator.

Another convention of the notation is the use of header comments. As already noted, comments are introduced by two consecutive dashes --. They may appear at any place in a class text where the class author feels that readers will benefit from an explanation. A special role is played by the **header comment** which, as a general style rule, should appear at the beginning of every routine, after the keyword **is**, indented as shown by the examples in class *POINT*. Such a header comment should tersely express the purpose of the routine.

Attributes should also have a header comment immediately following their declaration, aligned with routine's header comments, as illustrated here with *x* and *y*.

The indexing clause

At the beginning of the class comes a clause starting with the keyword **indexing**. It contains a single entry, labeled *description*. The indexing clause has no effect on software execution, but serves to associate information with the class. In its general form it contains zero or more entries of the form

See "A note about component indexing", page 78.

        index_word: *index_value*, *index_value*, …

where the *index_word* is an arbitrary identifier, and each *index_value* is an arbitrary language element (identifier, integer, string…).

The benefit is twofold:

- Readers of the class get a summary of its properties, without having to see the details.

Chapter 36 describes a general O-O browsing mechanism.

- In a software development environment supporting reuse, query tools (often known as *browsers*) can use the indexing information to help potential users find out about available classes; the tools can let the users enter various search words and match them with the index words and values.

The example has a single indexing entry, with *description* as index word and, as index value, a string describing the purpose of the class. All classes in this book, save for short examples, will include a *description* entry. You are strongly encouraged to follow this example and begin every class text with an **indexing** clause providing a concise overview of the class, in the same way that every routine begins with a header comment.

"Self-Documenta-tion", page 54.

Both indexing clauses and header comments are faithful applications of the Self-Documentation principle: as much as possible of a module's documentation should appear in the text of the module itself.

Denoting a function's result

We need another convention to understand the texts of the functions in class *POINT*: *rho*, *theta* and *distance*.

An "entity" is a name denoting a value. Full definition on page 213.

Any language that supports functions (value-returning routines) must offer a notation allowing the body of a function to set the value which will be returned by any particular call. The convention used here is simple: it relies on a predefined entity name, *Result*, denoting the value that the call will return. For example, the body of *rho* contains an assignment to *Result*:

$$Result := sqrt\ (x \wedge 2 + y \wedge 2)$$

Result is a reserved word, and may only appear in functions. In a function declared as having a result of type *T*, *Result* is treated in the same way as other entities, and may be assigned values through assignment instructions such as the above.

Initialization rules will be given in "The creation instruc-tion", page 232.

Any call to the function will return, as its result, the final value assigned to *Result* during the call's execution. That value always exists since language rules (to be seen in detail later) require every execution of the routine, when it starts, to initialize *Result* to a preset value. For a *REAL* the initialization value is zero; so a function of the form

```
non_negative_value (x: REAL): REAL is
        -- The value of x if positive; zero otherwise.
    do
        if x > 0.0 then
            Result := x
        end
    end
```

will always return a well-defined value (as described by the header comment) even though the conditional instruction has no **else** part.

The discussion section of this chapter examines the rationale behind the *Result* convention and compares it with other techniques such as return instructions. Although this convention addresses an issue that arises in all design and programming languages, it blends particularly well with the rest of the object-oriented approach.

See "Denoting the result of a function", page 210.

Style rules

The class texts in this book follow precise style conventions regarding indentation, fonts (for typeset output), choice of names for features and classes, use of lower and upper case.

The discussion will point out these conventions, under the heading "style rules", as we go along. They should not be dismissed as mere cosmetics: quality software requires consistency and attention to all details, of form as well as of content. The reusability goal makes these observations even more important, since it implies that software texts will have a long life, during which many people will need to understand and improve them.

You should apply the style rules right from the time you start writing a class. For example you should never write a routine without immediately including its header comment. This does not take long, and is not wasted time; in fact it is time saved for all future work on the class, whether by you or by others, whether after half an hour or after half a decade. Using regular indentation, proper spelling for comments and identifiers, adequate lexical conventions — a space before each opening parenthesis but not after, and so on — does not make your task any longer than ignoring these rules, but compounded over months of work and heaps of software produces a tremendous difference. Attention to such details, although not sufficient, is a necessary condition for quality software (and quality, the general theme of this book, is what defines software engineering).

The elementary style rules are clear from the preceding class example. Since our immediate goal is to explore the basic mechanisms of object technology, their precise description will only appear in a later chapter.

Chapter 26 is devoted to style rules.

Inheriting general-purpose facilities

Another aspect of class *POINT* which requires clarification is the presence of calls to the *sqrt* function (in *rho* and *distance*). This function should clearly return the square root of a real number, but where does it come from?

Since it does not seem appropriate to encumber a general-purpose language with specialized arithmetic operations, the best technique is to define such operations as features of some specialized class — say *ARITHMETIC* — and then simply require any class that needs these facilities to inherit from the specialized class. As will be seen in detail in a later chapter, it suffices then to write *POINT* as

```
class POINT inherit
    ARITHMETIC
feature
    ... The rest as before ...
end
```

See "FACILITY INHERITANCE", 24.9, page 847.

This technique of inheriting general-purpose facilities is somewhat controversial; one can argue that O-O principles suggest making a function such as *sqrt* a feature of the class representing the object to which it applies, for example *REAL*. But there are many operations on real numbers, not all of which can be included in the class. Square root may be sufficiently fundamental to justify making it a feature of class *REAL*; then we would write *a•sqrt* rather than *sqrt (x)*. We will return, in the discussion of design principles, to the question of whether "facilities" classes such as *ARITHMETIC* are desirable.

7.7 THE OBJECT-ORIENTED STYLE OF COMPUTATION

Let us now move to the fundamental properties of class *POINT* by trying to understand a typical routine body and its instructions, then studying how the class and its features may be used by other classes — clients.

The current instance

Here again is the text of one of our example routines, procedure *translate*:

> *translate* (*a*, *b*: *REAL*) **is**
>
> -- Move by *a* horizontally, *b* vertically
>
> **do**
>
> $x := x + a$
>
> $y := y + b$
>
> **end**

At first sight this text appears clear enough: to translate a point by *a* horizontally, *b* vertically, we add *a* to its *x* and *b* to its *y*. But if you look at it more carefully, it may not be so obvious anymore! Nowhere in the text have we stated what point we were talking about. To whose *x* and whose *y* are we adding *a* and *b*? In the answer to this question will lie one of the most distinctive aspects of the object-oriented development style. Before we are ready to discover that answer we must understand a few intermediate topics.

A class text describes the properties and behavior of objects of a certain type, points in this example. It does so by describing the properties and behavior of a typical instance of that type — what we could call the "point in the street" in the way newspapers report the opinion of the "man or woman in the street". We will settle for a more formal name: the **current instance** of the class.

Once in a while, we may need to refer to the current instance explicitly. The reserved word

> *Current*

will serve that purpose. In a class text, *Current* denotes the current instance of the enclosing class. As an example of when *Current* is needed, assume we rewrite *distance* so that it checks first whether the argument *p* is the same point as the current instance, in which case the result is 0 with no need for further computation. Then *distance* will appear as *distance (p: POINT): REAL* **is**

> -- Distance to *p*

do

> **if** *p* /= *Current* **then**
>
> > *Result* := *sqrt* $((x — p.x) \wedge 2 + (y — p.y) \wedge 2)$
>
> **end**

end

(/= is the inequality operator. Because of the initialization rule mentioned above, the conditional instruction does not need an **else** part: if *p* = *Current* the result is zero.)

In most circumstances, however, the current instance is implicit and we will not need to refer to *Current* by its name. For example, references to *x* in the body of *translate* and the other routines simply mean, if not further qualified: "the *x* of the current instance".

This only pushes back the mystery, of course: "who" really is *Current*? The answer will come with the study of routine calls below. As long as we only look at the routine text, it will suffice to know that all operations are relative, by default, to an implicitly defined object, the current instance.

Clients and suppliers

Ignoring for a few moments the enigma of *Current*'s identity, we know how to define simple classes. We must now study how to use their definitions. Such uses will be in other classes — since in a pure object-oriented approach every software element is part of some class text.

There are only two ways to use a class such as *POINT*. One is to inherit from it; this is studied in detail in later chapters. The other one is to become a **client** of *POINT*. *Chapters 14 to 16 study inheritance.*

The simplest and most common way to become a client of a class is to declare an entity of the corresponding type:

> ### Definition: client, supplier
>
> Let *S* be a class. A class *C* which contains a declaration of the form *a*: *S* is said to be a client of *S*. *S* is then said to be a supplier of *C*.

In this definition, *a* may be an attribute or function of *C*, or a local entity or argument of a routine of *C*.

For example, the declarations of *x*, *y*, *rho*, *theta* and *distance* above make class *POINT* a client of *REAL*. Other classes may in turn become clients of *POINT*. Here is an example:

```
class GRAPHICS feature
    p1: POINT

    ...

    some_routine is
            -- Perform some actions with p1.
        do
            ... Create an instance of POINT and attach it to p1 ...
            p1.translate (4.0, −1.5)                    --**
            ...
        end
    ...
end
```

Before the instruction marked --** gets executed, the attribute *p1* will have a value denoting a certain instance of class *POINT*. Assume that this instance represents the origin, of coordinates $x = 0$, $y = 0$:

The origin

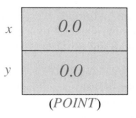

(*POINT*)

Entity *p1* is said to be **attached** to this object. We do not worry at this point about how the object has been created (by the unexplained line that reads "...Create object...") and initialized; such topics will be discussed as part of the object model in the next chapter. Let us just assume that the object exists and that *p1* is attached to it.

Feature call

The starred instruction,

   p1.translate (4.0, −1.5)

deserves careful examination since it is our first complete example of what may be called the **basic mechanism of object-oriented computation**: feature call. In the execution of an object-oriented software system, all computation is achieved by calling certain features on certain objects.

This particular feature call means: apply to *p1* the feature *translate* of class *POINT*, with arguments *4.0* and *−1.5*, corresponding to *a* and *b* in the declaration of *translate* as it appears in the class. More generally, a feature call appears in its basic form as one of

   x.f
   x.f (u, v, ...)

In such a call, x, called the **target** of the call, is an entity or expression (which at run time will be attached to a certain object). As any other entity or expression, x has a certain type, given by a class C; then f must be one of the features of C. More precisely, in the first form, f must be an attribute or a routine without arguments; in the second form, f must be a routine with arguments, and u, v, ..., called the **actual arguments** for the call, must be expressions matching in type and number the formal arguments declared for f in C.

In addition, f must be available (exported) to the client containing this call. This is the default; a later section will show how to restrict export rights. For the moment, all features are available to all clients.

*"SELECTIVE EX-
PORTS AND INFOR-
MATION HIDING",
7.8, page 191.*

The effect of the above call when executed at run time is defined as follows:

Effect of calling a feature f on a target x

Apply feature f to the object attached to x, after having initialized each formal argument of f (if any) to the value of the corresponding actual argument.

The Single Target principle

What is so special about feature call? After all, every software developer knows how to write a procedure *translate* which moves a point by a certain displacement, and is called in the traditional form (available, with minor variants, in all programming languages):

   translate $(p1, 4.0, -1.5)$

Unlike the object-oriented style of feature call, however, this call treats all arguments on an equal basis. The O-O form has no such symmetry: we choose a certain object (here the point *p1*) as target, relegating the other arguments, here the real numbers *4.0* and *–1.5*, to the role of supporting cast. This way of making every call relative to a single target object is a central part of the object-oriented style of computing:

Single Target principle

Every operation of object-oriented computation is relative to a certain object, the current instance at the time of the operation's execution.

To novices, this is often the most disconcerting aspect of the method. In object-oriented software construction, we never really ask: "Apply this operation to these objects". Instead we say: "Apply this operation to **this** object here." And perhaps (in the second form): "Oh, by the way, I almost forgot, you will need those values there as arguments".

What we have seen so far does not really suffice to justify this convention; in fact its negative consequences will, for a while, overshadow its advantages. An example of counter-intuitive effect appears with the function *distance* of class *POINT*, declared above as *distance* (*p*: *POINT*): *REAL*, implying that a typical call will be written

   $p1 \bullet distance (p2)$

which runs against the perception of *distance* as a symmetric operation on two arguments. Only with the introduction of inheritance will the Single Target principle be fully vindicated.

The module-type identification

"The class as module and type", page 170.
The Single Target principle is a direct consequence of the module-type merge, presented earlier as the starting point of object-oriented decomposition: if every module is a type, then every operation in the module is relative to a certain instance of that type (the current instance). Up to now, however, the details of that merge remained a little mysterious. A class, it was said above, is both a module and a type; but how can we reconcile the syntactic notion of module (a grouping of related facilities, forming a part of a software system) with the semantic notion of type (the static description of certain possible run-time objects)? The example of *POINT* makes the answer clear:

How the module-type merge works

The facilities provided by class *POINT*, viewed as a module, are precisely the operations available on instances of class *POINT*, viewed as a type.

This identification between the operations on instances of a type and the services provided by a module lies at the heart of the structuring discipline enforced by the object-oriented method.

The role of *Current*

With the help of the same example, we are now also in a position to clear the remaining mystery: what does the current instance really represent?

The form of calls indicates why the text of a routine (such as *translate* in *POINT*) does not need to specify "who" *Current* is: since every call to the routine will be relative to a certain target, specified explicitly in the call, the execution will treat every feature name appearing in the text of the routine (for example x in the text of *translate*) as applying to that particular target. So for the execution of the call

$p1 \bullet translate\ (4.0, -1.5)$

every occurrence of x in the body of *translate*, such as those in the instruction

$x := x + a$

means: "the x of $p1$".

The exact meaning of *Current* follows from these observations. *Current* means: "the target of the current call". For example, for the duration of the above call, *Current* will denote the object attached to $p1$. In a subsequent call, *Current* will denote the target of that new call. That this all makes sense follows from the extreme simplicity of the object-oriented computation model, based on feature calls and on the Single Target principle:

> ## Feature Call principle
>
> F1 • No software element ever gets executed except as part of a routine call.
>
> F2 • Every call has a target.

Qualified and unqualified calls

It was said above that all object-oriented computation relies on feature calls. A consequence of this rule is that software texts actually contain more calls than meet the eye at first. The calls seen so far were of one of the two forms introduced above:

$x \cdot f$

$x \cdot f (u, v, \ldots)$

Such calls use so-called dot notation (with the "$\cdot$" symbol) and are said to be **qualified** because the target of the call is explicitly identified: it is the entity or expression (x in both cases above) that appears before the dot.

Other calls, however, will be unqualified because their targets are implicit. As an example, assume that we want to add to class *POINT* a procedure *transform* that will both translate and scale a point. The procedure's text may rely on *translate* and *scale*:

transform $(a, b, factor: REAL)$ **is**
        -- Move by a horizontally, b vertically, then scale by *factor*.
   do
      translate (a, b)
      scale $(factor)$
   end

The routine body contains calls to *translate* and *scale*. Unlike the earlier examples, these calls do not show an explicit target, and do not use dot notation. Such calls are said to be **unqualified**.

Unqualified calls do not violate the property called F2 in the Feature Call principle: like qualified calls, they have a target. As you have certainly guessed, the target in this case is the current instance. When procedure *transform* is called on a certain target, its body calls *translate* and *scale* on the same target. It could in fact have been written

   do
      Current $\cdot$ *translate* (a, b)
      Current $\cdot$ *scale* $(factor)$

More generally, you may rewrite any unqualified call as a qualified call with *Current* as its target. The unqualified form is of course simpler and just as clear.

Strictly speaking, the equivalence only applies if the feature is exported.

The unqualified calls that we have just examined were calls to routines. The same discussion applies to attributes, although the presence of calls is perhaps less obvious in this case. It was noted above that, in the body of *translate*, the occurrence of x in the expression $x + a$ denotes the x field of the current instance. Another way of expressing this property is that x is actually a feature call, so that the expression as a whole could have been written as *Current.x + a*.

More generally, any instruction or expression of one of the forms

f

$f(u, v, …)$

is in fact an unqualified call, and you may also write it in qualified form as (respectively)

Current.f

Current.f (u, v, …)

although the unqualified forms are more convenient. If you use such a notation as an instruction, f must be a procedure (with no argument in the first form, and with the appropriate number and types of arguments in the second). If it is an expression, f may be an attribute (in the first form only, since attributes have no arguments) or a function.

Be sure to note that this syntactical equivalence only applies to a feature used as an instruction or an expression. So in the following assignment from procedure *translate*

$x := x + a$

only the occurrence of x on the right-hand side is an unqualified call: a is a formal argument, not a feature; and the occurrence of x on the left is not an expression (one cannot assign a value to an expression), so it would be meaningless to replace it by *Current.x*.

Operator features

A further look at the expression $x + a$ leads to a useful notion: operator features. This notion (and the present section) may be viewed as pure "cosmetics", that is to say, covering only a syntactical facility without bringing anything really new to the object-oriented method. But such syntactical properties can be important to make developers' life easier if they are present — or miserable if they are absent. Operator features also provide a good example of how successful the object-oriented paradigm can be at integrating earlier approaches smoothly.

Here is the idea. Although you may not have guessed it, the expression $x + a$ contains not just one call — the call to x, as just seen — but two. In non-O-O computation, we would consider $+$ as an operator, applied here to two values x and a, both declared of type *REAL*. In a pure O-O model, as noted, the only computational mechanism is feature call; so you may consider the addition itself, at least in theory, to be a call to an addition feature.

The Object rule was given on page 171.

To understand this better, consider how we could define the type *REAL*. The Object rule stated earlier implied that every type is based on some class. This applies to predefined types such as *REAL* as well as developer-defined types such as *POINT*. Assume you are requested to write *REAL* as a class. It is not hard to identify the relevant features: arithmetic operations (addition, subtraction, negation…), comparison operations (less than, greater than…). So a first sketch could appear as:

indexing
> *description: "Real numbers (not final version!)"*
class *REAL* **feature**
> *plus (other: REAL): REAL* **is**
>> -- Sum of current value and *other*
>
>> **do**
>>> ...
>
>> **end**
>
> *minus (other: REAL) REAL* **is**
>> -- Difference of current value and *other*
>
>> **do**
>>> ...
>
>> **end**
>
> *negated: REAL* **is**
>> -- Current value but with opposite sign
>
>> **do**
>>> ...
>
>> **end**
>
> *less_than (other: REAL): BOOLEAN* **is**
>> -- Is current value strictly less than *other*?
>
>> **do**
>>> ...
>
>> **end**
>
> ... Other features ...
end

With such a form of the class, you could not write an arithmetic expression such as $x + a$ any more; instead, you would use a call of the form

> *x.plus* (*a*)

Similarly, you would have to write *x.negated* instead of the usual $-x$.

One might try to justify such a departure from usual mathematical notation on the grounds of consistency with the object-oriented model, and invoke the example of Lisp to suggest that it is sometimes possible to convince a subset of the software development community to renounce standard notation. But this argument contains it owns limitations: usage of Lisp has always remained marginal. It is rather dangerous to go against notations which have been in existence for centuries, and which people have been using since elementary school, especially when there is nothing wrong with these notations.

A simple syntactical device reconciles the desire for consistency (requiring here a single computational mechanism based on feature call) and the need for compatibility with traditional notations. It suffices to consider that an expression of the form

> $x + a$

is in fact a call to the addition feature of class *REAL*; the only difference with the *plus* feature suggested above is that we must rewrite the declaration of the corresponding feature to specify that calls will use operator notation rather than dot notation.

Here is the form of a class that achieves this goal:

The next chapter will show how to declare this class as "expanded". See "The role of expanded types", page 256.

indexing
    description: "Real numbers"
class *REAL* **feature**
    infix "+" (*other*: *REAL*): *REAL* **is**
          -- Sum of current value and *other*
        do
           …
        end
    infix "−" (*other*: *REAL*) *REAL* **is**
          -- Difference of current value and *other*
        do
           …
        end
    prefix "−": *REAL* **is**
          -- Current value but with opposite sign
        do
           …
        end
    infix "<" (*other*: *REAL*): *BOOLEAN* **is**
          -- Is current value strictly less than *other*?
        do
           …
        end
    … Other features …
end

Two new keywords have been introduced: **infix** and **prefix**. The only syntactical extension is that from now on we may choose feature names which, instead of identifiers (such as *distance* or *plus*), are of one of the two forms

    infix "§"
    prefix "§"

where § stands for an operator symbol chosen from a list which includes +, −, $*$, <, <= and a few other possibilities listed below. A feature may have a name of the **infix** form only if it is a function with one argument, such as the functions called *plus*, *minus* and *less_than* in the original version of class *REAL*; it may have a name of the **prefix** form only if it is a function with no argument, or an attribute.

Infix and prefix features, collectively called **operator features**, are treated exactly like other features (called **identifier features**) with the exception of the two syntactical properties already seen:

- The name of an operator feature as it appears in the feature's declaration is of the form **infix** "§" or **prefix** "§", rather than an identifier.

- Calls to operator features are of the form *u* § *v* (in the infix case) or § *u* (in the prefix case) rather than using dot notation.

As a consequence of the second property, operator features only support qualified calls. If a routine of class *REAL* contained, in the first version given earlier, an unqualified call of the form *plus* (*y*), yielding the sum of the current number and *y*, the corresponding call will have to be written *Current* + *y* in the second version. With an identifier feature, the corresponding notation, *Current.plus* (*y*), is possible but we would not normally use it in practice since it is uselessly wordy. With an operator feature we do not have a choice.

Other than the two syntactical differences noted, operator features are fully equivalent to identifier features; for example they are inherited in the same way. Any class, not just the basic classes such as *REAL*, can use operator features; for example, it may be convenient in a class *VECTOR* to have a vector addition function called **infix** "+".

The following rule will apply to the operators used in operator features. An operator is a sequence of one or more printable characters, containing no space or newline, and beginning with one of

$$+ \ - \ * \ / \ < \ > \ = \ \backslash \ ^{\wedge} \ @ \ \# \ | \ \&$$

In addition, the following keywords, used for compatibility with usual boolean notation, are permitted as operators:

not and or xor and then or else implies

In the non-keyword case, the reason for restricting the first character is to preserve the clarity of software texts by ensuring that any use of an infix or prefix operator is immediately recognizable as such from its first character.

Basic classes (*INTEGER* etc.) use the following, known as standard operators:

- Prefix: + − **not**.
- Infix: + − * / < > <= >= // \\ ^ **and or xor and then or else implies**.

See "Non-strict boolean operators", page 454.

The semantics is the usual one. // is used for integer division, \\ for integer remainder, ^ as the power operation, **xor** as exclusive or. In class *BOOLEAN*, **and then** and **or else** are variants of **and** and **or**, the difference being explained in a later chapter, and **implies** is the implication operator, such that *a* **implies** *b* is the same as (**not** *a*) **or else** *b*.

Operators not in the "standard" list are called free operators. Here are two examples of possible operator features using free operators:

- When we later introduce an *ARRAY* class, we will use the operator feature **infix** "@" for the function that returns an array element given by its index, so that the *i*-th element of an array *a* may be written simply as *a* @ *i*.
- In class *POINT*, we could have used the name **infix** "|−|" instead of *distance*, so that the distance between *p1* and *p2* is written *p1* |−| *p2* instead of *p1.p2*.

The precedence of all operators is fixed; standard operators have their usual precedence, and all free operators bind tighter than standard operators.

The use of operator features is a convenient way to maintain compatibility with well-accepted expression notation while ensuring the goal of a fully uniform type system (as stated by the Object Rule) and of a single fundamental mechanism for computation. In the same way that treating *INTEGER* and other basic types as classes does not need to cause any performance problem, treating arithmetic and boolean operations as features does not need to affect efficiency. Conceptually, $a + x$ is a feature call; but any good compiler will know about the basic types and their features, and will be able to handle such a call so as to generate code at least as good as the code generated for $a + x$ in C, Pascal, Ada or any other language in which + is a special hard-wired language construct.

When using operators such as +, < and others in expressions, we may forget, most of the time, that they actually stand for feature calls; the effect of these operators is the one we would expect in traditional approaches. But it is pleasant to know that, thanks to the theoretical context of their definition, they do not cause any departure from object-oriented principles, and fit in perfectly with the rest of the method.

7.8 SELECTIVE EXPORTS AND INFORMATION HIDING

See "Information Hiding", page 51.
In the examples seen so far all the features of a class were exported to all possible clients. This is of course not always acceptable; we know from earlier discussion how important information hiding is to the design of coherent and flexible architectures.

"SELECTIVE EXPORTS", 23.5, page 796.
Let us take a look at how we can indeed restrict features to no clients, or to some clients only. This section only introduces the notation; the chapter on the design of class interfaces will discuss its proper use.

Full disclosure

By default, as noted, features declared without any particular precaution are available to all clients. In a class of the form

> **class** *S1* **feature**
>
> f ...
>
> g ...
>
>   ...
>
> **end**

features f, g, ... are available to all clients of $S1$. This means that in a class C, for an entity x declared of type $S1$, a call

> $x \cdot f$ ...

is valid, provided the call satisfies the other validity conditions on calls to f, regarding the number and types of arguments if any. (For simplicity the discussion will use identifier features as examples, but it applies in exactly the same way to operator features, for which the clients will use calls in infix or prefix form rather than dot notation.)

Restricting client access

To restrict the set of clients that can call a certain feature h, we will use the possibility for a class to have two or more **feature** clauses. The class will then be of the form

```
class S2 feature
    f ...
    g ...
feature {A, B}
    h ...
    ...
end
```

Features *f* and *g* have the same status as before: available to all clients. Feature *h* is available only to *A* and *B*, and to their descendants (the classes that inherit directly or indirectly from *A* or *B*). This means that with *x* declared of type *S2* a call of the form

$x.h$ ...

is invalid unless it appears in the text of *A*, *B*, or one of their descendants.

As a special case, if you want to hide a feature *i* from all clients, you may declare it as exported to an empty list of clients:

```
class S3 feature { }
    i ...
end
```

This is not the recommended style; see S5 below.

In this case a call of the form $x.i$ (...) is always invalid. The only permitted calls to *i* are unqualified calls of the form

i (...)

appearing in the text of a routine of *S3* itself, or one of its descendants. This mechanism ensures full information hiding.

The possibility of hiding a feature from all clients, as illustrated by *i*, is present in many O-O languages. But most do not offer the selective mechanism illustrated by *h*: exporting a feature to certain designated clients and their proper descendants. This is regrettable since many applications will need this degree of fine control.

The discussion section of the present chapter explains why selective exports are a critical part of the architectural mechanisms of the object-oriented approach, avoiding the need for "super-modules" that would hamper the simplicity of the method.

"The architectural role of selective exports", page 209.

We will encounter various examples of selective exports in subsequent chapters, and will study their methodological role in the design of good modular interfaces.

"SELECTIVE EXPORTS", 23.5, page 796.

Style for declaring secret features

A small point of style. A feature declared in the form used above for *i* is secret, but perhaps this property does not stand out strongly enough from the syntax. In particular, the difference with a public feature may not be visible enough, as in

Not the recom-
mended style; see S5
next.

class *S4* **feature**
      exported...
feature { }

    secret ...

end

where feature *exported* is available to all clients whereas *secret* is available to no client. The difference between **feature** { }, with an empty list in braces, and **feature**, with no braces, is a little weak. For that reason, the recommended notation uses not an empty list but a list consisting of the single class *NONE*, as in

The recommended
style.

class *S5* **feature**
      ... Exported ...
feature {*NONE*}
      ... Secret ...

end

"The bottom of the
pit", page 582.

Class *NONE*, which will be studied in a later chapter in connection with inheritance, is a Base library class which is so defined as to have no instances and no descendants. So exporting a feature to *NONE* only is, for all practical purposes, the same as keeping it secret. As a result there is no meaningful difference between the forms illustrated by *S4* and *S5*; for reasons of clarity and readability, however, the second form is preferred, and will be employed in the rest of this book whenever we need to introduce a secret feature.

Exporting to yourself

A consequence of the rules seen so far is that a class may have to export a secret feature. Assume the declaration

```
indexing
    note: "Invalid as it stands (see explanations below)"
class S6 feature
    x: S6
    my_routine is do ... print (x.secret) ... end
feature {NONE}
    secret: INTEGER
end -- class S6
```

By declaring *x* of type *S6* and making the call *x.secret*, the class becomes its own client. But this call is invalid, since *secret* is exported to no class! That the unauthorized client is *S6* itself does not make any difference: the {*NONE*} export status of *secret* makes any call *x.secret* invalid. Permitting exceptions would damage the simplicity of the rule.

The solution is simple: instead of **feature** {*NONE*} the header of the second **feature** clause should read **feature** {*S6*}, exporting the feature to the class itself and its descendants.

Be sure to note that this is only needed if you want to use the feature in a qualified call such as appears in *print* (*x.secret*). If you are simply using *secret* by itself, as in the instruction *print (secret)*, you of course do not need to export it at all. Features declared in a class must be usable by the routines of the class and its descendants; otherwise we could never do anything with a secret feature! Only if you use the feature indirectly in a qualified call do you need to export it to yourself.

7.9 PUTTING EVERYTHING TOGETHER

The previous discussions have introduced the basic mechanisms of object-oriented computation, but we are still missing the big picture: how does anything ever get executed?

Answering this question will help us piece everything together and understand how to build executable systems from individual classes.

General relativity

What is a little mind-boggling is that every description given so far of what happens at run time has been relative. The effect of a routine such as *translate* is relative to the current instance; within the class text, as noted, the current instance is not known. So we can only try to understand the effect of a call with respect to a specific target, such as *p1* in

$p1.translate\ (u, v)$

But this brings the next question: what does *p1* actually denote? Here again the answer is relative. The above call must appear in the text of some class such as *GRAPHICS*. Assume that *p1* is an attribute of class *GRAPHICS*. Then the occurrence of *p1* in the call, as noted above, may be viewed as a call: *p1* stands for *Current.p1*. So we have only pushed the problem further, as we must know what object *Current* stood for at the time of the above call! In other words, we must look at the client that called the routine of class *GRAPHICS* containing that call.

So this attempt at understanding a feature call starts off a chain of reasoning, which we will not be able to follow to the end unless we know where execution started.

The Big Bang

To understand what is going on let us generalize the above example to an arbitrary call. If we do understand that arbitrary call, we will indeed understand all of O-O computation, thanks to the Feature Call principle which stated that

> F1 • No software element ever gets executed except as part of a routine call.
>
> F2 • Every call has a target.

See page 186.

Any call will be of one of the following two forms (the argument list may be absent in either case):

- Unqualified: $f\ (a, b, \ldots)$
- Qualified: $x.g\ (u, v, \ldots)$

The call appears in the body of a routine r. It can only get executed as part of a call to r. Assume we know the target of that call, some object OBJ. Then the target t is easy to determine in each case:

T1 • For the unqualified form, t is simply OBJ. Cases T2, T3 and T4 will apply to the qualified form.

T2 • If x is an attribute, the x field of OBJ has a value which must be attached to some object; t is that object.

T3 • If x is a function, we must first execute the (unqualified) call to x; the result gives us t.

T4 • If x is a local entity of r, earlier instructions will have given x a value, which at the time of the call must be attached to a certain object; t is that object.

The only problem with these answers is of course that they are relative: they only help us if we know the current instance OBJ. What is OBJ? Why, the target of the current call, of course! As in the traditional song (the kid was eaten by the cat, the cat was bitten by the dog, the dog was beaten by the stick…), we do not see the end of the chain.

To transform these relative answers into absolute ones, then, we must know what happened when everything started — at Big Bang time. Here is the rule:

Definition: system execution

Execution of an object-oriented software system consists of the following two steps:

• Create a certain object, called the **root object** for the execution.

• Apply a certain procedure, called a **creation procedure**, to that object.

At Big Bang time, an object gets created, and a creation procedure gets started. The root object is an instance of a certain class, the system's **root class**; the creation procedure is one of the procedures of the root class. In all but trivial systems, the creation procedure will itself create new objects and call routines on them, triggering more object creations and more routine calls. System execution as a whole is the successive deployment of all the pieces in a giant and complex firework, all resulting directly or indirectly from the initial lighting of a minuscule spark.

Once we know where everything starts, it is not difficult to trace the fate of *Current* throughout this chain reaction. The first current object, at the start of everything (Big Bang time, when the root's creation procedure is called), is the root object. Then at any stage during system execution let r be the latest routine to have been called; if OBJ was the current object at the time of the call to r, here is what becomes of *Current* during the execution of r:

C1 • If r executes an instruction which does not call a routine (for example an assignment), we keep the same object as current object.

C2 • Starting an unqualified call also keeps the same object as current object.

C3 • Starting a qualified call $x \cdot f$ ... causes the target object of that call, which is the object attached to x (determined from OBJ through the rules called T1 to T4 at the top of the previous page), to become the new current object. When the call terminates, OBJ resumes its role as current object.

In cases C2 and C3 the call may be to a routine that itself includes further calls, qualified or not; so this rule must be understood recursively.

There is nothing mysterious or confusing, then, in the rule for determining the target of any call, even though that rule is relative and in fact recursive. What is mind-boggling is the power of computers, the power we use to play sorcerer's apprentice by writing a deceptively small software text and then executing it to create objects and perform computations on them in numbers so large — number of objects, number of computations — as to appear almost infinite when measured on the scale of human understanding.

Systems

The emphasis in this chapter is on classes: the individual components of object-oriented software construction. To obtain executable code, we must assemble classes into systems.

The definition of a system follows from the previous discussion. To make up a system we need three things:

- A set CS of classes, called the system's **class set**.
- The indication of which class in CS is the **root class**.
- The indication of which procedure of the root class is the **root creation procedure**.

To yield a meaningful system, these elements must satisfy a consistency condition, **system closure**: any class needed directly or indirectly by the root class must be part of CS.

Let us be a little more precise:

- A class C **needs directly** a class D if the text of C refers to D. There are two basic ways in which C may need directly D: C may be a client of D, as defined earlier in this chapter, and C may inherit from D, according to the inheritance relation which we will study later.
- A class C **needs** a class E, with no further qualification, if C is E or C needs directly a class D which (recursively) needs E.

With these definitions we may state the closure requirement as follows:

Definition: system closure

A system is closed if and only if its class set contains all classes needed by the root class.

If the system is closed, a language-processing tool, such as a compiler, will be able to process all its classes, starting with the root class, and recursively handling needed classes as it encounters their names. If the tool is a compiler, it will then produce the executable code corresponding to the entire system.

This act of tying together the set of classes of a system, to generate an executable result, is called **assembly** and is the last step in the software construction process.

Not a main program

The discussions in the previous chapters repeatedly emphasized that systems developed with the object-oriented method have no notion of main program. By introducing the notion of root class, and requiring the system specification to indicate a particular creation procedure, have we not brought main programs back through a side door?

Not quite. What is wrong with the traditional notion of main program is that it merges two unrelated concepts:

- The place where execution begins.

- The top, or fundamental component of the system's architecture.

The first of these is obviously necessary: every system will begin its execution somewhere, so we must have a way to let developers specify the starting point; here they will do so by specifying a root class and a creation procedure. (In the case of concurrent rather than sequential computation we may have to specify several starting points, one per independent thread of computation.)

On the concept of top, enough abuse has been heaped in earlier chapters to make further comments unnecessary.

But regardless of the intrinsic merit of each of the two notions, there is no reason to merge them: no reason to assume that the starting point of a computation will play a particularly important role in the architecture of the corresponding system. Initialization is just one of many aspects of a system. To take a typical example, the initialization of an operating system is its booting procedure, usually a small and relatively marginal component of the OS; using it as the top of the system's design would not lead to an elegant or useful architecture. The notion of system, and object technology in general, rely in fact on the reverse assumption: that the most important property of a system is the set of classes that it contains, the individual capabilities of these classes, and their relationships. In this view the choice of a root class is a secondary property, and should be easy to change as the system evolves.

For a critique of function-based decomposition see "FUNCTIONAL DECOMPOSITION", 5.2, page 103

As discussed extensively in an earlier chapter, the quest for extendibility and reusability requires that we shed the practice of asking "what is the main function?" at an early stage of the system's design and of organizing the architecture around the answer. Instead, the approach promotes the development of reusable software components, built as abstract data type implementations — classes. Systems are then built as reconfigurable assemblies of such components.

In fact, you will not always build systems in the practice of O-O software development. An important application of the method is to develop **libraries** of reusable components — classes. A library is not a system, and has no root class. When developing a library, you may of course need to produce, compile and execute one or more systems along the way, but such systems are a means, not an end: they help test the components, and will usually not be part of the library as finally delivered. The actual delivered product is the set of classes making up the library, which other developers will then use to produce their own systems — or again their own libraries.

Assembling a system

The process of putting together a number of classes (one of which is designated as root) to produce an executable system was called "assembly" above. How in practice do we assemble a system?

Let us assume an operating system of the usual form, where we will keep our class texts stored in files. The language processing tool in charge of this task (compiler, interpreter) will need the following information:

A1 • The name of the root class.

A2 • A **universe**, or set of files which may contain the text of classes needed by the root (in the above precise sense of "needed").

This information should not be included in the class texts themselves. Identifying a class as root in its own text (A1) would violate the "no main program" principle. Letting a class text include information about the files where the needed classes reside would tie the class to a particular location in the file system of a given installation; this would prevent use of the class by another installation and is clearly inappropriate.

These observations suggest that the system assembly process will need to rely on some information stored outside of the text of the classes themselves. To provide this information we will rely on a little control language called Lace. Let us observe the process, but not until we have noted that the details of Lace are not essential to the method; Lace is just an example of a control language, allowing us to keep the O-O components (the classes) autonomous and reusable, and to rely on a separate mechanism for their actual assembly into systems.

A typical Lace document, known as an **Ace file**, might appear as follows:

system *painting* **root**
        GRAPHICS *("painting_application")*
cluster
        base_library: *"\library\base"*;
        graphical_library: *"\library\graphics"*;
        painting_application: *"\user\application"*
end -- system *painting*

The **cluster** clause defines the universe (the set of files containing class texts). It is organized as a list of clusters; a cluster is a group of related classes, representing a subsystem or a library.

Chapter 28 discusses the cluster model.

In practice, an operating system such as Windows, VMS or Unix provides a convenient mechanism to support the notion of cluster: directories. Its file system is structured as a tree, where only the terminal nodes (leaves), called "plain files", contain directly usable information; the internal nodes, called directories, are sets of files (plain files or again directories).

A directory structure

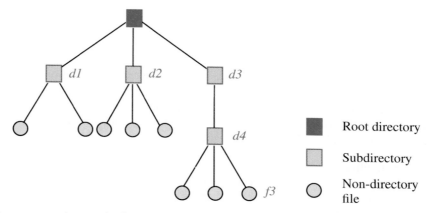

We may associate each cluster with a directory. This convention is used in Lace as illustrated above: every cluster, with a Lace name such as *base_library*, has an associated directory, whose name is given as a string in double quotes, such as "*library**base*". This file name assumes Windows conventions (names of the form *dir1**dir2*\\...), but this is just for the sake of the example. You can obtain the corresponding Unix names by replacing the backslash characters \\ by slashes /.

> Although by default you may use the hierarchical structure of directories to represent cluster nesting, Lace has a notion of subcluster through which you can define the logical structure of the cluster hierarchy, regardless of the clusters' physical locations in the file system.

The directories listed in the **cluster** clause may contain files of all kinds. To determine the universe, the system assembly process will need to know which ones of these files may contain class texts. A simple convention is to require the text of any class of name *NAME* to be stored in a file of name *name*.e (lower case). Let us assume this convention (which can easily be extended for more flexibility) for the rest of this discussion. Then the universe is the set of files having names of the form *name*.e in the list of directories appearing in the **cluster** clause.

The **root** clause of Lace serves to designate the root class of the system. Here the root class is *GRAPHICS* and, as indicated in parentheses, it appears in the *painting_application* cluster. If there is only one class called *GRAPHICS* in the universe, it is not necessary to specify the cluster.

Assume that you start a language processing tool, for example a compiler, to process the system described by the above Ace. Assume further that none of the classes in the system has been compiled yet. The compiler finds the text of the root class, *GRAPHICS*, in the file *graphics*.e of the cluster *painting_application*; that file appears in the directory

\user\application. By analyzing the text of class *GRAPHICS*, the compiler will find the names of the classes needed by *GRAPHICS* and will look for files with the corresponding .e names in the three cluster directories. It will then apply the same search to the classes needed by these new classes, repeating the process until it has located all the classes needed directly or indirectly by the root.

An important property of this process is that it should be **automatic**. As a software developer, you should not have to write lists of dependencies between modules (known as "Make files"), or to indicate in each file the names of the files that will be needed for its compilation (through what is known in C and C++ as "Include directives"). Not only is it tedious to have to create and maintain such dependency information manually; this process also raises the possibility of errors when the software evolves. All that the Ace requires you to provide is the information that no tool can find by itself: the name of the root class, and the list of locations in the file system where needed classes — what earlier was called the *class set* of the system — may appear.

To simplify the work of developers further, a good compiler will, when called in a directory where no Ace is present, construct a template Ace whose **cluster** clause includes the basic libraries (kernel, fundamental data structures and algorithms, graphics etc.) and the current directory, so that you will only have to fill in the name of the system and of its root class, avoiding the need to remember the syntax of Lace.

The end result of the compilation process is an executable file, whose name is the one given after **system** in the Ace — *painting* in the example.

The Lace language includes a few other simple constructs, used to control the actions of language processing tools, in particular compiler options and assertion monitoring levels. We will encounter some of them as we explore further O-O techniques. Lace, as noted, also supports the notion of logical subcluster, so that you can use it to describe complex system structures, including the notions of subsystem and multi-level libraries.

Using a system description language such as Lace, separate from the development language, allows classes to remain independent from the system or systems in which they intervene. Classes are software components, similar to chips in electronic design; a system is one particular assembly of classes, similar to a board or a computer made by assembling a certain set of chips.

Printing your name

Reusable software components are great, but sometimes all you want to do is just a simple task, such as printing a string. You may have been wondering how to write a "program" that will do it. Having introduced the notion of system, we can answer this burning question. (Some people tend to be nervous about the whole approach until they see how to do this, hence this little digression.)

The following little class has a procedure which will print a string:

```
class SIMPLE creation
    make
feature
    make is
                -- Print an example string.
        do
                print_line ("Hello Sarah!")
        end
end
```

On *GENERAL* see
"Universal classes",
page 580.
The procedure *print_line* can take an argument of any type; it prints a default representation of the corresponding object, here a string, on a line. Also available is *print* which does not go to a new line after printing. Both procedures are available to all classes, coming from a universal ancestor, *GENERAL*, as explained in a later chapter.

To obtain a system that will print the given string, do the following:

E1 • Put the above class text in a file called *simple*.e in some directory.

E2 • Start the compiler.

E3 • If you have not provided an Ace, you will be prompted to edit a new one, automatically generated from a template; just fill in the name of the root class, *SIMPLE*, the name of the system — say *my_first* — and the cluster directory.

E4 • Exit from the editor; the compiler will assemble the system and produce an executable file called *my_first*.

E5 • Execute the result. On platforms such as Unix with a notion of command-line execution a command will have been generated, of name *my_first*; simply type that name. On graphical platforms such as Windows and OS/2, a new icon will have appeared, labeled *my_first*; just double-click on that icon.

The result of the last step will be, as desired, to print on your console the message

---

Hello Sarah!

Structure and order: the software developer as arsonist

We now have an overall picture of the software construction process in the object-oriented method — assembling classes into systems. We also know how to reconstruct the chain of events that will lead to the execution of a particular operation. Assume this operation is

[A]
$$x \bullet g \ (u, v, \ldots)$$

appearing in the text of a routine *r* of a class *C*, of which we assume *x* to be an attribute. How does it ever get executed? Let us recapitulate. You must have included *C* in a system, and assembled that system with the help of an appropriate Ace. Then you must have started an execution of that system by creating an instance of its root class. The root's creation procedure must have executed one or more operations which, directly or indirectly, caused the creation of an instance C_OBJ of C, and the execution of a call of the form

[B]

$$a \cdot r \, (\ldots)$$

where a was at the time attached to C_OBJ. Then the call shown as [A] will execute g, with the arguments given, using as target the object attached to the x field of C_OBJ.

So by now we know (as well we should) how to find out the exact sequence of events that will occur during the execution of a system. But this assumes we look at the entire system. In general we will not be able, just by examining the text of a given class, to determine the order in which clients will call its various routines. The only ordering property that is immediately visible is the order in which a given routine executes the instructions of its body.

Even at the system level, the structure is so decentralized that the task of predicting the precise order of operations, although possible in principle, is often difficult. More importantly, it is usually not very interesting. Remember that we treat the root class as a somewhat superficial property of the system — a particular choice, made late in the development process, of how we are going to combine a set of individual components and schedule their available operations.

This downplaying of ordering constraints is part of object technology's constant push for decentralization in system architectures. The emphasis is not on "the" execution of "the" program (as in Pascal or C programming and many design methods) but on the services provided by a set of classes through their features. The *order* in which the services will be exercised, during the execution of a particular system built from these classes, is a secondary property.

The method goes in fact further by prescribing that *even if you know* the order of execution you should not base any serious system design decision on it. The reason for this rule was explored in earlier chapters: it is a consequence of the concern for extendibility and reusability. It is much easier to add or change services in a decentralized structure than to change the order of operations if that order was one of the properties used to build the architecture. This reluctance of the object-oriented method to consider the order of operations as a fundamental property of software systems — what an earlier discussion called the shopping list approach — is one of its major differences with most of the other popular software design methods.

See "Premature ordering", page 110.

These observations once again evoke the picture of the software developer as firework expert or perhaps arsonist. He prepares a giant conflagration, making sure that all the needed components are ready for assembly and all the needed connections present. He then lights up a match and watches the blaze. But if the structure has been properly set up and every component is properly attached to its neighbors, there is no need to follow or even try to predict the exact sequence of lightings; it suffices to know that every part that must burn will burn, and will not do so before its time has come.

7.10 DISCUSSION

As a conclusion to this chapter, let us consider the rationale behind some of the decisions made in the design of the method and notation, exploring along the way a few alternative paths. Similar discussion sections will appear at the end of most chapters introducing new constructs; their aim is to spur the reader's own thinking by presenting a candid, uncensored view of a few delicate issues.

Form of declarations

To hone our critical skills on something that is not too life-threatening, let us start with a syntactical property. One point worth noting is the notation for feature declarations. For routines, there are none of the keywords **procedure** or **function** such as they appear in many languages; the form of a feature determines whether it is an attribute, a procedure or a function. The beginning of a feature declaration is just the feature name, say

f ...

When you have read this, you must still keep all possibilities open. If a list of arguments comes next, as in

$g\ (a1\colon A;\ b1\colon B;\ \dots)$ ...

then you know g is a routine; it could still be either a function or a procedure. Next a type may come:

$f\colon T$ ...
$g\ (a1\colon A;\ b1\colon B;\ \dots)\colon T$ ...

In the first example, f can still be either an attribute or a function without arguments; in the second, however, the suspense stops, as g can only be a function. Coming back to f, the ambiguity will be resolved by what appears after T: if nothing, f is an attribute, as in

my_file: *FILE*

But if an **is** is present, followed by a routine body (**do** or the variants **once** and **external** to be seen later), as in

$f\colon T$ **is**

       -- ...

    do ... **end**

f is a function. Yet another variant is:

$f\colon T$ **is** *some_value*

Chapter 18 discusses constant attributes.

which defines f as a **constant attribute** of value *some_value*.

The syntax is designed to allow easy recognition of the various kinds of feature, while emphasizing the fundamental similarities. The very notion of feature, covering routines as well as attributes, is in line with the Uniform Access principle — the goal of providing clients with abstract facilities and downplaying their representation differences. The similarity between feature declarations follows from the same ideas.

Attributes vs. functions

Let us explore further the consequences of the Uniform Access principle and of grouping attributes and routines under a common heading — features.

"Uniform Access", page 55; see also, in the present chapter, "Uniform access", page 175.

The principle stated that clients of a module should be able to use any service provided by the module in a uniform way, regardless of how the service is implemented — through storage or through computation. Here the services are the features of the class; what is meaningful for clients is the availability of certain features and their properties. Whether a given feature is implemented by storing appropriate data or by computing the result on demand is, for most purposes, irrelevant.

Assume for example a class *PERSON* containing a feature *age* of type *INTEGER*, with no arguments. If the author of a client class writes the expression

> *Isabelle.age*

the only important information is that *age* will return an integer, the age field of an instance of *PERSON* attached, at run-time, to the entity *Isabelle*. Internally, *age* may be either an attribute, stored with each object, or a function, computed by subtracting the value of a *birth_date* attribute from the current year. But the author of the client class does not need to know which one of these solutions was chosen by the author of *PERSON*.

The notation for *accessing* an attribute, then, is the same as for calling a routine; and the notations for *declaring* these two kinds of feature are as similar as conceptually possible. Then if the author of a supplier class reverses an implementation decision (implementing as a function a feature that was initially an attribute, or conversely), clients will not be affected; they will require neither change, possibly not even recompilation.

The contrast between the supplier's and client's view of the features of a module was apparent in the two figures which helped introduce the notion of feature earlier in this chapter. The first used as its primary criterion the distinction between routines and attributes, reflecting the internal (implementation) view, which is also the supplier's view. In the second figure, the primary distinction was between commands and queries, the latter further subdivided into queries with and without arguments. This is the external view — the client's view.

The figures appeared on pages 174 and 175.

The decision to treat attributes and functions without arguments as equivalent for clients has two important consequences, which later chapters will develop:

- The first consequence affects software documentation. The standard client documentation for a class, known as the **short form** of the class, will be devised so as not to reveal whether a given feature is an attribute or a function (in cases for which it could be either).

"Using assertions for documentation: the short form of a class", page 389.

- The second consequence affects inheritance, the major technique for adapting software components to new circumstances without disrupting existing software. If a certain class introduces a feature as a function without arguments, descendant classes will be permitted to **redefine** the feature as an attribute, substituting memory for computation.

"Redeclaring a function into an attribute", page 491.

Exporting attributes

The class text was on page 176. A consequence of the preceding observations is that classes may export attributes. For example, class *POINT*, in the cartesian implementation introduced earlier, has attributes x and y, and exports them to clients in exactly the same way as the functions *rho* and *theta*. To obtain the value of an attribute for a certain object, you simply use feature call notation, as in *my_point.x* or *my_point.theta*.

This ability to export attributes differs from the conventions that exist in many O-O languages. Typical of these is Smalltalk, where only routines (called "methods") may be exported by a class; attributes ("instance variables") are not directly accessible to clients.

A consequence of the Smalltalk approach is that if you want to obtain the effect of exporting an attribute you have to write a small exported function whose only purpose is to return the attribute's value. So in the *POINT* example we could call the attributes *internal_x* and *internal_y*, and write the class as follows (using the notation of this book rather than the exact Smalltalk syntax, and calling the functions *abscissa* and *ordinate* rather than x and y to avoid any confusion):

```
class POINT feature -- Public features:
    abscissa: REAL is
            -- Horizontal coordinate
        do Result := internal_x end

    ordinate: REAL is
            -- Vertical coordinate
        do Result := internal_y end
    … Other features as in the earlier version …
feature {NONE} -- Features inaccessible to clients:
    internal_x, internal_y: REAL
end
```

This approach has two drawbacks:

• It forces authors of supplier classes to write many small functions such as *abscissa* and *ordinate*. Although in practice such functions will be short (since the syntax of Smalltalk is terse, and makes it possible to give the same name to an attribute and a function, avoiding the need to devise special attribute names such as *internal_x* and *internal_y*), writing them is still a waste of effort on the part of the class author, and reading them is a useless distraction for the class reader.

• The method entails a significant performance penalty: every access to a field of an object now requires a routine call. No wonder object technology has developed a reputation for inefficiency in some circles. (It is possible to develop an optimizing compiler which will expand calls to *abscissa*-style functions in-line, but then what is the role of these functions?)

The technique discussed in this chapter seems preferable. It avoids the need for cluttering class texts with numerous little extra functions, and instead lets the class designers export attributes as needed. Contrary to what a superficial examination might suggest, this policy does not violate information hiding; it is in fact a direct implementation of this principle and of the associated principle of Uniform Access. To satisfy these requirements it suffices to make sure that attributes, as seen by clients, are indistinguishable from functions without arguments, and that they have the same properties for inheritance and class documentation.

This technique reconciles the goals of Uniform Access (essential for the clients), ease of writing class texts (essential for the suppliers), and efficiency (essential for everyone).

The client's privileges on an attribute

Exporting an attribute, using the techniques just discussed, allows clients to access the value of an attribute for a certain object, as in *my_point.x* It does not allow clients to modify that value. You may not assign to an attribute; the assignment

> *my_point.x := 3.7*

Warning: illegal construct — for illustration only.

is syntactically illegal. The syntax rule is simple: *a.attrib*, if *attrib* is an attribute (or for that matter a function) is an expression, not an entity, so you cannot assign to it, any more than you can assign to the expression *a + b*.

To make *attrib* accessible in modification mode, you must write and export an appropriate procedure, of the form:

> *set_attrib* (*v*: *G*) **is**
>
>> -- Set to *v* the value of *attrib*.
>
> **do**
>
>> *attrib := v*
>
> **end**

Instead of this convention, one could imagine a syntax for specifying access rights, such as

> **class** *C* **feature** [*AM*]
>
>> ...
>
> **feature** [*A*] {*D, E*}
>
>> ...

Warning: not a retained notation. For discussion only.

where *A* would mean access and *M* modification. (Specifying *A* could be optional: if you export something you must at least allow clients to access it in read mode). This would avoid the frequent need for writing procedures similar to *set_attrib*.

Besides not justifying the extra language complication, this solution is not flexible enough. In many cases, you will want to export *specific* ways of modifying an attribute. For example, the following class exports a counter, and the right to modify it not arbitrarily but only by increments of +1 or −1:

class *COUNTING* **feature**

    counter: *INTEGER*

    increment **is**

            -- Increment counter

      do

            count := count + 1

      end

    decrement **is**

            -- Decrement counter

      do

            count := count — 1

      end

end

Similarly, class *POINT* as developed in this chapter does not let its clients set the x and y of a point directly; clients can change the values of these attributes, but only by going through the specific mechanisms that have been exported for that purpose, procedures *translate* and *scale*.

When we study assertions we will see another fundamental reason why it is inappropriate to let clients perform direct assignments of the $a \bullet attrib := some\_value$ form: not all *some_value* are acceptable. You may define a procedure such as

set_polygon_size (*new_size*: *INTEGER*) **is**

            -- Set the number of polygon vertices to *new_size*.

  require

    new_size >= 3

  do

    size := new_size

  end

requiring any actual argument to be 3 or more. Direct assignments would make it impossible to enforce this constraint; a call could then produce an incorrect object.

These considerations show that a class writer must have at his disposal, for each attribute, *five* possible levels for granting access privileges to clients:

Possible client privileges on an attribute

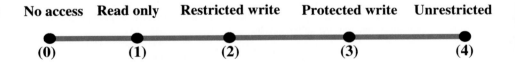

No access	Read only	Restricted write	Protected write	Unrestricted
(0)	**(1)**	**(2)**	**(3)**	**(4)**

Level 0 is total protection: clients have no way of accessing the attribute. At level 1 and above, you make the attribute available for access, but at level 1 you do not grant any modification right. At level 2, you let clients modify the attribute through specific algorithms. At level 3, you let them set the value, but only if it satisfies certain constraints, as in the polygon size example. Level 4 removes the constraints.

The solution described in this chapter is a consequence of this analysis. Exporting an attribute only gives clients access permission (level 1); permission to modify is specified by writing and exporting appropriate procedures, which give clients restricted rights as in the counter and point examples (level 2), direct modification rights under some constraints (3) or unrestricted rights (4).

This solution is an improvement over the ones commonly found in O-O languages:

- In Smalltalk, as noted, you have to write special encapsulation functions, such as the earlier *abscissa* and *ordinate*, just to let clients access an attribute at level 1; this may mean both extra work for the developer and a performance overhead. Here there is no need to write routines for attribute access; only for attribute modifications (levels 2 and above) do we require writing a routine, since it is conceptually necessary for the reasons just seen.

- C++ and Java are the other extreme: if you export an attribute then it is up for grabs at level 4: clients can set it through direct assignments in the *my_point.x := 3.7* style as well as access its value. The only way to achieve level 2 (not 3 in the absence of an O-O assertion mechanism in these languages) is to hide the attribute altogether, and then write exported routines, both procedures for modification (levels 2 or 4) and functions for access (level 1). But then you get the same behavior as with the Smalltalk approach.

This discussion of a fairly specific language trait illustrates two of the general principles of language design: do not needlessly bother the programmer; know when to stop introducing new language constructs at the point of diminishing returns.

Optimizing calls

At levels 2 and 3 of the preceding discussion, the use of explicit procedure calls such as *my_polygon.set_size (5)* to change an attribute value is inevitable. At level 4, one could fear the effect on performance of using the *set_attrib*-style. The compiler, however, can generate the same code for *my_point.set_x (3.7)* as it would for *my_point.x := 3.7* had this last phrasing been legal.

> ISE's compiler achieves this through a general in-line expansion mechanism, which eliminates certain routine calls by inserting the routine body directly, with appropriate argument substitutions, into the caller's code.

In-line expansion is indeed one of the transformations that we may expect from an optimizing compiler for an object-oriented language. The modular style of development fostered by object technology produces many small routines. It would be unacceptable for developers to have to worry about the effect of the corresponding calls on performance. They should just use the clearest and most robust architecture they can devise, according to the modularity principles studied in this book, and expect the compiler to get rid of any calls which may be relevant to the design but not necessary for the execution.

In some programming languages, notably Ada and C++, developers specify what routines they want expanded in-line. I find it preferable to treat this task as an automatic optimization, for several reasons:

- It is not always correct to expand a call in-line; since the compiler must, for correctness, check that the optimization applies, it may just as well spare developers the trouble of requesting it in the first place.

- With changes in the software, in particular through inheritance, a routine which was inlinable may become non-inlinable. A software tool is better than a human at detecting such cases.

- On a large system, compilers will always be more effective. They are better equipped to apply the proper heuristics — based on routine size and number of calls — to decide what routines should be inlined. This is again especially critical as the software changes; we cannot expect a human to track the evolution of every piece.

- Software developers have better things to do with their time.

"Garbage collector requirements", page 305, and "The C++ approach to binding", page 513.

The modern software engineering view is that such tedious, automatable and delicate optimizations should be handled by software tools, not people. The policy of leaving them to the responsibility of developers is one of the principal criticisms that have been leveled at C++ and Ada. We will encounter this debate again in studying two other key mechanisms of object technology: memory management, and dynamic binding.

The architectural role of selective exports

The selective export facility is not just a convenience; it is essential to object-oriented architecture. It enables a set of conceptually related classes to make some of their features accessible to each other without releasing them to the rest of the world, that is to say, without violating the rule of Information Hiding. It also helps us understand a frequently debated issue: whether we need modules above the level of classes.

Without selective exports, the only solution (other than renouncing Information Hiding altogether) would be to introduce a new modular structure to group classes. Such super-modules, similar to Ada's or Java's packages, would have their own rules for hiding and exporting. By adding a completely new and partly incompatible module level to the elegant framework defined by classes, they would yield a bigger, hard-to-learn language.

Rather than using a separate package construct, the super-modules could themselves be classes; this is the approach of Simula, which permits class nesting. It too brings its share of extra complexity, for no clear benefit.

We have seen that the simplicity of object technology relies for a good part on the use of a single modular concept, the class; its support for reusability relies on our ability to extract a class from its context, keeping only its logical dependencies. With a super-module concept we run the risk of losing these advantages. In particular, if a class belongs to a package or an enclosing class we will not be able to reuse it by itself; if we want to include it in another super-module we will need either to import the entire original super-module, or to make a copy of the class — not an attractive form of reuse.

The need will remain to group classes in structured collections. This will be addressed in a later chapter through the notion of *cluster*. But the cluster is a management and organizational notion; making it a language construct would jeopardize the simplicity of the object-oriented approach and its support for modularity.

Chapter 28.

When we want to let a group of classes grant each other special privileges, we do not need a super-module; selective exports, a modest extension to basic information hiding, provide a straightforward solution, allowing classes to retain their status of free-standing software components. This is, in my opinion, a typical case of how a simple, low-tech idea can outperform the heavy artillery of a "powerful" mechanism.

Listing imports

Each class lists, in the headers of its **feature** clauses, the features that it makes available to others. Why not, one might ask, also list features obtained from other classes? The encapsulation language Modula-2 indeed provides an **import** clause.

In a typed approach to O-O software construction, however, such a clause would not serve any purpose other than documentation. To use a feature f from another class C, you must be a client or (through inheritance) a descendant of that class. In the first case, the only one seen so far, this means that every use of f is of the form

$a.f$

where, since our notation is typed, a must have been declared:

$a: C$

showing without any ambiguity that f came from the C. In the descendant case the information will be available from the official class documentation, its "flat-short form".

"The flat-short form", page 543.

So there is no need to bother developers with import clauses.

There is a need, however, to *help* developers with import documentation. A good graphical development environment should include mechanisms that enable you, by clicking a button, to see the suppliers and ancestors of a class, and follow the import chain further by exploring their own suppliers and ancestors.

See chapter 36.

Denoting the result of a function

An interesting language issue broached earlier in this chapter is how to denote function results. It is worth exploring further although it applies to non-O-O languages as well.

Consider a function — a value-returning routine. Since the purpose of any call to the function is to compute a certain result and return it to the caller, the question arises of how to denote that result in the text of the function itself, in particular in the instructions which initialize and update the result.

The convention introduced in this chapter uses a special entity, *Result*, treated as a local entity and initialized to the appropriate default value; the result returned by a call is the final value of *Result*. Because of the initialization rules, that value is always defined even if the routine body contains no assignment to *Result*. For example, the function

> *f: INTEGER* **is**
> > **do**
> > > **if** *some_condition* **then** *Result* := *10* **end**
> > **end**

will return the value 10 if *some_condition* is satisfied at the time of the call, and 0 (the default initialization value for *INTEGER*) otherwise.

The technique using *Result* originated, as far as I know, with the notation developed in this book. (Since the first edition it has found its way into at least one other language, Borland's Delphi.) Note that it would not work in a language allowing functions to be declared within functions, as the name *Result* would then be ambiguous. Among the techniques used in earlier languages, the most common are:

A • Explicit return instructions (C, C++/Java, Ada, Modula-2).

B • Treating the function name as a variable (Fortran, Algol 60, Simula, Algol 68, Pascal).

Convention A relies on an instruction of the form **return** *e* whose execution terminates the current execution of the enclosing function, returning *e* as the result. This technique has the benefit of clarity, since it makes the returned value stand out clearly from the function text. But it suffers from several drawbacks:

A1 • Often, the result must in practice be obtained through some computation: an initialization and a few subsequent updates. This means you must introduce and declare an extraneous variable (an entity in the terminology of this chapter) just for the purpose of holding the intermediate results of the computation.

A2 • The technique tends to promote multiple-exit modules, which are contrary to the principles of good program structuring.

A3 • The language definition must specify what will happen if the last instruction executed by a call to the function is not a **return**. The Ada result in this case is to raise … a run-time exception! (This may be viewed as the ultimate in buck-passing, the language designers having transferred the responsibility for language design issues not just to software developers, but finally to the *end-users* of the programs developed in the language!)

Note that it is possible to solve the last two problems by treating **return** not as an instruction, but as a syntactic clause which would be a required part of any function text:

> **function** *name* (*arguments*): *TYPE* **is**
> > **do**
> > > …
> > **return**
> > > *expression*
> > **end**

This solution remains compatible in spirit with the idea of a **return** instruction while addressing its most serious deficiencies. No common language, however, uses it, and of course it still leaves problem A1 open.

The second common technique, B, treats a function's name as a variable within the text of the function. The value returned by a call is the final value of that variable. (This avoids introducing a special variable as mentioned under A1.)

The above three problems do not arise in this approach. But it raises other difficulties because the same name now ambiguously denotes both a function and a variable. This is particularly confusing in a language allowing recursion, where a function body may use the function's name to denote a recursive call. Because an occurrence of the function's name now has two possible meanings, the language must define precise conventions as to when it denotes the variable, and when it denotes a function call. Usually, in the body of a function f, an occurrence of the name f as the target of an assignment (or other contexts implying a value to be modified) denotes the variable, as in

$f := x$

and an occurrence of f in an expression (or other contexts implying a value to be accessed) denotes a recursive function call, as in

$x := f$

which is valid only if f has no arguments. But then an assignment of the form

$f := f + 1$

will be either rejected by the compiler (if f has arguments) or, worse, understood as containing a recursive call whose result gets assigned to f (the variable). The latter interpretation is almost certainly not what the developer had in mind: if f had been a normal variable, the instruction would simply have increased its value by one. Here the assignment will usually cause a non-terminating computation. To obtain the desired effect, the developer will have to introduce an extra variable; this takes us back to problem A1 above and defeats the whole purpose of using technique B.

The convention introduced in this chapter, relying on the predefined entity *Result*, avoids the drawbacks of both A and B. An extra advantage, in a language providing for default initialization of all entities including *Result*, is that it simplifies the writing of functions: if, as often happens, you want the result to be the default value except in specific cases, you can use the scheme

> **do**
>> **if** *some_condition* **then** *Result* := "Some specific value" **end**
>
> **end**

Page 233.

without worrying about an **else** clause. The language definition must, of course, specify all default values in an unambiguous and platform-independent way; the next chapter will introduce such conventions for our notation.

Chapter 11.

A final benefit of the *Result* convention will become clear when we study Design by Contract: we can use *Result* to express an abstract property of a function's result, independent of its implementation, in the routine's postcondition. None of the other conventions would allow us to write

infix "|_" (*x: REAL): INTEGER* **is**
        -- Integer part of x
   do
        … Implementation omitted …
   ensure
      no_greater: Result <= x
      smallest_possible: Result + 1 > x
   end

The postcondition is the **ensure** clause, stating two properties of the result: that it is no greater than the argument; and that adding 1 to it yields a result greater than the argument.

Complement: a precise definition of entities

It will be useful, while we are considering notational problems, to clarify a notion that has repeatedly been used above, but not yet defined precisely: entities. Rather than a critical concept of object technology, this is simply a technical notion, generalizing the traditional notion of variable; we need a precise definition.

Entities as used in this book cover names that denote run-time values, themselves attached to possible objects. We have now seen all three possible cases:

Definition: entity

An entity is one of the following:

E1 • An attribute of a class.

E2 • A routine's local entity, including the predefined entity *Result* for a function.

E3 • A formal argument of a routine.

Case E2 indicates that the entity *Result* is treated, for all purposes, as a local entity; other local entities are introduced in the **local** clause. *Result* and other local entities of a routine are initialized anew each time the routine is called.

All entities except formal arguments (E3) are writable, that is to say may appear as the target x of an assignment $x := some\_value$.

7.11 KEY CONCEPTS INTRODUCED IN THIS CHAPTER

- The fundamental concept of object technology is the notion of class. A class is an abstract data type, partially or fully implemented.

- A class may have instances, called objects.

- Do not confuse objects (dynamic items) with classes (the static description of the properties common to a set of run-time objects).

- In a consistent approach to object technology, every object is an instance of a class.

- The class serves as both a module and a type. The originality and power of the O-O model come in part from the fusion of these two notions.

- A class is characterized by features, including attributes (representing fields of the instances of the class) and routines (representing computations on these instances). A routine may be a function, which returns a result, or a procedure, which does not.

- The basic mechanism of object-oriented computation is feature call. A feature call applies a feature of a class to an instance of that class, possibly with arguments.

- Feature call uses either dot notation (for identifier features) or operator notation, prefix or infix (for operator features).

- Every operation is relative to a "current instance" of a class.

- For clients of a class (other classes which use its features), an attribute is indistinguishable from a function without arguments, in accordance with the Uniform Access principle.

- An executable assembly of classes is called a system. A system contains a root class and all the classes which the root needs directly or indirectly (through the client and inheritance relations). To execute the system is to create an instance of the root class and to call a creation procedure on that instance.

- Systems should have a decentralized architecture. Ordering relations between the operations are inessential to the design.

- A small system description language, Lace, makes it possible to specify how a system should be assembled. A Lace specification, or Ace, indicates the root class and the set of directories where the system's clusters reside.

- The system assembly process should be automatic, with no need for Make files or Include directives.

- The Information Hiding mechanism needs flexibility: besides being hidden or generally available, a feature may need to be exported to some clients only; and an attribute may need to be exported for access only, access and restricted modification, or full modification.

- Exporting an attribute gives clients the right to access it. Modifying it requires calling the appropriate exported procedure.

- Selective exports are necessary to enable groups of closely related classes to gain special access to each other's features.

- There is no need for a super-module construct above classes. Classes should remain independent software components.

- The modular style promoted by object-oriented development leads to many small routines. Inlining, a compiler optimization, removes any potential efficiency consequence. Detecting inlinable calls should be the responsibility of the compiler, not software developers.

7.12 BIBLIOGRAPHICAL NOTES

Chapter 35, bibliography on page 1138. The notion of class comes from the Simula 67 language; see the bibliographical references of the corresponding chapter. A Simula class is both a module and a type, although this property was not emphasized in the Simula literature, and was dropped by some successors of Simula.

The Single Target principle may be viewed as a software equivalent of a technique that is well known in mathematical logic and theoretical computing science: **currying**. To curry a two-argument function f is to replace it by a one-argument function g yielding a one-argument function as a result, such that for any applicable x and y:

$$(g\ (x))\ (y) = f\ (x,\ y)$$

To curry a function, in other words, is to specialize it on its first argument. This is similar to the transformation described in this chapter to replace a traditional two-argument routine *rotate*, called under the form

rotate (some_point, some_angle)

by a one-argument function with a target, called under the form

some_point.rotate (some_angle)

Chapter 32 (discussion on the CD). [M 1990]describes currying and some of its applications to computing science, in particular the formal study of programming language syntax and semantics. We will encounter currying again in the discussion of graphical user interfaces.

A few language designs have used the concept of object as a software construct rather than just a run-time notion as described in this chapter. In such approaches, meant for exploratory programming, there may be no need for a notion of class. The most notable representative of this school of thought is the Self language [Chambers 1991], which uses "prototypes" rather than classes.

The detail of the conventions for infix and prefix operators, in particular the precedence table, is given in [M 1992].

James McKim brought to my attention the final argument for the *Result* convention (its use for postconditions).

EXERCISES

E7.1 Clarifying the terminology

[This exercise requires two well-sharpened pencils, one *blue* and the other *red*.]

Study the textbook extract used earlier in this chapter to illustrate the confusion between objects and classes; for each use of the word "object", "thing" or "user" in that extract, underline the word in *blue* if you think that the authors really meant object; underline the word in *red* if you think that they really meant class.

See "What would you think of this?", page 166.

E7.2 *POINT* as an abstract data type

Write an abstract data type specification for the notion of two-dimensional point, as suggested in the informal introduction of that notion.

E7.3 Completing *POINT*

Complete the text of class *POINT* by filling in the missing details and adding a procedure *rotate* (to rotate a point around the origin) as well as any other feature that you feel is necessary.

Page 176.

E7.4 Polar coordinates

Write the text of class *POINT* so as to use a polar, rather than cartesian, representation.

8

The run-time structure: objects

*I*n the previous chapter we saw that classes may have instances, called objects. We must now turn our attention to these objects and, more generally, to the run-time model of object-oriented computation.

Where the previous chapters were mostly concerned with conceptual and structural issues, the present one will, for the first time in this book, include implementation aspects. In particular it will describe how the execution of object-oriented software uses memory — a discussion continued by the study of garbage collection in the next chapter. As already noted, one of the benefits of object technology is to restore implementation issues to their full status; so even if your interest is mostly in analysis and design topics you should not be afraid of this excursion into implementation territory. It is impossible to understand the method unless you have some idea of its influence on run-time structures.

The study of object structures in this chapter indeed provides a particularly good example of how wrong it is to separate implementation aspects from supposedly higher-level issues. Throughout the discussion, whenever we realize the need for a new O-O technique or mechanism, initially introduced for some implementation-related purpose, the real reason will almost always turn out to be deeper: we need the facility just as much for purely descriptive, abstract purposes. A typical example will be the distinction between references and expanded values, which might initially appear to be an obscure programming technique, but in reality provides a general answer to the question of sharing in whole-to-parts relations, an issue that figures prominently in many discussions of object-oriented analysis.

This contribution of implementation is sometimes hard to accept for people who have been influenced by the view, still prevalent in the software literature, that all that counts is analysis. But it should not be so surprising. To develop software is to develop models. A good implementation technique is often a good modeling technique as well; it may be applicable, beyond software systems, to systems from various fields, natural and artificial.

More than implementation in the strict sense of the term, then, the theme of this chapter is modeling: how to use object structures to construct realistic and useful operational descriptions of systems of many kinds.

8.1 OBJECTS

At any time during its execution, an O-O system will have created a certain number of objects. The run-time structure is the organization of these objects and of their relations. Let us explore its properties.

What is an object?

First we should recall what the word "object" means for this discussion. There is nothing vague in this notion; a precise technical definition was given in the previous chapter:

The definition appeared on page 166. See also the Object rule, page 171.

Definition: object

An object is a run-time instance of some class.

A software system that includes a class C may at various points of its execution create (through creation and cloning operations, whose details appear later in this chapter) instances of C; such an instance is a data structure built according to the pattern defined by C; for example an instance of the class *POINT* introduced in the previous chapter is a data structure consisting of two fields, associated with the two attributes x and y declared in the class. The instances of all possible classes constitute the set of objects.

The above definition is the official one for object-oriented software. But "object" also has a more general meaning, coming from everyday language. Any software system is related to some external system, which may contain "objects": points, lines, angles, surfaces and solids in a graphics system: employees, pay checks and salary scales in a payroll system; and so on. Some of the objects created by the software will be in direct correspondence with such external objects, as in a payroll system that includes a class *EMPLOYEE*, whose run-time instances are computer models of employees.

This dual use of the word "object" has some good consequences, which follow from the power of the object-oriented method as a modeling tool. Better than any other method, object technology highlights and supports the modeling component of software development. This explains in part the impression of naturalness which it exudes, the attraction it exerts on so many people, and its early successes — still among the most visible — in such areas as simulation and user interfaces. The method here enjoys the *direct mapping* property which an earlier chapter described as a principal requirement of good modular design. With software systems considered to be direct or indirect models of real systems, it is not surprising that some classes will be models of external object types from the problem domain, so that the software objects (the instances of these classes) are themselves models of the corresponding external objects.

"Direct Mapping", page 47.

But we should not let ourselves get too carried away by the word "object". As always in science and technology, it is a bit risky to borrow words from everyday language and give them technical meanings. (The only discipline which seems to succeed in this delicate art is mathematics, which routinely hijacks such innocent words as "neighborhood", "variety" or "barrel" and uses them with completely unexpected meanings — perhaps the reason why no one seems to have any trouble.) The term "object" is so overloaded with everyday meanings that in spite of the benefits just mentioned its use in a technical software sense has caused its share of confusion. In particular:

- As pointed out in the discussion of direct mapping, not all classes correspond to object types of the problem domain. The classes introduced for design and implementation have no immediate counterparts in the modeled system. They are often among the most important in practice, and the most difficult to find.

See chapter 20 about the form-based system. About the notion of command, see chapter 21.

- Some concepts from the problem domain may yield classes in the software (and objects in the software's execution) even though they would not necessarily be classified as objects in the usual sense of the term if we insist on a concrete view of objects. A class such as *STATE* in the discussion of the form-based interactive system, or *COMMAND* (to be studied in a later chapter in connection with undo-redo mechanisms) fall in this category.

When the word "object" is used in this book, the context will clearly indicate whether the usual meaning or (more commonly) the technical software meaning is intended. When there is a need to distinguish, one may talk about *external objects* and *software objects*.

Basic form

A software object is a rather simple animal once you know what class it comes from.

Let O be an object. The definition on the previous page indicates that it is an instance of some class. More precisely, it is a **direct instance** of just one class, say *C*.

Because of inheritance, O will then be an instance, direct or not, of other classes, the ancestors of *C*; but that is a matter for a future chapter, and for the present discussion we only need the notion of direct instance. The word "direct" will be dropped when there is no possible confusion.

C is called the generating class, or just **generator**, of O. *C* is a software text; O is a run-time data structure, produced by one of the object creation mechanisms studied below.

Among its features, *C* has a certain number of attributes. These attributes entirely determine the form of the object: O is simply a collection of components, or **fields**, one for each attribute.

Consider class *POINT* from the previous chapter. The class text was of the form:

For the text of class POINT see page 176.

class *POINT* **feature**
    x, y: *REAL*
    … Routine declarations …
end

The routines have been omitted, and for good reason: the form of the corresponding objects (the direct instances of the class) is solely determined by the attributes, although the *operations* applicable to the objects depend on the routines. Here the class has two attributes, *x* and *y*, both of type *REAL*, so a direct instance of *POINT* is an object with two fields containing values of that type, for example:

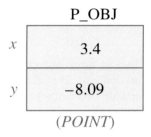

(*POINT*)

Notice the conventions used here and in the rest of this book for representing an object as a set of fields, shown as adjacent rectangles containing the associated values. Below the object the name of the generating class, here *POINT*, appears in parentheses and in italics; next to each field, also in italics, there appears the name of the corresponding attribute, here x and y. Sometimes a name in roman (here P_OBJ) will appear above the object; it has no counterpart in the software but identifies the object in the discussion.

See "Graphical conventions", page 271.

In diagrams used to show the structure of an object-oriented system, or more commonly of some part of such a system, classes appear as ellipses. This convention, already used in the figures of the previous chapter, avoids any confusion between classes and objects.

Simple fields

Both attributes of class *POINT* are of type *REAL*. As a consequence, each of the corresponding fields of a direct instance of *POINT* contains a real value.

This is an example of a field corresponding to an attribute of one of the "basic types". Although these types are formally defined as classes, their instances take their values from predefined sets implemented efficiently on computers. They include:

- *BOOLEAN*, which has exactly two instances, representing the boolean values true and false.

- *CHARACTER*, whose instances represent characters.

- *INTEGER*, whose instances represent integers.

- *REAL* and *DOUBLE*, whose instances represent single-precision and double-precision floating-point numbers.

Another type which for the time being will be treated as a basic type, although we will later see that it is actually in a different category, is *STRING*, whose instances represent finite sequences of characters.

"STRINGS", 13.5, page 456.

For each of the basic types we will need the ability to denote the corresponding values in software texts and on figures. The conventions are straightforward:

- For *BOOLEAN*, the two instances are written *True* and *False*.

- To denote an instance of *CHARACTER* you will write a character enclosed in single quotes, such as '*A*'.

- To denote an instance of *STRING*, write a sequence of characters in double quotes, as in *"A STRING"*.

- To denote an instance of *INTEGER*, write a number in an ordinary decimal notation with an optional sign, as in *34*, *–675* and *+4*.

- You can also write an instance of *REAL* or *DOUBLE* in ordinary notation, as in *3.5* or *–0.05*. Use the letter *e* to introduce a decimal exponent, as in *–5.e‑2* which denotes the same value as the preceding example.

A simple notion of book

Here is a class with attribute types taken from the preceding set:

class *BOOK1* **feature**

    title: *STRING*

    date, *page_count*: *INTEGER*

end

A typical instance of class *BOOK1* may appear as follows:

An object representing a book

title	"The Red and the Black"
date	1830
page_count	341

(*BOOK1*)

Since for the moment we are only interested in the structure of objects, all the features in this class and the next few examples are attributes — none are routines.

This means that our objects are similar at this stage to the records or structure types of non-object-oriented languages such as Pascal and C. But unlike the situation in these languages there is little we can do with such a class in a good O-O language: because of the information hiding mechanisms, a client class has no way of assigning values to the fields of such objects. In Pascal, or in C with a slightly different syntax, a record type with a similar structure would allow a client to include the declaration and instruction

    b1: *BOOK1*

    ...

    b1.*page_count* := *355*

Warning: not permitted in the O-O notation! For discussion only.

which at run time will assign value 355 to the *page_count* field of the object attached to *b1*. With classes, however, we should not provide any such facility: letting clients change object fields as they please would make a mockery of the rule of information hiding, which implies that the author of each class controls the precise set of operations that clients may execute on its instances. No such direct field assignment is possible in an O-O context; clients will perform field modifications through procedures of the class. Later in this chapter we will add to *BOOK1* a procedure that gives clients the effect of the above assignment, if the author of the class indeed wishes to grant them such privileges.

> We have already seen that C++ and Java actually permit assignments of the form *b1.page_count := 355*. But this simply reflects the inherent limits of attempts to integrate object technology in a C context.

> As the designers of Java themselves write in their book about the language: *"A programmer could still mess up the object by setting [a public] field, because the field [is] subject to change"* through direct assignment instructions. Too many languages require such "don't do this" warnings. Rather than propose a language and then explain at length how not to use it, it is desirable to define hand in hand the method and a notation that will support it.

[Arnold 1996], page 40.

See also "If it is baroque, fix it", page 670.

In proper O-O development, classes without routines, such as *BOOK1*, have little practical use (except as ancestors in an inheritance hierarchy, where descendants will inherit the attributes and provide their own routines; or to represent external objects which the O-O part can access but not modify, for example sensor data in a real-time system). But they will help us go through the basic concepts; then we will add routines.

Writers

Using the types mentioned above, we can also define a class *WRITER* describing a simple notion of book author:

class *WRITER* **feature**
    name, real_name: *STRING*
    birth_year, death_year: *INTEGER*
end

name	"Stendhal"
real_name	"Henri Beyle"
birth_year	1783
death_year	1842

A "writer" object

(*WRITER*)

References

Objects whose fields are all of basic types will not take us very far. We need objects with fields that represent other objects. For example we will want to represent the property that a book has an author — denoted by an instance of class *WRITER*.

A possibility is to introduce a notion of subobject. For example we might think of a book object, in a new version *BOOK2* of the book class, as having a field *author* which is itself an object, as informally suggested by the following picture:

Two "book" objects with "writer" subobjects

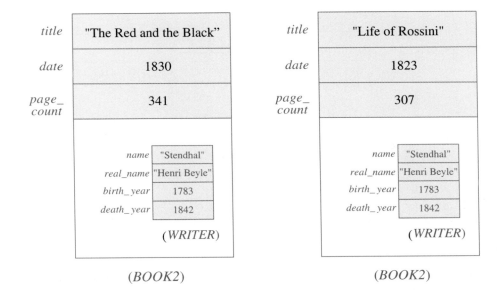

Such a notion of subobject is indeed useful and we will see, later in this chapter, how to write the corresponding classes.

But here it is not exactly what we need. The example represents two books with the same author; we ended up duplicating the author information, which now appears as two subobjects, one in each instance of *BOOK2*. This duplication is probably not acceptable:

- It wastes memory space. Other examples would make this waste even more unacceptable: imagine for example a set of objects representing people, each one with a subobject representing the country of citizenship, where the number of people represented is large but the number of countries is small.

- Even more importantly, this technique fails to account for the need to express **sharing**. Regardless of representation choices, the *author* fields of the two objects refer to the same instance of *WRITER*; if you update the *WRITER* object (for example to record an author's death), you will want the change to affect all book objects associated with the given author.

Here then is a better picture of the desired situation, assuming yet another version of the book class, *BOOK3*:

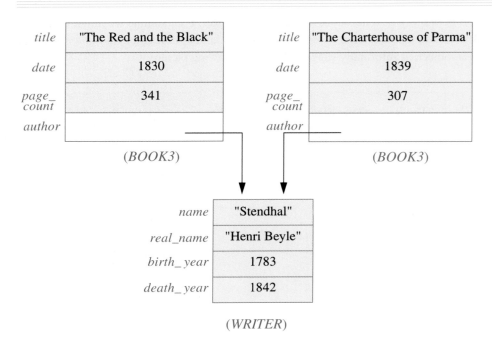

The *author* field of each instance of *BOOK3* contains what is known as a **reference** to a possible object of type *WRITER*. It is not difficult to define this notion precisely:

Definition: reference

A reference is a run-time value which is either **void** or **attached**.

If attached, a reference identifies a single object. (It is then said to be attached to that particular object.)

In the last figure, the *author* reference fields of the *BOOK3* instances are both attached to the *WRITER* instance, as shown by the arrows, which are conventionally used on such diagrams to represent a reference attached to an object. The following figure has a void reference (perhaps to indicate an unknown author), showing the graphical representation of void references:

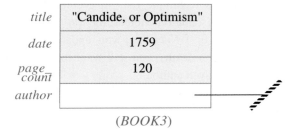

An object with a void reference field

("Candide" was published anonymously.)

The definition of references makes no mention of implementation properties. A reference, if not void, is a way to identify an object; an abstract *name* for the object. This is similar to a social security number that uniquely identifies a person, or an area code that identifies a phone area. Nothing implementation-specific or computer-specific here.

The reference concept of course has a counterpart in computer implementations. In machine-level programming it is possible to manipulate addresses; many programming languages offer a notion of pointer. The notion of reference is more abstract. Although a reference may end up being represented as an address, it does not have to; and even when the representation of a reference includes an address, it may include other information.

Another property sets references apart from addresses, although pointers in typed languages such as Pascal and Ada (not C) also enjoy it: as will be explained below, a reference in the approach described here is typed. This means that a given reference may only become attached to objects of a specific set of types, determined by a declaration in the software text. This idea again has counterparts in the non-computer world: a social security number is only meant for persons, and area codes are only meant for phone areas. (They may look like normal integers, but you would not *add* two area codes.)

Object identity

The notion of reference brings about the concept of object identity. Every object created during the execution of an object-oriented system has a unique identity, independent of the object's value as defined by its fields. In particular:

I1 • Two objects with different identities may have identical fields.

I2 • Conversely, the fields of a certain object may change during the execution of a system; but this does not affect the object's identity.

These observations indicate that a phrase such as "*a* denotes the same object as *b*" may be ambiguous: are we talking about objects with different identities but the same contents (I1)? Or about the states of an object before and after some change is applied to its fields (I2)? We will use the second interpretation: a given object may take on new values for its constituent fields during an execution, while remaining "the same object". Whenever confusion is possible the discussion will be more explicit. For case I1 we may talk of equal (but distinct) objects; equality will be defined more precisely below.

A point of terminology may have caught your attention. It is not a mistake to say (as in the definition of I2) that the fields of an object may change. The term "field" as defined above denotes one of the values that make up an object, not the corresponding field identifier, which is the name of one of the attributes of the object's generating class.

For each attribute of the class, for example *date* in class *BOOK3*, the object has a field, for example *1832* in the object of the last figure. During execution the attributes will never change, so each object's division into fields will remain the same; but the fields themselves may change. For example an instance of *BOOK3* will always have four fields, corresponding to attributes *title*, *date*, *page_count*, *author*; these fields — the four values that make up a given object of type *BOOK3* — may change.

"Object identity", page 1052. The study of how to make objects *persistent* will lead us to explore further properties of object identity.

Declaring references

Let us see how to extend the initial book class, *BOOK1*, which only had attributes of basic types, to the new variant *BOOK3* which has an attribute representing references to potential authors. Here is the class text, again just showing the attributes; the only difference is an extra attribute declaration at the end:

> **class** *BOOK3* **feature**
>   *title*: *STRING*
>   *date*, *page_count*: *INTEGER*
>   *author*: *WRITER*   -- This is the new attribute.
> **end**

The type used to declare *author* is simply the name of the corresponding class: *WRITER*. This will be a general rule: whenever a class is declared in the standard form

> **class** *C* **feature** … **end**

then any entity declared of type *C* through a declaration of the form

> *x*: *C*

denotes values that are **references** to potential objects of type *C*. The reason for this convention is that using references provides more flexibility, and so are appropriate in the vast majority of cases. You will find further examination of this rule (and of the other possible conventions) in the discussion section of this chapter.

See page 272.

Self-reference

Nothing in the preceding discussion precludes an object O1 from containing a reference field which (at some point of a system's execution) is attached to O1 itself. This kind of self-reference can also be indirect. In the situation pictured below, the object with "Almaviva" in its *name* field is its own landlord (direct reference cycle); the object "Figaro" loves "Susanna" which loves "Figaro" (indirect reference cycle).

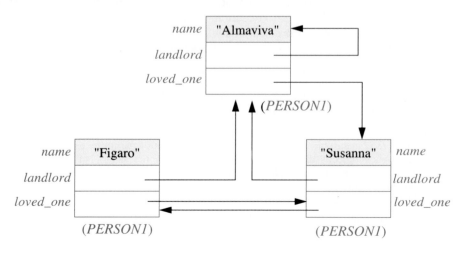

Direct and indirect self-reference

Such cycles in the dynamic structure can only exist if the client relation among the corresponding classes also has direct or indirect cycles. In the above example, the class declaration is of the form

> **class** *PERSON1* **feature**
>> *name*: *STRING*
>> *loved_one*, *landlord*: *PERSON1*
> **end**

showing a direct cycle (*PERSON1* is a client of *PERSON1*).

The reverse property is not true: the presence of a cycle in the client relation does not imply that the run-time structure will have cycles. For example you may declare a class

> **class** *PERSON2* **feature**
>> *mother*, *father*: *PERSON2*
> **end**

which is a client of itself; but if this models the relations between people suggested by the attributes' names, there can be no reference cycle in the run-time structure, as it would imply that a certain person is his own parent or indirect ancestor.

A look at the run-time object structure

From what we have seen so far emerges a first picture of the structure of an object-oriented system during its execution.

A possible run-time object structure

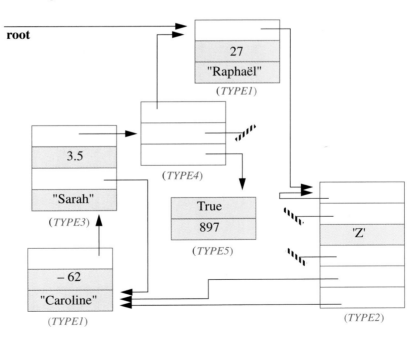

The system is made of a certain number of objects, with various fields. Some of these fields are values of basic types (integer fields such as *27*, character fields such as *'Z'* and so on); others are references, some void, others attached to objects. Each object is an instance of some type, always based on a class and indicated below the object in the figure. Some types may be represented by just one instance, but more commonly there will be many instances of a given type; here *TYPE1* has two instances, the others only one. An object may have reference fields only; this is the case here with the *TYPE4* instance, or basic fields only, as with the *TYPE5* instance. There may be self-references: direct, as with the top field of the *TYPE2* instance, or indirect, as with the clock-wise reference cycle starting from and coming back to the *TYPE1* instance at the top.

This kind of structure may look unduly complicated at first — an impression reinforced by the last figure, which is meant to show many of the available facilities and does not purport to model any real system. The expression "spaghetti bowl" comes to mind.

But this impression is not justified. The concern for simplicity applies to the software text and not necessarily to the run-time object structure. The text of a software system embodies certain relations (such as "is child of", "loves", "has as landlord"); a particular run-time object structure embodies what we may call an instance of these relations — how the relations hold between members of a certain set of objects. The relations modeled by the software may be simple even if their instances for a particular set of objects are complex. Someone who considers the basic idea behind the relation "loves" fairly simple might find the instance of the relation for a particular group of people — the record of who loves whom — hopelessly entangled.

So it is often impossible to prevent the run-time object structures of our O-O systems from becoming big (involving large numbers of objects) and complex (involving many references with a convoluted structure). A good software development environment will provide tools that help explore object structures for testing and debugging.

Such run-time complexity does not have to affect the static picture. We should try to keep the software itself — the set of classes and their relations — as simple as possible.

The observation that simple models can have complex instances is in part a reflection on the power of computers. A small software text can describe huge computations; a simple O-O system can at execution time yield millions of objects connected by many references. A cardinal goal of software engineering is to keep the software simple even when its instances are not.

8.2 OBJECTS AS A MODELING TOOL

We can use the techniques introduced so far to improve our understanding of the method's modeling power. It is important in particular two clarify two aspects: the various worlds touched by software development; and the relationship of our software to external reality.

The four worlds of software development

From the preceding discussions it appears that when talking about object-oriented software development we should distinguish between four separate worlds:

- The modeled system, also known as the external system (as opposed to the software system) and described through object types and their abstract relations.

- A particular instantiation of the external system, made of objects between which relations may hold.

- The software system, made of classes connected by the relations of the object-oriented method (client and inheritance).

- An object structure, as may exist during the execution of the software system, made of software objects connected through references.

The following picture suggests the mappings that exist between these worlds.

Molds and their instances

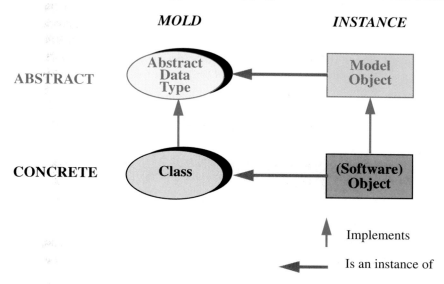

On both the software level (lower part of the picture) and the external level (higher part) it is important to distinguish between the general notions (classes and abstract relations, appearing on the left) and their specific instances (objects and relation instances, appearing on the right). This point has already been emphasized in the previous chapter's discussion of the comparative role of classes and objects. It also applies to relations: we must distinguish between the abstract relation *loved_one* and the set of *loved_one* links that exist between the elements of a certain set of objects.

This distinction is emphasized neither by the standard mathematical definitions of relations nor, in the software field, by the theory of relational databases. Limiting ourselves to binary relations, a relation is defined in both mathematics and relational databases as a set of pairs, all of the form $<x, y>$ where every x is a member a given set TX

and every *y* is a member of a given set *TY*. (In software terminology: all *x* are of type *TX* and all *y* are of type *TY*.) Appropriate as such definitions may be mathematically, they are not satisfactory for system modeling, as they fail to make the distinction between an abstract relation and one of its particular instances. For system modeling, if not for mathematics and relational databases, the *loves* relation has its own general and abstract properties, quite independent of the record of who loves whom in a particular group of people at a particular time.

> This discussion will be extended in a later chapter when we look at *transformations* on both abstract and concrete objects and give a name to the vertical arrows of the preceding figure: the *abstraction function*.

"The abstraction function", page 375.

Reality: a cousin twice removed

You may have noted how the above discussion (and previous ones on neighboring topics) stayed clear of any reference to the "real world". Instead, the expression used above in reference to what the software represents is simply "the modeled system".

This distinction is not commonly made. Many of the discussions in information modeling talk about "modeling the real world", and similar expressions abound in books about O-O analysis. So we should take a moment to reflect on this notion. Talking about the "reality" behind a software system is deceptive for at least four reasons.

First, reality is in the eyes of the beholder. Without being accused of undue chauvinism for his profession, a software engineer may with some justification ask his customers why *their* systems are more real than his. Take a program that performs mathematical computations — proving the four-color conjecture in graph theory, integrating some differential equations, or solving geometrical problems in a four-dimensional Riemann surface. Are we, the software developers, to quarrel with our mathematician friends (and customers) as to whose artefacts are more real: a piece of software written in some programming language, or a complete subspace with negative curvature?

Second, the notion of real world collapses in the not infrequent case of software that solves software problems — reflexive applications, as they are sometimes called. Take a C compiler written in Pascal. The "real" objects that it processes are C programs. Why should we consider these programs more real than the compiler itself? The same observation applies to other systems handling objects that only exist in a computer: an editor, a CASE tool, even a document processing system (since the documents it manipulates are computer objects, the printed version being only their final form).

The third reason is a generalization of the second. In the early days of computers, it may have been legitimate to think of software systems as being superimposed on a pre-existing, independent reality. But today the computers and their software are more and more a part of that reality. Like a quantum physicist finding himself unable to separate the measure from the measurement, we can seldom treat "the real world" and "the software" as independent entities. The MIS field (Management Information Systems, that is to say, business data processing) provides some of the most vivid evidence: although it may have been the case with the first MIS applications, a few decades ago, that companies

See also "DISCUS-SION", 20.6, page 693 on the dangers of staying too close to reality.

introduced computers and the associated software simply with the aim of automating existing procedures, the situation today is radically different, as many existing procedures already involve computers and their software. To describe the operations of a modern bank is to describe mechanisms of which software is a fundamental component. The same is true of most other application areas; many of the activities of physicists and other natural scientists, for example, rely on computers and software not as auxiliary tools but as a fundamental part of the operational process. One may reflect here about the expression "virtual reality", and its implication that what software produces is no less real than what comes from the outside world. In all such cases the software is not disjoint from the reality, as if we had a feedback loop in which operating the software injects some new and important inputs into the model.

The last reason is even more fundamental. A software system is not a model of reality; it is at best a model of a model of some part of some reality. A hospital's patient monitoring system is not a model of the hospital, but the implementation of someone's view of how certain aspects of the hospital management should be handled — a *model* of a *model* of a *subset* of the hospital's reality. An astronomy program is not a model of the universe; it is a software model of someone's model of some properties of some part of the universe. A financial information system is not a model of the stock exchange; it is a software transposition of a model devised by a certain company to describe those aspects of the stock exchange which are relevant to the company's goals.

See "BEYOND SOFTWARE", 6.6, page 147.
The general theme of the object-oriented method, abstract data types, helps understand why we do not need to delude ourselves with the flattering but illusory notion that we deal with the real world. The first step to object orientation, as expressed by the ADT theory, is to toss out reality in favor of something less grandiose but more palatable: a set of abstractions characterized by the operations available to clients, and their formal properties. (This gave the ADT modeler's motto — tell me not what you are but what you have.) Never do we make any pretense that these are the only possible operations and properties: we choose the ones that serve our purposes of the moment, and reject the others. *To model is to discard.*

To a software system, the reality that it addresses is, at best, a cousin twice removed.

8.3 MANIPULATING OBJECTS AND REFERENCES

Let us come back to more mundane matters and see how our software systems are going to deal with objects so as to create and use flexible data structures.

Dynamic creation and reattachment

What the description of the run-time object structure has not yet shown is the highly dynamic nature of a true object-oriented model. As opposed to static and stack-oriented policies of object management, illustrated at the programming language level by Fortran and Pascal respectively, the policy in a proper O-O environment is to let systems create objects as needed at run time, according to a pattern which is usually impossible to predict by a mere static examination of the software text.

From an initial state in which (as described in the previous chapter) only one object has been created — the root object — a system will repetitively perform such operations on the object structure as creating a new object, attach a previously void reference to an object, make a reference void, or reattach a previously attached reference to a different object. The dynamic and unpredictable nature of these operations is part of the reason for the flexibility of the approach, and its ability to support the dynamic data structures that are necessary if we are to use advanced algorithms and model the fast-changing properties of many external systems.

The next sections explore the mechanisms needed to create objects and manipulate their fields, in particular references.

The creation instruction

Let us see how to create an instance of a class such as *BOOK3*. This can only be done by a routine of a class which is a client of *BOOK3*, such as

> **class** *QUOTATION* **feature**
>
>> *source*: *BOOK3*
>>
>> *page*: *INTEGER*
>>
>> *make_book* **is**
>>
>>> -- Create a *BOOK3* object and attach *source* to it.
>>>
>>> **do**
>>>
>>>> ... See below ...
>>>
>>> **end**
>
> **end**

which might serve to describe a quotation of a book, appearing in another publication and identified by two fields: a reference to the quoted book and the number of the page which quotes the book.

The (soon to be explained) mechanism that creates an instance of type *QUOTATION* will also by default initialize all its fields. An important part of the default initialization rule is that any reference field, such as the one associated with attribute *source*, will be initialized to a void reference. In other words, creating an object of type *QUOTATION* does not by itself create an object of type *BOOK3*.

The general rule is indeed that, unless you do something to it, a reference remains void. To change this, you may create a new object through a creation instruction. This can be done by procedure *make_book*, which should then read as follows:

make_book **is**

> -- Create a *BOOK3* object and attach *source* to it.

do

> !! *source*

end

This illustrates the simplest form of the creation instruction: !! *x*, where *x* is an attribute of the enclosing class or (as will be seen later) a local entity of the enclosing routine. We will see a few extensions to this basic notation later.

The symbol ! is usually read aloud as "bang", so that !! is "bang bang". The entity *x* named in the instruction (*source* in the above example) is called the **target** of the creation instruction.

This form of the creation instruction is known as a "basic creation instruction". (Another form, involving a call to a procedure of the class, will appear shortly.) Here is the precise effect of a basic creation instruction:

Effect of a basic creation instruction

The effect of a creation instruction of the form !! *x*, where the type of the target *x* is a reference type based on a class *C*, is to execute the following three steps:

C1 • Create a new instance of *C* (made of a collection of fields, one for each attribute of *C*). Let OC be the new instance.

C2 • Initialize each field of OC according to the standard default values.

C3 • Attach the value of *x* (a reference) to OC.

The "standard default values" mentioned in step C2 appear in the next box.

Step C1 will create an instance of *C*. Step C2 will set the values of each field to a predetermined value, which depends on the type of the corresponding attribute. Here are these values:

Default initialization values

For a reference, the default value is a void reference.

For a *BOOLEAN*, the default value is *False*.

For a *CHARACTER*, the default value is the null character.

For a number (of type *INTEGER*, *REAL* or *DOUBLE*), the default value is zero (that is to say, the zero value of the appropriate type).

So for a target *source* of type *BOOK3*, where the above class declaration read

class *BOOK3* **feature**
    title: *STRING*
    date, page_count: *INTEGER*
    author: *WRITER*
end

the creation instruction !! *source*, executed as part of a call to procedure *make_book* of class *QUOTATION*, will yield an object of the following form:

A newly created and initialized object

The integer fields have been initialized to zero. The reference field for *author* has been initialized to a void reference. The field for *title*, a *STRING*, also shows a void reference. This is because type *STRING* (of which the above initialization rules said nothing) is in fact a reference type too, although as noted we may for most practical purposes treat it as a basic type.

"STRINGS", 13.5, page 456.

The global picture

It is important not to lose track of the order in which things happen. For the above instance of *BOOK3* to be created, the following two events must occur:

B1 • An instance of *QUOTATION* gets created. Let Q_OBJ be that instance and let *a* be an entity whose value is a reference attached to Q_OBJ.

B2 • Some time after step B1, a call of the form *a.make_book* executes procedure *make_book* with Q_OBJ as its target.

It is legitimate of course to ask how we ever get to step B1 — how Q_OBJ itself will be created. This only pushes the problem further. But by now you know the answer to this question: it all comes back to the Big Bang. To execute a system, you must provide a root class and the name of a procedure of that class, the creation procedure. At the start of the execution, you are automatically provided with one object, the root object — an instance of the root class. The root object is the only one that does not need to be created by the software text itself; it comes from the outside, as an *objectus ex machina*. Starting with that one providential object, the software can now create other objects in the normal way, through routines that execute creation instructions. The first routine to be executed is the creation procedure, automatically applied to the root object; in all but the most trivial cases it will include at least one creation instruction so as to start what the previous chapter compared to a giant firework: the process of producing as many new objects as a particular execution will need.

See "PUTTING EVERYTHING TOGETHER", 7.9, page 194.

Why explicit creation?

Object creation is explicit. Declaring an entity such as

> *b*: *BOOK3*

does not cause an object to be created at run time: creation will only occur when some element of the system executes an operation

> !! *b*

You may have wondered why this was so. Should the declaration of *b* not be sufficient if we need an object at run time? What good is it to declare an entity if we do not create an object?

A moment's reflection, however, shows that the distinction between declaration and creation is actually the only reasonable solution.

The first argument is by *reductio ad absurdum*. Assume that somehow we start processing the declaration of *b* and immediately create the corresponding book object. But this object is an instance of class *BOOK3*, which has an attribute *author*, itself of a reference type *WRITER*, so that the *author* field is a reference, for which we must create an object right away. Now this object has reference fields (remember that *STRING* is in fact a reference type) and they will require the same treatment: we are starting on a long path of recursive object creation before we have even begun any useful processing!

This argument would be even more obvious with a self-referential class, such as *PERSON1* seen above:

> **class** *PERSON1* **feature**
> > *name*: *STRING*
> > *loved_one*, *landlord*: *PERSON1*
> **end**

Treating every declaration as yielding an object would mean that every creation of an instance of *PERSON1* would cause creation of two more such objects (corresponding to *loved_one* and *landlord*), entering into an infinite loop. Yet we have seen that such self-referential definitions, either direct as here or indirect, are common and necessary.

Another argument simply follows from a theme that runs through this chapter: the use of object technology as a powerful modeling technique. If every reference field were initialized to a newly created object, we would have room neither for void references nor for multiple references attached to a single object. Both are needed for realistic modeling of practical systems:

See the figure on page 226.

- In some cases the model may require that a certain reference be left not attached to any object. We used this technique when leaving the *author* field void to indicate that a book is by an unknown author.

- In other cases two references should be attached, again for conceptual reasons coming from the model, to the same object. In the self-reference example we saw the *loved_one* fields of two *PERSON1* instances attached to the same object. It would not make sense in that case to create an object for each field on creation; what you need is, rather than a creation instruction, an assignment operation (studied later in this chapter) that attaches a reference to an already existing object. This observation applies even more clearly to the self-referential field from the same example (field *landlord* for the top object).

The object management mechanism never attaches a reference implicitly. It creates objects through creation instructions (or *clone* operations, seen below and explicit too), initializing their reference fields to void references; only through explicit instructions will these fields, in turn, become attached to objects.

In the discussion of inheritance we will see that a creation instruction may use the syntax ! *T* ! *x* to create an object whose type *T* is a descendant of the type declared for *x*.

"Polymorphic creation", page 479.

8.4 CREATION PROCEDURES

All the creation instructions seen so far relied on default initializations. In some cases, you may be unhappy with the language-defined initializations, wanting instead to provide specific information to initialize the created object. Creation procedures address this need.

Overriding the default initializations

To use an initialization other than the default, give the class one or more creation procedures. A creation procedure is a procedure of the class, which is listed in a clause starting with the keyword **creation** at the beginning of the class, before the first feature clause. The scheme is this:

> **indexing**
>
>   …
>
> **class** *C* **creation**
>
>   *p1, p2, …*
>
> **feature**
>
>   … Feature declarations, including declarations for procedures *p1, p2, …*
>
> **end**

A style suggestion: the recommended name for creation procedures in simple cases is *make*, for a class that has only one creation procedure; for a class that has two or more creation procedures it is generally desirable to give them a name starting with *make_* and continuing with some qualifying word, as in the *POINT* example that follows.

"CHOOSING THE RIGHT NAMES", 26.2, page 879.

The corresponding creation instruction is not just !! *x* any more, but of the form

> !! *x.p* (…)

where *p* is one of the creation procedures listed in the **creation** clause, and (…) is a valid actual argument list for *p*. The effect of such an instruction is to create the object using the default values as in the earlier form, and to apply *p*, with the given arguments, to the result. The instruction is called a **creation call**; it is a combination of creation instruction and procedure call.

We can for example add creation procedures to the class *POINT* to enable clients to specify initial coordinates, either cartesian or polar, when they create a point object. We will have two creation procedures, *make_cartesian* and *make_polar*. Here is the scheme:

Original version of POINT in "The class", page 176.

class *POINT1* **creation**

      make_cartesian, make_polar

feature

      … The features studied in the preceding version of the class:

         x, y, ro, theta, translate, scale, …

feature {*NONE*} -- See explanations below about this export status.

      make_cartesian (*a, b*: *REAL*) **is**

            -- Initialize point with cartesian coordinates *a* and *b*.

        do

           $x := a; y := b$

        end

      make_polar (*r, t*: *REAL*) **is**

            -- Initialize point with polar coordinates *r* and *t*.

        do

           $x := r * cos\ (t); y := r * sin\ (t)$

        end

end -- class *POINT1*

With this class text, a client will create a point through such instructions as

!! *my_point.make_cartesian* (*0, 1*)

!! *my_point.make_polar* (*1, Pi/2*)

both having the same effect if *Pi* has the value suggested by its name.

Here is the rule defining the effect of such creation calls. The first three steps are the same as for the basic form seen earlier:

Effect of a creation call

The effect of a creation call of the form !! $x \bullet p$ (…), where the type of the target x is a reference type based on a class C, p is a creation procedure of class C, and (…) represents a valid list of actual arguments for this procedure if necessary, is to execute the following four steps:

C1 • Create a new instance of C (made of a collection of fields, one for each attribute of C). Let OC be the new instance.

C2 • Initialize each field of OC according to standard default values.

C3 • Attach the value of x (a reference) to OC.

The new step → C4 • Call procedure p, with the arguments given, on OC.

The export status of creation procedures

In *POINT1* the two creation procedures have been declared in a feature clause starting with **feature** {*NONE*}. This means they are secret, but only for normal calls, not for creation calls. So the two example creation calls just seen are valid; normal calls of the form *my_point.make_cartesian* (*0, 1*) or *my_point.make_polar* (*1, Pi/2*) are invalid since the features have not been made available for calling by any client.

On the {*NONE*} *construct see "Style for declaring secret features", page 192.*

The decision to make the two procedures secret means we do not want clients, once a point object exists, to set their coordinates directly, although they may set them indirectly through the other procedures of the class such as *translate* and *scale*. Of course this is only one possible policy; you may very well decide to export *make_cartesian* and *make_polar* in addition to making them creation procedures.

It is possible to give a procedure a selective creation status as well by including a set of classes in braces in its **creation** clause, as in

> **class** *C* **creation** {*A, B, ...*}
>   *p1, p2,*
> ...

although this is less frequent than limiting the export status of a feature through the similar syntax **feature** {*A, B, ...*} or **feature** {*NONE*}. Remember in any case that the creation status of a procedure is independent of its call export status.

Rules on creation procedures

The two forms of creation instructions, the basic form !! *x* and the creation call !! *x.p* (...), are mutually exclusive. As soon as a class has a **creation** clause, then only the creation call is permitted; the basic form will be considered invalid and rejected by the compiler.

This convention may seem strange at first, but is justified by considerations of object consistency. An object is not just a collection of fields; it is the implementation of an abstract data type, which may impose consistency constraints on the fields. Here is a typical example. Assume an object representing a person, with a field for the birth year and another for the age. Then you cannot set these two fields independently to arbitrary values, but must ensure a consistency constraint: the sum of the age field and the birth year field must equal either the current year or the one before. (In a later chapter we will learn how to express such constraints, often reflecting axioms from the underlying ADT, as **class invariants**.) A creation instruction must *always* yield a consistent object. The basic form of the creation instruction — !! *x* with no call — is only acceptable if setting all the fields to the default values yields a consistent object. If this is not the case, you will need creation procedures, and should disallow the basic form of the creation instruction.

See "CLASS INVARIANTS", 11.8, page 363, in particular "The role of creation procedures", page 371.

In some infrequent cases you may want to accept the default initializations (as they satisfy the class invariant) while also defining one or more creation procedures. The technique to apply in this case is to list *nothing* among the creation procedures. Feature *nothing* is a procedure without arguments, inherited from the universal class *ANY*, which has an empty body (the feature declaration is simply: *nothing* **is do end**) so that it does exactly what the name indicates. Then you can write:

class *C* **creation**

    nothing, some_creation_procedure, some_other_creation_procedure…

feature

    …

Although the form !! *x* is still invalid in this case, clients can achieve the intended effect by writing the instruction as !! *x.nothing*

Finally, note that as a special case the rule on creation instructions gives a way to define a class that *no client* will be permitted to instantiate. A class declaration of the form

class *C* **creation**

    -- There is nothing here!

feature

    … Rest of class text …

end

has a creation clause — an empty one. The above rule states that if there is a **creation** clause the only permitted creation instructions are creation calls using a creation procedure; here, since there are no creation procedures, no creation call is permitted.

Being able to disallow class instantiation is of little interest if we limit ourselves to the object-oriented mechanisms seen so far. But when we move on to inheritance this little facility may prove handy if we want to specify that a certain class should only be used as ancestor to other classes, never directly to create objects.

See "What to do with deferred classes", page 487 and exercise E14.5, page 518.

Another way to achieve this is to make the class *deferred*, but a deferred class must have at least one deferred feature, and we will not always have a role for such a feature.

Multiple creation and overloading

In advance of the discussion section, it is illuminating to compare the mechanism of multiple creation procedures with the C++/Java approach. The need is universal: providing several ways to initialize an object on creation. C++ and Java, however, rely on a different technique, name overloading.

In these languages all the creation procedures of a class (its "constructors") have the same name, which is in fact the class name; if a class *POINT* contains a constructor with two real arguments corresponding to *make_cartesian*, the expression **new** *POINT* (0, 1) will create a new instance. To differentiate between two constructors, the languages rely on the signatures (the types of the arguments).

See "Syntactic overloading", page 93.

The problem is of course, as we saw in the discussion of overloading, that the argument signature is not the appropriate criterion: if we also want a constructor providing the equivalent of *make_polar* we are stuck, since the arguments would be the same, two real numbers. This is the general problem of overloading: using the same name for different operations, thereby causing potential ambiguity — compounded here by the use of that name as a class name as well as a procedure name.

The technique developed earlier seems preferable in all respects: minimum hassle (no creation procedure) if default initializations suffice; prevent creation, if desired, through an empty **creation** clause; to provide several forms of creation, define as many creation procedures as needed; do not introduce any confusion between class names and feature names; let the effect of every operation stand out clearly from its names, as with *make_polar*.

8.5 MORE ON REFERENCES

The run-time model gives an important role to references. Let us examine some of their properties, in particular the notion of void reference, and some of the issues they raise.

States of a reference

A reference may be in either of two states: void and attached. We have seen that a reference is always void initially and can be come attached through creation. Here is a more complete picture.

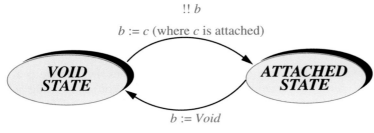

The possible states of a reference

Other than creation, a reference may change state through assignment, as will be studied shortly. For the moment, please make sure you understand the difference between the three notions — object, reference and entity — which recur through this chapter:

- "Object" is a run-time notion; any object is an instance of a certain class, created at execution time and made of a number of fields.

- "Reference" is also a run-time notion: a reference is a value that is either void or attached to an object. We have seen a precise definition of "attached": a reference is attached to an object if it identifies that object unambiguously.

- In contrast, "entity" is a static notion — that is to say, applying to the software text. An entity is an identifier appearing in the text of a class, and representing a run-time value or a set of successive run-time values. (Readers used to traditional forms of software development may think of the notion of entity as covering variables, symbolic constants, routine arguments and function results.)

Full definition of "entity": page 213.

If b is an entity of reference type, its run-time value is a reference, which may be attached to an object O. By an abuse of language we can say that b itself is attached to O.

Void references and calls

In most situations we expect a reference to be attached to an object, but the rules also permit a reference to be void. Void references play an important role — if only by making a nuisance of themselves — in the object-oriented model of computation. As discussed extensively in the previous chapter, the fundamental operation in that model is feature call: apply to an instance of a class a feature of that class. This is written *some_entity.some_feature (arg1, ...)*

where *some_entity* is attached to the desired target object. For the call to work, *some_entity* must indeed be attached to an object. If *some_entity* is of a reference type and happens to have a void value at the time of the call, the call cannot proceed, as *some_feature* needs a target object.

See chapter 12, in particular "Sources of exceptions", page 412.

To be correct, an object-oriented system must never attempt at run time to execute a feature call whose target is void. The effect will be an **exception**; the notion of exception, and the description of how it is possible to recover from an exception, will be discussed in a later chapter.

It would be desirable to let compilers check the text of a system to guarantee that no such event will occur at run time, in the same way that they can check the absence of type incompatibilities by enforcing type rules. Unfortunately such a general goal is currently beyond the reach of compilers (unless we place unacceptable restrictions on the language). So it remains the software developer's responsibility to ensure that the execution will never attempt a feature call on a void target. There is of course an easy way to do so: always write $x.f(...)$ as

The test "x is not void" may be written simply as x /= Void. See below.

if "*x* is not void" **then**

   $x.f(...)$

else

   ...

end

but this is too unwieldy to be acceptable as a universal requirement. Sometimes (as when a call $x.f$ immediately follows a creation !! *x*) it is clear from the context that *x* is not void, and you do not want to test.

The question of non-vacuity of references is part of the larger question of software correctness. To prove a system correct, it is necessary to prove that no call is ever applied to a void reference, and that all the software's assertions (as studied in a later chapter) are satisfied at the appropriate run-time instants. For non-vacuity as well as for assertion correctness, it would be desirable to have an automatic mechanism (a program prover, either integrated with the compiler or designed as a separate software tool) to ascertain that a software system is correct. In the absence of such tools, the result of a violation is a run-time error — an exception. Developers may protect their software against such situations in two ways:

• When writing the software, trying to prevent the erroneous situations from arising at run time, using all means possible: systematic and careful development, class inspections, use of tools that perform at least partial checks.

• If any doubt remains and run-time failures are unacceptable, equipping the software with provisions for handling exceptions.

8.6 OPERATIONS ON REFERENCES

We have seen one way of changing the value of a reference x: using a creation instruction of the form !! x, which creates a new object and attaches x to it. A number of other interesting operations are available on references.

Attaching a reference to an object

So far the classes of this chapter have had attributes but no routines. As noted, this makes them essentially useless: it is not possible to change any field in an existing object. We need ways to modify the value of references, without resorting to instructions of the Pascal-C-Java-C++ form *my_beloved.loved_one := me* (to set the *loved_one* field of an object directly), which violates information hiding and is syntactically illegal in our notation.

To modify fields of foreign objects, a routine will need to call other routines that the authors of the corresponding classes have specifically designed for that purpose. Let us adapt class *PERSON1* to include such a procedure, which will change the *loved_one* field to attach it to a new object. Here is the result:

> **class** *PERSON2* **feature**
>
> > *name*: *STRING*
> >
> > *loved_one, landlord*: *PERSON2*
> >
> > *set_loved* (*l*: *PERSON2*) **is**
> >
> > > -- Attach the *loved_one* field of current object to *l*.
> >
> > **do**
> >
> > > *loved_one* := *l*
> >
> > **end**
>
> **end**

Procedure *set_loved* assigns to the *loved_one* field of the current instance of *PERSON2*, a reference field, the value of another reference, *l*. Reference assignments (like assignments of simple values such as integers) rely on the := symbol, with the assignment's source on the right and the target on the left. In this case, since both source and target are of reference types, the assignment is said to be a reference assignment.

The effect of a reference assignment is exactly what the name suggests: the target reference gets reattached to the object to which the source reference is attached — or becomes void if the source was void. Assume for example that we start with the situation shown at the top of the facing page; to avoid cluttering the picture, the *landlord* fields and the irrelevant *loved_one* fields have been left blank.

Assume that we execute the procedure call

a.*set_loved* (*r*)

***Before
reference
assignment***

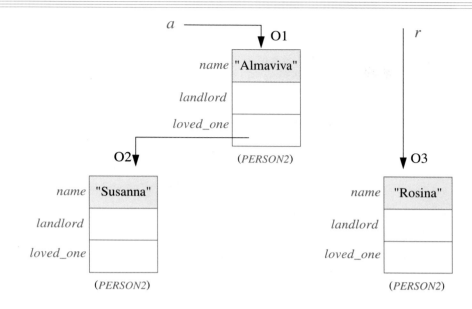

where *a* is attached to the top object (O1) and *r* to the bottom-right object (O3). From the way *set_loved* has been written, this will execute the assignment

> *loved_one* := *l*

with O1 as the current object and *l* having the same value as *r*, a reference to O3. The result is to reattach the *loved_one* field of O1:

***After
reference
assignment***

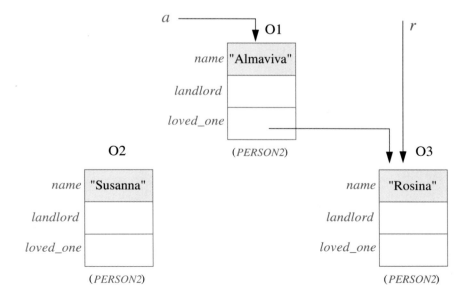

If *r* had been a void reference, the assignment would have made the *loved_one* field of O1 void too.

> A natural question at this stage is: what happens to the object to which the modified field was initially attached — O2 in the figure? Will the space it occupies be automatically recycled for use by future creation instructions?

> This question turns out to be so important as to deserve a chapter of its own — the next chapter, on memory management and garbage collection. So please hold your breath until then. But it is not too early for a basic observation: regardless of the final answer, a policy that would always recycle the object's space would be incorrect. In the absence of further information about the system from which the above run-time structure is extracted, we do not know whether some other reference is still attached to O2. So a reference assignment by itself does not tell us what to do with the previously attached object; any mechanism for recycling objects will need more context.

Reference comparison

In the same way that we have an operation (the := assignment) to attach a reference to an object, we need a way to test whether two references are attached to the same object. This is simply provided by the usual equality operator =.

> If *x* and *y* are entities of reference types, the expression

$$x = y$$

is true if and only if the corresponding references are either both void or both attached to the same objects. The opposite operator, "not equal", is written /= (a notation borrowed from Ada).

> For example, the expression

$$r = a.loved\_one$$

has value true on the last figure, where both sides of the = sign denote references attached to the object O3, but not on the next-to-last figure, where *a.loved_one* is attached to O2 and *r* is attached to O3.

> In the same way that an assignment to a reference is a reference operation, not an operation on objects, the expressions *x = y* and *x /= y* compare references, not objects. So if *x* and *y* are attached to two distinct objects, *x = y* has value false even if these objects are field-by-field identical. Operations which compare objects rather than reference will be introduced later.

The void value

Although it is easy to get a void reference — since all reference fields are by default initialized to *Void* –, we will find it convenient to have a name for a reference value accessible in all contexts and known always to be void. The predefined feature

> *Void*

will play that role.

Two common uses of *Void* are to test whether a certain reference is void, as in

if $x = Void$ **then** …

and to make a reference void, using the assignment

$x := Void$

This last assignment has the effect of putting the reference back to the void state, and so of de-attaching it from the attached object, if any:

De-attaching a reference from an object

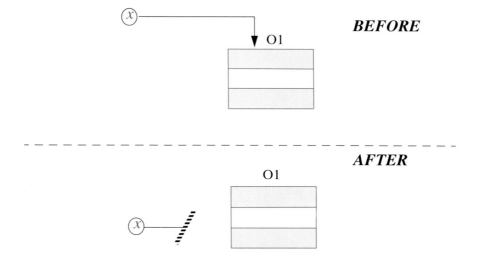

The comment made in the general discussion of reference assignment is worth repeating here: the assignment of *Void* to x has no immediate effect on the attached object (O1 in the figure); it simply cuts the link between the reference and the object. It would be incorrect to understand it as freeing the memory associated with O1, since some other reference may still be attached to O1 even after x has been de-attached from it. See the discussion of memory management in the next chapter.

Object cloning and equality

Reference assignments may cause two or more references to become attached to a single object. Sometimes you will need a different form of assignment, which works on the object itself: rather than attaching a reference to an existing object, you will want to create a new copy of an existing object.

This goal is achieved through a call to a function called *clone*. If y is attached to an object OY, the expression

clone (y)

denotes a new object OX, such that OX has the same number of fields as OY, each field of OX being identical to the corresponding field of OY. If y is void, the value of $clone\ (y)$ is also void.

To duplicate the object attached to y and attach the resulting object to x (or make x void if y is void), you may use a call to $clone$ in an assignment:

[1]

    $x := clone\ (y)$

Here is an illustration of this mechanism.

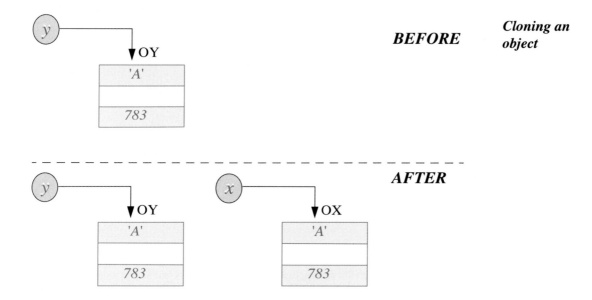

Cloning an object

We similarly need a mechanism to compare two objects. The expression $x = y$, as noted, fulfills another purpose: comparing references. For objects, we will use function $equal$. The call

    $equal\ (x, y)$

returns a boolean value, true if and only if x and y are either both void, or attached to two objects whose corresponding fields have the same values. If a system executes the clone assignment [1], the state immediately following that assignment will satisfy $equal\ (x, y)$.

You may wonder why function $clone$ has an argument, and $equal$ two arguments treated symmetrically, rather than being called under forms closer to the usual object-oriented style, for example $y.twin$ and $x.is\_equal\ (y)$. The answer appears in the discussion section, but it is not too early to try to guess it.

"The form of clone and equality operations", page 274.

Object copying

Function *clone* creates a new object as a carbon copy of an existing one. Sometimes the target object already exists; all we want to do is to overwrite its fields. Procedure *copy* achieves this. It is called through the instruction

$$x.copy\ (y)$$

for *x* and *y* of the same type; its effect is to copy the fields of the object attached to *y* onto the corresponding ones of the object attached to *x*.

As with all feature calls, any call to *copy* requires the target *x* to be non-void. In addition, *y* must also be non-void. This inability to deal with void values distinguishes *copy* from *clone*.

See chapter 11 about assertions.

The requirement that *y* must be non-void is so important that we should have a way to express it formally. The problem is in fact more general: how a routine can state the **preconditions** on the arguments passed by its callers. Such preconditions, a case of the more general notion of assertion, will be discussed in detail in a later chapter. Similarly, we will learn to express as **postconditions** such fundamental semantic properties as the observation made above that the result of a *clone* will satisfy *equal*.

Procedure *copy* may be considered more fundamental than function *clone* in the sense that we can, at least for a class with no creation procedure, express *clone* in terms of *copy* through the following equivalent function:

> *clone* (*y*: *SOME_TYPE*) **is**
>
>   -- Void if *y* is void; otherwise duplicate of object attached to *y*
>
>   **do**
>
>   **if** *y* /= *Void* **then**
>
>   !! *Result*   -- Valid only in the absence of creation procedures
>
>   *Result*.*copy* (*y*)
>
>   **end**
>
>   **end**

On execution of a function call, *Result* is automatically initialized using the same rules defined above for attributes. This is the reason why the **if** needs no **else**: since *Result* is initialized to *Void*, the result of the above function is a void value if *y* is void.

Deep clone and comparison

The form of copy and comparison achieved by routines *clone*, *equal* and *copy* may be called **shallow** since these operations work on an object at the first level only, never trying to follow references. There will also be a need for **deep** variants which recursively duplicate an entire structure.

To understand the differences assume for example that we start with the object structure appearing in black (except for the attribute and class names) under **A** in the figure on the facing page, where the entity a is attached to the object labeled O1.

For purposes of comparison, consider first the simple reference assignment

$b := a$

As pictured under **B**, this simply attaches the assignment's target b to the same object O1 to which the source a was attached. No new object is created.

Next consider the cloning operation

$c := clone\ (a)$

This instruction will, as shown under **C**, create a single new object O4, field-by-field identical to O1. It copies the two reference fields onto the corresponding fields of O4, yielding references that are attached to the same objects O1 and O3 as the originals. But it does not duplicate O3 itself, or any other object other than O1. This is why the basic *clone* operation is known as shallow: it stops at the first level of the object structure.

Note that a self-reference has disappeared: the *landlord* field of O1 was attached to O1 itself. In O4 this field becomes a reference to the original O1.

In other cases, you may want to go further and duplicate a structure recursively, without introducing any sharing of references such as occurred in the creation of O4. The function *deep_clone* achieves this. Instead of stopping at the object attached to y, the process of creating *deep_clone* (y) recursively follows any reference fields contained in that object and duplicates the entire structure. (If y is void the result is void too.) The function will of course process cyclic reference structures properly.

The bottom part of the figure, labeled **D**, illustrates the result of executing

$d := deep\_clone\ (a)$

This case introduces no new sharing; all the objects accessible directly or indirectly from O1 (the object attached to a) will be duplicated, yielding new objects O5, O6 and O7. There is no connection between the old objects (O1, O2 and O3) and the new. Object O5, mimicking O1, has a self-reference.

In the same way that we need both deep and shallow clone operations, equality must have a deep variant. The *deep_equal* function compares two object structures to determine whether they are structurally identical. In the figure's example, *deep_equal* holds between any two of a, b and d; but whereas *equal* (a, c) is true, since the corresponding objects O1 and O4 are field-by-field identical, *equal* (a, d) is false. In fact *equal* does not hold between d and any of the other three. (Both *equal* (a, b) and *equal* (b, c) hold.) In the general case we may note the following properties:

- After an assignment $x := clone\ (y)$ or a call $x.copy\ (y)$, the expression *equal* (x, y) has value true. (For the first assignment this property holds whether or not y is void.)

- After $x := deep\_clone\ (y)$, the expression *deep_equal* (x, y) has value true.

These properties will be expressed as postconditions of the corresponding routines.

Various forms of assignment and cloning

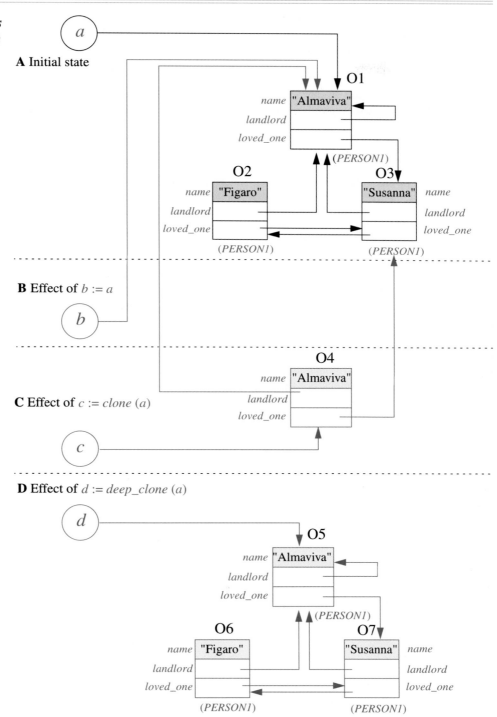

A Initial state

B Effect of *b* := *a*

C Effect of *c* := *clone* (*a*)

D Effect of *d* := *deep_clone* (*a*)

Deep storage: a first view of persistence

The study of deep copy and equality leads to another mechanism which, in environments where it is available, provides one of the great practical advantages of the O-O method.

So far, the discussion has not examined the question of input and output. But of course an object-oriented system will need to communicate with other systems and with the rest of the world. Since the information it manipulates is in the form of objects, this means it must be able to write and read objects to and from files, databases, communication lines and various devices.

> For simplicity this section will assume that the problem is to write to and write from files, and will use the terms "storage" and "retrieval" for these operations ("input" and "output" would also be adequate.) But the mechanisms studied must also be applicable for exchanging objects with the outside world through other means of communication, for example by sending and receiving objects through a network.

For instances of such classes as *POINT* or *BOOK1*, storage and retrieval of objects raise no particular novelty. These classes, used as the first examples at the beginning of this chapter, have attributes of types such as *INTEGER*, *REAL* and *STRING*, for which well-understood external representations are available. Storing an instance of such a class into a file, or retrieving it from that file, is similar to performing an output or input operation on a Pascal record or a C structure. Account must be taken, of course, of the peculiarities of data representations on different machines and in different languages (C, for example, has a special convention for strings, which the language expects to be terminated by a null character); but these are well-known technical problems for which standard solutions exist. So it is reasonable to expect that for such objects a good O-O environment could provide general-purpose procedures, say *read* and *write*, which, in the manner of *clone*, *copy* and consorts, would be available to all classes.

But such mechanisms will not take us very far because they do not handle a major component of the object structure: references. Since references can be represented in memory (as addresses or otherwise) it is possible to find an external representation as well. That is not the difficult part of the problem. What matters is the meaning of these references. A reference attached to an object is worthless without that object.

So as soon as we start dealing with non-trivial objects — objects that contain references — we cannot satisfy ourselves any more with a storage and retrieval mechanism that would just work on individual objects; the mechanism must process, together with an object, all its dependents according to the following definition:

Definition: direct dependents, dependents

The direct dependents of an object are the objects attached to its reference fields, if any.

The dependents of an object are the object itself and (recursively) the dependents of its direct dependents

---

With the object structure shown below (identical to earlier examples), it would be meaningless to store into a file, or transmit over a network, just the object O1. The operation must also include the dependents of O1: O2 and O3.

Three mutually dependent objects

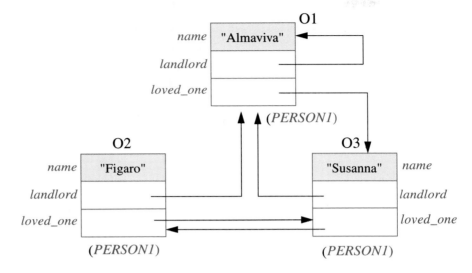

In this example any one of the three objects has the other two as dependents. In the *BOOK3* example reproduced below, we may store W1 by itself, and whenever we store B1 or B2 we must store W1 as well.

"Book" and "Writer" objects

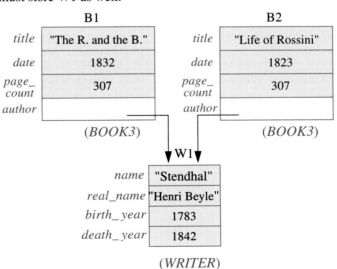

The notion of dependent was implicitly present in the presentation of *deep_equal*. Here is the general rule:

> ## Persistence Closure principle
>
> Whenever a storage mechanism stores an object, it must store with it the dependents of that object. Whenever a retrieval mechanism retrieves a previously stored object, it must also retrieve any dependent of that object that has not yet been retrieved.

The basic mechanism which will achieve this for our purposes is known as the *STORABLE* facility from the name of the Base library class which includes the corresponding features. The basic features of *STORABLE* are of the form:

store (f: IO_MEDIUM)

retrieved (f: IO_MEDIUM): STORABLE

The effect of a call of the form $x \bullet store\ (f)$ is to store the object attached to x, together with all its dependents, in the file associated with f. The object attached to x is said to be the **head object** of the stored structure. The generating class of x must be a descendant of *STORABLE* (that is to say, it must inherit directly or indirectly from *STORABLE*); so you will have to add *STORABLE* to the list of its parents if it is not already there. This applies only to the generating class of the head object; there is no particular requirement on the generating classes of the dependent objects — fortunately, since a head object can have an arbitrary number of direct and indirect dependents, instances of arbitrary classes.

Class *IO_MEDIUM* is another Base library class, covering not only files but also structures for network transmission. Clearly f must be non-void and the attached file or transmission medium must be writable.

The result of a call *retrieved (f)* is an object structure recursively identical, in the sense of *deep_clone*, to the complete object structure stored in f by an earlier call to *store*. Feature *retrieved* is a function; its result is a reference to the head object of the retrieved structure.

If you have already acquired a basic understanding of inheritance and of the associated type rules, you may have noted that *retrieved* raises a typing problem. The result of this function is of type *STORABLE*; but it seems that its normal use will be in assignments of the form $x := retrieved\ (f)$ where the type of x is a proper descendant of *STORABLE*, not *STORABLE* itself, even though the type rules will permit $x := y$ only if the type of y is a descendant of the type of x — not the other way around. The key to this problem will be an important construct, the **assignment attempt**. All this will be examined in detail when we study inheritance and the associated type rules.

See "ASSIGNMENT ATTEMPT", 16.5, page 591.

The *STORABLE* mechanism is our first example of what is known as a **persistence** facility. An object is persistent if it survives individual sessions of the systems that manipulate it. *STORABLE* only provides a partial solution to the persistence problem, suffering from several limitations:

- In the structure stored and retrieved, only one object is known individually: the head object. It may be desirable to retain the identity of other objects too.

- As a consequence, the mechanism is not directly usable to retrieve objects selectively through contents-based or keyword-based queries as in database management systems.

- A call to *retrieved* recreates the entire object structure. This means that you cannot use two or more such calls to retrieve various parts of a structure, unless they are disjoint.

Chapter 31.   To address this problem is to move from a mere persistence mechanism to the notion of object-oriented database, presented in a later chapter, which also discusses a number of issues associated with *STORABLE* and other persistence mechanisms, such as schema evolution (what happens when you retrieve an object and its class has changed?) and persistent object identity.

But the above limitations should not obscure the considerable practical benefits of the *STORABLE* mechanism as described above. In fact one may conjecture that the absence of such a mechanism has been one of the major obstacles to the use of sophisticated data structures in traditional development environments. Without *STORABLE* or its equivalent, storing a data structure becomes a major programming effort: for every kind of structure that you want to endow with persistence properties you must write a special input and output mechanism, including a set of mutually recursive procedures (one for each type) and special-purpose traversal mechanisms (which are particularly tricky to write in the case of possibly cyclic structures). But the worst part is not even the work that you have to do initially: as usual, the real trouble comes when the structure changes and you have to update the procedures.

With *STORABLE* a predefined mechanism is available regardless of your object structure, its complexity, and the software's evolution.

A typical application of the *STORABLE* mechanism is a SAVE facility. Consider an interactive system, for example a text editor, a graphical editor, a drafting program or a computer-aided design system; it needs to provide its users with a SAVE command to store the state of the current session into a file. The information stored should be sufficient to restart the session at any later time, so it must include all the important data structures of the system. Writing such a procedure in an ad hoc fashion suffers from the difficulties mentioned; in particular, you will have to update it whenever you change a class during development. But with the *STORABLE* mechanism and a good choice of head object, you can implement the SAVE facility using a single instruction:

> *head*.*store* (*save_file*)

Just by itself, this mechanism would suffice to recommend an object-oriented environment over its more traditional counterparts.

8.7 COMPOSITE OBJECTS AND EXPANDED TYPES

The preceding discussion described the essentials of the run-time structure. It gives an important role to references. To complete the picture, we must see how to handle values which are *not* references to objects, but the objects themselves.

References are not sufficient

The values considered so far, save for integers, booleans and the like, were references to objects. Two reasons suggest that we may also need entities whose values are objects:

- An important goal announced in the last chapter is to have a completely uniform type system, in which basic types (such as *BOOLEAN* and *INTEGER*) are handled in the same way as developer-defined types (such as *POINT* or *BOOK*). But if you use an entity n to manipulate an integer, you will almost always want the value of n to be an integer, for example 3, not a reference to an object containing the value 3. The reason is partly efficiency — think of the penalty in both time and space that we would have to incur if every integer access were indirect; just as important in this case is the goal of faithful modeling. An integer is conceptually not the same thing as a reference to an integer.

- Even with complex, developer-defined objects, we may prefer in some cases to consider that object O1 contains a subobject O2, rather than a reference to another object O2. The reason again may be efficiency, faithful modeling or both.

Expanded types

The answer to the need for modeling composite objects is simple. Let C be a class declared, as all classes so far, under the form

> **class C feature**
>
>   . . .
>
> **end**

C may be used as a type. Any entity declared of type C represents a reference; for that reason C is called a **reference type**.

Now assume that we need an entity x whose value at run time will be an instance of C — not a reference to such an instance. We may obtain this effect by declaring x as

> x : **expanded** C

This notation uses a new keyword, **expanded**. The notation **expanded** C denotes a type. The instances of this type are exactly the same as the instances of C. The only difference affects declarations using these types: an entity of type C denotes a reference which may become attached to an instance of C; an entity of type **expanded** C, such as x above, directly denotes an instance of C.

This mechanism adds the notion of composite object to the structure defined in the preceding sections. An object O is said to be composite if one or more of its fields are themselves objects — called **subobjects** of O. The following example class (routines again omitted) shows how to describe composite objects:

> **class** *COMPOSITE* **feature**
>   *ref*: *C*
>   *sub*: **expanded** *C*
> **end**

This class relies on *C* declared as above. *COMPOSITE* has two attributes: *ref*, denoting a reference, and *sub*, denoting a subobject; *sub* is what makes the class composite. Any direct instance of *COMPOSITE* may look like this:

A composite object with one subobject

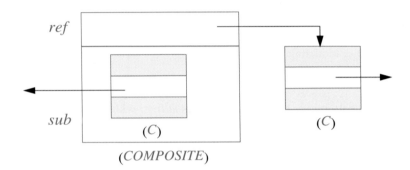

(COMPOSITE)

The *ref* field is a reference attached to an instance of *C* (or void). The *sub* field (which cannot be void) contains an instance of *C*.

A notational extension is convenient here. You may sometimes write a class *E* with the intention that all entities declared of type *E* should be expanded. To make this intention explicit, declare the class as

> **expanded class** *E* **feature**
>   … The rest as for any other class …
> **end**

A class defined in this manner is said to be an expanded class. Here too the new declaration changes nothing for instances of *E*: they are the same as if the class had been declared as just **class** *E* … But an entity declared of type *E* will now denote an object, not a reference. As a consequence of this new possibility, the notion of "expanded type" includes two cases:

Definition: expanded type

A type is said to be expanded in the following two cases:

- It is of the form **expanded** *C*.
- It is of the form *E*, where *E* is an expanded class.

It is not a mistake to declare an entity x as being of type **expanded** E if E is an expanded class, just useless, since the result in this case is the same as if you declare x to be just of type E.

We now have two kinds of type; a type which is not expanded is a **reference type** (a term already used in this chapter). We may apply the same terminology to the entities correspondingly declared: reference entities and expanded entities. Similarly, a class is an expanded class if it has been declared as **expanded class**..., a reference class otherwise.

The role of expanded types

Why do we need expanded types? They play three major roles:

- Improving efficiency.

- Providing better modeling.

- Supporting basic types in a uniform object-oriented type system.

The first application may be the most obvious at first: without expanded types, you would have to use references every time you need to describe composite objects. This means that accessing their subobjects would require an operation to follow a reference — "dereferencing", as it is sometimes called – which implies a time penalty. There is also a space penalty, as the run-time structure must devote space to the references themselves.

This performance argument is not, however, the prime justification. The key argument, in line with this chapter's general emphasis on object-oriented software construction as a modeling activity, is the need to model composite objects separately from objects that contain references to other objects. This is not an implementation issue but a conceptual one.

Consider the two attribute declarations

D1 • *ref*: *S*

D2 • *exp*: **expanded** *S*

appearing in a class C (and assuming that S is a reference class). Declaration D1 simply expresses that every instance of C "knows about" a certain instance of S (unless *ref* is void). Declaration D2 is more committing: it states that every instance of **C** **contains** an instance of S. Aside from any implementation issue, this is a quite different relation.

In particular, the "contains" relation as provided by expanded types does not allow any **sharing** of the contained elements, whereas the "knows about" relation allows two or more references to be attached to the same object.

You may apply this property to ensure proper modeling of relations between objects. Consider for example this class declaration:

*All classes shown
are assumed to be
reference (non-
expanded) classes.*

class *WORKSTATION* **feature**

    k: **expanded** *KEYBOARD*

    c: **expanded** *CPU*

    m: **expanded** *MONITOR*

    n: *NETWORK*

    . . .

end

Under this model a computer workstation has a keyboard, a CPU (central processing unit) and a monitor, and is attached to a network. The keyboard, CPU and monitor are part of a single workstation, and cannot be shared between two or more workstations. The network component, however, is shared: many workstations can be hooked up to the same network. The class definition reflects these properties by using expanded types for the first three attributes, and a reference type for the network attribute.

***"Knows about"
and "contains"
relations
between
objects***

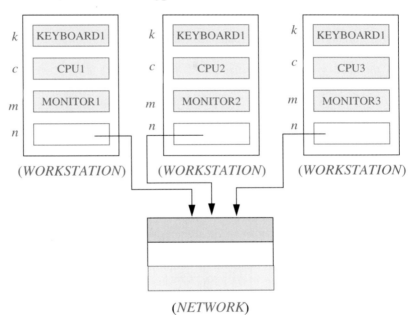

(NETWORK)

So the concept of expanded type, which at first sight appears to be an implementation-level technique, actually helps describe some of the relations used in information modeling. The "contains" relation, and its inverse often known as "is-part-of", are central to any effort at building models of external systems; they appear in analysis methods and in database modeling.

*See "A UNIFORM
TYPE SYSTEM", 7.4,
page 171. The outline
of class REAL was on
page 189.*

The third major application of expanded types is in fact a special case of the second. The previous chapter emphasized the desirability of a uniform type system, based on the notion of class, which must encompass both developer-defined types and basic types. The example of *REAL* was used to show how, with the help of infix and prefix features, we can indeed model the notion of real number as a class; we can do the same for the other basic types *BOOLEAN*, *CHARACTER*, *INTEGER*, *DOUBLE*. But a problem remains. If these classes were treated as reference classes, an entity declared of a basic type, such as

> *r*: *REAL*

would at run time denote a reference to a possible object containing a value (here of type *REAL*). This is unacceptable: to conform to common practice, the value of *r* should be the real value itself. The solution follows from the earlier discussion: define class *REAL* as expanded. Its declaration will be

> **expanded class** *REAL* **feature**
>   … Feature declarations exactly as given earlier (see page 189) …
> **end**

All the other basic types are similarly defined by expanded classes.

Aggregation

In some areas of computing science — databases, information modeling, requirements analysis — authors have developed a classification of the relations that may hold between elements of a modeled system. Often mentioned in this context is the "aggregation" relation, which serves to express that every object of a certain type is a combination (an aggregate) of zero or more objects, each of a specified type. For example we might define "car" as an aggregation of "engine", "body" etc.

Expanded types provide the equivalent mechanism. We may for example declare class *CAR* with features of types **expanded** *ENGINE* and **expanded** *BODY*. Another way to express this observation is to note that aggregation is covered by the "expanded client" relation, where a class *C* is said to be an expanded client of a class *S* if it contains a declaration of a feature of type **expanded** *S* (or just *S* if *S* is expanded). One advantage of this modeling approach is that "expanded client" is just a special case of the general client relation, so that we can use a single framework and notation to combine aggregation-like dependencies (that is to say, dependencies on subobjects, such as the relation between *WORKSTATION* and *KEYBOARD* in the earlier example) with dependencies that permit sharing (such as the relation between *WORKSTATION* and *NETWORK*).

With the object-oriented approach, one can avoid the multiplicity of relations found in the information modeling literature, and cover all possible cases with just two relations: client (expanded or not) and inheritance.

Properties of expanded types

Consider an expanded type *E* (of either form) and an expanded entity *x* of type *E*.

Since the value of *x* is always an object, it can never be void. So the expression

> *x* = *Void*

will always yield the value false, and a call of the form $x \bullet some\_feature\ (arg1, …)$ will never raise the exception "call on void target" that was possible in the case of references.

"Void references and calls", page 240.

Let object O be the value of x. As with the case of a non-void reference, x is said to be attached to O. So for any non-void entity we may talk of the attached object, whether the entity is of reference or expanded type.

What about creation? The instruction

!! x

See "Effect of a basic creation instruction", page 233.

may be applied to an expanded x. For reference x, its effect was to perform three steps: (C1) create a new object; (C2) initialize its fields to the default values; (C3) attach it to x. For expanded x, step C1 is inappropriate, and step C3 is unneeded; so the only effect is to set all fields to their default values.

More generally, the presence of expanded types affects the default initialization performed as part of C2. Assume a class, expanded or not, having one or more expanded attributes:

    class F **feature**
        u: *BOOLEAN*
        v: *INTEGER*
        w: *REAL*
        x: C
        y: **expanded** C
        z: E
        …

    end

where E is expanded but C is not. The initialization of a direct instance of F involves setting the u field to false, the v field to 0, the w field to 0.0, the x field to a void reference, and the y and z to instances of C and E respectively, whose fields are themselves initialized according to the standard rules. This initialization process is to be applied recursively, since C and E may themselves include expanded fields.

Cycles in the client relation were studied in "Self-reference", page 226.

As you may have realized, a restriction is necessary for expanded types to be usable (to ensure that the recursive process just defined always remains finite): although, as discussed earlier, the client relation may in general include cycles, such cycles must make no use of expanded attributes. For example it is not permitted for class C to have an attribute of type **expanded** D if class D has an attribute of type **expanded** C; this would mean that every object of type C includes a subobject of type D and conversely — a clear impossibility. Hence the following rule, based on the notion of "expanded client" already introduced informally above:

Expanded Client rule

Let "expanded client" the relation between classes be defined as follows: C is an expanded client of S if some attribute of C is of an expanded type based on S (that is to say **expanded** S, or just S if S is an expanded class).

Then the expanded client relation may not include any cycles.

In other words there may not be a set of classes A, B, C, ... N such that A is an expanded client of B, B an expanded client of C etc., with N being an expanded client of A. In particular, A may not have an attribute of type **expanded** A, as this would make A an expanded client of itself.

No references to subobjects

A final comment about expanded types will answer the question of how to mix references and subobjects. An expanded class, or an expanded type based on a reference class, may have reference attributes. So a subobject may contain references attached to objects:

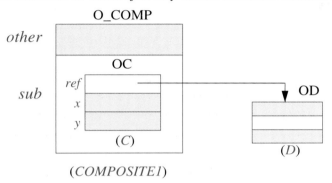

A subobject with a reference to another object

The situation pictured assumes the following declarations:

class *COMPOSITE1* **feature**
    other: *SOME_TYPE*
    sub: **expanded** *C*
end

class *C* **feature**
    ref: *D*
    x: *OTHER_TYPE*; *y*: *YET_ANOTHER_TYPE*
end

class *D* **feature**
    ...
end

Each *COMPOSITE* instance, such as O_COMP in the figure, has a subobject (OC in the figure) containing a reference *ref* which may be attached to an object (OD in the figure).

But the reverse situation, where a reference would become attached to a subobject, is impossible. (This will follow from the rules on assignment and argument passing, studied in the next section.) So the run-time structure can never come to the state described by the picture on the facing page, where OE contains a reference to OC, a subobject of O_CMP1, and OC similarly contains a reference to itself.

A reference to
a subobject

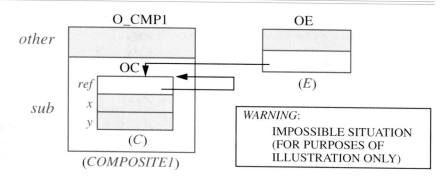

This rule is open to criticism since it limits the modeling power of the approach. Earlier versions of this book's notation did in fact permit references to subobjects. But this possibility was found to cause more problems than it was worth:

Garbage collection is studied in the next chapter.

• From the implementation's perspective, the garbage collection mechanism must be prepared to deal with subobject references even if in a given execution there are few such references, or none at all. This caused a significant performance degradation.

• From the viewpoint of modeling, excluding subobject references actually turned out to simplify system descriptions by defining a single unit of referencing, the object.

The discussion will point out what precise attachment rule would have to be modified to revert to the scheme in which references may be attached to subobjects.

8.8 ATTACHMENT: REFERENCE AND VALUE SEMANTICS

If skipping, go to "DEALING WITH REFERENCES: BENEFITS AND DANGERS", 8.9, page 265.

(This section covers more specialized information and you may skip it on first reading.)

The introduction of expanded types means that we must take a second look at two fundamental operations studied earlier in this chapter: assignment, written :=, which attaches a reference to an object, and the associated comparison operation, written =. Since entities may now denote objects as well as references to objects, we must decide what assignment and equality will mean in the first of these cases.

Attachment

The semantics of assignment will actually cover more than this operation. Another case in which the value of an entity may change is argument passing in routine calls. Assume a routine (procedure or function) of the form

$r (\ldots, x: SOME\_TYPE, \ldots)$

Here entity x is one of the **formal arguments** of r. Now consider a particular call to r, of one of the possible two forms (unqualified and qualified):

$r (\ldots, y, \ldots)$
$t \bullet r (\ldots, y, \ldots)$

where expression y is the **actual argument** having the same position in the list of actual arguments as x has in the list of formal arguments.

Whenever r gets started as a result of one of these calls, it initializes each of its formal arguments with the value of the corresponding actual argument, such as y for x.

For simplicity and consistency, the rules governing such actual-formal argument associations are the same as the rules governing assignment. In other words, the initial effect on x of such a call is exactly as if x were the target of assignment of the form

$x := y$

This rule yields a definition:

Definition: attachment

An attachment of y to x is either of the following two operations:

- An assignment of the form $x := y$.
- The initialization of x at the time of a routine call, where x is a formal argument of a routine and y is the corresponding actual argument in the call.

In both cases, x is the **target** of the attachment and y its **source**.

Exactly the same rules will be applicable in both cases to determine whether an attachment is valid (depending on the types of its target and source) and, if it is, what effect it will have at execution time.

Reference and copy attachment

We have seen a first rule for the effect of attachment when studying reference assignment. If both source and target are references, then the effect of an assignment

$x := y$

and of the corresponding argument passing is to make x denote the same reference as y. This was illustrated through several examples. If y is void prior to the attachment, the operation will make x void too; if y is attached to an object, x will end up attached to the same object.

What now if the types of x and y are expanded? Reference assignment would not make sense, but a copy (the shallow form) is possible. The meaning of an attachment of an expanded source to an expanded target will indeed be a copy. With the declarations

x, y: **expanded** *SOME_CLASS*

the assignment $x := y$ will copy every field of the object attached to y onto the corresponding field of the object attached to x, producing the same effect as

$x.copy\ (y)$

which of course is still legal in this case. (In the case of reference types, $x := y$ and $x.copy\ (y)$ are both legal but have different effects.)

This copy semantics for expanded types yields the expected effect in the case of the basic types which, as noted above, are all expanded. For example if m and n have been declared of type *INTEGER*, you will expect the assignment $m := n$, or a corresponding argument passing, to copy the value of n onto that of m.

The analysis just applied to attachment transposes immediately to a related operation: comparison. Consider the boolean expressions $x = y$ and $x \mathbin{/=} y$, which will have opposite values. For x and y of reference types, as already noted, the tests compare references: $x = y$ yields true if and only if x and y are either both void or both attached to the same object. For expanded x and y, this would not make sense; the only acceptable semantics is to use field-by-field comparison, so that in this case $x = y$ will have the same value as *equal* (x, y).

"Fixed semantics for copy, clone and equality features", page 583.

It is possible, as we will see in the discussion of inheritance, to adapt the semantics of *equal* to support a specific notion of equality for the instances of some class. This has no effect on the semantics of =, which, for safety and simplicity, is always that of the original function *standard_equal*.

The basic rule for attachment and comparison, then, is summarized by the following observation:

> An attachment of y to x is a copy of objects x if x and y are of expanded types (including any of the basic types). It is a reference attachment if x and y are of reference types.
>
> Similarly, an equality or inequality test $x = y$ or $x \mathbin{/=} y$ is a comparison of objects for x and y of expanded types; it is a comparison of references if x and y are of reference types.

Hybrid attachments

In the cases seen so far, the source and target types of an attachment are of the same category — both expanded or both reference. What if they are of different categories?

See chapter 12, in particular "Sources of exceptions", page 412.

First consider $x := y$ where the target x is of an expanded type and the source y is of a reference type. Because reference assignment does not make sense for x, the only acceptable semantics for this attachment is copy semantics: copy the fields of the object attached to y onto the corresponding fields of the object attached to x. This is indeed the effect of the assignment in this case; but it only makes sense if y is non-void at the time of execution (otherwise there is no attached object). If y is void, the result will be to trigger an exception. The effect of exceptions, and the specification of how to recover from an exception, are discussed in a later chapter.

For expanded x, the test $x = Void$ does not cause any abnormal event; it simply yields the result false. But there is no way we can find an acceptable semantics for the assignment $x := Void$, so any attempt at executing it causes an exception.

Now consider the other case: $x := y$ where x is of a reference type and y is of an expanded type. Then at run time y is always attached to an object, which we may call OY, and the attachment should also attach x an object. One possibility would be to attach x to OY. This convention, however, would introduce the possibility of references to subobjects, as in routine *reattach* below:

class *C* **feature**

   ...

end

class *COMPOSITE2* **feature**

    x: *C*

    y: **expanded** *C*

    reattach **is**

        do $x := y$ **end**

end

If, as suggested earlier, we prohibit references to subobjects, we may in such a case prescribe that the attachment perform a **clone** of OY. This will indeed be the effect of the attachment for expanded source and reference target: attach the target to a clone of the source object.

The following table summarizes the semantics of attachment in the cases studied:

Type of source $y \rightarrow$ $\downarrow$ *Type of target* x	**Reference**	**Expanded**
Reference	Reference attachment	Clone; effect of $x := clone\ (y)$
Expanded	Copy; effect of $x.copy\ (y)$ (will fail if *y* is void)	Copy; effect of $x.copy\ (y)$

Effect of attachment

$x := y$

To allow references to subobjects, it would suffice to replace the clone semantics defined in the top-right entry by the semantics of reference attachment.

Equality comparison

The semantics of equality comparison (the = and /= signs) should be compatible with the semantics of attachment: if $y\ /= z$ is true and you execute $x := y$, then both $x = y$ and $x\ /= z$ should be true immediately after the assignment.

Besides =, we have seen that there is an operation *equal* applicable to objects. Which of these operations is available depends on the circumstances:

E1 • If x and y are references, you can test both for reference equality and, if the references are not void, for object equality. We have defined the operation $x = y$ as denoting reference equality in this case. The *equal* function was introduced to cover object equality; for completeness it also applies when x or y is void (returning true in this case only if both are).

E2 • If x and y are expanded, the only operation that makes sense is object comparison.

E3 • If x is a reference and y is expanded, object equality is also the only meaningful operation — again extended to accept void x, in which case it will return false since y cannot be void.

This analysis yields the desirable interpretation for = in all cases. For object comparison, *equal* is always available, conveniently extended to deal with cases in which one or both operands are void. = serves to apply reference comparison when it makes sense, defaulting to *equal* in other cases:

Meaning of comparison

$x = y$

Type of y → ↓ *Type of x*	**Reference**	**Expanded**
Reference	Reference comparison	*equal* (x, y) i.e. object comparison if x non-void, false if x void.
Expanded	*equal* (x, y) i.e. object comparison if y non-void, false if y void.	*equal* (x, y) i.e. object comparison.

By comparing with the preceding table, you may check that = and /= are indeed compatible with := in the sense defined above. Recall in particular that *equal* (x, y) will be true as a result of $x := clone\ (y)$ or $x.copy\ (y)$.

This issue that we have just settled arises in any language which includes pointer or references (such as Pascal, Ada, Modula-2, C, Lisp etc.), but is particularly acute in an object-oriented language in which all non-basic types are reference types; in addition, for reasons explained in the discussion section, the syntax does not explicitly show them to be references, so we need to be particularly careful.

8.9 DEALING WITH REFERENCES: BENEFITS AND DANGERS

Two properties of the run-time model, as introduced in the preceding sections, deserve further examination. One is the important role of references; the other is the dual semantics of basic operations such as assignment, argument passing and equality tests which, as we have seen, produce different effects for reference and expanded operands.

Dynamic aliasing

If x and y are of reference types and y is not void, the assignment $x := y$, or the corresponding attachment in a call, causes x and y to be attached to the same object.

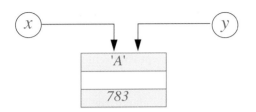

*Sharing as a
result of an
attachment*

The result is to bind *x* and *y* in a durable way (until any further assignment to any of them). In particular, an operation of the form *x•f*, where *f* is some feature of the corresponding class, will have the same effect as *y•f* since they affect the same object.

The attachment of *x* to the same object as *y* is known as dynamic aliasing: aliasing because the assignment makes an object accessible through two references, like a person known under two names; dynamic because the aliasing occurs at run time.

Static aliasing, where a software text specifies that two names will always denote the same value regardless of what happens at execution time, is also possible in some programming languages: the Fortran *EQUIVALENCE* directive states that two variables will always denote the contents of the same memory location; and the C preprocessor directive *#define x y* specifies that any further occurrence of *x* in the program text means exactly the same thing as *y*.

Because of dynamic aliasing, attachment operations have a more far-reaching effect on entities of reference types than on those of expanded types. If *x* and *y* are of type *INTEGER*, an example of expanded type, the assignment *x := y* only resets the value of *x* using that of *y*; but it does not durably bind *x* and *y*. For reference types, the assignment causes *x* and *y* to become aliases for the same object.

The semantics of aliasing

A somewhat shocking consequence of aliasing (static or dynamic) is that an operation may affect an entity that it does not even cite.

Models of computation that do not involve aliasing enjoy a pleasant property: the correctness of such extracts as

[NO SURPRISE]

            -- Assume that here *P* (*y*) holds

    x := *y*

    C (*x*)

            -- Then here *P* (*y*) still holds.

This example assumes that *P* (*y*) is an arbitrary property of *y*, and *C* (*x*) some operation whose textual description in the software may involve *x* but does not involve *y*. Correctness here means that the property of "NO SURPRISE" expressed by the comments is indeed satisfied: if *P* (*y*) is true initially, then no action on *x* can invalidate this property. An operation on *x* does not affect a property of *y*.

With entities of expanded types, property NO SURPRISE indeed holds. Here is s typical example, assuming x and y of type *INTEGER*:

-- Assume that here $y \geq 0$

$x := y$

$x := -1$

-- Then here $y \geq 0$ still holds.

In no way can the assignment to x have any effect on y in this case. But now consider a similar one involving dynamic aliasing. Let x and y be of type C, where class C is of the form

class C **feature**

    boolattr: *BOOLEAN*

        -- Boolean attribute, modeling some object property.

    set_true **is**

        -- Make *boolattr* true.

      do

        boolattr := *True*

      end

    … Other features …

end

Assume that y is of type C and that its value at some run-time instant is not void. Then the following instance of the above scheme violates property NO SURPRISE:

[SURPRISE, SURPRISE!]

        -- Assume that $y.boolattr$ is false.

    $x := y$

        -- Here it is still true that $y.boolattr$ is false.

    $x.set\_true$

        -- But then here $y.boolattr$ is true!

The last instruction of this extract does not involve y in any way; yet one of its effects is to change the properties of y, as indicated by the final comment.

Coming to terms with dynamic aliasing

Having seen the disturbing consequences of reference assignments and dynamic aliasing, one may legitimately ask why we should keep such a facility in our model of computation.

The answer is twofold — partly theoretical and partly practical:

• We need reference assignments if we are to benefit from the full power of the object-oriented method, in particular to describe complex data structures. The issue here is again to make sure that our tools are versatile enough for our modeling needs.

• In the practice of object-oriented software construction, encapsulation makes it possible to avoid the dangers of reference manipulations.

Let us examine these two important aspects in turn.

Aliasing in software and elsewhere

The first observation is simply that many of the data structures we will need require references and reference sharing. Some standard data structures, for example, include cyclically chained elements, which you cannot implement without references. In representing list and tree structures, it is often convenient to let every node contain a reference to its neighbor or parent. The figure below shows a circular list representation, combining both of these ideas. Open any textbook on fundamental data structures and algorithms, as used in introductory computing science courses, and you will find many such examples. With object technology we will want, if anything, to use even more sophisticated structures.

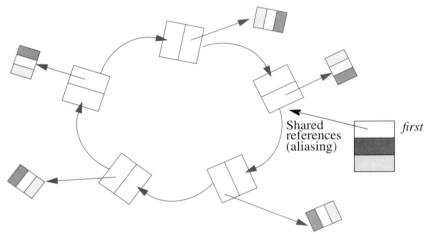

A linked circular list

In fact the need for references, reference attachment and reference sharing already arises with quite unsophisticated data structures. Recall the classes used above to describe books; one of the variants was

class *BOOK3* **feature**

    … Other features; …

    author: *WRITER*

end

Page 226.

Here the need for reference sharing is simply a consequence of the property that two or more books may have the same author. Many of the examples of this chapter also cause sharing; in the *PERSON* case, several people may have the same landlord. The question, as already noted, is modeling power, not just the requirements of implementation.

But then if *b1* and *b2* are two instances of *BOOK3* with the same author, we have a case of aliasing: *b1*.*author* and *b2*.*author* are two references attached to the same object, and using any of them as target of a feature call will have exactly the same effect as using the other. Seen in this light, dynamic aliasing appears less as a potentially dangerous software facility than as a fact of life, the price to pay for the convenience of being able to refer to things under more than one name.

It is indeed easy to find violations of the above NO SURPRISE property without ever entering the software field. Consider the following property and operation, defined for any book *b*:

* *NOT_NOBEL* (*b*) stands for: "the author of *b* has never received the Nobel prize".

* *NOBELIZE* (*b*) stands for: "Give the Nobel prize to the author of *b*".

Now assume *rb* denotes the book *The Red and the Black* and *cp* denotes *The Charterhouse of Parma*. Then the following is a correct development:

Stendhal lived prior to the establishment of the prize, of course — and would probably not have got it anyway; he did not even make it to the Académie.

[SURPRISE IN OSLO]
     -- Assume that here *NOT_NOBEL* (*rb*) holds
   NOBELIZE (*cp*)
     -- Then here *NOT_NOBEL* (*rb*) does not hold any more!

An operation on *cp* has changed a property of a different entity, *rb*, not even named in the instruction! The consequences on *rb* may actually be quite significant (with a Nobel author an out-of-print book will be reprinted, its price may rise etc.). In this non-software case exactly the same thing happens as when the operation *x.set_true*, in the earlier software example, produced an important effect on *y* even though it did not refer to *y*.

So dynamic aliasing is not just a consequence of programmers' dirty tricks with references or pointers. It is a consequence of the human ability to *name* things ("objects" in the most general sense of the word), and to give many names to one thing. In classical rhetoric, this was known as a *polyonymy*, as with the use of "Cybele", "Demeter" and "Ceres" for the same goddess, and *antonomasia*, the ability to refer to an object through indirect phrases, as with "The beautiful daughter of Agammemnon" for Helena of Troy. Polyonymy, antonomasia and the resulting dynamic aliasing are not restricted to gods and heroes; if in the cafeteria you overhear two conjectures from separate conversations, one stating that the spouse of the engineering Vice President just got a big promotion and the other that the company has fired its accountant, you will not realize the contradiction — unless you know that the accountant is the VP's husband.

Encapsulating reference manipulations

By now we have accumulated enough evidence that any realistic framework for modeling and software development must support the notion of reference, and consequently dynamic aliasing. How then do we cope with the unpleasant consequences of these mechanisms? The inability to ensure the NO SURPRISE property illustrates how references and aliasing endanger our ability to reason systematically about our software, that is to say, to infer run-time properties of the software's execution, in a safe and simple way, by examining the software text.

To find an answer it helps to understand first how much of this issue is specific to the object-oriented method. If you are familiar with such programming languages as Pascal, C, PL/I, Ada and Lisp you will probably have noted that much of the above discussion applies to them as well. They all have a way of allocating objects dynamically (although in C the corresponding function, *malloc*, is in the library rather than the language proper) and of letting objects contain references to other objects. The level of abstraction of the language mechanisms varies significantly: C and PL/I pointers are scantily dressed machine addresses; Pascal and Ada use typing rules to wrap pointers in more respectable attire, although they do not need much prompting to return to their original state.

What then is new with object-oriented development? The answer lies not in the theoretical power of the method (whose run-time structures are similar to those of Pascal or Ada, with the important difference of garbage collection, studied in the next chapter) but in the practice of software construction. O-O development implies reuse. In particular, any project in which many application classes perform tricky manipulations (such as reference manipulation) is a flawed use of the object-oriented approach. Such operations should be encapsulated once and for all in library classes.

Regardless of the application domain, if a system includes object structures requiring non-trivial reference operations, the vast majority of these structures are not application-specific but merely instances of such frequently needed and well-known structures as lists of various kinds, trees under various representations, graphs, hash tables and a few others. In a good O-O environment a library will be readily available, offering many implementations of these structures; appendix A will sketch an example, the Base library. The classes of such a library may contain many operations on references (think for example of the reference manipulations needed to insert or delete an element in a linked list, or a node in a tree using linked representation). The library should have been patiently crafted and validated, so as to take care of the tricky problems once and for all.

If, as you are building the application, you recognize the need for complex object structures which are not adequately covered by the available libraries, you should look at them as requiring new general-purpose classes. You should design and check them carefully, under the expectation that in due time they will become part of some library. Using the terminology introduced in an earlier chapter, such a case is an example of moving from a consumer's to a producer's view of reuse.

"Reuse consumers, reuse producers", page 69.

The remaining reference manipulations in application-dependent classes should be restricted to simple and safe operations. (The bibliographical notes cite an article by Suzuki which explores this idea further.)

8.10 DISCUSSION

This chapter has introduced a number of rules and notations for manipulating objects and the corresponding entities. Some of these conventions may have surprised you. So it is useful to conclude our exploration of objects and their properties by examining the issues involved and the reasons behind the choices made. Although I hope you will in the end agree with these choices, the more important goal of this discussion is to make sure that you fully understand the underlying problems, so that even if you prefer a different solution you choose it with your eyes open.

Graphical conventions

To warm up let us begin with a little notational issue — a detail, really, but software is sometimes in the details. This particular detail is the set of conventions used to illustrate classes and objects in graphical representations.

"The mold and the instance", page 167.

The previous chapter emphasized the importance of not confusing the notions of class and object. Accordingly, the graphical representations are different. Objects are represented as rectangles. Classes, as they appear in system architecture diagrams, are represented by ellipses (connected by arrows representing the relations between classes: single arrow for the inheritance relation, double arrow for the client relation).

Class and object representations appear in different contexts: a class ellipse will be part of a diagram representing the structure of a software system; an object rectangle will be part of a diagram representing a snapshot of the state of a system during its execution. Because these two kinds of diagram address completely different purposes, there is usually no opportunity in paper presentations such as the present book for having both class and object representations appear in the same context. But the situation is different with interactive CASE tools: during the execution of a software system, you may want (for example for debugging purposes) to look at an object, and then display its generating class to examine the features, parents or other properties of that class.

On BON see the bibliographical notes and chapter 27.

The graphical conventions used for classes and objects are compatible with the standard established by Nerson and Waldén's BON method. In BON (Business Object Notation), which is meant for use in interactive CASE tools as well as for paper documentation, class bubbles can be stretched vertically so as to reveal a class's features, invariant, indexing words, and other properties.

As with any choice of graphical representation, there is no absolute justification for the conventions used in BON and in this book. But if the graphical symbols at our disposal are ellipses and rectangles, and the elements to be represented are classes and objects, then it does appear preferable to assign rectangles to objects: an object is a set of fields, so we can represent each field by a small rectangle and glue together a set of fields to make up a bigger rectangle which represents an object.

From a review of Martin and Odell's "Object-Oriented Analysis and Design", in OOPS (British Computer Society O-O interest group newsletter), 16, Winter 1992, pages 35-37.

A further convention, illustrated by the figures of this chapter, is to make expanded fields appear shaded, whereas references fields are blank; subobjects appear as smaller embedded rectangles, containing their own fields. All these conventions follow from the decision to use rectangles for objects.

On the lighter side, it is hard to resist quoting the following non-scientific argument, from Ian Graham's critique of an O-O analysis book that uses a different convention:

> *Nor do I like showing classes as sharp cornered triangles. I like to think that instances have sharp corners because if you drop them on your foot they hurt, whereas classes can't hurt anyone and therefore have rounded corners.*

References and simple values

An important syntactical question is whether we should deal differently with references and simple values. As noted, assignment and equality test have different meanings for references and for values of expanded types — the latter including values of basic types: integers and the like. Yet the same symbols are used in both cases: :=, =, /=. Is this not dangerous? Would it not be preferable to use different sets of symbols to remind the reader that the meanings are different?

Using two sets of symbols was indeed the solution of Simula 67. Transposing the notation slightly so as to make it compatible with those of the present book, the Simula solution is to declare an entity of a reference type C as

Simula, covered in chapter 35, abbreviates **reference** *to* **ref***.*

   x: **reference** C

where the keyword **reference** reminds the reader that instances of x will be references. Assuming the declarations

   m, n: *INTEGER*
   x, y: **reference** C

then different notations are used for operations on simple and reference types, as follows:

OPERATION	EXPANDED OPERANDS	REFERENCE OPERANDS
Assignment	$m := n$	$x := y$
Equality test	$m = n$	$x == y$
Inequality test	$m /= n$	$x =/= y$

Simula-style notations for operations on reference and expanded values

The Simula conventions remove any ambiguity. Why not keep them then? The reason is that in practice they turn out in spite of the best intentions to cause more harm than help. The problems begin with a mundane matter: typing errors. The two sets of symbols are so close that one tends to make syntactical oversights, such as using := instead of :–. Such errors will be caught by the compiler. But although compiler-checkable restrictions in programming languages are meant to help programmers, the checks are of no use here: either you know the difference between reference and value semantics, in which case the obligation to prove again, each time you write an assignment or equality, that you did understand this difference, is rather annoying; or you do not understand the difference, but then the compiler message will not help you much!

The remarkable aspect of the Simula convention is that you do not in fact have a choice: for references, no predefined construct is available that would give value semantics. It might have seemed reasonable to allow two sets of operations on entities a and b of reference types:

• $a :– b$ for reference assignment, and $a == b$ for reference comparison.

• $a := b$ for copy assignment (the equivalent, in our notation, of either $a := clone(b)$ or $a.copy(b)$), and $a = b$ for object comparison (the equivalent of our $equal(a, b)$).

But this is not the case; for operands of reference types, with one exception, Simula only provides the first set of operations, and any attempt to use := or = will produce a syntactical error. If you need operations of the second set (copy or clone, object comparison), you must write specific routines corresponding to our *clone*, *copy* and *equal* for each target class. (The exception is the *TEXT* type, representing character strings, for which Simula does offer both sets of operations.)

On further examination, by the way, the idea of allowing both sets of operations for all reference types does not appear so clever. It would mean that a trivial oversight such as typing := for :– would now go undetected by the compiler but produce an effect quite different from the programmer's intent, for example a *clone* where a reference assignment was intended.

As a result of this analysis, the notation of this book uses a different convention from Simula's: the same symbols apply for expanded and reference types, with different semantics (value in one case, reference in the other). You can achieve the effect of value semantics for objects of reference types by using predefined routines, available on all types:

- *a* := *clone* (*b*) or *a*.*copy* (*b*) for object assignment.

- *equal* (*a*, *b*) for object (field-by-field) comparison.

These notations are sufficiently different from their reference counterparts (:= and =, respectively) to avert any risk of confusion.

Beyond the purely syntactical aspects, this issue is interesting because it typifies some of the tradeoffs that arise in language design when a balance must be found between conflicting criteria. One criterion, which won in the Simula case, may be stated as:

- "Make sure different concepts are expressed by different symbols".

But the opposing forces, which dominated in the design of our notation, say:

- "Avoid bothering the software developer."

- "Weigh carefully any new restriction against the actual benefits that it will bring in terms of security and other quality factors." Here the restriction is the prohibition of := and similar operators for references.

- "Make sure that the most common operations can be expressed by short and simple notations." The application of this principle requires some care, as the language designer may be wrong in his guesses of what cases will be the most common. But in the present example it seems clear that on entities of expanded types (such as *INTEGER*) value assignment and comparison are the most frequent operations, whereas on references entities reference assignment and comparison are more frequent than clone, copy and object comparison. So it is appropriate to use := and = for the fundamental operations in both cases.

- "To keep the language small and simple, do not introduce new notations unless they are absolutely necessary". This applies in particular if, as in this example, existing notations will do the job and there is no danger of confusion.

- "If you know there is a serious risk of confusion between two facilities, make the associated notations as different as possible." This leads us to avoid making both :– and := available for the same operands with different semantics.

One more reason plays a role in the present case, although it involves mechanisms that we have not yet studied. In later chapters we will learn to write generic classes, such as *LIST* [*G*], where *G*, known as a formal generic parameter, stands for an arbitrary type. Such a class may manipulate entities of type *G* and use them in assignments and equality tests. Clients that need to use the class will do so by providing a type to serve as actual generic parameter; for example they may use *LIST* [*INTEGER*] or *LIST* [*POINT*]. As these examples indicate, the actual generic parameter may be an expanded type (as in the first case) as well as a reference type (as in the second case). In the routines of such a generic class, if *a* and *b* are of type *G*, it is often useful to use assignments of the form $a := b$ or tests of the form $a = b$ with the intent of obtaining value semantics if the actual generic parameter is expanded (as with *INTEGER*) and reference semantics if it is a reference type (as with *POINT*).

> An example of a routine which needs such dual behavior is a procedure for inserting an element *x* into a list. The procedure creates a new list cell; if *x* is an integer, the cell must contain a copy of that integer, but if *x* is a reference to an object the cell will contain a reference to the same object.

In such a case the rules defined above ensure the desired dual behavior, which would have been impossible to achieve if a different syntax had been required for the two kinds of semantics. If, on the other hand, you want a single identical behavior in all cases, you can specify it too: that behavior can only be value semantics (since reference semantics does not make sense for expanded types); so in the appropriate routines you should use not := and = but *clone* (or *copy*) and *equal*.

The form of clone and equality operations

A small point of style which may have surprised you is the form under which routines *clone* and *equal* are called. The notations

clone (*x*)

equal (*x*, *y*)

do not look very O-O at first; a dogmatic reading of the previous chapter would suggest conventions that seem more in line with what was there called "the object-oriented style of computation"; for example:

"THE OBJECT-ORI-ENTED STYLE OF COMPUTATION", 7.7, page 181.

x.*twin*

x.*is_equal* (*y*)

In a very early version of the notation, these were indeed the conventions. But they raise the problem of void references. A feature call of the form $x.f(...)$ cannot be executed correctly if, at run time, the value of x is void. (In that case the call will trigger an exception which, unless the class contains specific provisions to recover from the exception, will cause the execution of the entire system to terminate abnormally.) So the second set of conventions would only work for non-void x. Because in many cases x may indeed be void, this would mean that most uses of *twin* would in practice be of the form

if $x = Void$ **then**

    $z := Void$

else

    $z := x.twin$

end

and most uses of *is_equal* of the form

and then *is a variant of* **and**. *See "Non-strict boolean operators", page 454.*

if

    $((x = Void)$ **and** $(y = Void))$ **or**

    $((x /= Void)$ **and then** $x.is\_equal\ (y))$

then

    ...

Needless to say, these conventions were not kept for long. We quickly became tired of having to write such convoluted expressions — and even more of having to face the consequences (run-time errors) when we forgot. The conventions finally retained, described earlier in this chapter, have the pleasant property of giving the expected results for void x: in that case *clone* (x) is a void value, and *equal* (x, y) is true if and only if y is also void.

Procedure *copy*, called under the form $x.copy\ (y)$, raises no particular problem: it requires x (and also y) to be non-void, but this requirement is acceptable because it is a consequence of the semantics of *copy*, which copies an object onto another and so does not makes sense unless both objects exist. The condition on y, as explained in a later chapter, is captured by an official precondition on *copy* and so is present in a clear form in the documentation for this procedure.

It should be noted that a function *is_equal* as introduced above exists. The reason is that it is often convenient to define specific variants of equality, adapted to a class and overriding the default semantics of field-by-field comparison. To obtain this effect it suffices to redefine function *is_equal* in the desired classes. Function *equal* is defined in terms of *is_equal* (through the expression shown above to illustrate the use of *is_equal*), and so will follow its redefinitions.

See also "Fixed semantics for copy, clone and equality features", page 583.

In the case of *clone*, there is no need for *twin*. This is because *clone* is simply defined as a creation plus a call to *copy*. So to adapt the meaning of *clone* to the specific needs of a class it suffices to redefine procedure *copy* for that class; *clone* will automatically follow.

The status of universal operations

The last comments have partly lifted the veil on a question that have may caught your attention: what is the status of the universal operations *clone*, *copy*, *equal*, *is_equal*, *deep_clone*, *deep_equal*?

Although fundamental in practice, these operations are not language constructs. They come from a Kernel library class, *ANY*, which has the special property that every class written by a software developer automatically inherits (directly or indirectly) from *ANY*. This is why it is possible to redefine the features mentioned to support a particular view of equality or copying.

"THE GLOBAL INHERITANCE STRUCTURE", 16.2, page 580.

We need not concern ourselves with the details here, as they will be studied together with inheritance. But it is useful to know that, thanks to the inheritance mechanism, we can rely on library classes to provide facilities that are then made available to any class — and can be adapted by any class to suit its own specific purposes.

8.11 KEY CONCEPTS INTRODUCED IN THIS CHAPTER

- Object-oriented computation is characterized by a highly dynamic run-time structure, where objects are created on demand rather than pre-allocated.

- Some of the objects manipulated by the software are (usually quite indirect) models of outside objects. Others serve design and implementation purposes only.

- An object is made of a number of values called fields. Each field corresponds to an attribute of the object's generator (the class of which the object is a direct instance).

- A value, in particular a field of an object, is either an object or a reference.

- A reference is either void or attached to an object. The test $x = Void$ tells which of the two cases holds. A call with target x, such as $x.f$ (...), can only be executed correctly if x is non-void.

- If the declaration of a class begins with **class** C ..., an entity declared of type C will denote a reference, which may become attached to instances of C. If the declaration begins with **expanded class** D ..., an entity declared of type D will denote an object (an instance of D), and will never be void.

- The basic types (*BOOLEAN*, *CHARACTER*, *INTEGER*, *REAL*, *DOUBLE*) are defined by expanded classes.

- Expanded declarations also make it possible to define composite objects: objects with subobjects.

- Object structures may contain cyclic chains of references.

- The creation instruction !! x creates an object, initializes its field to default values (such as void for references and zero for numbers), and attaches x to it. If the class has defined creation procedures, The instruction will also perform, in the form !! $x.creatproc$ (...), any desired specific initializations.

- On entities of reference types, assignment (:=) and equality test (=) are reference operations. On entities of expanded types, they represent copy and field-by-field comparison. They also have the appropriate semantics for mixed operands.

- Reference operations cause dynamic aliasing, which makes it more difficult to reason formally about software. In practice, most non-trivial reference manipulations should be encapsulated in library classes.

8.12 BIBLIOGRAPHICAL NOTES

The notion of object identity plays an important role in databases, especially object-oriented databases. See chapter 31 and its bibliographical notes.

The graphical conventions of the BON method (Business Object Notation), designed by Jean-Marc Nerson and Kim Waldén, appear in [Waldén 1995]. James McKim and Richard Bielak expound the merits of multiple creation procedures in [Bielak 1994].

The risks caused by unfettered pointer or reference operations have worried software methodologists for a long time, prompting the inevitable suggestion that they are the data equivalent of what abhorred **goto** instructions represent on the control side. A surprisingly little-known article by Nori Suzuki [Suzuki 1982] explores whether a disciplined approach, using higher-level operations (in the same way that one avoids **goto** by sticking to the "structured programming" constructs of sequence, conditional and loop), could avoid the troubles of dynamic aliasing. Although the results are somewhat disappointing — by the author's own admission — the article is useful reading.

I am indebted to Ross Scaife from the University of Kentucky for help with rhetorical terms. See his page at *http://www.uky.edu/ArtsSciences/Classics/rhetoric.html*.

EXERCISES

E8.1 Books and authors

Starting from the various sketches given in this chapter, write classes *BOOK* and *WRITER* covering a useful view of books and their authors. Be sure to include the relevant routines (not just the attributes as in most of this chapter).

E8.2 Persons

Write a class *PERSON* covering a simple notion of person, with attributes *name* (a *STRING*), *mother*, *father* and *sibling* (describing the next older sibling if any). Include routines which will find (respectively) the list of names of ancestors, direct cousins, cousins direct or indirect, uncles or aunts, siblings-in-laws, parents-in-laws etc. of a given person. **Hint**: write recursive procedures (but make sure to avoid infinite recursion where the relations, for example direct or indirect cousin, are cyclic.).

E8.3 Notation design

Assume you are frequently using comparisons of the form *x•is_equal* (*y*) and want to simplify the notation to take advantage of infix features (applicable here since *is_equal* is a function with one argument). With an infix feature using some operator §, the call will be written *x* § *y*. This little exercise asks you to invent a symbol for §, compatible with the rules on infix operators. There are of course many possible answers, and deciding between them is partly (but only partly) a matter of taste.

See "Operator features", page 187 about infix features and permissible operators.

Hint: The symbol should be easy to remember and somehow suggest equality; but perhaps even more importantly it should be different enough from = to avoid mistakes. Here you can benefit from the study of C and C++ which, departing from mathematical tradition, use = for assignment rather than equality comparison, but for the latter operation introduce a similar-looking symbol, ==. The matter is made even more delicate by the rule that permits treating an assignment as an expression, whose value is the value being assigned to the target, and by the rule accepting values such as integers as boolean expressions, meaning true if non-zero, so that compilers will accept a text of the form

> **if** (*x* = *y*) **then** ...

although in most practical cases it is in error (mistakenly using = for ==), and will have the probably incorrect effect of assigning the value of *y* to *x*, returning true if and only if that value is non-zero.

9

Memory management

$\mathcal{F}$rankly, it would be nice to forget about memory.

Our programs would just create objects as they please. One after the other, unused objects would vanish into abysses, while those most needed would slowly move closer to the top, like meritorious employees of a large corporation who manage once in a while to catch the attention of a higher officer, and by making themselves indispensable to their immediate superiors will with a bit of luck, at the end of a busy career, be admitted into the inner circle.

But it is not so. Memory is not infinite; it does not harmoniously organize itself into a continuous spectrum of storage layers with decreasing access speeds, to which objects would naturally distribute. We do need to fire our useless employees, even if we must call it early retirement imposed with regret because of the overall economic situation. This chapter examines who should be thus downsized, how, and by whom.

9.1 WHAT HAPPENS TO OBJECTS

Object-oriented programs create objects. The previous chapter showed how useful it is to rely on dynamic creation to obtain flexible object structures, which automatically adapt to the needs of a system's execution in any particular case.

Object creation

We have seen the basic operation for allocating space to new objects. In its simplest form it appears as

> $!!\ x$

and its effect was defined as threefold: create a new object; attach it to the reference x; and initialize its fields.

A variant of the instruction calls an initialization procedure; and you can also create new objects through routines *clone* and *deep_clone*. Since all these forms of allocation internally rely on basic creation instructions, we can restrict our attention to the form $!!\ x$ without fear of losing generality.

We will now study the effect of such instructions on memory management.

Three modes of object management

First it is useful to broaden the scope of the discussion. The form of object management used for object-oriented computation is only one of three commonly found modes: **static**, **stack-based** and **free**. The choice between these modes determines how an entity can become attached to an object.

> Recall that an entity is a name in the software text representing a run-time value, or a succession of run-time values. Such values are either objects or (possibly void) references to objects. Entities include attributes, formal routine arguments, local entities of routines and *Result*. The term **attached** describes associations between entities and objects: at some stage during execution, an entity x is attached to an object O if the value of x is either O (for x of expanded type) or a reference to O (for x of reference type). If x is attached to O, it is sometimes convenient to say also that O is attached to x. But whereas a reference is attached to at most one object, an object may be attached to two or more references; this is the problem of dynamic aliasing, discussed in the previous chapter.

In the static mode, an entity may become attached to at most one run-time object during the entire execution of the software. This is the scheme promoted by languages such as Fortran, designed to allow an implementation technique which will allocate space for all objects (and attach them to the corresponding entities) once and for all, at program loading time or at the beginning of execution.

The static mode

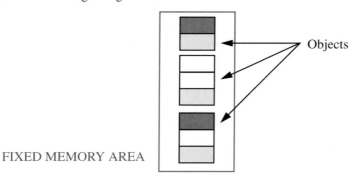

FIXED MEMORY AREA

The static mode is simple and supports efficient implementation on the usual computer architectures. But it presents serious limitations:

- It precludes recursion, since a recursive routine must be permitted to have several incarnations active at once, each with its own incarnations of the routine's entities.

- It also precludes dynamically created data structures, since the compiler must be able to deduce the exact size of every data structure from the software text. Each array, for example, must be statically declared with its exact size. This seriously limits the modeling power of the language: it is impossible to handle structures that grow and shrink in response to run-time events, except by allocating the maximum possible space for each of them — a technique that wastes memory, and is rather dangerous since just one data structure may cause the whole system execution to fail if its size has been underestimated.

The second scheme of object allocation is the stack-based mode. Here an entity may at run time become attached to several objects in succession, and the run-time mechanisms allocate and deallocate these objects in last-in, first-out order. When an object is deallocated, the corresponding entity becomes attached again to the object to which it was previously attached, if any.

The stack-based mode

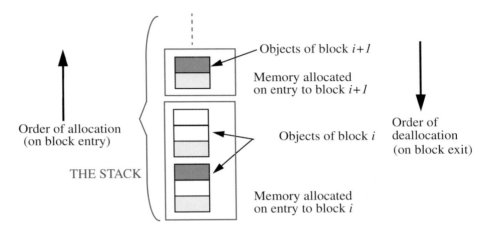

Order of allocation (on block entry)

THE STACK

Objects of block $i+1$

Memory allocated on entry to block $i+1$

Objects of block i

Order of deallocation (on block exit)

Memory allocated on entry to block i

Dynamic arrays can be created in C through the malloc function, a mechanism of the "free" kind, the mode studied next; some Pascal extensions support dynamic arrays.

Stack-based object management was made popular by Algol 60 and is supported (often in conjunction with one or both of the other two modes) in most posterior programming languages. Stack-based allocation supports recursion and, if the language permits it, arrays whose bounds only become known at run time. In Pascal and C, however, the mechanism only applies to variables of basic types and record types — not to arrays as it did in Algol. In practice the data structures that developers would most often want to allocate in this fashion are precisely arrays. Even when it applies to arrays, stack-based allocation still does not support complex data structures in their full generality.

To obtain such general data structures, we need the third and last scheme: the free mode, also called heap-based because of the way it is implemented. This is the fully dynamic mode in which objects are created dynamically through explicit requests. An entity may become successively attached to any number of objects; the pattern of object creations is usually not predictable at compile time. Objects may, furthermore, contain references to other objects.

The free (heap-based) mode

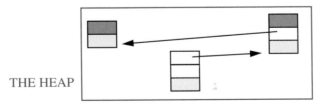

THE HEAP

The free mode allows us to create the sophisticated dynamic data structures which we will need if, as discussed in the previous chapter, we are to take our software systems to their full modeling power.

Using the free mode

The free mode is clearly the most general, and is required for object-oriented computation. Many non-O-O languages use it too. In particular:

- Pascal uses the static mode for arrays, the stack-based mode for variables of type other than array or pointer, and the free mode for pointer variables. In the last case object creation is achieved by a call to a special creation procedure, *new*.

- C is similar to Pascal but in addition offers static non-array variables and free arrays. Dynamic allocation of pointer variables and arrays relies on a library function, *malloc*.

- PL/I supports all modes.

- Lisp systems have traditionally been highly dynamic, relying for the most part on the free mode. One of the most important Lisp operations, used repeatedly to construct lists, is *CONS*, which creates a two-field cell, ready to serve as a list element with the element's value in the first field and a pointer to the next element in the second field. Here *CONS*, rather than explicit creation instructions, will be the principal source of new objects

Space reclamation in the three modes

The ability to create objects dynamically, as in the stack-based and free modes, raises the question of what to do when an object becomes unused: is it possible to reclaim its memory space, so as to use it again for one or more new objects in later creation instructions?

In the static mode, the problem does not exist: for every object, there is exactly one attached entity; execution needs to retain the object's space as long as the entity is active. So there is no possibility for reclamation in the proper sense. A related technique is, however, sometimes used. If you are convinced that the objects attached to two entities will never be needed at the same time, if these entities need not retain their values between successive uses, and if space efficiency is a critical problem, you can assign the same memory location to two or more entities — if you are really sure of what you are doing. This technique, known as **overlay** is still, appallingly enough, practiced manually.

> If used at all, overlay should clearly be handled by automatic software tools, as the potential for errors is too high when programmers control the process themselves. Once again a major problem is change: a decision to overlay two variables may be correct at a certain stage of the program's evolution, but an unexpected change may suddenly make it invalid. We will encounter similar problems below, in a more modern context, with garbage collection.

With the stack-based mode, the objects attached to an entity may be allocated on a stack. Block-structured language make things particularly simple: object allocation occurs at the same time for all entities declared in a given block, allowing the use of a single stack for a whole program. The scheme is elegant indeed, as it just involves two sets of concomitant events:

Allocation and deallocation in a block-structured language

Dynamic Property (event at execution time)	Static Property (location in the software text)	Implementation Technique
Object allocation	Block entry.	Push objects (one for each of the entities local to the block) onto stack.
Object deallocation	Block exit.	Pop stack.

The simplicity and efficiency of this implementation technique are part of the reason why block-structured languages have been so successful.

With the free mode, things cease to be so simple. The problem comes from the very power of the mechanism: since the pattern of object creation is unknown at compile time, it is not possible to predict when a given object may become useless.

Detachment

Objects may indeed, in the free mode, become useless to the software at unpredictable times during execution, so that some mechanism (to be determined later in this discussion) may reclaim the memory they occupy.

The reason is the presence in our execution mode of operations performing what may be called **detachment** — the reverse of attachment. The previous chapter studied at length how entities can become attached to objects, but did not examine in any detail the consequences of detachments. Now is the time to correct this.

Detachment only affects entities x of reference types. If x is of expanded type, the value of x is an object O, and there is no way to detach x from O. Note, however, that if x is an expanded attribute of some class, O represents a subobject of some bigger object BO; then BO, and with it O, may become unreachable for any of the reasons studied below. So for the rest of this chapter we may confine our attention to entities of reference types.

Detachment

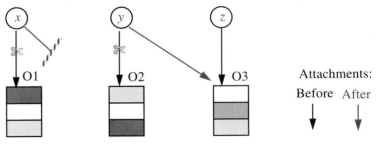

The principal causes of detachment are the following, assuming x and y, entities of reference type, were initially attached to objects O1 and O2. The figure illustrates cases D1 and D2.

D1 • An assignment of the form $x := Void$, or $x := v$ where v is void, detaches x from O1.

D2 • An assignment of the form $y := z$, where z is attached to an object other than O2, detaches y from *O2*.

D3 • Termination of a routine detaches formal arguments from any attached objects.

D4 • A creation instruction !! x, attaches x to a newly created object, and hence detaches x if it was previously attached to an object O1.

Case D3 corresponds to the rule given earlier that the semantics of an assignment $a := b$ is exactly the same as that of initializing a formal argument a of a routine r at the time of a call $t.r (..., b, ...)$, where the position of b in the call corresponds to that of a in the declaration of r.

Unreachable objects

Does detachment mean that the detached object — O1 or O2 on the preceding figure — becomes useless and hence that the runtime mechanisms can reclaim the memory space it occupies, then recycle it for other objects? That would be too easy! The entity for which an object was initially created may have lost all interest in it, but because of dynamic aliasing other references may still be attached to it. For example the last figure may have shown only a partial view of attachments; looking at a broader context might reveal that O1 and O2 are still reachable from other objects:

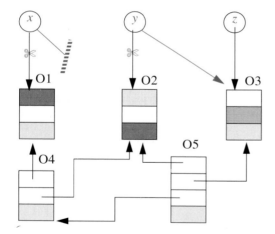

Detachment is not always death

But this is still not the entire object structure. By getting even more context, we might now discover that O4 and O5 are themselves useless, so that in the absence of other references O1 and O2 are not needed after all.

So the answer to the question "what objects can we reclaim?" must follow from a global analysis of the entire set of objects created so far. We can identify three kinds of object:

C1 • Objects directly attached to entities of the software text, known (from the language rules) to be needed.

C2 • Dependents of objects of category C1. (Recall that the direct dependents of an object are those to which it has references; here we are considering both direct and indirect dependents.)

C3 • Objects which are in neither of the preceding two categories.

The objects of category C1 may be called the **origins**. Together with those of category C2, the origins make up the set of **reachable** objects. Those of category C3 are **unreachable**. They correspond to what was informally called "useless objects" above. A more lively if somewhat macabre terminology uses the term "dead objects" for C3, the origins and their dependents being then called "live objects". (Computing scientists, however, have not quite managed to reconcile their various metaphors, as the process of reclaiming dead objects, studied below, is called "garbage collection".)

> The term "root" is also used for "origin". But here the latter is preferable because an O-O system also has a "root object" and a root class. The resulting ambiguity would not be too damaging since the root object, as seen below, is indeed one of the origins.

The first step towards addressing the problem of memory management under the free mode is to separate the reachable objects from the unreachable ones. To identify reachable objects, we must start from the origins and repeatedly follow all references. So the first question is to identify the origins; the answer depends on the run-time structure defined by the underlying language.

Reachable objects in classical approaches

Because the unreachability problem is already present in the run-time structure of such classical approaches as Pascal, C and Ada, it is interesting to start with this case. (More accurately, this is interesting for the reader who is familiar with one of these approaches. If you are not in this category, you may prefer to skip this section and go directly to the next one, which moves right on to the run-time structure of O-O software.)

The approaches quoted combine the stack-based and free modes of allocation. C and Ada also support the static mode, but to keep things simple we may ignore static allocation by viewing it as a special case of stack-based allocation: we treat static objects as if they were allocated once and for all, when execution starts, at the bottom of the stack. (This is indeed the way Pascal developers emulate static entities: they declare them in the outermost block.)

Another common property of these approaches is that entities may denote pointers. To provide a better preparation for the object-oriented approach of this book, where instead of pointers we use references (a more abstract notion, as discussed in the previous chapter), let us pretend that the pointers in question are actually references. This means in particular that we disregard the weakly typed nature of pointers in C.

With these assumptions and simplifications the origins, shown with thick borders on the following figure, are all the objects which are either allocated on the stack or attached to references allocated on the stack. The reachable objects (including the origins) appear in color, the unreachable objects in black.

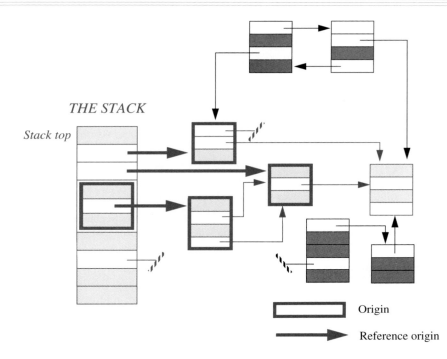

THE STACK

Stack top

Origin

Reference origin

Live objects (in color) and dead objects (in black) in a combined stack-based and free model

Because the unreachability problem only arises for objects allocated under the free mode, and such objects are always attached to entities of reference types, it is convenient to ignore the reclamation problem for objects allocated on the stack (which can be handled simply by popping the stack at the time of block exit) and to start from the references coming from the stack. We may call these references **reference origins**. They are shown with thick arrows in the figure. A reference origin is either:

O1 • The value of a local entity or routine argument of reference type (as with the top two reference origins in the figure).

O2 • A field of reference type, in an object allocated on the stack (as with the lowest reference origin in the figure).

As an example, consider the following type and procedure declarations, written in a syntax half-way between Pascal and the notation of the rest of this book (an entity of type **reference** G is a reference that may become attached to objects of type G):

type
    COMPOSITE =
        record
            m: *INTEGER*
            r: **reference** *COMPOSITE*
        end
    ...

procedure p **is**

   local

       n: *INTEGER*

       c: *COMPOSITE*

       s: **reference** *COMPOSITE*

  do

      …

  end

Every execution of p allocates three values on the stack:

Entity allocation for a procedure

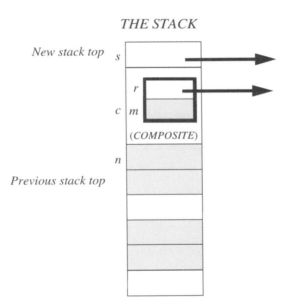

The three new values are an integer n, which does not affect the problem of object management (since it will disappear when the procedure terminates, and does not refer to any other object); a reference s, which is an example of category O1; and an object c of type *COMPOSITE*. This object is itself stack-based and its allocated memory may be reclaimed on procedure termination; but it contains a reference field for r, which is an example of category O2.

In summary, to determine the reachable objects in a classical approach combining the stack-based and free modes, you can start from the references on the stack (variables of reference types, and reference fields of composite objects), and repeatedly follow all reference fields of the attached objects if any.

Reachable objects in the object-oriented model

The object-oriented run-time structure presented in the preceding chapter has a few differences from the one just discussed.

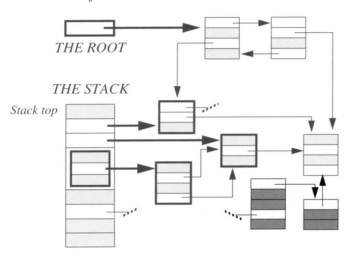

Reachability
in the object-
oriented model

The execution of any system starts with the creation of one object, called the root object of the system, or just its root (when there is no confusion with the root class, a static notion). Clearly, the root is one of the origins in this case.

Another set of origins arises because of the possible presence of local entities in a routine. Assume a routine of the form

> *some_routine* **is**
> > **local**
> > > *rb1, rb2: BOOK3*
> > > *eb*: **expanded** *BOOK3*
> > **do**
> > > ...
> > > *!! rb1*
> > > ... Operations possibly involving *rb1*, *rb2* and *eb* ...
> > **end**

Whenever a call to *some_routine* is executed, and for the duration of that execution, the instructions in the routine's body may refer to *rb1*, *rb2* and *eb*, and hence to the attached objects if any. (For *eb* there is always an attached object, but at various points *rb1* and *rb2* may be void.) This means that such objects must be part of the reachable set, even though they are not necessarily dependents of the root.

Local entities of reference types, such as *rb1* and *rb2*, are similar to the local routine variables which, in the previous model, were allocated on the stack. Local entities of expanded types, such as *eb*, are similar to the stack-based objects.

When a call to *some_routine* terminates, the current incarnations of entities *rb1*, *rb2* and *eb* disappear. As a result, any attached objects cease to be part of the origin set. This does not necessarily mean that they become unreachable, as they may in the meantime have become dependents of the root object or other origins.

Assume for example that *a* is an attribute of the enclosing class and that the whole text of the routine is:

> *some_routine* **is**
> > **local**
> > > *rb1*, *rb2*: *BOOK3*
> > > *eb*: **expanded** *BOOK3*
> > **do**
> > > !! *rb1*; !! *rb2*
> > > *a* := *rb1*
> > **end**

The following figure shows in color the objects that a call to *some_routine* will create and the references that it will reattach.

Objects attached to local entities

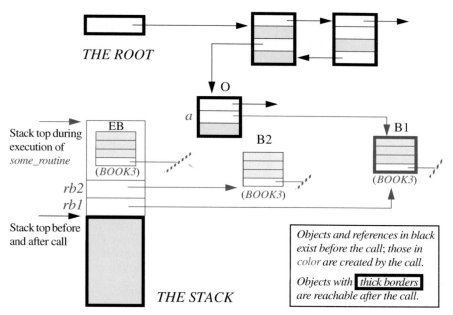

When a call to *some_routine* terminates, the object O that served as target of the call is still reachable (otherwise there would have been no call!). The *a* field of O is now attached to the *BOOK3* object B1 created by the first creation instruction (the one of target *rb1*), which, then, remains reachable. In contrast, the objects B2 and EB that were attached to *rb2* and *eb* during the call now become unreachable: with the routine text as given there is no possibility that any of the other objects of the system, reachable or not, could "remember" B2 or EB.

The memory management problem in the object-oriented model

We may summarize the preceding analysis by defining the origins, and hence of the reachable objects, in the object-oriented framework:

Definition: origins, reachable and unreachable objects

At any point during the execution of a system, the set of **origins** is made of the following objects:

- The system's root object.

- Any object attached to a local entity or formal argument of a routine currently being executed (including the local entity *Result* for a function).

Any dependent, direct or indirect, of these origins is **reachable**. Any other object is unreachable; it is possible to reclaim the memory it occupies (for example to recycle it for other objects) without affecting the correct semantics of the system's execution.

The problem of memory management arises from the unpredictability of the operations which affect the set of reachable objects: creation and detachment. Because these operations are instructions, appearing as part of a system's control structures, there is usually no way to determine with certainty, from a mere examination of the software text, the pattern of object creation and detachment at run time.

More precisely, such a prediction is possible in some cases, for data structures managed in a strictly controlled way. An example is the *LINKED_LIST* library class studied in a later chapter, with the associated class *LINKABLE* which describes linked list elements. Instances of *LINKABLE* are only created through specific procedures of *LINKED_LIST*, and can only become unreachable as a result of executing the *remove* procedure of that class. For such classes one might envision specific reclamation procedures. (This approach will be explored later in this chapter.)

About linked lists see "Linked list representation", page 774, and subsequent sections.

But such examples, although important, are only special cases. In the most general case we must face a difficult question: what do we do about unreachable objects?

The three answers

Three general attitudes are possible as to objects that become unreachable:

- Ignore the problem and hope that there will be enough memory to accommodate all objects, reachable or not. This may be called the **casual approach**.

- Ask developers to include in every application an algorithm that looks for unreachable objects, and give them mechanisms to free the corresponding memory. This approach is called **manual reclamation**.

• Include in the development environment (as part of the so-called runtime system) automatic mechanisms that will detect and reclaim unreachable objects. This is called **automatic garbage collection**.

The rest of this chapter discusses these approaches.

9.2 THE CASUAL APPROACH

The first approach consists in forgetting about the problem: abandon dead objects to their fate. Execute creation instructions as needed, and do not worry about what may later happen to those objects that have thus been allocated.

Can the casual approach be justified?

One case in which the casual approach presents no particular problem is that of systems that do not create many objects, such as small-scale tests or experiments.

More interesting is the case of systems that may in fact create many objects, but in such a way that it is possible to guarantee that none or very few of them become unreachable. As with the static allocation scheme, no objects are ever retired; the difference is that creation occurs at execution time.

This case provides a good justification for the casual approach, as there is no need for reclamation. The number of objects created may still be too big for the available memory, but no reclamation policy would alleviate the problem if there is nothing to reclaim.

Some real-time programs follow this scheme: for efficiency reasons, they create all needed objects statically or at initialization time, avoiding any non-predictable patterns of dynamic object creation.

This method has its advocates, who usually are involved in the construction of "hard-real-time" systems demanding guaranteed sub-millisecond response times to external events (such as a missile detection), and who as a consequence insist that the time to execute every operation must be fully predictable. But then memory management is only a small part of what we must give up: predictability requires the absence of any kind of object allocation (creation instruction, *malloc*, recursion, possibly any call of a routine with local entities) after initialization; and it assumes a dedicated, single-user, single-processing machine, with no preemptive operating system call and in fact no operating system in the usual sense of the term. In such environments people sometimes choose to program in assembly language, as they fear the additional unpredictability of compiler-generated code. All this, of course, restricts the discussion to a tiny (although strategic) part of the software development world.

Do we care about memory any more?

Another argument sometimes heard to justify the casual approach is the increasing availability of large memory spaces, and the decreasing cost of memory.

The memory involved may be virtual as well as real. On a virtual memory system, both primary and secondary memory are divided into blocks called pages; when primary memory is needed, blocks of primary memory that have not been frequently used are moved to secondary memory ("paged out"). If such a system is used to run object-oriented systems, pages that contain reachable objects will tend to be paged out and leave main memory space to frequently used ones.

If we indeed had almost infinite amounts of almost free memory, we could satisfy ourselves (as suggested at the very beginning of this chapter) with the casual approach. Unfortunately this is not the case.

One reason is that in practice virtual memory is not really equivalent to real memory. If you store large numbers of objects in virtual memory, where a minority of reachable objects are interspersed with a majority of unreachable ones, the system's execution will constantly cause pages to be moved in and out, a phenomenon known as **thrashing** which leads to dramatic degradation of time performance. Indeed, virtual memory systems make it harder to separate the space and time aspects of efficiency.

But there is a more serious limitation to the casual approach. Even systems with a large memory have limits; it is always surprising to see how quickly programmers will reach them. And as was pointed out in the more general discussion of efficiency, hardware advances — in time or in space — should be put to good use. Larger memories are bought to be used, not wasted. *See "Efficiency", page 9.*

As soon as you move beyond the case discussed above in which it is possible to prove that only a small number of objects will become unreachable, you will have to face the reclamation problem.

A byte here, a byte there, and soon we will be talking real corpses

It is time to lend our ears to the sad and edifying story of the London Ambulance Service.

The London Ambulance Service, said to be the largest in the world, serves an area of about 1500 square kilometers, a resident population of almost seven million people and an even larger daytime population. Every day it handles over five thousand patients and receives between two and three thousand calls. *For the source of this information and of the quotes which follow, see the bibliographic notes, page 315.*

As you may have guessed from the somber tone of this introduction, computers (and more to the point computer software) got involved at some stage. At more than one stage, in fact: several attempted systems were discarded as inadequate without being ever put into actual use, the latest in 1991, having burned seven and half million pounds. Then in 1992 a new system, developed at a cost of a million pounds, was put into operation. It soon made headlines again; on October 28 and 29, television and press reports were announcing that twenty lives had been lost because of the system's inadequacy; in one particular case an ambulance crew is said to have radioed base on reaching the location of their call, to ask why the undertaker had got there first. The Service's chief executive resigned and an inquiry commission was appointed.

The Service did not immediately scrap the computerized system but switched to a hybrid mode — partly manual, partly relying on the system. According to the official report:

> *This [hybrid] system operated with reasonable success from the afternoon of 27 October 1992 up to the early hours of 4 November. However, shortly after 2AM on 4 November the system slowed significantly and, shortly after this, locked up altogether. Attempts were made to re-boot (switch off and restart workstations) in the manner that staff had previously been instructed by XX to do in these circumstances. This re-booting failed to overcome the problem with the result that calls in the system could not be printed out and mobilizations via [the system] from incident summaries could not take place. Management and staff [...] reverted fully to a manual, paper-based system with voice or telephone mobilization.*

What caused the system to fail in such a dismal way that it could not be kept even as an adjunct to a manual operation? The inquiry report identifies several reasons, but here is the clincher:

> *The Inquiry Team has concluded that the system crash was caused by a minor programming error.*
>
> *In carrying out some work on the system some three weeks previously the XX programmer had inadvertently left in the system a piece of program code that caused a small amount of memory within the file server to be used up and not released every time a vehicle mobilization was generated by the system.*
>
> *Over a three week period these activities had gradually used up all available memory thus causing the system to crash. This programming error should not have occurred and was caused by carelessness and lack of quality assurance of program code changes. Given the nature of the fault it is unlikely that it would have been detected through conventional programmer or user testing.*

The reader will be the judge of how accurate it is to call the programming error "minor", especially in view of the crucial last comments (that the error would have been hard to find through testing), which will be discussed again below.

For anyone wondering whether the casual approach may be good enough, and more generally for anyone who may be tempted to dismiss memory management as "just an implementation issue", the twenty victims of the London Ambulance Service will serve as a sobering reminder of the seriousness of the problems covered by this chapter.

9.3 RECLAIMING MEMORY: THE ISSUES

If we go beyond the casual approach and its simplistic assumptions, we must find how and when to reclaim memory. This in fact involves two issues:

- How we will find out about dead elements (**detection**).

- How the associated memory is actually reclaimed (**reclamation**).

For each of these tasks, we may look for a solution at any one of two possible levels:

- The language implementation level — compiler and runtime system, providing the support common to all software written in a certain language in a certain computing environment.

- The application level — application programs, intended to solve specific problems.

In the first case the selected memory management functions will be handled automatically by the hardware-software machine. In the second case, each application developer has to take care of these functions on his own.

There is in fact a third possible level, in-between these two: working at the **component manufacturing** level, that is to say handling memory management functions in the general-purpose reusable library classes in an object-oriented environment. As at the application level, you can only use the programming language's official mechanisms (rather than enjoying direct access to hardware and operating system facilities); but as at the language implementation level, you can address the memory management problem, or part of it, once and for all for all applications.

Given two tasks and three possibilities for each, we are in principle faced with nine possibilities. Actually, only four or so make sense. We will review those which are actually available in existing systems.

9.4 PROGRAMMER-CONTROLLED DEALLOCATION

One popular solution is to provide a reclamation facility at the implementation level, while passing on the detection problem to software developers.

This is certainly the easiest solution for language implementers: all they have to do is to provide a primitive, say *reclaim*, such that *a . reclaim* tells the runtime system that the object attached to *a* is no longer needed and the corresponding memory cells may be recycled for new objects.

This is the solution adopted by such non object-oriented languages as Pascal (*dispose* procedure), C (*free*), PL/I (*FREE*), Modula-2 and Ada; you will also find it in most of the "hybrid object-oriented languages", in particular C++ and Objective-C.

This solution is favored by many programmers, especially in the C world, who like to feel in full control of what happens. As a typical reaction here is a Usenet message, posted on the *comp.lang.objective-c* discussion group in response to a suggestion that Objective-C could benefit from automatic reclamation:

> *I say a big NO! Leaving an unreferenced object around is BAD PROGRAMMING. Object pointers ARE like ordinary pointers — if you [allocate an object] you should be responsible for it, and free it when its finished with (didn't your mother always tell you to put your toys away when you'd finished with them?).*

Posting by Ian Stephenson, 11 May 1993.

For serious software development this attitude is not defensible. Grown-up developers must be prepared let someone else play with their "toys" for two reasons: reliability and ease of development.

The reliability issue

Assume developers are in control of deallocating objects with a *reclaim* mechanism. The possibility of an erroneous *reclaim* is always lurking, especially in the presence of complex data structures. In particular, as the software evolves, a *reclaim* that used to be justified may become incorrect.

Such a mistake causes what is known as the *dangling reference* problem: the case in which an object keeps, in one of its fields, a reference to another object which has been reclaimed. If the system then tries to use the reference after that object's memory area has been recycled to hold wholly unrelated information, the result will usually be a run-time crash or (worse yet) erroneous and erratic behavior.

This type of error is known to be the source of some of the most common and nasty bugs in the practice of C and derived languages. Programmers in these languages particularly fear such bugs because of the difficulty of tracing down their source, a difficulty that is easy to understand: if the programmer forgot to note that a certain reference was still attached to an object, and as a result wrongly issued a *reclaim* on the object, it is often because the missed reference came from a completely different part of the software. If so there will be a great conceptual and physical distance between the error (the wrong *reclaim*) and its manifestation (a crash or other abnormal behavior due to an attempt to follow an incorrect reference); the latter may occur long after the former, and in a seemingly unrelated part of the system. In addition the bug may be hard to reproduce if the operating system does not always allocate memory in the same way.

Dismissing the issue, as in the Usenet message reproduced above, by claiming that only "BAD PROGRAMMING" leads to such situations, does nothing to help. To err is human; to err when programming a computer is inevitable. Even in a moderately complex application, no developer can be trusted, or trust himself, to keep track of all run-time objects. This is a task for computers, not people.

Many a C or C++ programmer has spent many a night trying to figure out what in the world could have happened to one of his "toys". It is not rare to see a project repeatedly delayed by such mysterious memory bugs.

The ease of development issue

Even if we were able to avoid erroneous *reclaim* calls, the question remains of how realistic it would be to ask developers to handle object reclamation. The snag is that, assuming you have positively identified an object that is up for reclamation, just releasing that object is usually not sufficient, as it may itself contain references to other objects.

This figure originally appeared on page 226. dispose, as noted, is the name of the Pascal procedure for what is called reclaim in this discussion.

Take the structure shown by the figure at the top of the next page, the same one used in the previous chapter to describe the dynamic nature of object structures. Assume you have correctly deduced that you may reclaim the top object. Then in the absence of any other references you may also reclaim the other two objects, which it references directly in one case and indirectly in the other. Not only may you reclaim them, you *should* do so: how good would it be to reclaim only part of a structure? In Pascal terminology this is sometimes called the **recursive dispose** problem: if the reclaim operations are to make any sense, they must recursively apply to a whole data structure, not just to an individual object. But of course you need to make sure that no references remain to the other objects from the outside. This is an arduous and error-prone task.

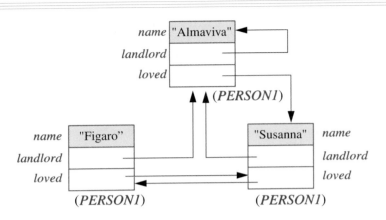

In this figure all the objects are of the same type. Consider now an entity *x* attached to an object O of type *MY_TYPE*, with the class declaration

class *MY_TYPE* **feature**
    attr1: *TYPE_1*
    attr2: *TYPE_2*
end

Every object of type *MY_TYPE*, such as O, contains references which (unless void) are attached to objects of types *TYPE_1* and *TYPE_2*. Reclaiming O may imply that these two objects should also be reclaimed, as well as any of their own direct or indirect dependents. Implementing the recursive dispose in this case means writing a set of reclamation procedures, one for each type of objects that may contain references to other objects. The result will be a set of mutually recursive procedures of great complication.

All this leads to disaster. It is indeed not uncommon, in languages that do not support automatic garbage collection, to see a large part of the text of an "application" system, and a large part of the development effort, being devoted to memory management. Such a situation is unacceptable. As an application developer, you should be able to concentrate on your job — solving application problems —, not become a bookkeeper or garbage collector (whichever metaphor is more appropriate).

Needless to say, the increased software complexity resulting from manual memory management results in decreased quality. In particular, it hampers readability and such other properties as ease of error detection and ease of modification. The resulting complexity further compounds the problem highlighted in the previous section — reliability. The more complex a system, the more likely it is to contain errors. The sword of Damocles of a possible erroneous *reclaim* is always hanging over your head, likely to fall at the worst possible time: when the system goes from testing to production and, as a result, starts creating bigger and more intricate object structures.

The conclusion is clear. Except in tightly controlled situations (as discussed in the next section), manual memory management is not appropriate for serious software development — at least if there is any concern for quality.

9.5 THE COMPONENT-LEVEL APPROACH

The next section is "AUTOMATIC MEMORY MANAGEMENT", 9.6, page 301.

(This section describes a solution useful in a specific case only; you may skip it on first reading.)

Before we move on to more ambitious schemes such as automatic garbage collection, it is interesting to look at a solution which may be described as a responsible alternative to the previous one, avoiding some of its drawbacks.

This solution is only applicable within an object-oriented, bottom-up approach to software design, where data structures are not developed "on the spot" as programs need them, but built as reusable classes: general-purpose implementations of abstract data types, with all the associated operations — features.

What sets the object-oriented approach apart with respect to memory management? Part of the novelty, rather than technical, is organizational: with the method's emphasis on reuse of libraries, there now stands between the application developers and the implementers of the base technology (compiler and development tools), a third group of people responsible for writing reusable components that implement the main data structures. Its members — who may of course participate at times in the other two activities — may be called the **component manufacturers**.

The component manufacturers have total control over all uses of a given class, and so are in a better position to find an acceptable solution to the memory management problem for all instances of that class.

If the pattern of allocation and deallocation for the class is simple enough, the component manufacturers may be able to find an efficient solution which does not even require the underlying runtime system to provide a specific *reclaim* routine; they can express everything in terms of higher-level concepts. This may be called the component-level approach.

Managing space for a linked list

See illustrations of linked lists and LINKABLE objects on the next page.

Here is an example of the component-level approach. Consider a class *LINKED_LIST*, describing lists that consist of a header and any number of linked cells, themselves instances of a class *LINKABLE*. The allocation and deallocation pattern for linked lists is simple. The objects of concern are the "linkable" cells. In this example, the component manufacturers (the people responsible for classes *LINKED_LIST* and *LINKABLE*) know exactly how linkables are created — by the insertion procedures — and how linkables may become dead — as a result of the deletion procedures. So they can manage the corresponding space in a specific way.

Let us assume that *LINKED_LIST* has only two insertion procedures, *put_right* and *put_left*, which insert a new element at the left and right of the current cursor position. Each will need to create exactly one new *LINKABLE* object; they are the basic source of allocation due to *LINKED_LIST*. A typical implementation is:

put_right (*v*: *ELEMENT_TYPE*) **is**

      -- Insert an element of value *v* to the right of cursor position.

  require

       . . .

  local

      new: *LINKABLE*

  do

      !! *new*.*make* (*v*)

      active. *put_linkable_right* (*new*)

      . . . Instructions to update other links . . .

  end

The creation instruction !! *new*.*make* (*v*) directs the language implementation level to allocate memory for a new object.

In the same way that we control where objects are created, we know exactly where they can become unreachable: through one of the deletion procedures. Let us assume three such procedures *remove*, *remove_right*, *remove_left*; there may also be others such as *remove_all_occurrences* (which removes all occurrences of a certain value) and *wipe_out* (which remove all elements), but we may assume that they internally rely on the first three, each of which makes exactly one *LINKABLE* unreachable. Procedure *remove*, for example, may have the following form:

remove **is**

      -- Delete element at cursor position.

  do

      . . .

      previous. *put_linkable_right* (*next*)

      . . . Instructions to update other links . . .

      active := *next*

  end

These deletion procedures provide the exact context for detecting unreachable objects and, if desired, putting them aside for later reuse. In the absence of any automatic scheme for releasing memory, the component manufacturer may safely conserve memory, by avoiding the allocation requested by an insertion when previous deletions have created unreachable *LINKABLE* objects and stored them somewhere for later reuse.

Assume we keep these instances of *LINKABLE* in a data structure called *available*; we will see below how to represent it. Then we may replace the creation instructions such as !! *new*.*make* (*v*) in *put_right* and *put_left* by

  new := *fresh* (*v*)

where *fresh* is a new secret function of *LINKED_LIST*, which will return a ready-for-use linkable. Function *fresh* will attempt to obtain its result from the *available* list, and will only perform a creation if the list is empty.

Elements will be fed into *available* by the deletion procedures. For example, the body of *remove* should now be of the form

do

    recycle (*active*)

        -- The rest as before:

        ... Instructions to update links: *previous, next, first_element, active* ...

where *recycle*, a new procedure of *LINKED_LIST*, plays the opposite role of *fresh*: adding its argument to the list of available objects. This procedure will be secret (not exported to any client) since it is for internal use only.

Dealing with recycled objects

To implement *fresh* and *recycle*, we may, among other possible choices, represent *available* as a stack: *fresh* will pop from and *recycle* will push onto the stack. Let us introduce a class *STACK_OF_LINKABLES* for the occasion and add the following secret features to *LINKED_LIST*:

available: *STACK_OF_LINKABLES*

Exercise E23.1, page 807 (based on later methodological discussions), asks you to discuss whether it is proper for function fresh to produce a side effect.

fresh (*v*: *ELEMENT_TYPE*): *LINKABLE* **is**

    -- A new element with value *v*, for reuse in an insertion

do

    if *available.empty* **then**

        -- No choice but to perform an actual allocation

    !! *Result.make* (*v*)

    else

        -- Reuse previously discarded linkable

        Result := *available.item*; *Result.put* (*v*); *available.remove*

    end

end

recycle (*dead*: *LINKABLE*) **is**

    -- Return *dead* to the available list.

require

    dead /= *Void*

do

    available.put (*dead*)

end

We may declare class *STACK_OF_LINKABLES* as follows:

class
  STACK_OF_LINKABLES
feature {*LINKED_LIST*}
  item: *LINKABLE*
        -- Element at top
  empty: *BOOLEAN* **is**
              -- Is there no item?
     do
              Result := (*item* = *Void*)
     end
  put (*element*: *LINKABLE*) **is**
              -- Add *element* on top.
     require
                element /= *Void*
     do
                element.*put_right* (*item*); *item* := *element*
     end
  remove **is**
              -- Remove last item added.
     require
                not *empty*
     do
                item := *item*.*right*
     end
end

The stack representation, as pictured, takes advantage of the *right* field already present in every *LINKABLE* to link all recycled elements without using any extra space. *LINKABLE* must export *right* and *put_right* to *STACK_OF_LINKABLES* as well as *LINKED_LIST*.

Feature *available*, as declared, is an attribute of the class. This means that each linked list will have its own stack of linkables. It is of course a better use of space, if a given system contains several lists, to share the pool of recycled linkables over the whole system. The technique to do this, *once functions*, will be introduced later; making *available* a once function means that only one instance of the class will exist throughout a given system execution, achieving the desired goal.

Exercise E9.3, page 316, and E9.4. On once functions see "CONSTANTS OF CLASS TYPES", 18.3, page 646.

Discussion

This example shows what the component-level approach can do to alleviate the problem of space reclamation by treating it at the component manufacturing level. It assumes that the underlying language implementation does not offer the automatic mechanisms described in the next sections; rather than burdening application programs with memory management problems, with all the risks discussed earlier, the solution presented assigns both detection and reclamation to the basic reusable classes.

The drawbacks and benefits are clear. Problems of manual memory management (reliability risks, tediousness) do not magically vanish; coming up with a foolproof memory management scheme for a particular data structure, as done above for linked lists, is hard. But instead of letting each application developer cope with the issue, we assign this job to component manufacturers; it should fit well in their general task of chiseling out high-quality reusable components. The extra effort is justified by the benefits of having good components available for frequent use by many different applications.

The component-level approach assumes a data structure whose patterns of creation and obsolescence are simple and perfectly understood. This covers only certain cases; for many structures the pattern is unpredictable or too complicated. When the approach is applicable, it provides a better solution, when the underlying language system does not offer automatic memory management, than letting each application developer try to handle the problem manually, or not handle it at all.

9.6 AUTOMATIC MEMORY MANAGEMENT

None of the approaches seen so far is fully satisfactory. A general solution to the problem of memory management for objects involves doing a serious job at the language implementation level.

The need for automatic techniques

A good O-O environment should offer an automatic memory management mechanism which will detect and reclaim unreachable objects, allowing application developers to concentrate on their job — application development.

The preceding discussion should suffice to show how important it is to have such a facility available. In the words of Michael Schweitzer and Lambert Strether:

From [Schweitzer 1991], *page 57.*

> *An object-oriented program without automatic memory management is roughly the same as a pressure cooker without a safety valve: sooner or later the thing is sure to blow up*!

Many development environments advertized as O-O still do not support such mechanisms. They may have other features which make them attractive at first; and indeed they may work nicely on small systems. But for serious development you run the risk that they will let you down as soon as the application reaches real size. To summarize in the form of concrete advice:

> In choosing an O-O environment — or just an O-O language compiler — for production development, restrict your attention to solutions that offer automatic memory management.

Two major approaches are applicable to automatic memory management: reference counting and garbage collection. They are both worth examining, although the second one is by far the more powerful and generally applicable.

What exactly is reclamation?

One technical point before we look at reference counting and garbage collection. With any form of automatic storage management, the question arises of what it concretely means for the mechanism to "reclaim" an object which it has detected as being unreachable. Two interpretations are possible:

- The mechanism may add the object's memory to a "free cell list" which it constantly maintains, in line with the techniques used by the earlier component-level scheme. A subsequent creation instruction (!! x...) will then look first in this list to find space for the desired new object; only if the list is empty, or contains no appropriate cell, will the instruction require memory from the underlying operating system. This may be called the **internal free list** approach.

- Alternatively, reclaiming an object may mean returning the associated memory to the operating system. In practice, this solution will usually include some aspects of the first: to avoid the overhead of repeated system calls, reclaimed objects will temporarily be kept in a list, whose contents are returned to the operating system whenever their combined size reaches a certain threshold. This may be called the **actual reclamation** approach.

Although both solutions are possible, long-running systems (in particular systems that must run forever) require actual reclamation. The reason is easy to understand: assume an application which never stops creating objects, of which a large proportion will eventually become unreachable, so that there is an upper bound on the total number of objects reachable at any one time, even though the total number of created objects since the beginning of a session is unbounded. Then with the internal free list approach it is possible to have a situation where the application will forever keep asking for more memory even though its actual memory needs are not growing. An exercise at the end of this chapter asks you to construct a pattern that will exhibit this behavior.

Exercise E9.1, page 316.

It would be frustrating to have automatic memory management and still find ourselves in the London Ambulance Service situation — encroaching byte by byte on the available memory for no good reason, until execution runs out of space and ends in disaster.

9.7 REFERENCE COUNTING

The idea behind the first automatic memory management technique, reference counting, is simple. In every object, we keep a count of the number of references to the object; when this count becomes null, the object may be recycled.

This solution is not hard to implement (at the language implementation level). We must update the reference count of any object in response to all operations that can create the object, attach a new reference to it and detach a reference from it.

Any operation that creates an object must initialize its reference count to one. This is the case in particular with the creation instruction !! a, which creates an object and attaches it to a. (The case of *clone* will be studied shortly.)

Any operation that attaches a new reference to an object O must increase O's reference count by one. Such attachment operations are of two kinds (where the value of a is a reference attached to O):

A1 • $b := a$ (assignment).

A2 • $x \bullet r\ (\ldots, a, \ldots)$, where r is some routine (argument passing).

Any operation which detaches a reference from O must decrease its reference count by one. Such detachment operations are of two kinds:

D1 • Any assignment $a := b$. Note that this is also an attachment operation (A1) for the object attached to b. (So if b was also attached to O we will both increment and decrement O's count, leaving it unchanged — the desired outcome.)

D2 • Termination of a routine call of the form $x \bullet r\ (\ldots, a, \ldots)$. (If a occurs more than once in the list of actual arguments we must count one detachment per occurrence.)

After such an operation, the implementation must also check whether O's reference count has reached value zero; if so, it may reclaim the object.

Finally the case of *clone* must be handled carefully. The operation $a := clone\ (b)$, which duplicates the object OB attached to b, if any, and attaches the resulting new object OA to a, must not duplicate the reference count. Instead, it must initialize the reference count of OA to one; in addition, if OB had any non-void reference fields, it must increase by one, for every such field, the reference count of the attached object. (If two or more fields are attached to a single object, its reference count will be increased as many times.)

One obvious drawback of reference counting is the performance overhead in both time and space. For every operation on references the implementation will now execute an arithmetic operation — and, in the detachment case, a conditional instruction. In addition, every object must be extended with an extra field to hold the count.

But there is an even more serious problem which makes reference counting, unfortunately, of little practical use. ("Unfortunately" because this technique is not too hard to implement.) The problem is cyclic structures. Consider once again our staple example of a structure with mutually referring objects:

Uncollectible cyclic structure

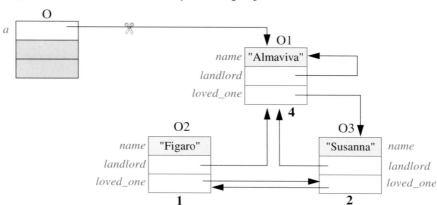

The objects in the right part of the figure, O1, O2 and O3, contain cyclic references to each other; assume that no outside object other than O contains a reference to any of these objects. The corresponding reference counts have been displayed below each object.

Now assume that (as suggested by the ✂) the reference from O to O1 is detached, for example because a routine call with target O executes the instruction

   $a := Void$

Then the three objects on the right have become unreachable. But the reference counting mechanism will never detect this situation: the above instruction decreases O1's count to three; after that the reference counts of the three colored objects will stay positive forever, preventing them from being reclaimed.

Because of this problem, reference counting is only applicable to structures which are guaranteed never to include any cycle. This makes it unsuitable as a general-purpose mechanism at the language implementation level, since it is impossible to guarantee that arbitrary systems will not create cyclic structures. So the only application that would seem to remain is as a technique to be used by library developers at the component manufacturing level. Unfortunately if the component-level techniques of the previous section are not applicable it is usually because the structures at hand are too complex, and in particular because they contain cycles.

9.8 GARBAGE COLLECTION

The most general technique, and in fact the only fully satisfactory one, is automatic garbage collection, or just garbage collection for short.

The garbage collection mechanism

A garbage collector is a facility included in the runtime system for a programming language. (The runtime system, or just runtime for short, is a component of the programming language's implementation; it complements the compiler by providing the mechanisms needed at execution time to support the execution of software systems written in the language.) The garbage collector will take care of both detecting and reclaiming unreachable objects, without the need for explicit handling by application software — although application software may have various facilities at its disposal to control the collector's operation.

A detailed exploration of garbage collection techniques would justify a book of its own (which remains to be written). Let us take a look at the general principles of garbage collectors and the problems that they raise, focusing on the properties that are directly relevant to application developers.

See the bibliographi-cal notes on page 315 for references on garbage collection.

Garbage collector requirements

A garbage collector should, of course, be correct. This is actually two requirements:

> ### Garbage collector properties
>
> **Soundness**: every collected object is unreachable.
>
> **Completeness**: every unreachable object will be collected.

It is just as easy to write a sound collector (never collect any object) as a complete one (collect all objects); the difficulty is of course to achieve both properties in a single product.

Soundness is an absolute requirement: better no garbage collector than one which, once in a while, steals an active object from your application! You must be able to trust memory management blindly; in fact, you should be able to forget about it most of the time, being content enough to know that someone, somehow, collects the mess in your software the same way someone, somehow, collects the garbage in your office while you are gone — but does not take away your books, your computer, or the family pictures on your desk.

Completeness is desirable too, since without it you may still face the problem that the garbage collector was supposed to solve: memory wasted on useless objects. But here we may be able to accept less than perfection: a quasi-complete collector could still be useful if it collects the bulk of the garbage while occasionally missing an object or two.

Let us refine and improve this observation. In reality you *will* want any industrial-grade collector to be complete, lest you get back to the uncertainties of environments with no memory management. Completeness is in practice just as necessary as soundness, but less pressing if we rephrase the definition as: "every unreachable object will *ultimately* be collected". Suppose that we can make the collection process more efficient overall through an algorithm that eventually collects every unreachable object but may lag in getting to some of them: such a scheme would be acceptable for most applications. This is the idea of "generation scavenging" algorithms discussed below, which for efficiency's sake spend most of their efforts scanning the memory areas most likely to contain unreachable objects, and take care of the remaining areas at less frequent intervals.

> If we start considering such tradeoffs it will be necessary to characterize a garbage collector, beyond the yes-no criteria of soundness and completeness, by a more quantitative property which we may call **timeliness**: the time it takes — both the average value and the upper bound will be interesting — between the moment an object becomes unreachable and the moment the collector, assumed to be both sound and complete, reclaims it.

The definition of soundness illuminates the difficulties associated with garbage collection for some languages, and the respective roles of a language and its implementation. Why, for example, is garbage collection usually not available for C++? The reasons most commonly cited are cultural: in the C world each developer is supposed to take care of his toys (in Stephenson's words); he simply does not trust any automatic mechanism to manage his own business. But if this were the true reason, rather than a posteriori justification, C++ environments could at least offer garbage collection as an option, and most do not.

The real issue is language design, not compiling technology or even cultural attitudes. C++, in the C tradition, is rather weakly typed, providing *casts* — type conversions — through which you can refer to an object of a certain type through an entity of another type, with few restrictions on possible type combinations. The syntax

(*OTHER_TYPE*) *x*

denotes *x* viewed as an entity of type *OTHER_TYPE*, related or not to the true type of *x*. Good C++ books censure the wilder applications of this common practice, but methodological aspersions are of no use to the compiler writer, who must deal with the language as defined. Now imagine the following scenario: a reference to an object of some useful type, say *NUCLEAR_SUBMARINE*, is temporarily cast into an integer; the garbage collector jumps in and examines the value, seeing nothing but the most innocent-looking of integers; finding no other reference to the object, it reclaims it; but now the program casts the integer back to its true vocation of nuclear submarine reference; and it tries to access the now inexistent object, with consequences of great sorrow to all affected.

Various techniques have been proposed around this problem. Because they usually involve some restrictions on the use of the language, they have not found their ways into common commercial offerings. The Java language may be viewed as a form of C++ which has dramatically restricted the type system — going so far as to remove genericity and multiple inheritance — to make garbage collection possible at last in a C-based world.

With a carefully designed type system, it is of course possible to provide the whole power of multiple inheritance and genericity while ensuring type safety and language support for efficient garbage collection.

Garbage collection basis

Let us come now to how a garbage collector works.

The basic algorithm usually includes two phases, at least conceptually: mark and sweep. The mark phase, starting from the origins, follows references recursively to traverse the active part of the structure, marking as reachable all the objects it encounters. The sweep phase traverses the whole memory structure, reclaiming unmarked elements and unmarking everything.

The origins are the objects directly attached to entities of the software text. See "Reachable objects in the object-oriented model", page 288.

As with reference counting, objects must include an extra field, used here for the marking; but the space overhead is negligible, since one bit suffices per object. As will be seen when we study dynamic binding, implementation of O-O facilities requires that every object carry some extra internal information (such as its type) in addition to its official fields corresponding to the attributes of the generating class. This information typically occupies one or two words per object; the marking bit can usually be squeezed into one of these extra words, so that in practice there is no observable overhead.

All-or-nothing collection

When should the garbage collector be triggered?

Classical garbage collectors are activated on demand and run to completion. In other words the garbage collector is inactive as long as there is some memory left to the application; when the application runs out of memory, it triggers an entire garbage collection cycle — mark phase followed by sweep phase.

This technique may be called the all-or-nothing approach. Its advantage is that it causes no overhead as long as there is enough memory; the program is only penalized by memory management when it has exceeded available resources.

But all-or-nothing garbage collection has a serious potential drawback: a complete mark-sweep cycle may take a long time — especially in a virtual memory environment in which filling the memory means filling a very large virtual address space, which the garbage collector will then have to traverse entirely, all that time preventing the application from proceeding.

This scheme may be acceptable for batch applications, although with a high ratio of virtual to real memory thrashing may cause serious performance degradation if a system creates many objects and a large proportion of them become unreachable. All-or-nothing garbage collection will not work, however, for interactive or real-time systems. Imagine a missile interception system which has a 50-millisecond window to react when an enemy missile is fired. Assume everything works fine until the software runs out of memory, at which stage it defers to the garbage collector; but — bad luck — this is precisely when the missile comes in! Even in less life-threatening applications, such as a interactive systems, it is not pleasant to use a tool (for example a text editor) which, once in a while, gets unpredictably hung for ten minutes or so because the underlying implementation has entered a garbage collection cycle.

In such cases the problem is not necessarily the global effect of garbage collection on efficiency: a certain overall performance penalty may be perfectly tolerable to users and developers as the price to pay for the gain in reliability and convenience afforded by automatic garbage collection. But such a penalty should be evenly spread; what will usually not be acceptable is the unpredictable bursts of memory management activity caused by the all-or-nothing approach. Better a tortoise than a hare which, once in a while and without warning, takes a half-hour nap. Reference counting, were it not for its fatal flaw, would satisfy this observation that uniformly slow is often preferable to usually fast but occasionally unpredictable.

Of course the penalty, besides being uniform, must also be small. If the application without a garbage collector is a indeed a hare, no one will really settle for a tortoise; what we can accept is a somewhat less agile hare. A good garbage collector will have an overhead of 5% to 15%. Although some managers, developers and users will scream that this is unacceptable, I know very few applications that cannot tolerate this kind of cost, especially in light of the obvious observation that in the absence of garbage collection the software will have to perform manual reclamation, which does not come for free either (even if we concentrate on execution overhead only and disregard the overhead on development time and the reliability problems). Unfortunately most of the few benchmarks that exist in this area end up, in their effort to measure the measurable, comparing the incomparable: a system executed with no garbage collection and no manual reclamation, versus one running with garbage collection. Even under this unfavorable light, however, a performance cost in the quoted range makes garbage collection shine.

This discussion has identified the two complementary efficiency issues for garbage collectors: *overall performance* and *incrementality*.

Advanced approaches to garbage collection

A good collector should provide good performance both overall and incrementally, making itself suitable for interactive or even real-time applications.

A first requirement is to give developers some control over the activation and de-activation of collector cycles. In particular, the environment's libraries should offer procedures

> *collection_off*
> *collection_on*
> *collect_now*

such that a call to the first specifies that no collector cycle should start until further notice; a call to the second resumes normal operation; and a call to the third immediately triggers a complete cycle. Then if a system contains a time-critical section, which must not be subject to any unpredictable delay, the developer will put a call to *collection_off* at the beginning of the section and a call to *collection_on* at the end; and at any point where the application is known to be idle (for example during certain input or output operations) the developer may, if useful, include a call to *collect_now*.

A more advanced technique, used in some form by most modern garbage collectors, is known as **generation scavenging**. It follows from the experimental observation that "old objects will stay around": the more garbage collection cycles an object has survived, the better chance it has of surviving many more cycles or even remaining forever reachable. This property is precious since the sweep part of garbage collection tends to consume a considerable amount of time, so that the collector will greatly benefit from any information allowing it to examine certain categories less frequently than others.

Generation scavenging will detect objects that have existed for more than a certain number of cycles. This is called **tenuring** (by analogy with the mechanisms that protect instances of the real-life class *PROFESSOR* once they have survived a few cycles of university politics). Tenured objects will be set aside and handled by a separate collection process, which will run less frequently than the collector of "young" objects.

Generation scavenging helps incrementality, but does not fully achieve it, since there remains a need to perform full collections occasionally.

Practical implementations of generation scavenging use many variations on this basic idea. In particular, it is common to divide objects not just into young and old, but into several generations, with different policies for collecting the various generations. These ideas have a considerable effect on the overall performance of garbage collection.

Parallel garbage collection algorithms

To obtain a full solution to the incrementality problem, an attractive idea (if the underlying operating system supports multiprocessing) is to assign garbage collection to a separate thread of control. This is known as **on-the-fly**, or **parallel**, garbage collection.

With on-the-fly garbage collection, execution of an O-O system involves two separate threads (often corresponding to two separate processes of the operating system): the application and the collector. Only the application can allocate memory, through creation instructions; only the collector can free memory, through *reclaim* operations.

The collector will run continuously, repeatedly executing a mark phase followed by a sweep phase to detect and pick up the application's unreachable objects. Think of an endless New York ticker-tape parade, forever marching through the streets of the city. The application is the parade, generously scattering, wherever it passes, objects of all kinds; the garbage collector is the cleaning squad which follows at a short distance, gathering all that has been left.

The notion of corou-tine will be intro-duced in the concurrency chap-ter. See "Corou-tines", page 1012.

The separate threads of control need not be physically distinct processes. With modern operating systems they can be threads; or, to avoid the overhead of switching between processes or even threads, they may be plain coroutines. Even so, however, on-the-fly garbage collection tends in practice to have unsatisfactory overall performance. This is regrettable since the method's incrementality is indeed (with Dijkstra's algorithm, see the reference in the bibliographic notes) quite good.

In my opinion (the proper word here, since this comment reflects hope, not a scientifically established result) parallel garbage collection remains the solution of the future, but will require cooperation from the hardware. Rather than stealing time from the processor which handles the application, garbage collection should be handled by a separate processor, entirely devoted to that task and designed so as to interfere as little as possible with the processor or processors devoted to the application.

This idea requires changes to the dominant hardware architectures and so is not likely to be widely implemented soon. But in an answer to the sometimes asked question

"*What kind of hardware support would be most useful for object technology?*"

the presence of a separate garbage collection processor should, I believe, be the first item on the wish list.

9.9 PRACTICAL ISSUES OF GARBAGE COLLECTION

An environment providing automatic memory management through garbage collection must not only use excellent garbage collection algorithms but also provide a few facilities which, although not central to a theory of memory management, are essential for the practical use of the environment.

Class *MEMORY*

See "ADVANCED EXCEPTION HAN-DLING", 12.6, page 431 about EXCEP-TIONS and "REQUESTING SPECIAL SER-VICE", 30.8, page 998 about CON-CURRENCY.

Several of the required facilities can be provided in the form of features callable by application software. As always in such cases (facilities to be used by developers who need to tune or adapt a basic mechanism of the method and language) the most convenient approach is to group these features in a class, which we will call *MEMORY*. Then any class that needs these facilities will inherit from *MEMORY*.

A similar approach will be used for adapting the exception handling mechanism (class *EXCEPTIONS*) and the concurrency mechanism (class *CONCURRENCY*).

Among the features of class *MEMORY* will be the procedures discussed earlier for stopping the collection mechanism, resuming it, and triggering a full collection: *collection_off*, *collection_on*, *collect_now*.

A disposal mechanism

Another important procedure of *MEMORY* is *dispose* (not to be confused with its Pascal namesake, which frees memory). It addresses an important practical problem sometimes called *finalization*. If the garbage collector reclaims an object that is associated with some external resources, you may wish to specify a certain action — such as freeing the resources — to be executed at reclamation time. A typical example is a class *FILE*, whose instances will represent files of the operating system. It is desirable to have a way of specifying that whenever the garbage collector reclaims an instance of *FILE* that has become unreachable it will call a certain procedure to close the associated physical file.

More generally let us assume a procedure *dispose* which executes the operations needed at the time an instance of the class is reclaimed. With a manual approach to memory management no particular problem would arise: it would suffice to include a call to *dispose* just before every call to *reclaim*. The "destructors" of C++ take care of both operations: *dispose* and *reclaim*. With a garbage collector, however, the software does not directly control (for all the good reasons that we have explored) the moment at which an object is reclaimed; so it is impossible to include explicit calls to *dispose* at the right places.

The answer relies on the power of object technology and in particular on inheritance and redefinition. (These techniques are studied in later chapters but their application here is simple enough to be understandable without a detailed grasp of their principles.) Class *MEMORY* has a procedure *dispose*, whose body performs no action at all:

> *dispose* **is**
> > -- Action to be taken in case of reclamation by garbage collector;
> > -- nothing by default.
> > -- Called automatically by garbage collector.
>
> **do**
> **end**

Then any class which requires special dispose actions whenever the collector reclaims one of its instances will redefine procedure *dispose* to perform these actions. For example, assuming that class *FILE* has a boolean attribute *opened* and a procedure *close*, both with the obvious semantics, it will redefine *dispose* appropriately:

> *dispose* **is**
> > -- Action to be taken in case of reclamation by garbage collector:
> > -- close the associated file if open.
> > -- Called automatically by garbage collector.
>
> **do**
> > **if** *opened* **then**
> > > *close*
> > **end**
> **end**

As the comments indicate, the rule is that any object reclamation will cause a call to *dispose* — either the original empty procedure for the (by far commonest) case in which no redefinition has occurred in the generating class, or the redefined version.

Garbage collection and external calls

See "INTERFAC-ING WITH NON-O-O SOFTWARE", 13.1, page 439.

A well-engineered object-oriented environment with garbage collection must address another practical problem. O-O software will in many cases have to interact with software written in other languages. In a later chapter we will see how best to ensure this interaction with the non-O-O world.

If your software indeed uses calls to routines written in other languages (called *external routines* in the rest of this discussion), you may have to pass to these routines references to objects. This causes a potential danger with respect to memory management. Assume that an external routine is of the following form (transposed to the appropriate foreign language):

> *r* (*x*: *SOME_TYPE*) **is**
> > **do**
> > > ...
> > > *a* := *x*
> > > ...
> > **end**

where *a* is an entity which may retain its value between successive activations of *r*; for example *a* could be a global or "static" variable in traditional languages, or a class attribute in our O-O notation. Consider a call *r* (*y*), where *y* is attached to some object O1. Then it is possible that some time after the call O1 becomes unreachable from the object-oriented side while there is still a reference to it (from *a*) in the external software. The garbage collector could — and eventually should — reclaim O1, but this is wrong.

For such cases we must provide procedures, callable from the external software, which will protect a retained object from the collector, and terminate such protection. These procedures may be called under the form

> *adopt* (*a*)
> *wean* (*a*)

and should be part of any interface library supporting the communication between object-oriented and external software. The C interface library of the mechanism described in the next section supports such a facility. "Adopting" an object takes it off the reach of the reclamation mechanism; "weaning" it makes it reclaimable again.

Passing objects to non-object-oriented languages and retaining references to them from the foreign side of the border is of course risky business. But it is not always possible to avoid it. For example an object-oriented project may need a special interface between the O-O language and an existing database management system; in such cases you may need to let the other side retain information about your objects. Such low-level manipulations should never appear in normal application software, but should be encapsulated in utility classes, written with particular care so as to hide the details from the rest of the software and protect it against possible trouble.

9.10 AN ENVIRONMENT WITH MEMORY MANAGEMENT

As a conclusion let us take a peek at how one particular environment — the one presented more broadly in the last chapter of this book — handles memory management. This will give an example of practical, state-of-the-art approaches to the problem.

Basics

Memory management is automatic. The environment includes a garbage collector, which is always on by default. It is sufficiently unobtrusive to have caused users to call and ask *"what should I do to turn on the garbage collector?"*, only to be told that it is already on! In normal usage, including interactive applications, you will not notice it. You can turn it off through *collection_off* as discussed earlier.

Unlike the collectors found in many other environments, the garbage collector does not just free memory for reuse by further object allocations in the same system execution, but actually returns it to the operating system for use by other applications (at least on operating systems that do provide a mechanism to free memory for good). We have seen how essential that property was, especially for systems that must run permanently or for a long time.

Additional engineering goals presided over the garbage collector design: efficient memory collection; small memory overhead; incremental behavior (avoiding blocking the application for any significant period of time).

Challenges

The garbage collector must face the following issues, following from the practical constraints on object allocation in a modern, O-O environment:

- O-O routines can call external functions, in particular C functions, which have their own needs for memory allocation. We must therefore consider that there are two distinct kinds of memory: object memory and external memory.

- All objects are not created equal. Arrays and strings have a variable size; instances of other classes have a fixed size.

- Finally, as noted, it is not enough to free memory for reuse by the O-O application: we must also be able to give it back for good to the operating system.

For these reasons, memory allocation cannot rely on the standard *malloc* system call which, among other limitations, does not return memory to the operating system. Instead, the environment asks the operating system's kernel for memory chunks and allocates objects in these chunks using its own mechanisms.

Object movement

The need to return memory to the operating system is the source of one of the most delicate parts of the mechanism: garbage collection can move objects around.

This property has by far caused the most headaches in the implementation of the collector. But it has also made the mechanism robust and practical; without it there would be no way to use garbage collection for long-running, mission-critical systems.

If you stay within the O-O world you need not think about object movement, except as a guarantee that your system will not expand forever, even if it keeps creating new objects (provided the total size of reachable objects is bounded). But you will need to consider this property if you also use external routines, written for example in C, and pass objects to them. If the C side stores somewhere, in the form of a plain address (a C pointer), a reference to an object from the O-O world, you may be in trouble if it tries to use it without protection ten minutes later: by then the object may have moved elsewhere, and the address may contain something completely different, or nothing at all. A simple library mechanism solves the issue: the C function should "access" the object and access it through the appropriate macro, which will find the object wherever it is.

Garbage collection mechanism

Here is an outline of the algorithm used by the garbage collector.

Rather than a single algorithm the solution actually relies on a combination of basic algorithms, used together (for some of them) or independently. Each activation of the collector selects an algorithm or algorithm combination based on such criteria as the urgency of the memory need. The basic algorithms include generation scavenging, mark-and-sweep and memory compaction, plus a few others less relevant to this discussion.

The idea behind **generation scavenging** was described earlier in this chapter: concentrate on young objects, since they have the greatest likelihood of yielding collectable garbage. A main advantage of this algorithm is that it need not explore all the objects, but only those which can be reached from local entities, and from old objects containing references to young objects. Each time the algorithm processes a generation, all the surviving objects become older; when they reach a given age, they are tenured to the next generation. The algorithm looks for the right tradeoff between low tenure age (too many old objects) and high tenure age (too frequent scavengings).

The algorithm still needs, once in a while, to perform a full **mark-and-sweep** to find any unreachable objects that generation scavenging may have missed. There are two steps: *mark* recursively explores and marks the reachable objects; *sweep* traverses applicable memory and collects the marked objects.

Memory compaction compacts memory, returning unused parts to the operating system, at the lowest possible cost. The algorithm divides the memory into n blocks and takes $n-1$ cycles to compact them all.

Bulimia and anorexia

Since operating system calls (allocate memory, return memory) are expensive, the memory compaction algorithm is conservative: rather than returning all the blocks that have been freed, it will keep a few of them around to build a small reserve of available memory. This way if the application starts shortly afterwards to allocate objects again the memory will be readily available, without any need to call the operating system.

Without this technique, the fairly frequent case of a bulimic-anorexic application — an application that regularly goes into a mad allocation binge, followed by a purge period during which it gets rid of many objects — would cause the memory management mechanism constantly to get memory from the operating system, return it, then ask again.

Garbage collector operation

The garbage collector gets into action when one of the two operations that request memory, a creation instruction (!! x...) or a clone, triggers it. The trigger criterion is not just that the application has run out of memory: preferring prevention to cure, the mechanism may activate itself when it detects various conditions in advance of actual memory exhaustion.

If the primary allocation area is full, the collector will execute a scavenging cycle. In most cases this will free enough memory for the current needs. If not, the next step is to go through a full mark-and-sweep collection cycle, generally followed by memory compaction. Only if all this fails to provide the required space will the application, as a last resort, ask the operating system for more memory, if it is still not possible to allocate a new object.

The main algorithms are incremental, and their time consumption is a few percent of the application's execution time. Internal statistics keep track of the memory allocated and help determine the proper algorithm to call.

You can tune the collector's behavior by setting various parameters; in particular, selecting the *speed* option will cause the algorithms not to try to collect all available memory (through the compaction mechanism described above) but instead to call the operating system's allocation facilities earlier. This optimizes speed over compactness. The various parameter-setting mechanisms are obtained, like *collection_off*, *collect_now* and *dispose*, from class *MEMORY*.

The memory management mechanism resulting from the combination of all these techniques has made it possible to develop and run successfully the kind of large, ambitious applications which need to create many objects, create them fast, and (while remaining careful about overall usage of space) let someone else worry about the mundane consequences.

9.11 KEY CONCEPTS INTRODUCED IN THIS CHAPTER

- There are three basic modes of object creation: static, stack-based and free. The last is characteristic of object-oriented languages but also occurs elsewhere, for example in Lisp, Pascal (pointers and *new*), C (*malloc*), Ada (access types).

- In programs that create many objects, objects may become unreachable; their memory space is lost, leading to memory waste and, in extreme cases, failure from lack of space even though some space is not used.

- The issue may be safely ignored in the case of programs that create few unreachable objects, or few objects altogether as compared to the available memory size.

- In all other cases (highly dynamic data structures, limited memory resources), any solution will involve two components: *detection* of dead objects, and *reclamation* of the associated space.

- Either task may be handled by the language implementation, the component manufacturing level or application programs.

- Leaving application programs in charge of detection is cumbersome and dangerous. So is a memory reclamation operation in a high-level language.

- In some contexts, it is possible to provide simple memory management at the component level. Detection is handled by the components; reclamation, by either the components or the language implementation.

- Reference counting is inefficient, and does not work for cyclic structures.

- Garbage collection is the most general technique. It is possible to keep its potential overhead on normal system execution acceptably low and, through sufficiently incremental algorithms, not visible in normal interactive applications.

- *Generation scavenging* improves the efficiency of garbage collection algorithms by using the observation that many objects die (become unreachable) young.

- A good memory management mechanism should return unused space not just to the current application but to the operating system.

- A practical memory management scheme was described, offering a combination of algorithms and ways for application developers to tune the mechanism, including turning garbage collection off and on in sensitive sections.

9.12 BIBLIOGRAPHICAL NOTES

A broader perspective on the different models of object creation, discussed at the beginning of this chapter, is provided by the "**contour model**" of programming language execution, which may be found in [Johnston 1971].

The information about the London Ambulance Service fiasco comes from an extensive set of messages posted on the Risks forum (*comp.risks* Usenet newsgroup) moderated by Peter G. Neumann, in April and October of 1992. I relied particularly on several messages by Brian Randell — quoting journal articles (*The Independent*, 29 and 30 October 1992) and BBC bulletins — as well as Trevor Jenkins, Jean Ramaekers, John

Jones, Tony Lezard, and Paul Johnson (to whom I am grateful for bringing this example to my attention). The primary *comp.risks* issue on this topic is 14.48; see also 13.38, 13.42, 13.43, 14.02. The newsgroup archives are accessible through the World-Wide Web at *http://catless.ncl.ac.uk/Risks*.

A parallel garbage collection algorithm was introduced in [Dijkstra 1978]. [Cohen 1984] discusses the performance issues of such algorithms. Generation scavenging was introduced in [Ungar 1984].

The garbage collection mechanism of ISE's environment sketched at the end of this chapter was built by Raphaël Manfredi and refined by Fabrice Franceschi (whose technical report served as the basis for the presentation here) and Xavier Le Vourch.

EXERCISES

E9.1 Patterns of object creation

In the discussion of automatic memory management it was pointed out that the "internal free list" approach (in which the space of reclaimed objects is not physically returned to the operating system, but kept in a list for use by future creation instructions) may cause the memory allocated to an application to grow forever even though the actual memory requirement is bounded, whereas the "actual reclamation" approach (in which a reclaim operation actually returns memory) would result in bounded memory usage. Devise a pattern of object creation and reclamation which exhibits this problem.

> *"What exactly is reclamation?", page 302.*

You may describe such a pattern as a sequence $o_1\ o_2\ o_3\ \ldots$ where each o_i is either 1, indicating the allocation of one memory unit, or $-n$ (for some integer n), indicating the reclamation of n memory units.

E9.2 What level of reclamation?

The component level policy, if implemented in a language like Pascal or C where an operating system *dispose* or *free* facility is available, could use this facility directly rather than managing its own free list for every type of data structure. Discuss the pros and cons of both approaches.

> *"THE COMPO-NENT-LEVEL APPROACH", 9.5, page 297.*

E9.3 Sharing the stack of available elements

(This exercise assumes familiarity with the results of chapter 18.) Rewrite the feature *available*, giving the stack of available elements in the component-level approach, so that the stack will be shared by all linked lists of a certain type. (**Hint**: use a once function.)

E9.4 Sharing more

(This exercise assumes that you have solved the previous one, and that you have read up to chapter 18.) Is it possible to make the *available* stack shared by linked lists of all types?

10

Genericity

$\mathcal{F}$rom the merging of module and types concepts, we have been able to develop a powerful notion of class, which serves as the basis of the object-oriented method and can already, as it stands, enable us to do much. But to achieve our goals of extendibility, reusability and reliability we must make the class construct more flexible, an effort that will proceed in two directions. One, vertical in the figure below, represents abstraction and specialization; it will give rise to the study of inheritance in subsequent chapters. The present chapter studies the other dimension, horizontal in the figure: type parameterization, also known as genericity.

Dimensions of generalization

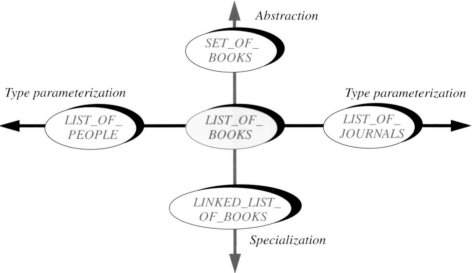

10.1 HORIZONTAL AND VERTICAL TYPE GENERALIZATION

With the mechanisms studied so far we have all that we need to write the class at the center of the figure, *LIST_OF_BOOKS*, of which an instance represents a list of book objects. We know what kinds of feature it would have: *put* to add an element, *remove* to delete an element, *count* to find out how many elements are present and so on. But it is easy to see two ways of generalizing the notion of *LIST_OF_BOOKS*:

- Lists are a special case of "container" structure, of which other examples (among many) include trees, stacks and arrays. A more abstract variant might be described by a class *SET_OF_BOOKS*. A more specialized variant, covering a particular choice of list representation, might be described by a class *LINKED_LIST_OF_BOOKS*. This is the vertical dimension of our figure — the dimension of inheritance.

- Lists of books are a special case of lists of objects of any particular kind, of which other examples (among many) include lists of journals, lists of people, lists of integers. This is the horizontal dimension of our figure — the dimension of genericity, our topic for the rest of this chapter. By giving classes parameters representing arbitrary types, we will avoid the need to write many quasi-identical classes — such as *LIST_OF_BOOKS* and *LIST_OF_PEOPLE* — without sacrificing the safety afforded by static typing.

The relation between these two mechanisms is an elusive question for students of object-oriented concepts. Should inheritance and genericity be viewed as comrades or competitors in the rush towards more flexible software? That question is the subject of an appendix. In the present chapter we concentrate on genericity; this will also enable us to take a closer look at one of the most common examples of generic structure: arrays.

Appendix B.

10.2 THE NEED FOR TYPE PARAMETERIZATION

Genericity is not really a new concept in this discussion, although we have not yet seen it applied to classes. We encountered the idea a first time when reviewing traditional approaches to reusability; and when we studied the mathematical model — abstract data types — we saw the need to define an ADT as parameterized by types.

See "Genericity", page 96, and again "Genericity", page 131.

Generic abstract data types

Our working ADT example, *STACK*, was declared as *STACK* [*G*], meaning that any actual use requires you to specify an "actual generic parameter" representing the type of the objects stored in a particular stack. The name *G* as used in the ADT's specification stands for any possible type that these stack elements may have; it is called the **formal generic parameter** of the class. With this approach you can use a single specification for all possible stacks; the alternative, hard to accept, would be to have a class *INTEGER_STACK*, a class *REAL_STACK* and so on.

Any ADT describing "container" structures — data structures such as sets, lists, trees, matrices, arrays and many others that serve to keep objects of various possible types — will be similarly generic.

The same concerns, applied to the container classes of our software systems rather than to the container ADTs of our mathematical models, will yield a similar solution.

The issue

Let us keep the stack example, no longer as a mathematical ADT but as a software class. We know how to write a class *INTEGER_STACK* describing the notion of stack of integers. Features will include *count* (number of elements), *put* (push a new element), *item* (top element), *remove* (pop the top element), *empty* (is this stack empty?).

Type *INTEGER* will be used frequently in this class. For example it is the type of the argument of *put* and of the result of *item*:

> *put* (*element*: <u>*INTEGER*</u>) **is**
> > -- Push *element* on top.
>
> **do** … **end**
>
> *item*: <u>*INTEGER*</u> **is**
> > -- Item at top
>
> **do** … **end**

These appearances of type *INTEGER* follow from the rule of explicit declaration that we have used in developing the notation: any time you introduce an entity, denoting possible run-time objects, you must write an explicit type declaration for it, such as *element*: *INTEGER*. Here this means that you must specify a type for the query *item*, for the argument *element* of procedure *put*, and for other entities denoting possible stack elements.

But as a consequence you must write a different class for every sort of stack: *INTEGER_STACK*, *REAL_STACK*, *POINT_STACK*, *BOOK_STACK*… All such stack classes will be identical except for the type declarations of *item*, *element* and a few other entities: since the basic operations on a stack are the same regardless of the type of stack elements, nothing in the bodies of the various routines depends on the choice of *INTEGER*, *REAL*, *POINT* or *BOOK* as the type of stack element. For anyone concerned with reusability, this is not attractive.

The issue, then, is the contradiction that container classes seem to cause between two of the fundamental quality goals introduced at the beginning of this book:

• Reliability: retaining the benefits of type safety through explicit type declarations.

• Reusability: being able to write a single software element covering variants of a given notion.

The role of typing

Chapter 17.

Why insist on explicit type declarations (the first of the two requirements)? This is part of the general question of typing, to which an entire chapter is devoted later in this book. It is not too early to note the two basic reasons why an O-O notation should be statically typed:

• The *readability* reason: explicit declarations tell the reader, loud and clear, about the intended use of every element. This is precious to whoever — the original author, or someone else — needs to understand the element, for example to debug or extend it.

• The *reliability* reason: thanks to explicit type declarations, a compiler will be able to detect erroneous operations before they have had a chance to strike. In the fundamental operations of object-oriented computation, feature calls of the general form $x.f(a, \ldots)$, where x is of some type TX, the potential for mischief is manyfold: the class corresponding to TX might not have a feature called f; the feature might exist but be secret; the number of arguments might not coincide with what has been declared for f in the class; the type for a or another argument might not be compatible with what f expects. In all such cases, letting the software text go through unopposed — as in a language without static typechecking — would usually mean nasty consequences at run time, such as the program crashing with a diagnostic of the form "*Message not understood*" (the typical outcome in Smalltalk, a non-statically-typed O-O language). With explicit typing, the compiler will not let the erroneous construct through.

The key to software reliability, as was pointed out in the discussion of that notion, is prevention more than cure. Many studies have found that the cost of correcting an error grows astronomically when the time of detection is delayed. Static typing, which enables the early detection of type errors, is a fundamental tool in the quest for reliability.

Without these considerations we would not need explicit declarations, and so we would not need genericity. As a consequence the rest of this chapter only applies to *statically typed* languages, that is to say languages which require all entities to be declared and enforce rules enabling compilers to detect type inconsistencies prior to execution. In a non-statically-typed language such as Smalltalk, there is no role for genericity; this removes a language construct, but also removes any protection against schemes such as

my_stack.put (*my_circle*)

my_account := *my_stack.item*

my_account.withdraw (*5000*)

where an element is retrieved from the top of the stack and treated as if it were a bank account even though it is in reality (because of the first instruction) a circle, so that the software ends up trying to withdraw five thousand dollars from a circle on the screen.

Static typing protects us against such mishaps; combining it with the reusability requirement implies that we develop a mechanism for genericity.

10.3 GENERIC CLASSES

Reconciling static typing with the requirement of reusability for classes describing container structures means, as illustrated by the stack example, that we want both to:

- Declare a type for every entity appearing in the text of a stack class, including entities representing stack elements.

- Write the class so that it does not give out any clue about the elements' type, and hence that it can be used to build stacks of arbitrary elements.

At first sight these requirements seem irreconcilable but they are not. The first one commands us to declare a type; it does not assume that the declaration is exact! As soon as we have provided a type name, we will have pacified the type checking mechanism. ("Name your fear, and it will go away".) Hence the idea of genericity: to obtain a type-parameterized class, equip it with the name of a fictitious type, called the formal generic parameter.

Declaring a generic class

By convention the generic parameter will use the name G for Generic; this is a style recommendation, not a formal rule. If we need more generic parameters they will be called H, I and so on.

The syntax will include the formal generic parameters in square brackets after the class name, as with generic ADTs in a previous chapter. Here is an example:

indexing
        description: *"Stacks of elements of an arbitrary type G"*
class *STACK* [*G*] **feature**
        count: *INTEGER*
                    -- Number of elements in stack
        empty: *BOOLEAN* **is**
                    --Are there no items?
            do ... **end**
        full: *BOOLEAN* **is**
                    -- Is representation full?
            do ... **end**
        item: *G* **is**
                    -- Top element
            do ... **end**
        put (*x*: *G*) **is**
                    -- Add *x* on top.
            do ... **end**
        remove **is**
                    -- Remove top element.
            do ... **end**
    end -- class *STACK*

In the class, you may use a formal generic parameter such as G in declarations: not only for function results (as in *item*) and formal arguments of routines (as in *put*), but also for attributes and local entities.

Using a generic class

A client may use a generic class to declare entities of its own, such as an entity representing a stack. In such a case, the declaration must provide types, called **actual generic parameters** — as many as the class has formal generic parameters, here just one:

    sp: *STACK* [*POINT*]

Providing an actual generic parameter to a generic class so as to produce a type, as here, is called a **generic derivation**, and the resulting type, such as *STACK* [*POINT*], is said to be generically derived.

A generic derivation both produces and requires a type:

- The result of the derivation, *STACK* [*POINT*] in this example, is a type.

- To produce this result, you need an existing type to serve as actual generic parameter, *POINT* in the example.

The actual generic parameter is an arbitrary type. Nothing prevents us, in particular, from choosing a type that is itself generically derived; assuming another generic class *LIST* [*G*], we can define a stack of lists of points:

   slp: *STACK* [*LIST* [*POINT*]]

or even, using *STACK* [*POINT*] itself as the actual generic parameter, a stack of stacks of points:

   ssp: *STACK* [*STACK* [*POINT*]]

There is no limit — other than suggested by the usual guideline that software texts should remain simple — to the depth of such nesting.

Terminology

To discuss genericity, we need to be precise about the terms that we use:

- To produce a type such as *STACK* [*POINT*] by providing a type, here *POINT*, as actual generic parameter for a generic class, here *STACK*, is to perform a generic derivation. You may encounter the term "generic instantiation" for that process, but it is confusing because "instantiation" normally denotes a run-time event, the production of an object — an instance — from its mold (a class). Generic derivation is a static mechanism, affecting the text of the software, not its execution. So it is better to use completely different terms.

- This book uses the term "parameter" exclusively to denote the types that parameterize generic classes, never to denote the values that a routine call may pass to that routine, called *arguments*. In traditional software parlance "parameter" and "argument" are synonymous. Although the decision of which term to use for routines and which for generic classes is a matter of convention, it is desirable to stick to a consistent rule to avoid any confusion.

Type checking

Using genericity, you can guarantee that a data structure will only contain elements of a single type. Assuming a class contains the declarations

   sc: *STACK* [*CIRCLE*]; *sa*: *STACK* [*ACCOUNT*]; *c*: *CIRCLE*; *a*: *ACCOUNT*

then the following are valid instructions in routines of that class:

   sc.*put* (*c*)   -- Push a circle onto a stack of circles
   sa.*put* (*a*)   -- Push an account onto a stack of accounts
   c := *sc*.*item*   -- Assign to a circle entity the top of a stack of circles

but each of the following is invalid and will be rejected:

> *sc.put* (*a*);   -- Attempt to push an account onto a stack of circles
> *sa.put* (*c*);   -- Attempt to push a circle onto a stack of accounts
> *c* := *sa.item*   -- Attempt to access as a circle the top of a stack of accounts

This will rule out erroneous operations of the kind described earlier, such as attempting to withdraw money from a circle.

The type rule

The type rule that makes the first set of examples valid and the second invalid is intuitively clear but let us make it precise.

First the basic non-generic rule. Consider a feature declared as follows, with no use of any formal generic parameter, in a non-generic class C

> *f* (*a*: *T*): *U* **is** …

This will be the Feature Application rule, page 473.

Then a call of the form $x.f(d)$, appearing in an arbitrary class B where x is of type C, will be typewise correct if and only if: f is available to B — that is to say, generally exported, or exported selectively to a set of classes including B; and d is of type T. (When we bring inheritance into the picture we will also accept d if its type is based on a descendant of T.) The result of the call — there is a result since the example assumes that f is a function — is of type U.

Now assume that C is generic, with G as formal generic parameter, and has a feature

> *h* (*a*: *G*): *G* **is** …

A call to h will be of the form $y.h(e)$ for some entity y that has been declared, for some type V, as

> *y*: *C* [*V*]

The counterpart of the non-generic rule is that e must now be of type V (or a compatible type in the sense of inheritance), since the corresponding formal argument a is declared as being of type G, the formal generic parameter, and in the case of y we may consider G, wherever it appears in class C, as a placeholder for V. Similarly, the result of the call will be of type V. The earlier examples all follow this model: a call of the form $s.put(z)$ requires an argument z of type *POINT* if s is of type *STACK* [*POINT*], *INTEGER* if s is of type *STACK* [*INTEGER*]; and $s.item$ returns a result of type *POINT* in the first case and *INTEGER* in the second.

These examples involve features with zero or one argument, but the rule immediately extends to an arbitrary number of arguments.

Operations on entities of generic types

In a generic class C [$G, H, …$] consider an entity whose type is one of the formal generic parameters, for example x of type G. When the class is used by a client to declare entities, G may ultimately represent any type. So any operation that the routines of C perform on x must be applicable to all types. This leaves only five kinds of operation:

> ## Uses of entities of a formal generic type
>
> The valid uses for an entity x whose type G is a formal generic parameter are the following:
>
> G1 • Use of x as left-hand side in an assignment, $x := y$, where the right-hand side expression y is also of type G.
>
> G2 • Use of x as right-hand side of an assignment $y := x$, where the left-hand side entity y is also of type G.
>
> G3 • Use of x in a boolean expression of the form $x = y$ or $x /= y$, where y is also of type G.
>
> G4 • Use of x as actual argument in a routine call corresponding to a formal argument declared of type G, or of type ANY.
>
> G5 • Use as target of a call to a feature of ANY.

In particular, a creation instruction of the form $!! \; x$ is illegal, since we know nothing about the creation procedures, if any, defined for possible actual generic parameters corresponding to G.

Cases G4 and G5 refer to class ANY. Mentioned a few times already, this class contains features that all classes will inherit. So you can be assured that whatever actual type G represents in a particular generic derivation will have access to them. Among the features of ANY are all the basic operations for copying and comparing objects: *clone*, *copy*, *equal*, *copy*, *deep_clone*, *deep_equal* and others. This means it is all right, for x and y of a formal generic type G, to use instructions such as

See "THE GLOBAL INHERITANCE STRUCTURE", 16.2, page 580.

$x \text{.} copy \; (y)$

$x := clone \; (y)$

if $equal \; (x, y)$ **then** …

Ignoring ANY, case G4 permits a call $a \text{.} f(x)$ in a generic class $C \; [G]$ if f takes a formal argument of type G. In particular a could be of type $D \; [G]$, where D is another generic class, declared as $D \; [G]$ with a feature f that takes an argument of type G, here denoting D's own formal generic parameter. (If the preceding sentence does not immediately make sense, please read it once more and it will, I hope, soon seem as clear as a mountain creek!)

To check creek-clarity do exercise E10.3, page 330.

Types and classes

We have learned to view the class, the central notion in object technology, as the product of the corporate merger between the module and type concepts. Until we had genericity, we could say that every class is a module and is also a type.

With genericity, the second of these statements is not literally true any more, although the nuance will be small. A generic class declared as $C \; [G]$ is, rather than a type, a type pattern covering an infinite set of possible types; you can obtain any one of these by providing an actual generic parameter — itself a type — corresponding to G.

This yields a more general and flexible notion. But for what we gain in power we have to pay a small price in simplicity: only through a small abuse of language can we continue talking, if x is declared of type T, about "the features of T" or "the clients of T"; other than a class, T may now be a generically derived type $C[U]$ for some generic class C and some type U. Of course there is still a class involved — class C —, which is why the abuse of language is acceptable.

When we need to be rigorous the terminology is the following. Any type T is associated with a class, the **base class** of T, so that it is always correct to talk about the features or clients of T's base class. If T is a non-generic class, then it is its own base class. If T is a generic derivation of the form $C[U, \ldots]$, then the base class of T is C.

"ANCHORED DECLARATION", 16.7, page 598.

The notion of base class will again be useful when we introduce yet another kind of type, also (like all others in the O-O approach) based on classes, but indirectly: anchored types.

10.4 ARRAYS

As a conclusion to this discussion it is useful to take a look at a very useful example of container class: *ARRAY*, which represents one-dimensional arrays.

Arrays as objects

The notion of array is usually part of a programming language's definition. But with object technology we do not need to burden the notation with special predefined constructs: an array is just a container object, an instance of a class which we may call *ARRAY*.

ARRAY is a good example of generic class. Here is a first outline:

A better version of the class, relying on assertions, appears in "Arrays revisited", page 372.

indexing
    description: "*Sequences of values, all of the same type or of a conforming one, %*
        %*accessible through integer indices in a contiguous interval*"
class *ARRAY* [*G*] **creation**
    make
feature
    make (*minindex, maxindex: INTEGER*) **is**
        -- Allocate array with bounds *minindex* and *maxindex*
        -- (empty if *minindex > maxindex*)
      do ... **end**
    lower, upper, count: INTEGER
        -- Minimum and maximum legal index; array size.
    put (*v: G; i: INTEGER*) **is**
        -- Assign *v* to the entry of index *i*
      do ... **end**
    infix "@", *item* (*i: INTEGER*): *G* **is**
        -- Entry of index *i*
      do ... **end**
end -- class *ARRAY*

To create an array of bounds m and n, with a declared of type $ARRAY\ [T]$ for some type T, you will execute the creation instruction

> !! $a.make\ (m,\ n)$

To set the value of an array element you will use procedure put: the call $a.put\ (x,\ i)$ sets the value of the i-th element to x. To access the value of an element you will use function $item$ (the synonym **infix** "@" will be explained shortly), as in

> $x := a.item\ (i)$

Here is a sketch of how you might use the class from a client:

> pa: $ARRAY\ [POINT]$; $p1$: $POINT$; i, j: $INTEGER$
>
> $\dots$
>
> !! $pa.make\ (-32,\ 101)$ -- Allocate array with the bounds shown.
> $pa.put\ (p1,\ i)$ -- Assign $p1$ to entry of index i.
> $\dots$
> $p1 := pa.item\ (j)$ -- Assign to $p1$ the value of entry of index j.

In conventional (say Pascal) notation, you would write

> $pa\ [i] := p1$ for $pa.put\ (i,\ p1)$
> $p1 := pa\ [i]$ for $p1 := pa.item\ (i)$

Array properties

A few observations on the preceding class:

- Similar classes exist for arrays with more dimensions: $ARRAY2$ etc.

- Feature $count$ may be implemented as either an attribute or a function, since it satisfies $count = upper - lower+1$. This is expressed in the actual class by an invariant, as explained in the next chapter.

- More generally, assertion techniques will allow us to associate precise consistency conditions with put and $item$, expressing that calls are only valid if the index i is between $lower$ and $upper$.

The idea of describing arrays as objects and $ARRAY$ as a class is a good example of the unifying and simplifying power of object technology, which helps us narrow down the notation (the design or programming language) to the bare essentials and reduce the number of special-purpose constructs. Here an array is simply viewed as an example of a container structure, with its own access method represented by features put and $item$.

Since $ARRAY$ is a normal class, it can fully participate in what an earlier chapter called the object-oriented games; in particular other classes can inherit from it. A class $ARRAYED\_LIST$ describing the implementation of the abstract notion of list by arrays can be a descendant of both $LIST$ and $ARRAY$. We will study many such constructions.

As soon as we learn about assertions we will take this unifying approach even further; thanks to preconditions, we will be able to handle through the normal concepts of the object-oriented method one more problem traditionally thought to require special-purpose mechanisms: run-time bounds checking (monitoring array accesses to enforce the rule that all indices must lie between the bounds).

Efficiency considerations

The fear may arise that all this elegance and simplicity could cause performance to take a hit. One of the primary reasons developers use arrays in traditional approaches is that the basic operations — accessing or modifying an array element known through its index — are fast. Are we now going to pay the price of a routine call every time we use *item* or *put*?

We do not need to. That *ARRAY* looks to the unsuspecting developer as a normal class does not prevent the compiler from cheating — from relying on some insider information. This information enables the compiler to detect calls to *item* and *put* and hijack them so as to generate exactly the same code that a Fortran, Pascal or C compiler would produce for equivalent instructions as shown above ($p1 := pa[i]$ and $pa[i] := p1$ in Pascal syntax). So the developer will gain the best of both worlds: the uniformity, generality, simplicity, and ease of use of the O-O solution; and the performance of the traditional solution.

> The compiler's job is not trivial. As will be clear in the study of inheritance, it is possible for a descendant of class *ARRAY* to redefine any feature of the class, and such redefinitions may be called indirectly through dynamic binding. So compilers must perform a thorough analysis to check that the replacement is indeed correct. Today's compilers from ISE and other companies can indeed, for a typical array-intensive computation typical of large scientific software, generate code whose efficiency matches that of hand-written C or Fortran code.

An infix synonym

Class *ARRAY* provides the opportunity to introduce a small facility that, although not directly related to the other topics of this chapter, will be useful in practice. The declaration of feature *item* actually reads

> **infix** "@", *item* (*i*: *INTEGER*): *G* **is** …

This introduces two feature names **infix** "@" and *item* as synonyms, that is to say as denoting the same feature, given by the declaration that follows. In general, a feature declaration of the form

> *a, b, c,* … "Feature description"

is considered as an abbreviation for a sequence of declarations of the form

> *a* "Feature description"
> *b* "Feature description"
> *c* "Feature description"
>
> …

all for the same "Feature description". This is applicable to attributes (where the "Feature description" is of the form : *some_type*) as well as routines (where it reads **is** *routine_body*).

The notion of infix feature was introduced in "Operator features", page 187.

The benefit in this example is that you have a simpler notation for array access. Although consistent with the access mechanisms for other data structures, the notation $a.item(i)$ is more wordy than the traditional $a[i]$ found, with some variants, in Pascal, C,

Fortran and so on. By defining **infix** "@"as a synonym, you can actually beat traditional languages at their own terseness game by writing an array element as $a @ i$ (the supreme dream: undercutting — by one keystroke — even C!). Note again that this is not a special language mechanism but the straightforward application of a general O-O concept, operator features, combined here with the notion of synonym.

10.5 THE COST OF GENERICITY

As always, we need to make sure that the object-oriented techniques that we introduce for reusability, extendibility and reliability do not imply a performance overhead. The question has just been raised and answered for arrays; but we need to examine it for the genericity mechanism at large. How much will genericity cost?

The concern arises in particular because of the experience of C++, where genericity (known as the *template* mechanism) was a late addition to the language, causing performance difficulties. It appears that some compiler implementations take the idea of parameterization literally, generating a different copy of the class features for each actual generic parameter! As a consequence the literature warns C++ programmers of the dangers of using templates too generously:

> *Template instantiation time is already an issue for some C++ users... If a user creates a List<int>, a List<String>, a List<Widget>, and a List<Blidget> (where Widget and Blidget are user-defined classes), and calls head, tail, and insert on all four objects, then each of these functions will be instantiated* [in the sense of generically derived] *four times. A widely useful class such as List might be instantiated in user programs with many different types, causing many functions to be instantiated. Thus, a significant amount of code might be generated for the* [features of] *the List template* [class].

From: Martin Carroll & Margaret Ellis, "Reducing Instantiation Time", in "C++ Report", vol. 6, no. 5, July-August 1994, pages 14, 16 and 64. List<T> would be LIST [T] in the notation of this book.

The authors of this advice (both with respected C++ expertise from the original AT&T group, one of them co-author of the official C++ reference [Ellis 1990]) go on proposing various techniques for avoiding template derivation. But developers should of course be protected from such concerns. Genericity should not imply code duplication; it is possible, with appropriate language design and a good compiler, to generate a single target code for any generic class, so that all of the following will be small or zero:

- Effect on compilation time.

- Effect on the size of the generated code.

- Effect on execution time.

- Effect on execution space.

When working in such an environment, you can use the full power of genericity without any fear of unpleasant effects on either compile-time or at run-time performance.

10.6 DISCUSSION: NOT DONE YET

The presentation of genericity has introduced the basic ideas. But, as you may have noticed, it leaves two important questions unanswered.

First, in our effort to guarantee type safety, we may have erred on the conservative side. We will be prevented from pushing a bank account onto a *STACK* [*CIRCLE*], or a point onto a *STACK* [*ACCOUNT*]. This is what we want: it is hard to imagine what kind of application — other than general-purpose utilities such as a database management system — would need to handle a stack containing both points and bank accounts. But what about a graphics application asking for a stack that contains a few circles, a few rectangles, a few points? This request seems quite reasonable, and we cannot accommodate it; the type system defined so far will reject the call *figure_stack.put* (*that_point*) if *figure_stack* has been declared of type *STACK* [*FIGURE*] and *that_point* of any type other than *FIGURE*. We can give a name to such structures: **polymorphic data structures**. The challenge will be to support them without renouncing the benefits of type safety.

Second, our generic parameters represent arbitrary types. This is fine for stacks and arrays, since any object is by essence "stackable" and storable into an array. But when we come to structures such as vectors, we will want to be able to add two vectors, requiring that we can also add two vector elements; and if we want to define a hash table class, we will need the certainty that a hash function is applicable to every table element. Such a form of genericity, whereby the formal generic parameter does not any more stand for an arbitrary type, but represents a type guaranteed to offer certain operations, will be called **constrained genericity**.

For both of these problems, the object-oriented method will provide simple and elegant solutions, both based on combining genericity with inheritance.

10.7 KEY CONCEPTS INTRODUCED IN THIS CHAPTER

- Classes may have formal generic parameters representing types.
- Generic classes serve to describe general container data structures, implemented in the same way regardless of the elements they contain.
- Genericity is only needed in a typed language, to ensure statically checkable type safety.
- A client of a generic class must provide actual types for the formal parameters.
- The only permitted operations on an entity whose type is a formal generic parameter are operations applicable to every type. The entity may serve as left- or right-hand side of an assignment, actual routine argument, or operand of an equality or inequality test. It may also participate in universally applicable features such as cloning and object equality testing.
- The notion of array can be covered by a generic library class, without any specific language mechanism but also without any loss in run-time performance.
- More flexible advanced uses of genericity — polymorphic data structures, constrained genericity — require the introduction of inheritance.

10.8 BIBLIOGRAPHICAL NOTES

An early language supporting genericity was LPG [Bert 1983]. Ada made the concept widely known through its generic package mechanism.

For references on Ada see chapter 33.

Genericity has also been introduced in formal specification languages such as Z, CLEAR and OBJ-2, to which references appear in the chapter on abstract data types. The generic mechanism described here was derived from the mechanism introduced in an early version of Z [Abrial 1980] [Abrial 1980a] and extended in M [M 1985b].

Page 160.

Aside from the notation of this book, one of the first object-oriented languages to offer genericity was DEC's Trellis language [Schaffert 1986].

EXERCISES

E10.1 Constrained genericity

This exercise is a little peculiar since it asks you a question to which a detailed answer appears later in the book. Its aim is to get you thinking about the proper language structures, and compare your answer to what will be introduced later. It will only be worthwhile if you are new to this problem and have not yet seen the object-oriented solution. Familiarity with how the problem is handled in other approaches, notably Ada, may be helpful but is not required.

The question is about constrained genericity, a need that was presented in the discussion section. Devise a language mechanism, compatible with the spirit of the object-oriented approach and with the notations seen so far, that will address constrained genericity by enabling the author of a generic class to specify that valid actual generic parameters must possess certain operations.

E10.2 Two-dimensional arrays

Using class *ARRAY* both as inspiration and as basis for the implementation, write a generic class *ARRAY2* describing two-dimensional arrays.

E10.3 Using your own formal generic parameter as someone else's actual

Construct an example in which a routine of a generic class $C [G]$ calls a routine declared in another generic class $D [G]$ as taking a formal argument of type G.

11

Design by Contract: building reliable software

Equipped with the basic concepts of class, object and genericity, you can by now write software modules that implement possibly parameterized types of data structures. Congratulations. This is a significant step in the quest for better software architectures.

But the techniques seen so far are not sufficient to implement the comprehensive view of quality introduced at the beginning of this book. The quality factors on which we have concentrated — reusability, extendibility, compatibility — must not be attained at the expense of reliability (*correctness* and *robustness*). Although, as recalled next, the reliability concern was visible in many aspects of the discussion, we need more.

> The need to pay more attention to the semantic properties of our classes will be particularly clear if you remember how classes were defined: as implementations of abstract data types. The classes seen so far consist of attributes and routines, which indeed represent the functions of an ADT specification. But an ADT is more than just a list of available operations: remember the role played by the semantic properties, as expressed by the axioms and preconditions. They are essential to capture the true nature of the type's instances. In studying classes, we have — temporarily — lost sight of this semantic aspect of the ADT concept. We will need to bring it back into the method if we want our software to be not just flexible and reusable, but also correct and robust.

Assertions and the associated concepts, explained in this chapter, provide some of the answer. Although not foolproof, the mechanisms presented below provide the programmer with essential tools for expressing and validating correctness arguments. The key concept will be **Design by Contract**: viewing the relationship between a class and its clients as a formal agreement, expressing each party's rights and obligations. Only through such a precise definition of every module's claims and responsibilities can we hope to attain a significant degree of trust in large software systems.

In reviewing these concepts, we shall also encounter a key problem of software engineering: how to deal with run-time errors — with contract violations. This leads to the subject of *exception handling*, covered in the next chapter. The distribution of roles between the two chapters roughly reflects the distinction between the two components of reliability; as you will recall, correctness was defined as the software's ability to perform according to its specification, and robustness as its ability to react to cases not included in the specification. Assertions (this chapter) generally cover correctness, and exceptions (next chapter) generally cover robustness.

Some important extensions to the basic ideas of Design by Contract will have to wait until the presentation of inheritance, polymorphism and dynamic binding, enabling us to go from contracts to *subcontracting*.

11.1 BASIC RELIABILITY MECHANISMS

The preceding chapters already introduced a set of techniques that directly address the goal of producing reliable software. Let us review them briefly; it would be useless to consider more advanced concepts until we have put in place all the basic reliability mechanisms.

First, the defining property of object technology is an almost obsessive concern with the *structure* of software systems. By defining simple, modular, extendible architectures, we make it easier to ensure reliability than with contorted structures as often result from earlier methods. In particular the effort to limit inter-module communication to the strict minimum was central to the discussion of modularity that got us started; it resulted in the prohibition of such common reliability risks as global variables, and in the definition of restricted communication mechanisms, the client and inheritance relations. The general observation is that the single biggest enemy of reliability (and perhaps of software quality in general) is complexity. Keeping our structures as simple as possible is not enough to ensure reliability, but it is a necessary condition. So the discussion of the previous chapters provides the right starting point for the systematic effort of the present one.

Also necessary if not sufficient is the constant emphasis on making our software *elegant* and *readable*. Software texts are not just written, they are read and rewritten many times; clarity and simplicity of notation, such as have been attempted in the language constructs introduced so far, are a required basis for any more sophisticated approach to reliability.

Another indispensable weapon is automatic memory management, specifically *garbage collection*. The chapter on memory management explained in detail why, for any system that creates and manipulates dynamic data structures, it would be dangerous to rely on manual reclamation (or no reclamation). Garbage collection is not a luxury; it is a crucial reliability-enhancing component of any O-O environment.

The same can be said of another technique presented (in connection with genericity) in the last chapter: static typing. Without statically enforced type rules, we would be at the mercy of run-time typing errors.

All these techniques provide the necessary basis, from which we can now take a closer look at what it will take for a software system to be correct and robust.

11.2 ABOUT SOFTWARE CORRECTNESS

We should first ask ourselves what it *means* for a software element to be correct. The observations and deductions that will help answer this question will seem rather trivial at first; but let us not forget the comment (made once by a very famous scientist) that scientific reasoning is nothing but the result of starting from ordinary observations and continuing with simple deductions — only very patiently and stubbornly.

Assume someone comes to you with a 300,000-line C program and asks you "Is this program correct?". There is not much you can answer. (If you are a consultant, though, try answering "no" and charging a high fee. You might just be right.)

To consider the question meaningful, you would need to get not only the program but also a precise description of what it is supposed to do — a *specification*.

The same comment is applicable, of course, regardless of the size of a program. The instruction $x := y + 1$ is neither correct nor incorrect; these notions only make sense with respect to a statement of what one expects from the instruction — what effect it is intended to have on the state of the program variables. The instruction is correct for the specification

"Make sure that x and y have different values"

but it is incorrect vis-à-vis the specification

"Make sure that x has a negative value"

(since, assuming that the entities involved are integers, x may end up being non-negative after the assignment, depending on the value of y).

These examples illustrate the property that must serve as the starting point of any discussion of correctness:

> ## Software Correctness property
>
> Correctness is a relative notion.

A software system or software element is neither correct nor incorrect per se; it is correct or incorrect with respect to a certain specification. Strictly speaking, we should not discuss whether software elements are *correct*, but whether they are *consistent* with their specifications. This discussion will continue to use the well-accepted term "correctness", but we should always remember that the question of correctness does not apply to software elements; it applies to pairs made of a software element and a specification.

In this chapter we will learn how to express such specifications through **assertions**, to help us assess the correctness of our software. But we will go further. It turns out (and only someone who has not practiced the approach will think of this as a paradox) that just writing the specification is a precious first step towards *ensuring* that the software actually meets it. So we will derive tremendous benefits from writing the assertions at the same time as we write the software — or indeed before we write the software. Among the consequences we will find the following:

- Producing software that is correct from the start because it is designed to be correct.   [Mills 1975]. The title of an article written by Harlan D. Mills (one of the originators of "Structured Programming") in the nineteen-seventies provides the right mood: *How to write correct programs and know it*. To "know it" means to equip the software, at the time you write it, with the arguments showing its correctness.

- Getting a much better understanding of the problem and its eventual solutions.

- Facilitating the task of software documentation. As we will see later in this chapter, assertions will play a central part in the object-oriented approach to documentation.

- Providing a basis for systematic testing and debugging.

The rest of this chapter explores these applications.

A word of warning: C, C++ and some other languages (following the lead of Algol W) have an "assert" instruction that tests whether a certain condition holds at a certain stage of the software's execution, and stops execution if it does not. Although relevant to the present discussion, this concept represents only a small part of the use of assertions in the object-oriented method. So if like many other software developers you are familiar with such instructions but have not been exposed to the more general picture, almost all the concepts of this chapter will be new.

11.3 EXPRESSING A SPECIFICATION

We can turn the preceding informal observations into a simple mathematical notation, borrowed from the theory of formal program validation, and precious for reasoning about the correctness of software elements.

Correctness formulae

Let A be some operation (for example an instruction or a routine body). A **correctness formula** is an expression of the form

$$\{P\}\, A\, \{Q\}$$

denoting the following property, which may or may not hold:

> ## Meaning of a correctness formula $\{P\}\ A\ \{Q\}$
>
> *"Any execution of* A, *starting in a state where* P *holds, will terminate in a state where* Q *holds."*

Correctness formulae (also called *Hoare triples*) are a mathematical notation, not a programming construct; they are not part of our software language, but only designed to guide us through this discussion by helping to express properties of software elements.

In $\{P\}\ A\ \{Q\}$ we have seen that A denotes an operation; P and Q are properties of the various entities involved, also called assertions (the word will be defined more precisely later). Of the two assertions, P is called the precondition and Q the postcondition. Here is a trivial correctness formula (which, assuming that x is an integer entity, holds):

> $$\{x >= 9\}\ \ x := x + 5\ \ \{x >= 13\}$$

The use of correctness formulae is a direct application of the Software Correctness Property. What the Property stated informally — that correctness is only meaningful relative to a particular specification — correctness formulae turn into a form that is directly usable for working on the software: from now on the discourse about software correctness will not be about individual software elements A, but about triples containing a software element A, a precondition P and a postcondition Q. The sole aim of the game is to establish that the resulting $\{P\}\ A\ \{Q\}$ correctness formulae hold.

> The number *13* appearing in the postcondition is not a typo! Assuming a correct implementation of integer arithmetic, the above formula holds: if $x >= 9$ is true before the instruction, $x >= 13$ will be true after the instruction. Of course we can assert more interesting things: with the given precondition, the most interesting postcondition is the strongest possible one, here $x >= 14$; with the given postcondition, the most interesting precondition is the *weakest* possible one, here $x >= 8$. From a formula that holds, you can always get another one by strengthening the precondition or weakening the postcondition. We will now examine more carefully these notions of "stronger" and "weaker".

Weak and strong conditions

One way to look at a specification of the form $\{P\}\ A\ \{Q\}$ is to view it as a job description for A — an ad in the paper, which states "We are looking for someone whose work will be to start from initial situations as characterized by P, and deliver results as defined by Q".

Here is a small quiz to help you sharpen your understanding of the concepts.

Assume one of your friends is looking for a job and comes across several such ads, all with similar salary and benefits, but differing by their Ps and Qs. (Tough times have encouraged the companies that publish the ads to resort to this notation, which they like for its mathematical compactness since the newspaper charges by the word.) Like everyone else, your friend is lazy, that is to say, wants to have the easiest possible job. He is asking for your advice, always a dangerous situation. What should you recommend for P: choose a job with a *weak* precondition, or a *strong* one? Same question for the postcondition Q. (The answers appear right after this, but do take the time to decide the issue for yourself before turning the page.)

The precondition first. From the viewpoint of the prospective employee — the person who has to perform what has been called A — the precondition P defines the conditions under which the required job will start or, to put it differently, the set of cases that have to be handled. So a strong P is good news: it means that you only have to deal with a limited set of situations. The stronger the P, the easier for the employee. In fact, the perfect sinecure is the job defined by

Sinecure 1
{False} A *{...}*

The postcondition has been left unspecified because it does not matter what it is. Indeed if you ever see such an ad, do not even bother reading the postcondition; *take the job right away*. The precondition *False* is the strongest possible assertion, since it is never satisfied in any state. Any request to execute A will be incorrect, and the fault lies not with the agent responsible for A but with the requester — the client — since it did not observe the required precondition, for the good reason that it is impossible to observe it. Whatever A does or does not do may be *useless*, but is always *correct* — in the sense, defined earlier, of being consistent with the specification.

> The above job specification is probably what a famous police chief of a Southern US city had in mind, a long time ago, when, asked by an interviewer why he had chosen his career, he replied: "Obvious — it is the only job where the customer is always wrong".

For the postcondition Q, the situation is reversed. A strong postcondition is bad news: it indicates that you have to deliver more results. The weaker the Q, the better for the employee. In fact, the second best sinecure in the world is the job defined, regardless of the precondition, by

Sinecure 2
{...} A *{True}*

The postcondition *True* is the weakest possible assertion, satisfied by all states.

> The notions of "stronger" and "weaker" are formally defined from logic: $P1$ is said to be stronger than $P2$, and $P2$ weaker than $P1$, if $P1$ implies $P2$ and they are not equal. As every proposition implies *True*, and *False* implies every proposition, it is indeed legitimate to speak of *True* as the weakest and *False* as the strongest of all possible assertions.

Why, by the way, is Sinecure 2 only the "second best" job in the world? The reason has to do with a fine point that you may have noticed in the definition of the meaning of $\{P\}\ A\ \{Q\}$ on the preceding page: termination. The definition stated that the execution must *terminate* in a state satisfying Q whenever it is started in a state satisfying P. With Sinecure 1 there are no states satisfying P, so it does not matter what A does, even if it is a program text whose execution would go into an infinite loop or crash the computer. Any A will be "correct" with respect to the given specification. With Sinecure 2, however, there must be a final state; that state does not need to satisfy any specific properties, but it must exist. From the viewpoint of whoever has to perform *A*: you need to do nothing, *but you must do it in finite time*.

> Readers familiar with theoretical computing science or program proving techniques will have noted that the *{P} A {Q}* notation as used here denotes **total correctness**, which includes termination as well as conformance to specification. (The property that a program will satisfy its specification if it terminates is known as partial correctness.) See [M 1990] for a detailed presentation of these concepts.

The discussion of whether a stronger or weaker assertion is "bad news" or "good news" has taken the viewpoint of the prospective employee. If, changing sides, we start looking at the situation as if we were the employer, everything is reversed: a weaker precondition will be good news, as it means a job that handles a broader set of input cases; so will be a stronger postcondition, as it means more significant results. This reversal of criteria is typical of discussions of software correctness, and will reappear as the central notion of this chapter: *contracts* between client and supplier modules, in which a benefit for one is an obligation for the other. To produce effective and reliable software is to draw up the contract representing the best possible compromise in all applicable client-supplier communications.

11.4 INTRODUCING ASSERTIONS INTO SOFTWARE TEXTS

Once we have defined the correctness of a software element as the consistency of its implementation with its specification, we should take steps to include the specification, together with the implementation, in the software itself. For most of the software community this is still a novel idea: we are accustomed to programs as defining the operations that we command our hardware-software machines to execute for us (the *how*); it is less common to treat the description of the software's purposes (the *what*) as being part of the software itself.

To express the specification, we will rely on assertions. An assertion is an expression involving some entities of the software, and stating a property that these entities may satisfy at certain stages of software execution. A typical assertion might express that a certain integer has a positive value or that a certain reference is not void.

Mathematically, the closest notion is that of predicate, although the assertion language that we shall use has only part of the power of full predicate calculus.

Syntactically, the assertions of our notation will simply be boolean expressions, with a few extensions. One of these extensions, the **old** notation, is introduced later in this chapter. Another is the use of the semicolon, as in

n > 0 ; x /= Void

The meaning of the semicolon is equivalent to that of an **and**. As between declarations and instructions, the semicolon is actually optional, and we will omit it when assertion clauses appear on separate lines; just consider that there is an implicit **and** between successive assertion lines. These conventions facilitate identification of the individual components of an assertion. It is indeed possible, and usually desirable, to label these components individually, as in

Positive: $n > 0$
Not_void: $x /= Void$

If present, the labels (such as *Positive* and *Not_void* in this example) will play a role in the run-time effect of assertions — to be discussed later in this chapter — but for the moment they are mainly there for clarity and documentation.

The next few sections will review this principal application of assertions: as a conceptual tool enabling software developers to construct correct systems and to document *why* they are correct.

11.5 PRECONDITIONS AND POSTCONDITIONS

The first use of assertions is the semantic specification of routines. A routine is not just a piece of code; as the implementation of some function from an abstract data type specification, it should perform a useful task. It is necessary to express this task precisely, both as an aid in designing it (you cannot hope to ensure that a routine is correct unless you have specified what it is supposed to do) and, later, as an aid to understanding its text.

You may specify the task performed by a routine by two assertions associated with the routine: a *precondition* and a *postcondition*. The precondition states the properties that must hold whenever the routine is called; the postcondition states the properties that the routine guarantees when it returns.

A stack class

An example will enable us to become familiar with the practical use of assertions. In the previous chapter, we saw the outline of a generic stack class, under the form

```
class STACK [G] feature
        … Declaration of the features:
        count, empty, full, put, remove, item
end
```

An implementation will appear below. Before considering implementation issues, however, it is important to note that the routines are characterized by strong semantic properties, independent of any specific representation. For example:

- Routines *remove* and *item* are only applicable if the number of elements is not zero.

- *put* increases the number of elements by one; *remove* decreases it by one.

Such properties are part of the abstract data type specification, and even people who do not use any approach remotely as formal as ADTs understand them implicitly. But in common approaches to software construction software texts reveal no trace of them. Through routine preconditions and postconditions you can turn them into explicit elements of the software.

We will express preconditions and postconditions as clauses of routine declarations introduced by the keywords **require** and **ensure** respectively. For the stack class, leaving the routine implementations blank for the time being, this gives:

indexing

 description: "*Stacks*: *Dispenser structures with a Last-In, First-Out %*
 %access policy"

class *STACK1* [*G*] **feature** -- Access

 count: *INTEGER*
 -- Number of stack elements

 item: *G* **is**
 -- Top element
 require
 not *empty*
 do
 …
 end

feature -- Status report

 empty: *BOOLEAN* **is**
 -- Is stack empty?
 do … **end**

 full: *BOOLEAN* **is**
 -- Is stack representation full?
 do
 …
 end

feature -- Element change

 put (*x*: *G*) **is**
 -- Add *x* on top.
 require
 not *full*
 do
 …
 ensure
 not *empty*
 item = *x*
 count = **old** *count* + *1*
 end

 remove **is**
 -- Remove top element.
 require
 not *empty*
 do
 …
 ensure
 not *full*
 count = **old** *count* – *1*
 end

end

Both the **require** and the **ensure** clauses are optional; when present, they appear at the places shown. The **require** appears before the **local** clause, if present. The next sections explain in more detail the meaning of preconditions and postconditions.

> Note the division into several **feature** clauses, useful to group the features into categories indicated by the clauses' header comments. Access, Status report and Element change are some of a dozen or so standard categories used throughout the libraries and, whenever applicable, subsequent examples in this book.

More on feature categories in "A stack class", page 348.

Preconditions

A precondition expresses the constraints under which a routine will function properly. Here:

- *put* may not be called if the stack representation is full.
- *remove* and *item* may not be applied to an empty stack.

A precondition applies to all calls of the routine, both from within the class and from clients. A correct system will never execute a call in a state that does not satisfy the precondition of the called routine.

Postconditions

A postcondition expresses properties of the state resulting from a routine's execution. Here:

- After a *put*, the stack may not be empty, its top is the element just pushed, and its number of elements has been increased by one.
- After a *remove*, the stack may not be full, and its number of elements has been decreased by one.

The presence of a postcondition clause in a routine expresses a guarantee on the part of the routine's implementor that the routine will yield a state satisfying certain properties, assuming it has been called with the precondition satisfied.

A special notation, **old**, is available in postconditions; *put* and *remove* use it to express the changes to *count*. The notation **old** *e*, where *e* is an expression (in most practical cases an attribute), denotes the value that *e* had on routine entry. Any occurrence of *e* not preceded by **old** in the postcondition denotes the value of the expression on exit. The postcondition of *put* includes the clause

$$count = \textbf{old } count + 1$$

to state that *put*, when applied to any object, must increase by one the value of the *count* field of that object.

A pedagogical note

If you are like most software professionals who get exposed to these ideas for the first time, you may be itching to know what effect, if any, the assertions have on the execution of the software, and in particular what happens if one of them gets violated at run time — if *full* is true when someone calls *put*, or *empty* is true when *put* terminates one of its executions. It is too early to give the full answer but as a preview we can use the lawyer's favorite: *it depends*.

More precisely, it depends on what you want. You may decide to treat assertions purely as comments, with no effect on the software's execution; then a run-time assertion violation will remain undetected. But it is also possible to use assertions to check that everything goes according to plan; then during execution the environment will automatically monitor that all assertions hold when they should, and if one does not it will trigger an exception, usually terminating execution and printing a message indicating clearly what happened. (It is also possible to include an exception handling clause that will try to recover from the exception and continue execution; exception handling is discussed in detail in the next chapter.) To specify the policy that you want — no assertion checking, or assertion monitoring at one of various possible levels — you will use a compilation option, which you can set separately for each class.

See "Monitoring assertions at run time", page 392.

The full details of run-time assertion monitoring do appear later in this chapter. But it would be a mistake to attach too much importance to this aspect at this stage (one of the reasons why you were warned earlier not to think too much about the C notion of assertion if that has been your only exposure to the concept). Other aspects of assertions demand our attention first. We have only started to see assertions as a technique to help us get our software right in the first place; we still have much to discover of their *methodological* role as built-in guardians of reliability. The question of what happens if we do fail (in particular if an assertion, in spite of all our efforts, is not satisfied at some execution instant) is important too, but only after we have done all we could to prevent it from arising.

So (although it is never bad to think ahead) you do not need at this point to be too preoccupied by such questions as the possible performance penalty implied by the **old** construct. Must the run-time system preserve values before we start a routine, just to be able to evaluate an **old** expression appearing in the postcondition? *It depends*: in some circumstances (for example testing and debugging) it will indeed be useful to evaluate assertions; in others (for example production runs of fully validated systems) you can treat them as mere annotations to the software text.

All that counts for the next few sections is the methodological contribution of assertions, and of the associated method of Design by Contract: as a conceptual tool for analysis, design, implementation and documentation, helping us to build software in which **reliability is built-in**, rather than achieved or attempted after the fact through debugging; in Mills's terms, enabling us to build correct programs and know it.

11.6 CONTRACTING FOR SOFTWARE RELIABILITY

Defining a precondition and a postcondition for a routine is a way to define a *contract* that binds the routine and its callers.

Rights and obligations

By associating clauses **require** *pre* and **ensure** *post* with a routine *r*, the class tells its clients:

> "If you promise to call *r* with *pre* satisfied then I, in return, promise to deliver a final state in which *post* is satisfied."

In relations between people or companies, a contract is a written document that serves to clarify the terms of a relationship. It is really surprising that in software, where precision is so important and ambiguity so risky, this idea has taken so long to impose itself. A precondition-postcondition pair for a routine will describe the contract that the routine (the *supplier* of a certain service) defines for its callers (the *clients* of that service).

Perhaps the most distinctive feature of contracts as they occur in human affairs is that any good contract entails obligations as well as benefits for both parties — with an obligation for one usually turning into a benefit for the other. This is true of contracts between classes, too:

- The precondition binds the client: it defines the conditions under which a call to the routine is legitimate. It is an *obligation* for the client and a *benefit* for the supplier.

- The postcondition binds the class: it defines the conditions that must be ensured by the routine on return. It is a benefit for the client and an obligation for the supplier.

The benefits are, for the client, the guarantee that certain properties will hold after the call; for the supplier, the guarantee that certain assumptions will be satisfied whenever the routine is called. The obligations are, for the client, to satisfy the requirements as stated by the precondition; for the supplier, to do the job as stated by the postcondition.

Here is the contract for one of the routines in our example:

put	**OBLIGATIONS**	**BENEFITS**
Client	**(*Satisfy precondition:*)** Only call *put* (*x*) on a non-full stack.	**(*From postcondition:*)** Get stack updated: not empty, *x* on top (*item* yields *x*, *count* increased by 1).
Supplier	**(*Satisfy postcondition:*)** Update stack representation to have *x* on top (*item* yields *x*), *count* increased by 1, not empty.	**(*From precondition:*)** Simpler processing thanks to the assumption that stack is not full.

A routine contract: routine put *for a stack class*

Zen and the art of software reliability: guaranteeing more by checking less

Although you may not have noticed it yet, one of the contract rules given goes against the generally accepted wisdom in software engineering; shocking at first to many, it is among the method's main contributions to software reliability and deserves emphasis.

The rule reflects the above observation that the precondition is a *benefit* for the supplier and is expressed in the bottom-right box of the table: if the client's part of the contract is not fulfilled, that is to say if the call does not satisfy the precondition, then the class is not bound by the postcondition. In this case the routine may do what it pleases: return any value; loop indefinitely without returning a value; or even crash the execution in some wild way. This is the case in which (in reference to the discussion at the beginning of this chapter) "the customer is wrong".

The first advantage of this convention is that it considerably simplifies the programming style. Having specified as a precondition the constraints which calls to a routine must observe, you, the class developer, may assume when writing the routine body that the constraints are satisfied; you do not need to test for them in the body. So if a square root function, meant to produce a real number as a result, is of the form

> *sqrt* (*x*: *REAL*): *REAL* **is**
>   -- Square root of *x*
>   **require**
>   *x* >= *0*
>   **do** ... **end**

you may write the algorithm for computing the square root without any concern for the case in which *x* is negative; this is taken care of by the precondition and becomes the responsibility of your clients. (At first sight this may appear dangerous; but read on.)

Actually the method of Design by Contract goes further. Writing the **do** clause of the routine under the form

> **if** *x* < *0* **then**
>   "Handle the error, somehow"
> **else**
>   "Proceed with normal square root computation"
> **end**

is not just unnecessary but unacceptable. This may be expressed as a methodological rule:

Non-Redundancy principle

Under no circumstances shall the body of a routine ever test for the routine's precondition.

This rule is the reverse of what many software engineering or programming methodology textbooks advocate, often under the name *defensive programming* — the idea that to obtain reliable software you should design every component of a system so that it protects itself as much as possible. Better check too much, this approach holds, than not enough; one is never too careful when dealing with strangers. A redundant check might not help, but at least it will not hurt.

Design by Contract follows from the opposite observation: redundant checks can and indeed will hurt. Of course this will at first seem strange; the natural reaction is to think that an extra check — for example routine *sqrt* containing the above conditional instruction testing for *x* < *0* even though callers have been instructed to ensure *x* >= *0* —

may at worst be useless, but cannot possibly cause any damage. Such a comment, however, comes from a microscopic understanding of reliability, focused on individual software elements such as the *sqrt* routine. If we restrict our view to the narrow world of *sqrt*, then the routine seems more robust with the extra test than without it. But the world of a system is not restricted to a routine; it contains a multitude of routines in a multitude of classes. To obtain reliable systems we must go from the microscopic view to a macroscopic view encompassing the entire architecture.

If we take this global view, *simplicity* becomes a crucial criterion. As was noted at the beginning of this chapter, complexity is the major enemy of quality. When we bring in this concern, possibly redundant checks do not appear so harmless any more! Extrapolated to the thousands of routines of a medium-size system (or the tens or hundreds of thousands of routines of a larger one), the **if** $x < 0$ **then** ... of *sqrt*, innocuous at first sight, begins to look like a monster of useless complexity. By adding possibly redundant checks, you add more software; more software means more complexity, and in particular more sources of conditions that could go wrong; hence the need for more checks, meaning more software; and so on ad infinitum. If we start on this road only one thing is certain: we will *never* obtain reliability. The more we write, the more we will have to write.

To avoid this infinite chase we should never start it. With Design by Contract you are invited to identify the consistency conditions that are necessary to the proper functioning of each client-supplier cooperation (each contract); and to specify, for each one of these conditions, **whose responsibility it is** to enforce it: the client's, or the supplier's. The answer may vary, and is partly a matter of design style; advice will be given below on how best to choose it. But once you have made the decision, you should stick to it: if a correctness requirement appears in the precondition, indicating that the requirement is part of the client's responsibility, there must not be a corresponding test in the routine; and if it is not in the precondition, then the routine must check for the requirement.

Defensive programming appears in contrast to cover up for the lack of a systematic approach by blindly putting in as many checks as possible, furthering the problem of reliability rather than addressing it seriously.

Redundant checking, it should be noted, is a standard technique in hardware. The difference is that in a hardware system some object that was found to be in a correct state at some point may later have its integrity destroyed because of reasons beyond the control of the system itself, such as interference from another system, harmful external event, or simply wear and tear. For that reason it is normal practice, for example, to have both the sender and the receiver of an electronic signal check its integrity.

But no such phenomenon occurs in software: if I can prove or check in some way that a is non-negative whenever *sqrt* (a) is called, I do not need to insert a check for $x \geq 0$, where x is the corresponding formal argument, in the body of *sqrt*. Nothing will happen to a between the time it is "sent" by the caller and the time it is "received" (under the name x) by the routine. Software does not wear out when used for too long; it is not subject to line loss, to interference or to noise.

Also note that in most cases what is called redundant checking in hardware is not really redundant: one actually applies *different* and complementary verifications, such as a parity check and some other test. Even when the checks are the same they are often applied by different devices, as in the just mentioned case of a sender and receiver that both check a signal, or in a redundant computer system where several computers perform the same computation, with a voting mechanism to resolve discrepancies.

Another drawback of defensive programming is its costs. Redundant checks imply a performance penalty — often enough in practice to make developers wary of defensive programming regardless of what the textbooks say. If they do make the effort to include these checks, removing some of them later to improve performance will be tedious. The techniques of this chapter will also leave room for extra checks, but if you choose to enable them you will rely on the development environment to carry them out for you. To remove them, once the software has been debugged, it suffices to change a compilation option (details soon). The software itself does not contain any redundant elements.

Aside from performance considerations, however, the principal reason to distrust defensive programming is simply our goal of getting the best possible reliability. For a system of any significant size the individual quality of the various elements involved is not enough; what will count most is the guarantee that for every interaction between two elements there is an explicit roster of mutual obligations and benefits — the contract. Hence the Zen-style paradox of our conclusion: that to get *more* reliability the best policy is often to check *less*.

Assertions are not an input checking mechanism

It is useful here to emphasize a few properties of the approach which, although implicit in the preceding discussion, have been shown by experience to require further explanations. The following comments should help address some of the questions that may have been forming in your mind as you were reading about the basic ideas of Design by Contract.

To avoid a common misunderstanding, make sure to note that each of the contracts discussed holds between a routine (the supplier) and another routine (its caller): we are concerned about software-to-software communication, not software-to-human or software-to-outside-world. A precondition will not take care of correcting user input, for example in a *read_positive_integer* routine that expects the interactive user to enter a positive number. Including in the routine a precondition of the form

require

   input > 0

would be wishful thinking, not a reliability technique. Here there is no substitute for the usual condition-checking constructs, including the venerable **if** … **then** …; the exception handling mechanism studied in the next chapter may also be helpful.

"Modular protec-tion", page 45. Assertions do have a role to play in a solution to this problem of input validation. In line with the criterion of Modular Protection, the method encourages validating any objects obtained from the outside world — from sensors, from user input, from a network… — as close to the source of the objects as possible, using "filter" modules if necessary:

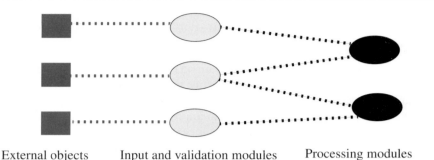

Using filter modules

External objects   Input and validation modules   Processing modules

In obtaining information from the outside (communication paths shown in color) you cannot rely on preconditions. But part of the task of the input modules shown in grey in the middle of the figure is to guarantee that no information is passed further to the right — to the modules responsible for the system's actual computations — unless it satisfies the conditions required for correct processing. In this approach there will be ample use of assertions in the software-to-software communication paths represented by the black dotted lines on the right. The postconditions achieved by the routines of the input modules will have to match (or exceed, in the sense of "stronger" defined earlier) the preconditions imposed by the processing routines.

> The routines of the filter classes may be compared to security officers in, say, a large government laboratory. To meet experts from the laboratory and ask them technical questions, you must submit to screening procedures. But it is not the same person who checks your authorization level and answers the questions. The physicists, once you have been officially brought into their offices, assume you satisfy the preconditions; and you will not get much help from the guards on theoretical physics.

Assertions are not control structures

Another common misunderstanding, related to the one just discussed, is to think of assertions as control structures — as techniques to handle special cases. It should be clear by now that this is not their role. If you want to write a routine *sqrt* that will handle negative arguments a certain way, and non-negative arguments another way, a **require** clause is not what you need. Conditional instructions (**if** … **then** … **else** …) and related constructs to deal with various cases (such as Pascal's **case** … **of** … or the **inspect** instruction of this book's notation) are perfectly appropriate for such purposes.

Assertions are something else. They express correctness conditions. If *sqrt* has its precondition, a call for which $x < 0$ is not a special case: it is a bug, plain and simple.

> ### Assertion Violation rule (1)
>
> A run-time assertion violation is the manifestation of a bug in the software.

"Bug" is not a very scientific word but is clear enough to anyone in software; we will look for more precise terminology in the next section. For the moment we can pursue the assertion violation rule further by noting a consequence of the contract view:

> ### Assertion violation rule (2)
>
> A precondition violation is the manifestation of a bug in the client.
>
> A postcondition violation is the manifestation of a bug in the supplier.

A precondition violation means that the routine's caller, although obligated by the contract to satisfy a certain requirement, did not. This is a bug in the client itself; the routine is not involved. ("The customer is wrong".) An outside observer might of course criticize the contract as too demanding, as with the unsatisfiable **require** *False* precondition or our fictitious *Sinecure 1* example ("the customer is *always* wrong"), but this is too late to argue over the contract: it is the contract, and the client did not observe its part of the deal. So if there is a mechanism for monitoring assertions during execution — as will be introduced shortly — and it detects such a precondition violation, the routine should not be executed at all. It has stated the conditions under which it can operate, and these conditions do not hold; trying to execute it would make no sense.

A postcondition violation means that the routine, presumably called under correct conditions, was not able to fulfill its contract. Here too the distribution of guilt and innocence is clear, although it is the reverse of the previous one: the bug is in the routine; the caller is innocent.

Errors, defects and other creeping creatures

The appearance of the word "bug" in the preceding analysis of assertion violation causes is a good opportunity to clarify the terminology. In Edsger W. Dijkstra's view, using the word "bug" is a lame attempt by software people to blame someone else by implying that mistakes somehow creep into the software from the outside while the developers are looking elsewhere — as if were not the developers who made the mistakes in the first place.

Yet the term enjoys enduring success, if only because it is colorful and readily understood. Like the rest of the software literature, this book uses it freely. But it is appropriate to complement it by more specific (if more stodgy) terms for cases in which we need precise distinctions.

> ### Terms to denote software woes
>
> An *error* is a wrong decision made during the development of a software system.
>
> A *defect* is a property of a software system that may cause the system to depart from its intended behavior.
>
> A *fault* is the event of a software system departing from its intended behavior during one of its executions.

The causal relation is clear: faults are due to defects, which result from errors.

"Bug" usually has the meaning of defect ("are you sure there remains no other bug in this routine?"). This is the interpretation in this book. But in informal discussions it is also used in the sense of fault ("We have had bug-free operation for the last three weeks") or error ("the bug was that I used an unsorted list").

11.7 WORKING WITH ASSERTIONS

Let us now probe further the use of preconditions and postconditions, continuing with fairly elementary examples. Assertions, some simple, some elaborate, will be pervasive in the examples of the following chapters.

A stack class

The assertion-equipped *STACK* class was left in a sketchy form (*STACK1*). We can now come up with a full version including a spelled out implementation.

For an effective (directly usable) class we must choose an implementation. Let us use the array implementation illustrated at the beginning of the discussion of abstract data types:

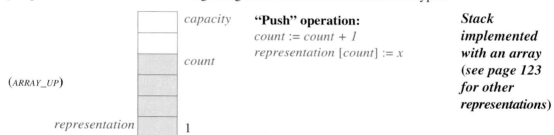

"Push" operation:
$count := count + 1$
$representation\ [count] := x$

Stack implemented with an array (see page 123 for other representations)

The array will be called *representation* and will have bounds 1 and *capacity*; the implementation also uses an integer, the attribute *count*, to mark the top of the stack.

Note that as we discover inheritance we will see how to write deferred classes that cover several possible implementations rather than just one. Even for a class that uses a particular implementation, for example by arrays as here, we will be able to *inherit* from the implementation class *ARRAY* rather than use it as a client (although some object-oriented developers will still prefer the client approach). For the moment, however, we can do without any inheritance-related technique.

For an array-based stack implementation using inheritance, see "IMPLEMENTATION INHERITANCE", 24.8, page 844.

Here is the class. Recall that if a is an array then the operation to assign value x to its i-th element is $a.put\ (x, i)$, and the value of its i-th element is given by $a.item\ (i)$ or, equivalently, $a\ @\ i$. If, as here, the bounds of the array are 1 and *capacity*, then i must in all cases lie between these bounds.

indexing

> *description*: "*Stacks*: *Dispenser structures with a Last-In, First-Out %*
> *%access policy, and a fixed maximum capacity*"

class *STACK2* [*G*] **creation**

> *make*

feature -- Initialization

> *make* (*n*: *INTEGER*) **is**
>> -- Allocate stack for a maximum of *n* elements
>
>> **require**
>>> *positive_capacity*: *n* >= *0*
>>
>> **do**
>>> *capacity* := *n*
>>> !! *representation*•*make* (*1*, *capacity*)
>>
>> **ensure**
>>> *capacity_set*: *capacity* = *n*
>>> *array_allocated*: *representation* /= *Void*
>>> *stack_empty*: *empty*
>>
>> **end**

feature -- Access

On the export status of capacity *see exercise E11.4, page 409.*

> *capacity*: *INTEGER*
>> -- Maximum number of stack elements
>
> *count*: *INTEGER*
>> -- Number of stack elements
>
> *item*: *G* **is**
>> -- Top element
>
>> **require**
>>> *not_empty*: **not** *empty* -- i.e. *count* > *0*
>>
>> **do**
>>> *Result* := *representation* @ *count*
>>
>> **end**

feature -- Status report

> *empty*: *BOOLEAN* **is**
>> -- Is stack empty?
>
>> **do**
>>> *Result* := (*count* = *0*)
>>
>> **ensure**
>>> *empty_definition*: *Result* = (*count* = *0*)
>>
>> **end**

full: *BOOLEAN* **is**
          -- Is stack full?
     do
          Result := (*count* = *capacity*)
     ensure
          full_definition: *Result* = (*count* = *capacity*)
     end

feature -- Element change

put (*x*: *G*) **is**
          -- Add *x* on top
     require
          not_full: **not** *full*   -- i.e. *count* < *capacity* in this representation
     do
          count := *count* + *1*
          representation.*put* (*count*, *x*)
     ensure
          not_empty: **not** *empty*
          added_to_top: *item* = *x*
          one_more_item: *count* = **old** *count* + *1*
          in_top_array_entry: *representation* @ *count* = *x*
     end

remove **is**
          -- Remove top element
     require
          not_empty: **not** *empty* -- i.e. *count* > *0*
     do
          count := *count* – *1*
     ensure
          not_full: **not** *full*
          one_fewer: *count* = **old** *count* – *1*
     end

feature {*NONE*} -- Implementation

representation: *ARRAY* [*G*]
          -- The array used to hold the stack elements

invariant
     … To be filled in later (see page 364) …
end -- class *STACK2*

This class text illustrates the simplicity of working with assertions. It is complete except for the **invariant** clause, which will be added later in this chapter. Let us explore its various properties.

*Invariants are intro-
duced in "CLASS
INVARIANTS",
11.8, page 363.*

This is the first full-fledged class of this chapter, not too far from what you will find in professional libraries of reusable object-oriented components such as the Base libraries. (Apart from the use of inheritance and a few extra features, what still distinguishes this class from its real-life counterparts is the absence of the **invariant** clause.)

On multiple feature clauses and exporting to NONE see "SELECTIVE EXPORTS AND INFORMATION HIDING", 7.8, page 191.
Before studying the assertions, a general note about the structure of the class. As soon as a class has more than two or three features, it becomes essential to organize its features in a coherent way. The notation helps by providing the possibility of including multiple **feature** clauses. An earlier chapter introduced this facility as a way to specify a different export status for certain features, as done here for the last part of the class, labeled -- Implementation to specify that feature *representation* is secret. But as already previewed in *STACK1* you can take advantage of multiple feature clauses even when the export status is the same. The purpose is to make the class easier to read, and easier to manage, by grouping features into general categories. After each **feature** keyword appears a comment (known as the Feature Clause Comment) defining the general role of the features that follow. The categories used in the example are those of *STACK1*, plus *Initialization* for the creation procedure.

"Feature clause header comments", page 889.
The standard feature categories and associated Feature Clause Comments are part of the general rules for consistency and organization of reusable library classes. A more complete list appears in the chapter on style rules.

The imperative and the applicative

"Introducing a more imperative view", page 145.
The assertions of *STACK2* illustrate a fundamental concept of which we got a first glimpse when we studied the transition from abstract data types to classes: the difference between imperative and applicative views.

The assertions in *empty* and *full* may have caused you to raise an eyebrow. Here again is the text of *full*:

> *full*: *BOOLEAN* **is**
>
> -- Is stack full?
>
> **do**
>
> *Result* := (*count* = *capacity*)
>
> **ensure**
>
> *full_definition*: *Result* = (*count* = *capacity*)
>
> **end**

The postcondition expresses that *Result* has the same value as *count = capacity*. (Since both sides of the equality, the entity *Result* and the expression *count = capacity*, are boolean, this means that the function returns **true** if and only if *count* is equal to *capacity*.) But what is the point of writing this postcondition, one may ask, since the body of the routine (the **do** clause) says exactly the same thing through the instruction *Result* := (*count = capacity*), whose only difference with the postcondition clause is its use of := rather than =? Is the postcondition not redundant?

Actually, there is a big difference between the two constructs, and no redundancy at all. The instruction *Result* := (*count = capacity*) is a command that we give to our virtual computer (the hardware-software machine) to change its state in a certain way; it performs an action. The assertion *Result* = (*count = capacity*) does not do anything: it specifies a property of the expected end state, as visible to the routine's caller.

The instruction is *prescriptive*; the assertion is *descriptive*. The instruction describes the "how"; the assertion describes the "what". The instruction is part of the implementation; the assertion is an element of specification.

The instruction is *imperative*; the assertion is *applicative*. These two terms emphasize the fundamental difference between the worlds of computing and mathematics:

- Computer operations may change the state of the hardware-software machine. Instructions of common programming languages are commands (imperative constructs) directing the machine to execute such operations.

- Mathematical reasoning never changes anything; as noted in the presentation of abstract data types, taking the square root of the number 2 does not change that number. Mathematics instead describes how to use properties of known objects, such as the number 2, to infer properties of others, such as $\sqrt{2}$, obtained from the former by *applying* (hence the name) certain mathematical derivations such as square root.

That the two notations are so close in our example — assignment := and equality = — should not obscure this fundamental difference. The assertion describes an intended result, and the instruction (the loop body) prescribes a particular way to achieve that result. Someone using the class to write a client module will typically be interested in the assertion but not in the implementation.

The reason for the closeness of notations for assignment and equality is that assignment is indeed in many cases the straightforward way to achieve equality; in our example the chosen implementation, *Result* := (*count = capacity*), is indeed the obvious one. But as soon as we move on to more advanced examples the conceptual difference between the specification and the implementation will be much larger; even in the simple case of a function to compute the square root of a real number *x*, where the postcondition is just something like *abs* (*Result* ^ 2 − *x*) <= *tolerance* with *abs* denoting absolute value and *tolerance* a tolerance value, the instructions in the function's body will be far less trivial since they have to implement a general algorithm for the computation of square roots.

> Even for *put* in class *STACK2*, the same specification could have led to different implementations, although the differences are minor; for example the body could be
>
>> **if** *count = capacity* **then** *Result* := *True* **else** *Result* := *False* **end**
>
> perhaps simplified (thanks to the rules of default initialization) into
>
>> **if** *count = capacity* **then** *Result* := *True* **end**

So the presence of related elements in the body and the postcondition is not evidence of redundancy; it is evidence of consistency between the implementation and the specification — that is to say, of correctness as defined at the beginning of this chapter.

In passing, we have encountered a property of assertions that will merit further development: their relevance for authors of client classes, whom we should not ask to read routine implementations, but who need a more abstract description of the routine's role. This idea will lead to the notion of **short form** discussed later in this chapter as the basic class documentation mechanism.

See "Including functions in assertions", page 400.

A caveat: for practical reasons we will allow assertions to include some seemingly imperative elements (functions). This issue will be explored at the end of this chapter.

As a summary of this discussion it is useful to list the words that have been used to contrast the two categories of software elements:

The imperative-applicative opposition

Implementation	Specification
Instruction	Expression
How	What
Imperative	Applicative
Prescription	Description

A note on empty structures

The precondition of the creation procedure *make* in class *STACK1* requires a comment. It states $n >= 0$, hence allowing empty stacks. If n is zero, *make* will call the creation procedure for arrays, also named *make*, with arguments *1* and *0* for the lower and upper bounds respectively. This is not an error, but follows from a convention regarding *ARRAY*'s creation procedure: using a first argument greater than the second by one creates an empty array.

A zero n for a stack, or a first creation argument greater than the second for an array, is not wrong but simply means that this particular stack or array should be empty. An error would only occur out of a call attempting to access an element from the structure, for example a *put* for the stack or an *item* for the array, both of whose preconditions will always be false for an empty structure ("my customer is always wrong").

When you define a general data structure such as a stack or array, you should determine whether the case of an empty structure is conceptually meaningful. In some cases it is not: for example most definitions of the notion of *tree* start from the assumption that there is at least one node, the root. But if the empty case raises no logical impossibility, as with arrays and stacks, you should plan for it in the design of your data structure, acknowledging that clients will, every once in a while, create empty instances, and should not suffer for it. An application system may for example need a stack for n elements, where n is an upper bound on the number of elements to be stacked, computed by the application just before it creates the stack; in some runs that number may be zero. This is not an error, simply an extreme case.

The array mechanism of Algol W provides a counter-example. When a dynamically allocated array has an empty range, the program terminates in error — even if it was a perfectly valid array which simply happened to be empty on that particular run. This is too restrictive: an array with zero size is valid, it simply does not allow access to any element.

Precondition design: tolerant or demanding?

Central to Design by Contract is the idea, expressed as the Non-Redundancy principle, *The principle was on* that for any consistency condition that could jeopardize a routine's proper functioning you *page 343.* should assign enforcement of this condition to only one of the two partners in the contract.

Which one? In each case you have two possibilities:

- Either you assign the responsibility to clients, in which case the condition will appear as part of the routine's precondition.

- Or you appoint the supplier, in which case the condition will appear in a conditional instruction of the form **if** *condition* **then** ..., or an equivalent control structure, in the routine's body.

We can call the first attitude *demanding* and the second one *tolerant*. The *STACK2* class illustrates the demanding style; a tolerant version of the class would have routines with no preconditions, such as

```
remove is
                                                    Warning: not the
                                                    recommended style.
        -- Remove top element

    do

        if empty then

            print ("Error: attempt to pop an empty stack")

        else

            count := count – 1

        end

    end
```

In the analogy with human contracts we can think of the demanding style as characterizing an experienced contractor who expects his clients to "do their homework" before calling on him; he has no trouble finding business, and will reject requests that appear too broad or unreasonable. The tolerant style evokes the image of a freshly established consulting practice, whose owner is so desperate for business that he will take anything, having put in his driveway a big sign:

Which is the better style? To a certain extent this is a matter of personal choice (as opposed to the Non-Redundancy principle, which was absolute in stating that it is *never* acceptable to deal with a correctness condition on both the client and supplier sides). A strong case can be made, however, for the demanding style illustrated by *STACK2*, especially in the case of software meant to be reusable — and in O-O development we should always write our software with the goal of ultimately making it reusable.

At first the tolerant style might appear better for both reusability and reliability; after all the demanding approach appears to put more responsibility on the clients, and there are typically many clients for a single supplier — even more so for a reusable class. Is it not preferable, then, to let the supplier take care of the correctness conditions once and for all, rather than require every client to do it for itself?

If we look more closely at the issue this reasoning does not hold. The correctness conditions describe what the routine requires to be able to do its job properly. The tolerant *remove* on the facing page is a good counter-example: what can a poor stack-popping routine do for an empty stack? It makes a brave attempt by outputting an error message, but this is clearly inadequate: a specialized utility module such as a stack handler has no business messing up the system's user output. We could try something more sophisticated, but *remove* simply does not have the proper context; the focus of class *STACK2* is too narrow to determine what to do in the case of an empty stack. **Only the client** — a module using stacks in some application, for example the parsing module in a compiler — has enough information to decide what an attempt to pop an empty stack really means: is it a normal although useless request that we should simply ignore, executing a null operation? Or is it an error, and if so, how should we handle it: raise an exception, correct the situation before trying again, or (the least likely answer) output a user-visible error message?

In the square root example, you may remember the fictitious routine text quoted in the discussion preceding the Non-Redundancy principle:

Page 343.

if $x < 0$ **then**
    "Handle the error, somehow"
else
    "Proceed with normal square root computation"
end

The operative word is "somehow". The **then** clause is incantation more than software: there is really no good general-purpose technique for handling the $x < 0$ case. Here again a general-purpose routine has no clue. Only the client author can know what the call means in this case — an error in the software, a case in which the expected result is 0, a reason to trigger an exception…

In this case as in the attempt at a tolerant *remove*, the position of the routine is not unlike that of a postman asked to deliver a postcard with no delivery address and no return address: the case falls outside of the contract, and there is no good way to decide what to do.

In the spirit of Design by Contract, the demanding approach to precondition design does not attempt to produce routines that are all things to all clients. Instead, it insists that each routine do a well-defined job and do it well (correctly, efficiently, generally enough to be reusable by many clients…), and specify clearly what cases it cannot handle. In fact you cannot hope that the routine will do its job well *unless* you have carefully circumscribed that job. A factotum routine, which wants to do a computation and check for abnormal cases and take corrective actions and notify the client and produce a result anyway, will most likely fail to fulfill any of these goals properly.

The routine author does not try to outsmart his clients; if he is not sure of what the routine is supposed to do in a certain abnormal situation, he excludes it explicitly through the precondition. This attitude is more generally a consequence of the overall theme in this book: building software systems as sets of modules that mind their own business.

If you read the supplementary mathematical section in the chapter on abstract data types, you may have noted the similarity between the present discussion and the arguments for using partial functions in the mathematical model, rather than special error values such as $\omega_{INTEGER}$. The two ideas are indeed very close, and Design by Contract is in part the application to software construction of the concept of partial function, so remarkably flexible and powerful in formal specification.

"Alternatives to partial functions", page 151.

A word of caution: the demanding approach is only applicable if the preconditions remain reasonable. Otherwise the job of writing a module would become easy: start every routine with **require** *False* so that, as we have seen, any routine body will be correct. What does "reasonable" concretely mean for the precondition of a routine? Here is a more precise characterization:

Reasonable Precondition principle

Every routine precondition (in a "demanding" design approach) must satisfy the following requirements:

- The precondition appears in the official documentation distributed to authors of client modules.

- It is possible to justify the need for the precondition in terms of the specification only.

The first requirement will be supported by the notion of short form studied later in this chapter. The second requirement excludes restrictions meant only for the supplier's convenience in implementing the routine. For example when you want to pop a stack the precondition **not** *empty* is a logical requirement that can be justified "in terms of the specification only", through the simple observation that in an empty stack there is nothing to pop; and when you want to compute the real square root of a number, the precondition $x >= 0$ is a direct result of the mathematical property that negative real numbers do not have real square roots.

The general stack ADT was studied in chapter 6; the bounded stack ADT was the subject of exercise E6.9, page 162.

Some restrictions may arise from the general kind of implementation selected. For example the presence of **require not** *full* as precondition to the push operation *put* in *STACK2* is due to the decision of using an array for the implementation of stacks. But such a case does not violate the principle, as the bounded nature of *STACK2* stacks has been made part of the specification: the class does not claim to represent arbitrary stacks, but only stacks of finite maximum capacity (as expressed for example in the **indexing** clause of the class). The abstract data type serving as specification of this class is not the most general notion of stack, but the notion of bounded stack.

> In general, it is desirable to avoid bounded structures; even a stack implemented by arrays can use array resizing. This is the case with the most commonly used stack class in the Base libraries, which follows the *STACK2* style but without a notion of *capacity*; a stack that overflows its current capacity resizes itself silently to accommodate the new elements.

Preconditions and export status

You may have noted the need for a supplementary requirement on preconditions, which does not figure in the Reasonable Precondition principle: to be satisfiable by the clients, the precondition must not use features that are hidden from the clients as a result of export restrictions.

Assume for example the following situation:

```
                    -- Warning: this is an invalid class, for purposes of illustration only.
class SNEAKY feature

    tricky is
            require
                    accredited
            do
                    ...
            end

feature {NONE}

    accredited: BOOLEAN is do ... end

end -- class SNEAKY
```

The specification for *tricky* states that any call to that procedure must satisfy the condition expressed by the boolean function *accredited*. But whereas the class exports *tricky* to all clients, it keeps *accredited* secret, so that clients have no way of finding out, before a call, whether the call is indeed correct. This clearly unacceptable situation is akin, in human contracts, to a deal in which the supplier would impose some conditions not stated explicitly in the contract, and hence could reject a client's request as incorrect without giving the client any way to determine in advance whether it is correct.

The reason why the Reasonable Precondition principle does not cover such cases is that here a methodological principle does not suffice: we need a language rule to be enforced by compilers, not left to the decision of developers.

The rule must take into account all possible export situations, not just those illustrated above in which a feature is available to all clients (*tricky*) or to no client (*accredited*). As you will recall from the discussion of information hiding, it is also possible to make a feature available to some clients only, by declaring it in a feature clause appearing as **feature** {*A*, *B*, ...}, which makes it available only to *A*, *B*, ... and their descendants. Hence the language rule:

"SELECTIVE EXPORTS AND INFORMATION HID-ING", 7.8, page 191.

Precondition Availability rule

Every feature appearing in the precondition of a routine must be available to every client to which the routine is available.

With this rule every client that is in a position to call the feature will also be in a position to check for its precondition. The rule makes class *SNEAKY* invalid, since *tricky* is generally exported (available to all clients); you can turn it into a valid class by making *accredited* also generally exported. If *tricky* had appeared in a feature clause starting with **feature** {*A*, *B*, *C*}, then *accredited* would have to be exported at least to *A*, *B* and *C* (by appearing in the same feature clause as *tricky*, or by appearing in a clause of the form **feature** {*A*, *B*, *C*}, or **feature** {*A*, *B*, *C*, *D*, ...}, or just **feature**). Any violation of this rule is a compile-time error. Class *SNEAKY*, for example, will be rejected by the compiler.

There is no such rule for postconditions. It is not an error for some clauses of a postcondition clause to refer to secret features, or features that are not as broadly exported as the enclosing routine; this simply means that you are expressing properties of the routine's effect that are not directly usable by clients. This was the case with the *put* procedure in *STACK2*, which had the form

```
put (x: G) is
            -- Add x on top
    require
            not full
    do
            ...
    ensure
            ... Other clauses ...
            in_top_array_entry: representation @ count = x
    end
```

For the Other clauses *see page 350.*

The last postcondition clause indicates that the array entry at index *count* contains the element just pushed. This is an implementation property; even though *put* is generally available (exported to all clients), array *representation* is secret. But there is nothing wrong with the postcondition; it simply includes, along with properties that are directly useful to clients (the "Other clauses"), one that is only meaningful for someone who reads the entire class text. Such secret clauses will not appear in the "short" form of the class — the documentation for client authors.

A tolerant module

(On first reading you may skip this section or just look through it quickly.)

For filters of the first kind see "Assertions are not an input checking mechanism", page 345.
The simple but unprotected basic modules may not be robust enough for use by arbitrary clients. In some cases there will be a need for new classes to serve as filters, interposed not between the software and the external world (as with filters of the kind discussed earlier in this chapter) but between software and other software: possibly careless clients on one side, unprotected classes on the other.

Although we have seen that this is generally not the right approach, it is useful to examine how classes will look if we do decide to use the tolerant style in a specific case. Class *STACK3*, appearing next, illustrates the idea. Because the class needs to set integer error codes, it is convenient to rely on a property of the notation that has not been introduced yet: "unique" integer constants. If you declare a set of attributes as

a, *b*, *c*, …: *INTEGER* **is unique**

"UNIQUE VALUES", 18.6, page 654.
the effect is to define *a*, *b*, *c* … as integer constants with consecutive positive values. These values will be assigned by the compiler, and are guaranteed to be different for all constants thus declared, relieving you of having to invent separate codes. By convention, constant attributes such as these have names beginning with an upper-case letter, with the rest in lower case, as in *Underflow*.

Here, using this technique, is a tolerant version of our earlier stack class. Make sure to note that this class text (which you may just skim through on first reading) is included here only to make sure you understand the tolerant style; it is **not** an example of the generally recommended design — for reasons that will be discussed below, but will probably be clear enough as you browse through the text.

indexing
  description: "*Stacks*: *Dispenser structures with a Last-In, First-Out %*
      %access policy, and a fixed maximum capacity; *%*
      %tolerant version, setting an error code in case %
      %of impossible operations."

class *STACK3* [*G*] **creation**
  make

feature -- Initialization

    make (*n*: *INTEGER*) **is**

        -- Allocate stack for a maximum of *n* elements if $n > 0$;

        -- otherwise set *error* to *Negative_size*.

        -- No precondition!

    do

        if *capacity* $>= 0$ **then**

            capacity := *n*

            !! *representation* •*make* (*capacity*)

        else

            error := *Negative_size*

        end

    ensure

        error_code_if_impossible: $(n < 0) = (error = Negative\_size)$

        no_error_if_possible: $(n >= 0) = (error = 0)$

        capacity_set_if_no_error: $(error = 0)$ **implies** $(capacity = n)$

        allocated_if_no_error: $(error = 0)$ **implies** $(representation \mathrel{/=} Void)$

    end

feature -- Access

    item: *G* **is**

        -- Top element if present; otherwise the type's default value.

        -- with *error* set to *Underflow*.

        -- No precondition!

    do

        if not *empty* **then**

                         check *representation* $\mathrel{/=}$ *Void* **end**

            Result := *representation*•*item*

            error := *0*

        else

            error := *Underflow*

                -- In this case the result is the default value

        end

    ensure

        error_code_if_impossible: (**old** *empty*) $= (error = Underflow)$

        no_error_if_possible: (**not** (**old** *empty*)) $= (error = 0)$

    end

feature -- Status report

    empty: *BOOLEAN* **is**

        -- Number of stack elements

    do

        Result := $(capacity = 0)$ **or else** *representation*•*empty*

    end

error: *INTEGER*
> -- Error indicator, set by various features to a non-zero value
> -- if they cannot do their job

full: *BOOLEAN* **is**
> -- Number of stack elements
> **do**
>> *Result* := (*capacity* = *0*) **or else** *representation*.*full*
> **end**

Overflow, *Underflow*, *Negative_size*: *INTEGER* **is unique**
> -- Possible error codes

feature -- Element change

put (*x*: *G*) **is**
> -- Add *x* on top if possible; otherwise set error code.
> -- No precondition!
> **do**
>> **if** *full* **then**
>>> *error* := *Overflow*
>> **else**
>>>> **check** *representation* /= *Void* **end**
>>> *representation*.*put* (*x*); *error* := *0*
>> **end**
> **ensure**
>> *error_code_if_impossible*: (**old** *full*) = (*error* = *Overflow*)
>> *no_error_if_possible*: (**not old** *full*) = (*error* = *0*)
>> *not_empty_if_no_error*: (*error* = *0*) **implies not** *empty*
>> *added_to_top_if_no_error*: (*error* = *0*) **implies** *item* = *x*
>> *one_more_item_if_no_error*: (*error* = *0*) **implies** *count* = **old** *count* + *1*
> **end**

remove **is**
> -- Remove top element if possible; otherwise set error.
> -- No precondition!
> **do**
>> **if** *empty* **then**
>>> *error* := *Underflow*
>> **else**
>>>> **check** *representation* /= *Void* **end**
>>> *representation*.*remove*
>>> *error* := *0*
>> **end**
> **ensure**
>> *error_code_if_impossible*: (**old** *empty*) = (*error* = *Underflow*)
>> *no_error_if_possible*: (**not old** *empty*) = (*error* = *0*)
>> *not_full_if_no_error*: (*error* = *0*) **implies not** *full*
>> *one_fewer_item_if_no_error*: (*error* = *0*) **implies** *count* = **old** *count* – *1*
> **end**

feature {*NONE*} -- Implementation

    representation: *STACK2* [*G*]

        -- The unprotected stack used as implementation

    capacity: *INTEGER*

        -- The maximum number of stack elements

end -- class *STACK3*

The operations of this class have no preconditions (or, more accurately, have *True* as their preconditions). For those that may result in abnormal situations, the postcondition has been refined to distinguish between correct and erroneous processing. An operation such as *s.remove*, where *s* is a *STACK3*, will set *s.error* to 0 or to *Underflow* (which, from the rules on unique values, is known to be strictly positive) and, in the latter case, do nothing else. It is still the caller's responsibility to check for *s.error* after the call. As noted, a general-purpose module such as *STACK3* has no way to decide what to do in the case of an erroneous popping attempt: produce an error message, take corrective action...

Such filter modules serve to separate algorithmic techniques to deal with normal cases and techniques for handling errors. This is the distinction between correctness and robustness explained at the beginning of this book: writing a module that performs correctly in legal cases is one task; making sure that other cases are also processed decently is another. Both are necessary, but they should be handled separately. Failure to do so is one of the principal reasons why so many software systems are hopelessly complex: any algorithm that does anything useful also takes care of checking that it is applicable, and for good measure tries to handle the cases in which it is not. Such software soon mushrooms into a total mess.

See "A REVIEW OF EXTERNAL FAC-TORS", 1.2, page 4.

A few technical comments apply to this example:

- An instance of *STACK3* is not an array but a structure containing a reference (*representation*) to an instance of *STACK2*, itself containing a reference to an array. These two indirections, detrimental to efficiency, can be avoided through inheritance as studied in later chapters.

- The boolean operator **or else** is similar to **or** but ignores the second operand if it does not affect the result and trying to evaluate it could cause trouble.

*On **or else** see "Non-strict boolean operators", page 454.*

- The **check** instruction used in *put* and *remove* serves to state that a certain assertion is satisfied. It will be studied later in this chapter.

Finally, you will have noted the heaviness of *STACK3*, especially if you compare it to the simplicity that *STACK2* achieves with its precondition. *STACK3* is good evidence that a tolerant style may lead to uselessly complex software. The demanding style, in contrast, follows from the general spirit of Design by Contract. Trying to handle all possible (and impossible) cases is not necessarily the best way to help your clients. If instead you build classes that impose possibly strict but reasonable usage conditions, and describe these conditions precisely as part of the official documentation for the class, you actually make life easier for the clients. This has been called the **tough love** approach: you can often serve your clients better by being more restrictive.

Better an efficient supplier that states its functionally justified limitations than a overzealous one that tries to second-guess its clients, making possibly inappropriate decisions for abnormal cases, and sacrificing simplicity and efficiency.

For modules whose clients are other software modules, the demanding approach is usually the right one. A possible exception is the case of modules intended for clients whose authors use a non-O-O language and may not have understood the basic concepts of Design by Contract.

"Assertions are not an input checking mechanism", page 345. The tolerant approach remains useful for software elements that deal not with other software elements but with data coming from the outside world, such as user input, or sensor data. Then, as noted earlier, filter modules are often necessary to separate the actual processing modules (the physicists in our metaphor) from those which simply qualify data and reject anything that is not appropriate (the guards). This separation of concerns is essential for maintaining the simplicity of software elements on both sides. *STACK3* provides an idea of what such modules may look like.

11.8 CLASS INVARIANTS

Preconditions and postconditions describe the properties of individual routines. There is also a need for expressing global properties of the instances of a class, which must be preserved by all routines. Such properties will make up the class invariant, capturing the deeper semantic properties and integrity constraints characterizing a class.

Definition and example

Consider again the earlier implementation of stacks by arrays, the one without the protections (*STACK2*):

Page 349.

> **class** *STACK2* [*G*] **creation**
>   *make*
> **feature**
>   ... *make, empty, full, item, put, remove* ...
>   *capacity*: *INTEGER*
>   *count*: *INTEGER*
> **feature** {*NONE*} -- Implementation
>   *representation*: *ARRAY* [*G*]
> **end**

The attributes of the class — array *representation* and integers *capacity* and *count* — constitute the stack representation. Although routine preconditions and postconditions, given earlier, express some of the semantic properties of stacks, they fail to express other important consistency properties linking the attributes. For example, *count* should always remain between 0 and *capacity*:

> *0 <= count; count <= capacity*

(implying also that *capacity >= 0*), and *capacity* should be the array size:

capacity = representation.capacity

A class invariant is such an assertion, expressing general consistency constraints that apply to every class instance as a whole; this is different from preconditions and postconditions, which characterize individual routines.

The above assertions involve only attributes. Invariants may also express the semantic relations between functions, or between functions and attributes. For example the invariant for *STACK2* may include the following property describing the connection between *empty* and *count*:

empty = (count = 0)

In this example, the invariant assertion links an attribute and a function; it is not particularly interesting as it merely repeats an assertion that appears in the postcondition of the function (here *empty*). More useful assertions are those which involve either only attributes, as above, or more than one function.

Here is another typical example. Assume — in line with previous examples dealing with the notion of bank account — that we have a class *BANK_ACCOUNT* with features *deposits_list*, *withdrawals_list* and *balance*. Then the invariant for such a class could include a clause of the form:

This example was first discussed in "Uniform Access", page 55. It will serve again to illustrate persistence issues: "Correction", page 1045.

consistent_balance: *deposits_list.total – withdrawals_list.total = balance*

where the function *total* gives the cumulated value of a list of operations (deposits or withdrawals). This states the basic consistency condition between the values accessible through features *deposits_list*, *withdrawals_list* and *balance*.

Form and properties of class invariants

Syntactically, a class invariant is an assertion, appearing in the **invariant** clause of the class, after the features and just before the **end**, as in

class *STACK4 [G]* **creation**

     … As in *STACK2* …

feature

     … As in *STACK2* …

invariant

     count_non_negative: *0 <= count*

     count_bounded: *count <= capacity*

     consistent_with_array_size: *capacity = representation.capacity*

     empty_if_no_elements: *empty = (count = 0)*

     item_at_top: *(count > 0)* **implies** *(representation.item (count) = item)*

end

For the features of STACK2 see page 349.

An invariant for a class *C* is a set of assertions that every instance of *C* will satisfy at all "stable" times. Stable times are those in which the instance is in an observable state:

- On instance creation, that is to say after execution of !! *a* or !! *a*.*make* (…), where *a* is of type *C*.

- Before and after every remote call *a*.*r* (…) to a routine *r* of the class.

The following figure, showing the life of an object, helps put the notions of invariant and stable time in place.

The life of an object

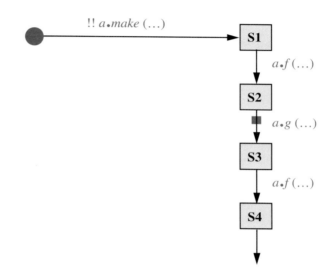

Life as an object, to tell the truth, is not that thrilling (in case you ever wondered). At the beginning — left of the figure — you do not exist. You are begot by a creation instruction !! *a* or !! *a*.*make* (…), or a *clone*, and reach your first station in life. Then things get quite boring: through some reference *a*, clients use you, one after the other, by applying operations of the form *a*.*f* (…) where *f* is a feature of your generating class. And so on forever, or at least until execution terminates.

The invariant is the characteristic property of the states represented by gray squares in the figure — S1 etc. These are the "stable times" mentioned above: those at which the object is observable from the outside, in the sense that a client can apply a feature to it. They include:

- The state that results from the creation of an object (S1 in the figure).

Chapter 30 covers concurrency; see in particular "Concurrent accesses to an object", page 982.

- The states immediately before and after a call of the form *a*.*some_routine* (…) executed by a client.

Here the context is sequential computation, but the ideas will transpose to concurrent systems in a later chapter.

An invariant that varies

In spite of its name, the invariant does not need to be satisfied at all times, although in the *STACK4* example it does remain true after the initial creation. In the more general case, it is perfectly acceptable for a procedure *g* to begin by trying to work towards its goal — its postcondition — and in the process to destroy the invariant (as in human affairs, trying to do something useful may disrupt the established order of things); then it spends the second part of its execution scurrying to restore the invariant without losing too much of whatever ground has been gained. At some intermediate stages, such as the instant marked ■ in the figure, the invariant will not hold; this is fine as long as the procedure reestablishes the invariant before terminating its execution.

Who must preserve the invariant?

Qualified calls, of the form $a.f\,(\ldots)$, executed on behalf of a client, are the only ones that must always start from a state satisfying the invariant and leave a state satisfying the invariant; there is no such rule for unqualified calls of the form $f\,(\ldots)$, which are not directly executed by clients but only serve as auxiliary tools for carrying out the needs of qualified calls. As a consequence, the obligation to maintain the invariant applies only to the body of features that are exported either generally or selectively; a secret feature — one that is available to no client — is not affected by the invariant.

From this discussion follows the rule that precisely defines when an assertion is a correct invariant for a class:

Invariant rule

An assertion *I* is a correct class invariant for a class *C* if and only if it meets the following two conditions:

E1 • Every creation procedure of *C*, when applied to arguments satisfying its precondition in a state where the attributes have their default values, yields a state satisfying *I*.

E2 • Every exported routine of the class, when applied to arguments and a state satisfying both *I* and the routine's precondition, yields a state satisfying *I*.

Note that in this rule:

- Every class is considered to have a creation procedure, defined as a null operation if not explicitly specified.

- The state of an object is defined by all its fields (the values of the class attributes for this particular instance).

- The precondition of a routine may involve the initial state and the arguments.

- The postcondition may only involve the final state, the initial state (through the **old** notation) and, in the case of a function, the returned value, given by the predefined entity *Result*.

- The invariant may only involve the state.

   Assertions may use functions, but such functions are an indirect way of referring to the attributes — to the state.

   A mathematical statement of the Invariant rule appears later in this chapter.

This is the topic of exercise E11.8, page 409. The reasoning for preconditions and postconditions was in "Assertions are not control structures", page 346
You can use the Invariant rule as a basis for answering a question that comes up in light of earlier discussions: what would it mean if an invariant clause turned out to be violated during system execution? We saw before that a precondition violation signals an error (a "bug") in the client, a postcondition violation an error in the supplier. The answer will be for invariants as for postconditions; you have all the elements for deriving this property by yourself.

The role of class invariants in software engineering

Property E2 indicates that we may consider the invariant as being implicitly added (**and**ed) to both the precondition and postcondition of every exported routine. So in principle the notion of invariant is superfluous: we could do without it by enriching the preconditions and postconditions of all routines in the class.

Such a transformation is of course not desirable. It would complicate the routine texts; but more importantly, we would lose the deeper meaning of the invariant, which transcends individual routines and applies to the class as a whole. One should in fact consider that the invariant applies not only to the routines actually written in the class, but also to any ones that might be added later, thus serving as control over future evolution of the class. This will be reflected in the inheritance rules.

In the view of software development introduced at the beginning of this book, we accept that change is inevitable, and we try to control it. Some aspects of a software system, and of its individual components — classes — may be expected to change faster than others. Adding, removing or changing features, in particular, is a frequent and normal event. In this volatile process one will want to cling to properties that, although they may change too — for we can hardly guarantee that any aspect of a system will remain set for eternity — will change far less often. Invariants, because they capture the fundamental semantic constraints applying to a class, play this role.

The *STACK2* example illustrates the basic ideas, but to appreciate the full power of the concept of invariant you should be on the lookout for further examples of invariants in the rest of this book. To me the notion of the invariant is one of the most illuminating concepts that can be learned from the object-oriented method. Only when I have derived the invariant (for a class that I write) or read and understood it (for someone else's class) do I feel that I know what the class is about.

Invariants and contracting

Invariants have a clear interpretation in the contract metaphor. Human contracts often contain references to general clauses or regulations that apply to all contracts within a certain category; think of a city's zoning regulations, which apply to all house-building contracts. Invariants play a similar role for software contracts: the invariant of a class affects all the contracts between a routine of the class and a client.

Let us probe further. It was noted above that we may consider the invariant as being added to both the precondition and postcondition of every exported routine. Let *body* be the body of a routine (the set of instructions in its **do** clause), *pre* its precondition, *post* its postcondition and *INV* the class invariant. The correctness requirement on the routine may be expressed, using the notation introduced earlier in this chapter, as:

$$\{INV \text{ and } pre\} \ body \ \{INV \text{ and } post\}$$

The notation was defined on page 335.

(As you will remember this means: any execution of *body*, started in any state in which *INV* and *pre* both hold, will terminate in a state in which both *INV* and *post* hold.)

For the supplier author — the person who writes *body* — is the invariant good news or bad news, that is to say, does it make the job easier or harder?

The answer, as you will have figured out from the earlier discussion, is: both. Remember our lazy job applicant, who wanted a *strong* precondition and a *weak* postcondition. Here adding *INV* makes stronger or equal both the precondition and the postcondition. (From the rules of logic, *a* **and** *b* always implies *a*, that is to say, is stronger than or equal to *a*.) So, if you are in charge of implementing the *body*, the invariant:

- Makes your job easier: in addition to the official precondition *pre*, you may assume that the initial state satisfies *INV*, further restricting the set of cases that you must handle.

- Makes your job harder: in addition to your official postcondition *post*, you must ensure that the final state satisfies *INV*.

These observations are consistent with the view of the invariant as a general consistency condition that applies to the class as a whole, and hence to all of its routines. As the author of such a routine, you have the benefit of being permitted to take this condition for granted at the start of the routine; but you have the obligation to ensure that the routine will satisfy it again on termination — so that the next routine to be executed on the same object can in turn take it for granted.

The class *BANK_ACCOUNT* mentioned above, with the invariant clause

$$deposits\_list \bullet total - withdrawals\_list \bullet total = balance$$

provides a good example. If you have to add a routine to the class, this clause gives you the guarantee that the features *deposits_list*, *withdrawals_list* and *balance* have consistent values, so you do not need to check this property (and then, as we have seen, you **must not** check it). But it also means that you must write the routine so that, whatever else it does, it will leave the object in a state that again satisfies the property. So a procedure *withdraw*, used to record a withdrawal operation, should not just update *withdrawals_list*: it must also, if *balance* is an attribute, update the value of *balance* to take the withdrawal into account and restore the invariant, enabling any other routine called later on the same object to benefit from the same original assumption that facilitated the work of *withdraw*.

See "Uniform Access", page 55.

Rather than an attribute, *balance* could be a function, whose body computes and returns the value of *deposits_list.total – withdrawals_list.total*; in this case procedure *withdraw* does not need to do anything special to maintain the invariant. The ability to switch at will between the two representations without affecting the client is an illustration of the principle of Uniform Access.

This example shows the idea of class invariant as a transposition to software of one of the rules of polite behavior: that if you use a shared facility — say an office kitchen — you should leave it for others, after each use, in the state in which you would like to find it when you start.

11.9 WHEN IS A CLASS CORRECT?

If you prefer to skip the theory you should turn to "AN ASSERTION INSTRUCTION", 11.11, page 378.

Although we still have to see a few more constructs involving assertions, it is useful to take a brief pause and examine some of the implications of what we have learned about preconditions, postconditions and invariants. This section does not introduce any new constructs, but describes some of the theoretical background. Even on your first reading I think you should get familiar with these ideas as they are central to a proper understanding of the method, and will be precious when we try to figure out how to use inheritance well.

The correctness of a class

With preconditions, postconditions and invariants, we can now define precisely what it means for a class to be correct.

The basis for the answer appeared at the beginning of this chapter: a class, like any other software element, is correct or incorrect not by itself but with respect to a specification. By introducing preconditions, postconditions and invariants we have given ourselves a way to include some of the specification in the class text itself. This provides a basis against which to assess correctness: the class is correct if and only if its implementation, as given by the routine bodies, is consistent with the preconditions, postconditions and invariant.

The notation $\{P\}\ A\ \{Q\}$ introduced at the beginning of this chapter helps express this precisely. Remember that the meaning of such a correctness formula is: whenever A is executed in a state satisfying P, the execution will terminate in a state satisfying Q.

Let C be a class, *INV* its class invariant. For any routine r of the class, call $pre_r\ (x_r)$ and $post_r\ (x_r)$ its precondition and postcondition; x_r denotes the possible arguments of r, to which both the precondition and the postcondition may refer. (If the precondition or postcondition is missing from the routine text, then pre_r or $post_r$ is just *True*.) Call $Body_r$ the body of routine r.

Finally, let $Default_C$ be the assertion expressing that the attributes of C have the default values of their types. For example $Default_{STACK2}$, referring to the earlier stack class, is the assertion

representation = Void
capacity = 0
count = 0

These notations permit a general definition of class correctness:

Definition: class correctness

A class is correct with respect to its assertions if and only if:

C1 • For any valid set of arguments x_p to a creation procedure p:

$\{Default_C$ **and** $pre_p(x_p)\}$ $Body_p$ $\{post_p(x_p)$ **and** $INV\}$

C2 • For every exported routine r and any set of valid arguments x_r:

$\{pre_r(x_r)$ **and** $INV\}$ $Body_r$ $\{post_r(x_r)$ **and** $INV\}$

This rule — previewed informally in the *BANK_ACCOUNT* example — is a mathematical statement of the earlier informal diagram showing the lifecycle of a typical object, which is worth looking at again:

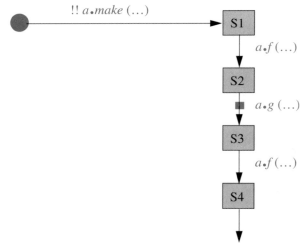

The life of an object

(*This figure first appeared on page 365.*)

Condition C1 means that any creation procedure (such as *make* in the figure), when called with its precondition satisfied, must yield an initial state (S1 in the figure) that satisfies the invariant and the procedure's postcondition. Condition C2 expresses that any exported routine r (such as f or g in the figure), if called in a state (S1, S2 or S3) satisfying both its precondition and the invariant, must terminate in a state that satisfies both its postcondition and the invariant.

If we focus on invariants, we may look at the preceding definition of class correctness as working by induction on the set of instances of a class. Rule C1 is the base step of the induction, stating that the invariant holds for all newborn objects — those which directly result from a creation instruction. Rule C2 is the induction step, through which we determine that if a certain generation of instances satisfies the invariant, then the next generation — the set of instances obtained by applying exported features to the members of the current generation — will also satisfy it. Since by starting from newborn objects and going from generation to generation through exported features we obtain all possible instances of the class, the mechanism enables us to determine that all instances satisfy the invariant.

Two practical observations:

- If the class has no **creation** clause, we may consider that it has a single implicit creation procedure *nothing* with an empty body. Applying rule C1 to $B_{nothing}$ then means that $Default_C$ must imply INV: the default values must satisfy the invariant.

- A requirement of the form $\{P\}\ A\ \{Q\}$ does not commit A in any way for cases in which P is not initially satisfied. So the notation is in line with the property discussed in detail earlier in this chapter: the contract is not binding on the routine if the client fails to observe its part of the deal. Accordingly, the definition of class correctness leaves the routines of the class free to do as they please for any call that violates the precondition or the invariant.

What has just been described is how to *define* the correctness of a class. In practice, we may also want to *check* whether a given class is indeed correct. This issue will be discussed later in this chapter.

The role of creation procedures

See "CREATION PROCEDURES", 8.4, page 236, in particular "Rules on creation procedures", page 238

The discussion of invariants yields a better understanding of the notion of creation procedure.

A class invariant expresses the set of properties that objects (instances of the class) must satisfy in what has been called the stable moments of their lifetime. In particular, these properties must hold upon instance creation.

The standard object allocation mechanism initializes fields to the default values of the corresponding attribute types; these values may or may not satisfy the invariant. If not, a specific creation procedure is required; it should set the values of the attributes so as to satisfy the invariant. So creation may be seen as the operation that ensures that all instances of a class start their lives in a correct mode — one in which the invariant is satisfied.

The first presentation of creation procedures introduced them as a way to answer a more mundane (and obvious) question: how do I override the default initialization rules if they do not suit me for a particular class, or if I want to provide my clients with more than one initialization mechanism? But with the introduction of invariants and the theoretical discussion summarized by rule C1, we also see the more profound role of creation procedures: they are here to make sure that any instance of the class, when it starts its life, already satisfies the fundamental rules of its caste — the class invariant.

Arrays revisited

The library class *ARRAY* was sketched in the previous chapter. Only now, however, are we in a position to give its definition properly. The notion of array fundamentally requires preconditions, postconditions and an invariant.

See "ARRAYS", 10.4, page 325.

Here is a better sketch with assertions. Preconditions express the basic requirement on array access and modification: indices should be in the permitted range. The invariant shows the relation between *count*, *lower* and *upper*; it would allow *count* to be implemented as a function rather than an attribute.

> **indexing**
>> *description*: "*Sequences of values, all of the same type or of a conforming one, %*
>>> *%accessible through integer indices in a contiguous interval*"
>
> **class** *ARRAY* [*G*] **creation**
>> *make*
>
> **feature** -- Initialization
>> *make* (*minindex, maxindex*: *INTEGER*) **is**
>>> -- Allocate array with bounds *minindex* and *maxindex*
>>> -- (empty if *minindex* > *maxindex*).
>>
>> **require**
>>> *meaningful_bounds*: *maxindex* >= *minindex* – *1*
>>
>> **do**
>>> . . .
>>
>> **ensure**
>>> *exact_bounds_if_non_empty*: (*maxindex* >= *minindex*) **implies**
>>>> ((*lower* = *minindex*) **and** (*upper* = *maxindex*))
>>> *conventions_if_empty*: (*maxindex* < *minindex*) **implies**
>>>> ((*lower* = *1*) **and** (*upper* = *0*))
>>
>> **end**
>
> **feature** -- Access
>> *lower, upper, count*: *INTEGER*
>>> -- Minimum and maximum legal indices; array size.
>>
>> **infix** "@", *item* (*i*: *INTEGER*): *G* **is**
>>> -- Entry of index *i*
>>
>> **require**
>>> *index_not_too_small*: *lower* <= *i*
>>> *index_not_too_large*: *i* <= *upper*
>>
>> **do** ... **end**

feature -- Element change

put (v: G; i: $INTEGER$) **is**

-- Assign v to the entry of index i

require

$index\_not\_too\_small$: $lower <= i$

$index\_not\_too\_large$: $i <= upper$

do

…

ensure

$element\_replaced$: $item$ (i) = v

end

invariant

$consistent\_count$: $count = upper - lower + 1$

$non\_negative\_count$: $count >= 0$

end -- class $ARRAY$

The only part left blank is the implementation of routines *item* and *put*. Because efficient array manipulation will require low-level system access, the routines will actually be implemented using **external** clauses, introduced in a later chapter.

11.10 THE ADT CONNECTION

This section explores the implications of previous concepts. Some readers may prefer to skip to "AN ASSERTION INSTRUCTION", 11.11, page 378

A class — you have heard this quite a few times by now — is an implementation of an abstract data type, whether formally specified or (as in many cases) just implicitly understood. As noted at the beginning of this chapter, we may view assertions as a way to re-introduce into the class the semantic properties of the underlying ADT. Let us perfect our understanding of assertion concepts by clarifying the connection of assertions to the components of an abstract data type specification.

Not just a collection of functions

As studied in the ADT chapter, an abstract data type is made of four elements:

- The name of the type, possibly with generic parameters (TYPES paragraph).
- The list of functions with their signatures (FUNCTIONS paragraph).
- The axioms (AXIOMS paragraph) expressing properties of the functions' results.
- The restrictions on the functions' applicability (PRECONDITIONS paragraph)

Simple-minded applications of abstract data types often overlook the last two parts. This removes much of the appeal of the approach, since preconditions and axioms express the semantic properties of the functions. If you omit them and simply view "stack" as encapsulating the (not specified further) operations *put*, *remove* etc., you retain the benefits of information hiding, but that is all. The notion of stack becomes an empty shell, with no semantics other than suggested by the operation names. (And in the approach of this book that is of little comfort, since for reasons of structure, consistency and reusability we deliberately choose general names — *put*, *remove*, *item* ... — rather than concrete, type-specific names such as *push*, *pop* and *top*.)

This risk transposes to programming in an O-O language: the routines which are supposed to implement the operations of the corresponding abstract data types could in principle perform just about any operations. Assertions avert that risk by bringing the semantics back in.

Class features *vs.* ADT functions

See "Function categories", page 134.

To understand the relation between assertions and ADTs we need first to establish the relation between class features and their ADT counterparts — the ADT's functions. An earlier discussion introduced three categories of function: creators, queries and commands. As you will recall, the category of a function

$$f : A \times B \times \ldots \to X$$

depended on where the ADT, say T, appeared among the types A, B, ... X involved in this signature:

- If T appears on the right only, f is a creator; in the class it yields a creation procedure.

- If T appears only on the left of the arrow, f is a query, providing access to properties of instances of the class. The corresponding features are either attributes or functions (collectively called queries, for classes as well as ADTs). *See "Attributes and routines", page 173.*

- If T appears on both the left and the right, f is a command function, which yields a new object from one or more existing objects. Often f will be expressed, at the implementation stage, by a procedure (also called a command) which modifies an object, rather than creating a new object as a function would do.

Expressing the axioms

From the correspondence between ADT functions and class features we can deduce the correspondence between semantic ADT properties and class assertions:

- A precondition for one of the specification's functions reappears as precondition clauses for the corresponding routine.

- An axiom involving a command function, possibly with one or more query functions, reappears as postcondition clauses of the corresponding procedure.

- Axioms involving only query functions reappear as postconditions of the corresponding functions or (especially if more than one function is involved, or if at least one of the queries is implemented as an attribute) as clauses of the invariant.

- Axioms involving constructor functions reappear in the postcondition of the corresponding creation procedure.

Exercise E11.2, page 408. The ADT specification is on page 139.

At this point you should go back to the preconditions and axioms of the ADT *STACK* and compare them with the assertions of class *STACK4* (including those of *STACK2*).

Non-mathematical readers may skip this section

The abstraction function

It is instructive to think of the preceding observations in terms of the following figure, inspired by the discussion in [Hoare 1972a], which pictures the notion "*C* is a correct implementation of *A*".

Transformations on abstract and concrete objects

(See also the figure on page 229.)

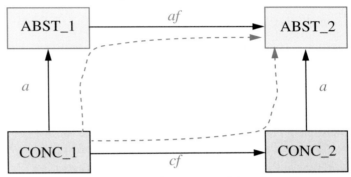

Abstract objects (instances of the ADT *A*)

Concrete objects (instances of the class *C*)

A is an abstract data type, and *C* as a class implementing it. For an abstract function *af* of the ADT specification — of which we assume for simplicity that it yields a result also of type *A* — there will be a concrete feature *cf* in the class.

The arrows labeled *a* represent the **abstraction function** which, for any instance of the class, or "concrete object", yields the abstract object (instance of the ADT) that it represents. As will be seen, this function is usually partial, and the inverse relation is usually not a function.

The implementation is correct if (for all functions *af* applicable to abstract data types, and their implementations *cf*) the diagram is commutative, that is to say:

> ### Class-ADT Consistency property
>
> $$(cf \,\mathbf{;}\, a) = (a \,\mathbf{;}\, af)$$

where **;** is the composition operator between functions; in other words, for any two functions *f* and *g*, *f* **;** *g* is the function *h* such that $h(x) = g(f(x))$ for every applicable *x*. (The composition *f* **;** *g* is also written $g \circ f$ with the order of the operands reversed.)

The property states that for every concrete object CONC_1, it does not matter in which order you apply the transformation (abstract *af* or concrete *cf*) and the abstraction; the two paths, represented by dotted lines, lead to the same abstract object ABST_2. The result is the same whether you:

- Apply the concrete transformation *cf*, then abstract the result, yielding *a* (*cf* (CONC_1)).

- Abstract first, then apply the abstract transformation *af*, yielding *af* (*a* (CONC_1)).

Implementation invariants

Certain assertions appear in invariants although they have no direct counterparts in the abstract data type specifications. These assertions involve attributes, including some secret attributes which, by definition, would be meaningless in the abstract data type. A simple example is the following properties appearing in the invariant of *STACK4*:

STACK4 and its invariant appeared on page 364.

> *count_non_negative*: *0 <= count*
>
> *count_bounded*: *count <= capacity*

Such assertions constitute the part of the class invariant known as the **implementation invariant**. They serve to express the consistency of the representation chosen in the class (here by attributes *count*, *capacity* and *representation*) vis-à-vis the corresponding abstract data type.

The figure on the previous page helps understand the concept of implementation invariant. It illustrates the characteristic properties of the abstraction function *a* (represented by the vertical arrows), which we should explore a little further.

First, is it correct to talk about *a* as being the abstraction *function*, as suggested by the upwards arrows representing *a* in the preceding figure? Recall that a function (partial or total) maps every source element to at most one target element, as opposed to the more general case of a relation which has no such restriction. If we go downwards rather than upwards in the figure and examine the inverse of *a*, which we may call the **representation relation**, we will usually find it not to be a function, since there are in general many possible representations of a given abstract object. In the array implementation that represents every stack as a pair *<representation, count>*, an abstract stack has many different representations, as illustrated by the figure on the facing page; they all have the same value for *count* and for the entries of array *representation* between indices *1* and *count*, but the size *capacity* of the array can be any value greater than or equal to *count*, and the array positions beyond index *count* may contain arbitrary values.

Since the class interface is restricted to the features directly deduced from the ADT's functions, clients have no way of distinguishing between the behaviors of several concrete objects that all represent the same abstract object (that is to say, all have the same *a* value). Note in particular that procedure *remove* in *STACK4* does its job simply by executing

> *count := count – 1*

without bothering to clear the previous top entry, now at index *count + 1*; changing an entry of index higher than *count* modifies a concrete stack object CS, but has no effect on the associated abstract stack *a* (CS).

So the implementation relation is usually not a function. But its inverse the abstraction function *a* (the upwards arrows in both figures) is indeed a function since every concrete object represents at most one abstract object. In the stack example, every valid *<representation, count>* pair represents just one abstract stack (the stack with *count* elements, given, from the bottom up, by the entries of *representation* at indices *1* to *count*).

Same abstract object, two representations

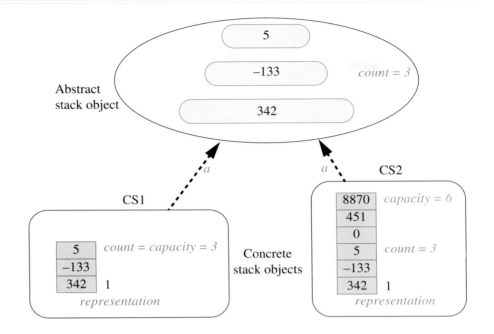

Both of the concrete stacks in this figure are implementations of the abstract stack consisting of three elements of values 342, –133 and 5 from the bottom up. That a is a function is a universal requirement: if the same concrete object could be interpreted as implementing more than one abstract object, the chosen representation would be ambiguous and hence inadequate. So it is proper that the arrow associated with a points up in all the figures depicting connections between abstract and concrete types. (The discussion for inheritance will suggest a similar convention.)

The abstraction function a is usually a *partial* function: not every possible concrete object is a valid representation of an abstract object. In the example, not every *<representation, count>* pair is a valid representation of an abstract stack; if *representation* is an array of capacity three and *count* has value 4, they do not together represent a stack. Valid representations (members of the domain of the abstraction function) are those pairs for which *count* has a value between zero and the size of the array. This property is the implementation invariant.

In mathematical terms, the implementation invariant is the characteristic function of the **domain** of the abstraction function, that is to say, the property that defines when that function is applicable. (The characteristic function of a subset A is the boolean property that is true on A and false elsewhere.)

The implementation invariant is the one part of the class's assertions that has no counterpart in the abstract data type specification. It relates not to the abstract data type, but to its representation. It defines when a candidate concrete object is indeed the implementation of one (and then only one) abstract object.

11.11 AN ASSERTION INSTRUCTION

The uses of assertions seen so far — preconditions, postconditions and class invariants — are central components of the method. They establish the connection between object-oriented software construction and the underlying theory (abstract data types). Class invariants, in particular, cannot be understood, or even discussed, in a non-O-O approach.

Some other uses of assertions, although less specific to the method, are also precious in a systematic software development process and should be part of our notation. They include the **check** instruction, as well as loop correctness constructs (loop invariant and variant) which will be reviewed in the next section.

The **check** instruction serves to express the software writer's conviction that a certain property will be satisfied at certain stages of the computation. Syntactically, the construct is an instruction, written under the form

> **check**
>   *assertion_clause*$_1$
>   *assertion_clause*$_2$
>   …
>   *assertion_clause*$_n$
> **end**

Including this instruction in the text of a routine is a way to state that:

"Whenever control reaches this instruction at execution time, the assertion shown (as given by its assertion clauses) will hold."

This is a way to reassure yourself that certain properties are satisfied, and (even more importantly) to make explicit for future readers of your software the hypotheses on which you have been relying. Writing software requires making frequent assumptions about properties of the objects of your system; as a trivial but typical example, any function call of the form *sqrt* (x), where *sqrt* is a routine requiring a non-negative argument, relies on the assumption that x is positive or zero. This assumption may be immediately obvious from the context, for example if the call is part of a conditional instruction of the form

> **if** $x >= 0$ **then** $y := sqrt\ (x)$ **end**

but the justification may also be more indirect, based for example on an earlier instruction that computed x as the sum of two squares:

> $x := a\ \wedge 2 + b \wedge 2$

The **check** instruction makes it possible to express such an assumption if it is not immediately obvious from the context, as in

> $x := a \wedge 2 + b \wedge 2$
> … Other instructions …
>   **check**
> $x >= 0$
>   -- Because x was computed above as a sum of squares.
>   **end**
> $y := sqrt\ (x)$

No **if** … **then** … protects the call to *sqrt* in this example; the **check** indicates that the call is correct. It is good practice to include, as here, a comment stating the reason invoked to support the assumption ("-- Because *x*..."). The extra two steps of indentation for the instruction are also part of the recommended style; they suggest that the instruction is not meant, in normal circumstances, to affect the algorithmic progression of the routine.

This example is typical of what is probably the most useful application of the **check** instruction: adding such an instruction just before a call to a routine that has a certain precondition (here we may assume that *sqrt* has a precondition requiring its argument to be non-negative), when you are convinced that the call satisfies the precondition but this is not immediately obvious from the context. As another example assume *s* is a stack and you include in your code a call

> *s*•*remove*

at a position where you are certain that *s* is not empty, for example because the call has been preceded by *n* "*put*" and *m* "*remove*" instructions with $n > m$. Then there is no need to protect the call by an **if not** *s*•*empty* **then**...; but if the reason for the correctness of the call is not immediately obvious from the context, you may want to remind the reader that the omission of any protection was a conscious decision, not an oversight. You can achieve this by adding before the call the instruction

> **check not** *s*•*empty* **end**

A variant of this case occurs when you write a call of the form *x*•*f* with the certainty that *x* is not void, so that you do not need to enclose this call in a conditional instruction **if** *x* /= *Void* **then** …, but the non-vacuity argument is not obvious from the context. We encountered this in the procedures *put* and *remove* of our "protected stack" class *STACK3*. The body of *put* used a call to the corresponding procedure in *STACK2*, as follows:

This is from the body of put on page 361.

```
if full then
        error := Overflow
else
                check representation /= Void end
        representation.put (x); error := 0
end
```

Exercise E11.5, page 409, asks you for the implementation invariant of STACK3

Here a reader might think the call *representation*•*put* (*x*) in the **else** potentially unsafe since it is not preceded by a test for *representation* /= *Void*. But if you examine the class text you will realize that if *full* is false then *capacity* must be positive and hence *representation* cannot be void. This is an important and not quite trivial property, which should be part of the implementation invariant of the class. In fact, with a fully stated implementation invariant, we should rewrite the **check** instruction as:

```
check
        representation_exists: representation /= Void
                -- Because of clause representation_exists_if_not_full of the
                -- implementation invariant.
end
```

In ordinary approaches to software construction, although calls and other operations often (as in the various preceding examples) rely for their correctness on various assumptions, these assumptions remain largely implicit. The developer will convince himself that a certain property always holds at a certain point, and will put this analysis to good use in writing the software text; but after a while all that survives is the text; the rationale is gone. Someone — even the original author, a few months later — who needs to understand the software, perhaps to modify it, will not have access to the assumption and will have to figure out from scratch what in the world the author may have had in mind. The **check** instruction helps avoid this problem by encouraging you to document your non-trivial assumptions.

> As with the other assertion mechanisms of this chapter, the benefit goes beyond helping you get things *right* in the first place, to helping you find that you got them *wrong*. You can, using a compilation option, turn the **check** into a true executable instruction, which will do nothing if all its assertion clauses are true, but will produce an exception and stop execution if any of them is false. So if one of your assumptions was actually not justified you should find out quickly. The mechanisms for enabling **check**-checking will be reviewed shortly.

11.12 LOOP INVARIANTS AND VARIANTS

Our last assertion constructs help us get loops right. They nicely complement the mechanisms seen so far, but are not really specific to the object-oriented method, so it is all right to skip this section on first reading.

If skipping, go to "USING ASSER-TIONS", 11.13, page 389.

Loop trouble

The ability to repeat a certain computation an arbitrary number of times without succumbing to exhaustion, indeed without experiencing any degradation whatsoever, is the principal difference between the computational abilities of computers and those of humans. This is why loops are so important; just imagine what you could do in a language that only has the other two principal control structures, sequencing and conditional instructions, but no loops (and no support for recursive routine calls, the other basic mechanism permitting iterative computations).

But with power comes risk. Loops are notoriously hard to get right. Typical trouble includes:

- "Off-by-one" errors (performing one iteration too many or too few).

- Improper handling of borderline cases such as empty structures: for example a loop may work properly on a large array, but fail when the array has zero or one element.

- Failure to terminate ("infinite looping") in some cases.

Binary search — a staple of Computing Science 101 courses — is a good illustration of how tricky loops can be even when they appear trivial. Consider an array t of integers assumed to be in increasing order and indexed from 1 to n; binary search is a way to decide whether a certain integer value x appears in the array: if the array has no elements, the

See exercise E11.7, page 409.

answer is no; if the array has one element, the answer is yes if and only if that element has value x; otherwise compare x to the element at the array's middle position, and repeat on the lower or higher half depending on whether that element is greater or lesser than x. The four loop algorithms below all attempt to implement this simple idea; unfortunately all are wrong, as you are invited to check by yourself by finding, for each of them, a case in which it will not work properly.

Recall that $t @ m$ denotes the element at index i in array t. The // operator denotes integer division, for example $7 // 2$ and $6 // 2$ have value 3. The loop syntax is explained next but should be self-explanatory; the **from** clause introduces the loop initialization.

Four (wrong) attempts at binary search. From [M 1990]

BS1	**BS2**

from
    $i := 1; j := n$
until $i = j$ **loop**
    $m := (i + j) // 2$
    if $t @ m <= x$ **then**
        $i := m$
    else
        $j := m$
    end
end
$Result := (x = t @ i)$
	from
	    $i := 1; j := n; found :=$ **false**
	until $i = j$ **and not** *found* **loop**
	    $m := (i + j) // 2$
	    if $t @ m < x$ **then**
	        $i := m + 1$
	    elseif $t @ m = x$ **then**
	        $found :=$ **true**
	    else
	        $j := m - 1$
	    end
	end
	$Result := found$

BS3	**BS4**

from
$i := 0; j := n$
until $i = j$ **loop**
    $m := (i + j + 1) // 2$
    if $t @ m <= x$ **then**
        $i := m + 1$
    else
        $j := m$
    end
end
if $i >= 1$ **and** $i <= n$ **then**
    $Result := (x = t @ i)$
else
    $Result :=$ **false**
end
	from
	    $i := 0; j := n + 1$
	until $i = j$ **loop**
	    $m := (i + j) // 2$
	    if $t @ m <= x$ **then**
	        $i := m + 1$
	    else
	        $j := m$
	    end
	end
	if $i >= 1$ **and** $i <= n$ **then**
	    $Result := (x = t @ i)$
	else
	    $Result :=$ **false**
	end

Getting loops right

The judicious use of assertions can help avoid such problems. A loop may have an associated assertion, the *loop invariant* (not to be confused with the class invariant for the enclosing class); it may also have a *loop variant*, not an assertion but an integer expression. The invariant and variant will help us guarantee that a loop is correct.

To understand these notions it is necessary to realize that a loop is always a way to compute a certain result by **successive approximations**.

Take the trivial example of computing the maximum value of an array of integers using the obvious algorithm:

maxarray (*t*: *ARRAY* [*INTEGER*]): *INTEGER* **is**

        -- The highest of the values in the entries of *t*

  require

      t.*capacity* >= *1*

  local

      i: *INTEGER*

  do

    from

        i := *t*.*lower*

        Result := *t* @ *lower*

    until *i* = *t*.*upper* **loop**

        i := *i* + *1*

        Result := *Result*.*max* (*t* @ *i*)

    end

  end

We initialize *i* to the array's lower bound *i* := *t*.*lower* and the entity *Result* representing the future result to the value of the associated entry *t* @ *lower*. (We know that this entry exists thanks to the routine's precondition, which states that the array has at least one element.) Then we iterate until *i* has reached the upper bound, at each stage increasing *i* by one and replacing *Result* by the value of *t* @ *i*, the element at index *i*, if higher than the previous value of *Result*. (We rely on a *max* function for integers: *a*.*max* (*b*), for two integers *a* and *b*, is the maximum of their values.)

This computation works by successive approximations. We approach the array by its successive slices: [*lower,lower*], [*lower,lower+1*], [*lower,lower+2*] and so on up to the full approximation [*lower, upper*].

***Approximating
an array by
successive slices***

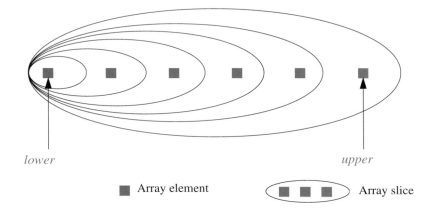

lower   *upper*

■ Array element   ⬭ ■ ■ ■ ⬭ Array slice

The invariant property is that at each stage through the loop *Result* is the maximum of the current approximation of the array. This is true after the initialization, since the instructions in the **from** clause ensure that *Result* is the maximum of the first approximation, the trivial slice [*lower, lower*] consisting of just one element. Then on each iteration we extend the slice by one element — improving our approximation of the array — and make sure to maintain the invariant by updating *Result* if the new value is higher than the previous maximum. At the end, the approximation covers the entire array, and since we have maintained invariant the property that *Result* is the maximum of the current approximation we know that it now is the maximum of the array as a whole.

Ingredients for a provably correct loop

The simple example of computing an array's maximum illustrates the general scheme of loop computation, which applies to the following standard situation. You have determined that the solution to a certain problem is an element belonging to an n-dimensional surface *POST*: to solve the problem is to find an element of *POST*. In some cases *POST* has just one element — *the* solution — but in general there may be more than one acceptable solution. Loops are useful when you have no way of shooting straight at *POST* but you see an indirect strategy: aiming first into an m-dimensional surface *INV* that includes *POST* (for $m > n$); then approaching *POST*, iteration by iteration, without ever leaving *INV*. The following figure illustrates this process.

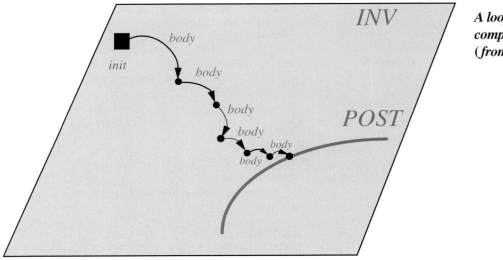

A loop computation (from [M 1990])

A loop computation has the following ingredients:

- A goal *post*, the postcondition, defined as a property that any satisfactory end state of the computation must satisfy. Example: "*Result* is the maximum value in the array". The goal is represented in the figure by the set of states *POST* satisfying *post*.

- An invariant property *inv*, which is a generalization of the goal, that is to say includes the goal as a special case. Example: "*Result* is the maximum value in a non-empty array slice beginning at the lower bound". The invariant is represented in the figure by the set of states *INV* satisfying *inv*.

- An initial point *init* which is known to be in *INV*, that is to say to satisfy the invariant. Example: the state in which the value of *i* is the array's lower bound and the value of *Result* is that of the array element at that index, satisfying the invariant since the maximum of a one-element slice is the value of the element.

- A transformation *body* which, starting from a point in *INV* but not in *POST*, yields a point closer to *POST* and still in *INV*. In the example this transformation extends the array slice by one element, and replaces *Result* by the value of that element if higher than the previous *Result*. The loop body in function *maxarray* is an implementation of that transformation.

- An upper bound on the number of applications of *body* necessary to bring a point in *INV* to *POST*. This will be the variant, as explained next.

Computations by successive approximations are a mainstay of numerical analysis, but the idea applies more broadly. An important difference is that in pure mathematics we accept that a series of approximations may have a limit even though it cannot reach it through a finite number of approximations: the sequence *1, 1/2, 1/3, 1/4, …, 1/n, …* has limit 0 but no element of the sequence has value zero. In computing, we want to see the results on our screen during our lifetime, so we insist that all approximation sequences reach their goal after a finite number of iterations.

> Computer implementations of numerical algorithms also require finite convergence: even when the mathematical algorithm would only converge at infinity, we cut off the approximation process when we feel that we are close enough.

The practical way to guarantee termination of a loop process is to associate with the loop an integer quantity, the loop variant, which enjoys the following properties:

- The variant is always non-negative.

- Any execution of the loop body (the transformation called *body* in the figure) decreases the variant.

Since a non-negative integer quantity cannot decrease forever, your ability to exhibit such a variant for one of your loops guarantees that the loop will always terminate. The variant is an upper bound, for each point in the sequence, of the maximum number of applications of *body* that will land the point in *POST*. In the array maximum computation, a variant is easy to find: $t.upper - i$. This satisfies both conditions:

The invariant of class ARRAY appeared on page 373.

- Because the routine precondition requires $t.capacity$ to be positive (that is to say, the routine is only applicable to non-empty arrays) and the invariant of class *ARRAY* indicates that $capacity = upper - lower + 1$, the property $i <= t.upper$ (part of the loop's invariant) will always be satisfied when i is initialized to $t.lower$.

- Any execution of the loop body performs the instruction $i := i + 1$, reducing the variant by one.

In this example the loop is simply an iteration over a sequence of integer values in a finite interval, known in common programming languages as a "for loop" or a "DO loop"; termination is not difficult to prove, although one must always check the details (here, for example, that i always starts no greater than $t.upper$ because of the routine's precondition). For more sophisticated loops, the number of iterations is not that easy to determine in advance, so ascertaining termination is more of a challenge; the only universal technique is to find a variant.

One more notion is needed to transform the scheme just outlined into a software text describing a loop: we need a simple way of determining whether a certain iteration has reached the goal (the postcondition) *post*. Because the iteration is constrained to remain within *INV*, and *POST* is part of *INV*, it is usually possible to find a condition *exit* such that an element of *INV* belongs to *POST* if and only if it satisfies *exit*. In other words, the postcondition *post* and the invariant *inv* are related by

> $post = inv$ **and** $exit$

so that we can stop the loop — whose intermediate states, by construction, always satisfy *inv* — as soon as *exit* is satisfied. In the *maxarray* example, the obvious *exit* condition is $i = t.upper$: if this property is true together with the invariant, which states that *Result* is the maximum value in the array slice $[t.lower, i]$, then *Result* is the maximum value in the array slice $[t.lower, t.upper]$, hence in the entire array — the desired postcondition.

Loop syntax

The syntax for loops follows directly from the preceding rationale. It will include the elements listed as necessary:

- A loop invariant *inv* — an assertion.

- An exit condition *exit*, whose conjunction with *inv* achieves the desired goal.

- A variant *var* — an integer expression.

- A set of initialization instructions *init*, which always produces a state that satisfies *inv* and makes *var* non-negative.

- A set of body instructions *body* which, when started in a state where *inv* holds and *var* is non-negative, preserves the invariant and decreases the variant while keeping it non-negative (so that the resulting state still satisfies *inv* and has for *var* a value that is less than before but has not gone below zero).

The loop syntax combining these ingredients is straightforward:

from
     init
invariant
     inv
variant
     var
until
     exit
loop
     body
end

The **invariant** and **variant** clauses are optional. The **from** clause is required (but the *init* instructions may be empty). The effect of this instruction is to execute the *init* instructions and then, zero or more times, the *body* instructions; the latter are executed only as long as *exit* is false.

In Pascal, C etc. the loop would be a "while" loop, since the loop body is executed zero or more times, unlike the "**repeat** … **until**" loop for which the body is always executed at least once. Here the test is an exit condition, not a continuation condition, and the loop syntax includes room for initialization. So the equivalent in Pascal of **from** *init* **until** *exit* **loop** *body* **end** is

    init;
    while not *exit* **do** *body*

Warning: this is Pascal, not the O-O notation.

With a variant and an invariant the loop for *maxarray* appears as

> **from**
>> $i := t.lower; Result := t @ lower$
>
> **invariant**
>> -- *Result* is the maximum of the elements of *t* at indices *t.lower* to *i*.
>
> **variant**
>> $t.lower - i$
>
> **until**
>> $i = t.upper$
>
> **loop**
>> $i := i + 1$
>>
>> $Result := Result.max (t @ i)$
>
> **end**

"The expressive power of assertions", page 399.   Note that the invariant is expressed informally as a comment; the discussion section of this chapter will explain this limitation of the assertion language.

Here is another example, first shown without variant or invariant. The purpose of the following function is to compute the greatest common divisor (gcd) of two positive integers *a* and *b* with Euclid's algorithm:

> $gcd (a, b: INTEGER): INTEGER$ *is*
>> -- Greatest common divisor of *a* and *b*
>
> **require**
>> $a > 0; b > 0$
>
> **local**
>> $x, y: INTEGER$
>
> **do**
>> **from**
>>> $x := a; y := b$
>>
>> **until**
>>> $x = y$
>>
>> **loop**
>>> **if** $x > y$ **then** $x := x - y$ **else** $y := y - x$ **end**
>>
>> **end**
>>
>> $Result := x$
>
> **ensure**
>> -- *Result* is the greatest common divisor of *a* and *b*
>
> **end**

How do we know that function *gcd* ensures its postcondition — that it indeed computes the greatest common divisor of *a* and *b*? One way to check this is to note that the following property is true after loop initialization and preserved by every iteration:

$x > 0; y > 0$

-- The pair $<x, y>$ has the same greatest common divisor as the pair $<a, b>$

This will serve as our loop invariant *inv*. Clearly, *INV* is satisfied after execution of the **from** clause. Also, if *inv* is satisfied before an execution of the loop body

if $x > y$ **then** $x := x - y$ **else** $y := y - x$ **end**

under the loop continuation condition $x \mathrel{/=} y$, then *inv* will still be satisfied after execution of this instruction; this is because replacing the greater of two positive non-equal numbers by their difference leaves them positive and does not change their gcd.

We have shown *inv* to be satisfied before the first iteration and preserved by every iteration. It follows that on loop exit, when $x = y$ becomes true, *inv* still holds; that is to say:

$x = y$ **and** "The pair $<x, y>$ has the same greatest common divisor as the pair $<a, b>$"

which implies that the gcd is x because of the mathematical property that the gcd of any integer x and itself is x.

How do we know that the loop will always terminate? We need a variant. If x is greater than y, the loop body replaces x by $x - y$; if y is greater than x, it replaces y by $y - x$. We cannot choose x as a variant, because we cannot be sure that an arbitrary loop iteration will decrease x; nor can we be sure that it will decrease y, so y is also not an appropriate variant. But we can be sure that it will decrease *either* x or y, and hence their maximum $x.max\ (y)$; this maximum will never become negative, so it provides the sought variant. We may now write the loop with all its clauses:

from

        $x := a; y := b$

invariant

    $x > 0; y > 0$

    -- The pair $<x, y>$ has the same greatest common divisor as the pair $<a, b>$

variant

    $x.max\ (y)$

until

    $x = y$

loop

    if $x > y$ **then** $x := x - y$ **else** $y := y - x$ **end**

end

As noted, the **invariant** and **variant** clauses in loops are optional. When present, they help clarify the purpose of a loop and check its correctness. Any non-trivial loop may be characterized by an interesting invariant and variant; many of the examples in subsequent chapters include variants and invariants, providing insights into the underlying algorithms and their correctness.

11.13 USING ASSERTIONS

We have now seen all the constructs involving assertions and should review all the benefits that we can derive from them. There are four main applications:

- Help in writing correct software.
- Documentation aid.
- Support for testing, debugging and quality assurance.
- Support for software fault tolerance.

Only the last two assume the ability to monitor assertions at run time.

Assertions as a tool for writing correct software

The first use is purely methodological and perhaps the most important. It has been explored in detail in the preceding sections: spelling out the exact requirements on each routine, and the global properties of classes and loops, helps developers produce software that is correct the first time around, as opposed to the more common approach of trying to debug software into correctness. The benefits of precise specifications and a systematic approach to program construction cannot be overemphasized. Throughout this book, whenever we encounter a program element, we shall seek to express as precisely as possible the formal properties of that element.

The key idea runs through this chapter: the principle of **Design by Contract**. To use features from a certain module is to contract out for services. Good contracts are those which exactly specify the rights and obligations of each party, and the *limits* to these rights and obligations. In software design, where correctness and robustness are so important, we need to spell out the terms of the contracts as a prerequisite to enforcing them. Assertions provide the means to state precisely what is expected from and guaranteed to each side in these arrangements.

Using assertions for documentation: the short form of a class

The second use is essential in the production of reusable software elements and, more generally, in organizing the interfaces of modules in large software systems. Preconditions, postconditions and class invariants provide potential clients of a module with basic information about the services offered by the module, expressed in a concise and precise form. No amount of verbose documentation can replace a set of carefully expressed assertions, appearing *in the software itself.*

"POSTSCRIPT: THE ARIANE 5 CRASH", page 410.

To learn how a particular project ignored this rule and lost an entire space mission at a cost of $500 million, see the very last section of this chapter.

The automatic documentation tool **short** uses assertions as an important component in extracting from a class the information that is relevant to potential clients. The short form of a class is a high-level view of the class. It only includes the information that is useful to authors of client classes; so it does not show anything about secret features and, for public features, it does not show the implementation (the **do** clauses). But the short

Chapter 23 discusses **short** *in detail.*

form does retain the assertions, which provide essential documentation by stating the contracts that the class offers to its clients.

Here is the short form of class *STACK4*:

indexing

    description: *"Stacks: Dispenser structures with a Last-In, First-Out %*

        %access policy, and a fixed maximum capacity"

STACK4 appeared on page 364, based on STACK2 from page 349.

class interface *STACK4* [*G*] **creation**

    make

feature -- Initialization

    make (*n*: *INTEGER*) **is**

        -- Allocate stack for a maximum of *n* elements

      require

        non_negative_capacity: $n >= 0$

      ensure

        capacity_set: *capacity* = *n*

      end

feature -- Access

    capacity: *INTEGER*

        -- Maximum number of stack elements

    count: *INTEGER*

        -- Number of stack elements

    item: *G* **is**

        -- Top element

      require

        not_empty: **not** *empty* -- i.e. *count* > 0

      end

feature -- Status report

    empty: *BOOLEAN* **is**

        -- Is stack empty?

      ensure

        empty_definition: *Result* = (*count* = 0)

      end

    full: *BOOLEAN* **is**

        -- Is stack full?

      ensure

        full_definition: *Result* = (*count* = *capacity*)

      end

feature -- Element change

put (*x*: *G*) **is**

-- Add *x* on top

require

not_full: **not** *full*

ensure

not_empty: **not** *empty*

added_to_top: *item* = *x*

one_more_item: *count* = **old** *count* + *1*

end

remove **is**

-- Remove top element

require

not_empty: **not** *empty* -- i.e. *count* > *0*

ensure

not_full: **not** *full*

one_fewer: *count* = **old** *count* – *1*

end

invariant

count_non_negative: *0* <= *count*

count_bounded: *count* <= *capacity*

empty_if_no_elements: *empty* = (*count* = *0*)

end -- class interface *STACK4*

This short form is not a syntactically valid class text (hence the use of **class interface** rather than the usual **class** to avoid any confusion), although it is easy to turn it into a valid *deferred* class, a notion to be seen in detail in our study of inheritance.

See chapter 36 about the environment.

In the ISE environment, you obtain the short form of a class by clicking on the corresponding button in a Class Tool displaying a class; you can generate plain text, as well as versions formated for a whole host of formats such as HTML (for Web browsing), RTF (Microsoft's Rich Text Format), FrameMaker's MML, T$_E$X, troff and others. You can also define your own format, for example if you are using some text processing tool with its specific conventions for specifying fonts and layout.

If you compare the short form's assertions to those of the class, you will notice that all the clauses involving *representation* have disappeared, since that attribute is not exported.

The **short** form of documentation is particularly interesting for several reasons:

- The documentation is at a higher level of abstraction than what it describes, an essential requirement for quality documentation. The actual implementation, describing the *how*, has been removed, but the assertions, explaining the *what* (or in some cases the *why*) are still there. Note that the header comments of routines, which complement assertions by giving a less formal explanation of each routine's purpose, are retained, as well as the *description* entry of the **indexing** clause.

- A direct consequence of the Self-Documentation principle studied in our review of modularity concepts, the short form treats documentation not as a separate product but as information contained in the software itself. This means that there is only one product to maintain, a requirement that runs through this book. There is also, as a result, a much better chance that the documentation will be correct, since by having everything at the same place you decrease the risk of forgetting to update the documentation after a change to the software, or conversely.

"Self-Documenta-tion", page 54.

- The short form can be extracted from the class by automatic tools. So the documentation is not something that you have to write; instead it is something that you ask "the computer" to produce, at the click of a mouse button, when you need it.

It is interesting to compare this approach with the notion of package interface present in Ada ("specification part"), where you write a module (package) in two parts: the interface and the implementation. Java uses a similar mechanism. The interface of a package has some similarities to the short form of a class, but also significant differences:

- There are no assertions, so all the "specification" that you can give is in the form of type declarations and comments.

- The interface is not produced by a tool but written separately. So the developer has to state many things twice: the headers of routines, their signatures, any header comments, declarations of public variables. This forced redundancy is tedious (it would be even more so with assertions) and, as always, raises the risk of inconsistency, as you may change one of the two parts and forget to update the other.

The short form (complemented by its variant the flat-short form, which deals with inheritance and is studied in a later chapter) is a principal contribution of the object-oriented method. In the daily practice of O-O development it appears all the time not just as a tool for documenting software, particularly reusable libraries, but also as the standard format in which developers and managers study existing designs, prepare new designs, and discuss proposed designs.

"The flat-short form", page 543.

The reason for the central role of the short form in O-O development is that it finally fulfills the goal defined by the analysis of reusability requirements at the beginning of this book. There we arrived at the requirement for *abstracted modules* as the basic unit of reuse. A class in its short (or flat-short) form is the abstracted module that we have been seeking.

"Reuse of abstracted mod-ules", page 73.

Monitoring assertions at run time

It is time now to deal in full with the question "what is the effect of assertions at run time?". As previewed at the beginning of this chapter, the answer is up to the developer, based on a compilation option. To set that option, you should not, of course, have to change the actual class texts; you will rely instead on the Ace file. Recall that an Ace file, written in Lace, allows you to describe how to assemble and compile a system.

Lace and Ace files were introduced in "Assembling a sys-tem", page 198.

> Recall too that Lace is just one possible control language for assembling O-O systems, not an immutable component of the method. You will need something like Lace, even if it is not exactly Lace, to go from individual software components to complete compilable systems.

Here is how to adapt a simple Ace (the one used as example in the original presentation of Lace) to set some assertion-monitoring options:

Warning: this text is in Lace, not in the O-O notation.

system *painting* **root**
> *GRAPHICS*

default
> *assertion* (**require**)

cluster
> *base_library*: "*\library\base*"
> *graphical_library*: "*\library\graphics*"
>> **option**
>>> *assertion* (**all**): *BUTTON, COLOR_BITMAP*
>> **end**
> *painting_application*: "*\user\application*"
>> **option**
>>> *assertion* (**no**)
>> **end**

end -- system *painting*

The **default** clause indicates that for most classes of the system only preconditions will be checked (**require**). Two clusters override this default: *graphical_library*, which will monitor all assertions (**all**), but only for classes *BUTTON* and *COLOR_BITMAP*; and *painting_application*, which has disabled any assertion checking for all its classes. This illustrates how to define an assertion monitoring level for the system as a whole, for all the classes of a cluster, or for some classes only.

The following assertion checking levels may appear between parentheses in *assertion* (…):

- **no**: do not execute anything for assertions. In this mode assertions have no more effect on execution than comments.
- **require**: check that preconditions hold on routine entry.
- **ensure**: check that postconditions hold on routine exit.

A qualified call is a call from the outside, as in x.f, as opposed to a plain internal call f. See "Qualified and unqualified calls", page 186.

- **invariant**: check that class invariants hold on routine entry and exit for qualified calls.
- **loop**: check that loops invariants hold before and after every loop iteration, and that variants decrease while remaining non-negative.
- **check**: execute **check** instructions by checking that the corresponding assertions hold. **all** is a synonym for **check**.

Excluding **no**, each of these levels implies the previous ones; in particular it does not make sense to monitor postconditions unless you also monitor preconditions, since the principles of Design by Contract indicate that a routine is required to ensure its postcondition only if it was called with its precondition satisfied (otherwise "the customer is wrong"). This explains why **check** and **all** are synonyms.

If turned on, assertion monitoring will have no visible effect, except for the CPU cycles that it takes away from your computation, as long as the assertions that it monitors all evaluate to true. But having any assertion evaluate to false is a rather serious event which will usually lead to termination. Actually it will trigger an exception, but unless you have taken special measures to catch the exception (see next) everything will stop. An *exception history table* will be produced, of the general form

> Failure: object: O2 class: *YOUR_CLASS* routine: *your_routine*
>
>> Cause: precondition violation, clause: *not_too_small*
>
> Called by: object: O2 class: *YOUR_CLASS* routine: *his_routine*
>
> Called by: object: O1 class: *HER_CLASS* routine: *her_routine*
>
> . . .

This gives the call chain, starting from the routine that caused the exception, the object to which is was applied and its generating class. Objects are identified by internal codes. The form shown here is only a sketch; the discussion of exceptions will give a more complete example of the exception history table.

See page 421 for the detailed form.

The optional labels that you can add to the individual clauses of an assertion, such as *not_too_small* in

> *your_routine* (*x*: *INTEGER*) **is**
>
>> **require**
>
>>> *not_too_small*: $x >= Minimum\_value$
>
>> . . .

prove convenient here, since they will be listed in the exception trace, helping you identify what exactly went wrong.

How much assertion monitoring?

What level of assertion tracing should you enable? The answer is a tradeoff between the following considerations: how much you trust the correctness of your software; how crucial it is to get the utmost efficiency; how serious the consequences of an undetected run-time error can be.

In extreme cases, the situation is clear:

- When you are debugging a system, or more generally testing it prior to release, you should enable assertion monitoring at the highest level for the classes of the system (although not necessarily for the libraries that it uses, as explained next). This ability is one of the principal contributions to software development of the method presented in this book. Until they have actually had the experience of testing a large, assertion-loaded system using the assertion monitoring mechanisms described in this section, few people realize the power of these ideas and how profoundly they affect the practice of software development.

- If you have a fully trusted system in an efficiency-critical application area — the kind where every microsecond counts — you may consider removing all monitoring.

The last advice is somewhat paradoxical since in the absence of formal proving techniques (see the discussion section of this chapter) it is seldom possible to "trust a system fully" — except by monitoring its assertions. This is a special case of a general observation made with his customary eloquence by C.A.R. Hoare:

From [Hoare 1973].

> *It is absurd to make elaborate security checks on debugging runs, when no trust is put in the results, and then remove them in production runs, when an erroneous result could be expensive or disastrous. What would we think of a sailing enthusiast who wears his life-jacket when training on dry land but takes it off as soon as he goes to sea?*

An interesting possibility is the option that only checks preconditions: *assertion* (**require**). In production runs — that is to say, past debugging and quality assurance — it has the advantage of avoiding catastrophes that would result from undetected calls to routines outside of their requirements, while costing significantly less in run-time overhead than options that also check postconditions and invariants. (Invariants, in particular, can be quite expensive to monitor since the method suggests writing rich invariants that include all relevant consistency conditions on a class, and the invariant is checked on entry and exit for every qualified call.)

Precondition checking is indeed the default compilation option if you do not include a specific *assertion* option in your Ace, so that the clause **default** *assertion* (**require**) appearing in the example Ace for system *painting* was not necessary.

Second Assertion Violation rule, page 347.

This option is particularly interesting for libraries. Remember the basic rule on assertion violations: a violated precondition indicates an error in the client; a violated postcondition or invariant indicates an error in the supplier. So if you are relying on reusable libraries that you assume to be of high quality, it is generally not desirable to monitor their postconditions and invariants: this would mean that you suspect the libraries themselves, and although the possibility of a library error is of course always open it should only be investigated (for a widely used library coming from a reputable source) once you have ruled out the presence, *a priori* much more likely, of an error in your own client software. But even for a perfect library it is useful to check **preconditions**: the goal is to find errors in client software.

See the class text starting on page 372.

Perhaps the most obvious example is array bound checking. In the *ARRAY* class we saw that *put*, *item* and the latter's synonym **infix** *"@"* all had the precondition clauses

index_not_too_small: *lower* <= *i*

index_not_too_large: *i* <= *upper*

Enabling precondition checking for the class solves a well-known problem of any software that uses arrays: the possibility of an out-of-bounds array access, which will usually scoop some memory area containing other data or code, causing ravages. Many compilers for conventional programming languages offer special compilation options to monitor array access at run time. But in object technology, just as we treat arrays through general notions of class and object rather than special constructs, we can handle array bound monitoring through the general mechanism for precondition checking. Just use a version of *ARRAY* compiled with *assertion* (**require**).

Should bounds always be checked? Hoare thinks so:

In our Algol compiler every occurrence of every subscript of every array element
was on every occasion checked at run time against the declared bounds. Many
years later we asked our customers whether they wished us to provide an option
to switch off these checks in the interest of efficiency in production runs.
Unanimously they urged us not to — they already knew how frequently index
errors occur on production runs where failure could be disastrous. I note with
fear and horror that even today, language designers and users have not learned
this lesson. In any respectable branch of engineering, failure to observe such
elementary precautions would have long been against the law.

From [Hoare 1981];
slightly abridged.

These comments should be discussed not just for arrays but for preconditions in general. If indeed "index errors frequently occur on production runs" this must be true of other precondition violations too.

One may defend a less extreme position. (Some might of course see here an attempt at self-preservation, coming from a "language designer" who has provided a way to turn off assertion checking, through Lace options such as *assertion* (**no**), and presumably does not like being branded as acting "against the law".) First, a company which delivers software in which precondition errors "frequently occur on production runs" probably has a problem with its software quality practices, which run-time assertion monitoring will not solve. Monitoring addresses the symptoms (*faults* in the terminology introduced earlier in this chapter), not the cause (defects and errors). True, assertion monitoring is in such a case beneficial to the software's end-users: however unpleasant it is to have a system end its interruption with some message spouting insults about preconditions and other venomous beasts unknown to a layman, this is better than continuing operation and producing bad results. But in the long term a practice of always delivering systems with some level of assertion monitoring also has negative effects: it can encourage among developers, even unconsciously, a happy-go-lucky attitude towards correctness, justified by the knowledge that if an error remains it will be caught by the users through an assertion violation, reported to the supplier, and fixed for the following release. So can't we stop testing right now and start shipping?

It is hard to give an absolute answer to the question "should we leave some assertion monitoring on?" without some knowledge of the performance overhead of assertion monitoring. If adding some monitoring multiplied the execution time by ten, few people outside of the mission-critical-computing community would support Hoare's view; if the overhead were two percent, few people would disagree with it. In practice, of course, the penalty will be somewhere in-between.

How much is it, by the way? This clearly depends on what the software does and how many assertions it has, but it is possible to give empirical observations. In ISE's experience the cost for monitoring preconditions (the default option, including of course array bounds checking) is on the order of 50%. What is frustrating is that more than 75% of that cost is due not to precondition checking per se but to the supporting machinery of monitoring calls — recording every routine entry and every routine exit — so that if a precondition fails the environment can say which one and where. (A message of the form *Execution stopped because some assertion was violated somewhere* would not be very useful.) This may be called the Precondition Checking Paradox: precondition checking is by itself cheap enough, but to get it you have to pay for something else. As to postcondition and invariant checking, they can bring the penalty to 100% to 200%. (Although circumstances vary, preconditions are often relatively simple consistency conditions such as $x > 0$ or $a /= Void$, whereas many postconditions and invariants express more advanced semantic properties.)

One might fear that bringing performance into this discussion may lead to compromising on correctness, against the principle expressed at the beginning of this book:

Page 15.
> *Necessary as tradeoffs between quality factors may be, one factor stands out from the rest: correctness. There is never any justification for compromising on correctness for the sake of other concerns, such as efficiency. If the software does not perform its function, the rest is useless.*

Considering performance when we decide whether to leave assertion monitoring on is not, however, a violation of this principle. The point is not to sacrifice correctness for efficiency, but to determine what we should do for systems that are *not* correct — obviously because we have not worked hard enough at making them correct.

In fact, efficiency may be part of correctness. Consider a meteorological system that takes twelve hours to predict the next-day's weather (two hours would be more useful, of course). The system has been thoroughly optimized; in particular it does not have run-time checking for array bound violations or other such faults. It has also undergone careful development and extensive testing. Now assume that adding the run-time checks multiplies the execution time by two, giving a forecasting system that takes 24 hours to predict tomorrow's weather. Would you enable these checks? No.

> Although the examples that first come to mind when discussing such performance *vs.* safety issues tend to be of the Patriot-against-Scud variety, I prefer the weather forecasting example because here one cannot dismiss the efficiency issue offhand by saying "just buy a faster microprocessor". In meteorological computing, the hardware tends *already* to be the fastest parallel computer available on the market.

Let us not stop here but ask the really hard questions. Assume the original running time of twelve hours was with checking *enabled*. Would you disable it to get a six-hour forecast? Now assume that you also have the option of applying the improved efficiency to keep the same running time but use a more accurate forecasting model (since you can afford more grid points); would you do it? I think that in either case, if offered "*an option to switch off the checks in the interest of efficiency in production runs*", almost everyone will say yes.

So in the end the choice of assertion monitoring level at production time is not as simple as Hoare's rule suggests. But a few precise and strict principles do hold:

- Remember that a software system should be made reliable *before* it begins operation. The key is to apply the reliability techniques described in the software engineering literature, including those which appear in this chapter and throughout this book.

- If you are a project manager, *never let the developers assume* that the production versions will have checks turned on. Make everyone accept that — especially for the biggest production runs, those which by nature make the consequences of potential errors most frightening — all checks may be off.

- Make sure that during development assertion checking is always turned on at least at the precondition level.

- Perform extensive testing with *all* the checks enabled. Also turn all checks on as soon as any bug is encountered during development.

- For the standard production versions, decide whether to choose a no-check version or a protected version (usually at the precondition level) based on your assessment, from an engineering perspective, of the relative weight of the three factors cited at the beginning of this discussion: how much you trust the correctness of your software (meaning in part how hard you have *worked* at making it correct and convincing yourself and others that it is); how crucial it is to get the utmost efficiency; and how serious the consequences of an undetected run-time error can be.

- If you decide to go for a no-check version, also include in your delivery a version that checks at least for preconditions. That way, if the system starts exhibiting abnormal behavior against all your expectations, you can ask the users — those at least who have not been killed by the first erroneous production runs — to switch to the checking version, helping you find out quickly what is wrong.

Used in this way, run-time assertion monitoring provides a remarkable aid for quickly weeding out any errors that may have survived a systematic software construction process.

11.14 DISCUSSION

The assertion mechanism presented in this chapter raises some delicate issues, which we must now examine.

Why run-time monitoring?

Should we really have to check assertions at run time? After all we were able, using assertions, to give a theoretical definition of what it means for a class to be correct: every creation procedure should ensure the invariant, and every routine body, when started in a state satisfying the precondition and the invariant, should maintain the invariant and ensure the postcondition. This means that we should simply *prove* the $m + n$ corresponding properties mathematically (for m creation procedures and n exported routines), and then do away with run-time assertion monitoring.

See "WHEN IS A CLASS COR-RECT?", 11.9, page 369.

We should, but we cannot. Although mathematical program proving has been an active area of research for many years, and has enjoyed some successes, it is not possible today to prove the correctness of realistic software systems written in full-fledged programming languages.

We would also need a more extensive assertion language. The IFL sublanguage, discussed below, could be used as part of a multi-tier proof strategy.

Even if proof techniques and tools eventually become available, one may suspect that run-time checks will *not* go away, if only to cope with hard-to-predict events such as hardware faults, and to make up for possible bugs in the proof software itself — in other words to apply the well-known engineering technique of multiple independent checking.

The expressive power of assertions

As you may have noted, the assertion language that we have used is essentially the language of boolean expressions, extended with a few concepts such as **old**. As a result, we may find it too restrictive when we would like to include in our classes some of the properties that were easy to express in the mathematical notation for abstract data types.

The assertions for stack classes provide a good example of what we can and cannot say. We found that many of the preconditions and axioms from the original ADT specification of chapter 6 gave assertion clauses; for example the axiom

A4 • **not** *empty* (*put* (*s*, *x*))

gives the postcondition **not** *empty* in procedure *put*. But in some cases we do not have the immediate counterpart in the class. None of the postconditions for *remove* in the stack classes given so far includes anything to represent the axiom

A2 • *remove* (*put* (*s*, *x*)) = *s*

We can of course add an informal property to the postcondition by resorting to a comment:

    remove **is**

                -- Remove top element

       require

             not_empty: **not** *empty* -- i.e. *count* > *0*

       do

             count := *count* – *1*

       ensure

             not_full: **not** *full*

             one_fewer: *count* = **old** *count* – *1*

             LIFO_policy: -- *item* is the last element pushed (by *put*)

                         -- and not yet removed, if any.

       end

Both on page 387.   Similar informal assertions, syntactically expressed as comments, appeared in the loop invariants for *maxarray* and *gcd*.

In such a case, two of the principal uses of assertions discussed earlier remain applicable at least in part: help in composing correct software, and help in documentation (an assertion clause that is syntactically a comment will appear in the short form). The other uses, in particular debugging and testing, assume the ability to evaluate assertions and do not apply any more.

It would be preferable to express all assertions formally. The best way to reach this goal is to extend the assertion language so that it can describe arbitrary properties; this requires the ability to describe complex mathematical objects such as sets, sequences, functions and relations, and including the full power of first-order predicate calculus, which allows quantified expressions ("for all" and "there exists"). Formal specification languages exist which provide at least part of this expressive power. The best known are Z, VDM, Larch and OBJ-2; both Z and VDM have had object-oriented extensions, such as Object-Z, in recent years, and the last two were close to O-O concepts already. The bibliographic notes to chapter 6 provide references.

Including a full specification language into the language of this book would have completely changed its nature. The language is meant to be simple, easy to learn, applicable to all areas of software construction, and implementable efficiently (with a final run-time performance similar to that of Fortran and C, and a fast compilation process).

Instead, the assertion mechanism is an engineering tradeoff: it includes enough formal elements to have a substantial effect on software quality; but stops at the point of diminishing return — the threshold beyond which the benefits of more formality might start being offset by the decrease of learnability, simplicity and efficiency.

> Determining that threshold is clearly a matter of personal judgment. I have been surprised that, for the software community at large, the threshold has not moved since the first edition of this book. Our field needs more formality, but the profession has not realized it yet.

So for the time being, and probably for quite a while, assertions will remain boolean expressions extended with a few mechanisms such as the **old** expression in postconditions. The limitation is not as stringent as it seems at first, because boolean expressions can use *function calls*.

Including functions in assertions

A boolean expression is not restricted to using attributes or local entities. We have already used the possibility of calling *functions* in assertions: the precondition for *put* in our stack classes was **not** *full*, were *full* is the function

> *full*: *BOOLEAN* **is**
>> -- Is stack full?
>
> **do**
>> *Result* := (*count* = *capacity*)
>
> **ensure**
>> *full_definition*: *Result* = (*count* = *capacity*)
>
> **end**

This is our little assertion secret: we get out of the stranglehold of propositional calculus — basic boolean expressions involving attributes, local entities and boolean operators such as **and, or, not** — thanks to function routines, which give us the power to compute a boolean value in any way we like. (You should not be troubled by the presence of a postcondition in *full* itself, as it does not create any harmful circularity. Details shortly.)

Using function routines is a way to obtain more abstract assertions. For example, some people may prefer replacing the precondition of the array operations, expressed earlier as

> *index_not_too_small*: *lower* <= *i*
> *index_not_too_large*: *i* <= *upper*

by a single clause of the form

> *index_in_bounds*: *correct_index* (*i*)

with the function definition

> *correct_index* (*i*: *INTEGER*): *BOOLEAN* **is**
>   -- Is *i* within the array bounds?
>   **do**
>   *Result* := (*i* >= *lower*) **and** (*i* <= *upper*)
>   **ensure**
>   *definition*: *Result* = ((*i* >= *lower*) **and** (*i* <= *upper*))
>   **end**

Another advantage of the use of functions in assertions is that it may provide a way to circumvent the limitations on expressive power arising from the absence of first-order predicate calculus mechanisms. The informal invariant of our *maxarray* loop

> -- *Result* is the maximum of the elements of *t* at indices *t.lower* to *i*

may be expressed formally as

> *Result* = (*t.slice* (*lower*, *i*)).*max*

assuming a function *slice* which yields the set of elements between two indices of an array, and a function *max* which yields the maximum element in a set.

> This approach has been explored in [M 1995a] as a way to extend the power of the assertion mechanism, possibly leading to a fully formal development method (that is to say, to software that may be *proven* correct mathematically). Two central ideas in this investigation are the use of libraries in any large-scale proof process, so that one could prove real, large-scale systems in a multi-tier proof structure using conditional proofs, and the definition of a restricted language of a purely applicative nature — IFL, for Intermediate Functional Language — in which to express the functions used in assertions. IFL is a subset of the notation of this book, which excludes some imperative constructs such as arbitrary assignments.

"The imperative and the applicative", page 351.

The risk that such efforts try to address is clear: as soon as we permit functions in assertions, we introduce potentially imperative elements (routines) into the heretofore purely applicative world of assertions. Without functions, we had the clear and clean separation of roles emphasized in the earlier discussion: instructions prescribe, assertions describe. Now we open the gates of the applicative city to the imperative hordes.

Yet it is hard to resist the power of using functions, as the alternatives are not without their drawbacks either:

- Including a full specification sublanguage could, as noted, cause problems of ease of learning and efficiency.

- Perhaps worse, it is not even clear that commonly accepted assertion languages would suffice. Take what most people versed in these topics would suggest as the natural candidate: first-order predicate calculus. This formalism will not enable us to express some properties of immediate interest to developers and common use in assertions, such as "the graph has no cycles" (a typical invariant clause). Mathematically this would be stated as $r^+ \cap r = \varnothing$ where r is the graph's relation and $^+$ is transitive closure. Although it is possible to conceive of a specification language that supports these notions, most do not.

The transitive closure of a relation is obtained by iterating it any number of times. For example "ancestor" is the transitive closure of "parent".

This is all the more troubling because, for a programmer, writing a boolean-valued function routine *cyclic* that explores the graph and returns true if and only if there is a cycle, is not particularly hard. Such examples provide a strong argument for contenting ourselves with a basic assertion language and using functions for anything beyond its expressive power.

But the need to separate applicative and imperative elements remains. Any function routine used in an assertion to specify the properties of a software element should be "beyond reproach", more precisely beyond imperative reproach; it should not cause any permanent change of the abstract state.

> This informal requirement is clear enough in practice; the IFL sublanguage formalizes it by excluding all the imperative elements which either change the global state of the system or do not have trivial applicative equivalents, in particular:
> - Assignments to attributes.
> - Assignments in loops.
> - Calls to routines not themselves in IFL.

If you exert the proper care by sticking to functions that are simple and self-evidently correct, the use of function routines in assertions can provide you with a powerful means of abstraction.

A technical point may have caught your attention. A function f used by an assertion for a routine r (or the invariant of the class containing r) may itself have assertions, as illustrated by both the *full* and *correct_index* examples. This raises a potential problem for run-time assertion monitoring: if as part of a call to r we evaluate an assertion and this causes a call to f, we do not want the call to evaluate any assertion that f itself may have. For one thing, it is easy to construct examples that would cause infinite recursion. But even without that risk it would be just wrong to evaluate the assertions of f. This would mean that we treat as peers the routines of our computation, such as r, and their assertions's functions, such as f — contradicting the rule that assertions should be on a higher plane than the software they protect, and their correctness crystal-clear. The rule is simple:

Assertion Evaluation rule

During the process of evaluating an assertion at run-time, routine calls shall be executed without any evaluation of the associated assertions.

If a call to *f* occurs as part of assertion checking for *r*, that is too late to ask whether *f* satisfies its assertions. The proper time for such a question is when you decide to use *f* in the assertions applicable to *r*.

We can use an analogy introduced earlier. Think of *f* as a security guard at the entrance of a nuclear plant, in charge of inspecting the credentials of visitors. There are requirements on guards too. But you will run the background check on a guard in advance; not while he is screening the day's visitors.

Class invariants and reference semantics

The object-oriented model developed so far includes two apparently unrelated aspects, both useful:

- The notion of class invariant, as developed in this chapter.

See chapter 8, in particular "DEALING WITH REFERENCES: BENEFITS AND DANGERS", 8.9, page 265.

- A flexible run-time model which, for various reasons detailed in an earlier chapter (in particular the modeling needs of realistic systems), makes considerable use of references.

Unfortunately these individually desirable properties cause trouble when put together.

The problem is, once again, dynamic aliasing, which prevents us from checking the correctness of a class on the basis of that class alone. We have seen that the correctness of a class means $m + n$ properties expressing that (if we concentrate on the invariant *INV*, ignoring preconditions and postconditions which play no direct role here):

P1 • Every one of the m creation procedures produces an object that satisfies *INV*.

P2 • Every one of the n exported routines preserves *INV*.

These two conditions seem sufficient to guarantee that *INV* is indeed invariant. The proof is apparently trivial: since *INV* will be satisfied initially, and preserved by every routine call, it should by induction be satisfied at all stable times.

This informal proof, however, is not valid in the presence of reference semantics and dynamic aliasing. The problem is that attributes of an object may be modified by an operation on another object. So even if all $a \cdot r$ operations preserve *INV* on the object OA attached to a, some operation $b \cdot s$ (for b attached to another object) may destroy *INV* for OA. So even with conditions P1 and P2 satisfied, *INV* may not be an invariant.

Here is a simple example. Assume classes *A* and *B*, each with an attribute whose type is the other's class:

class *A* ... **feature** *forward*: *B* ... **end**
class *B* ... **feature** *backward*: *A* ... **end**

We require that following the *forward* reference (if defined) from an instance of *A* and then the *backward* reference from the corresponding *B* will yield the original *A*. This may be expressed as an invariant property of *A*:

round_trip: (*forward* /= *Void*) **implies** (*forward*•*backward* = *Current*)

Here is a situation involving instances of both classes and satisfying the invariant:

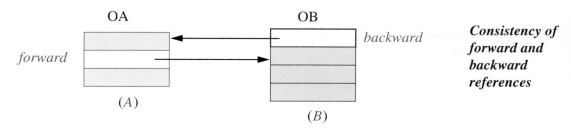

Consistency of forward and backward references

Invariant clauses of the *round_trip* form are not uncommon; think of *forward* in class *PERSON* denoting a person's residence, and *backward* in class *HOUSE* denoting a house's resident. Then *round_trip* states that the resident of any person's residence is that person, a simple consistency requirement. Another example is the linked implementation of trees, where the attributes of a tree node include references to its first child and to its parent, introducing the following *round_trip*-style property in the invariant:

($first\_child$ /= *Void*) **implies** ($first\_child$•*parent* = *Current*)

Assume, however, that the invariant clause of *B*, if any, says nothing about the attribute *backward*. The following version of *A* appears consistent with the invariant:

class *A* **feature**

    forward: *B*

    attach (*b1*: *B*) **is**

            -- Link *b1* to current object.

      do

            forward := *b1*

                -- Update *b1*'s backward reference for consistency:

            if *b1* /= *Void* **then**

                b1•*attach* (*Current*)

            end

      end

invariant

    round_trip: (*forward* /= *Void*) **implies** (*forward*•*backward* = *Current*)

end

The call *b1*•*attach* is meant to restore the invariant after an update of *forward*. Class *B* must provide its own *attach* procedure:

class *B* **feature**

    backward: *B*

> *attach* (*a1*: *A*) **is**
>
>> -- Link *a1* to current object.
>
> **do**
>
>> *backward* := *a1*
>
> **end**

end

Class *A* appears to be correct: a procedure-less creation instruction ensures the invariant *round_trip* (since it initializes *forward* to a void reference), and its sole procedure will always preserve *round_trip*. But consider execution of the following:

a1: *A*; *b1*: *B*

...

!! *a1*; !! *b1*

a1.*attach* (*b1*)

b1.*attach* (*Void*)

Here is the situation after the last instruction:

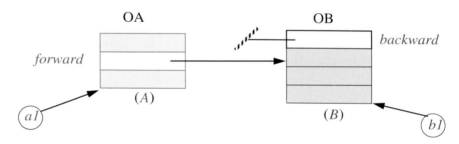

The invariant is violated on OA! This object is now linked to OB, but OB is not linked to OA since its *backward* field is void. (A call to *b1*.*attach* (...) could also have linked OB to an instance of *A* other than OA, which would be equally incorrect.)

What happened? Dynamic aliasing has struck again. The proof of correctness of class *A* outlined above is valid: every operation of the form *a1*.*r*, where *a1* is a reference to object OA, will preserve *round_trip* since the corresponding features of *A* (here there is only one, *attach*) have been designed accordingly. But this is not sufficient to preserve the consistency of OA, since properties of OA may involve instances of other classes, such as *B* in the example, and the proof says nothing about the effect of these other classes' features on the invariant of *A*.

This problem is important enough to deserve a name: **Indirect Invariant Effect**. It may arise as soon as we allow dynamic aliasing, through which an operation may modify an object even without involving any entity attached to it. But we have seen how much we need dynamic aliasing; and the *forward-backward* scheme, far from being just an academic example, is as noted a useful pattern for practical applications and libraries.

What can we do? The immediate answer involves the conventions for run-time monitoring of assertions. You may have wondered why the effect of enabling assertion monitoring at the *assertion* (**invariant**) level was described as

> *"Check that class invariants hold on routine entry and exit for qualified calls."*   Page 393.

Why both entry and exit? Without the Indirect Invariant Effect, it would suffice to check the invariant when exiting qualified calls. (It is also checked at the end of creation calls.) But now we have to be more careful, since between the termination of a call and the beginning of the next one on the same object, some call may have affected that object even though its target was another object.

A more satisfactory solution would be to obtain a statically enforceable validity rule, which would guarantee that whenever the invariant of a class A involves references to instances of a class B, the invariant of B includes a mirror clause. In our example we can avoid trouble by including in B an invariant clause *trip_round* mirroring *round_trip*:

$$trip\_round: (backward \mathrel{/=} Void) \textbf{ implies } (backward\textbf{.}forward = Current)$$

It may be possible to generalize this observation to a universal mirroring rule. Whether such a rule indeed exists, solving the Indirect Invariant Effect and removing the need for double run-time monitoring, requires further investigation.

More to come

We are not done with Design by Contract. Two important consequences of the principles remain to be studied:

- How they lead to a disciplined exception handling mechanism; this is the topic of the next chapter.

- How they combine with inheritance, allowing us to specify that any semantic constraints that apply to a class also apply to its descendants, and that semantic constraints on a feature apply to its eventual redeclarations; this will be part of our study of inheritance.   *"INHERITANCE AND ASSER-TIONS", page 569.*

More generally, assertions and Design by Contract will accompany us throughout the rest of this book, enabling us to check, whenever we write software elements, that we know what we are doing.

11.15 KEY CONCEPTS INTRODUCED IN THIS CHAPTER

- Assertions are boolean expressions expressing the semantic properties of classes and reintroducing the axioms and preconditions of the corresponding abstract data types.

- Assertions are used in preconditions (requirements under which routines are applicable), postconditions (properties guaranteed on routine exit) and class invariants (properties that characterize class instances over their lifetime). Other constructs that involve assertions are loop invariants and the **check** instruction.

- A precondition and a postcondition associated with a routine describe a contract between the class and its clients. The contract is only binding on the routine inasmuch as calls observe the precondition; the routine then guarantees the postcondition on return. The notion of contracting provides a powerful metaphor for the construction of correct software.

- The invariant of a class expresses the semantic constraints on instances of the class. The invariant is implicitly added to the precondition and the postcondition of every exported routine of the class.

- A class describes one possible representation of an abstract data type; the correspondence between the two is expressed by the abstraction function, which is usually partial. The inverse relation is in general not a function.

- An implementation invariant, part of the class invariant, expresses the correctness of the representation vis-à-vis the corresponding abstract data type.

- A loop may have a loop invariant, used to deduce properties of the result, and a variant, used to ascertain termination.

- If a class is equipped with assertions, it is possible to define formally what it means for the class to be correct.

- Assertions serve four purposes: aid in constructing correct programs; documentation aid; debugging aid; basis for an exception mechanism.

- The assertion language of our notation does not include first-order predicate calculus, but can express many higher-level properties through function calls, although the functions involved must be simple and of unimpeachable correctness.

- The combination of invariants and dynamic aliasing raises the Indirect Invariant Effect, which may cause an object to violate its invariant through no fault of its own.

11.16 BIBLIOGRAPHICAL NOTES

According to Tony Hoare:

From [Hoare 1981].

An early advocate of using assertions in programming was none other than Alan Turing himself. On 24 June 1950 at a conference in Cambridge, he gave a short talk entitled "Checking a Large Routine" which explains the idea with great clarity. "How can one check a large routine in the sense that it's right? In order that the man who checks may not have too difficult a task, the programmer should make a number of definite assertions which can be checked individually, and from which the correctness of the whole program easily follows."

The notion of assertion as presented in this chapter comes from the work on program correctness pioneered by Bob Floyd [Floyd 1967], Tony Hoare [Hoare 1969] and Edsger Dijkstra [Dijkstra 1976], and further described in [Gries 1981]. The book *Introduction to the Theory of Programming Languages* [M 1990] presents a survey of the field.

The notion of class invariant comes from Hoare's work on data type invariants [Hoare 1972a]. See also applications to program design in [Jones 1980] [Jones 1986]. A formal theory of morphisms between abstract data types may be found in [Goguen 1978].

Formal specification languages include Z, VDM, OBJ-2 and Larch; see the bibliographical references to chapter 6. Object-oriented formal specification languages include Object Z, Z++, MooZ, OOZE, SmallVDM and VDM++, all of which are described in [Lano 1994] which gives many more references.

The IEEE Computer Society publishes standards for the terminology of software errors, defects, failures [IEEE 1990] [IEEE 1993]. Its Web page is at *http://www.computer.org*.

Surprisingly, few programming languages have included syntactical provision for assertions; an early example (the first to my knowledge) was Hoare's and Wirth's Algol W [Hoare 1966], the immediate precursor of Pascal. Others include Alphard [Shaw 1981] and Euclid [Lampson 1977], which were specifically designed to allow the construction of provably correct programs. The connection with object-oriented development introduced by the notation developed in this book was foreshadowed by the assertions of CLU [Liskov 1981] which, however, are not executable. Another CLU-based book by Liskov and Guttag [Liskov 1986], one of the few programming methodology texts to discuss in depth how to build reliable software, promotes the "defensive programming" approach of which the present chapter has developed a critique.

The notion of Design by Contract presented in this chapter and developed in the rest of this book comes from [M 1987a] and was further developed in [M 1988], [M 1989c], [M 1992b] and [M 1992c]. [M 1994a] discusses the tolerant and demanding approaches to precondition design, with particular emphasis on their application to the design of reusable libraries, and introduces the "tough love" policy. Further developments of the ideas have been contributed by James McKim in [McKim 1992a] (which led to some of the initial ideas for IFL), [McKim 1995], [McKim 1996], [McKim 1996a]; see also [Henderson-Sellers 1994a] which examines the viewpoint of the supplier.

EXERCISES

E11.1 Complex numbers

Write the abstract data type specification for a class *COMPLEX* describing the notion of complex number with arithmetic operations. Assume perfect arithmetic.

E11.2 A class and its ADT

The ADT specification appears on page 139. STACK4 is on page 364 and includes STACK2, page 349

Examine all the preconditions and axioms of the *STACK* abstract data type introduced in an earlier chapter and study whether and how each is reflected in class *STACK4*.

E11.3 Complete assertions for stacks

Show that by introducing a secret function *body* which returns the body of a stack, it is possible to make the assertions in a *STACK* class reflect the full corresponding abstract data type specification. Discuss the theoretical and practical value of this technique.

E11.4 Exporting the size

Page 349.

Why is *capacity* exported for the bounded implementation of stacks, class *STACK2*?

E11.5 An implementation invariant

"A tolerant module", page 359.

Write the implementation invariant for class *STACK3*.

E11.6 Assertions and exports

Page 401.

The discussion of using functions in assertions introduced a function *correct_index* for the precondition of *item* and *put*. If you add this function to class *ARRAY*, what export status must you give it?

E11.7 Finding the bugs

Page 381.

Show that each of the four attempts at binary search algorithms advertized as "wrong" is indeed incorrect. (**Hint**: unlike proving an algorithm correct, which requires showing that it will work for all possible cases, proving it incorrect only requires that you find *one* case in which the algorithm will produce a wrong result, fail to terminate, or execute an illegal operation such as an out-of-bounds array access or other precondition violation.)

E11.8 Invariant violations

The discussion in this chapter has shown that a precondition violation indicates an error in the client, and a postcondition violation indicates an error in the supplier. Explain why an invariant violation also reflects a supplier error.

E11.9 Random number generators

Write a class implementing pseudo-random number generation, based on a sequence $n_i = f(n_{i-1})$ where f is a given function and the seed n_0 will be provided by clients of the class. Functions should have no side effects. (Assume f is known; you can find such functions in textbooks such as [Knuth 1981], and in numerical libraries.)

E11.10 A queue module

Write a class implementing queues (first-in, first-out policy), with appropriate assertions, in the style of the *STACK* classes of this chapter.

E11.11 A set module

Write a class implementing sets of elements of an arbitrary types, with the standard set operations (membership test, addition of a new element, union, intersection etc.). Be sure to include the proper assertions. Any correct implementation, such as linked lists or arrays, is acceptable.

POSTSCRIPT: THE ARIANE 5 CRASH

As this book was being printed, the European Space Agency released the report of the international investigation into the test flight of the Ariane 5 launcher, which crashed on June 4, 1996, 40 seconds after lift-off, at a reported cost of 500 million dollars (uninsured).

For a more detailed discussion see [M 1997a].

The cause of the crash: a failure of the on-board computer systems. The cause of that failure: a conversion from a 64-bit floating-point number (the mission's "horizontal bias") to a 16-bit signed integer produced an exception because the number was not representable with 16 bits. Although some other possible exceptions were monitored (using the Ada mechanisms described in the next chapter) prior analysis had shown that this particular one could not occur; so it was decided not to encumber the code with an extra exception handler.

The real cause: insufficient specification. The analysis that the value would always fit in 16 bits was in fact correct — but for the Ariane 4 flight trajectory! The code was reused for Ariane 5, and the assumption, although stated in an obscure part of some technical document, was simply forgotten. It did not apply any more to Ariane 5.

With the Design by Contract approach, it would have been stated in a precondition:

require

> *horizontal_bias <= Maximum_horizontal_bias*

naturally prompting the quality assurance team to check all uses of the routine and to detect that some could violate the assertion. Although we will never know, it seems almost certain that the mistake would have been caught, probably through static analysis, and at worst during testing thanks to the assertion monitoring mechanisms described in this chapter.

The lesson is clear: **reuse without contracts is folly**. The "abstracted modules" that we have defined as our units of reuse must be equipped with clear specifications of their operating conditions — preconditions, postconditions, invariants; and these specifications must be *in the modules themselves*, not in external documents. The principles that we have learned, particularly Design by Contract and Self-Documentation, are a required condition of any successful reusability policy. Even if your mistakes would cost less than half a billion dollars, remember this rule as you go after the great potential benefits of reuse: to be reusable, a module must be specified; and the programming language must support assertion mechanisms that will put the specification in the software itself.

12

When the contract is broken: exception handling

$\mathcal{L}$ike it or not, it is no use pretending: in spite of all static precautions, some unexpected and undesired event will sooner or later occur while one of your systems is executing. This is known as an exception and you must be prepared to deal with it.

12.1 BASIC CONCEPTS OF EXCEPTION HANDLING

The literature on exception handling is often not very precise about what really constitutes an exception. One of the consequences is that the exception mechanisms present in such programming languages as PL/I and Ada are often misused: instead of being reserved for truly abnormal cases, they end up serving as inter-routine **goto** instructions, violating the principle of Modular Protection.

Fortunately, the Design by Contract theory introduced in the preceding chapter provides a good framework for defining precisely the concepts involved.

Failures

Informally, an exception is an abnormal event that disrupts the execution of a system. To obtain a more rigorous definition, it is useful to concentrate first on a more elementary concept, failure, which follows directly from the contract idea.

A routine is not just some arbitrary sequence of instructions but the implementation of a certain specification — the routine's contract. Any call must terminate in a state that satisfies the precondition and the class invariant. There is also an implicit clause in the contract: that the routine must not have caused an abnormal operating system signal, resulting for example from memory exhaustion or arithmetic overflow and interrupting the normal flow of control in the system's execution.

It *must* refrain from causing such events, but of course not everything in life is what it must be, and we may expect that once in a while a routine call will be unable to satisfy its contract — triggering an abnormal signal, producing a final state that violates the postcondition or the invariant, or calling another routine in a state that does not satisfy that routine's precondition (assuming run-time assertion monitoring in the last two cases).

Such a case will be called a failure.

> ## Definitions: success, failure
>
> A routine call succeeds if it terminates its execution in a state satisfying the routine's contract. It fails if it does not succeed.

The discussion will use the phrase "routine failure", or just "failure", as an abbreviation for "failure of a routine call". Of course what succeeds or fails is not a routine (an element of the software text) but one particular call to that routine at run time.

Exceptions

From the notion of failure we can derive a precise definition of exceptions. A routine fails because of some specific event (arithmetic overflow, assertion violation…) that interrupts its execution. Such an event is an exception.

> ## Definition: exception
>
> An exception is a run-time event that may cause a routine call to fail.

Often an exception *will* cause failure of the routine. But you can prevent this from occurring by writing the routine so that it will catch the exception and try to restore a state from which the computation will proceed. This is the reason why failure and exception are different concepts: every failure results from an exception, but not every exception results in failure.

The study of software anomalies in the previous chapter introduced the terms *fault* (for a harmful execution event), *defect* (for an inadequacy of system, which may cause faults) and *error* (for a mistake in the thinking process, which may lead to defects). A failure is a fault; an exception is often a fault too, but not if its possible occurrence has been anticipated so that the software can recover from the exception.

See "Errors, defects and other creeping creatures", page 347.

Sources of exceptions

The software development framework introduced so far opens the possibility of specific categories of exception, listed at the top of the facing page.

Case E1 reflects one of the basic requirements of using references: a call $a.f$ is only meaningful if a is attached to an object, that is to say non-void. This was discussed in the presentation of the dynamic model.

"Void references and calls", page 240.

Case E2 also has to do with void values. Remember that "attachment" covers assignment and argument passing, which have the same semantics. We saw in the discussion of attachment that it is possible to attach a reference to an expanded target, the result being to copy the corresponding object. This assumes that the object exists; if the source is void, the attachment will trigger an exception.

"Hybrid attachments", page 263.

> ### Definition: exception cases
>
> An exception may occur during the execution of a routine r as a result of any of the following situations:
>
> E1 • Attempting a qualified feature call $a.f$ and finding that a is void.
>
> E2 • Attempting to attach a void value to an expanded target.
>
> E3 • Executing an operation that produces an abnormal condition detected by the hardware or the operating system.
>
> E4 • Calling a routine that fails.
>
> E5 • Finding that the precondition of r does not hold on entry.
>
> E6 • Finding that the postcondition of r does not hold on exit.
>
> E7 • Finding that the class invariant does not hold on entry or exit.
>
> E8 • Finding that the invariant of a loop does not hold after the **from** clause or after an iteration of the loop body.
>
> E9 • Finding that an iteration of a loop's body does not decrease the variant.
>
> E10 • Executing a **check** instruction and finding that its assertion does not hold.
>
> E11 • Executing an instruction meant explicitly to trigger an exception.

Case E3 follows from signals that the operating system sends to an application when it detects an abnormal event, such as a fault in an arithmetic operation (underflow, overflow) or an attempt to allocate memory when none is available.

Case E4 arises when a routine fails, as a result of an exception that happened during its own execution and from which it was not able to recover. This will be seen in more detail below, but be sure to note the rule that results from case E4:

> ### Failures and exceptions
>
> A *failure* of a routine causes an *exception* in its caller.

See "Monitoring assertions at run time", page 392.

Cases E5 to E10 can only occur if run-time assertion monitoring has been enabled at the proper level: at least *assertion* (**require**) for E5, *assertion* (**loop**) for E8 and E9 etc.

Case E11 assumes that the software may include calls to a procedure *raise* whose sole goal is to raise an exception. Such a procedure will be introduced later.

Causes of failure

Along with the list of possible exception cases, it is useful for the record to define when a *failure* (itself the source of an exception in the caller, as per case E4) can occur:

<table>
<tr><td>

Definition: failure cases

A routine call will fail if and only if an exception occurs during its execution and the routine does not recover from the exception.

</td></tr>
</table>

We have yet to see what it means for a routine to "recover" from an exception.

The definitions of failure and exception are mutually recursive: a failure arises from an exception, and one of the principal sources of exceptions in a calling routine (E4) is the failure of a called routine.

12.2 HANDLING EXCEPTIONS

We now have a definition of what may happen — exceptions — and of what we would prefer not to happen as a result — failure. Let us equip ourselves with ways to deal with exceptions so as to avoid failure. What can a routine do when its execution is suddenly interrupted by an unwelcome diversion?

As so often in this presentation, we can get help towards an answer by looking at examples of how *not* to do things. Here the C mechanism (coming from Unix) and an Ada textbook will oblige.

How not to do it — a C-Unix example

The first counter-example mechanism (most notably present on Unix, although it has been made available on other platforms running C) is a procedure called *signal* which you can call under the form

> *signal* (*signal_code*, *your_routine*)

with the effect of planting a reference to *your_routine* into the software, as the routine that should be called whenever a signal of code *signal_code* occurs. A signal code is one of a number of possible integers such as *SIGILL* (illegal instruction) and *SIGFPE* (floating-point exception). You may include as many calls to *signal* as you like, so as to associate different routines with different signals.

Then assume some instruction executed after the call to *signal* triggers a signal of code *signal_code*. Were it not for the *signal* call, this event would immediately terminate the execution in an abnormal state. Instead it will cause a call to *your_routine*, which presumably performs some corrective action, and then will … resume the execution exactly at the point where the exception occurred. This is dangerous, as you have no guarantee that the cause of the trouble has been addressed at all; if the computation was interrupted by a signal it was probably impossible to complete it starting from its initial state.

What you will need in most cases is a way to correct the situation and then **restart** the routine in a new, improved initial state. We will see a simple mechanism that implements this scheme. Note that one can achieve it in C too, on most platforms, by combining the *signal* facility with two other library routines: *setjmp* to insert a marker into the execution record for possible later return, and *longjmp* to return to such a marker, even if several calls have been started since the *setjmp*. The *setjmp-longjmp* mechanism is, however, delicate to use; it can be useful in the target code generated by a compiler — and can indeed serve, together with *signal*, to implement the high-level O-O exception mechanism introduced later in this chapter — but is not fit for direct consumption by human programmers.

How not to do it — an Ada example

Here is a routine taken from an Ada textbook:

From Sommerville and Morrison, "Software Development with Ada", Addison-Wesley, 1987. Letter case, indentation, semicolon usage and the name of the floating-point type have been adapted to the conventions of the present book; Non_ positive has been changed to Negative.

```
sqrt (n: REAL) return REAL is
    begin
        if x < 0.0 then
            raise Negative
        else
            normal_square_root_computation
        end
    exception
        when Negative =>
            put ("Negative argument")
            return
        when others => ...
end -- sqrt
```

This example was probably meant just as a syntactical illustration of the Ada mechanism, and was obviously written quickly (for example it fails to return a value in the exceptional case); so it would be unfair to criticize it as if it were an earnest example of good programming. But it provides a useful point of reference by clearly showing an undesirable way of handling exceptions. Given the intended uses of Ada — military and space systems — one can only hope that not too many actual Ada programs have taken this model verbatim.

The goal is to compute the real square root of a real number. But what if the number is negative? Ada has no assertions, so the routine performs a test and, if it finds *n* to be negative, raises an exception.

The Ada instruction **raise** *Exc* interrupts execution of the current routine, triggering an exception of code *Exc*. Once raised, an exception can be caught, through a routine's (or block's) **exception** clause. Such a clause, of the form

```
exception
    when code_a1, code_a2, ...=> Instructions_a;
    when code_b1, ... => Instructions_b;
    ...
```

is able to handle any exception whose code is one of those listed in the **when** subclauses; it will execute *Instructions_a* for codes *code_a1*, *code_a2*, ... and so on for the others. One of the subclauses may, as in the example, start with **when others**, and will then handle any exception not explicitly named in the other subclauses. If an exception occurs but its code is not listed (explicitly or through **when others**), the routine will pass it to its caller; if there is no caller, meaning that the failed routine is the main program, execution terminates abnormally.

In the example there is no need to go to the caller since the exception, just after being raised, is caught by the **exception** clause of the routine itself, which contains a subclause **when** *Negative* => ...

But what then do the corresponding instructions do? Here they are again:

put ("Negative argument")

return

In other words: print out a message — a delicate thought, considering was happens next; and then return to the caller. The caller will not be notified of the event, and will continue its execution as if nothing had happened. Thinking again of typical applications of Ada, we may just wish that artillery computations, which can indeed require square root computations, do not follow this scheme, as it might direct a few missiles to the wrong soldiers (some of whom may, however, have the consolation of seeing the error message shortly before the encounter).

This technique is probably worse than the C-Unix *signal* mechanism, which at least picks up the computation where it left. A **when** subclause that ends with **return** does not even continue the current routine (assuming there are more instructions to execute); it gives up and returns to the caller as if everything were fine, although everything is *not* fine. Managers — and, to continue with the military theme, officers — know this situation well: you have assigned a task to someone, and are told the task has been completed — but it has not. This leads to some of the worst disasters in human affairs, and in software affairs too.

This counter-example holds a lesson for Ada programmers: under almost no circumstances should a **when** subclause terminate its execution with a **return**. The qualification "almost" is here for completeness, to account for a special case, the *false alarm*, discussed below; but that case is very rare. Ending exception handling with a **return** means pretending to the caller that everything is right when it is not. This is dangerous and unacceptable. If you are unable to correct the problem and satisfy the Ada routine's contract, you should make the routine fail. Ada provides a simple mechanism to do this: in an **exception** clause you may execute a **raise** instruction written as just

   raise

whose effect is to re-raise the original exception to the caller. This is the proper way of terminating an execution that is not able to fulfill its contract.

Ada Exception rule

The execution of any Ada exception handler should end by either executing a **raise** instruction or retrying the enclosing program unit.

Exception handling principles

These counter-examples help show the way to a disciplined use of exceptions. The following principle will serve as a basis for the discussion.

The classification of exception cases, including E3, is on page 413.

> ### Disciplined Exception Handling principle
>
> There are only two legitimate responses to an exception that occurs during the execution of a routine:
>
> R1 •**Retrying**: attempt to change the conditions that led to the exception and to execute the routine again from the start.
>
> R2 •**Failure** (also known as **organized panic**): clean up the environment, terminate the call and report failure to the caller.
>
> In addition, exceptions resulting from some operating system signals (case E3 of the classification of exceptions) may in rare cases justify a **false alarm** response: determine that the exception is harmless and pick up the routine's execution where it started.

Let us do away first with the false alarm case, which corresponds to the basic C-Unix mechanism as we have seen it. Here is an example. Some window systems will cause an exception if the user of an interactive system resizes a window while some process is executing in it. Assume that such a process does not perform any window output; then the exception was harmless. But even in such case there are usually better ways, such as disabling the signals altogether, so that no exception will occur. This is how we will deal with false alarms in the mechanism of the next sections.

False alarms are only possible for operating system signals — in fact, only for signals of the more benign kind, since you cannot ignore an arithmetic overflow or an inability to allocate requested memory. Exceptions of all the other categories indicate trouble that cannot be ignored. It would be absurd, for example, to proceed with a routine after finding that its precondition does not hold.

So much for false alarms (unfortunately, since they are the easiest case to handle). For the rest of this discussion we concentrate on true exceptions, those which we cannot just turn off like an oversensitive car alarm.

Retrying is the most hopeful strategy: we have lost a battle, but we have not lost the war. Even though our initial plan for meeting our contract has been disrupted, we still think that we can satisfy our client by trying another tack. If we succeed, the client will be entirely unaffected by the exception: after one or more new attempts following the initial failed one, we will return normally, having fulfilled the contract. ("Mission accomplished, Sir. The usual little troubles along the way, Sir. All fine by now, Sir.")

What is the "other tack" to be tried on the second attempt? It might be a different algorithm; or it might be the same algorithm, executed again after some changes have been brought to the state of the execution (attributes, local entities) in the hope of preventing the exception from occurring again. In some cases, it may even be the original routine tried again without any change whatsoever; this is applicable if the exception was due to some external event — transient hardware malfunction, temporarily busy device or communication line — which we do not control although we expect it will go away.

With the other response, *failure*, we accept that we not only have lost the battle (the current attempt at executing the routine body) but cannot win the war (the attempt to terminate the call so as to satisfy the contract). So we give up, but we must first ensure two conditions, explaining the use of "organized panic" as a more vivid synonym for "failure":

- Making sure (unlike what happened in the *sqrt* counter-example) that the caller gets an exception. This is the *panic* aspect: the routine has failed to live up to its contract.
- Restoring a consistent execution state — the *organized* aspect.

What is a "consistent" state? From our study of class correctness in the previous chapter we know the answer: a state that satisfies the invariant. We saw that in the course of its work a routine execution may temporarily violate the invariant, with the intention of restoring it before termination. But if an exception occurs in an intermediate state the invariant may be violated. The routine must restore it before returning control to its caller.

The call chain

To discuss the exception handling mechanism it will be useful to have a clear picture of the sequence of calls that may lead to an exception. This is the notion of call chain, already present in the explanation of the Ada mechanism.

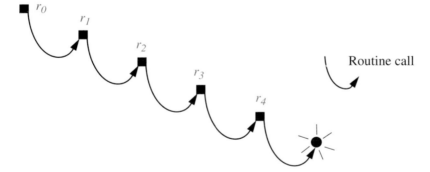

The call chain

Let r_0 be the root creation procedure of a certain system (in Ada r_0 would be the main program). At any time during the execution, there is a *current routine*, the routine whose execution was started last; it was started by the execution of a certain routine; that routine was itself called by a routine; and so on. If we follow this called-to-caller chain all the way through we will end up at r_0. The reverse chain (r_0, the last routine r_1 that it called, the last routine r_2 that r_1 called, and so on down to the current routine) is the call chain.

If a routine produces an exception (as pictured at the bottom-right of the figure), it may be necessary to go up the chain until finding a routine that is equipped to handle the exception — or stop execution if we reach r_0, not having found any applicable exception handler. This was the case in Ada when no routine in the call chain has an **exception** clause with a **when** clause that names the exception type or **others**.

12.3 AN EXCEPTION MECHANISM

From the preceding analysis follows the exception mechanism that fits best with the object-oriented approach and the ideas of Design by Contract.

The basic properties will follow from a simple language addition — two keywords — to the framework of the preceding chapters. A library class, *EXCEPTIONS*, will also be available for cases in which you need to fine-tune the mechanism.

Rescue and Retry

First, it must be possible to specify, in the text of a routine, how to deal with an exception that occurs during one of its calls. We need a new clause for that purpose; the most appropriate keyword is **rescue**, indicating that the clause describes how to try to recover from an undesirable run-time event. Because the **rescue** clause describes operations to be executed when the routine's behavior is outside of the standard case described by the precondition (**require**), body (**do**) and postcondition (**ensure**), it will appear, when present, after all these other clauses:

>   *routine* **is**
>
>   **require**
>
>   *precondition*
>
>   **local**
>
>   … Local entity declarations …
>
>   **do**
>
>   *body*
>
>   **ensure**
>
>   *postcondition*
>
>   **rescue**
>
>   *rescue_clause*
>
>   **end**

The *rescue_clause* is a sequence of instructions. Whenever an exception occurs during the execution of the normal *body*, this execution will stop and the *rescue_clause* will be executed instead. There is at most one **rescue** clause in a routine, but it can find out what the exception was (using techniques introduced later), so that you will be able to treat different kinds of exception differently if you wish to.

The other new construct is the retry instruction, written just **retry**. This instruction may only appear in a **rescue** clause. Its execution consists in re-starting the routine body from the beginning. The initializations are of course not repeated.

These constructs are the direct implementation of the Disciplined Exception Handling principle. The **retry** instruction provides the mechanism for retrying; a **rescue** clause that does not execute a **retry** leads to failure.

How to fail without really trying

The last observation is worth emphasizing:

Failure principle

Execution of a **rescue** clause to its end, not leading to a **retry** instruction, causes the current routine call to fail.

So if you have wondered how routines can fail in practice — causing case E4 of the exception classification — this is it.   *See page 413.*

As a special case, consider a routine which does *not* have a **rescue** clause. In practice this will be the case with the vast majority of routines since the approach to exception handling developed here suggests equipping only a select few routines with such a clause. Ignoring possible local entity declarations, arguments, precondition and postcondition, the routine appears as

> *routine* **is**
>> **do**
>>> *body*
>> **end**

Then if we consider — as a temporary convention — that the absence of a **rescue** clause is the same thing as an empty rescue clause, that is to say

> *routine* **is**
>> **do**
>>> *body*
>> **rescue**
>>> -- Nothing here (empty instruction list)
>> **end**

the Failure principle has an immediate consequence: if an exception occurs in a routine without **rescue** clause it will cause the routine to fail, triggering an exception in its caller.

Treating an absent **rescue** clause as if it were present but empty is a good enough approximation at this stage of the discussion; but we will need to refine this rule slightly when we start looking at the effect of exceptions on the class invariant.   *For the exact convention see "When there is no rescue clause", page 430.*

An exception history table

If a routine fails, either because it has no **rescue** clause at all or because its **rescue** clause executes to the end without a **retry**, it will interrupt the execution of its caller with a "Routine failed" (E4) exception. The caller is then faced with the same two possibilities: either it has a **rescue** clause that can execute a successful **retry** and get rid of the exception, or it will fail too, passing the exception one level up the call chain.

If in the end no routine in the call chain is able to recover from the exception, the execution as a whole will fail. In such a case the environment should print out a clear description of what happened, the exception history table. Here is an example:

An exception history table

Object	Class	Routine	Nature of exception	Effect
O4	*Z_FUNCTION*	*split* (from *E_FUNCTION*)	Feature *interpolate*: Called on void reference.	Retry
O3	*INTERVAL*	*integrate*	*interval_big_enough*: Precondition violated.	Fail
O2	*EQUATION*	*solve* (from *GENERAL_EQUATION*)	Routine failure	Fail
O2	*EQUATION*	*filter*	Routine failure	Retry
O2	*MATH*	*new_matrix* (from *BASIC_MATH*)	*enough_memory*: Check violated.	Fail
O1 (root)	*INTERFACE*	*make*	Routine failure	Fail

This is a record not only of the exceptions that directly led to the execution's failure but of all recent exceptions, up to a limit of 100 by default, including those from which the execution was able to recover through a **retry**. From top to bottom the order is the reverse of the order in which calls were started; the creation procedure is on the last line.

The **Routine** column identifies, for each exception, the routine whose call was interrupted by the exception. The **Object** column identifies the target of that call; here the objects have names such as O1, but in a real trace they will have internal identifiers, useful to determine whether two objects are the same. The **Class** column gives the object's generating class.

The **Nature of exception** column indicates what happened. This is where, for a assertion violation as in the second entry from the top, the environment can take advantage of assertion labels, *interval_big_enough* in the example, to identify the precise clause that was violated.

The last column indicates how the exception was handled: Retry or Fail. The table consists of a sequence of sections separated by thick lines; each section except the last led to a Retry. Since a Retry enables the execution to restart normally, an arbitrary number of calls may have occurred between two calls separated by a thick line.

Ignoring any such intermediate calls — successful and as such uninteresting for the purposes of this discussion — here is the call and return chain corresponding to the above exception history table. To reconstruct the action you should follow the arrows counter-clockwise from the call to *make* at the top left.

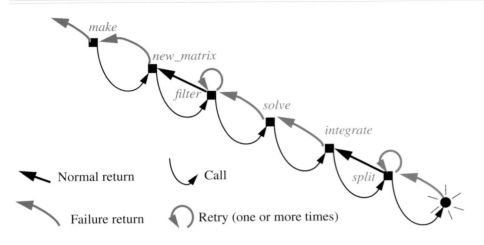

A failed execution

Normal return   Call

Failure return   Retry (one or more times)

12.4 EXCEPTION HANDLING EXAMPLES

We now have the basic mechanism. Let us see how to apply it to common situations.

Fragile input

Assume that in an interactive system you need to prompt your system's user to enter an integer. Assume further that the only procedure at your disposal to read the integer, *read_one_integer*, leaving its result in the attribute *last_integer_read*, is not robust: if provided with something else than integer input, it may fail, producing an exception. Of course you do not want your own system to fail in that case, but since you have no control over *read_one_integer* you must use it as it is and try to recover from the exception if it occurs. Here is a possible scheme:

```
get_integer is
        -- Get integer from user and make it available in last_integer_read.
        -- If input initially incorrect, ask again as many times as necessary.
    do
        print ("Please enter an integer: ")
        read_one_integer
    rescue
        retry
    end
```

This version of the routine illustrates the retry strategy: we just keep retrying.

An obvious criticism is that if a user keeps on entering incorrect input, the routine will forever keep asking for a value. This is not a very good solution. We might put an upper bound, say five, on the number of attempts. Here is the revised version:

Maximum_attempts: *INTEGER* **is** *5*
    -- Number of attempts before giving up getting an integer.

get_integer **is**
    -- Attempt to read integer in at most *Maximum_attempts* attempts.
    -- Set value of *integer_was_read* to record whether successful.
    -- If successful, make integer available in *last_integer_read*.
  local
    attempts: *INTEGER*
  do
    if *attempts* < *Maximum_attempts* **then**
      print ("*Please enter an integer*: ")
      read_one_integer
      integer_was_read := *True*
    else
      integer_was_read := *False*
      attempts := *attempts* + *1*
    end
  rescue
    retry
  end

This assumes that the enclosing class has a boolean attribute *integer_was_read* which will record how the operation went. Callers should use the routine as follows to try to read an integer and assign it to an integer entity *n*:

get_integer
if *integer_was_read* **then**
  n := *last_integer_read*
else
  "Deal with case in which it was impossible to obtain an integer"
end

Recovering from hardware or operating system exceptions

Among the events that trigger exceptions are signals sent by the operating system, some of which may have originated with the hardware. Examples include: arithmetic overflow and underflow; impossible I/O operations; "illegal instruction" attempts (which, with a good object-oriented language, will come not from the O-O software but from companion routines, written in lower-level languages, which may overwrite certain areas of memory); creation or clone operations that fail because no memory is available; user interrupts (a user hitting the "break" key or equivalent during execution).

Theoretically you may view such conditions as assertion violations. If $a + b$ provokes overflow, it means that the call has not observed the implicit precondition on the + function for integer or real numbers, stating that the mathematical sum of the two arguments should be representable on the computer. A similar implicit precondition on the allocation of a new object (creation or clone) is that enough memory is available; if a write fails, it is because the environment — files, devices, users — did not meet the applicability conditions. But in such cases it is impractical or impossible to express the assertions, let alone check them: the only solution is to attempt the operation and, if the hardware or operating system signals an abnormal condition, to treat it as an exception.

Consider the problem of writing a function *quasi_inverse* which for any real number x must return either its inverse $\frac{1}{x}$ or, if that is impossible to compute because x is too small, the value 0. This type of problem is essentially impossible to solve without an exception mechanism: the only practical way to know whether x has a representable inverse is to attempt the division $\frac{1}{x}$; but if this provokes overflow and you cannot handle exceptions, the program will crash and it will be too late to return 0 as a result.

> On some platforms it may be possible to write a function *invertible* such that *invertible* (x) is true if and only if the inverse of x can be computed. You can then use *invertible* to write *quasi_inverse*. But this is usually not a practical solution since such a function will not be portable across platforms, and in time-sensitive numerical computations will cause a serious performance overhead, a call to *invertible* being at least as expensive as the inversion itself.

With the **rescue-retry** mechanism you can easily solve the problem, at least on hardware that triggers a signal for arithmetic underflow:

```
quasi_inverse (x: REAL): REAL is
            -- 1/x if possible, otherwise 0
      local
            division_tried: BOOLEAN
      do
            if not division_tried then
                  Result := 1/x
            end
      rescue
            division_tried := True
            retry
      end
```

The initialization rules set *division_tried* to false at the start of each call. The body does not need any **else** clause because these rules also initialize *Result* to 0.

Retrying for software fault tolerance

Assume you have written a text editor and (shame on you) you are not quite sure it is entirely bug-free, but you already want to get some initial user feedback. Your guinea pigs are willing to tolerate a system with some remaining errors; they might accept for example that once in a while it will be unable to carry out a command that they have requested; but they will not use it to enter serious texts (which is what you want them to do, to test your editor under realistic conditions) if they fear that a failure may result in a catastrophe, such as brutal exit and loss of the last half-hour's work. With the Retrying mechanism you can provide a defense against such behavior.

Assume that the editor, as will usually be the case, contains a basic command execution loop of the form

> **from** … **until** *exit* **loop**
>
>   *execute_one_command*
>
> **end**

where the body of routine *execute_one_command* is of the form

> "Decode user request"
>
> "Execute appropriate command in response to request"

Chapter 21.

The "Execute…" instruction chooses among a set of available routines (for example delete a line, change a word etc.) We will see in a later chapter how the techniques of inheritance and dynamic binding yield simple, elegant structures for such multi-way decisions.

The assumption is that the different routines are not entirely safe; some of them may fail at unpredictable times. You can provide a primitive but effective protection against such an event by writing the routine as

> *execute_one_command* **is**
>
>   -- Get a request from the user and, if possible,
>
>   -- execute the corresponding command.
>
>   **do**
>
>   "Decode user request"
>
>   "Execute appropriate command in response to request"
>
>   **rescue**
>
>   *message* ("*Sorry, this command failed*")
>
>   *message* ("*Please try another command*")
>
>   *message* ("*Please report this failure to the author*")
>
>   "Instructions to patch up the state of the editor"
>
>   **retry**
>
>   **end**

This scheme assumes in practice that the types of supported user request include "save current state of my work" and "quit", both of which had better work correctly. A user who sees the message *Sorry, this command failed* will most likely want to save the results of the current session and get out as quickly as possible.

Some of the routines implementing individual operations may have their own **rescue** clauses, leading to failure (so that the above **rescue** clause of *execute_one_command* takes over) but only after printing a more informative, command-specific message.

N-version programming

Another example of retrying for software fault tolerance is an implementation of the "N-version programming" approach to improving software reliability.

N-version programming was inspired by redundancy techniques that have proved their usefulness in hardware. In mission-critical setups it is frequent to encounter redundant hardware configurations, where several devices — for example computers — perform an identical function, and an arbitrating mechanism compares the results, deciding for the majority in case of discrepancy. This approach guards against single-component failures and is common in aerospace applications. (In a famous incident, an early space shuttle launch had to be delayed because of a bug in the software for the *arbitrating* computer itself.) N-version programming transposes this approach to software by suggesting that for a mission-critical development two or more teams, working in environments as distinct as possible, should produce alternative systems, in the hope that errors, if any, will be different.

See A. Avizienis, "The N-Version Approach to Fault-Tolerant Software", IEEE Trans. on Soft. Eng., SE-11, 12, Dec. 1985, pp. 1491-1501.

This is a controversial idea; one may argue that the money would be better spent in improving the correctness and robustness of a single version than in financing two or more imperfect implementations. Let us, however, ignore these objections and refrain from any judgment on the idea itself, but see how the **retry** mechanism would support the idea of using several implementations where one takes over if the others fail:

```
do_task is
            -- Solve a problem by applying one of several possible implementations.
    require
        …
    local
        attempts: INTEGER
    do
        if attempts = 0 then
            implementation_1
        elseif attempts = 1 then
            implementation_2
        end
    ensure
        …
    rescue
        attempts := attempts + 1
        if attempts < 2 then
            "Perhaps some instructions to reset to stable state"
            retry
        end
    end
```

The generalization to more than two alternative implementations is immediate.

This example is typical of the use of **retry**. The rescue clause *never* attempts to reach the original goal using a substitute implementation; reaching this goal, as expressed by the postcondition if there is one, is the privilege of the normal body. Note that after two attempts (or *n* in the general case) the routine simply executes its **rescue** clause to the end and so fails.

Let us look more closely at what happens when an exception is triggered during the execution of *r*. The normal execution (the body) stops; the rescue clause is executed instead. Then two cases may occur:

- The rescue clause may execute a **retry**, usually after some other instructions. In this case, execution of the routine will start anew. This new attempt may succeed; then the routine will terminate normally and return to its client. The call is a success; the contract has been fulfilled. Execution of the client is not affected, except of course that the call may have taken longer than normal. If, however, the retry attempt again causes an exception, the process of executing the rescue clause will start anew.

- If the rescue clause does not execute a **retry**, it will continue to its end. (This happens in the last example when *attempts* $>= 2$.) In this case the routine fails: it returns control to its caller, signaling an exception. Because the caller gets an exception, the same rule determines how its own execution continues.

This mechanism strictly adheres to the Disciplined Exception Handling principle: either a routine succeeds, that is to say its body executes to the end and satisfies the postcondition, or it fails. When interrupted by an exception, you may either report failure or try your normal body again; in no way can you exit through the rescue clause and pretend to your caller that you succeeded.

12.5 THE TASK OF A RESCUE CLAUSE

The last comments get us started towards a better understanding of the exception mechanism by suggesting the theoretical role of rescue clauses. Some formal reasoning will help us obtain the complete picture.

The correctness of a rescue clause

See "WHEN IS A CLASS COR-RECT?", 11.9, page 369.

The formal definition of class correctness stated two requirements on the features of a class. One (C1) requires creation procedures to start things off properly. The other (C2), more directly relevant for the present discussion, states that to satisfy its contract, every routine, started with its precondition and the class invariant both satisfied, must preserve the invariant and ensure its postcondition. This was illustrated by the diagram depicting the typical object lifecycle:

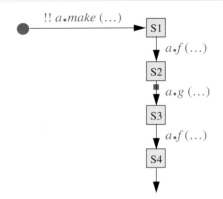

The life of an object

(*Original page 365.*)

The formal rule read:

> C2 • For every exported routine r and any set of valid arguments x_r:
>
> $\{pre_r(x_r) \textbf{ and } INV\} \; Body_r \; \{post_r(x_r) \textbf{ and } INV\}$

This rule appeared on page 370.

where pre_r is the precondition, INV the class invariant, $Body_r$ the body of the routine, and $post_r$ the postcondition. To keep things simple let us ignore the arguments x_r.

Let $Rescue_r$ be the rescue clause of a routine, ignoring any branch that leads to a **retry** — that is to say keeping only those branches that will result in failure if executed. Rule C2 is a specification of the body $Body_r$ of the routine, in terms of what initial states it assumes and what final states it can guarantee. Can we obtain a similar specification for $RESCUE_r$? It should be of the form

$$\{ \; ? \; \} \; Rescue_r \; \{ \; ? \; \}$$

with the question marks replaced by actual assertions. (Here it is useful to try answering the question for yourself before reading on: how would you fill in the question marks?)

Consider first the input assertion — the question mark on the left of $Rescue_r$. **Anything** non-trivial that we write there would be wrong! Remember the discussion of attractive job offers: for whoever implements the task A in $\{P\} \; A \; \{Q\}$, the stronger the precondition P, the easier the job, since a precondition restricts the set of input cases that you must handle. Any precondition for $Rescue_r$ would make the job easier by restricting the set of states in which $Rescue_r$ may be called to action. But we may not assume any such restriction since exceptions, by their very nature, may happen at any time. If we knew when an exception will happen, it probably would not be an exception any more. Think of hardware failures: we have no clue as to when a computer can start to malfunction. Nor do we know, in an interactive system, when a user will feel like hitting the "break" key.

See "Weak and strong conditions", page 335.

So the only P assertion that we can afford here (to replace the question mark on the left) is the one that asserts nothing at all: *True*, the assertion that all states satisfy.

For a lazy $Rescue_r$ implementor — again in reference to the discussion of job offers in the previous chapter — this is bad news; in fact the precondition *True* is always the worst possible news for a supplier, the case in which "the customer is always right"!

What about the output assertion (the Q)? As discussed earlier, a rescue clause that leads to a failure must, before returning control to its caller with an exception, restore a stable state. This means reestablishing the invariant.

Hence the rule that we seek, with no more question marks:

Correctness rule for failure-inducing rescue clauses

C3 • $\{True\}\ Rescue_r\ \{INV\}$

Similar reasoning yields the corresponding rule for any branch $Retry_r$ of the rescue clause leading to a **retry** instruction:

Correctness rule for retry-inducing rescue clauses

C4 • $\{True\}\ Retry_r\ \{INV \textbf{ and } pre_r\}$

A clear separation of roles

It is interesting to contrast the formal roles of the body and the rescue clause:

C2 • $\{pre_r \textbf{ and } INV\}\ Body_r\ \{post_r\ (x_r)\ INV\}$

C3 • $\{True\}\ Rescue_r\ \{INV\}$

The input assertion is stronger for $Body_r$: whereas the rescue clause is not permitted to assume anything at all, the routine's body may assume the precondition and the invariant. This makes its job easier.

The output assertion, however, is also stronger for $Body_r$: whereas the rescue clause is only required to restore the invariant, the normal execution must also ensure the postcondition — the official job of the routine. This makes its job harder.

These rules reflect the separation of roles between the body (the **do** clause) and the rescue clause. The task of the body is to ensure the routine's contract; not directly to handle exceptions. The task of the rescue clause is to handle exceptions, returning control to the body or (in the failure case) to the caller; not to ensure the contract.

As an analogy — part of this book's constant effort to provide readers not just with theoretically attractive concepts but also with practical skills that they can apply to the pursuit of their careers — consider the difficulty of choosing between two noble professions: *cook* and *firefighter*. Each has its grandeur, but each has its servitudes. A gratifying quality of the cook's job is that he may assume, when he shows up at work in the morning, that the restaurant is not burning (satisfies the invariant); presumably his contract does not specify any cooking obligation under burning circumstances. But with a non-burning initial state the cook must prepare meals (ensure the postcondition); it is also a component of his contract, although perhaps an implicit one, that throughout this endeavor he should maintain the invariant, if he can, by not setting the restaurant on fire.

The firefighter, for his part, may assume nothing as to the state in which he finds the restaurant when he is called for help at any time of day or night. There is not even any guarantee that the restaurant is indeed burning — no precondition of the form *is_burning*, or of any other form save for *True* — since any call may be a false alarm. In some cases, of course, the restaurant will be burning. But then a firefighter's only duty is to return it to a non-burning state; his job description does not require that he also serve a meal to the assembly of patiently waiting customers.

When there is no rescue clause

Having formalized the role of rescue clauses we can take a second look at what happens when an exception occurs in a routine that has no such clause. The rule introduced earlier — with a warning that it would have to be revised — stated that an absent rescue clause was equivalent to a present but empty one (**rescue end**). In light of our formal rules, however, this is not always appropriate. C3 requires that

$\{True\}\ \ Rescue_r\ \ \{INV\}$

If $Rescue_r$ is an empty instruction and the invariant *INV* is anything other than *True*, this will not hold.

Hence the exact rule. The class *ANY* — mother of all classes — includes a procedure

default_rescue **is**

           -- Handle exception if no Rescue clause.

           -- (Default: do nothing)

   do

   end

We will study ANY, whose features are present in all classes, in "THE GLOBAL INHERITANCE STRUCTURE", 16.2, page 580.

A routine that does not have a Rescue clause is considered to have one that, rather than being empty as first suggested, has the form

rescue

   default_rescue

Every class can redefine *default_rescue* (using the feature redefinition mechanism studied as part of inheritance in a later chapter) to perform some specific action, instead of the default empty effect defined in *GENERAL*.

Rule C3 indicates the constraint on any such action: starting in any state, it must restore the class invariant *INV*. Now you will certainly remember that producing a state that satisfies the invariant was also the role of the **creation procedures** of a class, as expressed by the rule labeled C1. In many cases, you will be able to write the redefinition of *default_rescue* so that it relies on a creation procedure.

See "The role of creation procedures", page 371. Rule C1 was on page 370.

12.6 ADVANCED EXCEPTION HANDLING

The extremely simple mechanism developed so far handles most of the needs for exception handling. But certain applications may require a bit of fine-tuning:

- You may need to find out the nature of the latest exception, so as to handle different exceptions differently.

- You may want to specify that certain signals should not trigger an exception.

- You may decide to trigger an exception yourself.

We could extend the language mechanism accordingly, but this does not seem the right approach, for at least three reasons: the facilities are needed only occasionally, so that we would be needlessly burdening the language; some of them (in particular anything that has to do with signals) may be platform-dependent, whereas a language definition should be portable; and when you select a set of these facilities it is hard to be sure that you will not at some later time think of other useful ones, which would then force a new language modification — not a pleasant prospect.

For such a situation we should turn not to the language but to the supporting library. We introduce a library class *EXCEPTIONS*, which provides the necessary fine-tuning capabilities. Classes that need these capabilities will inherit *EXCEPTIONS*, using the inheritance mechanism detailed in later chapters. (Some developers may prefer to use the client relation rather than inheritance.)

Exception queries

Class *EXCEPTIONS* provides a number of queries for obtaining some information about the last exception. You can find out the integer code of that exception:

> *exception*: *INTEGER*
>
> > -- Code of last exception that occurred
>
> *original_exception*: *INTEGER*
>
> > -- Original code of last exception that triggered current exception

The difference between *exception* and *original_exception* is significant in the case of an "organized panic" response: if a routine gets an exception of code *oc* (indicating for example an arithmetic overflow) but has no rescue clause, its caller will get an exception whose own code, given by the value of *exception*, indicates "failure of a called routine". It may be useful at that stage, or higher up in the call chain, to know what the original cause was. This is the role of *original_exception*.

The exception codes are integers. Values for the predefined exceptions are given by integer constants provided by *EXCEPTIONS* (which inherits them from another class *EXCEPTION_CONSTANTS*). Here are some examples:

Check_instruction: *INTEGER* **is** 7
        -- Exception code for violated check

Class_invariant: *INTEGER* **is** …
        -- Exception code for violated class invariant

Incorrect_inspect_value: *INTEGER* **is** …
        -- Exception code for inspect value which is not one
        -- of the inspect constants, if there is no Else_part

Loop_invariant: *INTEGER* **is** …
        -- Exception code for violated loop invariant

Loop_variant: *INTEGER* **is** …
        -- Exception code for non-decreased loop variant

No_more_memory: *INTEGER* **is** …
        -- Exception code for failed memory allocation

Postcondition: *INTEGER* **is** …
        -- Exception code for violated postcondition

Precondition: *INTEGER* **is** …
        -- Exception code for violated precondition

Routine_failure: *INTEGER* **is** …
        -- Exception code for failed routine

Void_assigned_to_expanded: *INTEGER* **is** …

Since the integer values themselves are irrelevant, only the first one has been shown.

A few other self-explanatory queries provide further information if needed:

meaning (*except*: *INTEGER*)
        -- A message in English describing the nature of exceptions
        -- of code *except*

is_assertion_violation: *BOOLEAN*
        -- Is last exception originally due to a violated assertion
        -- or non-decreasing variant?
    ensure
        Result = (*exception* = *Precondition*) **or** (*exception* = *Postcondition*) **or**
                (*exception* = *Class_invariant*) **or**
                (*exception* = *Loop_invariant*) **or** (*exception* = *Loop_variant*)

is_system_exception: *BOOLEAN*
        -- Is last exception originally due to external event (operating system error)?

is_signal: *BOOLEAN*
        -- Is last exception originally due to an operating system signal?

tag_name: *STRING*
        -- Tag of last violated assertion clause

original_tag_name: *STRING*
        -- Assertion tag for original form of last assertion violation.

recipient_name: *STRING*
>> -- Name of routine whose execution was interrupted by last exception

class_name: *STRING*
>> -- Name of class including recipient of last exception

original_recipient_name: *STRING*
>> -- Name of routine whose execution was interrupted by
>> -- original form of last exception

original_class_name: *STRING*
>> -- Name of class including recipient of original form of last exception

With these features a rescue clause can handle different kinds of exception in different ways. For example you can write it, in a class inheriting from *EXCEPTIONS*, as

rescue
>> **if** *is_assertion_violation* **then**
>>> "Process assertion violation case"
>> **else if** *is_signal* **then**
>>> "Process signal case"
>> **else**
>>> ...
>> **end**

or, with an even finer grain of control, as

rescue
>> **if** *exception = Incorrect_inspect_value* **then**
>>> "Process assertion violation case"
>> **else if** *exception = Routine_Failure* **then**
>>> "Process signal case"
>> **else**
>>> ...
>> **end**

quasi_inverse was on page 424. Using class *EXCEPTIONS*, we can modify the *quasi_inverse* example so that it will only attempt the **retry** if the exception was overflow. Other exceptions, such as one generated when the interactive user presses the Break key, will not cause the retry. The instruction in the rescue clause becomes:

>> **if** *exception = Numerical_error* **then**
>>> *division_tried := True*; **retry**
>> **end**

Since there is no **else** clause, exceptions other than *Numerical_error* will result in failure, the correct consequence since the routine has no provision for recovery in such cases. When writing a rescue clause specifically to process a certain kind of possible exception, you may use this style to avoid lumping other, unexpected kinds with it.

How fine a degree of control?

One may express reservations about going to the level of specific exception handling illustrated by the last two extracts. This chapter has developed a view of exceptions as undesired events; when one happens, the reaction of the software and its developer is "I don't want to be here! Get me out as soon as possible!". This seems incompatible with exerting fine control, depending on the exception's source, over what happens in a rescue clause.

For that reason, I tend in my own work to avoid using detailed case analysis on exception sources, and stick to exception clauses that try to fix things if they can, and then fail or retry.

This style is perhaps too austere, and some developers prefer a less restricted exception handling scheme that makes full use of the query mechanisms of class *EXCEPTIONS* while remaining disciplined. If you want to use such a scheme you will find in *EXCEPTIONS* all that you need. But do not lose sight of the following principle, a consequence of the discussion in the rest of this chapter:

> ### Exception Simplicity principle
>
> All processing done in a rescue clause should remain simple, and focused on the sole goal of bringing the recipient object back to a stable state, permitting a retry if possible.

Developer exceptions

All the exceptions studied so far resulted from events caused by agents external to the software (such as operating system signals) or from involuntary consequences of the software's action (as with assertion violations). It may be useful in some applications to cause an exception to happen on purpose.

Such an exception is called a developer exception and is characterized by an integer code (separate from the general exception code, which is the same for all developer exceptions) and an associated string name, which may be used for example in error messages. You can use the following features to raise a developer exception, and to analyze its properties in a rescue clause:

trigger (*code*: *INTEGER*; *message*: *STRING*)
-- Interrupt execution of current routine with exception
-- of code *code* and associated text *message*.

developer_exception_code: *INTEGER*
-- Code of last developer exception

developer_exception_name: *STRING*
-- Name associated with last developer exception

is_developer_exception: *BOOLEAN*
>>> -- Was last exception originally due to a developer exception?

is_developer_exception_of_name (*name*: *STRING*): *BOOLEAN*
>>> -- Is the last exception originally due to a developer
>>> -- exception of name *name*?

ensure
>>> *Result* := *is_developer_exception* **and then**
>>>>> *equal* (*name*, *developer_exception_name*)

It is sometimes useful to associate with a developer exception a *context* — any object structure that may be useful to the software element handling the exception:

set_developer_exception_context (*c*: *ANY*)
>>> -- Define *c* as the context associated with subsequent developer
>>> -- exceptions (as caused by calls to *trigger*).

require
>>> *context_exists*: *c* /= *Void*

developer_exception_context: *ANY*
>>> -- Context set by last call to *set_developer_exception_context*
>>> -- void if no such call.

These facilities enable a style of development that heavily relies on some software elements triggering exceptions that others will process. In one compiler that I have seen, the developers took advantage of this mechanism, in the parsing algorithm, to stick to a relatively linear control structure, recognizing the various elements of the input text one after the other. Such sequential treatment is only possible if the elements parsed are the expected ones; any syntactical error disrupts the process. Rather than complicating the control structure by adding possibly nested **if** ... **then** ... **else** constructs, the developers chose to raise a developer exception whenever encountering an error, then dealt with it separately in the calling routine. As hinted earlier, this is not my favorite style, but there is nothing inherently wrong with it, so the developer exception mechanisms are there for those who want them.

12.7 DISCUSSION

We have now completed the design of an exception mechanism for object-oriented software construction, compatible with the rest of the approach and resulting directly from the ideas of Design by Contract developed in the preceding chapter. Thanks in particular to the **retry** instructions the mechanism is more powerful than what you will find in many languages; at the same time it may appear stricter because of its emphasis on retaining the ability to reason precisely about the effect of each routine.

Let us explore a few alternative design ideas that could have been followed, and why they were not retained.

Disciplined exceptions

Exceptions, as they have been presented, are a technique to deal with erroneous conditions that may be arise at run time: assertion violations, hardware signals, attempts to access void references.

The approach we have explored is based on the contracting metaphor: under no circumstances should a routine pretend it has succeeded when in fact it has failed to achieve its purpose. A routine may only succeed (perhaps after experiencing some exceptions but recovering from them through one or more **retry**, unbeknownst to the client) or fail.

Exceptions in Ada, CLU or PL/I do not follow this model. Using the Ada model, and instruction

> **raise** *exc*

cancels the routine that executed it and returns control to its caller, which may handle the exception *exc* in a special handler clause or, if it has no such handler, will itself return control to its caller. But there is no rule as to what a handler may do. Hence it is perfectly possible to ignore an exception, or to return an alternate result. This explains why some developers use this exception mechanism simply to deal with cases other than the easiest one for an algorithm. Such applications of exceptions really use **raise** as a **goto** instruction, and a fairly dangerous one since it crosses routine boundaries. In my opinion, they are abuses of the mechanism.

There have traditionally been two viewpoints on exceptions: many practicing programmers, knowing how essential it is to retain control at run time whenever an abnormal condition is detected (whether due to a programming error or to an unforeseeable hardware event, say numerical overflow or hardware failure), consider them an indispensable facility. Computing scientists preoccupied with correctness and systematic software construction have often for their part viewed exceptions with suspicion, as an unclean facility used to circumvent the standard rules on control structures. The mechanism developed above will, it is hoped, appeal to both sides.

Should exceptions be objects?

An object-oriented zealot (and who, having discovered and mastered the beauty of the approach, does not at times risk succumbing to zeal?) may criticize the mechanism presented in this chapter for not treating exceptions as first-class citizens of our software society. Why is an exception not an object?

One recent language, the object-oriented extension of Pascal for Borland's Delphi environment has indeed taken the attitude that exceptions should be treated as objects.

It is not clear that such a solution would bring any benefit. The reasoning is in part a preview of the more general discussion that will help us, in a later chapter, tackle the question "how do we find the objects and classes?" An object is an instance of an abstractly defined data type, characterized by features. An exception has some features, of

"No-command classes", page 729.
See exercise E12.2, page 438.

course, which we saw in class *EXCEPTIONS*: its type, which was given by an integer code; whether it is a signal, an assertion violation, a developer exception; its associated message if it is a developer exception. But these features are *queries*; in most classes describing true "objects" there should also be *commands* changing the objects' state. Although one might conceive of commands applicable to exception objects, for example to disarm an exception after it has occurred, this seems incompatible with reliability requirements. Exceptions are not under the control of the software system; they are triggered by events beyond its reach.

Making their properties accessible through the simple queries and commands of the class *EXCEPTIONS* seems enough to satisfy the needs of developers who want fine-grain access to the exception handling mechanism.

The methodological perspective

"DEALING WITH ABNORMAL CASES", 23.6, page 797.

A final note and preview. Exception handling is not the only answer to the general problem of *robustness* — how to deal with special or undesired cases. We have gained a few methodological insights, but a more complete answer will appear in the chapter discussing the design of module interfaces, allowing us to understand the place of exception handling in the broader arsenal of robustness-enhancing techniques.

12.8 KEY CONCEPTS INTRODUCED IN THIS CHAPTER

- Exception handling is a mechanism for dealing with unexpected run-time conditions.

- A failure is the impossibility, for a routine execution, to fulfill the contract.

- A routine gets an exception as a result of the failure of a routine which it has called, of an assertion violation, of an abnormal condition signaled by the hardware or operating system.

- It is also possible for a software system to trigger a "developer exception" explicitly.

- A routine will deal with an exception by either Retry or Organized Panic. Retry reexecutes the body; Organized Panic causes a routine failure and sends an exception to the caller.

- The formal role of an exception handler not ending with a **retry** is to restore the invariant — not to ensure the routine's contract, as that is the task of the body (the **do** clause). The formal role of a branch ending with **retry** is to restore the invariant and the precondition so that the routine body can try again to achieve its contract.

- The basic language mechanism for handling exceptions should remain simple, if only to encourage straightforward exception handling — organized panic or retrying. For applications that need finer control over exceptions, their properties and their processing, a library class called *EXCEPTIONS* is available; it provides a number of mechanisms for distinguishing between exception types, as well as for triggering developer-defined exceptions.

12.9 BIBLIOGRAPHICAL NOTES

[Liskov 1979] and [Cristian 1985] offer other viewpoints on exceptions. Much of the work on software fault tolerance derives from the notion of "recovery block" [Randell 1975]; a recovery block for a task is used when the original algorithm for the task fails to succeed. This is different from rescue clauses which never by themselves attempt to achieve the original goal, although they may restart the execution after patching up the environment.

[Hoare 1981] contains a critique of the Ada exception mechanism.

The approach to exception handling developed in this chapter was first presented in [M 1988e] and [M 1988].

EXERCISES

E12.1 Largest integer

Assume a machine that generates an exception when an integer addition overflows. Using exception handling, write a reasonably efficient function that will return the largest positive integer representable on the machine.

E12.2 Exception objects

Notwithstanding the skeptical comments expressed in the discussion section as to the usefulness of treating exceptions as objects, press the idea further and discuss what a class *EXCEPTION* would look like, assuming an instance of that class denotes an exception that has occurred during execution. (Do not confuse this class with *EXCEPTIONS*, the class, meant to be used through inheritance, which provides general exception properties.) Try in particular to include commands as well as queries.

13

Supporting mechanisms

*E*xcept for one crucial set of mechanisms, we have now seen the basic techniques of object-oriented software construction. The major missing piece is inheritance and all that goes with it. Before moving to that last component of the approach, we should review a few mechanisms that will be important to the writing of actual systems: external routines and the encapsulation of non-O-O software; argument passing; control structures; expressions; string manipulation; input and output.

These are technical aspects, not essential to the understanding of the method; but we will need them for some later examples, and they blend well with the fundamental concepts. So even on your first reading you should spend some time getting at least generally familiar with them.

13.1 INTERFACING WITH NON-O-O SOFTWARE

So far, we have expressed software elements entirely in the object-oriented notation. But the software field grew up long before object technology became popular, and you will often need to interface your software with non-O-O elements, written in such languages as C, Fortran or Pascal. The notation should support this process.

We will first look at the language mechanism, then reflect on its broader significance as a part of the object-oriented software development process.

External routines

Our object-oriented systems are made of classes, consisting of features, particularly routines, that contain instructions. What is, among these three, the right level of granularity for integrating external software?

The construct must be common to both sides; this excludes classes, which exist only in object-oriented languages. (They may, however, be the right level of integration between two different O-O languages.) Instructions are too low-level; a sequence in which two object-oriented instructions bracket a C instruction:

Warning: this style is neither supported nor recommended. For purposes of discussion only.

```
!! x.make (clone (a))
(struct A) *x = &y;  /* A piece of C */
x.display
```

would be very hard to understand, validate and maintain.

This leaves the feature level, the right one since encapsulating features is compatible with O-O principles: a class is an implementation of a data type protected by information hiding; features are the unit of interaction of the class with the rest of the software; since clients rely on the features' official specification (the short form) independently of their implementation, it does not matter to the outside world whether a feature is internally written in the object-oriented notation or in another language.

Hence the notion of external routine. An external routine will have most of the trappings of a normal routine: name, argument list, result type if it is a function, precondition and postcondition if appropriate. Instead of a **do** clause it will have an **external** clause stating the language used for the implementation. Here is an example, extracted from a class describing character files:

```
put (c: CHARACTER) is
            -- Add c to end of file.
      require
            write_open: open_for_write
      external
            "C" alias "_char_write";
      ensure
            one_more: count = old count + 1
      end
```

The **alias** clause is optional, useful only if the name of the external routine, in its language of origin, is different from the name given in the class. This happens for example when the external name would not be legal in the object-oriented notation, as here with a name beginning with an underscore (legal in C).

Advanced variants

The mechanism just described covers most cases and will suffice for the purposes of this book. In practice some refinements are useful:

- Some external software elements may be *macros* rather than routines. They will appear to the O-O world as routines, but any call will be expanded in-line. This may be achieved by varying the language name (as in "*C*:[**macro**]... ").

- It is also necessary to permit calls to routines of "Dynamic Link Libraries" (DLL) available on Windows and other platforms. Instead of being a static part of the system, a DLL routine is loaded at run time, on the first call. It is even possible to define the routine and library names at run time. DLL support should include both a way to specify the names statically (as in **external** "*C*:[**dll**]...") and a completely dynamic approach using library classes *DYNAMIC_LIBRARY* and *DYNAMIC_ROUTINE* which you can instantiate at run time, to create objects representing dynamically determined libraries and routines.

- You may also need communication in the reverse direction, letting non-O-O software create objects and call features on them. For example you may want the *callback mechanism* of a non-O-O graphical toolkit to call certain class features.

All these facilities are present in the O-O environment described in the last chapter. Their detailed presentation, however, falls beyond the scope of this discussion.

Uses of external routines

External routines are an integral part of the method, fulfilling the need to combine old software with new. Any software design method emphasizing reusability must allow accessing code written in other languages. It would be hard to convince potential users that reusability begins this minute and that all existing software must be discarded.

Openness to the rest of the world is a requirement for most software. This might be termed the **Principle of Modesty**: authors of new tools should make sure that users can still access previously available facilities.

External routines are also necessary to provide access to machine-dependent or operating system capabilities. The file class is a typical example. Another is class *ARRAY*, whose interface was presented in earlier chapters but whose implementation will rely on external routines: the creation procedure *make* use a memory allocation routine, the access function *item* will use an external mechanism for fast access to array elements, and so on.

"Polite society" is not classless.

This technique ensures a clean interface between the object-oriented world and other approaches. To clients, an external routine is just a routine. In the example, the C routine *_char_write* has been elevated to the status of a feature of a class, complete with precondition and postcondition, and the standard name *put*. So even facilities which internally rely on non-O-O mechanisms get repackaged in data abstractions; the rest of the object-oriented software will see them as legitimate members of the group, their lowly origins never to be mentioned in polite society.

Object-oriented re-architecturing

The notion of external routine fits well with the rest of the approach. The method's core contribution is architectural: object technology tells us how to devise the structure of our systems to ensure extendibility, reliability and reusability. It also tells us how to fill that structure, but what fundamentally determines whether a system is object-oriented is its modular organization. It is often appropriate, then, to use an O-O architecture — what is sometimes called a **wrapper** — around internal elements that are not all O-O.

One extreme but not altogether absurd way to use the notation would rely solely on external routines, written in some other language, for all actual computation. Object technology would then serve as a pure packaging tool, using its powerful encapsulation mechanisms: classes, assertions, information hiding, client, inheritance.

In general there is no reason to go that far, since the notation is perfectly adequate to express computations of all kinds and execute them as efficiently as older languages such as Fortran or C. But object-oriented encapsulation of external software is useful in several cases. We have seen one of them: providing access to platform-specific operations. Another is to address a problem that faces many organizations: managing so-called *legacy software*. During the sixties, seventies and eighties, companies have accumulated a legacy of Cobol, Fortran, PL/I and C code, which is becoming harder and harder to maintain, and not just because the original developers are gone or going. Object technology offers an opportunity to re-engineer such systems by re-architecturing them, without having to rewrite them completely.

> Think of this process as the reverse of turkey stuffing: instead of keeping the structure and changing the internals, you keep the entrails and replace the skeleton, as if repackaging the content of a turkey into the bones of a zebra or a mouse. It must be noted, however, that such non-software applications of the idea appear neither useful nor appetizing.

This technique, which we may call **object-oriented re-architecturing**, offers an interesting solution for preserving the value of existing software assets while readying them for future extension and evolution.

It will only work, however, under specific conditions:

* You must be able to identify good abstractions in the existing software. Since you are not dealing with object-oriented software, they will typically be function abstractions, not data abstractions; but that is normal: it is your task to find the underlying data abstractions and repackage the old software's routines into the new software's classes. If you cannot identify proper abstractions already packaged in routines, you are out of luck, and no amount of object-oriented re-architecturing attempts will help.

* The legacy software must be of good quality. Re-architectured junk is still junk — possibly worse than the original, in fact, as the junkiness will be hidden under more layers of abstraction.

These two requirements are partly the same, since quality in software, O-O or not, is largely determined by quality of structure.

When they are satisfied, it is possible to use the **external** mechanism to build some very interesting object-oriented software based on earlier efforts. Here are two examples, both part of the environment described in the last chapter.

* The *Vision* library provides portable graphics and user interface mechanisms, enabling developers to write graphical applications that will run on many different platforms, with the native look-and-feel, for the price of a recompilation. Internally, it relies on the native mechanisms, used through external routines. More precisely, its lower level — WEL for Windows, MEL for Motif, PEL for OS/2 Presentation Manager — encapsulates the mechanisms of the corresponding platforms. WEL, MEL, PEL and consorts are also usable directly, providing developers who do not care about portability with object-oriented encapsulations of the Windows, Motif and Presentation Manager Application Programming Interfaces.

On these libraries see "PORTABILITY AND PLATFORM ADAPTATION", 32.2, page 1066.

* Another library, *Math*, provides an extensive set of facilities for numerical computation in such areas as probability, statistics, numerical integration, linear and non-linear equations, ordinary differential equations, eigenproblems, fitting and interpolation, orthogonal factorizations, linear least squares, optimization, special functions, Fast Fourier Transforms and time series analysis. Internally, it is based

on a commercial subroutine library, the NAG library from Nag Ltd. of Oxford, but it provides a completely object-oriented interface to its users. The library hides the underlying routines and instead is organized around such abstract concepts as integrator, matrix, discrete function, exponential distribution and many others; each describes "objects" readily understandable to a mathematician, physicist or economist, and is represented in the library by a class: *INTEGRATOR, BASIC_ MATRIX, DISCRETE_FUNCTION, EXPONENTIAL_DISTRIBUTION*. The result builds on the quality of the external routines — NAG is the product of hundreds of person-years of devising and implementing numerical algorithms — and adds the benefits of O-O ideas: classes, information hiding, multiple inheritance, assertions, systematic error handling through exceptions, simple routines with short argument lists, consistent naming conventions.

These examples are typical of how one can combine the best of traditional software and object technology.

The compatibility issue: hybrid software or hybrid languages?

Few people would theoretically disagree with the principle of modesty and deny the need for some integration mechanism between O-O developments and older software. The matter becomes more controversial when it comes to deciding on the level of integration.

See chapter 35.   A whole set of languages — the best known are Objective-C, C++, Java, Object Pascal and Ada 95 — have taken the approach of adding O-O constructs to an existing non-O-O language (respectively C in the first three cases, Pascal and Ada). Known as *hybrid languages*, they are discussed in varying degree of detail in a later chapter.

The integration technique described above, relying on external routines and object-oriented re-architecturing, follows from a different principle: that the need for *software* compatibility does not mean that we should burden the *language* with mechanisms that may be at odds with the principles of object technology. In particular:

• A hybrid adds a new language level to the weight of an existing language such as C. The result can be quite complex, limiting one of the principal attractions of object technology — the essential simplicity of the ideas.

• Beginners as a result often have trouble mastering a hybrid language, since they do not clearly see what is truly O-O and what comes from the legacy.

• Some of the older mechanisms may be incompatible with at least some aspects of object-oriented ideas. We have seen how the type concepts inherited from C make it hard to equip C++ environments with garbage collection, even though automatic memory management is part of the appeal of object technology. There are many other examples of clashes between the C or Pascal type system and the O-O view.

- The non-O-O mechanisms are still present, often in apparent competition with their higher-level object-oriented counterparts. For example C++ offers, along with dynamic binding, the ability to choose a function at run time through arithmetic on function pointers. This is disconcerting for the non-expert who lacks guidance on which approach to choose in a particular case. The resulting software, although compiled by an O-O environment, is still, deep-down, C code, and does not yield the expected quality and productivity benefits — giving object technology a bad name through no fault of its own.

If the aim is to obtain the best possible software process and products, compromising at the language level does not seem the right approach. *Interfacing* object-oriented tools and techniques with previous achievements is not the same thing as *mixing* widely different levels of technology.

> With the usual precautions about attaching too much weight to a metaphor, we can think of the precedent of electronics. It is definitely useful to combine different technology levels in a single system, as in an audio amplifier which still includes a few diodes together with transistors and integrated circuits. But the levels remain separate: there is little use for a basic component that would be half-diode, half-transistor.

O-O development should provide compatibility with software built with other approaches, but not at the expense of the method's power and integrity. This is what the **external** mechanism achieves: separate worlds, each with its own consistency and benefits, and clear interfaces between these worlds.

13.2 ARGUMENT PASSING

One aspect of the notation may require some clarification: what may happen to values passed as arguments to routines?

Consider a routine call of the form

$$r\ (a_1, a_2, ..., a_n)$$

corresponding to a routine

$$r\ (x_1: T_1, x_2: T_2, ..., x_n: T_n)\ \textbf{is}\ ...$$

where the routine could be a function as well as a procedure, and the call could be qualified, as in $b.r\ (...)$. The expressions $a_1, a_2, ..., a_n$ are called actual arguments, and the x_i are called formal arguments. (Recall that we reserve the term "parameter" for generic type parameters.)

The relevant questions are: what is the correspondence between actual and formal arguments? What operations are permitted on formal arguments? What effect will they have on the corresponding actuals? For all three we should stick to simple and safe rules.

We already know the answer to the first question: the effect of actual-formal argument association is the same as that of a corresponding assignment. Both operations are called **attachments**. For the above call we can consider that the routine's execution starts by executing instructions informally equivalent to the assignments

$$x_1 := a_1; \ x_2 := a_2; \ \ldots \ x_n := a_n$$

On the second question: within the routine body, any formal argument x is protected. The routine may not apply to it any direct modification, such as:

- An assignment to x, of the form $x := \ldots$

- A creation instruction with x as its target: !! x.*make* $(\ldots)$

Readers familiar with the passing mechanism known as *call by value* will note that the restriction is harsher here: with call by value, formals are initialized to actuals but may then be the target of arbitrary operations.

"ATTACHMENT: REFERENCE AND VALUE SEMAN-TICS", 8.8, page 261, in particular table on page 264.

The answer to the third question — what can the routine actually do to the actuals? — follows from the use of attachment to define the semantics of actual-formal association Attachment means copying either a reference or an object. As you will remember from the discussion of attachment, this depends on whether the types involved are expanded:

- For reference types (the more common case), argument passing will copy a reference, either void or attached to an object.

- For expanded types (which include in particular the basic types: *INTEGER*, *REAL* and the like), argument passing will actually copy an object.

In the first case, the prohibition of direct modification operations means that you cannot modify the **reference** through reattachment or creation; but if the reference is not void you can modify the attached **object** through appropriate routines.

Permissible operations on a reference argument

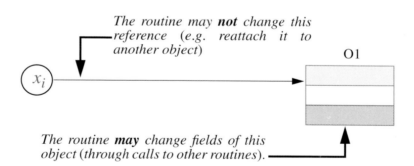

*The routine may **not** change this reference (e.g. reattach it to another object)*

O1

*The routine **may** change fields of this object (through calls to other routines).*

If x_i is one of the formal arguments to routine r, the body of the routine could contain a call of the form

$$x_i \cdot p \ (\ldots)$$

where p is a procedure applicable to x_i, meaning a procedure declared in the base class of x_i's type T_i. This routine may modify the fields of the object attached to x_i at execution time, which is the object attached to the corresponding actual argument a_i.

So although a call $q (a)$ can never change the value of a — the corresponding object if a is expanded, the reference otherwise — it can, in the reference case, change the attached object.

There are many reasons for not permitting routines to modify their arguments directly. One of the most striking is the *Conflicting Assignments To Actual* trick. Assume a language that permits assignments to arguments, and a procedure

> $dont\_I\_look\_innocuous$ $(a, b: INTEGER)$ **is**
>
> > -- But do not trust me too much.
>
> **do**
>
> > $a := 0; b := 1$
>
> **end**

WARNING: invalid routine text. For purposes of illustration only.

Then consider the call $dont\_I\_look\_innocuous$ (x, x) for some entity x. What is the value of x on return: 0 or 1? The answer depends on how the compiler implements formal-to-actual update on routine exit. This has fooled more than a few Fortran programmers, among others.

Permitting argument-modifying routines would also force us to impose restrictions on actual arguments: the actual corresponding to a modifiable formal must be an element that can change its value (a writable entity); this allows variable attributes, but not constant attributes, *Current*, or general expressions such as $a + b$. By precluding argument-modifying routines we can avoid imposing such restrictions and accept any expression as actual argument.

On constant attributes see chapter 18.

As a consequence of these rules, there are only three ways to modify the value of a reference x: through a creation instruction $!! \ x...$; through an assignment $x := y$; and through a variant of assignment, assignment attempt $x \ ?= y$, studied in a later chapter. Passing x as actual argument to a routine will never modify x.

This also means that a routine returns at most one result: none if it is a procedure; the official result (represented in the routine's body by the entity *Result*) if it is a function. To achieve the effect of multiple results, you can either:

- Use a function that returns an object with several fields (or more commonly a reference to such an object).

- Use a procedure that sets several fields of an object, corresponding to attributes that the client may then query.

The first technique is appropriate when the result is truly made of several components; a function may not for example return two values corresponding to the title and publication year of a book, but it may return a single value of type $BOOK$, with attributes *title* and *publication_year*. The second technique is applicable for a routine that, besides its principal job, sets some status indicators. We will study it, as well as the more general question of *side effects*, in the discussion of module design principles.

See chapter 23, especially "The a posteriori scheme", page 800.

13.3 INSTRUCTIONS

The object-oriented notation developed in this book is imperative: we specify computations through commands, also called instructions. (The word "statement" is commonly used in this sense but we will steadfastly avoid it since it is misleading: a statement is an expression of facts, not a command.)

Except for some specific properties of loops, intended to make their verification easier, instructions will look familiar to anyone who has had some experience with a modern language of the Algol line such as Pascal, Ada or Modula, or even just with C or a derivative. They include: Procedure call; Assignment; Creation; Conditional; Multi_branch; Loop; Check; Debug; Retry; Assignment attempt.

Procedure call

A routine call involves a routine, possibly with actual arguments. In a call instruction, the routine must be a procedure; if it is a function, the call is an expression. Although for the moment we are interested in instructions, the following rules apply to both cases.

A call is either qualified or unqualified. An unqualified call to a routine of the enclosing class uses the current instance as target; it appears under the form

r (without arguments), or

$r (x, y, \ldots)$ (with arguments)

A qualified call explicitly names its target, denoted by an expression: if a is an expression of a certain type, C is the base class of that type, and q is one of the routines of C, then a qualified call is of the form $a \cdot q$. Again, q may be followed by a list of actual arguments; a may be an unqualified function call with arguments, as in $p (m) \cdot q (n)$ where the target is $p (m)$. You may also use as target a more complex expression, provided you enclose it in parentheses, as in $(vector1 + vector2) \cdot count$.

Multidot qualified calls, of the form $a \cdot q_1 \cdot q_2 \ldots \cdot q_n$ are also permitted, where a as well as any of the q_i may include a list of actual arguments.

Export controls apply to qualified calls. Recall that a feature f declared in a class B is **available** to a class A if the feature clause declaring f begins with **feature** (without further qualification) or **feature** $\{X, Y, \ldots\}$ where one of $X, Y, \ldots$ is A or an ancestor of A. Then:

Qualified Call rule

A qualified call of the form $b \cdot q_1 \cdot q_2 \ldots \cdot q_n$ appearing in a class C is valid only if it satisfies the following conditions:

R1 • The feature appearing after the first dot, q_1, must be available to C.

R2 • In a multidot call, every feature after the second dot, that is to say every q_i for $i > 1$, must also be available to C.

To understand the reason for the second rule, note that $a \cdot q \cdot r \cdot s$ is a shorthand for

$b := a \bullet q; \; c := b \bullet r; \; c \bullet s$

which is only valid if q, r and s are all available to C, the class where this fragment appears. Whether r is available to the base class of q's type, and s available to the base class of r's type, is irrelevant.

As you will remember it is also possible to express calls in infix or prefix form; an expression such as $a + b$ is a different syntax for a call that would otherwise be written $a \bullet plus \, (b)$. The same validity rules apply to such expressions as to the dot form.

See "Operator features", page 187.

Assignment

The assignment instruction is written

$x := e$

where x is a writable entity and e an expression of compatible type. A writable entity is either:

- A non-constant attribute of the enclosing class.

- A local entity of the enclosing routine, including *Result* for a function.

Other, non-writable kinds of entity include constant attributes (introduced in declarations such as *Zero*: *INTEGER* **is** *0*) and formal arguments of a routine — to which, as we just saw, the routine may not assign a new value.

Chapter 18 discusses constant attributes.

Creation instruction

The creation instruction was studied in an earlier chapter in its two forms: without a creation procedure, as in !! x, and with a creation procedure, as in !! $x \bullet p \, (\ldots)$. In both cases, x must be a writable entity.

See "The creation instruction", page 232 and "CREATION PROCEDURES", 8.4, page 236. A variant will be seen in "Polymorphic creation", page 479.

Conditional

A conditional instruction serves to specify that different forms of processing should be applied depending on certain conditions. The basic form is

> **if** *boolean_expression* **then**
>   *instruction*; *instruction*; ...
> **else**
>   *instruction*; *instruction*; ...
> **end**

where each branch may have an arbitrary number of instructions (possibly none).

This will execute the instructions in the first branch if the *boolean_expression* evaluates to true, and those in the second branch otherwise. You may omit the **else** part if the second instruction list is empty, giving:

> **if** *boolean_expression* **then**
>   *instruction*; *instruction*; ...
> **end**

When there are more than two relevant cases, you can avoid nesting conditional instructions in **else** parts by using one or more **elseif** branches, as in

> **if** c_1 **then**
>> *instruction*; *instruction*; …
>
> **elseif** c_2 **then**
>> *instruction*; *instruction*; …
>
> **elseif** c_3 **then**
>> *instruction*; *instruction*; …
>
> …
>
> **else**
>> *instruction*; *instruction*; …
>
> **end**

where the **else** part remains optional. This avoids the repeated nesting of

> **if** c_1 **then**
>> *instruction*; *instruction*; …
>
> **else**
>> **if** c_2 **then**
>>> *instruction*; *instruction*; …
>>
>> **else**
>>> **if** c_3 **then**
>>>> *instruction*; *instruction*; …
>>>
>>> …
>>>
>>> **else**
>>>> *instruction*; *instruction*; …
>>>
>>> **end**
>>
>> **end**
>
> **end**

For handling a set of cases defined by the possible values of a certain expression, the multi-branch **inspect**, studied next, may be more convenient than the plain conditional.

The object-oriented method, in particular through polymorphism and dynamic binding, tends to reduce the need for explicit conditional and multi-branch instructions by supporting an implicit form of choice: you apply a feature to an object, and if the feature has several variants the right one automatically gets selected at run time on the basis of the object's type. When applicable, this implicit style is usually preferable. But of course some of your algorithms will still require explicit choice instructions.

Multi-branch

The multi-branch (also known as a Case instruction because of the corresponding keyword in Pascal, where it was first introduced based on a design by Tony Hoare) discriminates between a set of conditions that are all of the form $e = v_i$ where x is an expression and the v_i are constants of the same type. Although a conditional instruction (**if** $e = v_1$ **then** …

elseif $e = v_2$ **then** …) would do the job, two reasons justify a special instruction, departing from the usual rule that if the notation offers one good way to do something it does not need to offer two:

- This case is so common as to justify specific syntax, which will enhance clarity by avoiding the useless repetition of "$e =$".

- Compilers can use a particularly efficient implementation technique, the *jump table*, not applicable to general conditional instructions and avoiding explicit tests.

For the type of the discriminated values (the type of e and the v_i), the multi-branch instruction only needs to support two possibilities: integers and booleans. The rule will indeed be that e and the v_i must be declared as either all *INTEGER* or all *CHARACTER*. The general form of the instruction is:

> **inspect**
>> e
>
> **when** v_1 **then**
>> *instruction*; *instruction*; …
>
> **when** v_2 **then**
>> *instruction*; *instruction*; …
>
> …
>
> **else**
>> *instruction*; *instruction*; …
>
> **end**

All the v_i values must be different. The **else**… part is optional. Each of the branches may have an arbitrary number of instructions, possibly none.

The effect of the instruction is the following: if the value of e is equal to one of the v_i (this can be the case for at most one of them), execute the instructions in the corresponding branch; otherwise, execute the instructions in the **else** branch if any.

If there is no **else** branch and the value of e does not match any of the v_i, the effect is to raise an exception (of code *Incorrect_inspect_value*). This policy may seem surprising, since the corresponding conditional instruction would simply do nothing in this case. But it highlights the specificity of the multi-branch. When you write an **inspect** with a set of v_i values, you should include an **else** branch, empty or not, if you are prepared for run-time values of e that match none of the v_i. If you do not include an **else**, you are making an explicit statement: that you expect the value of e always to be one of the v_i. By checking this expectation and raising an exception if it is not met, the implementation is providing a service. Doing nothing would be the worst possible response, since this case usually reflects a bug (forgetting a possible case to be handled in its own specific way), which in any case should be fixed as early as possible.

A typical application of the multi-branch is to decode a single-character user input:

This is an elementary scheme. See chapter 21 for more sophisticated user command processing techniques.

inspect
> *first_input_letter*

when *'D'* **then**
> "Delete line"

when *'I'* **then**
> "Insert line"

> …

else
> *message* ("*Unrecognized command; type* H *for help*")

end

"UNIQUE VALUES", 18.6, page 654. Do and Si are also known as Ut and Ti.

In the integer case, the v_i can be Unique values, a concept detailed in a later chapter. This makes it possible to define a number of abstract constants, in a declaration such as *Do, Re, Mi, Fa, Sol, La, Si*: *INTEGER* **is unique**, and then discriminate among them in an instruction such as **inspect** *note* **when** *Do* **then**… **when** *Re* **then**… **end**.

The Discrimination principle appears on page 655.

Like conditionals, multi-branch instructions should not be used as a substitute for the implicit discrimination techniques of object technology, based on dynamic binding. The restriction to integer and character values helps avoid misuse; the Discrimination principle, introduced together with unique values, will provide further guidance.

Loop

See "LOOP INVARI-ANTS AND VARI-ANTS", 11.12, page 380.

The syntax of loops was introduced in the presentation of Design by Contract:

from
> *initialization_instructions*

invariant
> *invariant*

variant
> *variant*

until
> *exit_condition*

loop
> *loop_instructions*

end

The **invariant** and **variant** clauses are optional. The **from** clause is required (but may be empty); it specifies the loop initialization instructions. Leaving aside the optional clauses, the execution of such a loop consists of executing the *initialization_instructions* followed by the "loop process", itself defined as follows: if the *exit_condition* is true, the loop process is a null instruction; if it is false, the loop process is the execution of the *loop_instructions* followed (recursively) by a new loop process.

Check

The **check** instruction was also seen in the discussion of assertions. It serves to express that certain assertions must be satisfied at certain points:

See "LOOP INVARI-
ANTS AND VARI-
ANTS", 11.12, page
380.

> **check**
>
> > *assertion* -- One or more clauses
>
> **end**

Debug

The ***debug*** instruction is a facility for conditional compilation. It is written

> **debug** *instruction*; *instruction*; ... **end**

For every class, you may turn on or off the corresponding *debug* option of the control file (the Ace). If on, any debug instruction in the class is equivalent to the instructions it contains; if off, it has no effect on the execution.

You can use this instruction to include special actions that should only be executed in debugging mode, for example instructions to print out some values of interest.

Retry

The last instruction is **retry**, introduced in the discussion of exceptions. It may only appear in a **rescue** clause, and will restart the body of a routine that was interrupted by an exception.

See "AN EXCEP-
TION MECHA-
NISM", 12.3, page
419.

13.4 EXPRESSIONS

An expression serves to denote a computation that yields a value — an object, or a reference to an object. Expressions include the following varieties:

- Manifest constants.
- Entities (attributes, local routine entities, formal routine arguments, *Result*).
- Function calls.
- Expressions with operators (technically are a special case of function calls).
- *Current*.

*Entities were defined
on page 213.*

Manifest constants

A manifest constant is a value that denotes itself (such as the integer value written 0) — as opposed to a symbolic constant, whose name is independent of the denotation of the value.

There are two boolean manifest constants, written *True* and *False*. Integer constants follow the usual form and may be preceded by a sign. Examples are

> *453 –678 +66623*

Real constants use a decimal point. Either the integer part or the fractional part may be absent; you may include a sign, and specify an integer power of 10 by *e* followed by the exponent value. Examples are:

52.5 –54.44 +45.01 .983 –897. 999.e12

Character constants consist of a single character written in quotes, as in *'A'*; they describe single characters. For strings of more than one character we will use the library class *STRING*, discussed later in this chapter.

Function calls

Function calls follow the same syntax as procedure calls studied earlier in this chapter. They may be qualified or unqualified; in the qualified case, multidot notation is available. Assuming the proper class and function declarations, examples are:

> *b.f*
> *b.g (x, y, …)*
> *b.h (u, v).i.j (x, y, …)*

The Qualified Call rule introduced for procedures applies to function calls as well.

Current object

The reserved word *Current* denotes the current instance of the class and may be used in an expression. Note that *Current* itself is an expression, not a writable entity; thus an assignment to *Current*, such as *Current := some_value*, would be syntactically illegal.

When referring to a feature (attribute or routine) of the current instance, it is not necessary to write *Current. f*; just *f* suffices. Because of this rule, we will use *Current* less frequently than in object-oriented languages where every feature reference must be explicitly qualified. (In Smalltalk, for example, there is no such convention; a feature is always qualified, even when it applies to the current instance, written *self*.) Cases in which you will need to name *Current* explicitly include:

- Passing the current instance as argument to a routine, as in *a.f (Current)*. A common application is to create a duplicate of the current instance, as in *x := clone (Current)*.

- Testing whether a reference is attached to the current instance, as in the test *x = Current*.

- Using *Current* as anchor in an "anchored declaration" of the form **like** *Current*, as will be seen in the study of inheritance.

"ANCHORED DECLARATION", 16.7, page 598.

Expressions with operators

Operators are available to construct composite expressions.

Unary operators are + and –, applicable to integer and real expressions, and **not**, applicable to boolean expressions.

Binary operators, which take exactly two operands, include the relational operators

> = /= < > <= >=

where /= is "not equal". The relational operators yield boolean results.

Multiary expressions involve one or more operands, combined with operators. Numerical operands may be combined using the following operators:

    + − * / ^ // \\

where // is integer division, \\ is integer remainder and ^ is power (exponentiation).

Boolean operands may be combined with the operators **and, or, xor, and then, or else, implies**. The last three are explained in the next section; **xor** is exclusive or.

The precedence of operators, based on the conventions of ordinary mathematics, has been devised according to the "Principle of Least Surprise". To avoid any uncertainty or confusion, this book makes generous use of parentheses even where they are not needed, as in the examples of the next section.

Non-strict boolean operators

The operators **and then** and **or else** (whose names have been borrowed from Ada) as well as **implies** are not commutative, and are called *non-strict* boolean operators. Here is their semantics:

For an explanation of the word "non-strict" see e.g. [M 1990] *or* [M 1992].

Non-strict boolean operators

- *a* **and then** *b* has value false if *a* has value false, and otherwise has the value of *b*.

- *a* **or else** *b* has value true if *a* has value true, and otherwise has the value of *b*.

- *a* **implies** *b* has the same value as: (**not** *a*) **or else** *b*.

The boolean values from mathematics are written in regular font: true and false; *True* and *False* are predefined language constants and hence written in color italics.

The first two definitions at first seem to yield the same semantics as **and** and **or**. But the difference is what happens when *b* is not defined. In that case the expressions using the standard boolean operators are mathematically undefined, but the above definitions may still yield a result: if *a* is false, *a* **and then** *b* is false regardless of *b*; and if *a* is true, *a* **or else** *b* is true regardless of *b*. Similarly, *a* **implies** *b* is true if *a* is false, even if *b* is undefined. So the non-strict operators may yield a result when the standard ones do not.

A typical application is the boolean expression (using integer division //)

    (*i* /= *0*) **and then** (*j* // *i* = *k*)

which, from the above definition, has value false if *i* is equal to zero (as the first operand is then false). If the expression had been written using **and** rather than **and then**, then its second operand would be undefined when *i* is zero, so that the status of the whole expression is unclear in this case. This uncertainty is reflected in what may happen at run time:

B1 • If the compiler generates code that evaluates both operands and then takes their boolean "and", a division by zero will result at run time, producing an exception.

B2 • If, on the other hand, the generated code only evaluates the second operand when the first is true, otherwise returning false as the value of the expression, then the expression will indeed evaluate to false.

To guarantee interpretation B2, use **and then**. Similarly,

$(i = 0)$ **or else** $(j \,/\!/\, i \,/\!=\, k)$

will evaluate to true if i is zero, whereas the **or** variant could produce a run-time error.

An expression using **and then** always yields the same value as the corresponding expression written using **and** if both are defined. But the **and then** form may yield a value (false) in cases when the **and** form does not. The same holds with **or else** (and the value true) with respect to **or**. In this sense, the non-commutative operators may be said to be "more defined than or equal to" their respective counterparts. This also means that the non-strict interpretation — strategy B2 — is a correct implementation for the ordinary operators: a compiler writer may decide to implement **and** as **and then** and **or** as **or else**. But he does not have to, so the software developer may not rely on the assumption that **and** and **or** will be non-strict; only **and then** and **or else** guarantee the correct behavior in cases such as the last two examples.

One might wonder why two new operators are needed; would it not be simpler and safer to just keep the standard operators **and** and **or** and take them to mean **and then** and **or else**? This would not change the value of any boolean expression when both operands are defined, but would extend the set of cases in which expressions may be given a consistent value. This is indeed the way some programming languages, notably ALGOL W and C, interpret boolean operators. There are, however, both theoretical and practical reasons for keeping two sets of distinct operators:

• On the theoretical side, the standard mathematical boolean operators are commutative: a **and** b always has the same value as b **and** a, whereas a **and then** b may be defined when b **and then** a is not. When the order of operands does not matter it is preferable to use a commutative operator.

• In practice, some compiler optimizations become impossible if we require the compiler to evaluate the operands in a given sequence, as is the case with the non-commutative operators. So it is better to use the standard operators if both operands are known to be defined.

Note that it is possible to simulate the non-strict operators through conditional instructions in a language that does not include such operators. For example, instead of

$b := ((i \,/\!=\, 0)$ **and then** $(j \,/\!/\, i \,=\, k))$

one may write

if $i = 0$ **then** $b :=$ **false else** $b := (j \,/\!/\, i = k)$ **end**

The non-strict form is of course simpler. This is particularly clear when it is used as the exit condition of a loop, such as the following iteration on an array:

from
    $i := a.lower$
invariant
    -- For all elements in the interval $[a.lower .. i -- 1]$, $(a @ i) /= x$
variant
    $a.upper -- i$
until
    $i > a.upper$ **or else** $(a @ i = x)$
loop
    $i := i + 1$
end;
$Result := (i <= a.upper)$

whose purpose is to make *Result* true if and only if the value x appears in the array a. The use of **or** would be incorrect here: a compiler may generate code that will always evaluate both operands, so that for the last index examined ($i > a.upper$) if no array value equals x, there will be an erroneous attempt at run time to access the non-existent array item $a @$ ($a.upper + 1$), causing a run-time error (a precondition violation if assertion checking is on).

It is possible to program this example safely without non-strict operators, but the result is heavy and inelegant (try it).

Another example is an assertion — appearing for example in a class invariant — expressing that the first value of a certain list l of integers is non-negative — provided, of course, that the list is not empty. You may express this as

$l.empty$ **or else** $l.first >= 0$

Using **or** would have been incorrect. Here there is no way to write the condition without non-strict operators (except by writing a special function and calling it in the assertion). The Base libraries of algorithms and data structures contain many such cases.

The **implies** operator, describing implication, is also non-strict. Mathematical logic defines "a implies b" as "**not** a **or** b"; but in practical uses property b is often meaningless for false a, so that it is appropriate to use **or else** rather than **or**; this is the official definition given above. In this case there is no need for a strict variant.

The **implies** form does not always come first to mind when you are not used to it, but it is often clearer; for example you might like the last example better under the form

(**not** $l.empty$) **implies** ($l.first >= 0$)

13.5 STRINGS

Class *STRING* describes character strings. It enjoys a special status since the notation permits manifest string constants, understood as denoting instances of *STRING*.

A string constant is written enclosed in double quotes, as in

"*ABcd Ef ~*_ 01*"

The double quote character must be preceded by a percent % if it appears as one of the characters of the string.

Non-constant character strings are also instances of class *STRING*, whose creation procedure *make* takes as argument the expected initial length of the string, so that

> *text1*, *text2*: *STRING*; *n*: *INTEGER*;
>
> …
>
> !! *text1*•*make* (*n*)

will dynamically allocate a string *text1*, reserving the space for *n* characters. Note that *n* is only an initial size, not a maximum; any string can grow or shrink to an arbitrary size.

Numerous features are available on instances of *STRING*: concatenation, character or substring extraction, comparison etc. (They may change the size of the string, automatically triggering re-allocation if it becomes greater than the currently allocated size.)

Assignment of a *STRING* to another implies sharing: after *text2* := *text1*, any modification to the contents of *text1* will also affect the contents of *text2* and conversely. To duplicate rather than share, use by *text2* := *clone* (*text1*).

You can declare a constant string attribute:

> *message*: *STRING* **is** "*Your message here*"

13.6 INPUT AND OUTPUT

Two Kernel Library classes provide basic input and output facilities: *FILE* and *STD_FILES*.

Among the operations defined on an object *f* declared of type *FILE* are the following:

!! *f*•*make* ("*name*")	--Associate *f* with a file of name *name*.
f•*open_write*	-- Open *f* for writing
f•*open_read*	-- Open *f* for reading
f•*put_string* ("*A_STRING*")	--Write the given string on *f*

For I/O operations on the standard input, output and error files, you can inherit from *STD_FILES*, which defines the features *input*, *output* and *error*. Alternatively you can use the predefined value *io*, as in *io*•*put_string* ("*ABC*"), bypassing inheritance.

13.7 LEXICAL CONVENTIONS

Identifiers are sequences of characters, all of which must be letters, digits or underscore characters (_); the first character of an identifier must be a letter. There is no limit to the length of identifiers, and all the characters of identifiers are significant. This can be used to make both feature names and class names as clear as possible.

Letter case is not significant in identifiers, so that *Hi*, *hi*, *HI* and *hI* all denote the same identifier. The reason is that it would be dangerous to allow two identifiers that differ from each other by just one character, say *Structure* and *structure*, to denote different elements. Better ask developers to use some imagination than risk mistakes.

Chapter 26.   The notation, however, comes with a set of precise standard style conventions, detailed in a later chapter entirely devoted to style: classes (*INTEGER*, *POINT*…) and formal generic parameters (*G* in *LIST* [*G*]) in all upper case; predefined entities and expressions (*Result*, *Current*...) and constant attributes (*Pi*) start with an upper-case letter and continue in lower case; all other identifiers (non-constant attributes, formal routine arguments, local entities) in all lower case. Although compilers do not enforce them since they are not part of the notation's specification, these rules are essential to the readability of software texts; the libraries and this book apply them consistently.

13.8 KEY CONCEPTS INTRODUCED IN THIS CHAPTER

- External routines are accessible through a well-defined interface.
- Object technology can serve as a wrapping mechanism for legacy software.
- Routines may not directly modify their arguments, although they may change the *objects* associated with these arguments.
- The notation includes a small set of instructions: assignment, conditional, loop, call, debug, check.
- Expressions follow common usage. *Current* is an expression denoting the current instance. Not being an entity, *Current* may not be the target of an assignment.
- Non-strict boolean operators yield the same values as the standard boolean operators when both operands are defined, but are defined in some cases when the standard operators are not.
- Strings, input and output are covered by simple library classes.
- Letter case is not significant in identifiers, although the style rules include recommended conventions

EXERCISES

E13.1 External classes

The discussion of how to integrate external software mentioned that although features are the right level of integration for non-O-O software elements, interaction with another object-oriented language might take place at the class level. Discuss a notion of "external class" meant for that purpose, and its addition to the notation of this book.

E13.2 Avoiding non-strict operators

Write a loop that determines if an element x appears in an array a, similar to the algorithm given in this chapter but not using any of the non-strict operators.   *Page 456.*

14

Introduction to inheritance

*I*nteresting systems are seldom born into an empty world.

Almost always, new software expands on previous developments; the best way to create it is by imitation, refinement and combination. Traditional design methods largely ignored this aspect of system development. In object technology it is an essential concern.

The techniques studied so far are not enough. Classes do provide a good modular decomposition technique and possess many of the qualities expected of reusable components: they are homogeneous, coherent modules; you may clearly separate their interface from their implementation according to the principle of information hiding; genericity gives them some flexibility; and you may specify their semantics precisely thanks to assertions. But more is needed to achieve the full goals of reusability and extendibility.

For *reusability*, any comprehensive approach must face the problem of repetition and variation, analyzed in an earlier chapter. To avoid rewriting the same code over and over again, wasting time, introducing inconsistencies and risking errors, we need techniques to capture the striking commonalities that exist within groups of similar structures — all text editors, all tables, all file handlers — while accounting for the many differences that characterize individual cases.

For *extendibility*, the type system described so far has the advantage of guaranteeing type consistency at compile time, but prohibits combination of elements of diverse forms even in legitimate cases. For example, we cannot yet define an array containing geometrical objects of different but compatible types such as *POINT* and *SEGMENT*.

Progress in either reusability or extendibility demands that we take advantage of the strong conceptual relations that hold between classes: a class may be an extension, specialization or combination of others. We need support from the method and the language to record and use these relations. Inheritance provides this support.

A central and fascinating component of object technology, inheritance will require several chapters. In the present one we discover the fundamental concepts. The next three chapters will describe more advanced consequences: multiple inheritance, renaming, subcontracting, influence on the type system. Chapter 24 complements these technical presentations by providing the methodological perspective: how to use inheritance, and avoid misusing it.

14.1 POLYGONS AND RECTANGLES

To master the basic concepts we will use a simple example. The example is sketched rather than complete, but it shows the essential ideas well.

Polygons

Assume we want to build a graphics library. Classes in this library will describe geometrical abstractions: points, segments, vectors, circles, ellipses, general polygons, triangles, rectangles, squares and so on.

Consider first the class describing general polygons. Operations will include computation of the perimeter, translation, rotation. The class may look like this:

> **indexing**
> > *description*: "*Polygons with an arbitrary number of vertices*"
> **class** *POLYGON* **creation**
> > …
> **feature** -- Access
> > *count*: *INTEGER*
> > > -- Number of vertices
> >
> > *perimeter*: *REAL* **is**
> > > -- Length of perimeter
> > > **do** … **end**
> **feature** -- Transformation
> > *display* **is**
> > > -- Display polygon on screen.
> > > **do** … **end**
> >
> > *rotate* (*center*: *POINT*; *angle*: *REAL*) **is**
> > > -- Rotate by *angle* around *center*.
> > > **do**
> > > > … See next …
> > > **end**
> >
> > *translate* (*a*, *b*: *REAL*) **is**
> > > -- Move by *a* horizontally, *b* vertically.
> > > **do** … **end**
> >
> > … Other feature declarations …
> **feature** {*NONE*} -- Implementation
> > *vertices*: *LINKED_LIST* [*POINT*]
> > > -- Successive points making up polygon
> **invariant**
> > *same_count_as_implementation*: *count* = *vertices*.*count*
> > *at_least_three*: *count* >= *3*
> > > -- A polygon has at least three vertices (see exercise 14.2)
> **end**

The attribute *vertices* yields the list of vertices; the choice of a linked list is only one possible implementation. (An array might be better.)

See also exercise E24.4, page 869.

Here is a possible implementation for a typical procedure, *rotate*. The procedure performs a rotation by a certain angle around a certain rotation center. To rotate a polygon, it suffices to rotate every vertex in turn:

rotate (*center*: *POINT*; *angle*: *REAL*) **is**
     -- Rotate around *center* by *angle*.
do
    from
        vertices.*start*
    until
        vertices.*after*
    loop
        vertices.*item*.*rotate* (*center*, *angle*)
        vertices.*forth*
    end
end

The text of class POINT appeared on page 176.

To understand this procedure, note that feature *item* from *LINKED_LIST* yields the value of the currently active list element (where the cursor is). Since *vertices* is of type *LINKED_LIST* [*POINT*], *vertices*.*item* denotes a point, to which we may apply procedure *rotate* defined for class *POINT* in an earlier chapter. It is valid — and common — to give the same name, here *rotate*, to features of different classes, as the target of any feature always has a clearly defined type. (This is the O-O form of overloading.)

Another routine, more important for our immediate purposes, is the function to compute the perimeter of a polygon. Since our polygons have no special properties, the only way to compute their perimeter is to loop through their vertices and sum the edge lengths. Here is an implementation of *perimeter*:

perimeter: *REAL* **is**
     -- Sum of edge lengths
local
    this, *previous*: *POINT*
do
    from
        vertices.*start*; *this* := *vertices*.*item*
            check not *vertices*.*after* **end** -- A consequence of *at_least_three*
    until
        vertices.*is_last*
    loop
        previous := *this*
        vertices.*forth*
        this := *vertices*.*item*
        Result := *Result* + *this*.*distance* (*previous*)
    end
    Result := *Result* + *this*.*distance* (*vertices*.*first*)
end

this   (*is_last*)

previous

first

(*start*)

The loop simply adds the successive distances between adjacent vertices. Function *distance* was defined in class *POINT*. *Result*, representing the value to be returned by the function, is automatically initialized to 0 on routine entry. From class *LINKED_LIST* we use features *first* to get the first element, *start* to move the cursor to that first element, *forth* to advance it to the next, *item* to get the value of the element at cursor position, *is_last* to know whether the current element is the last one, *after* to know if the cursor is past the last element. As recalled by the **check** instruction the invariant clause *at_least_three* will guarantee that the loop starts and terminates properly: since it starts in a **not** *after* state, *vertices*.*item* is defined, and applying *forth* one or more time is correct and will eventually yield a state satisfying *is_last*, the loop's exit condition.

The list interface will be discussed in "ACTIVE DATA STRUCTURES", 23.4, page 774.

Rectangles

Now assume we need a new class representing rectangles. We could start from scratch. But rectangles are a special kind of polygon and many of the features are the same: a rectangle will probably be translated, rotated or displayed in the same way as a general polygon. Rectangles, on the other hand, also have special features (such as a diagonal), special properties (the number of vertices is four, the angles are right angles), and special versions of some operations (to compute the perimeter of a rectangle, we can do better than the above general polygon algorithm).

We can take advantage of this mix of commonality and specificity by defining class *RECTANGLE* as an **heir** to class *POLYGON*. This makes all the features of *POLYGON* — called a **parent** of *RECTANGLE* — by default applicable to the heir class as well. It suffices to give *RECTANGLE* an **inheritance clause**:

class *RECTANGLE* **inherit**
    POLYGON
feature
    … Features specific to rectangles …
end

The **feature** clause of the heir class does not repeat the features of the parent: they are automatically available because of the inheritance clause. It will only list features that are specific to the heir. These may be new features, such as *diagonal*; but they may also be redefinitions of inherited features.

The second possibility is useful for a feature that was already meaningful for the parent but requires a different form in the heir. Consider *perimeter*. It has a better implementation for rectangles: no need to compute four vertex-to-vertex distances; the result is simply twice the sum of the two side lengths. An heir that redefines a feature for the parent must announce it in the inheritance clause through a **redefine** subclause:

class *RECTANGLE* **inherit**
    POLYGON
        redefine *perimeter* **end**
feature
    …
end

This allows the **feature** clause of *RECTANGLE* to contain a new version of *perimeter*, which will supersede the *POLYGON* version for rectangles. If the **redefine** subclause were not present, a new declaration of *perimeter* among the features of *RECTANGLE* would be an error: since *RECTANGLE* already has a *perimeter* feature inherited from *POLYGON*, this would amount to declaring a feature twice.

The *RECTANGLE* class looks like the following:

indexing
    description: "*Rectangles, viewed as a special case of general polygons*"
class *RECTANGLE* **inherit**
      POLYGON
          redefine *perimeter* **end**
creation
    make
feature -- Initialization
    make (*center*: *POINT*; *s1*, *s2*, *angle*: *REAL*) **is**
          -- Set up rectangle centered at *center*, with side lengths
          -- *s1* and *s2* and orientation *angle*.
      do ... **end**
feature -- Access
    side1, *side2*: *REAL*
      -- The two side lengths

    diagonal: *REAL*
      -- Length of the diagonal

    perimeter: *REAL* **is**
      -- Sum of edge lengths
      -- (Redefinition of the *POLYGON* version)
      do
        Result := 2 $*$ (*side1* + *side2*)
      end
invariant
    four_sides: *count* = 4
    first_side: (*vertices*.*i_th* (*1*)).*distance* (*vertices*.*i_th* (*2*)) = *side1*
    second_side: (*vertices*.*i_th* (*2*)).*distance* (*vertices*.*i_th* (*3*)) = *side2*
    third_side: (*vertices*.*i_th* (*3*)).*distance* (*vertices*.*i_th* (*4*)) = *side1*
    fourth_side: (*vertices*.*i_th* (*4*)).*distance* (*vertices*.*i_th* (*1*)) = *side2*

end

For a list, i_th (i) gives the element at position i (the i-th element, hence the name of the query).

Because *RECTANGLE* is an heir of *POLYGON*, all features of the parent class are still applicable to the new class: *vertices, rotate, translate, perimeter* (in redefined form) and any others. They do not need to be repeated in the new class.

This process is transitive: any class that inherits from *RECTANGLE*, say *SQUARE*, also has the *POLYGON* features.

Basic conventions and terminology

The following terms will be useful in addition to "heir" and "parent".

Inheritance terminology

A **descendant** of a class C is any class that inherits directly or indirectly from C, including C itself. (Formally: either C or, recursively, a descendant of an heir of C.)

A **proper descendant** of C is a descendant other than C itself.

An **ancestor** of C is a class A such that C is a descendant of A. A **proper ancestor** of C is a class A such that C is a proper descendant of A.

In the literature you will also encounter the terms "subclass" and "superclass", but we will stay away from them because they are ambiguous; sometimes "subclass" means heir (immediate descendant), sometimes it is used in the more general sense of proper descendant, and it is not always clear which. In addition, we will see that the "subset" connotation of this word is not always justified.

Associated terminology applies to the features of a class: a feature is either *inherited* (coming from a proper ancestors) or *immediate* (introduced in the class itself).

In graphical representations of object-oriented software structures, where classes are represented by ellipses ("bubbles"), inheritance links will appear as single arrows. This distinguishes them from links for the other basic inter-class relation, client, which as you will recall uses a double arrow. (For further distinction this book uses black for client and color for inheritance.)

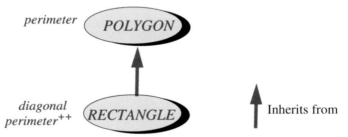

An inheritance link

A redefined feature is marked $^{++}$, a convention from the Business Object Notation (B.O.N.).

The arrow points upward, from the heir to the parent; the convention, easy to remember, is that it represents the relation "inherits from". In some of the literature you will find the reverse practice; although in general such choices of graphical convention are partly a matter of taste, in this case one convention appears definitely better than the other — in the sense that one suggests the proper relationship and the other may lead to confusion. An arrow is not just an arbitrary pictogram but indicates a unidirectional link, between the two ends of the arrow. Here:

- Any instance of the heir may be viewed (as we shall see in more detail) as an instance of the parent, but not conversely.

- The text of the heir will always mention the parent (as in the **inherit** clause above), but not conversely; it is in fact an important property of the method, resulting among others from the Open-Closed principle, that a class does not "know" the list of its heirs and other proper descendants.

Mathematically, the direction of the relationship is reflected in algebraic models for inheritance, which use a *morphism* (a generalization of the notion of function) from the heir's model to the parent's model — not the other way around. One more reason for drawing the arrow from the heir to the parent.

Although with complex systems we cannot have an absolute rule for class placement in inheritance diagrams, we should try whenever possible to position a class above its heirs.

Invariant inheritance

You will have noticed the invariant of class *RECTANGLE*, which expresses that the number of sides is four and that the successive edge lengths are *side1*, *side2*, *side1* and *side2*.

Class *POLYGON* also had an invariant, which still applies to its heir:

> ### Invariant inheritance rule
>
> The invariant property of a class is the boolean **and** of the assertions appearing in its **invariant** clause and of the invariant properties of its parents if any.

Because the parents may themselves have parents, this rule is recursive: in the end the full invariant of a class is obtained by **and**ing the invariant clauses of all its ancestors.

The rule reflects one of the basic characteristics of inheritance: to say that *B* inherits from *A* is to state that one may view any instance of *B* also as an instance of *A* (more on this property later). As a result, any consistency constraint applying to instances of *A*, as expressed by the invariant, also applies to instances of *B*.

In the example, the second clause (*at_least_three*) invariant of *POLYGON* stated that the number of sides must be at least three; this is subsumed by the *four_sides* subclause in *RECTANGLE*'s invariant clause, which requires it to be exactly four.

You may wonder what would happen if the heir's clause, instead of making the parent's redundant as here (since *count = 4* implies *count >= 3*), were incompatible with it, as with an heir of *POLYGON* that would introduce the invariant clause *count = 2*. The result is simply an inconsistent invariant, not different from what you get if you include, in the invariant of a single class, two separate subclauses that read *count >= 3* and *count = 2*.

Inheritance and creation

Although it was not shown, a creation procedure for *POLYGON* might be of the form

make_polygon (*vl*: *LINKED_LIST* [*POINT*]) **is**
> -- Set up with vertices taken from *vl*.

require
> *vl.count* >= *3*

do
> ... Initialize polygon representation from the items of *vl* ...

ensure
> -- *vertices* and *vl* have the same items (can be expressed formally)

end

This procedure takes a list of points, containing at least three elements, and uses it to set up the polygon.

The procedure has been given a special name *make_polygon* to avoid any name conflict when *RECTANGLE* inherits it and introduces its own creation procedure *make*. This is not the recommended style; in the next chapter we will learn how to give the standard name *make* to the creation procedure in *POLYGON*, and use renaming in the inheritance clause of *RECTANGLE* to remove any name clash.

See "FEATURE RENAMING", 15.2, page 535.

The creation procedure of class *RECTANGLE*, shown earlier, took four arguments: a point to serve as center, the two side lengths and an orientation. Note that feature *vertices* is still applicable to rectangles; as a consequence, the creation procedure of *RECTANGLE* should set up the *vertices* list with the appropriate point values (the four corners, to be computed from the center, side lengths and orientation given as arguments).

The creation procedure for general polygons is awkward for rectangles, since only lists of four elements satisfying the invariant of class *RECTANGLE* would be acceptable. Conversely, the creation procedure for rectangles is not appropriate for arbitrary polygons. This is a common case: a parent's creation procedure is not necessarily right as creation procedure for the heir. The precise reason is easy to spot; it follows from the observation that a creation procedure's formal role is to establish the class invariant. The parent's creation procedure was required to establish the parent's invariant; but, as we have seen, the heir's invariant may be stronger (and usually is); we cannot then expect that the original procedure will guarantee the new invariant.

In the case of an heir adding new attributes, the creation procedures might need to initialize these attributes and so require extra arguments. Hence the general rule:

Creation Inheritance rule

An inherited feature's creation status in the parent class (that is to say, whether or not it is a creation procedure) has no bearing on its creation status in the heir.

An inherited creation procedure is still available to the heir as a normal feature of the class (although, as we shall see, the heir may prefer to make it secret); but it does not by default retain its status as a creation procedure. Only the procedures listed in the heir's own **creation** clause have that status.

In some cases, of course, a parent's creation procedure may still be applicable as a creation procedure; then you will simply list it in the creation clause:

class *B* **inherit**
    A
creation
    make
feature
     . . .

where *make* is inherited — without modification — from *A*, which also listed it in its own **creation** clause.

An example hierarchy

For the rest of the discussion it will be useful to consider the *POLYGON-RECTANGLE* example in the context of a more general inheritance hierarchy of geometrical figure types, such as the one shown on the next page.

Figures have been classified into open and closed variants. Along with polygons, an example of closed figure is the ellipse; a special case of the ellipse is the circle.

Various features appear next to the applicable classes. The symbol $^{++}$, as noted, means "redefined"; the symbols $^{+}$ and * will be explained later.

In the original example, for simplicity, *RECTANGLE* was directly an heir of *POLYGON*. Since the sketched classification of polygons is based on the number of vertices, it seems preferable to introduce an intermediate class *QUADRANGLE*, at the same level as *TRIANGLE*, *PENTAGON* and similar classes. Feature *diagonal* can be moved up to the level of *QUADRANGLE*.

Note the presence of *SQUARE*, an heir to *RECTANGLE*, characterized by the invariant *side1 = side2*. Similarly, an ellipse ⬬ has two focuses (or foci), which for a circle ⊙ are the same point, giving *CIRCLE* an invariant property of the form *equal (focus1 = focus2)*.

14.2 POLYMORPHISM

Inheritance hierarchies will give us considerable flexibility for the manipulation of objects, while retaining the safety of static typing. The supporting techniques, polymorphism and dynamic binding, address some of the fundamental issues of software architecture discussed in part B of this book. Let us begin with polymorphism.

Polymorphic attachment

"Polymorphism" means the ability to take several forms. In object-oriented development what may take several forms is a variable entity or data structure element, which will have the ability, at run time, to become attached to objects of different types, all controlled by the static declaration.

Figure type hierarchy

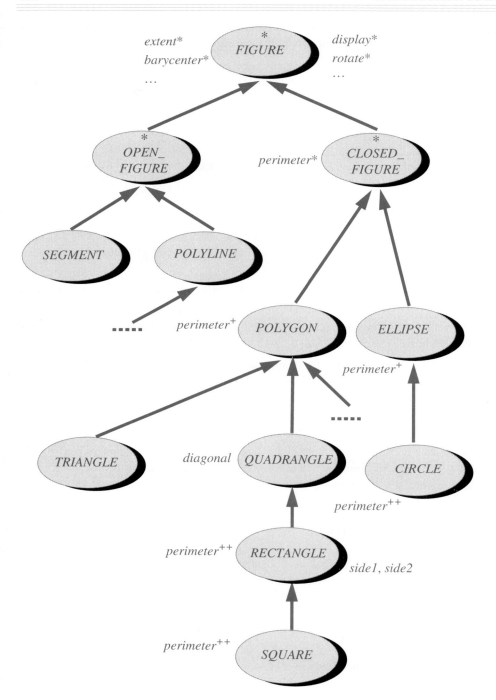

Assume, with the inheritance structure shown in the figure, the following declarations using short but mnemonic entity names:

p: POLYGON; r: RECTANGLE; t: TRIANGLE

Then the following assignments are valid:

p := r

p := t

These instructions assign to an entity denoting a polygon the value of an entity denoting a rectangle in the first case, a triangle in the second.

Such assignments, in which the type of the source (the right-hand side) is different from the type of the target (the left-hand side), are called **polymorphic assignments**. An entity such as *p* which appears in some polymorphic assignment is a **polymorphic entity**.

Before the introduction of inheritance, all our assignments were monomorphic (non-polymorphic): we could assign — in the various examples of earlier chapters — a point to a point, a book to a book, an account to an account. With polymorphism, we are starting to see more action on the attachment scene.

The polymorphic assignments taken as example are legitimate: the inheritance structure permits us to view an instance of *RECTANGLE* or *TRIANGLE* as an instance of *POLYGON*. We say that the type of the source **conforms to** the type of the target. In the reverse direction, as with *r := p*, the assignment would not be valid. This fundamental type rule will be discussed in more detail shortly.

Instead of an assignment, you may achieve polymorphism through argument passing, as with a call of the form *f (r)* or *f (t)* and a feature declaration of the form

f (p: POLYGON) **is do** … **end**

As you will remember, assignment and argument passing have the same semantics, and are together called *attachment*; we can talk of *polymorphic* attachment when the source and target have different types.

What exactly happens during a polymorphic attachment?

All the entities appearing in the preceding cases of polymorphic attachment are of reference types: the possible values for *p*, *r* and *t* are not objects but references to objects. So the effect of an assignment such as *p := r* is simply to reattach a reference:

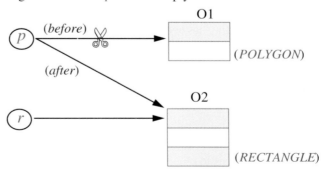

Polymorphic reference reattachment

So in spite of the name you should not imagine, when thinking of polymorphism, some run-time transmutation of objects. Once created, an object never changes its type. Only references do so by getting reattached to objects of different types. This also means that polymorphism does not carry any efficiency penalty; a reference reattachment — a very fast operation — costs the same regardless of the objects involved.

Polymorphic attachments will only be permitted for targets of a reference type — not for the other case, expanded types. Since a descendant class may introduce new attributes, the corresponding instances may have more fields; the last figure suggested this by showing the *RECTANGLE* object bigger than the *POLYGON* object. Such differences in object size do not cause any problem if all we are reattaching is a reference. But if instead of a reference p is of an expanded type (being for example declared as **expanded** *POLYGON*), then the value of p is directly an object, and any assignment to p would overwrite the contents of that object. No polymorphism is possible in that case.

See "COMPOSITE OBJECTS AND EXPANDED TYPES", 8.7, page 254.

Polymorphic data structures

Consider an array of polygons:

> *poly_arr*: *ARRAY* [*POLYGON*]

When you assign a value x to an element of the array, as in

> *poly_arr*.*put* (*x*, *some_index*)

(for some valid integer index value *some_index*), the specification of class *ARRAY* indicates that the assigned value's type must conform to the actual generic parameter:

> **class** *ARRAY* [*G*] **creation**
>
>   . . .
>
> **feature** -- Element change
>
>   *put* (*v*: *G*; *i*: *INTEGER*) **is**
>
>   -- Assign *v* to the entry of index *i*
>
>   . . .
>
> **end** -- class *ARRAY*

This is extracted from class ARRAY as it appears on page 372.

Because v, the formal argument corresponding to x, is declared of type G in the class, and the actual generic parameter corresponding to G is *POLYGON* in the case of *poly_arr*, the type of x must conform to *POLYGON*. As we have seen, this does not require x to be of type *POLYGON*: any descendant of *POLYGON* is acceptable.

So assuming that the array has bounds 1 and 4, that we have declared some entities as

> *p*: *POLYGON*; *r*: *RECTANGLE*; *s*: *SQUARE*; *t*: *TRIANGLE*

and created the corresponding objects, we may execute

> *poly_arr*.*put* (*p*, *1*)
> *poly_arr*.*put* (*r*, *2*)
> *poly_arr*.*put* (*s*, *3*)
> *poly_arr*.*put* (*t*, *4*)

yielding an array of references to objects of different types:

A polymorphic array

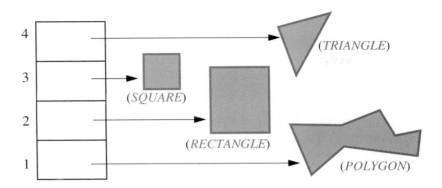

The graphical objects have been represented by the corresponding geometrical shapes rather than the usual multi-field object diagrams.

Such a data structure, containing objects of different types (all of them descendants of a common type), are called **polymorphic data structures**. We will encounter many examples in later discussions. The use of arrays is just one possibility; any other container structure, such as a list or stack, can be polymorphic in the same way.

The introduction of polymorphic data structures achieves the aim, stated at the beginning of chapter 10, of combining genericity and inheritance for maximum flexibility and safety. It is worth recalling the figure that illustrated the idea:

Dimensions of generalization

(See page 317.)

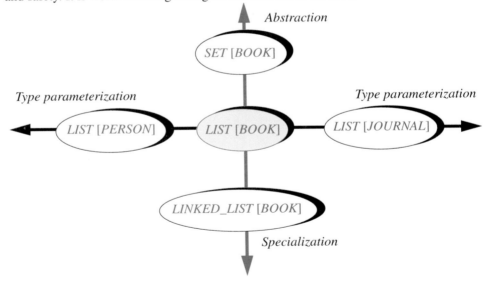

Types that were informally called *SET_OF_BOOKS* and the like on the earlier figure have been replaced with generically derived types, such as *SET* [*BOOK*].

This combination of genericity and inheritance is powerful. It enables you to describe object structures that are as general as you like, but no more. For example:

- *LIST* [*RECTANGLE*]: may contain squares, but not triangles.

- *LIST* [*POLYGON*]: may contain squares, rectangles, triangles, but not circles.

- *LIST* [*FIGURE*]: may contain instances of any of the classes in the *FIGURE* hierarchy, but not books or bank accounts.

- *LIST* [*ANY*]: may contain objects of arbitrary types.

The last case uses class *ANY*, which by convention is an ancestor to all classes.

By choosing as actual generic parameter a class at a varying place in the hierarchy, you can set the limits of what your container will accept.

We will study ANY in "Universal classes", page 580.

14.3 TYPING FOR INHERITANCE

That the remarkable flexibility provided by inheritance does not come at the expense of reliability follows from the use of a *statically typed* approach, in which we guarantee at compile time that no incorrect run-time type combination can occur.

Type consistency

Inheritance is consistent with the type system. The basic rules are easy to explain on the above example. Assume the following declarations:

p: *POLYGON*
r: *RECTANGLE*

referring to the earlier inheritance hierarchy, of which the relevant extract is this:

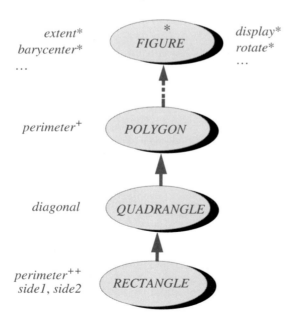

Then the following are valid:

- *p.perimeter*: no problem, since *perimeter* is defined for polygons.

- *p.vertices*, *p.translate* (…), *p.rotate* (…) with valid arguments.

- *r.diagonal*, *r.side1*, *r.side2*: the three features considered are declared at the *RECTANGLE* or *QUADRANGLE* level.

- *r.vertices*, *r.translate* (…), *r.rotate* (…): the features considered are declared at the *POLYGON* level or above, and so are applicable to rectangles, which inherit all polygon features.

- *r.perimeter*: same case as the previous one. The version of the function to be called here is the redefinition given in *RECTANGLE*, not the original in *POLYGON*.

The following feature calls, however, are illegal since the features considered are not available at the polygon level:

p.side1

p.side2

p.diagonal

These cases all result from the first fundamental typing rule:

Feature Call rule

In a feature call $x.f$, where the type of x is based on a class C, feature f must be defined in one of the ancestors of C.

Recall that the ancestors of C include C itself. The phrasing "where the type of x is based on a class C" is a reminder that a type may involve more than just a class name if the class is generic: *LINKED_LIST* [*INTEGER*] is a class type "based on" the class name *LINKED_LIST*; the generic parameters play no part in this rule.

Like all other validity rules reviewed in this book, the Feature Call rule is static; this means that it can be checked on the sole basis of a system's text, rather than through run-time controls. The compiler (which typically is the tool performing such checking) will reject classes containing invalid feature calls. If we succeed in defining a set of tight-proof type rules, there will be no risk, once a system has been compiled, that its execution will ever apply a feature to an object that is not equipped to handle it.

Chapter 17 discusses typing.

Static typing is one of object technology's main resources for achieving the goal of software reliability, introduced in the first chapter of this book.

It has already been mentioned that not all approaches to object-oriented software construction are statically typed; the best-known representative of *dynamically typed* languages is Smalltalk, which has no static Feature Call rule but will let an execution terminate abnormally in the case of a "message not understood" run-time error. The chapter on typing will compare the various approaches further.

Limits to polymorphism

Unrestrained polymorphism would be incompatible with a static notion of type. Inheritance governs which polymorphic attachments are permissible.

The polymorphic attachments used as examples, such as $p := r$ and $p := t$, all had as source type a descendant of the target's class. We say that the source type *conforms* to the target class; for example *SQUARE* conforms to *RECTANGLE* and to *POLYGON* but not to *TRIANGLE*. This notion has already been used informally but we need a precise definition:

Definition: conformance

A type U conforms to a type T only if the base class of U is a descendant of the base class of T; also, for generically derived types, every actual parameter of U must (recursively) conform to the corresponding formal parameter in T.

Why is the notion of descendant not sufficient? The reason is again that since we encountered genericity we have had to make a technical distinction between types and classes. Every type has a *base class*, which in the absence of genericity is the type itself (for example *POLYGON* is its own base class), but for a generically derived type is the class from which the type is built; for example the base class of *LIST* [*POLYGON*] is *LIST*. The second part of the definition indicates that B [Y] will conform to A [X] if B is a descendant of A and Y a descendant of X.

See "Types and classes", page 324.

Note that, as every class is a descendant of itself, so does every type conform to itself.

With this generalization of the notion of descendant we get the second fundamental typing rule:

Type Conformance rule

An attachment of target x and source y (that is to say, an assignment $x := y$, or the use of y as an actual argument to a routine call where the corresponding formal argument is x) is only valid if the type of y conforms to the type of x.

The Type Conformance rule expresses that you can assign from the more specific to the more general, but not conversely. So $p := r$ is valid but $r := p$ is invalid.

The rule may be illustrated like this. Assume I am absent-minded enough to write just "Animal" in the order form I send to the Mail-A-Pet company. Then, whether I receive a dog, a ladybug or a killer whale, I have no right to complain. (The hypothesis is that classes *DOG* etc. are all descendants of *ANIMAL*.) If, on the other hand, I specifically request a dog, and the mailman brings me one morning a box with a label that reads *ANIMAL*, or perhaps *MAMMAL* (an intermediate ancestor), I am entitled to return it to the sender — even if from the box come unmistakable sounds of yelping and barking. Since my order was not fulfilled as specified, I shall owe nothing to Mail-A-Pet.

Instances

The original discus-
sion was "The mold
and the instance",
page 167.

With the introduction of polymorphism we need a more specific terminology to talk about instances. Informally, the instances of a class are the run-time objects built according to the definition of a class. But now we must also consider the objects built from the definition of its proper descendants. Hence the more precise definition:

Definition: direct instance, instance

A direct instance of a class C is an object produced according to the exact definition of C, through a creation instruction `!! x...` where the target x is of type C (or, recursively, by cloning a direct instance of C).

An instance of C is a direct instance of a descendant of C.

The last part of this definition implies, since the descendants of a class include the class itself, that a direct instance of C is also an instance of C.

So the execution of

p1, p2: POLYGON; r: RECTANGLE
...
`!! p1 ...; !! r ...; p2 := r`

will create two instances of *POLYGON* but only one direct instance (the one attached to *p1*). The other object, to which the extract attaches both *p2* and *r*, is a direct instance of *RECTANGLE* — and so an instance of both *POLYGON* and *RECTANGLE*.

Although the notions of instance and direct instance are defined above for a class, they immediately extend to any type (with a base class and possible generic parameters).

Polymorphism means that an entity of a certain type may become attached not only to direct instances of that type, but to arbitrary instances. We may indeed consider that the role of the type conformance rule is to ensure the following property:

Static-dynamic type consistency

An entity declared of a type T may at run time only become attached to instances of T.

Static type, dynamic type

The name of the last property suggests the concepts of "static type" and "dynamic type". The type used to declare an entity is the *static type* of the corresponding reference. If, at run time, the reference gets attached to an object of a certain type, this type becomes the *dynamic type* of the reference.

So with the declaration *p: POLYGON*, the static type of the reference that *p* denotes is *POLYGON*; after the execution of `!! p`, the dynamic type of that reference is also *POLYGON*; after the assignment *p := r*, with *r* of type *RECTANGLE* and non-void, the dynamic type is *RECTANGLE*.

The Type Conformance rule states that the dynamic type must always conform to the static type.

To avoid any confusion remember that we are dealing with three levels: an *entity* is an identifier in the class text; at run time its value is a *reference* (except in the expanded case); the reference may get attached to an *object*. Then:

See "States of a reference", page 240.

- An object only has a dynamic type, the type with which it has been created. That type will never change during the object's lifetime.

- At any time during execution, a reference has a dynamic type, the type of the object to which it is currently attached (or the special type *NONE* if the reference is void). The dynamic type may change as a result of reattachment operations.

NONE will be seen in "The bottom of the pit", page 582.

- Only an entity has both a static type and dynamic types. Its static type is the type with which it was declared: *T* if the declaration was *x: T*. Its dynamic type at some execution-time instant is the type of its reference value, meaning the type of the attached object.

  In the expanded case there is no reference; the value of *x* is an object of type *T*, and *x* has *T* as both its static type and as its only possible dynamic type.

Are the restrictions justified?

The two typing rules may sometimes seem too restrictive. For example, the second instruction in both of the following sequences will be statically rejected:

R1 •   *p:= r; r := p*

R2 •   *p := r; x := p.diagonal*

In R1, we refuse to assign a polygon to a rectangle entity even though that polygon happens at run time to be a rectangle (like refusing to accept a dog because it comes in a box marked "animal"). In R2, we decide that *diagonal* is not applicable to *p* even though at run time it would in fact be — as it were by accident.

But closer examination of these examples confirms that the rules are justified. If you attach a reference to an object, better avoid later problems by making sure that they are of compatible types. And if you want to apply a rectangle operation, why not declare the target as a rectangle?

In practice, cases of the form R1 and R2 are unlikely. Assignments such as *p := r* will normally occur as part of some control structure that depends on run-time conditions, such as user input. A more realistic polymorphic scheme may look like this:

```
!! r.make (…); …
screen.display_icons                -- Display icons representing various polygons
screen.wait_for_mouse_click         -- Wait for the user to click the mouse button
x := screen.mouse_position          -- Find out at what position
                                    -- the mouse was clicked
chosen_icon := screen.icon_where_is (x)   -- Find out what icon appears at the
                                          -- mouse's position
```

> **if** *chosen_icon = rectangle_icon* **then**
>   *p := r*
> **elseif** …
>   *p :=* "Some other type of polygon" …
>   ◦
> **end**
> … Uses of *p*, for example *p•display, p•rotate, …*

On the last line, *p* can denote arbitrary polygons, so you should only apply general *POLYGON* features. Clearly, operations valid for rectangles only, such as *diagonal*, should be applied to *r* only (for example in the first clause of the **if**). Where *p* as such is going to be used, in the instructions following the **if** instruction, only operations defined for all variants of polygons are applicable to it.

In another typical case, *p* could just be a formal routine argument:

   some_routine (*p: POLYGON*) **is**…

and you execute a call *some_routine* (*r*), valid as per the Type Conformance rule; but when you write the routine you do not know about this call. In fact a call *some_routine* (*t*) for *t* or type *TRIANGLE*, or any other descendant of *POLYGON* for that matter, would be equally valid, so all you can assume is that *p* represents some kind of polygon — *any* kind of polygon. It is quite appropriate, then, that you should be restricted to applying *POLYGON* features to *p*.

It is in this kind of situation — where you cannot predict the exact type of the attached object — that polymorphic entities such as *p* are useful.

Can ignorance be bliss?

It is worthwhile reinforcing the last few points a bit since the concepts now being introduced will be so important in the rest of our discussion. (There will be nothing really new in this short section, but it should help you understand the basic concepts better, preparing you for the more advanced ones which follow.)

If you are still uneasy at the impossibility of writing *p•diagonal* even after a call *p :=r* — case R2 — you are not alone; this is a shock to many people when they start grappling with these concepts. We know that *p* is a rectangle because of the assignment, so why may we not access its diagonal? For one thing, that would be useless. After the polymorphic assignment, as shown in the following extract from an earlier figure, the same *RECTANGLE* object now has two names, a polygon name *p* and a rectangle name *r*:

After a polymorphic attachment

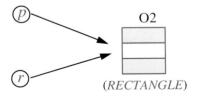

(*RECTANGLE*)

In such a case, since you do know that the object O2 is a rectangle and have access to it through its rectangle name *r*, why would you write a diagonal access operation in the form *p.diagonal*? This is uninteresting since you can just write it as *r.diagonal*; using the object's official rectangle name removes any doubt as to the validity of applying a rectangle operation. Using the polygon name *p*, which could just as well denote a triangle object, brings nothing and introduces uncertainty.

Polymorphism, in fact, *loses* information: when as a result of the assignment *p := r* you are able to refer to the rectangle object O2 under its polygon name *p*, you have lost something precious: the ability to use rectangle-specific features. What then is the purpose? In this case, there is none. The only interesting application, as noted, arises when you do not know for sure what kind of polygon *p* is, as a result of a conditional instruction **if** *some_condition* **then** *p:= r* **else** *p := something_else* ..., or because *p* is a formal routine argument and you do not know what the actual argument will be. But then in such cases it would be incorrect and dangerous to apply to *p* anything else than *POLYGON* features.

> To continue with the animal theme, imagine that someone asks "do you have a pet?" and you answer "yes, a cat!". This is similar to a polymorphic assignment, making a single object known through two names of different types: "*my_pet*" and "*my_cat*" now denote the same animal. But they do not serve the same purpose; the first has less information than the second. You can use either name if you call the post-sales division of Mail-A-Pet, Absentee Owner Department ("*I am going on holiday; what's your price for keeping my_pet* [or: *my_cat*] *for two weeks*"); but if you phone their Destructive Control Department to ask "*Can I bring my_pet for a de-clawing Tuesday?*", you probably will not get an appointment until the employee has made you confirm that you really mean *my_cat*.

When you want to force a type

In some special cases there may be a need to try an assignment going against the grain of inheritance, and accept that the result is not guaranteed to yield an object. This does not normally occur, when you are properly applying the object-oriented method, with objects that are internal to a certain software element. But you might for example receive over the network an object advertized to be of a certain type; since you have no control over the origin of the object, static type declarations will guarantee nothing, and you must *test* the type before accepting it.

> When we receive that box marked "Animal" rather than the expected "Dog", we might be tempted to open the "Animal" box anyway and take our chances, knowing that if its content is not the expected dog we will have forfeited our right to return the package, and depending on what comes out of it we may not even live to tell the story.

Such cases require a new mechanism, **assignment attempt**, which will enable us to write instructions of the form *r ?= p* (where *?=* is the symbol for assignment attempt, versus := for assignment), meaning "do the assignment if the object type is the expected one for *r*, otherwise make *r* void". But we are not equipped yet to understand how this instruction fits in the proper use of the object-oriented method, so we will have to return to it in a subsequent chapter. (Until then, you did not read about it here.)

See "ASSIGNMENT ATTEMPT", 16.5, page 591.

Polymorphic creation

The introduction of inheritance and polymorphism suggests a small extension to the mechanism for creating objects, allowing direct creation of objects of a descendant type.

See "The creation instruction", page 232, and "CREATION PROCEDURES", 8.4, page 236.

The basic creation instruction, as you will recall, is of one of the forms

!! *x*

!! *x*.*make* (…)

where the second form both assumes and requires that the base class of *x*'s type *T* contain a **creation** clause listing *make* as one of the creation procedures. (A creation procedure may of course have any name; *make* is the recommended default.) The effect of the instruction is to create a new object of type *T*, initialize it to the default values, and attach it to *x*. In addition, the second form will apply *make*, with the arguments given, to the just created and initialized object.

Assume that *T* has a proper descendant *U*. We may want to use *x* polymorphically and, in some cases, make it denote a newly created direct instance of *U* rather than *T*. A possible solution uses a local entity of type *U*:

> *some_routine* (…) **is**
>
> > **local**
> >
> > > *u_temp*: *U*
> >
> > **do**
> >
> > > …; !! *u_temp*.*make* (…); *x* := *u_temp*; …
> >
> > **end**

This works but is cumbersome, especially in a multi-choice context where we may want to attach *x* to an instance of one of several possible descendant types. The local entities, *u_temp* above, play only a temporary part; their declarations and assignments clutter up the software text. Hence the need for a variant of the creation instruction:

! *U* ! *x*

! *U* ! *x*.*make* (…)

The effect is the same as with the !! forms, except that the created object is a direct instance of *U* rather than *T*. The constraint on using this variant is obvious: type *U* must conform to type *T* and, in the second form, *make* must be defined as a creation procedure in the base class of *U*; if that class indeed has one or more creation procedures, only the second form is valid. Note that whether *T*'s own base class has creation procedures is irrelevant here; all that counts is what *U* requires.

A typical use involves creation of an instance of one of several possible types:

f: *FIGURE*

...

"Display a set of figure icons"

if *chosen_icon* = *rectangle_icon* **then**

    ! *RECTANGLE* ! *f*

else if *chosen_icon* = *circle_icon* **then**

    ! *CIRCLE* ! *f*

else

    ...

end

This new form of creation instruction suggests introducing the notion of **creation type** of a creation instruction, denoting the type of the object that will be created:

- For the implicit-type form !! *x* ..., the creation type is the type of *x*.

- For the explicit-type form ! *U* ! *x* ..., the creation type is *U*.

14.4 DYNAMIC BINDING

Dynamic binding will complement redefinition, polymorphism and static typing to make up the basic tetralogy of inheritance.

Using the right variant

Operations defined for all polygons need not be *implemented* identically for all variants. For example, *perimeter* has different versions for general polygons and for rectangles; let us call them $perimeter_{POL}$ and $perimeter_{RECT}$. Class *SQUARE* will also have its own variant (yielding four times the side length). You may imagine further variants for other special kinds of polygon. This immediately raises a fundamental question: what happens when a routine with more than one version is applied to a polymorphic entity?

In a fragment such as

!! *p*.*make* (...); *x* := *p*.*perimeter*

it is clear that $perimeter_{POL}$ will be applied. It is just as clear that in

!! *r*.*make* (...); *x* := *r*.*perimeter*

$perimeter_{RECT}$ will be applied. But what if the polymorphic entity *p*, statically declared as a polygon, dynamically refers to a rectangle? Assume you have executed

!! *r*.*make* (...)

p := *r*

x := *p*.*perimeter*

The rule known as **dynamic binding** implies that **the dynamic form of the object** determines which version of the operation to apply. Here it will be $perimeter_{RECT}$.

As noted, of course, the more interesting case arises when we cannot deduce from a mere reading of the software text what exact dynamic type *p* will have at run time, as in

    -- Compute perimeter of figure built according to user choice

p: *POLYGON*

  ...

if *chosen_icon = rectangle_icon* **then**
    ! *RECTANGLE* ! *p*•*make* (...)
elseif *chosen_icon = triangle_icon* **then**
    ! *TRIANGLE* ! *p*•*make* (...)
elseif

    ...

end

  ...

x := p•*perimeter*

or after a conditional polymorphic assignment **if** ... **then** *p := r* **elseif**... **then** *p := t*...; or if *p* is an element of a polymorphic array of polygons; or simply if *p* is a formal argument, declared of type *POLYGON*, of the enclosing routine — to which callers can pass actual arguments of any conforming type.

Then depending on what happens in any particular execution, the dynamic type of *p* will be *RECTANGLE*, or *TRIANGLE*, and so on. You have no way to know which of these cases will hold. But thanks to dynamic binding you do not *need* to know: whatever *p* happens to be, the call will execute the proper variant of *perimeter*.

This ability of operations to adapt automatically to the objects to which they are applied is one of the most important properties of object-oriented systems, directly addressing some of the principal quality issues discussed at the beginning of this book. We will examine its consequences in detail later in this chapter.

Dynamic binding also gives the full story about the information-loss aspects of polymorphism discussed earlier. Now we really understand why it is not absurd to lose information about an object: after an assignment *p := q*, or a call *some_routine* (*q*) where *p* is the formal argument, we have lost the type information specific to *q* but we can rest assured that if we apply an operation *p*•*polygon_feature* where *polygon_feature* has a special version applicable to *q*, that version will be the one selected.

> It is all right to send your pets to an Absentee Owner Department that caters to all kinds — *provided* you know that when meal time comes your cat will get cat food and your dog will get dog food.

Redefinition and assertions

If a client of *POLYGON* calls *p*•*perimeter*, it expects to get the value of *p*'s perimeter, as defined by the specification of function *perimeter* in the definition of the class. But now, because of dynamic binding, the client may well be calling another routine, redefined in some descendant. In *RECTANGLE*, the redefinition, while improving efficiency, preserves the result; but what prevents you from redefining *perimeter* to compute, say, the area?

This is contrary to the spirit of redefinition. Redefinition should change the implementation of a routine, not its semantics. Fortunately we have a way to constrain the semantics of a routine — assertions. The basic rule for controlling the power of redefinition and dynamic binding is simple: the precondition and postcondition of a routine will apply (informally speaking) to any redefinition; and, as we have already seen, the class invariant automatically carries over to all the descendants.

The exact rules will be given in chapter 16. But you should already note that redefinition is not arbitrary: only semantics-preserving redefinitions are permitted. It is up to the routine writer to express the semantics precisely enough to express his intent, while leaving enough freedom to future reimplementers.

On the implementation of dynamic binding

One might fear that dynamic binding could be a costly mechanism, requiring a run-time search of the inheritance graph and hence an overhead that grows with the depth of that graph and becomes unacceptable with multiple inheritance (studied in the next chapter).

Fortunately this is not the case with a properly designed (and statically typed) O-O language. This issue will be discussed in more detail at the end of this chapter, but we can already reassure ourselves that efficiency consequences of dynamic binding should not be a concern for developers working with a decent environment.

14.5 DEFERRED FEATURES AND CLASSES

Polymorphism and dynamic binding mean that we can rely on abstractions as we design our software, and rest assured that execution will choose the proper implementations. But so far everything was fully implemented.

We do not always need everything to be fully implemented. Abstract software elements, partially implemented or not implemented at all, help us for many tasks: analyzing the problem and designing the architecture (in which case we may keep them in the final product to remind ourselves of the analysis and design); capturing commonalities between implementations; describing the intermediate nodes in a classification.

Deferred features and classes provide the needed abstraction mechanism.

Moving arbitrary figures

To understand the need for deferred routines and classes, consider again the *FIGURE* hierarchy, reproduced for convenience on the facing page.

The most general notion is that of *FIGURE*. Relying on the mechanisms of polymorphism and dynamic binding, you may want to apply the general scheme described earlier, as in:

The *FIGURE* **hierarchy** **again**

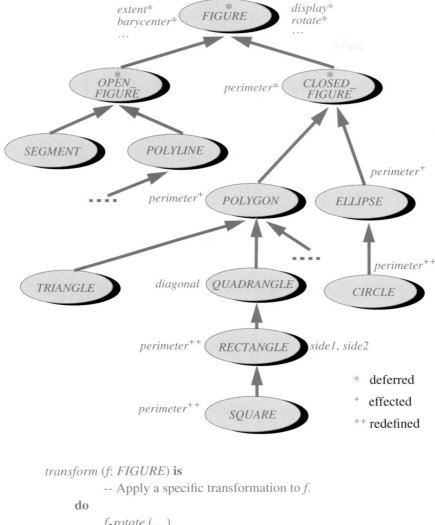

```
transform (f: FIGURE) is
        -- Apply a specific transformation to f.
    do
        f.rotate (…)
        f.translate (…)
    end
```

with appropriate values for the missing arguments. Then all the following calls are valid:

```
transform (r)                    -- with r: RECTANGLE
transform (c)                    -- with c: CIRCLE
transform (figarray.item (i))    -- with figarray: ARRAY [POLYGON]
```

In other words, you want to apply *rotate* and *translate* to a figure *f*, and let the underlying dynamic binding mechanism pick the appropriate version (different for classes *RECTANGLE* and *CIRCLE*) depending on the actual form of *f*, known only at run time.

This should work, and is a typical example of the elegant style made possible by polymorphism and dynamic binding, applying the Single Choice principle. You should simply have to redefine *rotate* and *translate* for the various classes involved.

But there is nothing to redefine! *FIGURE* is a very general notion, covering all kinds of two-dimensional figure. You have no way of writing a general-purpose version of *rotate* and *translate* without more information on the figures involved.

So here is a situation where routine *transform* would execute correctly thanks to dynamic binding, but is statically illegal since *rotate* and *translate* are not valid features of *FIGURE*. Type checking will catch *f.rotate* and *f.translate* as invalid operations.

You could, of course, introduce at the *FIGURE* level a *rotate* procedure which would do nothing. But this is a dangerous road to follow; *rotate* (*center, angle*) has a well-defined intuitive semantics, and "do nothing" is not a proper implementation of it.

Deferring a feature

What we need is a way to specify *rotate* and *translate* at the *FIGURE* level, while making it incumbent on descendants to provide actual implementations. This is achieved by declaring the features as "deferred". We replace the whole instruction part of the body (**do** *Instructions*) by the keyword **deferred**. Class *FIGURE* will declare:

> *rotate* (*center: POINT; angle: REAL*) **is**
>   -- Rotate by *angle* around *center*.
>   **deferred**
>   **end**

and similarly for *translate*. This means that the feature is *known* in the class where this declaration appears, but *implemented* only in proper descendants. Then a call such as catch *f.rotate* in procedure *transform* becomes valid.

With such a declaration, *rotate* is said to be a deferred feature. A non-deferred feature — one which has an implementation, such as all the features that we had encountered up to this one — is said to be **effective**.

Effecting a feature

In some proper descendants of *FIGURE* you will want to replace the deferred version by an effective one. For example:

> **class** *POLYGON* **inherit**
>   *CLOSED_FIGURE*
> **feature**
>   *rotate* (*center: POINT; angle: REAL*) **is**
>   -- Rotate by *angle* around *center*.
>   **do**
>   ... Instructions to rotate all vertices (see page 461) ...
>   **end**
>   ...
> **end** -- class *POLYGON*

Note that *POLYGON* inherits the features of *FIGURE* not directly but through *CLOSED_FIGURE*; procedure *rotate* remains deferred in *CLOSED_FIGURE*.

This process of providing an effective version of a feature that is deferred in a parent is called **effecting**. (The term takes some getting used to, but is consistent: to effect a feature is to make it effective.)

A class that effects one or more inherited features does not need to list them in its **redefine** subclause, since there was no true definition (in the sense of an implementation) in the first place. It simply provides an effective declaration of the features, which must be type-compatible with the original, as in the *rotate* example.

Effecting is of course close to redefinition, and apart from the listing in the **redefine** subclause will be governed by the same rules. Hence the need for a common term:

Definition: redeclaration

To redeclare a feature is to redefine or effect it.

The examples used to introduce redefinition and effecting illustrate the difference between these two forms of redeclaration:

- When we go from *POLYGON* to *RECTANGLE*, we already had an implementation of *perimeter* in the parent; we want to offer a new implementation in *RECTANGLE*. This is a redefinition. Note that the feature gets redefined again in *SQUARE*.

- When we go from *FIGURE* to *POLYGON*, we had no implementation of *rotate* in the parent; we want to offer an implementation in *POLYGON*. This is an effecting. Proper descendants of *POLYGON* may of course redefine the effected version.

There may be a need to change some properties of an inherited deferred feature, while leaving it deferred. These properties may not include the feature's implementation (since it has none), but they may include the signature of the feature — the type of its arguments and result — and its assertions; the precise constraints will be reviewed in the next chapter. In contrast with a redeclaration from deferred to effective, such a redeclaration from deferred to deferred is considered to be a redefinition and requires the **redefine** clause. Here is a summary of the four possible cases of redeclaration:

Redeclaring from → to ↓	Deferred	Effective
Deferred	Redefinition	Undefinition
Effective	Effecting	Redefinition

"Conflicts under sharing: undefinition and join", page 551.

This shows one case that we have not seen yet: *undefinition*, or redeclaration from effective to deferred — forgetting one's original implementation to start a new life.

Deferred classes

A feature, as we have seen, is either deferred or effective. This distinction extends to classes:

Definition: deferred, effective class

A class is deferred if it has a deferred feature. A class is effective if it is not deferred.

So for a class to be effective, all of its features must be effective. One or more deferred features make the class deferred. In the latter case you must mark the class:

Deferred class declaration rule

The declaration of a deferred class must use the juxtaposed keywords **deferred class** (rather than just **class** for an effective class).

So *FIGURE* will be declared (ignoring the **indexing** clause) as:

deferred class *FIGURE* **feature**
> *rotate* (…) **is**
>> … Deferred feature declaration as shown earlier …
>
> … Other feature declarations …

end -- class *FIGURE*

Conversely, if a class is marked as **deferred** it must have at least one deferred feature. But a class may be deferred even if it does not declare any deferred feature of its own: it might have a deferred parent, from which it inherits a deferred feature that it does not effect. In our example, the class *OPEN_FIGURE* most likely does not effect *display*, *rotate* and other deferred features that it inherits from *FIGURE*, since the notion of open figure is still not concrete enough to support default implementations of these operations. So the class is deferred, and will be declared as

> **deferred class** *OPEN_FIGURE* **inherit**
>> *FIGURE*

…

even if it does not itself introduce any deferred feature.

A descendant of a deferred class is an effective class if it provides effective definitions for all features still deferred in its parents, and does not introduce any deferred feature of its own. Effective classes such as *POLYGON* and *ELLIPSE* must provide implementations of *display*, *rotate* and any other routines that they inherit deferred.

For convenience we will say that a type is deferred if its base class is deferred. So *FIGURE*, viewed as a type, is deferred; and if the generic class *LIST* is deferred — as it should be if it represents general lists regardless of the implementation — the type *LIST* [*INTEGER*] is deferred. Only the base class counts here: *C* [*X*] is effective if class *C* is effective and deferred if *C* if is deferred, regardless of the status of *X*.

Graphical conventions

The graphical symbols that have illustrated inheritance figures can now be fully explained. An asterisk marks a deferred feature or class:

*FIGURE**

*display**

*perimeter** -- At the level of *OPEN_FIGURE* in the illustration of page 483

A plus sign means "effective" and marks the effecting of a feature:

perimeter[+] -- At the level of *POLYGON* in the illustration of page 483

You may mark a class with a plus sign [+] to indicate that it is effective. This is only used for special emphasis; an unmarked class is by default understood as effective, like a class declared as just **class** *C* …, without the **deferred** keyword, in the textual notation.

You may also attach a single plus sign to a feature, to indicate that it is being effected. For example *perimeter* appears, deferred and hence in the form *perimeter**, as early as class *CLOSED_FIGURE*, since every closed figure has a perimeter; then at the level of *POLYGON* the feature is effected to indicate the polygon algorithm for computing a perimeter, and so appears next to *POLYGON* as *perimeter*[+].

Finally, two plus signs (informally suggesting double effecting) mark redefinition:

perimeter[++] -- At the level of *RECTANGLE* and *SQUARE* in the figure of page 483

What to do with deferred classes

The presence of deferred elements in a system prompts the question "what happens if we apply *rotate* to an object of type *FIGURE*?"; more generally, if we apply a deferred routine to a direct instance of a deferred class. The answer is draconian: there is no such thing as an object of type *FIGURE* — no such thing as a direct instance of a deferred class.

> ### Deferred Class No-Instantiation rule
>
> The creation type of a creation instruction may not be deferred

Recall that the creation type of a creation instruction is the type of *x* in the form !! *x*, and is *U* in the explicit-type form ! *U* ! *x*. A type is deferred if its base class is.

So the creation instruction !! *f*… is invalid, and will be rejected by the compiler, if the type of *f* is one of *FIGURE*, *OPEN_FIGURE*, *CLOSED_FIGURE*, all deferred. This rule removes any danger of causing erroneous feature calls.

Note, however, that even though *f*'s type is deferred you can still use *f* as target in the type-explicit form of the creation instruction, as in ! *RECTANGLE* ! *f*, as long as the creation type, here *RECTANGLE*, is one of the effective descendants of *FIGURE*. We saw how to use this technique in a multi-branch instruction to create a *FIGURE* object which, depending on the context, will be a direct instance of *RECTANGLE*, or of *CIRCLE*, etc.

At first the rule may appear to limit the usefulness of deferred classes to little more than a syntactic device to fool the static type system. This would be true but for polymorphism and dynamic binding. You cannot create an **object** of type *FIGURE*, but you can declare a polymorphic **entity** of that type, and use it without knowing the type (necessarily based on an effective class) of the attached object in a particular execution:

See also exercise E14.5, page 518.

> *f: FIGURE*
>
> …
>
> *f :=* "Some expression of an effective type, such as *CIRCLE* or *POLYGON*"
>
> …
>
> *f.rotate* (*some_point, some_angle*)
>
> *f.display*
>
> …

f could also be a formal argument, as in some_routine
(f: FIGURE) **is** …

Such examples are the combination and culmination of the O-O method's unique abstraction facilities: classes, information hiding, Single Choice, inheritance, polymorphism, dynamic binding, deferred classes (and, as seen next, assertions). You manipulate objects without knowing their exact types, specifying only the minimum information necessary to ensure the availability of the operations that you require (here, that these objects are figures, so that they can be rotated and displayed). Having secured the type checker's stamp of approval, certifying that these operations are consistent with your declarations, you rely on a benevolent power — dynamic binding — to apply the correct version of each operation, without having to find out what that version will be.

Specifying the semantics of deferred features and classes

Although a deferred feature has no implementation, and a deferred class has either no implementation or a partial implementation only, you will often need to express their abstract semantic properties. You can use assertions for that purpose.

Like any other class, a deferred class can have a class invariant; and a deferred feature can have a precondition, a postcondition or both.

Consider the example of sequential lists, described independently of any particular implementation. As with many other such structures, it is convenient to associate with each list a cursor, indicating a currently active position:

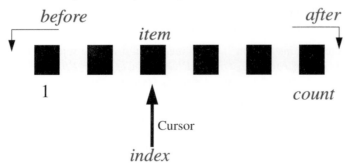

List with cursor

The class is deferred:

indexing
    description: "*Sequentially traversable lists*"
deferred class
    LIST [*G*]
feature -- Access
    count: *INTEGER* **is**
            -- Number of items
        deferred
        end

    index: *INTEGER* **is**
            -- Cursor position
        deferred
        end

    item: *G* **is**
            -- Item at cursor position
        deferred
        end

feature -- Status report
    after: *BOOLEAN* **is**
            --Is cursor past last item?
        deferred
        end

    before: *BOOLEAN* **is**
            --Is cursor before first item?
        deferred
        end

feature -- Cursor movement
    forth **is**
            --Advance cursor by one position.
        require
            not *after*
        deferred
        ensure
            index = **old** *index* + *1*
        end
    … Other features …
invariant
    non_negative_count: *count* >= *0*
    offleft_by_at_most_one: *index* >= *0*
    offright_by_at_most_one: *index* <= *count* + *1*
    after_definition: *after* = (*index* = *count* + *1*)
    before_definition: *before* = (*index* = *0*)
end -- class *LIST*

The invariant expresses the relations between the various queries. The first two clauses state that the cursor may only get off the set of items by one position left or right:

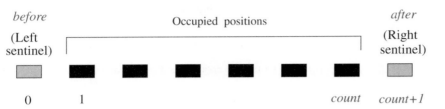

Cursor positions

The last two clauses of the invariant could also be expressed as postconditions: **ensure** *Result* = (*index* = *count* + *1*) in *after* and **ensure** *Result* = (*index* = *0*) in *before*. This choice always arises for a property involving argumentless queries only. In such a case I prefer to use an invariant clause, treating the property as applying globally to the class, rather than attaching it to any particular feature.

The assertions of *forth* express precisely what this procedure must do: advance the cursor by one position. Since we want to maintain the cursor within the range of list elements, plus two "sentinel" positions as shown on the last figure, application of *forth* requires **not** *after*; the result, as stated by the postcondition, is to increase *index* by one.

Here is another example, our old friend the stack. Our library will need a general *STACK* [*G*] class, which we now know will be deferred since it should cover all possible implementations; proper descendants such as *FIXED_STACK* and *LINKED_STACK* will describe specific implementations. One of the deferred procedures of *STACK* is *put*:

```
put (x: G) is
            -- Add x on top.
    require
            not full
    deferred
    ensure
            not_empty: not empty
            pushed_is_top: item = x
            one_more: count = old count + 1
    end
```

The boolean functions *empty* and *full* (also deferred at the *STACK* level) express whether the stack is empty, and whether its representation is full.

Only with assertions do deferred classes attain their full power. As noted (although the details will wait until two chapters from now), preconditions and postconditions apply to all redeclarations of a routine. This is especially significant in the deferred case: these assertions, if present, will set the limits for all permissible effectings. So the above specification constrains all variants of *put* in descendants of *STACK*.

Thanks to these assertion techniques you can make deferred classes informative and semantics-rich, even though they do not prescribe any implementation.

"THE ROLE OF DEFERRED CLASSES", 14.8, page 500.

At the end of this chapter we will come back to deferred classes and explore further their many roles in the object-oriented process of analysis, design and implementation.

14.6 REDECLARATION TECHNIQUES

The possibility of redeclaring a feature — redefining or effecting it — provides us with a flexible, incremental development style. Two techniques add to its power:

- The ability to redeclare a function into an attribute.

- A simple notation for referring to the original version in the body of a redefinition.

Redeclaring a function into an attribute

Redeclaration techniques provide an advanced application of one of the central principles of modularity that led us to the object-oriented method: uniform access.

See "Uniform Access", page 55.

As you will recall, the Uniform Access principle stated (originally in less technical terms, but we can afford to be precise now) that there should not be any fundamental difference, from a client's perspective, between an attribute and an argumentless function. In both cases the feature is a query; all that differs is its internal representation.

The first example was a class describing bank accounts, where the *balance* feature can be implemented as a function, which adds all the deposits and subtracts all the withdrawals, or as an attribute, updated whenever necessary to reflect the current balance. To the client, this makes no difference except possibly for performance.

With inheritance, we can go further, and allow a class that inherits a routine to redefine it as an attribute.

Our old example is directly applicable. Assume an original *ACCOUNT1* class:

class *ACCOUNT1* **feature**
    balance: *INTEGER* **is**
            -- Current balance
        do
            Result := list_of_deposits.total – list_of_withdrawals.total
        end

    ...

end -- class *ACCOUNT1*

Then a descendant can choose the second implementation of our original example, redefining *balance* as an attribute:

class *ACCOUNT2* **inherit**
    ACCOUNT1
                redefine *balance* **end**
feature
    balance: *INTEGER*
            -- Current balance

    ...

end -- class *ACCOUNT2*

ACCOUNT2 will likely have to redefine certain procedures, such as *withdraw* and *deposit*, so that on top of their other duties they update *balance*, maintaining invariant the property *balance = list_of_deposits.total – list_of_withdrawals.total*.

In this example the redeclaration is a redefinition. An effecting can also turn a deferred feature into an attribute. For example a deferred *LIST* class may have a feature

> *count*: *INTEGER* **is**
>
>> -- Number of inserted items
>
> **deferred**
>
> **end**

Then an array implementation may effect this feature as an attribute:

> *count*: *INTEGER*

If we are asked to apply the classification that divides features into attributes and routines, we will by convention consider a deferred feature as a routine — even though, for a deferred feature with a result and no argument, the very notion of deferment means that we have not yet chosen between routine and attribute implementations. The phrase "deferred feature" is suitably vague and hence preferable to "deferred routine".

Combined with polymorphism and dynamic binding, such redeclarations of routines into attributes carry the Uniform Access principle to its extreme. Not only can we implement a client's request of the form *a.service* through either storage or computation, without requiring the client to be aware of our choice (the basic Uniform Access idea): we now have a situation where the same call could, in successive executions of the request during a single session, trigger a field access in some cases and a routine call in some others. This could for example happen with successive executions of the same *a.balance* call, if in the meantime *a* is polymorphically reattached to different objects.

Not the other way around

You might expect to be able to redefine an attribute into an argumentless function. But no. Assignment, an operation applicable to attributes, makes no sense for functions. Assume *x* is an attribute of a class *C*, and a routine of *C* contains the instruction

> *a := some_expression*

Were a descendant of *C* to redefine *a*, then the routine — assuming it is not also redefined — would become inapplicable, since one cannot assign to a function.

The lack of symmetry (redeclaration permitted from function to attribute but not conversely) is unfortunate but inevitable, and not a real impediment in practice. It makes the use of an attribute a final, non-reversible implementation choice, whereas using a function still leaves room for later storage-based (rather than computation-based) implementations.

Using the original version in a redefinition

Consider a class that redefines a routine inherited from a parent. A common scheme for the redefinition is to perform what the original version did, preceded or followed by some other specific actions.

For example, a class *BUTTON* inheriting from *WINDOW* might redefine procedure *display* to indicate that to display a button is to display it as a window, then draw the border:

```
class BUTTON inherit
        WINDOW
                redefine display end
feature -- Output
        display is
                        -- Display as a button.
                do
                        "Display as a normal window"; -- See below
                        draw_border
                end
        ... Other features ...
end -- class BUTTON
```

where *draw_border* is a procedure of the new class. What we need to "Display as a normal window" is a call to the original, pre-redefinition version of *display*, known technically as the **precursor** of *draw_border*.

This case is common enough to justify a specific notation. The construct

Precursor

may be used in lieu of a feature name, but only in the body of a redefined routine. A call to this feature, with arguments if required, is a call to the parent's version of the routine (the precursor).

So in the last example the "Display as a normal window" part may be written as just

Precursor

meaning: call the version of this feature in class *WINDOW*. This would be illegal in any context other than the redefinition of a routine inherited from *WINDOW*, where *WINDOW* is a direct parent. *Precursor* is a reserved entity name, such as *Result* or *Current*, and like them is written in italics with an upper-case first letter.

In this example the redefined routine is a procedure, and so a call to the *Precursor* construct is an instruction. The call would be an expression in the redefinition of a function:

```
some_query (n: INTEGER): INTEGER is
                -- Value returned by parent version if positive, otherwise zero
        do
                Result := (Precursor (n)).max (0)
        end
```

In cases of multiple inheritance studied in the next chapter, a routine may have several precursors (enabling you to join several inherited routines into one). Then you will need to remove the ambiguity by specifying the parent, as in {{*WINDOW*}} *Precursor*.

"Keeping the original version of a redefined feature", page 555.

Note that the use of the *Precursor* construct does not make the precursor feature a feature of the class; only the redefined version is. (For one thing, the precursor version might fail to maintain the new invariant.) The only effect of the construct is to facilitate the task of the redefiner if the new job includes the old.

For any more complicated case, and in particular if you want to use both the precursor and the redefined version as features of the class, you will rely on a technique based on repeated inheritance, which actually *duplicates* a parent feature, yielding two full-fledged features in the heir. This will be part of the discussion of repeated inheritance.

14.7 THE MEANING OF INHERITANCE

We have now seen the basic techniques of inheritance. More remains to be studied, in particular how to deal with multiple inheritance, and the details of what happens to assertions in the context of inheritance (the notion of subcontracting).

But first we must reflect on the fundamental concepts and understand what they mean in the quest for software quality and an effective software development process.

The dual perspective

Nowhere perhaps does the dual role of classes as modules and types, defined when we first encountered the notion of class, appear more clearly than in the study of inheritance. In the module view, an heir describes an extension of the parent module; in the type view, it describes a subtype of the parent type.

Although some aspects of inheritance belong more to the type view, most are useful for both views, as suggested by the following approximate classification (which refers to a few facilities yet to be studied: renaming, descendant hiding, multiple and repeated inheritance). No aspect seems to belong exclusively to the module view.

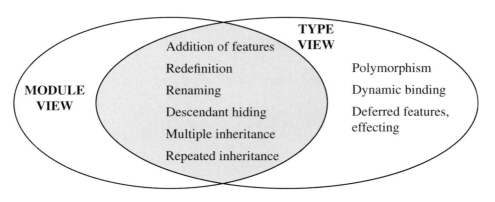

Inheritance mechanisms and their role

*See "ONE MECHA-
NISM, OR MORE?",
24.6, page 833.*
The two views reinforce each other, giving inheritance its power and flexibility. The power can in fact be intimidating, prompting proposals to separate the mechanism into two: a pure module extension facility, and a subtyping mechanism. But when we probe further (in the chapter on the methodology of inheritance) we will find that such a separation would have many disadvantages, and bring no recognizable benefit. Inheritance is a unifying principle; like many of the great unifying ideas of science, it brings together phenomena that had hitherto been treated as distinct.

The module view

From the module viewpoint, inheritance is particularly effective as a reusability technique.

A module is a set of services offered to the outside world. Without inheritance, every new module must itself define all the services it offers. Of course, the *implementations* of these services may rely on services provided by other modules: this is the purpose of the client relation. But there is no way to define a new module as simply adding new services to previously defined modules.

Inheritance gives that possibility. If B inherits from A, all the services (features) of A are automatically available in B, without any need to define them further. B is free to add new features for its own specific purposes. An extra degree of flexibility is provided by redefinition, which allows B to take its pick of the implementations offered by A, keeping some as they are while overriding others by locally more appropriate versions.

This leads to a style of software development which, instead of trying to solve every new problem from scratch, encourages building on previous accomplishments and extending their results. The spirit is one of both economy — why redo what has already been done? — and humility, in line with Newton's famous remark that he could reach so high only because he stood on the shoulders of giants.

*"The Open-Closed
principle", page 57.*
The full benefit of this approach is best understood in terms of the **Open-Closed principle** introduced in an earlier chapter. (It may be worthwhile to reread the corresponding section now in light of the concepts just introduced.) The principle stated that a good module structure should be both closed and open:

- Closed, because clients need the module's services to proceed with their own development, and once they have settled on a version of the module should not be affected by the introduction of new services they do not need.

- Open, because there is no guarantee that we will include right from the start every service potentially useful to some client.

This double requirement looks like a dilemma, and classical module structures offer no clue. But inheritance solves it. A class is closed, since it may be compiled, stored in a library, baselined, and used by client classes. But it is also open, since any new class may use it as a parent, adding new features and redeclaring inherited features; in this process there is no need to change the original or to disturb its clients. This property is fundamental in applying inheritance to the construction of reusable, extendible software.

If the idea were driven to the extreme, every class would add just one feature to those of its parents! This, of course, is not recommended. The decision to close a class should not be taken lightly; it should be based on a conscious judgment that the class as it stands already provides a coherent set of services — a coherent data abstraction — to potential clients.

See "Single-routine classes", page 728.

Also remember that the Open-Closed principle does not cover late hacking of inadequate services. If bad judgment resulted in a poor feature specification we cannot update the class without affecting its clients. Thanks to redefinition, however, the Open-Closed principle remains applicable if the change is compatible with the advertized specification.

Among one of the toughest issues in designing reusable module structures was the necessity to take advantage of commonalities that may exist between groups of related data abstractions — all hash tables, all sequential tables etc. By using class structures connected by inheritance, we can benefit from the logical relationships that exist between these implementations. The diagram below is a rough and partial sketch of a possible structure for a table management library. The scheme naturally uses multiple inheritance, discussed in more detail in the next chapter.

"Factoring Out Common Behaviors", page 85.

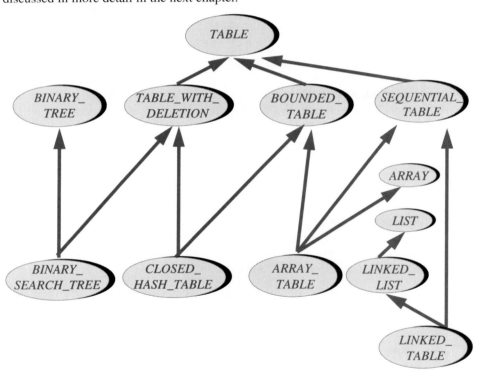

Draft structure for a table library

This inheritance diagram is only a draft although it shows inheritance links typical of such a structure. For a systematic inheritance-based classification of tables and other containers, see [M 1994a].

With this view we can express the reusability requirement quite concretely: the idea is to move the definition of every feature **as far up** in the diagram as possible, so that it may be shared by the greatest possible number of descendant classes. Think of the process as the *reusability game*, played on boards that represent inheritance hierarchies such as the one on the last figure, with tokens that represent features. He who moves the most features the highest, as a result of discovering higher-level abstractions, and along the way merges the most tokens, as a result of discovering commonalities, wins.

The type view

From the type perspective, inheritance addresses both reusability and extendibility, in particular what an earlier discussion called continuity. The key is dynamic binding.

A type is a set of objects characterized (as we know from the theory of abstract data types) by certain operations. *INTEGER* describes a set of numbers with arithmetic operations; *POLYGON*, a set of objects with operations *vertices*, *perimeter* and others.

For types, inheritance represents the *is* relation, also known as *is-a*, as in "every dog is a mammal", "every mammal is an animal". Similarly, every rectangle is a polygon.

What does this relation mean?

"Instances", page 475.

- If we consider the values in each type, the relation is simply set inclusion: dogs make up a subset of the set of animals; similarly, instances of *RECTANGLE* make up a subset of the instances of *POLYGON*. (This comes from the definition of "instance" earlier in this chapter; note that a direct instance of *RECTANGLE* is not a direct instance of *POLYGON*).

- If we consider the operations applicable to each type, saying that every *B* is an *A* means that every operation applicable to instances of *A* is also applicable to instances of *B*. (With redefinition, however, *B* may provide its own implementation, which for instances of *B* overrides the implementation given in *A*.)

Using this relation, you can describe *is-a* networks representing many possible type variants, such as all the variants of *FIGURE*. Each new version of a routine such as *rotate* and *display* is defined in the class that describes the corresponding type variant. In the table example, each class in the graph will provide its own implementation of *search*, *insert*, *delete*, except of course when the parent's version is still appropriate.

A caveat about the use of "*is*" and "*is-a*". Beginners — but, I hope, no one who has read so far with even a modicum of attention — sometimes misuse inheritance to model the instance-to-mold relation, as with a class *SAN_FRANCISCO* inheriting from *CITY*. This is most likely a mistake: *CITY* is a class, which may have an instance representing San Francisco. To avoid such mistakes, it suffices to remember that the term *is-a* does not stand for "*x* is an *A*" (as in "*San_francisco* is a *CITY*"), a relation between an instance and a category, but for "every *B* is an *A*" (as in "Every *CITY* is a *GEOGRAPHICAL_UNIT*"), a relation between two categories — two classes in software terms. Some authors prefer to call this relation "*is-a-kind-of*" or, like [Gore 1996], "*can act as a*". This is partly a matter of taste (and partly a matter of substance, to be discussed in the chapter on inheritance methodology); once we have learned to avoid the trivial mistake, we can continue to use the well-accepted "*is*" or "*is-a*" terminology, never forgetting that it describes a relation between categories.

Inheritance and decentralization

With dynamic binding we can produce the **decentralized software architectures** necessary to achieve the goals of reusability and extendibility. Compare the O-O approach — self-contained classes each providing its set of operation variants — with classical approaches. In Pascal or Ada, you may use a record type with variants

> **type** *FIGURE* =
>   **record**
>   "Common fields if any"
>   **case** *figtype*: (*polygon, rectangle, triangle, circle, …*) **of**
>   *polygon*: (*vertices*: *LIST_OF_POINTS*; *count*: *INTEGER*);
>   *rectangle*: (*side1, side2*: *REAL*; …);
>   …
>   **end**

See "Single Choice", page 61.

to define the various forms of figures. But this means that every routine that does something to figures (*rotate* and the like) must discriminate between possibilities:

> **case** *f*.*figure_type* **of**
>   *polygon*: …
>   *circle*: …
>   …
> **end**

Routines *search* and others in the table case would use the same structure. The trouble is that all these routines possess far too much **knowledge** about the overall system: each must know exactly what types of figure are allowed in the system. Any addition of a new type, or change in an existing one, will affect every routine.

Ne sutor ultra crepidam, the shoemaker should not look beyond the sandal, is a software design principle: a rotation routine has no business knowing the exhaustive list of figure types. It should be content enough with the information necessary to do its job: rotating certain kinds of figure.

This distribution of knowledge among too many routines is a major source of inflexibility in classical approaches to software design. Much of the difficulty of modifying software may be traced to this problem. It also explains in part why software projects are so difficult to keep under control, as apparently small changes have far-reaching consequences, forcing developers to reopen modules that were thought to have been closed for good.

Object-oriented techniques deal with the problem head-on. A change in a particular implementation of an operation will only affect the class to which the implementation applies. Addition of a new type variant will in many cases leave the others completely unaffected. Decentralization is the key: classes manage their own implementations and do not meddle in each other's affairs. Applied to humans, this would sound like Voltaire's *Cultivez votre jardin*, tend your own garden. Applied to modules, it is an essential requirement for obtaining decentralized structures that will yield gracefully to requests for extension, modification, combination and reuse.

Representation independence

"Representation Independence", *page 84.*

Dynamic binding also addresses one of the principal reusability issues: representation independence — the ability to request an operation with more than one variant, without having to know which variant will be applied. The discussion of this notion in an earlier chapter used the example of a call

$$present := has\ (x,\ t)$$

which should use the appropriate search algorithm depending on the run-time form of t. With dynamic binding, we have exactly that: if t is declared as a table, but may be instantiated as any of binary search tree, closed hash table etc. (assuming all needed classes are available), then the call

$$present := t.has\ (x)$$

will find, at run time, the appropriate version of *has*. Dynamic binding achieves what the earlier discussion showed to be impossible with overloading and genericity: a client may request an operation, and let the underlying language system automatically find the appropriate implementation.

So the combination of classes, inheritance, redefinition, polymorphism and dynamic binding provides a remarkable set of answers to the questions raised at the beginning of this book: requirements for reusability; criteria, principles and rules of modularity.

The extension-specialization paradox

Inheritance is sometimes viewed as extension and sometimes as specialization. Although these two interpretations appear contradictory, there is truth in both — but not from the same perspective.

It all depends, again, on whether you look at a class as a type or a module. In the first case, inheritance, or *is*, is clearly specialization; "dog" is a more specialized notion than "animal", and "rectangle" than "polygon". This corresponds, as noted, to subset inclusion: if B is heir to A, the set of run-time objects represented by B is a subset of the corresponding set for A.

But from the module perspective, where a class is viewed as a provider of services, B implements the services (features) of A plus its own. *Fewer* objects often allows *more* features, since it implies a higher information value; going from arbitrary animals to dogs we can add the specific property of barking, and from arbitrary polygons to rectangles we can add the feature *diagonal*. So with respect to features implemented the subsetting goes the other way: the features applicable to instances of A are a subset of those for instances of B.

> Features *implemented* rather than services *offered* (to clients) because of the way information hiding combines with inheritance: as we will see, B may hide from its clients some of the features exported by A to its own.

Inheritance, then, is specialization from the type viewpoint and extension from the module viewpoint. This is the extension-specialization paradox: more features to apply, hence fewer objects to apply them to.

The extension-specialization paradox is one of the reasons for avoiding the term "subclass", which suggests "subset". Another, already noted, is the literature's sometimes confusing use of "subclass" to indicate direct as well as indirect inheritance. No such problem arises for the precisely defined terms *heir*, *descendant* and *proper descendant* and their counterparts *parent*, *ancestor* and *proper ancestor*.

14.8 THE ROLE OF DEFERRED CLASSES

Among the inheritance-related mechanisms addressing the problems of software construction presented at the beginning of this book, deferred classes are prominent.

Back to abstract data types

Loaded with assertions, deferred classes come close to representing abstract data types. A deferred class covering the notion of stack provides an excellent example. Procedure *put* has already been shown; here is a possible version for the full class.

> **indexing**
>> *description*:
>>> "*Stacks* (*Last-in, First-Out dispenser structures*), *independently of %*
>>>> *%any representation choice*"
>
> **deferred class**
>> *STACK* [*G*]
>
> **feature** -- Access
>> *count*: *INTEGER* **is**
>>> -- Number of elements inserted.
>>
>> **deferred**
>> **end**
>
>> *item*: *G* **is**
>>> -- Last element pushed.
>>
>> **require**
>>> *not_empty*: **not** *empty*
>>
>> **deferred**
>> **end**
>
> **feature** -- Status report
>> *empty*: *BOOLEAN* **is**
>>> -- Is stack empty?
>>
>> **do**
>>> *Result* := (*count* = *0*)
>>
>> **end**
>
>> *full*: *BOOLEAN* **is**
>>> -- Is stack full?
>>
>> **deferred**
>> **end**

feature -- Element change

   put (*x*: *G*) **is**

          -- Push *x* onto top.

     require

        not *full*

     deferred

     ensure

        not_empty: **not** *empty*

        pushed_is_top: *item* = *x*

        one_more: *count* = **old** *count* + *1*

     end

   remove **is**

          -- Pop top element.

     require

        not *empty*

     deferred

     ensure

        not_full: **not** *full*

        one_less: *count* = **old** *count* — *1*

     end

   change_top (*x*: *T*) **is**

          -- Replace top element by *x*

     require

        not_empty: **not** *empty*

     do

        remove; *put* (*x*)

     ensure

        not_empty: **not** *empty*

        new_top: *item* = *x*

        same_number_of_items: *count* = **old** *count*

     end

   wipe_out **is**

          -- Remove all elements.

     deferred

     ensure

        no_more_elements: *empty*

     end

invariant

   non_negative_count: *count* >= *0*

   empty_count: *empty* = (*count* = *0*)

end

The class shows how you can implement effective routines in terms of deferred ones: for example, *change_top* has been implemented as a *remove* followed by a *put*. (This implementation may be inefficient in some representations, for example with arrays, but effective descendants of *STACK* may redefine the routine.)

If you compare class *STACK* with the abstract data type specification given in the chapter on ADTs, you will find the similarities striking. Note in particular how the ADT functions map to features of the class, and the PRECONDITIONS paragraph to routine preconditions. Axioms are reflected in routine postconditions and in the class invariant. *Full specification page 139; also "FROM ABSTRACT DATA TYPES TO CLASSES", 6.5, page 142.*

The addition of operations *change_top*, *count* and *wipe_out* is not an important difference since they could be specified as part of the abstract data type. Also minor is the absence of an explicit equivalent of the abstract data type function *new*, since creation instructions (which may rely on creation procedures introduced by effective descendants) will take care of object creation. There remain three significant differences. *See exercise E6.8, page 162: "more stack operations".*

The first is the introduction of a function *full*, accounting for implementations that will only accept a limited number of successive insertions, for example array implementations. This is typical of constraints that are irrelevant at the specification level but necessary in the design of practical systems. Note, however, that this is not an intrinsic difference between abstract data types and deferred classes, since we may adapt the ADT specification to cover the notion of bounded stack. Also, no generality is lost since some implementations (linked, for example) may have a version of *full* that always returns false. *See exercise E6.9, page 162: "bounded stacks".*

The second difference, mentioned in the discussion of Design by Contract, is that an ADT specification is purely applicative (functional): it only includes functions, without side effects. A deferred class is imperative (procedural) in spite of its abstractness; *put*, for example, is specified as a procedure that will modify a stack, not as a function that takes a stack and returns a new stack. *"The imperative and the applicative", page 351.*

Finally, as also noted in the earlier discussion, the assertion mechanism is not expressive enough for some ADT axioms. Of the four stack axioms

> For any x: G, s: *STACK* [G]
>
> A1 • *item* (*put* (*s*, x)) = x
>
> A2 • *remove* (*put* (*s*, x)) = s
>
> A3 • *empty* (*new*)
>
> A4 • **not** *empty* (*put* (*s*, x))

all but A2 have a direct equivalent in the assertions. (For A3 we assume that descendants' creation procedures will state **ensure** *empty*.) An earlier discussion explained the reasons for this limitation, and hinted at possible ways — formal specification languages, IFL — to remove it. *"The expressive power of assertions", page 399, and subsequent section.*

Deferred classes as partial implementations: the notion of behavior class

Not all deferred classes are as close as *STACK* to an abstract data type. In-between a fully abstract class like *STACK*, where all the fundamental features are deferred, and an effective class such as *FIXED_STACK*, describing just one implementation of an abstract data type, there is room for all degrees of partial ADT implementations or, said differently, groups of possible implementations.

See "Factoring Out Common Behaviors", page 85; figure on page 86.

The review of table implementation variants, which helped us understand the role of partial commonality in our study of reusability issues, provides a typical example. The original figure showing the relations between the variants can now be redrawn as an inheritance diagram:

Variants of the notion of table

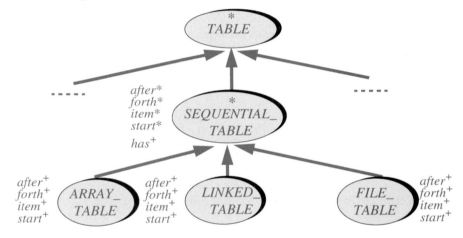

The most general class, *TABLE*, is fully or almost fully deferred, since at that level we may specify a few features but not provide any substantial implementation. Among the variants is *SEQUENTIAL_TABLE*, representing tables in which elements are inserted sequentially. Examples of sequential tables include array, linked list and sequential file implementations. The corresponding classes, in the lowest part of the figure, are effective.

Classes such as *SEQUENTIAL_TABLE* are particularly interesting. The class is still deferred, but its status is intermediate between full deferment, as with *TABLE*, and full effecting, as with *ARRAY_TABLE*. It has enough information to allow implementing some specific algorithms; for example we can implement sequential search fully:

```
has (x: G): BOOLEAN is
            -- Does x appear in table?
    do
            from start until after or else equal (item, x) loop
                forth
            end
            Result := not after
    end
```

This function is effective, although it relies for its algorithm on deferred features. The features *start* (bring the cursor to the first position), *forth* (advance the cursor by one position), *item* (value of element at cursor position), *after* (is the cursor after the last element?) are deferred in *SEQUENTIAL_TABLE*; each of the heirs of this class shown in the figure effects them in a different way, corresponding to its choice of implementation. These various effectings were given in the discussion of reusability. *ARRAY_TABLE*, for example, can represent the cursor as an integer *i*, so that the procedure *start* is implemented as *i := 1*, *item* as *t @ i* and so on.

See the table on page 88 (which uses found in lieu of item).

Note how important it is to include the precondition and postcondition of *forth*, as well as the invariant of the enclosing class, to make sure that all future effectings observe the same basic specification. These assertions appeared earlier in this chapter (in a slightly different context, for a class *LIST*, but directly applicable here).

"Specifying the semantics of deferred features and classes", page 488.

This discussion shows the correspondence between classes and abstract data types in its full extent:

- A fully deferred class such as *TABLE* corresponds to an ADT.

- A fully effective class such as *ARRAY_TABLE* corresponds to an implementation of an ADT.

- A partially deferred class such as *SEQUENTIAL_TABLE* corresponds to a family of related implementations (or, equivalently, a partial implementation) of an ADT.

A class such as *SEQUENTIAL_TABLE*, which captures a behavior common to several ADT variants, may be called a **behavior class**. Behavior classes provide some of the fundamental design patterns of object-oriented software construction.

Don't call us, we'll call you

SEQUENTIAL_TABLE is representative of how object technology, through the notion of behavior class, answers the last one among the major reusability issues still open from the discussion in chapter 4: *Factoring out common behaviors*.

"Factoring Out Common Behaviors", page 85.

Particularly interesting is the possibility for an effective routine of a behavior class to rely on deferred routines for its implementation, as illustrated by *has*. This is how you may use partially deferred classes to capture common behaviors in a set of variants. The deferred class only describes what is common; variations are left to descendants.

Several of the design examples of later chapters rely on this technique, which plays a central role in the application of object-oriented techniques to building reusable software. It is particularly useful for domain-specific libraries and has been applied in many different contexts. A typical example, described in [M 1994a], is the design of the Lex and Parse libraries, a general-purpose solution to the problem of analyzing languages. Parse, in particular, defines a general parsing scheme, which will process any input text whose structure conforms to a certain grammar (for a programming language, some data format etc.). The higher-level behavior classes contain a few deferred features such as *post_action* describing semantic actions to be executed just after a certain construct has been parsed. To define your own semantic processing, you just effect these features.

This scheme is broadly applicable. Business applications, in particular, often follow standard patterns — process all the day's invoices, perform appropriate validation on a payment request, enter new customers … — with individual components that may vary.

In such cases we may provide a set of behavior classes with a mix of effective features to describe the known part and deferred features to describe the variable elements. Typically, as in the preceding example, the effective features call the deferred ones. Then descendants can provide the effectings that satisfy their needs.

> Not all the variable elements need to be deferred. If a default implementation is available, include it in the ancestor as an effective feature, which descendants may still redefine; this facilitates the work on the descendants, since they only need to provide new versions for features that depart from the default. (Recall that to become effective, that is, directly usable, a class must effect *all* its parents' deferred features.) Apply this technique only if a sound default exists; if not, as with *display* for *FIGURE*, the feature should be deferred.

This technique is part of a general approach that we may dub *don't call us, we'll call you*: rather than an application system that calls out reusable primitives, a general-purpose scheme lets application developers "plant" their own variants at strategic locations.

The idea is not entirely new. IBM's ancient and venerable database management system, IMS, already relied on something of the sort. In more recent software, a common structure for graphics systems (such as X for Unix) has an "event loop" which at each iteration calls specific functions provided by each application developer. This is known as a **callback** scheme.

What the O-O method offers, thanks to behavior classes, is systematic, safe support for this technique, through classes, inheritance, type checking, deferred classes and features, as well as assertions that enable the developer of the fixed part to specify what properties the variable replacements must always satisfy.

Programs with holes

With the techniques just discussed we are at the heart of the object-oriented method's contribution to reusability: offering not just frozen components (such as found in subroutine libraries), but flexible solutions that provide the basic schemes and can be adapted to suit the needs of many diverse applications.

One of the central themes of the discussion of reusability was the need to combine this goal with adaptability — to get out of the *reuse or redo* dilemma. This is exactly the effect of the scheme just described, for which we can coin the name "programs with holes". Unlike a subroutine library, where all is fixed except for the values of the actual arguments that you can pass, programs with holes, using classes patterned after the *SEQUENTIAL_TABLE* model, have room for user-contributed parts.

These observations help to put in perspective the "Lego block" image often used to discuss reusability. In a Lego set, the components are fixed; the child's creativity goes towards arranging them into an interesting structure. This exists in software, but sounds more like the traditional idea of subroutines. Often, software development needs to do exactly the reverse: keep the structure, but change the components. In fact the components may not be there at all yet; in their place you find placeholders (deferred features), useful only when you plug in your own variants.

In analogies with child games, we can go back to a younger age and think of those playboards where toddlers have to match shapes of blocks with shapes of holes — to realize that the square block goes into the square hole and the round block into the round hole.

You can also picture a partially deferred behavior class (or a set of such classes, called a "library" or a "framework") as having a few electrical outlets — the deferred features — into which the application developer will plug compatible devices. The metaphor nicely suggests the indispensable safeguards: the assertions, which express the requirements on acceptable pluggable devices, in the same way that an outlet's specification would prescribe a range of acceptable voltages, currents and other electrical parameters.

Deferred classes for analysis and global design

Deferred classes are also a key tool for using the method not just for implementation but also at the earliest and highest levels of system building — analysis and global design. The aim is to produce a system specification and architecture; for design, we also need an abstract description of each module, without implementation details.

The advice commonly given is to use separate notations: some analysis "method" (a term that in many cases just covers a graphical notation) and a PDL (Program Design Language, again often graphical). But this approach has many drawbacks:

- By introducing a gap between the successive steps, it poses a grave threat to software quality. The necessity of translating from one formalism to another may bring in errors and endangers the integrity of the system. Object technology, instead, offers the promise of a seamless, continuous software process.

  "Seamless development", page 931.

- The multi-tiered approach is particularly detrimental to maintenance and evolution. It is very hard to guarantee that design and implementation will remain consistent throughout the system's evolution.

- Finally, most existing approaches to analysis and design offer no support for the formal specification of functional properties of modules independently of their implementation, in the form of assertions or a similar technique.

The last comment gives rise to the **paradox of levels**: precise notations such as the language of this book are sometimes dismissed as "low-level" or "implementation-oriented" because they externally look like programming languages, whereas thanks to assertions and such abstraction mechanisms as deferred classes they are actually *higher-level* than most of the common analysis and design approaches. Many people take a while to realize this, so early have they been taught the myth that high-level must mean vague; that to be abstract one has to be imprecise.

The use of deferred classes for analysis and design allows us to be both abstract and precise, and to keep the same language throughout the software process. We avoid conceptual gaps ("impedance mismatches"); the transition from high-level module descriptions to implementations can now proceed smoothly, within one formalism. But even unimplemented operations of design modules, now represented by deferred routines, may be characterized quite precisely by preconditions, postconditions and invariants.

The notation which we have by now almost finished developing covers analysis and design as well as implementation. The same concepts and constructs are applied at all stages; only the level of abstraction and detail differs.

14.9 DISCUSSION

This chapter has introduced the basic concepts of inheritance. Let us now assess the merits of some of the conventions introduced. Further comments on the inheritance mechanism (in particular on multiple inheritance) appear in the next chapter.

Explicit redefinition

The role of the **redefine** subclause is to enhance readability and reliability. Compilers do not really need it: since a class may have at most one feature of a given name, a feature declared in a class with the same name as an ancestor's feature can only be a redefinition of that feature — or a mistake.

The possibility of a mistake should not be taken lightly, as a programmer may be inheriting from a class without being aware of all the features declared in its ancestors. To avoid this dangerous case, any redefinition must be explicitly requested. This is the aim of the **redefine** subclause, which is also helpful to a reader of the class.

Accessing the precursor of a routine

You will have noted the rule on the *Precursor* (…) construct: it may only appear in the redefined version of a routine.

This ensures that the construct serves its purpose: enabling a redefinition to rely on the original implementation. The explicit naming of the parent avoids any ambiguity (in particular with multiple inheritance). Allowing arbitrary routines to access arbitrary ancestor features could make a class text very hard to understand, all the time forcing the reader to go the text of many other classes.

Dynamic binding and efficiency

One might fear that dynamic binding, for all its power, would lead to unacceptable run-time overhead. The danger exists, but careful language design and good implementation techniques avert it.

The problem is that dynamic binding requires some more work to be done at run time. Compare the usual routine call of traditional programming languages (Pascal, Ada, C…)

[1]

$$f(x, a, b, c…)$$

with the object-oriented form

[2]

$$x{\scriptstyle\bullet}f(a, b, c…)$$

"The Single Target principle", page 184.

The difference between the two was explained, in the introduction to the notion of class, as a consequence of the module-type identification. But now we know that more than style is at stake: there is also a difference of semantics. In [1], it is known statically

— at compile time, or at worst at link time, if you use a linker to combine separately compiled modules — what exact feature the name f denotes. With dynamic binding, however, no such information is available statically for f in [2]: the feature to be selected depends on the type of the object to which x will be attached during a particular execution. What that type will be cannot, in the general case at least, be predicted from the text of the software; this is the source of the flexibility of the mechanism, touted earlier.

Let us think for a moment of a naïve implementation. We keep at run time a copy of the class hierarchy. Each object contains information about its type — a node in that hierarchy. To interpret $x.f$, the run-time environment looks at that node to see if the corresponding class has a feature f. If so, great, we have found what we need. If not, we look at the node's parent, and repeat the operation. We may have to go all the way to the topmost class (or the topmost classes in the case of multiple inheritance).

> In a typed language we have the guarantee that somewhere along the way we will find a suitable feature; in an untyped language such as Smalltalk we may fail to do so, and have to terminate the execution with a "message not understood" diagnostic.

This scheme is still applied, with various optimizations, in many implementations of non-statically typed languages. It implies a considerable performance penalty. Worse, that penalty is not predictable, and it *grows with the depth of the inheritance structure*, as the algorithm may have to go back all the way to the root of the inheritance hierarchy. This means introducing a direct conflict between reusability and efficiency, since working harder at reusability often leads to introducing more levels of inheritance. Imagine the plight of the poor designer who, whenever tempted to add an inheritance link, must assess whether it is really worth the resulting performance hit. No software developer should be forced into such choices.

This approach is one of the primary sources of inefficiency in Smalltalk environments. It also explains why Smalltalk does not (in common commercial implementations at least) support multiple inheritance, since the penalty in this case would be enormous, due to the need to traverse an entire graph, not just a linear chain.

Fortunately, the use of static typing avoids such unpleasantness. With the proper type system and compiling algorithms, there is no need ever to traverse the inheritance structure at run time. Because in a statically typed O-O language the possible types for x are not arbitrary but confined to descendants of x's original type, the compiler can prepare the work of the run-time system by building arrayed data structures that contain all the needed type information. With these data structures, the overhead of dynamic binding becomes very small: *an index computation and an array access*. Not only is this penalty small; even more importantly, it is **constant** (more precisely, bounded by a constant), so that there is no need to worry about any reusability-efficiency tradeoff as discussed above. Whether the deepest inheritance structure in your system is 2 or 20, whether you have 100 classes or 10,000, the maximum overhead is exactly the same. This is true for both single and multiple inheritance.

> The discovery, in 1985, of this property — that even in the presence of multiple inheritance it was possible to implement a dynamically-bound feature call in constant time — was the key impetus for the project that, among other things, yielded both the first

and the present editions of this book: to build a modern software development environment, starting from the ideas brilliantly introduced by Simula 67 and extending them to multiple inheritance (prolonged experience with Simula having shown that the limitation to single inheritance was unacceptable, as explained in the next chapter), reconciling them with modern principles of software engineering, and combining them with the most directly useful results of formal approaches to software specification, construction and verification. The design of an efficient, constant-time dynamic binding mechanism, which may at first sight appear to be somewhat peripheral in this set of goals, was in reality an indispensable enabler.

These observations will be surprising to anyone who has been introduced to object technology through the lens of O-O analysis and design presentations that treat implementation and efficiency as mundane issues to be addressed after one has solved everything else. In the reality of industrial software development — the reality of engineering tradeoffs — efficiency is one of the key factors that must be considered at every step. (As noted in an earlier chapter, if you dismiss efficiency, efficiency will dismiss you.) Object technology is much more than constant-time dynamic binding; but without constant-time dynamic binding there can be no successful object technology.

Estimating the overhead

With the techniques described so far, it is possible to give rough figures on the overhead of dynamic binding. The following figures are drawn from ISE's experience, using dynamic binding (that is to say, disabling the static binding optimization explained next).

For a procedure that does nothing — a procedure declared as *p1* **is do end** — the penalty for dynamic binding over static binding (that is to say, over the equivalent procedure in C) is about 30%.

This is of course an upper bound, since real-life procedures do something. The price for dynamic binding is the same for any routine call regardless of what it does; so the more a routine does, the smaller the relative penalty. If instead of *p1* we use a procedure that performs some arbitrary but typical operations, as in

> *p2* (*a*, *b*, *c*: *INTEGER*) **is**
> > **local**
> > > *x*, *y*
> > **do**
> > > $x := a$; $y := b + c + 1$; $x := x * y$; *p2*
> > > **if** $x > y$ **then** $x := x + 1$ **else** $x := x - 1$ **end**
> > **end**

then the overhead goes down to about 15%. For a routine that does anything more significant (for example by executing a loop), it can become very small.

Static binding as an optimization

In some cases you need the utmost in efficiency, and even the small overhead just discussed may be undesirable. Then you will notice that the overhead is not always justified. A call $x.f(a, b, c...)$ need not be dynamically bound when either:

S1   • *f* is not redeclared anywhere in the system (it has only one declaration).

S2   • *x* is not polymorphic, that is to say is not the target of any attachment whose source has a different type.

In any such case — detectable by a good compiler — the code generated for *x*.*f* (*a*, *b*, *c*...) can be identical to what a compiler for C, Pascal, Ada or Fortran would generate for *f* (*x*, *a*, *b*, *c*...). No overhead of any kind is necessary.

ISE's compiler, part of the environment described in the last chapter of this book, currently applies optimization S1; the addition of S2 is planned. (S2 analysis is in fact a consequence of the type analysis mechanisms described in the chapter on typing.)

Although S1 is interesting in itself, its direct benefit is limited by the relatively low cost of dynamic binding given in the preceding statistics. The real payoff is indirect, since S1 enables a third optimization:

S3   • Apply **automatic routine inlining** when appropriate

Routine inlining means expanding the body of a routine within the text of its caller, eliminating the need for any actual call. For example, with a routine

> *set_a* (*x*: *SOME_TYPE*) **is**
>> -- Make *x* the new value of attribute *a*.
>
> **do**
>> *a* := *x*
>
> **end**

the compiler may generate, for the call *s*.*set_a* (*some_value*), the same code that a Pascal compiler would generate for the assignment *s*.*a* := *some_value* (not permitted by our notation, of course, since it violates information hiding). In this case there is no overhead at all, since the generated code does not use a routine call.

Inline expansion has traditionally been viewed as an optimization that **programmers** should specify. Ada includes the provision for an **inline** pragma (directive to the compiler); C and C++ offer similar mechanisms. But this approach suffers from inherent limitations. Although for a small, stationary program a competent developer can have a good idea of what should be inlined, this ceases to be true for large, evolutionary developments. In that case, a compiler with a decent inlining algorithm will beat the programmers' guesses 100% of the time.

For any call to which automatic static binding (S1) is applicable, an O-O compiler can (as in the case of ISE's) determine whether automatic routine inlining (S3) is worthwhile, based on an analysis of the space-time tradeoffs. This is one of the most dramatic optimizations — one of the reasons why it is possible to match the efficiency of hand-crafted C or Fortran code and sometimes, especially on large systems, exceed it.

To the efficiency advantage, which grows with the size and complexity of the software, the automatic approach to inlining adds the advantage of safety and flexibility. As you will have noted, inlining is semantically correct only for a routine that can be statically bound, as in cases S1 and S2. It is not only common but also consistent with the method, in particular the Open-Closed principle, to see a developer, midway through the development of a large system, add a redefinition of a feature which until then had only one implementation. If that routine has been inlined manually, the result is erroneous semantics (since dynamic binding is now required, and inlining of course means static binding). Developers should concentrate on building correct software, not performing optimizations that are tedious, error-prone when done manually, and automatable.

> There are some other correctness requirements for inlining; in particular, it is only applicable to non-recursive calls. When correct, inlining should only be applied when the space-time tradeoff makes sense: the inlined routine should be small, and should be called from only one place or a small number of places.

A final note on efficiency. Published statistics for object-oriented languages show that somewhere between 30% and 60% of calls truly need dynamic binding, depending on how extensively the developers use the method's specific facilities. (In ISE's software the proportion is indeed around 60%.) With the optimizations just described, you will only pay the price of dynamic binding for calls that need it. For the remaining dynamic calls, the overhead is not only small and constant-bounded, it is *logically necessary*; in most cases, achieving the equivalent effect without O-O mechanisms would have required the use of conditional instructions (**if** … **then** … or **case** … **of** …), which can be more costly than the simple array-indirection mechanism outlined above. So it is not surprising that O-O software, processed by a good compiler, can compete with hand-produced C code.

A button by any other name: when static binding is wrong

By now the reader will have understood a key consequence of the principles of inheritance presented in this chapter:

Dynamic Binding principle

Static binding is semantically incorrect unless its effect is identical to that of dynamic binding.

In the call $x.r$, if x is declared of type A but ends up at run time attached to an object of type B, and you have redefined r in B, calling the original version (say r_A) is not a choice; it is a bug!

No doubt you had a reason for redefining r. The reason may have been optimization, as with *perimeter* for *RECTANGLE*; but it may have been that the original version r_A was simply incorrect for B. Consider the example, sketched earlier, of a class *BUTTON* that inherits from a class *WINDOW* in a window system, because buttons are a special kind of window; the class redefines procedure *display* because displaying a button is a little different from displaying an ordinary window (for example you must display the border). Then if w is of type *WINDOW* but dynamically attached, through polymorphism, to an object of type *BUTTON*, the call $w.display$ **must** execute the button version! Using $display_{WINDOW}$ would result in garbled display on the screen.

As another example, assume a video game with a data structure *LIST* [*AIRCRAFT*] — a polymorphic data structure, as we have learned to use them — and a loop that executes *item.land* on each element of the list. Each aircraft type may have a different version of *land*, the landing procedure. Executing the default version is not an option but a mistake. (We may of course imagine real flight control software rather than just a game.)

We should not let the flexibility of the inheritance-based type system — specifically, the type conformance rule — fool us here: the ability to declare an entity at a level of abstraction (*WINDOW, AIRCRAFT*) higher than the actual type of the attached object during one particular execution (*BUTTON* or *BOEING_747_400*) is only a facility for the *engineering* of the software, at system writing time. During program *execution* the only thing that matters is the objects to which we apply features; entities — names in the text of the software — have long been forgotten. A button by any other name is still a button; whether the software called it a button, or for generality treated it as a window, does not change its nature and properties.

Mathematical analysis supports and explains this reasoning. From the chapter on assertions you may remember the correctness condition for a routine:

$$\{pre_r(x_r) \text{ \textbf{and} } INV\} \ Body_r \ \{post_r(x_r) \text{ \textbf{and} } INV\}$$

From the definition of class correctness on page 370.

which we can simplify for the benefit of this discussion (keeping the part relative to the class invariant only, ignoring the arguments, and using as subscript the name *A* of the enclosing class) as

[A-CORRECT]

$$\{INV_A\} \ r_A \ \{INV_A\}$$

meaning in plain English: any execution of routine *r* from class *A* will preserve the invariant of class *A*. Now assume that we redefine *r* in a proper descendant *B*. The corresponding property will hold if the new class is correct:

[B-CORRECT]

$$\{INV_B\} \ r_B \ \{INV_B\}$$

As you will recall, invariants accumulate as we go down an inheritance structure: so INV_B implies INV_A, but usually not the other way around.

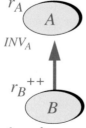

r_A preserves the invariant of *A*…

… and r_B preserves the invariant of *B*…

… but r_A has no particular reason to preserve the invariant of *B*!

$INV_B = INV_A$ \textbf{and} other_clauses

A parent version may fail to satisfy the new invariant

*On the ACCOUNT
example see "CLASS
INVARIANTS",
11.8, page 363.*

Remember for example how *RECTANGLE* added its own clauses to the invariant of *POLYGON*. Another example, studied in the presentation of invariants, is a class *ACCOUNT1* with features *withdrawals_list* and *deposits_list*; then, perhaps for efficiency reasons, a proper descendant *ACCOUNT2* adds an attribute *balance* to store an account's current balance at all time, with the new invariant clause given in the earlier discussion:

$$\textit{consistent\_balance: deposits\_list} \bullet \textit{total} - \textit{withdrawals\_list} \bullet \textit{total} = \textit{current\_balance}$$

As a result, we may have to redefine some of the routines of *ACCOUNT1*; for example a procedure *deposit* that merely used to add a list element to *deposits_list* must now update *balance* as well. Otherwise the class is simply wrong. This is similar to *WINDOW*'s version of the *display* procedure not being correct for an instance of *BUTTON*.

Now assume static binding applied to an object of type *B*, accessible through an entity of type *A*. Because the corresponding routine version, r_A, will usually not preserve the needed invariant — as with $deposit_{ACCOUNT1}$ for an object of type *ACCOUNT2*, or $display_{WINDOW}$ for an object of type *BUTTON* — the result will be to produce an inconsistent object, such as an *ACCOUNT2* object with an incorrect *balance* field, or a *BUTTON* object improperly displayed on the screen.

Such a result — an object that does not satisfy the invariant of its generating class, that is to say, the fundamental and universal constraints on all objects of its kind — is one of the worst events that could occur during the execution of a software system. If such a situation can arise, we can no longer hope to predict what execution will do.

*Cases S1 and S2
appeared were
defined on page 510.*

To summarize: **static binding is either an optimization or a bug**. If it has the same semantics as dynamic binding (as in cases S1 and S2), it is an optimization, which compilers may perform. If it has a different semantics, it is a bug.

The C++ approach to binding

Given its widespread use and its influence on other languages, it is necessary to explain how the C++ language addresses some of the issues discussed here.

The C++ convention is surprising. By default, binding is static. To be dynamically bound, a routine (function or method in C++ terms) must be specially declared as **virtual**.

Two decisions are involved here:

C1 • Making the programmer responsible for selecting static or dynamic binding.

C2 • Using static binding as the default.

Both are damaging to object-oriented software development, but there is a difference of degree: C1 is arguable; C2 is hard to defend.

*"PROGRAMMER-
CONTROLLED
DEALLOCA-
TION", 9.4, page
294*

Compared to the approach of this book, C1 results from a different appreciation of which tasks should be handled by humans (software developers), and which by computers (more precisely, compilers). This is the same debate that we encountered with automatic memory management. The C++ approach, in the C tradition, is to give the programmer full control over the details of what happens at run time, be it object deallocation or routine call. The spirit of object technology instead suggests relying on compilers for tasks that are tedious and error-prone, if algorithms are available to handle them. On a large scale and in the long run, compilers always do a better job.

Developers are responsible for the efficiency of their software, of course, but they should direct their efforts to the area where they can make a real difference: the choice of proper software structures and algorithms. Language designers and compilers writers are responsible for the rest.

Hence the disagreement on decision C1: C++ considers that static binding, as well as inlining, should be specified by developers; the O-O approach developed in this book, that it is the responsibility of the compiler, which will optimize calls behind the scenes. Static binding is an optimization, not a semantic choice.

C1 has another negative consequence on the application of the method. Whenever you declare a routine you must specify a binding policy: virtual or not, that is to say dynamic or static. This policy runs against the Open-Closed principle since it forces you to guess from the start what will be redefinable and what will not. This is not how inheritance works in practice: you may have to redefine a feature in a distant descendant, without having ever foreseen the need for such a redefinition in the original. With the C++ approach, if the original designer did not have enough foresight, you need to go back to the ancestor class to change the declaration to **virtual**. (This assumes that you can modify its source text. If it is not available, or you are not entitled to change it, tough luck.)

Because of all this, decision C1 — requiring programmers to specify a binding policy — impedes the effectiveness of the object-oriented method.

C2 — the use of static binding as the default in the absence of a special "virtual" marker — is worse. Here it is hard to find justifications for the language design. Static binding, as we have seen, is always the wrong choice when its semantics differs from that of dynamic binding. There can be not reason for choosing it as the default.

Making programmers rather than compilers responsible for optimization when things are safe (that is to say, asking them to request static binding explicitly when they think it is appropriate) is one thing; forcing them to write something special to *get the correct semantics* is quite another. When the concern for efficiency, misplaced or not, starts to prevail over the basic requirement of correctness, something is wrong.

Even in a language that makes the programmer responsible for choosing a binding policy (decision C1), the default should be the reverse: instead of requiring dynamically bound functions to be declared as **virtual**, the language should by default use dynamic binding and allow programmers to mark as **static**, or some such keyword, those features for which they want to request the optimization — trusting them, in the C-C++ tradition, to ascertain that it is valid.

The difference is particularly important for beginners, who naturally tend to stick with the default. Even with less intimidating a language than C++, no one can be expected to master all the details of inheritance right away; the responsible policy is to guarantee the correct semantics for novices (and more generally for developers starting a new project, who will "want to make it right before making it faster"), then provide an optimization facility for people who need it and understand the issues.

Given the software industry's widespread concern for "upward compatibility", getting the C++ committee to change the language's binding policy, especially C2, will be hard, but it is worth trying in light of the dangers of the current conventions.

> The C++ approach has regrettably influenced other languages; for example the dynamic binding policy of Borland's Delphi language, continuing earlier Pascal extensions, is essentially that of C++. Note, however, that Java, a recent derivative of C++, has adopted dynamic binding as its policy.

These observations call for some practical advice. What can the developer do in C++ or a language that follows its policy? The best suggestion — for developers who do not have the option of switching to better tools, or waiting for the language to change — is to declare **all** functions as virtual, hence allowing for arbitrary redeclarations in the spirit of object-oriented software development. (Some C++ compilers unfortunately put a limit on the number of virtuals in a system, but one may hope that such limitations will go away.)

The paradox of this advice is that it takes you back to a situation in which all calls are implemented through dynamic binding and require a bit of extra execution time. In other words, language conventions (C1 and C2) that are promoted as enhancing efficiency end up, at least if one follows correctness-enhancing rules, working against performance!

Not surprisingly, C++ experts have come to advise against becoming "too much" object-oriented. Walter Bright, author of a best-selling C++ compiler, writes

[Bright 1995].

> *It's generally accepted that the more C++ [mechanisms] you use in a class, the slower your code will be. Fortunately, you can do a few things to tip the scales in your favor. First, don't use virtual functions [i.e. dynamic binding], virtual base classes [deferred classes], destructors, and the like, unless you need them. [...] Another source of bloat is multiple inheritance [...] For a complex class hierarchy with only one or two virtual functions, consider removing the virtual aspect, and maybe do the equivalent with a test and branch.*

"Modular decomposability", page 40.

In other words: avoid using object-oriented techniques. (The same text also advocates *"grouping all the initialization code"* to favor locality of reference — an invitation to violate elementary principles of modular design which, as we have seen, suggest that each class be responsible for taking care of its own initialization needs.)

This chapter has suggested a different approach: let the O-O software developer rely on the guarantee that the semantics of calls will always be the correct one — dynamic binding. Then use a compiler sophisticated enough do generate statically bound or inlined code for those calls that have been determined, on the basis of rigorous algorithmic analysis, not to require a d ynamically bound implementation.

14.10 KEY CONCEPTS INTRODUCED IN THIS CHAPTER

- With inheritance, you can define new classes by extension, specialization and combination of previously defined ones.

- A class inheriting from another is said to be its heir; the original is the parent. Taken to an arbitrary number of levels (including zero), these relations yield the notion of descendant and ancestor.

- Inheritance is a key technique for both reusability and extendibility.

- Fruitful use of inheritance requires redefinition (the possibility for a class to override the implementation of some of its proper ancestors' features), polymorphism (the ability for a reference to become associated at run time with instances of different classes), dynamic binding (the dynamic selection of the appropriate variant of a redefined feature), type consistency (the requirement that an entity be only attached to instances of descendant types).

- From the module perspective, an heir extends the services of its parents. This particularly serves reusability.

- From the type perspective, the relation between an heir and a parent of the original class is the *is* relation. This serves both reusability and extendibility.

- You may redefine an argumentless function into an attribute, but not the other way around.

- Inheritance techniques, especially dynamic binding, permit highly decentralized software architectures where every variant of an operation is declared within the module that describes the corresponding data structure variant.

- With a typed language it is possible to achieve dynamic binding at low run-time cost. Associated optimizations, in particular compiler-applied static binding and automatic in-line expansion, help O-O software execution match or surpass the efficiency of traditional approaches.

- Deferred classes contain one or more deferred (non-implemented) features. They describe partial implementations of abstract data types.

- The ability of effective routines to call deferred ones provides a technique for reconciling reusability with extendibility, through "behavior classes".

- Deferred classes are a principal tool in the use of object-oriented methods at the analysis and design stages.

- Assertions are applicable to deferred features, allowing deferred classes to be precisely specified.

- When the semantics is different, dynamic binding is always the right choice; static binding is incorrect. When they have the same abstract effect, using static binding as the implementation is an optimization technique, best left to the compiler to detect and apply safely, together with inlining when applicable.

14.11 BIBLIOGRAPHICAL NOTES

The concepts of (single) inheritance and dynamic binding were introduced by Simula 67, on which references may be found in chapter 35. Deferred routines are also a Simula invention, under a different name (virtual procedures) and different conventions.

The *is-a* relation is studied, more with a view towards artificial intelligence applications, in [Brachman 1983].

A formal study of inheritance and its semantics is given in [Cardelli 1984].

The double-plus graphical convention to mark redefinition comes from Nerson's and Waldén's Business Object Notation for analysis and design; references in chapter 27.

Some elements of the discussion of the role of deferred features come from [M 1996].

The *Precursor* construct (similar to the Smalltalk **super** construct, but with the important difference that its use is limited to routine redefinitions) is the result of unpublished work with Roger Browne, James McKim, Kim Waldén and Steve Tynor.

EXERCISES

E14.1 Polygons and rectangles

Complete the versions of *POLYGON* and *RECTANGLE* sketched at the beginning of this chapter. Include the appropriate creation procedures.

E14.2 How few vertices for a polygon?

The invariant of class *POLYGON* requires every polygon to have at least three vertices; note that function *perimeter* would not work for an empty polygon. Update the definition of the class so that it will cover the degenerate case of polygons with fewer than three vertices.

E14.3 Geometrical objects with two coordinates

Write a class *TWO_COORD* describing objects that are characterized by two real coordinates, having among its heirs classes *POINT*, *COMPLEX* and *VECTOR*. Be careful to attach each feature to its proper level in the hierarchy.

E14.4 Inheritance without classes

This chapter has presented two views of inheritance: as a module, an heir class offers the services of its parent plus some; as a type, it embodies the *is-a* relation (every instance of the heir is also an instance of each of the parents). The "packages" of modular but not object-oriented languages such as Ada or Modula-2 are modules but not types; inheritance in its first interpretation might still be applicable to them. Discuss how such a form of inheritance could be introduced in a modular language. Be sure to consider the Open-Closed principle in your discussion.

E14.5 Non-creatable classes

It is not permitted to create an instance of a deferred class. In an earlier chapter we saw another way to make a class non-creatable: include an empty creation clause. Are the two mechanisms equivalent? Can you see cases for using one rather than the other? (**Hint**: a deferred class must have at least one deferred feature.)

"Rules on creation procedures", page 238.

E14.6 Deferred classes and rapid prototyping

Deferred classes may not be instantiated. It was argued, on the other hand, that a first version of a class design might leave all the features deferred. It may be tempting to attempt the "execution" of such a design: in software development, one sometimes wishes, early in the game, to execute incomplete implementations, so as to get an early hands-on experience of some aspects of the system even though other aspects have not been finalized. Discuss the pros and cons of having a "prototype" option in the compiler, which would allow instantiating a deferred class and executing a deferred feature (amounting to a null operation). Discuss the details of such an option.

E14.7 Table searching library (term project)

Based on the discussion of tables in this chapter and the chapter on reusability, design a library of table classes covering various categories of table representations, such as hash tables, sequential tables, tree tables etc.

E14.8 Kinds of deferred feature

Can an attribute be deferred?

E14.9 Complex numbers

(This exercise assumes that you have read up to at least chapter 23.) An example in the discussion of module interfaces uses complex numbers with two possible representations, changes in representations being carried out behind the scenes. Study whether it is possible to obtain equivalent results through inheritance, by writing a class *COMPLEX* and its heirs *CARTESIAN_COMPLEX* and *POLAR_COMPLEX*.

"Legitimate side effects: an example", page 759.

15

Multiple inheritance

$\mathcal{F}$ull application of inheritance requires an important extension to the framework defined in the preceding chapter. In studying the basics of the mechanism we have encountered the notion that a class may need more than one parent. Known as multiple inheritance (to distinguish it from the more restrictive case of *single* inheritance), this possibility is necessary to build robust object-oriented architectures by combining different abstractions.

Multiple inheritance, in its basic form, is a straightforward application of the principles of inheritance already seen; you just allow a class to include an arbitrary number of parents. More detailed probing brings up two interesting issues:

- The need for feature renaming, which in fact has useful applications in single inheritance too.

- The case of *repeated* inheritance, in which the ancestor relation links two classes in more than one way.

15.1 EXAMPLES OF MULTIPLE INHERITANCE

The first task is to form a good idea of when multiple inheritance is useful. Let us study a few typical examples from many different backgrounds; a few will be shown in some detail, others only sketched.

This review is all the more necessary that in spite of the elegance, necessity and fundamental simplicity of multiple inheritance, obvious to anyone who cares to study the concepts, this facility has sometimes been presented (often, as one later finds out, based solely on experience with languages or environments that cannot deal with it) as complex, mysterious, error-prone — as the object-oriented method's own "goto". Although it has no basis in either fact or theory, this view has been promoted widely enough to require that we take the time to review a host of cases in which multiple inheritance is indispensable.

As it will turn out, the problem is not to think of valuable examples, but to stop the flow of examples that will start pouring in once we open the tap.

What not to use as an introductory example

To dispel a frequent confusion, we must first consider an example whose use (with some variants) by many introductory papers, books and lectures may account for some of the common mistrust of multiple inheritance. Not that there is anything fundamentally wrong with the example; it is simply inadequate for an introductory presentation, since it is not typical of simple, straightforward uses of multiple inheritance.

The standard form of this example involves classes *TEACHER* and *STUDENT*, part of the model for some university system; you will be invited to note that some students are also teachers, prompting a new class *TEACHING_ASSISTANT* that inherits from both *TEACHER* and *STUDENT*.

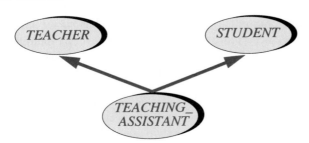

A case of multiple inheritance ...

Is this example an improper use of inheritance? Not necessarily. But as an introduction to multiple inheritance it is about as bad as they can get. The problem is that *TEACHER* and *STUDENT* are not separate abstractions but variations on a common theme: person, or more accurately *UNIVERSITY_PERSON*. So if we draw the full picture we see a case of not just multiple but **repeated** inheritance — the scheme, studied later in this chapter, in which a class is a proper descendant of another through two paths or more:

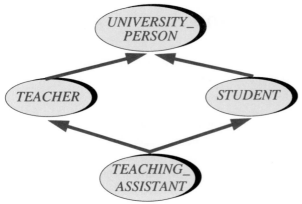

... that is a case of repeated inheritance

Repeated inheritance is a special case; as will be noted when we get to it, using this facility requires good experience with the more elementary forms of inheritance, single and multiple. So it is not a matter for beginners, if only because it seems to create conflicts (what about a feature *name* or *subscribe_to_health_plan* which *TEACHING_ASSISTANT* inherits

For details see "REPEATED INHERITANCE", 15.4, page 543.

from both of its parents, even though they are really in each case a single feature coming from the common ancestor *UNIVERSITY_PERSON*?). With a well-reasoned approach we will be able to remove these conflicts simply. But it is a serious mistake to begin with such exceptional and seemingly tricky cases as if they were typical of multiple inheritance.

The truly common cases do not raise any such problem. Instead of dealing with variants of a single abstraction, they combine **distinct abstractions**. This is the form that you will need most often in building inheritance structures, and the one that introductory discussions should describe. The following examples belong to that pattern.

Can an airplane be an asset?

Our first proper example belongs to system modeling more than to software construction in the strict sense. But it is typical of situations that require multiple inheritance.

Assume a class *AIRPLANE* describing the abstraction suggested by its name. Queries may include *passenger_count*, *altitude*, *position*, *speed*; commands may include *take_off*, *land*, *set_speed*.

In a different domain, we may have a class *ASSET* describing the accounting notion of an asset — something which a company owns, although it may still be paying installments on it, and which it can depreciate or resell. Features may include *purchase_price*, *resale_value*, *depreciate*, *resell*, *pay_installment*.

You must have guessed where we are heading: companies may own company planes. For the pilot, a company plane is just a plane with its usual features: it takes off, lands, has a certain speed, flies somewhere. From the viewpoint of the accountant (the one who grumbles that the money would have been better kept in the bank or spent on more productive ventures) it is an asset, with a purchase value (too high), an estimated resale value (too low), and the need to pay interest on the loan each month.

To model the notion of company plane we can resort to multiple inheritance:

Company planes

class *COMPANY_PLANE* **inherit**
    PLANE
    ASSET
feature
    … Any feature that is specific to company planes
        (rather than applying to all planes or all assets) …
end

To specify multiple parents in the **inherit** clause, just list them one after the other. (As usual, you can use semicolons as optional separators.) The order in which you list parents is not significant.

Cases similar to *COMPANY_PLANE* abound in system modeling. Here are a few:

- Wristwatches (a special case of the notion of watch, itself specializing the general notion of clock — there are a few inheritance links here) provide commands such as setting the time, and queries such as the current time and date. Electronic calculators provide arithmetic features. There also exist some (quite handy) watch-calculators, elegantly modeled through multiple inheritance.

- Boats; trucks; *AMPHIBIOUS_VEHICLE*. A variant is: boats; planes; *HYDROPLANE*. (There is a hint of repeated inheritance here, as with *TEACHING_ASSISTANT*, since both parents may themselves be descendants of some *VEHICLE* class.)

- You eat in a restaurant; you travel in a train car. To make your trip more enjoyable, the railway company may let you eat in an instance of *EATING_CAR*. A variant of this example is *SLEEPING_CAR*.

- On an instance of *SOFA_BED* you may not only read but also sleep.

- A *MOBILE_HOME* is a *VEHICLE* and a *HOUSE*.

And so on. Multiple inheritance is the natural tool to help model the endless combinations that astute people never tire of concocting.

For a software engineer the preceding examples may at first appear academic, since we get paid not to model the world but to build systems. In many practical applications, however, you will encounter similar combinations of abstractions. A detailed example, from ISE's own graphical development environment appears later in this chapter.

Numeric and comparable values

The next example is much more directly useful to the daily practice of object-oriented software construction. It is essential to the buildup of the Kernel library.

Some of the Kernel library's classes — that is to say, classes describing abstractions of potential use to all applications — require arithmetic features: operations such as **infix** "+", **infix** "−", **infix** "∗", **prefix** "−" as well as special values *zero* (identity element for "+") and *one* (identity element for "∗"). Kernel library classes that use these features include *INTEGER*, *REAL* and *DOUBLE*; but many non-predefined classes may need them too, for example a class *MATRIX* describing matrices of some application-specific kind. It is appropriate to capture the corresponding abstraction through a deferred class *NUMERIC*, itself a part of the Kernel library:

> **deferred class** *NUMERIC* **feature**
>
> ... **infix** "+", **infix** "−", **infix** "∗", **prefix** "−", *zero, one* ...
>
> **end**

Mathematically, *NUMERIC* has a precise specification: its instances represent members of a ring (a set equipped with two operations, both of which separately give it the structure of a group, one commutative, with distributivity between the two operations).

Some classes also need an order relation, with features for comparing arbitrary elements: **infix** "<", **infix** "<=", **infix** ">", **infix** ">=". Again this is useful not only to some Kernel library classes, such as *STRING* whose instances are comparable through lexical ordering, but also to many application classes; for example you may write a class *TENNIS_CHAMPION* which takes into account the ranking of professional tennis players, with a feature "<" such that *tc1* < *tc2* tells us whether *tc2* is ranked ahead of *tc1*. So it is appropriate to capture the corresponding abstraction through a deferred class *COMPARABLE*, itself a part of the Kernel library:

> **deferred class** *COMPARABLE* **feature**
>> … **infix** "<", **infix** "<=", **infix** ">", **infix** ">=" …
>
> **end**

Technically the exact model is that of a "preorder".

COMPARABLE has a precise mathematical model: its instances represent members of a set ordered by a total order relation.

Not all descendants of *COMPARABLE* should be descendants of *NUMERIC*: in class *STRING*, we need the order features for lexicographical ordering but not the arithmetic features. Conversely, not all descendants of *NUMERIC* should be descendants of *COMPARABLE*: the set of real matrices has addition, multiplication, zero and one, giving it a ring structure, but no total order relation. So it is appropriate that *COMPARABLE* and *NUMERIC*, representing completely different abstractions, should remain distinct classes, neither of them a descendant of the other.

Objects of certain types, however, are both comparable and numeric. (In mathematical terms. the structures modeled by their generating classes are totally ordered rings.) Example classes include *REAL* and *INTEGER*: integers and real numbers can be compared for "<=" as well as added and multiplied. These classes should be defined through multiple inheritance, as in (see the figure on the next page):

> **expanded class** *REAL* **inherit**
>> *NUMERIC*
>> *COMPARABLE*
>
> **feature**
>> …
>
> **end**

Types of objects that need to be both comparable and numeric are sufficiently common to suggest a class *COMPARABLE_NUMERIC*, still deferred, covering the merged abstraction by multiply inheriting from *COMPARABLE* and *NUMERIC*. So far this solution has not been adopted for the library because it does not bring any obvious advantage and seems to open the way to endless combinations: why not *COMPARABLE_HASHABLE*, *HASHABLE_ADDABLE_SUBTRACTABLE*? Basing such deferred classes on well-accepted mathematical abstractions, such as ring or totally ordered set, seems to yield the right level of granularity. Related issues in the methodology of inheritance are discussed in detail in chapter 16.

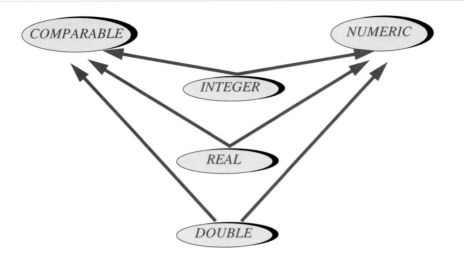

Multiple structure inheritance

Windows are trees and rectangles

Assume a window system that allows nesting windows to an arbitrary depth:

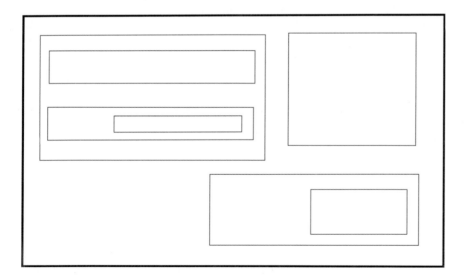

Windows and subwindows

In the corresponding class *WINDOW*, we will find features of two general kinds:

- Some deal with a window as a member of a hierarchical structure: list of subwindows, parent window, number of subwindows, add or remove a subwindow.

- Others cover its properties as a graphical object occupying a graphical area: height, width, *x* position, *y* position, display, hide, translate.

It is possible to write the class as a single piece, with all these features mixed together. But this would be bad design. To keep the structure manageable we should separate the two aspects, treating class *WINDOW* as the combination of two abstractions:

- Hierarchical structures, which should be covered by a class *TREE*.
- Rectangular screen objects, covered by a class *RECTANGLE*.

In practice we may need more specific class names (describing some particular category of trees, and a graphical rather than purely geometrical notion of rectangle), but the ones above will be convenient for this discussion. *WINDOW* will appear as:

class *WINDOW* **inherit**
    TREE [*WINDOW*]
    RECTANGLE
feature
    … Specific window features …

end

Note that class *TREE* will be generic, so we need to specify an actual generic parameter, here *WINDOW* itself. The recursive nature of this definition reflects the recursion in the situation modeled: a window is a tree of windows.

> This example will, later on in the discussion, help us understand the need for a feature renaming mechanism associated with inheritance.

A further refinement might follow from the observation that some windows are purely text windows. Although we might represent this property by introducing a class *TEXT_WINDOW* as a client of *STRING* with an attribute

text: *STRING*

we may prefer to consider that each text window *is* also a string. In this case we will use multiple inheritance from *WINDOW* and *STRING*. (If all windows of interest are text windows, we might directly use triple inheritance from *TREE*, *RECTANGLE* and *STRING*, although even in that case it is probably better to work in two successive stages.)

See "WOULD YOU RATHER BUY OR INHERIT?", 24.2, page 812.

The general question of how to choose between heir and client relations, as in the case of *TEXT_WINDOW*, is discussed in detail in the chapter on inheritance methodology.

Trees are lists and list elements

Class *TREE* itself provides a striking example of multiple inheritance.

A tree is a hierarchical structure made of nodes, each containing some information. Common definitions tend to be of the form "A tree is either empty or contains an object called the root, together with (recursively) a list of trees, called the children of the root", complemented by a definition of *node*, such as "An empty tree has no nodes; the nodes of a non-empty tree comprise its root and (recursively) the nodes of its children". Although useful, and reflective of the recursiveness inherent in the notion of tree, these definitions fail to capture its essential simplicity.

To get a different perspective, observe that there is no significant distinction between the notion of tree and that of node, as we may identify a node with the subtree of which it is the root. This suggests aiming for a class *TREE* [*G*] that describes both trees and nodes. The formal generic parameter *G* represents the type of information attached to every node; the tree below, for example, is an instance of *TREE* [*INTEGER*].

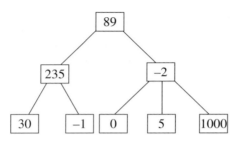

A tree of integers

Now consider a notion of *LIST*, with a class that has been sketched in earlier chapters. A general implementation (linked, for example) will need an auxiliary class *CELL* to describe the individual elements of a list.

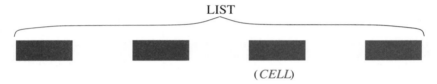

These notions suggest a simple definition of trees: a tree (or tree node) is a list, the list of its children; but it is also a potential list element, as it can be made into a subtree of another tree.

Definition: tree

A tree is a list that is also a list element.

Although this definition would need some refinement to achieve full mathematical rigor, it directly yields a class definition:

deferred class *TREE* [*G*] **inherit**
    LIST [*G*]
    CELL [*G*]
feature

        ...

end

From *LIST* come the features to find out the number of children (*count*), add a child, remove a child and so on.

From *CELL* come the features having to do with a node's siblings and parents: next sibling, add a sibling, reattach to a different parent node.

This example is typical of the reusability benefits of multiple inheritance. Writing specific features for subtree insertion or removal would needlessly replicate the work done for lists. Writing specific features for sibling and parent operations would needlessly replicate the work done for list elements. Only a facelift is needed in each case.

In addition you will have to take care, in the **feature** clause, of the specific features of trees and of the little mutual compromises which, as in any marriage, are necessary to ensure that life together is harmonious and prolific. In a class *TREE* derived from these ideas, which has been used in many different applications (from graphics to structural editing), these specific features fit on little more than a page; for the most part, the class is simply engendered as the legitimate fruit of the union between lists and list elements.

> This process is exactly that used in mathematics to combine theories: a *topological vector space*, for example, is a *vector space* that also is a *topological space*; here too, some connecting axioms need to be added to finish up the merger.

Composite figures

The following example is more than an example; it is a design pattern useful in many different contexts.

Consider an inheritance structure containing classes for various graphical figures, such as the one used in the preceding chapter to introduce some of the fundamental concepts of inheritance — *FIGURE*, *OPEN_FIGURE*, *POLYGON*, *RECTANGLE*, *ELLIPSE* and so on. So far, as you may have noted, that structure used single inheritance.

Assume that we have included in this hierarchy all the basic figure patterns that we need. That is not enough yet: many figures are not basic. Of course we could build any graphical illustration from elementary shapes, but that is not a convenient way to work; instead, we will want to build ourselves a library of figures, some basic, some constructed from the basic ones. For example, from basic segment and circle figures

Elementary figures

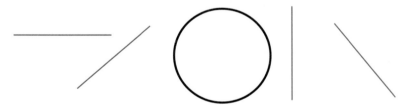

we may assemble a composite figure, representing a wheel

A composite figure

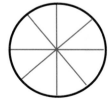

which someone may in turn use as a predefined pattern to draw, say, a bicycle; and so on.

We need a general mechanism for adding a new figure type which will be built from previously defined ones but, once defined, will be on a par with them. Computer drawing tools provide a Group command for this purpose.

Let us call the corresponding notion *COMPOSITE_FIGURE*. A composite figure is clearly a figure; so *COMPOSITE_FIGURE* should inherit from *FIGURE*, achieving the goal of treating composite figures "on a par" with basic ones. A composite figure is also a list of figures — its constituents; each of them may be basic or itself composite. Hence the use of multiple inheritance:

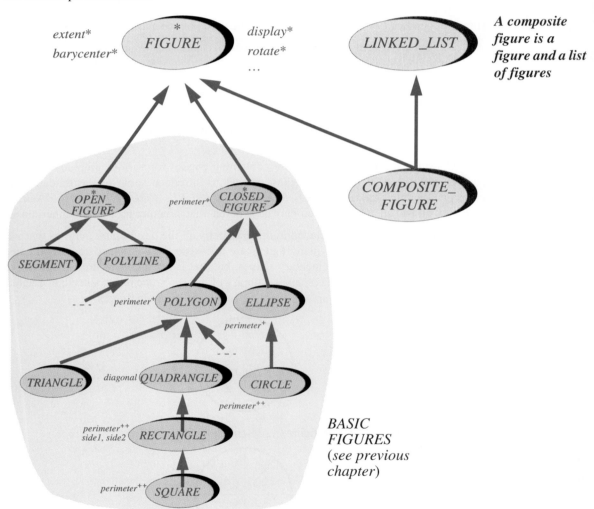

A composite figure is a figure and a list of figures

To get an effective class for *COMPOSITE_FIGURE* we choose an implementation of lists; *LINKED_LIST* is just one possibility. The class declaration will look like this:

```
class COMPOSITE_FIGURE inherit
    FIGURE
    LINKED_LIST [FIGURE]
feature
    ...
end
```

The **feature** clause is particularly pleasant to write. An operation on a composite figure is, in many cases, an operation on all of its constituents taken in sequence. For example, procedure *display* will be effected as follows in *COMPOSITE_FIGURE*:

```
display is
        -- Display figure by displaying all its components in turn.
    do
        from
            start
        until
            after
        loop
            item.display
            forth
        end
    end
```

For the details see "ACTIVE DATA STRUCTURES", 23.4, page 774.

As in earlier discussions, we assume that our list classes offer traversal mechanisms based on the notion of cursor: *start* moves the cursor to the first element if any (otherwise *after* is immediately true), *after* indicates whether the cursor is past all elements, *item* gives the value of the element at cursor position, and *forth* advances the cursor by one position.

I find this scheme admirable and hope its beauty will strike you too. Almost everything is concentrated here: classes, multiple inheritance, polymorphic data structures (*LINKED_LIST [FIGURE]*), dynamic binding (the call *item.display* will apply the proper variant of *display* based on the type of each list element), recursion (note that any list element — any *item* — may itself be a composite figure, with no limit on the degree of nesting). To think that some people will live an entire life and never see this!

Exercise E15.4, page 567.

It is in fact possible to go further. Consider other *COMPOSITE_FIGURE* features such as *rotate* and *translate*; because they all must apply the corresponding operation to every member figure in turn, their body will look very much like *display*. For an object-oriented designer this is cause for alert: we do not like repetition; we transform it, through encapsulation, into reuse. (This could yield a good motto.) The technique to use here is to define a deferred "iterator" class, whose instances are little machines able to iterate over a *COMPOSITE_FIGURE*. Its effective descendants may include *DISPLAY_ITERATOR* and so on. This is a straightforward scheme and is left to the reader as an exercise.

Exercises E15.8, page 568, and E21.6, page 716.

The technique describing composite structures through multiple inheritance, using a list or other container class as one of the parents, is a general **design pattern**, directly useful in widely different areas. Make sure to look at the exercise asking you to apply similar reasoning to the notion of *submenu* in a window system: a submenu is a menu, but it is also a menu entry. Another deals with *composite commands* in an interactive system.

The marriage of convenience

In the preceding examples the two parents played a symmetric role. This is not always the case; sometimes each parent brings a contribution of a different nature.

An important application of multiple inheritance is to provide an implementation of an abstraction defined by a deferred class, using facilities provided by effective class.

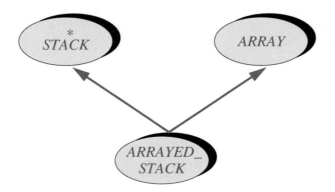

A marriage of convenience

Consider the implementation of stacks as arrays. Since classes are available to cover stacks as well as arrays (deferred for *STACK*, effective for *ARRAY*, both seen in earlier chapters), the best way to implement class *ARRAYED_STACK*, describing stacks implemented as arrays, is to define it as an heir to both *STACK* and *ARRAY*. This is conceptually right: an arrayed stack is a stack (as seen by clients) and is also an array (internally). The general form is:

The deferred STACK class appeared on page 500; class ARRAY was sketched on page 372.

    indexing
        description: "*Stacks implemented as arrays*"
    class *ARRAYED_STACK* [*G*] **inherit**
        STACK [*G*]
        ARRAY [*G*]
                  … A **rename** subclause will be added here (see page 540) …
    feature
        … Implementation of the deferred routines of *STACK*
          in terms of *ARRAY* operations (see below)…
    end

ARRAYED_STACK offers the same functionality as *STACK*, effecting its deferred features such as *full*, *put*, *count* through implementations relying on array operations.

Here is an outline of some typical features: *full*, *count* and *put*. The condition under which a stack is full is given by

full: *BOOLEAN* **is**
-- Is stack representation full?
do
Result := (count = capacity)
end

Here *capacity*, inherited from class *ARRAY*, is the number of positions in the array. For *count* we need an attribute:

count: *INTEGER*

This is a case of effecting a deferred feature into an attribute. Here finally is *put*:

put (*x*: *G*) **is**
-- Push *x* on top.
require
not *full*
do
count := count + 1
array_put (*x*, *count*)
end

Procedure *array_put*, inherited from *ARRAY*, assigns a new value to an array element given by its index.

See "Using a parent's creation procedure", page 539.

The array features *capacity* and *array_put* had different names in class *ARRAY*: *count* and *put*. The name change is explained later in this chapter.

ARRAYED_STACK is representative of a common kind of multiple inheritance, called the *marriage of convenience*. It is like a marriage uniting a rich family and a noble family. The bride, a deferred class, belongs to the aristocratic family of stacks: it brings prestigious functionality but no practical wealth — no implementation worth speaking of. (What good is an effective *change_top* with a deferred *put* and *remove*?) The groom comes from a well-to-do bourgeois family, arrays, but needs some luster to match the efficiency of its implementation. The two make a perfect match.

Besides providing effective implementations of routines deferred in *STACK*, class *ARRAYED_STACK* may also redefine some which were not deferred. In particular, with an array representation, *change_top* (*x*: *G*), implemented in *STACK* as *remove* followed by *put* (*x*), may be implemented more efficiently as

array_put (*x*, *count*)

To make this redefinition valid, do not forget to announce it in the inheritance clause:

class *ARRAYED_STACK* [*G*] **inherit**
STACK [*G*]
redefine *change_top* **end**
… The rest as before …

The invariant of the class might read

invariant

> *non_negative_count*: *count* >= 0
> *bounded*: *count* <=*capacity*

The two parts of the assertion are of a different nature. The first expresses a property of the abstract data type. (It was in fact already present in the parent class *STACK*, and so is redundant; it is included here for pedagogical purposes, but should not appear in a final version of the class.) The second line involves *capacity*, that is to say the array representation: it is an **implementation invariant**.

"Implementation invariants", page 376.

You might take a minute to compare *ARRAYED_STACK*, as sketched here, with *STACK2* of an earlier discussion, and see how dramatically inheritance simplifies the class. This comparison will be pursued in the discussion of the methodology of inheritance, which will also address some of the criticisms occasionally heard against marriage-of-convenience inheritance and, more generally, against what is sometimes called *implementation inheritance*.

The methodological discussion is "It feels so good, but is it wrong?", page 844. STACK2 appeared on page 349.

Structure inheritance

Multiple inheritance is indispensable when you want to state explicitly that a certain class possesses some properties beyond the basic abstraction that it represents.

Consider for example a mechanism that makes object structures persistent (storable on long-term storage). You may have to request that the lead object in a storable structure be equipped with the corresponding store and retrieve operations: in addition to its other properties such an object is "storable". In the Kernel library, as we have seen, this property is captured by a class *STORABLE*, from which any other class can inherit. Clearly, such classes may have other parents as well, so this would not work without multiple inheritance. This form of inheritance, from a class that describes a general structural property — often with a name that ends with *-ABLE* — is similar to inheritance from classes *COMPARABLE* and *NUMERIC* seen earlier in this chapter. The discussion of inheritance methodology will define it as inheritance of the *structural* kind.

On STORABLE see "Deep storage: a first view of persistence", page 250.

For a more detailed discussion of this form of inheritance: "Structure inheritance", page 831.

Without multiple inheritance, there would be no way to specify that a certain abstraction must possess two structural properties — numeric and storable, comparable and hashable. Selecting one of them as *the* parent would be like having to choose between your father and your mother.

Facility inheritance

Here is another typical case. Many tools need "history" facilities, enabling their users to perform such operations as:

- Viewing the list of recent commands.

- Executing again a recent command.

- Executing a new command defined by editing a recent one and changing a few details.

- Undoing the effect of the last command not yet undone

Such a mechanism makes any interactive tool nicer to use. But it is a chore to write. As a result, only a few tools (such as certain "shells" under Unix and Windows) support it, often partially. Yet the general techniques are tool-independent. They can be encapsulated in a class, from which a session-control class for any tool can then inherit. (A solution based on the client relation may be possible, but is less attractive.) Once again, without multiple inheritance such an inheritance link would conflict with other possible parents.

A similar case is that of a class *TEST* encapsulating a number of mechanisms useful for testing a class: getting and storing user input, printing and storing output, comparing with expected values, recording all the results, comparing with earlier test runs (*regression testing*), managing the testing process. Although a client-based solution may be preferable in some cases, it is convenient to have the possibility, for testing a class *X*, of defining a class *X_TEST* that inherits from *X* and from *TEST*.

In later chapters we will encounter other cases of such *facility* inheritance, whereby a class *F* encapsulates a set of related facilities, such as constants or routines from a mathematical library, which any class can then obtain by inheriting from *F*.

See chapter 24.   Although the use of inheritance in such cases is sometimes viewed with suspicion, it is in fact a perfectly legitimate application of the concept. It does differ in one respect from the other examples of multiple inheritance reviewed in this chapter: in the cases just reviewed, we could achieve our goals, albeit less conveniently, with a client rather than inheritance link.

Buttonholes

Here is a case in which, as in earlier ones, multiple inheritance is indispensable. It is similar in spirit to "company planes", "sleeping cars" and other examples of the combination-of-abstractions type encountered earlier. Rather than using concepts from some external model, however, this one deals with genuine software abstractions. The reason why it has been moved to the end of this review of multiple inheritance examples is that understanding it requires a little background preparation.

See chapter 36.   Like other graphical applications, many tools of the development environment presented in the last chapter offer "buttons", on which you can click to trigger certain operations. They also use a "pick and throw" mechanism (a variation on traditional "drag-and-drop"), through which you can select a visual object, causing the mouse cursor to change into a "pebble" that indicates the type of the object, and bring it to a **hole** of a matching shape. You can "throw" the pebble into the hole by right-clicking; this causes some operation to occur. For example, a Class Tool, which you use to explore the properties of a class in the development environment, has a "class hole" into which you can drag-and-drop a class pebble; this causes the tool to retarget itself to the selected class.

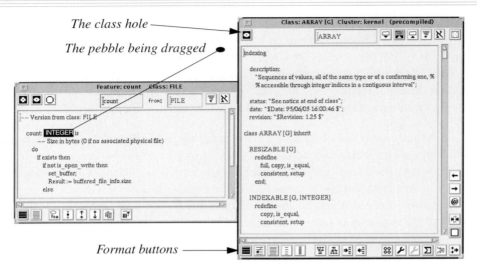

Pick-and-throw

In the figure, a user has picked somewhere — in a Feature Tool — the class *INTEGER*, by right-clicking on its name. He is moving it towards the class hole of the Class Tool currently targeted to (showing the text of) class *ARRAY*. Note the row of format buttons at the bottom; clicking on one of them will show other information for *ARRAY*, for example if you left-click on ≡ you will get the short form. The pick-and-throw (unless canceled by a left-click) will end when the user right-clicks on the class hole, whose shape, representing Class, matches that of the pebble. This will retarget the Class Tool on the right to the selected class — *INTEGER*.

In some cases it may be convenient to let a hole act as button too, so that you can not only throw an object into it but also, independently of any pick-and-throw, left-click on it to produce a certain effect. For example the class hole, in which the small dot suggests the presence of a current target (first *ARRAY*, then *INTEGER*) can serve as a button; left-clicking on it retargets the tool to its current target, which is useful if the display was overwritten. Such holes which double up as buttons are called buttonholes.

As you will have guessed, class *BUTTONHOLE* multiply inherits from *BUTTON* and from *HOLE*. The new class simply combines the features and properties of its parents, since a buttonhole reacts like a button to the operations on buttons, and like a hole to the operations on holes.

An assessment

The examples accumulated so far are representative of the power and usefulness of multiple inheritance. Experience in building general-purpose libraries confirms that multiple inheritance is needed throughout.

See [M 1994a] *on library design.*

Whenever you must combine two abstractions, not having multiple inheritance would mean that you choose one of them as the official parent, and duplicate all the other's features by copy-and-paste — making the new class, as it were, an illegitimate child. On the illegitimate side, you lose polymorphism, the Open-Closed principle, and all the reusability benefits of inheritance. This is not acceptable.

15.2 FEATURE RENAMING

Multiple inheritance raises an interesting technical problem: name clashes. The solution, feature renaming, turns out to have applications far beyond that original problem, and leads to a better understanding of the nature of classes.

Name clashes

A class has access to all the features of its parents. It can use them without having to indicate where they come from: past the **inherit** clause in **class** C **inherit** A ..., a feature f of C is known just as f. The same is true of clients of C: for x of type C in some other class, a call to the feature is written just $x \bullet f$, without any reference to the A origin of f. If the metaphors were not so incompatible, we could view inheritance as a form of adoption: C adopts all the features of A.

It adopts them under their assigned names: the set of feature names of a class includes all of its parents' feature name sets.

What then if two or more parents have used the same name for different features? We have relied on the rule of no intra-class overloading: within a class, a feature name denotes only one feature. This could now be violated because of the parents. Consider

> **class** *SANTA_BARBARA* **inherit**
>   *LONDON*
>   *NEW_YORK*
> **feature**
>   . . .
> **end**-- class *SANTA_BARBARA*

What can we do if both *LONDON* and *NEW_YORK* had a feature named the same, say *foo* (for some reason a favorite name in programming examples)?

> Do not attach too much importance to the names in this example, by the way. No useful abstraction is assumed behind the class names, especially none that would justify the inheritance structure. The names simply make the example easier to follow and remember than if we called our classes A, B and C.

Under no circumstances should we renounce the no-overloading rule, essential to keep classes simple and easy to understand. Within a class, a name should mean just one thing. So class *SANTA_BARBARA* as shown is invalid and the compiler must reject it.

This rule seems rather harsh. In an approach emphasizing construction-box-like combination of modules from several sources, we may expect attempts to combine separately developed classes that contain identically named features.

> As an example, we saw earlier a version of class *TREE* that inherits from *CELL* and *LIST*, both of which have a feature called *item*; for a cell, it returns the value stored in the cell, and for a list it returns the value at the current cursor position. Both also have a feature called *put*. These choices of name are all reasonable, and we would not like to have to change the original classes just because someone got a clever idea for defining trees by combining them.

What can be done? You should not have to go back to the parents. You may not have access to the source text of *LONDON* and *NEW_YORK*; you may have access to it, but not be permitted to change it; you may be permitted but unwilling, as *LONDON* comes from an external supplier and you know there will be new releases, which would force you to do the work all over again; and most importantly you know about the Open-Closed principle, which says one should not disturb modules when reusing them for new extensions, and you are rightly wary of changing the interface of classes (*LONDON* and *NEW_YORK*) which may already have numerous clients that rely on the old names.

It is a mistake to blame the parents for a name clash occurring in inheritance: the problem is in the would-be heir. There too should the solution be.

The language solution to name clashes follows from these observations. A class that inherits different but identically named features from different parents is invalid, but will become valid by including one or more **rename** subclauses in the inheritance clause. A **rename** subclause gives a new local name to one or more inherited features. For example:

> **class** *SANTA_BARBARA* **inherit**
>
> > *LONDON*
> >
> > > **rename** *foo* **as** *fog* **end**
> >
> > *NEW_YORK*
>
> **feature**
>
> > ...
>
> **end** -- class *SANTA_BARBARA*

Both within *SANTA_BARBARA* and in its clients, the *foo* feature from *LONDON* will be referred to as *fog*, and the one from *NEW_YORK* as *foo*. Clients of *LONDON*, of course, will still know the feature as *foo*.

This is enough (assuming there is no other clash, and no other feature of *LONDON* or *NEW_YORK* is called *fog*) to remove the clash. Of course, we could have renamed the *NEW_YORK* feature instead; or we could have renamed both for symmetry:

> **class** *SANTA_BARBARA* **inherit**
>
> > *LONDON*
> >
> > > **rename** *foo* **as** *fog* **end**
> >
> > *NEW_YORK*
> >
> > > **rename** *foo* **as** *zoo* **end**
>
> **feature**
>
> > ...
>
> **end** -- class *SANTA_BARBARA*

The **rename** subclause follows the name of a parent and comes before the **redefine** subclause if any. It can of course rename several features, as in

> class *TREE* [*G*] **inherit**
>
> > *CELL* [*G*]
> >
> > > **rename** *item* **as** *node_item*, *put* **as** *put_right* **end**

which removes clashes between features of *CELL* and their namesakes in the other parent, *LIST*. The clause renames the *item* feature from *CELL* as *node_item*, since this feature denotes the item attached to the current node, and similarly renames *put* as *put_right*.

Effects of renaming

Let us make sure we fully understand the results of a renaming. Assume the last form of class *SANTA_BARBARA* (the one that renames both inherited versions of *foo*):

A name clash, removed

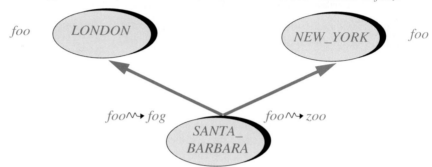

(Note the graphical symbol for renaming: ⤳.) Assume entities of the three types:

l: *LONDON*; *n*: *NEW_YORK*; *s*: *SANTA_BARBARA*

Then *l*.*foo* and *s*.*fog* are both valid; after a polymorphic assignment *l* := *s* they would have the same effect, since the feature names represent the same feature. Similarly *n*.*foo* and *s*.*zoo* are both valid, and after *n* := *s* they would have the same effect.

None of the following, however, is valid:

- *l*.*zoo*, *l*.*fog*, *n*.*zoo*, *n*.*fog* since neither *LONDON* nor *NEW_YORK* has a feature called *fog* or *zoo*.

- *s*.*foo* since as a result of the renaming *SANTA_BARBARA* has no feature called *foo*.

Artificial as the names are, this example also illustrates the nature of the name clash issue. Believe it or not, I have heard it presented as a "deep semantic problem". It is neither semantic nor deep; rather, a simple syntactical problem. Had one of the class authors been led by the local context to choose the name *fog* in the first class or *zoo* in the second, no clash would have occurred; yet in each case the change is just one letter. The name clash is, as it were, a case of bad luck; it does not reveal any intrinsic problem with the classes or their ability to be combined. If you think of multiple inheritance as marriage, this is not a dramatic case, discovered at the last minute, of a rare blood incompatibility; it is more like realizing that the spouses' mothers are both called Tatiana, making life a little more complicated for their grandchildren to come, but easy to solve through proper naming conventions.

Renaming and redeclaration

In the last chapter we studied another inheritance mechanism: redeclaration of an inherited feature. (Remember that redeclaration includes the redefinition of an already effective feature, and the effecting of a deferred one.) It is illuminating to compare the effect of renaming and redeclaring a feature:

- Redeclaration changes the feature, but keeps its name.

- Renaming changes the name but keeps the feature.

With redeclaration you can ensure that the *same* feature name refers to *different* actual features depending on the type of the object to which it is applied (that is to say, the dynamic type of the corresponding entity). This is a semantic mechanism.

Renaming is a syntactic mechanism, allowing you to refer to the *same* feature under *different* names in different classes.

In some cases you may want to do both:

class *SANTA_BARBARA* **inherit**
    LONDON
        rename
            foo **as** *fog*
        redefine
            fog
        end
     ...

Then assuming *l*: *LONDON*; *s*: *SANTA_BARBARA* as before, and the polymorphic assignment *l := s*, the calls *l.foo* and *s.fog* will both trigger the redefined version (whose declaration must appear in a **feature** clause of the class).

You will have noted that the **redefine** subclause uses the new name. This is normal since that name is the only one under which the feature is known in the class. Accordingly, the **rename** clause appears before all other inheritance subclauses (**redefine**, and others yet to be studied: **export**, **undefine**, **select**). Past the **rename** clause, the feature — like an immigrant given a new identity at Ellis Island by a customs officer who found the old name too hard to pronounce — has shed its ancestral name and will be known under its new one to class, clients and descendants alike.

Local name adaptation

The ability to rename an inherited feature is interesting even in the absence of a name clash. It allows the designer of a class to define the appropriate name for every feature, whether immediate (declared in the class itself) or inherited.

The name under which a class inherits a facility from an ancestor is not necessarily the most telling one for its clients. The original name may have been well adapted to the ancestor's clients, but the new class has its own context, its own abstraction, which may suggest its own naming conventions. To provide this abstraction it finds the ancestor's *features* useful, but not necessarily the feature names. Renaming, which enables us to distinguish features from feature names, provides the solution.

The construction of class *WINDOW* as an heir of *TREE* provides a good example. *TREE* describes the hierarchical structure, common to general trees and windows; but the tree names may not be desirable for the interface that *WINDOW* presents to its clients. Renaming provides the ability to put these names in tune with the local context:

> **class** *WINDOW* **inherit**
>
> > *TREE* [*WINDOW*]
> >
> > > **rename**
> > >
> > > > *child* **as** *subwindow*, *is_leaf* **as** *is_terminal*, *root* **as** *screen*,
> > > >
> > > > *arity* **as** *child_count*, …
> > >
> > > **end**
> >
> > *RECTANGLE*
>
> **feature**
>
> > … Specific window features …
>
> **end**

Similarly, *TREE* inheriting from *CELL* may rename *right* as *right_sibling* and so on. Through renaming, a class may offer its clients a consistent set of names for the services it offers, regardless of how these services were built from facilities provided by ancestors.

The game of the name

The use of renaming for local name adaptation highlights the importance of naming — feature naming, but also class naming — in object-oriented software construction. A class is formally a mapping from feature names to features; the feature names determine how it will be known to the rest of the world.

See "Standard names", page 882.

In a later chapter we will see a number of systematic rules for choosing feature names. Interestingly, they promote a set of across-the-board names — *count*, *put*, *item*, *remove*, … — to emphasize commonalities between abstractions over the inevitable differences. This style, which increases the likelihood of name clashes under multiple inheritance, decreases the need for "vanity" renaming of the kind illustrated with *WINDOW*. But whatever general naming conventions we follow, we must have the flexibility to adapt the names to the local needs of each class.

Using a parent's creation procedure

Let us see one more example of renaming, illustrating a typical scheme where the renamed feature is a creation procedure. Remember *ARRAYED_STACK*, obtained by inheritance from *STACK* and *ARRAY*; the creation procedure of *ARRAY* allocates an array with given bounds:

make (*minb*, *maxb*: *INTEGER*) **is**
            -- Allocate array with bounds *minb* and *maxb*
            -- (empty if *minb* > *maxb*)
      do ... **end**

To create a stack, we must allocate the array so that it will accommodate a given number of items. The implementation will rely on the creation procedure of *ARRAY*:

class *ARRAYED_STACK* [*G*] **inherit**
      STACK [*G*]
                  redefine *change_top* **end**
      ARRAY [*G*]
            rename
                  count **as** *capacity*, *put* **as** *array_put*, *make* **as** *array_make*
            end
creation
      make
feature -- Initialization
      make (*n*: *INTEGER*) **is**
                  -- Allocate stack for at most *n* elements.
            require
                  non_negative_size: *n* >= *0*
            do
                  array_make (*1*, *n*)
            ensure
                  capacity_set: *capacity* = *n*
                  empty: *count* = *0*
            end
      ... Other features (see "The marriage of convenience", page 530) ...

invariant
                  count >= *0*; *count* <= *capacity*
end -- class *ARRAYED_STACK*

Note that here our naming conventions — the use of *make* as the standard name for basic creation procedures — would cause a name clash, which, however, does not occur thanks to renaming.

We also need to remove ambiguities for *count* and *put*, both used for features of *ARRAY* as well as *STACK*. Query *count*, by convention, denotes the number of items in a structure; for *ARRAYED_STACK*, the relevant count is the number of elements pushed, that is to say, *count* from *STACK*; the other *count*, from *ARRAY*, becomes the stack's capacity — the maximum number of pushable items — and so is renamed *capacity*. Similarly, *put* for stacks is the push operation; we keep the array *put* (the operation that replaces the element at a certain array position) under the new name *array_put*. It is used, as you will remember, in the effecting of the other *put*, the stack pushing procedure.

15.3 FLATTENING THE STRUCTURE

Renaming is only one of the tools that the inheritance craftsman can use to build rich classes satisfying the needs of his clients. Another is redefinition. Later in this chapter, and in the next one, we will see a few more mechanisms: undefinition, join, **select**, descendant hiding. The power of these combined mechanisms makes inheritance sometimes obtrusive, and suggests the need for a special, inheritance-free version of a class: the flat form.

The flat form

In the view that we see emerging, inheritance is a *supplier* technique more than a client technique. It is primarily an internal tool for constructing classes effectively. True, the client side will need to know about the inheritance structure if it is to use polymorphism and dynamic binding (with *a1*: *A*; *b1*: *B* you need to know that *B* is a descendant of *A* if you are to use the assignment *a1* := *b1*); apart from that case, however, the inheritance structure that led to a particular class is none of the clients' business.

> Like a good car mechanic, we are entirely led by the needs of our customers, but how we go about taking care of them in the back of the garage is our responsibility.

As a consequence, it should be possible to present a class in a self-contained manner, independent from any knowledge of its ancestry. This is particularly important in the case of using inheritance to separate various components of a composite abstraction, such as the tree and rectangle parts of the window concept.

The flat form of a class serves that purpose. It is not something you will ever write; instead, you will rely on a tool of the software development environment to produce it for you, through a command-line script (**flat** *class_name*) or when you click on a certain icon.

The flat form of a class *C* is a valid class text which has exactly the same semantics as *C* when viewed from a client, except for polymorphic uses, but includes no inheritance clause. It is what the class would have looked like had its author not been able to use inheritance. To produce a flat form means:

- Removing the entire **inherit** clause if any.

- Keeping all the feature declarations or redeclarations of *C*.

- Adding declarations for all inherited features, copied from the declarations in the applicable parents and taking into account all the inheritance transformations that were specified in the **inheritance** clause: renaming, redefinition, undefinition, **select**, feature join.

- Adding to each inherited feature a comment line of the form **from** *ANCESTOR* indicating the name of the proper ancestor from which the current version is derived: the closest one that declared or redeclared the feature (and, in the case of a feature join, described later in this chapter, the winning side).

- Reconstructing the full preconditions and postconditions of inherited routines (according to the rules on assertion inheritance explained in the next chapter).

- Reconstructing the full invariant, by **and**ing all the parents' invariants, after applying the proper transformations if they use any renamed or selected feature.

The resulting class text shows all the features of the class at the same level, not making any difference (except for the **from** *ANCESTOR* comments) between immediate and inherited features. If present, the labels of feature clauses — as in **feature** -- Access — are retained; clauses with identical labels, whether from parents or the class itself, are merged. Within each feature clause the features appear alphabetically.

An "immediate" feature is one introduced in the class itself.

The illustration below shows the beginning of the flat form of the Base library class *LINKED_TREE*, produced in a Class Tool of ISE's development environment (and scrolled past the **indexing** clause). To obtain this result, you target the Class Tool to the class, and click on the Flat format button.

Displaying a flat form

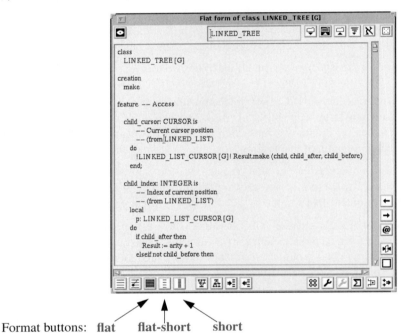

Format buttons: **flat**   **flat-short**   **short**

Uses of the flat form

The flat form is a precious tool for developers: it enables them to see the full set of properties of a class, all together in one place, ignoring how these features were derived in the inheritance games. A potential drawback of inheritance is that when reading a class text you may not immediately see what a feature name means, since the declaration can be in any ancestor. The flat form solves this problem by giving you the full picture.

The flat form may also be useful to deliver a stand-alone version of a class, not encumbered by the class history. That version will not be usable polymorphically.

The flat-short form

*See "Using asser-
tions for documen-
tation: the short
form of a class",
page 389.*

The flat form is a valid class text. So in its just mentioned role as documentation, it is of interest for the supplier side — for developers working on the class itself or a new descendant. The client side needs more abstraction.

In an earlier chapter we saw the tool that provides this abstraction: **short** (corresponding in the last figure to the second button to the right of **flat**.)

Combining the two notions yields the notion of flat-short form. Like the short form, the flat-short form of a class only includes public information, removing any non-exported feature and, for exported features, removing any implementation aspects, **do** clauses in particular. But like the flat form, it treats all features, immediate or inherited, as peers — whereas for a class with parents the non-flat short form only shows information about immediate features.

The flat-short form is the primary mechanism for documenting classes, in particular reusable library classes, for the benefits of their users (client authors). The book presenting the Base libraries [M 1994a] provides all the class specifications in that form.

15.4 REPEATED INHERITANCE

As noted at the beginning of this chapter, repeated inheritance arises whenever a class is a descendant of another in more than one way. This case causes some potential ambiguities, which we must resolve.

Repeated inheritance will only arise explicitly in advanced development; so if you are only surveying the key components of the method you may skip directly to the next chapter.

Sharing ancestors

As soon as multiple inheritance is allowed into a language, it becomes possible for a class D to inherit from two classes B and C, both of which are heirs, or more generally descendants, of the same class A. This situation is called repeated inheritance.

*Repeated
inheritance*

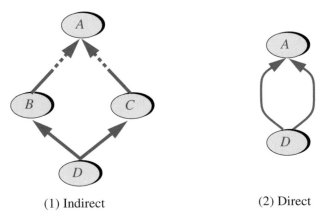

(1) Indirect   (2) Direct

If *B* and *C* are heirs of proper descendants of *A* (case 1 in the figure), the repeated inheritance is said to be indirect. If *A*, *B* and *C* are all the same class (case 2), the repeated inheritance is direct; this is achieved by writing

class *D* **inherit**
    A
    A
    ...
feature
    ...
end

Intercontinental drivers

The following system modeling example will enable us to see under what circumstances repeated inheritance may occur and to study the problem that it raises. Assume a class *DRIVER* with attributes such as

age: *INTEGER*
address: *STRING*
violation_count: *INTEGER*   -- The number of recorded traffic violations

and routines such as

pass_birthday **is do** *age := age + 1* **end**
pay_fee **is**
                -- Pay the yearly license fee.
      do ... **end**

An heir of *DRIVER*, taking into account the specific characteristics of US tax rules, may be *US_DRIVER*. Another may be *FRENCH_DRIVER* (with reference to places where cars are driven, not citizenship).

Now we may want to consider people who drive in both France and the US, perhaps because they reside in each country for some part of the year. A simple way to express this situation is to use multiple inheritance: class *FRENCH_US_DRIVER* will be declared as heir to both *US_DRIVER* and *FRENCH_DRIVER*. As shown by the figure at the top of the facing page, this causes repeated inheritance.

> To make sure that the example is a proper use of inheritance we assume that *US_DRIVER* and *FRENCH_DRIVER* are not just distinguished by the value of some attribute representing the country of driving, but are indeed distinct abstraction variants, each with its specific features. Chapter 24 discusses in depth the methodology of using inheritance.

Sharing and replication

The first and principal problem of repeated inheritance appears clearly in the intercontinental driver example:

> *What is the meaning in the repeated descendant (FRENCH_US_DRIVER in the example) of a feature inherited from the repeated ancestor (DRIVER)?*

Kinds of driver

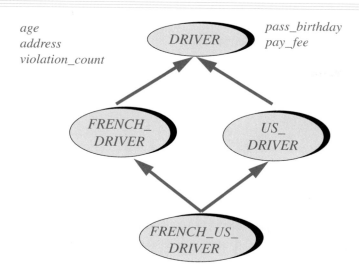

Consider a feature such as *age*. It is inherited from *DRIVER* by both *US_DRIVER* and *FRENCH_DRIVER*; so at first sight the name clash rule seems to require renaming. But this would be too stringent: there is no real conflict since *age* from *US_DRIVER* and *age* from *FRENCH_DRIVER* are not really different features: they are one feature, from *DRIVER*. Unless you are trying to hide something from someone, you have the same age wherever you happen to be driving. The same applies to procedure *pass_birthday*.

If you read carefully the rule about name clashes, you will have noted that it does not preclude such cases. It stated:

Page 536.

> *A class that inherits different but identically named features from different parents is invalid.*

Here the versions of *age* and *pass_birthday* that *FRENCH_US_DRIVER* inherits from its two parents are not "*different*" features, but a single feature in each case. So there is no real name clash. (An ambiguity could still exist if one of the features was redeclared in an intermediate ancestor; we will see shortly how to resolve it. For the moment we assume that nothing is redeclared.)

In such cases, when a feature coming from a repeated ancestor is inherited under the same name from two or more parents, the clear rule is that it should give a single feature in the repeated descendant. This case will be called **sharing**.

Is sharing always appropriate? No. Consider *address*, *pay_fee*, *violation_count*: our dual drivers will most likely declare two different addresses to the respective Departments of Motor Vehicles; paying the yearly fee is a separate process for each country; and traffic violations are distinct. For each of these features inherited from *DRIVER*, class *FRENCH_US_DRIVER* needs not one but two different features. This case will be called **replication**.

What the example — and many others — also shows is that we could not get what we need with a policy that would either share all features of a repeated ancestor or replicate all of them. This is too coarse a level of granularity. We need the ability to tune the policy *separately for each repeatedly inherited feature*.

We have seen how to obtain sharing: just do nothing — inherit the original version from both parents under the same name. How do we obtain replication? By doing the reverse: inheriting it under two different names.

This idea is consistent with the general rule, simple and clear, that we apply to features and their names: within a class, a feature name denotes only one feature; two separate names denote two separate features. So to replicate a repeatedly inherited feature we simply make sure that some renaming occurs along the way.

> ### Repeated Inheritance rule
>
> In a repeated descendant, versions of a repeatedly inherited feature inherited under the same name represent a single feature. Versions inherited under different names represent separate features, each replicated from the original in the common ancestor.

This rule applies to attributes as well as routines. It gives us a powerful replication mechanism: from one feature of a class, it is possible in a descendant to get two or more features. For an attribute, this means an extra field in all the instances; for a routine, it means a new routine, initially with the same algorithm.

Except in special cases involving redeclaration, the replication can be conceptual only: no code actually gets duplicated, but the repeated descendant has access to two features.

The rule gives us the desired flexibility for combining classes. For example the class *FRENCH_US_DRIVER* may look like this:

```
class FRENCH_US_DRIVER inherit
    FRENCH_DRIVER
        rename
            address as french_address,
            violation_count as french_violation_count,
            pay_fee as pay_french_fee
        end
    US_DRIVER
        rename
            address as us_address,
            violation_count as us_violation_count,
            pay_fee as pay_us_fee
        end
feature
    ...
end -- class FRENCH_US_DRIVER
```

Sharing and
replication

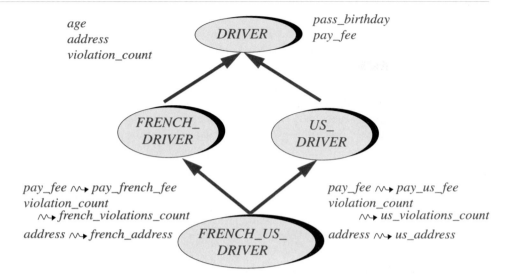

The renaming occurs here at the last stage — in the repeated descendant — but some or all of it could also have been done by intermediate ancestors *FRENCH_DRIVER* and *US_DRIVER*; all that counts is whether in the end a feature is repeatedly inherited under one name or more.

The features *age* and *pass_birthday*, which have not been renamed along any of the inheritance paths, will remained shared, as desired.

A replicated attribute such as *address* will, as noted, yield a new field in each of the instances of the repeated descendant. So assuming there are no other features than the ones listed, here is how instances of the classes will look:

Attribute
replication

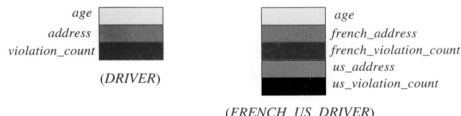

(*DRIVER*)

(*FRENCH_US_DRIVER*)

(Instances of *FRENCH_DRIVER* and *US_DRIVER* have the same composition as those of *DRIVER* as shown.)

This is the conceptual picture, but with a good implementation it must be the concrete representation too. Particularly important is the ability not to replicate the fields for shared attributes such as *age* in *FRENCH_US_DRIVER*. A naïve implementation would replicate all fields anyway; some fields, such as the duplicate *age* field, would simply never be used. Such waste of space is not acceptable, since it would accumulate as we go down inheritance hierarchies, and lead to catastrophic space inefficiency. (As a general rule, one must be very careful with attributes, as every attribute field will be present at run time in each one of the potentially many instances of a class and its descendants.)

The compiling mechanism of the development environment described at the end of this book indeed makes sure that no attribute space is lost: conceptually shared attributes are shared physically too. This is one of the most difficult parts of implementing inheritance and the calling machinery of dynamic binding, especially under the additional requirement that repeated inheritance must not affect the performance achievements described in earlier chapters:

- Zero cost for genericity.

- Small, constant-bounded cost for dynamic binding (that cost must be the same whether or not a system includes repeated inheritance).

The implementation meets these goals, making repeated inheritance a technique that any system can use at no extra cost.

> Repeated inheritance in C++ follows a different pattern. The level of granularity for deciding to share or duplicate is the class. So if you need to duplicate one field from the repeated ancestor, you will need to duplicate all. For that reason, C++ users tend to stay away from this mechanism altogether. Java has eliminated the problem — by eliminating multiple inheritance.

Unobtrusive repeated inheritance

Cases of repeated inheritance similar to the "transcontinental drivers", with duplicated features as well as shared ones, do occur in practice, but not frequently. They are not for beginners; only after you have reached a good level of sophistication and practice in object technology should you encounter any need for them.

If you are writing a straightforward application and end up using repeated inheritance, you are probably making things more complicated than you need to.

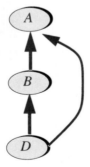

Redundant inheritance

The figure shows a typical beginner's (or absent-minded developer's) mistake: *D* is made an heir of *B*, and also needs facilities from *A*; but *B* itself inherits from *A*. Forgetting that inheritance is transitive, the developer wrote

> class *D*… **inherit**
>
> > *B*
> >
> > *A*
> >
> > …

This case causes repeated inheritance, but what it really shows is *redundant* inheritance. One of the pleasant consequences of the conventions discussed so far, and of the corresponding implementation, is that they will yield the expected behavior in such a case: in the absence of renaming, all features will be shared; no new features will be introduced, and there will be no performance overhead. Even if *B* renames some attributes, the only consequence will be some waste of space.

The only exception is the case in which *B* has redefined a feature of *A*, which causes an ambiguity in *D*. But then, as explained below, you will get an error message from the compiler, inviting you to select one of the two versions for use in *D*.

A case of redundant but harmless inheritance may occur when *A* is a class implementing general-purpose facilities like input or output (such as the class *STD_FILES* from the Kernel library), needed by *D* as well as *B*. It is enough for *D* to inherit from *B*: this makes *D* a descendant of *A*, giving it access to all the needed features. Inheriting redundantly will not, however, have any harmful consequences — in fact, it will have no consequences at all.

See "THE GLOBAL INHERITANCE STRUCTURE", 16.2, page 580.
Such involuntary and innocuous cases of repeated inheritance may also occur as a result of inheritance from universal classes *ANY* and *GENERAL*, studied in the next chapter.

The renaming rule

(This section introduces no new concept but gives a more precise formulation of the rules seen so far, and an explanatory example.)

We can now give a precise working of the rule prohibiting name clashes:

Definition: final name

The final name of a feature in a class is:

- For an immediate feature (that is to say, a feature declared in the class itself), the name under which it is declared.

- For an inherited feature that is not renamed, its final name (recursively) in the parent from which it is inherited.

- For a renamed feature, the name resulting from the renaming.

Single Name rule

Two different effective features of a class may not have the same final name.

A name clash occurs if two different features, both effective, still have the same name even after renaming subclauses have been taken into account. Such a name clash makes the class invalid, but is easy to correct by adding the proper renaming subclause.

The key word is *different* features. If a feature from a repeated ancestor is inherited from both parents under the same name, the sharing rule applies: only **one feature** is being inherited, so there is no name clash.

The prohibition of name clashes only applies to effective features. If one or more homonymous features are deferred, you can actually *merge* them since there is no incompatibility between implementations; the details will be seen shortly.

The rules are simple, intuitive and straightforward. To check our understanding one final time, let us build a simple example showing a legitimate case and an invalid case:

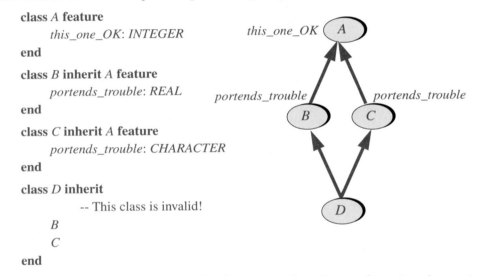

class *A* **feature**
      this_one_OK: *INTEGER*
end

class *B* **inherit** *A* **feature**
      portends_trouble: *REAL*
end

class *C* **inherit** *A* **feature**
      portends_trouble: *CHARACTER*
end

class *D* **inherit**
      -- This class is invalid!
    B
    C
end

That class *D* inherits *this_one_OK* twice — once from *B*, once from *C* — does **not** cause a name clash, since the feature will be shared; it is indeed the same feature, coming from *A*, in each case.

The two features called *portends_trouble*, however, deserve their name: they are different features, and so they cause a name clash, making class *D* invalid. (They have different types, but giving them the same type would not affect this discussion.)

It is easy to make class *D* valid through renaming; for example:

class *D* **inherit**
      -- This class is now quite valid.
    B
        rename *portends_trouble* **as** *does_not_portend_trouble_any_more* **end**
    C
end

Conflicting redefinitions

In the cases seen so far only names could change along the various inheritance paths. What if some intermediate ancestor, such as B or C on the last figure, redeclares a feature that is then repeatedly inherited? Under dynamic binding there may be an ambiguity in D.

Two simple mechanisms, undefinition and selection, will solve the issue. As usual you will be invited to participate in the development of these mechanisms and will see that once a problem is stated clearly the language solution follows immediately.

Assume that somewhere along the way a repeatedly inherited feature gets redefined:

Redefinition causing potential ambiguity

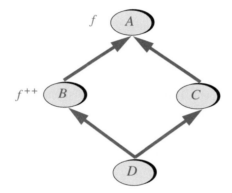

Class B redefines feature C (this is the conventional meaning of the $^{++}$ symbol, as you will recall). So now you have two variants of f available in D: the redefined version from B, and the version from C, which here is the original version from A. (We might assume that C also redefines f in its own way, but this would bring nothing to the discussion except more symmetry.) This is different from all the previous cases, in which there was only one version of the feature, possibly inherited under different names.

What are the consequences? The answer depends on whether D inherits the two versions of f under the same name or different names, that is to say whether the repeated inheritance rule implies sharing or replication. Let us review the two cases in turn.

Conflicts under sharing: undefinition and join

Assume first that the two versions are inherited under the same name. This is the sharing case: with just one feature name, there must be exactly one feature. Three possibilities:

S1 • If one of the two versions is deferred and the other effective, there is no difficulty: the effective version will serve to effect the other. Note that in the Single Name rule this case was explicitly permitted: the rule only prohibited name clashes between two effective features.

S2 • If both versions are effective, but each of them appears in a **redefine** subclause, there is no problem either: both inherited versions are merged into a new version, whose redefinition appears in the class.

S3 • But if the versions are both effective and not both redefined, we have a true name clash: class D will be rejected as violating the Single Name rule.

Often S3 will indeed reflect an error: you have created an ambiguity for a certain feature name, and you must resolve it. The usual resolution is to **rename** one of the two variants; then instead of sharing you get replication — two different features. This is the other main case, replication, studied next.

In some situations, however, you may want a more sophisticated resolution of the S3 conflict: letting one of the two variants, say the one from B, take over. Then the obvious solution is to transform this case into S1 by making one of the two variants deferred.

The rules on redefinition allow us to redefine an effective f into a deferred version; but they would force us to introduce an intermediate class, say C', an heir of C whose only role is to redefine f into a deferred version; then we would make D inherit from C' rather than C. This is heavy and inelegant. Instead, we need a simple language mechanism: **undefine**. It will yield a new subclause in the inheritance part:

class D **inherit**

   B

   C

       undefine f **end**

feature

   ...

end

If more than one subclause is present, **undefine** naturally comes after **rename** (since any undefinition should apply to the final name of a feature) but before **redefine** (since we should take care of any undefinition before we redefine anything).

A sign that a proposed language mechanism is desirable is, almost always, that it should solve several problems rather than just one. (Conversely, *bad* language mechanisms tend to cause as many problems, through their interactions with other language traits, as they purport to solve.) The undefinition mechanism satisfies this property: it gives us the ability to **join** features under multiple — not necessarily repeated — inheritance. Assume that we wish to combine two abstractions into one:

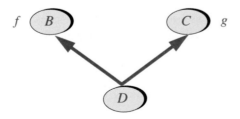

Two parents with features to be merged

We want D to treat the two features f and g as a single feature; this clearly requires that they have compatible signatures (number and types of arguments and result if any), and compatible semantics. Assuming that they have different names, and that we want to keep the f name, we can achieve the desired result by combining renaming with undefinition:

class D **inherit**
    B
    C
        rename
            g **as** f
        undefine
            f
        end
feature
    …
end

Here the victory of B is total: it imposes both the feature and the feature name. All other combinations are possible: we may get the feature from one of the parents and the name from the other; or we may rename both features to an entirely new name for D.

Another way to join features is more symmetric: replace both inherited versions by a new one. To achieve this, simply make sure that the features have the same final name, adding a **rename** subclause if necessary, and list them both in **redefine** subclauses, with a new declaration in the class. Then there is no illicit name clash (this is case S2 above), and both features are joined into the new version.

Note the versatility of the renaming mechanism (showing that it satisfies the just introduced criterion for good language traits): originally introduced as a technique for removing name clashes, it now enables us to *introduce* name clashes — name clashes of a desirable kind, resolved by undefining one of the inherited versions to let the other take over.

Conflicts under replication: selection

There remains to consider the case of conflicting redefinitions under replication, that is to say when the repeated descendant inherits the separately redefined features with different names, and they are both effective.

The need for selection

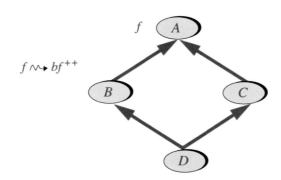

On the B branch in the figure, feature f is renamed bf and is also redefined. Favoring again simplicity over symmetry we assume no change in the C branch; renaming or redefining f in C would not affect the discussion. Also, note that the result would be the same if B redefined the feature without renaming it, the renaming then occurring at the D level. Let us assume this is not a case of join (which would arise if we redefined both features, under S2 above, or undefined one of them).

Because the features are inherited under different names bf and f, replication applies: D gets two separate features from the feature f of A. In contrast with previous cases of replication, these are not duplicates of the same feature, but different features.

Here, unlike in the sharing case, there is no name clash. But as the careful reader will have noted, a different problem arises (the last issue of repeated inheritance), due to dynamic binding. Assume that a polymorphic entity $a1$ of type A, the common ancestor, becomes attached at run time to an instance of D, the common descendant. What then should the call $a1.f$ do?

The rule of dynamic binding states that the version of f to apply is the one deduced from the type of the target object, here D. But now for the first time that rule is ambiguous: D has two versions — known locally as bf and f — of the original f of A.

The observation made in the case of name clashes, which led to the renaming mechanism, applies here too: we cannot, in an approach favoring clarity and reliability, let the compiler make the choice behind the scenes through some default rule. The author of the software must be in control.

This shows the need for a simple language mechanism to resolve the ambiguity:

```
class D inherit
        B

        C
            select f end
    feature
        ...
    end
```

to trigger C's version under dynamic binding for an entity of type A, and

```
class D inherit
        B
            select bf end
        C
    feature
        ...
    end
```

to select B's version instead. The **select** clause will naturally appear after **rename**, **undefine** and **redefine** if present (you select variants once everything has been named and defined). Here is the rule governing its usage:

The case in which both are redefined corresponds to S2, page 552.

> ## Select rule
>
> A class that inherits two or more different effective versions of a feature from a repeated ancestor, and does not redefine them both, must include exactly one of them in a **select** clause.

The **select** resolves the ambiguity once and for all: proper descendants of the class do not need to repeat it (and should not).

Selecting everything

Every redefinition conflict must be resolved through **select**. When combining two classes that cause several such conflicts, you may want one of the classes to win all or most of these conflicts. This happens in particular with inheritance of the "marriage of convenience" form, as illustrated by *ARRAYED_STACK* inheriting from *STACK* and *ARRAY*, if the parents have a common ancestor. (In the Base libraries, both classes cited are indeed distant descendants of a general *CONTAINER* class.) In such a case, since one of the parents — what has been called the noble parent, here *STACK* — provides the specification, you will probably want to resolve all conflicts, or most of them, in its favor.

The following important notational facility simplifies your task in such cases, by avoiding the need to list all conflicting features individually. At most one of the parent listings in the **inherit** clause may be of the form

> *SOME_PARENT*
>   **select all end**

The effect is simply, as suggested by the keyword **all**, to resolve in favor of *SOME_PARENT* all redefinition conflicts — more precisely all the conflicts that might remain after the application of other **select** subclauses. This last qualification means that you can still request some other parent's version for certain features.

Keeping the original version of a redefined feature

(This section describes a more specialized technique and may be skipped on first reading.)

"Using the original version in a redefinition", page 493.

In the introduction to inheritance we saw a simple construct allowing a redefined feature to call the original version: *Precursor*. The repeated inheritance mechanism, through its support for feature duplication, provides a more general (but also heavier) solution in those rare cases for which the basic mechanism does not suffice.

Consider again the earlier example: *BUTTON* inheriting from *WINDOW* and redefining *display* as

> *display* **is**
>   -- Display button on the screen.
>   **do**
>   *window_display*
>   *special_button_actions*
>   **end**

where *window_display* takes care of displaying the button as if it were a normal window, and *special_button_actions* adds button-specific elements such as displaying the button's border. Feature *window_display* is exactly the same as the *WINDOW* version of *display*.

We have seen how to write *window_display* simply as *Precursor*. (If there is any ambiguity, that is to say if two or more parents redefine their *display* routine into the new one, the selected parent will appear in double braces, as in {{*WINDOW*}} *Precursor*.) We can achieve the same goal, although less simply, through repeated inheritance:

> **indexing**
> > *WARNING*: "*This is a first attempt — this version is invalid!*"
>
> **class** *BUTTON* **inherit**
> > *WINDOW*
> > > **redefine** *display* **end**
> >
> > *WINDOW*
> > > **rename** *display* **as** *window_display* **end**
>
> **feature**
> > ...
>
> **end** -- class *BUTTON*

Because one of the branches renames *display*, the repeated inheritance rule indicates that *BUTTON* will have two versions of that feature, one redefined and keeping the original name, the other not redefined but having the name *window_display*.

As indicated, this is almost valid but not quite: we need a **select**. If (as will usually be the case) we want to select the redefined version, this will give:

> **indexing**
> > *note*: "*This the (valid!) repeated inheritance scheme for continuing to use %*
> > > *%the original version of a redefined feature*"
>
> **class** *BUTTON* **inherit**
> > *WINDOW*
> > > **redefine**
> > > > *display*
> > >
> > > **select**
> > > > *display* ←——————————— *The selection*
> > >
> > > **end**
> >
> > *WINDOW*
> > > **rename**
> > > > *display* **as** *window_display*
> > >
> > > **export**
> > > > {*NONE*} *window_display*
> > >
> > > **end**
>
> **feature**
> > ...
>
> **end** -- class *BUTTON*

If several features need this scheme, you can list them together (in other words, you do not need to inherit more than twice from the parent). Often you will want to resolve all conflicts in favor of the redefined versions; in that case, use **select all**.

> The **export** clause (studied only in the next chapter, although there is little more to it than shown here) changes the export status of an inherited feature: *WINDOW* probably exported the original *display*, now known as *window_display*, but *BUTTON* makes it secret. Although *window_display* is a full-fledged feature of the class, which needs it for its internal purposes, clients have no use for it. As discussed in earlier examples, exporting the original version of an inherited feature might make the class formally incorrect if that version does not satisfy the new class invariant.

> To apply hiding to all features inherited along a certain branch you can, here too, use the keyword **all**, as in **export** {*NONE*} **all**.

This pattern of exporting only the redefined version, making the original secret under a new name, is the most common. It is not universal; the heir class sometimes needs to export both versions (assuming the original does not violate the invariant), or to hide both.

How useful is this technique using repeated inheritance to keep the original version of a redefined feature? Usually you do not need it: the *Precursor* construct suffices. You should use repeated inheritance when you do not just require the old version for implementing the redefined one, but want to keep it, along with the redefined version, as one of the features of the new class.

Remember that if both are exported they must both make sense for the corresponding abstraction; in particular, they must preserve the invariant.

An advanced example

Here is an extensive example showing various aspects of repeated inheritance at work.

The problem, similar in spirit to the last example, comes from an interesting discussion in the basic book on C++ [Stroustrup 1991].

Consider a class *WINDOW* with its *display* procedure and two heirs, *WINDOW_WITH_BORDER* and *WINDOW_WITH_MENU* representing the abstractions suggested by their names. Each redefines *display* so that it will first perform the standard window display, and then display the border in the first case, and the menu cells in the second.

We may want to describe windows that have both a border and a menu; hence the use of repeated inheritance for class *WINDOW_WITH_BORDER_AND_MENU*.

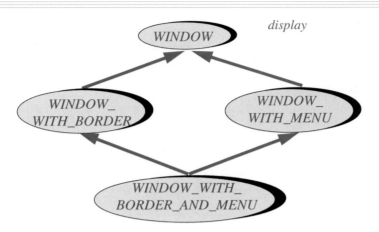

In class *WINDOW_WITH_BORDER_AND_MENU* we will again redefine *display*; here the redefined version should apply the standard window display, then display the border, then display the menu.

The original *WINDOW* class has the following form:

class *WINDOW* **feature**

    display **is**

             -- Display window (general algorithm)

        do

            …

        end

    … Other features …

end

For an heir such as *WINDOW_WITH_BORDER* we need to apply the original *display* and add border display. We do not need repeated inheritance here, but can simply rely on the *Precursor* construct:

class *WINDOW_WITH_BORDER* **inherit**

    WINDOW

        redefine *display* **end**

feature -- Output

    display **is**

             -- Draw window and its border.

        do

            Precursor

            draw_border

        end

feature {*NONE*} -- Implementation

    draw_border **is do** … **end**

    …

end

Note the addition of a procedure *draw_border* which displays the border. It has been hidden from clients (exported to *NONE*), since from the outside it makes no sense to display the border only. Class *WINDOW_WITH_MENU* is exactly symmetrical:

class *WINDOW_WITH_MENU* **inherit**
  WINDOW
    redefine *display* **end**
feature -- Output
  display **is**
      -- Draw window and its menu.
    do
      Precursor
      draw_menu
    end
feature {*NONE*} -- Implementation
  draw_menu **is do** … **end**
   …
end

It remains to write the common heir *WINDOW_WITH_BORDER_AND_MENU* of these two classes, a repeated descendant of *WINDOW*. Here is a first attempt:

indexing
  WARNING: "This is a first attempt — this version will not work properly!"
class *WINDOW_WITH_BORDER_AND_MENU* **inherit**
  WINDOW_WITH_BORDER
    redefine *display* **end**
  WINDOW_WITH_MENU
    redefine *display* **end**
feature
  display **is**
      -- Draw window and its border.
    do
      {{*WINDOW_WITH_BORDER*}} *Precursor*
      {{*WINDOW_WITH_MENU*}} *Precursor*
    end
   …
end

Note the need to name the parent in each use of *Precursor*: each parent has a *display* feature, each redefined into the same new *display* (otherwise we would have an invalid name clash, of course), so in each case we must say which one we want.

But, as Stroustrup notes (for a different solution), this is not correct: both parent versions call the original *WINDOW* version, which will end up being called twice, possibly producing garbled output. To get a correct form, we may among other solutions let the new class inherit directly from *WINDOW*, making it a triple descendant of that class:

indexing
    note: "*This is a correct version*"
class *WINDOW_WITH_BORDER_AND_MENU* **inherit**
    WINDOW_WITH_BORDER
        redefine
            display
        export {*NONE*}
            draw_border
        end
    WINDOW_WITH_MENU
        redefine
            display
        export {*NONE*}
            draw_menu
        end
    WINDOW
        redefine *display* **end**
feature
    display **is**
        -- Draw window and its border.
        do
            {{*WINDOW*}} *Precursor*
            draw_border
            draw_menu
        end
    ...
end

Note that for good measure we have made features *draw_border* and *draw_menu* hidden in the new class, as there does not seem to be any reason for clients of *WINDOW_WITH_BORDER_AND_MENU* to call them directly.

In spite of its lavish use of repeated inheritance, this class does not need any **select** since it redefines all inherited versions of *display* into one. This is the benefit of using *Precursor* rather than feature replication.

A good way to test your understanding of repeated inheritance is to rewrite this example without making use of the *Precursor* construct, that is to say by using repeated inheritance to obtain feature replication at the level of the two intermediate classes. You will, of course, need **select** subclauses.

Exercise E15.10, page 568.

In the version obtained above, there is sharing only, no replication. Let us extend Stroustrup's example by assuming that *WINDOW* also has a query *id* (perhaps an integer) used to identify each window. If each window is identified at most once, then *id* will be shared and we do not need to change anything. But if we want to keep track separately of instances of each window type, an instance of *WINDOW_WITH_BORDER_AND_MENU* will have three separate identifiers. The new class combines sharing with replication:

The only changes are the additions marked with an arrow.

indexing
    note: "*More complete version with separate identifiers*"
class *WINDOW_WITH_BORDER_AND_MENU* **inherit**
    WINDOW_WITH_BORDER
        rename
            id **as** *border_id*   ◄————
        redefine
            display
        export {*NONE*}
            draw_border
        end
    WINDOW_WITH_MENU
        rename
            id **as** *menu_id*   ◄————
        redefine
            display
        export {*NONE*}
            draw_menu
        end
    WINDOW
        rename
            id **as** *window_id*   ◄————
        redefine
            display
        select
            window_id
        end
feature
    …. The rest as before …
end

Note the need for **select**ing one of the versions of *id*.

Repeated inheritance and genericity

To finish this review of repeated inheritance, we must consider a specific case which could cause trouble if left unchecked. It arises for features involving formal generic parameters. Consider the following scheme (which could also arise with indirect repeated inheritance):

class *A* [*G*] **feature**

    f: *G*; ...

end

class *B* **inherit**

    A [*INTEGER*]

    A [*REAL*]

end

In class *B*, the repeated inheritance rule would imply that *f* is shared. But this leaves an ambiguity on its type: does it return an integer or a real? The same problem would occur if *f* were a routine with an argument of type *G*.

Such an ambiguity is not acceptable. Hence the rule:

Genericity in Repeated Inheritance rule

The type of any feature that is shared under the repeated inheritance rule, and the type of any of its arguments if it is a routine, may not be a generic parameter of the class from which the feature is repeatedly inherited.

You can remove the ambiguity by renaming the offending feature at the point of inheritance, to get duplication rather than renaming.

Rules on names

(This section only formalizes previously seen rules, and may be skipped on first reading.)

We have seen that name clashes are prohibited when they could cause ambiguity, but that some cases are valid. To finish off this presentation of multiple and repeated inheritance without leaving any ambiguity, it is useful to summarize the constraints on name clashes with a single rule:

Name clashes: definition and rule

In a class obtained through multiple inheritance, a *name clash* occurs when two features inherited from different parents have the same final name.

A name clash makes the class invalid *except* in any of the following cases:

N1 • The two features are inherited from a common ancestor, and none has been redeclared from the version in that ancestor.

N2 • Both features have compatible signatures, and at least one of them is inherited in deferred form.

N3 • Both features have compatible signatures, and they are both redefined in the class.

Case N1 is the sharing case under repeated inheritance.

In case N2, a feature is "inherited in deferred form" if it was deferred in the parent, or if it was effective but the class **undefines** it.

Cases N2 and N3 have been separated but can be merged into a single case, the **join** case. Considering *n* features (*n* >= 2) rather than just two, these cases arise when the class gets *n* features with the same name, and compatible signatures, from its various parents. The name clash is valid if we can let the inheritance join all of these features into one, without any ambiguity. This means that:

- You can have any number of deferred features among the lot since they will not cause any conflicting definitions. (As noted, a deferred feature is either one that was already deferred, or one that the class undefines.)

- If exactly one of the features is effective, it imposes its implementation to the others.

- If two or more features are effective, the class must provide a common redefinition for all of them. (An example was the joining in *WINDOW_WITH_BORDER_AND_ MENU* of the *display* procedures of the three parents.) The redefinition will also, of course, serve as effecting for any deferred feature participating in the clash.

Here then is the precise rule on the *Precursor* (…) construct. If a redefinition uses a precursor version, case N3 is the only one causing ambiguity as to whose version is intended. Then you must resolve the ambiguity by writing the precursor call as {{*PARENT*}} *Precursor* (…) where *PARENT* is the name of the desired class. In all other cases (simple inheritance, or multiple outside of N3) naming the parent is optional.

15.5 DISCUSSION

Let us probe further the consequences of some of the decisions made in this chapter.

Renaming

Any language that has multiple inheritance must deal with the problem of name clashes. Since we cannot and should not require developers to change the original classes, only two conventions are possible besides the solution described in this chapter:

- Require clients to remove any ambiguity.

- Choose a default interpretation.

With the first convention, a class *C* inheriting two features called *f*, one from *A* and one from *B*, would be accepted by the compiler, possibly with a warning message. Nothing bad would happen unless a client of *C* contained something like

x: *C*
… *x*.*f* …

which would be invalid. The client would have to qualify the reference to *f*, with a notation such as *x* . *f* | *A* or *x* . *f* | *B*, to specify one of the variants.

This solution, however, runs contrary to one of the principles emphasized in this chapter: that the inheritance structure leading to a class is a private affair between the class and its ancestors, not relevant for clients except through its influence on polymorphic uses. When I use service *f* from *C*, I should not need to know whether *C* introduced it itself or got it from *A* or *B*.

With the second convention, $x.f$ is valid; the underlying language mechanisms select one of the variants, based on some criterion such as the order in which *C* lists its parents; a notation may be available for requesting another variant explicitly.

This approach has been implemented in several Lisp-based languages supporting multiple inheritance. But it is dangerous to let some underlying system choose a default semantics. The solution is also incompatible with static typing: there is no reason why two features with the same name in different parents should be typewise compatible.

The renaming mechanism solves these problems; it brings other benefits, such as the ability to rename inherited features with names that are meaningful to clients.

O-O development and overloading

This chapter's discussion of the role of names brings the final perspective on the question of in-class name overloading, complementing the preliminary observations made in earlier chapters.

Recall that in languages such as Ada (83 and 95) you can give the same name to different features within the same syntactical unit, as in

>   **infix** "+" (*a, b*: *VECTOR*) **is** ...
>   **infix** "+" (*a, b*: *MATRIX*) **is** ...

which could both appear in the same Ada package. C++ and Java have made the same possibility available within a single class.

An earlier presentation called this facility **syntactic** overloading. It is a static mechanism: to disambiguate a given call, such as $x + y$, it suffices to look at the types of the arguments *x* and *y*, which are apparent from the program text.

"Syntactic overloading", page 93.

Object technology introduces a more powerful of overloading: **semantic** (or *dynamic*) overloading. If classes *VECTOR* and *MATRIX* both inherit a feature

>   **infix** "+" (*a*: *T*) **is** ...

from a common ancestor *NUMERIC*, and each redeclares it in the appropriate way, then a call $x + y$ will have a different effect depending on the dynamic type of *x*. (Infix features are just a notational convenience: with a non-infix feature the call $x + y$ would be written something like $x.plus$ (*y*).) Only at run time will the ambiguity be resolved. As we know, this property is key to the flexibility of O-O development.

Semantic overloading is the truly interesting mechanism. It allows us to use the same name, in different classes, for variants of what is essentially **the same operation** — such as addition from *NUMERIC*. The next chapter's rules on assertions will make it even more clear that a feature redeclaration must keep the same fundamental semantics.

Does this leave a role for syntactic overloading in object technology? It is hard to find any. One can understand why Ada 83, which does not have classes, should use syntactic overloading. But in an object-oriented language, to let developers choose the same name for **two different operations** is to create the possibility of confusion.

The problem is that the syntactic form of overloading clashes with the semantic form provided by polymorphism and dynamic binding. Consider a call $x.f(a)$. If it follows the possibly polymorphic assignments $x := y$ and $a := b$, the result is exactly the same, in the absence of renaming, as that of $y.f(b)$, even if y and b have other types than x and a. But with overloading this property is not true any more! f may be the overloaded name of two features, one for the type of a and one for the type of b. Which rule takes precedence, syntactic overloading or the O-O concept of dynamic binding? (Probably the former, but not until it has fooled a few developers, novice or not.) To make things worse, the base class of y's type may redefine either or both of the overloaded features. The combinations are endless; so are the sources of confusion and error.

What we are witnessing here is the unpleasant consequences of the interaction between two separate language traits. (A language addition, as noted earlier in this chapter on another topic, should whenever possible *solve* new problems beyond its original purpose — not create new problems through its interaction with other mechanisms.) A prudent language designer, having toyed with a possible new facility, and encountering such incompatibilities with more important properties of the design, quickly retreats.

What, against these risks, is the potential benefit of syntactic overloading? On careful examination it seems dubious to start with. A simple principle of readability holds that within the same module a reader should have absolutely no hesitation making the connection between a name and the meaning of that name; with in-class overloading, this property collapses.

A typical example — sometimes mentioned in favor of overloading — is that of features of a *STRING* class. To append another string or a single character you will, in the absence of overloading, use different feature names, as in $s1.add\_string(s2)$ and $s1.add\_character('A')$, or perhaps, using infix operators, $s := s1 ++ s2$ and $s := s1 + 'A'$. With overloading, you can use a single name for both operations. But is this really desirable? Objects of types *CHARACTER* and *STRING* have quite different properties; for example appending a character will always increase the length by 1; appending a string may leave the length unchanged (if the appended string was empty) or increase it by any amount. It seems not only reasonable but desirable to use different names — especially since the confusions cited above are definitely possible (assume that *CHARACTER* inherits from *STRING* and that another descendant redefines *add_string* but not *add_character*.)

*"Multiple creation
and overloading",
page 239.*

Finally, we have already encountered the observation that even if we wanted overloading we would in general need a different disambiguating criterion. Syntactic overloading distinguishes competing routines by looking at their signatures (numbers and types of arguments); but this is often not significant. The typical example was the creation procedures for points, or complex numbers: *make_cartesian* and *make_polar* both take two arguments of type *REAL* — to mean completely different things. You cannot use overloading here! The routines' signatures are irrelevant. To express that two features are different, we should use the obvious technique, the same that we apply in everyday life to express that two things or concepts are different: give them different names.

> For creation operations ("constructors") such as *make_cartesian* and *make_polar* the Java and C++ solution is particularly ironic: you **may not** give them different names but are forced to rely on overloading, using the class name. I have been unable to find a good solution to this problem other than adding an artificial third argument.

In summary: syntactic (in-class) overloading appears in an object-oriented context to create many problems for no visible benefit. (Some methodological advice to users of languages such as C++, Java and Ada 95: do not use this facility at all, except for cases such as multiple constructor functions in which the language leaves no other choice.) In a consistent and productive application of object technology we should stick to the rule — simple, easy to teach, easy to apply and easy to remember — that, within a class, every feature has a name and every feature name denotes one feature.

15.6 KEY CONCEPTS INTRODUCED IN THIS CHAPTER

- The construction-box approach to software construction favored by object technology requires the ability to combine several abstractions into one. This is achieved by multiple inheritance.

- In the simplest and most common cases of multiple inheritance, the two parents represent disjoint abstractions.

- Multiple inheritance is frequently needed, both for system modeling and for everyday software development, in particular the construction of reusable libraries.

- Name clashes under multiple inheritance should be removed through renaming.

- Renaming also serves to provide classes with locally adapted terminology for inherited features.

- Features should be distinguished from feature names. The same feature can be known under different names in different classes. A class defines a mapping from feature names to features.

- Repeated inheritance, an advanced technique, arises as a result of multiple inheritance when a class is a descendant of another through two or more paths.

- Under repeated inheritance, a feature from the common ancestor yields a single feature if it is inherited under a single name, separate features otherwise.

- Competing versions from a common ancestor must be disambiguated, for dynamic binding, through a **select** subclause.

- The replication mechanism of repeated inheritance should not replicate any feature involving generic parameters.

- In an object-oriented framework, the semantic form of overloading provided by dynamic binding is more useful than syntactic overloading.

15.7 BIBLIOGRAPHICAL NOTES

The renaming mechanism and the repeated inheritance rules originated with the notation of this book. The undefinition mechanism is an invention of Michael Schweitzer, and the selection mechanism an invention of John Potter, both in unpublished correspondence.

Exercise E15.8, page 568.

The walking menu example comes from [M 1988c].

EXERCISES

E15.1 Windows as trees

Class *WINDOW* inherits from *TREE* [*WINDOW*]. Explain the generic parameter. Show that it yields an interesting clause in the class invariant.

E15.2 Is a window a string?

A window has an associated text, described by an attribute *text* of type *STRING*. Rather than having this attribute, should *WINDOW* be declared as an heir to *STRING*?

E15.3 Doing windows fully

Complete the design of the *WINDOW* class, showing exactly what is needed from the underlying terminal handling mechanism.

E15.4 Figure iterators

See also "Iterators", page 848.

The presentation of class *COMPOSITE_FIGURE* mentioned the possibility of using iterator classes for all operations that perform a certain operation on a composite figure. Develop the corresponding iterator classes. (**Hint**: [M 1994a] presents library iterator classes which provide the basic pattern.)

E15.5 Linked stacks

Write the class *LINKED_STACK* which describes a linked list implementation of stacks, as an heir to both *STACK* and *LINKED_LIST*.

E15.6 Circular lists and chains

Explain why the *LIST* class may not be used for circular lists. (**Hint**: a look at the assertions, benefiting from the discussion at the beginning of the next chapter, may help.). Define a class *CHAIN* that can be used as parent both to *LIST* and to a new class *CIRCULAR* describing circular lists. Update *LIST* and if necessary its descendants accordingly. Complete the class structure to provide for various implementations of circular lists.

E15.7 Trees

One way to look at a tree is to see it as a recursive structure: a list of trees. Instead of the technique described in this chapter, where *TREE* is defined as heir to both *LINKED_LIST* and *LINKABLE*, it seems possible to define

> **class** *TREE* [*G*] **inherit**
>   *LIST* [*TREE* [*G*]]
> **feature** … **end**

Can you expand this definition into a usable class? Compare it with the method used in the discussion of this chapter.

E15.8 Walking menus

Window systems offer a notion of menu, which we can cover through a class *MENU*, with a query giving the list of entries and commands to display the menu, move to the next entry etc. Since menus are made of entries we also need a class *MENU_ENTRY* with queries such as *parent_menu* and *operation* (the operation to execute when a user selects the entry), and commands such as *execute* (which executes *operation*).

Many systems offer cascading menus, also called "walking menus", where selecting an entry causes the display of a submenu. The figure illustrates a walking menu under Sun's Open Windows manager, where selecting the entry **Programs** brings up a submenu:

Walking menus

(*The last entry of the submenu,* **Demos**, *denotes in turn a submenu.*)

Show how to define the class *SUBMENU*. (**Hint**: a submenu is a menu and a menu entry, whose *operation* must display the submenu.)

Could this notion be described elegantly in a language with no multiple inheritance?

E15.9 The flat precursor

What should the flat form of a class show for an instruction using the *Precursor* construct?

E15.10 Repeated inheritance for replication

Write the *WINDOW_WITH_BORDER_AND_MENU* class without recourse to the *Precursor* construct, using replication under repeated inheritance to gain access to the parent version of a redefined feature. Make sure to use the proper **select** subclauses and to give each feature its proper export status.

16

Inheritance techniques

*F*rom the last two chapters we have learned to appreciate inheritance as a key ingredient in the object-oriented approach to reusability and extendibility. To complete its study we must explore a few more facilities — something of a mixed bag, but all showing striking consequences of the beauty of the basic ideas:

- How the inheritance mechanism relates to assertions and Design by Contract.
- The global inheritance structure, where all classes fit.
- Frozen features: when the Open-Closed principle does not apply.
- Constrained genericity: how to put requirements on generic parameters.
- Assignment attempt: how to force a type — safely.
- When and how to change type properties in a redeclaration.
- The mechanism of anchored declaration, avoiding redeclaration avalanche.
- The tumultuous relationship between inheritance and information hiding.

Two later chapters will pursue inheritance-related topics: the review of *typing* issues in chapter 17, and a detailed methodological discussion of *how to use inheritance* (and how not to misuse it) in chapter 24.

Most of the following sections proceed in the same way: examining a consequence of the inheritance ideas of the last two chapters; discovering that it raises a challenge or an apparent dilemma; analyzing the problem in more depth; and deducing the solution. The key step is usually the next-to-last one: by taking the time to pose the problem carefully, we will often be led directly to the answer.

16.1 INHERITANCE AND ASSERTIONS

Because of its very power, inheritance could be dangerous. Were it not for the assertion mechanism, class developers could use redeclaration and dynamic binding to change the semantics of operations treacherously, without much possibility of client control. But assertions will do more: they will give us deeper insights into the nature of inheritance. It is in fact not an exaggeration to state that only through the principles of Design by Contract can one finally understand what inheritance is really about.

The basic rules governing the rapport between inheritance and assertions have already been sketched: in a descendant class, all ancestors' assertions (routine preconditions and postconditions, class invariants) still apply. This section gives the rules more precisely and uses the results obtained to take a new look at inheritance, viewed as subcontracting.

Invariants

We already encountered the rule for class invariants:

Parents' Invariant rule

The invariants of all the parents of a class apply to the class itself.

The parents' invariants are added to the class's own, "addition" being here a logical **and then**. (If no invariant is given in a class, it is considered to have *True* as invariant.) By induction the invariants of all ancestors, direct or indirect, apply.

As a consequence, you should not repeat the parents' invariant clauses in the invariant of a class (although such redundancy would be semantically harmless since *a* **and then** *a* is the same thing as *a*).

The flat and flat-short forms of the class will show the complete reconstructed invariant, all ancestors' clauses concatenated.

See "FLATTENING THE STRUCTURE", 15.3, page 541.

Preconditions and postconditions in the presence of dynamic binding

The case of routine preconditions and postconditions is slightly more delicate. The general idea, as noted, is that any redeclaration must satisfy the assertions on the original routine. This is particularly important if that routine was deferred: without such a constraint on possible effectings, attaching a precondition and a postcondition to a deferred routine would be useless or, worse, misleading. But the need is just as bad with redefinitions of effective routines.

The exact rule will follow directly from a careful analysis of the consequences of redeclaration, polymorphism and dynamic binding. Let us construct a typical case and deduce the rule from that analysis.

Consider a class and one of its routines with a precondition and a postcondition:

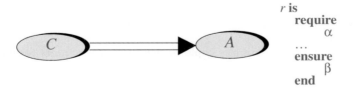

The routine, the client and the contract

The figure also shows a client *C* of *A*. The typical way for *C* to be a client is to include, in one of its routines, a declaration and call of the form

$a1: A$

...

$a1.r$

For simplicity, we ignore any arguments that r may require, and we assume that r is a procedure, although the discussion applies to a function just as well.

Of course the call will only be correct if it satisfies the precondition. One way for C to make sure that it observes its part of the contract is to protect the call by a precondition test, writing it (instead of just $a1.r$) as

if $a1.\alpha$ **then**
    $a1.r$
        check $a1.\beta$ **end**   -- i.e. the postcondition holds
    ... Instructions that may assume $a1.\beta$ ...
end

(As noted in the discussion of assertions, this is not required: it suffices to guarantee, with or without an **if** instruction, that α holds before the call. We will assume the **if** form for simplicity, and ignore any **else** clause.)

Having guaranteed the precondition, the client C is entitled to the postcondition on return: after the call, it may expect that $a1.\beta$ will hold.

All this is the basics of Design by Contract: the client *must* ensure the precondition on calling the routine and, as a recompense, *may* count on the postcondition being satisfied when the routine exits.

What happens when inheritance enters the picture?

The routine, the client, the contract and the descendant

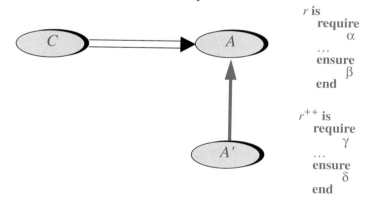

Assume that a new class A' inherits from A and redeclares r. How, if at all, can it change the precondition α into a new one γ and the postcondition β into a new one δ?

To decide the answer, consider the plight of the client. In the call $a1.r$ the target $a1$ may now, out of polymorphism, be of type A' rather than just A. But C does not know about this! The only declaration for $a1$ may still be the original one:

$a1: A$

which names *A*, not *A'*. In fact *C* may well use *A'* without its author ever knowing about the existence of such a class; the call to *r* may for example be in a routine of *C* of the form

> *some_routine_of_C* (*a1*: *A*) **is**
>> **do**
>>> …; *a1*.*r*; …
>> **end**

Then a call to *some_routine_of_C* from another class may use an actual argument of type *A'*, even though the text of *C* contains no mention of class *A'*. Dynamic binding means that the call to *r* will in that case use the redefined *A'* version.

So we can have a situation where *C* is only a client of *A* but in fact will at run time use the *A'* version of some features. (We could say that *C* is a "dynamic client" of *A'* even though its text does not show it.)

What does this mean for *C*? The answer, unless we do something, is: trouble. *C* can be an honest client, observing its part of the deal, and still be cheated on the result. In

> **if** *a1*.α **then** *a1*.*r* **end**

if *a1* is polymorphically attached to an object of type *A'*, the instruction calls a routine that expects γ and guarantees δ, whereas the client has been told to satisfy α and expect β. So we have a potential discrepancy between the client's and supplier's views of the contract.

How to cheat clients

To understand how to satisfy the clients' expectations, we have to play devil's advocate and imagine for a second how we could fool them. It is all for a good cause, of course (as with a crime unit that tries to emulate criminals' thinking the better to fight it, or a computer security expert who studies the techniques of computer intruders).

If we, the supplier, wanted to cheat our poor, honest *C* client, who guarantees α and expects β, how would we proceed? There are actually two ways to evil:

- We could *require more* than the original precondition α. With a stronger precondition, we allow ourselves to exclude (that is to say, not to guarantee any specific result) for cases that, according to the original specification, were perfectly acceptable.

  > Remember the point emphasized repeatedly in the discussion of Design by Contract: making a precondition stronger facilitates the task of the supplier ("the client is more often wrong"), as illustrated by the extreme case of precondition **false** ("the client is always wrong").

- We could *ensure less* than the original postcondition β. With a weaker postcondition, we allow ourselves to produce less than what the original specification promised.

As we saw, an assertion is said to be stronger than another if it logically implies it, and is different; for example, *x* >= 5 is stronger than *x* >= 0. If *A* is stronger than *B*, *B* is said to be weaker than *A*.

How to be honest

From understanding how to cheat we deduce how to be honest. When redeclaring a routine, we may keep the original assertions, but we may also:

- Replace the precondition by a *weaker* one.

- Replace the postcondition by a *stronger* one.

The first case means being more generous than the original — accepting more cases. This can cause no harm to a client that satisfies the original precondition before the call. The second case means producing more than what was promised; this can cause no harm to a client call that relies on the original postcondition being satisfied after the call.

Hence the basic rule:

Assertion Redeclaration rule (1)

A routine redeclaration may only replace the original precondition by one equal or weaker, and the original postcondition by one equal or stronger.

The rule expresses that the new version must accept all calls that were acceptable to the original, and must guarantee at least as much as was guaranteed by the original. It may — but does not have to — accept more cases, or provide stronger guarantees.

As its name indicates, this rule applies to both forms of redeclaration: redefinitions and effectings. The second case is particularly important, since it allows you to take seriously the assertions that may be attached to a deferred feature; these assertions will be binding on all effective versions in descendants.

For a more rigorous definition see "A mathematical note", page 580

The assertions of a routine, deferred or effective, specify the essential semantics of the routine, applicable not only to the routine itself but to any redeclaration in descendants. More precisely, they specify a **range of acceptable behaviors** for the routine and its eventual redeclarations. A redeclaration may specialize this range, but not violate it.

A consequence for the class author is the need to be careful, when writing the assertions of an effective routine, not to *overspecify*. The assertions must characterize the intent of the routine — its abstract semantics —, not the properties of the original implementation. If you overspecify, you may be closing off the possibility for a future descendant to provide a different implementation.

An example

Assume I write a class *MATRIX* implementing linear algebra operations. Among the features I offer to my clients is a matrix inversion routine. It is actually a combination of a command and two queries: procedure *invert* inverts the matrix, and sets attribute *inverse* to the value of the inverse matrix, as well as a boolean attribute *inverse_valid*. The value of *inverse* is meaningful if and only if *inverse_valid* is true; otherwise the inversion has failed because the matrix was singular. For this discussion we can ignore the singularity case.

Of course I can only compute an approximation of the inverse of a matrix. I am prepared to guarantee a certain precision of the result, but since I am not very good at numerical analysis, I shall only accept requests for a precision not better than 10^{-6}. The resulting routine will look like this:

```
invert (epsilon: REAL) is
            -- Inverse of current matrix, with precision epsilon
      require
            epsilon >= 10 ^ (–6)
      do
            "Computation of inverse"
      ensure
            ((Current * inverse) |–| One) <= epsilon
      end
```

The postcondition assumes that the class has a function **infix** "|–|" such that $m1$ |–| $m2$ is $|m1 - m2|$, the norm of the matrix difference of $m1$ and $m2$, and a function **infix** "*" which yields the product of two matrices; One is assumed to denote the identity matrix.

I am not too proud of myself, so for the summer I hire a bright young programmer-numerician who rewrites my *invert* routine using a much better algorithm, which approximates the result more closely and accepts a smaller *epsilon*:

```
      require
            epsilon >= 10 ^ (–20)
      ...
      ensure
            ((Current * inverse) |–| One) <= (epsilon / 2)
```

Warning: syntactically not valid as a redefinition. See next.

The author of this new version is far too clever to rewrite a full *MATRIX* class; only a few routines need adaptation. They will be included in a descendant of *MATRIX*, say *NEW_MATRIX*.

If the new assertions are in a redefinition, they must use a different syntax than shown above. The rule will be given shortly.

The change of assertions satisfies the Assertion Redeclaration rule: the new precondition *epsilon* >= $10 ^ (–20)$ is weaker than (that is to say, implied by) the original *epsilon* >= $10 ^ (–6)$; and the new postcondition is stronger than the original.

This is how it should be. A client of the original *MATRIX* may be requesting a matrix inversion but, through dynamic binding, actually calling the *NEW_MATRIX* variant. The client could contain a routine

```
some_client_routine (m1: MATRIX; precision: REAL) is
      do
            ... ; m1.invert (precision); ...
                  -- May use either the MATRIX or the NEW_MATRIX version
      end
```

to which one of its own clients passes a first argument of type *NEW_MATRIX*.

NEW_MATRIX must be able to accept and handle correctly any call that *MATRIX* would accept. If we made the precondition of the new *invert* stronger than the original (as in *epsilon* >= ^ (−5)), calls which are correct for *MATRIX* would now be incorrect; if we made the postcondition weaker, the result returned would not be as good as guaranteed by *MATRIX*. By using a weaker precondition and a stronger postcondition we correctly treat all calls from clients of *MATRIX*, while offering a better deal to our own clients.

Cutting out the middleman

The last comment points to an interesting consequence of the Assertion Redeclaration rule. In our general scheme

The routine, the client and the sub-contractor

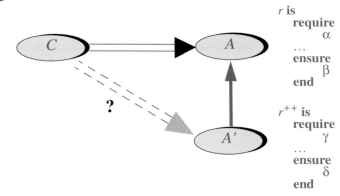

r **is**
    require
        α
    ...
    ensure
        β
    end

r^{++} **is**
    require
        γ
    ...
    ensure
        δ
    end

the assertions of the redeclared version, γ and δ, if different from α and β, are more favorable to the clients, in the sense explained earlier (weaker precondition, stronger postcondition). But a client of *A* which uses *A′* through polymorphism and dynamic binding cannot make good use of this improved contract, since its only contract is with *A*.

Only by becoming a direct client of *A′* (the shaded link with a question mark on the last figure) can you take advantage of the new contract, as in

    a1: *A′*

    ...

    if *a1*.γ **then** *a1*.*r* **end**
        check *a1*.δ **end**   -- i.e. the postcondition holds

But then of course you have specialized *a1* to be of type *A′*, not the general *A*; you have lost the polymorphic generality of going through *A*.

The tradeoff is clear. A client of *MATRIX* must satisfy the original (stronger) precondition, and may only expect the original (weaker) postcondition; even if its request gets served dynamically by *NEW_MATRIX* it has no way of benefiting from the broader tolerance of inputs and tighter precision of results. To get this improved specification it must declare the matrix to be of type *NEW_MATRIX*, thereby losing access to other implementations represented by descendants of *MATRIX* that are not also descendants of *NEW_MATRIX*.

Subcontracting

The Assertion Redeclaration rule fits nicely in the Design by Contract theory introduced in the chapter bearing that title.

We saw that the assertions of a routine describe the contract associated with that routine: the client is bound by the precondition and entitled to the postcondition, and conversely for the class implementer.

Inheritance, with redeclaration and dynamic binding, means *sub*contracting. When you have accepted a contract, you do not necessarily want to carry it out yourself. Sometimes you know of somebody else who can do it cheaper and perhaps better. This is exactly what happens when a client requests a routine from *MATRIX* but, through dynamic binding, may actually call at run time a version redefined in a proper descendant. Here "cheaper" refers to routine redefinition for more efficiency, as in the rectangle perimeter example of an earlier chapter, and "better" to improved assertions in the sense just seen.

The Assertion Redeclaration rule simply states that if you are an honest subcontractor and accept a contract, you must be willing to do the job originally requested, or better than the requested job, but not less.

> The scheme described in the last section — declaring $a1$ of type A' to benefit from the improved contract — is similar to the behavior of a customer who tries to get a better deal by bypassing his contractor to work directly with the contractor's own subcontractor

In the Design by Contract view, class invariants are general constraints applying to both contractors and clients. The parents' invariant rule expresses that all such constraints are transmitted to subcontractors.

It is only with assertions, and with the two rules just seen, that inheritance takes on its full meaning for object-oriented design. The contracting-subcontracting metaphor is a powerful analogy to guide the development of correct object-oriented software; certainly one of the central deas.

Abstract preconditions

The rule on weakening preconditions may appear too restrictive in the case of an heir that restricts the abstraction provided by its parent. Fortunately, there is an easy workaround, consistent with the theory.

A typical example arises if you want to make a class *BOUNDED_STACK* inherit from a general *STACK* class. In *BOUNDED_STACK* the procedure for pushing an element onto the stack, *put*, has a precondition, which requires $count <= capacity$, where *count* is the current number of stack elements and *capacity* is the physically available size.

For the general notion of *STACK*, however, there is no notion of *capacity*. So it seems we need to *strengthen* the precondition when we move down to *BOUNDED_STACK*. How do we build this inheritance structure without violating the Assertion Redeclaration rule?

The answer is straightforward if we take a closer look at client needs. What needs to be kept or weakened is not necessarily the concrete precondition as implemented by the supplier (which is the supplier's business), but the precondition *as seen by the client*. Assume that we write *put* in *STACK* as

    put (*x*: *G*) **is**
             -- Push *x* on top.
      require
         not *full*
      deferred
      ensure

          . . .

      end

with a function *full* defined always to return false, so that by default stacks are never full:

    full: *BOOLEAN* **is**
          -- Is representation full?
          -- (Default: no)
      do *Result* := *False* **end**

Then it suffices in *BOUNDED_STACK* to redefine *full*:

    full: *BOOLEAN* **is**
          -- Is representation full?
          -- (Answer: if and only if number of items is capacity)
      do *Result* := (*count* = *capacity*) **end**

A precondition such as **not** *full*, based on a property that is redefinable in descendants, is called an abstract precondition.

This use of abstract preconditions to satisfy the Assertion Redeclaration rule may appear to be cheating, but it is not: although the concrete precondition is in fact being strengthened, the abstract precondition remains the same. What counts is not how the assertion is implemented, but how it is presented to the clients as part of the class interface (the short or flat-short form). A protected call of the form

    if not *s*.*full* **then** *s*.*put* (*a*) **end**

will be valid regardless of the kind of *STACK* attached to *s*.

There is, however, a valid criticism of this approach: it goes against the Open-Closed principle. We must foresee, at the *STACK* level, that some stacks will have a bounded capacity; if we have not exerted such foresight, we must go back to *STACK* and change its interface. But this is inevitable. Of the following two properties

- A bounded stack is a stack.

- It is always possible to add an element to a stack.

one must go. If we want the first property, permitting *BOUNDED_STACK* to inherit from *STACK*, we must accept that the general notion of stack includes the provision that a *put* operation is not always possible, expressed abstractly by the presence of the query *full*.

    It would clearly be a mistake, in class *STACK*, to include *Result* = *False* as a postcondition for *full* or (equivalently but following the recommended style) an invariant clause **not** *full*. This would be a case of overspecification as mentioned earlier, hampering the descendants' freedom to adapt the feature.

The language rule

The Assertion Redeclaration rule as given so far is a conceptual guideline. How do we transform it into a safe, checkable language rule?

We should in principle rely on a logical analysis of the old and new assertions, to verify that the old precondition logically implies the new one, and that the new postcondition implies the old one. Unfortunately, such a goal would require a sophisticated *theorem prover* which, if at all feasible, is still far too difficult (in spite of decades of research in artificial intelligence) to be integrated routinely among the checks performed by a compiler.

Fortunately a low-tech solution is available. We c' n enforce the rule through a simple language convention, based on the observation that for any assertions α and β:

- α implies α **or** γ, regardless of what γ is.

- β **and** δ implies β, regardless of what δ is.

So to be sure that a new precondition is weaker than or equal to an original α, it suffices to accept it *only* if it is of the form α **or** γ; and to be sure that a new postcondition is stronger than or equal to an original β, it suffices to accept it only if it is of the form β **and** δ. Hence the language rule implementing the original methodological rule:

Assertion Redeclaration rule (2)

In the redeclared version of a routine, it is not permitted to use a **require** or **ensure** clause. Instead you may:

- Use a clause introduced by **require else**, to be or-ed with the original precondition.

- Use a clause introduced by **ensure then**, to be and-ed with the original postcondition.

In the absence of such a clause, the original assertion is retained.

Note that the operators used for or-ing and for and-ing are the non-strict boolean operators **or else** and **and then** rather than plain **or** and **and**, although in most cases the difference is irrelevant.

See "Non-strict boolean operators", page 454

Sometimes the resulting assertions will be more complicated than strictly necessary. For example in our matrix routine, where the original read

> *invert* (*epsilon*: *REAL*) **is**
>
> -- Inverse of current matrix, with precision *epsilon*
>
> **require**
>
> *epsilon* >= *10* ^ (*–6*)
>
> …
>
> **ensure**
>
> ((*Current* * *inverse*) |–| *One*) <= *epsilon*

the redefined version may not use **require** and **ensure** but will appear as

> …
>
> **require else**
>
> *epsilon* >= *10* ^ (*–20*)
>
> …
>
> **ensure then**
>
> ((*Current* * *inverse*) |–| *One*) <= (*epsilon* / 2)

so that formally the precondition is (*epsilon* >= *10* ^ (*–20*)) **or else** (*epsilon* >= *10* ^ (*–6*)), and similarly for the postcondition. But this does not really matter, since a weaker precondition or a stronger postcondition takes over: if α implies γ, then α **or else** γ has the same value as γ; and if δ implies β, then β **and then** δ has the same value as δ. So mathematically the precondition of the redefined version is *epsilon* >= *10* ^ (*–20*) and its postcondition is ((*Current* * *inverse*) |–| *One*) <= (*epsilon* / 2), even though the software assertions (and probably, in the absence of a symbolic expression simplifier, their evaluation at run time if assertion checking is enabled) are more complicated.

Redeclaring into attributes

See "Redeclaring a function into an attribute", page 491.

The Assertion Redeclaration rule needs a small complement because of the possibility of redeclaring a function into an attribute. What happens to the original's precondition and postcondition, if any?

An attribute is always accessible, and so may be considered to have precondition *True*. This means that we may consider the precondition to have been weakened, in line with the Assertion Redeclaration rule.

An attribute, however, does not have a postcondition. Since it is necessary to guarantee that the attribute satisfy any property ensured by the original function, the proper convention (an addition to the Assertion Redeclaration rule) is to consider that the postcondition is automatically added to the class invariant. The flat form of the class will include the condition in its invariant.

> When expressing a property of the value of a function without arguments, you always have the choice between including it in the postcondition or in the invariant. As a matter of style it is considered preferable to use the invariant. If you follow this rule there will not be any change of assertions if you later redeclare the function as an attribute.

A mathematical note

An informal comment on the Assertion Redeclaration rule stated: "A redeclaration may specialize the range of acceptable behaviors, but not violate it". Here, to conclude this discussion, is a rigorous form of that property (for mathematically inclined readers only). *Page 573.*

Consider that a routine implements a partial function r from the set of possible input states I to the set of possible output states O. The routine's assertions define rules as to what r and its possible redeclarations may and may not do:

- The precondition specifies the domain DOM of r (the subset of I in which r is guaranteed to yield a result).
- The postcondition specifies, for each element x of DOM, a subset $RESULTS\ (x)$ of O such that $r\ (x) \in RESULTS\ (x)$. This subset may have more than one element, since a postcondition does not have to define the result uniquely.

The Assertion Redeclaration rule means that a redeclaration may broaden the domain and restrict the result sets; writing the new sets in primed form, the rule requires that

$$DOM' \supseteq DOM$$
$$RESULTS'\ (x) \subseteq RESULTS\ (x) \text{ for any } x \text{ in } DOM$$

A routine's precondition specifies that the routine and its eventual redeclarations *must at least* accept certain inputs (DOM), although redeclarations may accept more. The postcondition specifies that the outputs produced by the routine and its eventual redeclarations *may at most* include certain values ($RESULTS\ (x)$), although redeclarations' postconditions may include fewer.

In this description a state of a system's execution is defined by the contents of all reachable objects; in addition, input states (elements of I) also include the values of the arguments. For a more detailed introduction to the mathematical description of programs and programming languages see [M 1990].

16.2 THE GLOBAL INHERITANCE STRUCTURE

A few references have been made in earlier discussions to the universal classes *GENERAL* and *ANY* and to the objectless class *NONE*. It is time to clarify their role and present the global inheritance structure.

Universal classes

It is convenient to use the following convention.

Universal Class rule

Any class that does not include an inheritance clause is considered to include an implicit clause of the form

    inherit *ANY*

referring to a Kernel library class *ANY*.

This makes it possible to define a certain number of features that will be inherited by all classes. These features provide operations of universal interest: copy, clone, comparison, basic input and output.

For more flexibility, we will not put these features in *ANY* but in a class *GENERAL* of which *ANY* itself is an heir. *ANY*, in its default form, will have no features (being simply of the form **class** *ANY* **inherit** *GENERAL* **end**); but then a project leader or corporate reuse manager who wants to make a certain number of features available across the board can adapt *ANY* for local purposes without touching *GENERAL*, which should be the same in Versailles, Vanuatu, Venice and Veracruz.

> To build a non-trivial *ANY*, you may want to use inheritance. You can indeed make *ANY* inherit from some class *HOUSE_STYLE*, or several such classes, without introducing any cycles in the inheritance hierarchy or violating the universal class rule: just make *HOUSE_STYLE* and its consorts explicit heirs of *GENERAL*. In the following figure, "All developer-written classes" means more precisely: all developer-written classes that do not explicitly inherit from *GENERAL*.

Here then is a picture of the general structure:

The global inheritance structure

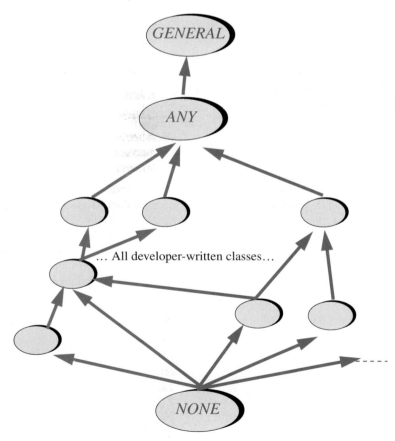

The bottom of the pit

Also included in the figure is a class *NONE*, the nemesis of *ANY*: it inherits from any class that does not have any other heir and makes the global inheritance class a lattice. You probably do not want to see the **rename** subclauses of *NONE* and, be relieved, you will not. (It changes anyway each time someone writes a new class.) *NONE* is just a convenient fiction. But its theoretical existence serves two practical purposes:

- The type of *Void*, the void reference used among other things to terminate linked structures, is by convention *NONE*. (*Void* is in fact one of the features of *GENERAL*.)

- To hide a feature from all clients, export it to *NONE* only (in a feature clause of the form **feature** {*NONE*}, equivalent in practice to **feature** { } but more explicit, or in an inheritance subclause **export** {*NONE*}, also with the same practical effect as **export** { }). This will make it unavailable to any developer class, since *NONE* has no proper descendants. Note that *NONE* hides all its features.

On the first property, note that you may assign the value *Void* to an entity of any reference type; so until now the status of *Void* was a little mysterious, since it had somehow to be compatible to all types. Making *NONE* the type of *Void* makes this status clear, official, and consistent with the type system: by construction, *NONE* is a descendant of all classes, so that we can use *Void* as a valid value of any reference type without any need to tamper with the type rules.

On the second property note that, symmetrically, a feature clause beginning with just **feature**, which exports its features to all developer classes, is considered a shorthand for **feature** {*ANY*}. To reexport to all classes a parent feature which had tighter availability, you may use **export** {*ANY*}, or the less explicit shorthand **export**.

ANY and *NONE* ensure that our type system is closed and our inheritance structure complete: the lattice has a top and it has a bottom.

Universal features

Here is a small sampling of the features found in *GENERAL* and hence available to all classes. Several of them were introduced and used in earlier chapters:

- *clone* for duplicating an object, and its deep variant *deep_clone* for recursively duplicating an entire object structure.

  See "Object cloning and equality", page 245, and subsequent sections.

- *copy* for copying the contents of an object into another.

- *equal* for field-by-field object comparison, and its deep variant *deep_equal*.

Other features include:

- *print* and *print_line* to print a simple default representation of any object.

- *tagged_out*, a string containing a default representation of any object, each field accompanied by its tag (the corresponding attribute name).

- *same_type* and *conforms_to*, boolean functions that compare the type of the current object to the type of another.

- *generator*, which yields the name of an object's generating class — the class of which it is a direct instance.

16.3 FROZEN FEATURES

The presentation of inheritance has repeatedly emphasized the Open-Closed principle: the ability to take any feature from an ancestor class and redefine it to do it something different. Can there be any reason for shutting off this possibility?

Prohibiting redefinition

The discussion of assertions at the beginning of this chapter has provided us with the theoretical understanding of redefinition: the "open" part of the Open-Closed principle — the ability to change features in descendants — is kept in check by the original assertions. The only permitted redefinitions change the implementation while remaining consistent with the specification given by the precondition and postcondition of the original.

In some rare cases, you may want to guarantee to your clients, and to the clients of your descendants, not only that a feature will satisfy the official specification, but also that it will use the exact original implementation. The only way to achieve this goal is to forbid redeclarations altogether. A simple language construct provides this possibility:

> **frozen** *feature_name* … **is** … The rest of the feature declaration as usual …

With this declaration, no descendant's **redefine** or **undefine** subclause may list the feature, whether under its original name or (since renaming remains of course permitted) another. A deferred feature — meant, by definition, for redeclaration — may not be frozen.

Fixed semantics for copy, clone and equality features

The most common use of frozen features is for general-purpose operations of the kind just reviewed for *GENERAL*. For example there are two versions of the basic copy procedure:

> *copy,* **frozen** *standard_copy (other:* …*)* **is**
>   -- Copy fields of *other* onto fields of current object.
>   **require**
>   *other_not_void: other* /= *Void*
>   **do**
>   …
>   **ensure**
>   *equal (Current, other)*
>   **end**

This declares two features as synonyms. (A general convention allows us to declare two features together so that they can share the same declaration; just separate their names with commas as here. The effect is as if there had been two separate declarations with identical declaration bodies.) But only one of the features is redefinable. So a descendant class can redefine *copy*; this is necessary for example for classes *ARRAY* and *STRING*, which redefine *copy* so as to compare actual array and string contents, not the array or string descriptors. It is convenient in such cases to have a frozen version as well, so that we can use the default operation, *standard_copy*, guaranteed to be the original.

In class *GENERAL*, feature *clone* also has a similar doppelgänger *standard_clone*, but here both versions are frozen. Why should *clone* be frozen? The reason is not to prevent the definition of a different cloning operation, but to ensure that clone and copy semantics remain compatible, and as a side benefit to facilitate the redefiner's task. The declaration of *clone* is of the general form

frozen *clone* (*other*: ...): ... **is**
        -- Void if *other* is void; otherwise new object with contents copied from *other*.
  do
      if *other* /= *Void* **then**
            Result := "New object of the same type as *other*"
            Result.*copy* (*other*)
      end
  ensure
      equal (*Result*, *other*)
  end

If other is void the default initializations yield Void for Result.

"New object of the same type as *other*" informally denotes a call to some function that creates and returns such an object, as provided by the implementation.

So even though *clone* is frozen, it will follow any redefinition of *copy*, for example in *ARRAY* and *STRING*. This is good for safety, as it would be a mistake to have different semantics for these operations, and convenience, as you will only need to redefine *copy* to change the copy-clone semantics in a descendant.

Although you need not (and cannot) redefine *clone*, you will still need, in step with a redefinition of *copy*, to redefine the semantics of equality. As indicated by the postconditions given for *copy* and *clone*, a copy must yield equal objects. Function *equal* itself is in fact frozen in the same way that *clone* is — to ensure its dependency on another, redefinable feature:

frozen *equal* (*some*, *other*: ...): *BOOLEAN* **is**
        -- Are *some* and *other* either both void
        -- or attached to objects considered equal?
  do
      Result := ((*some* = *Void*) **and** (*other* = *Void*)) **or else** *some*.*is_equal* (*other*)
  ensure
      Result = ((*some* = *Void*) **and** (*other* = *Void*)) **or else** *some*.*is_equal* (*other*)
  end

Function *equal* is called under the form *equal* (*a*, *b*), which does not quite enjoy the official O-O look of *a*.*is_equal* (*b*) but has the important practical advantage of being applicable when *a* or *b* is void. The basic feature, however, is *is_equal*, not frozen, which you should redefine in any class that redefines *copy*, to keep equality semantics compatible with copy and clone semantics — so that the postconditions of *copy* and *clone* remain correct.

The matter was discussed in "The form of clone and equality operations", page 274.

Besides *equal* there is a function *standard_equal* whose semantics is not affected by redefinitions of *is_equal*. (It uses the above algorithm but using *standard_is_equal*, frozen, rather than *is_equal*.)

Freeze only when needed

The examples of freezing that have just been given are typical of the use of this mechanism: guaranteeing the exact semantics of the original.

See "Static binding as an optimization", page 509.

It is never appropriate to freeze a feature out of efficiency concerns. (This is a mistake sometimes made by developers with a C++ or Smalltalk background, who have been told that dynamic binding is expensive and that they must manually avoid it if possible.) Clearly, a call to a frozen feature will never need dynamic binding; but this is a side effect of the **frozen** mechanism rather than its purpose. As discussed in detail in an earlier chapter, applying static binding safely is a compiler optimization, not a concern for software developers. In a well-designed language the compiler will have all it needs to perform this optimization when appropriate, along with even more far-reaching optimizations such as routine inlining. Determining the appropriate cases is a job for machines, not humans. Use **frozen** in the rare although important cases in which you need it for conceptual purposes — to guarantee the exact semantics of the original implementation — and let the language and the compiler do their job.

16.4 CONSTRAINED GENERICITY

"Polymorphic data structures", page 470.

Inheritance and genericity have been presented as the two partners in the task of extending the basic notion of class. We have already studied how to combine them through the notion of *polymorphic data structure*: into a container object described by an entity of type *SOME_CONTAINER_TYPE* [*T*] for some *T*, we can insert objects whose type is not just *T* but any descendant of *T*. But there is another interesting combination, in which inheritance serves to define what is and is not acceptable as actual generic parameter to a certain class.

Addable vectors

A simple and typical example will allow us to see the need for constrained genericity — and, as everywhere else in this book, to deduce the method and language construct as a logical consequence of the problem's statement.

Assume we want to declare a class *VECTOR* to describe vectors of elements, with an addition operation. There are vectors of elements of many different types, so we clearly need a generic class. A first sketch may look like

```
indexing
        description: "Addable vectors"
class
        VECTOR [G]
feature -- Access
        count: INTEGER
                -- Number of items

        item, infix "@" (i: INTEGER): G is
                        -- Vector element of index i (numbering starts at 1)
                require ... do
                        ...
                end
```

feature -- Basic operations

    infix "+" (*other*: *VECTOR* [*G*]): *VECTOR* **is**

            -- The sum, element by element, of current vector and *other*

        require ... **do**

          ...

        end

    ... Other features ...

invariant

    non_negative_count: *count* >= *0*

end -- class *VECTOR*

The use of an infix feature is convenient for this class, but does not otherwise affect the discussion. Also for convenience, we have two synonyms for the basic access feature, so that we can denote the i-th element of a vector (as in the *ARRAY* class, which could be used to provide an implementation) as either $v.item\ (i)$ or just $v\ @\ i$.

Now let us see how we could write the "+" function. At first it seems straightforward: to add two vectors, we just add one by one their elements at corresponding positions. The general scheme is

    infix "+" (*other*: *VECTOR* [*G*]): *VECTOR* **is**

            -- The sum, element by element, of current vector and *other*

    require

        count = *other.count*

    local

        i: *INTEGER*

    do

        "Create *Result* as an array of *count* items"

        from $i := 1$ **until** $i > count$ **loop**

            Result.put ($\boxed{item\ (i) + other.item\ (i)}$, *i*)

            $i := i + 1$

        end

    end

The boxed expression is the sum of the items at index i in the current vector and *other*, as illustrated by the figure on the facing page. The enclosing call to *put* assigns its value to the i-th item of *Result*. (Procedure *put* has not been shown in class *VECTOR*, but must obviously appear there, like its counterpart in *ARRAY*.)

But this does not work! The + operation in the boxed expression is an addition of vector elements (not vectors); it is intended to add values of type G, the generic parameter. By definition a generic parameter represents an unknown type — the actual generic parameter, to be provided only when we decide to use the generic class for good, through what has been called a **generic derivation**. If the generic derivation uses, as actual generic

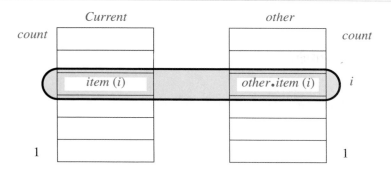

Adding two vectors, item by item

parameter, a type such as *INTEGER*, or some other class which includes a function **infix** "+" with the right signature, everything will work fine. But what if the actual generic parameter is *ELLIPSE*, or *STACK* [*SOME_TYPE*], or *EMPLOYEE*, or any other type that does not have an addition operation?

We did not have such a problem with the generic classes encountered previously — general container classes such as *STACK*, *LIST* and *ARRAY* — since the only operations they needed to apply to container elements (represented by entities of type *G*, the formal generic parameter) were universal, type-independent operations: assignment, comparison, use as argument in feature calls. But for an abstraction such as addable vectors we need to restrict the permissible actual generic parameters to make sure certain operations are available.

This is by no means an exceptional example. Here are two other typical ones:

• Assume you want to describe sortable structures, with a procedure *sort* that will order the elements according to some criterion. You need to ensure the availability of a comparison operation **infix** "<=", representing a total order, on the corresponding objects.

• In building basic data structures such as dictionaries, you may want to use a *hash-table*, where the position of each element is determined by a key derived from the value of the element. This assumes the availability of a "hashing function" which computes the key (also known as the "hash value") of any element.

A non-O-O approach

The hurried reader may skip directly to the O-O solution in the next section, "Constraining the generic parameter", page 588.

Although there have been enough hints in the preceding paragraphs to suggest the almost inevitable solution to our problem, it is useful to pause for a moment and examine how another approach, not object-oriented, has addressed the same problem.

Ada does not have classes, but has packages which serve to group related operations and types. A package may be generic, with generic parameters representing types. So the same problem arises: a package *VECTOR_PROCESSING* might include a declaration of type *VECTOR* and the equivalent of our **infix** "+" function.

The solution in Ada is to treat the needed operations, such as **infix** "+", as generic parameters themselves. The parameters of a package may include not only types, as in the object-oriented approach, but also routines (called subprograms). For example:

> **generic**
> > **type** *G* **is private**;
> > **with function** "+" (*a*, *b*: *G*) **return** *G* **is** <>;
> > **with function** "∗" (*a*, *b*: *G*) **return** *G* **is** <>;
> > *zero*: *G*; *unity*: *G*;
> **package** *VECTOR_HANDLING* **is**
> > … Package interface …
> **end** *VECTOR_HANDLING*

Note that along with the type *G* and the subprograms the package also uses, as generic parameter, a value *zero* representing the zero element of addition. A typical use of the package will be

> **package** *BOOLEAN_VECTOR_HANDLING* **is**
> > **new** *VECTOR_HANDLING* (*BOOLEAN*, "**or**", "**and**", **false**, **true**);

which uses boolean "or" as the addition and boolean "and" as the multiplication, with corresponding values for zero and unity. We will study a more complete solution to this example in a later chapter, as part of a systematic discussion of genericity *vs.* inheritance.

See "Constrained genericity", page 1170.

Although appropriate for Ada, this technique is not acceptable in an O-O context. The basic idea of object technology is the primacy of data types over operations in software decomposition, implying that there is no such thing as a stand-alone operation. *Every operation belongs to some data type, based on a class.* So it would be inconsistent with the rest of the approach to let a function such as **infix** "+", coming out of nowhere, serve as actual generic parameter along with types such as *INTEGER* and *BOOLEAN*. The same holds for values such as *zero* and *unity*, which will have to find their place as features of some class — respectable members of object-oriented society.

Constraining the generic parameter

These observations yield the solution. We must work entirely in terms of classes and types.

What we are requiring is that any actual parameter used for *VECTOR* (and similarly for the other examples) be a type equipped with a set of operations: **infix** "+", perhaps *zero* to initialize sums, and possibly a few others. But since we studied inheritance we know how to equip a type with certain operations: just make it a descendant of a class, deferred or effective, that has these operations.

A simple syntax is

> **class** *C* [*G* –> *CONSTRAINING_TYPE*] … The rest as for any other class …

where *CONSTRAINING_TYPE* is an arbitrary type. The –> symbol, made of a hyphen and a "greater than", evokes the arrow of inheritance diagrams. *CONSTRAINING_TYPE* is called the generic constraint. The consequences of such a declaration are two-fold:

*Conformance was
defined in "Limits to
polymorphism",
page 474.*

- Only types that conform to *CONSTRAINING_TYPE* will be acceptable as actual generic parameters; remember that a type conforms to another if, roughly speaking, it is based on a descendant.

- Within the text of class *C*, the operations permitted on an entity of type *G* are those which would be permitted on an entity of *CONSTRAINING_TYPE*, that is to say features of the base class of that type.

*See "Numeric and
comparable val-
ues", page 522.*

In the *VECTOR* case, what should we use as a generic constraint? A class introduced in the discussion of multiple inheritance, *NUMERIC*, describes the notion of objects to which basic arithmetic operations are applicable: addition and multiplication with zero and unity. (The underlying mathematical structure, as you may recall, is the ring.) This seems appropriate even though for our immediate purposes we only need addition. So the class will be declared as

indexing

> *description*: *"Addable vectors"*

class

> *VECTOR [G –> NUMERIC]*

… The rest as before (but now valid!) …

Then within the class text, the loop instruction that was previously invalid

> *Result*.*put* ($\boxed{item\ (i)\ +\ other.item\ (i)}$, *i*)

has become valid since *item* (*i*) and *other*.*item* (*i*) are both of type *G*, so that all *NUMERIC* operations such as **infix** "+" are applicable to them.

Generic derivations such as the following are all correct, assuming the classes given as actual generic parameters are all descendants of *NUMERIC*:

> *VECTOR* [*NUMERIC*]
>
> *VECTOR* [*REAL*]
>
> *VECTOR* [*COMPLEX*]

If, however, you try to use the type *VECTOR* [*EMPLOYEE*] you will get a compile-time error, assuming class *EMPLOYEE* is not a descendant of *NUMERIC*.

NUMERIC is a deferred class; this causes no particular problem. A generic derivation can use an effective actual parameter, as in the preceding examples, or a deferred one, as in *VECTOR* [*NUMERIC_COMPARABLE*], assuming the class given is a deferred heir of *NUMERIC*.

Similarly, a dictionary class could be declared as

class *DICTIONARY* [*G, H –> HASHABLE*] …

where the first parameter represents the type of the elements and the second represents the type of their keys. A class supporting sorting may be declared as

class *SORTABLE* [*G –> COMPARABLE*] …

Playing it recursively

A nice twist of the *VECTOR* example appears if we ask whether it is possible to have a vector of vectors. Is the type *VECTOR* [*VECTOR* [*INTEGER*]] valid?

The answer follows from the preceding rules: only if the actual generic parameter conforms to *NUMERIC*. Easy — just make *VECTOR* itself inherit from *NUMERIC*:

Exercise E16.2, page 610.

indexing
> *description*: "*Addable vectors*"

class
> *VECTOR* [*G –> NUMERIC*]

inherit
> *NUMERIC*

… The rest as before …

It is indeed justified to consider vectors "numeric", since addition and multiplication operations give them a ring structure, with *zero* being a vector of *G* zeroes and *unity* a vector of *G* ones. The addition operation is precisely the vector **infix** "+" discussed earlier.

We can go further and use *VECTOR* [*VECTOR* [*VECTOR* [*INTEGER*]]] and so on — a pleasant recursive application of constrained genericity.

Unconstrained genericity revisited

Not all cases of genericity are constrained, of course. The original form of genericity, as in *STACK* [*G*] or *ARRAY* [*G*], is still available and is called unconstrained genericity. As the example of *DICTIONARY* [*G, H –> HASHABLE*] shows, a class can have both constrained and unconstrained generic parameters.

The discussion of constrained genericity enables us to understand the unconstrained case better. You have certainly come up with the rule by yourself as you were reading the above: from now on, **class** *C* [*G*] will be understood as a shorthand for **class** *C* [*G –> ANY*]. So if *G* is an unconstrained generic parameter (say in *STACK*) and *x* is an entity of type *G*, we know exactly what we can do with *x*: assign to or from it, compare it through = and /=, pass it as argument, and apply to it any of the universal features *clone*, *equal*, *deep_clone* and the like.

16.5 ASSIGNMENT ATTEMPT

Our next technique addresses regions of Object Land in which, for fear of tyrannical behavior, we cannot let simplistic type rules reign without opposition.

When type rules become obnoxious

The aim of the type rules introduced with inheritance is to yield statically verifiable dynamic behavior, so that a system that passes the compiler's checks will not end up applying inadequate operations to objects at run time.

See "TYPING FOR INHERITANCE", 14.3, page 472.

The two basic rules were introduced in the first inheritance chapter:

- The *Feature Call rule*: $x.f$ is only valid if the base class of x's type includes and exports a feature f.

- The *Type Conformance rule*: to pass a as argument to a routine, or to assign it to a certain entity, requires that a's type conform to the expected type, that is to say, be based on a descendant class.

The Feature Call rule will not cause any problem; it is the fundamental condition for doing business with objects. Certainly, if we call a feature on an object, we need the reassurance that the corresponding class offers and exports such a feature.

The Type Conformance rule requires more attention. It assumes that we have all the type information that we need about the objects that we manipulate. Usually that is the case; after all, we create the objects, so we know who they are. But sometimes part of the information may be missing. In particular:

- In a polymorphic data structure we are only supposed to know the information that is common to all objects in the structure; but we may need to take advantage of some specific information that applies only to a particular object.

- If an object comes to our software from the outside world — a file, a network — we usually cannot trust that it has a certain type.

Let us explore examples of these two cases. First consider a polymorphic data structure such as a list of figures:

figlist: *LIST* [*FIGURE*]

This refers to the figure inheritance hierarchy of earlier chapters. What if someone asks us to find out what is the longest diagonal of all rectangles in the list (with some convention, say −1, if there are no rectangles)? We have no easy way of answering the request, since the expression *item* (*i*).*diagonal*, where *item* (*i*) is the *i*-th list element for some integer *i*, violates the Feature Call rule; *item* (*i*) is of type *FIGURE*, and there is no feature *diagonal* in class *FIGURE* — only in its proper descendant *RECTANGLE*.

The only solution with what we have seen so far is to change the class definitions so as to associate with each *FIGURE* class a code, different for each class, indicating the figure type. This is not an attractive approach.

Now for an example of the second kind. Assume a mechanism to store objects into a file, or transmit them over a network, such as the general-purpose *STORABLE* facility described in an earlier chapter. To retrieve an object or object structure you would use

See "Deep storage: a first view of persistence", page 250.

> *my_last_book*: *BOOK*
>
> ...
>
> *my_last_book* := *retrieved* (*my_book_file*)

WARNING: type-invalid assignment.

The result of function *retrieved* is of the Kernel library type *STORABLE*, but it might just as well be of type *ANY*; in either case it is only an ancestor of the object's generating type (that is to say, the type of which it is a direct instance), presumably *BOOK* or a descendant. But you are not expecting an *ANY* or a *STORABLE*: you are expecting a *BOOK*. The assignment to *my_last_book* violates the Type Conformance rule.

Even if instead of a general-purpose mechanism *retrieved* were a retrieval function specific to your application and declared with the intended type, you could still not trust its result blindly. Unlike an object that the software creates and then uses during the same session, guaranteeing type consistency thanks to the type rules, this one comes from the outside world. You may have chosen the wrong file name and retrieved an *EMPLOYEE* object rather than a *BOOK* object; or someone may have tampered with the file; or, if this is a network access, the transmission may have corrupted the data.

The challenge

It is clear from such examples that we may need a way to ascertain the type of an object.

The challenge is to satisfy this need — which arises only in specific cases, but in those cases is crucial — without sacrificing the benefits of the object-oriented style of development. In particular, we do not want to go back to the decried scheme

> **if** "f is of type *RECTANGLE*" **then**
>
> ...
>
> **elseif** "f is of type *CIRCLE*" **then**
>
> ...
>
> etc.

the exact antithesis of such principles of modularity as Single Choice and Open-Closed. Two insights will help us avoid this risk:

- We do not need a general mechanism to determine the type of an object, at least not for the purposes described. In the cases under discussion we *know the expected type* of the object. So all we require is a way to test our expectation. We will check an object against a designated type; this is much more specific than asking for the object's type. It also means that we do *not* need to introduce into our language any operations on types, such as type comparisons — a frightening thought.

- As already noted, we should not tamper with the Feature Call rule. Under no circumstances is there any justification for applying a feature ("sending a message") to an object unless we have statically ascertained that the corresponding class is equipped to deal with it. All that we will need is a looser version of the other rule, type conformance, allowing us to "try a type" and check the result.

The mechanism

Once again the notational mechanism follows directly from the analysis of the issue. We will use a new form of assignment, called **assignment attempt**, and written

> *target* ?= *source*

to be compared with the usual assignment, *target* := *source*. The question mark indicates the tentative nature of the assignment. The effect of the assignment attempt, assuming that the entity *target* has been declared with type T, is the following:

- If *source* is attached to an object of a type conforming to T, attach that object to *target* exactly as a normal assignment would do.

- Otherwise (that is to say if the value of *source* is void, or is a reference to an object of a non-conforming type), make *target* void.

There is no type constraint on the instruction, except that the type T of the target must be a reference type. (Assignment attempt is polymorphic by nature, so an expanded target would not make sense.)

This instruction immediately and elegantly solves problems of the kind mentioned above. First, type-specific access to objects of a polymorphic structure:

maxdiag (*figlist*: *LIST* [*FIGURE*]): *REAL* **is**
        -- Maximum value of diagonals of rectangles in list; −1 if none
  require
      list_exists: *figlist* /= *Void*
  local
      r: *RECTANGLE*
  do
      from
          figlist.*start*; *Result* := −1.0
      until
          figlist.*after*
      loop
          r ?= *figlist*.*item* ◄────── (The assignment attempt)
          if *r* /= *Void* **then**
              Result := *Result*.*max* (*r*.*diagonal*)
          end
          figlist.*forth*
      end
  end

See "ACTIVE DATA STRUCTURES", 23.4, page 774.

This routine uses the usual iteration mechanisms on sequential structures: *start* to position the traversal on the first element if any, *after* to determine whether there is any element left to examine, *forth* to advance by one position, *item* (defined if **not** *after*) to yield the element at the current cursor position.

The assignment attempt uses a local entity *r* of the appropriate type *RECTANGLE*. We know whether it succeeded by testing *r* against *Void*. Only if *r* is not void do we have a rectangle; then we can safely access *r.diagonal*. This scheme of testing for *Void* right after an assignment attempt is typical.

Note again that we never violate the Feature Call rule: any call of the form *r.diagonal* is guarded, statically, by a compiler check that *diagonal* is a feature of class *RECTANGLE*, and, dynamically, by a guarantee that *r* is not void — has an attached object.

A list element of type *SQUARE*, or some other descendant of *RECTANGLE*, will make *r* non-void, so that its diagonal will, rightly, participate in the computation.

The other example, using a general-purpose object retrieval function, is immediate:

```
my_last_book: BOOK
...
my_last_book ?= retrieved (my_book_file)
if my_last_book /= Void then
        ... "Proceed normally with operations on my_last_book" ...
else
        ... "What we expected is not what we got"...
end
```

Compare with := in the first try (page 592)

Using assignment attempt properly

Assignment attempt is an indispensable tool for those cases — typically of the two kinds shown: elements of polymorphic data structures, and objects coming from the outside world — in which you cannot trust the statically declared type of an entity but need to ascertain at run time the type of the object actually attached to it.

Note how carefully the mechanism has been designed to discourage developers from using it to go back to the old case-by-case style. If you really want to circumvent dynamic binding, and test separately for each type variant, you can — but you have to work really hard at it; for example instead of the normal *f.display*, using the O-O mechanisms of polymorphism and dynamic binding, you would write

```
display (f: FIGURE) is
            -- Display f, using the algorithm adapted to its exact nature.
    local
            r: RECTANGLE; t: TRIANGLE; p: POLYGON; s: SQUARE
            sg: SEGMENT; e: ELLIPSE; c: CIRCLE; ...
    do
            r ?= f; if r /= Void then "Apply the rectangle display algorithm" end
            t ?= f; if t /= Void then "Apply the triangle display algorithm" end
            c ?= f; if c /= Void then "Apply the circle display algorithm" end
            ... etc ...
    end
```

*Warning: this is **not** the recommended style!*

This scheme will in practice be even worse than it seems because the inheritance structure has several levels; for example an object of type *SQUARE* will make an assignment attempt *x ?= f* succeed for *x* of type *POLYGON* and *RECTANGLE* as well as *SQUARE*. So you must complicate the control structure to avoid multiple matches.

Because of the difficulty of writing such contorted uses of the assignment attempt, there is little risk that novice developers will mistakenly use it instead of the normal O-O scheme. But even advanced developers must remain alert to the possibility for misuse.

> Java offers a mechanism called "narrowing" similar in some respects to assignment attempt. But in case of a type mismatch, instead of yielding a void value, it produces an exception. This looks like overkill, since an unsuccessful assignment is not an abnormal case, simply one of several possible and expected cases; it does not justify adding exception-handling code and setting in motion the exception machinery. Java also offers the *instanceof* operator to test for type conformance.

> These mechanisms are used particularly extensively in Java because of the absence of genericity: you may have to rely on them, when retrieving elements from container data structures (even single-type), to check the elements' type against an expected type. Part of the reason may be that, in the absence of multiple inheritance, Java has no *NONE* class and hence no easy way to give the equivalent of *Void* a stable place in the type system.

16.6 TYPING AND REDECLARATION

When you redeclare a feature, you are not constrained to keep exactly the same signature. The precise rule will give us a further degree of flexibility.

So far we have seen redeclaration as a mechanism for substituting an algorithm for another — or, in the case of effecting a previously deferred routine, providing an algorithm where only a specification was originally given.

But we may also need to change the types involved, to support the general idea that a class may offer a more specialized version of an element declared in an ancestor. Let us study two typical examples, which will suggest the precise Type Redeclaration rule.

Devices and printers

Here is a simple example of type redefinition. Consider a notion of device including the provision that for every device there is an alternate, to be used if for some reason the first one is not available:

```
class DEVICE feature
    alternate: DEVICE

    set_alternate (a: DEVICE) is
            -- Designate a as alternate.
        do
            alternate := a
        end
    … Other features …
end -- class DEVICE
```

Printers are a special kind of device, justifying the use of inheritance. But the alternate of a printer can only be a printer — not a CD-ROM reader or a network transceiver! — so we must redefine the types:

class *PRINTER* **inherit**

    DEVICE

        redefine *alternate, set_alternate*

feature

    alternate: *PRINTER*

    set_alternate (*a*: *PRINTER*) **is**

        -- Designate *a* as alternate.

      … Body as in *DEVICE* …

    … Other features …

end -- class *DEVICE*

These redefinitions reflect the specializing nature of inheritance.

Linkable and bi-linkable elements

Here is another example, involving fundamental data structures. Consider the library class *LINKABLE* describing the linked list elements used in *LINKED_LIST*, one of the implementations of lists. A partial view of the class is:

indexing

    description: "*Cells to be linked in a list*"

class *LINKABLE* [*G*] **feature**

    item: *G*

    right: *LINKABLE* [*G*]

    put_right (*other*: *LINKABLE* [*G*]) **is**

        -- Put *other* to the right of current cell.

      do *right* := *other* **end**

    … Other features …

end -- class *LINKABLE*

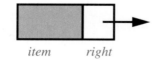

item   *right*

A linkable cell

Some applications need lists chained both ways (each element linked to its successor and its predecessor). The corresponding class, *TWO_WAY_LIST*, is an heir of *LINKED_LIST*, and will need an heir *BI_LINKABLE* of *LINKABLE*:

Parallel hierarchies

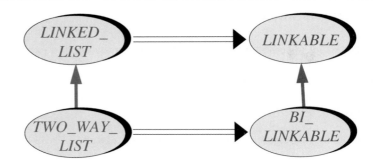

A bi-linkable element is like a linkable but with one more field:

A bi-linkable cell

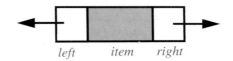

left   item   right

In a two-way list, bi-linkables should only be chained to bi-linkables (although it is harmless to introduce bi-linkables in a one-way list: this is polymorphism). So we should redefine *right* and *put_right* to guarantee that two-way lists remain homogeneous.

> **indexing**
> > *description*: *"Cells to be linked both ways in a list"*
>
> **class** *BI_LINKABLE* [*G*] **inherit**
> > *LINKABLE* [*G*]
> > > **redefine** *right*, *put_right* **end**
>
> **feature**
> > *left*, *right*: *BI_LINKABLE* [*G*]
> >
> > *put_right* (*other*: *BI_LINKABLE* [*G*]) **is**
> > > -- Put *other* to the right of current element.
> > >
> > > **do**
> > > > *right* := *other*
> > > > **if** *other* /= *Void* **then** *other*.*put_left* (*Current*) **end**
> > >
> > > **end**
> >
> > *put_left* (*other*: *BI_LINKABLE* [*G*]) **is**
> > > -- Put *other* to the left of current element
> > > … Left to the reader …
> >
> > … Other features …
>
> **invariant**
> > *right* = *Void* **or else** *right*.*left* = *Current*
> > *left* = *Void* **or else** *left*.*right* = *Current*
>
> **end**

(Try writing *put_left*. There is a pitfall! See appendix A.)

The Type Redeclaration rule

Although addressing abstractions of widely different kinds, the two examples show the same need for type redeclaration. Going down an inheritance hierarchy means specializing, and some types will follow that change pattern: types of routine arguments, such as *a* in *set_alternate* and *other* in *put_right*; types of queries, such as the attributes *alternate* and *right*, as well as functions.

The following rule captures this type aspect of redeclaration:

> ### Type Redeclaration rule
>
> A redeclaration of a feature may replace the type of the feature (if an attribute or function), or the type of a formal argument (if a routine), by any type that conforms to the original.

Here "conforms to" refers to the notion of type conformance, as defined on the basis of the descendant relation. The rule uses "or" non-exclusively: a function redeclaration may change both the type of the function's result and the type of one or more arguments.

The permitted forms of redeclaration all go in the same direction: the direction of specialization. As illustrated by the last inheritance diagram, when you go down from *LINKED_LIST* to *TWO_WAY_LIST*, arguments and results will concomitantly go down from *LINKABLE* to *BI_LINKABLE*. In the first example, when you go from *DEVICE* to *PRINTER*, the attribute *alternate* and the argument of *set_alternate* follow. This explains the name often use to characterize this type redeclaration policy: **covariant typing**, where the "co" indicates that as we descend the inheritance diagram all the types go down in step.

The diagram is on page 597.

Covariant typing, as we will see in the next chapter, creates for the compiler writer a few headaches which, fortunately, he can often avoid passing on to the software developer.

16.7 ANCHORED DECLARATION

The Type Redeclaration rule could make life quite unpleasant in some cases, and even cancel some of the benefits of inheritance. Let us see how and discover the solution — anchored declaration.

Type inconsistencies

As an example of the problems that may arise with the Type Redeclaration rule, consider the following example from *LINKED_LIST*. Here is the procedure for inserting a new element with a given value to the right of the current cursor position. Although there is nothing mysterious with the details, all you need to note at this stage is the need for a local entity *new* of type *LINKABLE*, representing the list cell to be created and added to the list.

> *put_right* (*v*: *G*) **is**
>> -- Insert an element of value *v* to the right of cursor position.
>> -- Do not move cursor.
>
> **require**
>> **not** *after*
>
> **local**
>> *new*: *LINKABLE* [*T*]
>
> **do**
>> !! *new*.*make* (*v*)
>>
>> *put_linkable_right* (*new*)
>>
>> …
>
> **ensure**
>> … See appendix A …
>
> **end**

To insert a new item of value *v*, we must create a cell of type *LINKABLE* [*G*]; the actual insertion is carried out by the secret procedure *put_linkable_right*, which takes a *LINKABLE* as argument (and chains it to the cursor item using the *put_right* procedure of class *LINKABLE*.) This procedure performs the appropriate reference manipulations.

In proper descendants of *LINKED_LIST*, such as *TWO_WAY_LIST* or *LINKED_TREE*, procedure *put_right* should still be applicable. Unfortunately, it will not work as given: although the algorithm is still correct, the entity *new* should be declared and created as a *BI_LINKABLE* or a *LINKED_TREE* rather than a *LINKABLE*. So we must redefine and rewrite the whole procedure for each descendant — a particularly wasteful task since the new body will be identical to the original except for a single declaration (for *new*). For an approach meant to solve the reusability issue, this is a serious deficiency.

Application-oriented examples

It would be a mistake to believe that the spurious redefinition problem only arises for implementation-oriented structures such as *LINKED_LIST*. With any scheme of the form

> *some_attribute*: *SOME_TYPE*
>
> *set_attribute* (*a*: *SOME_TYPE*) **is do** … **end**

BI_LINKABLE's put_right (not to be confused with *put_right* for *LINKED_LIST*) was on page 597.

a redefinition of *some_attribute* will imply the corresponding redefinition of *set_attribute*. In the case of *put_right* for *BI_LINKABLE*, the redefinition actually changed the algorithm (because of the necessity, if you chain O1 right to O2, also to chain O2 left to O1), but in many other cases, such as *set_alternate*, the new algorithm is identical to the original. This pattern is so common that we may expect to have to write many redundant routine bodies.

Here is one more example, showing how general the problem is (and not just tied to *set_xxx* procedures, themselves a result of information hiding principles). Assume we add to class *POINT* a function yielding the conjugate of a point, that is to say its mirror image across the horizontal axis:

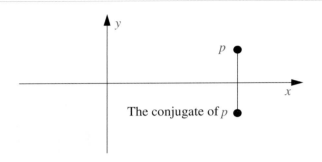

*A point and its
conjugate*

The function may appear as follows in *POINT*:

conjugate: *POINT* **is**
            -- Conjugate of current point
    do
            Result := *clone* (*Current*)   -- Get a copy of current point
            Result•*move* (0, −2∗*y*)   -- Translate result vertically
    end

Now consider a descendant of *POINT*, perhaps *PARTICLE*, where particles have
attributes other than *x* and *y*: perhaps a mass and a speed. Conceptually, *conjugate* is still
applicable to particles; it should yield a particle result when applied to a particle argument.
The conjugate of a particle is identical to that particle except for the *y* coordinate. But if
we leave the function as it stands, it will not work for particles, since instructions such as
the following violate the conformance rule:

    p1, *p2*: *PARTICLE*; !! *p1*•*make* (…); …
    p2 := *p1*•*conjugate*

In the <u>underlined</u> assignment, the source (right-hand side) is of type *POINT*, but the
target is of type *PARTICLE*; the Type Conformance rule would require the reverse. So we
must redefine *conjugate* in *PARTICLE*, for no purposes but type conformance.

> Assignment attempt is not the solution here: although valid, it will result in a void *p2*,
> since the source object's type will, at execution time, be of type *POINT*, not *PARTICLE*.

A serious problem

If you look more closely at class *LINKED_LIST* in appendix A you will realize that the
problem is of even greater scope. *LINKED_LIST* contains more than a few declarations
referring to type *LINKABLE* [*G*], and most will need to be redefined for two-way lists. For
example a possible representation of a list keeps four references to linkable elements:

    first_element, *previous*, *active*, *next*: *LINKABLE* [*G*]

All of these must be redefined in *TWO_WAY_LIST*, and similarly for other
descendants. Many routines such as *put_right* take linkables as arguments, and must also
be redefined. It seems that we will end up repeating in *TWO_WAY_LIST*, for purposes of
declaration only, most of the features written for *LINKED_LIST*.

The notion of anchor

Unlike other type-related problems solved earlier in this chapter — such as the problems whose analysis led to constrained genericity and assignment attempt — the Case of the Useless Code Duplication is not that the type system prevents us from doing something that we need: thanks to the covariant Type Redeclaration rule we can redefine types to our heart's content, but this forces us to perform tedious code duplication.

To obtain a solution, we may note that the examples do require a type redefinition, but only one: all others ensue from it. The answer follows: provide a mechanism to declare an entity's type not absolutely, but *relative* to another entity.

This will be called an anchored declaration. An anchored type has the form

like *anchor*

where *anchor*, called the anchor of the declaration, is either a query (attribute or function) of the current class or the predefined expression *Current*. To declare *my_entity*: **like** *anchor* in a class *A*, where *anchor* is a query, means to declare it as being of the same type as *anchor*, but with the provision that any redefinition of *anchor* in a proper descendant will implicitly cause the same redefinition for *my_entity*.

So, assuming that *anchor* has been declared of some type *T*, the anchored declaration will cause *my_entity* to be treated within the text of class *A* as if it too had been declared of type *T*. If you only consider *A* there is no difference between the two declarations

- *my_entity*: **like** *anchor*

- *my_entity*: *X*

The difference only comes up in descendant classes of *A*. Being declared "like" *anchor*, *my_entity* will automatically follow any redefinition of the type of *anchor*, without the need for explicit redefinition by the author of the descendant class.

So if you find that a class includes a group of entities — attributes, function results, formal routine arguments, local entities — which descendants will have to redefine identically, you can dispense with all but one of the redefinitions: just declare all elements **like** the first one, and redefine only that first one. All others will automatically follow.

Let us apply this technique to *LINKED_LIST*. We can choose *first_element* as anchor for the other entities of type *LINKABLE* [*G*]. The attribute declarations become:

first_element: *LINKABLE* [*G*]
previous, *active*, *next*: **like** *first_element*

put_right from LINKED_LIST is on page 599.

In the *put_right* procedure of *LINKED_LIST*, the local entity *new* should also be declared of type **like** *first_element*; this is the only change to the procedure. With these declarations, it suffices to redefine *first_element* as a *BI_LINKABLE* in class *TWO_WAY_LIST*, as a *LINKED_TREE* in class *LINKED_TREE* etc.; all entities declared **like** it follow automatically and need not be listed in the **redefine** clause. Neither is redefinition necessary any more for procedure *put_right*.

Anchored declarations are an essential tool to preserve reusability in a statically typed object-oriented context.

Current **as anchor**

Instead of the name of a query you can use *Current* as anchor. The expression *Current*, as you know, denotes the current instance. An entity declared **like** *Current* in a class *A* will be treated within the class as being of type *A* and, in any descendant *B* of *A*, as being of type *B* — without any need for redefinition.

See "The current instance", page 181.

This form of anchored declaration addresses the remaining examples. To get the correct type for function *conjugate* in class *POINT*, amend its declaration to read

Original: page 600.

> *conjugate*: **like** *Current* **is**
>   … The rest exactly as before …

Then the result type of *conjugate* gets automatically redefined, in every descendant, to the associated type, for example type *PARTICLE* in class *PARTICLE*.

In class *LINKABLE*, you should similarly, in the earlier declarations

> *right*: *LINKABLE* [*G*]
> *put_right* (*other*: *LINKABLE* [*G*]) **is**…

replace *LINKABLE* [*G*] by **like** *Current*. Feature *left* in *BI_LINKABLE* should also be declared as **like** *Current*.

This scheme applies to many *set_attribute* procedures. In the *DEVICE* case we get:

Class DEVICE, followed by PRINTER, appeared on page 595.

> **class** *DEVICE* **feature**
>   *alternate*: **like** *Current*
>
>   *set_alternate* (*a*: **like** *Current*) **is**
>   -- Designate *a* as alternate.
>   **do**
>   *alternate* := *a*
>   **end**
>   … Other features …
> **end** -- class *DEVICE*

No redefinition is then necessary in a descendant such as *PRINTER*.

Base classes revisited

With the introduction of anchored types, we need to extend the notion of base class of a type.

You will remember the idea. At the beginning, classes and types were a single concept. That property, the starting point of the object-oriented method, remains *essentially* true, but we have had to extend the type system a little by adding generic parameters to classes. Every type is still fundamentally based on a class; for a generically derived type such as *LIST* [*INTEGER*] you obtain the base class by removing the actual generic parameters, giving *LIST* in this example. We also added expanded types, again based on classes; the base type of **expanded** *SOME_CLASS* […] is *SOME_CLASS*.

See "Types and classes", page 324.

With anchored types we have another extension of the type system which, like the previous two, leaves intact the property that each type directly follows from a class. The base class of **like** *anchor* is the base class of the type of *anchor* in the current class; if *anchor* is *Current*, the base class is the enclosing class.

Rules on anchored types

There is no theoretical obstacle to accepting **like** *anchor* for an *anchor* that is itself of an anchored type; we must simply add a rule that prohibits cycles in declaration chains.

> Initially the notation disallowed anchored anchors; although this rule is acceptable, the more liberal one that only prohibits anchor cycles allows more flexibility.

Let T be the type of *anchor* (given by the current class if *anchor* is *Current*). The type **like** *anchor* conforms to itself, and to T.

In the other direction, the only type that conforms to **like** *anchor* is itself. In particular T does not conform to **like** *anchor*. If we allowed

anchor, other: T; *x*: **like** *anchor*

...

!! *other*

x := *other*

WARNING: invalid assignment.

then in a descendant class where *anchor* is redefined to be of type U (conforming to T but based on a proper descendant) the assignment would attach x to an object of type T, whereas we should only accept objects of type U or conforming to U.

Of course you may assign to and from the anchor, as in $x := anchor$ and $anchor := x$, and more generally between anchor-equivalent elements, defining x to be anchor-equivalent to y if it is y or declared as **like** z where z is (recursively) anchor-equivalent to y.

In the case of anchoring a formal argument or result of a routine, as in

r (*other*: **like** *Current*)

the actual argument in a call, such as b in $a.r(b)$, must be anchor-equivalent to the target a.

The discussion of typing issues in chapter 17 will further explore the conformance properties of anchored types.

When not to use anchored declaration

Not every declaration of the form x: A within a class A should be replaced by x: **like** *Current*, and not every pair of features with the same type should be declared **like** one another.

An anchored declaration is a commitment: it indicates that whenever the anchor changes types in the future, the anchored entity must change too. As we just saw with the type rules, this commitment is not reversible: once you have declared an entity of type **like** *anchor* you cannot redefine its type any further (since the new type would have to conform to the original, and no type conforms to an anchored type but itself). As long as you have not chosen an anchored type, everything is still possible: if *x* is of type *T*, you can redeclare *x* as being of a conforming type *U* in a descendant; and you can in fact redeclare it as **like** *anchor* for some compatible *anchor* to close off further variations.

The pros and cons are clear. Anchoring an entity guarantees that you will never have to redeclare it for type purposes; but it binds it irrevocably to the type of the anchor. It is a typical case of trading freedom for convenience — like signing up with the military, or taking vows. (In a certain sense Faust declared himself **like** *Mephistopheles*.)

As an example of when anchoring may not be desirable, consider a feature *first_child* of trees, describing the first child of a given tree node. (In the construction of trees explained in the last chapter it comes from *first_element* of lists, originally of type *CELL* [*G*] or *LINKABLE* [*G*].) In a tree class it must be declared or redeclared to denote a tree. It may seem appropriate to use an anchored declaration:

> *first_child*: **like** *Current*

This may, however, be too restrictive in practice. The tree class may have descendants, representing various kinds of tree (or tree node). Examples may include *UNARY_TREE* (nodes with just one child), *BINARY_TREE* (nodes with two children) and *BOUNDED_ARITY_TREE* (nodes with a bounded number of children). If *first_child* is anchored to *Current*, every node must have children of the same type: unary if it is unary, and so on.

This is probably not the desired effect, since you may want more flexible structures, permitting for example a binary node to have a unary child. This is obtained by declaring the feature not by an anchored declaration but simply as

> *first_child*: *TREE* [*G*]

This solution is not restrictive: if you later need trees with nodes guaranteed to be all of the same type, you may leave *TREE* as it is and give it a new descendant *HOMOGENEOUS_TREE* which redefines *first_child* as

> *first_child*: **like** *Current*

ensuring consistency of all the nodes in a tree.

To facilitate such a redefinition the other features of *TREE* representing nodes, such as *parent* and *current_child*, may and probably should be declared as **like** *first_child*; but *first_child* itself is not anchored in *TREE*.

A static mechanism

One last comment on anchored declaration, to dispel any possible misunderstanding that might remain about this mechanism: it is a purely static rule, not implying any change of object forms at run-time. The constraints may be checked at compile time.

Anchored declaration may be viewed as a syntactic device, avoiding many spurious redeclarations by having the compiler insert them. As it stands, it is an essential tool for reconciling reusability and type checking.

16.8 INHERITANCE AND INFORMATION HIDING

One last question needs to be answered to complete this panorama of inheritance issues: how inheritance interacts with the principle of information hiding.

For the other intermodule relation, client, the answer is clear: the author of each class is responsible for granting access privileges to the clients of the class. He specifies a policy for every feature: exported (generally available); selectively available; secret.

The policies

What happens to the export status of a feature when it is passed on to a descendant? Whatever you want to happen. Information hiding and inheritance are orthogonal mechanisms. A class B is free to export or hide any feature f that it inherits from an ancestor A. All possible combinations are indeed open:

- f exported in both A and B (although not necessarily to the same clients).

- f secret in both A and B.

- f secret in A, but exported, generally or selectively, in B.

- f exported in A, but secret in B.

The language rule is the following. By default — reflecting the most common case — f will keep the export status it had in A. But you may change this by adding an **export** subclause to the **inheritance** clause for A, as in

    class B **inherit**

        A

                export {*NONE*} f **end** -- Makes f secret (it may have been exported in A)

        ...

or

    class B **inherit**

        A

                export {*ANY*} f **end** -- Makes f exported (it may have been secret in A)

        ...

or

    class B **inherit**

        A

                export {*X, Y, Z*} f **end** -- Makes f selectively available to certain classes

        ...

Applications

A typical application of this flexibility is to provide several views of a certain basic notion.

Imagine a class *GENERAL_ACCOUNT* containing all the necessary tools for dealing with bank accounts, with procedures such as *open*, *withdraw*, *deposit*, *code* (for withdrawal from automatic teller machines), *change_code* etc.; but this class is not meant to be used directly by clients and so does not export anything. Descendants provide various views: they do not add any features, but simply differ in their export clauses. One will export *open* and *deposit* only, another will also include *withdraw* and *code*, and so on.

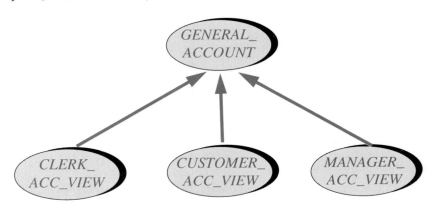

Views of a basic abstraction

See "Facility inheritance", page 832.

This scheme belongs to what the discussion of inheritance methodology will call "facility inheritance".

The notion of view is a classical one in databases, where it is often necessary to provide different users with different abstract notions of an underlying set of data.

"Trees are lists and list elements", page 525.

Classes sketched the discussion of multiple inheritance provide another application. Feature *right* of class *CELL* is secret in this class or, more precisely, is exported only to *LIST*; this is in fact true of all the features of *CELL*, since this class was initially designed only for the purpose of lists. But in class *TREE*, implemented as heir to *CELL* as well as *LIST*, *right* now denotes access to the right sibling of a node, a respectable public feature which should be exported.

Why the flexibility?

The policy of letting each descendant choose its own export policy (only by overriding the default, which keeps the parent's policy) makes type checking more difficult, as discussed in the next chapter, but provides the necessary flexibility to the class developer. Anything more restrictive hinders the goals of object-oriented software development.

Other solutions have been tried. Some O-O languages, beginning with a revision of Simula, let a class specify not only whether a feature will be exported to its clients, but whether it will be available to its descendants. The benefits are not clear. In particular:

- I am not aware of any published methodological advice on how to use this facility: when to bequeath a feature to descendants, when to hide it from them. A notational mechanism with no accompanying theory is of dubious value. (In comparison, the methodological rule governing information hiding policy for clients is limpid: what belongs to the underlying ADT should be exported; the rest should be secret.)

- More pragmatically, it seems that few developers in Simula and languages offering similar descendant restriction mechanisms bother to use them.

On closer examination, the lack of clear methodological guidelines is not surprising. Inheritance is the embodiment of the Open-Closed principle: a mechanism that enables you to pick an existing class, written yesterday or twenty years ago by you or by someone else, and discover that you can do something useful with it, far beyond what had been foreseen by the original design. Letting a class author define what eventual descendants may or may not use would eliminate this basic property of inheritance.

The example of *CELL* and *TREE* is typical: in the design of *CELL*, the only goal was to satisfy the needs of *LIST* classes, so *right* and *put_right* served only internal purposes. Only later did these features suddenly find a new application for a descendant, *TREE*. Without such openness, inheritance would lose much of its appeal.

If a class designer has no basis for deciding which features the class should pass on to its descendants, it would be even more preposterous for him to predict what they may or may not export to their *own clients*. Any such attempt is guesswork, with the knowledge that a wrong guess will make the descendant developers' task impossible.

These descendant developers have only one task: to provide their clients with the best possible class. In such an effort, inheritance is only a tool, enabling the developers to get a good result faster and better. The only rules of the game are the typing constraints and the assertions. Beyond that, anything goes. A useful ancestor feature is a godsend; whether the ancestor exported it or not is a matter between the ancestor and its own clients: the descendant developer could not care less.

In summary, the only policy compatible with the fundamental openness of inheritance seems to be the one described: let every descendant developer take its pick of ancestor features, and decide on its own export policy in the interest of its own clients.

Interface and implementation reuse

If you have read some of the more superficial O-O presentations, or follow newsgroup discussions, you may have been subjected to warnings against "inheriting implementation". But (as we shall see in more detail in the inheritance methodology chapter) there is nothing wrong about using inheritance for implementation.

See the figure on page 144.
There are two forms of reuse: reuse through interface, and reuse of implementation. We can understand them as follows from the theoretical picture. Any class is an implementation (possibly partial) of an abstract data type. It contains both the interface, as expressed by the ADT specification — the tip of the iceberg, if you remember the pictures that accompanied the presentation of information hiding and ADTs — and a set of implementation choices. Interface reuse means that you are content to rely on the specification; implementation reuse, that you need to rely on properties that belong to the class but not to the ADT.

You will not use these two possibilities for the same purposes. If you can reuse a certain set of facilities through their abstract properties only, and want to be protected against future changes in the reused elements, go for interface reuse. But in some cases you will just fall in love with a certain implementation because it provides the right basis for what you are building.

These forms of reuse are complementary, and are both perfectly legitimate.

The two inter-module relations of object-oriented software construction cover them: client provides interface reuse, inheritance supports implementation reuse.

Reusing an implementation is, of course, a more committing decision than just reusing an interface: you cannot reasonably expect, as in the other case, to be protected against changes in implementation! For that reason, inheriting is a more committing decision than just being a client. But in some cases it is what you need.

It is not always easy in practice to determine which one of the client and inheritance relations is appropriate in a certain case. A later chapter contains a detailed discussion of how to choose between them.

"WOULD YOU RATHER BUY OR INHERIT?", 24.2, page 812.

Rehabilitating implementation

Why the distrust of implementation inheritance? I have come to think that the answer is less technical than psychological. A thirty-year legacy of less-than-pristine programming has left us with a distrust of the very idea of implementation. The word itself has in some circles come to take on an almost indecent character, as if it were an insult to abstraction. (H.L. Mencken, in *The American Language*, similarly tells of how words such as *leg* came to be banished from late-nineteenth-century polite conversation for fear of the immodest connotations they evoke, even when the matter was limbs of a piano or of a chicken.) So we talk of analysis and design, and when we mention implementation at all we make sure to precede it by "but", "just" or "only", as in "this is just an implementation issue".

Object technology, of course, is the reverse of all that: producing implementations that are so elegant, useful and clearly correct that we do not have to watch our language. What for us is a program is often more abstract, more high-level, more understandable than much of what the analysis and design view presents as the highest of the high.

The two styles

In the picture that comes out of this discussion, we merge a set of originally separate distinctions.

We have two relations, client and inheritance; two forms of reuse, interface and implementation; information hiding, or not; protection against internal changes in provider modules, or not.

In each case the existence of a choice is not controversial, and both of the opposing options are defensible depending on the context. The slightly bolder step is to treat all these oppositions as just one:

Merging four
oppositions

Client	::	Inheritance
Reuse through interface	::	Reuse of implementation
Information hiding	::	No information hiding
Protection against changes in original implementation	::	No protection against original's changes

Other approaches may be possible. But I do not know of any that is as simple, easy to teach and practical.

Selective exports

As a consequence of the information hiding properties of inheritance we must clarify the effects of selective exports. A class A which exports f selectively to B, as in

> **class** A **feature** $\{B, \ldots\}$
> $f \ldots$
> $\ldots$

makes f available to B for the implementation of B's own features. What about the descendants of B? As we have just seen, they have access to B's implementation; so they should be able to access whatever is accessible to B — for example f.

Experimental observation confirms this theoretical reasoning: what a class needs, its descendants tend to need too. But we do not want to have to come back and modify A (to extend its export clause) whenever a new descendant is added to B.

Here the principle of information hiding should be combined with the Open-Closed principle. The designer of A is entitled to decide whether or not to make f available to B; but he has no right to limit the freedom of the designer of the B line of classes to provide new extensions and implementation variants. In fact, what descendants B has, if any, is none his business. Hence the rule:

> **Selective Export Inheritance rule**
>
> A feature selectively exported to a class is available to all its descendants.

16.9 KEY CONCEPTS INTRODUCED IN THIS CHAPTER

- Invariants of parents are automatically added to a class's invariant.
- In the Design by Contract approach, inheritance, redefinition and dynamic binding introduce the concept of subcontracting.
- A routine redeclaration (redefinition or effecting) may keep or weaken the precondition; it may keep or strengthen the postcondition.
- An assertion redeclaration may only use **require else** (for or-ing of preconditions) and **and then** (for and-ing of postconditions). It may not use just **require** or **ensure**. In the absence of these clauses the routine keeps the original assertions.

- The universal class *GENERAL* and its customizable heir *ANY* provide redefinable features of interest to all developer-defined classes. *NONE* closes down the lattice.

- It is possible to freeze a feature to guarantee eternal semantic uniqueness.

- To entrust generic parameters with specific features, use constrained genericity.

- Assignment attempt makes it possible to verify dynamically that an object has the expected type. It should not be used as a substitute for dynamic binding.

- A descendant may redefine the type of any entity (attribute, function result, formal routine argument). The redefinition must be covariant, that is to say replace the original type with a conforming one, based on a descendant.

- Anchored declaration (**like** *anchor*) is an important part of the type system. facilitating the application of covariant typing and avoiding redundant redeclarations.

- Inheritance and information hiding are orthogonal mechanisms. Descendants may hide features that were exported by their ancestors, and export features that were secret.

- A feature available to a class is available to its descendants.

16.10 BIBLIOGRAPHICAL NOTE

See [Snyder 1986] for a different viewpoint on the relationship between inheritance and information hiding.

EXERCISES

E16.1 Inheriting for simplicity and efficiency

Rewrite and simplify the protected stack example of an earlier chapter, making class *STACK3* a descendant rather than a client of *STACK* to avoid unneeded indirections. (**Hint**: see the rules governing the relationship between inheritance and information hiding.)

"A tolerant module", page 359.

E16.2 Vectors

Write a class *VECTOR* describing vectors of a numeric type (ring), with the usual mathematical operations, and itself treated recursively as a numeric type. You may have to complete class *NUMERIC* for yourself (or get a version from [M 1994a]).

E16.3 Extract?

The assignment $y1 := x1$ is not permitted if $x1$ is of a type X, $y1$ of type Y, and X is a proper ancestor of Y. It might seem useful, however, to include a universal feature *extract* such that the instruction $y1.extract(x1)$ copies the values of the fields of the object attached to $x1$ to the corresponding fields in the object attached to $y1$, assuming neither reference is void.

Explain why the notation does not include such an *extract* feature. (**Hint**: examine correctness issues, in particular the notion of invariant.) Examine whether it is possible to design a satisfactory mechanism that achieves the same general goal in a different way.

17

Typing

$\mathcal{E}$ffective use of object technology requires that we clearly specify, in the texts of our systems, the types of all objects that they will manipulate at run time. This rule, known as static typing — a notion defined precisely in the next sections — makes our software:

- More *reliable*, by enabling compilers and other tools to suppress discrepancies before they have had time to cause damage.

- More *readable*, by providing precious information to authors of client systems, future maintainers of our own software, and other readers.

- More *efficient*, since this information helps a good compiler generate better code.

Although the typing issue has been extensively discussed in non-O-O contexts, and static typing applied to many non-O-O languages, the concepts are particularly clear and relevant in object technology since the approach as a whole is largely based on the idea of type, merged with the idea of module to yield the basic O-O construct, the class.

The desire to provide static typing has been a major influence on the mechanisms discussed in earlier chapters. Here we need to take a comprehensive look at typing and devise solutions to the remaining difficulties raised by this concept.

17.1 THE TYPING PROBLEM

One nice thing can be said about the typing issue in object-oriented software construction: it may not be an easy problem, but it is a *simple* problem — simple, that is, to state.

The Basic Construct

The problem's simplicity comes from the simplicity of the object-oriented model of computation. If we put aside some of the details, only one kind of event ever occurs during the execution of an object-oriented system: feature call, of the general form

$x \cdot f(arg)$

which executes on the object attached to x the operation f, using the argument arg, with the understanding that in some cases arg stands for several arguments, or no argument at all. Smalltalk programmers would say "pass to the object x the message f with argument arg", and use another syntax, but those are differences of style, not substance.

That everything relies on this Basic Construct accounts in part for the general feeling of beauty that object-oriented ideas arouse in many people.

From the Basic Construct follows the basic kind of abnormal event that might occur at execution time:

> ### Definition: type violation
>
> A run-time type violation (or just type violation for short) occurs in the execution of a call $x.f(arg)$, where x is attached to an object OBJ, if either:
>
> V1 • There is no feature corresponding to f and applicable to OBJ.
>
> V2 • There is such a feature, but *arg* is not an acceptable argument for it.

The typing problem is the need to avoid such events:

> ### Object-oriented typing problem
>
> When do we know whether the execution of an object-oriented system may produce a type violation?

The key word is *when*. If the feature or arguments do not match, you will find out sooner or later: applying the feature "raise salary" to an instance of *SUBMARINE* or "fire the torpedoes" to an instance of *EMPLOYEE* will not work; somehow the execution will fail. But you may prefer to find out sooner rather than later.

Static and dynamic typing

Although intermediate variants are possible, two main approaches present themselves:

- *Dynamic typing*: wait until the last possible moment, the execution of each call.

- *Static typing*: rely on a set of rules that determine, from the text of a system, whether its executions may cause type violations. Only execute systems for which the rules guarantee that no violation will ever occur.

The names are easy to explain: with dynamic typing, type verification occurs at execution time (dynamically); with static typing, it is performed on the text of the software (statically, that is to say before any execution).

> The terms "typed" and "untyped" are sometimes used for "statically typed" and "dynamically typed". To avoid any confusion we will stick to the full names.

Static typing is only interesting if the rules can be checked automatically. Since software texts are usually processed by a compiler before being executed, it is convenient to have the compiler, rather than a separate tool, take care of these checks. The rest of the discussion will indeed assume for simplicity that the compiler and the type checker are the same tool. This assumption yields a simple definition:

> ### Definition: statically typed language
>
> An object-oriented language is statically typed if it is equipped with a set of consistency rules, enforceable by compilers, whose observance by a system text guarantees that no execution of the system can cause a type violation.

In the literature you will encounter the term "*strong* typing". It corresponds to the all-or-nothing nature of this definition, which demands rules that guarantee the absence of type violations. *Weak* forms of static typing, whose rules eliminate certain type violations but not all, are also possible, and some O-O languages are indeed weakly-statically-typed in this sense. We shall strive, however, for the strongest possible form.

Some authors also talk about strong forms of dynamic typing. But this is a contradiction.

In a dynamically typed language (also known as an "untyped" language), there are no type declarations; entities simply become associated with whatever values the execution of the software attaches to them. No static type checking is possible.

Typing rules

Our object-oriented notation is statically typed. Its type rules have been introduced in earlier chapters; they boil down to three simple constraints:

- Every entity or function must be declared as being of a certain type, as in *acc*: *ACCOUNT*; every routine declares zero or more formal arguments, with a type for each, as in *put* (*x*: *G*; *i*: *INTEGER*).

Type Conformance rule, page 474.

- In any assignment *x* := *y*, and in any routine call using *y* as the actual argument for the formal argument *x*, the type of the source *y* must conform to the type of the target *x*. The definition of conformance is based on inheritance — *B* conforms to *A* if it is a descendant of *A* — complemented by rules for generic parameters.

Feature Call rule, page 473.

- In a call of the form *x* • *f* (*arg*), *f* must be a feature of the base class of *x*'s type, and must be available to the class in which the call appears.

Realism

Although the definition of "statically typed language" is precise, it also highlights the need for informal criteria in devising type rules. Consider the following two extreme cases:

- An *all-valid language* in which every syntactically correct system is also typewise-valid, with no need for type rules. Such languages are possible (imagine for example a small notation for Polish-style additions and subtractions with integers); unfortunately, as readers familiar with the theory of computation will know, no useful general-purpose language can meet that criterion.

- An *all-invalid language*, easy to devise: just take any existing language and add a type rule that makes *any* system invalid! This makes the language typed according to the definition: since no system passes the rules, no system that passes the rules can cause a type violation.

We may say that an all-valid language is **usable**, but not **useful** for general-purpose development; an all-invalid language may be useful, but it is not usable.

What we need in practice is a type system that makes the language both useful and usable: powerful enough to express the computations we need; convenient enough not to force us into undue complications to satisfy the type rules.

We will say that a language is **realistic** if it is both useful and usable. Unlike the definition of static typing, which always yields an indisputable answer to the question "*Is language X statically typed?*", the definition of realism is partly subjective; reasonable people may disagree on whether a language, equipped with certain type rules, is still useful and usable.

In this chapter we will check that the typed notation defined in the preceding chapters is realistic.

Pessimism

In discussing approaches to O-O typing we should keep in mind another general property of static typing: it is always, by nature, a pessimistic policy. Trying to guarantee that *no computation shall ever fail*, you disallow *some computations that might succeed*.

To see this, consider a trivial non-O-O language, Pascal-like, with distinct types *INTEGER* and *REAL*. With the declaration *n: INTEGER*, the assignment *n := r* will be rejected as violating the type rules. So all the following will be considered type-invalid and rejected by the compiler:

n := 0.0	[A]
n := 1.0	[B]
n := —3.67	[C]
n := 3.67 — 3.67	[D]

Of these invalid operations, [A], if permitted to execute, would always work since any number system will provide an exact representation for the floating-point number 0.0, which can be transformed unambiguously to the integer 0. [B] would almost certainly work too. [C] is ambiguous (do we want the rounded version, the truncated version of the number?) But [D] would work. So would

if $n \wedge 2 < 0$ **then** $n := 3.67$ **end** [E]

because the assignment will never be executed ($n \wedge 2$ denotes the square of *n*). If we replace $n \wedge 2$ by just *n*, where *n* is read from user input just before the test, some executions would work (those for which *n* is non-negative), others would not. Assigning to *n* a very large real number, not representable as an integer, would not work.

In a typed language, all these examples — those which would always work, those which would never work, and those which would work some of the time — are equally and mercilessly considered violations of the type rules, and any compiler will reject them.

The question then is not *whether* to be pessimistic but *how* pessimistic we can afford to be. We are back to the realism requirement: if the type rules are so pessimistic as to bar us from expressing in a simple way the computations that we need, we will reject them. But if they achieve type safety with little loss of expressive power, we will accept them and enjoy the benefits. For example making *n := r* invalid turns out to be good news if the environment provides functions such as *round* and *truncate*, enabling you to convert a real into an integer in exactly the way you want, without the ambiguity of an implicit conversion.

17.2 STATIC TYPING: WHY AND HOW

Although the advantages of static typing seem obvious, it is necessary to review the terms of the debate.

The benefits

The reasons for using a statically typed form of object technology were listed at the very beginning of this chapter: reliability, readability and efficiency.

The **reliability** value comes from the use of static typing to detect errors that would otherwise manifest themselves only at run time, and only in certain runs. The rule that forces you to declare entities and functions — the first of our three type rules above — introduces redundancy into the software text; this enables the compiler, through the other two rules, to detect inconsistencies between the purpose and actual use of an entity, feature or expression.

Catching errors early is essential, as correction cost grows quickly with the detection delay. This property, intuitively clear to all software professionals, is confirmed quantitatively, for specification errors, by Boehm's well-known studies, plotting the cost of correcting an error against the time at which it is found (base 1 if found at requirements time), for both a set of large industrial projects and a controlled small project experiment:

Relative cost of correcting errors

After [Boehm 1981]. Reproduced with permission.

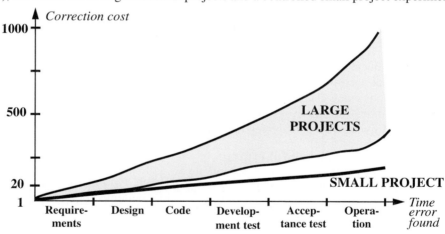

The **readability** benefit is also appreciable. As the examples appearing throughout this book should show convincingly, declaring every entity and function with a certain type is a powerful way of conveying to the software reader some information about its intended uses. This is particularly precious for maintainers of the software.

> If readability were not part of the goal we might be able to obtain some of the other benefits of typing without explicit declarations. It is possible indeed, under certain conditions, to use an implicit form of typing in which the compiler, instead of requiring software authors to declare entity types, attempts to determine the type of each entity automatically from its uses. This is known as *type inference*. But from a software engineering perspective explicit declarations are a help, not a penalty; types should be clear not just to the compiler but to the human reader.

Finally, the **efficiency** benefit can make the difference between success and failure of object technology in practice. Without static typing, the execution of $x \cdot f\,(arg)$ can take an arbitrary long time: as we saw in the discussion of inheritance, the basic algorithm looks for a feature f in the base class C of x's type; if it does not find it, it looks in C's parents, and so on. This is a fatal source of inefficiency. It can be mitigated by improvements to the basic algorithm, and the authors of the Self language have done extensive work to enable better code generation for a dynamically typed language. But it is through static typing that O-O software has been able to approach or equal the efficiency of traditional software.

For more details on the implementation techniques discussed in this section see "Dynamic binding and efficiency", page 507. On Self, see the bibliographical notes.

The key idea was explained in the earlier discussion. When the compiler generates the code for $x \cdot f\,(arg)$, it knows the type of x. Because of polymorphism, this is not necessarily the type of the attached run-time object OBJ, and so does not uniquely determine the proper version of f. But the declaration restricts the set of possible types, enabling the compiler to generate tables providing run-time access to the right f at minimum — and **constant-bounded** — expense. Further optimizations of *static binding* and *inlining*, also facilitated by typing, eliminate the expense altogether in applicable cases.

Arguments for dynamic typing

In spite of these benefits of static typing, dynamic typing keeps its supporters, found in particular in the Smalltalk community. Their argument mainly follows from the realism issue cited above: they contend that static typing is too constraining, preventing the unfettered expression of software ideas. Terms such as "stranglehold" and "chastity belt" are often heard in such discussions.

This argument can be correct, but only for a statically typed language that misses some important facilities. It is indeed remarkable that all the type-related concepts introduced in preceding chapters are necessary; remove any of them, and the straitjacket comment becomes valid in at least some cases. But by including them all we obtain enough flexibility to make static typing both practical and pleasurable.

The ingredients of successful typing

Let us review the mechanisms which permit realistic static typing. They have all been introduced in earlier chapters, so that we only need a brief reminder for each; listing them all together shows the consistency and power of their combination.

Our type system is entirely based on the notion of **class**. Even basic types such as *INTEGER* are defined by classes. So we do not need special rules for predefined types. (Here the notation departs from "hybrid" languages such as Object Pascal, Java and C++, which retain the type system of an older language along with the class-based system of object technology.)

Expanded types give us more flexibility by allowing types whose values denote objects along with types whose values denote object references.

"COMPOSITE OBJECTS AND EXPANDED TYPES", 8.7, page 254..

Crucial flexibility is afforded by **inheritance** and the associated notion of **conformance**. This addresses the major limitation of traditional typed languages such as Pascal and Ada, where an assignment $x := y$ requires the types of x and y to be identical.

"Limits to polymorphism", page 474.

This rule is too strict: it prevents you from using an entity that may denote objects of various related types, such as a *SAVINGS_ACCOUNT* and a *CHECKING_ACCOUNT*. With inheritance, all we require is that the type of *y* conform to the type of *x*; this is the case if *x* is of type *ACCOUNT*, *y* of type *SAVINGS_ACCOUNT*, and the latter class is a descendant of the former.

Chapter 15.

To be practical, a statically typed language requires its inheritance scheme to support **multiple inheritance**. A principal part of common objections against static typing is that it prevents you from looking at objects in different ways. For example an object of type *DOCUMENT* might need to be transmitted over a network, and so will need the features associated with objects of type *MESSAGE*. But this is only a problem with a language that is restricted to single inheritance; with multiple inheritance you can introduce as many viewpoints as you need.

Multiple inheritance

Chapter 10.

We also need **genericity**, to define flexible yet type-safe container data structures. For example a list class will be defined as **class** *LIST* [*G*] … Without this mechanism, static typing would force us to declare a different class for each type of list element — an obviously unsustainable solution.

"CONSTRAINED GENERICITY", 16.4, page 585.

Genericity needs in some cases to be **constrained**, allowing us to apply certain operations to entities of a generic type. For example if a generic class *SORTABLE_LIST* has a sort operation, it requires a comparison operation on entities of type *G*, the generic parameter. This is achieved by associating with *G* a generic constraint *COMPARABLE*:

class *SORTABLE_LIST* [*G* –> *COMPARABLE*] …

meaning that any actual generic parameter used for *SORTABLE_LIST* must be a descendant of class *COMPARABLE*, which has the required comparison features.

"ASSIGNMENT ATTEMPT", 16.5, page 591.

Another indispensable mechanism is **assignment attempt**, to access objects whose type the software does not control. If *y* denotes an object obtained from a database or a network, you cannot be sure it has the expected type; the assignment attempt *x* ?= *y* will assign to *x* the value of *y* if it is of a compatible type, but otherwise will make *x* void. Without assignment attempt we could not abide by the type rules in such cases.

Chapter 11.

Assertions — associated, as part of the idea of Design by Contract, with classes and features in the form of preconditions, postconditions and class invariants — allow you to describe semantic constraints which cannot be captured by type specifications. Although with the "interval types" of such languages as Pascal and Ada you can declare, for example, that a certain entity takes its values between 10 and 20, no type mechanism will enable you to state that i must be either in that interval or negative, and always twice as much as j. Here class invariants come to the rescue, by letting you specify exactly what you need, however sophisticated the constraint.

Anchored declarations are essential in practice to avoid redeclaration avalanche. By declaring y: **like** x you make sure that y will follow any redeclaration of the type of x in a descendant. Without this mechanism developers would be endlessly redeclaring routines for type purposes only.

"ANCHORED DECLARATION", 16.7, page 598.

Anchored declarations are a specific case of our last required language mechanism: **covariance**, which will be discussed in more detail later in this chapter.

A practical property of the environment is also essential: **fast incremental recompilation**. When you write a system or (more commonly) modify an existing system, you will want to see the effect soon. With static typing you must first let the compiler re-typecheck the system. Traditional compiling techniques require recompiling the whole system (and going through a *linking* process); the time may be painfully long, especially for a proportionally small change to a large system. This phenomenon has been a major *a contrario* argument for **interpreted** approaches, such as those of early Lisp and Smalltalk environments, which execute systems with no or little processing, hence no type checking. But modern compiler technology removes this argument. A good compiler will detect what has changed since the last compilation, and reprocess only that part, keeping the recompilation time small — and proportional to the size of the change, not of the system.

> The *Melting Ice Technology* described in the last chapter of this book achieves this goal, typically permitting recompilation in a matter of seconds after a small change even to a large system.

"A little bit typed"?

It was noted above that we should aim for a *strong* form of static typing. This means that we should avoid any loopholes in the static requirements — or, if any such loopholes remain, identify them clearly, if possible providing tools to flag any software using them.

The most common loophole, in languages that are otherwise statically typed, is the presence of conversions that disguise the type of an entity. In C and its derivatives, conversions are called "casts" and follow a simple syntax: (*OTHER_TYPE*) x denotes the value of x presented to the compiler as if it were of type *OTHER_TYPE*; there are few limitations on what that type may be, regardless of x's actual type.

Such mechanisms evade the constraints of type checking; casting is indeed a pervasive feature of C programming, including in the ANSI C variant (which is "more" typed than its precursor, the so-called Kernighan and Ritchie version). Even in C++, examination of published software shows that casts, although less frequent, remain an accepted and possibly indispensable occasional practice.

It seems difficult to accept claims of static typing if at any stage the developer can eschew the type rules through casts. Accordingly, the rest of this chapter will assume that the type system is strict and allows no casts.

You may have noted that assignment attempts, mentioned above as an essential component of a realistic type system, superficially resemble casts. But there is a fundamental difference: an assignment attempt does not blindly force a different type; it *tries* a candidate type, and enables the software to check whether the object actually matches that type. This is safe, and indispensable in some circumstances. The C++ literature sometimes includes assignment attempts ("downcasts") in its definition of casts; clearly, the above prohibition of casts only covers the harmful variant, and does not extend to assignment attempts.

Typing and binding: avoiding the confusion

Although as a reader of this book you will have no difficulty distinguishing static typing from static *binding*, you may meet people who confuse the two notions. This may be due in part to the influence of Smalltalk, whose advocacy of a dynamic approach to both typing and binding may leave the inattentive observer with the incorrect impression that the answer to both questions must be the same. (The analysis developed in this book suggests that to achieve reliability and flexibility it is preferable to combine dynamic binding with static typing.) Let us carefully compare the two concepts.

Both have to do with the semantics of the Basic Construct $x.f(arg)$; they cover the two separate questions that it raises:

Typing and binding

- **Typing question**: When do we know for sure that at run time there will be an operation corresponding to f and applicable to the object attached to x (with the argument arg)?
- **Binding question**: Which operation will the call execute?

Typing addresses the existence of **at least one** operation; binding addresses the choice of **the right one** among these operations, if there is more than one candidate.

In object technology:

- The typing question follows from *polymorphism*: since x may denote run-time objects of several possible types, we must make sure that an operation representing f is available in all cases.

- The binding question follows from *redeclaration*: since a class can change an inherited feature — as with *RECTANGLE* redefining *perimeter* inherited from *POLYGON* — there may be two or more operations all vying to be the one representing f for a particular call.

Both answers can be dynamic, meaning at execution time, or static, meaning before execution. All four possibilities appear in actual languages:

- Some non-O-O languages, such as Pascal and Ada, have both static typing and static binding. In these languages each entity represents objects of only one type, specified statically; the approach yields reliability at the expense of flexibility.

- Smalltalk and other O-O languages influenced by it have dynamic binding and dynamic typing. This is the reverse choice: favoring flexibility at the expense of reliability enforcement.

- Some non-O-O languages are untyped (really meaning, as we have seen, dynamically typed) and statically bound. They include assembly languages and some scripting languages.

- The notation developed in this book supports static typing and dynamic binding.

Note the peculiarity of C++ which supports static typing (although in a non-strong form because of the presence of casts) and, for binding, a static policy by default, while permitting dynamic binding at the price of explicit **virtual** declarations.

The C++ policy was discussed in "The C++ approach to binding", page 513.

The reason choosing static typing and dynamic binding is clear. To the first question, "when do we know we have a feature?", the most attractive answer for reliable software engineering is the static one: "*at the earliest possible time*" — compilation time, to catch errors before they catch you. To the second question, "what feature do we use?", the most attractive answer is the dynamic one: "*the right feature*" — the feature directly adapted to the object's type. As discussed in detail in the presentation of inheritance, this is the only acceptable solution unless static and dynamic binding have the same effect.

The following fictitious inheritance hierarchy helps make these notions more vivid.

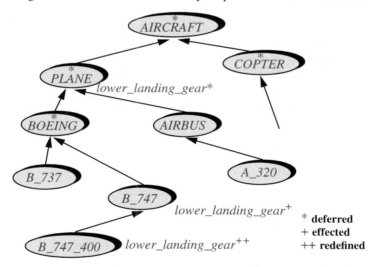

Kinds of flying object

For a call of the form

my_aircraft.lower_ landing_gear

the typing question is when to ascertain that there will be a feature *lower_ landing_gear* applicable to the object (for a *COPTER* there would not be any); the binding question is which version to choose (since we have several versions, as shown).

Static binding would mean that we disregard the object type and believe the entity declaration, leading us for example to apply to a Boeing 747-400 the version of a feature, such as *lower_landing_gear*, that has been defined for the standard Boeing 747 planes, instead of the version specially redefined for the 747-400 variant; this is clearly wrong if the object is of the latter type. Dynamic binding will apply the operation that the object demands, based on its type; this is the right approach.

With static typing we will refuse the call at compile time unless we can guarantee that whatever happens to *my_aircraft* at run time the type of the attached object will be equipped with a feature corresponding to *lower_landing_gear*. The basic technique for obtaining this guarantee is simple: since we must declare *my_aircraft*, we require that its type's base class include such a feature. This means that the declared type cannot be *AIRCRAFT* since there is no *lower_landing_gear* at that level; helicopters, for example, have no landing gears, for the purpose of this example at least. With such a declaration the compiler would reject our software with no possibility of appeal. But if we declare the entity as being of type *PLANE*, which has the required feature, all is well.

Smalltalk-style ynamic typing would mean waiting until execution to find out if there is an applicable feature; acceptable perhaps for prototypes and experimental software, but not for production systems. Run time is a little late to ask whether you have a landing gear.

17.3 COVARIANCE AND DESCENDANT HIDING

In a simple world a discussion of typing would stop here: we have defined the goals and advantages of static typing; examined the constraints that a realistic type system must meet; and reviewed the typing techniques of the object-oriented framework developed in the preceding chapters, checking that they satisfy the stated criteria.

The world is not simple. The combination of static typing with some of the software engineering requirements of object technology makes the issues more difficult than they appear at first. Two techniques raise difficulties: covariance, the change of argument types in redefinitions; and descendant hiding, the ability for a class to restrict the export status of an inherited feature.

Covariance

See the original discussions in "TYPING AND REDECLARATION" 16.6, page 595 and "ANCHORED DECLARATION", 16.7, page 598.

The principal problem is what happens to arguments when we redefine a feature's type. We have encountered several cases already: devices and printers, linkable and bi-linkable elements, points and their conjugates.

To understand the general nature of the issue let us use a fresh example. Being non-technical, it carries the usual risks of metaphors; but the closeness to software schemes is obvious, and we will frequently come back to actual software examples.

The example involves a high-school ski team preparing for a trip to a minor-league championship, and the team members' concerned parents. For brevity and simplicity it uses the class names *GIRL* as an abbreviation for "member of the girls' ski team" and *BOY* as an abbreviation for "member of the boys' ski team". Some skiers on each team are ranked, that is to say have already recorded good results in earlier championships. This is an important notion: ranked skiers will start first in a slalom, thus gaining a considerable advantage over the others since a slalom run is much harder to negotiate after too many competitors have already worked it. (This rule that ranked skiers go first is a way to privilege the already privileged, and may be the reason why skiing exerts such a fascination over many people: that it serves as an apt metaphor for life itself.) We get two new classes, *RANKED_GIRL* and *RANKED_BOY*.

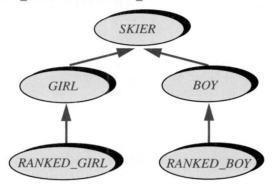

Kinds of skier

Some rooms are reserved for boys only, girls only, ranked girls only; we may use a class hierarchy parallel to the one above: *ROOM*, *GIRL_ROOM*, *RANKED_GIRL_ROOM* etc. The discussion will omit *RANKED_BOY* which is parallel to *RANKED_GIRL*.

Here is an outline of class *SKIER*:

class *SKIER* **feature**
    roommate: *SKIER*
        -- This skier's roommate
    share (*other*: *SKIER*) **is**
        -- Choose *other* as roommate.
      require
        other /= *Void*
      do
        roommate := *other*
      end
    … Other possible features omitted in this class and the following ones …
end -- class *SKIER*

We have two features of interest: the attribute *roommate*; and the procedure *share*, which assigns a certain skier as roommate to the current skier, as in

s1, *s2*: *SKIER*
…
s1 • *share* (*s2*)

Rather than *SKIER*, you may have thought of using for *other* the anchored type **like** *roommate* (or **like** *Current* for both *roommate* and *other*). If so, you are most likely right, but let us forget for a while that we know about anchored types: this will enable us to understand the covariance problem in its bare form; anchored types will soon come back.

How does type redefinition get into the picture? Assume the rules require girls to share rooms only with girls, and ranked girls only with other ranked girls. We will redefine the type of feature *roommate*, as shown below (in this class text and the next, the redefined elements appear <u>underlined</u>).

> **class** *GIRL* **inherit**
> > *SKIER*
> > > **redefine** <u>*roommate*</u> **end**
>
> **feature**
> > *roommate*: <u>*GIRL*</u>
> > > -- This skier's roommate.
>
> **end** -- class *GIRL*

We should correspondingly redefine the argument to procedure *share*, so that a more complete version of the class text is:

> **class** *GIRL* **inherit**
> > *SKIER*
> > > **redefine** <u>*roommate*</u>, <u>*share*</u> **end**
>
> **feature**
> > *roommate*: <u>*GIRL*</u>
> > > -- This skier's roommate.
> > *share* (*other*: <u>*GIRL*</u>) **is**
> > > -- Choose *other* as roommate.
> > > **require**
> > > > *other* /= *Void*
> > > **do**
> > > > *roommate* := *other*
> > > **end**
>
> **end** -- class *GIRL*

All proper descendants must be adapted in this way (remember, we are depriving ourselves from anchored types for the moment). The general picture is this:

Skier hierarchy and redefinitions

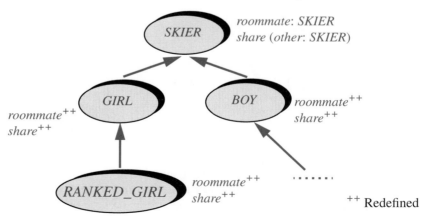

Since inheritance is specialization, the type rules require that if we redefine the result of a feature, here *roommate*, the new type must always be a descendant of the original one. This also applies to the redefined type for the argument *other* of routine *share*. This policy, as we know, is called covariance, where the "co" indicates that the argument and result vary together; the reverse policy is termed *contravariance*.

Type Redeclaration rule, page 598.

Covariance is, according to all available evidence, what we need in practice. Our earlier software examples illustrate this clearly:

- A *LINKABLE* list element may be chained to any other linkable; a *BI_LINKABLE* must be chained to another *BI_LINKABLE*. So the argument of procedure *put_right* should be redefined covariantly.

"Type inconsistencies", page 598.

- In the same example, any routine of *LINKED_LIST* that uses an argument of type *LINKABLE* will most likely need it to be of type *BI_LINKABLE* in *TWO_WAY_LIST*.

Figure "Parallel hierarchies", page 597.

- Procedure *set_alternate* takes a *DEVICE* argument in class *DEVICE*, a *PRINTER* argument in class *PRINTER*.

Covariant redefinition is particularly common because of the O-O method's emphasis on information hiding, which leads to procedures of the form

set_attrib (*v*: *SOME_TYPE*) **is**
        -- Set *attrib* to *v*.
   ...

with *attrib* of type *SOME_TYPE*; such procedures are naturally covariant (and in practice, as we know, will usually rely on anchored types) since any class that changes the type of *attrib* will need to redefine *set_attrib*'s argument in the same way. The preceding examples mostly belonged to this scheme, but it is by no means the only one requiring covariance. Think for example of a procedure or function for concatenating a *LINKED_LIST* to another: its argument will have to be redefined as a two-way-list in *TWO_WAY_LIST*. The general addition operation, **infix** "+", takes a *NUMERIC* argument in *NUMERIC*, a *REAL* argument in *REAL*, an *INTEGER* argument in *INTEGER*. In the parallel hierarchies

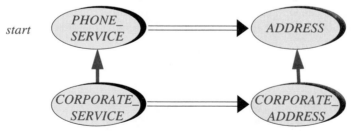

start

Phone service and billing addresses

procedure *start*, which starts a phone service, may need an argument of type *ADDRESS* representing the billing address; for a corporate account you will need a corporate address.

What about a contravariant solution? In the skier example, contravariance would mean that if we go to class *RANKED_GIRL*, where the result of *roommate* is redefined to be of type *RANKED_GIRL*, we may for the argument of routine *share* use type *GIRL*, or *SKIER* of the most general kind. One type that is *not* permitted under contravariance is *RANKED_GIRL*! Enough to justify the parents' worst fears.

Parallel hierarchies

To leave no stone unturned, it is useful to consider a variant of the *SKIER* example with two parallel hierarchies, rather than just one. This will model the situation evidenced in software examples already cited: *TWO_WAY_LIST* → *LINKED_LIST* parallel to *BI_LINKABLE* → *LINKABLE*, or the *PHONE_SERVICE* hierarchy. Just assume that we have a *ROOM* hierarchy with descendants such as *GIRL_ROOM* (*BOY* variants omitted):

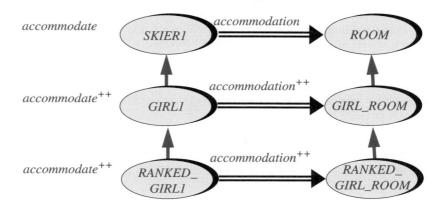

Then instead of *roommate* and *share*, the skier classes will have features *accommodation* and *accommodate*:

indexing
> *description*: *"New variant with parallel hierarchies"*

class *SKIER1* **feature**
> *accommodation*: *ROOM*
>
> *accommodate* (*r*: *ROOM*) **is** … **require** … **do**
> > *roommate* := *other*
>
> > **end**

end -- class *SKIER1*

Here too we need covariant redefinition: in class *GIRL1* both *accommodation* and the argument of *accommodate* should be redeclared of type *GIRL_ROOM*, in *BOY1* they should be of type *BOY_ROOM*, and so on. (Remember again that for the time being we are working without anchored types.) A contravariant policy would be as useless as in the preceding form of the example.

Polymorphic perversity

Enough covariant examples. Why would anyone consider contravariance, which goes against what we need in practice (not to mention proper behavior for young people)? To understand, we have to consider the problems that polymorphism may cause under a covariant policy. A harmful scheme is easy to make up, and you may have thought of it yourself already:

s: *SKIER*; *b*: *BOY*; *g*: *GIRL*

...

!! *b*; !! *g*;   -- Creation of a *BOY* and *GIRL* objects.

s := *b*;   -- Polymorphic assignment.

s.*share* (*g*)

The effect of the last call, although possibly to the boys' liking, is exactly what the type definitions were attempting to exclude. A room assignment makes a boy object, known as *b* but also disguising itself polymorphically under the *SKIER* pseudonym *s*, the roommate of the *GIRL* object attached to *g*. Yet the call appears type-correct, since *share* is an exported feature of class *SKIER*, and *GIRL*, the type of argument *g*, conforms to *SKIER*, the type declared for the formal argument of *share* in *SKIER*.

The corresponding scheme with the parallel hierarchy variant is just as simple: just replace *SKIER* by *SKIER1* etc., and the call to *share* by a a call *s*.*accommodate* (*gr*), where *gr* is of type *GIRL_ROOM*: at run time this will assign a boy to a girl room.

With contravariance one would not have these problems: as you specialize the target of a call (*s* in the example), you would generalize the argument. Contravariance, as a result, leads to simpler mathematical models of the inheritance-redefinition-polymorphism mechanism. For that reason a number of theoretical articles have advocated contravariance. But the argument is not very convincing, since, as we have seen and as the literature readily admits, contravariance is of essentially no practical use.

> An argument often encountered in the programming literature is that one should strive for techniques that have simple mathematical models. Mathematical elegance, however, is only one of several design criteria; we should not forget to make our designs realistic and useful too. In computing science as in other disciplines, it is after all much easier to devise dramatically simple theories if we neglect to make them agree with reality.

So rather than trying to force a covariant body into a contravariant suit, we should accept the reality for what it is, covariant, and study ways to remove the unpleasant effects.

Descendant hiding

Before looking for solutions to the covariance problem, let us examine the other mechanism that can cause type violations through polymorphism. Descendant hiding is the ability for a class not to export a feature that was exported by one of its parents.

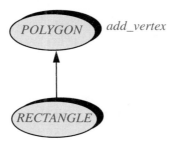

A typical example is a feature *add_vertex*, which class *POLYGON* exports but its descendant *RECTANGLE* hides, because it would violate the invariant of the class:

class *RECTANGLE* **inherit**
    POLYGON
            export {*NONE*} *add_vertex* **end**
feature
    …
invariant
    vertex_count = 4
end

A non-software counterpart is the well-known example of *OSTRICH* inheriting from a class *BIRD* equipped with a feature *fly*, which *OSTRICH* should not export.

*"SUBTYPE INHER-
ITANCE AND
DESCENDANT
HIDING", 24.7,
page 835.*

Let us for the moment accept this scheme at face value, setting aside the question, discussed in detail later, of whether such forms of inheritance are methodologically legitimate. The modeling power of descendant hiding, like that of covariance, clashes with the tricks made possible by polymorphism. An example is trivial to build:

p: *POLYGON*; *r*: *RECTANGLE*
…
!! *r*;   -- Creation of a *RECTANGLE* object.
p := *r*;   -- Polymorphic assignment.
p.*add_vertex* (…)

Since *add_vertex* is an exported feature of *POLYGON*, the call appears type-correct; if accepted, it would on execution add a vertex to a rectangle, producing an inconsistent object.

Class and system validity

Some terminology will be useful to discuss the issues raised by covariance and descendant hiding. A system is **class-valid** if it satisfies the type rules summarized at the beginning of this chapter: every entity declared with a type; every assignment and actual-formal argument association satisfies conformance; and every call uses a feature of the target's type, exported to the caller.

The system is **system-valid** if no type violation can occur at run time.

*For an explanation of
the names see end of
17.6, page 636.*

Ideally these two notions (whose names will be justified later in this chapter) should be equivalent. What we have seen through the preceding examples is that with covariance and descendant hiding a system can be class-valid without being system-valid. Such an error — making a system invalid although it is class-valid — will be called a **system validity error**.

Practical scope

The simplicity of the examples of system validity error, resulting from covariance or descendant hiding, makes up what we may call the static typing paradox. On being introduced to object-oriented typing, an inquisitive newcomer can make up such a counter-example in a few minutes; yet in actual development, while violations of class-level validity rules are common (and, caught by the compiler, provide tremendous help in getting the software right), system validity errors are exceedingly rare, even in large, multi-year projects.

This is not an excuse for ignoring them. The rest of this chapter investigates three possible solutions.

An important note: because the problems discussed next are both delicate and infrequent, it is reasonable and indeed suggested, if this is your first reading, that you skip the rest of this chapter unless you are already well-versed in the practical and theoretical aspects of object technology. If you are relatively new to the approach, you will understand the discussion much better after reading the methodological chapters of part D, in particular chapter 24 on the methodology of inheritance.

SUGGESTED SHORTCUT: skip to next chapter.

17.4 FIRST APPROACHES TO SYSTEM VALIDITY

Let us concentrate first on the covariance issue, the more challenging of the two. There is an abundant literature on the subject and we can take a look at various proposed solutions.

Contravariance and novariance

Adopting a contravariant policy removes the theoretical problem of system validity errors. But this approach makes the type system unrealistic, so we need not examine it further.

C++ is original in using a *novariant* policy: when you redefine a routine, you cannot change the types of its arguments! If C++ were a strongly typed language, this would make the type system quite unusable. The easiest solution, as with other such limitations of C++ (such as the absence of constrained genericity), is to use casts, and so to bypass the typing mechanism altogether. This solution is not particularly attractive. Note, however, that some of the proposals discussed next rely on a form of novariance, made meaningful by the introduction of new type mechanisms to replace covariant redefinition.

Using generic parameters

An interesting idea, originally introduced by Franz Weber, relies on genericity. We can declare our class *SKIER1* with a generic parameter representing the room: **class** *SKIER1* [*G*] or rather, using constrained genericity,

> **class** *SKIER1* [*G* –> *ROOM*] **feature**
> > *accommodation*: *G*
> > *accommodate* (*r*: *G*) **is** … **require**… **do** *accommodation* := *r* **end**
>
> **end**

Then class *GIRL1* will inherit from *SKIER1* [*GIRL_ROOM*] and so on. The same technique may be applied to the variant without parallel hierarchies, although it seems stranger at first: **class** *SKIER* [*G* –> *SKIER*].

This approach solves the covariance problem. In any use of the class you need to specify an actual generic parameter — such as *ROOM* or *GIRL_ROOM* —, so the invalid combinations become impossible. The language would become novariant, and systems would satisfy their covariance needs entirely through generic parameters.

Unfortunately, the generic parameter technique is not really acceptable as a general solution. It will lead to inflated generic parameter lists, with one parameter for each type of a possibly covariant argument. To use the class, a developer will have to provide as many types as there are parameters; this will make classes hard to understand.

Worse, adding a covariant routine with an argument of a type not yet covered would require adding a generic parameter to the class, and hence changing its interface, thereby invalidating all client classes. This is not acceptable.

Type variables

Several authors (including Kim Bruce, David Shang, Tony Simons) have proposed solutions based on the introduction of type variables. Although it is impossible to summarize these sophisticated proposals without being unfair, the basic idea is simple: instead of covariant redefinition, permit type declarations to use type variables rather than actual types; extend the conformance rules to handle type variables; make the language otherwise novariant; provide a facility to assign a type value to a type variable.

Instead of *ROOM*, the declarations for attribute *accommodation* and for the argument of *accommodate* would use a type variable, to which an actual type value can be assigned separately.

These proposals are worth considering, and the interested reader should consult the corresponding articles, as well as complementary publications by Cardelli, Castagna, Weber and others, starting from the paper and Web references cited in the bibliographical notes to this chapter. We will not, however, pursue this line, for two reasons:

- The type variable mechanism, if designed properly, should subsume genericity and anchored declarations, the two existing mechanisms for using a type without fully specifying it. At first this can be construed as an argument in favor of type variables, as they might enable us to replace two language constructs by one, and solve other problems at the same time. But the result may not be satisfactory in practice since both genericity and anchored types are simple, widely accepted and easy to explain; it is not clear that an all-encompassing type variable mechanism can do as well.

- Assuming we can indeed devise a type variable mechanism that solves the technical difficulties of combining covariance and polymorphism (still ignoring descendant hiding for the moment), it will require *perfect foresight* from the class designer: knowing in advance which features are subject to type redefinition in descendants, and which are not. The following section will further discuss this problem, which arises from a practical software engineering concern and, unfortunately, hampers the credibility of many theoretically satisfying schemes.

These considerations suggest trying a different approach: examining the mechanisms that we already have at our disposal — constrained and unconstrained genericity, anchored types, and of course inheritance — to see how they can be further constrained to remove the possibility of system validity errors.

17.5 RELYING ON ANCHORED TYPES

We can actually find an almost satisfactory solution to the covariance problem by taking a closer look at a mechanism that we already know well: anchored declarations.

You must indeed have been itching, in the *SKIER* and *SKIER1* examples, to use anchored declarations, removing most of the need for type redefinitions. Anchoring is the covariant mechanism *par excellence*: by declaring y: **like** x, you make y vary with x whenever x gets redefined to descendant-based types in descendant classes. Our examples become:

> **class** *SKIER* **feature**
>
>   *roommate*: **like Current**
>
>   *share* (*other*: **like Current**) **is** … **require** … **do**
>   *roommate* := *other*
>   **end**
>
>   …
>
> **end** -- class *SKIER*
>
> **class** *SKIER1* **feature**
>
>   *accommodation*: *ROOM*
>
>   *accommodate* (*r*: **like** *accommodation*) **is** … **require** … **do**
>   *accommodation* := *r*
>   **end**
>
> **end** -- class *SKIER1*

Underlining indicates the change from earlier versions.

Then descendants need no redefinition in the *SKIER* version, and in the *SKIER1* version they only need to redefine attribute *accommodation*. The anchored entities — *roommate* and the arguments of *share* and *accommodate* — will automatically follow the anchors' redefinitions. This tremendous simplification, in line with what we saw in the original examples of anchored declaration, confirms that without anchoring (or some alternate mechanism such as type variables) it would be impossible to write realistic typed object-oriented software.

But does this eliminate system validity violations? No! At least not without a further restriction. We can still cheat the type checker into letting pass polymorphic assignments that will cause run-time type violations.

True, the original examples will be rejected. In

s: *SKIER*; *b*: *BOY*; *g*: *GIRL*

º

!! *b*;!! *g*;   -- Creation of a *BOY* and *GIRL* objects.

s := *b*;   -- Polymorphic assignment.

s . *share* (*g*)

"Rules on anchored types", page 603.
the argument *g* to *share* is not valid, since we need something of type **like** *s*, and *GIRL* does not conform to **like** *s*. The conformance rule for anchored types stated that no type conforms to **like** *s* other than this type itself.

The relief is short-lived, however, The same rule stated that, in the other direction of conformance, **like** *s* conforms to the type of *s*. So we can fool the type checker, although we have to be pretty devious, by using polymorphism not just on the target *s* of the call but on its argument *g*:

s: *SKIER*; *b*: *BOY*; *g*: **like** *s*; *actual_g*: *GIRL*;

º

!! *b*; !! *actual_g*   -- Creation of a *BOY* and *GIRL* objects.

s := *actual_g*; *g* := *s*   -- Go through *s* to attach *g* to the *GIRL* object.

s := *b*   -- Polymorphic assignment.

s . *share* (*g*)

The effect is exactly the same as before.

There is a way out. If we are serious about using anchored declarations as the sole covariance mechanism, then we can get rid of system validity errors by prohibiting polymorphism altogether on anchored entities. This requires a language change: we would introduce a new keyword **anchor**, used in such declarations as

Warning: hypothetical construct, for purposes of discussion only.
anchor *s*: *SKIER*

Then we would permit a declaration of the form **like** *s* only if *s* is declared in this form, and adapt the conformance rule to make sure that *s* as well as elements of type **like** *s* can be attached (assigned or argument-passed) only to each other.

In the original rule there was a notion of **anchor-equivalent** elements: with *x* declared of some non-anchored type *T* and *y* declared **like** *x*, then *x* and *y* are anchor-equivalent to each other and to any other entity anchor-equivalent to either of them. An attachment to an anchored target was valid only if the source was anchor-equivalent to the target (which makes the assignment *g*:= *s* valid even though *g* is anchored and *s* is not); but there was no such restriction the other way around: *z* := *y* was valid for any *z* of type *T*. With the new approach this would not be permitted any more; in any attachment involving an entity that is either anchor or anchored, the source and the target must be anchor-equivalent.

With this approach, we would remove from the language the possibility of redefining the type of any routine argument. (We could also prohibit redefining the result type, but this is not necessary. We must retain, of course, the possibility of redefining an attribute type.) *All* such redefinitions will now be obtained indirectly, through the anchoring mechanism, which enforces covariance. Where with the earlier approach a class *D* redefined an inherited feature as

$r (u: Y) \ldots$

from an original version, in a proper ancestor C of D, that read

$r (u: X) \ldots$

with Y conforming to X, you should now define the original in C as

$r (u:$ **like** *your_anchor*$) \ldots$

and only redefine in D the type of *your_anchor*.

This solution to the covariance-polymorphism issue will be called the **Anchoring** approach (short for the more accurate "Covariance through anchoring only"). Its properties make it particularly attractive:

- It is based on a clear concept: strictly separating the *covariant* elements from the *potentially polymorphic* ones (just "polymorphic" for short). Any entity declared as **anchor** or as **like** *some_anchor* is covariant; any other is polymorphic. You can have attachments within each category; but no entity or expression will cross the boundary. For example you cannot assign a polymorphic source to a covariant target.

- The solution is simple, elegant, easy to explain even to relative beginners.

- It appears completely tight, removing any possibility of covariance-related system validity violation.

- It retains the framework defined in the preceding chapters, in particular the notions of genericity, constrained or not. (As a result it is, in my opinion, preferable to the introduction of type variables covering both covariance and genericity, since these two mechanisms address clearly distinct practical needs.)

- It entails a small language change — adding one keyword, reinforcing a conformance rule — and no foreseeable implementation difficulty.

- It is, at least in a theoretical sense, **realistic**: any system that was previously possible can be rewritten using the transformation just outlined, replacing covariant redefinitions by anchored redeclarations in the original. True, some attachments will become invalid as a result; but they correspond to cases that could have led to type violations, and can be replaced by assignment attempts, whose result the software can then check to ascertain at run time that everything is fine.

With such arguments we would seem to be at the end of the discussion. Why then is the Anchoring solution not fully satisfactory? First, it still leaves us with the descendant hiding issue. But the fundamental reason is the software engineering concern already voiced during our brief encounter with the notion of type variables. The Yalta-like division of the world into a polymorphic part and a covariant part assumes that the designer of a class always has perfect foresight: for every entity that he introduces, in particular every routine argument, he must decide once and for all between one of two possibilities:

- The entity is potentially polymorphic: now or later, it may become attached (through argument passing if it is a formal argument of a routine, through assignment otherwise) to objects of types other than its declared type. Then no descendant will be permitted to redefine that type.

- The entity is subject to type redefinition: then it is either anchored or an anchor itself.

Page 57.

But how can the designer be sure in each case? Much of the attraction of the object-oriented method, captured at the beginning of this book by the Open-Closed principle, comes from its support for late adaptation of original choices; from the way it accepts that designers of general-purpose modules need *not* have infinite wisdom, since authors of descendants can adapt some of their decisions.

In this imperfection-tolerant approach, both type redefinition and descendant hiding are a safety valve, which enables us to reuse an existing, almost-suitable class:

- With type redefinition, you can adapt the type declaration in the descendant without touching the original (to which, of course, you may lack source access or modification privileges). With the covariance-only solution you would need to change the original, using the transformation outlined earlier.

See "SUBTYPE INHERITANCE AND DESCENDANT HIDING", 24.7, page 835, which discusses taxonomy exceptions.

- Descendant hiding similarly preserves you from suffering too much from the bumps of the design process. True, one may criticize a design which has *RECTANGLE* inherit from *POLYGON* and still want *add_vertex* in *POLYGON*; instead, you may devise an inheritance structure that removes this problem, separating fixed polygons from variable ones. It is indeed preferable to stay away from *taxonomy exceptions* in designing inheritance structures. But can we eliminate them altogether? The discussion of descendant hiding in a later chapter (where we will encounter examples that cannot be restructured as easily as polygons and rectangles) suggests that we cannot, for two reasons. First, various classification criteria may compete: for example we may prefer to classify our polygons into regular and irregular ones. Second, we have to accept that even where an ideal solution is possible some designers will not have seen it, although we may still try to inherit from their classes.

If we want to preserve the flexibility of descendant adaptation, we will need to permit covariant type redefinition — not just through anchoring — and descendant hiding. The next sections describe how.

17.6 GLOBAL ANALYSIS

Skip to "BEWARE OF POLYMOR- PHIC CAT- CALLS!", 17.7, page 636.

(This section describes an intermediate approach; readers interested in an overview of the main practical solutions may skip to the next section.)

In studying the Anchoring solution we noted that the basic idea was to separate the covariant part from the polymorphic part. Indeed, if you consider the two instructions in

$s := b \dots$

$s \boldsymbol{.} share\ (g)$

each is a legitimate application of an important O-O mechanism: the first applies polymorphism; the second uses type redefinition. Things start to go wrong when you combine these operations for the same *s*. Similarly, in

$p := r \dots$

$p \boldsymbol{.} add\_vertex\ (\dots)$

the problem arises from the combination of two individually blameless operations. Here too you can use either instruction by itself without a hitch; include both and you are in trouble.

The type violations follow from erroneous calls. In the first example, the polymorphic assignment attaches *s* to a *BOY* object, making *g* an illegal argument to *share* since *g* is attached to a *GIRL* object. In the second example the assignment attaches *r* to a *RECTANGLE* object, making *add_vertex* a non-exported feature.

Hence an idea for a new solution: determine in advance — statically, as part of the type checking performed by the compiler or set of tools — the **typeset** of each entity, short for "dynamic type set", comprising the types of all objects to which the entity might become attached at run time. Then verify, still statically, that each call is valid for each element of the typesets of the target and arguments.

In our examples, the assignment $s := b$ indicates that *BOY* is in the typeset of *s* (because *BOY* is in the typeset of *b* as a result of the creation instruction !! *b*); *GIRL* is in the typeset of *g* because of the instruction !! *g*; but then the call to *share* would not be valid for a target *s* of type *BOY* and an argument *g* of type *GIRL*. Similarly, *RECTANGLE* is in the typeset of *p* because of the polymorphic assignment, but the call to *add_vertex* would not be valid for *p* of type *RECTANGLE*.

These observations lead to what we may call the **Global** approach, based on a new typing rule:

System Validity rule

A call $x . f (arg)$ is system-valid if and only if it is class-valid for x having any type in its own typeset, and *arg* having any type in its own typeset.

In this definition a call is "class-valid" if it is valid according to the Feature Call rule recalled at the beginning of this chapter: if C is the base class of x's type, f must be an exported feature of C, and the type of *arg* must conform to the type of the formal argument of f. (Remember that for simplicity we assume that each routine has exactly one argument; the rule is trivially transposed to an arbitrary number of arguments.)

System validity is the same thing as ordinary class validity, except that we do not just consider the type declared for the target x and the arguments *arg*: we apply class validity to every possible type in their typesets.

Here is the basic rule for determining the typeset of all entities:

T1 • Start out with an empty typeset for every entity.

T2 • For every creation instruction of the form ! *SOME_TYPE* ! *a*, add *SOME_TYPE* to the typeset of *a*. (For simplicity, assume that any instruction !! *a* has been replaced by ! *ATYPE* ! *a*, where *ATYPE* is the type declared for *a*.)

T3 • For every assignment of the form $a := b$, add all the elements of the typeset of *b* to the typeset of *a*.

T4 • If *a* is a formal argument of a routine, for every corresponding actual argument *b* in a call, add all the elements of the typeset of *b* to the typeset of *a*.

T5 • Repeat steps T3 and T4 until no typeset changes.

This description does not take genericity into account, but the extension is not hard. The repetition (T5) is necessary because of the possibility of attachment chains (an attachment of b to a, of c to b and so on). It is easy to see, however, that the process will terminate after a finite number of steps.

> The number of steps is bounded by the maximum length of attachment chains, that is to say the maximum n such that the system contains attachments of x_{i+1} to x_i for $i = 1, 2, \ldots$ $n-1$. The repetition of T3 and T4 is known as a "fixpoint" technique.

As you may have noted, the rule does not consider instruction sequencing. For example, in

> ! *TYPE1* ! t; $s := t$;   ! *TYPE2* ! t

we will include both *TYPE1* and *TYPE2* into the typeset of s, even though s can only, with the instructions given, become attached to an object of type *TYPE1*. Taking instruction sequencing into account would force the compiler to perform extensive flow analysis, leading to undue complexity. Instead, the rules are more pessimistic: they will flag any occurrence of all three operations

> !! b
>
> $s := b$
>
> $s \cdot share\ (g)$

as system-invalid, even if their possible run-time sequencing cannot possibly lead to a type violation.

The global analysis approach was presented (with more details) in chapter 22 of [M 1992]. It solves both the covariance problem and the descendant hiding problem. It suffers, however, from an annoying practical deficiency: although it does not require flow analysis, it assumes that you are checking an **entire system** at once, rather than each class incrementally. The killer rule is T4, which for any call $x \cdot f(b)$ corresponding to a routine $f(a: ARG\_TYPE)$, adds the typeset of b to that of a. If f is a routine from a library class, this means that adding a call to f in a new client can affect the typesets of f's formal arguments, and ripple over to existing calls in other clients.

Although there have been proposals for incremental algorithms [M 1989b], their practicality has not been established. This means that in a development environment supporting incremental compilation the global analysis technique would need to be implemented as a check on an entire system, rather than as part of the local (and fast) operations that the compiler performs each time a user changes a few classes. Even though there are precedents for such an approach — C developers, for example, sometimes rely on a tool called **lint**, separate from the compilation process, to look for inconsistencies — it is not really attractive, especially in today's sophisticated environments whose users expect the tools to provide fast and complete responses.

As a result, the global validity approach has not to my knowledge been implemented. (Another reason is probably that the rule may appear difficult to teach, especially when given with all the details of genericity etc.)

In passing we have seen the reason for some terminology used since the beginning of this discussion. A system was said to be **class-valid** if it satisfied the basic type rules according to each entity's type declaration; the name indicates that, as we just saw, this can be checked (and checked fast) by an incremental compiler working class-by-class. A system may be class-valid but not yet **system-valid** if its execution can still cause type violations. With the techniques seen so far, detecting this possibility seems to require a global (system-wide) analysis. *"Class and system validity", page 627.*

In spite of the name, however, it is in fact possible to avoid system validity errors through completely incremental checking. This will be our final tack on the issue.

17.7 BEWARE OF POLYMORPHIC CATCALLS!

The System Validity rule of global analysis, it was noted, is pessimistic: to simplify type rules and their enforcement, it may reject harmless combinations. Paradoxical as this may seem, we will obtain our last solution by turning to an even **more pessimistic** rule. This will of course raise the question of how realistic the result is. *Pessimism in type checking was discussed in "Pessimism", page 614.*

Back to Yalta

The gist of the **Catcall** solution — the name, to be explained shortly, for the new approach — is to come back to the Yalta-like character of the Anchoring solution, dividing the world into a polymorphic part and a covariant part (the latter also having, as its satellite, a descendant hiding part), but to remove the need for perfect foresight.

As before we narrow down the covariance issue to two operations: in our main example, the polymorphic assignment, $s := b$, and the call to a covariant routine, $s.share\ (g)$. Analyzing what is truly wrong, we note that the argument g is not an issue in itself; any other argument, which has to be of type *SKIER* or a descendant, would be just as bad since s is polymorphic and *share* covariantly redefines its argument. So with *other* statically declared of type *SKIER* and dynamically attached to a *SKIER* object, the call $s.share\ (other)$, which would seem to be ideally valid on its static face, will cause a type violation if s has been polymorphically assigned the value of b.

The fundamental problem, then, is that we are trying to use s in two incompatible ways: as a polymorphic entity; and as the target of a call to a covariant routine. (In the other working example, the problem is that we use p as both polymorphic entity and target of a call to a descendant-hidden routine *add_vertex*.)

The Catcall solution is drastic, in line with the Anchoring solution: it prohibits using an entity both polymorphically and covariantly. Like the Global solution, it will determine statically which entities can be polymorphic, but it will not try to be smart: instead of finding out the typeset, it just treats any polymorphic entity as suspect enough to warrant lifetime exclusion from any covariance or descendant hiding establishment.

Rule and definitions

The type rule of the Catcall approach is simple:

Catcall type rule

Polymorphic catcalls are invalid.

This is based on equally simple definitions. First, polymorphic entity:

Definition: Polymorphic entity

An entity x of reference (non-expanded) type is polymorphic if it satisfies any of the following properties:

P1 • It appears in an assignment $x := y$ where y is of a different type or (recursively) polymorphic.

P2 • It appears in a creation instruction ! *OTHER_TYPE* ! x where *OTHER_TYPE* is not the type declared for x.

P3 • It is a formal routine argument.

P4 • It is an external function.

The aim of the definition is to capture as polymorphic ("potentially polymorphic" would be more accurate) any entity that may at run time become attached to objects of more than one type. The definition only applies to reference types, since expanded entities cannot by nature be polymorphic.

In our examples, the skier s and the polygon p are both polymorphic from rule P1, since they appear in assignments, the first with a boy b and the second with a rectangle r.

If you have read the definition of the typeset concept in the Global approach, note how much more pessimistic the notion of polymorphic entity is, and simpler to check. Instead of trying to find out all the possible dynamic types of an entity, we settle for a binary property: can it be polymorphic, or can it not? Most strikingly (rule P3), we consider that **any formal argument of a routine is polymorphic** (unless it is expanded, as with integers and the like). We do not even bother to consider the calls to a routine: if you are an argument, you are at the beck and call of any client, so we cannot trust your type. This rule is closely tied to the reusability goal of object technology, where any class has the potential, ultimately, to become part of a reusable library where any client software will be able to call it.

The distinctive feature of this rule is that it does not require any global check. To determine whether an entity is polymorphic, it suffices to examine the text of a class. There is not even any need to examine proper ancestors' texts, provided we record, for each query (attribute or function) of each class, whether it is polymorphic. (We need this information since under P1 the assignment $x := f$ will make x polymorphic if f is polymorphic, whether or not it comes from the same class.) Unlike the computation of typesets in the Global approach, the detection of polymorphic entities can proceed class by class, as part of the checks performed by an incremental compiler.

As discussed in the presentation of inheritance, this analysis can also be precious for optimization purposes *See optimization S2, page 510.*

Calls, as well as entities, may be polymorphic:

> ### Definition: Polymorphic call
>
> A call is polymorphic if its target is polymorphic.

The calls of both examples are polymorphic: $s \cdot share (g)$ since s is polymorphic, and $p \cdot add\_vertex (\ldots)$ since p is polymorphic. The definition implies that only qualified calls $a \cdot f (\ldots)$ can be polymorphic. (Writing an unqualified call $f (\ldots)$ as $Current \cdot f (\ldots)$ changes nothing since $Current$, to which no assignment is possible, cannot be polymorphic.)

Next we need the notion of catcall, based on the notion of CAT. A routine is a CAT (short for Changing Availability or Type) if some redefinition of the routine, in a descendant, makes a change of one of the two kinds we have seen as potentially troublesome: retyping an argument (covariantly), or hiding a previously exported feature.

> ### Definition: CAT (Changing Availability or Type)
>
> A routine is a CAT if some redefinition changes its export status or the type of any of its arguments.

This property is again incrementally checkable: any argument type redefinition or change of export status makes a routine a CAT. It yields the notion of catcall: any call that a CAT change could make invalid. This completes the set of definitions used by the Catcall type rule:

> ### Definition: Catcall
>
> A call is a catcall if some redefinition of the routine would make it invalid because of a change of export status or argument type.

The Catcall type rule promotes our Yalta view by separating calls into two disjoint *Page 637.* categories: polymorphic calls and catcalls. Polymorphic calls yield some of the expressive power of the O-O method; catcalls yield the ability to redefine types and hide features. Using terminology introduced at the beginning of this chapter: polymorphism enhances the *usefulness* of the approach; type redefinition enhances its *usability*.

The calls of our examples are catcalls since *share* redefines its argument covariantly, and *add_vertex*, exported in *RECTANGLE*, is hidden in *POLYGON*. Since they are also polymorphic, they are prime examples of polymorphic catcalls and hence made invalid by the Catcall type rule.

17.8 AN ASSESSMENT

Before trying to summarize what we have learned on the covariance and descendant hiding issues, we should recall once more that system validity violations arise extremely rarely. The most important properties of static O-O typing are the ones summarized at the beginning of this chapter: the impressive array of type-related mechanisms which, with class-level validity, open the way to a safe and flexible method of software construction.

We have seen three solutions to the covariance problem, two of them also addressing descendant hiding. Which one is right?

The answer may not be final. The consequences of subtle interactions between O-O typing and polymorphism are not as well understood as the topics of the preceding chapters. The past few years have seen the appearance of numerous publications on the question, to which the bibliographical notes give the basic pointers. I hope that the present chapter has provided the elements for a definitive solution or something close to it.

The Global solution seems impractical because of the implied need for system-wide checking. But it helps understand the issue.

The Anchoring solution is extremely tempting. It is simple, intuitive, easy to implement. We must all the more regret its failure to support some of the key software engineering requirements of the object-oriented method, as summarized by the Open-Closed principle. If you have perfect foresight, then the Anchoring solution is great; but what designer can promise to have perfect foresight, or assume perfect foresight from the authors of the library classes he reuses through inheritance?

> This assumption limits the usefulness of many of the published approaches, such as those relying on type variables. If we can be assured that the developer always knows in advance which types may change, the theoretical problem becomes much easier, but it does not accurately model the practical problem of typed object-oriented software construction.

If we must give up the Anchoring approach, the Catcall type rule seems to be the appropriate one, easy enough to explain and enforce. Its pessimism should not exclude useful combinations. If a case that appears legitimate yields a polymorphic catcall, it is always possible to let it through safely by introducing an assignment attempt; this is a way to transfer some of the checks to run time. This should only happen in a marginal number of cases.

As a caveat, I should note that at the time of writing the Catcall solution has not yet been implemented. Until a compiler has been adapted to enforce the Catcall type rule and applied successfully to many representative systems, small and large, where success means evidence that the rule is realistic (that all useful systems will pass muster, possibly at the expense of a few easily justifiable changes) and that checking it imposes no significant penalty on incremental recompilation times, we must refrain from proclaiming that on the problem of reconciling static typing and polymorphism with covariance and descendant hiding we have heard the last word.

17.9 THE PERFECT FIT

As a complement to the discussion of covariance it is useful to study a general technique addressing a common problem. This technique was devised as a result of the Catcall theory, but it can be used in the basic language framework without any new rule.

Assume that we have two lists of skiers, where the second list includes the roommate choice of each skier at the corresponding position in the first list. We want to perform the corresponding *share* operations, but only if they are permitted by the type rules, that is to say girls with girls, ranked girls with ranked girls and so on. Problems of this kind are presumably frequent.

A simple solution is possible, based on the preceding discussion and on assignment attempt. Consider the following general-purpose function:

```
fitted (other: GENERAL): like other is
            -- Current object if its type conforms to that of object attached to
            -- other; void otherwise.
      do
            if other /= Void and then conforms_to (other) then
                  Result ?= Current
            end
      end
```

Function *fitted* returns the current object, but known through an entity of a type anchored to the argument; if this is not possible, that is to say if the type of the current object does not conform to that of the object attached to the argument, it returns void. Note the role of assignment attempt. The function relies on *conforms_to*, a feature of class *GENERAL* that determines whether the type of an object conforms to that of another.

On GENERAL, conforms_to and same_type, see "Universal features", page 582.

Replacing *conforms_to* by *same_type*, another *GENERAL* feature, yields a function *perfect_fitted* that returns void unless the types are exactly the same.

Function *fitted* gives us a simple solution to the problem of matching skiers without violating type rules. We can for example add the following procedure to class *SKIER* and use it in lieu of *share* (perhaps making *share* a secret procedure for more control):

```
safe_share (other: SKIER) is
            -- Choose other as roommate if permissible.
      local
            gender_ascertained_other: like Current
      do
            gender_ascertained_other := other . fitted (Current)
            if gender_ascertained_other /= Void then
                  share (gender_ascertained_other)
            else
                  "Report that matching is impossible for other"
            end
      end
```

For *other* of arbitrary *SKIER* type — not just **like** *Current* — we define a version *gender_ascertained_other* which has a type anchored to *Current*. To enforce identical types — so that a *RANKED_GIRL* goes only with another *RANKED_GIRL*, not with a mere *GIRL* — use *perfect_fitted* instead of *fitted*.

If you have two parallel lists of skiers, representing planned roommate assignments:

occupant1, occupant2: *LIST* [*SKIER*]

you can iterate over the lists, applying at each stage

occupant1 . item . safe_share (*occupant2 . item*)

to match elements at corresponding positions if and only if their types are compatible.

I find this technique elegant; I hope you will too. And of course parents anxious about what really happens during the ski trip should breathe a sigh of relief.

17.10 KEY CONCEPTS STUDIED IN THIS CHAPTER

- Static typing is essential for reliability, readability and efficiency.

- Static typing, to be realistic, requires a combination of mechanisms, including assertions, multiple inheritance, assignment attempt, constrained and unconstrained genericity, anchored declarations. The type system must not allow loopholes ("casts").

- Practical rules for routine redeclarations should permit covariant redeclaration: both results and arguments may be redefined to types conforming to the originals.

- Covariance, as well as the ability to hide in a descendant a feature that was exported in an ancestor, raise the rare but serious possibility of type violations when combined with polymorphism.

- Such type violations can be avoided through global analysis (impractical), limiting covariance to anchored types (conflicting with the Open-Closed principle), or the "catcall" technique which bars any covariance or descendant hiding for any routine used with a polymorphic target.

17.11 BIBLIOGRAPHICAL NOTES

Some of the material of this chapter originated with a keynote talk given at the OOPSLA 95 and TOOLS PACIFIC 95 conferences and published as [M 1996a]. Some of the overview material has been drawn from a journal article, [M 1989e].

The notion of automatic type inference was introduced by [Milner 1989], which describes an inference algorithm for the functional language ML. The connection between polymorphism and type checking is further explored in [Cardelli 1984a].

Techniques for improving the efficiency of dynamically typed language implementations are described, in the context of the Self language, in [Ungar 1992].

Luca Cardelli and Peter Wegner are the authors of an influential theoretical article on types in programming languages [Cardelli 1985]; using lambda calculus as the mathematical framework, it has served as a basis for much of the subsequent work. It followed another foundational article by Cardelli [Cardelli 1984].

For an introduction to lambda calculus see [M 1990].

An ISE manual [M 1988a] included a brief presentation of the issues raised by the combination of polymorphism with covariance and descendant hiding. The absence of such an analysis in the first edition of this book led to some critical discussions (predated by comments in a student's bachelor thesis report by Philippe Élinck), notably [Cook 1989] and [America 1989a]. Cook's paper showed several examples of the covariance problem and attempted a solution. At TOOLS EUROPE 1992, Franz Weber proposed a solution based on the use of generic parameters for covariant entities [Weber 1992]. [M 1992] defines precisely the notions of class-level and system-level validity, and proposes a solution based on system-wide analysis. The Catcall solution described in the present chapter was first presented in [M 1996a]; see also on-line material [M-Web].

Ph. Élinck: *"De la Conception-Prog- rammation par Objets"*, *Mémoire de licence, Université Libre de Bruxelles (Belgium), 1988.*

The Anchoring solution was presented in a talk I gave at a TOOLS EUROPE 1994 workshop. I had, however, overlooked the need for **anchor** declarations and the associated restriction on conformance. Paul Dubois and Amiram Yehudai immediately pointed out that the covariance problem could still arise under these conditions. Along with others including Reinhardt Budde, Karl-Heinz Sylla, Kim Waldén and James McKim, they provided many further comments that were fundamental to the work leading to the present chapter (without being committed to its conclusions).

There is an abundant literature on the covariance issue; [Castagna 1995] and [Castagna 1996] provide both a bibliography and a mathematical overview. For a list of links to on-line articles on O-O type theory and researchers' Web pages, see Laurent Dami's page [Dami-Web]. The terms "covariance" and "contravariance" come, by the way, from category theory; it appears that their introduction into discussions of software typing is due to Luca Cardelli, who started to use them in talks in the early eighties, although they seem not to have appeared in print until the end of that decade.

Techniques based on type variables are described in [Simons 1995], [Shang 1996], [Bruce 1997].

The Sather language uses contravariance. [Szypersky 1993] presents the rationale.

18

Global objects and constants

$\mathcal{L}$ocal knowledge is not always enough; components of a software system may need to access global information. It is easy to think of examples: a shared value, such as the size of available memory; an error window, to which all the components of an interactive system must be able to output messages; the gateway to a database or network.

In classical approaches, it is not difficult to provide for global objects; you just declare them as global variables, owned by the main program. In the modular style of design made possible by object-oriented techniques, there is neither a main program nor global variables. But even if our software texts do not include global variables our software executions may still need to share objects.

Such global objects pose a challenge to the method. Object technology is all about decentralization, all about modularity, all about autonomy. It has developed from the beginning of this presentation as a war of independence for the modules, each fighting for its freedom from the excesses of central authority. In fact, there is no central authority any more. How then do we satisfy the need for common institutions? In other words, how do we allow components to share data in a simple way, without jeopardizing their autonomy, flexibility and reusability?

It will not work, of course, to pass shared objects as arguments to the modules that need them. This would soon become clumsy if too many components need them. Besides, argument passing assumes that one module owns the value and then passes it on to others; in the case of a truly shared value no one module can claim ownership.

To find a better answer we will start from a well-known notion, which we need in object-oriented software construction just as much as we did in more traditional approaches: constants. What is, after all, a constant such as Pi if not a simple object shared by many modules? Generalizing this notion to more complex objects will provide a first step towards fully general constant and shared objects.

18.1 CONSTANTS OF BASIC TYPES

Let us start with a simple notation to denote constant values.

Using symbolic constants

A rule of software style, the **Symbolic Constant principle**, states that when an algorithm refers to a certain value — a number, a character, a string… — it should almost never use it directly. Instead, a declaration should associate a name with the value, so that the algorithm can use the name (known as a *symbolic* constant) rather than the value (known as a *manifest* constant). Two reasons justify this principle:

"Manifest and symbolic constants", page 884. See also "Modular continuity", page 44.

- Readability: someone who reads your software may not understand what the value 50 is doing in a certain algorithm; if instead you use the symbolic constant *US_states_ count* everything is clear.

- Extendibility: in practice, with a few exceptions (such as the value of π, unlikely to change soon), the only constant thing about constants is change. To update the value of a constant it suffices, if you have been using symbolic constants, to change one declaration. This is much nicer than having to chase throughout the software for all the places that may have relied on the earlier value.

The principle permits using manifest constants (hence the word "almost" above) for zero elements of various operations, as in a loop **from** $i := 1$ **until** $i > n$ … iterating over the elements of an array whose numbering follows the default convention of starting at 1. (But n should be symbolic, not manifest.)

Although few software developers apply the Symbolic Constant principle as systematically as they should, the benefits of declaring a symbolic constant are well worth the small extra effort. So we need a clear and simple way of defining symbolic constants in an O-O framework.

Constant attributes

A symbolic constant, like everything else, will be defined in a class. We will simply treat a constant value as an attribute which happens to have a fixed value, the same for all instances of the class.

For the syntax, we can reuse the keyword **is** which already serves to introduce routines; only here it will be followed by a value of the appropriate type, rather than by an algorithm. The following examples include one for each of the basic types *INTEGER*, *BOOLEAN*, *REAL* and *CHARACTER*:

> *Zero*: *INTEGER* **is** *0*
> *Ok*: *BOOLEAN* **is** *True*
> *Pi*: *REAL* **is** *3.1415926524*
> *Backslash*: *CHARACTER* **is** '\'

> *Backslash* is of type *CHARACTER*, its value a single character. Constants of string type, denoting character strings of arbitrary length, will be discussed below.

As these examples illustrate, the recommended style convention for names of constant attributes is to start with a capital letter, with the rest in lower case.

A descendant may not redefine the value of a constant attribute.

Like other attributes, constant attributes are either exported or secret; if they are exported, clients of the class may access them through feature calls. So if *C* is the class containing the above declarations and *x*, declared of type *C*, has a non-void value, then *x*. *Backslash* denotes the backslash character.

Unlike variable attributes, constant attributes do not occupy any space at run time in instances of the class. So there is no run-time penalty for adding as many constant attributes as you need.

18.2 USE OF CONSTANTS

Here is an example showing how clients may use constant attributes defined in a class:

```
class FILE feature
        error_code: INTEGER;      -- Variable attribute

        Ok: INTEGER is 0

        Open_error: INTEGER is 1
        …
        open (file_name: STRING) is
                    -- Open file of name file_name
                    -- and associate it with current file object
            do
                    error_code := Ok
                    …
                    if "Something went wrong" then
                            error_code := Open_error
                    end
            end
        … Other features …
end
```

A client may call *open* and compare the resulting error code to any of the constants to test how the operation went:

```
f: FILE; …
f. open
if f. error_code = f. Open_error then
        "Appropriate action"
else
        …
end
```

Often, however, a group of constants is needed without being attached to any particular object. For example, a system performing physics computations may use some numerical constants; or a text editor may need character constants describing the character keys associated with various commands. In such a case, the constants will still be grouped in a class (where else could they be?), but there will not be any instances of that class; it is simply used as parent for the classes that need to access the constants, as in

class *EDITOR_CONSTANTS* **feature**

     Insert: *CHARACTER* **is** '*i*'

     Delete: *CHARACTER* **is** '*d*'; -- etc.

     …

end

class *SOME_CLASS_FOR_THE_EDITOR* **inherit**

     EDITOR_CONSTANTS

     … Other possible parents …

feature …

     … Routines of the class have access to the constants

         declared in *EDITOR_CONSTANTS* …

end

A class such as *EDITOR_CONSTANTS* is used only to host a group of related constants, and its role as an "abstract data type implementation" (our working definition of the notion of class) is less obvious than in earlier examples. But it definitely serves a useful purpose. We will examine its theoretical justification in a later chapter.

See "FACILITY INHERITANCE", 24.9, page 847.

The scheme shown would not work without multiple inheritance, since *SOME_CLASS_FOR_THE_EDITOR* may need other parents, either for access to other constants or for more standard uses of inheritance.

18.3 CONSTANTS OF CLASS TYPES

Symbolic constants, allowing you to use identifiers to denote certain constant values, are not just useful for predefined types such as *INTEGER*; the need also arises for types that developers have defined, through classes. Here the solution is less obvious.

Manifest constants are inappropriate for class types

A typical example in which you may need to define a constant for a non-basic types is that of a class describing complex numbers:

class *COMPLEX* **creation**

     make_cartesian, *make_polar*

feature

     x, y: *REAL*

         -- Real and imaginary parts

> *make_cartesian* (*a*, *b*: *REAL*) **is**
>
> > -- Initialize with real part *a*, imaginary part *b*.
>
> > **do**
>
> > > *x* := *a*; *y* := *b*
>
> > **end**
>
> … Other routines (*x* and *y* are the only attributes) …
>
> **end**

You may want to define the complex number *i*, with real part 0 and imaginary part 1. The first idea that comes to mind is a manifest constant notation such as

> *i*: *COMPLEX* **is** "Expression specifying the complex number (0, 1)"

How can you write the expression after **is**? For simple types, the manifest constants were self-evident: *345* is a constant of type integer, '*A*' of type character. But no such predefined notation is available for developer-defined class types.

One could imagine a notation based on the attributes of the class; something like

Not a retained nota-tion. For purposes of illustration only.

> *i*: *COMPLEX* **is** *COMPLEX* (*0*, *1*)

But such an approach (although present in some O-O languages) is incompatible with the principles of modularity which serve as the basis for object technology. It would mean requiring clients of *COMPLEX* to describe constants in terms of the implementation. This breaks information hiding. You could not add an attribute, even a secret one, without invalidating client code; neither could you re-implement an attribute such as *x* as a function (to switch internally to a polar representation).

Besides, how could you make sure that such manifest constants will satisfy the class invariant if there is one?

This last remark opens the way to a correct solution. An earlier chapter noted that it is the responsibility of the **creation procedures** to make sure that every object satisfies the invariant immediately upon creation. Creating objects in any other way (apart from the safe companion mechanism, *clone*) would lead to error situations. So we should look for a mechanism that, rather than manifest objects in the above style, will rely on the usual technique for object creation.

Once functions

We may view a constant object as a function. For example *i* could be defined within class *COMPLEX* itself as

> *i*: *COMPLEX* **is**
>
> > -- Complex number with real part 0 and imaginary part 1
>
> > **do**
>
> > > !! *Result*•*make_cartesian* (*0*, *1*)
>
> > **end**

This almost does the job, since the function will always return a reference to an object of the desired form. Since we rely on normal creation procedures, the invariant will be satisfied, so we will only produce consistent objects.

The result, however, is not exactly what we need: each client use of *i* in the client produces a new object, identical to all the others. This is a waste of time and space:

To get the proper behavior, we need a special kind of function: one which executes its body only the first time it is called. We can call this a **once function**. A once function is otherwise similar to a normal function; syntactically, it will be distinguished by the keyword **once**, replacing the usual **do**, to introduce the body:

> *i*: *COMPLEX* **is**
> > -- Complex number with real part 0 and imaginary part 1
>
> **once** ◄─────────────────────────────────────(The only change)
> > !! *Result.make_cartesian* (*0, 1*)
>
> **end**

The first time a once function is called during a system's execution, it executes its body. In the example this creates an object representing the desired complex number, and returns a reference to that object. Every subsequent call executes no instruction at all, but terminates immediately, returning the result computed the first time around.

Regarding efficiency: a call to *i* other than the first should take only marginally longer than an attribute access.

The result computed by the first call to a once function is applicable to all instances of a class, in the general sense of the word "instance" covering instances of descendants as well, except of course for any descendant that redefines the function. As a consequence you can freely redefine functions from once to non-once and conversely. Here if a descendant *COMPLEX1* of *COMPLEX* redefines *i*, a call to *i* on an instance of *COMPLEX1* will use the redefined version (whether once or non-once); a call on a direct instance of *COMPLEX* or a descendant other than *COMPLEX1* will use the once function, that is to say the value computed by the first such call.

18.4 APPLICATIONS OF ONCE ROUTINES

The notion of once routine extends beyond examples such as *i* to more general applications: shared objects, global system parameters, initialization of common properties.

Shared objects

For reference types such as *COMPLEX*, as you may have noted, the "once" mechanism actually offers constant *references*, not necessarily constant *objects*. It guarantees that the body of the function is executed only once, to compute a result, which later calls will also return without further computation.

If the function returns a value of a reference type, its body will usually contain a creation instruction, as in the example of *i*. All calls will return a reference to the object created by the first. Although the creation will never be executed again, nothing prevents callers from modifying the object through the reference. Therefore the mechanism provides **shared** objects rather than constant ones.

An example of a shared object, cited at the beginning of this chapter, is a window showing error messages in an interactive system. Assume we have decided that any component of the system that detects a user error may output a message to that window, through a call of the form

Message_window.*put_text* ("*Appropriate error message*")

Here *message_window* is of type *WINDOW*, with class *WINDOW* declared as

class *WINDOW* **creation**
    make
feature
    make (…) **is**
            -- Create window at size and position indicated by arguments.
      do … **end**
    text: *STRING*
        -- Text to be displayed in window
    put_text (*s*: *STRING*) **is**
        -- Make *s* the text to be displayed in window.
      do
        text := *s*
      end
    … Other features …
end -- class *WINDOW*

Obviously *Message_window* must be the same for all components of the system. This is achieved by declaring the corresponding feature as a once function:

Message_window: *WINDOW* **is**
      -- Window where error messages will be output
    once
        !! *Result*.*make* ("…Size and position arguments…")
    end

In this case the message window object must be shared by all its users, but it is not a constant object: each call to *put_text* changes the object by putting its own chosen text in it. The best place to declare *Message_window* is a class from which all system components needing access to the message window will inherit.

In the case of a shared object that denotes a constant, such as *i*, you may want to disallow calls of the form *i*.*some_procedure* that might change the fields. To achieve this, simply include clauses *i*.*x* = *0* and *i*.*y* = *1* in the class invariant.

Once functions returning results of basic types

Another application of once functions is to represent global values — "system parameters" — used by several classes in a system. Such values will usually be constant over a given system execution; they are initially computed from user input, or from some information obtained from the environment. For example:

- The components of a low-level system may need to know the available memory space, obtained from the environment at initialization time.

- A terminal handler may start by querying the environment about the number of terminal ports: once obtained, these data elements are then used by several modules of the application.

Such global values are similar to shared objects such as *Message_window*; but in general they are values of basic types rather than class instances. You may represent them through once functions. The scheme is:

Const_value: *T* **is**
> -- A system parameter computed only once

> **local**
>> *envir_param*: *T'*   -- Any type (*T* or another)

> **once**
>> "Get the value of *envir_param* from the environment"
>> *Result* := "Some value computed from *envir_param*"

> **end**

Such once functions of basic types describe dynamically computed constants.

Assume the above declaration is in a class *ENVIR*. A class needing to use *Const_value* will get it simply by listing *ENVIR* among its parents. There is no need here for an initialization routine as might be used in classical approaches to compute *Const_value*, along with all other global parameters, at the beginning of system execution. As was seen in an earlier chapter, such a routine would have to access the internal details of many other modules, and hence would violate the criteria and principles of modularity: decomposability, few interfaces, information hiding etc. In contrast, classes such as *ENVIR* may be designed as coherent modules, each describing a set of logically related global values. The first component that requests the value of a global parameter such as *Const_value* at execution time will trigger its computation from the environment.

See "Modular decomposability", page 40.

Although *Const_value* is a function, components that use it may treat it as if it were a constant attribute.

The introduction to this chapter mentioned that none of the modules that use a shared value has more claim to own it than any of the others. This is especially true in the cases just seen: if, depending on the order of events in each execution of the system, any one among a set of modules may trigger the computation of the value, it would be improper to designate any single one among them as the owner. The modular structure reflects this.

Once procedures

> *The function close should only be called once. We recommend using a global variable in your application to check that close is not called more than once.*

(From the manual for a commercial C library.)

The "once" mechanism is interesting not just for functions but for procedures as well.

A once procedure is appropriate when some facility used on a system-wide basis must be initialized, but it is not known in advance which system component will be the first to use the facility. It is like having a rule that whoever comes in first in the morning should turn on the heating.

A simple example is a graphics library providing a number of display routines, where the first display routine called in any system execution must set up the terminal. The library author could of course require every client to perform a setup call before the first display call. This is a nuisance for clients and does not really solve the problem anyway: to deal properly with errors, any routine should be able to detect that it has been called without proper setup; but if it is smart enough to detect this case, the routine might just as well do the setup and avoid bothering the client!

Once procedures provide a better solution:

```
check_setup is
        -- Perform terminal setup if not done yet.
    once
        terminal_setup -- Actual setup action
    end
```

Then every display routine in the library should begin with a call to *check_setup*. The first call will do the setup; subsequent ones will do nothing. Note that *check_setup* does not have to be exported; client authors do not need to know about it.

This is an important technique to improve the usability of any library or other software package. Any time you can remove a usage rule — such as "Always call procedure *xyz* before the first operation" — and instead take care of the needed operations automatically and silently, you have made the software better.

Arguments

Like other routines, once routines — procedures and functions — can have arguments. But because of the definition of the mechanism, these arguments are only useful in the call that gets executed first.

In the earlier analogy, imagine a thermostat dial which anyone coming into the building may turn to any marking, but such that only the first person to do so will set the temperature: subsequent attempts have no effect.

Once functions, anchoring and genericity

(This section addresses a specific technical point and may be skipped on first reading.)

Once functions of class types carry a potential incompatibility with anchored types and genericity.

Let us start with genericity. In a generic class *EXAMPLE* [*G*] assume a once function returning a value whose type is the formal generic parameter:

f: *G* **is once** … **end**

Warning: not valid. See below.

and consider a possible use:

character_example: *EXAMPLE* [*CHARACTER*]
…
print (*character_example*.*f*)

So far so good. But you also try to do something with another generic derivation:

integer_example: *EXAMPLE* [*INTEGER*]
…
print (*integer_example*.*f* + *1*)

The last instruction adds two integer values. Unfortunately, the first of them, the result of calling *f*, has already been computed since *f* is a once function; and it is a character, not an integer. The addition is not valid.

The problem is that we are sharing a value between different generic derivations which expect the type of that value to depend on the actual generic parameter.

A similar issue arises with anchored types. Assume a class *B* which adds an attribute to the features of its parent *A*:

class *B* **inherit** *A* **feature**
    attribute_of_B: *INTEGER*
end

Assume that *A* had a once function *f*, returning a result of anchored type:

f: **like** *Current* **is once** !! *Result*.*make* **end**

Warning: not valid. See below.

and that the first evaluation of *f* is in

a2 := *a1*.*f*

with *a1* and *a2* of type *A*. The evaluation of *f* creates a direct instance of *A*, and attaches it to entity *a2*, also of type *A*. Fine. But assume now that a subsequent use of *f* is

b2 := *b1*.*f*

where *b1* and *b2* are of type *B*. If *f* were a non-once function, this would not cause any problem, since the call would now produce and return a direct instance of *B*. Since here we have a once function, the result has already been computed through the first call; and that result is a direct instance of *A*, not *B*. So an instruction such as

print (*b2*.*attribute_of_B*)

will try to access a non-existent field in an object of type *A*.

The problem is that anchoring causes an implicit redefinition. Had *f* been explicitly redefined, through a declaration appearing in *B* under the form

> *f*: *B* **is once** !! *Result*. *make* **end**

assuming that the original in class *A* similarly returned a result of type *A* (rather than **like** *Current*), then we would not have any trouble: direct instances of *A* use the *A* version, direct instances of *B* use the *B* version. Anchoring, of course, was introduced precisely to rid us of such explicit redefinitions serving type needs only.

These two cases are evidence of incompatibilities between the semantics of once functions (procedures are fine) and the results of either anchored or formal generic types.

One way out, suggested by the last observation on implicit *vs*. explicit redefinition, would be to treat such cases as we would explicit redefinitions: to specify that the result of a once function will be shared only within each generic derivation of a generic class, and, if the result is anchored, only within the direct instances of the class. The disadvantage of this solution, however, is that it goes against the expected semantics of once functions, which from a client's viewpoint should be the conceptual equivalent of a shared attribute. To avoid confusion and possible errors it seems preferable to take a more draconian attitude by banning such cases altogether:

Once Function rule

The result type of a once function may not be anchored, and may not involve any formal generic parameter.

18.5 CONSTANTS OF STRING TYPE

The beginning of this chapter introduced character constants, whose value is a single character. The example was

> *Backslash*: *CHARACTER* **is** '\'

Often, classes will also need symbolic constants representing multi-character strings.The notation for manifest string constants will use double quotes:

[S1]

> *Message*: *STRING* **is** "*Syntax error*"

Recall that *STRING* is a class of the library, not a simple type. So the value associated at run time with an entity such as *Message* is an object (an instance of *STRING*). As you may have guessed, the above declaration is a shorthand for the declaration of a once function, here of the form:

Message: *STRING* **is**
           -- String of length 12, with successive characters
           -- S, y, n, t, a, x, , e, r, r, o, r
    once
        !! *Result*•*make* (*12*)
        Result•*put* ('*S*', *1*)
        Result•*put* ('*y*', *2*)
        …
        Result•*put* ('*r*', *12*)
  end

The creation procedure for strings takes as argument the initial expected length of the string; *put* (*c*, *i*) replaces the *i*-th character with *c*.

Such string values are therefore not constants but references to shared objects. Any class that has access to *Message* may change the value of one or more of its characters.

You can also use string constants as expressions, for argument passing or assignment:

Message_window•*display* ("*CLICK LEFT BUTTON TO CONFIRM EXIT*")
greeting := "*Hello!*"

18.6 UNIQUE VALUES

It is sometimes necessary to define an entity that has several possible values denoting possible cases. For example a read operation may produce a status code whose possible values are codes meaning "successful", "error on opening" and "error on reading".

A simple solution is to use a variable integer attribute

code: *INTEGER*

with a set of associated integer constants, such as

[U1]
    Successful: *INTEGER* **is** *1*
    Open_error: *INTEGER* **is** *2*
    Read_error: *INTEGER* **is** *3*

so that you can write conditional instructions of the form

[U2]
    if *code* = *Successful* **then** …

or multi-branch instructions of the form

*See "Multi-branch",
page 449.*

[U3]
    inspect
        code
    when *Successful* **then**
        …
    when …
    end

It is tedious, however, to have to come up with the individual constant values. The following notation has the same practical effect as [U1]:

[U4]

Successful, Open_error, Read_error: *INTEGER* **is unique**

A **unique** value specification, coming in lieu of a manifest integer value in the declaration of a constant integer attribute, indicates that the value is chosen by the compiler rather than the developer. So the conditional instruction [U2] and the multi-branch [U3] are still applicable.

All **unique** values within a class are guaranteed to be positive and different; if they are declared together, as the three in [U4], they are also guaranteed to be consecutive. So if you want to express that *code* will only receive one of their values, you can include the invariant clause

code >= *Successful*; *code* <= *Read_error*

With this invariant, a descendant — which, as we know, may change the invariant only by strengthening it — may constrain the possible values of *code* further, for example to just two possibilities; it may not extend the set of possibilities.

You should only use Unique values to represent a fixed set of possible values. As soon as this set is open to variation, or the instructions in a structure such as [U3] are non-trivial, it is preferable to devise a set of classes which variously redefine some features, and then to rely on dynamic binding, satisfying the Open-Closed principle. More generally, do not use unique values for classification since the object-oriented method has better techniques. The preceding example is typical of good uses of the mechanism; others would be traffic light states (*green, yellow, red*: *INTEGER* **is unique**) or, as seen earlier, notes on the scale (*do, re, mi, …*: *INTEGER* **is unique**). But a declaration *savings, checking, money_market*: *INTEGER* **is unique** is probably a misuse if the various kinds of account have different features or different implementations of a common feature; here inheritance and redefinition will most likely provide a better solution.

These observations can be summed up as a methodological rule:

> ## Discrimination principle
>
> Use unique values to describe a fixed number of possible cases. For classification of data abstractions with varying features, use inheritance.

Although similar in some respects to the "enumerated types" of Pascal and Ada, unique declarations do not introduce new types, only integer values. The discussion section will explore the difference further.

18.7 DISCUSSION

In this discussion, the term "global object" refers both to global constants of basic types and to shared complex objects; their "initialization" includes object creation in the latter case.

Initializing globals and shared objects: language approaches

The principal problem addressed by this chapter is an instance of a general software issue: how to deal with global constant and shared objects, and particularly their initialization in libraries of software components.

Since the initialization of a global object should be done just once, the more general issue is how to enable a library component to determine whether it is the first to request a certain service.

This boils down to an apparently simple question: how to share a boolean variable and initialize it consistently. We can associate with a global object p, or any group of global objects that need to be initialized at the same time, a boolean indicator, say *ready*, which has value true if and only if initialization has been performed. Then we may include before any access to p the instruction

if not *ready* **then**
>   "Create or compute p"
>   *ready* := *True*

end

The initialization problem still applies to *ready*, itself a global object that must somehow be initialized to false before the first attempt to access it.

This problem has not changed much since the dawn of programming languages, and the early solutions are still with us. A common technique in block-structured languages such as Algol or Pascal is to use for *ready* a global variable, declared at the highest syntactical level. The main program will do the initialization. But this does not work for a library of autonomous modules which, by definition, is not connected to any main program.

In Fortran, a language designed to allow routines to be compiled separately (and hence to enjoy a certain degree of autonomy), the solution is to include all global objects, and in particular *ready* indicators, in a shared data area called a common block, identified by its name; every subroutine accessing a common block must include a directive of the form

>   *COMMON /common_block_name/ data_item_names*

There are two problems with this approach:

• Two sets of routines may use a common block of the same name, triggering a conflict if an application needs them both. Changing one of the names to remove the conflict may cause trouble since common blocks, by nature, are shared by many routines.

• How do we initialize the entities of a common block, such as our *ready* indicators? Because there is no default initialization rule, any data in a common block must be initialized in a special module called a "block data" unit. Fortran 77 allows named block data units, so that developers can combine global data from various contexts — provided they do not forget to include all the relevant block data units. A serious risk of accidental inconsistency exists.

The C solution is conceptually the same as in Fortran 77. The *ready* indicator should be declared in C as an "external" variable, common to more than one "file" (the C compilation unit). Only one file may contain the declaration of the variable with its initial value (false in our case); others will use an **extern** declaration, corresponding to Fortran's *COMMON* directive, to state that they need the variable. The usual practice is to group such definitions in special "header" files, with names conventionally ending with **.**h; they correspond to the block data units of Fortran. The same problems arise, partially alleviated by "Make" utilities which help programmers keep track of dependencies.

A solution would appear to be at hand with modular languages such as Ada or Modula 2 where routines may be gathered in a higher-level module, a "package" in Ada terms: if all the routines using a group of related global objects are in the same package, the associated *ready* indicators may be declared as boolean variables in that package, which will also contain the initialization. But this approach (also applicable in Fortran 77 and C using techniques described in chapter 18) does not solve the problem of initialization in autonomous library components. The more delicate question discussed in this chapter is what to do for global objects that must be shared between routines in **different** and independent modules. Ada and Modula provide no simple answer in this case.

In contrast, the "once" mechanism preserves the independence of classes, but allows context-dependent initializations.

Manifest string constants

The notation allows string constants (or more properly, as we have seen, shared objects) to be declared in manifest form, using double quotes: "...". A consequence of this policy is that the language definition, and any compiler, must rely on the presence of class *STRING* in the library. This is a compromise between two extreme solutions:

- *STRING* could have been a predefined basic type, as is the case in many languages. This, however, would have meant adding all string operations (concatenation, substring extraction, comparison etc.) as language constructs, making the language considerably more complex, even though only few applications require all these operations; some do not even need strings at all. Among the advantage of using a class is the ability to equip its operations with precise specifications through assertions, and to allow other classes to inherit from it.

- Treating *STRING* as just any other class would preclude manifest constants of the "..." form [S1], requiring developers always to enter the characters individually as in form [S2]. It might also prevent the compiler from applying optimizations for time-sensitive operations such as character access.

On the ARRAY case see "Efficiency consid- erations", page 327. So *STRING*, like its companion *ARRAY*, leads a double life: predefined type when you need manifest constants and optimization, class when you need flexibility and generality. All this, of course, is part of the general effort to have a single, universal, consistent type system entirely based on the notion of class.

Unique values and enumerated types

Pascal and derivatives allow declaring a variable as

code: *ERROR*

where *ERROR* is declared as an "enumerated type":

type *ERROR* = (*Normal*, *Open_error*, *Read_error*)

Being declared of type *ERROR*, variable *code* may only take the values of this type: the three symbolic codes given.

We have seen how to obtain the equivalent effect in the O-O notation: define the symbolic codes as **unique** integer constants, and *code* as an integer attribute, possibly with an invariant clause stating that its value must lie between *Normal* and *Read_error*. The result at execution time is almost identical, since Pascal compilers typically implement values of an enumerated type by integers. (A good compiler may take advantage of the small number of possible values to represent entities such as *code* by short integers.)

The **unique** technique involves no new type. It seems indeed hard to reconcile the notion of enumerated type with object technology. All our types are based on classes, that is to say abstractly characterized by the applicable operations and their properties. No such characterization exists for enumerated types, which are mere sets of values. Enumerated types actually raise problems even in non-O-O languages:

- The status of the symbolic names is not clear. Can two enumerated types share one or more symbolic names (as *Orange* both in type *FRUIT* and in type *COLOR*)? Are they exportable and subject to the same visibility rules as variables?

- It is difficult to pass values of an enumeration type to and from routines written in other languages, such as C or Fortran, which do not support this notion. Since **unique** values are plain integers they cause no such problem.

- Enumerated values may require special operators. For example you will expect a **next** operator yielding the next value, but it will not be defined for the last enumeration element. You will also need an operator to associate an integer with every enumerated value (its index in the enumeration). To go the other way around requires more operators since we must know the bounds of the enumeration to restrict applicable integer values. The resulting syntactic and semantic complexity seems out of proportion with the mechanism's contribution to the language.

Uses of enumeration types in Pascal and Ada tend to be of the form

type *FIGURE_SORT* = (*Circle*, *Rectangle*, *Square*, ...)

to be used in connection with variant record types of the form

FIGURE =
    record
        perimeter: *INTEGER*;
        ... Other attributes common to figures of all types ...
        case *fs*: *FIGURE_SORT* **of**
            Circle: (*radius*: *REAL*; *center*: *POINT*);
            Rectangle: ... Attributes specific to rectangles ...;
            ...
        end
    end

themselves used in **case** discrimination instructions:

procedure *rotate* (*f*: *FIGURE*)
   begin case *f* **of**
      Circle: … Appropriate actions to rotate a circle …;
      Rectangle: …;
   …

which we have learned to handle in a better way to preserve extendibility: by defining a different version of procedures such as *rotate* for each new variant, represented by a class.

When this most important application of enumerated types disappears, all that remains is the need, in some cases, to select integer codes having a fixed number of possible values. Defining them as integers avoids many of the semantic ambiguities associated with enumerated types; for example there is nothing mysterious about the expression *Circle + 1* if *Circle* is officially an integer. The only unpleasantness of integers would be to have to assign the values yourself; **unique** values solve that problem.

18.8 KEY CONCEPTS INTRODUCED IN THIS CHAPTER

- A challenging problem in any approach to software construction is how to allow for global data: objects that must be shared by various modular components, and initialized at run time by whatever component happens to need them first.

- A constant can be *manifest* (expressed as a self-describing representation of its value) or *symbolic* (expressed by a name).

- You can declare manifest constants of basic types as constant attributes, occupying no space in objects.

- Except for strings, developer-defined types have no manifest constants, which would damage information hiding and extendibility.

- A once routine, which differs from a normal function by one keyword, **once** instead of **do**, is evaluated only once during a system's execution: the first time any component of the system calls it. For a function, subsequent calls return the same value as the first; for a procedure, subsequent calls have no effect.

- Shared objects may be implemented as once functions. You can use the invariant to specify that they are constant.

- Use once procedures for operations to be performed only once over the execution of a system, such as initializations of global parameters.

- The type of a once function may not be anchored or generic.

- Constants of string types are treated internally as once functions, although they look like manifest constants written in double quotes.

- Enumerated types à la Pascal do not go well with the object-oriented method, but to represent codes with several possible values there is a need for "unique" attributes: symbolic constants of type *INTEGER*, whose value is chosen by the compiler rather than by the software writer.

18.9 BIBLIOGRAPHICAL NOTES

[Welsh 1977] and [Moffat 1981] study the difficulties raised by enumerated types.

Some of the techniques of this chapter were introduced in [M 1988b].

EXERCISES

E18.1 Emulating enumerated types with once functions

Show that in the absence of Unique types a Pascal enumerated type of the form

    type *ERROR* = (*Normal*, *Open_error*, *Read_error*)

could be represented by a class with a once function for each value of the type.

E18.2 Emulating unique values with once functions

Show that in a language that does not support the notion of **unique** declaration it is possible to obtain the effect of

    value: *INTEGER* **is unique**

by a declaration of the form

    value: *INTEGER* **is once** … **end**

where you are requested to fill in the body of the once function and anything else that may be needed.

E18.3 Once functions in generic classes

Give an example of a once function whose result involves a generic parameter and, if not corrected, would yield a run-time error.

See "Once functions, anchoring and genericity", page 652

E18.4 Once attributes?

Examine the usefulness of a notion of "once attribute", patterned after once routines. A once attribute would be common to all instances of the class. Issues to be considered include: how does a once attribute get initialized? Is the facility redundant with once functions without arguments and, if not, can you explain clearly under what conditions each facility is appropriate? Can you think of a good syntax for declaring once attributes?

Part D:

Object-oriented methodology: applying the method well

Part D will cover the methodology of object orientation: how to apply, for the benefit of our projects and the success of our organizations, the powerful set of concepts and techniques reviewed in the preceding chapters.

19

On methodology

*E*ntirely devoted to methodology, the next few chapters — making up part D of this book — examine how to address the issues facing object-oriented projects: how to find the classes; how not to misuse inheritance; the place of object-oriented analysis; fundamental design ideas ("patterns"); how to teach the method; the new software lifecycle. The result will, I hope, help you understand how best to take advantage of the techniques that we have now finished exploring.

It is appropriate, before going into the study of the rules, to reflect on the role of methodology in software. This will be an opportunity to define meta-rules — rules on how to make rules — which will help us devise sound methodological advice and separate the best from the rest in the methodological literature. In passing we will devise a taxonomy of rules, finding out that certain kinds are more desirable than others. Finally we will reflect on the attractive and dangerous role of *metaphors*, and take a short lesson in modesty.

19.1 SOFTWARE METHODOLOGY: WHY AND WHAT

People want guidance. The quest for Principles of Truth, which one only has to follow to succeed, is neither new nor specific to software.

The software literature, including for the past few years its object-oriented branch, has capitalized on this eagerness and attempted to offer recipes. This has resulted in much useful advice being made available (along with some more questionable ideas).

We must remember, however, that there is no easy path to quality software. Earlier chapters have pointed out several times that software construction is a challenging task. In the past few years our grasp of the issues has vastly improved, as illustrated in particular by the techniques presented in this book, but at the same time the size and ambition of what we are trying to do has been growing even faster, so the problem remains as difficult as it ever was.

It is important, then, to know the benefits and limitations of software methodology. From the following chapters and from the rest of the object-oriented literature, you are entitled to expect good advice, and the benefit of other people's experience. But neither here nor there will you find a sure-fire way to produce good software.

A comparison made in an earlier chapter helps set the limits of what you can expect. In many respect, building a software system is similar to developing a mathematical theory. Mathematics, as software construction, can be taught, including the general principles that help talented students produce brilliant results; but no teaching can guarantee success.

Not all recipe-style approaches are doomed. If you sufficiently restrict the application domain until you are left with a basic set of problem patterns, then it may be possible to define a teachable step-by-step process; this has occurred in some areas of business data processing, where methodologists have identified a small number of widely applicable solution schemes. The eventual fate of such schemes, of course, is to be subsumed by software packages or reusable libraries. But as soon as you open up the problem domain, no simplistic approach will work; the designer must exert his best powers of invention. A method will help through general guidelines, through the example of previous successful designs — also the example of what does *not* work — but not much more.

Keep these observations in mind both when reading part D and when going on to the methodology literature, where some methods make exaggerated claims. That is not necessarily a reason for rejecting them wholesale, as they may still include some useful advice; but they should be taken with a grain of salt.

> A point of terminology: it has become customary in some of the literature to talk about specific "methodologies", really meaning methods (actually even less: variants of a single general method, the object-oriented method). This practice may be viewed as just another mildly irritating example of verbal inflation — such as talking of repairmen as *maintenance engineers* — but is damaging since it leads readers to suspect that if the label is inflated the contents must be oversold. This book only uses the word *methodology* in the singular and sticks to the meanings that common dictionaries give for it: the study of methods; the "application of the principles of reasoning to scientific and philosophical inquiry"; and a system of methods.

19.2 DEVISING GOOD RULES: ADVICE TO THE ADVISORS

Before going into specific rules for using object-oriented techniques, it is necessary to ask ourselves what we should be looking for. The methodologist is entrusted with a serious responsibility: telling software developers how to write their software, and how not to write it. In a field where religious metaphors come up so often, it is hard to avoid the comparison with preachers or directors of conscience. Such a position, as is well known, is subject to abuse; it is appropriate, then, to define a few rules on rules: advice for the advisors.

The need for methodology guidelines

The field of software development methodology is not new. Its origins may be traced to   [Dijkstra 1968]. Dijkstra's famous *Go To Statement Considered Harmful* letter and subsequent publications by the same author and his colleagues on structured programming. But not all subsequent methodological work has upheld their standards.

It is relatively easy indeed to legislate about software construction, but the danger is great of producing rules that are useless, poorly thought out, or even harmful. The following guidelines, based on an analysis of the role of methodology in software, may help us avoid such pitfalls.

Theory

The first duty of an advisor is to base his advice on a consistent view of the target area:

> #### *Theoretical Basis* **methodology principle**
>
> Software methodology rules must be based on a theory of the underlying subject.

Dijkstra's example is still a good guide here. He did not just attack the Goto instruction for reasons of taste or opinion, but supported his suggested ban by a carefully woven chain of reasoning. One may disagree with some of that argument, but not deny that the conclusion is backed by a well thought-out view of the software development process. To counter Dijkstra's view you must find a flaw in his theory and provide your own replacement for that theory.

Practice

The theory is the deductive part of software methodology. But rules that would only be rooted in theory could be dangerous. The empirical component is just as important:

> #### *Practical Basis* **methodology principle**
>
> Software methodology rules should backed by extensive practical experience.

Perhaps one day someone will disprove this principle by devising a brilliant and applicable method of software construction through the sole power of abstract reasoning. In physics, after all, some of the most directly practical advances originated with theoreticians who never came close an experiment. But in software engineering the case has not occurred — all the great methodologists have also been programmers and project leaders on large developments — and seems unlikely to occur. Object technology in particular is among other things, an intellectual tool to build large and complex systems; the only approach, in fact, that has attempted consistently and comprehensively to reach this goal. One can master the essential concepts through taking classes, reading the literature, performing small-scale experiments and thinking further, but that is not preparation enough to give good methodological advice. The experience of playing a key role in the building of large systems — thousands of classes, hundreds of thousands of lines — is indispensable.

Such an experience must include all activities of the software lifecycle: analysis, design, implementation, and of course maintenance (the final reckoning, at which one recognizes whether the solution adopted at earlier stages stands the test of time and change, or collapses miserably).

Analysis experience, or even analysis and design experience, is not enough. More than once I have seen analysis consultants who do their job, charge their fees, and leave the company with no more than "bubbles and arrows" — an analysis document. The company then has to pick up the pieces and do the hard work; sometimes the analyst's work turns out to be totally useless as it has missed some of the most important practical constraints. An "analysis only" approach belies the fundamental ideas of *seamlessness* and *reversibility*, the integrated lifecycle that characterizes object technology, where analysis and design are interwoven with implementation and maintenance. Someone who misses part of this picture is not equipped to give methodological advice.

Reuse

Having played a key part in some large projects is necessary but not sufficient. In the object-oriented field the Practical Basis precept yields a corollary: the need for practical *reusability* experience.

Among the distinctive properties of the method is its ability to yield reusable components. No one can claim to be an expert who has not produced a *reused* O-O library; not just components claimed to be reusable, but a library that has actually been reused by a substantial number of people outside of the original group. Hence the next precept:

> ### *Reuse Experience* methodology principle
>
> To claim expert status in the object-oriented field, one must have played a key role in the development of a class library that has successfully been reused by widely different projects in widely different contexts.

A typology of rules

Next we should turn to the form of methodology rules. What kind of advice is effective in software development methodology?

A rule may be *advisory* (inviting you to follow a certain style) or *absolute* (enjoining you to work in a certain way); and it may be phrased in a *positive* form (telling you what you should do) or in *negative* form (telling you what you should not do). This gives four kinds:

> ### Classification of methodological rules
>
> - Absolute positive: "Always do *a*".
> - Absolute negative: "Never use *b*".
> - Advisory positive: "Use *c* whenever possible".
> - Advisory negative: "Avoid *d* whenever possible".

The requirements are slightly different in each case.

Absolute positives

Rules of the absolute positive kind are the most useful for software developers, since they provide precise and unambiguous guidance.

Unfortunately, they are also the least common in the methodological literature, partly for a good reason (for such precise advice, it is sometimes possible to write tools that carry out the desired tasks automatically, removing the need for methodological intervention), but mostly because advisors are too cautious to commit themselves, like a lawyer who never quite answers "yes" or "no" to a question for fear of being blamed for the consequences if his client does act on the basis of the answer.

Yet such rules are badly needed:

> ### *Absolute Positives* **methodology principle**
>
> In devising methodological rules, favor absolute positives, and for each such rule examine whether it is possible to enforce the rule automatically through tools or language constructs.

Absolute negatives

Absolute negatives are a sensitive area. One wishes that every methodologist who followed in Dijkstra's footsteps had taken the same care to justify his negatives as Dijkstra did with the Goto. The following precept applies to such rules:

> ### *Absolute Negatives* **methodology principle**
>
> Any absolute negative must be backed by a precise explanation of why the author considers the rejected mechanism bad practice, and accompanied by a precise description of how to substitute other mechanisms for it.

Advisories

Advisory rules, positive or negative, are fraught with the risk of uselessness.

It is said that to distinguish between a *principle* and a *platitude* you must consider the negation of the property: only if it is a principle does the negation still make sense, whether or not you agree with it. For example the often quoted software methodology advice "Use variable names that are meaningful" is a platitude, not a principle, since no one in his right mind would suggest using meaningless variable names. To turn this rule into a principle, you must define precise standards for naming variables. Of course in so doing you may find that some readers will disagree with those standards, which is why platitudes are so much more comfortable; but it is the role of a methodological advisor to take such risks.

Advisory rules, by avoiding absolute injunctions, are particularly prone to becoming platitudes, as especially reflected in qualifications of the form "*whenever possible*" or, for advisory negatives, "*unless you absolutely need to*", the most dishonest formula in software methodology.

The next precept helps avoid this risk by keeping us honest:

> ### *Advisory Rules* **methodology principle**
>
> In devising advisory rules (positive or negative), use principles, not platitudes.
>
> To help make the distinction, examine the rules' negation.

Here is an example of advisory negative, extracted from the discussion of type conversions (*casts*) in the C++ reference book:

> *Explicit type conversion is best avoided. Using a cast suppresses the type checking provided by the compiler and will therefore lead to surprises unless the programmer really was right.*   *From* [Ellis 1990].

This is accompanied by no explanation of how the programmer can find out whether he "*really was right*". So the reader is introduced to a certain language mechanism (type casts); warned, rightly, that it is dangerous and will "*lead to surprises*"; advised implicitly that the mechanism may sometimes be needed; but given no clue as to how to spot the legitimate uses.

Such advice is essentially useless; more precisely, it has a *negative* effect — impressing on the reader that the tool being described, in this case a programming language, is marred by areas of insecurity and uncertainty, and should not be trusted at all.

Exceptions

Many rules have exceptions. But if you present a software methodology rule and wish to indicate that it may not always apply, you should say precisely what cases justify exceptions. Otherwise the rule will be ineffective: each time a developer runs into a delicate case (that is to say, each time he truly needs your advice), he will be entitled to think that the rule does not apply.

Consider the following paragraph from an article about software methodology, coming after the presentation of a rather strict set of rules:

> *The strict version of the class form of the Law of Demeter is intended to be a guideline, not an absolute restriction. The minimization version of the law's class form gives you a choice of how strongly you want to follow the strict version of the law: the more nonpreferred acquaintance classes you use, the less strongly you adhere to the strict version. In some situations, the cost of obeying the strict version may be greater than the benefits.*   *From* [Lieberherr 1989].

It is difficult, after reading this extract, to decide how serious the authors are about their own rule; when should you apply it, and when is it OK to violate it?

What is wrong in not the presence of exceptions in a general guideline. Because software design is a complex task, it is sometimes inevitable (although always undesirable) to add to an absolute positive "*Always do X in situation A*" or an absolute negative "*Never do Y in situation A*" the qualification "*except in cases B, C and D*". Such a qualified rule remains an absolute positive or negative: simply, its domain of application is not the whole of *A*, but *A* deprived of *B*, *C* and *D*. What is unacceptable, however, is the contrast between a precise, prescriptive rule, and a vague provision for exceptions ("*in some situations, the cost may be greater than the benefits*" — what situations?). Later in the cited article, an example is shown that violates the rule, but the exception is justified in terms of ad hoc arguments. It should have been part of the rule:

Exceptions Included methodology principle

If a methodological rule presents a generally applicable guideline which may suffer exceptions, the exceptions must be stated as part of the rule.

If exceptions to a rule are included in the rule, they cease to be exceptions to the rule! This is why the principle talks about the "guideline" associated with a rule. There may be exceptions to the guideline, but they are not exceptions to the rule if the rule observes the above principle. In "*Cross the street only when the traffic lights are red, except if the lights are out of order*", the guideline "cross only on red" has an exception, but the rule as a whole does not.

This principle turns every rule of the form "Do this..." into an absolute positive, and every rule of the form "Do not do that..." into an absolute negative.

Self-doubt is an admirable quality in many circumstances of life, but not one that we expect to find in software methodology rules. One could almost argue that a wishy-washy methodologist is worse than a brilliant one who is occasionally wrong. The wishy-washy advice is largely useless, as it comes with so many blanket qualifications that you are never sure if it applies to your case of the moment; whereas if you study a methodological precept and decide that you disagree with it, you must try to refute the author's arguments with your own, and regardless of the outcome you will have learned something: either you fail, and gain a deeper, more personal appreciation of the rule and its relevance to your problem; or you succeed, and discover the rule's limitations, gaining some insights that the rule's author may have missed.

Abstraction and precision

A common theme of the last few principles is that methodological advice should be precise and directive.

This is of course more fully applicable for precise rules than for general design guidelines. When looking for advice on how to discover the right classes or how to devise the best inheritance hierarchy, you cannot expect step-1-step-2-step-3 recipes.

But even then generality and abstraction do not necessarily mean vagueness. Many of the principles of object-oriented design cover high-level issues; they will not do your work for you. Yet they are precise enough to be directly applicable, and to allow deciding without ambiguity whether they apply in any particular case.

If it is baroque, fix it

The advice on C++ type casts quoted earlier illustrates a general problem of advisory negatives: recommendations of this kind owe their existence to limitations of the underlying tool or language. For a perfect tool we would never have to give advisory negatives; every facility would be accompanied by a clear definition of when it is appropriate and when it is not — a criterion of the absolute kind, not advisory. No tool is perfect, but for a decent one the number of advisory negatives should remain very small. If in teaching the proper use of the tool you find yourself frequently resorting to comments of the form "Try to stay away from this mechanism unless you absolutely need it", then most likely the problem is what you are teaching about, not your teaching of it.

In such a case one should abandon trying to give advice, and improve the tool instead, or build a better one.

Typical phrases that signal this situation are

... unless you know what you are doing.

... unless you absolutely have to.

Avoid ... if you can.

Try not to ...

It is generally preferable not to ...

Better stay away from ...

The C/C++/Java literature has a particular fondness for such formulae. Typical is this advice: "*Don't write to your data structure unless you have to*", from the same C++ expert who in an earlier chapter was warning us against too much use of O-O mechanisms.

Advice from [Bright 1995]. *See page 515.*

This advice is puzzling. Why would developers write to a data structure for no reason?

***Rampant Problem of Programmers Writing to Data Structures When They Don't Have To Worries US Software Industry**. Why do they do it? Says Jill Kindsoul (not her real name), a Senior Software Engineer in Santa Barbara, California: "My heart goes out to the poor things. It can feel so lonely out there in swap space! I consider it my duty to write to each one of my objects' fields at least once a day, even if it's just with its own previous value. Sometimes I come back during the week-end just for it." The actions of programmers like Jill are a growing concern for the principal software vendors, all rumored to have set up special task forces to deal with the issue.*

(Imaginary media report.)

Another case of trying to address language flaws through methodological advice — making language users responsible for someone else's errors — was cited in an earlier chapter: the Java designers' recommendation ("*a programmer could still mess up the object…*") against using direct field assignments $a.x := y$, in violation of basic information hiding principles. It is a surprising approach, if you think a construct is bad, and just happen to be designing a programming language, to include the construct anyway and then write a book enjoining the language's future users to avoid it.

"A simple notion of book", page 221.

The "Law of Demeter" cited earlier also provides an example. It restricts the type of x, in a call $x.f(...)$ appearing in a routine r of a class C, to: types of arguments of r; types of attributes of C; creation types (types of u in $!! u ...$) for creation instructions appearing in

"Exceptions", page 668.

r. Such a rule, if justified, should be made part of the language. But as the authors themselves imply in the quoted excerpt this would be too harsh. The rule would make it impossible, for example, to write a call *my_stack.item.some_routine* which applies *some_routine* to the topmost element of *my_stack*; yet any alternative phrasing is heavier and less clear.

> For the first few weeks after the initial design of the notation of this book, years ago, multi-dot calls of the form *a.b.c* were not supported. This limitation proved insufferable and we did not rest until it was removed.

"SELECTIVE EX-PORTS AND INFOR-MATION HIDING", 7.8, page 191. Examination of the rationale for the Law, and for its exceptions, suggests that the authors may not have considered the notion of *selective export*, through which one can export a feature of a class *C* to specific clients having a close relation to *C*, while keeping it away from all other clients. With this mechanism, there may be no need for a Demeter-like law.

These observations yield our last precept:

Fixing What Is Broken methodology principle

If you encounter the need for many advisory negatives:

- Examine the supporting tool or language to determine if this reflects deficiencies in the underlying design.
- If so, consider the possibility of shifting over some of the effort from documenting that design to correcting it.
- Also consider the possibility of eliminating the problem altogether by switching to a better tool.

19.3 ON USING METAPHORS

> *ANDROMAQUE*:
> > *I do not understand abstractions.*
>
> *CASSANDRA*:
> > *As you like. Let us resort to metaphors.*
>
> Jean Giraudoux, *The Trojan War Will Not Happen*, Act I.

In this meta-methodological discussion it is useful to reflect briefly on the scope and limits of a powerful expository tool: metaphors.

Everyone uses metaphors — analogies — to discuss and teach technical topics. This book is no exception, with such central metaphors as inheritance and Design by Contract. The name of our entire subject, indeed, is a metaphor: when we use the word "object" to talk about some computing concept, we rely on a term loaded with everyday connections, which we hijack for a very specific purpose.

In scientific discourse metaphors are powerful, but they are dangerous. This is particularly applicable to software, and even more to software methodology.

A colleague with whom I used to attend software engineering conferences once swore that he would walk out the next time he heard an automotive comparison ("*if programs were like cars…*"). Had he kept the pledge, he would not have attended many talks.

Are metaphors good or bad? They can be very good, or very bad, depending on the purposes for which they are used.

Scientists use metaphors to guide their research; many have reported how they rely on concrete, visual images to explore the most abstract concepts. The great mathematician Hadamard, for example, describes the vivid images — clouds, red balls colliding, "*a kind of ribbon, which is thicker or darker at the place corresponding to the possibly important terms*" of a mathematical series — to which he and his peers have resorted to solve difficult problems in the most abstract realms of analysis and algebra.

[Hadamard 1945].

Metaphors can be excellent teaching tools. The great scientist-expositors — the Einsteins, Feynmans, Sagans — are peerless in conveying difficult ideas by appealing to analogies with concepts from everyday's experience. This is the best.

But the worst also exists. If we start taking metaphors at their face value, and deducing properties of the domain under study from properties of the metaphor, we are in serious trouble. A pseudo-syllogism ("*Proof by analogy*") of the form

$$\frac{A \; resembles \; B}{\textit{B has property p}}$$

Ergo: *A has property p*

is usually fallacious because the conclusion (*A has property p*) is precise whereas the first premise (*A resembles B*) is not. What matters is how exactly *A* is like *B*, and, even more, how *A* is *un*like *B*; clearly some properties of *B* must be different from those of *A*, otherwise *A* and *B* would be the same thing (as in those stories by Borges or Pérec in which a novel or painting is about itself, or in the language that the academicians of Laputa in *Gulliver's Travels* devised from the observation that "*since words are only names for things, it would be more convenient for all men to carry about them such things as were necessary to express the particular business they are to discourse on*"). A metaphor is defined by what differs as much as by what is common. But then to justify the conclusion we have to check that *p* only involves the common part. Once Hadamard had intuited his result, he knew he had to prove it step by step using the austere rites of mathematics; and many a student of a Feynman or Laurent Schwartz has realized, when faced with the week's homework, that brilliant images are only the beginning of the process.

Swift, Gulliver's Travels, *Part 3, "A Voyage to Laputa, etc.", chapter 5.*

The more alluring the metaphor, the greater the danger of falling into twisted reasoning of the above form. Think for example of the analogy so commonly used in the reusability literature, this book included, between software components and the "chips" of our hardware colleagues, through such terms as "software IC" (coined and trademarked by Brad Cox). Up to where do we use the metaphor to help us gain insights, and where do we start confusing the real thing *A* with the metaphor *B*?

Bachelard's fascinating book on the *Formation of the Scientific Mind*, which shows some of the best minds of the eighteenth century struggling with the transition from magical modes of reasoning to the scientific method, tells a story that anyone who is ever tempted to use a metaphor in scientific discourse should keep in mind. In trying to

[Bachelard 1960].

understand the nature of air, the great physicist-philosopher Réaumur used the then common metaphor of a sponge — which, as Bachelard shows, goes back at least to Descartes. Why not? Many good physics teachers occasionally resort to such gimmicks to capture students' attention and convey a point, supported or not by a bit of clowning in the classroom or the TV studio. But then things start to go wrong: the sponge *becomes* the air!

Réaumur, in Memoirs of the [French] Royal Academy of Sciences, 1731. Quoted by Bachelard, p. 74.

A very common idea is to consider air as being like cotton, like wool, like a sponge, and much more spongious even than any other bodies or collections of bodies to which they may be compared. This idea is particularly adequate to explain why air can also become extremely rarefied, and occupy a volume considerably bigger than what we had seen it occupy a moment before.

Air is like a sponge, so air expands like a sponge! And now comes none other than Benjamin Franklin, who finds sponges so convincing as to use them to explain … electricity. If matter is like a sponge, electric current must of course be *like* a liquid that flows through a sponge:

B. Franklin, in "Experiences and observations on electricity, expressed in several letters to P. Collinson of London's Royal Society". Translated back from the 1752 French text quoted in Bachelard, p. 77.

Common matter is a kind of sponge for the electric fluid. A sponge could not receive water if the parts which make up the water were bigger than the pores of the sponge; it would only receive it very slowly if there was no mutual attraction between its parts and the sponge's parts; the sponge would fill up faster if the mutual attraction between the water's parts did not create an obstacle, requiring that some force be applied to separate them; finally, the filling up would be very fast if, instead of attraction, there was mutual repulsion between the water's parts, concurring with the sponge's attraction. This is the precise situation with electrical matter and common matter.

Comments Bachelard: "*Franklin only thinks in sponge terms. The sponge, for him,* [*has become*] *an* empirical category." He adds, with a touch of mockery: "*Perhaps, in his youth,* [Franklin] *had marveled at such a simple object* [the sponge]. *I have often surprised children being fascinated by the sight of a blotter «drinking» ink*".

The Réaumur and Franklin quotations were not culled from a Usenet posting by an undergraduate who has yet to be taught to pour a few drops of intellectual rigor into his enthusiasm. They emanate from intellectual giants of their time, each of them responsible for decisive scientific advances. They should serve as a sobering influence when we discuss software concepts, and help us keep things in perspective the next time we see an author getting a bit carried away by his own analogies.

19.4 THE IMPORTANCE OF BEING HUMBLE

One final word of general advice as we prepare to study specific rules of design. To produce great products, designers, even the best ones, should never overestimate the value of their experience. Every ambitious software project is a new challenge: there are no sure recipes.

The design of a large software product is an intellectual adventure. Too much self-confidence can hurt. The more books you have read (or written), the more classes you have taken (or taught), the more programming languages you know (or designed), the more O-O software you have examined (or produced), the more requirements documents you have tried to decipher (or make decipherable), the more design patterns you have learned (or devised), the more design meetings you have attended (or led), the more talented co-workers you have met (or hired), the more projects you have helped (or managed), the better you will be equipped to deal with a new development. But do not think that your experience makes you infallible. In advanced software design there is no substitute for fresh thinking and creative insights. Every new problem calls for new ideas; everyone, from the seasoned project leader to the latest recruit, can have the right insight on any particular issue; and everyone can go wrong. What distinguishes the great designer is not necessarily that he has fewer bad ideas, but that he knows how to discard them, swallow his pride, and retain the good ideas whether or not he originated them. Incompetence and inexperience are obvious obstacles in the quest for the right solution; conceit can be just as bad.

No one will be surprised by these comments who has heard (although not necessarily believed) Luciano Pavarotti stating that he faces stage fright every night. One of the reasons the best people are best is that they are toughest with themselves. This rule is particularly relevant in software design, where there is always the risk of lapsing into intellectual laziness and making easy but wrong decisions, which may later be sorely regretted.

19.5 BIBLIOGRAPHICAL NOTES

The "advice to the advisors" part of this chapter is based on [M 1995b].

I first heard the definition of the difference between principles and platitudes from a talk by Joseph Gurvets at TOOLS EUROPE 1992. I owe to Éric Bezault the comment on the relevance of selective exports to the Law of Demeter.

EXERCISES

E19.1 Self-applying the rules

Perform a critique of the methodological rules of this book in the light of the precepts of this chapter. The list of all rules appears in Appendix C.

E19.2 Library rules

[M 1994a] contains an extensive set of rules, both design principles and style standards, for building library classes. Perform a critique of these rules in the light of the precepts of this chapter.

E19.3 Application of the rules

Examine the software methodology book of your choice, and the rules it gives, in the light of this chapter's precepts.

E19.4 Metaphors on the Net

Follow for a week or two the discussions of object technology in the Usenet newsgroup devoted to it, *comp.object*. Track the use of metaphors to talk about software concepts. Examine whether these metaphors are valuable, and whether any of them leads its author to make improper "proof by analogy" inferences.

20

Design pattern: multi-panel interactive systems

*I*n our first example we will devise a design pattern which, in addition to illustrating some typical properties of the object-oriented method, provides an excellent opportunity to contrast it with other approaches, in particular top-down functional decomposition.

Because this example nicely captures on a small scale some of the principal properties of object-oriented software construction, I have often used it when requested to introduce an audience to the method in a few hours. By showing concretely (even to people who have had very little theoretical preparation) how one can proceed from a classical decomposition to an O-O view of things, and the benefits gained in this transformation, it serves as a remarkable pedagogical device. This chapter has been written so that it could play the same role for readers who have been directed to it by the reference they found in the "spoiler" chapter at the beginning of this book.

To facilitate their task, it has been made as self-contained as possible; this is why you will find a few repetitions with previous chapters, in particular a few short definitions of concepts which you already know inside out if you have been reading this book sequentially and carefully from the start.

20.1 MULTI-PANEL SYSTEMS

The problem is to write a system covering a general type of interactive system, common in business data processing, in which users are guided at each step of a session by a full-screen panel, with predefined transitions between the available panels.

The general pattern is simple and well defined. Each session goes through a certain number of *states*. In each state, a certain panel is displayed, showing questions to the user. The user will fill in the required answer; this answer will be checked for consistency (and questions asked again until an acceptable answer is found); then the answer will be processed in some fashion; for example the system will update a database. A part of the user's answer will be a choice for the next step to perform, which the system will interpret as a transition to another state, where the same process will be applied again.

A typical example would be an airline reservation system, where the states might represent such steps of the processing as User Identification, Enquiry on Flights (for a certain itinerary on a certain date), Enquiry on Seats (for a certain flight) and Reservation.

A typical panel, for the Enquiry on Flights state, might look like the following (only intended, however, to illustrate the ideas, and making no claim of realism or good ergonomic design). The screen is shown towards the end of a step; items in *color italics* are the user's answers, and items in **bold color** show an answer displayed by the system.

A panel

```
┌─────────────────────────────────────────────────────────┐
│              – Enquiry on Flights –                       │
│                                                           │
│   Flight sought from: │ Santa Barbara │   To: │ Paris │   │
│                                                           │
│   Departure on or after:│ 21 Nov │  On or before:│ 22 Nov │ │
│                                                           │
│   Preferred airline (s):                                  │
│   Special requirements:  ─────────────────────            │
│                                                           │
│   AVAILABLE FLIGHTS: 1                                     │
│   Flt# AA 42      Dep 8:25      Arr 7:45    Thru: Chicago  │
│                                                           │
│   Choose next action:                                     │
│               0 — Exit                                    │
│               1 — Help                                    │
│               2 — Further enquiry                         │
│               3 — Reserve a seat                          │
└─────────────────────────────────────────────────────────┘
```

The session begins in an initial state, and ends whenever it reaches a final state. We can represent the overall structure by a transition graph showing the possible states and the transitions between them. The edges of the graph are labeled by integers corresponding to the possible user choices for the next step at the end of a state. At the top of the facing page is a graph for a simple airline reservation system.

The figure also include state numbers, for use later in the discussion.

The problem is to come up with a design and implementation for such applications, achieving as much generality and flexibility as possible. In particular:

G1 • The graph may be large. It is not uncommon to see applications with several hundred states and correspondingly many transitions.

G2 • The structure is subject to change. The designers are unlikely to foresee all the possible states and transitions. As users start exercising the system, they will come up with requests for changes and additions.

G3 • Nothing in the given scheme is specific to the choice of application: the airline reservation mini-system is just a working example. If your company needs a number of such systems, either for its own purposes or (in a software house) for various customers, it will be a big benefit to define a general design or, better yet, a set of modules that you can reuse from application to application.

A transition diagram

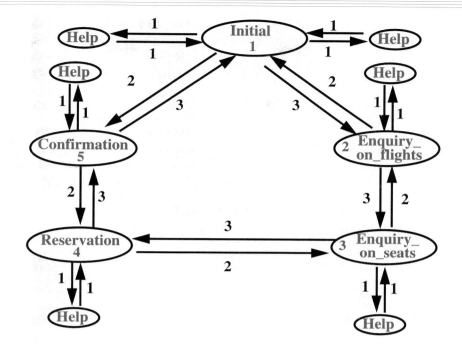

20.2 A SIMPLE-MINDED ATTEMPT

Let us begin with a straightforward, unsophisticated program scheme. This version is made of a number of blocks, one for each state of the system: $B_{Enquiry}$, $B_{Reservation}$, $B_{Cancellation}$ etc. A typical block (expressed in an ad hoc notation, not the object-oriented notation of this book although it retains some of its syntactic conventions) looks like this:

$B_{Enquiry}$:
    "Display *Enquiry on flights* panel"
    repeat
        "Read user's answers and choice C for the next step"
        if "Error in answer" **then** "Output appropriate message" **end**
    until not error in answer **end**
    "Process answer"
    case C **in**
        C_0: **goto** *Exit*,
        C_1: **goto** B_{Help},
        C_2: **goto** $B_{Reservation}$,
        …
    end

and similarly for each state.

This structure has something to speak for it: it is not hard to devise, and it will do the job. But from a software engineering viewpoint it leaves much to be desired.

The most obvious criticism is the presence of **goto** instructions (implementing conditional jumps similar to the **switch** of C and the "Computed Goto" of Fortran), giving the control structure that unmistakable "spaghetti bowl" look.

But the **goto**s are the symptom, not the real flaw. We have taken the superficial structure of the problem — the current form of the transition diagram — and hardwired it into the algorithm; the branching structure of the program is an exact reflection of the structure of the transition graph. This makes the software's design vulnerable to any of the simple and common changes cited above: any time someone asks us to add a state or change a transition, we will have to change the system's central control structure. And we can forget, of course, any hope of reusability across applications (goal G3 in the above list), as the control structure would have to cover all applications.

> This example is a sobering reminder that we should never get carried away when we hear about the benefits of "modeling the real world" or "deducing the system from the analysis of the reality". Depending on how you describe it, the real world can be simple or messy; a bad model will give bad software. What counts is not how close the software is to the real world, but how good the description is. More on this topic at the end of this chapter.

To obtain not just a system but a good system we must think a little harder.

20.3 A FUNCTIONAL, TOP-DOWN SOLUTION

Repeating on this particular example the evolution of the programming species as a whole, we will go from a low-level **goto**-based structure to a top-down, hierarchically organized solution, analyze its own limitations, and only then move on to an object-oriented version. The hierarchical solution belongs to a general style also known as "structured", although this term should be used with care.

> For one thing, an O-O solution is certainly structured too, although more in the sense of "structured programming" as originally introduced in the seventies by Dijkstra and others than relative to the quite distinct notion of "structured design".

The transition function

The first step towards improving the solution is to get rid of the central role of the traversal algorithm in the software's structure. The transition diagram is just one property of the system and it has no reason to rule over everything else. Separating it from the rest of the algorithm will, if nothing else, rid us of the **goto** instructions. And we should also gain generality, since the transition diagram depends on the specific application, such as airline reservation, whereas its traversal may be described generically.

What is the transition diagram? Abstractly, it is a function *transition* taking two arguments, a state and a user choice, such that *transition* (s, c) is the state obtained when the user chooses c when leaving state s. Here the word "function" is used in its mathematical sense; at the software level we can choose to implement *transition* either by a function in the software sense (a routine returning a value) or by a data structure such as an array. For the moment we can afford to postpone the choice between these solutions and just rely on *transition* as an abstract notion.

In addition to the function *transition* we also need to designate one of the states, say state *initial*, as the place where all sessions start, and to designate one or more states as final through a boolean-valued function *is_final*. Again this is a function in the mathematical sense, regardless of its eventual implementation.

We can picture the *transition* function in tabular form, with rows representing states and columns representing choices, as shown below.

Conventions used in this table: there is just one *Help* state, **0**, with a special transition *Return* which goes back to the state from which *Help* was reached, and just one final state, **−1**. These conventions will not be necessary for the rest of the discussion but help keep the table simple.

A transition table

Choice → ↓ State	0	1	2	3
1 (*Initial*)	−1	0	5	2
2 (*Flights*)		0	1	3
3 (*Seats*)		0	2	4
4 (*Reserv.*)		0	3	5
5 (*Confirm*)		0	4	1
0 (*Help*)		Return		
−1 (*Final*)				

The routine architecture

Following the traditional precepts of top-down decomposition, we choose a "top" (the main program) for our system. This should clearly be the routine *execute_session* that describes how to execute a complete interactive session.

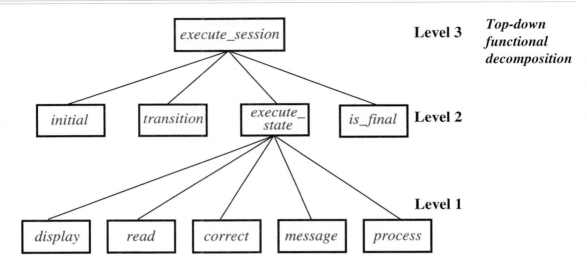

Top-down functional decomposition

Immediately below (level 2) we will find the operations relative to states: definition of the initial and final states, transition structure, and *execute_state* which prescribes the actions to be executed in each state. Then at the lowest level (1) we will find the constituent operations of *execute_state*: display a screen and so on. Note how such a solution may be described, as well as anything object-oriented that we may later see, to "reflect the real world": the structure of the software perfectly mirrors the structure of an application, which involves states, which involve elementary operations. Real-worldliness is not, in this example and many others, a significant difference between O-O and other approaches; what counts is *how* we model the world.

In writing *execute_session* let us try to make it as application-independent as possible. (The routine is again expressed in an ad hoc notation imitated from the O-O notation of the rest of this book. The **repeat** … **until** … loop is borrowed from Pascal.)

```
execute_session is
            -- Execute a complete session of the interactive system
      local
            state, choice: INTEGER
      do
            state := initial
            repeat
                  execute_state (state, →next)
                        -- Routine execute_state updates the value of next.
                  state := transition (state, next)
            until is_final (state) end
      end
```

This is a typical transition diagram traversal algorithm. (The reader who has written a lexical analyzer will recognize the pattern.) At each stage we are in a state *state*, originally set to *initial*; the process terminates when *state* satisfies *is_final*. For a non-final state we execute *execute_state*, which takes the current state and returns the user's transition choice through its second argument *next*, which the function *transition* uses, together with *state*, to determine the next state.

The → notation is a temporary convention, used only for this particular procedure and for read below.

The technique using a procedure *execute_state* that changes the value of one of its arguments would never be appropriate in good O-O design, but here it is the most expedient. To signal it clearly, the notation flags an "out" argument such as *next* with an arrow →. Instead of a procedure which modifies an argument, C developers would make *execute_state* a side-effect-producing function called as *next := execute_state (state)*; we will see that this practice is subject to criticism too.

Since *execute_state* does not show any information about any particular interactive application, you must fill in the application-specific properties appearing on level 2 in the figure: *transition* function; *initial* state; *is_final* predicate.

To complete the design, we must refine the *execute_state* routine describing the actions to be performed in each state. Its body is essentially an abstracted form of the contents of the successive blocks in the initial **goto**-based version:

```
execute_state (in s: INTEGER; out c: INTEGER) is
            -- Execute the actions associated with state s,
            -- returning into c the user's choice for the next state.
    local
        a: ANSWER; ok: BOOLEAN
    do
        repeat
            display (s)
            read (s, →a)
            ok := correct (s, a)
            if not ok then message (s, a) end
        until ok end
        process (s, a)
        c := next_choice (a)
    end
```

This assumes level 1 routines with the following roles:

* *display (s)* outputs the panel associated with state *s*.

* *read (s, →a)* reads into *a* the user's answer to the display panel of state *s*.

* *correct (s, a)* returns true if and only if *a* is an acceptable answer to the question displayed in state *s*; if so, *process (s, a)* processes answer *a*, for example by updating a database or displaying more information; if not, *message (s, a)* outputs the relevant error message.

The type *ANSWER* of the object representing the user's answer has not been refined further. A value *a* of that type globally represents the input entered by the user in a given state; it is assumed to include the user's choice for the next step, written *next_choice* (*a*). (*ANSWER* is in fact already very much like a class, even though the rest of the architecture is not object-oriented at all.)

To obtain a working application, you will need to fill in the various level 1 features: *display*, *read*, *correct*, *message* and *process*.

20.4 A CRITIQUE OF THE SOLUTION

Have we now a satisfactory solution? Not quite. It is better than the first version, but still falls short of our goals of extendibility and reusability.

Statism

Although on the surface it seems we have been able to separate the generic from the application-specific, in reality the various modules are still tightly coupled with each other and with the choice of application. The main problem is the data transmission structure of the system. Consider the signatures (argument and result types) of the routines:

execute_state	(**in** *s*: *STATE*; **out** *c*: *CHOICE*)
display	(**in** *s*: *STATE*)
read	(**in** *s*: *STATE*; **out** *a*: *ANSWER*)
correct	(**in** *s*: *STATE*; *a*: *ANSWER*): *BOOLEAN*
message	(**in** *s*: *STATE*; *a*: *ANSWER*)
process	(**in** *s*: *STATE*; *a*: *ANSWER*)

State intervention

The observation (which sounds like an economist's lament) is that the role of the state is too pervasive. The current state appears under the name *s* as an argument in all the routines, coming from the top module *execute_session*, where it is known as *state*. So the hierarchical structure shown in the last figure, seemingly simple and manageable, is a lie, or more precisely a façade. Behind the formal elegance of the functional decomposition lies a jumble of data transmission. The true picture, shown at the top of the facing page, must involve the data.

The architectural figure is on page 680.

The background for object technology, as presented at the beginning of this book, is the battle between the *function* and *data* (object) aspects of software systems for control of the architecture. In non-O-O approaches, the functions rule unopposed over the data; but then the data take their revenge.

The revenge comes in the form of sabotage. By attacking the very foundations of the architecture, the data make the system impervious to change — until, like a government unable to handle its *perestroika*, it will crumble under its own weight.

***The flow of
data***

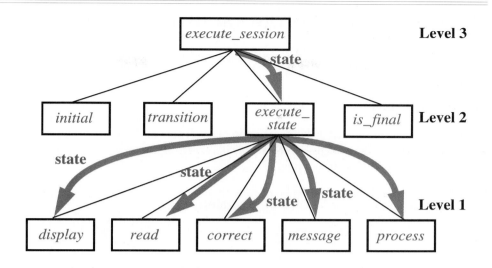

In this example the subversion of the structure comes in particular from the need to discriminate on states. All the level 1 routines must perform different actions depending on s: to display the panel for a certain state; to read and interpret a user answer (made of a number of input fields, different for each state); to determine whether the answer is correct; to output the proper error message; to process a correct answer — you must know the state. The routines will perform a discrimination of the form

> **inspect**
>
>> s
>
> **when** *Initial* **then**
>
>> ...
>
> **when** *Enquiry_on_flights* **then**
>
>> ...
>
> ...
>
> **end**

This means long and complex control structures and, worse yet, a fragile system: any addition of a state will require changes throughout the structure. This is a typical case of unbridled knowledge distribution: far too many modules of the system rely on a piece of information — the list of all possible states — which is subject to change.

The situation is in fact even worse than it appears if we are hoping for general reusable solutions. There is an extra implicit argument in all the routines considered so far: the *application* — airline reservation or anything else we are building. So to make routines such as *display* truly general we would have to let them know about all states of all possible applications in a given computing environment! Function *transition* would similarly contain the transition graph for all applications. This is of course unrealistic.

20.5 AN OBJECT-ORIENTED ARCHITECTURE

The very deficiencies of top-down functional decomposition point to what we must do to obtain a good object-oriented version.

The law of inversion

What went wrong? Too much data transmission in a software architecture usually signals a flaw in the design. The remedy, which leads directly to object-oriented design, may be expressed by the following design rule:

> ### Law of inversion
>
> If your routines exchange too many data, put your routines in your data.

Instead of building modules around operations (such as *execute_session* and *execute_state*) and distributing the data structures between the resulting routines, with all the unpleasant consequences that we have seen, object-oriented design does the reverse: it uses the most important data types as the basis for modularization, attaching each routine to the data type to which it relates most closely. When objects take over, their former masters, the functions, become their vassals.

The law of inversion is the key to obtaining an object-oriented design from a classical functional (procedural) decomposition, as in this chapter. Such a need arises in cases of *reverse-engineering* an existing non-O-O system to make it more maintainable and prepare its evolution; it is also frequent in teams that are new to object-oriented design and think "functional" first.

It is of course best to design in an object-oriented fashion from the beginning; then no inversion is needed. But the law of inversion is useful beyond cases of reverse-engineering and novice developers. Even someone who has been exposed to the principles of object-oriented software construction may come up with an initial design that has pockets of functional decomposition in an object landscape. Analyzing data transmission is a good way to detect and correct such design flaws. If you see — even in a structure intended as O-O — a data transmission pattern similar to what happens with states in the example of this chapter, it should catch your attention. Probing further will in most cases lead you to the discovery of a data abstraction that has not received its proper due in the software's architecture.

State as a class

The "state" example is typical. Such a data type, appearing so pervasively in the data transmissions between routines, is a prime candidate for serving as one of the modular components of an object-oriented architecture, which must be based on classes (abstractly described data types).

The notion of state was important in the original problem statement, but in the functional architecture that importance was lost: the state was just represented by a variable, passed from routine to routine as if it were some kind of lowlife. We have seen how it avenged itself. Now we are ready to give it the status it deserves. *STATE* should be a class, one of the principals in the structure of our new object-oriented system.

In that class we will find all the operations that characterize a state: displaying the corresponding screen (*display*), analyzing a user's answer (*read*), checking the answer (*correct*), producing an error message for an incorrect answer (*message*), processing a correct answer (*process*). We must also include *execute_state*, expressing the sequence of actions to be performed whenever the session reaches a given state; since the original name would be over-qualifying in a class called *STATE*, we can replace it by just *execute*.

Starting from the original top-down functional decomposition picture, we can highlight the set of routines that should be handed over to *STATE*:

STATE
features

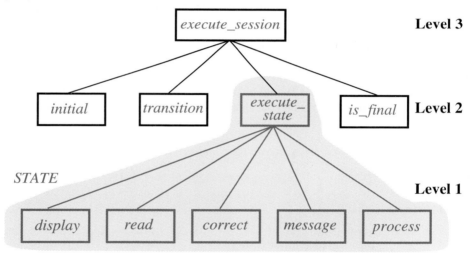

The class will have the following form:

... **class** *STATE* **feature**

    input: *ANSWER*

    choice: *INTEGER*

    execute **is do** ... **end**

    display **is** ...

    read **is** ...

    correct: *BOOLEAN* **is** ...

    message **is** ...

    process **is** ...

end

Features *input* and *choice* are attributes; the others are routines. Compared to their counterparts in the functional decomposition, the routines have lost their explicit state arguments, although the state will reappear in calls made by clients, such as *s.execute*.

In the previous approach, *execute* (formerly *execute_state*) returned the user's choice for the next step. But such a style violates principles of good design. It is preferable to treat *execute* as a command, whose execution determines the result of the query "what choice did the user make in the last state?", available through the attribute *choice*. Similarly, the *ANSWER* argument to the level 1 routines is now replaced by the secret attribute *input*. The reason is information hiding: client code does not need to look at answers except through the interface provided by the exported features.

See "SIDE EFFECTS IN FUNCTIONS", 23.1, page 748.

Inheritance and deferred classes

Class *STATE* does not describe a particular state, but the general notion of state. Procedure *execute* is the same for all states, but the other routines are state-specific.

Inheritance and deferred classes ideally address such situations. At the *STATE* level, we know the procedure *execute* in full detail and the attributes. We also know the existence of the level 1 routines (*display* etc.) and their specifications, but not their implementations. These routines should be deferred; class *STATE*, which describes a set of variants, rather than a fully spelled out abstraction, is itself a deferred class. This gives:

```
indexing
        description: "States for interactive panel-driven applications"
deferred class
        STATE
feature -- Access
        choice: INTEGER
                -- User's choice for next step

        input: ANSWER
                -- User's answer to questions asked in this state.
feature -- Status report
        correct: BOOLEAN is
                        -- Is input a correct answer?
                deferred
                end
feature -- Basic operations
        display is
                        -- Display panel associated with current state.
                deferred
                end
```

execute **is**
> -- Execute actions associated with current state
> -- and set *choice* to denote user's choice for next state.

local
> *ok*: *BOOLEAN*

do
> **from** *ok* := *False* **until** *ok* **loop**
> > *display*; *read*; *ok* := *correct*
> > **if not** *ok* **then** *message* **end**
>
> **end**
> *process*

ensure
> *ok*

end

It is easy to remove the test from within the loop for better efficiency.

message **is**
> -- Output error message corresponding to *input*.

require
> **not** *correct*

deferred
end

read **is**
> -- Obtain user's answer into *input* and choice into *next_choice*.

deferred
end

process **is**
> -- Process *input*.

require
> *correct*

deferred
end

end -- class *STATE*

To describe a specific state you will introduce descendants of *STATE* providing effectings (implementations) of the deferred features:

**State class
hierarchy**

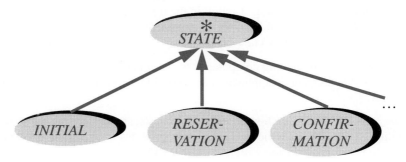

An example would look like:

class *ENQUIRY_ON_FLIGHTS* **inherit**
>   *STATE*

feature
>   *display* **is**
>>   **do**
>>>   ... Specific display procedure ...
>>   **end**
>   ... And similarly for *read*, *correct*, *message* and *process* ...

end -- class *ENQUIRY_ON_FLIGHTS*

This architecture separates, at the exact grain of detail required, elements common to all states and elements specific to individual states. The common elements, such as procedure *execute*, are concentrated in *STATE* and do not need to be redeclared in descendants such as *ENQUIRY_ON_FLIGHTS*. The Open-Closed principle is satisfied: *STATE* is closed in that it is a well-defined, compilable unit; but it is also open, since you can add any number of descendants at any time.

STATE is typical of **behavior classes** — deferred classes capturing the common behavior of a large number of possible objects, implementing what is fully known at the most general level (*execute*) in terms of what depends on each variant. Inheritance and the deferred mechanism are essential to capture such behavior in a self-contained reusable component.

"Don't call us, we'll call you", page 504.

Describing a complete system

To complete the design we must still take care of managing a session. In the functional decomposition this was the task of procedure *execute_session*, the main program. But now we know better. As discussed in an earlier chapter, the "topmost function of a system" as posited in the top-down method is mythical. A large software system performs many equally important functions. Here again, the abstract data type approach is more appropriate; it considers the system, taken as a whole, as a set of abstract objects capable of rendering a certain number of services.

"Finding the top", page 107

We have captured one key abstraction: *STATE* (along with *ANSWER*). What abstraction is our design still missing? Central in the understanding of the problem is the notion of *APPLICATION*, describing specific interactive systems such as the airline reservation system. This will yield a new class.

It turns out that the remaining components of the functional decomposition, shown in the figure, are all features of an application and will find their true calling as features of class *APPLICATION*:

• *execute_session*, describing how to execute an application. Here the name will be simplified to *execute* since the enclosing class provides qualification enough (and there is no possible confusion with *execute* of *STATE*).

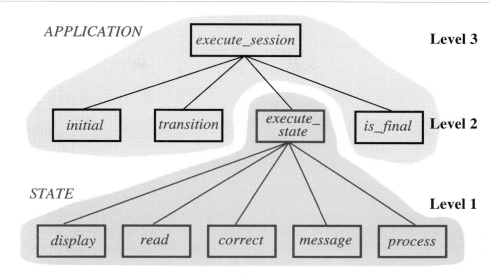

STATE and APPLICATION features

• *initial* and *is_final*, indicating which states have special status in an application. Note that it is proper to have these features in *APPLICATION* rather than *STATE* since they describe properties of applications rather than states: a state is not initial or final per se, but only with respect to an application. (If we reuse states between applications, a state may well be final in a certain application but not in another.)

• *transition* to describe the transition between states in the application.

The components of the functional decomposition have all found a place as features of the classes in the O-O decomposition — some in *STATE*, some in *APPLICATION*. This should not surprise us. Object technology, as has been repeatedly emphasized in this book, is before anything else an *architectural* mechanism, primarily affecting how we organize software elements into coherent structures. The elements themselves may be, at the lowest level, the same ones that you would find in a non-O-O solution, or at least similar (data abstraction, information hiding, assertions, inheritance, polymorphism and dynamic binding help make them more simple, general and powerful).

A panel-driven system of the kind studied in this chapter will always need to have operations for traversing the application graph (*execute_session*, now *execute*), reading user input (*read*), detecting final states (*is_final*). Deep down in the structure, then, we will find some of the same building blocks regardless of the method. What changes is how you group them to produce a modular architecture.

Of course we do not need to limit ourselves to features that come from the earlier solution. What for the functional decomposition was the end of the process — building *execute* for applications and all the other mechanisms that it needs — is now just a beginning. There are many more things we may want to do on an application:

- Add a new state.

- Add a new transition.

- Build an application (by repeated application of the preceding two operations).

- Remove a state, a transition.

- Store the complete application, its states and transitions, into a database.

- Simulate the application (for example on a line-oriented display, or with stubs replacing the routines of class *STATE*, to check the transitions only).

- Monitor usage of the application.

All these operations, and others, will yield features of class *APPLICATION*. They are no less and no more important than our former "main program", procedure *execute*, now just one of the features of the class, *inter pares* but not even *primus*. By renouncing the notion of top, we make room for evolution and reuse.

The application class

To finish class *APPLICATION* here are a few possible implementation decisions:

- Number states 1 to *n* for the application. Note that these numbers are not absolute properties of the states, but only relative to a certain application; so there is no "state number" attribute in class *STATE*. Instead, a one-dimensional array *associated_state*, an attribute of *APPLICATION*, yields the state associated with a given number.

- Represent the *transition* function by another attribute, a two-dimensional array of size $n \times m$, where *m* is the number of possible exit choices.

- The number of the initial state is kept in the attribute *initial* and set by the routine *choose_initial*. For final states we can use the convention that a transition to pseudo-state 0 denotes session termination.

- The creation procedure of *APPLICATION* uses the creation procedures of the library classes *ARRAY* and *ARRAY2*. The latter describes two-dimensional classes and is patterned after *ARRAY*; its creation procedure *make* takes four arguments, as in !! *a.make* (*1, 25, 1, 10*), and its *item* and *put* routines use two indices, as in *a.put* (*x, 1, 2*). The bounds of a two-dimensional array *a* are *a.lower1* etc.

Here is the class resulting from these decisions:

indexing

    description: "*Interactive panel-driven applications*"

class *APPLICATION* **creation**

    make

feature -- Initialization

    make (*n, m*: *INTEGER*) **is**

        -- Allocate application with *n* states and *m* possible choices.

      do

        !! *transition*.*make* (*1, n, 1, m*)

        !! *associated_state*.*make* (*1, n*)

      end

feature -- Access

    initial: *INTEGER*

        -- Initial state's number

feature -- Basic operations

    execute **is**

        -- Perform a user session

      local

        st: *STATE*; *st_number*: *INTEGER*

      do

        from

          st_number := *initial*

        invariant

          $0 <= st\_number$; $st\_number <= n$

        until *st_number* = *0* **loop**

          st := *associated_state*.*item* (*st_number*)

          ⟨ *st*.*execute* ⟩

            -- This refers of course to the *execute* procedure of *STATE*

            -- (see next page for comments on this key instruction).

          st_number := *transition*.*item* (*st_number*, *st*.*choice*)

        end

      end

feature -- Element change

    put_state (*st*: *STATE*; *sn*: *INTEGER*) **is**

        -- Enter state *st* with index *sn*.

      require

        $1 <= sn$; $sn <= associated\_state.upper$

      do

        associated_state.*put* (*st*, *sn*)

      end

    choose_initial (*sn*: *INTEGER*) **is**

        -- Define state number *sn* as the initial state.

      require

        $1 <= sn$; $sn <= associated\_state.upper$

      do

        initial := *sn*

      end

put_transition (*source, target, label*: *INTEGER*) **is**
    -- Enter transition labeled *label*
    -- from state number *source* to state number *target*.
  require
    1 <= source; *source <= associated_state•upper*
    0 <= target; *target <= associated_state•upper*
    1 <= label; *label <= transition•upper2*
  do
    transition•put (*source, label, target*)
  end

feature {*NONE*} -- Implementation

  transition: *ARRAY2* [*STATE*]

  associated_state: *ARRAY* [*STATE*]

  … Other features …

invariant

  transition•upper1 = associated_state•upper

end -- class *APPLICATION*

Note how simply and elegantly the highlighted call on the preceding page, *st•execute*, captures some of the problem's essential semantics. The feature called is *execute* from *STATE*; although effective because it describes a known general behavior, *execute* relies on deferred features *read, message, correct, display, process*, deferred at the level of *STATE* and effected only in its proper descendants such as *RESERVATION*. When we place the call *st•execute* in *APPLICATION*'s own *execute*, we have no idea what kind of state *st* denotes — although we do know that it is a state (this is the benefit of static typing). To come to life, the instruction needs the machinery of dynamic binding: when *st* becomes attached at run time to a state object of a particular kind, say *RESERVATION*, calls to *read, message* and consorts will automatically trigger the right version.

The value of *st* is obtained from *associated_state*, a **polymorphic data structure** which may contain objects of different types, all conforming to *STATE*. Whatever we find at the current index *st_number* will determine the next state operations.

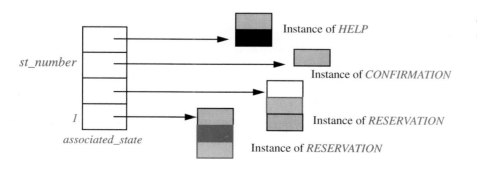

A polymorphic array of states

st_number

1

associated_state

Instance of *HELP*

Instance of *CONFIRMATION*

Instance of *RESERVATION*

Instance of *RESERVATION*

Here is how you build an interactive application. The application will be represented by an entity, say *air_reservation*, declared of type *APPLICATION*. You must create the corresponding object:

!! *air_reservation*.*make* (*number_of_states*, *number_of_possible_choices*)

You will separately define and create the application's states as entities of descendant types of *STATE*, either new or reused from a state library. You assign to each state *s* a number *i* for the application:

air_reservation.*put_state* (*s*, *i*).

You choose one of the states, say the state numbered i_0, as initial:

air_reservation.*choose_initial* (i_0)

To set up a transition from state number *sn* to state number *tn*, with label *l*, you use

air_reservation.*enter_transition* (*sn*, *tn*, *l*)

This includes exit transitions, for which *tn* is 0 (the default). You may now execute the application:

air_reservation.*execute_session*.

During system evolution you may at any time use the same routines to add a new state or a new transition.

It is of course possible to extend class *APPLICATION*, either by changing it or by adding descendants, to accommodate more features such as deletion, simulation, or any of the others mentioned in the course of the presentation.

20.6 DISCUSSION

This example provides a striking picture of the differences between object-oriented software construction and earlier approaches. It shows in particular the benefits of getting rid of the notion of main program. By focusing on the data abstractions and forgetting, for as long as possible, what is "the" main function of the system, we obtain a structure that is much more likely to lend itself gracefully to future changes and to reuse across many different variants.

This equalizing effect is one of the characteristic properties of the method. It takes some discipline to apply it consistently, since it means resisting the constant temptation to ask: "What does the system do?". This is one of the skills that sets the true object-oriented professional from people who (although they may have been using O-O techniques and an O-O language for a while) have not yet digested the method, and will still produce functional architectures behind an object façade.

We have also seen a heuristic that is often useful to identify key abstractions in an object-oriented (to "find the objects", or rather the classes, the topic of a subsequent chapter): analyzing data transmissions and being on the lookout for notions that show up in communications between numerous components of a system. Often this is an indication that the structure should be turned upside down, the routines becoming attached to the data abstraction rather than the reverse.

A final lesson of this chapter is that you should be wary of attaching too much importance to the notion that object-oriented systems are directly deduced from the "real world". The modeling power of the method is indeed impressive, and it is pleasant to produce software architectures whose principal components directly reflect the abstractions of the external system being modeled. But there are many ways to model the real world, and not all of them will lead to a good system. Our first, **goto**-filled version was as close to the real world as the other two — closer actually, since it is directly patterned after the structure of the transition diagram, whereas the other two require introducing intermediate concepts. But it is a software engineering disaster.

In contrast, the object-oriented decomposition that we finally produced is good because the abstractions that it uses — *STATE*, *APPLICATION*, *ANSWER* — are clear, general, manageable, change-ready, and reusable across a broad application area. Although once you understand them they appear as real as anything else, to a newcomer they may appear less "natural" (that is to say, less close to an informal perception of the underlying reality) than the concepts used in the inferior solutions studied first.

To produce good software, what counts is not how close you are to someone's perception of the real world, but how good are the abstractions that you choose both to model the external systems and to structure your own software. This is indeed the very definition of object-oriented analysis, design and implementation, the task that you will have to execute well, day in and day out, to make your project succeed, and the skill that distinguishes object experts from object amateurs: *finding the right abstractions*.

20.7 BIBLIOGRAPHICAL NOTE

Variants of the example discussed in this chapter were used to illustrate object-oriented concepts in [M 1983] and [M 1987].

21

Inheritance case study: "undo" in an interactive system

*F*or our second design example we examine a need that confronts the designers of almost any interactive system: how to provide a way to undo commands.

The discussion will show how inheritance and dynamic binding yield a simple, regular and general solution to an apparently intricate and many-faceted problem; and it will teach us a few general lessons about the issues and principles of object-oriented design.

21.1 PERSEVERARE DIABOLICUM

To err is human, it is said, but to foul things up for good takes a computer (aided, one should add, by humans). The faster and more powerful our interactive systems become, the easier it becomes to make them perform actions that we do not really want. This is why we all wish for a way to erase the recent past; not the "big red button" of computer jokes, but a Big Green Button that we can push to pretend that we did not do something that we did but wish we did not.

Undoing for fun and profit

In an interactive system, the equivalent of the Big Green Button is an Undo operation, which the system's designer has provided for the benefit of any user who, at some stage in a session, wants to cancel the effect of the last executed command.

The primary aim of an undo mechanism is to allow users to recover from potentially damaging input mistakes. It is all too easy to type the wrong character or click on "OK" instead of "Cancel". But a good undo facility goes further. It frees users from having to concentrate nervously on every key they type and button they click. Beyond this, it encourages a *What if… ?* style of interaction in which users try out various sorts of input, knowing that they can back up easily if the result is not what they expect.

Every good interactive system should provide such a mechanism. When present, it tends to be one of the most frequently used operations. (For that reason, the makers of the computer on my desk have wisely provided an Undo key on the keyboard, although it is neither green nor particularly big. It is only effective, of course, for those regrettably few software applications whose authors took notice of it.)

Multi-level undo and redo

Offering an undo mechanism is better than not offering one, but it is not enough. Most systems that provide Undo limit themselves to one level: you can only cancel the effect of the last command. If you never make two mistakes in a row, this is enough. But if you ever go off in the wrong direction, and wish you could go back several steps, you are in trouble. (Anyone having used Microsoft Word, the Unix Vi editor or FrameMaker, in the releases available at the time this book was published, will know exactly what I mean.)

There is really no excuse for the restriction to one level of undoing. Once you have set up the undoing machinery, going from one-level to multi-level undo is a simple matter, as we will see in this chapter. And, please (this is a potential customer speaking) do not, like so many application authors, limit the number of commands that can be undone to a ridiculously small value; if you must limit it at all, let the user choose his own limit (through a "preferences" setting that will apply to all future sessions) and set default to at least 20. The overhead is small if you apply the techniques below, and is well justified.

With multi-level undo, you will also need a Redo operation for users who get carried away and undo too much. With one-level undo no special Redo is required; the universally applied convention is that an Undo immediately following an Undo cancels it, so that Redo and Undo are the same operation. But this cannot work if you can go back more than one step. So we will have to treat Redo as a separate operation.

Practical issues

Although undo-redo can be retrofitted with reasonable effort into a well-written O-O system, it is best, if you plan to support this facility, to make it part of the design from the start — if only because the solution encourages a certain form of software architecture (the use of *command classes*) which, although beneficial in other respects, does not necessarily come to mind if you do not need undoing.

To make the undo-redo mechanism practical you will have to deal with a few practical concerns.

First you must include the facility in the user interface. For a start, we may just assume that the set of operations available to users is enriched with two new requests: Undo (obtained for example by typing control-U, although following the Macintosh convention control-Z seems to have become the standard on PC tools) and Redo (for example control-R). Undo cancels the effect of the last command not yet undone; Redo re-executes the last undone command not yet redone. You will have to define some convention for dealing with attempts to undo more than what has been done (or more than what is remembered), or to redo more than what has been undone: ignore the request, or bring up a warning message.

This is only a first shot at user interface support for undo-redo. At the end of this chapter we will see that a nicer, more visual interface is possible.

Second, not all commands are undoable. In some cases this is an impossibility of fact, as in the command "fire the missiles" (notwithstanding the televised comment of a then-in-office US president, who thought one could command a U-turn) or, less ominously, "print the page". In other cases, a command is theoretically undoable but the overhead is not worth the trouble; text editors typically do not let you undo the effect of a Save command, which writes the current document state into a file. The implementation of undoing will need to take into account such non-undoable commands, making this status clear in the user interface. Be sure to restrict non-undoable commands to cases for which this property is easily justifiable in user terms.

> As a counter-example, a document processing tool which I frequently use tells its user, once in a while, that in the current state of the document the command just requested is not undoable, with no other visible justification than the whim of the program. At least it says so in advance — in most cases.

> Interestingly, this warning is in a sense a lie: you *can* undo the effect if you want, although not through Undo but through "Revert to last saved version of the document". This observation yields a user interface rule: if there remains any case for which you feel justified to make a command non-undoable, do not follow the document processing system's example by just displaying a warning of the form "This command will not be undoable" and giving the choice between **Continue anyway** and **Cancel**. Give users *three* possibilities: save document, then execute command; execute without saving; cancel.

Finally, it may be tempting to offer, besides Undo and Redo, the more general "Undo, Skip and Redo" scheme, allowing users, after one or more Undo operations, to skip some of the commands before triggering Redo. The user interface shown at the end of this chapter could support this extension, but it raises a conceptual problem: after you skip some commands, the next one may not make sense any more. As a trivial example assume a text editor session, with a text containing just one line, and a user who executes the two commands

(1) Add a line at the end.

(2) Remove the second line.

Exercise E21.4, page 716.

Our user undoes both, then wants to skip (1) and redo (2). Unfortunately at this stage (2) is meaningless: there is no second line. This is less a problem in the user interface (you could somehow indicate to the user that the command is impossible) than in the implementation: the command Remove the second line was applicable to the object structure obtained as a result of (1), but applying it to the object structure that exists prior to (1) may be impossible (that is to say, cause a crash or other unpleasant results). Solutions are certainly possible, but they may not be worth the trouble.

Requirements on the solution

The undo-redo mechanism that we set out to provide should satisfy the following properties.

U1 • The mechanism should be applicable to a wide class of interactive applications, regardless of the application domain.

U2 • The mechanism should not require redesign for each new command.

U3 • It should make reasonable use of storage.

U4 • It should be applicable to both one-level and arbitrary-level Undo.

The first requirement follows from the observation that there is nothing application-specific about undoing and redoing. To facilitate the discussion, we will use as example a kind of tool familiar to everyone: a text editor (such as Notepad or Vi), which enables its users to enter texts and to perform such commands as INSERT_LINE, DELETE_LINE, GLOBAL_REPLACEMENT (of a word by another) and so on. But this is only an example and none of the concepts discussed below is specific to text editors.

The second requirement excludes treating Undo and Redo as just any other command in the interactive system. Were Undo a command, it would need a structure of the form

if "Last command was INSERT_LINE" **then**

   "Undo the effect of INSERT_LINE"

elseif "Last command was DELETE_LINE" **then**

   "Undo the effect of DELETE_LINE"

etc.

We know how bad such structures, the opposite of what the Single Choice principle directs us to use, are for extendibility. They have to be changed every time you add a command; furthermore, the code in each branch will mirror the code for the corresponding command (the first branch, for example, has to know a lot about what INSERT_LINE does), pointing to a flawed design.

See "Single Choice", page 61.

The third requirement directs us to be sparing in our use of storage. Supporting undo-redo will clearly force us to store *some* information for every Undo; for example when we execute a DELETE_LINE, we will not be able to undo it later unless we put aside somewhere, before executing the command, a copy of the line being deleted and a record of its position in the text. But we should store only what is logically necessary.

The immediate effect of this third requirement is to exclude an obvious solution: saving the whole system state — the entire object structure — before every command execution; then Undo would just restore the saved image. This would work but is terribly wasteful of space. Too bad, since the solution would be trivial to write: just use the *STORABLE* facilities for storing and retrieving an entire object structure in a single blow. But we must look for something a little more sophisticated.

On STORABLE see "Deep storage: a first view of persistence", page 250.

The final requirement, supporting an arbitrary depth of undoing, has already been discussed. It will turn out to be easier to consider a one-level mechanism first, and then to generalize it to multi-level.

These requirements complete the presentation of the problem. It may be a good idea, as usual, to spend a little time looking for a solution on your own before proceeding with the rest of this chapter.

21.2 FINDING THE ABSTRACTIONS

The key step in an object-oriented solution is the search for the right abstraction. Here the fundamental notion is staring us in the eyes.

Command as a class

The problem is characterized by a fundamental data abstraction: *COMMAND*, representing any editor operation other than Undo and Redo. Execution is only one of the features that may be applied to a command: the command might be stored, tested — or undone. So we need a class of the provisional form

deferred class *COMMAND* **feature**
    execute **is deferred end**
    undo **is deferred end**
end

COMMAND describes the abstract notion of command and so must remain deferred. Actual command types are represented by effective descendants of this class, such as

class *LINE_DELETION* **inherit**
    COMMAND
feature
    deleted_line_index: *INTEGER*

    deleted_line: *STRING*

    set_deleted_line_index (*n*: *INTEGER*) **is**
        -- Set to *n* the number of next line to be deleted.
    do
        deleted_line_index := *n*
    end

    execute **is**
        -- Delete line.
    do
        "Delete line number *deleted_line_index*"
        "Record text of deleted line in *deleted_line*"
    end

    undo **is**
        -- Restore last deleted line.
    do
        "Put back *deleted_line* at position *deleted_line_index*"
    end
end

And similarly for each command class.

What do such classes represent? An instance of *LINE_DELETION*, as illustrated below, is a little object that carries with it all the information associated with an execution of the command: the line being deleted (*deleted_line*, a string) and its index in the text (*deleted_line_index*, an integer). This is the information needed to undo the command should this be required later on, or to redo it.

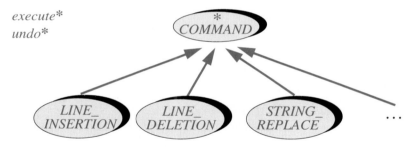

deleted_line_index   45
deleted_line   "Some text"

A command object

The exact attributes — such as *deleted_line* and *deleted_line_index* here — will differ for each command class, but they should always be sufficient to support the local variants of *execute* and *undo*. Such objects, conceptually describing the difference between the states that precede and follow the application of a command, will enable us to satisfy requirement U3 of the earlier list — storing only what is strictly necessary.

See "Requirements on the solution", page 697.

The inheritance structure of command classes may look like this:

execute*
undo*

COMMAND *

LINE_INSERTION   *LINE_DELETION*   *STRING_REPLACE*   ...

Command class hierarchy

The graph shown is flat (all proper descendants of *COMMAND* at the same level), but nothing precludes adding more structure by grouping command types into intermediate categories; this will be justified if such categories make sense as abstract data types, that is to say, have specific features.

When defining a notion, it is always important to indicate what it does not cover. Here the concept of command does not include Undo and Redo; for example it would not make sense to undo an Undo (except in the sense of doing a Redo). For this reason the discussion uses the term *operation* for Undo and Redo, reserving *command* for operations which can be undone and redone, such as line insertion. There is no need for a class covering the notion of operation, since non-command operations such as Undo have only one relevant feature, their ability to be executed.

> This is a good example of the limitations of simplistic approaches to "find the objects", such as the famous "Underline the nouns" idea studied in a later chapter. In the specification of the problem, the nouns *command* and *operation* are equally important; but one gives a fundamental class, the other does not give a class at all. Only the abstract data type perspective — studying abstractions in terms of the applicable operations and their properties — can help us find the classes of our object-oriented systems.

"The nouns and the verbs", page 720.

The basic interactive step

To get started we will see how to support one-level undo. The generalization to multi-level undo-redo will come next.

In any interactive system, there must be somewhere, in a module in charge of the communication with users, a passage of the form

> *basic_interactive_step* **is**
>
> -- Decode and execute one user request.
>
> **do**
>
> "Find out what the user wants us to do next"
>
> "Do it (if possible)"
>
> **end**

In a traditionally structured system, such as editor, these operations will be executed as part of a loop, the program's "basic loop":

> **from** *start* **until** *quit_has_been_requested_and_confirmed* **loop**
>
> *basic_interactive_step*
>
> **end**

whereas more sophisticated systems may use an event-driven scheme, in which the loop is external to the system proper (being managed by the underlying graphical environment). But in all cases there is a need for something like *basic_interactive_step*.

In light of the abstractions just identified, we can reformulate the body of the procedure as

> "Get latest user request"
>
> "Decode request"
>
> **if** "Request is a normal command (not Undo)" **then**
>
> "Determine the corresponding command in our system"
>
> "Execute that command"
>
> **elseif** "Request is Undo" **then**
>
> **if** "There is a command to be undone" **then**
>
> "Undo last command"
>
> **elseif** "There is a command to be redone" **then**
>
> "Redo last command"
>
> **end**
>
> **else**
>
> "Report erroneous request"
>
> **end**

This implements the convention suggested earlier that Undo applied just after Undo means Redo. A request to Undo or Redo is ignored if there is nothing to undo or redo. In a simple text editor with a keyboard interface, "Decode request" would analyze the user input, looking for such codes as control-I (for insert line), control-D (for delete line) and so on. With graphical interfaces you have to determine what input the user has entered, such as a choice in a menu, a button clicked in a menu, a key pressed.

Remembering the last command

With the notion of command object we can be more specific about the operations performed by *basic_interactive_step*. We will use an attribute

> *requested*: *COMMAND*
>> -- Command requested by interactive user

representing the latest command that we have to execute, undo or redo. This enables us to refine the preceding scheme of *basic_interactive_step* into:

> "Get and decode latest user request"
>
> **if** "Request is normal command (not Undo)" **then**
>> "Create appropriate command object and attach it to *requested*"
>>> -- *requested* is created as an instance of some
>>> -- descendant of *COMMAND*, such as *LINE_DELETION*
>>> -- (This instruction is detailed below.)
>>
>> | *requested*.*execute* | ; *undoing_mode* := False
>
> **elseif** "request is Undo" **and** *requested* /= *Void* **then**
>> **if** *undoing_mode* **then**
>>> "This is a Redo; details left to the reader"
>>
>> **else**
>>> | *requested*.*undo* | ; *undoing_mode* := True
>>
>> **end**
>
> **else**
>> "Erroneous request: output warning, or do nothing"
>
> **end**

Dynamic Binding

The boolean entity *undoing_mode* determines whether the last operation was an Undo. In this case an immediately following Undo request would mean a Redo, although the straightforward details have been left to the reader; we will see the full details of Redo implementation in the more interesting case of a multi-level mechanism.

Exercise E21.2, page 716.

The information stored before each command execution is an instance of some descendant of *COMMAND* such as *LINE_DELETION*. This means that, as announced, the solution satisfies the property labeled U3 in the list of requirements: what we store for each command is the difference between the new state and the previous one, not the full state.

See "Requirements on the solution", page 697.

The key to this solution — and its refinements in the rest of this chapter — is polymorphism and dynamic binding. Attribute *requested* is polymorphic: declared of type *COMMAND*, it will become attached to objects of one of its effective descendant types such as *LINE_INSERTION*. The calls *requested.execute* and *requested.undo* only make sense because of dynamic binding: the feature they trigger must be the version redefined for the corresponding command class, executing or undoing a *LINE_INSERTION*, a *LINE_DELETION* or a command of any other type as determined by the object to which *requested* happens to be attached at the time of the call.

The system's actions

No part of the structure seen so far is application-specific. The actual operations of the application, based on its specific object structures — for example the structures representing the current text in a text editor — are elsewhere; how do we make the connection?

The answer relies on the *execute* and *undo* procedures of the command classes, which must call application-specific features. For example procedure *execute* of class *LINE_DELETION* must have access to the editor-specific classes to call features that will yield the text of the current line, give its position in the text, and remove it.

As a result there is a clear separation between the user interaction parts of a system, largely application-independent, and the application-specific parts, closer to the model of each application's conceptual model — be it text processing, CAD-CAM or anything else. The first component, especially when generalized to a history mechanism as explained next, will be widely reusable between various application domains.

How to create a command object

After decoding a request, the system must create the corresponding command object. The instruction appeared abstractly as "Create appropriate command object and attach it to *requested*"; we may express it more precisely, using creation instructions, as

> **if** "Request is LINE INSERTION" **then**
>   ! *LINE_INSERTION* ! *requested.make* (*input_text, cursor_index*)
> **elseif** "Request is LINE DELETION" **then**
>   ! *LINE_DELETION* ! *requested.make* (*current_line, line_index*)
> **elseif**
>
>   ...

"Polymorphic creation", page 479.

This uses the ! *SOME_TYPE* ! *x* ... form of the creation instruction, which creates an object of type *SOME_TYPE* and attaches it to *x*; remember that *SOME_TYPE* must conform to the type declared for *x*, as is the case here since *requested* is of type *COMMAND* and all the command classes are descendants of *COMMAND*.

If each command type uses a **unique** integer or character code, a slightly simpler form relies on an **inspect**:

inspect

> *request_code*

when *Line_insertion* **then**

> ! *LINE_INSERTION* ! *requested*.*make* (*input_text*, *cursor_position*)

etc.

Both forms are multiple-branch choices, but they do not violate the Single Choice principle: as was pointed out in the discussion of that principle, if a system provides a number of alternatives some part of it *must* know the complete list of alternatives. The above extract, in either variant, is that point of single choice. What the principle precludes is spreading out such knowledge over many modules. Here, no other part of the system needs access to the list of commands; every command class deals with just one kind of command.

"Single Choice", page 61.

It is in fact possible to obtain a more elegant structure and get rid of the multi-branch choice totally; we will see this at the end of presentation.

"Precomputing command objects", page 708.

21.3 MULTI-LEVEL UNDO-REDO

Supporting an arbitrary depth of undoing, with the attendant redoing, is a straightforward extension of the preceding scheme.

The history list

What has constrained us to a single level of undoing was the use of just one object, the last created instance of *COMMAND* available through *requested*, as the only record of previously executed commands.

> In fact we create as many objects as the user executes commands. But because the software only has one command object reference, *requested*, always attached to the last command, every command object becomes unreachable as soon as the user executes a new command. It is part of the elegance and simplicity of a good O-O environment that we do not need to worry about such older command objects: the garbage collector will take care of reclaiming the memory they occupy. It would be a mistake to try to reclaim the command objects ourselves, since they may all be of different shapes and sizes.

See chapter 9 on garbage collection.

To provide more depth of undoing we need to replace the single command *requested* by a list of recently executed commands, the history list:

> *history*: *SOME_LIST* [*COMMAND*]

SOME_LIST is not a real class name; in true object-oriented, abstract data type style we will examine what features and properties we need from *SOME_LIST* and draw the conclusion as to what list class (from the Base library) we can use. The principal operations we need are straightforward and well known from previous discussions:

- *put* to insert an element at the end (the only place where we will need insertions). By convention, *put* will position the list cursor on the element just inserted.

- *empty* to find out whether the list is empty.

A history list

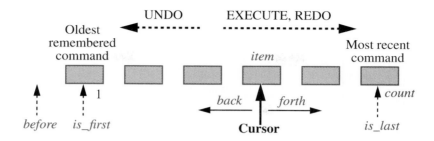

- *before*, *is_first* and *is_last* to answer questions about the cursor position.

- *back* to move the cursor back one position and *forth* to advance it one position.

- *item* to access the element at cursor position, if any; this feature has the precondition (**not** *empty*) **and** (**not** *before*), which we can express as a query *on_item*.

In the absence of undoing, the cursor will always be (except for an empty list) on the last element, making *is_last* true. If the user starts undoing, the cursor will move backward in the list (all the way to *before* if he undoes every remembered command); if he starts redoing, the cursor will move forward.

Skip is the subject of exercise E21.4, page 716.

The figure shows the cursor on an element other than the last; this means the user has just executed one or more Undo, possibly interleaved with some Redo, although the number of Undo must always be at least as much as the number of Redo (it is greater by two in the state captured in the figure). If at that stage the user selects a normal command — neither Undo nor Redo —, the corresponding object must be inserted immediately to the right of the cursor element. The remaining elements on the right are lost, since Redo would not make sense in that case; this is the same situation that caused us at the beginning of this chapter to relegate the notion of Skip operation to an exercise. As a consequence we need one more feature in *SOME_LIST*: procedure *remove_all_right*, which deletes all elements to the right of the cursor.

An Undo is possible if and only if the cursor is on an element, as stated by *on_item*. A Redo is possible if and only if there has been at least one non-overridden Undo, that is to say, (**not** *empty*) **and** (**not** *is_last*), which we may express through a query *not_last*.

Implementing Undo

With the history list, it is easy to implement Undo:

```
if on_item then
        history.item.undo
        history.back
else
        message ("Nothing to undo")
end
```

See once again how dynamic binding is essential. The *history* list is a polymorphic data structure:

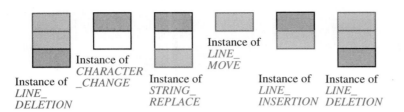

Instance of
*LINE_
DELETION*

Instance of
*CHARACTER
_CHANGE*

Instance of
*STRING_
REPLACE*

Instance of
*LINE_
MOVE*

Instance of
*LINE_
INSERTION*

Instance of
*LINE_
DELETION*

A history list with its various command objects

As the cursor moves left, each successive value of *history.item* may be attached to an object of any of the available command types; in each case, dynamic binding ensures that *history.item.undo* automatically selects the appropriate version of *undo*.

Implementing Redo

Redo is similar:

> **if** *not_last* **then**
>> *history.forth*
>> *history.item.redo*
> **else**
>> *message* ("*Nothing to redo*")
> **end**

This assumes a new procedure, *redo*, in class *COMMAND*. So far we had taken for granted that *redo* is the same thing as *execute*, and indeed in most cases it will be; but for some commands re-executing after an undo might be slightly different from executing from scratch. The best way to handle such situations — providing enough flexibility, without sacrificing convenience for the common cases — is to provide the default behavior in class *COMMAND*:

> *redo* **is**
>> -- Re-execute command that has been undone
>> -- by default, the same thing as executing it.
> **do**
>> *execute*
> **end**

This makes *COMMAND* a behavior class: along with deferred *execute* and *undo*, it has an effective procedure *redo* which defines a behavior based, by default, on the other two. Most descendants will keep this default, but some of them may redefine *redo* to account for special cases.

"Don't call us, we'll call you", page 504.

Executing a normal command

If a user operation is neither Undo nor Redo, it is a normal command identified by a reference that we may still call *requested*. In this case we must execute the command, but we must also insert it into the history list; we should also, as noted, forget any item to the right of the cursor. So the sequence of instructions is:

> **if not** *is_last* **then** *remove_all_right* **end**
>
> *history.put* (*requested*)
>
> > -- Recall that *put* inserts at the end of the list and moves
> > -- the cursor to the new element.
>
> *requested.execute*

With this we have seen all the essential elements of the solution. The rest of this chapter discusses a few implementation-related topics and draws the methodological lessons from the example.

21.4 IMPLEMENTATION ASPECTS

Let us examine a few details that help obtain the best possible implementation.

Command arguments

Some commands will need arguments. For example a *LINE_INSERTION* needs to know the text of the line to be inserted.

A simple solution is to add to *COMMAND* an attribute and a procedure:

> *argument*: *ANY*
>
> *set_argument* (*a*: **like** *argument*) **is**
> > **do** *argument* := *a* **end**

Then any command class can redefine *argument* to the proper type. To handle multiple arguments, it suffices to choose an array or list type. This was the technique assumed above when we passed various arguments to the creation procedures of command classes.

This technique is appropriate for all simple applications. Note, however, that the *COMMAND* class in ISE's libraries uses a different technique, slightly more complicated but more flexible: there is no *argument* attribute, but procedure *execute* takes an argument (in the usual sense of argument to a routine), representing the command argument:

> *execute* (*command_argument*: *ANY*) **is** …

The reason is that it is often convenient, in a graphical system, to let different instances of the same command type share the same argument; by removing the attribute we can reuse the same command object in many different contexts, avoiding the creation of a new command object each time a user requests a command.

The small complication is that the elements of the history list are no longer instances of *COMMAND*; they must instead be instances of a class *COMMAND_INSTANCE* with attributes

> *command_type*: *COMMAND*
>
> *argument*: *ANY*

For a significant system, the gain in space and time is worth this complication, since you will create one command object per command type, rather than one per command execution. This technique is recommended for production applications. You will only need to change a few details in the preceding class extracts.

Exercise E21.4, page 716.

Precomputing command objects

Before executing a command we must obtain, and in some cases create, the corresponding command object. The instruction was abstractly written as "Create appropriate command object and attach it to *requested*" and the first implementation draft was

Page 704.

> **inspect**
> > *request_code*
> **when** *Line_insertion* **then**
> > ! *LINE_INSERTION* ! *requested*.*make* (…)
> etc. (one branch for each command type)

As pointed out, this instruction does *not* violate the Single Choice principle: it is in fact the point of single choice — the only place in the entire system that knows what set of commands is supported. But we have by now developed a healthy loathing for **if** or **inspect** instructions with many branches, so even if this one appears inevitable at first let us see if perhaps we could get rid of it anyway.

We can — and the design pattern, which may be called **precomputing a polymorphic instance set**, is of wide applicability.

The idea is simply to create once and for all a polymorphic data structure containing one instance of each variant; then when we need a new object we simply obtain it from the corresponding entry in the structure.

Although several data structures would be possible for such as a list, it is most convenient to use an *ARRAY* [*COMMAND*], allowing us to identify each command type with an integer between 1 and *command_count*, the number of command types. We declare

> *commands*: *ARRAY* [*COMMAND*]

and initialize its elements in such a way that the *i*-th element ($1 <= i <= n$) refers to an instance of the descendant class of *COMMAND* corresponding to code *i*; for example, we create an instance of *LINE_DELETION*, associate it with the first element of the array (assuming line deletion has code 1), and so on.

The array of command templates

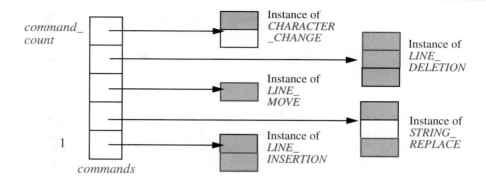

commands

A similar technique can be applied to the polymorphic array *associated_state* used in the O-O solution to the last chapter's problem (panel-driven applications).

The array *commands* is another example of the power of polymorphic data structures. Its initialization is trivial:

!! commands.make (1, command_count)

! LINE_INSERTION ! requested.make; commands.put (requested, 1)
! STRING_REPLACE ! requested.make; commands.put (requested, 2)
… And so on for each command type …

Note that with this approach the creation procedures of the various command classes should not have any arguments; if a command class has attributes, they should be set separately later on through specific procedures, as in *li.make (input_text, cursor_position)* where *li* is of type *LINE_INSERTION*.

Then there is no more need for any **if** or **inspect** multi-branch instruction. The above initialization serves as the point of single choice; you can now write the operation "Create appropriate command object and attach it to *requested*" as

requested := clone (commands @ code)

where *code* is the code of the last command. (Since each command type now has a code, corresponding to its index in the array, the basic user interface operation written earlier as "Decode request" analyzes the user's request and determines the corresponding code.)

The figure showing a history list example was on page 706.

The assignment to *requested* uses a *clone* of the command template from the array, so that you can have more than one instance of the same command type in the history list (as in the earlier example, where the history includes two *LINE_DELETION* objects).

If, however, you use the suggested technique of completely separating the command arguments from the command objects (so that the history list contains instances of *COMMAND_INSTANCE* rather than *COMMAND*), then the clone is not necessary any more, and you can go on using references to the original objects from the array, with just:

requested := commands @ code

In very long sessions the savings can be significant.

A representation for the history list

For the history list a type *SOME_LIST* was posited, with features *put*, *empty*, *before*, *is_first*, *is_last*, *back*, *forth*, *item* and *remove_all_right*. (There is also *on_item*, expressed in terms of *empty* and *before*, and *not_last*, expressed in terms of *empty* and *is_last*.)

Many of the classes in the Base libraries can be used to implement *SOME_LIST*; for example we could rely on *TWO_WAY_LIST* or one of the descendants of the deferred class *CIRCULAR_LIST*. To obtain a stand-alone solution let us devise an ad hoc class *BOUNDED_LIST*. Unlike a linked implementation such as *TWO_WAY_LIST*, this one will rely on an array, so it keeps only a bounded number of commands in the history. Let *remembered* be the maximum number of remembered commands. If you use this facility for a system to build, remember (if only to avoid receiving an angry letter from me should I ever become a user) to make this maximum user-settable, both during the session and in a permanent user profile consulted at the beginning of each session; and choose a default that is not too small, for example 20.

BOUNDED_LIST can use an array, managed circularly to enable reusing earlier positions as the number of commands goes beyond *remembered*. With this technique, common for representing bounded queues (it will show up again for bounded buffers in the discussion of concurrency), we can picture the array twisted into a kind of doughnut:

See "A buffer is a separate queue", page 990.

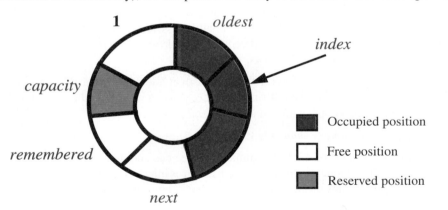

Bounded circular list implemented by an array

The size *capacity* of the array is *remembered* + *1*; this convention means setting aside one of the positions (the last, at index *capacity*) and is necessary if we want to be able to distinguish between an empty list and a full list (see below). The occupied positions are marked by two integer attributes: *oldest* is the position of the oldest remembered command, and *next* is the first free position (the one at which the next command will be inserted). The integer attribute *index* indicates the current cursor position.

An alternative to reserving a free position is to keep track of count, the number of elements, in an attribute. See "Unconstrained genericity", page 1181 for yet another variant.

Here is the implementation of the various features. For *put* (*c*), inserting command *c* at the end of the list, we execute

$$representation \bullet put\ (x, next); \qquad \text{-- where } representation \text{ is the name of the array}$$
$$next := (next \backslash\backslash\ remembered) + 1$$
$$index := next$$

where $\backslash\backslash$ is the integer remainder operation. The value of *empty* is true if and only if $next = oldest$; that of *is_first*, if and only if $index = oldest$; and that of *before* if and only if $(index \backslash\backslash\ remembered) + 1 = oldest$. The body of *forth* is

$$index := (index \backslash\backslash\ remembered) + 1$$

and the body of *back* is

$$index := ((index + remembered - 2)\ \backslash\backslash\ remembered) + 1$$

The +*remembered* term is mathematically redundant, but is included because of the lack of universal conventions as to the computer meaning of remainder operations for negative operands.

The query *item* giving the element at cursor position returns *representation @ index*, the array element at index *index*. Finally, the procedure *remove_all_right*, removing all elements to the right of the cursor position, is simply implemented as

$$next := (index \backslash\backslash\ remembered) + 1$$

21.5 A USER INTERFACE FOR UNDOING AND REDOING

Here is part of a possible user interface support for the undo-redo mechanism. It is taken from ISE's Case analysis and design workbench, but several of our other products use the same scheme.

Although keyboard shortcuts are available for Undo and Redo, the complete mechanism involves bringing up a **history window** (by clicking on a button in the interface, or selecting an item in the Tools menu). The history window is the exact user-visible equivalent of the *history* list as it exists inside the software. Once it is up, it will be regularly updated as you execute commands and other operations. In the absence of any undoing, it will look like this:

A history window, before any undoing

This shows the list of recent commands. As you execute new commands, they will appear at the end of the list. The currently active command (the one at cursor position) is highlighted in inverse video, like **change relation label** on the last figure.

To undo the active command, you can click on the up arrow button $\boxed{\uparrow}$ or use the keyboard shortcut (such as ALT-U). The cursor moves up (back) in the list; after a few such Undo, the window would look like this:

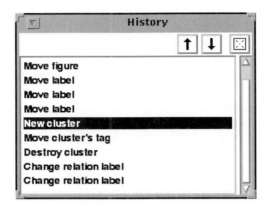

A history window, in the middle of an undo-redo process

As you know, this internally means that the software has been performing a few calls to *back*. At this stage you have a choice between several possibilities:

- You can perform more Undo operations by clicking on the up arrow button; the highlighting moves to the previous line.

- You can perform one or more Redo by clicking on the down arrow $\boxed{\downarrow}$ or using the equivalent keyboard shortcut; the highlighting goes to the next line, internally performing calls to *forth*.

- You can execute a normal command. As we have seen, this will remove from the history any commands that have been undone but not redone, internally performing a *remove_all_right*; in the interface, all the commands below the currently highlighted one disappear.

21.6 DISCUSSION

The design pattern presented in this chapter has an important practical role, as it will enable you to write significantly better interactive systems at little extra effort. It also brings an interesting theoretical contribution, by illuminating some aspects of object-oriented methodology worth exploring further.

The role of implementation

A striking property of the example user interface presented in the last section is that it was *directly deduced* from the implementation: we took the internal, developer-relevant notion of history list and translated it into an external, user-relevant history window, with the attendant user interaction mechanism.

> One may always imagine that someone could have devised the external view first, or at any rate independently from the implementation. But this is not the way it happened, either in this presentation or in history of our products' development.

Instituting such a relation between a system's functionality and its implementation goes against all that traditional software engineering methodology has taught. We have been told to deduce the implementation from the specification, not the reverse! Techniques of "iterative development" and "spiral lifecycle" change little to this fundamental rule that implementation is slave to prior concept, and that the software developers must do what the "users" (meaning, the customers, usually non-technical) tell them. Here we are violating every taboo by asserting that the *implementation* can tell us *what the system should be doing* in the first place. In earlier times questioning such time-honored definitions of what depends on what could have led one to the stake.

The legitimate emphasis on involving customers — meant to avoid the all too common horror stories of systems that do not do what their users need — has unfortunately led to downplaying the software developers' contribution, whose importance extends to the most external and application-related aspects. It is naïve to believe, for example, that customers will suggest the right interface facilities. Sometimes they will, but often they reason on the basis of the systems they know, and they will not see all the issues involved. That is understandable: they have their own jobs to do, and their own areas of expertise; getting everything right in a software system is not their responsibility. Some of the worst interactive interfaces in the world were designed with *too much* user influence. Where users are truly irreplaceable is for negative comments: they will see practical flaws in an idea which at first seems attractive to the developers. Such criticism must always be heeded. Users can make brilliant positive suggestions too, but do not depend on it. And once in a while, a developer's suggestion will seduce the users — possibly after a number of iterations taking their criticism into account — even though it draws its origin from a seemingly humble implementation technique, such as the history list.

More on seamlessness and reversibility in chapter 28.

This equalization of traditional relationships is one of the distinctive contributions of object technology. By making the development process seamless and reversible, we allow a great implementation idea to influence the specification. Instead of a one-way flow from analysis to design and "coding", we have a continuous process with feedback loops throughout. This assumes, of course, that implementation is no longer viewed as the messy, low-level component of system construction; its results, developed with the techniques described throughout this book, can and should be as clear, elegant and abstract as anything one can produce in the most implementation-abhorrent forms of traditional analysis and design.

Small classes

The design described in this chapter may, for a typical interactive system, involve a significant number of relatively small classes: one for each type of command. There is no reason, however, to be concerned about the effect on system size and complexity since the inheritance structure on these classes will remain simple, although it does not have to be as flat as the one sketched in this chapter. (You may want to group commands into categories.)

In a systematic O-O approach, similar questions arise whenever you have to introduce classes representing actions. Although some object-oriented languages make it possible to pass routines as arguments to other routines, such a facility contradicts the basic idea of the method — that a function (action, routine) never exists by itself but is always *relative to a certain data abstraction*. So instead of passing an operation we should pass an object equipped, through a routine of its generating class, with that operation, as with an instance of *COMMAND* equipped with the *execute* operation.

Sometimes the need to write a wrapper class seems artificial, especially to people used to passing routines around as arguments. But every time I have seen such a class legitimately being introduced, originally for the sole purpose (it was thought) of encapsulating an operation, it turned out to reveal a useful data abstraction, as evidenced by the later addition of other features beyond the one that served as the original incentive. Class *COMMAND* does not fall into this category, since right from the start it was conceived as a data abstraction, and had two features (*execute* and *undo*). But it is typical of the process, since if you start using commands seriously you will soon realize the need for even more features such as:

- *argument*: *ANY* to represent the command argument (as in one of the versions that we have encountered).

- *help*: *STRING*, to provide on-line help associated with each command.

- Logging and statistical features, to keep track of how often each command type is used.

Another example, drawn from the domain of numerical software, is more representative of situations where the introduction of a class may seem artificial at first, because the object-oriented designer will pass an object where a traditional approach would have passed a routine as argument. In performing scientific computation you will often need integration mechanisms, to which you give a mathematical function f to compute its integral on a certain interval. The traditional technique is to represent f as a routine, but in object-oriented design we recognize that "Integrable function" is an important abstraction, with many possible features. For someone coming from the functional world of C, Fortran and top-down design, the need to provide a class may at first appear to be a kind of programming trick: not finding in the language manual a way to pass a routine as argument, he asks his colleagues how to achieve this effect, and is told that he must write a class with the corresponding feature, then pass objects (instances of that class) rather than the feature itself.

He may at first accept this technique — perhaps grudgingly — as one of those quirks that programming languages impose on their users, as when you want a boolean variable in C and have to declare it of type integer, with 0 for false and 1 for true. But then as he continues his design he will realize that the technique was not a hack, simply the proper application of object-oriented principles: *INTEGRABLE_FUNCTION* is indeed one of the major abstractions of his problem domain, and soon new, relevant features (beyond the original one *item* (*a*: *REAL*): *REAL*, giving the value of the function at point *a*) will start piling up.

What was thought to be a trick turns out to yield a major component of the design.

21.7 BIBLIOGRAPHICAL NOTES

The undo-redo mechanism described in this chapter was present in the structural document constructor *Cépage* developed by Jean-Marc Nerson and the author in1982 [M 1984], and has been integrated into many of ISE's interactive tools (including ArchiText [ISE 1996], the successor to Cépage).

In [Cox 1986].   In a position paper for a panel at the first OOPSLA conference in 1986, Larry Tesler cites a mechanism based on the same ideas, part of Apple's *MacApp* interactive framework.

[Dubois 1997] explains in detail how to apply object-oriented concepts to the design of numerical software, with abstractions such as "Integrable function" (as mentioned in the last section), and describes in detail a complete object-oriented numerical library.

EXERCISES

E21.1 Putting together a small interactive system (programming project)

This small programming project is an excellent way to test your understanding of the topics of this chapter — and more generally of how to build a small system making full use of object-oriented techniques.

Write a line-oriented editor supporting the following operations:

- **p**: Print text entered so far.

- ↓: move cursor to next line if any. (Use the code **l**, for low, if that is more convenient.)

- ↑: move cursor to previous line if any. (Use **h**, for high, if that is more convenient.)

- **i**: insert a new line after cursor position.

- **d**: delete line at cursor position.

- **u**: Undo last operation if not Undo; if it was Undo, redo undone command.

You may add more commands, or choose a more attractive user interface, but in all cases you should produce a complete, workable system. (You may also apply right from the start the improvement described in the next exercise.)

E21.2 Multi-level Redo

Complete the previous exercise's one-level scheme by redefining the meaning of **u** as

- **u**: Undo last operation other than Undo and Redo.

and adding

- **r**: Redo last undone command (when applicable).

E21.3 Undo-redo in Pascal

Explain how to obtain a solution imitating the undo-redo technique of this chapter in non-O-O languages such as Pascal, Ada (using record types with variants) or C (using structure and union types). Compare with the object-oriented solution.

E21.4 Undo, Skip and Redo

Bearing in mind the issues raised early in the discussion, study how to extend the mechanism developed in this chapter so that it will support Undo, Skip and Redo, as well as making it possible to redo an undone command that has been followed by a normal command.

See "Practical issues", page 696 and "The history list", page 704.

Discuss the effect on both the user interface and the implementation.

E21.5 Saving on command objects

Adapt all the class extracts of this chapter to treat command arguments separately from commands (adding a routine argument to *execute*) and create only one command object per command type.

See "Command arguments", page 707.

If you have done the preceding exercise, apply this technique to its solution.

E21.6 Composite commands

For some systems it may be useful to introduce a notion of composite command, describing commands whose execution involves executing a number of other commands. Write the corresponding class *COMPOSITE_COMMAND*, an heir of *COMMAND*, making sure that composite commands can be undone, and that a component of a composite command may itself be composite.

Hint: use the multiple inheritance scheme presented for composite figures.

See "Composite figures", page 527.

E21.7 Non-undoable commands

A system may include commands that are not undoable, either by nature ("Fire the missiles") or for pragmatic reasons (when there is too much information to remember). Refine the solution of this chapter so that it will account for non-undoable commands. (**Hint**: introduce heirs *UNDOABLE* and *NON_UNDOABLE* to class *COMMAND*.) Study carefully the effect on the algorithms presented, and on the user interface, in particular for an interface using the history windows as presented at the end of the chapter.

E21.8 A command library (design and implementation project)

Write a general-purpose command library, meant to be used by an arbitrary interactive system and supporting an unlimited undo-redo mechanism. The library should integrate the facilities discussed in the last three exercises: separating commands from arguments; composite commands; non-undoable commands. (Integrating an "Undo, Skip and Redo" facility is optional.) Illustrate the applicability of your library by building three demonstration systems of widely different natures, such as a text editor, a graphics system and a training tool.

E21.9 A history mechanism

A useful feature to include in a command-oriented interactive tool is a history mechanism which remembers the last commands executed, and allows the user to re-execute a previous command, possibly modified, using simple mnemonics. Under Unix, for example, you may direct the C-shell (a command language) to remember the last few executed commands; then you may type !–2 to mean "re-execute the next-to-last command", or ^yes^no^ to mean "re-execute the last command, replacing the characters *yes* in the command text by *no*". Other environments offer similar facilities.

History mechanisms, when they exist, are built in an ad hoc fashion. On Unix, many interactive tools running under the C-shell, such as the Vi editor or various debuggers, would greatly benefit from such a mechanism but do not offer one. This is all the more regrettable that the same concept of command history and the same associated facilities are useful for any interactive tool independently of the functions it performs — command language, editor, debugger.

Design a class implementing a general-purpose history mechanism, in such a way that any interactive tool needing such a mechanism will obtain it by simply inheriting from that class. (Note that multiple inheritance is essential here.)

Discuss the extension of this mechanism to a general *USER_INTERFACE* class.

E21.10 Testing environment

Proper testing of a software component, for example a class, requires a number of facilities to prepare the test, input test data, run the test, record the results, compare them to expected results etc. Define a general *TEST* class that defines an appropriate testing environment and may be inherited by any class in need of being tested. (Note again the importance of multiple inheritance.)

E21.11 Integrable functions

(For readers familiar with the basics of numerical analysis.) Write a set of classes for integrating real functions of a real variable over arbitrary intervals. They should include a class *INTEGRABLE_FUNCTION*, as well as a deferred class *INTEGRATOR* to describe integration methods, with proper descendants such as *RATIONAL_FIXED_INTEGRATOR*.

See "Small classes", page 714. For a full-fledged solution see [Dubois 1997].

22

How to find the classes

$\mathcal{F}$oremost among the goals of object-oriented methodology, since the structure of O-O software is based on decomposition into classes, is that it should give us some advice on how to find these classes. Such is the purpose of the following pages. (In some of the literature you will see the problem referred to as "*finding the objects*", but by now we know better: what is at stake in our software architectures is not individual objects, but object types — classes.)

At first we should not expect too much. Finding classes is the central decision in building an object-oriented software system; as in any creative discipline, making such decisions right takes talent and experience, not to mention luck. Expecting to obtain infallible recipes for finding the classes is as unrealistic as would be, for an aspiring mathematician, expecting to obtain recipes for inventing interesting theories and proving their theorems. Although both activities — software construction and theory construction — can benefit from general advice and the example of successful predecessors, both also require creativity of the kind that cannot fully be covered by mechanical rules. If (like many people in the industry) you still find it hard to compare the software developer to a mathematician, just think of other forms of engineering design: although it is possible to provide basic guidelines, no teachable step-by-step rules can guarantee good design of buildings or airplanes.

In software too, no book advice can replace your know-how and ingenuity. The principal role of a methodological discussion is to indicate some good ideas, draw your attention to some illuminating precedents, and alert you to some known pitfalls.

This would be true with any other software design method. In the case of object technology, the observation is tempered by some good news, coming to us in the form of reuse. Because much of the necessary invention may already have been done, you can build on others' accomplishments.

There is more good news. By starting with humble expectations but studying carefully what works and also what does not, we will be able, little by little and against all odds, to devise what in the end deserves to be called a *method* for finding the classes. One of the key steps will be the realization that, as always in design, a selection technique is defined by two components: what to consider, and what to reject.

22.1 STUDYING A REQUIREMENTS DOCUMENT

To understand the problem of finding classes, it may be best to begin by assessing a widely publicized approach.

The nouns and the verbs

A number of publications suggest using a simple rule for obtaining the classes: start from the requirements document (assuming there is one, of course, but that is another story); in function-oriented design you would concentrate on the verbs, which correspond to actions ("do this"); in object-oriented design you underline the nouns, which describe objects. So according to this view a sentence of the form

See the bibliogra-phical notes.

> *The elevator will close its door before it moves to another floor.*

would lead the function-oriented designer to detect the need for a "move" function; but as an object-oriented designer you should see in it three object types, *ELEVATOR*, *DOOR* and *FLOOR*, which will give classes. Voilà!

Would it that life were that simple. You would bring your requirements documents home at night, and play *Object Pursuit* around the dinner table. A good way to keep the children away from the TV set, and make them revise their grammar lessons while they help Mom and Dad in their software engineering work.

But such a simple-minded technique cannot take us very far. Human language, used to express system requirements, is so open to nuance, personal variation and ambiguity that it is dangerous to make any important decision on the basis of a document which may be influenced as much by the author's individual style as by the actual properties of the projected software system.

Any useful result that the "underline the nouns" method would give us is obvious anyway. Any decent O-O design for an elevator control system will include an *ELEVATOR* class. Obtaining such classes is not the difficult part. To repeat an expression used in an earlier discussion, they are here for the picking. For the non-obvious classes a syntactic criterion — such as nouns versus verbs in a document that is by essence open to many possible stylistic variants — is close to useless.

Although by itself the "underline the nouns" idea would not deserve much more consideration, we can use it further, not for its own sake but as a foil; by understanding its limitations we can gain insights into what it truly takes to find the classes and how the requirements document can help us in this endeavor.

Avoiding useless classes

The nouns of a requirements document will cover some classes of the final design, but will also include many "false alarms": concepts that should *not* yield classes.

In the elevator example *door* was a noun. Do we need a class *DOOR*? Maybe, maybe not. It is possible that the only relevant property of elevator doors for this system is that they may be opened and closed. Then to express the useful properties of doors it suffices to include in class *ELEVATOR* the query and commands

> *door_open*: *BOOLEAN*;
>
> *close_door* **is**
>
> . . .
>
> **ensure**
>
>   **not** *door_open*
>
> **end**;
>
> *open_door* **is**
>
> . . .
>
> **ensure**
>
>   *door_open*
>
> **end**

In another variant of the system, however, the notion of door may be important enough to justify a separate class. The only resource here is the theory of abstract data types, and the only relevant question is:

> Is "door" a separate data type with its own clearly identified operations, or are all the operations on doors already covered by operations on other data types such as *ELEVATOR*?

Only your intuition and experience as a designer will tell you the answer. In looking for it, you will be aided by the requirements document, but do not expect grammatical criteria to be of more than superficial help. Turn instead to the ADT theory, which will help you ask customers or future users the right questions.

Chapter 21.   We encountered a similar case in the undo-redo mechanism design. The discussion distinguished between *commands*, such as the line insertion command in a text editor, and the more general notion of *operation*, which includes commands but also special requests such as Undo. Both of these words figured prominently in the statement of the problem; yet only *COMMAND* yielded a data abstraction (one of the principal classes of the design), whereas no class in the solution directly reflects the notion of operation. No analysis of a requirements document can suggest this striking difference of treatment.

Is a new class necessary?

Another example of a noun which may or may not give a class in the elevator example is *floor*. Here (as opposed to the *door* and *operation* cases) the question is not whether the concept is a relevant ADT: floors are definitely an important data abstraction for an elevator system. But this does not necessarily mean we should have a *FLOOR* class.

The reason is simply that the properties of floors may be entirely covered, for the purposes of the elevator system, by those of integers. Each floor has a floor number; then if a floor (as seen by the elevator system) has no other features than those associated with its floor number, you may not need a separate *FLOOR* class. A typical floor feature that comes from a feature of integers is the distance between two floors, which is simply the difference of their floor numbers.

Many hotels have no floor 13, so the arithmetic may be a bit more elaborate.

If, however, floors have properties other than those of their numbers — that is to say, according to the principles of abstract data types and object-oriented software construction, significant *operations* not covered by those of integers — then a *FLOOR* class will be appropriate. For example, some floors may have special access rights defining who can visit them; then the *FLOOR* class could include a feature such as

   rights: *SET* [*AUTHORIZATION*]

and the associated procedures. But even that is not certain: we might get away by including in some other class an array

   floor_rights: *ARRAY* [*SET* [*AUTHORIZATION*]]

which simply associates a set of *AUTHORIZATION* values with each floor, identified by its number.

Another argument for having a specific class *FLOOR* would be to limit the available operations: it makes sense to subtract two floors and to compare them (through the *infix* "<" function), but not to add or multiply them. Such a class may be written as an heir to *INTEGER*. The designer must ask himself, however, whether this goal really justifies adding a new class.

See exercise E22.1, page 745.

This discussion brings us once again to the theory of abstract data types. A class does not just cover physical "objects" in the naïve sense. It describes an abstract data type — a set of software objects characterized by well-defined operations and formal properties of these operations. A type of real-world objects may or may not have a counterpart in the software in the form of a type of software objects — a class. When you are assessing whether a certain notion should yield a class or not, only the ADT view can provide the right criterion: do the objects of the system under discussion exhibit enough specific operations and properties of their own, relevant to the system and not covered by existing classes?

The qualification "relevant to the system" is crucial. The aim of systems analysis is not to "model the world". This may be a task for philosophers, but the builders of software systems could not care less, at least for their professional activity. The task of analysis is to model that part of the world which is meaningful for the software under study or construction. This principle is reinforced by the ADT approach (that is to say, the object-oriented method), which holds that *objects are only defined by what we can do with them* — what the discussion of abstract data types called the Principle of Selfishness. If an operation or property of an object is irrelevant to the purposes of the system, then it should not be included in the result of your analysis — however interesting it may be for other purposes. For a census processing system, the notion of *PERSON* may have features *mother* and *father*; but for a payroll processing system which does not require information about the parents, every *PERSON* is an orphan.

"BEYOND SOFT-WARE", 6.6, page 147.

If all of the operations and properties that you can identify for a type of objects are irrelevant in this sense, or are already covered by the operations and properties of a previously identified class, the conclusion is that the object type itself is irrelevant: it must not yield a class.

This explains why an elevator system might not include *FLOOR* as a class because (as noted above) from the point of view of the elevator system floors have no relevant properties other than those of the associated integer numbers, whereas a Computer Aided Design system designed for architects will have a *FLOOR* class — since in that case the floor has several specific attributes and routines.

Missing important classes

Not only can nouns suggest notions which do not yield classes: they can also fail to suggest some notions which should definitely yield classes. There are at least three sources of such accidents.

> Do not forget that, as noted, the aim of this discussion is no longer to convince ourselves of the deficiencies of the "underline the nouns" approach, whose limitations are by now so obvious that the exercise would not be very productive. Instead, we are analyzing these limitations as a way to gain more insight into the process of discovering classes.

The first cause of missed classes is simply due to the flexibility and ambiguity of human language — the very qualities that make it suitable for an amazingly wide range of applications, from speeches and novels to love letters, but not very reliable as a medium for accurate technical documents. Assume the requirements document for our elevator example contains the sentence

> *A database record must be created every time the elevator moves from one floor to another.*

The presence of the noun "record" suggests a class *DATABASE_RECORD*; but we may totally miss a more important data abstraction: the notion of a *move* between two floors. With the above sentence in the requirements document, you will almost certainly need a *MOVE* class, which could be of the form

class *MOVE* **feature**
    initial, final: *FLOOR*;   -- Or *INTEGER* if no *FLOOR* class
    record (*d*: *DATABASE*) **is** ...
    ... Other features ...
end -- class *MOVE*

This will be an important class, which a grammar-based method would miss because of the phrasing of the above sentence. Of course if the sentence had appeared as

> *A database record must be created for every move of the elevator from one floor to another.*

then "move" would have been counted as a noun, and so would have yielded a class! We see once again the dangers of putting too much trust in a natural-language document, and the absurdity of making any serious property of a system design, especially its modular structure, dependent on such vagaries of style and mood.

The second reason for overlooking classes is that some crucial abstractions may not be directly deducible from the requirements. Cases abound in the examples of this book. It is quite possible that the requirements for a panel-driven system did not explicitly cite the notions of state and application; yet these are the key abstractions, which condition the entire design. It was pointed out earlier that some external-world object types may have no counterpart among the classes of the software; here we see the converse: classes of the software that do not correspond to any external-world objects. Similarly, if the author of the requirements for a text editor with undo-redo has written "*the system must support line insertion and deletion*", we are in luck since we can spot the nouns *insertion* and *deletion*; but the need for these facilities may just as well follow from a sentence of the form

Panel-driven system: chapter 20. Undo-redo: chapter 21.

> *The editor must allow its users to insert or delete a line at the current cursor position.*

leading the naïve designer to devote his attention to the trivial notions of "cursor" and "position" while missing the command abstractions (line insertion and line deletion).

The third major cause of missed classes, shared by any method which uses the requirements document as the basis for analysis, is that such a strategy overlooks reuse. It is surprising to note that much of the object-oriented analysis literature takes for granted the traditional view of software development: starting from a requirements document and devising a solution to the specific problem that it describes. One of the major lessons of object technology is the lack of a clear-cut distinction between problem and solution. Existing software can and should influence new developments.

When faced with a new software project, the object-oriented software developer does not accept the requirements document as the alpha and omega of wisdom about the problem, but combines it with knowledge about previous developments and available software libraries. If necessary, he will criticize the requirements document and propose updates and adaptations which will facilitate the construction of the system; sometimes a minor change, or the removal of a facility which is of limited interest to the final users, will produce a dramatic simplification by making it possible to reuse an entire body of existing software and, as a result, to decrease the development time by months. The corresponding abstractions are most likely to be found in the existing software, not in the requirements document for the new project.

See "THE CHANGING NATURE OF ANALYSIS", 27.2, page 906.

Classes *COMMAND* and *HISTORY_LOG* from the undo-redo example are typical. The way to find the right abstractions for this problem is not to rack one's brain over the requirements document for a text editor: either you come upon them through a process of intellectual discovery (a "Eureka", for which no sure recipe exists); or, if someone else has already found the solution, you reuse his abstractions. You may of course be able to reuse the corresponding implementation too if it is available as part of a library; this is even better, as the whole analysis-design-implementation work has already been done for you.

Discovery and rejection

> *It takes two to invent anything. One makes up combinations; the other chooses,*
> *recognizes what is important to him in the mass of things which the first has*
> *imparted to him. What we call genius is much less the work of the first than the*
> *readiness of the second to choose from what has been laid before him.*

> Paul Valéry (cited in [Hadamard 1945]).

Along with its straightforward lessons, this discussion has taught us a few more subtle consequences.

The simple lessons have been encountered several times: do not put too much trust in a requirements document; do not put *any* trust in grammatical criteria.

A less obvious lesson has emerged from the review of "false alarms": just as we need criteria for finding classes, we need criteria for **rejecting** candidate classes — concepts which initially appear promising but end up not justifying a class of their own. The design discussions of this book illustrate many such cases.

"Pseudo-random number generators: a design exercise", page 754.

To quote just one example: a discussion, yet to come, of how best to provide for pseudo-random number generation, starts naturally enough by considering the notion of random number, only to dismiss it as not the appropriate data abstraction.

The O-O analysis and design books that I have read include little discussion of this task. This is surprising because in the practice of advising O-O projects, especially with relatively novice teams, I have found that eliminating bad ideas is just as important as finding good ones.

It may even be more important. Sit down with a group of users, developers and managers trying to get started with object technology with a fresh new project and enthusiasm fresher yet. There will be no dearth of ideas for classes (usually proposed as "objects"). The problem is to dam the torrent before it damns the project. Although some class ideas will probably have been missed, many more will have to be examined and rejected. As in a large-scale police investigation, many leads come in, prompted or spontaneous; you must sort the useful ones from the canards.

So we must adapt and extend the question that serves as the topic for this chapter. "How to find the classes" means two things: not just how to come up with candidate abstractions but also how to unmask the inadequate among them. These two tasks are not executed one after the other; instead, they are constantly interleaved. Like a gardener, the object-oriented designer must all the time nurture the good plants and weed out the bad:

> ### Class Elicitation principle
>
> Class elicitation is a dual process: class suggestion, class rejection.

The rest of this chapter studies both components of the class elicitation process.

22.2 DANGER SIGNALS

To guide our search it is preferable to start with the rejection part. It will provide us with a checklist of typical pitfalls, alert us to the most important criteria, and help us keep our search for good classes focused on the most productive efforts.

Let us review a few signs that usually indicate a bad choice of class. Because design is not a completely formalized discipline, you should not treat these signs as *proof* of a bad design; in each case one can think of some circumstances that may make the original decision legitimate. So what we will see is not, in the terms of a previous chapter, "absolute negatives" (sure-fire rules for rejecting a design) but "advisory negatives": danger signals that alert you to the presence of a suspicious pattern, and should prompt you to investigate further. Although in most cases they should lead you to revise the design, you may occasionally decide in the end that it is right as it stands.

"A typology of rules", page 666.

The grand mistake

Many of the danger signals discussed below point to the most common and most damaging mistake, which is also the most obvious: designing a class that isn't.

The principle of object-oriented software construction is to build modules around object types, not functions. This is the key to the reusability and extendibility benefits of the approach. But beginners will often fall into the most obvious pitfall: calling "class" something which is in fact a routine. Writing a module as **class**… **feature** … **end** does not make it a true class; it may just be a routine in disguise.

This Grand Mistake is easy to avoid once you are conscious of the risk. The remedy is the usual one: make sure that each class corresponds to a meaningful data abstraction.

What follows is a set of typical traits alerting you to the risk that a module which presents itself as a candidate class, and has the syntactical trappings of a class, may be an illegal immigrant not deserving to be granted citizenship in the O-O society of modules.

My class performs…

In a design meeting, an architecture review, or simply an informal discussion with a developer, you ask about the role of a certain class. The answer: *"This class prints the results"* or *"this class parses the input"*, or some other variant of *"This class does…"*.

The answer usually points to a design flaw. A class is not supposed to *do* one thing but to offer a number of services (features) on objects of a certain type. If it really does just one thing, it is probably a case of the Grand Mistake: devising a class for what should just be a routine of some other class.

Perhaps the mistake is not in the class itself but in the way it is being described, using phraseology that is too operational. But you had better check.

In recent years the *"my class does…"* style has become widespread. A NeXT document describes classes as follows: *"The NSTextView class declares the programmatic interface to objects that display text laid out…"*; *"An NSLayoutManager coordinates the layout*

NeXT documentation for OpenStep, pre-release 4.0.

and display of characters..."; "*NSTextStorage is a semi-concrete subclass of NSMutableAttributedString that manages a set of client NSLayoutManagers, notifying them of any changes...*". Even if (as is most likely the case here) the classes discussed represent valuable data abstractions, it would be preferable to describe them less operationally by emphasizing these abstractions.

Imperative names

Assume that in a tentative design you find a class name such as *PARSE* or *PRINT* — a verb in the imperative or infinitive. It should catch your attention, as signaling again a probable case of a class that "does one thing", and should not be a class.

Occasionally you may find that the class is right. Then its name is wrong. This is an "absolute positive" rule:

Class Name rule

A class name must always be either:

• A noun, possibly qualified.

• (Only for a deferred class describing a structural property) an adjective.

Although like any other one pertaining to style this rule is partly a matter of convention, it helps enforce the principle that every class represents a data abstraction

The first form, nouns, covers the vast majority of cases. A noun may be used by itself, as in *TREE*, or with some qualifying words, as in *LINKED_LIST*, qualified by an adjective, and *LINE_DELETION*, qualified by another noun.

*"Structure inherit-
ance", page 831.*

The second case, adjectives, arises only for a specific case: *structural property* classes describing an abstract structural property, as with the Kernel Library class *COMPARABLE* describing objects on which a certain order relation is available. Such classes should be deferred; their names (in English or French) will often end with *ABLE*. They are meant to be used through inheritance to indicate that all instances of a class have a certain property; for example in a system for keeping track of tennis rankings class *PLAYER* might inherit from *COMPARABLE*. In the taxonomy of inheritance kinds, this scheme will be classified as *structure inheritance*.

See chapter 21.

The only case that may seem to suggest an exception to the rule is command classes, as introduced in the undo-redo design pattern to cover action abstractions. But even then you should stick to the rule: call a text editor's command classes *LINE_DELETION* and *WORD_CHANGE*, not *DELETE_LINE* and *REPLACE_WORD*.

English leaves you more flexibility in the application of this rule than many other languages, since its grammatical categories are more an article of faith than an observation of fact, and almost every verb can be nouned. If you use English as the basis for the names in your software it is fair to take advantage of this flexibility to devise shorter and simpler names: you may call a class *IMPORT* where other languages might treat the equivalent as a verb only, forcing you to use nouns such as *IMPORTATION*. But do not cheat: class

IMPORT should cover the abstraction "objects being imported" (nominal), not, except for a command class, the act of importing (verbal).

> It is interesting to contrast the Class Name rule with the discussion of the "underline the nouns" advice at the beginning of this chapter. "Underline the nouns" applied a formal grammatical criterion to an informal natural-language text, the requirements document; this is bound to be of dubious value. The Class Name rule, on the other hand, applies the same criterion to a *formal* text — the software.

Single-routine classes

A typical symptom of the Grand Mistake is an effective class that contains only one exported routine, possibly calling a few non-exported ones. The class is probably just a glorified subroutine — a unit of functional rather than object-oriented decomposition.

A possible exception arises for objects that legitimately represent abstracted actions, for example a command in an interactive system, or what in a non-O-O approach would have been represented by a routine passed as argument to another routine. But the examples given in an earlier discussion show clearly enough that even in such cases there will usually be several applicable features. We noted that a mathematical software object representing a function to be integrated will not just have the feature *item* (*a*: *REAL*): *REAL*, giving the value of the function at point *a*: others may include domain of definition, minimum and maximum over a certain interval, derivative. Even if a class does not yet have all these features, checking that it would make sense to add them later will reinforce your conviction that you are dealing with a genuine object abstraction.

See "Small classes", page 714.

In applying the single-routine rule, you should consider all the features of a class: those introduced in the class itself, and those which it inherits from its parents. It is not necessarily wrong for a class text to declare only one exported routine, if this is simply an addition to a meaningful abstraction defined by its ancestors. It may, however, point to a case of *taxomania*, an inheritance-related disease which will be studied as part of the methodology of inheritance.

See "TAXOMA-NIA", 24.4, page 820.

Premature classification

The mention of taxomania suggests a warning about another common mistake of novices: starting to worry about the inheritance hierarchy too early in the process.

As inheritance is central in the object-oriented method, so is a good inheritance structure — more accurately, a good modular structure, including both inheritance and client relations — essential to the quality of a design. But inheritance is only relevant as a relation among well-understood abstractions. When you are still looking for the abstractions, it is too early to devise the inheritance hierarchy.

The only clear exception arises when you are dealing with an application domain for which a pre-existing taxonomy is widely accepted, as in some branches of science. Then the corresponding abstractions will emerge together with their inheritance structure. (Before accepting the taxonomy as the basis for your software's structure, do check that it is indeed well recognized and stable, not just someone's view of things.)

In other cases, you should only design the inheritance hierarchy once you have at least a first grasp of the abstractions. (The classification effort may of course lead you to revise your choice of abstractions, prompting an iterative process in which the tasks of class elicitation and inheritance structure design feed each other.) If, early in a design process, you find the participants focusing on classification issues even though the classes are not yet well understood, they are probably putting the cart before the horse.

With novices, this may be a variant of the object-class confusion. I have seen people start off with inheritance hierarchies of the "*SAN_FRANCISCO* and *HOUSTON* inherit from *CITY*" kind — simply to model a situation where a single class, *CITY*, will have several instances at run time.

No-command classes

Sometimes you will find a class that has no routine at all, or only provides queries (ways to access objects) but no commands (procedures to modify objects). Such a class is the equivalent of a record in Pascal or a structure in Cobol or C. It may indicate a design mistake, but the mistake may be of two kinds and you will need to probe further.

First, let us examine three cases in which the class does *not* indicate improper design:

"FACILITY INHERIT-ANCE", 24.9, page 847.

- It may represent objects obtained from the outside world, which the object-oriented software cannot change. They could be data coming from a sensor in a process-control system, packets from a packet-switching network, or C structures that the O-O system is not supposed to touch.

- Some classes are meant not for direct instantiation, but for encapsulating facilities such as constants, used by other classes through inheritance. Such *facility inheritance* will be studied in the discussion of inheritance methodology.

Command functions were defined in "Function categories", page 134.

- Finally, a class may be *applicative*, that is to say describe non-modifiable objects; instead of commands to modify an object it will provide functions that produce new objects, usually of the same type. For example the addition operation in classes *INTEGER*, *REAL* and *DOUBLE* follows the lead of mathematics: it does not modify any value but, given two values x and y, produces a third one $x + y$. In the abstract data type specification such functions will, like others that yield commands, be characterized as command functions.

In all these cases the abstractions are easy to recognize, so you should have no difficulty identifying the two cases that may indeed point to a design deficiency.

See "A checklist", page 770.

Now for these suspicious cases. In the first one, the class is justified and would need commands; the designer has simply forgotten to provide mechanisms to modify the corresponding objects. A simple checklist technique presented in the discussion of class design will help avoid such mistakes.

In the second case, most directly relevant to this discussion, the class was not justified. It is not a real data abstraction, simply some piece of passive information which might have been represented by a structure such as a list or array, or just by adding more attributes to another class. This case sometimes happens when developers write a class for what would have been a simple record (structure) type in Pascal, Ada or C. Not all record types cover separate data abstractions.

You should investigate such a case carefully to try to understand whether there is room for a legitimate class, now or in the future. If the answer is unclear, you may be better off keeping the class anyway even if it risks being overkill. Having a class may imply some performance overhead if it means dealing with many small objects, dynamically created one by one and occupying more space than simple array elements; but if you do need a class and have not introduced it early enough, the adaptation may take some effort.

> We had such a false start in the history of ISE's compiler. A compiler for an O-O language needs some internal way to identify each class of a system it processes; the identification used to be an integer. This worked fine for several years, but at some point we needed a more elaborate class identification scheme, allowing us in particular to *renumber* classes when merging several systems. The solution was to introduce a class *CLASS_ IDENTIFIER*, and to replace the earlier integers by instances of that class. The conversion effort was more than we would have liked, as usually happens when you have missed an important abstraction. Initially *INTEGER* was a sufficient abstraction because no commands were applicable to class identifiers; the need for more advanced features, in particular renumbering commands, led to the recognition of a separate abstraction.

Mixed abstractions

Another sign of an imperfect design is a class whose features relate to more than one abstraction.

> In an early release of the NeXT library, the text class also provided full visual text editing capabilities. Users complained that the class, although useful, was too big. Large class size was the symptom; the true problem was the merging of two abstractions (character string, and interactively editable text); the solution was to separate the two abstractions, with a class *NSAttributedString* defining the basic string handling mechanism and various others, such as *NSTextView*, taking care of the user interface aspects.

Meilir Page-Jones uses the term *connascence* (defined in dictionaries as the property   [Page-Jones 1995]. of being born and having grown together) to describe the relation that exists between two features when they are closely connected, based on a criterion of simultaneous change: a change to one will imply a change to the other. As he points out, you should minimize connascence across class libraries; but features that appear within a given class should all be related to the same clearly identified abstraction.

This universal guideline deserves to be expressed as a methodological rule (presented in "positive" form although it follows a discussion of possible mistakes):

Class Consistency principle

All the features of a class must pertain to a single, well-identified abstraction.

The ideal class

This review of possible mistakes highlights, by contrast, what the ideal class will look like. Here are some of the typical properties:

- There is a clearly associated abstraction, which can be described as a data abstraction (or as an abstract machine).

- The class name is a noun or adjective, adequately characterizing the abstraction.

- The class represents a set of possible run-time objects, its instances. (Some classes are meant to have only one instance during an execution; that is acceptable too.)

- Several queries are available to find out properties of an instance.

- Several commands are available to change the state of an instance. (In some cases, there are no commands but instead functions producing other objects of the same type, as with the operations on integers; that is acceptable too.)

- Abstract properties can be stated, informally or (preferably) formally, describing: how the results of the various queries relate to each other (this will yield the invariant); under what conditions features are applicable (preconditions); how command execution affects query results (postconditions).

This list describes a set of informal goals, not a strict rule. A legitimate class may have only some of the properties listed. Most of the examples that play an important role in this book — from *LIST* and *QUEUE* to *BUFFER, ACCOUNT, COMMAND, STATE, INTEGER, FIGURE, POLYGON* and many others — have them all.

22.3 GENERAL HEURISTICS FOR FINDING CLASSES

Let us now turn to the positive part of our discussion: practical heuristics for finding classes.

Class categories

We may first note that there are three broad categories of classes: analysis classes, design classes and implementation classes. The division is neither absolute nor rigorous (for example one could find arguments to support attaching a deferred class *LIST* to any one of the three categories), but it is convenient as a general guideline.

An analysis class describes a data abstraction directly drawn from the model of the external system. *PLANE* in a traffic control system, *PARAGRAPH* in a document processing system, *PART* in an inventory control system are typical examples.

An implementation class describes a data abstraction introduced for the internal needs of the algorithms in the software, such as *LINKED_LIST* or *ARRAY.*

In-between, a design class describes an architectural choice. Examples included *COMMAND* in the solution to the undo-redo problem, and *STATE* in the solution to the problem of panel-driven systems. Like implementation classes, design classes belong to the *solution* space, whereas analysis classes belong to the problem space. But like analysis classes and unlike implementation classes they describe high-level concepts.

As we study how to obtain classes in these three categories, we will find that design classes are the most difficult to identify, because they require the kind of architectural insight that sets the gifted designer apart. (That they are the most difficult to find does not mean they are the most difficult to *build*, a distinction that usually belongs to the implementation classes, unless of course you come across a ready-to-be-reused implementation library.)

External objects: finding the analysis classes

Let us start with the analysis classes, modeled after external objects.

We use software to obtain answers to certain questions about the world (as in a program that computes the solution to a specific problem), to interact with the world (as in a process control system), or to add things to the world (as in a text processing system). In every case, the software must be based on some model of the aspects of the world that are relevant to the application, such as laws of physics or biology in a scientific program, the syntax and semantics of a computer language in a compiler, salary scales in a payroll system, and income tax regulations in tax processing software.

> To talk about the world being modeled we should avoid the term "real world", which is misleading, both because software is no less "real" than anything else and because many of the non-software "worlds" of interest are artificial, as in the case of a mathematical program dealing with equations and graphs. (An earlier chapter discussed this question in detail.) We should talk about the *external world*, as distinct from the internal world of the software that deals with it.

See "Reality: a cousin twice removed", page 230.

Any software system is based on an **operational model** of some aspect of the external world. Operational because it is used to generate practical results and sometimes to feed these results back into the world; model because any useful system must follow from a certain interpretation of some world phenomena.

Nowhere perhaps is this view of software as inescapable as in the area of *simulation*. It is no accident that the first object-oriented language, Simula 67, evolved from Simula 1, a language for writing discrete-event simulations. Although Simula 67 itself is a general-purpose programming language, it retained the name of its predecessor and includes a set of powerful simulation primitives. Well into the nineteen-seventies, simulation remained the principal application area of object technology (as a look into the proceedings of the annual Association of Simula Users conferences suffices to show). This attraction of O-O ideas for simulation is easy to understand: to devise the structure of a software system simulating the behavior of a set of external objects, what could be better than using software components which directly represent those objects?

See "SIMULA", 35.1, page 1113.

In a broad sense, of course, all software is simulation. Capitalizing on this view of software as operational modeling, object-oriented software construction uses as its first abstractions some types deduced from analyzing the principal types of objects, in the non-software sense of the term, in the external world: sensors, devices, airplanes, employees, paychecks, tax returns, paragraphs, integrable functions.

> These examples, by the way, suggest only part of the picture. As Waldén and Nerson note in their presentation of the B.O.N. method:

[Waldén 1995],
pages 182-183.

*A class representing a car is no more tangible than one that models the job
satisfaction of employees. What counts is how important the concepts are to
the enterprise, and what you can do with them.*

Keep this comment in mind when looking for external classes: they can be quite abstract.
SENIORITY_RULE for a parliament voting system and *MARKET_TENDENCY* for a
trading system may be just as real as *SENATOR* and *STOCK_EXCHANGE*. The smile of
the Cheshire Cat has as much claim to objectness as the Cheshire Cat.

Whether material or abstract, external classes represent the abstractions that
specialists of the external world, be they aerospace engineers, accountants or
mathematicians, constantly use to think and talk about their domain. There is always a
good chance — although not a certainty — that such an object type will yield a useful
class, because typically the domain experts will have associated significant operations and
properties with it.

The key word, as usual, is *abstraction*. Although it is desirable that analysis classes
closely match concepts from the problem domain, this is not what makes a candidate class
good. The first version of our panel-driven system dramatically showed why: there we had
a model directly patterned after some properties of the external system, but terrible from
a software engineering viewpoint because the selected properties were low-level and
subject to change. A good external class will be based on abstract concepts of the problem
domain, characterized (in the ADT way) through external features chosen because of their
lasting value.

For the object-oriented developer such pre-existing abstractions are precious: they
provide some of the system's fundamental classes; and, as we may note once more, the
objects are here for the picking.

Finding the implementation classes

Implementation classes describe the structures that software developers use to make their
systems run on a computer. Although the fashion in the software engineering literature has
been, for the past fifteen years, to downplay the role of implementation, developers know
the obvious — that implementation consumes a large part of the effort in building a
system, and much of the intelligence that goes into it.

The bad news is that implementation is difficult. The good news is that
implementation classes, although often hard to *build* in the absence of good reusable
libraries, are not the most difficult to *elicit*, thanks to the ample body of literature on the
topic. Since "Data Structures and Algorithms", sometimes known as "CS 2", is a required
component of computing science education, many textbooks survey the rich catalog of
useful data structures that have been identified over the years. Better yet, although most
existing textbooks do not explicitly use an object-oriented approach, many naturally
follow an abstract data type style, even if they do not use the phrase, to present data
structures; for example to introduce various forms of table such as binary search trees and
hash tables you have first to state the various operations (insert an element with its key,
search for an element through its key and so on) with their properties. The transition to
classes is fairly straightforward.

Recently, some textbooks have started to go further by applying a thoroughly object-oriented approach to the traditional CS 2 topics.

Whether or not he has gone through a Data Structures and Algorithms Course at school, every software engineer should keep a good textbook on the topic within reach of hand, and go back to it often. It is all too easy to waste time reinventing concepts that are well known, implement a less-than-optimal algorithm, or choose a representation that is not appropriate for the software's use of a data structure — for example a one-way linked list for a sequential structure that the algorithms must regularly traverse back and forth, or an array for a structure that constantly grows and shrinks in unpredictable ways. Note that here too the ADT approach reigns: the data structure and its representation follow from the services offered to clients.

Beyond textbooks and experience, the best hope for implementation classes is reusable libraries, as we will see at the end of this chapter.

Deferred implementation classes

Traditional data structures textbooks naturally emphasize effective (fully implemented) classes. In practice, much of the value of a set of implementation classes, especially if they are meant to be reusable, lies in the underlying taxonomy, as defined by an inheritance structure that will include deferred classes. For example, various queue implementations will be descendants of a deferred class *QUEUE* describing the abstract concept of sequential list.

"Deferred implementation class", then, is not an oxymoron. Classes such as *QUEUE*, although quite abstract, help build the taxonomies thanks to which we can keep the many varieties of implementation structures coherent and organized, assigning to every class a precise place in the overall scheme.

In another book [M 1994a] I have described a "Linnaean" taxonomy of the fundamental structures of computing science, which relies on deferred classes to classify the principal kinds of data structure used in software development.

Finding the design classes

Design classes represent architectural abstractions that help produce elegant, extendible software structures. *STATE*, *APPLICATION*, *COMMAND*, *HISTORY_LIST*, iterator classes, "controller" classes as in the Smalltalk MVC model are good examples of design classes. We will see other seminal ideas in subsequent chapters, such as active data structures and "handles" for platform-adaptable portable libraries.

About iterators and MVC see the bibliographical notes.

Although, as noted, there is no sure way to find design classes, a few guidelines are worth noting:

- Many design classes have been devised by others before. By reading books and articles that describe precise solutions to design problems, you will gain many fruitful ideas. For example the book *Object-Oriented Applications* contains chapters written by the lead designers of various industrial projects who describe their

[M 1993].

architectural solutions in detail, providing precious guidance to others faced with similar problems in telecommunications, Computer-Aided Design, artificial intelligence and other application areas.

[Gamma 1995].

- The book on "design patterns" by Gamma *et al.* has started an effort of capturing proven design solutions and is now being followed by several others.

- Many useful design classes describe abstractions that are better understood as machines than as "objects" in the common (non-software) sense.

- As with implementation classes, reuse is preferable to invention. One can hope that many of the "patterns" currently being studied will soon cease to be mere ideas, yielding instead directly usable library classes.

22.4 OTHER SOURCES OF CLASSES

A number of heuristics have proved useful in the quest for the right abstractions.

Previous developments

The advice of looking first at what is available does not just apply to library classes. As you write applications, you will accumulate classes which, if properly designed, should facilitate later developments.

See "GENERALI-ZATION", 28.5, page 928.

Not all reusable software was born reusable. Often, the first version of a class is produced to meet some immediate requirement rather than for posterity. If reusability is a concern, however, it pays to devote some time, after the development, to making the class more general and robust, improving its documentation, adding assertions. This is different from the construction of software meant from the start to be reusable, but no less fruitful. Having evolved from components of actual systems, the resulting classes have passed the first test of reusability, namely *usability*: they serve at least one useful purpose.

Adaptation through inheritance

When you discover the existence of a potentially useful class, you will sometimes find that it does not exactly suit your present need: some adaptation may be necessary.

Unless the adaptation addresses a deficiency which should be corrected in the original as well, it is generally preferable to leave the class undisturbed, preserving its clients according to the Open-Closed principle. Instead, you may use inheritance and redefinition to tune the class to your new need.

See "Variation inheritance", page 828.

This technique, which our later taxonomy of uses of inheritance will study in detail under the name *variation inheritance*, assumes that the new class describes a variant of the same abstraction as the original. If used properly (according to the guidelines of the later discussion) it is one of the most remarkable contributions of the method, enabling you to resolve the *reuse-redo* dilemma: combining reusability with extendibility.

Evaluating candidate decompositions

Criticism is said to be easier than art; a good way to learn design is to learn to analyze existing designs. In particular, when a certain set of classes has been proposed to solve a certain problem, you should study them from the criteria and principles of modularity given in chapter 3: do they constitute autonomous, coherent modules, with strictly controlled communication channels? Often, the discovery that two modules are too tightly coupled, that a module communicates with too many others, that an argument list is too long, will pinpoint design errors and lead to a better solution.

An important criterion was explored in the panel-driven system example: data flow. *Chapter 20.* We saw then how important it is to study, in a candidate class structure, the flow of objects passed as arguments in successive calls. If, as with the notion of State in that example, you detect that a certain item of information is transmitted over many modules, it is almost certainly a sign that you have missed an important data abstraction. Such an analysis, which we applied to obtain the class *STATE*, is an important source of abstractions.

It is of course preferable to find the classes right from the start; but better late than never. After such an a posteriori class discovery, you should take the time to analyze why the abstraction was initially missed, and to reflect on how to do better next time.

Hints from other approaches

The example of analyzing data flow in a top-down structure illustrates the general idea of deriving class insights from concepts of non-O-O decompositions. This will be useful in two non-disjoint cases:

- There may already exist a non-O-O software system which does part of the job; it may be interesting to examine it for class ideas. The same would apply if, instead of a working system, you can use the result of an analysis or design produced with another, older method.

- Some of the people doing the development may have had extensive experience with other methods, and as a consequence may initially think in terms of different concepts, some of which may be turned into class ideas.

Here are examples of this process, starting with programming languages and continuing with analysis and design techniques.

Fortran programs usually include one or more *common blocks* — data areas that can *On garbage common* be shared by several routines. A common block often hides one or more valuable data *blocks see "Small* abstractions. More precisely, good Fortran programmers know that a common block *Interfaces", page 48.* should only include a few variables or arrays, covering closely related concepts; there is a good chance that such a block will correspond to one class. Unfortunately, this is not universal practice, and even programmers who know better than to use the "garbage common block" mentioned at the beginning of this book tend to put too many things in one common block. In this case you will have to examine patterns of use of each block to discover the abstraction or abstractions that it covers.

Pascal and C programs use records, known in C as structures. (Pascal only has record *types*; in C you can have structure types as well as individual structures.) A record type often corresponds to a class, but only if you can find operations acting specifically on instances of the type, usually (as we saw) including commands as well as queries. If not, the type may just represent some attributes of another class.

Cobol also has structures, and its Data Division helps identify important data types.

In entity-relationship (ER) modeling, analysts isolate "entities" which can often serve as seeds for classes.

> People with a long practice of ER modeling are among those who sometimes find it initially hard to apply object-oriented ideas effecively, because they are used to treating the entities and relationships as being different in nature, and the "dynamic" behavior of the system as completely separate from them. With O-O modeling both the relationships and the behavior yield features attached to the types of objects (entities); thinking of relations and operations as variants of the same notion, and attaching them to entities, sometimes proves to be a little hard to swallow at first.

In dataflow design ("structured analysis and design") there is little that can be directly used for an object-oriented decomposition, but sometimes the "stores" (database or file abstractions) can suggest an abstraction.

Files

The comment about stores suggests a more general idea, useful again if you are coming from a non-O-O background. Sometimes much of the intelligence of a traditional system is to be found outside of the software's text, in the structure of the files that it manipulates.

To anyone with Unix experience, this idea will be clear: for some of the essential information that you need to learn, the essential documentation is the description not of specific commands but of certain key files and their formats: *passwd* for passwords, *printcap* for printer properties, *termcap* or *terminfo* for terminal properties. One could characterize these files as data abstractions without the abstraction: although documented at a very concrete level (*"Each entry in the printcap file describes a printer, and is a line consisting of a number of fields separated by : characters. The first entry for each printer gives the names which are known for the printer, separated by | characters"*, etc.), they describe important data types accessible through well-defined primitives, with some associated properties and usage conditions. In the transition to an object-oriented view, such files would play a central role.

A similar observation applies to many programs, whose principal files embody some of the principal abstractions.

I once participated in a consulting session with the manager of a software system who was convinced that the system — a collection of Fortran programs — could not lend itself to object-oriented decomposition. As he was describing what the programs did, he casually mentioned a few files through which the programs communicated. I started asking questions about these files, but initially he kept dismissing these questions as unimportant, immediately coming back to the programs. I insisted, and from his explanations realized that the files described complex data structures embodying the programs' essential information. The lesson was clear: as soon as the relevance of these files was recognized, they conquered the central place in the object-oriented architecture; in an upheaval typical of object-oriented rearchitecturing, the programs, formerly the key elements of the architecture, became mere features of the resulting classes.

Use cases

Ivar Jacobson has advocated relying on use cases as a way to elicit classes. A use case, called a *scenario* by some other analysis and design authors (and a *trace* in theoretical computing science, especially the study of concurrency), is a description of

> *a complete course of events initiated by a* [user of the future system] *and* [of] *the interaction between* [the user] *and the system.*

[Jacobson 1992], page 154. Jacobson uses the term "actor" for users of the future system.

In a telephone switching system, for example, the use case "customer-initiated call" has the sequence of events: customer picks handset, identification gets sent to the system, system sends dial tone, and so on. Other use cases for the system might include "caller-id service installation" and "customer disconnection".

Use cases are a not a good tool for finding classes. Relying on them in any significant way raises several risks:

- Use cases emphasize ordering ("*When a customer places an order over the phone, his credit card number is validated. Then the database is updated and a confirmation number is issued*", etc.). This is incompatible with object technology: the method shuns early reliance on sequentiality properties, because they are so fragile and subject to change. The competent O-O analyst and designer refuses to focus on properties of the form "The system does a, then b"; instead, he asks the question "What are the operations available on instances of abstraction A, and the constraints on these operations?". The truly fundamental sequentiality properties will emerge in the form of high-level constraints on the operations; for example, instead of saying that a stack supports alternating sequences of *push* and *pop* operations with never more *pop* than *push*, we define the preconditions attached with each of these operations, which imply the ordering property but are more abstract. Less fundamental ordering requirements simply have no place in the analysis model as they destroy the system's adaptability and hence its future survival. Early emphasis on ordering is among the worst mistakes an O-O project can make. If you rely on use cases for analysis, this mistake is hard to avoid.

See "Ordering and O-O development", page 111 and "Structure and order: the software developer as arsonist", page 201.

- Relying on a scenario means that you focus on how users see the system's operation. But the system does not exist yet. (A previous system might exist, but if it were fully satisfactory you would not be asked to change or rewrite it.) So the system picture that use cases will give you is based on existing processes, computerized or not. Your task as a system builder is to come up with *new*, better scenarios, not to perpetuate antiquated modes of operation. There are enough examples around of computer systems that slavishly mimic obsolete procedures.

- Use cases favor a functional approach, based on processes (actions). This approach is the reverse of O-O decomposition, which focuses on data abstractions; it carries a serious risk of reverting, under the heading of object-oriented development, to the most traditional forms of functional design. True, you may rely on several scenarios rather than just one main program. But this is still an approach that considers *what the system does* as the starting point, whereas object technology considers *what it does it to*. The clash is irreconcilable.

The practical consequences are obvious. A number of teams that have embraced use cases find themselves, without realizing it, practicing top-down functional design ("*the system must do a, then b, ...*") and building systems that are obsolete on the day they are released, yet hard to change because they are tied to a specific view of what the system does. I have sat, as an outside consultant, in design reviews for such projects, trying to push for more abstraction. But it is difficult to help, because the designers are convinced that they are doing object-oriented design; they expect the consultant to make a few suggestions, criticize a few details and give his blessing to the overall result. The designs that I saw were not object-oriented at all, and were bound to yield flawed systems; but trying to convey this observation politely was about as effective as telling the group that the sun was not shining outside — we work from use cases, and doesn't everyone know that use cases are O-O?

The risks are perhaps less severe with a very experienced object-oriented design team — experience being evidenced by the team's previous production of large and successful O-O systems, in the thousands of classes and hundreds of thousands of lines. Such a group might find use cases useful as a complement to other analysis techniques. But for a novice team, or one with moderate experience only, the benefits of use cases as an analysis tool are so uncertain, and the risk of destroying the quality of the future system so great, as to recommend staying away altogether from this technique:

Use Case principle

Except with a very experienced design team (having built several successful systems of several thousand classes each in a pure O-O language), do not rely on use cases as a tool for object-oriented analysis and design.

This principle does not mean that use cases are a worthless concept. They remain a potentially valuable tool but their role in object-oriented software construction has been misunderstood. Rather than an analysis tool they are a *validation* tool. If (as you should) you have a separate quality assurance team, it may find use cases useful as a way to inspect a proposed analysis model or tentative design for possibly missing features. The QA team can check that the system will be able to run the typical scenarios identified by the users. (In some cases of negative answer you may find that the model will support a different scenario that achieves the same or better results. This is of course satisfactory.)

Another possible application of use cases is to the final aspects of implementation, to make sure that the system includes routines for typical usage scenarios. Such routines will often be of the abstract behavior kind, describing a general effective scheme relying on deferred routines which various components of the system, and future additions to it, may redefine in different ways. ([Jacobson 1992] indeed mentions a notion of *abstract use case* that mirrors the object-oriented concept of behavior class.

In these two roles as a validation mechanism and an implementation guide, use cases can be beneficial. But in object technology they are not a useful analysis or design mechanism. The system analysts and builders should concentrate on the abstractions, not on particular ways of scheduling operations on these abstractions.

CRC cards

For completeness it is necessary to mention an idea that is sometimes quoted as a technique to find classes. CRC cards (*Class, Responsibility, Collaboration*) are paper cards, 4 inches by 6 inches (10.16 centimeters by 15.24 centimeters), on which designers discuss potential classes in terms of their responsibilities and how they communicate. The idea has the advantage of being easy on the equipment budget (a box of cards is typically cheaper than a workstation with CASE tools) and of fostering team interaction. Its technical contribution to the design process — to helping sort out and characterize valuable abstractions — is, however, unclear.

K. Beck and W. Cunningham: "A Laboratory for Teaching O-O Thinking", OOPSLA '89 Proceedings, pages 1-6.

22.5 REUSE

The easiest and most productive way of finding classes is not to have to invent them yourself, but to get them from a library, pre-written by other designers and pre-validated by the experience of earlier reusers.

The bottom-up component

The bottom-up nature of object-oriented development should apply throughout the software development process, starting with analysis. An approach that solely focuses on the requirements document and user requests (as reflected for example by use cases) is bound to lead to a one-of-a-kind system that will be expensive to build and may miss important insights obtained by previous projects. It is part of the task of a development team, beginning at the requirements capture phase, to look at what is already available and see how existing classes may help with the new development — even if, in some cases, this means adapting the original requirements.

Too often, when we talk about finding classes, we mean *devising* them. With the development of object technology, the growth of quality libraries and the penetration of reusability ideas, *finding* will more and more retain the dictionary's sense of *coming across*.

Class wisdom

There used to live in the province of Ood a young man who longed to know the secret of finding classes. He had approached all the local masters, but none of them knew.

Having attended the public penance of Yu-Ton, a former abbot of the Sacred Order of Arrows and Bubbles, he thought that perhaps this could mean the end of his search. Upon entering Yu's cell, however, he found him still trying to understand the difference between Classes and Objects. Realizing that no enlightenment would come from there, he left without asking any questions.

On his way home he overheard two donkey-cart pushers whispering about a famous elder who was said to know the secret of classes. The next day he set out to find that great Master. Many a road he walked, many a hill he climbed, many a stream he crossed, until at last he reached the Master's hideout. By then he had searched for so long that he was no longer a young man; but like all other pilgrims he had to undergo the thirty-three-month purification rite before being permitted to meet the object of his quest.

Finally, one black winter day as the snow was savagely hitting all the surrounding mountain peaks, he was admitted into the Master's audience room. With his heart beating at the pace of a boulder rolling down the bed of a dried-up torrent, he faintly uttered his question: "Master, how can I find the classes?".

The old sage lowered her head and answered in a slow, quiet tone. "Go back to where you came from. The classes were already there."

So stunned was the questioner that it took him a few moments to notice that the Master's attendants were already whisking her away. He barely had time to run after the frail figure now disappearing forever. "Master", he asked again (almost shouting this time), "Just one more question! Please! Tell me how this story is called!"

The old Teacher tiredly turned back her head. "Should you not already know? It is the story of reuse."

22.6 THE METHOD FOR OBTAINING CLASSES

Touch by touch, the ideas discussed in this chapter amount to what we may not too pretentiously call (provided we remember that a method is a way to incubate, nurture, channel and develop invention, not a substitute for invention) the method for obtaining the classes in object-oriented software construction.

The method recognizes that class identification requires two inextricably related activities: coming up with class suggestions; and weeding out the less promising among them. The two tables which follow summarize what we have learned about these two activities. Only a few of the entries cover specific kinds of class, such as analysis classes; the rest of the advice is applicable to all cases.

First, sources of class ideas:

Source of ideas	What to look for
Existing libraries	• Classes that address needs of the application. • Classes that describe concepts relevant to the application.
Requirements document	• Terms that occur frequently. • Terms to which the text devotes explicit definitions. • Terms that are not defined precisely but taken for granted throughout the presentation. • (Disregard grammatical categories.)
Discussions with customers and future users	• Important abstractions of the application domain. • Specific jargon of the application domain. • Remember that classes coming from the "external world" can describe *conceptual* objects as well as *material* objects.
Documentation (such as user manuals) for other systems (e.g. from competitors) in the same domain	• Important abstractions of the application domain. • Specific jargon of the application domain. • Useful design abstractions
Non-O-O systems or system descriptions	• Data elements that are passed as arguments between various components of the software, especially if they travel far. • Shared memory areas (*COMMON* blocks in Fortran). • Important files. • *DATA DIVISION* units (Cobol). • Record types (Pascal), structures and structure types (C, C++), playing an important role in the software, in particular if they are used by various routines or modules (files in C). • Entities in ER modeling.
Discussions with experienced designers	• Design classes having been successfully used in previous developments of a similar nature.
Algorithms and data structure literature	• Known data structures supporting efficient algorithms.
O-O design literature	• Applicable design patterns.

Then, criteria for investigating potential classes more carefully, and possibly rejecting them:

Reasons for rejecting a candidate class

Danger signal	Why suspicious
Class with verbal name (infinitive or imperative)	• May be a simple subroutine, not a class.
Fully effective class with only one exported routine	• May be a simple subroutine, not a class.
Class described as "performing" something	• May not be a proper data abstraction.
Class with no routine	• May be an opaque piece of information, not an ADT. Or may be an ADT, the routines having just been missed.
Class introducing no or very few features (but inherits features from parents)	• May be a case of "taxomania".
Class covering several abstractions	• Should be split into several classes, one per abstraction

22.7 KEY CONCEPTS INTRODUCED IN THIS CHAPTER

• Identifying the classes is one of the principal tasks of object-oriented software construction.

• To identify the classes is a dual process: class suggestion *and* class rejection. Just as important as identifying potential class candidates is the need to eliminate unsuitable ideas.

- To identify the classes is to identify the relevant abstractions in the modeled domain and the solution space.

- "Underlining the nouns in the requirements document" is not a sufficient technique for finding the classes, since its results are too dependent on stylistic issues. It may cause designers both to miss useful classes and to include unnecessary ones.

- A broad characterization of classes distinguishes analysis classes, tied to concepts of the external world being modeled, design classes, describing architectural decisions, and implementation classes, describing data structures and algorithms.

- Design classes tend to be the most difficult to invent.

- In designing external classes, remember that external objects include concepts as well as material things.

- To decide whether a certain notion justifies defining an associated class, apply the criteria of data abstraction.

- Implementation classes include both effective classes and their deferred counterparts, describing abstract categories of implementation techniques.

- Inheritance provides a way to reuse previous designs while adapting them.

- A way to obtain classes is to evaluate candidate designs and look for any unrecognized abstraction, in particular by analyzing inter-module data transmission.

- Use cases, or scenarios, may be useful as a validation tool and as a guide to finalize an implementation, but should not be used as an analysis and design mechanism.

- The best source of classes is reusable libraries.

22.8 BIBLIOGRAPHICAL NOTES

The advice to use nouns from the requirements as a starting point for finding object types was made popular by [Booch 1986], which credits the idea to an earlier article by Abbott. Further advice appears in [Wirfs-Brock 1990].

Russell J. Abbott in Comm. ACM, 26, 11, Nov. 1983, pp. 882-894.

An article on formal specification [M 1985a] analyzes the problems raised by natural-language requirements documents. Working from a short natural-language problem description which has been used extensively in the program verification literature, it identifies a large number of deficiencies and offers a taxonomy of such deficiencies (noise, ambiguity, contradiction, remorse, overspecification, forward reference); it discusses how formal specifications can remedy some of the problems.

[Waldén 1995] presents useful advice for identifying classes.

Appendix B of [Page-Jones 1995] lists numerous "problem symptoms" in candidate object-oriented designs (for example "*class interface supports illegal or dangerous behaviors*"), alerting designers to danger signals such as have been pointed out in the present chapter. The table, as well as the rest of Page-Jones's book, offers suggestions for correcting design deficiencies.

[Ong 1993] describes a tool for converting non-O-O programs (essentially Fortran) to an object-oriented form. The conversion is semi-automatic, that is to say relies on some manual effort. Relevant to the present chapter is the authors' description of some of the heuristics they use for identifying potential classes through analysis of the original code, in particular by looking at *COMMON* blocks.

Simula 1 (the simulation language that led to modern versions of Simula) is described in [Dahl 1966]. See chapter 35 for more Simula references.

Typical data structures books, providing a precious source of implementation classes, include Knuth's famous treatise [Knuth 1968] [Knuth 1981] [Knuth 1973] and numerous college textbooks such as [Aho 1974] [Aho 1983].

A recent text, [Gore 1996], presents fundamental data structures and algorithms in a thoroughly object-oriented way.

Sources of design classes include [Gamma 1995], presenting a number of "design patterns" for C++, and [M 1994a], a compendium of library design techniques and reusable classes, discussing in detail the notions of "handle class" and "iterator class". [Krief 1996] presents the Smalltalk MVC model.

EXERCISES

E22.1 Floors as integers

See "Is a new class necessary?", page 721.

Show how to define a class *FLOOR* as heir to *INTEGER*, restricting the applicable operations.

E22.2 Inspecting objects

Daniel Halbert and Patrick O'Brien discuss the following problem, arising in the design of software development environments:

> *Consider the design of an* **inspector** *facility, used to display information about an object in a debugger window: the contents of its fields, and perhaps some computed values. Different kinds of inspector are needed for different object types. For instance, all the relevant information about a point can be displayed at once in a simple format, while a large two-dimensional array might best be displayed as a matrix scrollable horizontally and vertically.*
>
> *You should first decide where to put the behavior of the inspector: in the [generating class] of the object to be inspected or in a new, separate class?*

From [Halbert 1987], *slightly abridged.*

Answer this question by considering the pros and cons of various alternatives. (*Note*: the inheritance-related discussions of the following chapters may be useful.)

23

Principles of class design

Experienced software developers know that few issues are more critical than the proper design of module interfaces. In a multi-person, or just multi-week software project, many of the decisions, discussions, disputes and confusions tend to revolve around matters of module interface specification: "Who takes care of making sure that…?", "But I thought you only passed me normalized input…", "Why are you processing this since I already took care of it?".

If there were just one advantage to expect from object technology, this would have to be it. From the outset of this presentation, object-oriented development has been described as an architectural technique for producing systems made of coherent, properly interfaced modules. We have now accumulated enough technical background to review the design principles through which you can take advantage of the best O-O mechanisms to develop modules with attractive interfaces.

In the following pages we will explore a set of class design principles which extensive practice has shown to yield quality and durability. Because what determines the success of a class is how it will look to its clients, the emphasis here is not on the internal implementation of a class but on how to make its interface simple, easy to learn, easy to remember, and able to withstand the test of time and change.

We will successively examine: whether functions should be permitted to have side effects; how many arguments a feature should reasonably have, and the associated notions of operand and option; whether you should be concerned about the size of your classes; making abstract structures active; the role of selective exports; how to document a class; how to deal with abnormal cases.

From this discussion will emerge an image of the class designer as a patient craftsman who chisels out and polishes each class to make it as attractive as possible to clients. This spirit of treating classes as carefully engineered products, aiming at perfection from the start and yet always perfectible, is a pervasive quality of well-applied object technology. For obvious reasons it is particularly visible in the construction of library classes, and indeed many of the design principles reviewed in this chapter originated in library design; in the same way that successful ideas first tried in Formula 1 racing eventually trickle down to the engineering of cars for the rest of us, a technique that has shown its value by surviving the toughest possible test — being applied to the development of a successful library of reusable components — will eventually benefit all object-oriented software, whether or not initially intended for reuse.

23.1 SIDE EFFECTS IN FUNCTIONS

The first question that we must address will have a deep effect on the style of our designs. Is it legitimate for functions — routines that return a result — also to produce a side effect, that is to say, to change something in their environment?

The gist of the answer is no, but we must first understand the role of side effects, and distinguish between good and potentially bad side effects. We must also discuss the question in light of all we now know about classes: their filiation from abstract data types, the notion of abstraction function, and the role of class invariants.

Commands and queries

A few reminders on terminology will be useful. The features that characterize a class are divided into *commands* and *queries*. A command serves to modify objects, a query to return information about objects. A command is implemented as a procedure. A query may be implemented either as an attribute, that is to say by reserving a field in each run-time instance of the class to hold the corresponding value, or as a function, that is to say through an algorithm that computes the value when needed. Procedures (which also have an associated algorithm) and functions are together called routines.

"Attributes and routines", page 173.

The definition of queries does not specify whether in the course of producing its result a query may change objects. For commands, the answer is obviously yes, since it is the role of commands (procedures) to change things. Among queries, the question only makes sense for functions, since accessing an attribute cannot change anything. A change performed by a function is known as a *side effect* to indicate that it is ancillary to the function's official purpose of answering a query. Should we permit side effects?

Forms of side effect

Let us define precisely what constructs may cause side effects. The basic operation that changes an object is an assignment $a := b$ (or an assignment attempt $a\ ?= b$, or a creation instruction $!!\ a$) where the target a is an attribute; execution of this operation will assign a new value to the field of the corresponding object (the target of the current routine call).

We only care about such assignments when a is an attribute: if a is a local entity, its value is only used during an execution of the routine and assignments to it have no permanent effect; if a is the entity *Result* denoting the result of the routine, assignments to it help compute that result but have no effect on objects.

Also note that as a result of information hiding principles we have been careful, in the design of the object-oriented notation, to avoid any indirect form of object modification. In particular, the syntax excludes assignments of the form $obj.attr := b$, whose aim has to be achieved through a call $obj.set\_attr\ (b)$, where the procedure $set\_attr\ (x:...)$ performs the attribute assignment $attr := x$.

"The client's privileges on an attribute", page 206.

The attribute assignment that causes a function to produce a side effect may be in the function itself, or in another routine that the function calls. Hence the full definition:

> ### Definition: concrete side effect
>
> A function produces a concrete side effect if its body contains any of the following:
>
> - An assignment, assignment attempt or creation instruction whose target is an attribute.
> - A procedure call.

(The term "concrete" will be explained below.) In a more fine-tuned definition we would replace the second clause by "A call to a routine that (recursively) produces a concrete side effect", the definition of side effects being extended to arbitrary routines rather than just functions. But the above form is preferable in practice even though it may be considered both too strong and too weak:

- The definition seems too strong because any procedure call is considered to produce a side effect whereas it is possible to write a procedure that changes nothing. Such procedures, however, are rarely useful — except if their role is to change something in the software's environment, for example printing a page, sending a message to the network or moving a robot arm; but then we do want to consider this a side effect even if it does not directly affect an object of the software itself.

- The definition seems too weak because it ignores the case of a function f that calls a side-effect-producing function g. The convention will simply be that f can still be considered side-effect-free. This is acceptable because the rule at which we will arrive in this discussion will prohibit *all* side effects of a certain kind, so we will need to certify each function separately.

The advantage of these conventions is that to determine the side-effect status of a function you only need to look at the body of the function itself. It is in fact trivial, if you have a parser for the language, to write a simple tool that will analyze a function and tell you whether it produces a concrete side effect according to the definition.

Referential transparency

Why should we be concerned about side effects in functions? After all it is in the nature of software execution to change things.

"Introducing a more imperative view", page 145.

The problem is that if we allow functions to change things as well as commands, we lose many of the simple mathematical properties that enable us to reason about our software. As noted in the discussion of abstract data types, when we first encountered the distinction between the applicative and the imperative, mathematics is change-free: it talks about abstract objects and defines operations on these objects, but the operations do not change the objects. (Computing $\sqrt{2}$ does not change the number two.) This immutability is the principal difference between the worlds of mathematics and computer software.

Some approaches to programming seek to retain the immutability of mathematics: Lisp in its so-called "pure" form, "Functional Programming" languages such as Backus's FP, and other *applicative* languages shun change. But they have not caught on for practical software development, suggesting that change is a fundamental property of software.

The object immutability of mathematics has an important practical consequence known as *referential transparency*, a property defined as follows:

> ### Definition: referential transparency
>
> An expression *e* is referentially transparent if it is possible to exchange any subexpression with its value without changing the value of *e*.

Definition from "The Free On-Line Dictionary of Computing", http://wombat. doc.ic.ac.uk

If *x* has value three, we can use *x* instead of *3*, or conversely, in any part of a referentially transparent expression. (Only Swift's Laputa academicians were willing to pay the true price of renouncing referential transparency: always carrying around all the things you will ever want to talk about.) As a consequence of the definition, if we know that *x* and *y* have the same value, we can use one interchangeably with the other. For that reason referential transparency is also called "substitutivity of equals for equals".

The Swift quotation was on page 672.

With side-effect-producing functions, referential transparency disappears. Assume a class contains the attribute and the function

attr: *INTEGER*

sneaky: *INTEGER* **is do** *attr* := *attr* + *1* **end**

Then the value of *sneaky* (meaning: of a call to that function) is always 0; but you cannot use *0* and *sneaky* interchangeably, since an extract of the form

Remember that Result in an integer function is initialized to zero.

attr := *0*; **if** *attr* /= *0* **then** *print* ("*Something bizarre!*") **end**

will print nothing, but would print *Something bizarre!* if you replaced *0* by *sneaky*.

Maintaining referential transparency in expressions is important to enable us to reason about our software. One of the central issues of software construction, analyzed clearly by Dijkstra many years ago, is the difficulty of getting a clear picture of the dynamic behavior (the myriad possible executions of even a simple software element) from its static description (the text of the element). In this effort it is essential to be able to rely on the proven form of reasoning, provided by mathematics. With the demise of referential transparency, however, we lose basic properties of mathematics, so deeply rooted in our practice that we may not even be aware of them. For example, it is no longer true that *n* + *n* is the same thing as *2* * *n* if *n* is the *sneaky*-like function

See [Dijkstra 1968].

n: *INTEGER* **is do** *attr* := *attr* + *1*; *Result* := *attr* **end**

since, with *attr* initially zero, *2* * *n* will return *2* whereas *n* + *n* will return *3*.

By limiting ourselves to functions that do not produce side effects, we will ensure that talking about "functions" in software ceases to betray the meaning of this term in ordinary mathematics. We will maintain a clear distinction between commands, which change objects but do not directly return results, and queries, which provide information about objects but do not change them.

Another way to express this rule informally is to state that *asking a question should not change the answer.*

Objects as machines

The following principle expresses the prohibition in more precise terms:

> ### Command-Query Separation principle
>
> Functions should not produce abstract side effects.

The definition of abstract side effects appears on page 757.

Note that we have only defined *concrete* side effects so far; for the moment you can ignore the difference.

As a result of the principle, only commands (procedures) will be permitted to produce side effects. (In fact, as noted, we not only permit but expect them to change objects — unlike in applicative, completely side-effect-free approaches.)

A list object as list machine

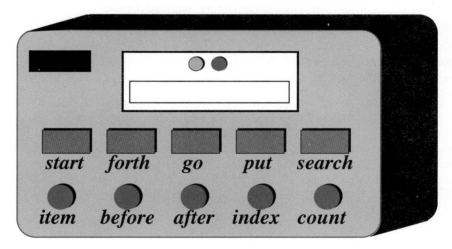

The view of objects that emerges from this discussion (a *metaphor*, to be treated with care as usual) is that of a machine, with an internal state that is not directly observable, and two kinds of button: command buttons, rectangular on the picture, and query buttons, round.

Object lifecycle picture: page 365.

Pressing a command button is a way to make the machine change state: it starts moving and clicking, then comes back to a new stable state (one of the states shown in the earlier picture of object lifecycle). You cannot directly see the state — open the machine — but you can press a query button. This does not change the state (remember: asking a question does not change the answer) but yields a response in the form of a message appearing in the display panel at the top; for boolean queries one of the two indicators in the display panel, representing true and false, will light up. If you press the button several times in a row, without touching the command buttons, you will get the same result each time. If, on the other hand, you push a command button and then a query button, the answer that you get will usually be different from what you would have obtained before the command.

Commands as well as queries may take arguments; these are figuratively entered in the slot at the top left.

The figure is based on the example of a list object with the kind of interface hinted at in earlier chapters and studied in more detail later in the present one. Commands include *start* (move the cursor to the first element), *forth* (advance the cursor one position), *search* (move the cursor to the next occurrence of the element entered into the top-left slot); queries include *item* (show in the display panel the value of the element at cursor position) and *index* (show the current cursor position). Note the difference between a notion such as "cursor", relative to the internal state and hence not directly visible, and *item* or *index* which provide more abstract, officially exported information about the state.

Functions that create objects

A technical point needs to be clarified before we examine further consequences of the Command-Query Separation principle: should we treat object creation as a side effect?

The answer is yes, as we have seen, if the target of the creation is an attribute a: in this case, the instruction !! a changes the value of an object's field. The answer is no if the target is a local entity of the routine. But what if the target is the result of the function itself, as in !! *Result* or the more general form !! *Result.make* (…)?

Such a creation instruction need not be considered a side effect. It does not change any existing object and so does not endanger referential transparency (at least if we assume that there is enough memory to allocate all the objects we need). From a mathematical perspective we may pretend that all of the objects of interest, for all times past, present and future, are already inscribed in the Great Book of Objects; a creation instruction is just a way to obtain one of them, but it does not by itself change anything in the environment. It is common, and legitimate, for a function to create, initialize and return such an object.

> These observations assume that in the second form the creation procedure *make* does not produce side effects on any object other than the one being created.

A clean style for class interfaces

From the Command-Query Separation principle follows a style of design that yields simple and readable software, and tremendously helps reliability, reusability and extendibility.

As you may have realized, this style is very different from the dominant practices of today, as fostered in particular by the C programming language. The predilection of C for side effects — for ignoring the difference between an action and a value — is not just a feature of the common C style (it sometimes seems just psychologically impossible for a C programmer to resist the temptation, when accessing a value, also to modify it a little in passing); it is embedded deeply into the language, with such constructs as $x++$, meaning: return the value of x, then increase it by one — saving a few keystrokes in $y = x++$ compared to $y = x$; $x := x+1$, and not to be confused with $++x$ which increments *before* computing the value. A whole civilization, in fact, is built on side effects.

It would be foolish to dismiss this side-effect-full style as thoughtless; its widespread use shows that many people have found it convenient, and it may even be part of the reason for the amazing success of C and its derivatives. But what was attractive in the nineteen-seventies and eighties — when the software development population was growing by an order of magnitude every few years, and the emphasis was on getting some kind of job done rather than on long-term quality — may not be appropriate for the software technology of the twenty-first century. There we want software that will grow with us, software that we can understand, explain, maintain, reuse and trust. The Command-Query Separation principle is one of the required conditions for these goals.

Applying a strict separation between commands and queries by prohibiting abstract side effects in functions is particularly appropriate for the development of large systems, where the key to success is to exert full control on every inter-module interaction.

If you have been used to the converse style, you may at first, like many people, find the new one too extreme. But after starting to practice it I think you will quickly realize its benefits.

Quietly, the preceding chapters have already applied Command-Query Separation to its full extent. You may remember for example that the interface for all our stack classes included a procedure *remove* describing the operation of popping a stack (removing the top element), and a function or attribute *item* which yields the top element. The first is a command, the second a query. In other approaches you might have seen a routine *pop* which both removes the element and returns it — a side-effect-producing function. This example has, I hope, been studied in enough depth to show the gains of clarity and simplicity that we achieve by keeping the two aspects cleanly separated.

Other consequences of the principles may seem more alarming at first. For reading input, many people are used to the style of using functions such as *getint* — the C name, but its equivalent exists in many other languages — whose effect is to read a new input element and return its value. This is a side-effect-producing function in all its splendor: a call to the function, written *getint* () — with the empty parentheses so unmistakably characteristic of the C look-and-feel — does not just return a value but affects the context ("asking a question changes the answer"); as typical consequences, excluding the chance case in which the input has two identical consecutive values:

• If you call *getint* () twice you will get different answers.

• *getint* () + *getint* () and *2 * getint* () will not yield the same value. (If an overzealous "optimizing" compiler treats the first expression like the second, you will report a bug to the compiler vendor, and you will be right.)

In other words, we lose the benefits of referential transparency — of reasoning about software functions as if they were mathematical functions, with a crystal-clear view of how we can build expressions from them and what values these expressions will denote.

The Command-Query Separation principle brings referential transparency back. Here this means that we will distinguish between the procedure that advances the input cursor to the next item and the function or attribute that yields the item last read. Assume *input* is of type *FILE*; the instructions to read the next integer from file *input* will be something like

> *input.advance*
> *n := input.last_integer*

If you call *last_integer* ten times in a row you will, unlike with *getint*, get ten times the same result. If you are new to this style, it may take some getting used to; but the resulting simplicity and clarity will soon remove any temptation to go back to side effects.

> In this example as in the *x++* case seen earlier, the traditional form beats the object-oriented one if the goal of the game is to minimize keystrokes. This illustrates a general observation: the productivity gains of object technology will not derive from trying to be as terse as possible on a microscopic scale (a game at which APL or modern "scripting languages" such as Perl will always win against a good O-O language). The achievements are on the global structure of a system: through reuse, through such mechanisms as genericity and garbage collection, through the use of assertions, you can decrease the size of your software by amounts far higher than anything you can achieve by skimping by a character here or a line there. Keystroke-wise is often system-foolish.

Pseudo-random number generators: a design exercise

An example sometimes quoted in favor of functions with side effects is that of pseudo-random number generators, which return successive values from a sequence enjoying adequate statistical properties. The sequence is initialized by a call of the form

> *random_seed* (*seed*)

where *seed* is a seed value provided by the client. A common way to get the successive pseudo-random values is by calling a function:

> *xx := next_random* ()

But here too there is no reason to make an exception to the command/query dichotomy. Before looking at the solution let us just forget that we have seen the above and restart from scratch by asking the question: how should we handle random generation in an object-oriented context? This will provide the opportunity of a little design exercise, and will enable us, if the need arises, to explain the results to someone whose view has not been unduly influenced by pre-O-O approaches.

As always in object technology, the relevant question — often the only one — is:

What are the data abstractions?

The relevant abstraction here is not "random number generation" or "random number generator", both of them quite functional in nature, focusing on *what the system does* rather than *what it does it to*.

Probing further, we might think "random number", but that is not the right answer yet. Remember, a data abstraction is characterized by features — commands and queries; it is hard to think of features applicable to "random number".

"Discovery and rejection", page 725. That "random number" leads to a dead end illustrates the Class Elicitation principle encountered when we studied the general rules for finding the classes: a key step may be to *reject* inappropriate candidates. And once again we see that not all promising nouns yield classes: were a "requirements document" written for this problem, the noun *random number* would certainly figure prominently in it.

A random number does not mean much by itself; it must be understood in relation to its predecessors and successors in the sequence.

Wait a minute — here we have it: *sequence*, more precisely pseudo-random number sequence. This is the abstraction we have been looking for; a perfectly legitimate data abstraction, similar to the cursor lists we have seen on a number of occasions, only infinite (do not look for an *after* boolean query!). Features will include:

- Commands: *make* — initialize with a certain seed; *forth* — advance to next element.

- Queries: *item* — return the element at cursor position.

An infinite list as a machine

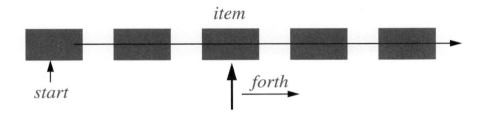

To get a new random number sequence *rand*, clients will use !! *rand.make* (*seed*); to advance to the next value, they will call *rand.forth*; and they will obtain the current value by *xx* := *rand.item*.

There is really nothing specific to *random number* sequences in the interface, except for the *seed* argument to the creation procedure. Adding a *start* procedure which brings the cursor to the first item (and which *make* may call for random number sequences), what we have is the framework for a deferred class *COUNTABLE_SEQUENCE* describing arbitrary infinite sequences. Think for example of how to model prime numbers in an object-oriented way; the answer is the same: define a class *PRIMES*, an heir to *COUNTABLE_SEQUENCE*, whose successive elements are the prime numbers. Other sequences — Fibonacci numbers and the like — will be modeled in the same way.

These examples illustrate in passing that contrary to popular belief it is quite possible, and even trivial, to represent infinite structures on a computer. Abstract data types provide the key: a structure is entirely defined by the applicable operations, of which there is of course a finite number, three in this case — *start, forth, item* — plus any auxiliary features we may want to add. The trick, of course, is that any execution will only try to evaluate a finite number of elements of an infinite structure.

[M 1994a]. *COUNTABLE_SEQUENCE* and its heirs such as *PRIMES* are part of the universal computing science hierarchy described in the companion guide to reusable components.

Abstract state, concrete state

From the discussion of referential transparency it would seem desirable to bar all concrete side effects from functions. Such a rule would have the advantage that — in line with one of our methodology precepts — we could build it into the language, since a compiler can easily detect concrete side effects (as we saw just after the definition of this notion).

"If it is baroque, fix it", page 670.

Unfortunately, this would be unacceptably restrictive, explaining why the Command-Query Separation principle only prohibits *abstract* side effects, a notion that will now be defined. The problem is that some concrete side effects are not only harmless but necessary. They are of two kinds.

The first category includes functions which, in the course of their execution, modify the state, sometimes drastically, and affecting very visible features; but then they restore the original state. Consider for example a class describing integer lists with cursor, and the following function for computing the maximum of a list:

```
max is
            -- The highest value of items in the list
    require
        not empty
    local
        original_index: INTEGER
    do
        original_index := index
        from
            start; Result := item
        until is_last loop
            forth; Result := Result.max (item)
        end
        go (original_index)
    end
```

To traverse the list, the algorithm needs to move the cursor over all elements. The function, calling such procedures as *start*, *forth* and *go*, is indeed full of concrete side effects on the cursor position; but it begins by noting the cursor position into *original_index* and ends by returning the cursor to that position through a call to *go*. All is well that ends well: the function leaves the list in exactly the state in which it found it. But no compiler in the world is going to detect that the side effect is only apparent.

Side effects of the second acceptable category may change the state of the object, but only affecting properties that are not visible to clients. To understand the concepts in depth, it will be useful to make sure that you are familiar with the discussion of "abstraction function" and "implementation invariants" in the presentation of Design by Contract. (In particular, take a look at the accompanying figures to refresh your memory.)

Pages 375 to 377.

We saw then that an object of our software (a *concrete* object) is the representation of an abstract object, and that two concrete objects may represent the same abstract object. For example two different stack representations, each made of an array and a top marker *count*, represent the same stack if they have the same value for *count* and the same array elements up to index *count*. They may differ in other properties, such as the array sizes and the values stored at indices above *count*. In mathematical terms, every concrete object belongs to the domain of the abstraction function a, and we can have $c1 \neq c2$ even with $a(c1) = a(c2)$.

What this means for us is that a function that modifies a concrete object is harmless if the result of this modification still represents the same abstract object — yields the same a value. For example assume in a function on stacks contains the operation

representation.put (some_value, count + 1)

(with the guarantee that the array's capacity is at least *count + 1*). This side effect changes a value above the stack-significant section of the array; it can do no ill.

More generally, a concrete side effect which changes the concrete state of an object c is an *abstract side effect* if it also changes its *abstract state*, that is to say the value of $a(c)$ (a more directly usable definition of abstract side effects will appear shortly). If a side effect is only concrete — does not affect the abstract state — it is harmless.

Figure page 751.   In the object-as-machine metaphor, functions producing concrete-only side effects correspond to query buttons that may produce an internal state change having absolutely no effect on the answers given by any query button. For example the machine might save energy by automatically switching off some internal circuits if nobody presses a button for some time, and turning them on again whenever someone presses any button, queries included. Such an internal state change is unnoticeable from the outside and hence legitimate.

The object-oriented approach is particularly favorable to clever implementations which, when computing a function, may change the concrete state behind the scenes without producing any visible side effect. The example of a stack function that changes array elements above the top is somewhat academic, but we will see below a practical and useful design that relies on this technique.

Since not every class definition is accompanied by a full-fledged specification of the underlying abstract data type, we need a more directly usable definition of "abstract side effect". This is not difficult. In practice, the abstract data type is defined by the interface offered by a class to its clients (expressed for example as the short form of the class). A side effect will affect the abstract object if it changes the result of any query accessible to these clients. Hence the definition:

> ### Definition: abstract side effect
>
> An abstract side effect is a concrete side effect that can change the value of a non-secret query.

This is the notion used by the Command-Query Separation principle — the principle that prohibits abstract side effects in functions. *The principle appears on page 751.*

The definition refers to "non-secret" rather than exported queries. The reason is that in-between generally exported and fully secret status, we must permit a query to be selectively exported to a set of clients. As soon as a query is non-secret — exported to any client other than *NONE* — we consider that changing its result is an abstract side effect, since the change will be visible to at least some clients.

The policy

As announced at the beginning of this discussion, abstract side effects are (unlike concrete side effects) not easily detectable by a compiler. In particular it does not suffice to check that a function preserves the values of all non-secret attributes: the effect on other queries might be indirect, or (as in the *max* example) several concrete side effects might in the end cancel out. The most a compiler can do would be to issue a warning if a function modifies an exported attribute.

So the Command-Query Separation principle is a methodological precept, not a language constraint. This does not, however, diminish its importance.

Past what for some people will be an initial shock, every object-oriented developer should apply the principle without exception. I have followed it for years, and would never write a side-effect-producing function. ISE applies it in all its O-O software (for the C part we have of course to adapt to the dominant style, although even here we try to apply the principle whenever we can). It has helped us produce much better results — tools and libraries that we can reuse, explain to others, extend and scale up.

Objections

It is important here two deal with two common objections to the side-effect-free style.

The first has to do with error handling. Sometimes a function with side effects is really a procedure, which in addition to doing its job returns a status code indicating how things went. But there are better ways to do this; roughly speaking, the proper O-O technique is to enable the client, after an operation on an object, to perform a query on the status, represented for example by an attribute of the object, as in

> *target.some_operation* (...)
> *how_did_it_go* := *target.status*

Note that the technique of returning a status as function result is lame anyway. It transforms a procedure into a function by adding the status as a result; but it does not work if the routine was already a function, which already has a result of its own. It is also problematic if you need more than one status indicator. In such cases the C approach is either to return a "structure" (the equivalent of an object) with several components, which is getting close to the above scheme, or to use global variables — which raises a whole set of new problems, especially in a large system where many modules can trigger errors.

The second objection is a common misconception: the impression that Command-Query Separation, for example the list-with-cursor type of interface, is incompatible with concurrent access to objects. That belief is remarkably widespread (this is one of the places where I know that, if I am lecturing on these topics, someone in the audience will raise his hand, and the question will be the same whether we are in Santa Barbara, Seattle, Singapore, Sydney, Stockholm or Saint-Petersburg); but it is incorrect nonetheless.

Chapter 30.

The misconception is that in a concurrent context it is essential to have atomic access-cum-modification operations, for example *get* on a buffer — the concurrent equivalent of a first-in, first out queue. Such a *get* function non-interruptibly performs, in our terminology, both a call to *item* (obtain the oldest element) and *remove* (remove that element), returning the result of *item* as the result of *get*. But using such an example as an argument for *get*-style functions with side effects is confusing two notions. What we need in a concurrent context is a way to offer a client exclusive access to a supplier object for certain operations. With such a mechanism, we can protect a client extract of the form

$x := buffer.item; \ buffer.remove$

thereby guaranteeing that the buffer element returned by the call to *item* is indeed the same one removed by the following call to *remove*. Whether or not we permit functions to have side effects, we will have to provide a mechanism to ensure such exclusive access; for example a client may need to dequeue two elements

$buffer.remove; \ buffer.remove$

with the guarantee that the removed elements will be consecutive; this requires exclusive access, and is unrelated to the question of side effects in functions.

Chapter 30. See in particular "Support for command-query separation", page 1029.

Later in this book we will have an extensive discussion of concurrency, where we will study a simple and elegant approach to concurrent and distributed computation, fully compatible with the Command-Query Separation principle — which in fact will help us arrive at it.

Legitimate side effects: an example

To conclude this discussion of side effects let us examine a typical case of legitimate side effects — functions that do not change the abstract state, but can change the concrete state, and for good reason. The example is representative of a useful design pattern.

Consider the implementation of complex numbers. As with points, discussed in an earlier chapter, two representations are possible: cartesian (by axis coordinates x and y) and polar (by distance to the origin ρ and angle θ). Which one do we choose? There is no easy answer. If we take, as usual, the abstract data type approach, we will note that what counts is the applicable operations — addition, subtraction, multiplication and division among others, as well as queries to access x, y, ρ and θ — and that for each of them one of the representations is definitely better: cartesian for addition, subtraction and such, polar for multiplication and division. (Try expressing division in cartesian coordinates!)

We could let the client decide what representation to use. But this would make our classes difficult to use, and violate information hiding: for the client author, the representation should not matter.

Alternatively, we could keep *both* representations up to date at all times. But this may cause unnecessary performance penalties. Assume for example that a client only performs multiplications and divisions. The operations use polar representations, but after each one of them we must recompute x and y, a useless but expensive computation involving trigonometric functions.

A better solution is to refuse to choose between the representations *a priori*, but update each of them only when we need it. As compared to the preceding approach, we do not gain anything in space (since we will still need attributes for each of x, y, ρ and θ, plus two boolean attributes to tell us which of the representations are up to date); but we avoid wasting computation time.

We may assume the following public operations, among others:

class *COMPLEX* **feature**

    … Feature declarations for:

                  infix "+", **infix** "–", **infix** "*", **infix** "/",

                  add, *subtract*, *multiply*, *divide*,

                  x, *y*, *rho*, *theta*, …

end

The queries *x*, *y*, *rho* and *theta* are exported functions returning real values. They are always defined (except *theta* for the complex number 0) since a client may request the *x* and *y* of a complex number even if the number is internally represented in polar, and its ρ and θ even if it is in cartesian. In addition to the functions "+" etc., we assume procedures *add* etc. which modify an object: *z1* + *z2* is a new complex number equal to the sum of *z1* and *z2*, whereas the procedure call *z1*·*add* (*z2*) changes *z1* to represent that sum. In practice, we might need only the functions or only the procedures.

Internally, the class includes the following secret attributes for the representation:

cartesian_ready: *BOOLEAN*

polar_ready: *BOOLEAN*

private_x, *private_y*, *private_rho*, *private_theta*: *REAL*

Not all of the four real attributes are necessarily up to date at all times; in fact only two need be up to date. More precisely, the following implementation invariant should be included in the class:

invariant

    cartesian_ready **or** *polar_ready*

    polar_ready **implies** ($0 <=$ *private_theta* **and** *private_theta* $<=$ *Two_pi*)

        -- *cartesian_ready* **implies** (*private_x* and *private_y* are up to date)

        -- *polar_ready* **implies** (*private_rho* and *private_theta* are up to date)

The value of *Two_pi* is assumed to be 2π. The last two clauses may only be expressed informally, in the form of comments.

At any time at least one of the representations is up to date, although both may be. Any operation requested by a client will be carried out in the most appropriate representation; this may require computing that representation if it was not up to date. If the operation produces a (concrete) side effect, the other representation will cease to be up to date.

Two secret procedures are available for carrying out representation changes:

prepare_cartesian **is**
>   -- Make cartesian representation available
>
> **do**
>> **if not** *cartesian_ready* **then**
>>> **check** *polar_ready* **end**
>>>   -- (Because the invariant requires at least one of the
>>>   -- two representations to be up to date)
>>
>> *private_x* := *private_rho* * *cos* (*private_theta*)
>> *private_y* := *private_rho* * *sin* (*private_theta*)
>> *cartesian_ready* := *True*
>>>   -- Here both *cartesian_ready* and *polar_ready* are true:
>>>   -- Both representations are available
>>
>> **end**
>
> **ensure**
>> *cartesian_ready*
>
> **end**

prepare_polar **is**
>   -- Make polar representation available
>
> **do**
>> **if not** *polar_ready* **then**
>>> **check** *cartesian_ready* **end**
>>
>> *private_rho* := *sqrt* (*private_x* ^ 2 + *private_y* ^ 2)
>> *private_theta* := *atan2* (*private_y*, *private_x*)
>> *polar_ready* := *True*
>>>   -- Here both *cartesian_ready* and *polar_ready* are true:
>>>   -- Both representations are available
>>
>> **end**
>
> **ensure**
>> *polar_ready*
>
> **end**

Functions *cos*, *sin*, *sqrt* and *atan2* are assumed to be taken from a standard mathematical library; *atan2* (*y*, *x*) should compute the arc tangent of *y* / *x*.

We will also need creation procedures *make_cartesian* and *make_polar*.

make_cartesian (*a*, *b*: *REAL*) **is**
>   -- Initialize with abscissa *a*, ordinate *b*.
>   **do**
>   *private_x* := *a*; *private_y* := *b*
>   *cartesian_ready* := *True*; *polar_ready* := *False*
>   **ensure**
>   *cartesian_ready*; **not** *polar_ready*
>   **end**

and symmetrically for *make_polar*.

The exported operations are easy to write; we can start for example with the procedure variants (we will see the function variants such as **infix** "+" next):

add (*other*: *COMPLEX*) **is**
>   -- Add the value of *other*.
>   **do**
>   *prepare_cartesian*; *polar_ready* := *False*
>   *private_x* := *x* + *other*$\bullet$*x*; *private_y* = *y* + *other*$\bullet$*y*
>   **ensure**
>   *x* = **old** *x* + *other*$\bullet$*x*; *y* = **old** *y* + *other*$\bullet$*y*
>   *cartesian_ready*; **not** *polar_ready*
>   **end**

(Note the importance in the postcondition of using *x* and *y*, not *private_x* and *private_y* which might not have been up to date before the call.)

divide (*z*: *COMPLEX*) **is**
>   -- Divide by *z*.
>   **require**
>   *z*$\bullet$*rho* /= *0*
>   -- (To be replaced by a numerically more realistic precondition)
>   **do**
>   *prepare_polar*; *cartesian_ready* := *False*
>   *private_rho* := *rho* / *other*$\bullet$*rho*
>   *private_theta* = (*theta* – *other*$\bullet$*theta*) \\ *Two_pi*
>   -- Using \\ as remainder operation
>   **ensure**
>   *rho* = **old** *rho* / *other*$\bullet$*rho*
>   *theta* = (**old** *theta* — *other*$\bullet$*theta*) \\ *Two_pi*
>   *polar_ready*; **not** *cartesian_ready*
>   **end**

and similarly for *subtract* and *multiply*. (The precondition and postcondition may need some adaptation to reflect the realities of floating-point computations on computers.) The function variants follow the same pattern:

infix "+" (*other*: *COMPLEX*): *COMPLEX* **is**

    -- Sum of current complex and *other*

do

    !! *Result*.*make_cartesian* (x + *other*.x, y + *other*.y)

ensure

    Result.x = x + *other*.x; *Result*.y = y + *other*.y

    Result.*cartesian_ready*

end

infix "/" (*z*: *COMPLEX*): *COMPLEX* **is**

    -- Quotient of current complex by *z*.

require

    z.*rho* /= *0*

        -- (To be replaced by a numerically more realistic condition)

do

    !! *Result*.*make_polar* (*rho* / *other*.*rho*, (*theta* − *other*.*theta*) \\ *Two_pi*)

ensure

    Result.*rho* = *rho* / *other*.*rho*

    Result.*theta* = (**old** *theta* — *other*.*theta*) \\ *Two_pi*

    Result.*polar_ready*

end

and similarly for **infix** "−" and **infix** "*".

> Note that for the last postcondition clauses of these functions to be valid, *cartesian_ready* and *polar_ready* must be exported to the class itself, by appearing in a clause of the form **feature** {*COMPLEX*}; they are not exported to any other class.

But where are the side effects? In the last two functions, they are not directly visible; this is because *x*, *y*, *rho* and *theta*, behind their innocent looks, are sneaky little side-effectors! Computing *x* or *y* will cause a secret change of representation (a call to *prepare_cartesian*) if the cartesian representation was not ready, and symmetrically for *rho* and *theta*. Here for example are *x* and *theta*:

x: *REAL* **is**

    -- Abscissa

do

    prepare_cartesian; *Result* := *private_x*

end

theta: *REAL* **is**

    -- Angle

do

    prepare_polar; *Result* := *private_theta*

end

Functions *y* and *rho* are similar. All these functions call a procedure which may trigger a change of state. Unlike *add* and consorts, however, they do not invalidate the previous representation when a new one is computed. For example, if *x* is called in a state where *cartesian_ready* is false, both representations (all four real attributes) will be up to date afterwards. This is because the functions may produce side effects on the concrete objects only, not on the associated abstract objects. To express this property more formally: computing $z \cdot x$ or one of the other functions may change the concrete object associated with z, say from c_1 to c_2, but always with the guarantee that

$$a (c_1) = a (c_2)$$

where a is the abstraction function. The computer objects c_1 and c_2 may be different, but they represent the same mathematical object, a complex number.

Such side effects are harmless, as they only affect secret attributes and hence cannot be detected by clients.

The object-oriented approach encourages such flexible, self-adapting schemes, which internally choose the best implementation according to the needs of the moment. As long as the resulting implementation changes affect the concrete state but not the abstract state, they can appear in functions without violating the Command-Query Separation principle or endangering referential transparency for clients.

23.2 HOW MANY ARGUMENTS FOR A FEATURE?

In trying to make classes — especially reusable classes — easy to use, you should devote special attention to the number of arguments of features. As we will see, well-understood object technology yields a style of feature interface radically different from what you typically get with traditional approaches; there will, in particular, be far fewer arguments.

The importance of argument counts

When your development relies on a supplier class, features are your day-to-day channel to it. The simplicity of the feature interfaces fundamentally determines the class's ease of use. Various factors influence this, in particular the consistency of the conventions; but in the end a simple numerical criterion dominates everything else: how many arguments do features have? The more arguments, the more you have to remember.

This is particularly true of library classes. The criterion for success there is simple: after a potential library user has taken the (preferably short) time to understand what a class is about and, if he decides to use it, selected the set of features that he needs for the moment, he should be able to learn these features quickly and, after as few uses as possible, remember them without having to go back to the documentation. This will only work if features — aside from all other qualities of consistency, proper naming conventions and general quality of the design — have very short argument lists.

If you examine a typical subroutine library you will commonly encounter subroutines with many arguments. Here for example is an integration routine from a mathematical library justly renowned for the excellence of its algorithms, but constrained in its interface by the use of traditional subroutine techniques:

Warning: this is not an object-oriented interface!

nonlinear_ode

    (*equation_count*: **in** *INTEGER*;

     epsilon: **in out** *DOUBLE*;

    func: **procedure**   (*eq_count*: *INTEGER*; *a*: *DOUBLE*; *eps*: *DOUBLE*;

                           b: *ARRAY* [*DOUBLE*]; *cm*: **pointer** *Libtype*)

    left_count, *coupled_count*: **in** *INTEGER*;

    …)

    [And so on. Altogether 19 arguments, including:

          - 4 **in out** values;

          - 3 arrays, used both as input and output;

          - 6 functions, each with 6 or 7 arguments of which 2 or 3 are arrays!]

Since the purpose of this example is not to criticize one particular numerical library but to emphasize the difference between O-O and traditional interfaces, the routine and arguments names have been changed and the syntax (in C in the original) has been adapted. The resulting notation resembles the notation of this book, which, however, would of course exclude such non-O-O mechanisms as **in out** arguments, explicit **pointer** manipulation, and arguments (such as *func* and 5 others) that are themselves routines.

Several properties make this scheme particularly complex to use:

- Many arguments are **in out**, that is to say must be initialized by the caller to pass a certain value and are updated by the routine to return some information. For example *epsilon* specifies on input whether continuation is required (yes if less than 0; if between 0 and 1, continuation is required unless $epsilon < \sqrt{precision}$, etc.). On output, it provides an estimate of the increment.

- Many arguments, both to the routine itself and to its own routine arguments, are arrays, which again serve to pass certain values on input and return others on output.

- Some arguments serve to specify the many possibilities for error processing (stop processing, write message to a file, continue anyway…).

Even though high-quality numerical libraries have been in existence for many years and, as mentioned in an earlier chapter, provide some of the most concrete evidence of real reuse, they are still not as widely used in scientific computation as they should be. The complexity of their interfaces, and in particular the large number of arguments illustrated by *nonlinear_ode*, are clearly a big part of the reason.

On the Math library and techniques of scientific object-oriented computing, see [Dubois 1997]. The earlier mention was in "Object-oriented re-architecturing", page 441.

Part of the complexity comes from the problems handled by these routines. But one can do better. An object-oriented numerical library, *Math*, offers a completely different approach, consistent with object technology concepts and with the principles of this book. An earlier discussion cited the Math library as an example of using object technology to re-architecture older software, and the library indeed uses an existing non-O-O library as its core engine, since it would have been absurd to duplicate the basic algorithmic work; but it provides a modern, O-O client interface. The basic non-linear ODE routine has the form

solve

    -- Solve the problem, recording the answer in *x* and *y*.

In other words it takes no argument at all! You simply create an instance of the class *GENERAL_BOUNDARY_VALUE_PROBLEM* to represent the mathematical problem to be solved, set its non-default properties through calls to the appropriate procedures, attach it to a "problem solver" object (an instance of the class in which the above routine appears: *GENERAL_BOUNDARY_VALUE_PROBLEM_SOLVER*), and call *solve* on that object. Attributes of the class, x and y, will provide the handle to the computed answer.

More generally, the thorough application of O-O techniques has a dramatic effect on argument counts. Measures on the ISE libraries, published in more detailed elsewhere, show an average number of arguments ranging from 0.4 for the Base libraries to 0.7 for the *Vision* graphical library. For the purposes of comparison with non-O-O libraries we should add 1 to all these figures, since we count two arguments for $x \cdot f (a, b)$ versus three for its non-O-O counterpart $f (x, a, b)$; but even so these averages are strikingly low when compared with the counts for non-O-O routines which, even when not reaching 19 as in the above numerical example, often have 5, 10 or 15 arguments.

See [M 1994a] *for detailed library measurements.*

These numbers are not a goal by themselves — and of course not by themselves an indicator of quality. Instead, they are largely the result of a deeper design principle that we will now examine.

Operands and options

An argument to a routine may be of two different kinds: *operands* and *options*.

To understand the difference, consider the example of a class *DOCUMENT* and a procedure *print*. Assume — just to make the example more concrete — that printing will rely on Postscript. A typical call illustrating a possible interface (*not* compatible with the principle stated below) would be

$my\_document \cdot print \quad (printer\_name, paper\_size, color\_or\_not,$
$postscript\_level, print\_resolution)$

Warning: this is not the recommended style!

Of the five arguments, which ones are truly indispensable? If you do not provide a Postscript level, the routine can use as a default the most commonly available option. The same applies to paper size: you can use LTR (8.5 by 11 inches) in the US, A4 (21 by 29.7 centimeters) elsewhere. 600 dots per square inch may be a reasonable default for the print resolution, and most printers are non-color. In all these cases, you might have a mechanism supporting installation-level or user-level defaults to override the universal ones (for example if your site has standardized on 1200 dpi resolution). The only argument that remains is the printer name; but here too you might have defined a default printer.

This example illustrates the difference between operands and options:

Definition: operand and option arguments

An operand argument to a routine represents an object on which the routine will operate.

An option argument represents a mode of operation.

This definition is too general to tell us unambiguously whether a proposed argument is an operand or an option, but here are two directly applicable criteria:

> ## How to distinguish options from operands
>
> - An argument is an option if, assuming the client had not supplied its value, it would have been possible to find a reasonable default.
>
> - In the evolution of a class, arguments tend to remain the same, but options may be added and removed.

According to the first criterion, all the arguments to *print* are options (with the possible exception of *printer_name* if you have not defined a default printer). Note, however, that the target of the call, an implicit argument (*my_document* in the example) is, as all targets should be, an operand: if you do not say what document you want to print, no one is going to choose a default for you.

The second criterion is less obvious since it requires some foresight, but it reflects the software engineering concerns that underlie all our discussions since the first chapters of this book. We know that a class is not an immutable product; like all software, it may change over its lifetime. Some properties of a class, however, change more often than others. Operands are there for the long term: adding or removing a operand is a major, incompatible change. Options, on the other hand, may come and go. For example one may imagine that support for colors was not part of the first version of the *print* procedure, a few years back, and was only added later. This is typical of an option.

The principle

The definition of operands and options yields the rule on arguments:

> ## Operand principle
>
> The arguments of a routine should only include operands (no options).

Two cases for loosening the rule, not quite qualifying as exceptions, are mentioned below.

In the style that this principle promotes, options to an operation are set not in calls to the operation but in calls to specific option-setting procedures:

```
my_document.set_printing_size ("A4")
my_document.set_color
my_document.print            -- No argument at all.
```

Once set, each option remains in force for the target object until reset by a new call. In the absence of any call to the corresponding procedures, and of any explicit setting at the time of object creation, options will have the default values.

For any type other than boolean, the option-setting procedure will take one argument of the appropriate type, as illustrated by *set_printing_size*; the standard name is of the form *set_property_name*. Note that the argument to a procedure such as *set_printing_size* itself satisfies the Operand principle: the page size, which was an option for the original *print*, is an operand for *set_printing_size* which by definition operates on page sizes.

For a boolean procedure, the same technique would yield a procedure taking either *True* or *False* as argument; since this is confusing (as users of the procedure may forget which ones of the two possibilities *True* represents), it is better to use a pair of procedures, with conventional names of the form *set_property_name* and *set_no_property_name*, for example *set_color* and *set_no_color*, although in this case it is probably just as well to call the second variant *set_black_and_white*.

Application of the Operand principle yields several benefits:

- You only specify what differs from the defaults. Any property for which you do not need any special setting will be handled with the settings that have proved to be most commonly appropriate.

- Novices need only learn the essentials and can ignore any advanced properties.

- As you get to know the class better and move on to sophisticated uses, you learn more properties; but you only have to remember what you use.

- Perhaps most importantly, the technique preserves extendibility and the Open-Closed principle: as you add more options to a certain facility, you do not need to change the interface of a routine and hence invalidate all existing callers. If the default value corresponds to the previous implicit setting, existing clients will not need to be changed.

Against the Operand principle, a possible objection comes to mind: does it not just trade argument complexity for call complexity (calls will be much simpler, but we will have more of them since we must include calls to option-setting procedures)? This is, however, not accurate. The only new calls will be for options that you want to set to values other than the default. Here the complexity is the same as with option arguments. (You may have a few more keystrokes to type, but what counts is the number of pieces of information you have to provide, and it is the same with both approaches.) The big difference is that you need only pay attention to the options that are relevant for your own use, whereas option arguments force you to specify *all* options explicitly.

Also note that frequently a certain option will apply to many successive calls. In that case, using option arguments forces you to specify it each time. With the style recommended here, you gain even if the value is not the default: you set it the first time around, and it stays in place until explicitly changed. The gain is particularly significant in cases such as the numerical library mentioned above where *every* call must include arguments indicating the desired error processing mode, the name of the file for error output and other general properties, which tend to remain applicable through many calls.

Some languages support the notion of *optional argument*, achieving some of the benefits of the Operand principle but not all. The comparison has been left as an exercise, but you may already note that the last point mentioned would not apply: any non-default argument must be specified each time.

See exercise E23.3, page 807.

Benefiting from the Operand principle

Comments made about the Command-Query Separation principle apply to the Operand principle too: it goes against today's dominant practices, and some readers will undoubtedly balk at it initially; but I can recommend it without any reservation, having applied it for many years and greatly benefited from it. It yields a simple, clear and elegant style, fostering clarity and extendibility.

That style soon becomes a natural one for developers who try it. (Predictably, we have made it part of our standard at ISE.) You create the required objects; set up any of their properties that differ from the defaults; then apply the operations that you need. This is the scheme sketched above for *solve* in the Math library. It certainly beats passing 19 arguments.

Exceptions to the Operand principle?

The Operand principle is of universal applicability. Rather than true exceptions, it requires adaptation in two specific cases.

First, we can take advantage of the flexibility of multiple creation procedures. Since a class can provide more than one way to initialize an object, through creation calls of the form !! *x.make*_specific (*argument*, …) where *make*_specific is any of the creation procedures, we can relax the Operand principle for such creation procedures, facilitating the client's task by offering various ways to set up objects with values other than the default. Two constraints, however:

- Remember that, as always, every creation procedure must ensure the class invariant.

- The set of creation procedures must include a minimal procedure (called *make* in the recommended style) which includes no option arguments and sets all option values to their defaults.

The other case for loosening the Operand principle follows from the last observation. If you have applied the principle, you may find that some operations (other than creation procedures) are often used with option-setting procedures according to a standard pattern; for example

> *my_document.set_printing_size* ("…")
> *my_document.set_printer_name* ("…")
> *my_document.print*

In such a case, it may be convenient, in the name of encapsulation and reusability, and in conformity to the Shopping List principle studied next, to provide an extra routine as a convenience for clients:

> *print_with_size_and_printer* (*printer_name*: STRING; *size*: SIZE_SPECIFICATION)

This assumes, of course, that the basic minimal routine (*print* in the example) remains available, and that the new routine is just a supplementary facility meant to simplify client text in cases that have been recognized as truly frequent.

> This is not really a violation of the principle, since the very nature of the new routine requires the arguments (printer and size in the example) to be present, making them operands.

A checklist

The Operand principle and its recognition of the need to pay attention to options suggest a technique that helps get a class right. For each class, list the supported options and produce a table with one row for each option, illustrated here by one of the rows for the *DOCUMENT* class:

Option	Initialized	Queried	Set
Paper size	default:A4 (international) *make_LTR*: LTR (US)	*size*	*set_size* *set_A4* *set_LTR*

The successive columns list: the role of the option; how it is initialized by the various creation procedures; how it can be accessed by clients; how it can be set to various values. This provides a useful checklist for frequent deficiencies:

- **Initialized** entries help spot a wrong initialization, especially when you rely on the defaults. (A boolean option, for example, is initialized to false; you should choose the corresponding attribute accordingly, so that the option for color support is *Black_and_white_only* if you wish the default, false, to represent full color support.)

- The **Queried** entries help spot the mistake of providing clients ways to set an option but not to access it. Note in particular that a routine that takes an object in a certain state may need to change some options for its own purposes, but then restore the initial state; this is only possible if the routine can query the initial value.

- The **Set** entries help spot missing option-setting procedures. For example if the default value for a boolean option is the usual false, and you provide a procedure to change it to true, you should not forget to provide another to reset it to false.

None of the rules suggested here is absolute; for example some options may never need to be returned to false. But they do apply in most cases, so it is important to check that the table's entries indicate the behavior that you expect from the class. The table, or extracts from it, can also help document the class.

23.3 CLASS SIZE: THE SHOPPING LIST APPROACH

We have learned to be paranoid about limiting the external size of features, as measured by the number of arguments, because it fundamentally affects the features' ease of use and hence the quality of a class interface. (We care less about the *internal* size of a feature, measured for example by the number of its instructions, since it simply reflects the complexity of the algorithm. But as you will certainly have noted most routine bodies in good O-O design will remain small anyway.)

Should we be similarly concerned about the size of each class as a whole? Here the answer will be much less drastic.

Class size definition

We must define how to measure the size of a class. It is possible to count the number of lines (or, preferably, the number of declarations and instructions, which is less subject to individual variations of textual layout, and just requires a simple parser). Although interesting for some applications, this is a supplier-side measure. If we are more interested in how much functionality a class provides to its clients, the appropriate criterion is the number of features.

This still leaves two questions:

- Information hiding: do we count all features (*internal* size) or only exported ones (*external*) size?

- Inheritance: do we count only the immediate features, that is to say those introduced in the class itself (*immediate* size), all the features of the class including those inherited from any proper ancestor (*flat* size, so called in reference to the notion of flat form of a class), or the immediate features plus those which the class inherits but somehow modifies through redefinition or effecting, although renaming does not count (*incremental* size)?

Various combinations may be interesting. For the present discussion the most interesting measure will be *external* and *incremental*: external size means that we take the client's view of the class, regardless of anything that is useful for internal purposes only; and incremental size means that we focus on the class's added value. With immediate size we would ignore the often important part of the functionality that is inherited; but with flat size we would be counting the same features again in every class and its descendants.

Maintaining consistency

Some authors, such as Paul Johnson, have argued for strong restraints on class size:

[Johnson 1995].

> *Class designers are often tempted to include lots of features (in both the language sense and system design sense of the word). The result is an interface where the few commonly used features are lost in a long list of strange routines. Worse yet, the list of possible features is infinite.*

ISE's experience suggests a different view. We have found that class size is not by itself a problem. Although most classes remain relatively small (a few features to a couple dozen), there is occasionally a need for bigger classes (up to 60 or even 80 features), and they do not raise any particular problem if they are otherwise well designed.

This experience leads to the **shopping list** approach: the realization that it does not hurt to add features to a class if they are conceptually relevant to it. If you hesitate to include an exported feature because you are not sure it is absolutely necessary, you should not worry about its effect on class size. The only criteria that matter involve whether the class fits in with the rest. These criteria can be expressed as a general guideline:

> ### Shopping List advice
>
> When considering the addition of a new exported feature to a class, observe the following rules:
>
> S1 • The feature must be relevant to the data abstraction represented by the class.
>
> S2 • It must be compatible with the other features of the class.
>
> S3 • It must not address exactly the same goal as another feature of the class.
>
> S4 • It must maintain the invariant of the class.

The first two requirements are related to the Class Consistency principle, which stated that all the features of a class must pertain to a single, well-identified abstraction The counter-example given there was that of a string class (from the original NEXTSTEP library) which actually covered several abstractions and, as a result, was eventually split into several classes. What is at issue here, however, is not size per se but design quality. *Page 730.*

It is interesting to note that the same example, string, is also one of the larger classes in ISE's libraries and has been criticized by Paul Johnson. But in fact the reaction from library users over the years has been the reverse: asking for more features. The class, although rich, is not particularly difficult to use because all the features clearly apply to the same abstraction, character string, and it is in the nature of that abstraction that many operations are applicable, from substring extraction and replacement to concatenation and global character substitution.

Class *STRING* shows that big does not mean complex. Some abstractions are just naturally endowed with many features. Quoting Waldén and Nerson:

> *A document handling class that contains 100 separate operations to set various font operations … may in fact only be dealing with one or a few underlying concepts which are quite familiar and easy to grasp. Ease of selecting the right operation is then reduced to having nicely organized manual pages.*

[Waldén 1995], *page 187.*

In such a case splitting the class would probably decrease rather than improve its ease of use.

An extreme "minimalist" view holds that a class should only include atomic features — those which cannot be expressed in terms of others. This would preclude some of the fundamental schemes of successful object-oriented software construction, in particular **behavior classes** in which an effective feature, for example a routine describing an iteration on a data structure, relies on other lower-level features of the class, often including some deferred ones. *"Don't call us, we'll call you", page 504.*

Minimalism would also prohibit including two theoretically redundant but practically complementary features. Consider a class *COMPLEX* to describe complex numbers, as developed earlier in this chapter. For arithmetic operations, some clients may need the function versions:

infix "+", infix "−", infix "∗", infix "/"

so that evaluating the expression $z1 + z2$ will create a new object representing the sum of $z1$ and $z2$, and similarly for the other functions. Other clients, or the same client in other contexts, may prefer the procedure versions, where the call $z1.add\ (z2)$ will update the $z1$ object to represent the result of the addition, and similarly for *subtract*, *multiply* and *divide*. In theory, it is redundant to include both the functions and the procedures, and either set can in fact be expressed in terms of the other. In practice, it is convenient to have both, for at least three reasons: client convenience; efficiency; and reusability.

Laxity and restrictiveness

In the last example the two sets of features, although theoretically redundant, are practically different. You should not, of course, introduce a feature if another already fills exactly the same need; this is covered by clause S3 of the Shopping List advice. That clause is more restrictive than it may seem at first. In particular:

*"CLASS EVOLU-TION: THE OBSO-LETE CLAUSE",
23.7, page 802.*

- Assume that you want to change the order of arguments of a routine, for compatibility with others in the same class or different ones. But you are concerned about compatibility with existing software. The solution in this case is *not* to keep both features with the same status; this would violate the advice. Instead, use the **obsolete** library evolution mechanism described later in this chapter.

- The same applies if you want to provide a default for an argument that used to be required for a certain routine. *Do not* provide two versions, one with the extra argument for compatibility, the other relying on a default along the lines discussed earlier in this chapter. Make one interface the official one; the other will be covered by the **obsolete** mechanism.

- If you hesitate between two possible names for a feature, you should almost always resist the temptation to provide both as synonyms. The only exceptions in ISE's libraries concern a handful of fundamental features for which it is convenient to have both an infix name and an identifier, for example array access which can be used as *my_array.item (some_index)* as well as *my_array @ some_index*, each form being preferable in some contexts. But this is a rare situation. As a general rule the class designer should choose a name, rather than passing the buck to client authors — penalizing them with the consequences of his indecision.

As you will have noted, the policy resulting from this discussion is a mix of laxity and restrictiveness. The policy seems lax because it explicitly encourages you to include acceptable features even if they have not yet proved to be essential. But it is in fact systematic and restrictive because it defines strong conditions for a feature to be considered acceptable. The features of a class should cover as many needs as possible; but they should only cover relevant needs and, for each distinct need, there should be just one feature.

> The Shopping List policy is only possible because we follow a systematic policy of keeping the *language* small. A minimalist attitude to language design — ensuring that we stick to a small number of extremely powerful constructs, and avoid redundancies — enables us to let class designers be non-minimalists. Every developer needs to learn the language and, if the language is minimalist enough, will know *all* of it. Classes, however, are only used by client authors, and they can skip what they do not use.

You should also relate the Shopping List advice to the preceding discussion of feature size. What might make a class difficult to use is not the number of its features but their individual complexity of use. More precisely, class size can only be a significant problem initially, by facilitating or hampering quick comprehension of the purpose and scope of a potentially reusable class which an application developer approaches for the first time. Even there, we have seen that size per se is less relevant than coherence (the Class Consistency principle). Past that stage, the reuser will, day in and day out, deal with the features of the class, or more commonly with a subset of these features. Feature size issues take precedence: a feature with many arguments to remember will make the task difficult. But class size has by then ceased to be relevant. Were you to rely on some arbitrary numerical criterion ("no class shall have more than m lines or n features"), the result could have been to split the class into several, in some cases making it *more* difficult to use.

The lesson for class developers, embodied in the Shopping List advice, is to worry about the quality of a class, in particular its conceptual integrity and the size of its features, but not about its size.

23.4 ACTIVE DATA STRUCTURES

Examples of this chapter and preceding ones have frequently relied on a notion of list or sequence characterized at any time by a "cursor position" indicating where accesses, insertions and deletions take place. This view of data structures, although different from most presentation in "algorithms and data structures" textbooks, is of broad applicability and deserves a more detailed explanation.

To understand the merits of this approach it will be useful to start with the more common one and assess its limitations.

Linked list representation

The discussion will be based on the example of lists. Although its results are independent of the choice of implementation, we need a specific representation to express the algorithms and illustrate the issues. Let us use a popular choice: linked lists. Our general-purpose library must have list classes and, among them, a class *LINKED_LIST*.

Here are a few basics about linked lists, applicable to all the interface styles discussed next — with and without cursors.

Linked lists are a useful representation of sequential structures because they facilitate operations of *insertion* and *deletion*. The successive elements will be housed in individual cells, or *linkables*, each containing a value and a reference to another linkable:

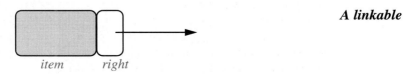

A linkable

item   *right*

The corresponding class, *LINKABLE*, should be generic, since we want the structure to be applicable to linked lists of any type. The cell value will be given by feature *item*, of type *G*, the generic parameter; this will be an in-place value if the actual generic parameter is expanded, for example for lists of integers or reals, and a reference otherwise. The other attribute, *right*, of type *LINKABLE* [*G*], always represents a reference.

The list itself is represented by a separate cell, the header, containing a reference *first_element* to the first linkable, and possibly some bookkeeping information such as the number of items, *count*. The figure shows the representation of a list of characters.

A linked list

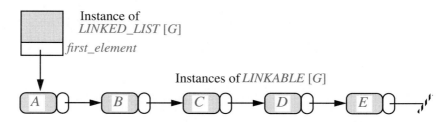

This representation makes insertion or deletion fast if you have a reference to the linkable immediately to the left of the operation's target: a few reference manipulations will do, as shown here for the deletion of the third element.

Deletion in a linked list

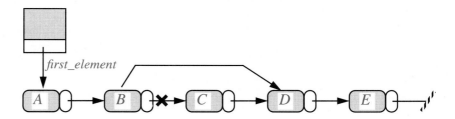

On the other hand, linked representation is not very good for finding an element known by its value or its position: these operations require sequential list traversal. Array representations, in contrast, are good for accessing by position, but poor for insertions and deletions. Many other representations exist, some of which manage to combine some of the best of both worlds. The basic linked list remains one of the most commonly used implementations, and is indeed an effective technique for applications that require many local insertions and deletions but few random accesses.

See "Uniform Access", page 55.
A technical point: the figure does not detail attributes of *LINKED_LIST* other than *first_element*, showing simply a shaded area. Although we could do with just *first_element*, the classes below will include an attribute *count* to record the number of elements of the list. This query could also be a function, but it would then be inefficient, requiring a traversal of the list to count its items each time a client asks us how many we have. Of course if you use an attribute you must make sure that every insertion or deletion updates it. The Uniform Access principle applies here: you can change the implementation without disturbing clients, which will in all cases use the same notation, *l•count*, to obtain the item count.

Passive classes

We clearly need two classes: *LINKED_LIST* for lists (more precisely, list headers), *LINKABLE* for list elements (linkables). Both are generic.

The notion of *LINKABLE* is essential for the implementation, but not relevant to most clients. We should strive for an interface that provides client modules with list primitives but does not bother them with such implementation details as the presence of linkable elements. The attributes, corresponding to the earlier figure, will appear as:

> **indexing**
>> *description*: *"Linkable cells, for use in connection with linked lists"*
>> *note*: *"Partial version, attributes only"*
>
> **class**
>> *LINKABLE1* [*G*]
>
> **feature** {*LINKED_LIST*}
>> *item*: *G*
>>> -- The cell value
>>
>> *right*: *LINKABLE* [*G*]
>>> -- The right neighbor
>
> **end** -- class *LINKABLE1*

For the type of *right* we might consider **like** *Current*, but it is preferable at this stage to keep more redefinition freedom as we do not know yet what may need to be changed by the possible descendants of *LINKABLE*.

To have a true class we need to add routines. What should clients be allowed to do on a linkable? They will need the ability to change the *item* and *right* fields. Also, we may expect that most clients creating a linkable will specify its initial value, requiring a creation procedure. This yields a proper version of the class:

> **indexing**
>> *description*: *"Linkable cells, for use in connection with linked lists"*
>
> **class** *LINKABLE* [*G*] **creation**
>> *make*
>
> **feature** {*LINKED_LIST*}
>> *item*: *G*
>>> -- The cell value
>>
>> *right*: *LINKABLE* [*G*]
>>> -- The right neighbor
>>
>> *make* (*initial*: *G*) **is**
>>> -- Initialize with item value *initial*.
>>
>>> **do** *put* (*initial*) **end**
>>
>> *put* (*new*: *G*) **is**
>>> -- Replace value with *new*.
>>
>>> **do** *item* := *new* **end**
>>
>> *put_right* (*other*: *LINKABLE* [*G*]) **is**
>>> -- Put *other* to the right of current cell.
>>
>>> **do** *right* := *other* **end**
>
> **end** -- class *LINKABLE*

For brevity the class omits the obvious procedure postconditions (such as **ensure** *item* = *initial* for *make*). There are no preconditions.

So much for *LINKABLE*. Now consider the linked lists themselves, to be accessed internally through their headers. Among others we need exported features to: obtain the number of elements (*count*); find out whether the list is empty (*empty*); obtain the value of the *i*-th element, for any legal index *i* (*item*); insert a new element at a certain position (*put*); change the value of the *i*-th element (*replace*); search for an element having a certain value (*occurrence*). We will also need a query returning a reference to the first element (void if the list is empty); it does not need to be exported.

Here is a sketch of a first version. Some of the routine bodies have been omitted.

```
indexing
        description: "One-way linked lists"
        note: "First version, passive"
class
        LINKED_LIST1 [G]
feature -- Access
        count: G
        empty: BOOLEAN is
                -- Is list empty?
            do
                Result := (count = 0)
            ensure
                empty_if_no_element: Result = (count = 0)
            end
        item (i: INTEGER): G is
                -- Value of i-th list element
            require
                1 <= i; i <= count
            local
                elem: LINKABLE [G]; j: INTEGER
            do
                from
                    j := 1; elem := first_element
                invariant j <= i; elem /= Void variant i — j until
                    j = i
                loop
                    j := j + 1; elem := elem.right
                end
                Result := elem.item
            end
        occurrence (v: G): INTEGER is
                -- Position of first element of value v in list (0 if none)
            do ... end
```

feature -- Element change

    put (*v*: *G*; *i*: *INTEGER*) **is**

                -- Insert a new element of value *v*

                -- so that it becomes the *i*-th element

        require

            1 <= i; *i <= count + 1*

        local

            previous, *new*: *LINKABLE* [*G*]; *j*: *INTEGER*

        do

                -- Create new cell

            !! *new•make* (*v*)

            if *i = 1* **then**

                -- Insert at head of list

                new•put (*first_element*); *first_element* := *new*

            else

                from

                    j := *1*; *previous* := *first_element*

                invariant

                    j >= 1; *j <= i — 1*; *previous /= Void*

                    -- *previous* is the *j*-th list element

                variant

                    i — j — 1

                until *j = i — 1* **loop**

                    j := *j + 1*; *previous* := *previous•right*

                end

previous

                    -- Insert after *previous*

                previous•put_right (*new*)

                new•put_right (*previous•right*)

            end

new

            count := *count + 1*

        ensure

            one_more: *count* = **old** *count + 1*

            not_empty: **not** *empty*

            inserted: *item* (*i*) = *v*

            -- For $1 <= j < i$, the element of index *j* has not changed its value

            -- For $i < j <= count$,

                -- the element of index *j* has the value

                -- that the element of index *j — 1* had before the call

        end

> *replace* (*i*: *INTEGER*; *v*: *G*) **is**
>> -- Replace by *v* the value of *i*-th list element.
>> **require**
>>> *1* <= *i*; *i* <= *count*
>> **do**
>>> ...
>> **ensure**
>>> *replaced*: *item* (*i*) = *v*
>> **end**

> **feature** -- Removal

>> *prune* (*i*: *INTEGER*) **is**
>>> -- Remove *i*-th list element
>>> **require**
>>>> *1* <= *i*; *i* <= *count*
>>> **do**
>>>> ...
>>> **ensure**
>>>> *one_less*: *count* = **old** *count* — *1*
>>> **end**

>> ... Other features ...

> **feature** {*LINKED_LIST*} -- Implementation

>> *first_element*: *LINKABLE* [*G*]
> **invariant**
>> *empty_definition*: *empty* = (*count* = *0*)
>> *empty_iff_no_first_element*: *empty* = (*first_element* = *Void*)
> **end** -- class *LINKED_LIST1*

It is a good idea to try to complete *occurrence*, *replace* and *prune* for yourself in this first version. (Make sure to maintain the class invariant.)

Encapsulation and assertions

Before we consider better versions, a few comments are in order on this first attempt.

Class *LINKED_LIST1* shows that even on fairly simple structures reference manipulations are tricky, especially when combined with loops. The use of assertions helps get them right (see procedure *put* and the invariant); but the sheer difficulty of this type of operations is a strong argument for encapsulating them once and for all in reusable modules, as promoted by the object-oriented approach.

Also note the application of the Uniform Access principle: although *count* is an attribute and *empty* a function, clients do not need to know these details. They are protected against any later reversal of these implementation decisions.

The assertions for *put* are complete, but, because of the limitations of the assertion language, not completely formal. Similarly extensive preconditions should be added to the other routines.

A critique of the class interface

How usable is *LINKED_LIST1*? Let us evaluate its design.

A worrying aspect is the presence of significant redundancies: *item* and *put* contain almost identical loops, and similar ones will need to be included in the routines whose code has been left to the reader (*occurrence*, *replace*, *remove*). Yet it does not seem possible to factor out the common part. Not a promising start.

This is an implementation problem, internal to the class: lack of reusability of the internal code. But it points to a more serious flaw — a poorly designed class interface.

Consider routine *occurrence*. It returns the index at which a given element has been found in the list, or zero if the element is not present. One drawback is that this only gives the first occurrence; what if the client wants to obtain the successive occurrences of a value? But there is a more serious difficulty. A client that has performed a successful search may, among other typical needs, want to change the value of the element found, to delete that element, or to insert a new one next to it. But any one of these operations requires traversing the list again! For example, *put* (*v, i*) goes through the first *i* elements, even if *i* is the result of *occurrence* — obtained by a similar traversal.

In the design of a general-purpose library component that will get used over and over, one cannot treat such inefficiencies lightly. Any performance overhead due to the increased generality of a reusable solution must remain negligible; otherwise developers will not accept paying the price, dooming any reuse policy. Here the price is not acceptable.

Simple-minded solutions

How can we remove the inefficiency? Two possible solutions come to mind:

- We could make *occurrence* return, instead of an integer, the *LINKABLE* reference to the cell where the requested value appears, or void for an unsuccessful search. Then the client has a direct handle on the actual linkable cell and may perform the needed operations without retraversal; it can for example use *LINKABLE*'s *put* procedure to change the value, and its *put_right* procedure to insert a new element. (Deletion is more delicate since the client would need the previous element too.)

- We could try to provide enough primitives to deal with various combinations of operations: search and replace, search and insert, search and delete and so on.

The first solution, however, defeats the whole idea of encapsulating data structures in classes: clients would directly manipulate the representations, with all the dangers involved. The notion of linkable is internal; we want client programmers to think in terms of lists and list values, not of list cells and pointers. Otherwise we lose data abstraction.

The second solution was attempted in an early version of ISE's libraries, which made an effort to provide routines covering common combinations of operations. To insert an element just before the occurrence of a known value, a client would use, rather than a call to *search* followed by a call to *put*, a single call to

insert_before_by_value (*v*: *G*; *v1*: *G*) **is**
                 -- Insert a new element of value *v* in front of first occurrence
                 -- of *v1* in list, or at end of list if no such occurrence
     do
         …
     end

This solution keeps the internal representation hidden from clients, while avoiding the inefficiencies of the initial version.

But we soon realized we were in for a long journey. Consider all the potentially useful variants: *search_and_replace*, *insert_before_by_value*, *insert_after_by_value*, *insert_after_by_position*, *insert_after_by_position*, *delete_before_by_value*, *insert_at_end_if_absent*, and more.

This raises troubling questions about the viability of the approach, forcing a reflection on library design. Writing general-purpose reusable software is a difficult task, and there is no guarantee that you will get everything right the first time — with a design that would follow the horizontal line in the figure below. You should be prepared to extend classes with new features as the library's usage reaches new users and new application domains. As represented by the colored line of the picture, however, the process must converge: after an initial tune-up period, the design should reach a stable state.

Evolution of a library class

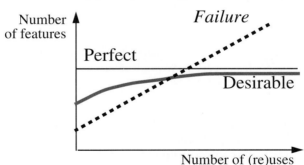

If not — that is to say, if almost every new use brings in the need for extension or modification, as represented by the dotted line in the figure — the approach to reusability is obviously flawed. This appeared to be the case with the list class we had at that point: it looked as if every time we put the list class to a new use the need would arise for yet another routine, representing a new combination of the basic operations.

To make matters worse, all such routines are rather complex, with loops similar to the one for *put*; they have much in common but all differ from each other by small details. The prospect of a robust, reusable linked list class seems to be receding.

Introducing a state

Fortunately, there is a way out. To find it requires taking a different view of the underlying abstract data type.

So far a list has been treated as a passive repository of information. To provide its clients with a better service, the list should become more active by "remembering" where the last operation was performed.

As noted earlier in this chapter, we should not hesitate to look at objects as machines with an internal state, and introduce both commands that change the state and queries on the state. In the first solution a list object already had a state, defined by its contents and modifiable by commands such as *put* and *remove*; but by adding more components to the state we will obtain a better interface, making the class both simpler and more efficient.

Besides the list contents, the state will include the notion of currently active position, or cursor; the interface will allow clients to move the cursor explicitly.

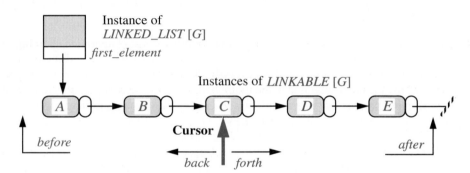

List with cursor

We permit the cursor to be on a list element (if any), or one position to the left of the first, in which case the boolean query *before* will return true, or one position to the right of the last, making *after* true.

An example of a command that may move the cursor is the procedure *search*, replacing the function *occurrence*. A call to *l.search* (*v*) will move the cursor to the first element of value *v* to the right of the current cursor position, or move it *after* if there is none. Note that in passing this solves the problem of finding multiple occurrences of *v*: just call *search* as many times as needed. (For symmetry we could also have *search_back*.)

The basic commands to manipulate the cursor are:

• *start* and *finish* to move the cursor to the first and last position if any.

• *forth* and *back* to move the cursor to the next and previous position.

• *go* (*i*) to move it to a stated position *i*.

Besides *before* and *after*, queries on the cursor position include *index*, its integer index (starting at 1 for the first element) as well as the booleans *is_first* and *is_last*.

The procedures to build and modify a list — insertion, deletion, replacement — become simpler because they do not have to worry about positions: they will simply act on elements at the current cursor position. All the loops disappear! For example, *remove* will not be called as *l•remove* (*i*) any more, but simply as *l•remove*, to delete the element at the current cursor position. We need to establish precise and consistent conventions about what happens to the cursor after each operation:

- *remove*, with no argument, deletes the element at cursor position and puts the cursor under its right neighbor (so that the value of *index* does not change in the end).

- *put_right* (*v*: *G*) inserts an element of value *v* to the right of the cursor and does not move the cursor (*index* is unchanged).

- *put_left* (*v*: *G*) inserts an element of value *v* to the left of the cursor and does not move the cursor (increasing the value of *index* by 1).

- *replace* (*v*: *G*) changes the value of the element at cursor position. The value of this element is given by the query function *item*, which now has no argument (and so could be implemented as an attribute).

Maintaining consistency: the implementation invariant

In building the class for such a fundamental data structure we must be careful to get everything right. Here assertions are indispensable. Without them we would be almost sure to miss some details. For example:

- Is a call to *start* permitted if the list is empty and, if so, what is its effect?

- What happens to the cursor after a *remove* if the cursor was on the last element? In other cases the cursor should go to the element immediately to the right of the deleted one, but here there is none. This is one of the reasons for the convention that was stated informally — allowing the cursor to move one position off to the right or to the left — but we need a more precise statement of this property, addressing all cases unambiguously.

Answers to questions of the first kind will be described by preconditions and postconditions.

See "Implementation invariants", page 376. For such properties as the permitted cursor positions, we should use the invariant, more precisely the clauses constituting the implementation invariant. Remember that an implementation invariant expresses the consistency of a representation, given by a class, vis-à-vis the underlying abstract data type. Here it will include the property

$0 <= index; index <= count + 1$

What about an empty list? We need to respect the symmetry between left and right. One solution, adopted in an earlier version of the library, is to consider that an empty list is both *before* and *after*, and constitutes the only case in which both of these properties may be true together. This works but leads, in the routines' algorithms, to frequent tests of the form **if** *after* **and not** *empty*… to distinguish between true cases of *after* and accidental ones resulting from *empty*. It turns out to be preferable to take the view that, conceptually, a list always has two extra *sentinel* elements, shown as 🖘 and 🖘 in the figure:

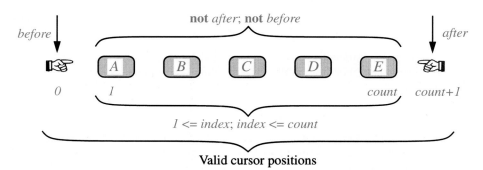

Valid cursor positions

The sentinel elements help us reason about the structure, but we will not necessarily store them in the representation. The implementation discussed next stores the left sentinel but not the right one; it is also possible to use an implementation that stores neither but still conforms to the conceptual model represented by the above figure.

Since we often want to state, for example as the precondition for an operation on an element given by its index, that the index indeed marks a position where the list has an element, we need a query to express this condition:

> *on_item* (*i*: *INTEGER*): *BOOLEAN* **is**
>
>> -- Is there an element at position *i*?
>
> **do**
>
>> *Result* := ((*index* >= *1*) **and** (*index* <= *count*))
>
> **ensure**
>
>> *within_bounds*: *Result* = ((*index* >= *1*) **and** (*index* <= *count*))
>>
>> *no_elements_if_empty*: *Result* **implies** (**not** *empty*)
>
> **end**

To state that there is an element at the cursor position, we may define query *readable*, whose value is that of *on_item* (*index*). This is a good example of the Shopping List principle: because *readable* is conceptually redundant, a minimalist policy would get rid of it; by including it we provide our clients with a better abstraction, freeing them from having to remember what exactly constitutes a valid item index at the implementation level.

The invariant will state that **not** (*after* **and** *before*). In the boundary case of an empty list, the picture becomes:

Empty list with sentinels

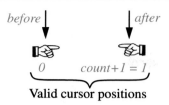

Valid cursor positions

So an empty list will have two possible states: *empty* and *before* and *empty* and *after*, corresponding to the two cursor positions in the figure. This seems strange at first but has no unpleasant consequence, and is in practice preferable to the earlier convention that *empty* = (*before* and *after*), now replaced by *empty* **implies** (*before* **or** *after*).

Note two general lessons here: the usefulness, as in many mathematics or physics problems, of checking boundary cases to verify that a general solution is sound; and the importance of relying on assertions to express the precise properties of a design. Here are some of the principal clauses of the invariant:

> $0 <= index$; $index <= count$
> $before = (index = 0)$; $after = (index = count + 1)$
> $is\_first = ((\textbf{not } empty) \textbf{ and } (index = 1))$; $is\_last = ((\textbf{not } empty) \textbf{ and } (index = count+1))$
> $empty = (count = 0)$
>   -- The next three clauses are theorems (deducible from the previous ones):
> $empty$ **implies** (*before* **or** *after*)
> **not** (*before* **and** *after*)
> $empty$ **implies** ((**not** is_first) **and** (**not** is_last))

For more clauses see page 791.

This example illustrates the general observation that writing the invariant is the best way to get a real understanding of what a class is about. The clauses seen so far apply equally to all implementations of sequential lists; they will shortly be complemented by a few others which are specific to the choice of a linked representation.

Exercise E23.6, page 807.

The last three clauses, as noted, are deducible from the others (prove them!). Invariants are not required to be minimal; it is often useful to list additional clauses such as these if they state important, non-trivial properties of the class. As we saw in the study of abstract data types, an ADT, and hence its implementation as a class, is a theory — here the theory of linked lists. The basic invariant clauses express the axioms of the theory; but any useful theory has interesting theorems too.

> Of course if you intend to monitor invariants at run time — meaning that you are not quite sure yet that the theory is sound! — you should also consider the effect of added clauses on execution time. But this only matters for development and debugging. In a usual production context there is no reason for monitoring the invariants.

The client's view

This design provides a simple and elegant interface to the implementation of linked lists. Operations such as "search and then insert" use two successive calls, although with no significant loss of efficiency:

l: LINKED_LIST [INTEGER]; m, n: INTEGER

...

l.search (m)

if not *after* **then** *l.put_right (n)* **end**

The call *search (m)* moves the cursor to the next occurrence of *m* after the current cursor position, or *after* if there is none. (The extract assumes that the cursor is initially known to be on the first element; if not, the client should execute *l.start* first.)

To delete the third occurrence of a certain value, a client will execute:

l.start; *l.search (m)*; *l.search (m)*; *l.search (m)*

if not *after* **then** *l.remove* **end**

To insert a value at position *i*:

l.go (i); *l.put_left (i)*

and so on. We have obtained a clear and easy to use interface by making the internal state explicit, and providing clients with the appropriate commands and queries on this state.

The internal view

The new solution simplifies the implementation just as it improves the interface. Most importantly, by giving each routine a simpler specification, concentrated on just one task, it removes unjustified redundancies, in particular all the unneeded loops. Insertion and deletion procedures no longer have to traverse the list; they just carry out a local modification. The responsibility of positioning the cursor now lies with other routines (*back, forth, go, search*), only some of which (*go* and *search*) need loops.

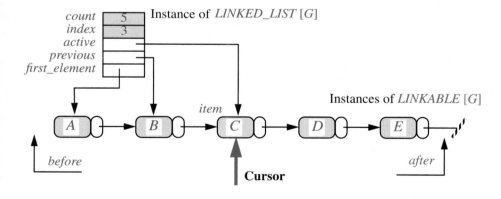

Cursor list representation (first variant)

Along with *first_element* it will be useful to keep two references in the list header, enabling us to perform insertions and deletions efficiently: *active*, attached to the cursor item at cursor position, and *previous* attached to the previous one.

Clients may know the state of the list by accessing public integer attributes *count* and *index* and boolean queries *before*, *after*, *is_first*, *is_last*, *item*. Here are two typical functions:

You should complete
before and is_last
based on this model.

after: BOOLEAN **is**

        -- Is there no valid position to right of cursor?

    do *Result* := (*index* = *count* + *1*) **end**

is_first: BOOLEAN **is**

        -- Is cursor on first item?

    do *Result* := (*index* = *1*) **end**

See "Routine header
comments: an exercise
in corporate downsiz-
ing", page 886.

Note the phrasing of the header comments. For *after*, "Is cursor to the right of last element?" would not be quite correct, since *after* may be true even if there is no element at all. Writing header comments so that they are clear, terse and accurate is an art form.

The query *item* returns the element at cursor position, if any:

item: G **is**

        -- Element at cursor position

    require

        readable: *readable*

    do

        Result := *active.item*

    end

Remember that *readable* indicates whether the cursor is on an element (*index* between 1 and *count*). Also note that *item* in *active.item* refers to the attribute in *LINKABLE*, not to the function of *LINKED_LIST* itself.

Here now are the basic cursor manipulation commands; they are fairly delicate to get right but, as a consolation, you may note that only a handful of routines, such as *start, forth, put_right, put_left* and *remove*, must perform non-trivial operations on references. Let us try *start* and *forth*. Procedure *start* must work for an empty list as well as a non-empty one; for an empty list the convention is that *start* brings the cursor to the second sentinel.

start1 **is**

        -- Move cursor to first position.

        -- (Provisional version; see next.)

    do

        index := *1*

        previous := *Void*

        active := *first_element*

    ensure

        moved_to_first: *index* = *1*

        empty_convention: *empty* **implies** *after*

    end

forth1 **is**

                    -- Move cursor to next position.

                    -- (Provisional version; see next.)

    require

        not_after: **not** *after*

    do

        index := *index* + *1*

        if *before* **then**

            active := *first_element*; *previous* := *Void*

        else

                check *active* /= *Void* **end**

            previous := *active*; *active* := *active*.*right*

        end

    ensure

        moved_by_one: *index* = **old** *index* + *1*

    end

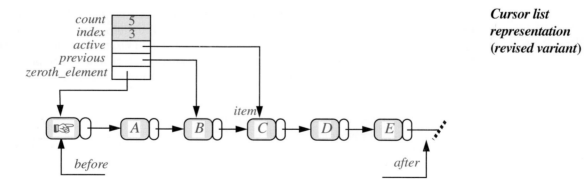

Here we stop! This is becoming too complicated and too inefficient. The performance of procedure *forth* is crucial, since a typical use of a list by a client is **from** *start* **until** *after* **loop** …; *forth* **end**. Can we get rid of the test?

We can, by taking the left sentinel seriously and always creating it when we create a list; the creation procedure *make* of *LINKED_LIST* is left as an exercise. We replace *first_element* by a reference *zeroth_element* to the sentinel:

Cursor list representation (revised variant)

The properties *zeroth_element* /= *Void* and *previous* /= *Void* will be part of the invariant (you must of course make sure that the creation procedure ensures them). They are precious since they will save many repeated tests.

Procedure *forth*, given here after the new *start*, is simpler and faster (no test!):

start **is**

  -- Move cursor to first position.

do

  index := 1

  previous := zeroth_element

  active := previous.right

ensure

  moved_to_first: *index = 1*

  empty_convention: *empty* **implies** *after*

  previous_is_zeroth: *previous = zeroth_element*

end

forth **is**

  -- Move cursor to next position.

  -- (Version revised for efficiency; no test!)

require

  not_after: **not** *after*

do

  index := index + 1

  previous := active

  active := active.right

ensure

  moved_by_one: *index =* **old** *index + 1*

end

It is convenient to define *go_before* which positions the cursor on the left sentinel:

go_before **is**

  -- Move cursor *before*.

do

  index := 0

  previous := zeroth_element

  active := zeroth_element

ensure

  before: *before*

  previous_is_zeroth: *previous = zeroth_element*

  previous_is_active: *active = previous*

end

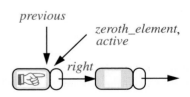

Procedure *go* is entirely defined in terms of *go_before* and *forth*:

go (*i*: *INTEGER*) **is**
                    -- Move cursor to *i*-th position.
    require
        not_offleft: *i* >= *0*
        not_offright: *i* <= *count* + *1*
    do
        from
            if *i* < *index* **then** *go_before* **end**
            invariant *index* <= *i* **variant** *i* – *index* **until** *index* = *i* **loop**
                forth
        end
    ensure
        moved_there: *index* = *i*
    end

Note the care exercised in avoiding useless traversal steps in *go*, the only one of procedures seen so far that needs a loop. For symmetry we should add *finish*, which brings the cursor to the last position and can be implemented as just *go* (*count* + *1*).

Although not really indispensable, it is convenient (Shopping List principle!) to export *go_before*. Then for symmetry we should also include and export *go_after*, which does *go* (*count* + *1*), and export it.

Also for symmetry is *back*, using *go*'s loop:

back **is**
                    -- Move cursor to previous position.
    require
        not_before: **not** *before*
    do
                        check *index* – *1* >= *0* **end**
        go (*index* – *1*)
    ensure
        index = **old** *index* – *1*
    end

However pleasing, the symmetry between *back* and *forth* is not without danger, since it may lead client authors to use both procedures freely even though *back*, which has to restart from the beginning of the list and perform *index* – *1* iterations of *forth*, is much more expensive. If you perform anything more than a few occasional *back*, the one-way linked list is inappropriate; you can for example use two-way linked lists. The corresponding class may be built as an heir to *LINKED_LIST* (a valid use of inheritance, since a list linked both ways is also linked one way) and is left as an exercise. Make sure to do this exercise at some stage if you want to reach a full mastery of the concepts.

Exercise E23.7, page 807.

The earlier invariant clauses, as noted, were implementation-independent. Here are a few more clauses capturing some of what we have learned about our implementation:

The first set of clauses was on page 785.

$empty = (zeroth\_element \boldsymbol{.} right = Void)$

$zeroth\_element /= Void; previous /= Void$

$(active = Void) = after; (active = previous) = before$
$(\textbf{not } before) \textbf{ implies } (previous \boldsymbol{.} right = active)$

$(previous = zeroth\_element) = (before \textbf{ or } is\_first)$
$is\_last = ((active /= Void) \textbf{ and then } (active \boldsymbol{.} right = Void))$

Most of the queries are straightforward. *before* should return the boolean value of $(index = 0)$ and *after* that of $(index = count + 1)$. The element at cursor position is given by

```
    item: G is
                -- Value of element at cursor position
        require
            readable: readable
        do
            Result := active.item
        end
```

Procedure *search* is similar to *go* and left to the reader. You should also write the procedure *i_th* (*i: INTEGER*) which returns the value of the element at position *i*; although concrete side effects are acceptable, be sure not to introduce any abstract side effect.

The last category of features includes procedures for insertion and deletion. The basic deletion operation is:

```
    remove is
                -- Delete element at cursor position and move cursor to its right neighbor.
                -- (If no right neighbor, list becomes after).
        require
            readable: readable
        do
            active := active.right
            previous.put_right (active)
            count := count — 1
        ensure
            same_index: index = old index
            one_less_element: count = old count – 1
            empty_implies_after: empty implies after
        end
```

The routine looks trivial; but this is only thanks to the technique of keeping the left sentinel around as a physical object, avoiding constant tests of the form *previous /= Void* and *first_element /= Void*. It is worth considering the more complicated and less efficient routine body that we would have obtained without this simplification:

Warning: rejected
version!

```
active := active.right
if previous /= Void then previous.put_right (active) end
count := count — 1
if count = 0 then
        first_element := Void
elseif index = 1 then
        first_element := active
-- else first_element does not change
end
```

In either case, the more you can express in assertions, the better you will understand what is going on and avoid mistakes.

You should exercise your understanding of these techniques by writing the insertion procedures *put_left* and *put_right*.

*Exercise E23.9,
page 808.*

Abstract data types and abstract machines

The notion of active data structure is widely applicable and in line with earlier principles of this chapter, Command-Query Separation in particular. Giving data structures an explicit state often yields simple, easy to document interfaces.

One might fear that the resulting structures would become less abstract, but this is not the case. Abstract does not mean passive. What the theory of abstract data types tells us is that our objects should be known through abstract descriptions of the applicable operations and their properties; but this does not imply treating them as mere repositories of data. By introducing a state and operations on that state, we actually make the abstract data type specification richer as it has more functions and more properties. The state itself is a pure abstraction, always accessed indirectly through commands and queries.

The view of objects as state machines reflects abstract data types which are more *imperative*, not less abstract.

Separating the state

It is possible to take the preceding techniques further. So far the cursor was just a concept, implemented indirectly through attributes *previous*, *active* and *index* rather than directly through one of the classes of the software. We can define a class *CURSOR* with descendants for various kinds of cursor structure. Then we can separate, for a structure such as a list, the attributes that describe the list contents (*zeroth_element*, *count*) from the traversal-related attributes, which will be stored in cursor objects.

Although we do not need to pursue this idea here, it is useful to note its possible application to a concurrent context. If a number of clients need to access a shared structure, they can each have their own cursors.

Merging the list and the sentinels

*Skip to "SELEC-
TIVE EXPORTS",
23.5, page 796.*

(This section describes an advanced optimization and may be skipped on first reading.)

The example of linked lists with the sentinels can benefit from one more optimization, which has indeed been applied to the latest versions of the ISE libraries. We will only take a peek at it because it is of a specialized nature and not relevant to normal application development. Such delicate optimizations should only be considered for widely used reusable components. (In other words: do not try this at home.)

Can we get the benefit of sentinels without wasting the corresponding space? As noted upon the introduction of the sentinel concept, we could treat the sentinels as fictitious; but then we would lose the crucial optimization which has enabled us to write the body of *forth* as just

index := *index* + *1*

previous := *active*

active := *active*.*right*

without the expensive tests of the earlier versions. We avoid these tests by making sure that, for a list in non-*after* state, *active* is never void (the corresponding invariant clause is (*active* = *Void*) = *after*); this is because we always have a real cell, the sentinel, available to serve as initialization for *active*, even for an empty list.

For a routine other than *forth*, the optimization would not be such a big deal. But *forth*, as noted, is the bread and butter of list processing by clients, resulting from the sequential nature of the lists; typical usage is of the form

from *your_list*.*start* **until** *your_list*.*after* **loop** …; *your_list*.*forth* **end**

and it is not uncommon, if you use a profiler tool to measure what happens during execution, to discover that the computation spends a good part of its time in *forth*. So it pays to optimize it, and the test-free form above indeed provides a dramatic improvement over the test-full one.

To get this time improvement, however, we pay a space penalty: each list now has an extra element, with no actual information. This would seem to cause a problem only if we have many short lists. But the problem can become more serious:

* In many cases, as hinted earlier, you will need two-way linked lists, fully symmetric, with *BI_LINKABLE* elements chained both ways. Class *TWO_WAY_LIST* (which, by the way, may be written as inheriting twice from *LINKED_LIST*, relying on repeated inheritance techniques) will need both a left and a right sentinel elements.

"Trees are lists and list elements", page 525.

* Linked trees present an even more serious problem. An important practical class is *TWO_WAY_TREE*, providing a convenient doubly-linked representation of trees. Building on ideas developed in the presentation of multiple inheritance, this class merges the notion of node and tree; it inherits from both *TWO_WAY_LIST* and *BI_LINKABLE*. But then every node is a list, a two-way one at that, and may have to carry both sentinels.

Although there are other ways to solve the second case — such as renouncing the inheritance structure — let us see if we can get the best of all worlds.

To find a solution let us ask an impertinent question. In the structure

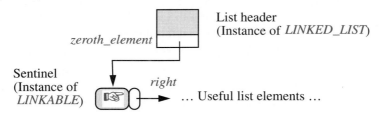

do we really need *two* bookkeeping-only objects? The truly useful information is in the part not shown on the figure, the actual list elements; to manage them we have added both a list header and a sentinel — two sentinels in the case of a two-way list. For long lists we are able to ignore this bloated bookkeeping structure, like a large company that has accumulated many layers of middle management in times of economic prosperity; but when the going gets tough it is time to take a closer look and see if we cannot merge a few of these management functions.

Can we indeed make the list header *itself* play the role of sentinel? It turns out we can. All that a *LINKABLE* needs is an *item* field and a *right* field. For a sentinel, in fact, only the *right* field. That field denotes the first of the list elements; so if we put it in the list header it will play the same role as what used to be called *first_element* in the first variant of the sentinel implementation. The problem, of course, was that *first_element* could be void, for an empty list, polluting all our algorithms with tests of the form **if** *before* **then**… We certainly do not want to go back to that situation. But we can keep the representation of the figure at the top of this page as the conceptual model, while getting rid of the sentinel object in the implementation. The concrete picture becomes

*first_element
appeared among
others in the figures
of page 786.*

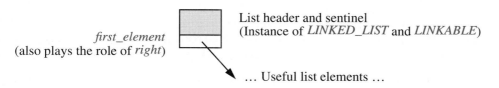

***Header as
sentinel (non-
empty list)***

The key to understanding this solution and getting things right is to remember that this solution is exactly the same conceptually as the last one, but replaces *zeroth_element* by a reference to the list header itself (*Current* in class *LINKED_LIST*), using *first_element* to represent what used to be *zeroth_element.right* (possibly void, but always defined since *zeroth_element* was never void). We still need a convention for the empty list, with no "Useful list elements"; in that case the last figure becomes

***Header as
sentinel
(empty list)***

with a simple convention: attaching *first_element* back to the list header itself. This way *first_element* will never be void — our crucial goal for keeping everything simple; we must just remember to replace, everywhere in class *LINKED_LIST*, any test of the form *zeroth_element.right* by *first_element = Current*.

We keep all the desirable invariant clauses of the previous sentinel versions:

> *previous /= Void*
> *(active = Void) = after*; *(active = previous) = before*
> (**not** *before*) **implies** (*previous.right = active*)
> *is_last = ((active /= Void)* **and then** *(active.right = Void))*

The clauses involving *zeroth_element*, which used to be

> *zeroth_element /= Void*
> *empty = (zeroth_element.right = Void)*
> *(previous = zeroth_element) = (before* **or** *is_first)*

now yield:

> *first_element /= Void*
> *empty = (first_element = Current)*
> *(previous = Current) = (before* **or** *is_first)*

All this is obtained simply (fasten your seat belts) by making *LINKED_LIST* inherit from *LINKABLE*:

class *LINKED_LIST* [*G*] **inherit**
> *LINKABLE* [*G*]
>> **rename** *right* **as** *first_element*, *put_right* **as** *set_first_element* **end**

… Rest of class as before, with the removal of *zeroth_element* as shown above …

Is it a kludge to let *LINKED_LIST* inherit from *LINKABLE*? Not at all! The whole idea was to merge the notions of list header and sentinel, that is to say, to consider a list header (an instance of *LINKED_LIST*) as a linkable too; so we have a perfect example of the "is-a" relation of inheritance. We have decided to treat every *LINKED_LIST* as a *LINKABLE*, so inheritance is the proper way to go. Here the client relation is not even in the race: not only would it not yield what we want, the removal of extra fat from our structures; it would *add* even more fields to our objects!

Make sure your seat belts are still securely fastened as we start considering what happens lower in the inheritance structure. *BI_LINKABLE* inherits twice from *LINKABLE*. Class *TWO_WAY_LIST* inherits from *LINKED_LIST* (once, or possibly twice depending on the implementation technique that we choose) and, in line with the technique just seen, from *BI_LINKABLE*. With all the repeated inheritance involved one might think that things would get out of hand and that our structures would start getting all kinds of unnecessary fields; but no, the rules on sharing and replication in repeated inheritance enable us to get exactly what we want.

The last step is *TWO_WAY_TREE* which, for good measure, inherits from both *TWO_WAY_LIST* and *BI_LINKABLE*. Enough, one might think, for a few heart attacks, but no; everything falls nicely into place. We get all the features we want, none of the features we do not want; all the sentinels are in place — conceptually — so that *forth*, *back* and all the consequent loops can be as fast as they need to be; and the sentinels do not take up any space at all.

This is indeed the scheme now applied to the affected classes in the Base libraries. Before we recover from the flight, a few observations are in order:

- Under no circumstance should this kind of work, involving tricky data structure manipulation, be undertaken without the full benefit of assertions. It is simply impossible to get them right without stating the invariant precisely, and checking that everything remains compatible with it.

- The machinery of repeated inheritance is essential. Without the techniques introduced by the notation of this book to enable a repeated descendant to obtain sharing or replication on a feature-by-feature basis, based on the simple criterion of feature names, it is impossible to handle effectively any situation involving serious use of repeated inheritance.

- To repeat the most important comment: such delicate optimizations are only worth considering in heavily used libraries of general-purpose reusable components. In normal application development, they are just too hairy to be worthwhile. The discussion has been included here to give the reader a glimpse of what it takes to craft professional components all the way to the end; but most developments will, happily, never have to undertake such efforts.

23.5 SELECTIVE EXPORTS

The relationship between classes *LINKABLE* and *LINKED_LIST* illustrates the importance, for a satisfactory application of the rule of Information Hiding, of supporting more than just two export modes, secret and generally available, for a feature.

Class *LINKABLE* should not make its features — *item*, *right*, *make*, *put*, *put_right* — generally available, since most clients have no business peeking into linkables, and should only use linked lists. But it cannot make them secret, for that would hide them from *LINKED_LIST*, their intended beneficiary. Such calls as *active.right*, essential to the operation of *forth* and other *LINKED_LIST* routines, would not be possible.

Selective exports provide the solution by enabling *LINKABLE* to select a set of classes to which, and to which only, it will export its features:

"SELECTIVE EXPORTS AND INFORMATION HID- ING", 7.8, page 191.

class
    LINKABLE [*G*]
feature {*LINKED_LIST*}
    item: *G*
    right: *LINKABLE* [*G*]
    etc.
end -- class *LINKABLE*

Remember that this makes the features available to all descendants of *LINKED_LIST*, as is indispensable if they need to redefine some inherited routines or add their own.

"Exporting to your-self", page 193.

Sometimes, as we saw in an earlier chapter, a class must export a feature selectively to itself. For example the heir *BI_LINKABLE* of *LINKABLE*, describing two-way linked lists with a field *left*, includes an invariant clause of the form

(*left* /= *Void*) **implies** (*left.right* = *Current*)

requiring *right* to be declared in a clause **feature** { ... Other classes ..., *BI_LINKABLE*}; otherwise the call *left.right* would be invalid.

Selective export clauses are essential when a group of related classes, as *LINKABLE* and *LINKED_LIST* here, need some of each other's features for their implementations, although these features remain private to the group and should not be made available to other classes.

"The architectural role of selective exports", page 209.

A reminder: in a discussion of an earlier chapter we saw that selective exports are a key requirement for the decentralized architectures of object-oriented software construction.

23.6 DEALING WITH ABNORMAL CASES

Our next interface design topic is a problem that affects every software development: how to handle cases that deviate from the normal, desired schemes.

Whether due to errors made by the system's users, to abnormal conditions in the operating environment, to irregular input data, to hardware malfunction, to operating system bugs or to incorrect behavior of other modules, special cases are the scourge of developers. The necessity to account for all possible situations, erroneous user input, failures of the hardware or of the operating system, and other modules' possibly improper processing, is a powerful impediment in the constant battle against software complexity.

This problem strongly affects the design of module interfaces What software developer has not wished that it would just go away? Then we could write clear, elegant algorithms for normal cases, and rely on external mechanisms to take care of all the others. Much of the hope placed in exception mechanisms results from this dream. In Ada, for example, you may deal with an abnormal case by writing something like

if *some_abnormal_situation_detected* **then**

    raise *some_exception*;

end;

"Go on with normal processing"

where execution of the **raise** instruction stops the execution of the current routine or block and transfers control to an "exception handler" written in one of the direct or indirect callers. But this is a control structure, not a method for dealing with abnormal cases. In the end you still have to decide what to do in these cases: is it possible to correct the situation? If so, how, and what should the system do next? If not, how quickly and gracefully can you terminate the execution?

We saw in an earlier chapter that a disciplined exception mechanism fits well with the rest of the object-oriented approach and in particular with the notion of Design by Contract. But not all special cases justify resorting to exceptions. The design techniques that we will now examine are perhaps less impressive at first — "low-tech" might be a good characterization — but they are remarkably powerful and address many of the possible practical situations. After studying them we will review the cases in which exceptions remain indispensable.

Chapter 12.

The a priori scheme

Perhaps the most important criterion in dealing with abnormal cases at the module interface level is specification. If you know exactly what inputs each software element is prepared to accept, and what guarantees it ensures in return, half the battle is won.

This idea was developed in depth as part of the study of Design by Contract. We saw in particular that, contrary to conventional wisdom, one does not obtain reliability by including many possible redundant checks, but by assigning every consistency constraint to the responsibility of just one class, either the client or the supplier.

"Zen and the art of software reliability: guaranteeing more by checking less", page 342.

Including the constraint in a routine precondition means assigning it to the clients. The precondition expresses what is required to make the routine's operation possible:

```
operation (x: …) is
    require
        precondition (x)
    do
        … Code that will only work if precondition is met …
    end
```

The precondition should, whenever possible, be complete, in the sense of guaranteeing that any call satisfying will succeed. If so, there are two ways to write the corresponding client extracts. One is to test explicitly:

```
if precondition (y) then
    operation (y)
else
    … Appropriate alternate action …
end
```

(For brevity this example uses an unqualified call, but of course most calls will be of the qualified form z.operation (y).) The other possibility avoids the **if…then…else** by ensuring that the context leading to the call ensures the precondition:

```
… Some instructions that, among other possible effects, ensure precondition (y) …
        check precondition (y) end
operation (y)
```

On **check** *see "AN ASSERTION INSTRUCTION", 11.11, page 378.*

As shown here and in many other examples throughout this book, it is desirable in this case to include a **check** instruction, with two benefits: making it immediately clear, for the reader of the software text, that you did not forget the precondition but instead checked that it would hold; and, in case your deduction was wrong, facilitating debugging when the software is executed with assertion monitoring on. (If you do not remember the details of the **check** instruction, make sure to re-read the corresponding section now.)

Such use of a precondition, which the client has to ensure beforehand — either by testing for it as in **if** *precondition* (*y*) ..., or by relying on other instructions —, may be called the a priori scheme: the client is asked to take advance measures to avoid any error.

With the a priori scheme, any remaining run-time failure signals a design error — a client not abiding by the rules. Then the only long-term solution is to correct the error, although we have seen that for mission-critical systems it is possible to devise software-fault-tolerant solutions which, on assertion violation, will attempt partial recovery through **retry**.

Obstacles to the a priori scheme

Because of its simplicity and clarity, the a priori scheme is ideal in principle. Three reasons, however, prevent it from being universally applicable:

A1 • Efficiency considerations make it impractical in some cases to test for the precondition before a call.

A2 • Limitations of practical assertion languages imply that some of the assertions of interest cannot be expressed formally.

A3 • Finally, some of the conditions required for the successful execution of a routine depend on external events and are not assertions at all.

An example of case A1, from numerical computation, is a linear equation solver. A function for solving an equation of the form $a\,x = b$, where a is a matrix, and x (the unknown) and b are vectors, might take the following form in an appropriately designed *MATRIX* class:

> *inverse* (*b*: *VECTOR*): *VECTOR*

so that a particular equation will be solved by $x := a.inverse\ (b)$. A unique solution only exists if the matrix is not "singular". (Singularity mans that one of the rows is a linear combination of others or, equivalently, that the determinant is zero.) We could make non-singularity the precondition of *inverse*, requiring client calls to be of the form

> **if** $a.singular$ **then**
>
>   ... Appropriate error action ...
>
> **else**
>
> $x := a.inverse\ (b)$
>
> **end**

This technique works but is very inefficient: determining whether a matrix is singular is essentially the same operation as solving the associated linear equation. Standard algorithms (Gaussian elimination) will at each step compute a divisor, called the pivot; if the pivot found at some step is zero or below a certain threshold, this shows that the matrix was singular. This result is obtained as a byproduct of the equation-solving algorithm; to obtain it separately would take almost as much computation time as to execute the entire algorithm. So doing the job in two steps — first finding out whether the matrix is singular, and then, if it is not, computing the solution — is a waste of effort.

Examples of A2 include cases in which the precondition is a global property of a data structure and would need to be expressed with quantifiers, for example the requirement that a graph contain no cycles or that a list be sorted. Our notation does not support this. As noted, we can usually rely on such assertions using functions; but then we might be back in case A1, as the precondition can be too costly to check before every call.

Finally, limitation A3 arises when it is impossible to test the applicability of the operation without attempting to execute it, because interaction with the outside world — a human user, a communication line, a file system — is involved.

The a posteriori scheme

When the a priori scheme does not work, a simple *a posteriori* scheme is sometimes possible. The idea is to try the operation first and then find out how it went; this will work if a failed attempt has no irrecoverable consequences.

The matrix equation problem provides a good example. With an a posteriori scheme, client code will now be of the form

```
a.invert (b)
if a.inverted then
        x := a.inverse
else
        … Appropriate error action …
end
```

Function *inverse* has been replaced by a procedure *invert*, for which a more accurate name might be *attempt_to_invert*. A call to this procedure sets the attribute *inverted* to true or false to indicate whether a solution was found; if it was, the procedure makes the solution itself available through attribute *inverse*. (An invariant clause in the matrix class may state that *inverted* = (*inverse* /= *Void*).)

With this method, any function that may produce an error condition is transformed into a procedure, the result being accessible, if it exists, through an attribute set by the procedure. To save space you may use a once function rather than an attribute if at most one answer is needed at any time.

This also works for input operations. For example a "read" function that may fail is better expressed as a procedure that attempts to read, and two attributes, one boolean indicating whether the operation succeeded and the other yielding the value read if any.

This technique, as you will have noted, is in line with the Command-Query Separation principle. A function that may fail to compute its intended result is not side-effect-free, and so is better decomposed into a procedure that attempts to compute the value and two queries (functions or attributes), one to ascertain success and the other to yield the value in case of success. The technique is also consistent with the idea of objects as machines, whose state can be changed by commands and accessed by queries.

The example of input functions is typical of cases that can benefit from this scheme. Most of the read functions provided by programming languages or the associated libraries are of the form "next integer", "next string" etc., requiring the client to state in advance the type of the element to be read. Inevitably, they will fail when the actual input does not match the expectation. A read procedure, on the other hand, can attempt to read the next input item without any preconception of what it will be, and then return information about its type through one of the queries available to clients.

This example highlights one of the constant rules for dealing with failure: whenever available, a method for engineering out failures is preferable to methods for recovering from failures.

The role of an exception mechanism

The preceding discussion has shown that in most cases methods based on standard control structures, principally essentially conditional instructions, are adequate for dealing with abnormal cases. Although the a priori scheme is not always practical, it is often possible to check success after attempting an operation.

There remain, however, cases in which both a priori and a posteriori techniques are inadequate. The above discussion leaves only three categories of such cases:

- Some abnormal events such as numerical failure or memory exhaustion can lead to preemptive action by the hardware or operating system, such as raising an exception and, unless the software catches the exception, terminating execution abruptly. This is often intolerable, especially in systems with continuous availability requirements (think of telephone switches and many medical systems).

- Some abnormal situations, although not detectable through a precondition, must be diagnosed at the earliest possible time; the operation must not be allowed to run to completion (for a posteriori checking) because it could lead to disastrous consequences, such as destroying the integrity of a database or even endanger human lives, as in a robot control system.

"Why run-time moni-toring?", page 398.

- Finally, the developer may wish to include some form of protection against the most catastrophic consequences of any remaining errors in the software; this is the use of exceptions for software fault tolerance.

Chapter 12.

In such cases, exception-based techniques appear necessary. The orderly exception mechanism presented in an earlier chapter provides the appropriate tools.

23.7 CLASS EVOLUTION: THE OBSOLETE CLAUSE

We try to make our classes perfect. All the techniques accumulated in this discussion tend towards that goal — unreachable, of course, but useful as an ever present ideal.

Unfortunately (with no intention of offending the reader) we are not ourselves perfect. What happens if, after a few months or a few years, we realize that some of the interface of a class could have been designed better? The dilemma is not pleasant:

- Favor the current users: this will mean continuing to live with an obsolete design whose unpleasant effects will be felt more and more sorely as time passes. This is known in the computer industry as *upward compatibility*. Compatibility, how many crimes have been committed in thy name! (as Victor Hugo almost wrote).

  The real Hugo quote is about Liberty.

  > According to Unix folklore, one of the less pleasant conventions of the Make tool, which has bothered quite a few novice users, was detected not too long after the first release. Since it implied a language change and the inconvenience was not a show-stopper, the decision was made to let things stand so as not to disturb the user community. The Make user community, at that time, must have included a dozen or two people at Bell Laboratories.

- Favor the future users: you cause trouble to the current ones, whose only sin was to trust you too early.

Sometimes — but sometimes only — there is a way out. We introduce into our notation the concept of **obsolete features** and **obsolete classes**. Here is an example of obsolete routine:

```
enter (i: INTEGER; v: G) is
        obsolete "Use put (value, index) instead"
    require
        correct_index (i)
    do
        put (v, i)
    ensure
        entry (i) = v
    end
```

This is a real example, although no longer current. Here is the context. Early in the evolution of the Base libraries, we realized that the names and conventions were not systematic enough; this is when the principles of style developed in chapter 26 of this book were codified. They entailed in particular using the name *put* rather than *enter* for the procedure that replaces an array element (and *item* rather than *entry* for the corresponding query) and, to make things worse, reversing the order of arguments, for compatibility with features of other classes in the library.

The above declaration smoothes out the evolution. Note how the old feature, *enter*, has a new implementation, relying on the new feature, *put*; you should normally use this scheme when making a feature obsolete, to avoid carrying along two competing implementations with the resulting reliability and extendibility risks.

What are the consequences of making a feature obsolete? Not much in practice. The tools of the environment must recognize this property, and output the corresponding warnings when a client system uses the class. The compiler, in particular, will output a message, which includes the string that has been included after the keyword **obsolete**, such as Use *put* (*value, index*) instead in our example. That is all. The feature otherwise continues to be normally usable.

Similar syntax enables you to declare an entire class as obsolete.

What you are providing your client developers, then, is a migration path. By telling them that a feature will be removed, you encourage them to adapt their software; but you are not putting a knife to their throat. If the change is justified — as it should be — users of the class will not resent having to update their part; what is unacceptable is, when they receive a new version, to be forced to do all the changes immediately. Given a little time, they will readily comply.

In practice, the migration period should be bounded. At the next major release — a few months later, a year at most — you should remove the obsolete features and classes for good. Otherwise no one will take obsolescence warnings seriously. This is why the example was mentioned above as "no longer current": *enter* and *entry* were removed several years ago. But in their short lives they helped keep more than one developer happy.

See "The module view", page 495.
Feature and class obsolescence only solve a specific problem. The comment made when we discussed the Open-Closed principle and how inheritance enables you to adapt a parent's design without disturbing the original is fully applicable here: when a design is *flawed*, the only reasonable approach is to correct it, while making your best efforts to help current users make the transition. Neither inheritance-cum-redefinition nor obsolescence should serve as cover-ups for bugs in existing software. But obsolescence is precious when the original design, while satisfactory in other respects, does not conform to your current views; it typically resulted from a narrower and less clear perspective than what you have gained now. Although there was nothing fundamentally wrong with the old design, you can do better: simpler interfaces, better consistency with the rest of the software, interoperability with other products, better naming conventions. In such cases, making a few features and classes obsolete is a remarkable way to protect the investment of your current users while moving ahead to an ever brighter future.

23.8 DOCUMENTING A CLASS AND A SYSTEM

Having mastered the most advanced techniques of class interface design, you build a set of great classes. To achieve the success they deserve, they will need good interface documentation. We have seen the basic documentation tool: the short form and its variant the flat-short form. Let us summarize their use and examine a complementary mechanism that works on entire systems rather than just classes.

See "Using assertions for documentation: the short form of a class", page 389, and "The flat-short form", page 543.
Mentions of the short form in this discussion will encompass the flat-short form as well. The difference between the two, as you will remember, is that the flat-short form takes inherited features into account, whereas the plain short form only relies on the immediate features introduced in the class itself. In most practical cases, the flat-short form is what client authors will need.

Showing the interface

The short form directly applies the rule of Information Hiding by removing all secret information from client view. Secret information includes:

- Any non-exported feature and anything having to do with it (for example, a clause of an assertion which refers to the feature).

- Any routine implementation, as given by the **do** ... clause.

What remains is abstract information about the class, providing authors of client classes, current or prospective, with the implementation-independent description that they need to use it effectively.

> Remember that the purpose is abstraction, not protection. We do not necessarily wish to prevent client authors from accessing secret class elements; we wish to relieve them from having to do so. By separating function from implementation, information hiding decreases the amount of information to be mastered; client authors should view it as help rather than hindrance.

See the "common misunderstanding" cited on page 52.

The short form avoids the technique (supported, without assertions, by Ada, Modula-2 and Java) of writing separate and partially redundant module interfaces, as this can mean trouble for evolution; as always in software engineering, repetition breeds inconsistency. Instead it puts everything into the class and relies on computer tools to extract abstract information.

The underlying principle was introduced at the beginning of this book: try to make the software as self-documenting as possible. In this effort, judiciously chosen assertions will play a fundamental part. Examining the examples of this chapter and constructing their short forms (at least mentally) should provide clear enough evidence.

"Self-Documenta-tion", page 54.

To help the short form deliver the best possible results, you should keep it in mind when writing your classes, and apply the following principle:

Documentation principle

Try to write the software so that it includes all the elements needed for its documentation, recognizable by the tools that are available to extract documentation elements automatically at various levels of abstraction.

This simply translates the more general Self-Documentation principle into a practical rule to be applied day to day by developers. Particularly important will be:

- Well-designed preconditions, postconditions and invariants.

- Careful choice of names for both classes and features.

- Informative indexing clauses.

Chapter 26.

The chapter on style will give precise guidelines on the last two points.

System-level documentation

The **short** and **flat-short** tools, when applied to software developed according to the rules developed in this book (assertions, Design by Contract, information hiding, clear and systematic naming conventions, header comments etc.) apply the Documentation principle at the module level. There is also a need for higher-level documentation — documentation on an entire system, or one of its subsystems — applying the same principle. But here textual output, although necessary, is not sufficient. To grasp the organization of a possibly complex system, you will want graphical descriptions.

The Case tool of ISE's environment, based on Business Object Notation concepts, provides such system views, as illustrated below for a session devoted to reverse-engineering of the Base libraries.

A system architecture diagram

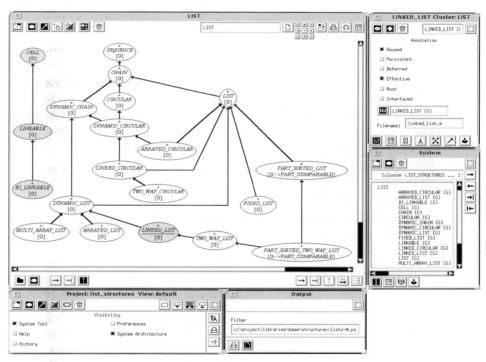

See [M 1995c].

Although further details fall beyond the scope of this discussion, we may note that the tool supports the exploration of large systems through zooming, unzooming and other abstraction mechanisms such as the ability to focus on a cluster (subsystem) or one of its subclusters as well as the entire system; also, it combines graphical views, essential to provide a general glimpse of an architecture, with textual information about the components of a system, dictionaries of abstractions etc.

All these tools are applications of the Documentation principle, tending towards the production of software which, thanks to carefully designed notations and with the help of advanced environments, should get us ever closer to the ideal of self-documentation.

23.9 KEY CONCEPTS INTRODUCED IN THIS CHAPTER

- A class should be known by its interface, which specifies the services offered independently of their implementation.

- Class designers should strive for simple, coherent interfaces.

- One of the key issues in designing modules is which features should be exported, and which should remain secret.

- The design of reusable modules is not necessarily right the first time, but the interface should stabilize after some use. If not, there is a flaw in the way the interface was designed. The mechanism of **obsolete** features and classes makes it possible to smooth over the transition to a better design.

- It is often fruitful to treat some data structures as active machines, with an internal state remembered from one feature call to the next.

- Proper use of assertions (preconditions, postconditions, invariants) is essential for documenting interfaces.

- Abnormal situations are best dealt with through standard control structures, either through the a priori scheme, which checks applicability before calling an operation, or through the a posteriori scheme, which attempts the operation and then examines whether it has succeeded. A disciplined exception mechanism remains necessary in cases when execution must immediately cancel a potential dangerous operation.

23.10 BIBLIOGRAPHICAL NOTES

The work of Parnas [Parnas 1972] [Parnas 1972a] introduced many seminal ideas on the design of interfaces.

The operand-option distinction, and the resulting principle, come from [M 1982a].

The notion of "active data structure" is supported in some programming languages by control abstractions called iterators. An iterator is a mechanism defined together with a data structure, which describes how to apply an arbitrary operation to every element of an instance of the data structure. For example, an iterator associated with a list describes a looping mechanism for traversing the list, applying a given operation to every list element; a tree iterator specifies a tree traversal strategy. Iterators are available in the programming language CLU [Liskov 1981]; [Liskov 1986] contains a detailed discussion of the concept. In object technology, we can implement iterators through classes rather than predefine them as language constructs; see [M 1994a], which applies to library design a number of ideas from the present chapter.

The example of the self-adaptive complex number implementation comes from [M 1979], where it was expressed in Simula.

Literate programming [Knuth 1984] emphasizes, like this chapter, that programs should contain their own documentation. Its concepts, however, are quite different from those of object technology; one of the exercises below invites you to compare the approaches.

Articles by James McKim and Richard Bielak [Bielak 1993], [McKim 1992a] [McKim 1995] present useful advice on class interface design based on the notion of Design by Contract.

EXERCISES

E23.1 A function with side effects

Function fresh appeared on page 299.

The example of component-level memory management for linked lists had a function *fresh* that calls a procedure, *remove* for stacks, and hence produces a side effect on the data structure. Discuss whether this is acceptable.

E23.2 Operands and options

Examine a class or routine library to which you have access and study its routines to determine, for each of them, which arguments are operands and which are options.

E23.3 Optional arguments

Some languages, such as Ada, offer the possibility for a routine of having optional arguments, each with an associated argument keyword; if the keyword is not included, the argument may be set to a default. Discuss which of the advantages of the Operand principle this technique retains, and which it fails to ensure.

E23.4 Number of elements as function

Adapt the definition of class *LINKED_LIST* [*G*] so that *count* is a function rather than an attribute, the interface of the class being unchanged.

E23.5 Searching in a linked list

Write the *LINKED_LIST* procedure *search* (*x*: *G*), searching for the next occurrence of *x*.

E23.6 Invariant theorems

Page 785.

Prove the three assertion clauses listed as theorems in the first part of the invariant for *LINKED_LIST*.

E23.7 Two-way lists

Write a class describing two-way linked lists, with the same interface as *LINKED_LIST*, but more efficient implementations of some operations such as *back*, *go* and *finish*.

E23.8 Alternative linked list class design

Devise a variant of the linked list class design using the convention that an empty list is considered both *after* and *before*. (This was the technique used in the first edition of this book.) Assess it against the approach developed in the present chapter.

See [M 1988], *sections 9.1 and A.5.*

E23.9 Insertion in a linked list

Drawing inspiration from *remove*, write the procedures *put_left* and *put_right* to insert an element to the left and right of the cursor position.

remove is on page 791.

E23.10 Circular lists

Explain why the *LINKED_LIST* class may not be used for circular lists. (Hint: show what assertions would be violated.) Write a class *CIRCULAR_LINKED* that implements circular lists.

E23.11 Side-effect-free input functions

Design a class describing input files, with input operations, without any side-effect-producing functions. Only the class interface (without the **do** clause describing the routine implementations, but with the routine headers and any appropriate assertions) is required.

E23.12 Documentation

Discuss, expand and refine the Self-Documentation principle and its various developments in this book, considering various kinds of documentation in software and examining what styles of documentation are appropriate in various circumstances and at various levels of abstraction.

E23.13 Self-documenting software

The approach to self-documenting software advocated in this chapter emphasizes terseness and does not readily support long explanations of design decisions. Knuth's "Literate programming" style of design combines techniques from programming, writing and text processing to integrate a program, its complete design documentation and its design history within a single document. The method relies on a classical paradigm: top-down development of a single program. Starting from Knuth's work, discuss how his method could be transposed to the object-oriented development of reusable components.

For references on literate programming see the bibliographic notes to this chapter.

24

Using inheritance well

*L*earning all the technical details of inheritance and related mechanisms, as we did in part C, does not automatically mean that we have fully grasped the methodological consequences. Of all issues in object technology, none causes as much discussion as the question of when and how to use inheritance; sweeping opinions abound, for example on Internet discussion groups, but the literature is relatively poor in precise and useful advice.

In this chapter we will probe further into the meaning of inheritance, not for the sake of theory, but to make sure we use it best to benefit our software development projects. We will in particular try to understand how inheritance differs from the other inter-module relation in object-oriented system structures, its sister and rival, the client relation: when to use one, when to use the other, when both choices are acceptable. Once we have set the basic criteria for using inheritance — identifying along the way the typical cases in which it is wrong to use it — we will be able to devise a classification of the various legitimate uses, some widely accepted (subtype inheritance), others, such as implementation or facility inheritance, more controversial. Along the way we will try to learn a little from the experience in taxonomy, or *systematics*, gained from older scientific disciplines.

24.1 HOW NOT TO USE INHERITANCE

To arrive at a methodological principle, it is often useful — as illustrated by so many other discussions in this book — to study first how *not* to do things. Understanding a bad idea helps find good ones, which we might otherwise miss. In too constantly warm a climate, a pear tree will not flower; it needs the jolt of Winter frost to attain full bloom in the Spring.

Extracts from "Software Engineering" by Ian Sommerville, Fourth edition, Addison-Wesley, 1993.

Here the jolt is obligingly provided by a widely successful undergraduate textbook, used throughout the world to teach software engineering to probably more computing science students than any other. Already in its fourth edition, it introduced some elements of object orientation, including a discussion of multiple inheritance. Here is the beginning:

> *Multiple inheritance allows several objects to act as base objects and is supported in object-oriented languages such as* [the notation of the present book] [M 1988].

The bibliographic reference is to the first edition of the present book. Apart from the unfortunate use of "objects" for classes, this is an auspicious start. The extract continues:

> *The characteristics of several different object classes*

(classes, good!)

can be combined to make up a new object.

(no luck). Then comes the example of multiple inheritance:

> *For example, say we have an object class CAR which encapsulates information about cars and an object class PERSON which encapsulates information about people. We could use both of these to define*

(will our worst fears come out true?)

> *a new object class CAR-OWNER which combines the attributes of CAR and PERSON.*

(They have.) We are invited to consider that every *CAR-OWNER* object may be viewed as not only a person but also a car. To anyone who has studied inheritance even at an elementary level, this will be a surprise.

As you will undoubtedly have figured out, the relation to use in the second case was client, not inheritance: a car owner *is* a person, but *has* a car. In pictures:

A proper model

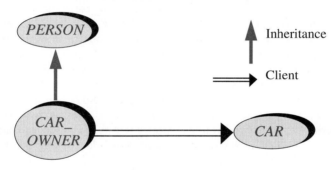

In formal words:

class *CAR_OWNER* **inherit**
    PERSON
feature
    my_car: *CAR*
    ...
end -- class *CAR_OWNER*

In the cited text, both links use the inheritance relation. The most interesting twist actually comes a little later in the discussion, when the author advises his reader to treat inheritance with caution:

> *Adaptation through inheritance tends to lead to extra functionality being inherited, which can make components inefficient and bulky.*

Bulky indeed; think of the poor car owner, loaded with his roof, engine and carburetor, not to mention four wheels plus a spare. This view might have been influenced by one of the picturesque phrases of Australian slang, about a car owner who does look as if he also *is* his car:

*"He has a head
like an Austin
Mini with the
doors open".*

Cartoon by Geoff
Hocking; from *The
Dictionary of
Aussie Slang*, The
Five Mile Press,
Melbourne,
Australia, reprinted
with permission.

Inheritance is a non-trivial concept, so we can forgive the author of this extract on the grounds that he was perhaps a little far from his home turf. But the example has an important practical benefit apart from helping us feel smarter: it reminds us of the basic rule on inheritance.

"Is-a" rule of inheritance

Do not make a class B inherit from a class A unless you can somehow make the argument that one can view every instance of B also as an instance of A.

In other words, we must be able to convince someone — if only ourselves to start with — that "every B is an A" (hence the name: "is-a").

In spite of what you may think at first, this is a loose rule, not a strict one. Here is why:

- Note the phrase "can somehow make the argument". This is voluntarily vague: we do not require a *proof* that every B is an A. Many cases will leave room for discussion. Is it true that "Every savings account is a checking account"? There is no absolute answer; depending on the bank's policies and your analysis of the properties of the various kinds of account, you may decide to make class *SAVINGS_ACCOUNT* an heir to *BANK_ACCOUNT*, or put it elsewhere in the inheritance structure, getting some help from the other criteria discussed in this chapter. Reasonable people might still disagree on the result. But for this to be the case the "is-a" argument must be sustainable. Once again our counter-example helps: the argument that a *CAR_OWNER* "is-a" *CAR* is *not* sustainable.

- Our view of what "is-a" means will be particularly liberal. It will not, for example, disallow *implementation inheritance* — a form of inheritance that many people view with suspicion — as long as the "is-a" argument can reasonably be made.

These observations define both the usefulness and the limitations of the Is-a rule. It is useful as a *negative* rule in the Popperian style, enabling you to detect and reject inappropriate uses of inheritance. But as a positive rule it is not sufficient; not all suggested uses that pass the rule's test will be appropriate.

Gratifying as the *CAR_OWNER* counter-example may be, then, any feeling of elation that we may have gained from it will be short-lived. It was both the beginning and the end of the unmitigated good news — the news that some proposed uses of inheritance are obviously wrong and easy to spot. The rest of this chapter has to contend with the bad or at least mixed news: that in just about all other cases the decision is a true design issue, that is to say hard, although we will fortunately be able to find some general guidelines.

24.2 WOULD YOU RATHER BUY OR INHERIT?

To choose between the two possible inter-module relations, client and inheritance, the basic rule is deceptively simple: client is *has*, inheritance is *is*. Why then is the choice not easy?

To have and to be

The reason is that whereas to have is not always to be, in many cases *to be is also to have*.

No, this is neither some cheap attempt at existentialist philosophy nor a pitch to make you buy a house if you are currently renting; rather, simple observations on the difficulty of system modeling. We have already encountered an illustration of the first property — to have is not always to be — in the preceding example: a car owner has a car, but by no twist of reasoning or exposition can we assert that he is a car.

What about the reverse situation? Take a simple statement about two object types from ordinary life, such as

> *Every software engineer is an engineer.*   [A]

whose truth we accept for its value as an example of the "is-a" relation (whatever our opinion may be as to the statement's accuracy). It seems hard indeed to think of a case which so clearly expresses "to be" rather than "to have". But now consider the following rephrasing of the property:

> *In every software engineer there is an engineer*   [B]

which can in turn be restated as

> *Every software engineer has an "engineer" component.*   [C]

Twisted, yes, and perhaps a trifle bizarre in its expression; but not fundamentally different from our premise [A]! So here it is: by changing our perspective slightly we can rephrase the "is" property as a "has".

*"COMPOSITE
OBJECTS AND
EXPANDED
TYPES", 8.7, page
254*

        If we look at the picture through the eyes of a programmer, we may summon an
object diagram, in the style of those which served to discuss the dynamic model in an
earlier chapter, showing a typical instance of a class and its components:

*A "software
engineer"
object as
aggregate*

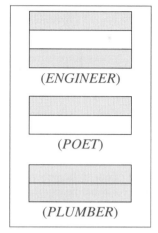

(*SOFTWARE_ENGINEER*)

        This shows an instance of *SOFTWARE_ENGINEER* with various subobjects,
representing the various posited aspects of a software engineer's personality and tasks.
Rather than subobjects (the expanded view) we might prefer to think in terms of references:

*Another
possible view*

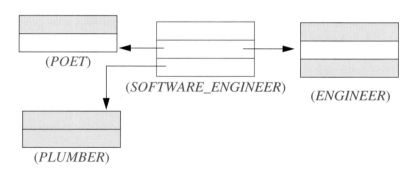

        Take both of these representations as ways to visualize the situation as seen from
an implementation-oriented mindset, nothing more. Both suggest, however, that a client,
or "has", interpretation — every software engineer has an engineer as one of his parts —
is faithful to the original statement. The same observation can be made for any similar
"is-a" relationship.

        So this is why the problem of choosing between client and inheritance is not trivial:
when the "is" view is legitimate, one can always take the "has" view instead.

The reverse is not true: when "has" is legitimate, "is" is not always applicable, as the *CAR_OWNER* example shows so clearly. This observation takes care of the easy mistakes, obvious to anyone having understood the basic concepts, and perhaps even explainable to authors of undergraduate texts. But whenever "is" does apply it is not the only contender. So two reasonable and competent people may disagree, one wanting to use inheritance, the other preferring client.

Two criteria fortunately exist to help in such discussions. Not surprisingly (since they address a broad design issue) they may sometimes fail to give a clear, single solution. But in many practical cases they do tell you, beyond any hesitation, which of the two relations is the right one.

Conveniently, one of these two criteria favors inheritance, and the other favors client.

The rule of change

The first observation is that the client relation usually permits change, while the inheritance relation does not. Here we must be careful with our use of the verbs "to be" and "to have" from ordinary language; so far they have helped us characterize the general nature of our two software relations, but software rules are, as always, more precise than their general non-software counterparts.

One of the defining properties of inheritance is that it is a relation between **classes**, not objects. We have interpreted the property "Class *B* inherits from class *A*" as meaning "every *B* object is an *A* object", but must remember that it is not in the power of any such object to change that property: only a change of the class can achieve such a result. The property characterizes the software, not any particular execution.

With the client relation, the constraints are looser. If an object of type *B* has a component of type *A* (either a subobject or an object reference), it is quite possible to change that component; the only restrictions are those of the type system, ensuring provably reliable execution (and governed, through an interesting twist, by the inheritance structure).

So even though a given inter-object relationship can result from either inheritance or client relationships between the corresponding classes, the effect will be different as to what can be changed and what cannot. For example our fictitious object structure

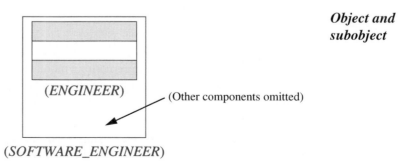

Object and subobject

(*ENGINEER*)

(Other components omitted)

(*SOFTWARE_ENGINEER*)

could result from an inheritance relationship between the corresponding classes:

class *SOFTWARE_ENGINEER_1* **inherit**

    ENGINEER

feature

    …

end -- class *SOFTWARE_ENGINEER_1*

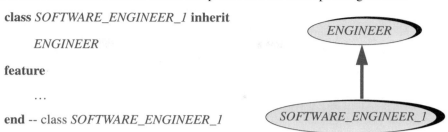

but it could just as well have been obtained through the client relation:

class *SOFTWARE_ENGINEER_2* **feature**

    the_engineer_in_me: *ENGINEER*

    …

end -- class *SOFTWARE_ENGINEER_2*

which could in fact be

class *SOFTWARE_ENGINEER_3* **feature**

    the_truly_important_part_of_me: *VOCATION*

    …

end -- class *SOFTWARE_ENGINEER_3*

provided we satisfy the type rules by making class *ENGINEER* a descendant of class *VOCATION*.

> Strictly speaking the last two variants represent a slightly different situation from the first if we assume that none of the given classes is expanded: instead of subobjects, the "software engineer" objects will in the last two cases contain *references* to "engineer" objects, as in the second figure of page 813. The introduction of references, however, does not fundamentally affect this discussion.

With the first class definition, because the inheritance relationship holds between the generating classes, it is not possible to modify the object relationship dynamically: once an engineer, always an engineer.

But with the other two definitions such a modification is possible: a procedure of the "software engineer" class can assign a new value to the corresponding object field (the field for *the_engineer_in_me* or *the_truly_important_part_of_me*). In the case of class *SOFTWARE_ENGINEER_2* the new value must be of type *ENGINEER* or compatible; but with class *SOFTWARE_ENGINEER_3* it may be of any type compatible with *VOCATION*. So our software can model the idea of a software engineer who, after many years of pretending to be an engineer, finally sheds that part of his personality in favor of something that he deems more representative of his work, such as poet or plumber.

This yields our first criterion:

> ### Rule of change
>
> Do not use inheritance to describe a perceived "is-a" relation if the corresponding object components may have to be changed at run time.

Only use inheritance if the corresponding inter-object relation is permanent. In other cases, use the client relation.

The really interesting case is the one illustrated by *SOFTWARE_ENGINEER_3*. With *SOFTWARE_ENGINEER_2* you can only replace the engineer component with another of exactly same type. But in the *SOFTWARE_ENGINEER_3* scheme, *VOCATION* should be a high-level class, most likely deferred; so the attribute can (through polymorphism) represent objects of many possible types, all conforming to *VOCATION*.

This also means that even though this solution uses client as the primary relation, in practice its final form will often use inheritance as a complement. This will be particularly clear when we come to the notion of handle.

The polymorphism rule

Now for a criterion that will require inheritance and exclude client. That criterion is simple: polymorphic uses. In our study of inheritance we have seen that with a declaration of the form

  x: *C*

x denotes at run time (assuming class C is not expanded) a potentially polymorphic reference; that is to say, x may become attached to direct instances not just of C but of any proper descendants of C. This property is of course a key contribution to the power and flexibility of the object-oriented method, especially through its corollary, the possibility of defining polymorphic data structures, such as a *LIST* [*C*] which may contains instances of any of C's descendants.

In our example, this means that with the *SOFTWARE_ENGINEER_1* solution — the form of the class which inherits from *ENGINEER* — a client can declare an entity

  eng: *ENGINEER*

which may become attached at run time to an object of type *SOFTWARE_ENGINEER_1*. Or we can have a list of engineers, or a database of engineers, which includes a few mechanical engineers, a few chemical engineers, and a few software engineers as well.

A reminder on methodology: the use of non-software words is a good help for understanding the concepts, but we should not let ourselves get carried away by such anthropomorphic examples; the objects of interest are software objects. So although we may loosely understand the words "a software engineer" for what they say, they actually denote an instance of *SOFTWARE_ENGINEER_1*, that is to say, a software object somehow modeling a real person.

Such polymorphic effects require inheritance: with *SOFTWARE_ENGINEER_2* or *SOFTWARE_ENGINEER_3* there is no way an entity or data structure of type *ENGINEER* can directly denote "software engineer" objects.

Generalizing these observations — which are not, of course, specific to the example — yields the complement of the rule of change:

Polymorphism rule

Inheritance is appropriate to describe a perceived "is-a" relation if entities or data structure components of the more general type may need to become attached to objects of the more specialized type.

Summary

Although it brings no new concept, the following rule will be convenient as a summary of this discussion of criteria for and against inheritance.

Choosing between client and inheritance

In deciding how to express the dependency of a class *B* on a class *A*, apply the following criteria:

CI1 • If every instance of *B* initially has a component of type *A*, but that component may need to be replaced at run time by an object of a different type, make *B* a client of *A*.

CI2 • If there is a need for entities of type *A* to denote objects of type *B*, or for polymorphic structures containing objects of type *A* of which some may be of type *B*, make *B* an heir of *A*.

24.3 AN APPLICATION: THE HANDLE TECHNIQUE

Here is an example using the preceding rule. It yields a design pattern of wide applicability: *handles*.

The first design of the *Vision* library for platform-independent graphics encountered a general problem: how to account for platform dependencies. The first solution used multiple inheritance in the following way: a typical class, such as the one describing windows, would have a parent describing the platform-independent properties of the corresponding abstraction, and another providing the platform-specific elements.

```
class WINDOW inherit
    GENERAL_WINDOW
    PLATFORM_WINDOW
feature
    ...
end -- class WINDOW
```

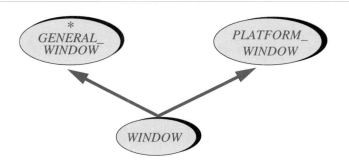

Platform
adaptation
through
inheritance

Class *GENERAL_WINDOW* and similar ones such as *GENERAL_BUTTON* are deferred: they express all that can be said about the corresponding graphical objects and the applicable operations without reference to a particular graphical platform. Classes such as *PLATFORM_WINDOW* provide the link to a graphical platform such as Windows, OS/2-Presentation-Manager or Unix-Motif; they give access to the platform-specific mechanisms (encapsulated through a library such as WEL or MEL).

On the platform-specific libraries WEL and MEL see "Object-oriented re-architecturing", page 441

A class such as *WINDOW* will then combine its two parents through features which effect (implement) the deferred features of *GENERAL_WINDOW* by using the implementation mechanisms provided by *PLATFORM_WINDOW*.

PLATFORM_WINDOW (like all other similar classes) needs several variants, one for each platform. These identically named classes will be stored in different directories; the Ace for a compilation (the control file) will select the appropriate one.

On the notion of Ace see "Assembling a system", page 198

This solution works, but it has the drawback of tying the notion of *WINDOW* closely to the chosen platform. To transpose an earlier comment about inheritance: once a Motif window, always a Motif window. This may not be too bad, as it is hard to imagine a Unix window which, suddenly seized by middle-age anxiety, decides to become an OS/2 window. The picture becomes less absurd if we expand our definition of "platform" to include formats such as Postscript or HTML; then a graphical object could change representation for purposes of printing or inclusion in a Web document.

The observation that we might need a looser connection between GUI objects such as a window and the underlying toolkit suggests trying the client relation. An inheritance link will remain, between *WINDOW* and *GENERAL_WINDOW*; but the platform dependency will be represented by a client link to a class *TOOLKIT* representing the underlying "toolkit" (graphical platform). The figure at the top of the facing page illustrates the resulting structure, involving both client and inheritance.

An interesting aspect of this solution is that it recognizes the notion of toolkit as a full-fledged abstraction, represented by a deferred class *TOOLKIT*. Each specific toolkit is then represented by an effective descendant of *TOOLKIT* such as *MOTIF* or *MS_WINDOWS*.

Here is how it works. Each class describing graphical objects, such as *WINDOW*, has an attribute providing access to the underlying platform:

handle: *TOOLKIT*

Platform adaptation through a handle

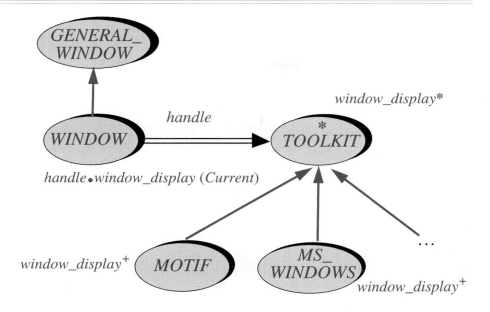

This will yield a field in each instance of the class. It is possible to change the handle:

set_handle (*new*: *TOOLKIT*) **is**
>   -- Make *new* the new handle for this object.
>   **do**
>>   *handle* := *new*
>   **end**

A typical operation inherited from *GENERAL_WINDOW* in deferred form will be effected through a call to the platform's mechanism:

display **is**
>   -- Display window on screen.
>   **do**
>>   *handle*.*window_display* (*Current*)
>   **end**

Through the handle, the graphical object asks the platform to perform the required operation. A feature such as *window_display* is deferred in class *TOOLKIT* and effected variously for its various descendants such as *MOTIF*.

Note that it would be inappropriate to draw from this example the conclusion "Aha! Another case in which inheritance was overused, and the final version stays away from it." The initial version was not wrong; in fact it works quite well, but is less flexible than the second one. And that second version fundamentally relies on inheritance and the consequent techniques of polymorphism and dynamic binding, which it combines with the client relation. Without the *TOOLKIT*-rooted inheritance hierarchy, the polymorphic entity *handle*, and dynamic binding on features such as *window_display*, it would not work. Far from being a rejection of inheritance, then, this technique illustrates a more sophisticated form of inheritance.

The handle technique is widely applicable to the development of libraries supporting multi-platform compatibility. Besides the *Vision* graphical library, we have applied it to the *Store* database library, where the notion of platform covers various SQL-based relational database interfaces such as Oracle, Ingres, Sybase and ODBC.

24.4 TAXOMANIA

For every one of the inheritance categories introduced later in this chapter, the heir redeclares (redefines or effects) some inherited features, or introduces features of its own, or adds to the invariant. (It may of course do several of these things.) A consequence is:

> ### Taxomania rule
>
> Every heir must introduce a feature, redeclare an inherited feature, or add an invariant clause.

This is actually a consequence of the Inheritance rule seen later in this chapter, page 822.

What this rule addresses is a foible sometimes found in newcomers who have been won over to the O-O method, and enthusiastically start seeing taxonomical divisions everywhere (hence the name of the rule, a shortcut for "taxonomy mania"). The result is over-complicated inheritance hierarchies. Taxonomy and inheritance are meant to *help* us master complexity, not to introduce complexity. Adding useless classification levels is self-defeating.

As is so often the case, you can gain the proper perspective — and bring the neophytes back to reason — by keeping in mind the ADT view at all times. A class is the implementation, partial or total, of an abstract data type. Different classes, in particular a parent and an heir, should describe different ADTs. Then, because an ADT is entirely characterized by the applicable features and their properties (captured in the class by assertions), a new class should change an inherited feature, introduce a new feature or change some assertion. Since you can only change a precondition or postcondition by redefining the enclosing feature, the last case means the addition of an invariant clause (as in *restriction inheritance*, one of the categories in our taxonomy).

You may occasionally justify a case of taxomania — a class that does not bring anything new of its own, apart from its existence — on the grounds that the heir class describes an important variant of the notion described by the parent, and that you are introducing it now to pave the way for future introduction or redeclaration of features, even if none has occurred so far. This may be valid when the inheritance structure corresponds to a generally accepted classification in the problem domain. But you should always be wary of such cases, and resist the introduction of new featureless classes unless you can find compelling arguments.

Here is an example. Assume a certain system or library includes a class *PERSON* and that you are considering adding heirs *MALE* and *FEMALE*. Is this justified? You will have to take a closer look. A personnel management system that includes gender-specific features, pertaining for example to maternity leave, may benefit from having heir classes *MALE* and *FEMALE*. But in many other cases the variants, if present, would have no specific features; for example statistical software that just records the gender of individuals may be better off with a single class *PERSON* and a boolean attribute

> *female*: BOOLEAN

or perhaps

> *Female*: INTEGER **is unique**
> *Male*: INTEGER **is unique**

rather than new heirs. Yet if there is any chance that specific features will be added later on, the corresponding classification is so clearly known in the problem domain that you may prefer to introduce these heirs anyway.

One guideline to keep in mind is the Single Choice principle. We have learned to distrust the use of explicit variant lists, as implemented by **unique** constants, for fear of finding our software polluted with conditional instructions of the form

> **if** *female* **then**
>
>   …
>
> **else**
>
>   …

or **inspect** instructions. This is, however, not too much of a concern here:

- One of the principal criticisms against this style was that any addition of a variant would cause a chain reaction of changes throughout the software, but in certain cases — such as the above example — we can be confident there will be no new variants.

- Even with a fixed set of variants, the explicit **if** … style is less effective than relying on dynamic binding through calls such as *this_person.some_operation* where *MALE* and *FEMALE* have different redeclarations of *some_operation*. But then if we do need to discriminate on a person's gender we violate the premise of this discussion — that there are no features specific to the variants. If such features do exist, inheritance is justified.

The last comment alerts us to the real difficulty. Simple cases of taxomania — in which the patient needlessly adds intermediate nodes all over the inheritance structure — are relatively easy to diagnose (by noticing classes that have no specific features) and cure. But what if the variants *do* have specific features, although the resulting classification conflicts with other criteria? A personnel management system for which we can justify a class *FEMALE_EMPLOYEE* because of a few specific features might have other distinctions as well, such as permanent versus temporary employees, or supervisory versus non-supervisory ones. Then we do not have taxomania any more, but face a general and delicate problem, *multi-criteria classification*, whose possible solutions are discussed later in this chapter.

24.5 USING INHERITANCE: A TAXONOMY OF TAXONOMY

The power of inheritance comes from its versatility. True, this also makes it scary at times, causing many authors to impose restrictions on the mechanism. While understanding these fears and even sometimes sharing them — do the boldest not harbor the occasional doubt and anxiety? — we should overcome them and learn to enjoy inheritance under all of its legitimate variants, which will now be explored.

After recalling some commonly encountered wrong uses of inheritance we will individually review the valid uses:

- Subtype inheritance.

- View inheritance.

- Restriction inheritance.

- Extension inheritance.

- Functional variation inheritance

- Type variation inheritance.

- Reification inheritance.

- Structure inheritance.

- Implementation inheritance.

- Facility inheritance (with two special variants: constant inheritance and machine inheritance).

Some of these categories (subtype, view, implementation, facility) raise specific issues and will be discussed in more detail in separate sections.

Scope of the rules

The relatively broad view of inheritance taken in this book in no way means that "anything goes". We accept and in fact encourage certain forms of inheritance on which some authors frown; but of course there are many ways to misuse inheritance, and not just *CAR_OWNER*. So the inevitable complement of our broad-mindedness is a particularly strict constraint:

Inheritance rule

Every use of inheritance should belong to one of the accepted categories.

This rule is stern indeed: it states that the types of use of inheritance are known and that if you encounter a case that is not covered by one of these types you should just *not* use inheritance.

What are "the accepted categories"? The implicit meaning is "the accepted categories, as discussed in the rest of this section". I indeed hope that all meaningful uses are covered. But the phrasing is a little more careful because the taxonomy may need further thinking. I found precious little in the literature about this topic; the most useful reference is an unpublished Ph. D. thesis [Girod 1991]. So it is quite possible that this attempt at classification has missed some categories. But the rule indicates that if you see a possible use of inheritance that does not fall into one of the following categories, you should give it serious thought. Most likely you should not use inheritance in that case; if after further reflection you are still convinced that inheritance is appropriate, and you are still unable to attach your example to one of the categories of this chapter, then you may have a new contribution to the literature.

Page 820.

> We already saw a consequence of the Inheritance rule: the Taxomania rule, which states that every heir class should redeclare or introduce a feature, or change some assertion. It follows directly from the observation that every legitimate form of inheritance detailed below requires the heir to perform at least one of these operations.

The Inheritance rule does not prohibit inheritance links that belong to *more than one* of the inheritance categories. Such practice is, however, not recommended:

Inheritance Simplicity rule

A use of inheritance should preferably belong to just one of the accepted categories.

See "Advisories", page 667.

This is not an absolute rule but what an earlier discussion called an "advisory positive". The rationale for the rule is once again the desire for simplicity and clarity: if whenever you introduce an inheritance link between two classes you apply explicit methodological principles, and in particular decide which one of the approved variants you will be using, you are less likely to make a design mistake or to produce a messy, hard-to-use and hard-to-maintain system structure.

A compelling argument does not seem to exist, however, for making the rule absolute, and once in a while it may be convenient to use a single inheritance link for two of the goals captured by the classification. Such cases remain a minority.

> Unfortunately I do not know of a simple criterion that would unambiguously tell us when it is all right to collapse several inheritance categories into one link. Hence the advisory nature of the Inheritance Simplicity rule. The reader's judgment, based on a clear understanding of the methodology of inheritance, should decide any questionable case.

Wrong uses

The preceding two rules confirm the obvious: that it is possible to misuse inheritance. Here is a list of typical mistakes, most of which have already been mentioned. Human ability for mischief being what it is, we can in no way hope for completeness, but a few common mistakes are easy to identify.

The first is **"has" relation with no "is" relation.** *CAR_OWNER* served as an example — extreme but not unique. Over the years I have heard or seen a few similar ones, often as purported examples of multiple inheritance, such as *APPLE_PIE* inheriting from *APPLE* and from *PIE*, or (this one reported by Adele Goldberg) *ROSE_TREE* inheriting from *ROSE* and from *TREE*.

Another is a typical case of **taxomania** in which a simple boolean property, such as a person's gender (or a property with a few fixed values, such as the color of a traffic light) is used as an inheritance criterion even though no significant feature variants depend on it.

A third typical mistake is **convenience inheritance**, in which the developer sees some useful features in a class and inherits from that class simply to reuse these features. What is wrong here is neither the act of "using inheritance for implementation", nor "inheriting a class for its features", both of which are acceptable forms of inheritance studied later in this chapter, but the use of a class as a parent *without the proper is-a relationship between the corresponding abstractions* — or in some cases without adequate abstractions at all.

General taxonomy

On now to the valid uses of inheritance. The list will include twelve different categories, conveniently grouped into three broad families:

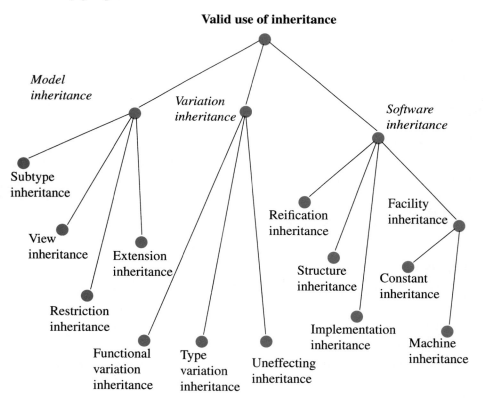

Valid use of inheritance

Classification of the valid categories of inheritance

The classification is based on the observation that any software system reflects a certain external model, itself connected with some outside reality in the software's application domain. Then we may distinguish:

- Model inheritance, reflecting "is-a" relations between abstractions in the model.

- Software inheritance, expressing relations within the software, with no obvious counterpart in the model.

- Variation inheritance — a special case that may pertain either to the software or to the model — serving to describe a class through its differences with another class.

These three general categories facilitate understanding, but the most important properties are captured by the final categories (the tree leaves on the preceding figure).

Exercise E24.2, page 869.

Since the classification is itself a taxonomy, you may want to ask yourself, out of curiosity, how the identified categories apply to it. This is the topic of an exercise.

The definitions which follow all use the names A for the parent class and B for the heir.

Naming convention for definitions of inheritance categories

Each definition will state which of A and B is permitted to be deferred, and which effective. A table at the end of the discussion recalls the applicable categories for each deferred-effective combination.

Subtype inheritance

We start with the most obvious form of model inheritance. You are modeling some external system where a category of (external) objects can be partitioned into disjoint subcategories — as with closed figures, partitioned into polygons, ellipses etc. — and you use inheritance to organize the corresponding classes in the software. A bit more formally:

Definition: subtype inheritance

Subtype inheritance applies if A and B represent certain sets A' and B' of external objects such that B' is a subset of A' and the set modeled by any other subtype heir of A is disjoint from B'. A must be deferred.

A' could be the set of closed figures, B' the set of polygons, A and B the corresponding classes. In most practical cases the "external system" will be non-software, for example some aspect of a company's business (where the external objects might be checking and savings accounts) or some part of the physical world (where they might be planets and stars).

Subtype inheritance is the form of inheritance that is closest to the hierarchical taxonomies of botany, zoology and other natural sciences (*VERTEBRATE* ◀— *MAMMAL* and the like). A typical software example (other than closed figures and polygons) is *DEVICE* ◀— *FILE*. We insist that the parent, *A*, be deferred, so that it describes a non-completely specified set of objects. *B*, the heir, may be effective, or it may still be deferred. The next two categories cover the case in which *A* may be effective.

A later section will explore in more detail this inheritance category, not always as straightforward as it would seem at first.

"SUBTYPE INHER-ITANCE AND DESCENDANT HIDING", 24.7, page 835.

Restriction inheritance

> ### Definition: restriction inheritance
>
> Restriction inheritance applies if the instances of *B* are those instances of *A* that satisfy a certain constraint, expressed if possible as part of the invariant of *B* and not included in the invariant of *A*. Any feature introduced by *B* should be a logical consequence of the added constraint. *A* and *B* should be both deferred or both effective.

Typical examples are *RECTANGLE* ◀— *SQUARE*, where the extra constraint is *side1 = side2* (included in the invariant of *SQUARE*), and *ELLIPSE* ◀— *CIRCLE*, where the extra constraint is that the two focuses (or *foci*) of an ellipse ⬯ are the same point for a circle ⊙; in the general case an ellipse is the set of points such that the sum of their distances to the two focuses ⬯ is equal to a certain constant. Many mathematical examples indeed fall into this category.

The last part of the definition is meant to avoid mixing this form of inheritance with others, such as extension inheritance, which may add completely new features in the heir. Here to keep things simple it is preferable to limit new features, if any, to those that directly follow from the added constraint. For example class *CIRCLE* will have a new feature *radius* which satisfies this property: in a circle, all points have the same distance from the merged center, and this distance deserves the status of a feature of the class, whereas the corresponding notion in class *ELLIPSE* (the average of the distances to the two focuses) was probably not considered significant enough to yield a feature.

Because the only conceptual change from *A* to *B* is to add some constraints, the classes should be both deferred or both effective.

Restriction inheritance is conceptually close to subtype inheritance; the later discussion of subtyping will for the most part apply to both categories.

Extension inheritance

> ### Definition: extension inheritance
>
> Extension inheritance applies when *B* introduces features not present in *A* and not applicable to direct instances of *A*. Class *A* must be effective.

The presence of both the restriction and extension variants is one of the paradoxes of inheritance. As noted in the discussion of inheritance, extension applies to features whereas restriction (and more generally specialization) applies to instances, but this does not completely eliminate the paradox.

The problem is that the added features will usually include attributes. So if we take the naïve interpretation of a type (as given by a class) as the set of its instances, then it seems the subset relation is the wrong way around! Assume for example

class *A* **feature** *a1*: *INTEGER* **end**

class *B* **inherit**
    A
feature
    b1: *REAL*
end

Non-mathematical readers may skip this one paragraph.

Then if we view each instance of *A* as representing a singleton, that is to say a set containing one integer (which we can write as *<n>* where *n* is the chosen integer) and each instance of *B* as a pair containing an integer and a real (such as the pair *<1, –2.5>*), the set of pairs *MB* is not a subset of the set of singletons *MA*. In fact, if we absolutely want a subset relation, it will be in the reverse direction: there is a one-to-one mapping between *MA* and the set of all pairs having a given second element, for example *0.0*.

This discovery that the subset relation seems to be the wrong way may make extension inheritance look suspicious. For example an early version of a respected O-O library (not from ISE) had *RECTANGLE* inheriting from *SQUARE*, not the other way around as we have learned. The reasoning was simple: *SQUARE* has a *side* attribute; *RECTANGLE* inherits from *SQUARE* and adds a new feature, *other_side*, so here is an inheritance link for you! Several people criticized the design and it was soon reversed.

But we cannot dismiss the general category of extension inheritance. In fact its equivalent in mathematics, where you specialize a certain notion by adding completely new operations, is frequently used and considered quite necessary. A typical example is the notion of *ring*, specializing the notion of *group*. A group has a certain operation, say +, with certain properties. A ring is a group, so it also has + with these properties, but it adds a new operation, say *, with extra properties of its own. This is not fundamentally different from introducing a new attribute in an heir software class.

The corresponding scheme is frequent in O-O software too. In most applications, of course, *SQUARE* should inherit from *RECTANGLE*, not the reverse; but it is not difficult to think of legitimate examples. A class *MOVING_POINT* (for kinematics applications) might inherit from a purely graphical class *POINT* and add a feature *speed* describing the speed's magnitude and direction; or, in a text processing application, a class *CHAPTER* might inherit from *DOCUMENT*, adding the specific features of a document which is a chapter in a book, such as its current position in the book and a procedure that will reposition it.

A proper mathematical model

(Non-mathematically-inclined readers should skip this section.)

For peace of mind we must resolve the apparent paradox noted earlier (the discovery that *MB* is not a subset of *MA*) since we do want some subset relation to hold between instances of an heir and instances of the parent. That relation does exist in the case of extension inheritance; what the paradox shows is that it is inappropriate to use cartesian product of the attribute types to model a class. Given a class

class *C* **feature**

    c1: *T1*

    c2: *T2*

    c3: *T3*

end

we should *not* take, as a mathematical model C' for the set of instances of C, the cartesian product $T'1 \times T'2 \times T'3$, where the prime signs ' indicate that we recursively use the model sets; this would lead to the paradox (among other disadvantages).

Instead, we should consider any instance as being a partial function from the set of possible attribute names *ATTRIBUTE* to the set of all possible values *VALUE*, with the following properties:

The functions of interest are not only partial but finite.

A1 • The function is defined for $c1$, $c2$ and $c3$.

A2 • The set *VALUE* (the target set of the function) is a superset of $T'1 \cup T'2 \cup T'3$.

A3 • The function's value for $c1$ is in $T'1$, and so on.

Then if we remember that a function is a special case of a relation, and that a relation is a set of pairs (for example an instance of class A may be modeled by the function $\{<a1, 25>\}$, and the instance of B cited on the preceding page by $\{<a1, 1>, <b1, -2.5>\}$), then we do have the expected property that B' is a subset of A.

> Note that it is essential to state the property A1 as "The function is defined for…", not "The function's domain is…" which would limit the domain to the set $\{c1, c2\ c3\}$, preventing descendants from adding their own attributes. As a result of this approach, every software object is modeled by an infinity of (finite) mathematical objects.

This discussion has only given a sketch of the mathematical model. For more details on using partial functions to model tuples, and the general mathematical background, see [M 1990].

Variation inheritance

(Non-mathematical readers, welcome back!) We now move to the second of our three broad groups of inheritance categories: variation inheritance.

Definition: functional and type variation inheritance

Variation inheritance applies if B redefines some features of A; A and B are either both deferred or both effective, and B must not introduce any features except for the direct needs of the redefined features. There are two cases:

- Functional variation inheritance: some of the redefinitions affect feature bodies, rather than just their signatures.
- Type variation inheritance: all redefinitions are signature redefinitions.

Variation inheritance is applicable when an existing class A, describing a certain abstraction, is already useful by itself, but you discover the need to represent a similar although not identical abstraction, which essentially has the same features with some different signatures or implementations.

The definition requires that both classes be effective (the more common case) or both deferred: variation inheritance does not cover the case of an effecting, where we transform a notion from abstract to concrete. A closely related category is uneffecting, studied next, in which some effective features are made deferred.

The definition stipulates that the heir should introduce no new features, except as directly needed by the redefined features. This clause distinguishes variation inheritance from extension inheritance.

In **type** variation inheritance you only change the signatures (argument and result types and number) of some features. This form of inheritance is suspect; it is often a sign of taxomania. In legitimate cases, however, it may be a preparation for extension inheritance or implementation variation inheritance. An example of type variation inheritance might be the heirs *MALE_EMPLOYEE* and *FEMALE_EMPLOYEE*.

Type variation inheritance is not necessary when the original signature used anchored (**like** …) declarations. For example in the *SEGMENT* class of an interactive drawing package you may have introduced a function

> *perpendicular*: *SEGMENT* **is**
>   -- Segment of same length and same middle point, rotated 90 degrees
>
>   …

and then want to define an heir *DOTTED_SEGMENT* to provide a graphical representation with a dotted line rather than a continuous one. In that class, *perpendicular* should return a result of type *DOTTED_SEGMENT*, so you will need to redefine the type. None of this would be needed if the original returned a result of type **like** *Current*, and if you have access to the source of the original and the authority to modify it you may prefer to update that type declaration, normally without any adverse effect on existing clients. But if for some reason you cannot modify the original, or if an anchored declaration is not appropriate in that original (perhaps because of the needs of other descendants), then the ability to redefine the type can save the day.

In **functional** variation inheritance we change some of the features' bodies; if, as is usually the case, the features were already effective, this means changing their implementation. The features' specification, as given by assertions, may also change. It is also possible, although less common, to have functional variation inheritance between two deferred classes; in that case the assertions will change. This may imply changes in some functions, deferred or effective, used by the assertions, or even the addition of new features as long as this is for the "direct needs of the redefined features" as the definition states.

Functional variation inheritance is the direct application of the Open-Closed principle: we want to adapt an existing class without affecting the original (of which we may not even have the source code) and its clients. It is subject to abuses since it may be a form of hacking: twisting an existing class so as to fit a slightly different purpose. At least this will be *organized* hacking, which avoids the dangers of directly modifying existing software, as analyzed in the discussion of the Open-Closed principle. But if you do have access to the source code of the original class, you should examine whether it is not preferable to reorganize the inheritance hierarchy by introducing a more abstract class of which both *A* (the existing variant) and *B* (the new one) will both be heirs, or proper descendants with peer status.

See "The Open-Closed principle", page 57.

Uneffecting

> ### Definition: uneffecting inheritance
>
> Uneffecting inheritance applies if *B* redefines some of the effective features of *A* into deferred features.

Uneffecting is not common, and should not be. Its basic idea goes against the normal direction of inheritance, since we usually expect *B* to be more concrete and *A* more abstract (as with the next category, reification, for which *A* is deferred and *B* effective or at least less deferred). For that reason beginners should stay away from uneffecting. But it may be justified in the following two cases:

- In multiple inheritance, you may want to merge features inherited from two different parents. If one is deferred and the other is effective, this will happen automatically: as soon as they have the same name (possibly after renaming), the effective version will serve as implementation. But if both are effective, you will need to uneffect one of them; the other's implementation will take precedence.

See "Rules on names", page 562.

- You may find a reusable class that is **too concrete** for your purposes, although the abstraction it describes serves your needs. Uneffecting will remove the unwanted implementations. Before using this solution, consider the alternatives: it is preferable to reorganize the inheritance hierarchy to make the more concrete class an heir of the new deferred class, rather than the reverse. But this is not always possible, for example if you do not have the authority to modify *A* and its inheritance hierarchy. Uneffecting may, in such cases, provide a useful form of generalization.

For a link of the uneffecting category, *B* will be deferred; *A* will normally be effective, but might be partially deferred.

Reification inheritance

We now come to the third and last general group, software inheritance.

> **Definition: reification inheritance**
>
> Reification inheritance applies if A represents a general kind of data structure, and B represents a partial or complete choice of implementation for data structures of that kind. A is deferred; B may still be deferred, leaving room for further reification through its own heirs, or it may be effective.

An example, used several times in earlier chapters, is a deferred class *TABLE* describing tables of a very general nature. Reification leads to heirs *SEQUENTIAL_TABLE* and *HASH_TABLE*, still deferred. Final reification of *SEQUENTIAL_TABLE* leads to effective classes *ARRAYED_TABLE*, *LINKED_TABLE*, *FILE_TABLE*.

The term "reification", from Latin words meaning "making into a thing", comes from the literary criticism of Georg Lukács. In computing science it is used as part of the VDM specification and development method.

Structure inheritance

> **Definition: structure inheritance**
>
> Structure inheritance applies if A, a deferred class, represents a general structural property and B, which may be deferred or effective, represents a certain type of objects possessing that property.

Usually A represents a mathematical property that a certain set of objects may possess; for example A may be the class *COMPARABLE*, equipped with such operations as **infix** "<" and **infix** ">=", representing objects to which a total order relation is applicable. A class that needs an order relation of its own, such as *STRING*, will inherit from *COMPARABLE*.

See "Numeric and comparable values", page 522.

It is common for a class to inherit from several parents in this way. For example class *INTEGER* in the Kernel Library inherits from *COMPARABLE* as well as from a class *NUMERIC* (with features such as **infix** "+" and **infix** "*") representing its arithmetic properties. (Class *NUMERIC* more precisely represents the mathematical notion of ring.)

What is the difference between the structure and reification categories? With reification inheritance B represents the same notion as A, with more implementation commitment; with structure inheritance B represents an abstraction of its own, of which A covers only one aspect, such as the presence of an order relation or of arithmetic operations.

Waldén and Nerson note that novices sometimes believe they are using a similar form of inheritance when they are in fact mistaking a "contains" relation for "is" — as with *AIRPLANE* inheriting from *VENTILATION_SYSTEM*, a variant of the "car-owner" scheme, and just as wrong. They point out that it is easy to avoid this mistake through a criterion of the "absolute" kind, leaving no room for hesitation or ambiguity:

*With the inheritance scheme, although the inherited properties are secondary, they are still properties of the **whole objects** described by the class. If we make AIRPLANE inherit COMPARABLE to take account of an ordering relation on planes, the inherited features apply to each airplane as a whole; but the features of VENTILATION_SYSTEM do not. Feature stop of VENTILATION_SYSTEM is not supposed to stop the plane.*

Cited (with change of example) from [Waldén 1995], pages 193-194.

The conclusion in this example is clear: *AIRPLANE* must be a client, not an heir, of *VENTILATION_SYSTEM*.

Implementation inheritance

> ### Definition: implementation inheritance
>
> Structural inheritance applies if *B* obtains from *A* a set of features (other than constant attributes and once functions) necessary to the implementation of the abstraction associated with *B*. Both *A* and *B* must be effective.

Implementation inheritance is discussed in detail later in this chapter. A common case is the "marriage of convenience", based on multiple inheritance, where one parent provides the specification (reification inheritance) and the other provides the implementation (implementation inheritance).

"IMPLEMENTA-TION INHERIT-ANCE", 24.8, page 844.

The case of inheriting constant attributes or once functions is covered by the next variant.

Facility inheritance

Facility inheritance is the scheme in which the parent is a collection of useful features meant only for use by descendants:

> ### Definition: facility inheritance
>
> Facility inheritance applies if *A* exists solely for the purpose of providing a set of logically related features for the benefit of heirs such as *B*. Two common variants are:
>
> - *Constant inheritance* in which the features of *A* are all constants or once functions describing shared objects.
>
> - *Machine inheritance* in which the features of *A* are routines, which may be viewed as operations on an abstract machine.

An example of facility inheritance was provided by class *EXCEPTIONS*, a utility class providing a set of facilities for detailed access to the exception handling mechanism.

See "ADVANCED EXCEPTION HAN-DLING", 12.6, page 431.

Sometimes, as in the examples given later in this chapter, a link of the facility kind uses only one of the two variants, constant or machine; but in others, such as *EXCEPTIONS*, the parent class provides both constants (such as the exception code

Incorrect_inspect_value) and routines (such as *trigger* to raise a developer exception). Since this discussion is meant to introduce disjoint inheritance categories, we should treat facility inheritance as a single category — with two (non-disjoint) variants.

With constant inheritance, both A and B are effective. With machine inheritance, there is more flexibility, but B should be at least as effective as A.

"FACILITY INHER-ITANCE", 24.9, page 847.

Facility inheritance is discussed in detail later in this chapter.

Using inheritance with deferred and effective classes

Each of the various categories reviewed places some requirements on which of the heir and the parent may be deferred and which may be effective. The following table summarizes the rules. "Variation" covers type variation and functional variation. Items marked •appear in more than one entry.

Deferred and effective heir and parent

Parent → Heir ↓	Deferred	Effective
Deferred	Constant• Restriction• Structure• Subtype• Uneffecting• Variation• View	Extension• Uneffecting•
Effective	Constant• Reification Structure• Subtype•	Constant• Extension• Implementation Restriction• Variation•

24.6 ONE MECHANISM, OR MORE?

"The dual perspective", page 494; "The two styles", page 608.

(Note: this discussion assumes as background the earlier presentation of "The meaning of inheritance", especially its section entitled "The dual perspective", and the presentation of descendant hiding, especially its section entitled "The two styles" with its summary table.)

The variety of uses of inheritance, evidenced by the preceding discussion, may lead to the impression that we should have several language mechanisms to cover the underlying notions. In particular, a number of authors have suggested separating between *module* inheritance, essentially a tool to reuse existing features in a new module, and *type* inheritance, essentially a type classification mechanism.

Such a division seems to cause more harm than good, for several reasons.

First, recognizing only two categories is not representative of the variety of uses of inheritance, reflected by the preceding classification. Since no one will advocate introducing ten different language mechanisms, the result would be too restrictive.

The practical effect would be to raise useless methodological discussions: assume you want to inherit from an iterator class such as *LINEAR_ITERATOR*; should you use module inheritance or type inheritance? One can find arguments to support either answer. You will waste your time trying to decide between two competing language mechanisms; the contribution of such reflections to the only goals that count — the quality of your software and the speed at which you produce it — is exactly zero.

An exercise asks you to analyze our categories to try to see for each of them whether it relates more to the "module" or "type" kind.

Exercise E24.8, page 870.

It is also interesting to think of the consequences that such a division will have on the complexity of the language. Inheritance comes with a number of auxiliary mechanisms. Most of them will be needed on both sides:

- *Redefinition* is useful both for subtyping (think of *RECTANGLE* redefining *perimeter* from *POLYGON*) and for module extension (the Open-Closed principle demands that when we inherit a module we keep the flexibility of changing what is not adapted any more to our new context — a flexibility without which we would lose one of the main attractions of the object-oriented method).

- *Renaming* is definitely useful for module inheritance. To present it as inappropriate for type inheritance (see [Breu 1995]) seems too restrictive. In the modeled external system, variants of a certain notion may introduce specific terminology, which it is often desirable for the software to respect. A class *STATE_INSTITUTIONS* in a geographical or electoral information system might have a descendant class *LOUISIANA_INSTITUTIONS* reflecting the peculiarities of Louisiana's political structures; it is not unreasonable to expect that the feature *counties*, giving the list of counties in a state, would be renamed *parishes* in the descendant, since parish is what Louisianians call what the rest of the US knows as a county.

- *Repeated inheritance* may occur with either form. Since we may expect that module-only inheritance will preclude polymorphic substitution, the problem of disambiguating dynamic binding, and hence the need for a **select** clause, will only arise for type inheritance; but all the other questions, in particular when to share repeatedly inherited features and when to replicate them, still arise.

- As always when we introduce new mechanisms into a language, they interact with the rest, and with each other. Do we prohibit a class from both module-inheriting and type-inheriting the same class? If so, we may be just vexing developers who have a good reason to use the same class in two different ways; if not, we open up a whole Pandora's box of new language issues — name conflicts, redefinition conflicts etc.

On Dijkstra's advice see "The need for methodology guidelines", page 664.

All this for the benefit of a purist's view of inheritance — restrictive and controversial. Not that there is anything wrong with defending controversial views; but one should be careful before imposing their consequences on language users — that is to say, on everyone. When in doubt, abstain. Once again, the contrast with Dijkstra's original **goto** excommunication is striking: Dijkstra took great care to explain in detail the drawbacks of the **goto** instruction, based on a theory of software construction and execution, and to explain what replacements were available. In the present case, no compelling argument — at least none that I have seen — shows why it is "bad" to use a single mechanism to cover both module and type inheritance.

Aside from blanket condemnations based on preconceived ideas of what inheritance should be, there is only one serious objection to the use of a single mechanism: the extra complication that this approach imposes on the task of **static type checking**. This issue was discussed at length in chapter 17; it places an extra burden on *compilers*, which is always justifiable (when the burden is reasonable, as here) if the effect is to facilitate the *developer*'s task.

In the end what all this discussion shows is that the ability to use only one inheritance mechanism for both module and type inheritance is not — as partisans of separate mechanisms implicitly consider — the result of a confusion of genres. It is the result of the *very first decision* of object-oriented software construction: the unification of module and type concepts into a single notion, the class. If we accept classes as both modules and types, then we should accept inheritance as both module accumulation and subtyping.

24.7 SUBTYPE INHERITANCE AND DESCENDANT HIDING

The first category on our list is probably the only form on which everyone agrees, at least everyone who accepts inheritance: what we may call pure subtype inheritance.

Most of the discussion will also apply to restriction inheritance, whose principal difference with subtype inheritance is that it does not require the parent to be deferred.

Defining a subtype

As was pointed out in the introduction of inheritance, part of the power of the idea comes from its fusion of a type mechanism, the definition of a new type as a special case of existing types, with a module mechanism, the definition of a module as extension of existing modules. Many of the controversial questions about inheritance come from perceived conflicts between these two views. With subtype inheritance there is no such question — although, as we shall see, this does not mean that everything becomes easy.

Subtype inheritance is closely patterned after the taxonomical principles of natural and mathematical sciences. Every vertebrate is an animal; every mammal is a vertebrate; every elephant is a mammal. Every group (in mathematics) is a monoid; every ring is a group; every field is a ring. Similar examples, of which we saw many in earlier chapters, abound in object-oriented software:

- *FIGURE* ◄— *CLOSED_FIGURE* ◄— *POLYGON* ◄— *QUADRANGLE* ◄— *RECTANGLE* ◄— *SQUARE*

- *DEVICE* ◄— *FILE* ◄— *TEXT_FILE*

- *SHIP* ◄— *LEISURE_SHIP* ◄— *SAILBOAT*

- *ACCOUNT* ◄— *SAVINGS_ACCOUNT* ◄— *FIXED_RATE_ACCOUNT*

and so on. In any one of these subtype links, we have clearly identified the set of objects that the parent type describes; and we have spotted a subset of these objects, characterized by some properties which do not necessarily apply to all instances of the parent. For example a text file is a file, but it has the extra property of being made of a sequence of characters — a property that some other files, such as executable binaries, do not possess.

A general rule of subtype inheritance is that the various heirs of a class represent disjoint sets of instances. No closed figure, for example, is both a polygon and an ellipse.

Several of the examples, such as *RECTANGLE* ◄— *SQUARE*, will most likely involve an effective parent, and so are cases of restriction inheritance.

Multiple views

Subtype inheritance is straightforward when a clear criterion exists to classify the variants of a certain notion. But sometimes several qualities vie for our attention. Even in such a seemingly easy example as the classification of polygons, doubt may arise: should we use the number of sides, leading to heirs such as *TRIANGLE*, *QUADRANGLE* etc., or should we divide our objects into regular polygons (*EQUILATERAL_POLYGON*, *SQUARE* and so on) and irregular ones?

Several strategies are available to address such conflicts. They will be reviewed as part of the study of view inheritance later in this chapter.

Enforcing the subtype view

A type is not just as a set of objects, of course: it is also characterized by the applicable operations (the features), and their semantic properties (the assertions: preconditions, postconditions, invariants). We expect the fate of features and assertions in the heir to be compatible with the concept of subtype — meaning that it must allow us to view any instance of the heir also as an instance of the parent.

The rules on assertions indeed support the subtype view:

- The parent's invariant is automatically part of the heir's invariant; so all the constraints that have been specified for instances of the parent also apply to instances of the heir.

- A routine precondition applies, possibly weakened, to any redeclaration of the routine: so any call which satisfies the requirement specified for instances of the parent will also satisfy the (equal or weaker) requirement specified for instances of the heir.

- A routine postcondition applies, possibly strengthened, to any redeclaration of the routine: so any property of the routine's outcome that has been specified for instances of the parent will be guaranteed to hold as a result of the (equal or stronger) properties specified for instances of the heir.

For features, the situation is a little more subtle. The subtype view implies that all operations applicable to an instance of the parent should be applicable to an instance of the heir. Internally, this is always true: even in the inheritance of *ARRAYED_STACK* from *ARRAY*, which seems far from subtype inheritance, the features of *ARRAY* were still available to the heir, and indeed were essential to the implementation of its *STACK* features. But in that case we had hidden all these *ARRAY* features from the heir's clients, and for good reason (we do not want a client of a stack class to perform arbitrary operations on the representation, such as directly modifying an array element, since this would be a violation of the class interface).

For pure subtype inheritance we might expect a much stronger rule: that *every* feature that a client can apply to instances of the parent class also be applicable, by that same client, to instances of the heir. In other words, no descendant hiding: if B inherits f from A, then the export status of f in B is at least as generous as in A. (That is to say: if f was generally exported, it still is; and if it was selectively exported to some classes, it is still exported to them, although it may be exported to more.)

The need for descendant hiding

In a perfect world we could indeed enforce the no-descendant-hiding rule; but not in the real world of software development. Inheritance must be usable even for classes written by people who do not have perfect foresight; some of the features they include in a class may not make sense in a descendant written by someone else, later and in a completely different context. We may call such cases **taxonomy exceptions**. (In a different context the word "exception" would suffice, but we do not want any confusion with the software notion of exception handling as studied in earlier chapters.)

Should we renounce inheriting from an attractive and useful class simply because of a taxonomy exception, that is to say because one or two of its features are inapplicable to our own clients? This would be unreasonable. We just hide the features from our clients' view, and proceed with our work.

The alternatives have been studied as part of one of the founding principles of object technology — **Open-Closed principle** — and they are not attractive:

- We might modify the original class. This means we may invalidate myriads of existing systems that relied on it — no, thanks. In most practical cases, anyway, the class will not be ours to modify; we may not even have access to its source form.

- We might write a new version of the class (or, if we are lucky and do have access to its source code, make a copy), and modify it. This approach is the reverse of everything that object technology promotes; it defeats any attempt at reusability and at an organized software process.

Avoiding descendant hiding

Before probing further why and when we may need descendant hiding, it is essential to note that most of the time we do not. Descendant hiding should remain a technique of last resort. When you have a full grasp of the inheritance structure sufficiently early in the design process, *preconditions* are a better technique to handle apparent taxonomy exceptions.

Consider class *ELLIPSE*. An ellipse has two focuses through which you can normally draw a line:

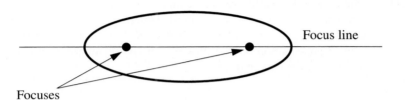

An ellipse and its focus line

Class *ELLIPSE* might correspondingly have a feature *focus_line*.

It is quite normal to define class *CIRCLE* as an heir to *ELLIPSE*: every circle is also an ellipse. But for a circle the two focuses are the same point — the circle's center — so there is no focus line. (It is perhaps more accurate to say that there is an infinity of focus lines, including any line that passes through the center, but in practice the effect is the same.)

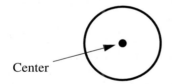

A circle and its center

Is this a good example of descendant hiding? In other words, should class *CIRCLE* make feature *focus_line* secret, as in

```
class CIRCLE inherit
    ELLIPSE
        export {NONE} focus_line end
    ...
```

Probably not. In this case, the designer of the parent class has all the information at his disposal to determine that *focus_line* is not applicable to all ellipses. Assuming the feature is a routine, it should have a precondition:

```
focus_line is
            -- The line through the two focuses
    require
        not equal (focus_1, focus_2)
    do
        ...
    end
```

(The precondition could also be abstract, using a function *distinct_focuses*; this has the advantage that *CIRCLE* can redefine that function once and for all to yield false.)

See page 61.

Here the need to support ellipses without a focus line follows from a proper analysis of the problem. Writing an ellipse class with a function *focus_line* that has no precondition would be a design error; addressing such an error through descendant hiding would be attempting to cover up for that error. As was pointed out at the end of the presentation of the Open-Closed principle, erroneous designs must be fixed, not patched in descendants.

Applications of descendant hiding

The *focus_line* example is typical of taxonomy exceptions arising in application domains such as mathematics which can boast a solid theory with associated classifications, patiently refined over a long period. In such a context, the proper answer is to use a precondition, concrete or abstract, at the place where the original feature appears.

But that technique is not always applicable, especially in domains that are driven by human processes, with their attendant capriciousness that often makes it hard to foresee all possible exceptions.

Consider as an example a class hierarchy, rooted in a class *MORTGAGE*, in a software system for managing mortgages. The descendants have been organized according to various criteria, such as fixed rate versus variable rate, business versus personal or any other that was found appropriate; we may assume for simplicity that this is a taxonomy of the pure subtype kind. Class *MORTGAGE* has a procedure *redeem*, which handles the mechanisms for paying off a mortgage at a certain time earlier than maturation.

Now assume that Congress, in a fit of generosity (or under the pressure of construction lobbies), introduces a new form of government-backed mortgage whose otherwise advantageous conditions carry a provision barring any early redemption. We have found a proper place in the hierarchy for the corresponding class *NEW_MORTGAGE*; but what about procedure *redeem*?

We could use the technique illustrated with *focus_line*: a precondition. But what if there has never before in banker's memory existed a mortgage that could not be redeemed? Then procedure *redeem* probably does not have a precondition. (The situation is the same if the precondition existed but was concrete, so that it cannot be redefined.)

So if we decide to use a precondition we must modify class *MORTGAGE*. As usual, this assumes that we have access to its source code and the right to modify it — often not true. Suppose, however, that this is not a problem. We will add to *MORTGAGE* a boolean-valued function *redeemable* and to *redeem* a clause

require
　　redeemable

But now we have changed the interface of the class. All the clients of the class and of its numerous descendants have instantly been made potentially incorrect; to observe the specification all calls $m.redeem\ (\ldots)$ should now be rewritten as

if *m.redeemable* **then**

    m.redeem (…)

else

    … (What in the world do we say here?) …

end

Initially this change is not urgent, since the incorrectness is only potential: existing software will only use the existing descendants of *MORTGAGE*, so no harm can result. But not fixing them means leaving a time bomb — unprotected calls to a precondition-equipped routine — ticking in our software. As soon as a client developer has the clever idea of using a polymorphic attachment with a source of type *NEW_MORTGAGE* but forgets the test we have a bug. And the compiler will not produce any diagnostic.

The absence of a precondition in the original version of *redeem* was not a design mistake on the part of the original designers: in their view of the world, until now correct, no precondition was needed. Every mortgage was redeemable. We cannot require every feature to have a precondition; imagine a world in which for every useful *f* there would be an accompanying boolean-valued function *f_feasible* serving as its bodyguard; then we would never be able to write a simple *x.f* for the rest of our lives; each call would be in an **if** … or equivalent as illustrated above for *m.redeem*. Not fun.

The *redeem* example is typical of taxonomy exceptions which, unlike *focus_line* and other cases of perfect-foresight classification, cannot be addressed through careful *a priori* precondition design. The observation made earlier fully applies: it would be absurd to renounce inheritance — the reuse of a rich class structure, lovingly developed and carefully validated — because a feature or two, out of dozens of useful ones, do not apply to our goal of the moment. We should just use descendant hiding:

    class *NEW_MORTGAGE* **inherit**

        MORTGAGE

            export {*NONE*} *redeem* **end**

      …

No error or anomaly will be introduced in existing software — the existing class structure or its clients. If someone modifies a client class to include a polymorphic attachment with source type *NEW_MORTGAGE*, and the target of that attachment is also used with *redeem*, as in

    m: *MORTGAGE*; *nm*: *NEW_MORTGAGE*

    …

    m := *nm*

    …

    m.redeem (…)

then the call becomes a catcall, and the potential error will be caught statically by the extended mechanism described in our discussion of typing.

"BEWARE OF POLYMORPHIC CATCALLS!", 17.7, page 636.

Taxonomies and their limitations

Taxonomy exceptions are not specific to software examples. Even — or perhaps especially — in the most established areas of natural science, it sometimes seems impossible to find a statement of the form *"members of the ABC phylum* [or genus, species etc.] *are characterized by property XYZ"* that is not prefaced by *"most"*, qualified by *"usually"* or followed by *"except in a few cases"*.This is true at all levels of the hierarchy, even the most fundamental categories, which a layman might naïvely believe to be established on indisputable criteria!

If you think for example that the distinction between the animal and plant kingdoms is simple, just ponder its definition in a popular reference text (italics added):

From: the New York Public Library Science Desk Reference, ed. Patricia Barnes-Svarney, 1995.

DISTINGUISHING PLANTS FROM ANIMALS

There are several *general* factors that distinguish plants from animals, *though* there are *numerous exceptions*.

Locomotion *Most* animals move about freely, *while* it is *rare* to find plants that can move around in their surrounding environments. *Most* plants are rooted in the soil, or attached to rocks, wood or *other materials*.

Food Green plants that contain chlorophyll manufacture food themselves, but *most* animals obtain nutrients by eating plants or other animals. [...]

Growth Plants *usually* grow from the tips of their branches and roots, and at the outer layer of their stems, for their entire life. Animals *usually* grow in all parts of their bodies and stop growing after maturity.

Chemical regulation Though both plants and animals *generally* have hormones and other chemicals that regulate *certain* reactions within the organism, the chemical composition of these hormones differ[s] in the two kingdoms.

The same comments apply to another area of study, cultural rather than natural, which has also contributed to the development of systematic taxonomy: the historical classification of human languages.

In zoology a common example, so famous in Artificial Intelligence circles as to have become a cliché, still provides a good illustration of taxonomy exceptions. (Remember, however, that this is only an *analogy*, not a software example, and so cannot prove anything; it can only help us understand ideas whose relevance has been demonstrated otherwise.) Birds fly; in software terms class *BIRD* would have a procedure *fly*. Yet if we wanted a class *OSTRICH* we would have to admit that ostriches, although among the birdest of birds, do not fly.

We could think of classifying birds into flying and non-flying categories. But this would conflict with other possible criteria including, most importantly, the commonly retained one, shown on the next page.

Kingdom: **Animalia** — multicellular organisms without chlorophyll

Phylum: **Chordata** —coelemic cavity, 3 germ layers, a notocord, an endoskeleton and a closed circulatory system

Class: **Aves** birds (there are 30 orders)

Order: Anseriformes — waterfowl

Order: Apodiformes — swifts and hummingbirds

Order: Caprimulgiformes — nightjars, potoos, frogmouths, owlet- frogmouths and oilbirds

Order: Casuariiformes cassowaries and emu

Order: Chardriiformes — shorebirds

Order: Ciconiiformes — long-legged wading birds

Order: Coliiformes — mousebirds

Order: Columbiformes — pigeons and doves

Order: Coraciiformes — kingfishers

Order: Cuciliformes — cuckoos

Order: Dinornithiformes — kiwis and moas

Order: Falconiformes — raptors

Order: Galliformes — gallinaceous birds (chickens, grouse, quail and pheasant)

Order: Gaviiformes — loons

Order: Gruiformes — terrestrial and marsh birds

Order: Musophagiformes — turacos

Order: Passeriformes — perching birds, songbirds and passerines

Order: Pelecaniformes — waterbirds with webbed feet

Order: Phoenicopteriformes — flamingos

Order: Piciformes — woodpeckers

Order: Podicipediformes — grebes

Order: Procellariiformes — tube-nosed seabirds

Order: Psittaciformes — parrots, macaws

Order: Pteroclidiformes — sandgrouse

Order: Rheiformes — rheas, nandus

Order: Sphenisciformes — penguins

Order: Strigiformes — owls

Order: Struthioniformes — ostrich

Order: Tinamiformes — tinamous

Order: Trogoniformes — trogons and quetzals

General classification of birds

(*Data from Ed Everham, at* www.runet.edu/ ~eeverham.) *Reproduced with the author's permission. Associated comments are reproduced in* "The arbitrariness of classifications", page 859.

The *OSTRICH* example has an interesting twist. Although regrettably most of them do not seem to be aware of it, ostriches really should fly. Younger generations lost this ancestral skill through an accident of evolutionary history, but anatomically ostriches have retained most of the aeronautical machinery of birds. This property, which makes the job of the professional taxonomist a little harder (although it may facilitate that of his colleague, the professional taxidermist), will not in the end prevent him from classifying ostriches among birds.

In software terms *OSTRICH* will simply inherit from *BIRD* and hide the inherited *fly* feature.

Using descendant hiding

> *All our efforts* [at classification] *are powerless against the multiple relations which from everywhere affect the living beings around us. This is the fight, described by the great botanist Goethe, between Man and Nature in her infinity. One can be sure that Man will always be defeated.*
>
> Henri Baillon, *General Study of the Euphorbiaceous Family* (1850). Quoted (in French) in Peter F. Stevens, *The Development of Biological Systematics*: *Antoine-Laurent de Jussieu, Nature, and the Natural System*, Columbia University Press, New York, 1994.

The preceding evidence, from both software practice and non-software analogies, suggests that even with a careful design some taxonomy exceptions may remain. Hiding *redeem* from *NEW_MORTGAGE* or *fly* from *OSTRICH* is not necessarily a sign of sloppy design or insufficient foresight; it is the recognition that other inheritance hierarchies that would not require descendant hiding could be more complex and less useful.

Such taxonomy exceptions have the precedent of centuries of effort by intellectual giants (including Aristotle, Linné, Buffon, Jussieu and Darwin). They may even signal some intrinsic limitation of the human ability to comprehend the world. Could they be related to the indeterminacy results that shook scientific thought in the twentieth century, uncertainty in physics and undecidability in mathematics?

All this assumes that descendant hiding remains, as already noted, a rare occurrence. If you design a taxonomy with taxonomy exceptions all over — well, they are not exceptions any more, so you do not really have much of a taxonomy.

In software, for those few cases in which conflicting classification criteria or massive previous work precludes the production of a perfect subtype hierarchy, descendant hiding is more than a convenient facility: it will save your neck.

24.8 IMPLEMENTATION INHERITANCE

A form of inheritance that has often been criticized but is in fact both convenient and conceptually valid is the use of an inheritance link between a class describing a certain implementation of an abstract data structure and the class providing the implementation.

The marriage of convenience

In the discussion of multiple inheritance we saw an example of the "marriage of convenience" kind, which combines a deferred class with a mechanism to implement it. The example was *ARRAYED_STACK*, of the general form

"The marriage of convenience", page 530.

> **class** *ARRAYED_STACK* [*G*] **inherit**
> > *STACK* [*G*]
> > > **redefine** *change_top* **end**
> > *ARRAY* [*G*]
> > > **rename**
> > > > *count* **as** *capacity*, *put* **as** *array_put*
> > > **export**
> > > > {*NONE*} **all**
> > > **end**
>
> **feature**
> > … Implementation of the deferred routines of *STACK*, such as *put*, *count*, *full*, and redefinition of *change_top*, in terms of *ARRAY* operations…
>
> **end**

It is interesting to compare *ARRAYED_STACK*, as sketched here, with the class *STACK2* of an earlier discussion — an array implementation of stacks defined without any use of inheritance. Note in particular how avoiding the need for the class to be a client of *ARRAY* simplifies the notation (the previous version had to use *implementation.put* where we can now just write *put*).

STACK2 appeared on page 349.

In the above inheritance part for *ARRAY* all features have been made secret. This is typical of marriage-of-convenience inheritance: all the features from the specification-providing parent, here *STACK*, are exported; all the features from the implementation-providing parent, here *ARRAY*, are hidden. This forces clients of class *ARRAY_STACK* to use the corresponding instances through stack features only; we do not want to let them perform arbitrary array operations on the representation, such as changing the value of an element other than the top one.

It feels so good, but is it wrong?

Implementation inheritance is not without its critics. That we hide many inherited features seems to some people a violation of the "is-a" principle of inheritance.

It is not. There are different forms of "is-a". By its behavior, an arrayed stack is a stack; but internally it is an array. In fact the representation of an instance of *ARRAYED_STACK* is exactly the same as that of an instance of *ARRAY*, enriched with one attribute (*count*).

Being made in the same way is a rather strong form of "is-a". And it is not just the representation: all the features of *ARRAY*, such as *put* (renamed *array_put*), **infix** *"@"* and *count* (renamed *capacity*) are available to *ARRAYED_STACK*, although not exported to its clients; the class needs them to implement the *STACK* features.

So there is nothing conceptually wrong with such implementation-only inheritance. The comparison with the counter-example studied at the beginning of this chapter is striking: for *CAR_OWNER* we had a gross misunderstanding of the concept; with *ARRAYED_STACK* we have a well-identified form of the "is-a" relationship.

There is one drawback: permitting the inheritance mechanism to restrict the export availability of an inherited feature — that is to say, permitting the **export** clause — makes static type checking more difficult, as we have studied in detail. But this difficulty is largely for the compiler writer, not for the software developer.

Doing without inheritance

Page 349.

Let us probe further and see what it would take to work without implementation inheritance in our example case. This has been seen already: class *STACK2* of an earlier chapter. It has an attribute *representation* of type *ARRAY* [*G*] and stack procedures implemented in the following style (assertions omitted):

```
put (x: G) is
            -- Add x on top.
     require
          ...
     do
          count := count + 1
          representation.put (count, x)
     ensure
          ...
     end
```

Every manipulation of the representation requires a call to a feature of *ARRAY* with *representation* as the target. There is a performance penalty: minor for space (the *representation* attribute), more serious for time (going through *representation*, that is to say adding an indirection, for each operation).

Assume we can ignore the efficiency issue. Tediousness is another, with all the "*representation.*" prefixes that you must add before every array operation. This will be true in all the classes that implement various data structures — stacks, but also lists, queues and others — through arrays.

The object-oriented designer hates tedious, repetitive tasks. "Encapsulate repetition" is our motto. If we see such a pattern occurring repeatedly throughout a set of classes, the natural and healthy reaction is to try to understand the common abstraction, and encapsulate it in a class. The abstraction here is something like "data structure that has access to an array and its operations". The class could be:

indexing
    description: "*Objects that have access to an array and its operations*"
class
    ARRAYED [*G*]
feature -- Access
    item (*i*: *INTEGER*): *G* **is**
          -- The representation's element at index *i*
      require
        …
      do
        Result := *representation*$\bullet$*item* (*i*)
      ensure
        …
      end
feature -- Element change
    put (*x*: *G*; *i*: *INTEGER*) **is**
          -- Replace by *x* the representation's element at index *i*.
      require
        …
      do
        representation$\bullet$*put* (*x*, *i*)
      ensure
        …
      end
feature {*NONE*} -- Implementation
    representation: *ARRAY* [*G*]
end -- class *ARRAYED*

The features *item* and *put* have been exported. Since *ARRAYED* only describes internal properties of a data structure, it does not really need exported features. So someone who disagrees with the very idea of letting a descendant hide some of its parents' exported features may prefer to make all the features of *ARRAYED* secret. They will then by default remain secret in descendants.

With this class definition it becomes quite uncontroversial to make classes such as *ARRAYED_STACK* or *ARRAYED_LIST* inherit from *ARRAYED*: they indeed describe "arrayed" structures. These classes can now use *item* instead of *representation*$\bullet$*item* and so on; we have rid ourselves of the tediousness.

But wait a minute! If it is right to inherit from *ARRAYED*, why can we not inherit directly from *ARRAY*? We gain nothing from the further layer or encapsulation that we have thrown over *ARRAY* — a form of encapsulation that starts looking more like obfuscation. By going through *ARRAYED* we are just pretending to ourselves that we are not using implementation inheritance, but for all practical purposes we are. We have just made the software more complex and less efficient.

There is indeed no reason in this example for class *ARRAYED*. Direct implementation inheritance from classes such as *ARRAY* is simpler and legitimate.

24.9 FACILITY INHERITANCE

With facility inheritance we are even less coy than with implementation inheritance about why we want the marriage: pure, greedy self-interest. We see a class with advantageous features and we want to use them. But there is nothing to be ashamed of: the class has no other *raison d'être*.

Using character codes

The Base Libraries include a class *ASCII*:

> **indexing**
> > *description*:
> > > *"The ASCII character set. %*
> > > *%This class may be used as ancestor by classes needing its facilities."*
>
> **class** *ASCII* **feature** -- Access
> > *Character_set_size*: *INTEGER* **is** *128*; *Last_ascii*: *INTEGER* **is** *127*
> > *First_printable*: *INTEGER* **is** *32*; *Last_printable*: *INTEGER* **is** *126*
> > *Letter_layout*: *INTEGER* **is** *70*
> > *Case_diff*: *INTEGER* **is** *32*
> > > *-- Lower_a – Upper_a*
> >
> > ...
> >
> > *Ctrl_a*: *INTEGER* **is** *1*; *Soh*: *INTEGER* **is** *1*
> > *Ctrl_b*: *INTEGER* **is** *2*; *Stx*: *INTEGER* **is** *2*
> >
> > ...
> >
> > *Blank*: *INTEGER* **is** *32*; *Sp*: *INTEGER* **is** *32*
> > *Exclamation*: *INTEGER* **is** *33*; *Doublequote*: *INTEGER* **is** *34*
> >
> > ...
> > ...
> >
> > *Upper_a*: *INTEGER* **is** *65*; *Upper_b*: *INTEGER* **is** *66*
> >
> > ...
> >
> > *Lower_a*: *INTEGER* **is** *97*; *Lower_b*: *INTEGER* **is** *98*
> > ... etc. ...
>
> **end** -- class *ASCII*

This class is a repertoire of constant attributes (142 features in all) describing properties of the ASCII character set. As the *description* entry states, it is meant to be inherited by classes needing access to such properties.

Consider for example a lexical analyzer — the part of a language analysis system that is responsible for identifying the basic elements, or *tokens*, of an input text; these tokens may be (assuming the input is a text in some programming language) integer constants, identifiers, symbols and so on. One of the classes of the system, say *TOKENIZER*, will need access to the character codes, to classify the input characters into digits, letters etc. Such a class will inherit these codes from *ASCII*:

class *TOKENIZER* **inherit** *ASCII* **feature**

    … Routines here may use such features as *Blank*, *Case_diff* etc. …

end

Classes such as *ASCII* have been known to raise a few eyebrows; before going into the methodological discussion of whether they are a proper application of inheritance, we will look at another example of facility inheritance.

Iterators

The second example will show a case in which the inherited features are not just constant attributes (as with *ASCII*) but routines of the most general kind.

Assume that we want to provide a general mechanism to iterate over data structures of a certain kind, for example linear structures such as lists. "Iterating" means performing a certain procedure, say *action*, on elements of such a structure, taken in their sequential order. We are asked to provide a number of iteration mechanisms, including: applying *action* to all the elements; applying it to all the elements that satisfy a certain criterion given by a boolean-valued function *test*; applying it to all the elements up to the first one that satisfies *test*, or the first one that does not satisfy this condition; and so on. A system that uses the mechanism must be able to apply it to any *action* and *test* of its choice.

At first it might seem that the iterating features should belong to the data structure classes themselves, such as *LIST* or *SEQUENCE*; but as an exercise invites you to determine for yourself this is not the right solution. It is preferable to introduce a separate hierarchy for iterators:

Exercise E24.7, page 870.

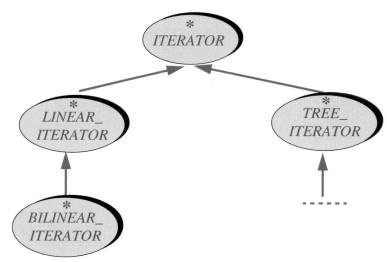

Class *LINEAR_ITERATOR*, the one of interest for this discussion, looks like this:

indexing

description:

"*Objects that are able to iterate over linear structures*"

names: *iterators, iteration, linear_iterators, linear_iteration*

deferred class *LINEAR_ITERATOR* [*G*] **inherit**

ITERATOR [*G*]

redefine *target* **end**

feature -- Access

invariant_value: BOOLEAN **is**

-- The property to be maintained by an iteration (default: true).

do

Result := *True*

end

target: *LINEAR* [*G*]

-- The structure to which iteration features will apply

test: *BOOLEAN* **is**

-- The boolean condition used to select applicable elements

deferred

end

feature -- Basic operations

action **is**

-- The action to be applied to selected elements.

deferred

end

do_if **is**

-- Apply *action* in sequence to every item of *target* that satisfies *test*.

do

from *start* **invariant** *invariant_value* **until** *exhausted* **loop**

if *test* **then** *action* **end**

forth

end

ensure then

exhausted

end

… And so on: *do_all, do_while, do_until* etc. …

end -- class *LINEAR_ITERATOR*

Now assume a class that needs to perform a certain operation on selected elements of a list of some specific type; for example a command class in a text processing system may need to justify all paragraphs in a document, excepted for preformated paragraphs (such as program texts and other display paragraphs). Then:

class *JUSTIFIER* **inherit**
   LINEAR_ITERATOR [*PARAGRAPH*]
     rename
       action **as** *justify*,
       test **as** *justifiable*,
       do_all **as** *justify_all*
     end
feature
  justify **is**
     do ... **end**
  justifiable **is**
     -- Is paragraph subject to justification?
    do
      Result := **not** *preformated*
    end

   ...
end -- class *JUSTIFIER*

The renaming was not indispensable but helps for clarity. Note that there is no need to declare or redeclare the procedure *justify_all* (the former *do_all*): as inherited, it does the expected job based on the effected versions of *action* and *test*.

Procedure *justify*, instead of being described in the class, could be inherited from another parent. In this case multiple inheritance would perform a "join" operation that effects the deferred *action*, inherited from one parent under the name *justify* (here the renaming is essential), with the effective *justify* inherited from the other parent. A form of marriage of convenience, in fact.

LINEAR_ITERATOR is a remarkable example of **behavior class**, capturing common behaviors while leaving specific components open so that descendants can plug in their specific variants.

"Don't call us, we'll call you", page 504.

Forms of facility inheritance

The two examples, *ASCII* and *LINEAR_ITERATOR*, are typical of the two main variants of facility inheritance:

* *Constant* inheritance, in which the parent principally yields constant attributes and shared objects.

* *Operation* inheritance, in which it yields routines.

As noted earlier, it is possible to combine both of these variants in a single inheritance link. That is why facility inheritance is one of our categories, not two.

Understanding facility inheritance

To some people facility inheritance appears to be an abuse of the mechanism — a form of hacking. But that is not necessarily the case.

The main question to consider in these examples is not about inheritance but about the classes that have been defined, *ASCII* and *LINEAR_ITERATOR*. As always when looking at a class design, we must ask ourselves: "Does this indeed describe a meaningful data abstraction?" — a set of objects characterized by their abstract properties.

With the examples the answer is less obvious than with a class *RECTANGLE*, *BANK_ACCOUNT* or *LINKED_LIST*, but it exists all the same:

"Objects as machines", page 751.

- Class *ASCII* represents the abstraction: "any object that has access to the properties of the ASCII character set".

- Class *LINEAR_ITERATOR* represents the abstraction: "any object that has the ability to perform sequential iterations on a linear structure". Such objects tend to be of the "machine" kind described in the preceding chapter.

Once these abstractions have been accepted, the inheritance links do not raise any problem: an instance of *TOKENIZER* does need "access to the properties of the ASCII character set", and an instance of *JUSTIFIER* does need "the ability to perform sequential iterations on a linear structure". In fact, we could classify such examples of inheritance links under the subtype kind. What distinguishes facility inheritance is the nature of the parent.

That the classes themselves are the issue, not the use of inheritance, is reinforced by the observation that an application class could rely on these classes as a client rather than heir. This would make things heavier, especially for *ASCII*: with

> *charset*: *ASCII*
>
> ...
>
> !! *charset*

On iterator objects see exercise E15.4, page 567.

every use of a character code would have to be written *charset.Lower_a* and the like. The object attached with *ASCII* does not play any useful role. With *LINEAR_ITERATOR* the same comments apply as long as a given class needs only one kind of iteration. If several are required, it becomes interesting to create iterator objects, each with its own version of *action* and *test*; then you can have as many iteration schemes as you need.

If it is appropriate to have iterator objects, we need iterator classes, and there is no reason to deny such classes the right to join the inheritance club.

24.10 MULTIPLE CRITERIA AND VIEW INHERITANCE

Perhaps the most difficult problem of using inheritance arises when alternative criteria are available to classify the abstractions of a certain application area.

Classifying through multiple criteria

The traditional classifications of the natural sciences use a single criterion (possibly involving several qualities) at each level: vertebrate versus invertebrate, leaves renewed each year or not, and so on. The result is what we would call single inheritance hierarchies, whose main advantage is their great simplicity. But there are problems too, since nature is definitely not single-criterion. This will be obvious to anyone who has ever tried to take a nature walk armed with a botanical book meant to enable plant recognition through the official Linnaean criteria. Species A is deciduous and species B is not, the book says; how long can you afford to wait, if this is July, to find out whether the leaves remain? You are told that June will bring bright purple flowers, but how can you tell in the midst of January? The roots of A are at most 7 meters deep, versus at least 9 for B — must you dig?

In software, when a single criterion seems too restrictive, we can use all the techniques of multiple and especially repeated inheritance that we have learned to master in earlier chapters. Assume for example a class *EMPLOYEE* in a personnel management system. Assume further that we have two separate criteria for classifying employees:

- By contract type, such as permanent *vs.* temporary.

- By job type, such as engineering, administrative, managerial.

and that both of these criteria have been recognized to lead to valid descendant classes; in other words you are not engaging in taxomania, since the classes that you have identified, such as *TEMPORARY_EMPLOYEE* for the first criterion and *MANAGER* for the second, are truly characterized by specific features not applicable to the other categories. What do you do?

A first attempt might introduce all the variants at the same level:

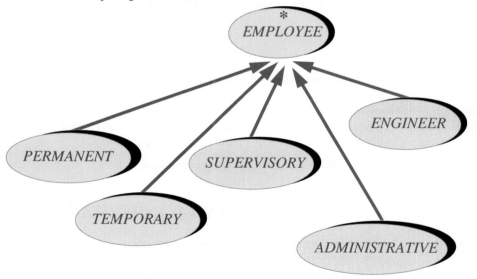

A messy classification

To keep this sketched example small and the figure simple, the class names have been abbreviated. To go from this example to a real system we would have to apply the usual naming guidelines, which suggest longer and more accurate names such as *PERMANENT_EMPLOYEE, ENGINEERING_EMPLOYEE* and so on.

This inheritance hierarchy is not satisfactory since widely different concepts are represented by classes at the same level.

View inheritance

Classification through views

If you retain the idea of using inheritance for the classification used in the example under discussion, you should introduce an intermediate level to describe the competing classification criteria:

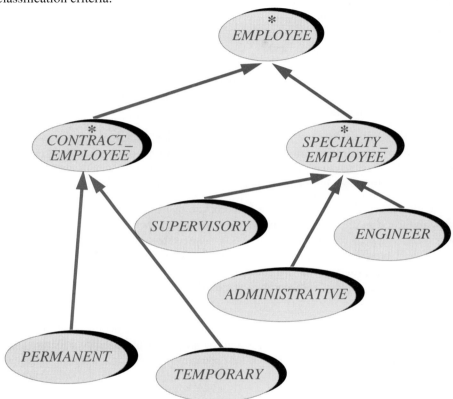

Note that the name *CONTRACT_EMPLOYEE* does not mean "employee that has a contract" (as opposed to employees who might not have one!), but "employee as characterized by his contract". The name of the sibling class similarly means "employee as characterized by his specialty".

That these names seem far-fetched reflects a certain uneasiness, typical of this kind of inheritance. In subtype inheritance we encountered the rule that the sets of instances represented by the various heirs to a class be disjoint. Here the rule does not apply: a permanent employee, for example, may be an engineer too. This means that such a classification is meant for repeated inheritance: some proper descendants of the classes shown in the figure will have both *CONTRACT_EMPLOYEE* and *SPECIALTY_EMPLOYEE* as ancestors — not directly, but for example by inheriting from both *PERMANENT* and *ENGINEER*. Such classes will be repeated descendants of *EMPLOYEE*.

This form of inheritance may be called view inheritance: various heirs of a certain class represent not disjoint subsets of instances (as in the subtype case) but various ways of classifying instances of the parent. Note that this only makes sense if both the parent and the heirs are deferred classes, that is to say, classes describing general categories rather than fully specified objects. Our first attempt at *EMPLOYEE* classification by views (the one that had all descendants at the same level) violated that rule; the second one satisfies it.

Is view inheritance appropriate?

View inheritance is relatively far from the more common uses of inheritance and is subject to criticism. The reader will be judge of whether to use it for his own purposes, but in any case we should examine the pros and cons.

It should be clear that — like repeated inheritance, which it requires — view inheritance is **not a beginner's mechanism**. The rule of prudence that was introduced for repeated inheritance holds here: if you have less than a few months' hands-on experience with O-O development of significant projects, better stay away from view inheritance.

The alternative to view inheritance is to choose one of the classification criteria as primary, and use it as the sole guide for devising the inheritance hierarchy; to address the other criteria, you will use specific features. It is interesting to note that many modern zoologists and botanists use this approach: their basic classification criterion is the reconstructed evolutionary history of the genera and species involved. Would it that we always had such a single, indisputable standard to guide us in devising software taxonomies.

To stick to a single primary criterion in our example we could decide that the job type is the factor of principal interest, and represent the employment status by a feature. As a first attempt, the feature (in class *EMPLOYEE*) could be

> *is_permanent*: *BOOLEAN*

but this is dangerously constraining; to extend the possibilities, we could have

> *Permanent*: *INTEGER* **is unique**
> *Temporary*: *INTEGER* **is unique**
> *Contractor*: *INTEGER* **is unique**
> ...

but then we have learned to be wary, for good reasons, of explicit enumerations. A better approach is to introduce a class *WORK_CONTRACT*, most likely deferred, with as many descendants as necessary to account for specific kinds of work contract. Then we can stay away from loathed explicit discriminations of the form

> **if** *is_permanent* **then** ... **else** ... **end**

or

inspect

> *contract_type*

when *Permanent* **then**

> ...

when ...

> ...

end

with their contingent of future extendibility troubles (stemming from their violation of just about every modularity principle: continuity, single choice, open-closedness); instead, we will equip class *WORK_CONTRACT* with deferred features representing contract-type-dependent operations, which will then be effected differently in descendants. Most of these features will need an argument of type *EMPLOYEE*, representing the employee to which the operation is being applied; examples might include *hire* and *terminate*.

The resulting structure will look like this:

Multi-criteria classification through separate, client-related hierarchies

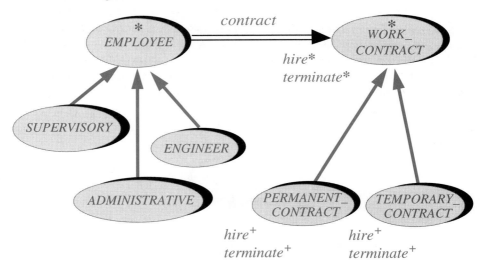

See *"AN APPLICA-TION: THE HAN-DLE TECHNIQUE"*, *24.3, page 817.*

This scheme, as you may have noted, is almost identical to the **handle**-based design pattern described earlier in this chapter.

Such a technique may be used in place of view inheritance. It does complicate the structure by introducing a separate hierarchy, a new attribute (here *contract*) and the corresponding client relations. It has the advantage that the abstractions in such a hierarchy are beyond question (work contract, permanent work contract); with the view inheritance solution, the abstractions are clear too but a little trickier to explain ("employee seen from the perspective of his work contract", "employee seen from the perspective of his specialty").

Criteria for view inheritance

It is not uncommon to think of view inheritance early in the analysis of a problem domain, while you are still struggling with the fundamental concepts and considering several possible classification criteria, all of which vie for your attention. As you improve your understanding of the application area, it will often happen that one of the criteria starts to dominate the others, imposing itself as the primary guide for devising the inheritance structure. In such cases, the preceding discussion strongly suggests that you should renounce view inheritance in favor of more straightforward techniques.

I still find view inheritance useful when the following three conditions are met:

- The various classification criteria are equally important, so any choice of a primary one would be arbitrary.

- Many possible combinations (such as, in the earlier example, permanent supervisor, temporary engineer, permanent engineer and so on) are needed.

- The classes under consideration are so important as to justify spending significant time to get the best possible inheritance structure. This applies in particular when the classes are part of a **reusable library** with large reuse potential.

An example of application of these criteria is the uppermost structure of the Base libraries, in the environment described in the last chapter of this book. The resulting classes followed from an effort, described in detail in the book [M 1994a], of applying taxonomical principles to the systematic classification of computing science's basic structures, in the tradition of the natural scientists. The highest part of the "container" structure looks like this:

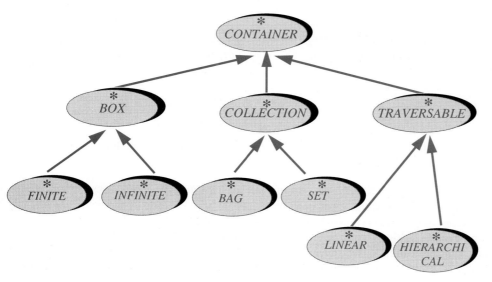

A view-based classification of fundamental computing structures

The first-level classification (*BOX*, *COLLECTION*, *TRAVERSABLE*) is view-based; the level below it (and many of those further below, not shown) is a subtype classification. A container structure is characterized through three criteria:

- How items will be accessed: *COLLECTION*. A *SET* makes it possible to find out whether an item is present, whereas a *BAG* also enables the client to find out the number of occurrences of a given element. Further refinements include such access abstractions as *SEQUENCE* (items are accessed sequentially), *STACK* (items are accessed in the reverse order of their insertion) and so on.

- How items will be represented: *BOX*. Variants include finite and infinite structures. A finite structure can be bounded or unbounded; a bounded structured can be fixed or resizable.

- How the structure can be traversed: *TRAVERSABLE*.

It is interesting to note that the hierarchy did not start out as view inheritance. The initial idea was to define *BOX*, *COLLECTION* and *TRAVERSABLE* as unrelated classes, each at the top of a separate hierarchy; then, when describing any particular data structure implementation, to use multiple inheritance to pick one parent from each of the three parts. For example a linked list is finite and unbounded (representation), sequentially accessed (access), and linearly traversable (traversal):

Building a data structure class by combination of abstractions through multiple inheritance

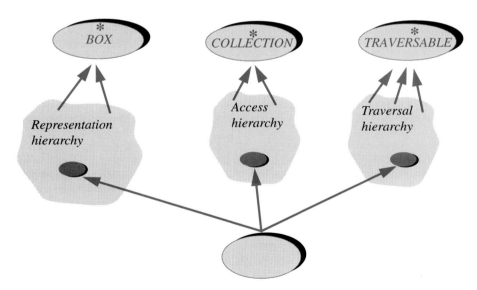

But then we realized that it was inappropriate to keep *BOX*, *COLLECTION* and *TRAVERSABLE* separate: they all needed a few common features, in particular *has* (membership test) and *empty* (test for no elements). This clearly indicated the need for a common ancestor — *CONTAINER*, where these common features now appear. Hence a structure that was initially designed as pure multiple inheritance, with three disjoint hierarchies at the top, turned out to be a view inheritance hierarchy with a considerable amount of repeated inheritance.

Although initially difficult to get right, this structure has turned out to be useful, flexible and stable, confirming both of the conclusions of this discussion: that view inheritance is not for the faint of heart; and that when applicable it can play a key role for complex problem domains where many criteria interact — if the effort is justified, as in a fundamental library of reusable components, which simply has to be done right.

24.11 HOW TO DEVELOP INHERITANCE STRUCTURES

When you read a book or pedagogical article on the object-oriented method, or when you discover a class library, the inheritance hierarchies that you see have already been designed, and the author does not always tell you how they got to be that way. How then do you go about designing your own structures?

Some of the material in this section is from [M 1995].

Specialization and abstraction

Voluntarily or not, many pedagogical presentations tend to create the impression that inheritance structures should be designed from the most general (the upper part) to the most specific (the leaves). This is in part because this is often the best way to *describe* a good structure once it exists: from the general to the particular; from the figures to the closed figures to the polygons to the rectangles to the squares. But the best way to describe a structure is not necessarily the best way to *produce* it.

> A similar comment, due to Michael Jackson, was mentioned in the discussion of top-down design.

See "Production and description", page 114.

In an ideal world populated with perfect people, we would always recognize the proper abstractions right away, and then draw the categories, their subcategories and so on. In the real world, however, we often see a specific case before we discover the general abstraction of which it is but a variant.

In many cases the abstraction is not unique; how best to generalize a certain notion depends on what you or your clients will most likely want to do with the notion and its variants. Consider for example a notion that we have often encountered in earlier discussion: points in a two-dimensional space. At least four generalizations are possible:

* Points in arbitrary-dimension space — leading to an inheritance structure where the sisters of class *POINT* will be classes *POINT_3D* and so on.

* Geometrical figures — the other classes in the structure being the likes of *FIGURE*, *RECTANGLE*, *CIRCLE* and so on.

* Polygons — with other classes such as *QUADRANGLE* (four vertices), *TRIANGLE* (three vertices) and *SEGMENT* (two vertices), *POINT* being the special polygon with just one vertex.

* Objects that are entirely determined by two coordinates — the other contenders here being *COMPLEX* and *VECTOR_2D*.

Although some of these generalizations may intuitively be more appealing than others, it is impossible to say in the absolute which one of them is the best. The answer will depend on how your software base evolves and what it will need. So a prudent process in which you sometimes abstract a bit too late, because you waited until you were sure that you had found the most useful path of generalization, may be preferable to one in which you might get too much untested abstraction too soon.

The arbitrariness of classifications

The *POINT* example is typical. When presented with two competing classifications of a certain set of abstractions, you will often be able to determine, based on rational arguments, which one is *better*; but seldom is one in a position to determine that a certain inheritance structure is the *best* possible one.

This situation is not specific to software. Do not believe, for example that the Linnaean classifications of natural science are universally accepted or eternal. The maintainers of the "Tree of Life" Internet archive mentioned earlier (see also the bibliographical notes) state at the outset that the project's classification — however collaborative and interdisciplinary — is controversial. And this is not just for weird smallish creatures too viscous to be discussed at lunch; Dr. Everham's Web classification of birds cited earlier comes with the comment

See page 842. Bibliographic references removed.

There are 174 Families, 2044 Genera and 9021 species of birds in the world! The most abundant species are in the order Passeriformes with 5276 species. The least number of species in an order is 1: the Ostrich in Struthioniformes. (I would have thought the Ostrich would be in an order with the Emus, Kiwis and Moas, all extinct, because they all are flightless with stout legs and longish necks.) The Linnaeus system groups organisms based on morphological similarities. Another classification of animals is based on DNA-DNA hybridization. This is highly complex; for example an American Cuckoo would be classified as: Kingdom, Animalia; Phylum, Chordata; Class, Aves; Subclass, Neornithes; Infraclass, Neoaves; Parvclass, Passerae; Superorder, Cuculimorphae; Order, Cuculiformes; Infraorder, Cuculides; Parvorder, Coccyzida; Family, Coccyzidae.

More on competing classification methods at the end of this chapter.

This shows the competition between two systems: the traditional one, based on morphology (and evolution); and a more inductive one based on DNA analysis. They lead to radically different results. Also note, as an aside, that here we see a zoologist who does think that flightlessness should be a significant taxonomical criterion — but the official classification disagrees.

Induction and deduction

To design software hierarchies, the proper process is a combination of the deductive and the inductive, of specialization and generalization: sometimes you see the abstraction first and then infer the special cases; sometimes you first build or find a useful class and then realize that there is a more abstract underlying concept.

If you find yourself not always using the first scheme, but once in a while discovering the abstract only after you have seen the concrete, *maybe there is nothing wrong with you.* You are simply using a normal "yoyo" approach to classification.

As you accumulate experience and insight, you should find that the share of (correct) a priori decisions grows. But an a posteriori component will always remain.

Varieties of class abstraction

> *This principle of Reversion is the most wonderful of all the attributes of inheritance.*
>
> Charles Darwin

Two forms of a posteriori parent construction are common and useful.

Abstracting is the late recognition of a higher-level concept. You find a class *B* which covers a useful notion, but whose developer did not recognize that it was actually a special case of a more general notion *A*, justifying an inheritance link:

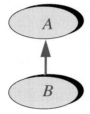

Abstraction

That this insight was initially missed — that is to say, that *B* was built without *A* — is not a reason to renounce the use of inheritance in this case. Once you recognize the need for *A*, you can, and in most cases should, write this class and adapt *B* to become one of its heirs. It is not as good as having written *A* earlier, but better than not writing it at all.

Factoring is the case in which you detect that two classes *E* and *F* actually represent variants of the same general notion:

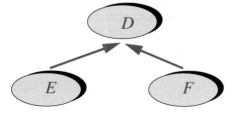

Factoring

If you recognize this commonality belatedly, the generalization step will enable you to add a common parent class *D*. Here again it would have been preferable to get the hierarchy right the first time around, but late is better than never.

Client independence

Abstracting and factoring may in many cases proceed without negative effects on the existing clients (an application of the Open-Closed principle).

This property results from the method's use of information hiding. Consider again the preceding schematic cases, but with a typical client class *X* added to the picture:

Abstraction, factoring and clients

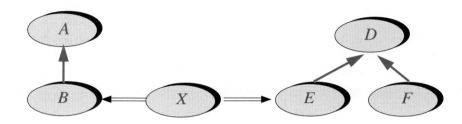

When *B* gets abstracted into *A*, or the features of *E* get factored with those of *F* into *D*, a class *X* that is a client of *B* or *E* (in the figure it is a client of both) will in many cases not feel any effect from the change. The ancestry of a class does not affect its clients if they are simply applying the features of the class on entities of the corresponding type. In other words, if *X* uses *B* and *E* as suppliers under the scheme

> *b1*: *B*; *e1*: *E*
>
> …
>
> *b1*.*some_feature_of_B*
>
> …
>
> *e1*.*some_feature_of_E*

then *X* is unaffected by any re-parenting of *B* or *E* arising from abstracting or factoring.

Elevating the level of abstraction

Abstracting and factoring are typical of the process of continuous improvement that characterizes a successful object-oriented software construction process. In my experience this is one of the most elating aspects of practicing the method: knowing that even though you are not expected to reach perfection the first time around, you are given the opportunity to improve your design continually, until it satisfies everyone.

In a development group that applies the method well, this regular elevation of the *level of abstraction* of the software, and as a corollary of its quality, is clearly perceptible to the project members, and serves as constant incentive and motivation.

24.12 A SUMMARY VIEW: USING INHERITANCE WELL

Inheritance will never cease to surprise us with its power and versatility. In this chapter we have tried to get a better handle at what inheritance really means and how we can use it to our best advantage. A few central conclusions have emerged.

First, we should not be afraid of the variety of ways in which we can use inheritance. Prohibiting multiple inheritance or facility inheritance achieves no other aim than to hurt ourselves. The mechanisms are there to help you: use them well, but use them.

Next, inheritance is for the most part a *supplier*'s technique. It is one weapon in our arsenal of techniques for fighting our adversaries (in particular complexity, the software developer's relentless foe). Inheritance may matter to *client* software as well, especially in the case of libraries, but its main goal is to help us building the thing in the first place.

Of course, all software is designed for its clients, and the clients' needs drive the process. A set of classes is good if it will offer excellent service to client software: interfaces and associated implementations that are complete, free from bad surprises (such as unexpected performance penalties), simple to use, easy to learn, easy to remember, extendible. To achieve these goals, the designer is free to use inheritance and other object-oriented techniques in any way he pleases. The end justifies the means.

Also remember, when designing an inheritance structure, that the goal is software construction, not philosophy. Seldom is there a single solution, or even a best one in the absolute. "Best" means best for the purposes of a certain class of client applications. This is particularly true as we move away from areas such as mathematics and fundamental computing science, where a widely accepted body of theory exists, towards business-driven application domains. To find out what class hierarchy best addresses the notion of company share, you probably need to know whether the software caters to individual investors, to a publicly traded company, to a stock broker, or to the Stock Exchange.

In a way, this is comforting. The naturalist who classifies a certain set of plants and animals must devise absolute categories. In software the equivalent only happens if you are in the business of producing general-purpose libraries (such as those covering fundamental data structures, graphics, databases). Most of the time, your aims will be more modest. You will need to design a *good* hierarchy, one that will satisfy the needs of a certain kind of client software.

The final lesson of this chapter generalizes a comment made in the discussion of facility inheritance: the principal difficulty of building class structures is not inheritance per se; it is the search for abstractions. If you have identified valid abstractions, their inheritance structure will follow. To find the abstractions, the guide you will use is the guide that we follow throughout this book: the theory of abstract data types.

24.13 KEY CONCEPTS INTRODUCED IN THIS CHAPTER

- Every use of inheritance should reflect some form of "is" relation between two categories of object, either in an external modeled domain or in the software itself.

- Do not use inheritance to model a "has this kind of component" relation; this is the province of the client relation. (Remember *CAR_OWNER*.)

- When inheritance is applicable, client is often potentially applicable too. If the corresponding view can change, use the client relation; if you foresee polymorphic uses, use inheritance.

- Do not introduce intermediate inheritance nodes unless they describe a well-identified abstraction, characterized by specific features.

- A classification of inheritance was defined, based on twelve kinds divided into three general categories: model inheritance (describing relations existing in the modeled domain), software inheritance (describing relations in the software itself), and variation inheritance (for class adaptation in either the model or the software).

- The power of inheritance comes from its combination of a type specialization and a module extension mechanism. It seems neither wise nor useful to use different language mechanisms.

- Implementation and facility inheritance require some care but can be powerful supplier-side techniques.

- View inheritance, a delicate technique involving repeated inheritance, allows classifying object types along several competing criteria. It is useful for professional libraries. In many cases a simpler handle technique is preferable.

- Although not theoretically ideal, the actual process of designing inheritance hierarchies is often yoyo-like — from the abstract to the concrete and back.

- Inheritance is primarily a supplier technique.

24.14 BIBLIOGRAPHICAL NOTES

The principal reference on the taxonomy of inheritance is [Girod 1991]. A book on O-O methodology [Page-Jones 1995], one of a very small number that provide useful methodological advice on object-oriented design, includes precious advice on uses and misuses of inheritance. Another useful reference is [McGregor 1992]; John McGregor has particularly explored the technique called view inheritance in this chapter.

[Breu 1995] also provides interesting concepts, based on a view of proper inheritance usage more restrictive than the one in this chapter.

A technique similar to this chapter's "handles" is described in [Gil 1994].

The preparation of this chapter benefited from the comments of several biologists who maintain Web-accessible resources on the taxonomy of living beings, in particular: the "tree of life" at the University of Arizona (*phylogeny.arizona.edu/tree/life.html*), courtesy of Professors David Maddison and, for birds, Michel Laurin (the latter from Berkeley). Professor Edwin Everham from Radford University was also very helpful.

General references on the theory of classification, or *systematics*, appear at the end of the next section.

24.15 APPENDIX: A HISTORY OF TAXONOMY

This Appendix is supplementary material, not used in the rest of this book. The study of taxonomic efforts in other disciplines is full of potential lessons for us object-oriented software developers. I hope to spur further interest in this fascinating area — possibly a topic for an inter-disciplinary Master's or Ph. D. thesis.

From Aristotle to Darwin

The classification of species began at least as early as Aristotle (384-322 B.C.E.), whose taxonomy of animals, *Historia Animalium*, continued for plants under the title *Historia Plantarum* by his student Theophrastus of Eresos (ca. 370-288 B.C.E.), was accepted as definitive for many centuries. Aristotle's criteria for classifying animals include both how they reproduce and where they live; from a modern viewpoint, only the first would be considered relevant, as we have come to accept that regardless of habitat considerations a dolphin is closer to a llama than to a shark. Theophrastus's classification was more systematically structural. Modern botanical terminology comes largely from Aristotle and Theophrastus through the Latin translation of the latter's terms in the *Natural History of* Pliny the Elder (23-79 C.E.) (Pliny was well aware of the need to avoid being misled by appearances: "*It was the plan* [of some Greek naturalists] *to delineate the various plants in colors, and then to add in writing a description of the properties which they possessed. Pictures, however, are very apt to mislead; … besides, it is not sufficient to delineate a plant as it appears at one period only, as it presents a different appearance at each of the four seasons of the year.*") A later important contributor was Dioscorides of Anazarbus (1st century C.E.), Nero's doctor, who classified plants according to their medicinal properties.

Several scholars took up the work at the time of the Renaissance, in particular Conrad Gessner, who was to influence Linné and Cuvier through his *Opera Botanica* and *Historia Plantarum* (1541-1571), distinguishing genus from species and order from class, and Caspar Bauhin, who devised a binomial system for the classification of plants in his *Pinax* (1596). In the next century, John Ray (1628-1705) removed some of the arbitrariness of prevailing classifications by taking into account several properties of plants' morphology, rather than just one feature. He established the basic division of flowering plants into monocots and dicots (foreseen by Theophrastus). That division, still in use today, is another example of the fuzziness of even some of the fundamental classification criteria of biology; the UC Berkeley Museum of Paleontology (see the bibliographical references at the end of this section) gives a list of seven factors distinguishing monocots from dicots — one *vs.* two cotyledons in the embryo, flower parts in multiples of three *vs.* multiples of four or five, etc. — but adds that no single factor in that list will infallibly identify a given flowering plant as a monocot or dicot.

Only in the eighteenth century, with the development of biology as a science and the fast growth in known species, did the problem of biological classification start to acquire a character of urgency. Whereas Theophrastus had identified five hundred plant species, Bauhin knew six thousand, and Linnaeus catalogued eighteen thousand; less than a century later Cuvier listed over fifty thousand! The philosopher-scientists of the Age of Enlightenment, aroused by Newton's classification of heavenly bodies in his *Principia Mathematica* (1687), were not content any more to list the species, but started to look for meaningful principles of grouping them into categories — for the proper abstraction mechanisms, as we software people would say. The roots of modern taxonomy can be traced to that collective effort of the early modern era.

The key contributor was the Swedish botanist Carl Linné (1701-1778), also known by the Latin name Carolus Linnaeus, who in 1737 published his taxonomic system, still the basis of all taxonomic systems used today. One of his major innovations, was — using software engineering terminology again — to discard the *top-down* approach used by previous taxonomists (who posited basic abstract categories and successively divided them into smaller groups) in favor of a *bottom-up* approach, well in line with the emphasis on pragmatism and experimentation that marked the beginnings of the scientific method; he started from the species themselves and grouped them into categories.

Both Ray and Linné were in search of a "natural system", that is to say an ideal classification that would reveal divine intentions.

Progress between Linné and Darwin was largely due to an astonishing succession of naturalists at the Paris *Jardin des Plantes*:

- Georges-Louis de Buffon (1707-1788) wrote the magnificent 44-volume *Histoire Naturelle*, bold enough to suggest a common ancestry for humans and apes.

- Antoine-Laurent de Jussieu (1748-1836) looked for a more natural and comprehensive system of plant classification than Linné's. Modern taxonomies of plants actually follow from Jussieu's work, itself based on Ray's. (Although modern classification systems are based on Linné's ideas, his actual taxonomy has largely been discarded — initially in part because of moral reasons, since he gave such importance to sexual features.)

- Jean-Baptiste Lamarck (1744-1829), whose theory of evolution announced Darwin's, published his *Flore française* in 1778 and almost single-handedly originated the classification of "invertebrates", a term he coined. In his *Histoire naturelle des Animaux sans Vertèbres* he was the first to separate the crustaceans from the insects.

- Georges Cuvier (1769-1832) did for vertebrates what Lamarck did for invertebrates. He was famous for his ability to reconstruct complete organisms from fossil fragments. He classified animals into four branches.

- Étienne Geoffroy Saint-Hilaire (1772-1844), another great taxonomist, was the adversary of Cuvier (whom he had brought to Paris) in a famous public debate about unity *vs.* diversity of life forms. The dispute reflected deeper questions: evolutionary *vs.* fixed views of species, and the issue, still open today, of formalism *vs.* functionalism. When we see Cuvier writing "*If there are resemblances between the organs of fishes and those of the other vertebrate classes, it is only insofar as there are resemblances between their functions*" in 1828, and Geoffroy responding "*Animals have no habits but those that result from the structure of their organs*" in 1829, it is hard for a software professional to avoid thinking "abstract data type" and "implementation".

The next revolution in taxonomical thought came with Charles Darwin (1809-1882), whose *Origin of Species* (1859) suggested a simple basis for taxonomy: use evolutionary history. The classification of organisms according to their origin in evolution is known as **cladistics**. For some biologists, this is the *only* criterion. The Berkeley Museum of Paleontology again:

> *For many years, since even before Darwin, it has been popular to tell "stories" about how certain traits of organisms came to be. With cladistics, it is possible to determine whether these stories have merit, or whether they should be abandoned in favor of a competing hypothesis. For instance, it was long said that the orb-weaving spiders, with their intricate and orderly webs, had evolved from spiders with cobweb-like webs. The cladistic analysis of these spiders showed that, in fact, orb-weaving was the primitive state, and that cobweb-weaving had evolved from spiders with more orderly webs.*

Biologists who use to this single, unimpeachable criterion, are in a way more fortunate than us poor software modelers: they can assume, or pretend, that there is a single taxonomical truth, and that the only problem is to reconstruct it. (In other words they have fulfilled Ray's, Linné's and Jussieu's quest for a single Natural System.) In software modeling we cannot postulate, let alone discover, such an underlying truth.

The modern scene

You would think that biological taxonomy, with its long and prestigious history, from Aristotle to Darwin and Huxley, would by now be a sedate field. Think again. Since the sixties, controversy has been raging. There are three main schools, the ardor of whose debates will seem thoroughly familiar to anyone who has heard software engineers debate their favorite programming languages. Here is — after the taxonomy of taxonomy which occupied our efforts at the beginning of this chapter — the taxonomy of taxonomists:

- The *numerical pheneticists* draw their classifications from the study of organisms' individual characters, using numerical measures of distance (and relying generously on computer algorithms) to group organisms that have the most characters in common. Sokal and Sneath are recognized as the founders of this approach.

- The *cladists* use evolutionary history as the sole criterion. The Berkeley extract reflected this view (more details below). Cladistics draws its inspiration from work by the German scientist Willi Hennig, first published in German in 1950 and in English in 1965.

- The *evolutionary taxonomists*, led by G.G. Simpson and Ernst Mayr, who claim Darwin's direct heritage, "*base* [their] *classifications on observed similarities and differences among groups of organisms, evaluated in the light of their inferred evolutionary history*" (as stated by Mayr, 1981, reference below).

It is next to impossible to find neutral accounts of the arguments for each approach in the literature. (Perhaps this sounds familiar.) It falls on the outsider to try to develop an impartial view. In this brief survey we will try to remain as close as possible to the software analogies.

Numerical phenetics — what we would call the bottom-up approach — has the advantage of being based on precise, repeatable measures. But the choice of measured characters and their weighting is subjective. And a purely external measure risks being influenced by chance factors; it is well known since Darwin that evolution involves not only divergence (species evolving from a common ancestor by developing different characters) but convergence (completely distinct species developing similar features to adapt to similar environments or by sheer coincidence). So there is a great danger of arbitrariness. One can also fear instability: the discovery of new species — which occurs all the time in biology — could, more than with the other approaches, put into question classifications drawn from the statistical analysis of the previously known species.

On the surface the other two schools would seem to be very close to each other. Why then do they keep arguing with each other from their respective journals and conferences? The reason is that the cladists are particularly rigorous, as they would see it, or dogmatic, as the other two schools might put it. They take evolution, and evolution only, as the classification criterion. The method is particularly strict: it examines the evolutionary history, as given by the fossil record, and decides which characters are *synapomorhic* and which ones *plesiomorphic*. A feature is plesiomorphic if it was already present in a common ancestor; then for the cladist it is not interesting at all! The useful features as the synapomorphic ones, which hold for two organisms but not their ancestors. Synapomorphies are the primary tool for positing new groups (*taxa*, the plural of *taxon*).

In the following situation, then, the cladists will see only two taxa:

A cladogram

After Mayr, 1961.

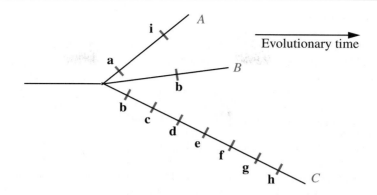

This is a *cladogram*, or record of the appearance of characters in the evolutionary history. The marks indicate new characters. *B* and *C* have a synapomorphy, character **b**, which was not in the ancestor and is not in *A*; so for a cladist *B* and *C* will form a taxon, and *A* another. For an evolutionary taxonomist, there would be three taxa, since *C* differs from *B* in many other characters (**c** to **h**). In its pure form cladistics is even more restrictive: like Roman Jakobson's phonology, it only considers *binary* characters; and it posits that when taxa evolve from a common ancestor the ancestor disappears.

Evolutionary taxonomy seems a more moderate approach, trying to draw from both cladistics and phenetics: evolution is the classification basis, but complemented by analysis of other characters, not necessarily synapomorphic.

Why then the restrictiveness of cladistics? The principal argument is epistemological: an attempt to satisfy Karl Popper's rules of falsifiability. Cladists argue that their approach is the only non-circular one; whereas the other two more or less assume (according to this view) what they are trying to deduce, a cladistic hypothesis can be refuted, in the same way that a single experiment can disprove a theory of physics, although no amount of experimentation will *prove* a theory.

The debate between these approaches is not closed. The progress of molecular biology will certainly affect it; in particular, by providing a link between observed characters and the evolutionary record, it may help achieve some reconciliation between phenetics and the other two methods.

We will stop here, with regret (more mundane software engineering topics are claiming our attention). For an O-O software developer, reading the taxonomy literature, although requiring a fair deal of attention in some cases ("*A phylogenetic definition of homology may be considered more falsifiable than a phenetic definition and therefore preferable if it leads to a hypothesis of homology which includes all the potential falsifiers provided by phenetic comparisons as well as the potential falsifiers provided by phylogeny…*") is rich in rewards. Our own work constantly subjects us, like our friends from the Biology department or the Herbarium, to two siren songs from opposite sides: the a priori form of classification, top-down, deductive and based on a "natural" order of things, coming to us through the cladists from Linné; and the empirical, inductive, bottom-up view of the pheneticists, telling us to observe and gather. Perhaps, like the evolutionary taxonomists, we will want a bit of both.

Bibliography on taxonomy

The following references — which have been separated from the main bibliography of this book to avoid too much *mélange des genres* — will be useful as a starting point on the subject of taxonomy history:

- The on-line material on evolution at the University of California Museum of Paleontology in Berkeley: **http://www.ucmp.berkeley.edu/clad/clad4.html** (authors: Allen G. Collins, Robert Guralnick, Brian R. Speer). Resolutely cladist. Some of the above presentation draws from the UCMP pages and from suggestions by their authors.

- A biography of Jussieu: *Antoine-Laurent de Jussieu, Nature and the Natural System* by Peter F. Stevens, Columbia University Press, New York, 1994. (I am grateful to Prof. Stevens for several important suggestions.)

- A collection of papers on cladistics: *Cladistic Theory and Methodology*, edited by Thomas Duncan and Tod F. Stuessy, Van Nostrand Reinhold, 1985. Quite cladist, but the end of the volume adds some interesting critical articles, one in particular by Ernst Mayr (*Cladistic analysis or cladistic classifications?*, pages 304-308, originally in *Zeitung Zool. Syst. Evolut.-Forsch.*, 19:94-128, 1974).

- Another volume of contributions: *Prospects in Systematics*, ed. D.L. Hawksworth, Systematics Association, Clarendon Press, Oxford, 1988.

- A textbook: *Biological Systematics* by Herbert H. Ross, Addison-Wesley, Reading (Mass.), 1973.

- The founding book of cladistics: *Phylogenetic Systematics* by Willi Hennig, English translation, University of Illinois Press, Urbana (Ill.), 1966. See also a shorter presentation by Hennig (adapted from his original 1950 article) in Duncan and Stuessy.

- A cladistic treatise, starting with the picture of Hennig: *Phylogenetics — The Theory and Practice of Phylogenetic Systematics* by E.O. Wiley, published by John Wiley and Sons, New York, 1981. By the same author, a Popperian argument for cladistics, *Karl R. Popper, Systematics, and Classification: A Reply to Walter Bock and Other Evolutionary Taxonomists*, pages 37-47 of Duncan and Stuessy, originally in *Syst. Zool* 24:233-243, 1975.

- A clear article by Ernst Mayr, leaning to evolutionary taxonomy but discussing the other approaches with some sympathy: *Biological Classification: Towards a Synthesis of Opposing Methodologies*, in *Science*, vol. 214, 1961, pages 510-516.

- The foundational text of the pheneticists: *Principles of Numerical Taxonomy*, by Robert P. Sokal and Peter H.A. Sneath, Freeman Publishing, San Francisco, 1963, revised edition 1973.

- A short and more recent book advocating *Transformed Cladistics* (subtitle: *Taxonomy and Evolution*) by N.R. Scott-Ram, Cambridge University Press, 1990.

EXERCISES

E24.1 Arrayed stacks

Write in full the *STACK* class and its heir *ARRAYED_STACK* sketched in this chapter, using the "marriage of convenience" technique.

E24.2 Meta-taxonomy

See "General taxonomy", page 824.

Imagine this chapter's classification of the forms of inheritance were an inheritance hierarchy. What kind or kinds would it involve?

E24.3 The stacks of Hanoï

The Towers of Hanoï problem, used in many computing science texts as an example of recursive procedure, comes from Édouard Lucas, "Récréations Mathématiques", Paris, 1883, reprinted by Albert Blanchard, Paris, 1975.

(This exercise comes from an example used by Philippe Drix on the French GUE electronic mailing list, late 1995 and early 1996.)

Assume a deferred class *STACK* with a procedure *put* to push an element onto the top, with a precondition involving the boolean-valued function *full* (which could also be called *extendible*; as you study the exercise you will note that the choice of name may affect the appeal of various possible solutions).

Now consider the famous problem of the Towers of Hanoï, where disks are stacked on piles — the towers — with the rule that a disk may only be put on a larger disk.

Is it appropriate to define the class *HANOÏ_STACK*, representing such piles, as an heir to *STACK*? If so, how should the class be written? If not, can *HANOÏ_STACK* still make use of *STACK*? Write the class in full for the various possible solutions; discuss the pros and cons of each, state which one you prefer, and explain the rationale for your choice.

E24.4 Are polygons lists?

"POLYGONS AND RECTANGLES", 14.1, page 460.

The implementation of our first inheritance example, class *POLYGON*, uses a linked list attribute *vertices* to represent the vertices of a polygon. Should *POLYGON* instead inherit from *LINKED_LIST* [*POINT*]?

E24.5 Functional variation inheritance

Provide one or more examples of functional variation inheritance. For each of them, discuss whether they are legitimate applications of the Open-Closed principle or examples of what the discussion called "organized hacking".

E24.6 Classification examples

For each of the following cases, indicate which one of the inheritance kinds applies:

- *SEGMENT* from *OPEN_FIGURE*.

- *COMPARABLE* (objects equipped with a total order relation) inheriting from *PART_COMPARABLE* (objects with a partial order relation).

"ADVANCED EXCEPTION HANDLING", 12.6, page 431.

- Some class from *EXCEPTIONS*.

E24.7 Where do iterators belong?

Would it be a good idea to have iterator features (*while_do* and the like) included in classes describing the data structures on which they iterate, such as *LIST*? Consider the following points:

- The ease of applying iterations to arbitrary *action* and *test* routines, chosen by the application.

- Extendibility: the possibility of adding new iteration schemes to the library.

- More generally, respect of object-oriented principles, in particular the idea that operations do not exist by themselves but only in relation to certain data abstractions.

E24.8 Module and type inheritance

Assume we devise a language with two kinds of inheritance: module extension and subtyping. Where would each of the inheritance kinds identified in this chapter fit?

E24.9 Inheritance and polymorphism

Of the kinds of inheritance reviewed in this chapter between a parent *A* and an heir *B*, which ones do you expect in practice to be used for polymorphic attachment, that is to say assignments $x := y$ or the corresponding argument passing with x of type *A* and y of type *B*?

25

Useful techniques

$\mathcal{E}$xamples of object-oriented design given in preceding chapters have illustrated a number of distinctive techniques. Although we are not done yet with our review of methodological issues — we must still explore style rules, O-O analysis concepts, teaching methods, and the software process — it is time to pause briefly to recapitulate some of the principal O-O techniques that we have learned.

This will be the tersest chapter of all: it just enumerates fruitful ideas, followed in a few cases by keywords meant to remind you of some of the examples in which we first encountered the ideas.

25.1 DESIGN PHILOSOPHY

General development scheme

Bottom-up development: build a solid basis, then apply it to specific cases.

Chapter 28 discusses seamlessness and reversibility. Seamlessness: apply consistent techniques and tools to analysis, design, implementation, maintenance.

Reversibility: let the functional specification benefit from the lessons of implementation.

Generalization: from specialized classes, derive reusable ones. Abstraction, factoring out commonalities.

The structure of systems

Systems are made of classes only.

The development style is bottom-up. Whenever possible, start from what you have.

Try to make classes as general as possible from the start.

Try to make classes as autonomous as possible.

Two inter-class relations: client (with "reference client" and "expanded client" variants); inheritance. Roughly correspond to "has" and "is".

Use multi-layer architectures to separate abstract interface from implementations for various platforms: Vision, WEL/PEL/MEL.

System evolution

Design for change and reuse.

When improving a design, use obsolete features and classes to facilitate the transition.

25.2 CLASSES

Class structure

Every class should correspond to a well-defined data abstraction.

Shopping List approach: if a feature is potentially useful, and fits in with the data abstraction of the class, put it in.

Facility classes: group related facilities (e.g. a set of constants).

Active data structures (object as abstract machine).

Key decision is what features to make secret and what to export.

Use selective exports for a group of intimately connected classes: *LINKED_LIST*, *LINKABLE*.

Re-engineer non-O-O software by encapsulating abstractions into classes (cf. *Math* library).

Class documentation

Put as much information as possible in the class itself.

Write header comments carefully and consistently; they will be part of the official interface.

Indexing clauses.

Designing feature interfaces

Command-Query Separation principle: a function should not produce any abstract side effect (concrete side effects are OK).

Use only operands as arguments.

Set status, then execute operation.

For each status-setting command, provide a status-returning query.

For argumentless queries, there should be no externally visible difference between an attribute implementation and a function implementation.

Let an object change representation silently as a result of requested operations (example of complex number class).

Cursor structures (*LIST*, *LINKED_LIST* and many others).

Using assertions

The precondition binds the client, the postcondition binds the supplier.

Make precondition strong enough to enable the routine to do its job well — but not stronger.

Two kinds of invariant clause: some clauses come from the underlying abstract data type; others (*representation invariant*) describe consistency properties of the implementation. Use implementation invariant to express and improve your understanding of the relationship between the different constituents of the class, attributes in particular.

For an argumentless query, include abstract properties in the invariant (even if, for a function, the property also appears in the postcondition).

Redeclarations can weaken the precondition to make the routine more tolerant.

To achieve the effect of strengthening the precondition, use an abstract precondition (based on a boolean function) in the original.

Even with no strengthening need, abstract preconditions are preferable.

Any precondition must be enforceable and testable by clients.

Do not overconstrain postcondition, to enable strengthening in a descendant (for example you may want to use one-way **implies** rather than equality).

Dealing with special cases

A priori checking: before operation, check if you can apply it.

A posteriori checking: try operation, then query an attribute (or higher-level function encapsulation) to find out whether it worked.

When everything else fails: use exception handling.

Organized failure: if a **rescue** executes to the end, do not forget to restore the invariant. The caller will get an exception too.

Retrying: try another algorithm, or (the strategy of hope) the same one again. Record what happened through an attribute or local entity; local entities are initialized only when the call starts, not after a **retry**.

25.3 INHERITANCE TECHNIQUES

Redeclaration

Redefining a routine to use a more specific algorithm, for more efficiency: *perimeter* in *POLYGON*, *RECTANGLE*, *SQUARE*.

Redefining a routine into an attribute: *balance* in *ACCOUNT*.

Effecting a feature that was deferred in the parent.

Joining two or more features through effecting (all but one inherited as deferred; the effective one takes over). Undefine some effective ones if needed.

Redefining two or more effective features together.

Accessing parent version in a redefinition: *precursor*.

Redeclarations preserve semantics (rules on assertions).

Deferred classes

Deferred classes capture high-level categories.

Deferred classes also serve as an analysis and design tool, to describe abstractions without commitment to an implementation.

Behavior classes: capture general behavior. Effective routines call deferred ones. Class will be partially deferred, partially implemented (covers partial choice of ADT implementation).

Polymorphism

Polymorphic data structures: through inheritance and genericity, combine right amount of similitude and variation.

Handles: describe a variable-type component through a polymorphic attribute.

Dynamic binding: avoid explicit discrimination.

Dynamic binding on a polymorphic data structure: apply to each element of a structure an operation that the element will apply in its own appropriate way.

For the point of single choice, pre-compute a data structure with one object of each possible type (as in the undoing pattern).

Forms of inheritance

Make sure all uses of inheritance belong to one of the categories in the taxonomy.

Inheritance for subtyping.

Inheritance for module extension.

Marriage of convenience: implement abstraction through concrete structure.

Restriction inheritance: add constraint.

Inheriting general-purpose mechanisms from facility classes.

Functional Variation inheritance: "organized hacking", Open-Closed principle.

Type Variation inheritance: covariance.

26

A sense of style

*I*mplementing the object-oriented method requires paying attention to many details of style, which a less ambitious approach might consider trifles.

26.1 COSMETICS MATTERS!

Although the rules appearing hereafter are not as fundamental as the principles of object-oriented software construction covered in earlier chapters, it would be foolish to dismiss them as just "cosmetics". Good software is good in the large *and* in the small, in its high-level architecture and in its low-level details. True, quality in the details does not guarantee quality of the whole; but sloppiness in the details usually indicates that something more serious is wrong too. (If you cannot get the cosmetics right, why should your customers believe that you can master the truly difficult aspects?) A serious engineering process requires doing *everything* right: the grandiose and the mundane.

So you should not neglect the relevance of such seemingly humble details as text layout and choice of names. True, it may seem surprising to move on, without lowering our level of attention, from the mathematical notion of sufficient completeness in formal specifications (in the chapter on abstract data types) to whether a semicolon should be preceded by a space (in the present chapter). The explanation is simply that both issues deserve our care, in the same way that when you write quality O-O software both the design and the realization will require your attention.

We can take a cue from the notion of style in its literary sense. Although the first determinant of good writing is the author's basic ability to tell a story and devise a coherent structure, no text is successful until everything works: every paragraph, every sentence and every word.

Applying the rules in practice

Some of the rules of this chapter can be checked or, better yet, enforced from the start by software tools. Tools will not do everything, however, and there is no substitute for care in writing every piece of the software.

There is often a temptation to postpone the application of the rules, writing things casually at first and thinking "I will clean up everything later on; I do not even know how much of this will eventually be discarded". This is not the recommended way. Once you get used to the rules, they do not add any significant delay to the initial writing of the software; even without special tools, it is always more costly to fix the text later than to write it properly from the start. And given the pressure on software developers, there is ever a risk that you will forget or not find the time to clean things up. Then someone who is asked later to take up your work will waste more time than it would have cost you to write the proper header comments, devise the right feature names, apply the proper layout. That someone may be you.

Terseness and explicitness

Software styles have oscillated between the terse and the verbose. In programming languages, the two extremes are perhaps APL and Cobol. The contrast between the Fortran-C-C++ line and the Algol-Pascal-Ada tradition — not just the languages themselves, but the styles they have bred — is almost as stark.

What matters for us is clarity and, more generally, quality. Extreme forms of terseness and verbosity can both work against these goals. Cryptic C programs are unfortunately not limited to the famous "obfuscated C" and "Obfuscated C++" contests; but the almost equally famous *DIVIDE DAYS BY 7 GIVING WEEKS* of Cobol is a waste of everyone's attention.

The style that follows from this chapter's rules is a particular mix of Algol-like explicitness (although not, it is hoped, verbosity) and telegram-style terseness. It never begrudges keystrokes, even lines, when they truly help make the software readable; for example, you will find rules that enjoin using clear identifiers based on full words, not abbreviations, as it is foolish to save a few letters by calling a feature *disp* (ambiguous) rather than *display* (clear and precise), or a class *ACCNT* (unpronounceable) rather than *ACCOUNT*. There is no tax on keystrokes. But at the same time when it comes to eliminating waste and unneeded redundancies the rules below are as pitiless as the recommendations of a General Accounting Office Special Commission on Improving Government. They limit header comments to indispensable words, getting rid of all the non-essential "the" and other such amenities; they proscribe over-qualification of feature names (as in *account_balance* in a class *ACCOUNT*, where *balance* is perfectly sufficient); against dominant mores, they permit the grouping of related components of a complex construct on a single line, as in **from** $i := 1$ **invariant** $i <= n$ **until** $i = n$ **loop**; and so on.

This combination of terseness and explicitness is what you should seek in your own texts. Do not waste space, as exaggerated size will in the end mean exaggerated complexity; but do not hesitate to use space when it is necessary to enhance clarity.

Also remember, if like many people you are concerned about how much smaller the text of an object-oriented implementation will be than the text of a comparable C, Pascal, Ada or Fortran program, that the only interesting answer will appear at the level of a significant system or subsystem. If you express a basic algorithm — at the level of

Quicksort, say, or Euclid's algorithm — in C and in the notation of this book, expect the O-O version to be at least as large. In many cases, if you apply the principles thoroughly, it will be larger, since it will include assertions and more type information. Yet in ISE's experience of looking at medium-scale systems we have sometimes found (without being able to give a general law, as the circumstances vary considerably) the object-oriented solution to be several times smaller. Why? This is not due to terseness at the "micro" level but to systemwide application of the architectural techniques of the O-O method:

- Genericity is one of the key factors. We have found C programs that repeated essentially the same C code many times to handle different types. With a generic class — or for that matter a generic Ada package — you immediately get rid of that redundancy. It is disturbing in this respect to see that Java, a recent O-O language based on C, does not support genericity.

- Inheritance is also fundamental in gathering commonalities and removing duplications.

- Dynamic binding replaces many complex decision structures by much shorter calls.

- Assertions and the associated idea of Design by Contract avoid redundant error checking, a principal source of bloat.

- The exception mechanism gets rid of some error code.

If you are concerned with source size, make sure to concentrate on these architectural aspects. You should also be terse in expressing algorithms, but never skimp on keystrokes at the expense of clarity.

The role of convention

Most rules define a single permissible form, with no variants. The few exceptions include font use, which is governed by external considerations (what looks good in a book may not be visible on overhead transparencies), and semicolons, for which there exist two opposite schools with equally forceful arguments (although we will have a few universal rules anyway). In all other cases, in line with the introductory methodology chapter's exhortations against wishy-washiness, the rules leave about as much room to doubt as a past due reminder from the Internal Revenue Service.

The rules are rooted in a careful analysis of what works and what works less well, resulting from many years of observation; some of the rationale will appear in the discussion. Even so, some rules may appear arbitrary at first, and indeed in a few cases the decision is a matter of taste, so that reasonable persons working from the same assumptions may disagree. If you object to one of the recommended conventions, you should define your own, provided you explain it in detail and document it explicitly; but do think carefully before making such a decision, so obvious are the advantages of abiding by a universal set of rules that have been systematically applied to thousands of classes over more than ten years, and that many people know and understand.

As noted in an earlier chapter (in the more general context of design principles), many of the style rules were originally developed for libraries, and then found their way into ordinary software development. In object technology, of course, all software is developed under the assumption that even if it is not reusable yet it *might* eventually be made reusable, so it is natural to apply the same style rules right from the start.

The comment was in the introduction to chapter 23.

Self-practice

Like the design rules of the preceding chapters, the style rules which follow have been carefully applied to the many examples of this book. The reasons are obvious: one should practice what one preaches; and, more fundamentally, the rules do support clarity of thought and expression, which can only be good for a detailed presentation of the object-oriented method.

The only exceptions are a few occasional departures from the rules on software text layout. These rules do not hesitate to spread texts over many lines, for example by requiring that every assertion clause have its own label. Lines are not a scarce resource on computer screens; it has been observed that with the computer age we are reversing the direction of the next-to-last revolution in written communication, the switch from papyrus rolls to page-structured books. But this text is definitely a book, structured into pages, and a constant application of the layout-related rules would have made it even bigger than it is.

The cases of self-dispensation affect only two or three layout-related rules, and will be noted in their presentation below. Any exception only occurs after the first few examples of a construct in the book have applied the rules scrupulously.

Such exceptions are only justified for a paper presentation. Actual software texts should apply the rules literally.

Discipline and creativity

It would be a mistake to protest against the rules of this chapter (and others) on the grounds that they limit developer creativity. A consistent style favors rather than hampers creativity by channeling it to where it matters. A large part of the effort of producing software is spent reading existing software and making others read what is being written. Individual vagaries benefit no one; common conventions help everyone.

Some of the software engineering literature of the nineteen-seventies propounded the idea of "egoless programming": developing software so that it does not reflect anything of its authors' personality, thereby making developers interchangeable. Applied to system design, this goal is clearly undesirable, even if some managers may sometimes long for it (as in this extract of a programming management book quoted by Barry Boehm: "…*the programmer*['*s*] <u>*creative instincts should be totally dulled*</u> *to insure uniform and understandable programming*", to which Boehm comments: "Given what we know about programmers and their growth motivation, such advice is a clear recipe for disaster").

Sentence in italics from D.H. Brandon, "Data Processing Organization and Manpower Planning", Petrocelli, 1974, emphasis in original. Quoted in [Boehm 1981], *p. 674.*

What quality software requires is **egoful design** with **egoless expression**.

More than style standards, what would seem to require justification is the current situation of software development, with its almost total lack of style standards. In no other discipline that demands to be called "engineering" is there such room for such broad personal variations of whim and fancy. To become more professional, software development needs to regulate itself.

26.2 CHOOSING THE RIGHT NAMES

The first aspect that we need to regulate is the choice of names. Feature names, in particular, will be strictly controlled for everyone's benefit.

General rules

What matters most is the names of **classes** and **features** which will be used extensively by the authors of classes that rely on yours.

For feature and class names, use full words, not abbreviations, unless the abbreviations are widely accepted in the application domain. In a class *PART* describing parts in an inventory control system, call *number*, not *num*, the feature (query) giving the part number. Typing is cheap; software maintenance is expensive. An abbreviation such as *usa* in a Geographical Information System or *copter* in a flight control system, having gained an independent status as a word of its own, is of course acceptable. In addition, a few standard abbreviations have gained recognition over the years, such as *PART* for *PARTIAL* in class names such as *PART_COMPARABLE* describing objects equipped with a partial order relation.

In choosing names, aim for clarity. Do not hesitate to use several words connected by underscores, as in *ANNUAL_RATE*, a class name, or *yearly_premium*, a feature name.

Although modern languages do not place any limit on the length of identifiers, and treat all letters as significant, name length should remain reasonable. Here the rule is not the same for classes and for features. Class names are input only occasionally (in class headers, type declarations, inheritance clauses and a few other cases) and should describe an abstraction as completely as possible, so *PRODUCT_QUANTITY_INDEX_EVALUATOR* may be fine. For features, there is seldom a need for more than two or possibly three underscore-connected words. In particular, *do not overqualify feature names*. If a feature name appears too long, it is usually because it is overqualified:

> ### Composite Feature Name rule
>
> Do not include in a feature name the name of the underlying data abstraction (which should serve as the class name).

The feature giving the part number in class *PART* should be called just *number*, not *part_number*. Such over-qualification is a typical beginner's mistake; the resulting names obscure rather than illuminate the text. Remember that every use of the feature will unambiguously indicate the class, as in *part1.number* where *part1* must have been declared with a certain type, *PART* or a descendant.

For composite names, it is better to avoid the style, popularized by Smalltalk and also used in such libraries as the X Window System, of joining several words together and starting the internal ones with an upper-case letter, as in *yearlyPremium*. Instead, separate components with underscores, as in *yearly_premium*. The use of internal upper-case letters is ugly; it conflicts with the conventions of ordinary language; and it leads to cryptic names, hence to possible errors (compare *aLongAndRatherUnreadableIdentifier* with *an_even_longer_but_perfectly_clear_choice_of_name*).

Sometimes, every instance of a certain class contains a field representing an instance of another class. This suggests using the class name also as attribute name. You may for example have defined a class *RATE* and, in class *ACCOUNT*, need one attribute of type *RATE*, for which it seems natural to use the name *rate* — in lower case, according to the rules on letter case stated below. Although you should try to find a more specific name, you may, if this fails, just declare the feature as *rate*: *RATE*. The rules on identifier choice explicitly permit assigning the same name to a feature and a class. Avoid the style of prefixing the name with *the*, as in *the_rate*, which only adds noise.

Local entities and routine arguments

The emphasis on clear, spelled-out names applies to features and classes. Local entities and arguments of a routine only have a local scope, so they do not need to be as evocative. Names that carry too much meaning might almost decrease the software's readability by giving undue weight to ancillary elements. So it is appropriate to declare local entities (here in routines of *TWO_WAY_LIST* in the Base libraries) as

> *move* (*i*: *INTEGER*) **is**
> > -- Move cursor *i* positions, or *after* if *i* is too large.
> > **local**
> > > *c*: *CURSOR*; *counter*: *INTEGER*; *p*: **like** *FIRST_ELEMENT*
> >
> > …
>
> *remove* **is**
> > -- Remove current item; move cursor to right neighbor (of *after* if none).
> > **local**
> > > *succ*, *pred*, *removed*: **like** *first_element*
> >
> > …

If *succ* and *pred* had been features they would have been called *successor* and *predecessor*. It is also common to use the names *new* for a local entity representing a new object to be created by a routine, and *other* for an argument representing an object of the same type as the current one, as in the declaration for *clone* in *GENERAL*:

> **frozen** *clone* (*other*: *GENERAL*): **like** *other* **is**…

Letter case

Letter case is not significant in our notation, as it is too dangerous to let two almost identical identifiers denote different things. But strongly recommended guidelines help make class texts consistent and readable:

- Class names appear in all upper case: *POINT, LINKED_LIST, PRICING_MODEL*. Formal generic parameters too, usually with just one letter: *G*.

- Names of non-constant attributes, routines other than once functions, local entities and routine arguments appear in all lower case: *balance, deposit, succ, i*.

- Constant attributes have their first letter in upper case and the rest in lower case: *Pi: INTEGER* **is** *3.1415926524*; *Welcome_message: STRING* **is** *"Welcome!"*. This applies to unique values, which are constant integers.

The example of i was on page 648.

- The same convention applies to once functions, the equivalent of constants for non-basic types: *Error_window, Io*. Our first example, the complex number *i*, remained in lower case for compatibility with mathematical conventions.

This takes care of developer-chosen names. For reserved words, we distinguish two categories. *Keywords* such as **do** and **class** play a strictly syntactic role; they are written in lower case, and will appear in boldface (see below) in printed texts. A few *reserved words* are not keywords because they carry an associated semantics; written with an initial upper case since they are similar to constants, they include *Current, Result, Precursor, True* and *False*.

Grammatical categories

Precise rules also govern the grammatical category of the words from which identifiers are derived. In some languages, these rules can be applied without any hesitation; in English, as noted in an earlier chapter, they will leave more flexibility.

See the Class Name rule on page 727.

The rule for class names has already been given: you should always use a noun, as in *ACCOUNT*, possibly qualified as in *LONG_TERM_SAVINGS_ACCOUNT*, except for the case of deferred classes describing a structural property, which may use an adjective as in *NUMERIC* or *REDEEMABLE*.

Routine names should faithfully reflect the Command-Query separation principle:

- Procedures (commands) should be verbs in the infinitive or imperative, possibly with complements: *make, move, deposit, set_color*.

- Attributes and functions (queries) should never be imperative or infinitive verbs; never call a query *get_value*, but just *value*. Non-boolean query names should be nouns, such as *number*, possibly qualified as in *last_month_balance*. Boolean queries should use adjectives, as in *full*. In English, because of possible confusions between adjectives and verbs (*empty*, for example, could mean "is this empty?" or "empty this!"), a frequent convention for boolean queries is the *is_* form, as in *is_empty*.

Standard names

You will have noted, throughout this book, the recurrence of a few basic names, such as *put* and *item*. They are an important part of the method.

Many classes will need features representing operations of a few basic kinds: insert an element into a structure, replace the value of an element, access a designated element… Rather than devising specific names for the variants of these operations in every class, it is preferable to apply a standard terminology throughout.

Here are the principal standard names. We can start with creation procedures, for which the recommended is *make* for the most common creation procedure of a class. Non-vanilla creation procedures may be called *make*_some_qualification, for example *make_polar* and *make_cartesian* for a *POINT* or *COMPLEX* class.

For commands the most common names are:

extend	Add an element.
replace	Replace an element.
force	Like *put* but may work in more cases; for example *put* for arrays has a precondition to require the index to be within bounds, but *force* has no precondition and will resize the array if necessary.
remove	Remove an (unspecified) element.
prune	Remove a specific element.
wipe_out	Remove all elements.

Standard command names

For non-boolean queries (attributes or functions):

item	The basic query for accessing an element: in *ARRAY*, the element at a given index; in *STACK* classes, the stack top; in *QUEUE* classes, the oldest element; and so on.
infix "@"	A synonym for *item* in a few cases, notably *ARRAY*.
count	Number of usable elements in a structure.
capacity	Physical size allocated to a bounded structure, measured in number of potential elements. The invariant should include $0 <= count$ **and** $count <= capacity$.

Standard names for non-boolean queries

For boolean queries:

empty	Is the structure devoid of elements?
full	Is there no more room in the representation to add elements? (Normally the same as $count = capacity$.)
has	Is a certain element present? (The basic membership test.)
extendible	Can an element be added? (May serve as a precondition to *extend*.)
prunable	Can an element be removed? (May serve as a precondition to *remove* and *prune*.)
readable	Is there an accessible element? (May serve as precondition to *item* and *remove*.)
writable	Is it possible to change an element? (May variously serve as precondition to *extend*, *replace*, *put* etc.)

A few name choices which may seem strange at first are justified by considerations of clarity and consistency. For example *prune* goes with *prunable* and *extend* with *extendible*; *delete* and *add* might seem more natural, but then *s.deletable* and *s.addable* would carry the wrong connotation, since the question is not whether *s* can be deleted or added but whether we can add elements to it or delete elements from it. The verbs *prune* and *extend*, with the associated queries, convey the intended meaning.

The benefits of consistent naming

The set of names sketched above is one of the elements that most visibly contribute to the distinctive style of software construction developed from the principles of this book.

Is the concern for consistency going too far? One could fear that confusion could result from routines that bear the same name but internally do something different. For example *item* for a stack will return the top element, and for an array will return an element corresponding to the index specified by the client.

With a systematic approach to O-O software construction, using static typing and Design by Contract, this fear is not justified. To learn about a feature, a client author can rely on four kinds of property, all present in the short form of the enclosing class:

F1 • Its name.

F2 • Its signature (number and type of arguments if a routine, type of result if a query).

F3 • Its precondition and postcondition if any.

F4 • Its header comment.

A routine also has a body, but that is not part of what client authors are supposed to use.

Three of these elements will differ for the variants of a basic operation. For example in the short form of class *STACK* you may find the feature

> *put (x: G)*
>> -- Push *x* on top.
>
> **require**
>> *writable*: **not** *full*
>
> **ensure**
>> *not_empty*: **not** *empty*
>>
>> *pushed*: *item = x*

whereas its namesake will appear in *ARRAY* as

> *put (x: G; i: INTEGER)*
>> -- Replace by *x* the entry of index *i*
>
> **require**
>> *not_too_small*: *i >= lower*
>>
>> *not_too_large*: *i <= upper*
>
> **ensure**
>> *replaced*: *item (i) = x*

The signatures are different (one variant takes an index, the other does not); the preconditions are different; the postconditions are different; and the header comments are different. Using the same name *put*, far from creating confusion, draws the reader's attention to the common role of these routines: both provide the basic element change mechanism.

This consistency has turned out to be one of the most attractive aspects of the method and in particular of the libraries. New users take to it quickly; then, when exploring a new class which follows the standard style, they feel immediately at home and can zero in on the features that they need.

26.3 USING CONSTANTS

Many algorithms will rely on constants. As was noted in an early chapter of this book, constants are widely known for the detestable practice of changing their values; we should prepare ourselves against the consequences of such fickleness.

Manifest and symbolic constants

The basic rule is that uses of constants should not explicitly rely on the value:

> ### Symbolic Constant principle
>
> Do not use a manifest constant, other than the zero elements of basic operations, in any construct other than a symbolic constant declaration.

In this principle, a **manifest constant** is a constant given explicitly by its value, as in *50* (integer constant) or *"Cannot find file"* (string constant). The principle bars using instructions of the form

population_array.*make* (*1, 50*)

or

print (*"Cannot find file"*)   -- See mitigating comment below about this case

Instead, you should declare the corresponding constant attributes, and then, in the bodies of the routines that need the values, denote them through the attribute names:

US_state_count: *INTEGER* **is** *50*
File_not_found: *STRING* **is** *"Cannot find file"*
...
population_array.*make* (*1, state_count*)
...
print (*file_not_found*)

The advantage is obvious: if a new state is added, or the message needs to be changed, you have only have to update one easy-to-locate declaration.

The use of *1* together with *state_count* in the first instruction is not a violation of the principle, since its prohibition applies to manifest constants "*other than zero elements of basic operations*". These zero elements, which you may use in manifest form, include the integers *0* and *1* (zero elements of addition and multiplication), the real number *0.0*, the null character written '*%0*', the empty string *""*. Using a symbolic constant *One* every time you need to refer to the lower bound of an array (1 using the default convention) would lead to an unsustainable style — pedantic, and in fact less readable because of its verbosity. Sometimes, Freud is supposed to have said, a cigar is just a cigar; sometimes *One* is just 1.

> Some other times *1* is just a system parameter that happens to have the value one today but could become 4,652 later — its role as addition's zero element being irrelevant. Then it should be declared as a symbolic constant, as in *Processor_count*: *INTEGER* **is** *1* in a system that supports multiple processors and is initially applied to one processor.

The Symbolic Constant principle may be judged too harsh in the case of simple manifest strings used just once, such as *"Cannot find file"* above. Some readers may want to add this case to the exception already stated in the principle (replacing the qualification by "*other than manifest string constants used only once in the same class, and zero elements of basic operations*"). This book has indeed employed a few manifest constants in simple examples. Such a relaxation of the rule is acceptable, but in the long run it is probably preferable to stick to the rule as originally given even if the result for string constants looks a little pedantic at times. One of the principal uses of string constants, after all, is for messages to be output to users; when a successful system initially written for the home market undergoes internationalization, it will be that much less translation work if all the user-visible message strings (at least any of them that actually appear in the software text) have been put in symbolic constant declarations.

Where to put constant declarations

If you need more than a handful of local constant attributes in a class, you have probably uncovered a data abstraction — a certain concept characterized by a number of numeric or character parameters.

It is desirable, then, to group the constant declarations into a class, which can serve as ancestor to any class needing the constants (although some O-O designers prefer to use the client relation in this case). An example in the Base libraries is the class *ASCII*, which declares constant attributes for the different characters in the ASCII character set and associated properties.

See "Facility inheritance", page 832.

26.4 HEADER COMMENTS AND INDEXING CLAUSES

Although the formal elements of a class text should give as much as possible of the information about a class, they must be accompanied by informal explanations. Header comments of routines and feature clause answer this need together with the indexing clause of each class.

Routine header comments: an exercise in corporate downsizing

Like those New York street signs that read "Don't even *think* of parking here!", the sign at the entrance of your software department should warn "Don't even think of writing a routine without a header comment". The header comment, coming just after the **is** for a routine, expresses its purpose concisely; it will be kept by the short and flat-short forms:

```
distance_to_origin: REAL is
            -- Distance to point (0, 0)
    local
        origin: POINT
    do
        !! origin
        Result := distance (origin)
    end
```

Note the indentation: one step further than the start of the routine body, so that the comment stands out.

Header comments should be informative, clear, and terse. They have a whole style of their own, which we can learn by looking at an initially imperfect example and improve it step by step. In a class *CIRCLE* we might start with

Warning: not the recommended style for header comments!

tangent_from (*p*: *POINT*): *LINE* **is**
> -- Return the tangent line to the current circle going through the point *p*,
> -- if the point is outside of the current circle.

   require
> *outside_circle*: **not** *has* (*p*)

    ...

There are many things wrong here. First, the comment for a query, as here, should not start with "Return the..." or "Compute the...", or in general use a verbal form; this would go against the Command-Query Separation principle. Simply name what the query returns, typically using a qualified noun for a non-boolean query (we will see below what to use for a boolean query and a command). Here we get:

Not the recommended style.

> -- The tangent line to the current circle going through the point *p*,
> -- if the point *p* is outside of the current circle

Since the comment is not a sentence but simply a qualified noun, the final period disappears. Next we can get rid of the auxiliary words, especially *the*, where they are not required for understandability. Telegram-like style is desirable for comments. (Remember that readers in search of literary frills can always choose Proust novels instead.)

Not yet...

> --Tangent line to current circle from point *p*,
> -- if point *p* is outside current circle

The next mistake is to have included, in the second line, the condition for the routine's applicability; the precondition, **not** *has* (*p*), which will be retained in the short form where it appears just after the header comment, expresses this condition clearly and unambiguously. There is no need to paraphrase it: this could lead to confusion, if the informal phrasing seems to contradict the formal precondition, or even to errors (a common oversight is a precondition of the form *x* >= *0* with a comment stating "applicable only to positive *x*", rather than "non-negative"); and there is always a risk that during the software's evolution the precondition will be updated but not the comment. Our example becomes:

Still not it...

> -- Tangent line to current circle from point *p*.

Yet another mistake is to have used the words line to refer to the result and point to refer to the argument: this information is immediately obvious from the declared types, *LINE* and *POINT*. With a typed notation we can rely on the formal type declarations — which again will appear in the short form — to express such properties; repeating them in the informal text brings nothing. So:

Almost there, but not quite...

> -- Tangent to current circle from *p*.

The mistakes of repeating type information and of duplicating the precondition's requirements point to the same general rule: in writing header comments, *assume the reader is competent in the fundamentals of the technology*; do not include information that is obvious from the immediately adjacent short form text. This does not mean, of course, that you should never specify a type; the earlier example, -- Distance to point (0,0), could be ambiguous without the word point.

When you need to refer to the current object represented by a class, use phrasing such as current circle, current number and so on as above, rather than referring explicitly to the entity *Current*. In many cases, however, you can avoid mentioning the current object altogether, since it is clear to everyone who can read a class text that features apply to the current object. Here, for example, we just need

> -- Tangent from *p*.   *This is it.*

At this stage — three words, starting from twenty-two, an 87% reduction that would make the toughest Wall Street exponent of corporate downsizing jealous — it seems hard to get terser and we can leave our comment alone.

A few more general guidelines. We have noted the uselessness of "Return the …" in queries; other noise words and phrases to be avoided in routines of all kinds include "This routine computes…", "This routine returns…"; just say what the routine does, not that it does it. Instead of

> -- This routine records the last outgoing call.

write

> -- Record outgoing call.

As illustrated by this example, header comments for commands (procedures) should be in the imperative or infinitive (the same in English), in the style of marching orders. They should end with a period. For boolean-valued queries, the comment should always be in the form of a question, terminated by a question mark:

> *has* (*v*: *G*): *BOOLEAN* **is**
>> -- Does *v* appear in list?

>   …

A convention governs the use of software entities — attributes, arguments — appearing in comments. In typeset texts such as the above they will appear in italics (more on font conventions below); in the source text they should always appear between an opening quote ("backquote") and a closing quote; the original text for the example is then:

> -- Does 'v' appear in list?

Tools such as the **short** class abstracter will recognize this convention when generating typeset output. Note that the two quotes should be different: 'v', not 'v'.

Be consistent. If a function of a class has the comment Length of string, a routine of the same class should not say Update width of string if it affects the same property.

All these guidelines apply to routines. Because an exported attribute should be externally indistinguishable from argumentless functions — remember the Uniform Access principle — it should also have a comment, which will appear on the line following the attribute's declaration, with the same indentation as for functions:

> *count*: *INTEGER*
>> -- Number of students in course

For secret attributes a comment is desirable too but the rule is less strict.

Feature clause header comments

As you will remember, a class may have any number of feature clauses:

indexing

...

class *LINKED_LIST* [*G*] **inherit** ... **creation**

...

feature -- Initialization
  make **is** ...
feature -- Access
  item: *G* **is** ...

...

feature -- Status report
  before: *BOOLEAN* **is** ...

...

feature -- Status setting

...

feature -- Element change
  put_left (*v*: *G*) **is** ...

...

feature -- Removal
  remove **is** ...

...

feature {*NONE*} -- Implementation
  first_element: *LINKABLE* [*G*].

...

end -- class *LINKED_LIST*

One of the purposes of having several feature clauses is to allow different features to have different export privileges; in this example everything is generally available except the secret features in the last clause. But another consequence of this convention is that you could, and should, group features by categories. A comment on the same line as the keyword **feature** should characterize the category. Such comments are, like header comments of routines, recognized an preserved by documentation tools such as **short**.

"Operands and options", page 766. Eighteen categories and the corresponding comments have been standardized for the Base libraries, so that every feature (out of about 2000 in all) belongs to one of them. The example above illustrates some of the most important categories. Status report corresponds to options (set by features in the Status setting category, not included in the example). Secret and selectively exported features appear in the Implementation category. These standard categories always appear in the same order, which the tools know (through a user-editable list) and will preserve or reinstate in their output. Within each category, the tools list the features alphabetically for ease of retrieval.

The categories cover a wide range of application domains, although for special areas you may need to add your own categories.

Indexing clauses

Similar to header comments but slightly more formal are indexing clauses, appearing at the beginning of a class:

Indexing clauses were previewed in "A note about component indexing", page 78.

> **indexing**
>
> > *description*: *"Sequential lists, in chained representation"*
> >
> > *names*: *"Sequence"*, *"List"*
> >
> > *contents*: *GENERIC*
> >
> > *representation*: *chained*
> >
> > *date*: *"$Date: 96/10/20 12:21:03 $"*
> >
> > *revision*: *"$Revision: 2.4$"*
> >
> > ...
>
> **class** *LINKED_LIST* [*G*] **inherit**
>
> > ...

Indexing clauses proceed from the same Self-Documentation principle that has led to built-in assertions and header comments: include as much as possible of the documentation in the software itself. For properties that do not directly appear in the formal text, you may include indexing entries, all of the form

"Self-Documentation", page 54.

> *indexing_term*: *indexing_value*, *indexing_value*, ...

where the *indexing_term* is an identifier and each *indexing_value* is some basic element such as a string, an integer and so on. Entries can indicate alternative names under which potential client authors might search for the class (*names*), contents type (*contents*), implementation choices (*representation*), revision control information, author information, and anything else that may facilitate understanding the class and retrieving it through keyword-based search tools — tools that support reuse and enable software developers to find their way through a potentially rich set of reusable components.

Both the indexing terms and the indexing values are free-form, but the possible choices should be standardized for each project. A set of standard choices has been used throughout the Base libraries; the above example illustrates six of the most common entry kinds. Every class must have a *description* entry, introducing as *index_value* a string describing the role of the class, always expressed in terms of the instances (as *Sequential lists...*, not "this class describes sequential lists", or "sequential list", or "the notion of sequential list" etc.). Most significant class texts in this book — but not short examples illustrating a specific point — include the *description* entry.

More details in [M 1994a].

Non-header comments

The preceding rules on comments applied to standardized comments, appearing at specific places — feature declarations and beginning of feature clauses — and playing a special role for class documentation.

As in all forms of software development, there is also a need for comments within routine bodies, to provide further explanations

> Another use of comments, although frequent in the practice of software development, does not figure much in software engineering and programming methodology textbooks. I am referring here to the technique of transforming some part of the code into comments, either because it does not work, or because it is not ready yet. This practice is clearly a substitute for better tools and techniques of configuration management. It has enriched the language with a new verb form, *comment out*, whose potential, surprisingly enough, has not yet been picked up by hip journalists, even though the non-technical applications seem attractive and indeed endless: "The last elections have enabled Congress to *comment out* the President", "Letterman was *commented out* of the Academy Awards", and so on.

Every comment should be of a level of abstraction higher than the code it documents. A famous counter-example is -- Increase *i* by *1* commenting the instruction $i := i + 1$. Although not always that extreme, the practice of writing comments that paraphrase the code instead of summarizing its effect is still common.

Low-level languages cry for ample commenting. It is a good rule of thumb, for example, that for each line of C there should be a comment line; not a negative reflection on C, but a consequence that in modern software development the role of C is to encapsulate machine-oriented and operating-system-level operations, which are tricky by nature and require a heavy explanatory apparatus. In the O-O part, non-header comments will appear much more sparsely; they remain useful when you need to explain some delicate operation or foresee possible confusion. In its constant effort to favor prevention over cure, the method decreases the need for comments through a modular style that yields small, understandable routines, and through its assertion mechanisms: preconditions and postconditions of routines, to express their semantics formally; class invariants; **check** instructions to express properties expected to hold at certain stages; the systematic naming conventions introduced earlier in this chapter. More generally, the secret of clear, understandable software is not adding comments after the fact but devising coherent and stable system structures right from the start.

26.5 TEXT LAYOUT AND PRESENTATION

The next set of rules affects how we should physically write our software texts on paper — real, or simulated on a screen. More than any others, they prompt cries of "Cosmetics!"; but such cosmetics should be as important to software developers as Christian Dior's are to his customers. They play no little role in determining how quickly and accurately your software will be understood by its readers — maintainers, reusers, customers.

Layout

The recommended layout of texts results from the general form of the syntax of our notation, which is roughly what is known as an "operator grammar", meaning that a class text is a sequence of symbols alternating between "operators" and "operands". An operator is a fixed language symbol, such as a keyword (**do** etc.) or a separator (semicolon, comma …); an operand is a programmer-chosen symbol (identifier or constant).

Based on this property, the textual layout of the notation follows the **comb-like structure** introduced by Ada; the idea is that a syntactically meaningful part of a class, such as an instruction or an expression, should either:

- Fit on a line together with a preceding and succeeding operators.

- Be indented just by itself on one or more lines — organized so as to observe the same rules recursively.

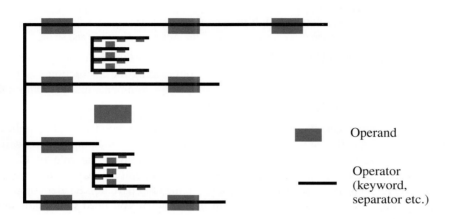

The comb-like structure of software texts

Each branch of the comb is a sequence of alternating operators and operands; it should normally begin and end with an operator. In the space between two branches you find either a single operand or, recursively, a similar comb-like structure.

As an example, depending on the size of its constituents a, b and c, you may spread out a conditional instruction as

> **if** c **then** a **else** b **end**

or

> **if**
> > c
>
> **then**
> > a
>
> **else**
> > b
>
> **end**

or

> **if** c **then**
> > a
>
> **else** b **end**

You would not, however, use a line containing just **if** *c* or *c* **end**, since they include an operand together with something else, and are missing an ending operator in the first case and a starting operator in the second.

Similarly, you may start a class, after the **indexing** clause, with

    class *C* **inherit**   -- [1]

or

    class *C* **feature**   -- [2]

or

    class   -- [3]
        C
    feature

but not

    class *C*   -- [4]
    feature

because the first line would violate the rule. Forms [1] and [2] are used in this book for small illustrative classes; since most practical classes have one or more labeled **feature** clauses, they should in the absence of an **inherit** clause use form [3] (rather than [2]):

    class
        C
    feature -- Initialization
        …
    feature -- Access
        etc.

Height and width

Like most modern languages, our notation does not attach any particular significance to line separations except to terminate comments, so that you can include two or more instructions (or two or more declarations) on a single line, separated by semicolons:

    count := count + 1; *forth*

This style is for some reason not very popular (and many tools for estimating software size still measure *lines* rather than syntactical units); most developers seem to prefer having one instruction per line. It is indeed not desirable to pack texts very tightly; but in some cases a group of two or three short, closely related instructions can be more readable if they all appear on one line.

In this area it is best to defer to your judgment and good taste. If you do apply intra-line grouping, make sure that it remains moderate, and consistent with the logical relations between instructions. The Semicolon Style principle seen later in this chapter requires any same-line instructions to be separated by a semicolon.

For obvious reasons of space, this book makes a fair use of intra-line grouping, consistent with these guidelines. It also avoids splitting multi-line instructions into more lines than necessary; on this point one can recommend the book's style for general use: there is really no reason to split **from** $i := 1$ **invariant** $i <= n$ **until** $i = n$ **loop** or **if** $a = b$ **then**. Whatever your personal taste, do observe the Comb structure.

Indenting details

The comb structure uses indentation, achieved through tab characters (**not** spaces, which are messy, error-prone, and not reader-parameterizable).

Here are the indentation levels for the basic kinds of construct, illustrated by the example on the facing page:

- Level 0: the keywords introducing the primitive clauses of a class. This includes **indexing** (beginning of an indexing clause), **class** (beginning of the class body), **feature** (beginning of a feature clause, except if on the same line as **class**), **invariant** (beginning of an invariant clause, not yet seen) and the final **end** of a class.
- Level 1: beginning of a feature declaration; indexing entries; invariant clauses.
- Level 2: the keywords starting the successive clauses of a routine. This includes **require, local, do, once, ensure, rescue, end**.
- Level 3: the header comment for a routine or (for consistency) attribute; declarations of local entities in a routine; first-level instructions of a routine.

Within a routine body there may be further indentation due to the nesting of control structures. For example the earlier **if** a **then** ... instruction contains two branches, each of them indented. These branches could themselves contain loops or conditional instructions, leading to further nesting (although the style of object-oriented software construction developed in this book leads to simple routines, seldom reaching high levels of nesting).

A **check** instruction is indented, together with the justifying comment that normally follows it, one level to the right of the instruction that it guards.

```
indexing
        description: "Example for formating"
class EXAMPLE inherit
        MY_PARENT
                redefine f1, f2 end
        MY_OTHER_PARENT
                rename
                        g1 as old_g1, g2 as old_g2
                redefine
                        g1
                select
                        g2
                end
creation
        make
```

A layout example

Note: this class has no useful semantics!

```
feature -- Initialization
    make is
            -- Do something.
        require
            some_condition: correct (x)
        local
            my_entity: MY_TYPE
        do
            if a then
                b; c
            else
                other_routine
                    check max2 > max1 + x ^ 2 end
                    -- Because of the postcondition of other_routine.
                new_value := old_value / (max2 - max1)
            end
        end
feature -- Access
    my_attribute: SOME_TYPE
            -- Explanation of its role (aligned with comment for make)

        … Other feature declarations and feature clauses …
invariant
    upper_bound: x <= y
end -- class EXAMPLE
```

Note the trailer comment after the **end** of the class, a systematic convention.

Spaces

White space contributes as much to the effect produced by a software text as silence to the effect of a musical piece.

The general rule, for simplicity and ease of remembering, is to follow as closely as possible the practice of standard written language. By default we will assume this language to be English, although it may be appropriate to adapt the conventions to the slightly different rules of other languages.

Here are some of the consequences. You will use a space:

- Before an opening parenthesis, but not after: $f\ (x)$ (not $f(x)$, the C style, or $f(\ x)$).
- After a closing parenthesis *unless* the next character is a punctuation sign such as a period or semicolon; but not before. Hence: $proc1\ (x); x := f1\ (x) + f2\ (y)$
- After a comma but not before: $g\ (x, y, z)$.
- After the two dash signs that start a comment: -- A comment.

Similarly, the default rule for semicolons is to use a space after but not before:

p1; *p2* (*x*); *p3* (*y, z*)

Here, however, some people prefer, even for English-based software texts, the French style of including a space both before and after, which makes the semicolon stand out and emphasizes the symmetry between the components before and after it:

p1 ; *p2* (*x*) ; *p3* (*y, z*)

Choose either style, but then use it consistently. (This book uses the English style.) English and French styles have the same difference for colons as for semicolons; since, however, the software notation only uses colons for declarations, in which the two parts — the entity being declared and its type — do *not* play a symmetric role, it seems preferable to stick to the English style, as in *your_entity*: *YOUR_TYPE*.

Spaces should appear before and after arithmetic operators, as in $a + b$. (For space reasons, this book has omitted the spaces in a few cases, all of the form $n+1$.)

For periods the notation departs from the conventions of ordinary written language since it uses periods for a special construct, as originally introduced by Simula. As you know, $a \cdot r$ means: apply feature r to the object attached to a. In this case there is a space neither before nor after the period. To avoid any confusion, this book makes the period bigger, as illustrated: **.** rather than just .

There is another use of the period: as decimal point in real numbers, such as *3.14*. Here, to avoid any confusion, the period is not made any bigger.

> Some European languages use a comma rather than a period as the separator between integral and fractional parts of numbers. Here the conflict is irreconcilable, as in English the comma serves to separate parts of big numbers, as in "300,000 dollars", where other languages would use a space. The committee discussions for Algol 60 almost collapsed when some continental members refused to bow to the majority's choice of the period; the stalemate was resolved when someone suggested distinguishing between a reference language, fixed, and representation languages, parameterizable. (In retrospect, not such a great idea, at least not if you ever have to compile the same program in two different countries!) Today, few people would make this a point of contention, as the spread of digital watches and calculators built for world markets have accustomed almost everyone to alternate between competing conventions.

Precedence and parentheses

The precedence conventions of the notation conform to tradition and to the "Principle of Least Surprise" to avoid errors and ambiguities.

Do not hesitate, however, to add parentheses for clarity; for example you may write $(a = (b + c))$ **implies** $(u \mathbin{/=} v)$ even though the meaning of that expression would be the same if all parentheses were removed. The examples in this book have systematically over-parenthesized expressions, in particular assertions, risking heaviness to avert uncertainty.

The War of the Semicolons

Two clans inhabit the computing world, and the hatred between them is as ferocious as it is ancient. The Separatists, following Algol 60 and Pascal, fight for the recognition of the semicolon as a separator between instructions; the Terminatists, rallied behind the contrasting flags of PL/I, C and Ada, want to put a semicolon behind every instruction.

Each side's arguments are endlessly relayed by its propaganda machine. The Terminatists worship uniformity: if every instruction is terminated by the same marker, no one ever has to ask the question "do I need a semicolon here?" (the answer in Terminatist languages is always yes, and anyone who forgets a semicolon is immediately beheaded for high treason). They do not want to have to add or remove a semicolon because an instruction has been moved from one syntactical location to another, for example if it has been brought into a conditional instruction or taken out of it.

The Separatists praise the elegance of their convention and its compatibility with mathematical practices. They see **do** *instruction1*; *instruction2*; *instruction3* **end** as the natural counterpart of f (*argument1, argument2, argument3*). Who in his right mind, they ask, would prefer f (*argument1, argument2, argument3,*) with a superfluous final comma? They contend, furthermore, that the Terminatists are just a front for the Compilists, a cruel people whose only goal is to make life easy for compiler writers, even if that means making it hard for application developers.

The Separatists constantly have to fight against innuendo, for example the contention that Separatist languages will *prevent* you from including extra semicolons. Again and again they must repeat the truth: that every Separatist language worthy of the name, beginning with the venerated Patriarch of the tribe, Algol 60, has supported the notion of empty instruction, permitting all of

```
a; b; c
a; b; c;
; a ;; b ;;; c;
```

to be equally valid, and to mean exactly the same thing, as they only differ by the extra empty instructions of the last two variants, which any decent compiler will discard anyway. They like to point out how much more tolerant this convention makes them: whereas their fanatical neighbors will use any missing semicolon as an excuse for renewed attacks, the Separatists will gladly accept as many extra semicolons as a Terminatist transfuge may still, out of habit, drop into an outwardly Separatist text.

The article is a study by Gannon and Horning [Gannon 1975]. Modern propaganda needs science and statistics, so the Terminatists have their own experimental study, cited everywhere (in particular as the justification for the Terminatist convention of the Ada language): a 1975 measurement of the errors made by two groups of 25 programmers each, using languages that, among other distinguishing traits, treated semicolons differently. The results show the Separatist style causing almost ten times as many errors! Starting to feel the heat of incessant enemy broadcasts, the Separatist leadership turned for help to the author of the present book, who remembered a long-forgotten principle: *quoting is good, but reading is better*. So he fearlessly went back to

the original article and discovered that the Separatist language used in the comparison —
a mini-language meant only for "teaching students the concepts of asynchronous
processes" — treats an extra semicolon after the final instruction of a compound, as in
begin a; b; **end**, as an error! No real Separatist language, as noted above, has ever had such
a rule, which would be absurd in any circumstance (as an extra semicolon is obviously
harmless), and is even more so in the context of the article's experiment since some of the
subjects apparently had Terminatist experience from PL/I and so would have been
naturally prone to add a few semicolons here and there. It then seems likely, although the
article gives no data on this point, that many of the semicolon errors were a result of such
normally harmless additions — enough to disqualify the experiment, once and for all, as
a meaningful basis for defending Terminatism over Separatism.

> On some of the other issues it studies, the article is not marred by such flaws in its test
> languages, so that it still makes good reading for people interested in language design.

All this shows, however, that it is dangerous to take sides in such a sensitive debate,
especially for someone who takes pride in having friends in both camps. The solution
adopted by the notation of this book is radical:

+---+
| ### Semicolon Syntax rule |
| |
| Semicolons, as markers to delimit instructions, declarations or assertion |
| clauses, are optional in almost all the positions where they may appear in the |
| notation of this book. |
+---+

"Almost" because of a few rare cases, not encountered in this book, in which omitting the
semicolon would cause a syntactical ambiguity.

*Exercise E26.2,
page 902.*

The Semicolon Syntax rule means you can choose your style:

- Terminatist: every instruction, declaration or assertion clause ends with a semicolon.

- Separatist: semicolons appear between successive elements but not, for example,
  after the last declaration of a **feature** or **local** clause.

- Moderately Separatist: like the Separatist style, but not worrying about extra
  semicolons that may appear as a result of habit or of elements being moved from one
  context to another.

- Discardist: no semicolons at all (except as per the Semicolon Style principle below).

This is one of the areas where it is preferable to let each user of the notation follow
his own inclination, as the choice cannot cause serious damage. But do stick, at least
across a class and preferably across an entire library or application, to the style that you
have chosen (although this will not mean much for the Moderately Separatist style, which
is by definition lax), and observe the following principle:

> ### Semicolon Style principle
>
> If you elect to include semicolons as terminators (Terminatist style), do so for all applicable elements.
>
> If you elect to forego semicolons, use them only when syntactically unavoidable, or to separate elements that appear on the same line.

The second clause governs elements that appear two or more to a line, as in

> *found := found + 1*; *forth*

which should always include the semicolon; omitting it would make the line quite confusing.

Just for once, this discussion has **no advice** here, letting you decide which of the four styles you prefer. Since the earliest version of the notation required semicolons — in other words, it had not yet been tuned to support the Semicolon Syntax rule — the first edition of this book used a Separatist style. For the present one I dabbled into a few experiments; after polling a sizable group of co-workers and experienced users of the notation, I found (apart from a handful of Terminatists) an almost equal number of Discardists and Separatists. Some of the Discardists were very forceful, in particular a university professor who said that the main reason his students loved the notation is that they do not need semicolons — a comment which any future language designer, with or without grandiose plans, should find instructive or at least sobering.

You should defer to your own taste as long as it is consistent and respects the Semicolon Style principle. (As to this book: for a while I stuck to the original Separatist style, more out of habit than of real commitment; then, hearing the approach of the third millenium and its call to start a new life free of antique superstitions, I removed all the semicolons over a single night of utter debauchery.)

Assertions

You should label assertion clauses to make the text more readable:

> **require**
>   *not_too_small*: *index >= lower*

See "Monitoring assertions at run time", page 392.
This convention also helps produce useful information during testing and debugging since, as you will remember, the assertion label will be included in the run-time message produced if you have enabled monitoring of assertions and one of them gets violated.

This convention will spread an assertion across as many lines as it has clauses. As a consequence, it is one of the rules to which the present book has made a few exceptions, again in the interest of saving space. When collapsing several clauses on one line, you should actually remove the labels for readability:

> **require**
>   *index >= lower*; *index <= upper*

In normal circumstances, that is to say for software texts rather than a printed textbook, better stick to the official rule and have one labeled clause per line.

26.6 FONTS

In typeset software texts, the following conventions, used throughout this book and related publications, are recommended.

Basic font rules

Print software elements (class names, feature names, entities…) in *italics* to distinguish them from non-software text elements. This facilitates their inclusion in sentences of the non-software text, such as "We can see that the feature *number* is a query, not an attribute". (The word *number* denotes the name of the feature; you do not want to mislead your reader into believing that you are talking about the number of features!)

Keywords, such as **class**, **feature**, **invariant** and the like, appear in **boldface**.

> This was also the convention of the first edition of this book. At some stage it seemed preferable to use ***boldface italics*** which blends more nicely with italics. What was esthetically pleasing, however, turned out to hamper quality; some readers complained that the keywords did not stand out clearly enough, hence the return to the original convention. This is a regrettable case of fickleness. [M 1994a] and a handful of books by other authors show the intermediate convention.

Keywords play a purely syntactic role: they have no semantics of their own but delimit those elements, such as feature and class names, that do carry a semantic value. As noted earlier in this chapter, there are also a few non-keyword reserved words, such as *Current* and *Result*, which have a denotation of their own — expressions or entities. They are written in non-bold italics, with an initial upper-case letter.

Following the tradition of mathematics, symbols — colons and semicolons ∶;, brackets [], parentheses (), braces { }, question and exclamation marks ?! and so on — should always appear in roman (straight), even when they separate text in italics. Like keywords, they are purely syntactic elements.

Comments appear in roman. This avoids any ambiguity when a feature name — which, according to the principles seen earlier, will normally be a word from ordinary language — or an argument name appears in a comment; the feature name will be in italics and hence will stand out. For example:

accelerate (*s*: *SPEED*; *t*: *REAL*) **is**

        -- Bring speed to *s* in at most *t* seconds.

…

set_number (*n*: *INTEGER*) **is**

        -- Make *n* the new value of *number*.

…

In the software text itself, where no font variations are possible, such occurrences of formal elements in comments should follow a specific convention already mentioned earlier: they will appear preceded by a back quote ' and followed by a normal quote ' , as in

-- Make 'n' the new value of 'number'.

(Remember that you must use two different quote characters for opening and closing.) Tools that process class texts and can produce typeset output, such as **short** and **flat**, know this convention and so can make sure the quoted elements are printed in italics.

Other font conventions

The preceding font conventions work well for a book, an article or a Web page. Some contexts, however, may call for different approaches. In particular, elements in plain italics, and sometimes even bold italics, are not always readable when projected on a projection screen, especially if what you are projecting is the output of a laptop computer with a relatively small display.

In such cases I have come to using the following conventions:

* Use non-italics boldface for everything, as this projects best.
* Choose a wide enough font, such as **Bookman** (for which boldface may be called "demibold").
* Instead of italics versus roman versus bold, use color to distinguish the various elements: keywords in black; comments in red; the rest (entities, feature names, expressions…) in blue. More colors can be used to highlight special elements.

These conventions seem to work well, although there is always room for improvement, and new media will undoubtedly prompt new conventions.

Color

The particularly attentive reader may by now have come to notice another convention used by this book: for added clarity, all formal elements — software texts or text extracts, but also mathematical elements — appear in color. This technique, which of course cannot be presented as a general requirement, enhances the effect of the rules seen so far on font usage.

26.7 BIBLIOGRAPHICAL NOTES

[Waldén 1995] is the source of the idea of showing by example that even a longer *separated_by_underscores* identifier is easier to read than an *internalUpperCase* identifier.

[Gannon 1975] is an experimental study of the effect of various language design choices on error rates.

The rules on standard feature names were first presented in [M 1990b] and are developed in detail in [M 1994a].

I received important comments from Richard Wiener on students' appreciation of the optionality of semicolons, and from Kim Waldén on the respective merits of bold italics and plain bold.

EXERCISES

E26.1 Header comment style

Rewrite the following header comments in the proper style:

> *reorder* (*s*: *SUPPLIER*; *t*: *TIME*) **is**
>
>   -- Reorders the current part from supplier s, to be delivered
>
>   -- on time t; this routine will only work if t is a time in the future.
>
>   **require**
>
>   *not_in_past*: *t* >= *Now*
>
>   ...
>
> *next_reorder_date*: *TIME* **is**
>
>   -- Yields the next time at which the current part is scheduled
>
>   -- to be reordered.

E26.2 Semicolon ambiguity

Can you think of a case in which omitting a semicolon between two instructions or assertions could cause syntactic ambiguity, or at least confuse a simple-minded parser? (**Hint**: a feature call can have as its target a parenthesized expression, as in (*vector1* + *vector2*).*count*.)

Object-oriented analysis

*F*ocused initially on the implementation aspects of software construction, the object-oriented method quickly expanded to cover the totality of the software lifecycle. Of particular interest has been the application of O-O ideas to the modeling of software systems, or even of non-software systems and issues. This use of object technology to present **problems** rather than solutions is known as object-oriented analysis.

In the past few years, many books have appeared on the topic and many specific methods of object-oriented analysis have been proposed. The bibliography section lists some of the best-known books, and Web addresses for some of the best-known methods.

Most of the concepts introduced in the preceding chapters are directly relevant to object-oriented analysis. Here we will briefly review what make object-oriented *analysis* special among other object-oriented topics, and what makes *object-oriented* analysis different from other analysis methods.

Two points of terminology to avoid imagining differences where none exist. First, you will encounter, as a synonym for "analysis", the term *system modeling*, or just *modeling*. Second, the computing science community tends to use the word *specification* where information modeling folks talk about analysis; in particular, computing scientists have devoted considerable efforts to devising methods and languages for *formal specification* using mathematical techniques for purposes of system modeling. The goals are the same, although the techniques may differ. In the past few years the two communities — information modelers and formal specifiers — have been paying more attention to each other's contributions.

27.1 THE GOALS OF ANALYSIS

To understand analysis issues we must be aware of the roles of analysis in software development and define requirements on an analysis method.

Tasks

By devoting time to analysis and producing analysis documents we pursue seven goals:

Goals of performing analysis

A1 • To understand the problem or problems that the eventual software system, if any, should solve.

A2 • To prompt relevant questions about the problem and the system.

A3 • To provide a basis for answering questions about specific properties of the problem and system.

A4 • To decide what the system should do.

A5 • To decide what the system should not do.

A6 • To ascertain that the system will satisfy the needs of its users, and define acceptance criteria (especially when the system is developed for an outside customer under a contractual relationship).

A7 • To provide a basis for the development of the system.

If analysis is being applied to a non-software system, or independently of a decision to build a software system, A1, A2 and A3 may be the only relevant goals.

For a software system, the list assumes that analysis follows a stage of *feasibility study* which has resulted in a decision to build a system. If, as sometimes happens, the two stages are merged into one (not an absurd proposition, since you may need an in-depth analysis to determine whether a satisfactory result is conceivable), the list needs another item: A0, deciding whether to build a system.

Although related, the goals listed are distinct, prompting us in the rest of this chapter to look for a set of complementary techniques; what is good for one of the goals may be irrelevant to another.

Goals A2 and A3 are the least well covered in the analysis literature and deserve all the emphasis they can get. One of the primary benefits of an analysis process, independently of any document that it produces in the end, is that it leads you to ask the relevant questions (A2): what is the maximum acceptable temperature? What are the recognized categories of employees? How are bonds handled differently from stocks? By providing you with a framework, which you will have to fill using input from people competent in the application domain, an analysis method will help spot and remove obscurities and ambiguities which can be fatal to a development. Nothing is worse than discovering, at the last stage of implementation, that the marketing and engineering departments of the client company have irreconcilable views of what equipment maintenance means, that one of these views was taken by default, and that no one cared to check what the actual order giver had in mind. As to A3, a good analysis document will be the place to which everyone constantly goes back if delicate questions or conflicting interpretations arise during the development process.

Requirements

The practical requirements on the analysis process and supporting notations follow from the above list of goals:

- There must be a way to let non-software people contribute input to the analysis, examine the results and discuss them (A1, A2).

- The analysis must also have a form that is directly usable by software developers (A7).

- The approach must *scale up* (A1).

- The analysis notation must be able to express precise properties unambiguously (A3).

- It must enable readers to get a quick glimpse of the overall organization of a system or subsystem (A1, A7)

Scaling up (the third point) means catering to systems that are complex, large or both — the ones for which you most need analysis. The method should enable you to describe the high-level structure of the problem or system, and to organize the description over several layers of abstraction, so that you can at any time focus on as big or as small a part of the system as you wish, while retaining the overall picture. Here, of course, the structuring and abstracting facilities of object technology will be precious.

Scaling up also means that the criteria of extendibility and reusability, which have guided much of our earlier discussions, are just as applicable to analysis as they are to software design and implementation. Systems change, requiring their descriptions to follow; and systems are similar to previous systems, prompting us to use *libraries* of specification elements to build their specifications, just as we use libraries of software components to build their implementations.

The clouds and the precipice

It is not easy to reconcile the last two requirements of the above list. The conflict, already discussed in the context of abstract data types, has plagued analysis methods and specification languages as long as they have existed. How do you "express precise properties unambiguously" without saying too much? How do you provide readable broad-brush structural descriptions without risking vagueness?

The analyst walks on a mountain path. On your left is the mountain top, deep ensconced in clouds; this is the realm of the fuzzy. But you must also stay away, on your right, from the precipice of overspecification, to which you might be perilously drawn if your attempts to be precise tempt you to say too much, especially by giving out *implementation* details instead of external properties of the system.

The risk of overspecification is ever present in the minds of people interested in analysis. (It is said that, to gain the upper hand in a debate in this field, you should try "*Approach X is nice, but isn't it a tad implementation-oriented* ?" The poor author of X, reputation lost, career shattered, will not dare show up in a software gathering for the next twenty years.) To avoid this pitfall, analysis methods have tended to err on the side of the clouds, relying on formalisms that do a good job of capturing overall structures, often through cloud-like graphical notations, but are quite limited when it comes to expressing the *semantic* properties of systems as required to address goal A2 (answering precise questions).

Many of the traditional analysis methods fit this description. Their success comes from their ability to list the components of a system and describe their relations graphically, making them the software equivalent of the *block diagrams* of other engineering disciplines. But they are not too good at capturing the semantics. For software projects this carries a risk: believing that you have completed a successful analysis when all you have really done is to define the major components and their relations, leaving out many deeper properties of the specification that may turn out to be critical.

Later in this chapter we will study ideas for reconciling the goals of structural description and semantic precision.

27.2 THE CHANGING NATURE OF ANALYSIS

Although the object-oriented analysis literature hardly mentions this point, the most significant contribution of object technology to analysis is not technical but organizational. Object technology does not just provide new ways of doing analysis; it affects the very nature of the task and its role in the software process.

This change follows from the method's emphasis on reusability. If instead of assuming that every new project must start from scratch, considering the customer's requirements as the Gospel, we bring into the picture the presence of a regularly growing repertory of software components, some obtained (or obtainable) from the outside and some developed as a result of in-house projects, the process becomes different: not the execution of an order from above, but a **negotiation**.

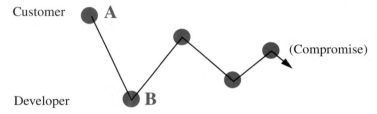

Requirements analysis as a negotiation

The figure suggests this process: the customer starts with a requirement at **A**; you counter with a proposal at **B**, covering perhaps only part of the requirements, or a slightly different form of the requirements, but based for a large part on existing reusable components and hence achievable at significantly less cost and sooner. The customer may initially find the sacrifice of functionality too large; this opens a haggling phase which should eventually lead to an acceptable compromise.

The haggling has always been there, of course. The customer's requirements were the Gospel only in some descriptions of the "software process" in the software engineering literature, presenting an ideal view for pedagogical purposes, and perhaps in some government contracts. In most normal situations, the developers had some freedom to discuss requirements. But with the advent of object technology this officious phenomenon becomes an official part of the software development process, and gains new prominence with the development of reusable libraries.

27.3 THE CONTRIBUTION OF OBJECT TECHNOLOGY

Object technology also affects, of course, the techniques of analysis.

Here the most important thing to learn is that we have almost nothing to learn. The framework defined in the preceding chapters has more than enough to get us started with modeling. "More than enough" actually means too much: the notation includes an *operational* part, made of two components which we do not need for analysis:

- Instructions (assignments, loops, procedure calls, …) and all that goes with them.

- Routine bodies of the **do** form (but we do need **deferred** routines to specify operations without giving out their implementation).

If we ignore these imperative elements, we have a powerful system modeling method and notation. In particular:

- **Classes** will enable us to organize our system descriptions around object types, in the broad sense of the word "object" defined in preceding chapters (covering not just physical objects but also important concepts of the application domain).

- The **ADT** approach — the idea of characterizing objects by the applicable operations and their properties — yields clear, abstract, evolutionary specifications.

- To capture inter-component relations, the two basic mechanisms of "client" and inheritance are appropriate. The **client** relation, in particular, covers such information modeling concepts as "part of", association and aggregation.

- As we saw in the discussion of objects, the distinction between **reference** and **expanded** clients corresponds to the two basic kinds of modeling association.

- **Inheritance** — single, multiple and repeated — addresses classification. Even such seemingly specialized inheritance mechanisms as renaming will be precious to model analysis concepts.

- **Assertions** are essential to capture what was called above the *semantics* of systems: properties other than structural. Design by Contract is a powerful guide to analysis.

- **Libraries** of reusable classes will provide us — especially through their higher-level deferred classes — with ready-made specification elements.

This does not necessarily mean that the approach seen so far covers all the needs of system analysis (a question that will be discussed further below); but it certainly provides the right basis. The following example will provide some evidence.

27.4 PROGRAMMING A TV STATION

Let us see concretely how to apply the O-O concepts that we know to pure modeling.

The example involves organizing the schedule of a television station. Because it is drawn from a familiar application area, we can start it (although we most likely could not complete it) without the benefit of input from "domain experts", future users etc.; we can just, for the analysis exercise, rely on every layperson's understanding of TV.

Although the effort may be the prelude to the construction of a computerized system to manage the station's programming automatically, this possibility is neither certain nor relevant here; we are just interested in modeling.

Schedules

We concentrate on the schedule for a 24-hour period; the class (data abstraction) *SCHEDULE* presents itself. A schedule contains a sequence of individual program segments; let us start with

>**class** *SCHEDULE* **feature**
>>*segments*: *LIST* [*SEGMENT*]
>
>**end**

When doing analysis we must constantly watch ourselves for fear of lapsing into overspecification. Is it overspecifying to use a *LIST*? No: *LIST* is a deferred class, describing the abstract notion of sequence; and television programming is indeed sequential, since one cannot broadcast two segments on the same station at the same time. By using *LIST* we capture a property of the problem, not the solution.

Note in passing the importance of reusability: by using classes such as *LIST* you immediately gain access to a whole set of features describing list operations: commands such as *put* for adding elements, queries such as the number of elements *count*. Reusability is as central to object-oriented analysis as it is to other O-O tasks.

What would be overspecifying here would be to *equate* the notion of schedule with that of list of segments. Object technology, as you will remember from the discussion of abstract data types, is implicit; it describes abstractions by listing their properties. Here there will certainly be more to a schedule than the list of its segments, so we need a separate class. Some of the other features of a schedule present themselves naturally:

See "More on implicitness", page 149.

>**indexing**
>>*description*: *"Twenty-four hour TV schedules"*
>
>**deferred class** *SCHEDULE* **feature**
>>*segments*: *LIST* [*SEGMENT*] **is**
>>>-- The successive segments
>>
>>>**deferred**
>>>**end**
>>
>>*air_time*: *DATE* **is**
>>>-- Twenty-four hour period for this schedule
>>
>>>**deferred**
>>>**end**
>>
>>*set_air_time* (*t*: *DATE*) **is**
>>>-- Assign this schedule to be broadcast at time *t*.
>>
>>>**require**
>>>>*t*.*in_future*
>>>
>>>**deferred**
>>>**ensure**
>>>>*air_time* = *t*
>>>
>>>**end**
>>
>>*print* **is**
>>>-- Print paper version of schedule.
>>
>>>**deferred**
>>>**end**
>
>**end**

See "Using assertions for documentation: the short form of a class", page 389.

Note the use of deferred bodies. This is appropriate since by nature an analysis document is implementation-independent and even design-independent; having no body, deferred features are the proper tool. You could, of course, dispense with writing the **deferred** specification and instead use a formalism such as that of short forms. But two important arguments justify using the full notation:

- By writing texts that conform to the syntax of the software notation, you can make use of all the tools of the supporting software development environment. In particular, the compiling mechanism will double up as a precious CASE (computer-aided software engineering) tool, applying type rules and other validity constraints to check the consistency of your specifications and detect contradictions and ambiguities; and the browsing and documentation facilities of a good O-O environment will be as useful for analysis as they are for design and implementation.

- Using the software notation also means that, should you decide to proceed to the design and implementation of a software system, you will be able to follow a smooth transition path; your work will be to add new classes, effective versions of the deferred features and new features. This supports the *seamlessness* of the approach, discussed in the next chapter.

The class assumes a boolean query *in_future* on objects of type *DATE*; it only allows setting air time for future dates. Note our first use of a precondition and postcondition to express semantic properties of a system during analysis.

Segments

Rather than continuing to refine and enhance *SCHEDULE*, let us at this stage switch to the notion of *SEGMENT*. We can start with the following features:

indexing

> *description*: "*Individual fragments of a broadcasting schedule*"

deferred class *SEGMENT* **feature**

> *schedule*: *SCHEDULE* **is deferred end**
> > -- Schedule to which segment belongs

> *index*: *INTEGER* **is deferred end**
> > -- Position of segment in its schedule

> *starting_time*, *ending_time*: *INTEGER* **is deferred end**
> > -- Beginning and end of scheduled air time

> *next*: *SEGMENT* **is deferred end**
> > -- Segment to be played next, if any

> *sponsor*: *COMPANY* **is deferred end**
> > -- Segment's principal sponsor

> *rating*: *INTEGER* **is deferred end**
>> -- Segment's rating (for children's viewing etc.)
>
> … Commands such as *change_next*, *set_sponsor*, *set_rating* omitted …
>
> *Minimum_duration*: *INTEGER* **is** *30*
>> -- Minimum length of segments, in seconds
>
> *Maximum_interval*: *INTEGER* **is** *2*
>> -- Maximum time between two successive segments, in seconds

invariant

> *in_list*: (*1 <= index*) **and** (*index <= schedule.segments.count*)
> *in_schedule*: *schedule.segments.item* (*index*) = *Current*
> *next_in_list*: (*next /= Void*) **implies** (*schedule.segments.item* (*index + 1*) = *next*)
> *no_next_iff_last*: (*next = Void*) = (*index = schedule.segments.count*)
> *non_negative_rating*: *rating >= 0*
> *positive times*: (*starting_time > 0*) **and** (*ending_time > 0*)
> *sufficient_duration*: *ending_time – starting_time >= Minimum_duration*
> *decent_interval*: (*next.starting_time*) *– ending_time <= Maximum_interval*

end

Each segment "knows" the schedule of which it is a part, expressed by the query *schedule*, and its position in that schedule, expressed by *index*. It has a *starting_time* and an *ending_time*; we could also add a query *duration*, with an invariant clause expressing its relation to the previous two. Redundancy is acceptable in system analysis provided redundant features express concepts of interest to users or developers, and the relations between redundant elements are stated clearly through the invariant. Here, clauses *in_list* and *in_schedule* of the invariant express the relation between a segment's own *index* and its position in the schedule's list of segments.

A segment also knows about the segment that will follow, *next*. Invariant clauses again express the consistency requirements: clause *next_in_list* indicates that if the segment is at position *i* the *next* one is at position *i +1*; clause *no_next_iff_last*, that there is a *next* if and only if the segment is not the last in its schedule.

The last two invariant clauses express constraints on durations: *sufficient_duration* defines a minimum duration of 30 seconds for a program fragment to deserve being called a segment, and *decent_interval* a maximum of two seconds for the time between two successive segments (when the TV screen may go blank).

The class specification has taken two shortcuts that would almost certainly have to be removed at the next iteration of the analysis process. First, times and durations have been expressed as integers, measured in seconds; this is not abstract enough, and we should be able to rely on library classes *DATE*, *TIME* and *DURATION*. Second, the notion of *SEGMENT* covers two separate notions: a TV program fragment, which can be defined independently of its scheduling time; and the scheduling of a certain program at a certain time slot. To separate these two notions is easy; just add to *SEGMENT* an attribute

content: *PROGRAM_FRAGMENT*

with a new class *PROGRAM_FRAGMENT* describing the content independently of its scheduling. Feature *duration* should then appear in *PROGRAM_FRAGMENT*, and a new invariant clause of *SEGMENT* should state

> *content.duration = ending_time – starting_time*

For brevity the rest of this sketch continues to treat the content as part of the segment. Such discussions are typical of what goes on during the analysis process, aided by the object-oriented method: we examine various abstractions, discuss whether they justify different classes, move features to other classes if we think they have been misassigned.

A segment has a primary sponsor, and a rating. Although here too we might benefit from a separate class, *rating* has just been specified as an integer, with the convention that a higher rating implies more restrictions; 0 means a segment accessible to all audiences.

Programs and commercials

Probing the notion of *SEGMENT* further, we distinguish two kinds: program segments and commercial breaks (advertizing segments). This immediately suggests using inheritance:

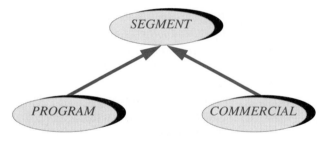

See "TAXOMA-NIA", 24.4, page 820.
This urge to use inheritance during analysis, by the way, is always suspect; you should be wary of bouts of taxomania, prompting you to create spurious classes where simple distinctive properties would suffice. The guiding criterion was given in the description of inheritance: does each proposed class really correspond to a separate abstraction, characterized by specific features and properties? Here the answer will be yes; it is not difficult to think of features for both programs and commercials, as will be listed in part below. Using inheritance will also yield the benefit of openness: we can add a new heir such as *INFOMERCIAL* later to describe segments of a different kind.

We can start *COMMERCIAL* as follows:

indexing
    description: "*Advertizing segment*"
deferred class *COMMERCIAL* **inherit**
    SEGMENT
        rename *sponsor* **as** *advertizer* **end**

feature

primary: *PROGRAM* **is deferred**
-- Program to which this commercial is attached

primary_index: *INTEGER* **is deferred**
-- Index of primary

set_primary (p: *PROGRAM*) **is**
-- Attach commercial to p.

require

program_exists: p /= Void
same_schedule: p.schedule = schedule
before: p.starting_time <= starting_time

deferred
ensure

index_updated: primary_index = p.index
primary_updated: primary = p

end

invariant

meaningful_primary_index: primary_index = primary.index
primary_before: primary.starting_time <= starting_time
acceptable_sponsor: advertizer.compatible (primary.sponsor)
acceptable_rating: rating <= primary.rating

end

Note the use of renaming, another example of a notational facility that at first sight might have appeared to be useful mostly for implementation-level classes, but turns out to be just as necessary for modeling. When a segment is a commercial, it is more appropriate to refer to its *sponsor* as being its *advertizer*.

Every commercial segment is attached to an earlier program segment (not a commercial), its *primary*, whose index in the schedule is *primary_index*. The first two invariant clauses express consistency conditions; the last two express compatibility rules:

- If a show has a sponsor, any advertizer during that show must be acceptable to it; you do not advertize for Pepsi-Cola during a show sponsored by Coca-Cola. The query *compatible* of class *COMPANY* might be given through some database.

- The rating of a commercial must be compatible with that of its primary program: you should not advertize for *Bulldozer Massacre III* on a toddlers' program.

The notion of *primary* needs refinement. It becomes clear at this stage of our analysis that we should really add a level: instead of a schedule being a succession of program segments and commercials, we should view it as a succession of shows, where each show (described by a class *SHOW*) has its own features, such as the show's sponsor, and a succession of show segments and commercials. Such improvement and refinement, developed as we gain more insight into the problem and learn from our first attempts, are a normal component of the analysis process.

Business rules

We have seen how invariant clauses and other assertions can cover semantic constraints of the application domain, also known in analysis parlance as *business rules*: in class *SCHEDULE*, that one can schedule a segment only in the future; in *SEGMENT*, that the interruption between two segments may not exceed a preset duration; in *COMMERCIAL*, that a commercial's rating must be compatible with that of the enclosing program.

It is indeed one of the principal contributions of the method that you can use assertions and the principles of Design by Contract to express such rules along with the structure, avoiding both the clouds and the precipice.

A practical warning however: even without any implementation commitment, there is a risk of overspecification. In assertions of the analysis text, you should only include business rules that have a high degree of certainty and durability. If any rule is subject to change, use abstraction to express what you need but leave room for adaptation. For example the rules on sponsor-advertizer compatibility can change; so the invariant of *COMMERCIAL* stays away from overspecification by simply postulating a boolean-valued query *compatible* in class *COMPANY*. One of the great advantages of analysis is that you choose what you say and what you say not. State what is known — if you specify nothing, the specification will not be of much interest — but no more. This is the same comment that we encountered in the discussion of abstract data types: we want the truth, all the relevant truth, but nothing *more* than the truth.

> That ADT comments should be directly applicable here is no surprise: ADTs are a high-level specification technique, and in fact the use of deferred classes with their assertions as a tool for analysis, illustrated by the TV station example, is conceptually a variant of ADT specification using software syntax.

Assessment

Although we have only begun the TV station programming example, we have gone far enough to understand the general principles of the approach. What is striking is how powerful and intuitive the concepts and notation are for general, software-independent system modeling, even though they were initially developed (in earlier chapters) for software purposes and, to the superficial observer, may even appear to address just *programming* issues. Here they come out in their full scope: as a general-purpose method and notation for describing systems of many kinds, covering the structure of systems as well as fine aspects of their semantics, and able to tackle complexity as well as evolution.

Nothing in a specification of the kind illustrated above is implementation-related, or even software-related, or even computer-related. We are using the concepts of object technology for purely descriptive purposes; no computer need enter the picture.

Of course if you or your customer do decide to go ahead and build a software system for managing TV station programming, you will have the tremendous advantage of a description that is already in a software-like form, syntactically and structurally. The transition to a design and implementation will proceed seamlessly in the same framework; you may even be able to retain many of the analysis classes *as is* in the final system, with implementations provided in proper descendants.

27.5 EXPRESSING THE ANALYSIS: MULTIPLE VIEWS

The use of specifications expressed in a software-like language, illustrated by the TV station example, raises an obvious question of practicality in normal industrial environments.

What can cause some skepticism is that the people who will have to review the analysis document may not all be comfortable with such notations; more than any other stage, analysis is the time for collaboration with application domain experts, future users, managers, contract administrators. Can we expect to them to read a specification that at first sight looks like a software text (although it is a pure model), and possibly contribute to it?

Surprisingly often, the answer is yes. Understanding the part of the notation that serves for analysis, as illustrated by the preceding example, does not require in-depth software expertise, simply an understanding of elements of the basic laws of logic and organized reasoning in any discipline. I can attest to having used such specifications successfully with people of widely different backgrounds and education.

But this is not the end of the story. A core of formalism-averse people may remain, whose input you will still need. And even those who appreciate the power of the formalism will need other views, in particular graphical representations. In fact the recurrent fights about graphics versus formalism, formalism versus natural language, are pointless. In practice the description of a non-trivial system requires **several** complementary views, such as:

- A formal text, as illustrated in the preceding example.

- A graphical representation, showing system structures in terms of "bubble and arrow" diagrams (also used in one instance for the example). Here the graphs will show classes, clusters, objects, and relations such as client and inheritance.

- A natural-language requirements document.

- Perhaps a tabular form, as appears in the presentation of the BON method below.

Each such view has its unique advantages, addressing some of the multiple goals of analysis defined at the beginning of this chapter; each has limitations that may make it irrelevant to other goals. In particular:

- Natural-language documents are irreplaceable for conveying essential ideas and explaining fine nuances. But they are notoriously prone to imprecision and ambiguity, as we saw in the critique of the "underline the nouns" approach.

  "STUDYING A REQUIREMENTS DOCUMENT", 22. 1, page 720.

- Tabular representations are useful to collect a set of related properties, such as the principal characteristics of a class — parents, features, invariant.

- Graphical representations are excellent for describing *structural* properties of a problem or system by showing the components and their relations. This explains the success of "bubble-and-arrow" descriptions as promoted by "structured analysis". But they are severely limited when it comes to expressing precise *semantic* properties, as required by item A3 of the list of analysis goals (answering specific questions). For example a graphical description is not the best place to look at for an answer to the question *"what is the maximum length of a commercial break?"*.

- Formal textual representations, such as the notation of this book, are the best tool for answering such precise questions, although they cannot compete with graphical representation when the goal is simply to get a quick understanding of how a system is organized.

> The usual argument for graphical representations over textual ones is the cliché that "a picture is worth a thousand words". It has its share of truth; block diagrams are indeed unsurpassed to convey to the reader the overall impression of a structure. But the proverb conveniently ignores the details that the words can carry, the imprecision that can affect the picture, and the *errors* that it can contain. The next time someone invites you to use a diagram as the final specification of some delicate aspect of a system, look at the comics page of the daily paper: the "find the differences between these two variants" teasers do not ask you to rack your eyes and brain over two sentences or two paragraphs, but to find the hidden differences between two deceptively similar *pictures.*

So what we need with a good analysis method is a way to use each one of these views as the need arises, switching freely from one to the other.

The question then arises of how to maintain consistency between the various views. The solution is to use one of the views as the reference, and to rely on software tools to make sure that additions and changes get propagated to all views. The best candidate to serve as reference — the only credible one, in fact — is the formal text, precisely because it is the only one that is both defined rigorously and able to cover semantics as well as structural properties.

With this approach, the use of formal software-like descriptions is not exclusive of other styles, and you can use a variety of tools adapted to the expertise levels and personal tastes of the analysis participants (software people, managers, end users). For the formal text, the software development environment may be appropriate: we have seen in particular that the compiler can double as an analysis support tool thanks to its facilities for checking type rules and other validity constraints, although its code generation mechanism is irrelevant at this stage. For the graphical notation, you will use a graphical CASE tool, apt at producing and manipulating structure charts. For the natural language texts, document manipulation and management systems can help. Tables can also have specific tool support. The various tools involved can be either separate or integrated in an analysis or development workbench.

Graphical or tabular input will immediately be reflected in the formal representation; for example if the graphical view showed a class C inheriting from a class A

Inheritance link

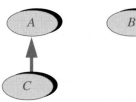

and you interactively redirect the arrow to point to *B*, the tools will automatically change the **inherit** clause of the formal text to reflect the change. Conversely, if you edit the formal description, the graphical and tabular representations will be updated.

It is more difficult for tools to process changes in natural-language descriptions. But if the document manipulation system enforces structured system descriptions, with chapters, sections and paragraphs, it is possible to keep links between the formal text and the natural-language requirements document, for example to indicate that a certain class or feature is connected to a certain paragraph of the requirements; this is particularly useful when the environment also provides configuration management tools, so that when something changes in the requirements the tools can, if not update the formal description, at least alert you to the change and produce a list of all the elements that depended, directly or indirectly, on the modified part.

The other direction is interesting too: producing natural-language descriptions from formal texts. The idea is simply to reconstruct, from a formal system description, a natural-language text that would express the same information in a form that will not scare the more formalism-averse members of the target readership. It is not hard indeed to think of a tool that, starting from our analysis sketch, would produce a fake English form such as

1. System concepts
>   The concepts of this system are:
>   *SCHEDULE, SEGMENT, COMMERCIAL, PROGRAM* …
>   *SCHEDULE* is discussed in section 2; *SEGMENT* is discussed in section 3; [etc.]

2. The notion of *SCHEDULE*
>   …

3. …

4. The notion of *COMMERCIAL*
>   **4.1 General description:**
>   Advertizing segments
>   **4.2 Source notions.**
>   The notion of *COMMERCIAL* is a specialized case of the notion
>   of *SEGMENT* and has all its operations and properties,
>   except for redefined ones as listed below.
>   **4.2 Renamed operations.**
>   What is called *sponsor* for *SEGMENT* is called *advertizer* for *COMMERCIAL*.
>   …
>   **4.3 Redefined operations**
>   …
>   **4.4 New operations**
>   The following operations characterize a *COMMERCIAL*:
>   *primary*, a query returning a *PROGRAM*
>   Needs: none   [Arguments, if any, would be listed here]
>   Description:
>   Program to which commercial is attached
>   Input conditions:

> ...
> Result conditions:
> ...
> ... Other operations ...
> **4.5 Constraints**
> ... An English-like rendition of the invariant properties ...
> **4. The notion of** *PROGRAM*
> ...

etc.

All the English sentences ("The concepts of this system are", "The following operations characterize a ..." and so on) are drawn from a standard set of predefined formulae, so they are not really "natural" language; but the illusion can be strong enough to make the result palatable to non-technical people, with the guarantee that it is consistent with the more formal view since it has been mechanically derived from it.

Although I do not know any tool that has explored this idea very far, the goal seems reachable. A project to build such a tool would be several orders of magnitude more realistic than long-going efforts in the reverse direction (attempts at automatic *analysis* of natural-language requirements documents) which have never been able to produce much, because of the inherent difficulty of analyzing natural language. Here we are interested in natural language *generation*, an easier task (in the same way that speech synthesis has progressed faster than speech recognition).

What makes this possible is the generality of the formal notation and, especially, its support for assertions, allowing us to include useful semantic properties in the generated natural-language texts. Without assertions we would remain in the vague — in the clouds.

27.6 ANALYSIS METHODS

Here is a list of some of the best-known methods of O-O analysis, listed in the approximate order of their public appearance. Although the description focuses on the analysis component of the methods, note that most of them also include design-related or even implementation-related components. The short summaries cannot do justice to the methods; to learn more, see the books and Web pages listed in the bibliographic notes to this chapter.

The **Coad-Yourdon** method initially resulted from an effort to objectify ideas coming from structured analysis. It involves five stages: finding classes and objects, starting from the application domain and analyzing system responsibilities; identifying structures by looking for generalization-specialization and whole-part relationships; defining "subjects" (class-object groups); defining attributes; defining services.

The **OMT** method (Object Modeling Technique) combines concepts of object technology with those of entity-relation modeling. The method includes a static model, based on the concepts of class, attribute, operation, relation and aggregation, and a dynamic model based on event-state diagrams, describing in an abstract way the intended behavior of the system.

The **Shlaer-Mellor** method is original in its emphasis on producing models that lend themselves to simulation and execution, making it possible to validate model behavior independently of any design or implementation. To separate concerns, it divides the problem into a number of domains: application domain, service domains (such as the user interface domain), software architecture domain, implementation domains (such as operating system or language). Rather than seamless development, its model for the development process uses translation to link the domains together into code for final system construction.

> The presence of architecture, design and implementation models in Shlaer-Mellor and some of the following methods illustrates the comment made above that the methods' ambition often extends beyond analysis to cover a large part of the lifecycle, or all of it.

In the **Martin-Odell** method, also known as OOIE (Object-Oriented Information Engineering), analysis consists of two parts: object structure analysis, which identifies the object types and their composition and inheritance relations; and object behavior analysis, which defines the dynamic model by considering object states and the events that may change these states. The events are considered first, leading to the identification of classes.

The **Booch** method uses a logical model (class and object structure) and a physical model (module and process architecture), including both static and dynamic components, and relying on numerous graphical symbols. It is intended to be subsumed by the "Unified Modeling Language" (see below).

The **OOSE** method (Object-Oriented Software Engineering), also known as Jacobson's method or as Objectory, the name of the original supporting tool, relies on use cases (scenarios) to elicit classes. It distinguishes five use case models: domain object model, analysis model (the use cases structured by the analysis), design model, implementation model, testing model.

See "Use cases", page 738.

The **OSA** method (for Object-oriented Systems Analysis) is meant to provide a general model of the analysis process rather than a step-by-step procedure. It consists of three parts: the object-relationship model, which describes objects and classes as well as their relations — with each other and with the "real world"; the object-behavior model, which provides the dynamic view through states, transitions, events, actions and exceptions; and the object-interaction model, specifying possible interactions between objects. The method also supports a notion of view, as well as generalization and specialization, which apply to both the interaction and behavior models.

The **Fusion** method seeks to combine some of the best ideas of earlier methods. For analysis it includes an object model, devoted to the problem domain, and an interface model, describing system behavior. The interface model is itself made of an operation model, specifying events and the resulting operations, and a lifecycle model, describing scenarios that guide the evolution of the system. Analysts should maintain a data dictionary which collects all the information from the various models.

The **Syntropy** method defines three models: the essential model "*is a model of a real or imaginary situation, [having nothing] to do with software: it describes the elements of the situation, their structure and behavior*". The specification model is an abstract model that treats the system as a stimulus-response mechanism, assuming unlimited hardware resources. The implementation model takes into account the actual computing environment. Each model may be expressed along several views: a type view describing object types and their static properties; state views, similar to the state transition diagrams of OMT, to

Citation from the Syntropy Web page listed in the bibliography section.

describe dynamic behavior; and mechanisms diagrams for implementation. The method also supports a notion of viewpoint to describe various interfaces to the same objects, going beyond the mere separation of interface and implementation provided by O-O languages.

The **MOSES** method involves five models: object-class; event, showing class collaboration by describing what messages are triggered as a result of calling a service on an object; "objectcharts", to model state-transition dynamics; inheritance; and service structure, to show data flow. Like the Business Object Notation reviewed in the next section, MOSES emphasizes the importance of contracts in specifying a class, using preconditions, postconditions and invariants in the style of the present book. Its "fountain" process model defines a number of standard documents to be produced at each stage.

The **SOMA** method (Semantic Object Modeling Approach) uses a "Task Object Model" to capture the requirements and transforms them into a "Business Object Model". It is one of the few methods to have benefited from formal approaches, using a notion of contract to describe business rules applying to objects.

At the time of writing, two separate efforts are progressing to unify existing methods. One, led by Brian Henderson-Sellers, Don Firesmith, Ian Graham and Jim Odell, is intended to produce an OPEN (the retained name) unified method. The other, by Rational Corporation, is starting from the OMT, Booch and Jacobson methods to define a "Unified Modeling Language".

27.7 THE BUSINESS OBJECT NOTATION

Each of the approaches listed in the preceding sections has its strong points. The method that seems to provide the most benefit for the least complexity is Nerson's and Waldén's Business Object Notation; let us take a slightly closer look at it to gain some insight into what a comprehensive approach to O-O analysis requires. This brief presentation will only sketch the principal features of the method, limiting itself to its contribution to analysis; for more details, and to explore design and implementation aspects, see the Waldén-Nerson book cited in the bibliography.

The Business Object Notation started as a graphical formalism for representing system structures. The original name was kept, even though BON has grown from just a notation to a complete development method. BON has been used in many different application areas for the analysis and development of systems, some very complex.

BON is based on three principles: *seamlessness*, *reversibility* and *contracting*. Seamlessness is the use of a continuous process throughout the software lifecycle. Reversibility is the support for both forward and backward engineering: from analysis to design and implementation, and back. Contracting (remember *Design by Contract*) is the precise definition, for each software element, of the associated semantic properties; BON is almost the only one among the popular analysis methods to use a full-fledged assertion mechanism, allowing analysts to specify not only the structure of a system but also its semantics (constraints, invariants, properties of the expected results).

Several other properties make BON stand out among O-O methods:

- It is meant to "scale up", in the sense explained at the beginning of this chapter. Various facilities and conventions enable you to choose the level of abstraction of a system or subsystem description, to zoom in on a component, to hide parts of a description. This selective hiding is preferable, in my opinion, to the use of multiple models illustrated by some of the preceding methods: here, for seamlessness and reversibility, you keep a single model; but you can at any time decide what aspects are relevant to your needs of the moment, and hide the rest.

- BON, created in the nineteen-nineties, was designed under the assumption that its users would have access to computing resources, not just paper and whiteboards. This makes it possible to use powerful tools to display complex information, free from the tyranny of fixed-size areas such as paper pages. Such a tool is sketched in the last chapter of this book. For small examples, the method can of course be used with pencil and paper.

- For all its ambition, especially its ability to cover large and complex systems, the method is notable for its simplicity. It only involves a small number of basic concepts. Note in particular that the formalism can be described over two pages; the most important elements appear below and on the facing page.

BON's support for large systems relies in part on the notion of **cluster**, denoting a group of logically related classes. Clusters can include subclusters, so that the result is a nested structure allowing analysts to work on various levels at different times. Some of the clusters may of course be libraries; the method puts a strong emphasis on reuse.

For further discussion of clusters see "CLUSTERS", 28. 1, page 923.

The static part of the model focuses on classes and clusters; the dynamic part describes objects, object interactions and possible scenarios for message sequencing.

BON recognizes the need for several complementary formalisms, explained earlier in this chapter. (The assumed availability of software tools is essential here: with a manual process, multiple views would raise the issue of how to maintain the *consistency* of the model; tools can ensure it automatically.) The formalisms include a textual notation, a tabular form and graphical diagrams.

The *textual notation* is similar to the notation of this book; but since it does not have to be directly compilable, it can use a few extensions in the area of assertions, including **delta** a to specify that a feature can change an attribute a, **forall** and **exists** to express logic formulae of first-order predicate calculus, and set operators such as **member_of**.

The *tabular form* is convenient to summarize the properties of a class compactly. Here is the general form of a tabular class chart:

CLASS	*Class_name*		Part:	
Short description		Indexing information		
Inherits from				
Queries				
Commands				
Constraints				

"Constraints" are invariants.

The graphical notation is extremely simple, so as to be easy to learn and remember. The principal conventions, static as well as dynamic, appear below.

Main diagram types of the Business Object Notation

(After [Waldén 1995], used with permission.)

STATIC DIAGRAMS

Cluster (with some classes)

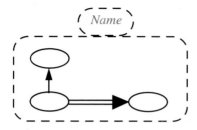

Inter-class relations

Inherits from

Client

Expanded client (aggregation)

Multiplicity of relations

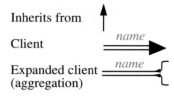

Class: generic,   effective,   deferred,   reused,   persistent,   interfaced,   root.

Class: detailed interface

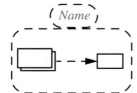

NAME
Inherits: *Parent classes*
Public features
— A, B, — *Features selectively exported to A, B*
— **Invariant** — *Class invariant*

Features

name*, *name*[+], *name*[++]   deferred, effective, redefined

→ *name*: *TYPE*   input argument

⟦?⟧ ⟦!⟧   precondition, postcondition

Assertion operators

Δ *name*   feature may change attribute *name*

@, ∅   current object, void reference

∃, ∀, |, •   symbols for predicate calculus operations

∈, ∉   membership operators

DYNAMIC DIAGRAMS

Object group (with some objects)

Object ⟦Name⟧

Objects (one or more) ⟦Name⟧

Inter-object relations

Message passing (with message number from scenario)   – – 7 – –▶

The method defines a precise process for analysis and development, consisting of seven tasks. The order of tasks corresponds to an ideal process, but the method recognizes that in practice it is subject to variation and iteration, as implied in fact by the very concept of reversibility. The standard tasks are:

B1 • **Delineate system borderline**: identify what the system will include and not include; define major subsystems, user metaphors, functionality, reused libraries.

B2 • **List candidate classes**: produce first list of classes based on problem domain.

B3 • **Select classes and group into clusters**: organize classes in logical groups, decide what classes will be deferred, persistent, externally interfaced etc.

B4 • **Define classes**: expand the initial definition of classes to specify each of them in terms of queries, commands and constraints.

B5 • **Sketch system behavior**: define charts for object creation, events and scenarios.

B6 • **Define public features**: finalize class interfaces.

B7 • **Refine system**.

Throughout the process, the method prescribes keeping a **glossary** of terms of the technical domain. Experience shows this to be an essential tool for any large application project, both to give non-experts a place to go when they do not understand some of the domain experts' jargon, and to make sure that the experts actually agree on the terms (it is surprising to see how often the process reveals that they do not!).

More generally, the method specifies for each step is a precise list of its deliverables: documents that the manager is entitled to expect as a result of the step's work. This precision in defining organizational responsibilities makes BON not only an analysis and design method but also a strategic tool for project management.

27.8 BIBLIOGRAPHY

The principal reference on the Business Object Notation is [Waldén 1995]. The basic concepts were introduced in [Nerson 1992]. A Web page is available at *www.tools.com/ products/bon/*.

*Add the ritual **http://** as a prefix to all Web addresses.*

Here are the principal references on other methods, with associated Web addresses. Coad-Yourdon: [Coad 1990], *www.oi.com*; OMT: [Rumbaugh 1991]; Shlaer-Mellor [Shlaer 1992], *www.projtech.com*; Martin-Odell, [Martin 1992]; Booch: [Booch 1994]; OOSE: [Jacobson 1992]; OSA: [Embley 1992], *osm7.cs.byu.edu/OSA.html*; Syntropy: [Cook 1994], *www.objectdesigners.co.uk/syntropy*; Fusion, [Coleman 1994]; MOSES: [Henderson-Sellers 1994], *www.csse.swin.edu.au/cotar/OPEN/OPEN.html*; SOMA, [Graham 1995].

On the OPEN method convergence project see [Henderson-Sellers 1996]; [Computer 1996] is a discussion of Rational's Unified Modeling Language effort (Booch-OMT-Jacobson).

Katsuya Amako maintains a set of descriptions of O-O methods, along with other useful O-O information, at *arkhp1.kek.jp/~amako/OOInfo.html*.

28

The software construction process

*F*oremost among the methodological issues of object technology is how it affects the broader picture of software development. We will now examine the consequences of object-oriented principles on the organization of projects and their division into phases.

[M 1995].

Such a presentation is part of a more general topic: the management perspective on object technology. Another book, *Object Success*, explores management issues in detail. The discussion which follows, drawing in part from *Object Success*, presents the essential ideas: **clusters**, the basic organizational unit; principles of **concurrent engineering** leading to the cluster model of the software lifecycle; steps and tasks of that model; the role of **generalization** for reusability; and the principles of **seamlessness** and **reversibility**.

28.1 CLUSTERS

The module structure of the object-oriented method is the class. For organizational purposes, you will usually need to group classes into collections, called clusters — a notion briefly previewed in the last chapter's sketch of the Business Object Notation.

A cluster is a group of related classes or, recursively, of related clusters.

The two cases are exclusive: for simplicity and ease of management, a cluster that contains subclusters should not have any classes of its own. So a cluster will be either a *basic cluster*, made of classes, or a *supercluster*, made of other clusters.

Typical basic clusters could include a parsing cluster for analyzing users' text input, a graphic cluster for graphical manipulations, a communications cluster. A basic cluster will typically have somewhere between five and forty classes; at around twenty classes, you should start thinking about splitting it into subclusters. The cluster is also the natural unit for single-developer mastery: each cluster should be managed by one person, and one person should be able to understand *all* of it — whereas in a large development no one can understand all of a system or even a major subsystem.

On super-modules see "The architectural role of selective exports", page 209.

Clusters are not super-modules. In an earlier chapter we saw the arguments for avoiding the introduction of units such as packages, and instead keeping a single module mechanism, the class.

Unlike packages, clusters are not a language construct, although they will appear in the Lace control files used to assemble systems out of components. They are a management tool. The responsibility for finding clusters will rest with the project leader; less challenging than the task of finding classes, studied in detail in a previous chapter, clustering classes mostly relies on common sense and the project leader's experience. This point actually deserves some emphasis, as it is sometimes misunderstood: the truly difficult job, which can launch a project on to an auspicious life or wreck it, and for which one can talk of right and wrong solutions, is to identify the classes (the proper data abstractions); grouping these classes into clusters is an organizational matter, for which many solutions are possible, depending on the resources available and on the expertise of the various team members. A less-than-optimal clustering decision may cause trouble and slow the development, but will not by itself bring the project down.

On Lace see "Assembling a system", page 198.

28.2 CONCURRENT ENGINEERING

One of the consequences of the division into clusters is that we can avoid the disadvantages of the all-or-nothing nature of traditional software lifecycle models. The well-known "waterfall" approach, introduced in 1970, was a reaction against the "code it now and fix it later" approach of that bygone era. It had the merit of separating concerns, of defining the principal tasks of software engineering, and of emphasizing the importance of up-front specification and design tasks.

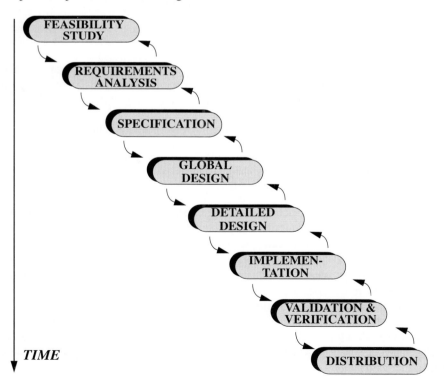

The waterfall model

(*WARNING: this is not the recommended process model for O-O development!*)

But the Waterfall Model also suffers (among other deficiencies) from the rigidity of its approach: taken literally, it would mean that no design can proceed until all the specification is complete, no implementation until all design is complete. This is a certain recipe for disaster: one grain of sand in the machine, and the whole project comes to a halt.

Various proposals such as the Spiral model have attempted to reduce this risk by providing a more iterative approach, But they retain the one-thread approach of the Waterfall, which hardly reflects the nature of today's software development, especially for large "virtual" teams that may be distributed over many sites, communicating through the Internet and other "electronic collocation" mechanisms.

Successful object-oriented development needs to support a **concurrent engineering** scheme, offering decentralization and flexibility, without losing the benefits of the waterfall's orderliness. We will in particular have to retain a sequential component, with well-defined activities. Object-oriented development does not mean that we can or should get rid of sound engineering practices. If anything, the added power of the method requires us to be *more* organized than before.

With a division into clusters we can achieve the right balance between sequentiality and concurrent engineering. We will have a sequential process, but subject to backward adjustments (this is the concept of reversibility, discussed in more detail at the end of this chapter), and applied to **clusters** rather than to the entire system.

The mini-lifecycle governing the development of a cluster may pictured as this:

*Individual
cluster
lifecycle*

The shape of the activity representations suggests the seamless nature of the development. Instead of separate steps as in the waterfall model, we see an accretion process — think of the figure as depicting a stalactite — in which every step takes over from the previous one and adds its own contribution.

28.3 STEPS AND TASKS

The steps listed in the mini-lifecycle of each cluster are:

- Specification: identify the classes (data abstractions) of the cluster and their major features and constraints (yielding invariant clauses).

- Design: define the architecture of the classes and their relations.

- Implementation: finalize the classes, with all details added.

- Verification & Validation: check that the cluster's classes perform satisfactorily (through static examination, testing and other techniques).

- Generalization: prepare for reuse (see below).

Given the high-level of abstraction of the method, the distinction between design and implementation is not always clear-cut. So a variant of the model merges these two steps into one, "design-implementation".

The need remains for two system-wide, cluster-independent phases. First, as with any other approach, you should perform a **feasibility study**, resulting in a go or no-go decision. Then, the project needs to be divided into clusters; this is, as noted, the responsibility of the project leader, who can of course rely on the help of other experienced team members.

28.4 THE CLUSTER MODEL OF THE SOFTWARE LIFECYCLE

The general development scheme, known as the Cluster Model, appears on the facing page. The vertical axis represents the sequential component of the process: a step that appears lower than another will be executed after it. The horizontal direction reflects concurrent engineering: tasks at the same level can proceed in parallel.

Various clusters, and various steps within each cluster, will proceed at their own pace depending on the difficulty of the task. The project leader is in charge of deciding when to start a new cluster or a new task.

The result is to give the project leader the right combination of order and flexibility. Order because the definition of cluster tasks provides a control framework and control points against which to assess progress and delays (one of the most difficult aspects of project management); flexibility because you can buffer unexpected delays, or take advantage of unexpectedly fast progress, by starting activities sooner or later. The project leader also controls the degree of concurrent engineering: for a small team, or in the early stages of a difficult project, there may be a small number of parallel clusters, or just one; for a larger team, or once the basic existential questions seems to be under control, you can start pursuing several clusters at once.

Better than traditional approaches, the cluster model enables project leaders to do their job to its full extent, exerting their decision power to devote resources where they are needed the most.

The cluster model of the software lifecycle

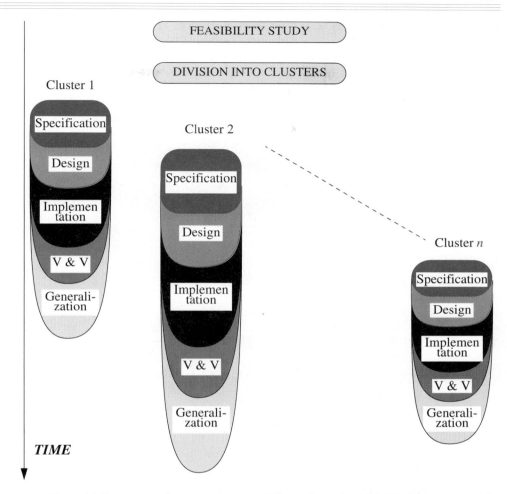

To avoid divergence, the current states of the various clusters' development must be regularly reconciled. This is the task of **integration**, best performed at preset intervals, for example once a week. It is the responsibility of the project leader, and ensures that at every stage after start-up there will be a **current demo**, not necessarily up to date for all aspects of the system, but ready to be showed to whoever — customers, managers... — needs reassurance about the project's progress. This also serves to remove any inconsistency between clusters before it has had the opportunity to cause damage, reassuring the project members themselves that the pieces fit together and that the future system is taking shape.

What makes possible the cluster model's form of concurrent engineering is the set of information hiding properties of the object-oriented method. Clusters may depend on each other; for example a graphical interface cluster may need, for remote display, classes of the communication cluster. Thanks to data abstraction, it is possible for a cluster to proceed even if the clusters on which it depends are not yet finished; it suffices that the *specification* phase of the needed classes be complete, so that you can proceed on the basis of their official interface, given as a short form or deferred version. This aspect of the model is perhaps easier to picture if we rotate the preceding figure, as illustrated below, to emphasize the software layers corresponding to the various clusters, with the more general clusters at the bottom and the more application-specific ones at the top. The design and implementation of each cluster depend only on the specifications of clusters below it, not on their own design and implementation. The figure only shows dependencies on the cluster immediately below, but a cluster may rely on any lower-level cluster.

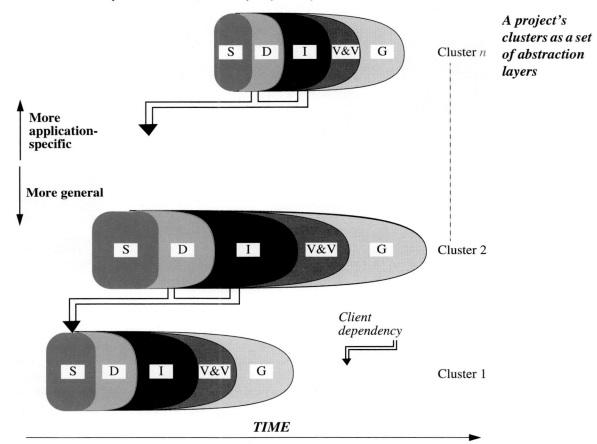

28.5 GENERALIZATION

The last task of cluster mini-lifecycles, generalization (the G on the above figure) has no equivalent in traditional approaches. Its goal is to polish the classes so as to turn them into potentially reusable software components.

Including a generalization step immediately suggests a criticism: instead of an a posteriori add-on, should reusability concerns not be part of the entire software process? How can one make software reusable after the fact? But this criticism is misplaced. The a priori view of software reuse ("to be reusable, software should be designed as reusable from the start") and the a posteriori view ("software will not be reusable the first time around") are complementary, not contradictory. The success of a reusability policy requires both instilling a *reusability culture* in the minds of everyone involved, and devoting sufficient resources to improving the reusability of classes' initial versions.

In spite of the best of intentions, software elements produced as part of an application-oriented project will usually not be fully reusable. This is due in part to the constraints affecting projects — the pressure of customers wanting the next version ASAP, of the competition putting out its own products, of shareholders eager to see results. We live in a hurried world and an even more hurried industry. But there is also an intrinsic reason for not always trusting reusability promises: until someone has reused it, you cannot be sure that a product has been freed of all its dependencies, explicit and (particularly) implicit, on its original developers' background, corporate affiliation, technical context, working practices, hardware resources and software environment.

The presence of a generalization step is not, then, an excuse for ignoring reusability until the last moment. The arguments of the a priori school are correct: you cannot add reusability as an afterthought. But do not assume that having a reusability policy is sufficient. Even with reusability built into everyone's mindset, you will need to devote some more time to your project's classes before you can call them software components.

Including a generalization step in the official process model is also a matter of policy. Very few corporate executives these days will take a public stand *against* reusability. Of course, my friend, we want our software to be reusable! The software people need to find out whether this is sincere commitment or lip service. Very easy. The commitment exists if management is ready to reserve *some* resources, on top of the money and time allocated to each project, for generalization. This is a courageous decision, because the benefits may not be immediate and other urgent projects may suffer a little. But it is the only way to guarantee that there will, in the end, be reusable components. If, however, the management is not ready to pledge such resources, even modest ones (a few percent above the normal project budget can make a world of difference), then you can listen politely to the grandiose speeches about reuse and read sympathetically about the "reuser of the month" award in the company's newsletter: in truth, the company is not ready for reusability and will not get reusability.

If, on the other hand, some resources are devoted to generalization, remember that this is not sufficient either. Success in reusability comes from a combination of a priori and a posteriori efforts:

The reusability culture

Develop all software under the assumption that it will be reused.

Do not trust that any software will be reusable until you have seen it reused.

The first part implies applying reusability concerns throughout development. The second implies not taking the result for granted, but performing a generalization step to remove any traces of context-specific elements.

The generalization task may involve the following activities:

- **Abstracting**: introducing a deferred class to describe the pure abstraction behind a certain class.

On abstracting and factoring see "Varieties of class abstraction", page 860.

- **Factoring**: recognizing that two classes, originally unrelated, are in fact variants of the same general notion, which can then be described by a common ancestor.

- Adding assertions, especially postconditions and invariant clauses which reflect increased understanding of the semantics of the class and its features. (You may also have to add a precondition, but this is more akin to correcting a bug, since it means the routine was not properly protected.)

- Adding rescue clauses to handle exceptions whose possibility may initially have been ignored.

- Adding documentation.

The first two of these activities, studied in the discussion of inheritance methodology, reflect the non-standard view of inheritance hierarchy construction that we explored then: the recognition that, although it would be nice always to go from the general to the specific and the abstract to the concrete, the actual path to invention is often more tortuous, and sometimes just the other way around.

The role of generalization is to improve classes that may be considered good enough for internal purposes — as long, that is, as they are only used within a particular system — but not any more when they become part of a library available to any client author who cares to use them for his own needs. Peccadillos that may have been forgivable in the first setting, such as insufficient specification or reliance on undocumented assumptions, become show-stoppers. This is why developing for reusability is more difficult than ordinary application development: when your software is available to anyone, working on applications of any kind for any platform anywhere in the world, everything starts to matter. Reusability breeds perfectionism; you cannot leave good enough alone.

28.6 SEAMLESSNESS AND REVERSIBILITY

The "stalactite" nature of the cluster lifecycle reflects one of the most radical differences between O-O development and earlier approaches. Instead of erecting barriers between successive lifecycle steps, well-understood object technology defines a single framework for analysis, design, implementation and maintenance. This is known as *seamless development*; one of its consequences, previewed in the last chapter's discussion of the Business Object Notation, is the need for a *reversible* software development process.

Seamless development

Different tasks will of course remain. To take extreme examples, you are not doing the same thing when defining general properties of a system that has yet to be built and performing the last rounds of debugging. But the idea of seamlessness is to downplay differences where the traditional approach exaggerated them; to recognize, behind the technical variations, the fundamental unity of the software process. Throughout development the same issues arise, the same intellectual challenges must be addressed, the same structuring mechanisms are needed, the same forms of reasoning apply and, as shown in this book, the same notation can be used.

The benefits of a seamless approach are numerous:

- You avoid costly and error-prone transitions between steps, magnified by changes in notation, mindset, and personnel (analysts, designers, implementers...). Such gaps are often called **impedance mismatches** by analogy with a circuit made of electrically incompatible elements; the mismatches between analysis and design, design and implementation, implementation and evolution, are among the worst causes of trouble in traditional software development.

"Direct Mapping",
page 47.
- By starting from the analysis classes as a basis for the rest of the development, you ensure a close correspondence between the description of the problem and the solution. This **direct mapping property** helps the dialog with customers and users, and facilitates evolution by ensuring that they all think in terms of the same basic concepts. It is part of the O-O method's support for extendibility.

- The use of a single framework facilitates the backward adjustments that will inevitably accompany the normally one-directional progress of the software development process.

Reversibility: wisdom sometimes blooms late in the season

The last benefit cited defines one of the principal contributions of object technology to the software lifecycle — reversibility.

Reversibility is the official acceptance of a characteristic of software development which, although inevitable and universal, is one of the most closely guarded secrets of the software literature: the influence of later stages of the software process on decisions made during initial stages.

We all wish, of course, that problems be fully defined before we get to solve them. That is the normal way to go, and in software it means that we complete the analysis before we engage in design, the design before we start implementation, the implementation before we deliver. But what if, during implementation, a developer suddenly realizes that the system could do something better, or should do something different altogether? Do we scold him for not minding his own business? What if his suggestion is indeed right?

The phrase *esprit de l'escalier*, "wit of the staircase", captures this phenomenon. Picture a pleasant dinner in an apartment on the second or fourth floor (the fashionable ones) of a Parisian building. Sharp comments fly back and forth over the veal Marengo, and you feel dumb. The soirée finishes and you take leave of your hosts, start walking down the stairs, when … there it is: the smashing repartee that would have made you the hero of the evening! But too late.

Are bouts of *esprit de l'escalier* too late in software also? They have existed ever since software projects have been told to freeze the specification before they start on a solution. Bad managers suppress them, telling the implementers, in effect, to code and shut up. Good managers try to see whether they can take advantage of belated specification ideas, without attracting the attention of whoever is in charge of enforcing the company's software quality plan and its waterfall-style ukases against changing the specification at implementation time.

The bad managers may be unconsciously applying another **escalier** *aphorism, Clemenceau's "in love, the best moment is in the stairs" — beforehand, that is.*

With O-O development it becomes clear that the *esprit de l'escalier* phenomenon is not just the result of laziness in analysis, but follows from the intrinsic nature of software development. Wisdom sometimes blooms late in the season. Nowhere more than with object technology do we see the intimate connection between problem and solution that characterizes our field. It is not just that we sometimes understand aspects of the problem only at the time of the solution, but more profoundly that the solution affects the problem and suggests better functionalities.

Remember the example of command undoing and redoing: an implementation technique, the "history list" — which someone trained in a more traditional approach would dismiss as irrelevant to the task of defining system functionality —, actually suggested a new way of providing end-users of our system with a convenient interface for undoing and redoing commands.

Chapter 21.

The introduction of reversibility suggests that the general forward thrust of our earlier cluster mini-lifecycle diagrams is actually tempered by the constant possibility of backward revisions and corrections:

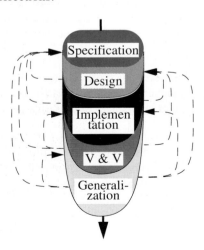

Individual cluster lifecycle, reversible

28.7 WITH US, EVERYTHING IS THE FACE

The stress on seamlessness and reversibility is perhaps the most potentially subversive component of object technology. It affects project organization, and the very nature of the software profession; in line with modern trends in other industries, it tends to remove barriers between narrow specialties — analysts who only deal in ethereal concepts, designers who only worry about structure, implementers who only write code — and to favor the emergence of a single category of generalists: *developers* in a broad sense of the term, people who are able to accompany part of a project from beginning to end.

The approach also departs from the dominant view in the current software engineering literature, which treats analysis and implementation (with design somewhere in the middle) as fundamentally different activities, susceptible to different methods, using different notations and pursuing different goals, often with the connotation that analysis and design are all that really matters, implementation being an inevitable chore. This view has historical justifications: from its infancy in the nineteen-seventies, software engineering was an attempt to put some order into the haphazard nature of program construction by teaching software people to think before they shoot. Hence the stress on early stages of software development, on the need to specify what you are going to implement. This is all justified, now as much as then. But some of the consequences of this essentially beneficial effort have gone too far, creating impedance mismatches between the different activities, and producing a strictly sequential model even though product and process quality demands seamlessness and reversibility.

With object technology we can remove the unnecessary differences between analysis, design and implementation — the necessary ones will manifest themselves clearly enough — and rehabilitate the much maligned task of implementation. It was natural for the pioneers of software engineering, when programming meant trying to solve many machine-dependent issues and explaining the result to the computer in a language that it could understand, usually low-level and sometimes inelegant, to detach themselves from these mundane aspects and stress instead the importance of studying abstract concepts from the problem domain. But we can retain these abstraction qualities without losing the link to the solution.

The secret is to make the concepts of programming, and the notations for programming, high-level enough that they can serve just as well as tools for *modeling*. This is what object technology achieves.

The following story, stolen from Roman Jakobson's *Essays on General Linguistics*, will perhaps help make the point clear:

> *In a far-away country, a missionary was scolding the natives. "You should not go around naked, showing your body like this!". One day a young girl spoke back, pointing at him: "But you, Father, you are also showing a part of your body!". "But of course", the missionary said with a dignified tone; "That is my face". The girl replied: "So you see, Father, it is really the same thing. Only, with us, everything is the face".*

So it is with object technology. With us, everything is the face.

28.8 KEY CONCEPTS COVERED IN THIS CHAPTER

• Object technology calls for a new process model, supporting seamless, reversible development.

• The unit for the sequential component of the lifecycle is the cluster, a set of logically related classes. Clusters can be arbitrarily nested.

• The lifecycle model relies on concurrent engineering: parallel development of several clusters, each permitted to rely on the specification of earlier ones.

• Object technology rehabilitates implementation.

28.9 BIBLIOGRAPHICAL NOTES

[M 1995] discusses further the topics of this chapter. It develops in detail the cluster model, and explores the consequences of the object-oriented software process on team organization, on the manager's role, and on the economics of software engineering.

[Baudoin 1996] is an extensive discussion of the lifecycle issues raised by object technology, also covering many other important topics such as project organization and the role of standards, and including several case studies.

The first presentation of the cluster model appeared in [Gindre 1989]. Another O-O lifecycle model, the *fountain model*, originally appeared in [Henderson-Sellers 1990] and is further developed in [Henderson-Sellers 1991], [Henderson-Sellers 1994]; it complements rather than contradicts the cluster model, emphasizing the need to iterate lifecycle activities.

A number of O-O analysis publications, in particular [Rumbaugh 1991] (the original text on the OMT method) and [Henderson-Sellers 1991], stress seamless development. For a detailed treatment of reversibility as well as seamlessness, see [Waldén 1995].

***

Wisdom sometimes blooms late in the season
Or half-way down the stairs.
Is it, my Lords, a crime of high treason
To trust the implementers?

29

Teaching the method

*E*nding our study of methodological issues, we turn our attention to one of the principal questions facing companies and universities that adopt object technology: how best to educate those who will have to apply it. This chapter presents teaching principles and points to common errors.

The first part of the discussion takes the view of someone who is in charge of organizing a training program in a company; the following parts take the view of a university or high school professor. All emphasize the pedagogical issues of O-O training, and so they should be relevant to you even if you are in neither of these positions — in particular if you are a trainee rather than a trainer.

29.1 INDUSTRIAL TRAINING

Let us start with a few general observations about how to teach object technology — either in public seminars or as part of an in-company training plan — to software professionals previously trained in other approaches.

Paradoxically, the trainer's task may be harder now than when object technology started to attract wide interest in the mid-eighties. It was new then to most people, and had an aura of heresy which made the audience listen. Today, no one will call security if one of the cocktail guests declares object-oriented tastes. This is the buzzword effect, which has been dubbed **mOOzak**: the omnipresence, in the computer press, of O-O this and O-O that, causing a general dilution of the concepts. The words flow so continuously from the loudspeakers — object, class, polymorphism… — as to seem familiar, but are the concepts widely understood? Often not. This puts a new burden on the trainer: convincing the trainees that they do not yet know everything, since no one can learn a subject who thinks he already knows it.

The only strategy guaranteed to overcome this problem applies the following plan:

Initial training: the "hit them twice" strategy

T1 • Take the initial training courses.

T2 • Try your hand at O-O development.

T3 • Take the initial training courses.

T3 is not a typo: after having tried to apply O-O ideas to real development, trainees take the class again. O-O training companies sometimes suggest this strategy to their customers, not always with success since it suspiciously looks like a marketing ploy to sell the same thing twice. But that is not the case.

The second iteration is what really gets the concepts through. Although the first is necessary to provide the right background, it may not be fully effective; partly because of the mOOzak effect, your students may not quite internalize the concepts. Only when they have grappled with the day-to-day challenges of object-oriented software construction — *Is a new class necessary for this concept? Is this a proper use of inheritance? Do these two features justify introducing a new node in the inheritance structure? Is this design pattern from the course relevant here?* — will they have the necessary preparation to listen properly. The second session will not, of course, be identical to the first (if anything, the audience's questions will be more interesting), and might straddle the border between training and consulting; but it is really a second presentation of the same basic material — not merely an advanced course following an elementary one.

> In practice only the more enlightened companies are ready to accept the "teach it once, then teach it again" strategy. Others will dismiss the idea as a waste of resources. In my experience, however, the result is well worth the extra effort. The strategy is the best I know to train developers who truly understand object technology and can apply it effectively to serve the company's needs.

The next principle addresses *what* should be taught:

Training Topics principle

Especially in initial training, focus on implementation and design.

Some people assume that the curriculum should start with object-oriented analysis. This is a grave mistake. A beginner in object technology cannot understand O-O analysis (except in the mOOzak sense of recognizing the buzzwords). To master O-O analysis, you must have learned the fundamental concepts — class, contracts, information hiding, inheritance, polymorphism, dynamic binding and the like — at the level of implementation, where they are immediately applicable, and you must have used them to build a few O-O systems, initially small and then growing in size; you must have taken these projects all the way to completion. Only after such a hands-on encounter with the operational use of the method will you be equipped to understand the concepts of O-O analysis and their role in the seamless process of object-oriented software construction.

Two more principles. First, do not limit yourselves to introductory courses:

Advanced Curriculum principle

At least 50% of a training budget should be reserved for non-introductory courses.

Finally, do not consider developers alone:

Manager Training principle

A training curriculum should include courses for managers as well as software developers.

It is unrealistic, for a company or group that is adopting object technology on any scale, to hope to succeed by training developers only. Managers, regardless of the depth of their technical background, must be introduced to the basic O-O ideas and apprised of their repercussions on distribution of tasks, team organization, project lifecycle, economics of software development. The lifecycle discussion of the next chapter and, more exhaustively, management-oriented books such as [Goldberg 1995], [Baudoin 1996] and [M 1995], are typical of the material to be covered in such (usually short) courses.

> Here is an example of what manager education must include to avoid potential trouble, allow effective development and benefit the bottom line. The industry's measures of productivity are still largely based, deep-down, on ratios of produced code to production effort. In a reuse-conscious software process, you may spend some time improving software elements that *already work well* to increase their potential for reuse in future projects. This is the generalization task, an important step of the lifecycle model presented in the next chapter. Often, such efforts will *remove* code, for example because you have given a common ancestor to two originally unrelated classes, moving commonality to that ancestor. In the productivity ratio, the numerator decreases (less code) and the denominator increases (more effort)! Managers must be warned that the old measures do not tell the whole story, and that the extra effort actually improves the software assets of the company. Without such preparation, serious misunderstandings may develop, jeopardizing the success of the best planned technical strategies.

29.2 INTRODUCTORY COURSES

Let us turn our attention now to the teaching of object technology in an academic environment (although many observations will also be applicable to industrial training).

As the software community recognizes the value of the object-oriented approach, the question increasingly arises of when, where and how to include object-oriented concepts, languages and tools in a software curriculum – university, college or even high school.

Phylogeny and ontogeny

When should we start?

The earlier the better. The object-oriented method provides an excellent intellectual discipline; if you agree with its goals and techniques, there is no reason to delay bringing it to your students; you should in fact teach it as the first approach to software development. Beginning students react favorably to O-O teaching, not because it is trendy, but because the method is clear and effective.

This strategy is preferable to a more conservative one whereby you would teach an older method first, then *unteach* it in order to introduce O-O thinking. If you think object-oriented development is the right way to go, there is no reason to make a detour first.

Teachers may unconsciously tend to apply an idea that was once popular in biology: that ontogeny (the story of the individual) repeats phylogeny (the story of the species); a human embryo, at various stages of its development, vaguely looks like a frog, a pig etc. Transposed to our subject, it means that a teacher who first learned Algol, then went on to structured design and finally discovered objects may want to take his students through the same path. There is little justification for such an approach, which in elementary education would make students first learn to count in Roman numerals, only later to be introduced to more advanced "methodologies" such as Arabic numerals. If you think you know what the right approach is, teach it first.

Paving the way for other approaches

One of the reasons for recommending (without fear of fanaticism or narrow-mindedness) the use of object technology right from the start is that, because the method is so general, it prepares students for the later introduction of other paradigms such as logic and functional programming – which should be part of any software engineer's culture. If your curriculum calls for the teaching of traditional programming languages such as Fortran, Cobol or Pascal, it is also preferable to introduce these later, as knowledge of the object-oriented method will enable students to use them in a safer and more reasoned way.

O-O teaching is also good preparation for a topic which will become an ever more prevalent part of software education programs: formal approaches to software specification, construction and verification, rooted in mathematics and formal logic. The use of assertions and more generally of the Design by Contract approach is, in my experience, an effective way to raise the students' awareness of the need for a sound, systematic, implementation-independent and at least partially formal characterization of software elements. Premature exposure to the full machinery of a formal specification method such as Z or VDM may overwhelm students and cause rejection; even if this does not occur, students are unlikely to appreciate the merits of formality until they have had significant software development experience. Object-oriented software construction with Design by Contract enables students to start producing real software and at the same time to gain a gentle, progressive exposure to formal techniques.

Language choice

Using the object-oriented method for introductory courses only makes sense if you can rely on a language and an environment that fully support the paradigm, and are not encumbered by ghosts of the past. Note in particular that "hybrid" approaches, based on object-oriented extensions of older languages, are unsuitable for beginning students, since they mix O-O concepts with unrelated remnants from other methods, forcing the teacher to spend much of the time on excuses rather than concepts.

In C-based languages, for example, just explaining why an array and a pointer have to be treated as the same notion — a property having its roots in optimization techniques for older hardware architectures — would consume precious time and energy, which will not be available for teaching the concepts of software design. More generally, students would be encouraged, at the very beginning of their training, to reason in terms of low-level mechanisms – addresses, pointers, memory, signals. They would inevitably spend much of their time, if they eventually produce a compilable program, chasing various bugs. The approach would leave the students perplexed and might end up in disaster.

An introductory course must do the reverse: present the students with a clear, coherent set of practical principles. The notation must directly support these principles, ensuring a one-to-one correspondence between method and language. Any time you spend explaining the language per se is time lost. With a good language, you explain the concepts, and use the notation as the natural way to apply them.

Although the main quality of an introductory language is its structural simplicity and its support of O-O ideas such as class-based modularization, design by contract, static typing and inheritance, you should not underestimate the role of syntactic clarity. C++ and Java texts are replete with lines such as

Examples from the basic book on Java, [Arnold 1996].

```
public static void main(String[] args {
if (this->fd == -1 && !open_fd(this))
if ((xfrm = (char *)malloc(xfrm_len + 1)) == NULL) {
```

showing cryptic and confusing syntax relying on many special operators. Beginners should not be subjected to such contortions, justified only by historical considerations; learning to program well is hard enough without the interposed obstacle of a hostile notation.

Exceprts from posting of 15 October 1996.

David Clark from the University of Canberra went through this experience and posted some of his conclusions on Usenet:

Last semester I taught the second half of a first year programming [course] using Java… My experience has been that students do not find Java easy to learn. Time and again the language gets in the way of what I want to teach. Here are some examples:

- *The first thing they see is public static void main (String [ ] args) throws IOException There are about 6 different concepts in that one line which students are not yet ready to learn…*

- *You get output for "free", but have to jump through several hoops to input anything. (import, declare, initialize.). The only way to read a number from the keyboard is to read a string and parse it. Again, this is something that crops up in the first lecture.*

- *Java treats the primitive data types (int, char, boolean, float, long,…) differently from other objects. There are Object-type equivalents (Integer, Boolean, Character etc.). There is no relation between int and Integer.*

- *The String class is a special case. (Again, for efficiency.) It is only used for strings that don't change. There is a StringBuffer class for strings that do change. Fair enough. but there is no relationship between String and StringBuffer. There are few features in common.*

- *The lack of generics means that you are forever casting if you want to use a collection of elements such as Stack or Hashtable. [These things] are hurdles for beginning students, and distract them from the main learning outcomes of the course.*

Prof. Clark goes on to compare this experience with his practice of teaching with the notation of this book, for which, he writes, "*I do virtually no language teaching beyond giving some examples of code*".

The initial notations taught to students, so important to their future vision, must always be simple and clear, to allow in-depth understanding of the basic concepts. Even Pascal, the traditional choice of computing science departments for introductory teaching, is preferable in this respect to a hybrid language since it provides a solid, consistent basis, from which students can later move to another solid, consistent approach. It is of course even better, as noted, if the basis can be solid, consistent *and* O-O.

Some hybrid languages are industrially important; but they should be taught later, when students have mastered the basic concepts. This is not a new idea: when computing science departments adopted Pascal in the nineteen-seventies, they also included service courses to teach Fortran, Cobol or PL/I as requested by industry then. Similarly, a modern object-based curriculum may include a C++ or Java service course to satisfy downstream requirements and enable the students to include the required buzzwords on their résumés. Students will understand C++ and Java better anyway after having been taught the principles of object technology using a pure O-O language. Introductory courses, which shape a student's mind forever, must use the best technical approach.

Some teachers are tempted to use C hybrids because of perceived industry pressures. But this is inappropriate for several reasons:

- Industry demands are notoriously volatile. A few years ago, ads were all for things like RPG and Cobol. In late 1996 they were all for Java, but in 1995 no one had heard of Java. What will they list in 2010 or 2020? We do not know, but we must endow our students with capabilities that will still be marketable then. For this we must emphasize long-term design skills and intellectual principles.

- Starting with these skills and principles does not exclude teaching specific approaches later. In fact it helps, as already noted. A student who has been taught O-O concepts in depth, using an appropriate notation, will be a better C++ or Java programmer than one whose first encounter with programming involved fighting with the language.

- The historical precedent of Pascal around 1975 shows that computing science teachers can succeed with their own choices. At that time, no one in industry requested Pascal; in fact, almost no one in industry had heard of Pascal. Industry, if anything, would have requested one of the Three Tenors of the moment: Fortran, Cobol and PL/I. The computing scientists chose to go with the best technical solution, corresponding to the state of the art in programming methodology (structured programming). The result proved them right, as they were able to teach students the abstract concepts and techniques of software development while preparing them for learning new languages and tools.

29.3 OTHER COURSES

Beyond introductory courses, the object-oriented method can play a role at many stages of a software curriculum. Let us review the corresponding uses.

Terminology

The organization of higher education differs widely among countries. To avoid any confusion we must first decide on a reasonably universal terminology to denote the various levels of study. Here is some attempt at common ground:

- High school (US), lycée, Gymnasium, called secondary education below.
- First few years of university or equivalent: this is called "undergraduate studies" in the US and other Anglo-Saxon countries (*Gakubu* in Japan). In France and countries influenced by its system it corresponds to either the combination of *classes préparatoires* with the first two years of engineering schools, or to the first and second *cycles* of universities. In the German system it is the *Grundstudium*. The term "undergraduate" will be retained below.
- Finally for the later years, leading to advanced degrees, we can use the US term "graduate". (The rough equivalents are "postgraduate" in the UK; third cycle, DEA, DESS, options of engineering schools in France; *Hauptstudium* in Germany; *Daigakuin* in Japan.)

Secondary and undergraduate studies

At the secondary or undergraduate level the object-oriented method can play a central role, as noted, in an introductory programming course. It can also help for many other courses. We may distinguish here between courses that can be entirely taught in an object-oriented way, and those which will benefit from some partial use of object-oriented ideas.

Here are some of the standard courses that can be taught in a fully O-O way:

- Data structures and algorithms. Here the techniques of Design by Contract are fundamental: characterizing routines by assertions, specifying data structures with class invariants, associating loop variants and invariants with algorithms. In addition, an innovative and powerful way to organize such a course is to design it around an existing **library** of software components from an existing object-oriented environment. Then instead of starting from scratch students can learn by imitation and improvement. (More on this topic below.)
- Software engineering. The object-oriented method provides an excellent framework to introduce students to the challenges of industrial, multi-person software development, and to evaluate the benefits and limitations of project management techniques, software metrics, software economics, development environments and the other techniques which the software engineering literature discusses (in complement to object orientation) as answers to this challenge.
- Analysis and design. Clearly this can be taught in a fully O-O way; again Design by Contract is central. Courses should emphasize the seamless transition to implementation and maintenance.
- Introduction to graphics; introduction to simulation; etc.

Courses that may benefit from heavier or lighter object doses include: operating systems (where the method helps understand the notion of process, the message passing paradigm, and the importance of information hiding, clearly defined interfaces and limited communication channels in the design of proper system architectures); introduction to formal methods (as noted above); functional programming; logic programming (where the connection with assertions should be emphasized); introduction to artificial intelligence (where inheritance is a key concept for knowledge representation); databases (which should reserve a central place for the notion of abstract data type, and include a discussion of object-oriented databases).

Even computer architecture courses are not immune from the influence of O-O ideas, as concepts of modularity, information hiding and assertions can serve to present the topic in a clear and convincing manner.

Graduate courses

At the graduate level, many O-O courses and seminars are possible, covering more advanced topics: concurrency, distributed systems, persistence, databases, formal specifications, advanced analysis and design methods, configuration management, distributed project management, program verification.

A complete curriculum

This incomplete list shows the method as being so ubiquitous that it would make sense to design an entire software curriculum around it. A few institutions have made some progress in that direction. No doubt in the years to come someone will jump and convince the management of some university to go all the way.

29.4 TOWARDS A NEW SOFTWARE PEDAGOGY

Not only does object technology affect what can be taught to students of software topics; the method also suggests new pedagogical techniques, which we will now explore.

An important note: the strategies described in the rest of this chapter are still somewhat futuristic. I believe that they must and will become prevalent for teaching software, but their full application will require an infrastructure which is not yet fully in place, in particular new textbooks and different administrative policies.

If you or your institution are not ready to apply such strategies, this does not mean that you should remove objects from your teaching. You can still, as described in the preceding sections, instill variable doses of object technology in your courses while retaining compatibility with your current way of teaching. And you should read the rest of this chapter anyway since, even if you do not follow its more radical suggestions, you might find an idea or two immediately applicable in a more conventional context.

The consumer-to-producer strategy

An O-O course on data structures and algorithms can, as noted above, be organized around a library. This idea actually has much broader applications.

A frustrating aspect of many courses is that teachers can only give introductory examples and exercises, so that students do not get to work on really interesting applications. One can only get so much excitement out of computing the first 25 Fibonacci numbers, or replacing all occurrences of a word by another in a text, two typical exercises of elementary programming courses.

With the object-oriented method, a good O-O environment and, most importantly, good libraries, a different strategy is possible if you give students access to the libraries early in the process. In this capacity students are just reuse consumers, and use the library components as black boxes in the sense defined above; this assumes that proper techniques are available for describing component usage without showing the components' internals. Then students can start building meaningful applications early: their task is merely to combine existing components and assemble them into systems. In many respects this is a better introduction to the challenges and rewards of software development than the toy examples which have been the mainstay of most introductory courses.

Almost on day one of the course, the students will be able to produce impressive applications by reusing existing software. Their first assignment may involve writing just a few lines — enough to call a pre-built application, and yielding striking results (devised by someone else!). It is desirable, by the way, to use libraries that include graphics or other multimedia components, so as to make the outcome truly dazzling.

Later, students will be invited to go further. First they will be shown, little by little, the internals of some of the components. *Then* they will be asked to make some extensions and modifications, either in the classes themselves or in new descendants. *Finally* they will write their own classes (the step that would have come first in a traditional curriculum, but should not occur until they have had ample exposure to the work of their elders).

This learning process may be called "progressive opening of the black boxes" or, using a shorter name, the consumer-to-producer strategy. ("Outside-in" would also be an appropriate name.)

Consumer-to-producer strategy

S1 • Learn to use library classes, solely through their abstract specifications.

S2 • Learn to understand the internals of selected classes.

S3 • Learn to extend selected classes.

S4 • Learn to modify selected classes.

S5 • Learn to add your own classes.

If you like automotive comparisons, think of someone who first learns to drive, then is invited to lift the hood and study, little by little, how the engine works, then will do repairs — and, much later, design his own cars.

For this process to work, good abstraction facilities must be present, allowing a consumer to understand the essentials of a component without understanding all of it. The notion of **short form** of a class supports this idea by listing the exported features with their assertions, but hiding implementation properties. After students have seen and understood the short form, they may selectively explore the internals of the class – again under the guidance of the instructor.

Abstraction

Most good introductory programming textbooks preach abstraction. Many in fact include the word "abstraction" in their titles. This is because the authors, being experienced software professionals and teachers, know that one cannot overcome the difficulties of large-scale software development without making constant efforts at abstraction.

Often, unfortunately, such preaching is lost on the students, who simply see it as another exhortation to "be good". You can indeed handle the small programming exercises favored by traditional teaching methods without too much abstraction effort. So why pay attention to the teacher's musings about the importance of abstraction? They will not, or so it seems, improve your Grade Point Average. Only when they have moved to larger developments would the students be in a position to benefit fully from this advice.

To preach is not the best way to teach. With the consumer-to-producer strategy, based on libraries, abstraction is not something to pontificate on: it is a practical and indispensable tool. Without abstraction, one cannot use libraries; the alternative would be to go into the source code, which is overwhelming (you would never get to do your own application) and may not be available anyway. Only through the short form with its high-level information and assertions — the library module in its abstract form — can the students take advantage of a library class.

Having become used, right from the start, to view classes through abstract interfaces, the students will much more easily apply the same principles when they start developing their own classes.

Note once again that these results are only possible in an environment supporting short forms, appropriate documentation and browsing tools, assertions, and distribution of libraries without the source.

Apprenticeship

The consumer-to-producer strategy is the application to software teaching of a time-honored technique: apprenticeship. As an apprentice you learn from the previous generation of master practitioners of your chosen craft, and once you have understood their techniques you try to do better if you can. For lack of available masters, one-on-one apprenticeship is necessarily of limited applicability; but here we do not need the masters themselves, just the results of their work, made available as reusable components.

This approach is the continuation of a trend that had already influenced the teaching of some topics in software education, such as compiler construction, before object technology became popular. In the seventies and early eighties, the typical term project for a compiler course was the writing of a compiler (or interpreter) from scratch. The front-end tasks of compiler construction, lexical analysis and parsing, require such a large effort that in practice the compiler could only be for a very small toy language. Even so, few students ever got past parsing to the really interesting parts: semantic analysis, code generation, optimization. Then tools for lexical analysis and parsing, such as Lex and Yacc, became widely available, enabling students to spend less time on these front-end tasks. The producer-consumer strategy generalizes this change.

The inverted curriculum

The consumer-to-producer strategy has an interesting counterpart in electrical engineering, where Bernard Cohen has suggested an "inverted curriculum". Criticizing the classical progression (field theory, then circuit theory, power, device physics, control theory, digital systems, VLSI design) as "reductionist", the proponents of this approach suggest a more systems-oriented progression, which would successively cover:

- Digital systems, using VLSI and CAD.

- Feedback, concurrency, verification.

- Linear systems and control.

- Power supply and transmission, impedance matching requirements.

- Device physics and technologies, using simulation and CAD techniques.

The software education strategy suggested above is similar: rather than repeating phylogeny, start by giving students a user's view of the highest-level concepts and techniques that are actually applied in industrial environments, then, little by little, unveil the underlying principles.

A long-term policy

The consumer-to-producer strategy has an interesting variant applicable, for application-oriented courses such as operating systems, graphics, compiler construction or artificial intelligence, by professors who are in a position to define a multi-year educational plan.

The idea is to let students build a system by successive enhancement and generalization, each year's class taking over the collective product of the previous year and trying to build on it. This method has some obvious drawbacks for the first class (which collectively serves as advanceman for future generations, and will not enjoy the same reuse benefits), and I must confess I have not yet seen it applied in a systematic way. But on paper at least it is attractive. There hardly seems to be a better way of letting the students weigh the advantages and difficulties of reuse, the need for building extendible software and the challenge of improving on someone else's work. The experience will prepare them for the reality of software development in their future company, where chances are they will be asked to perform maintenance work on an existing system long before they are asked to develop a brand new system of their own.

Even if the context does not permit such a multi-year strategy, instructors should try to avoid a standard pitfall. Many undergraduate curricula include a "software engineering" course, which often devotes a key role to a software project to be carried out by the students, often in groups. Such project work is necessary, but often disappointing because of the time limitations due to its inclusion in a one-trimester or one-semester course. When administratively possible, it is by far preferable to run such a project over an entire schoolyear, even if the total amount of allocated work is the same. Trimester projects, in particular, border on the absurd; they either stop at the analysis or design stage, or result over the last few weeks in a rush to code at any cost and using any technique that will produce a running program — often defeating the very purpose of software engineering education. You need more time, if only to let the students appreciate the depth of the issues involved in building serious software. A year-long project, whether or not it is part of a longer-term policy, favors this process. It is more difficult to fit into the typical curriculum than the standard course, but worth the fight.

29.5 AN OBJECT-ORIENTED PLAN

The idea of a long-term teaching strategy based on reuse, as well as the earlier suggestion of organizing an entire curriculum around object-oriented concepts, may lead to a more ambitious concept which goes beyond the scope of software education to encompass research and development. Although this concept will be appealing to certain institutions only, it deserves a little more thought.

Assume a university department (computing science, information systems or equivalent) in search of a long-term unifying project — the kind of project that produces better teaching, development of new courses, faculty research, sources of publication, Ph. D. theses, Master's theses, undergraduate projects, collaborations with industry and government grants. Many a now well-respected department originally "put itself on the map" through such a collective multi-year effort.

The object-oriented method provides a natural basis for such an endeavor. The focus of the work will not be compilers, interpreters and development tools (which may already be available from companies) but **libraries**. What object technology needs most to progress today is application-oriented reusable components, also called domain libraries. A good O-O environment will already provide, as noted, a set of general-purpose libraries covering such universal needs as the fundamental data structures and algorithms of computing science, graphics, user interface design, parsing. This leaves open entire application domains, from Web browsing to multimedia, from financial software to signal analysis, from computer-aided design to document processing, in which the need for quality software components is crying.

The choice of such a library development project as a unifying effort for a university department presents several advantages:

- Even though this is a long-term pursuit, partial results can start to appear early. Compilers and other tools tend to be of the all-or-nothing category: until they are reasonably complete, distributing them may damage your reputation more than it helps it. With libraries, this is not the case: just a dozen or two quality reusable classes can render tremendous services to their users, and attract favorable attention.

- Because an ambitious library is a large project, there is room for many people to contribute, from advanced undergraduates to Ph. D. candidates, researchers and professors. This assumes of course that the application domain and the breadth of the library's coverage have been chosen judiciously so as to match the size of the available resources in people, equipment and funds.

- Talking about resources, the project may start with relatively limited means but is a prime candidate to attract the attention of funding agencies. It also offers prospects of industry funding if the application domain is of direct interest to companies.

See "APPENDIX: A HISTORY OF TAXONOMY", 24.15, page 864.

- Building good libraries is a technically exciting task, which raises new scientific challenges, so that the output of a successful project may include theses and publications, not just software. The intellectual challenges are of two kinds. First the construction of reusable components is one of the most interesting and difficult problems of software engineering, for which the method brings some help but certainly does not answer all questions. Second, any successful application library must rest on a *taxonomy* of the application domain, requiring a long-term effort at classifying the known concepts in that area. As is well known in the natural sciences (remember the discussion of the history of taxonomy), classification is the first step towards understanding. Developed for a new application area, such an effort, known as **domain analysis**, raises new and interesting problems.

- The last comment suggests the possibility of inter-disciplinary cooperation with researchers in various application domains, usually non-software.

- Cooperation should begin with people working in neighboring fields. Many universities have two groups pursuing teaching and research in software issues, one (often *"computing science"*) having more of an engineering and scientific background, the other (often *"information systems"*) more oriented towards business issues. Whether these groups are administratively separate or part of the same structure — both cases are common — the project may appeal to both, and provides an opportunity for collaboration.

- Finally, a successful library providing components for an important application area will be widely used and bring much visibility to its originating institution.

No doubt in the years to come a number of universities will seize on these ideas, and that the "X University Reusable Financial Components" or "Y Polytechnic Object-Oriented Text Processing Library" will (with better names than these) bring to their institutions the modern equivalent of what UCSD Pascal, Waterloo Fortran and the MIT's X Window system achieved in earlier eras for their respective sponsors.

29.6 KEY CONCEPTS STUDIED IN THIS CHAPTER

- In object-oriented training, emphasize implementation and design.

- In initial training for professionals, do not hesitate to repeat a session, with some time in-between for actual practice.

- Training in a company should include courses for managers as well as developers.

- Beginning programming courses, and many others, may take advantage of O-O techniques.

- For teaching, use a pure O-O language, clear and simple, supporting the full extent of the technology, in particular assertions.

- Courses should, as much as possible, be based on libraries of reusable components.

- The consumer-to-producer strategy (similar to "inverted curriculum" ideas), presents students with existing components, enabling them to write advanced applications right from the start, then lets students open the components, extend them, and produce new components by imitation through an apprenticeship process.

- More generally, a long-term library effort can be a unifying project for a department.

29.7 BIBLIOGRAPHICAL NOTES

The material in this chapter is derived from an article in the *Journal of Object-Oriented Programming*, of which a revised version was presented at TOOLS USA 93 and appears in the proceedings (see [M 1993c] for the two references). Further material about education and training issues appears in the book *Object Success* [M 1995], from which the term *mOOzak* is taken, as well as some observations regarding industry training.

Important articles about teaching programming using O-O concepts include [McKim 1992] and [Heliotis 1996].

The notion of inverted curriculum for education in electrical engineering is due to Bernard Cohen [Cohen 1991]. I am grateful to Warren Yates, chairman of the Electrical Engineering Department at University of Technology, Sydney, for bringing it to my attention. This chapter also benefited from discussions with many educators, including Christine Mingins, James McKim, Richard Mitchell, John Potter, Robert Switzer, Jean-Claude Boussard, Roger Rousseau, David Riley, Richard Wiener, Fiorella De Cindio, Brian Henderson-Sellers, Pete Thomas, Ray Weedon, John Kerstholt, Jacob Gore, David Rine, Naftaly Minsky, Peter Löhr, Robert Ogor, Robert Rannou.

An ongoing project is intended to produce an introductory programming book-cum-CD applying the "consumer-to-producer strategy", or "inverted curriculum" principle [M 199?]. But there are already a number of good introductory programming textbooks based on O-O ideas; they were listed in an earlier chapter, but here they are again, for convenience, without further comments: [Rist 1995], [Wiener 1996], [Gore 1996], [Wiener 1997] and [Jézéquel 1996].

The books were listed in the bibliography to chapter 2, on page 35.

Part E:

Advanced topics

Part E complements our study of object technology basics by exploring some more leading-edge, but equally important topics: concurrency, distribution, client-server computing and the Internet; persistence and databases; graphical interfaces.

30

Concurrency, distribution, client-server and the Internet

*L*ike humans, computers can team up with their peers to achieve results that none of them could obtain alone; unlike humans, they can do many things at once (or with the appearance of simultaneity), and do all of them well. So far, however, the discussion has implicitly assumed that the computation is *sequential* — proceeds along a single thread of control. We should now see what happens when this assumption no longer holds, as we move to *concurrent* (also known as *parallel*) computation.

Concurrency is not a new subject, but for a long time interest in it remained mostly confined to four application areas: operating systems, networking, implementation of database management systems, and high-speed scientific software. Although strategic and prestigious, these tasks involve only a small subset of the software development community.

Things have changed. Concurrency is quickly becoming a required component of just about every type of application, including some which had traditionally been thought of as fundamentally sequential in nature. Beyond mere concurrency, our systems, whether or not *client-server*, must increasingly become *distributed* over networks, including the network of networks — the *Internet*. This evolution gives particular urgency to the central question of this chapter: can we apply object-oriented ideas in a concurrent and distributed context?

Not only is this possible: object technology can help us develop concurrent and distributed applications simply and elegantly.

30.1 A SNEAK PREVIEW

As usual, this discussion will not throw a pre-cooked answer at you, but instead will carefully build a solution from a detailed analysis of the problem and an exploration of possible avenues, including a few dead ends. Although necessary to make you understand the techniques in depth, this thoroughness might lead you to believe that they are complex; that would be inexcusable, since the concurrency mechanism on which we will finally settle is in fact characterized by almost incredible simplicity. To avoid this risk, we will begin by examining a summary of the mechanism, without any of the rationale.

Warning: SPOILER!
(The next section is 30.2, page 953.)

If you hate "spoilers", preferring to start with the full statement of the issues and to let the drama proceed to its dénouement step by step and inference by inference, ignore the one-page summary that follows and skip directly to the next section.

The extension covering full-fledged concurrency and distribution will be as minimal as it can get starting from a sequential notation: a single new keyword — **separate**. How is this possible? We use the fundamental scheme of O-O computation: feature call, $x.f(a)$, executed on behalf of some object O1 and calling f on the object O2 attached to x, with the argument a. But instead of a single processor that handles operations on all objects, we may now rely on different processors for O1 and O2 — so that the computation on O1 can move ahead without waiting for the call to terminate, since another processor handles it.

Because the effect of a call now depends on whether the objects are handled by the same processor or different ones, the software text must tell us unambiguously what the intent is for any x. Hence the need for the new keyword: rather than just x: *SOME_TYPE*, we declare x: **separate** *SOME_TYPE* to indicate that x is handled by a different processor, so that calls of target x can proceed in parallel with the rest of the computation. With such a declaration, any creation instruction $!!\ x.make\ (\dots)$ will spawn off a new processor — a new thread of control — to handle future calls on x.

Nowhere in the software text should we have to specify *which* processor to use. All we state, through the **separate** declaration, is that two objects are handled by different processors, since this radically affects the system's semantics. Actual processor assignment can wait until run time. Nor do we settle too early on the exact nature of processors: a processor can be implemented by a piece of hardware (a computer), but just as well by a task (process) of the operating system, or, on a multithreaded OS, just a thread of such a task. Viewed by the software, "processor" is an abstract concept; you can execute the same concurrent application on widely different architectures (time-sharing on one computer, distributed network with many computers, threads within one Unix or Windows task...) without any change to its source text. All you will change is a "Concurrency Configuration File" which specifies the last-minute mapping of abstract processors to physical resources.

We need to specify synchronization constraints. The conventions are straightforward:

- No special mechanism is required for a client to resynchronize with its supplier after a separate call $x.f(a)$ has gone off in parallel. The client will wait when and if it needs to: when it requests information on the object through a query call, as in *value* $:= x.some\_query$. This automatic mechanism is called *wait by necessity*.

- To obtain exclusive access to a separate object O2, it suffices to use the attached entity a as an argument to the corresponding call, as in $r(a)$.

- A routine precondition involving a separate argument such as a causes the client to wait until the precondition holds.

- To guarantee that we can control our software and predict the result (in particular, rest assured that class invariants will be maintained), we must allow the processor in charge of an object to execute at most one routine at any given time.

- We may, however, need to *interrupt* the execution of a routine to let a new, high-priority client take over. This will cause an exception, so that the spurned client can take the appropriate corrective measures — most likely retrying after a while.

This covers most of the mechanism, which will enable us to build the most advanced concurrent and distributed applications through the full extent of O-O techniques, from multiple inheritance to Design by Contract — as we will now study in detail, forgetting for a while all that we have read in this short preview.

A complete summary appears in 30.11, page 1025.

30.2 THE RISE OF CONCURRENCY

Back to square one. We must first review the various forms of concurrency, to understand how the evolution of our field requires most software developers to make concurrency part of their mindset. In addition to the traditional concepts of multiprocessing and multiprogramming, the past few years have introduced two innovative concepts: object request brokers and remote execution through the Net.

Multiprocessing

More and more, we want to use the formidable amount of computing power available around us; less and less, we are willing to wait for the computer (although we have become quite comfortable with the idea that the computer is waiting for us). So if one processing unit would not bring us quickly enough the result that we need, we will want to rely on several units working in parallel. This form of concurrency is known as multiprocessing.

Spectacular applications of multiprocessing have involved researchers relying on hundreds of computers scattered over the Internet, at times when the computers' (presumably consenting) owners did not need them, to solve computationally intensive problems such as breaking cryptographic algorithms. Such efforts do not just apply to computing research: Hollywood's insatiable demand for realistic computer graphics has played its part in fueling progress in this area; the preparation of the movie *Toy Story*, one of the first to involve artificial characters only (only the voices are human), relied at some point on a network of more than one hundred high-end workstations — more economical, it seems, than one hundred professional animators.

Multiprocessing is also ubiquitous in high-speed scientific computing, to solve ever larger problems of physics, engineering, meteorology, statistics, investment banking.

More routinely, many computing installations use some form of *load balancing*: automatically dispatching computations among the various computers available at any particular time on the local network of an organization.

Another form of multiprocessing is the computing architecture known as **client-server computing**, which assigns various specialized roles to the computers on a network: the biggest and most expensive machines, of which a typical company network will have just one or a few, are "servers" handling shared databases, heavy computations and other strategic central resources; the cheaper machines, ubiquitously located wherever there is an end user, handle decentralizable tasks such as the human interface and simple computations; they forward to the servers any task that exceeds their competence.

> The current popularity of the client-server approach is a swing of the pendulum away from the trend of the preceding decade. Initially (nineteen-sixties and seventies) architectures were centralized, forcing users to compete for resources. The personal computer and workstation revolution of the eighties was largely about empowering users with resources theretofore reserved to the Center (the "glass house" in industry jargon). Then they discovered the obvious: a personal computer cannot do everything, and some resources *must* be shared. Hence the emergence of client-server architectures in the nineties. The inevitable cynical comment — that we are back to the one-mainframe-many-terminals architecture of our youth, only with more expensive terminals now called "client workstations" — is not really justified: the industry is simply searching, through trial and error, for the proper tradeoff between decentralization and sharing.

Multiprogramming

The other main form of concurrency is multiprogramming, which involves a single computer working on several tasks at once.

If we consider general-purpose systems (excluding processors that are embedded in an application device, be it a washing machine or an airplane instrument, and single-mindedly repeat a fixed set of operations), computers are almost always multi-programmed, performing operating system tasks in parallel with application tasks. In a strict form of multiprogramming the parallelism is apparent rather than real: at any single time the processing unit is actually working on just one job; but the time to switch between jobs is so short that an outside observer can believe they proceed concurrently. In addition, the processing unit itself may do several things in parallel (as in the advance fetch schemes of many computers, where each clock cycle loads the next instruction at the same time it executes the current one), or may actually be a combination of several processing units, so that multiprogramming becomes intertwined with multiprocessing.

A common application of multiprogramming is *time-sharing*, allowing a single machine to serve several users at once. But except in the case of very powerful "mainframe" computers this idea is considered much less attractive now than it was when computers were a precious rarity. Today we consider our time to be the more valuable resource, so we want the system to do several things at once just for us. In particular, *multi-windowing* user interfaces allow several applications to proceed in parallel: in one window we browse the Web, in another we edit a document, in yet another we compile and test some software. All this requires powerful concurrency mechanisms.

Providing each computer user with a multi-windowing, multiprogramming interface is the responsibility of the operating system. But increasingly the users of the software we develop want to have concurrency *within one application*. The reason is always the same: they know that computing power is available by the bountiful, and they do not want to wait idly. So if it takes a while to load incoming messages in an e-mail system, you will want to be able to send an outgoing message while this operation proceeds. With a good Web browser you can access a new site while loading pages from another. In a stock trading system, you may at any single time be accessing market information from several stock exchanges, buying here, selling there, and monitoring a client's portfolio.

It is this need for intra-application concurrency which has suddenly brought the whole subject of concurrent computing to the forefront of software development and made it of interest far beyond its original constituencies. Meanwhile, all the traditional applications remain as important as ever, with new developments in operating systems, the Internet, local area networks, and scientific computing — where the continual quest for speed demands ever higher levels of multiprocessing.

Object request brokers

Another important recent development has been the emergence of the CORBA proposal from the Object Management Group, and the OLE 2/ActiveX architecture from Microsoft. Although the precise goals, details and markets differ, both efforts promise substantial progress towards distributed computing.

The general purpose is to allow applications to access each other's objects and services as conveniently as possible, either locally or across a network. The CORBA effort (more precisely its CORBA 2 stage, clearly the interesting one) has also placed particular emphasis on interoperability:

- CORBA-aware applications can coöperate even if they are based on "object request brokers" from different vendors.

- Interoperability also applies to the language level: an application written in one of the supported languages can access objects from an application written in another. The interaction goes through an intermediate language called IDL (Interface Definition Language); supported languages have an official IDL binding, which maps the constructs of the language to those of IDL.

IDL is a common-denominator O-O language centered on the notion of interface. An IDL interface for a class is similar in spirit to a short form, although more rudimentary (IDL in particular does not support assertions); it describes the set of features available on a certain abstraction. From a class written in an O-O language such as the notation of this book, tools will derive an IDL interface, making the class and its instances of interest to client software. A client written in the same language or another can, through an IDL interface, access across a network the features provided by such a supplier.

Remote execution

Another development of the late nineties is the mechanism for remote execution through the World-Wide Web.

The first Web browsers made it not just possible but also convenient to explore information stored on remote computers anywhere in the world, and to follow logical connections, or *hyperlinks*, at the click of a button. But this was a passive mechanism: someone prepared some information, and everyone else accessed it read-only.

The next step was to move to an active setup where clicking on a link actually triggers execution of an operation. This assumes the presence, within the Web browser, of an execution engine which can recognize the downloaded information as executable code, and execute it. The execution engine can be a built-in part of the browser, or it may be dynamically attached to it in response to the downloading of information of the corresponding type. This latter solution is known as a **plug-in** mechanism and assumes that users interested in a particular execution mechanism can download the execution engine, usually free, from the Internet.

This idea was first made popular by Java in late 1995 and 1996; Java execution engines have become widely available. Plug-ins have since appeared for many other mechanisms. An alternative to providing a specific plug-in is to generate, from any source language, code for a widely available engine, such as a Java engine; several compiler vendors have indeed started to provide generators of Java "bytecode" (the low-level portable code that the Java engine can execute).

> For the notation of this book the two avenues have been pursued: ISE has a free execution engine; and at the time of writing a project is in progress to generate Java bytecode.

Either approach raises the potential of **security** problems: how much do you trust someone's application? If you are not careful, clicking on an innocent-looking hyperlink could unleash a vicious program that destroys files on your computer, or steals your personal information. More precisely you should not, as a user, be the one asked to be careful: the responsibility is on the provider of an execution engine and the associated library of basic facilities. Some widely publicized Java security failures in 1996 caused considerable worries about the issue.

The solution is to use carefully designed and certified execution engines and libraries coming from reputable sources. Often they will have two versions:

- One version is meant for unlimited Internet usage, based on a severely restricted execution engine.

  > In ISE's tool the only I/O library facilities in this restricted tool only read and write to and from the terminal, not files. The "external" mechanism of the language has also been removed, so that a vicious application cannot cause mischief by going to C, say, to perform file manipulations. The Java "Virtual Machine" (the engine) is also draconian in what it permits Internet "applets" to do with the file system of your computer.

- The other version has fewer or no such restrictions, and provides the full power of the libraries, file I/O in particular. It is meant for applications that will run on a secure Intranet (internal company network) rather than the wilderness of the Internet.

In spite of the insecurity specter, the prospect of unfettered remote execution, a new step in the ongoing revolution in the way we distribute software, has generated enormous excitement, which shows no sign of abating.

30.3 FROM PROCESSES TO OBJECTS

To support all these mind-boggling developments, requiring ever more use of concurrent processing, we need powerful software support. How are we going to program these things? Object technology, of course, suggests itself.

Robin Milner is said to have exclaimed, in a 1991 workshop at an O-O conference, *Cited in* [Matsuoka 1993]. "*I can't understand why objects* [of O-O languages] *are not concurrent in the first place*". Even if only in the second or third place, how do we go about making objects concurrent?

If we start from non-O-O concurrency work, we will find that it largely relies on the notion of *process*. A process is a program unit that acts like a special-purpose computer: it executes a certain algorithm, usually repeating it until some external event triggers termination. A typical example is the process that manages a printer, repeatedly executing

"Wait until there is at least a job in the print queue"
"Get the next print job and remove it from the queue"
"Print the job"

Various concurrency models differ in how processes are scheduled and synchronized, compete for shared hardware resources, and exchange information. In some concurrent programming languages, you directly describe a process; in others, such as Ada, you may also describe process *types*, which at run time are instantiated into processes, much as the classes of object-oriented software are instantiated into objects.

Similarities

The correspondence seems indeed clear. As we start exploring how to combine ideas from concurrent programming and object-oriented software construction, it seems natural to identify processes with objects, and process types with classes. Anyone who has studied concurrent computing and discovers O-O development, or the other way around, will be struck by the similarities between these two technologies:

- Both rely on autonomous, encapsulated modules: processes or process types; classes.

- Like processes and unlike the subroutines of sequential, non-O-O approaches, objects will, from each activation to the next, retain the values they contain.

- To build reasonable concurrent systems, it is indispensable in practice to enforce heavy restrictions on how modules can exchange information; otherwise things quickly get out of hand. The O-O approach, as we have seen, places similarly severe restrictions on inter-module communication.

- The basic mechanism for such communication may loosely be described, in both cases, under the general label of "message passing".

So it is not surprising that many people have had a "Eureka!" when first thinking, Milner-like, about making objects concurrent. The unification, it seems, should come easily.

This first impression is unfortunately wrong: after the similarities, one soon stumbles into the discrepancies.

Active objects

Building on the analogies just summarized, a number of proposals for concurrent O-O mechanisms (see the bibliographical notes) have introduced a notion of "active object". An active object is an object that is also a process: it has its own program to execute. In a definition from a book on Java:

From: Doug Lea, "Concurrent Programming in Java", Addison-Wesley, 1996.

Each object is a single, identifiable process-like entity (not unlike a Unix process) with state and behavior.

This notion, however, raises difficult problems.

The most significant one is easy to see. A process has its own agenda: as illustrated by the printer example, it relentlessly executes a certain sequence of actions. Not so with classes and objects. An object does not *do* one thing; it is a repository of services (the features of the generating class), and just waits for the next client to solicit one of those services — chosen by the client, not the object. If we make the object active, it becomes responsible for the scheduling of its operations. This creates a conflict with the clients, which have a very clear view of what the scheduling should be: they just want the supplier, whenever they need a particular service, to be ready to provide it immediately!

The problem arises in non-object-oriented approaches to concurrency and has led to mechanisms for **synchronizing** processes — that is to say, specifying when and how each is ready to communicate, waiting if necessary for the other to be ready too. For example in a very simple, unbuffered producer-consumer scheme we may have a *producer* process that repeatedly executes

"Make it known that *producer* is not ready"
"Perform some computation that produces a value *x*"
"Make it known that *producer* is ready"
"Wait for *consumer* to be ready"
"Pass *x* to *consumer*"   ◄──────────────────────╮
                                                        ├── ⬭ *Handshake*
and a *consumer* process that repeatedly executes   │
                                                        │
"Make it known that *consumer* is ready"   │
"Wait for *producer* to be ready"   │
"Get *x* from *producer*"   ◄────────────────────╯
"Make it known that *consumer* is not ready"
"Perform some computation that uses the value *x*"

a scheme which we may also view pictorially:

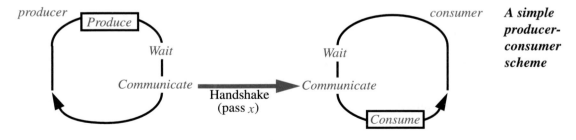

A simple producer-consumer scheme

Communication occurs when both processes are ready for each other; this is sometimes called a *handshake* or *rendez-vous*. The design of synchronization mechanisms — enabling us in particular to express precisely the instructions to "Make it known that *process* is ready" and "Wait for *process* to be ready" — has been a fertile area of research and development for several decades.

All this is fine for processes, the concurrent equivalent of traditional sequential programs which "do one thing"; indeed, a concurrent system built with processes is like a sequential system with several main programs. But in the object-oriented approach we have rejected the notion of main program and instead defined software units that stand ready to provide any one of a number of possible features.

Reconciling this view with the notion of process requires elaborate synchronization constructs to make sure that each supplier is ready to execute a feature when the client needs it. The reconciliation is particularly delicate when both client and supplier are active objects, since each has its own agenda.

All this does not make it *impossible* to devise mechanisms based on the notion of active object, as evidenced by the abundant literature on the subject (to which the bibliographical notes to this chapter give many references). But this evidence also shows the complexity of the proposed solutions, of which none has gained wide acceptance, suggesting that the active object approach is not the right one.

Active objects clash with inheritance

Doubts about the suitability of the active object approach grow as one starts looking at how it combines with other O-O mechanisms, especially inheritance.

If a class B inherits from a class A and both are active (that is to say, describe instances that must be active objects), what happens in B to the description of A's process? In many cases you will need to add some new instructions, but without special language mechanisms this means that you will almost always have to redefine and rewrite the entire process part — not an attractive proposition.

See "Sequencing and inheritance", page 1121, as part of the discussion of Simula.

Here is an example of special language mechanism. Although the Simula 67 language does not support concurrency, it has a notion of active object: a Simula class can, besides its features, include a set of instructions, called the body of the class, so that we can talk of executing an object — meaning executing the body of its generating class. The body of a class A can include a special instruction **inner**, which has no effect in the class itself but, in a proper descendant B, stands for the body of B. So if the body of A reads

some_initialization; **inner**; *some_termination_actions*

and the body of B reads

specific_B_actions

then execution of that body actually means executing

some_initialization; *specific_B_actions*; *some_termination_actions*

Although the need for a mechanism of this kind is clear in a language supporting the notion of active object, objections immediately come to mind: the notation is misleading, since if you just read the body of B you will get a wrong view of what the execution does; it forces the parent to plan in detail for its descendants, going against basic O-O concepts (the Open-Closed principle); and it only works in a single-inheritance language.

Even with a different notation, the basic problem will remain: how to combine the process specification of a class with those of its proper descendants; how to reconcile parents' process specifications in the case of multiple inheritance.

Later in this chapter we will see other problems, known as the "inheritance anomaly" and arising from the use of inheritance with synchronization constraints.

"Synchronization for concurrent O-O computation", page 980

Faced with these difficulties, some of the early O-O concurrency proposals preferred to stay away from inheritance altogether. Although justifiable as a temporary measure to help understand the issues by separating concerns, this exclusion of inheritance cannot be sustained in a definitive approach to the construction of concurrent object-oriented software; this would be like cutting the arm because the finger itches. (For good measure, some of the literature adds that inheritance is a complex and messy notion anyway, as if telling the patient, after the operation, that having an arm was a bad idea in the first place.)

The inference that we may draw is simpler and less extreme. The problem is not object technology per se, in particular inheritance; it is not concurrency; it is not even the combination of these ideas. What causes trouble is the notion of active object.

Processes programmed

As we prepare to get rid of active objects it is useful to note that we will not really be renouncing anything. An object is able to perform many operations: all the features of its generating class. By turning it into a process, we select one of these operations as the only one that really counts. There is absolutely no benefit in doing this! Why limit ourselves to one algorithm when we can have as many as we want?

Another way to express this observation is that the notion of process need not be a built-in concept in the concurrency mechanism; processes can be *programmed* simply as routines. Consider for example the concept of printer process cited at the beginning of this chapter. The object-oriented view tells us to focus on the object type, printer, and to treat the process as just one routine, say *live*, of the corresponding class:

> **indexing**
>   *description*: *"Printers handling one print job at a time"*
>   *note*: *"A better version, based on a general class PROCESS, %*
>   *%appears below under the name PRINTER"*
> **class**
>   *PRINTER_1*
> **feature** -- Status report
>   *stop_requested*: *BOOLEAN* **is do** … **end**
>   *oldest*: *JOB* **is do** … **end**
> **feature** -- Basic operations
>   *setup* **is do** … **end**
>   *wait_for_job* **is do** … **end**
>   *remove_oldest* **is do** … **end**
>   *print* (*j*: *JOB*) **is do** … **end**

feature -- Process behavior
    live **is**
        -- Do the printer thing.
    do
        from *setup* **until** *stop_requested* **loop**
            wait_for_job; *print* (*oldest*); *remove_oldest*
        end
    end
    … Other features …
end -- class *PRINTER_1*

Note the provision for Other features: although so far *live* and the supporting features have claimed all our attention, we can endow processes with many other features if we want to, encouraged by the O-O approach developed elsewhere in this book. Turning *PRINTER_1* objects into processes would mean limiting this freedom; that would be a major loss of expressive power, without any visible benefit.

By abstracting from this example, which describes a particular process type simply as a class, we can try to provide a more general description of all process types through a deferred class — a *behavior class* as we have often encountered in previous chapters. Procedure *live* will apply to all processes. We could leave it deferred, but it is not too much of a commitment to note that most processes will need some initialization, some termination, and in-between a basic step repeated some number of times. So we can already effect a few things at the most abstract level:

indexing
    description: *"The most general notion of process"*
deferred class
    PROCESS
feature -- Status report
    over: *BOOLEAN* **is**
        -- Must execution terminate now?
    deferred
    end
feature -- Basic operations
    setup **is**
        -- Prepare to execute process operations (default: nothing).
    do
    end
    step **is**
        -- Execute basic process operations.
    deferred
    end

> *wrapup* **is**
>
>> -- Execute termination operations (default: nothing).
>
>> **do**
>> **end**

feature -- Process behavior

> *live* **is**
>
>> -- Perform process lifecycle.
>
>> **do**
>>> **from** *setup* **until** *over* **loop**
>>>> *step*
>>> **end**
>>> *wrapup*
>> **end**

end -- class *PROCESS*

A point of methodology: whereas *step* is deferred, *setup* and *wrapup* are effective procedures, defined as doing nothing. This way we force every effective descendant to provide a specific implementation of *step*, the basic process action; but in the not infrequent cases that require no particular setup or termination operation we avoid bothering the descendants. This choice between a deferred version and a null effective version occurs regularly in the design of deferred classes, and you should resolve it based on your appreciation of the likely characteristics of descendants. A wrong guess is not a disaster; it will just lead to more effectings or more redefinitions in descendants.

From this pattern we may define a more specialized class, covering printers:

indexing

> *description*: "*Printers handling one print job at a time*"
>
> *note*: "*Revised version based on class PROCESS*"

class *PRINTER* **inherit**

> *PROCESS*
>
>> **rename** *over* **as** *stop_requested* **end**

feature -- Status report

> *stop_requested*: *BOOLEAN*
>
>> -- Is the next job in the queue a request to shut down?
>
> *oldest*: *JOB* **is**
>
>> -- The oldest job in the queue
>
>> **do** … **end**

feature -- Basic operations

> *step* **is**
>
>> -- Process one job.
>
>> **do**
>>> *wait_for_job*; *print* (*oldest*); *remove_oldest*
>> **end**

wait_for_job **is**
> -- Wait until job queue is not empty.

> **do**

> …

> **ensure**

> *oldest* /= *Void*

> **end**

remove_oldest **is**
> -- Remove oldest job from queue.

> **require**

> *oldest* /= *Void*

> **do**

> **if** *oldest*.*is_stop_request* **then** *stop_requested* := *True* **end**

> "Remove *oldest* from queue"

> **end**

print (*j*: *JOB*) **is**
> -- Print *j*, unless it is just a stop request.

> **require**

> *j* /= *Void*

> **do**

> **if not** *j*.*is_stop_request* **then** "Print the text associated with *j*" **end**

> **end**

end -- class *PRINTER*

*Exercise E30.1,
page 1035.*

The class assumes that a request to shut off the printer is sent as a special print job *j* for which *j*.*is_stop_request* is true. (It would be cleaner to avoid making *print* and *remove_oldest* aware of the special case of the "stop request" job; this is easy to improve.)

The benefits of O-O modeling are apparent here. In the same way that going from main program to classes broadens our perspective by giving us abstract objects that are not limited to "doing just one thing", considering a printer process as an object described by a class opens up the possibility of new, useful features. With a printer we can do more than execute its normal printing operation as covered by *live* (which we should perhaps have renamed *operate* when inheriting it from *PROCESS*); we might want to add such features as *perform_internal_test*, *switch_to_Postscript_level_1* or *set_resolution*. The equalizing effect of the O-O method is as important here as in sequential software.

More generally, the classes sketched in this section show how we can use the normal object-oriented mechanisms — classes, inheritance, deferred elements, partially implemented patterns — to implement processes. There is nothing wrong with the concept of process in an O-O context; indeed, we will need it in many concurrent applications. But rather than a primitive mechanism it will simply be covered by a **library class** *PROCESS* based on the version given earlier in this section, or perhaps several such classes covering variants of the notion.

For the basic new construct of concurrent object technology, we must look elsewhere.

30.4 INTRODUCING CONCURRENT EXECUTION

What — if not the notion of process — fundamentally distinguishes concurrent from sequential computation?

Processors

To narrow down the specifics of concurrency, it is useful to take a new look at the figure which helped us lay the very foundations of object technology by examining the three basic ingredients of computation:

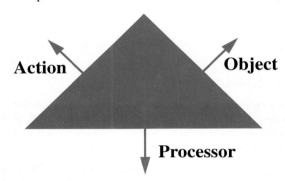

The three forces of computation

(*This figure first appeared on page 101.*)

To perform a computation is to use certain *processors* to apply certain *actions* to certain *objects*. At the beginning of this book we discovered how object technology addresses fundamental issues of reusability and extendibility by building software architectures in which actions are attached to objects (more precisely, object types) rather than the other way around.

What about processors? Clearly we need a mechanism to execute the actions on the objects. But in sequential computation there is just one thread of control, hence just one processor; so it is taken for granted and remains implicit most of the time.

In a concurrent context, however, we will have two or more processors. This property is of course essential to the idea of concurrency and we can take it as the definition of the notion. This is the basic answer to the question asked above: processors (not processes) will be the principal new concept for adding concurrency to the framework of sequential object-oriented computation. A concurrent system may have any number of processors, as opposed to just one for a sequential system.

The nature of processors

> **Definition: processor**
>
> A processor is an autonomous thread of control capable of supporting the sequential execution of instructions on one or more objects.

This is an abstract notion, it should not be confused with that of physical processing device, for which the rest of this chapter will use the term **CPU**, common in computer engineering to denote the processing units of computers. "CPU" is an abbreviation of "Central Processing Unit" even though there is most of the time nothing central about CPUs. You can use a CPU to implement a processor; but the notion of processor is much more abstract and general. A processor can be, for example:

- A computer (with its CPU) on a network.

- A task, also called process, as supported on operating systems such as Unix, Windows and many others.

- A coroutine. (Coroutines, covered in detail later in this chapter, simulate true concurrency by taking turns at execution on a single CPU; after each interruption, each coroutine resumes its execution where it last left it.)

- A "thread" as supported by such multi-threaded operating systems as Solaris, OS/2 and Windows NT.

  Threads are mini-processes. A true process can itself contain many threads, which it manages directly; the operating system (OS) only sees the process, not its threads. Usually the threads of a process will all share the same address space (in object-oriented terms, they potentially have access to the same set of objects), whereas each process has its own address space. We may view threads as coroutines within a process. The main advantage of threads is efficiency: whereas creating a process and synchronizing it with other processes are expensive operations, requiring direct OS intervention (to allocate the address space and the code of the process), the corresponding operations on threads are much simpler, do not involve any expensive OS operations, and so can be faster by a factor of several hundreds or even several thousands.

The difference between processors and CPUs was clearly expressed by Henry Lieberman (for a different concurrency model):

[Lieberman 1987], page 22. Square brackets signal differences in terminology.

The number of [processors] need not be bounded in advance, and if there are too many [processors] for the number of real physical [CPUs] you have on your computer system, they are automatically time-shared. Thus the user can pretend that processor resources are practically infinite.

To avoid any misunderstanding, be sure to remember that throughout this chapter the "processors" denote virtual threads of control; any reference to the physical units of computation uses the term CPU.

At some point before or during you will need to assign computational resources to the processors. The mapping will be expressed by a "Concurrency Control File", as described below, or associated library facilities.

Handling an object

Any feature call must be handled (executed) by some processor. More generally, any object O2 is *handled* by a certain processor, its *handler*; the handler is responsible for executing all calls on O2 (all calls of the form $x.f(a)$ where x is attached to O2).

We may go further and specify that the handler is assigned to the object at the time of creation, and remains the same throughout the object's life. This assumption will help keep the mechanism simple. It may seem restrictive at first, since some distributed systems may need to support *object migration* across a network. But we can address this need in at least two other ways:

- By allowing the reassignment of a processor to a different CPU (with this solution, all objects handled by a processor will migrate together).

- By treating object migration as the creation of a new object.

The dual semantics of calls

With multiple processors, we face a possible departure from the usual semantics of the fundamental operation of object-oriented computation, feature call, of one of the forms

$x.f(a)$ -- if *f* is a command
$y := x.f(a)$ -- if *f* is a query

As before, let O2 be the object attached to x at the time of the call, and O1 the object on whose behalf the call is executed. (In other words, the instruction in either form is part of a call to a certain routine, whose execution uses O1 as its target.)

We have grown accustomed to understanding the effect of the call as the execution of *f*'s body applied to O2, using a as argument, and returning a result in the query case. If the call is part of a sequence of instructions, as with

    ... previous_instruction; $x.f(a)$; *next_instruction*; *...*

(or the equivalent in the query case), the execution of *next_instruction* will not commence until after the completion of *f*.

Not so any more with multiple processors. The very purpose of concurrent architectures is to enable the client computation to proceed without waiting for the supplier to have completed its job, if that job is handled by another processor. In the example of print controllers, sketched at the beginning of this chapter, a client application will want to send a print request (a "job") and continue immediately with its own agenda.

So instead of one call semantics we now have two cases:

- If O1 and O2 have the same handler, any further operation on O1 (*next_instruction*) must wait until the call terminates. Such calls are said to be **synchronous**.

- If O1 and O2 are handled by different processors, operations on O1 can proceed as soon as it has initiated the call on O2. Such calls are said to be **asynchronous**.

The asynchronous case is particularly interesting for a command, since the remainder of the computation may not need any of the effects of the call on O2 until much later (if at all: O1 may just be responsible for spawning one or more concurrent computations and then terminating). For a query, we need the result, as in the above example where we assign it to y, but as explained below we might be able to proceed concurrently anyway.

Separate entities

A general rule of software construction is that a semantic difference should always be reflected by a difference in the software text.

Now that we have two variants of call semantics we must make sure that the software text incontrovertibly indicates which one is intended in each case. What determines the answer is whether the call's target, O2, has the same handler (the same processor) as the call's originator, O1. So rather than the call itself we should mark x, the entity denoting the target object. In accordance with the static typing policy, developed in earlier chapters to favor clarity and safety, the mark should appear in the declaration of x.

This reasoning yields the only **notational extension** supporting concurrency. Along with the usual

> x: *SOME_TYPE*

we allow ourselves the declaration form

> x: **separate** *SOME_TYPE*

to express that x may become attached to objects handled by a different processor. If a class is meant to be used only to declare separate entities, you can also declare it as

> **separate class** X ... The rest as usual ...

instead of just **class** X ... or **deferred class** X ....

"Expanded types",
page 254.
The convention is the same as for declaring an expanded status: you can declare y as being of type **expanded** T, or equivalently just as T if T itself is a class declared as **expanded class** T... The three possibilities — expanded, deferred, separate — are mutually exclusive, so at most one qualifying keyword may appear before **class**.

It is quite remarkable that this addition of a single keyword suffices to turn our sequential object-oriented notation into one supporting general concurrent computation.

Some straightforward terminology. We may apply the word "separate" to various elements, both static (appearing in the software text) and dynamic (existing at run time). Statically: a *separate class* is a class declared as **separate class** ...; a *separate type* is based on a separate class; a *separate entity* is declared of a separate type, or as **separate** T for some T; $x.f(...)$ is a *separate call* if its target x is a separate entity. Dynamically: the value of a separate entity is a *separate reference*; if not void, it will be attached to an object handled by another processor — a *separate object*.

Typical examples of separate class include:

- *BOUNDED_BUFFER*, to describe a buffer structure that enables various concurrent components to exchange data (some components, the producers, depositing objects into the buffer, and others, the consumers, acquiring objects from it).

- *PRINTER*, perhaps better called *PRINT_CONTROLLER*, to control one or more printers. By treating the print controllers as separate objects, applications do not need to wait for the print job to complete (unlike early Macintoshes, with which you were stuck until the last page had come out of the printer).

- *DATABASE*, which in the client part of a client-server architecture may serve to describe the database hosted by a distant server machine, to which the client may send queries through the network.

- *BROWSER_WINDOW*, in a Web browser that allows you to spawn a new window where you can examine different Web pages.

Obtaining separate objects

In practice, as illustrated by the preceding examples, separate objects will be of two kinds:

- In the first case an application will want to spawn a *new* separate object, grabbing the next available processor. (Remember that we can always get a new processor; since processors are not material resources but abstract facilities, their number is not bounded.) This is typically the case with *BROWSER_WINDOW*: you create a new window when you need one. A *BOUNDED_BUFFER* or *PRINT_CONTROLLER* may also be created in this way.

- An application may simply need to access an *existing* separate object, usually shared between many different clients. This is the case in the *DATABASE* example: the client application uses an entity *db_server*: **separate** *DATABASE* to access the database through such separate calls as *db_server.ask_query* (*sql_query*). The server must have at some stage obtained the value of *server* — the database handle — from the outside. Accesses to existing *BOUNDED_BUFFER* or *PRINT_CONTROLLER* objects will use a similar scheme.

The separate object is said to be **created** in the first case and **external** in the second.

To obtain a created object, you simply use the creation instruction. If x is a separate entity, the creation instruction

    !! x.make (…)

will, in addition to its usual effect of creating and initializing a new object, assign a new processor to handle that object. Such an instruction is called a *separate creation*.

To obtain an existing external object, you will typically use an external routine, such as

    server (*name*: *STRING*; … Other arguments …): **separate** *DATABASE*

where the arguments serve to identify the requested object. Such a routine will typically send a message over the network and obtain in return a reference to the object.

A word about possible implementations may be useful here to visualize the notion of separate object. Assume each of the processors is associated with a *task* (process) of an operating system such as Windows or Unix, with its own address space; this is of course just one of many concurrent architectures. Then one way to represent a separate object within a task is to use a small local object, known as a **proxy**:

***A proxy for a
separate object***

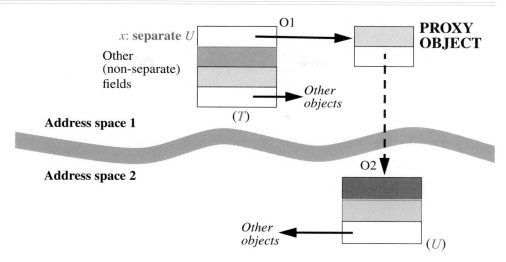

The figure shows an object O1, instance of a class T with an attribute x: **separate** U. The corresponding reference field in O1 is conceptually attached to an object O2, handled by another processor. Internally, however, the reference leads to a proxy object, handled by the same processor as O1. The proxy is an internal object, not visible to the author of the concurrent application. It contains enough information to identify O2: the task that serves as O2's handler, and O2's address within that task. All operations on x on behalf of O1 or other clients from the same task will go through the proxy. Any other processor that also handles objects containing separate references to O2 will have its own proxy for O2.

> Be sure to note that this is only one possible technique, not a required property of the model. Operating system tasks with separate address spaces are just one way to implement processors. With threads, for example, the techniques may be different.

Objects here, and objects there

When first presented with the notion of separate entity, some people complain that it is over-committing: "I do not want to know where the object resides! I just want to request the operation, $x_\bullet f\,(\ldots)$, and let the machinery do the rest — execute f on x wherever x is."

Although legitimate, this desire to avoid over-commitment does not obviate the need for **separate** declarations. It is true that the *precise* location of an object is often an implementation detail that should not affect the software. But one "yes or no" property of the object's location remains relevant: whether the object is handled by the *same* processor or by another. This is a fundamental semantic difference since it determines whether calls on the object are synchronous or asynchronous — cause the client to wait, or not. Ignoring this property in the software would not be a convenience; it would be a mistake.

Once we know the object is separate, it should not in most cases matter for the functionality of our software (although it may matter for its performance) whether the object belongs to another thread of the same process, another process on the same computer, another computer in the same room, another room in the same building, another site on the company's private network, or another Internet node half-way around the world. But it matters that it is separate.

A concurrency architecture

The use of **separate** declarations to cover the fundamental boolean property "is this object here, or is it elsewhere?" while leaving room for various physical implementations of concurrency suggests a two-level architecture, similar to what is available for the graphical mechanisms (with the *Vision* library sitting on top of platform-specific libraries):

General concurrency mechanism (*SCOOP*)

Process-based handle	Thread-based handle	CORBA-based handle	· · · · · · · · · · · · · · · ·

Two-level architecture for concurrency mechanism

(See a similar architecture for graphical libraries on page 1067.)

At the highest level the mechanism is platform-independent. This is the level which most applications use, and which this chapter describes. To perform concurrent computation, applications simply use the **separate** mechanism.

Internally, the implementation will rely on some practical concurrent architecture (lower level on the figure). The figure lists some possibilities:

• There may be an implementation using processes (tasks) as provided by the operating system. Each processor is associated with a process. This solution supports distributed computing: the process of a separate object can be on a remote machine as well as a local one. For non-distributed processing, it has the advantage that processes are stable and well known, and the disadvantage that they are CPU-intensive; both the creation of a new process and the exchange of information between processes are expensive operations.

• There may be an implementation using threads. Threads, as already noted, are a lighter alternative to processes, minimizing the cost of creation and context switching. Threads, however, have to reside on the same machine.

• A CORBA implementation is also possible, using CORBA distribution mechanisms as the physical layer to exchange objects across the network.

• Other possible mechanisms include PVM (Parallel Virtual Machine), the Linda language for concurrent programming, Java threads…

As always with such two-level architectures, the correspondence between high-level constructs and the actual platform mapping (the *handle* in terms of a previous chapter) is in most cases automatic, so that application developers will see the highest level only. But mechanisms must be available to let them access the lower level if they need to (and, of course, are ready to renounce platform-independence).

Mapping the processors: the Concurrency Control File

On Ace files see "Assembling a system", page 198.

If the software does not specify the physical CPUs, this specification must appear somewhere else. Here is a way to take care of it. This is only one possible solution, not a fundamental part of the approach; the exact format is not essential, but any configuration mechanism will somehow have to provide the same information.

Our example format is a "Concurrency Control File" (CCF) describing the concurrent computing resources available to our software. CCFs are similar in purpose and outlook to Ace files used to control system assembly. A typical CCF looks like this:

> **creation**
>> *local_nodes*:
>>> **system**
>>>> *"pushkin" (2)*: *"c:\system1\appl.exe"*
>>>> *"akhmatova" (4)*: *"/home/users/syst1"*
>>>> *Current*: *"c:\system1\appl2.exe"*
>>> **end**
>> *remote_nodes*:
>>> **system**
>>>> *"lermontov"*: *"c:\system1\appl.exe"*
>>>> *"tiuchev" (2)*: *"/usr/bin/syst2"*
>>> **end**
> **end**
>
> **external**
>> *Ingres_handler*: *"mandelstam"* **port** *9000*
>> *ATM_handler*: *"pasternak"* **port** *8001*
> **end**
>
> **default**
>> **port**: *8001*; **instance**: *10*
> **end**

Defaults are available for all properties of interest, so that each of the three possible parts (**creation**, **external**, **default**) is optional, as well as the CCF as a whole.

The **creation** part specifies what CPUs to use for separate creations (instructions of the form !! *x.make* (…) for separate *x*). The example uses two CPU groups: *local_nodes*, presumably covering local machines, and *remote_nodes*. The software can select a CPU group through a call such as

> *set_cpu_group* (*"local_nodes"*)

directing subsequent separate creations to use the CPU group *local_nodes* until the next call to *set_cpu_group*. This procedure comes from a class *CONCURRENCY* providing facilities for controlling the mechanism; we will encounter a few more of its features below.

The corresponding CCF entry specifies what CPUs to use for *local_nodes*: the first two objects will be created on machine *pushkin*, the next four on *akhmatova*, and the next ten on the current machine (the one which executes the creation instructions); after that the allocation scheme will repeat itself — two objects on *pushkin* and so on. In the absence of a processor count, as with *Current* here, the value is taken from the **instance** entry in the **default** part (here 10) if present, and is 1 otherwise. The system used to create each instance is an executable specified in each entry, such as *c:\system1\appl.exe* for *pushkin* (obviously a machine running Windows or OS/2).

In this example the processors are all mapped to processes. The CCF also supports assigning processors to threads (in the thread-based handle) or other concurrency mechanisms, although we need not concern ourselves with the details.

The **external** part specifies where to look for existing external separate objects. The CCF refers to these objects through abstract names, *Ingres_handler* and *ATM_handler* in the example, which the software will use as arguments to the functions that establish a connection with such an object. For example with the *server* function as assumed earlier

> *server* (*name*: *STRING*; ... Other arguments ...): **separate** *DATABASE*

a call of the form *server* ("*Ingres_handler*", ...) will yield a separate object denoting the Ingres database server. The CCF indicates that the corresponding object resides on machine *mandelstam* and is accessible on port 9000. In the absence of a port specification the value used is drawn from the **defaults** part or, barring that, a universal default.

The CCF is separate from the software. You may compile a concurrent or distributed application without any reference to a specific hardware and network architecture; then at run time each separate component of the application will use its CCF to connect to other existing components (**external** parts) and to create new components (**creation** parts).

This sketch of CCF conventions has shown how we can map the abstract concepts of concurrent O-O computation — processors, created separate objects, external separate objects — to physical resources. As noted, these conventions are only an example of what can be done, and they are not part of the basic concurrency mechanism. But they demonstrate that it is possible to decouple the software architecture of a concurrent system from the concurrent hardware architecture available at any particular stage.

Library mechanisms

With a CCF-like approach, the application software will, most of the time, not concern itself with the physical concurrency architecture. Some application developers may, however, need to exert a finer degree of control from within the application, at the possible expense of dynamic reconfigurability. Some CCF functionalities must then be accessible directly to the application, enabling it, for example, to select a specific process or thread for a certain processor. They will be available through libraries as part of the two-level concurrency architecture; it does not raise any difficult problem. We will encounter the need for more library mechanisms later in this chapter.

At the other extreme, some applications may want unlimited run-time reconfigurability. It is not enough then to have the ability to read a CCF or similar configuration information at start-up time and then be stuck with it. But we cannot either expect to re-read the configuration before each operation, as this would kill performance. The solution is once again to use a library mechanism: a procedure must be available to read or re-read the configuration information dynamically, allowing the application to adapt to a new configuration when (and only when) it is ready to do so.

Validity rules: unmasking traitors

Because the semantics of calls is different for separate and non-separate objects, it is essential to guarantee that a non-separate entity (declared as x: T for non-separate T) can never become attached to a separate object. Otherwise a call $x.f(a)$ would wrongly be understood — by the compiler, among others — as synchronous, whereas the attached object is in fact separate and requires asynchronous processing. Such a reference, falsely declared as non-separate while having its loyalties on the other side, will be called a **traitor**. We need a simple validity rule to guarantee that our software has no traitor — that every representative or lobbyist of a separate power is duly registered as such with the appropriate authorities.

The rule will have four parts. The first part eliminates the risk of producing traitors through attachment, that is to say assignment or argument passing:

> ### Separateness consistency rule (1)
>
> If the source of an attachment (assignment instruction or argument passing) is separate, its target entity must be separate too.

An attachment of target x and source y is either an assignment $x := y$ or a call $f(..., y, ...)$ where the actual argument corresponding to x is y. Having such an attachment with y separate but not x would make x a traitor, since we could use x to access a separate object (the object attached to y) under a non-separate name, as if it were a local object with synchronous call. The rule disallows this.

> Note that syntactically x is an entity but y may be any expression. This means that the rule assumes we have defined the notion of "separate expression", in line with previous definitions. A simple expression is an entity; more complex expressions are function calls (remember in particular that an infix expression such as $a + b$ is formally considered a call, similar to something like $a.plus(b)$). So the definition is immediate: an expression is separate if it is either a separate entity or a separate call.

As will be clear from the rest of the discussion, permitting an attachment of a non-separate source to a separate target is harmless — although usually not very useful.

We need a complementary rule covering the case in which a client passes to a separate supplier a reference to a local object. Assume the separate call

$$x.f(a)$$

where a, of type T, is not separate, although x is. The declaration of routine f, for the generating class of x, will be of the form

$$f(u: \dots \; SOME\_TYPE)$$

and the type T of a must conform to $SOME\_TYPE$. But this is not sufficient! Viewed from the supplier's side (that is to say, from the handler of x), the object O1 attached to a has a different handler; so unless the corresponding formal argument u is declared as separate it would become a traitor, giving access to a separate object as if it were non-separate:

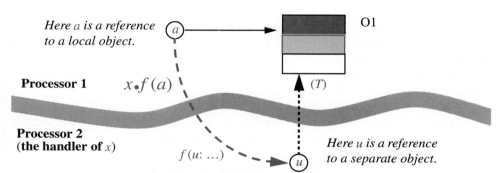

Here a is a reference to a local object.

O1

Processor 1 $x.f(a)$ (T)

Processor 2 (the handler of x)

$f(u: \dots)$

Here u is a reference to a separate object.

Passing a reference as argument to a separate call

So $SOME\_TYPE$ must be separate; for example it may be **separate** T. Hence the second consistency rule:

Separateness consistency rule (2)

If an actual argument of a separate call is of a reference type, the corresponding formal argument must be declared as separate.

The issue only arises for arguments of reference type. The other case, expanded types, including in particular the basic types such as *INTEGER*, is considered next.

As an application of the technique, consider an object that spawns several separate objects, giving them a way to rely later on its resources; it is saying to them, in effect, "*Here is my business card; call me if you need to*". A typical example would be an operating system's kernel that creates several separate objects and stands ready to perform operations for them when they ask. The creation calls will be of the form

$$!!\; subsystem.make \;(Current, \; \dots \; Other \; arguments \; \dots)$$

where *Current* is the "business card" enabling *subsystem* to remember its progenitor, and ask for its help in case of need. Because *Current* is a reference, the corresponding formal argument in *make* must be declared as separate. Most likely, *make* will be of the form

> *make* (*p*: **separate** *PROGENITOR_TYPE*; … Other arguments …) **is**
>> **do**
>>> *progenitor* := *p*
>>>
>>> … Rest of subsystem initialization operations …
>>
>> **end**

keeping the value of the progenitor argument in an attribute *progenitor* of the enclosing class. The second separateness consistency rule requires *p* to be declared as separate; so the first rule requires the same of attribute *progenitor*. Later calls for progenitor resources, of the form *progenitor.some_resource* (…) will, correctly, be treated as separate calls.

A similar rule is needed for function results:

Separateness consistency rule (3)

If the source of an attachment is the result of a separate call to a function returning a reference type, the target must be declared as separate.

Since the last two rules only apply to actual arguments and results of reference types, we need one more rule for the other case, expanded types:

Separateness consistency rule (4)

If an actual argument or result of a separate call is of an expanded type, its base class may not include, directly or indirectly, any non-separate attribute of a reference type.

In other words, the only expanded values that we can pass in a separate call are "completely expanded" objects, with no references to other objects. Otherwise we could again run into traitor trouble since attaching an expanded value implies copying an object:

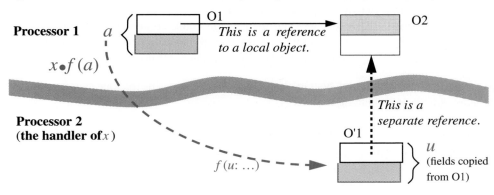

Passing to a separate call an object with references

The figure illustrates the case in which the formal argument u is itself expanded. Then the attachment is simply a copy of the fields of the object O1 onto those of the object O'1 attached to u. Permitting O1 to contain a reference would produce a traitor field in O'1. The problem would also arise if O1 had a subobject with a reference; hence the mention "directly or indirectly" in the rule.

The effect of reattachment in these cases was defined in "ATTACHMENT: REFERENCE AND VALUE SEMANTICS", 8.8, page 261.

If the formal argument u is a reference, the attachment is a clone; the call would create a new object O'1 similar to the one on the last figure and attach reference u to it. In this case the solution is to create the clone explicitly on the client's side, before the call:

a: **expanded** *SOME_TYPE*; $a1$: *SOME_TYPE*

...

$a1 := a$;   -- This clones the object and attaches $a1$ to the clone.

$x \bullet f (a1)$

As per the second validity rule, the formal argument u must be of a separate reference type, **separate** *SOME_TYPE* or conforming; the call on the last line makes u a separate reference attached to the newly created clone on the client's side.

Importing object structures

A consequence of the separateness consistency rules is that it is not possible to use the *clone* function (from the universal class *ANY*) to obtain an object handled by another processor. The function is declared as

See "Object cloning and equality", page 245.

clone (*other*: *GENERAL*): **like** *other* **is**

        -- New object, field-by-field identical to *other*

    ...

so that an attempt to use $y := clone\ (x)$ for separate x would violate part 1 of the rule: x, which is separate, does not conform to *other* which is not. This is what we want: a separate object running on a machine in Vladivostok may contain (non-separate) references to objects that are in Vladivostok too; but then if you could clone it in Kansas City, the resulting object would contain traitors — references to those objects, now separate, even though in the generating class the corresponding attributes are not declared as separate.

The following function, also in class *GENERAL*, enables us to clone separate object structures without producing traitors:

deep_import (*other*: **separate** *GENERAL*): *GENERAL* **is**

        -- New object, field-by-field identical to *other*

    ...

You should be familiar with the notions of shallow and deep clone; see "Deep clone and comparison", page 247.

The result is a non-separate object structure, recursively duplicated from the separate structure starting at *other*. For the reasons just explained, a *shallow* import operation could yield traitors; so what we need is the equivalent of *deep_clone* applied to a separate object. Function *deep_import* provides it. It will produce a copy of the entire structure, making all the object copies non-separate. (It may of course still contain separate references if the original structure contained references to objects handled by another processor.)

For the developers of distributed systems, *deep_import* is a convenient and powerful mechanism, through which you can transfer possibly large object structures across a network without the need to write any specialized software, and with the guarantee that the exact structure (including cycles etc.) will be faithfully duplicated.

30.5 SYNCHRONIZATION ISSUES

We have our basic mechanism for starting concurrent executions (separate creation) and for requesting operations from these executions (the usual feature call mechanism). Any concurrent computation, object-oriented or not, must also provide ways to **synchronize** concurrent executions, that is to say to define timing dependencies between them.

If you are familiar with concurrency issues, you may have been surprised by the announcement that a single language mechanism, **separate** declarations, is enough to add full concurrency support to our sequential object-oriented framework. Surely we need specific synchronization mechanisms too? Actually no. The basic O-O constructs suffice to cover a wide range of synchronization needs, provided we adapt the definition of their semantics when they are applied to separate elements. It is a testimony of the power of the object-oriented method that it adapts so simply and gracefully to concurrent computation.

Synchronization *vs*. communication

To understand how we should support synchronization in object-oriented concurrency, it is useful to begin with a review of non-O-O solutions. Processes (the concurrent units in most of these solutions) need mechanisms of two kinds:

- *Synchronization* mechanisms enforce timing constraints. A typical constraint might state that a certain operation of a process, such as accessing a database item, may only occur after a certain operation of another process, such as initializing the item.

- *Communication* mechanisms allow processes to exchange information, which in the object-oriented case will be in the form of objects (including the special case of simple values such as integers) or object structures.

A simple classification of approaches to concurrency rests on the observation that some of them focus on the synchronization mechanism and then use ordinary non-concurrent techniques such as argument passing for communication, whereas others treat communication as the fundamental issue and deduce synchronization from it. We may talk about *synchronization-based* and *communication-based* mechanisms.

Synchronization-based mechanisms

The best known and most elementary synchronization-based mechanism is the **semaphore**, a locking tool for controlling shared resources. A semaphore is an object on which two operations are available: *reserve* and *free* (traditionally called P and V, but more suggestive names are preferable). At any time the semaphore is either reserved by a certain client or free. If it is free and a client executes *reserve*, the semaphore becomes reserved by that client. If the client that has reserved it executes *free*, the semaphore becomes free. If the semaphore is reserved by a client and another executes *reserve*, the new client will wait until the semaphore is free again. The following table summarizes this specification:

STATE OPERATION	Free	Reserved by me	Reserved by someone else
reserve	Becomes reserved by me.		I wait.
free		Becomes free.	

Semaphore operations

Events represented by shaded entries are not supposed to occur; they can be treated either as errors or as having no effect.

The policy for deciding which client gets through when two or more are waiting for a semaphore that gets freed may be part of the semaphore's specification, or may be left unspecified. (Usually clients expect a *fairness* property guaranteeing that if everyone gaining access to the semaphore ultimately frees it no one will wait forever.)

This description covers *binary* semaphores. The *integer* variant lets at most n clients through at any given time, for some n, rather than at most one.

Although many practical developments still rely on them, semaphores are widely considered too low-level for building large, reliable systems. But they provide a good starting point for discussing more advanced techniques.

Critical regions are a more abstract approach. A critical region is a sequence of instructions that may be executed by at most one client at a time. To ensure exclusive access to a certain object a you may write something like

> **hold** a **then** ... Operations involving fields of a ...**end**

where the critical region is delimited by **then** ... **end**. Only one client can execute the critical region at any given time; others executing a **hold** will wait.

Most applications need a more general variant, the **conditional critical region**, in which execution of the critical region is subject to a boolean condition. Consider a buffer shared by a producer, which can only write into the buffer if it is not full, and a consumer, which can only read from it if it is not empty; they may use the two respective schemes

> **hold** *buffer* **when not** *buffer.full* **then** "Write into buffer, making it not empty" **end**

> **hold** *buffer* **when not** *buffer.empty* **then** "Read from buffer, making it not full" **end**

Such interplay between input and output conditions cries for introducing assertions and giving them a role in synchronization, an idea to be exploited later in this chapter.

Another well-known synchronization-based mechanism, combining the notion of critical region with the modular structure of some modern programming languages, is the **monitor**. A monitor is a program module, not unlike the packages of Modula or Ada. The basic synchronization mechanism is simple: mutual exclusion at the routine level. At most one client may execute a routine of the monitor at any given time.

Also interesting is the notion of **path expression**. A path expression specifies the possible sequencing of a set of processes. For example the expression

$$init \ ; \ (reader^* \mid writer)^+ \ ; finish$$

prescribes the following behavior: first an *init* process; then a state in which at any time either one *writer* process or any number of *reader* processes may be active; then a *finish* process. The asterisk $*$ means any number of concurrent instances; the semicolon $;$ indicates sequencing; $\mid$ means "either-or"; $^+$ means any number of successive repetitions. An argument often cited in favor of path expressions is that they specify the processes and the synchronization separately, avoiding interference between the description of individual algorithmic tasks and the description of their scheduling.

> Yet another category of techniques for specifying synchronization relies on analyzing the set of **states** through which a system or system component can go, and transitions between these states. **Petri nets**, in particular, rely on graphical descriptions of the transitions. Although intuitive for simple hardware devices, such techniques quickly yield a combinatorial explosion in the number of states and transitions, and make it hard to work hierarchically (specifying subsystems independently, then recursively embedding their specifications in those of bigger systems). So they do not seem applicable to large, evolutionary software systems.

Communication-based mechanisms

Starting with Hoare's "Communicating Sequential Processes" (CSP) in the late seventies, most non-O-O concurrency work has focused on communication-based approaches.

The rationale is easy to understand. If you have solved the synchronization problem, you must still find a way to make concurrent units communicate. But if you devise a good communication mechanism you might very well have solved synchronization too: because two units cannot communicate unless the sender is ready to send and the receiver ready to receive, communication implies synchronization; pure synchronization may be viewed as the extreme case of communicating an empty message. If your communication mechanism is general enough, it will provide *all* the synchronization you need.

CSP is based on this "I communicate, therefore I synchronize" view. The starting point is a generalization of a fundamental concept of computing, input and output: a process receives information v from a certain "channel" c through the construct $c \ ? \ v$; it sends information to a channel through the construct $c \ ! \ v$. Channel input and output are only two among the possible examples of *events*.

For more flexibility CSP introduces the notion of non-deterministic wait, represented by the symbol ▌, enabling a process to wait on several possible events and execute the action associated with the first that occurs. Assume for example a system enabling a bank's customers to make inquiries and transfers on their accounts, and the bank manager to check what is going on:

$(balance\_enquiry ? customer \rightarrow$
$\quad (ask\_password\bullet customer ? password \rightarrow$
$\quad\quad (password\_valid \rightarrow (balance\_out\bullet customer ! balance)$
$\quad\quad \blacksquare (password\_invalid \rightarrow (denial\bullet customer ! denial\_message)))$
$\quad \blacksquare transfer\_request ? customer \rightarrow ...$
$\quad \blacksquare control\_operation ? manager \rightarrow ...)$

In the initial state the system stands ready to accept one of three possible input events: a *balance_enquiry* or *transfer_request* from a *customer*, or a *control_operation* from a *manager*. The first event that occurs will trigger the behavior described, using the same mechanisms, on the right of the corresponding arrow.

The right side of the arrow has only been filled in for the first event: after getting a *balance_enquiry* relative to a certain *customer*, you send the *customer* an *ask_password* event from which you expect to get the *password*; you validate the password, as a result sending to the *customer* one of two possible messages: *balance_out*, with the *balance* as argument, or *denial*.

Once the event's processing is complete, the system returns to its initial state, listening to possible input events.

The original version of CSP was a major influence on the concurrency mechanism of Ada, whose "tasks" are processes able to wait on several possible "entries" through an "accept" instruction. The Occam language, a direct implementation of CSP, is the primary programming tool for the *transputer*, a family of microprocessors designed specifically by Inmos (now SGS-Thomson) for the construction of highly concurrent architectures.

The example reflects the most recent CSP rather than the original 1978 version; see bibliographical notes. On Ada concurrency see p. 1091.

Synchronization for concurrent O-O computation

Many of the ideas just reviewed will help us find the right approach to concurrency in an object-oriented context. In the final form of the solution you will recognize concepts coming from CSP as well as monitors and conditional critical regions.

The CSP emphasis on communication seems right for us, since the central technique of our model of computation — calling a feature, with arguments, on an object — is a communication mechanism. But there is another reason for preferring a communication-based solution: a synchronization-based mechanism can conflict with inheritance.

This conflict is most obvious if we consider path expressions. The idea of using path expressions has attracted many researchers on O-O concurrency as a way to specify the actual processing, given by the features of a class, separately from the synchronization constraints, given by path expressions. The purely computational aspects of the software, which may have existed prior to the introduction of concurrency, will thus remain untainted by concurrency concerns. So for example if a class *BUFFER* has the features *remove* (remove the oldest element of the buffer) and *put* (add an element), we may express the synchronization through constraints such as

Notation and example from [Matsuoka 1993], *which introduced the term "inheritance anomaly". For more details on the example see exercise E30.3, page 1035.*

empty: {*put*}
partial: {*put*, *remove*}
full: {*remove*}

using a path-expression-like notation which lists three possible states and, for each of them, the permitted operations. But then assume you want a descendant *NEW_BUFFER* to provide an extra feature *remove_two* which removes two buffer items at a time (with a buffer size of at least three). Then you need an almost completely new set of states:

empty: {*put*}

partial_one: {*put*, *remove*}   -- State in which the buffer contains exactly one item

partial_two_or_more: {*put*, *remove*, *remove_two*}

full: {*remove*, *remove_two*}

and if the routines specify what states they produce in each possible case, they must all be redefined from *BUFFER* to *NEW_BUFFER*, defeating the purpose of inheritance.

This problem, and similar ones identified by several researchers, have been dubbed the **inheritance anomaly**, and have led some concurrent O-O language designers to view inheritance with suspicion. The first versions of the POOL parallel object-oriented language, for example, excluded inheritance (see the bibliographical notes).

Concerns about the "inheritance anomaly" have sparked an abundant literature proposing solutions, which generally try to decrease the amount of redefinition by looking for modular ways of specifying the synchronization constraints, so that descendants can describe the changes more incrementally, instead of having to redefine everything.

On closer examination, however, the problem does not appear to be inheritance, or even any inherent conflict between inheritance and concurrency, but instead the idea of specifying synchronization constraints separately from the routines themselves. (The formalisms discussed actually do not quite meet this goal anyway, since the routines must specify their exit states.)

To the reader of this book, familiar with the principles of Design by Contract, the technique using explicit states and a list of the features applicable in each state will look too low-level. The specifications of *BUFFER* and *NEW_BUFFER* obscure fundamental properties that we have learned to characterize through preconditions: *put* should state **require not** *full*; similarly, *remove_two* should state **require** *count* >= *2*; and so on. This more compact and more abstract specification is easier to explain, to adapt (changing a routine's precondition does not affect any other routine), and to relate to the views of outsiders such as customers. State-based techniques appear more restrictive and error-prone. They also raise the risk of combinatorial explosion mentioned in relation to Petri nets and other state-based models: for the above elementary examples the number of states is already three in one case and four in the other, suggesting that in a complex system it might become unmanageable.

The "inheritance anomaly" only occurs because such specifications tend to be rigid and fragile: change anything, and the whole specification crumbles.

See "Active objects clash with inheritance", page 959.

At the beginning of this chapter we saw another apparent inheritance-concurrency clash; but the culprit turned out to be the notion of active object. In both cases inheritance is at odds not with concurrency but with a particular approach to concurrency (active objects, state-based specifications); rather than dismissing or limiting inheritance — cutting the arm whose finger itches — the solution is to look for better concurrency mechanisms.

One of the practical consequences of this discussion is that we should try to rely, for synchronization in concurrent computation, on what we already have in the object-oriented model, in particular assertions. Preconditions will indeed play a central role for synchronization, although we will need to adapt their semantics from the sequential case.

30.6 ACCESSING SEPARATE OBJECTS

We now have enough background to devise the proper synchronization mechanisms for our concurrent object-oriented systems.

Concurrent accesses to an object

The first question to address is how many executions may proceed concurrently on an object. The answer was in fact implicit in the definition of the notions of processor and handler: if all calls to features on an object are executed by its handler (the processor in charge of it), and a processor is a single thread of execution, it follows that at most one feature may be executing on a given object at any time.

Should we not allow several routines to execute concurrently on a given object? The main incentive for answering *no* is to retain the ability to reason on our software.

The study of class correctness in an earlier chapter provides the proper perspective. We saw the lifecycle of an object pictured as this:

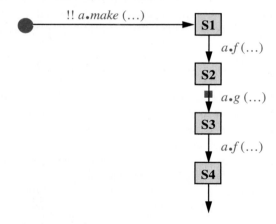

The life of an object

(*This figure first appeared on page 365.*)

In this view the object is externally observable only in the states marked as shaded squares: just after creation (S1), after every application of a feature by a client (S2 and subsequent states). These have been called the "stable times" of the object's life. A consequence was the formal rule: to prove the correctness of the class, we only have to verify one property for each creation procedure, and one property for each exported feature. If p is a creation procedure, the property to check is

These rules have been slightly simplified. The full versions appear in "WHEN IS A CLASS CORRECT?", 11.9, page 369.

$$\{Default \text{ and } pre_p\} \ Body_p \ \{post_p \text{ and } INV\}$$

meaning: if you execute the body of p when the object has been initialized to the default values and the precondition of p holds, you will end up satisfying the postcondition and the invariant. For an exported routine r, the property to check is

$$\{pre_r \text{ and } INV\} \quad Body_r \quad \{post_r \text{ and } INV\}$$

meaning: if you execute r when the precondition and the invariant are satisfied, you will end up satisfying the postcondition and the invariant.

So the number of things to check is very limited; there are no complicated run-time scenarios to analyze. This is important even in a somewhat informal approach to software development, which still requires the ability to reason about the software execution by examining the software text. The informal version of the preceding properties is that you can understand the class by looking at its routines separately from each other — convincing yourself, however informally, that each routine will deliver the intended final state starting from the expected initial state.

Introduce concurrent execution into this simple, consistent world, and all hell breaks loose. Even plain interleaving, in which we would start executing a routine, interrupt it in favor of another, switch back to the first and so on, would deprive us from any ability to use straightforward reasoning on our software texts. We simply would not have any clue as to what can happen at run-time; trying to guess would force us to examine all possible interleavings, immediately leading to a combinatorial explosion of cases to consider.

So for simplicity and consistency we will let at most one routine execute on any particular object at any particular time. Note, however, that in a case of emergency, or if a client keeps an object for too long, we should be able to **interrupt** the client, as long as we do so in a sufficiently violent way — triggering an exception — to ensure that the unfortunate client will receive a notification, enabling it to take corrective action if appropriate. The mechanism of *duels*, explained later, offers that possibility.

> The end of the discussion section examines whether any circumstances would allow us to relax the prohibition of concurrent accesses to a single object.

Reserving an object

We need a way for a client to obtain exclusive access to a certain resource, represented by a certain object.

An idea which seems attractive at first (but will not suffice) would be simply to rely on the notion of separate call. Consider, executed on behalf of a certain client object O1, the call $x.f(\ldots)$, for separate x attached at run time to O2. Once the call has started executing, we have seen that O1 can safely move to its next business without waiting for the call's termination; but this execution of the call cannot start until O2 is free for O1. So we might decide that before starting the call the client will wait until the target object is free.

Unfortunately this simple scheme is not sufficient, because it does not allow the client to decide how long to retain an object. Assume O2 is some shared data structure such as a buffer, and the corresponding class provides procedure *remove* to remove an element. A client O1 may need to remove two consecutive elements, but just writing *buffer.remove*; *buffer.remove*

will not do: between the two instructions, any other client can jump in and perform operations on the shared structure! So the two elements might not be adjacent.

One solution is to add to the generating class of *buffer* (or of a descendant) a procedure *remove_two* that removes two elements at once. But in the general case that is unrealistic: you cannot change your suppliers for every synchronization need of *your own client code*. There must be a way for the client to reserve a supplier object for as long as it needs, using the supplier class as it is.

In other words, we need something like a critical region mechanism. The syntax introduced earlier was

On critical regions see "Synchronization-based mechanisms", page 978.

    hold *a* **then** *actions_requiring_exclusive_access* **end**

or the conditional variant

    hold *a* **when** *a.some_property* **then** *actions_requiring_exclusive_access* **end**

We will, however, go for a simpler approach, perhaps surprising at first. The convention will simply be that if *a* is a non-void separate expression a call of the form

    actions_requiring_exclusive_access (*a*)

causes the caller to wait until the object attached to *a* is available. In other words, there is no need for a **hold** instruction; to reserve a separate object, you simply use it as actual argument in a call.

Note that waiting only makes sense if the routine contains at least one call *x.some_routine* on the formal argument *x* corresponding to *a*. Otherwise, for example if all it does is a "business card" assignment *some_attribute := x*, there is no need to wait. This is specified in the full form of the rule, also involving preconditions, which appears later in this chapter.

"Separate call semantics", page 996.

Other policies are possible, and indeed some authors have proposed retaining a **hold** instruction (see the bibliographical notes). But the use of argument passing as the object reservation mechanism helps keep the concurrency model simple and easy to learn. One of the observations justifying this policy is that with the **hold** scheme shown above it will be tempting for developers, in line with the general "Encapsulate Repetition" motto of O-O development, to gather in a routine the actions that require exclusive access to an object; this trend was foreseen in the above summary of the **hold** instruction, where the actions appear as a single routine *actions_requiring_exclusive_access*. But then such a routine will need an argument representing the object; here we go further and consider that the presence of such an argument suffices to achieve object reservation.

This convention also means that, paradoxically enough, *most separate calls do not need to wait*. When we are executing the body of a routine that has a separate formal argument *a*, we know that we have already reserved the attached object, so any call with target *a* can proceed immediately. As we have seen, there is no need to wait for the call to terminate. In the general case, with a routine of the form

```
r (a: separate SOME_TYPE) is
    do
            ...; a.r1 (...); ...
            ...; a.r2 (...); ...
    end
```

an implementation can continue executing the intermediate instructions without waiting for any of the calls to terminate, as long as it logs all the calls on a so that they will be executed in the order requested. (We have yet to see how to wait for a separate call to terminate if that is what we want; so far, we just start calls and never wait!)

> If a routine has two or more separate arguments, a client call will wait until it can reserve *all* the corresponding objects. This requirement is hard on the compiler, which will have to generate code using protocols for multiple simultaneous reservations; for that reason, an implementation might at first impose the restriction that a routine may have at most one separate formal argument. But if the full mechanism is implemented it provides considerable benefits to application developers; as a typical example, studied later in this chapter, the famous "dining philosophers" problem admits an almost trivial solution.

Accessing separate objects

The last example shows how to use, as the target of a separate call, a formal argument, itself separate, of the enclosing routine r. An advantage is that we do not need to worry about how to get access to the target object: this was taken care of by the call to r, which had to reserve the object — waiting if necessary until it is free.

We can go further and make this scheme the *only* one for separate calls:

Separate Call rule

The target of a separate call must be a formal argument of the routine in which the call appears.

Remember that a call $a.r$ (...) is separate if the target a is itself an entity or expression declared as separate. So if we have a separate entity a we cannot call a feature on it unless a is a formal argument of the enclosing routine. If, for example, *attrib* is an attribute declared as separate, we must use, instead of *attrib.r* (...), the call *rf* (*attrib*, ...) with

```
rf (x: separate SOME_TYPE; ... Other arguments ...) is
            -- Call r on x.
    do
            x.r (...)
    end
```

This rule may appear to place an undue burden on developers of concurrent applications, since it forces them to encapsulate all uses of separate objects in routines. It may indeed be possible to devise a variant of this chapter's model which does not include the Separate Call rule; but as you start using the model you will, I think, realize that the rule is in fact of great help. It encourages developers to identify accesses to separate objects and separate them from the rest of the computation. Most importantly, it avoids grave errors that would be almost bound to happen without it.

The following case is typical. Assume a shared data structure — such as, once again, a buffer — with features *remove* to remove an element and *count* to query the number of elements. Then it is quite "natural" to write

> **if** *buffer.count >= 2* **then**
>
> > *buffer.remove*; *buffer.remove*
>
> **end**

According to David Gries, "natural" is one of the most dangerous words in software discussions.

The intent is presumably to remove two elements. But, as we have already seen, this will not always work — at least not unless we have secured exclusive access to *buffer*. Otherwise between the time you test *count* and the time you execute the first *remove*, any other client can come in and remove an element, so that you will end up trying to apply *remove* to an empty structure.

Another example, assuming that we follow the style of previous chapters and include a feature *item*, side-effect-free, to return the element that *remove* removes, is

> **if not** *buffer.empty* **then**
>
> > *value* := *buffer.item*; *buffer.remove*
>
> **end**

Without a protection on *buffer*, another client may add or remove an element between the calls to *item* and *remove*. If the author of the above extract thinks that the effect is to access an element and remove it, he will be right some of the time; but if this is not your lucky day you will access an element and remove another — so that you may for example (if you repeat the above scheme) access the same element twice! Very wrong.

By making *buffer* an argument of the enclosing routine, we avoid these problems: *buffer* is guaranteed to be reserved for the duration of the routine's call.

Of course the fault in the examples cited lies with the developer, who was not careful enough. But without the Separate Call rule such errors are too easy to make. What makes things really bad is that the run-time behavior is non-deterministic, since it depends on the relative speed of the clients. The bug will be intermittent, here one minute, gone the next. Worse yet, it will probably occur rarely: after all (using the first example) a competing client has to be quite lucky to squeeze in between your test of *count* and your first call to *remove*. So the bug may be very hard to reproduce and isolate.

Such tricky bugs are responsible for the nightmarish reputation of concurrent system debugging. Any rule that can significantly decrease their likelihood of occurring is a big potential help.

With the Separate Call rule you will write the examples as the following procedures, assuming a separate type *BOUNDED_BUFFER* detailed below:

remove_two (*buffer*: *BOUNDED_BUFFER*) **is**
        -- Remove oldest two items.
  do
      if *buffer.count* >= *2* **then**
          buffer.remove; *buffer.remove*
      end
  end

get_and_remove (*buffer*: *BOUNDED_BUFFER*) **is**
        -- Assign oldest item to *value*, and remove it.
  do
      if not *buffer.empty* **then**
          value := *buffer.item*; *buffer.remove*
      end
  end

These procedures may be part of some application class; preferably, they will appear in a class *BUFFER_ACCESS* which encapsulates buffer manipulation operations, and serves as parent to application classes needing to use buffers of the appropriate type.

The procedures both seem to be crying for a precondition. We will shortly see to it that they can get one.

Wait by necessity

Assume that a separate call such as *buffer.remove* has been started, after waiting if necessary for any separate arguments to become available. We have seen that from then on it does not block the client, which can proceed with the rest of its computation. But surely the client may need to resynchronize with the supplier. When should we wait for the call to terminate?

See the bibliographi-cal notes.

It would seem that we need a special mechanism, as has indeed been proposed by some concurrent O-O languages such as Hybrid, to reunite the parent computation with its prodigal call. But instead we can use the idea of wait by necessity, due to Denis Caromel. The goal is to wait when we truly need to, but no earlier.

When does the client need to be sure that a call $a.r$ $(\ldots)$, for separate a attached to a separate object O1, is finished? Not when it is doing something else on other objects, separate or not; not even necessarily when it has started a new procedure call $a.r$ $(\ldots)$ on the same separate object since, as we have seen, a smart implementation can simply log such calls so that they will be processed in the order emitted (an essential requirement, of course); but when we need to access some property of O1. *Then* we require the object to be available, and all preceding calls on it to have been finished.

You will remember the division of features into *commands* (procedures), which perform some transformation on the target object, and *queries* (functions and attributes) which return information about it. Command calls do not need to wait, but query calls may.

Consider for example a separate stack s and the successive calls

$s.put(x1); \ldots$ Other instructions $\ldots; s.put(x2); \ldots$ Other instructions $\ldots; value := s.item$

(which because of the Separate Call rule must appear in a routine of which s is a formal argument). Assuming none of the Other instructions uses s, the only one that requires us to wait is the last instruction since it needs some information about the stack, its top value (which in this case should be $x2$).

These observations yield the basic concept of wait by necessity: once a separate call has started, a client only needs to wait for its termination if the call is to a query. A more precise rule will be given below, after we look at a practical example.

Wait by necessity (also called "lazy wait", and similar to mechanisms of "call by necessity" and "lazy evaluation" familiar to Lispers and students of theoretical computing science) is a convenient rule which allows you to start parallel computations as you need and avoid unnecessary waiting, but be reassured that the computation *will* wait when it must.

A multi-launcher

Here is a typical example showing the benefits of wait by necessity. Assume that a certain object must create a set of other objects, each of which goes off on its own:

```
launch (a: ARRAY [separate X]) is
        -- Get every element of a started.
    require
        -- No element of a is void
    local
        i: INTEGER
    do
        from i := a.lower until i > a.upper loop
            launch_one (a @ i); i := i + 1
        end
    end
launch_one (p: separate X) is
        -- Get p started.
    require
        p /= Void
    do
        p.live
    end
```

If, as may well be the case, procedure *live* of class X describes an infinite process, this scheme relies on the guarantee that each loop iteration will proceed immediately after starting *launch_one*, without waiting for the call to terminate: otherwise the loop would never get beyond its first iteration. One of the examples below uses this scheme.

"The dining philosophers", page 1003.

> Readers familiar with coroutine-based discrete event simulation, studied in a later chapter, will recognize a scheme very close to what happens when you start a simulated process and want to gain control back, as permitted by Simula's **detach** instruction.

"Coroutine concepts", page 1118.

An optimization

(This section examines a fine point and may be skipped on first reading.)

To wrap up this discussion of wait by necessity we need to examine more carefully when a client should wait for a separate call to terminate.

We have seen that only query calls should cause waiting. But we may go further by examining whether the query's result is of an expanded type or a reference type. (For the *s.item* example, assuming *s* of type *STACK* [*SOME_TYPE*], this is determined by *SOME_TYPE*.) If the type is expanded, for example if it is *INTEGER* or another of the basic types, there is no choice: we need the value, so the client computation must wait until the query has computed its result. But for a reference type, one can imagine that a smart implementation could still proceed while the result, a separate object, is being computed; in particular, if the implementation uses proxies for separate objects, the proxy object itself can be created immediately, so that the reference to it is available even if the proxy does not yet refer to the desired separate object.

This optimization, however, complicates the concurrency mechanism because it means proxies must have a "ready or not" boolean attribute, and all operations on separate references must wait until the proxy is ready. It also seems to prescribe a particular implementation — through proxies. So we will not retain it as part of the basic rule:

Wait by necessity

If a client has started one or more calls on a certain separate object, and it executes on that object a call to a query, that call will only proceed after all the earlier ones have been completed, and any further client operations will wait for the query call to terminate.

To account for the possible optimization just discussed, replace "*a call to a query*" by "*a call to a query returning of expanded type*".

Avoiding deadlock

Along with several typical and important examples of passing separate references to separate calls, we have seen that it is also possible to pass non-separate references, as long as the corresponding formal arguments are declared as separate (since, on the supplier's side, they represent foreign objects, and we do not want any traitors). Non-separate references raise a risk of deadlock and must be handled carefully.

The normal way of passing non-separate references is what we have called the *business card* scheme: we use a separate call of the form $x.f(a)$ where x is separate but a is not; that is to say, a is a reference to a local object of the client, possibly *Current* itself; on the supplier side, f is of the form

f (u: **separate** *SOME_TYPE*) **is**
    do
        local_reference := u
    end

where *local_reference*, also of type **separate** *SOME_TYPE*, is an attribute of the enclosing supplier class. Later on, in routines other than f, the supplier may use *local_reference* to request operations on objects on the original client's side, through separate calls of the form *local_reference*.*some_routine* (…)

This scheme is sound. Assume, however, that f did more, for example that it included a call of the form u.g (…) for some g. This is likely to produce deadlock: the client (the handler for the object attached to u and a) is busy executing f or, with wait by necessity, may be executing another call that has reserved the same object.

The following rule will avoid this kind of situation:

Business Card principle

If a separate call uses a non-separate actual argument of a reference type, the routine should only use the corresponding formal as source of assignments.

At present this is a only methodological guideline although it may be desirable to introduce a formal validity rule (an exercise asks you to explore this idea further.) Some more comments on deadlocks appear in the discussion section.

Exercise E30.4, page 1035; see also E30.13, page 1036.

30.7 WAIT CONDITIONS

One synchronization rule remains to be seen. It will deal with two questions at once:

- How can we make a client wait until a certain condition is satisfied, as in conditional critical regions?

- What is the meaning of assertions, in particular preconditions, in a concurrent context?

A buffer is a separate queue

We need a working example. To study what happens to assertions, it is interesting to take a closer look at a notion that is ubiquitous in concurrent application (and has already appeared informally several times in this chapter): **bounded buffers**. A bounded buffer, illustrated by the top figure on the facing page, allows different components of a concurrent system to exchange data, produced by some and consumed by others, without forcing each producer that has generated an object to wait until a consumer is ready to use it, and conversely. Instead, communication occurs through a shared structure, the buffer; producers deposit their wares into the buffer, and consumers get their material from it. In a bounded implementation the structure can only hold a certain number *maxcount* of items, and so it can get full. But waits will only occur when a consumer needs to consume and the buffer is empty, or when a producer needs to produce and the buffer is full. In a well-regulated system such events will be much more infrequent than with unbuffered communication, and their frequency will decrease as the buffer's capacity grows. True, a new source of delays arises because buffer access must be exclusive: at most one client may at any one time be performing a deposit (*put*) or retrieval (*item*, *remove*) operation. But these are very simple and fast operations, so any resulting wait is typically short.

In most cases the time sequence in which objects have been produced is relevant to the consumers, so the buffer must maintain a **first-in**, **first-out** policy (FIFO): an object deposited before another must be retrieved before it. The behavior is similar to that of train cars being added at one end of a single track and removed at the other end:

Bounded buffer

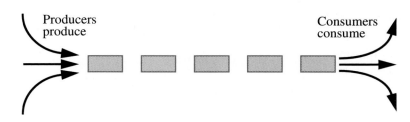

The bounded queue of the Undoing design pattern used a similar representation. See page 710.

A typical implementation — not essential to the discussion, but giving us a more concrete view — can use an array *representation* of size *capacity* = *maxcount* + *1*, managed circularly; the integer *oldest* will be the index of the oldest item, and *next* the index of the position to be used for inserting the next item that comes in. We can picture the array as being torn into a ring so that positions 1 and *capacity* are conceptually adjacent:

Bounded buffer implemented by an array

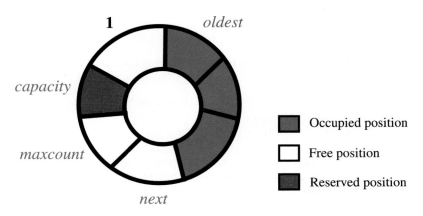

The procedure *put* used by a producer to add an item x will be implemented as

   representation.*put* (x, *next*); *next* := (*next* \\ *maxcount*) + *1*

where \\ is the integer remainder operation; the query *item* used by consumers to obtain the oldest element simply returns *representation* @ *oldest* (the array element at index *oldest*); and procedure *remove* simply executes *oldest*:= (*oldest* \\ *maxcount*) + *1*. The array entry at index *capacity*, shaded in gray on the figure, is kept free; this makes it possible to distinguish between the test for *empty*, expressed as $next = oldest$, and the test for *full*, expressed as $(next \backslash\backslash maxcount) + 1 = oldest$.

For an alternative technique see "Unconstrained genericity", page 1181.

The structure, with its FIFO policy, and the circular array representation, are of course not concurrency-specific: what we have is simply a **bounded queue** similar to many of the structures studied in preceding chapters. Writing the corresponding class — directly applicable to the Undoing design pattern — is not hard; here is a short form of the class, in simplified form (main features only, header comments removed, principal assertion clauses only):

class interface *BOUNDED_QUEUE* [*G*] **feature**

> *empty, full*: *BOOLEAN*
>
> *put* (*x*: *G*)
>> **require**
>>> **not** *full*
>> **ensure**
>>> **not** *empty*
>
> *remove*
>> **require**
>>> **not** *empty*
>> **ensure**
>>> **not** *full*
>
> *item*: *G*
>> **require**
>>> **not** *empty*

end -- class interface *BOUNDED_QUEUE*

Obtaining from this description a class describing bounded buffers is about as simple as we could dream:

separate class *BOUNDED_BUFFER* [*G*] **inherit**

> *BOUNDED_QUEUE* [*G*]

end

The **separate** qualifier applies only to the class where it appears, not its heirs. So a separate class may, as here, inherit from a non-separate one, and conversely. The convention is the same as with the other two qualifiers applicable to a class: **expanded** and **deferred**. As noted, the three properties are mutually exclusive, so that at most one of the qualifiers may appear before the keyword **class**.

We see once again the fundamental simplicity of concurrent O-O software development, and the smooth transition from sequential to concurrent concepts, made possible in particular by the method's focus on encapsulation. A bounded buffer (a notion for which you will find many complicated descriptions if you look at the concurrency literature) is nothing else than a bounded queue made separate.

Preconditions under concurrent execution

Let us examine a typical use of a bounded buffer *buffer* by a client, for example a producer that needs to deposit a certain object *y* using the procedure *put*. Assume that *buffer* is an attribute of the enclosing class, having been declared, for some type *T* which is also the type of *y*, as *buffer: BOUNDED_BUFFER* [*T*].

The client may for example have initialized *buffer* to a reference to the actual buffer passed by its creation procedure, using the *business card* scheme suggested earlier:

make (*b*: *BOUNDED_BUFFER* [*T*], …) **is do** …; *buffer* := *b*; … **end**

Because *buffer*, being declared of a separate type, is a separate entity, any call of the form *buffer*.*put* (*y*) is a separate call and has to appear in a routine of which *buffer* is an argument. So we should instead use *put* (*buffer*, *y*) where *put* (a routine of the client class, not to be confused with the *put* of *BOUNDED_BUFFER*, which it calls) is declared as

put (*b*: *BOUNDED_BUFFER* [*T*]; *x*: *T*) **is**
            -- Insert *x* into *b*. (First attempt.)
    do
        b.*put* (*x*)
    end

Well, this is not quite right. Procedure *put* of *BOUNDED_BUFFER* has a precondition, **not** *full*. Since it does not make sense to try to insert *x* into *b* if *b* is full, we should mimic this precondition for our new procedure in the client class:

put (*b*: *BOUNDED_BUFFER* [*T*]; *x*: *T*) **is**
            -- Insert *x* into *b*.
    require
        not *b*.*full*
    do
        b.*put* (*x*)
    end

Better. How can we call this procedure with a specific *buffer* and *y*? We must make sure, of course, that the precondition is satisfied on input. One way is to test:

if not *full* (*buffer*) **then** *put* (*buffer*, *y*)   -- [PUT1]

but we could also rely on the context of the call as in

remove (*buffer*); *put* (*buffer*, *y*)   -- [PUT2]

where the postcondition of *remove* includes **not** *full*. (Example PUT2 assumes that its initial state satisfies the appropriate precondition, **not** *empty*, for *remove* itself.)

Is this going to work? The answer, disappointing in light of the earlier comments about the unpredictability of bugs in concurrent systems, is *maybe*. Between the test for *full* and the call for *put* in the PUT1 variant, or between *remove* and *put* in PUT2, any other client may have interfered and made the buffer full again. This is the same flaw that required us, earlier on, to provide an object reservation mechanism through encapsulation.

We could try encapsulation again by writing PUT1 or PUT2 as a procedure to which *buffer* will be passed as argument, giving for PUT1:

> *put_if_possible* (*b*: *BOUNDED_BUFFER* [*T*]; *x*: *T*) **is**
> > -- Insert *x* into *b* if possible; otherwise set *was_full* to true.
>
> **do**
> > **if** *b*.*full* **then** *was_full*:= *True* **else**
> > > *put* (*b*, *x*); *was_full* := *False*
> >
> > **end**
>
> **end**

But this does not really help me as a client. First, having to check *was_full* on return is a nuisance; then, what do I do if it is true? Try again, probably — but with no more guarantee of result. What I probably want is a way to execute *put* when the buffer is indisputably non-full, even if I have to **wait** for this to be the case.

The precondition paradox

This situation that we have just uncovered is disturbing because it seems to invalidate, in a concurrent context, the basic methodological guideline for getting software right: Design by Contract. With a queue, that is to say in sequential computation, we have been used to precisely defined specifications of mutual obligations and benefits:

put	**OBLIGATIONS**	**BENEFITS**
Client	(***Satisfy precondition***:) Only call *put* (*x*) on a non-full queue.	(***From postcondition***:) Get new, non-empty queue with *x* added.
Supplier	(***Satisfy postcondition***:) Update queue to add *x* and ensure **not** *empty*.	(***From precondition***:) Processing protected by assumption that queue not full.

A contract:
routine put *for*
bounded
queues

(From the
example for stacks
on page 342.)

Implicit behind such contracts is a **no hidden clause** principle: the precondition is the only requirement that a client must satisfy to get served. If you call *put* with a non-full queue, you are entitled to the routine's result, as expressed by the postcondition.

But in a concurrent context, with a separate supplier such as a *BOUNDED_BUFFER*, things are rather distressing for the client: however hard we try to please the supplier by ensuring its stated precondition, we can never be sure to meet its expectations! To execute correctly, however, the suppliers still need the precondition. For example the body of routine *put* in class *BOUNDED_QUEUE* (which is the same as in *BOUNDED_BUFFER*) will most likely not work unless *full* is guaranteed to be false.

To summarize: suppliers cannot do their work without the guarantee that the precondition holds; but for separate arguments the clients are *unable* to ensure these preconditions. This may be called the **concurrent precondition paradox**.

> There is a similar *postcondition* paradox: on return from a separate call to *put*, we cannot any more be sure that **not** *empty* and other postcondition clauses hold for the client. These properties are satisfied just after the routine's termination; but some other client may invalidate them before the caller gets restarted. Because the problem is even more serious for preconditions, which determine the correct execution of suppliers, the rest of the discussion mainly considers preconditions.

The paradoxes only arise for separate formal arguments. For a non-separate argument — in particular for an expanded value such as an integer — we can continue to rely on the usual properties of assertions. But this not much consolation.

Although this has not yet been widely recognized in the literature, the concurrent precondition paradox is one of the central issues of concurrent O-O software construction, and the futility of trying to retain habitual assertion semantics is one of the principal factors distinguishing concurrent computation from its sequential variants.

Exercise E30.6, page 1036.

The precondition paradox may also arise in situations that are not ordinarily thought of as involving concurrency, such as accessing a file. This is explored in an exercise.

The concurrent semantics of preconditions

To resolve the concurrent precondition paradox we assess the situation through three observations:

A1 • Suppliers need the preconditions to protect their routine bodies. Here *put* will never work, in class *BOUNDED_BUFFER* as in *BOUNDED_QUEUE*, unless the routine has the guarantee that on entry the queue is non-full.

A2 • Separate clients cannot rely any more on the usual (sequential) semantics of preconditions. Testing for *full* before calling your buffer supplier gives you no guarantee at all.

A3 • Because each client may be vying with others for resource access, a client may be prepared to wait before it gets its resources — if this guarantees correct processing after the wait.

The conclusion seems inescapable: we still need preconditions, if only for the suppliers' sake, but they must be given a different semantics. Instead of being a *correctness condition*, as in the sequential context, a precondition applying to a separate argument will be a **wait condition**. This will apply to what we may call "separate precondition clauses": any precondition clause involving a call whose target is a separate argument. A typical separate precondition clause is **not** *b.full* for *put*.

Here is the rule:

Separate call semantics

Before it can start executing the routine's body, a separate call must wait until every blocking object is free and every separate precondition clause is satisfied.

In this definition, an object is *blocking* if it is attached to an actual argument, and the routine uses the corresponding formal as the target of at least one call.

A separate object is free if it is not being used as an actual argument of a separate call (implying that no routine is being executed on it).

The rule only causes waiting for separate arguments appearing as call targets somewhere in the routine's body (it uses the word "blocking" for the corresponding objects since they can block the call from proceeding). With a routine of the "business card" form

r (*x*: **separate** *SOME_TYPE*) **is do** *some_attribute* := *x* **end**

or some other scheme that does not contain a call of the form *x*.*some_routine*, there is no need to wait on the actual argument corresponding to *x*.

If there is such a call the short form of the class must reflect it for the benefit of client authors. It will present the routine header as *r* (*x*: **blocking** *SOME_TYPE*)…

With this rule the above version of *put* in a client class achieves the desired result:

put (*b*: *BOUNDED_BUFFER* [*T*]; *x*: *T*) **is**

    require
        not *b*.*full*

    do
        b.put (x)

    ensure
        not *b*.*empty*

    end

A call of the form *put* (*buffer, y*), from a producer client, will wait until *buffer* is free (available) and not full. If *buffer* is free but full, the call cannot be satisfied; but some other client, a consumer, may get access to it (since the precondition of interest to consumers, **not** *b*.*empty*, will be satisfied in this case); after such a client has removed an item, making the buffer non-full, the producer client can now have its call executed.

Which client should the implementation let through if two or more satisfy the conditions of the rule (blocking objects free, preconditions satisfied)? Some people, for fear of overspecifying, prefer to leave such decisions to the compiler, while providing library features allowing an application to specify a particular policy. It seems better to define a default first-in-first-out policy, which enhances portability and helps towards solving the issue of fairness. Library mechanisms can still be available to application writers who wish to override the default.

Be sure to note that the special semantics of preconditions as wait conditions only applies to what we have called separate precondition clauses, that is to say, clauses involving a condition of the form *b*.*some_property* where *b* is a separate argument. A non-separate clause, such as $i >= 0$ where i is an integer, or $b\ /= Void$ even if b is separate (this does not involve a call on b), will keep its usual correctness semantics since the concurrent precondition paradox does not apply in such cases: if the client ensures the stated condition before the call, it will still hold when the routine starts; if the condition does not hold, no amount of waiting would change the situation.

Assertions, sequential and concurrent

The idea that assertions, and in particular preconditions, may have two different semantics — sometimes correctness conditions, sometimes wait conditions — may have surprised you. But there is no way around it: the sequential semantics is inapplicable in the case of separate precondition clauses.

See "Monitoring assertions at run time", page 392.

One possible objection must be answered. We have seen that a mere compilation switch can turn run-time assertion checking on or off. Is it not dangerous, then, to attach that much semantic importance to preconditions in concurrent object-oriented systems? No, it is not. The assertions are an integral part of the software, whether or not they are enabled at run time. Because in a correct sequential system the assertions will always hold, we may turn off assertion checking for efficiency if we think we have removed all the bugs; but conceptually the assertions are still there. With concurrency the only difference is that certain assertions — the separate precondition clauses — may be violated at run time even for a correct system, and serve as wait conditions. So the assertion monitoring options must not apply to these clauses.

A validity constraint

To avert deadlock situations, we need to impose a validity constraint on precondition and postcondition clauses. Assume we permitted routines of the form

```
f (x: SOME_TYPE) is
    require
        some_property (separate_attribute)
    do
        ...
    end
```

where *separate_attribute* is a separate attribute of the enclosing class. Nothing in this example, save *separate_attribute*, need be separate. The evaluation of f's precondition, either as part of assertion monitoring for correctness, or as a synchronization condition if the actual argument corresponding to x in a call is itself separate, could cause blocking if the attached object is not available.

This is not acceptable and is prohibited by the following rule:

As a consequence, the assertion may not appear in a class invariant, which is not part of a routine.

Assertion Argument rule

If an assertion contains a function call, any actual argument of that call must, if separate, be a formal argument of the enclosing routine.

States and transitions

The following figure summarizes some of the preceding discussion by showing the various possible states in which objects and processors may be, and how they will change state as a result of calls.

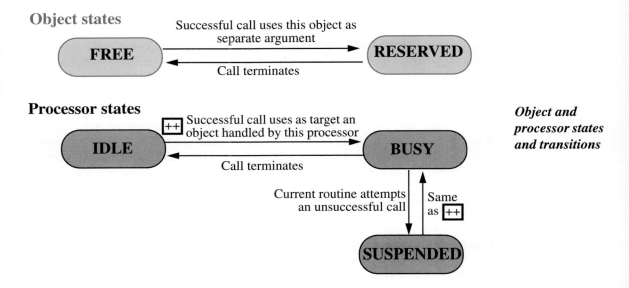

Object and processor states and transitions

A call is *successful* if the handler of its target is idle or suspended, all its non-void separate arguments are attached to free objects, and the corresponding separate precondition clauses, if any, are true. Note that this makes the definitions of object and processor states mutually dependent.

30.8 REQUESTING SPECIAL SERVICE

We have completed the review of the basic communication and synchronization policy. For more flexibility, it is useful to define a few mechanisms that will allow interrupting the normal processing in some cases.

Because these facilities are add-ons intended for convenience, rather than a part of the basic concurrency model, they are available not as language constructs but as library features. We will assume a class *CONCURRENCY*, which classes needing these special mechanisms can inherit. A similar approach has already been used twice in this book:

- To complement the basic exception handling rules when finer control is desired, through the library class *EXCEPTIONS*.

- To complement the default memory management and garbage collection mechanism when finer control is desired, through the library class *MEMORY*.

"ADVANCED EXCEPTION HAN-DLING", 12.6, page 431; "Class MEMORY", page 309.

Express messages

[Yonezawa 1987a]. The ABCL/1 concurrent language introduced the notion of "express message" for when we want to let a supplier object serve a certain VIP client immediately, even though the supplier may be busy with another client.

See "Concurrent accesses to an object", page 982.

The comments on static binding were on page 513.

In some approaches an express message will just interrupt the normal message, get serviced, and then let the normal message be resumed. But this is unacceptable, as we saw earlier in this chapter when we found out that at most one execution should be active on any object at any given time: the express message, like any exported feature, needs an initial state satisfying the invariant; but who knows in what state the interrupted routine will be when it is forced to yield to the express message? And who knows what state the express message will produce as a result? All this opens the way to what the discussion of static binding called "*one of the worst events that could occur during the execution of a software system*": producing an inconsistent object. As we saw then: "*if such a situation can arise, we can no longer hope to predict what execution will do*".

See also "Permitting concurrent access?", page 1031.

This does not mean, however, that we should reject the notion of express message altogether. We may indeed need to interrupt a client — either because we have something more important to do with the object it has reserved, or because it is overextending its welcome to retain it. But such an interruption is not a polite request to step aside for a while. It is *murder*, at least attempted murder. To take our rival's place we shoot at it, so that it will die unless it can recover in the hospital. In software terms, the interrupting client must cause an **exception** in its rival, which will either retry (the hospital) or fail.

Such behavior, however, assumes that the challenger is somehow stronger than the holder. If not, the one that will get an exception is the challenger.

Duels and their semantics

The almost inescapable metaphor suggests that instead of the "express message" terminology we talk about the attempt to snatch a shared object from its current holder as a *duel* (the result, in an earlier era, of trying to snatch away someone's legitimate spouse). An object has executed the instruction

$$r\ (b)$$

where b is separate. After possibly waiting for the object of its desires, b, to become free, and for separate precondition clauses to hold, it has captured b, becoming its current *holder*. The execution of r on b has started on behalf of the holder, but is not finished. Another separate object, the *challenger*, executes

$$s\ (c)$$

where c, also separate, is attached to the same object as the holder's b. Normally, the challenger will wait until the call to r is over. What if the challenger is impatient?

Through procedures in class *CONCURRENCY* we can provide the necessary flexibility. On the holder's side we have *yield*, which means: "I am willing to release my hold if someone more worthy comes along". Most holders, of course, are not so accommodating: unless it makes an explicit call to *yield*, a holder will retain its hold. To return to this default behavior, you may use the procedure *retain.*

On the challenger's side we can use two kinds of request to get special treatment:

- *demand* means "now or never!". If you cannot immediately capture the object of your dreams (that is to say, if the holder has not called *yield*), you will get an exception. (This is the old suicide threat trick, as in *Così fan tutte*.)

- *insist* is more gentle: you try to interrupt the holder's routine, but if that is impossible you accept the common lot — waiting until the object is freed.

To return to the default behavior of waiting for the holder to finish, use *wait_turn*.

A call to one of these *CONCURRENCY* procedures will retain its effect until another supersedes it. Note that the two sets of facilities are not exclusive; for example a challenger could use both *insist* to request special treatment and *yield* to accept being interrupted by another. A priority scheme can be added, so that challengers will only defer to others with higher priorities, but we can ignore this refinement here.

Exercise E30.5, page 1035, asks you to add priorities.

The following table shows the result of a duel — a conflict between a holder and a challenger — in all possible cases. The default options and behavior, in the absence of any call to *CONCURRENCY* procedures, are underlined.

Challenger → **↓ Holder**	*wait_turn*	*demand*	*insist*
retain	Challenger waits	Exception in challenger	Challenger waits
yield	Challenger waits	Exception in holder's routine.	Exception in holder's routine.

The semantics of duels

The "holder's routine" that gets an exception in the two rightmost bottom entries is the supplier routine being executed on behalf of the holder. In the absence of a `retry`, it will pass on the exception to the holder, and the challenger will get the object.

As you will remember, every kind of exception has a code, accessible through class *EXCEPTIONS*. To distinguish an exception caused by one of the situations appearing in the above table, *EXCEPTIONS* provides the boolean query *is_concurrency_interrupt*.

Interrupt handling: the Secretary-Receptionist Algorithm

Here is an example using duels. Assume a certain controller object has started off a number of partner objects, and then proceeds with its own work, which needs a certain resource *shared*. But the other objects may need access to the shared resource, and the controller is willing to interrupt its current task to let any of them proceed; when the partner is done, the controller resumes the last interrupted task.

This general description covers among others the case of an operating system kernel (the controller) which starts off input-output processors (the partners), but does not wait for an I/O operation to complete, since I/O is typically several orders of magnitude slower than computation. When an I/O operation terminates, its processor can interrupt the kernel to request attention. This is the traditional interrupt-driven scheme for handling I/O — and the problem which gave the original impetus, many years ago, to the study of concurrency.

The general scheme may be called the *Secretary-Receptionist Algorithm* by analogy with what you find in many organizations: a receptionist sits near the entrance to greet, register and direct visitors, but this is not a full-time job; the receptionist is also entrusted with some other work, usually secretarial. When a visitor shows up, the receptionist interrupts his work, takes care of the visitor, and then goes back to the interrupted task.

Restarting a task after it has been started and interrupted may require some cleanup; this is why the following procedure passes to *operate* the value of *interrupted*, which will enable *operate* to find out whether the current task has already been attempted. The first argument of *operate*, here *next*, identifies the task to perform. The procedure is assumed to be part of a class that inherits from both *CONCURRENCY* (for *yield* and *retain*) and *EXCEPTIONS* (for *is_concurrency_interrupt*). Procedure *operate* could take a long time to execute, and so is the interruptible part.

```
execute_interruptibly is
            -- Perform own set of actions, but take interrupts
            -- (the Secretary-Receptionist Algorithm).
      local
            done, next: INTEGER; interrupted: BOOLEAN
      do
            from done := 0 until termination_criterion loop
                  if interrupted then
                        process_interruption (shared); interrupted := False
                  else
                        next := done + 1; yield
                        operate (next, shared, interrupted)-- This is the interruptible part.
                        retain; done := next
                  end
            end
      rescue
            if is_concurrency_interrupt then
                  interrupted := True; retry
            end
      end
```

Some of the steps performed by the controller may actually have been requested by one of the interrupting partners. In an I/O interrupt, for example, the I/O processor will signal the end of an operation and (in the input case) the availability of the data just read.

The interrupting partner may use the object *shared* to deposit that information; to interrupt the controller, it will execute

> *insist*; *interrupt* (*shared*); *wait_turn*
> > -- Request controller's attention, interrupting it if necessary.
> > -- Deposit any needed information into the object *shared*.

This is the reason why *process_interruption*, like *operate*, uses *shared* as argument: it may have to analyze the *shared* object to detect information passed by the interrupting partner. This will allow it, if necessary, to set up one of its upcoming tasks, to be executed on behalf of that partner. Note that *process_interruption*, unlike *operate*, is not interruptible; any other partner that becomes ready while it is executing will have to wait (otherwise some partner requests might get lost). So *process_interruption* should only perform simple operations — registering information for future processing. If that is not possible, you may use a slightly different scheme in which *process_interruption* relies on a separate object other than *shared*.

We have one more precaution to take. Although partners' requests can be processed later (through calls to *operate* in upcoming steps), it is essential that none of these requests be lost. With the scheme as given, after a partner executes an *interrupt*, another one could do the same, overriding the information deposited by the first, before the controller has had the time to register that information by executing *process_interruption*. This case is not acceptable. To avoid it, we can just add to the generating class of *shared* a boolean attribute *deposited* with the associated setting and resetting procedures. Then *interrupt* will have the precondition **not** *shared.deposited*, so as to wait until the previous partner has been registered, and will execute the call *shared.set_deposited* before returning; *process_interruption* will execute *shared.set_not_deposited* before exiting.

The partners are initialized by "business card" calls of the form !! *partner.make* (*shared, ...*) which pass them a reference to *shared* to be retained for future needs.

> Procedure *execute_interruptibly* has been spelled out in full, with the application-specific elements represented by calls to routines *operate*, *process_interruption*, *termination_criterion* that are assumed to be deferred, in the behavior class style. This prepares for the procedure's possible inclusion into a concurrency library.

About the rest of this chapter

With the presentation of the duel mechanism we have finished defining the set of necessary concurrency tools. The rest of this chapter provides an extensive set of examples, from diverse application areas, illustrating the use of these tools. After the examples you will find:

30.9 EXAMPLES

To illustrate the mechanism, here now are a few examples chosen from diverse backgrounds — from traditional concurrent programming examples through large-scale multiprocessing to real-time applications.

The dining philosophers

The philosophers' spaghetti plate

Dijkstra's famous "dining philosophers", an artificial example meant to illustrate the behavior of operating system processes vying for shared resources, is an obligatory part of any discussion on concurrency. Five philosophers around a table spend their time thinking, then eating, then thinking again and so on. To eat the spaghetti, each needs access to the fork immediately to his left and to his right — creating contention and possible deadlock.

*The class is definitely **not** what people mean by "spaghetti code".*

The following class describes the philosopher's behavior. Thanks to the mechanism for reserving objects through separate arguments, there is essentially (in contrast with the usual solutions in the literature) no explicit synchronization code:

separate class *PHILOSOPHER* **creation**

    make

inherit

    GENERAL_PHILOSOPHER
    PROCESS
        rename *setup* **as** *getup* **undefine** *getup* **end**

feature {*BUTLER*}

    step **is**

        -- Perform a philosopher's tasks.

      do

        think

        eat (*left*, *right*)   ◄─────────── (The synchronization)

      end

feature {*NONE*}

    eat (*l*, *r*: **separate** *FORK*) **is**

        -- Eat, having grabbed *l* and *r*.

      do ... **end**

end -- class *PHILOSOPHER*

The entire synchronization requirement is embodied by the call to *eat*, which uses arguments *left* and *right* representing the two necessary forks, thus reserving these objects.

The simplicity of this solution comes from the mechanism's ability to reserve several resources through a single call having several separate arguments, here *left* and *right*. If we restricted the separate arguments to at most one per call, the solution would use one of the many published algorithms for getting hold of two forks one after the other without causing deadlock.

The principal procedure of class *PHILOSOPHER* does not appear above since it comes from the behavior class *PROCESS*: procedure *live*, which as given in *PROCESS* simply executes **from** *setup* **until** *over* **loop** *step* **end**, so all we need to redefine here is *step*. I hope you will enjoy the renaming of *setup* as *getup* — denoting the philosopher's initial operation.

Class PROCESS appeared on page 961. wrapup remains an empty procedure.

Thanks to the use of multiple object reservation through arguments, the solution described here does not produce deadlock; but it is not guaranteed to be fair. Some of the philosophers can conspire to starve the others. Here too the literature provides various solutions, which may be integrated into the above scheme.

To avoid confusion of genres the concurrency-independent features of a philosopher have been kept in a class *GENERAL_PHILOSOPHER*:

class *GENERAL_PHILOSOPHER* **creation**
   make

feature -- Initialization

   make (*l*, *r*: **separate** *FORK*) **is**
         -- Define *l* as left and *r* as right forks.
     do
       left := *l*; *right* := *r*
     end

feature {*NONE*} -- Implementation

   left, *right*: **separate** *FORK*
       -- The two required forks

   getup **is**
       -- Take any necessary initialization action.
     do ... **end**

   think **is**
       -- Any appropriate action or lack thereof.
     do ... **end**

end -- class *GENERAL_PHILOSOPHER*

The rest of the system simply takes care of initialization and of describing the auxiliary abstractions. Forks have no immediately relevant properties:

class *FORK* **end**

A butler is used to set up and start a session:

class *BUTLER* **creation**
   make

feature

   count: *INTEGER*
       -- The number of both philosophers and forks

   launch **is**
       -- Start a full session.
     local
       i: *INTEGER*
     do
       from *i* := *1* **until** *i* > *count* **loop**
         launch_one (*participants* @ *i*); *i* := *i* + *1*
       end
     end

feature {*NONE*}

    launch_one (*p*: *PHILOSOPHER*) **is**
             -- Let one philosopher start his actual life.
      do
          p•*live*
      end

    participants: *ARRAY* [*PHILOSOPHER*]

    cutlery: *ARRAY* [*FORK*]

feature {*NONE*} -- Initialization

    make (*n*: *INTEGER*) **is**
             -- Initialize a session with *n* philosophers.
      require
         n >= *0*
      do
         count := *n*
         !! *participants*•*make* (*1*, *count*); !! *cutlery*•*make* (*1*, *count*)
         make_philosophers
      ensure
         count = *n*
      end

    make_philosophers **is**
             -- Set up philosophers.
      local
         i: *INTEGER*; *p*: *PHILOSOPHER*; *left*, *right*: *FORK*
      do
         from *i* := *1* **until** *i* > *count* **loop**
            p := *philosophers* @ *i*
            left := *cutlery* @ *i*
            right := *cutlery* @ ((*i* \\ *count*) + *1*)
            !! *p*•*make* (*left*, *right*)
            i := *i* + *1*
         end
      end

invariant

    count >= *0*; *participants*•*count* = *count*; *cutlery*•*count* = *count*

end

Note how *launch* and *launch_one*, using a pattern discussed in the presentation of wait by necessity, rely on the property that the call *p*•*live* will not cause waiting, allowing the loop to proceed to the next philosopher.

See "A multi-launcher", page 988.

Making full use of hardware parallelism

The following example illustrates how to use wait by necessity to draw the maximum benefit from any available hardware parallelism. It shows a sophisticated form of *load balancing* in which we offload computation to many different computers on a network. Thanks to the notion of processor, we can rely on the concurrency mechanism to choose these computers automatically for us.

The example itself — computing the number of nodes in a binary tree — is of little practical value, but illustrates a general scheme that may be extremely useful for large, heavy computations such as those encountered in cryptography or advanced computer graphics, for which developers need all the resources they can get, but do not want to have to take care manually of the assignment of abstract computing units to actual computers.

Consider first a class extract that does not involve concurrency:

class *BINARY_TREE* [*G*] **feature**

> *left, right*: *BINARY_TREE* [*G*]

> … Other features …

> *nodes*: *INTEGER* **is**

> > -- Number of nodes in this tree

> > **do**

> > > *Result* := *node_count* (*left*) + *node_count* (*right*) + *1*

> > **end**

feature {*NONE*}

> *node_count* (*b*: *BINARY_TREE* [*G*]): *INTEGER* **is**

> > -- Number of nodes in *b*

> > **do**

> > > **if** *b* /= *Void* **then** *Result* := *b*•*nodes* **end**

> > **end**

end -- class *BINARY_TREE*

Function *nodes* uses recursion to compute the number of nodes in a tree. The recursion is indirect, through *node_count*.

In a concurrent environment offering many processors, we could offload all the separate node computations to different processors. Declaring the class as **separate**, replacing *nodes* by an attribute and introducing procedures does the job:

```
separate class BINARY_TREE1 [G] feature
        left, right: BINARY_TREE1 [G]
        … Other features …
        nodes: INTEGER
        update_nodes is
                -- Update nodes to reflect the number of nodes in this tree.
            do
                nodes := 1
                compute_nodes (left); compute_nodes (right)
                adjust_nodes (left); adjust_nodes (right)
            end
feature {NONE}
        compute_nodes (b: BINARY_TREE1 [G]) is
                -- Update information about the number of nodes in b.
            do
                if b /= Void then
                        b.update_nodes
                end
            end
        adjust_nodes (b: BINARY_TREE1 [G]) is
                -- Adjust number of nodes from those in b.
            do
                if b /= Void then nodes := nodes + b.nodes end
            end
end -- class BINARY_TREE1
```

The recursive calls to *compute_nodes* will now be started in parallel. The addition operations wait for these two parallel computations to complete.

If an unbounded number of CPUs (physical processors) are available, this solution seems to make the optimal possible use of the hardware parallelism. If there are fewer CPUs than nodes in the tree, the speedup over sequential computation will depend on how well the implementation allocates CPUs to the (virtual) processors.

The presence of two tests for vacuity of *b* may appear unpleasant. It results, however, from the need to separate the parallelizable part — the procedure calls, launched concurrently on *left* and *right* — from the additions, which by nature must wait for their operands to become ready.

On how to specify the mapping see "Mapping the processors: the Concurrency Control File", page 971.

An attractive property of the solution is that it ignores the practical problem of assigning the actual computers. The software just allocates processors as it needs to. (This is done in the creation instructions, not shown, which will appear in particular in the insertion procedure: to insert a new element into a binary tree you create a new node through !! *new_node.make* (*new_element*) which here, *new_node* being of the separate type *BINARY_TREE1*[*G*], will allocate a new processor to it.) The mapping of these virtual processors to the available physical resources is entirely automatic.

Locks

Assume you want to allow a number of clients (the "lockers") to obtain exclusive access to certain resources (the "lockables") without having to enclose the exclusive access sections in routines. This will provide us with a semaphore-like mechanism. Here is a solution:

```
class LOCKER feature
    grab (resource: separate LOCKABLE) is
            -- Request exclusive access to resource.
        require
            not resource.locked
        do
            resource.set_holder (Current)
        end
    release (resource: separate LOCKABLE) is
        require
            resource.is_held (Current)
        do
            resource.release
        end
end

class LOCKABLE feature {LOCKER}
    set_holder (l: separate LOCKER) is
            -- Designate l as holder.
        require
            l /= Void
        do
            holder := l
        ensure
            locked
        end
    locked: BOOLEAN is
            -- Is resource reserved by a locker?
        do
            Result := (holder /= Void)
        end
```

> *is_held* (*l*: **separate** *LOCKER*): *BOOLEAN* **is**
>> -- Is resource reserved by *l*?
>
> **do**
>> *Result* := (*holder* = *l*)
>
> **end**
>
> *release* **is**
>> -- Release from current holder.
>
> **do**
>> *holder* := *Void*
>
> **ensure**
>> **not** *locked*
>
> **end**

feature {*NONE*}

> *holder*: **separate** *LOCKER*

invariant
> *locked_iff_holder*: *locked* = (*holder* /= *Void*)

end

Any class describing resources will inherit from *LOCKABLE*. The proper functioning of the mechanism assumes that every locker performs sequences of *grab* and *release* operations, in this order. Other behavior will usually result in deadlock; this problem was mentioned in the discussion of semaphores as one of the major limitations of this technique. But we can once again rely on the power of object-oriented computation to enforce the required protocol; rather than trusting every locker to behave, we may require lockers to go through procedure *use* in descendants of the following behavior class:

deferred class *LOCKING_PROCESS* **feature**

> *resource*: **separate** *LOCKABLE*
>
> *use* **is**
>> -- Make disciplined use of *resource*.
>
> **require**
>> *resource* /= *Void*
>
> **do**
>> **from** !! *lock*; *setup* **until** *over* **loop**
>>> *lock*•*grab* (*resource*)
>>> *exclusive_actions*
>>> *lock*•*release* (*resource*)
>>
>> **end**
>> *finalize*
>
> **end**

```
set_resource (r: separate LOCKABLE) is
        -- Select r as resource for use.
    require
        r /= Void
    do
        resource := r
    ensure
        resource /= Void
    end
feature {NONE}
    lock: LOCKER

    exclusive_actions
            -- Operations executed while resource is under exclusive access
        deferred
        end

    setup
            -- Initial action; by default: do nothing.
        do
        end

    over: BOOLEAN is
            -- Is locking behavior finished?
        deferred
        end

    finalize
            -- Final action; by default: do nothing.
        do
        end
end -- class LOCKING_PROCESS
```

Exercise E30.7, page 1036.

An effective descendant of *LOCKING_PROCESS* will effect *exclusive_actions* and *over*, and may redefine *setup* and *finalize*. Note that it is desirable to write *LOCKING_PROCESS* as a descendant of *PROCESS*.

Whether or not we go through *LOCKING_PROCESS*, a *grab* does not take away the corresponding lockable from all possible clients: it only excludes other lockers that observe the protocol. To exclude any client from accessing a resource, you must enclose the operations accessing the resource in a routine to which you pass it as an argument.

Routine *grab* of class *LOCKER* is an example of what has been called the business card scheme: passing to *resource* a reference to the *Current* locker, which the resource will keep as a separate reference.

Exercise E30.7, page 1036.

Based on the pattern provided by these classes, it is not difficult to write others implementing semaphores under their various forms. Object-oriented mechanisms help us help users of our classes avoid the classic danger of semaphores: executing a *reserve* on a resource and forgetting to execute the corresponding *free*. A developer using a behavior class such as *LOCKING_PROCESS* will fill in the deferred operations to cover the needs of his application, and can rely on the predefined general scheme to guarantee that each *reserve* will be properly followed by the corresponding *free*.

Coroutines

Although not truly concurrent, at least not in its basic form, our next example is essential as a way to test the general applicability of a concurrent mechanism.

> The first (and probably the only) major programming language to include a coroutine construct was also the first object-oriented language, Simula 67; we will study its coroutine mechanism as part of the presentation of Simula. That discussion will also present some examples of the practical use of coroutines.

"Coroutine concepts", page 1118 (in the Simula chapter). The **resume** *instruction comes from Simula.*

Coroutines emulate concurrency on a sequential computer. They provide a form of program unit that, although similar to the traditional notion of routine, reflects a more symmetric form of communication:

- With a routine call, there is a master and a slave; the caller starts a routine, waits for its termination, and picks up where it left; the routine, however, always starts from the beginning. The caller *calls*; the routine *returns*.

- With coroutines, the relationship is between peers; coroutine *a* gets stuck in its work and calls coroutine *b* for help; *b* restarts where it last left, and continues until it is its turn to get stuck or it has proceeded as far as needed for the moment; then *a* picks up its computation. Instead of separate call and return mechanisms, there is a single operation **resume** *c*, meaning: restart coroutine *c* where it was last interrupted; I will wait until someone else **resume**s me.

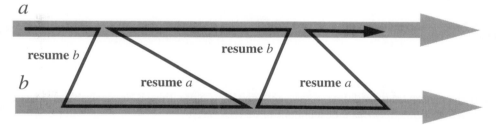

Coroutine sequencing

This is all strictly sequential and meant to be executed on a single process (task) of a single computer. But the ideas are clearly drawn from concurrent computation; in fact an operating system running on a single CPU will internally use a coroutine-like mechanism to implement such schemes as time-sharing, multitasking and multithreading.

Coroutines may be viewed as a boundary case of concurrency: the poor man's substitute to concurrent computation when only one thread of control is available. It is always a good idea to check that a general-purpose mechanism degrades gracefully to boundary cases; so let us see how we can represent coroutines. The following two classes will achieve this goal.

separate class *COROUTINE* **creation**

    make

feature {*COROUTINE*}

    resume (*i*: *INTEGER*) **is**

        -- Wake up coroutine of identifier *i* and go to sleep.

      do

        actual_resume (*i*, *controller*)

      end

feature {*NONE*} -- Implementation

    controller: *COROUTINE_CONTROLLER*

    identifier: *INTEGER*

    actual_resume (*i*: *INTEGER*; *c*: *COROUTINE_CONTROLLER*) **is**

        -- Wake up coroutine of identifier *i* and go to sleep.

        -- (Actual work of *resume*).

      do

        c•*set_next* (*i*); *request* (*c*)

      end

    request (*c*: *COROUTINE_CONTROLLER*) **is**

        -- Request eventual re-awakening by *c*.

      require

        c•*is_next* (*identifier*)

      do

        -- No action necessary

      end

feature {*NONE*} -- Creation

    make (*i*: *INTEGER*; *c*: *COROUTINE_CONTROLLER*) **is**

        -- Assign *i* as identifier and *c* as controller.

      do

        identifier := *i*

        controller := *c*

      end

end -- class *COROUTINE*

separate class *COROUTINE_CONTROLLER* **feature** {*NONE*}

    next: *INTEGER*

feature {*COROUTINE*}

    set_next (*i*: *INTEGER*) **is**

        -- Select *i* as the identifier of the next coroutine to be awakened.

      do

        next := *i*

      end

    is_next (*i*: *INTEGER*): *BOOLEAN* **is**

        -- Is *i* the index of the next coroutine to be awakened?

      do

        Result := (*next* = *i*)

      end

end -- class *COROUTINE_CONTROLLER*

One or more coroutines will share one coroutine controller (created through a "once" function not shown here). Each coroutine has an integer identifier. To resume a coroutine of identifier *i*, procedure *resume* will, through *actual_resume*, set the *next* attribute of the controller to *i*, and then block, waiting on the precondition *next* = *j*, where *j* is the coroutine's own identifier. This ensures the desired behavior.

Exercise E30.10, page 1036.

Although it looks like normal concurrent software, this solution ensures that (if all coroutines have different identifiers) at most one coroutine may proceed at any time, making it useless to allocate more than one physical CPU. (The controller could actually make use of its own CPU, but its actions are so simple as not to warrant it.)

The recourse to integer identifiers is necessary since giving *resume* an argument of type *COROUTINE*, a separate type, would cause deadlock. In practice, you should probably use **unique** declarations to avoid having to choose the values manually. This use of integers also has an interesting consequence: if we allow two or more coroutines to have the same identifier, then with a single CPU we obtain a **non-deterministic** mechanism: a call *resume* (*i*) will permit restarting any coroutine whose identifier has value *i*. With more than one CPU a call *resume* (*i*) will allow all coroutines of identifier *i* to proceed in parallel.

So the above scheme, which for a single CPU provides a coroutine mechanism, doubles up in the case of several CPUs as a mechanism for controlling the maximum number of processes of a certain type which may be simultaneously active.

An elevator control system

The following example shows a case where object technology and the mechanism defined in this chapter can be used to achieve a pleasantly decentralized event-driven architecture for a real-time application.

The example describes software for an elevator control system, with several elevators serving many floors. The design below is somewhat fanatically object-oriented in that every significant type of component in the physical system — for example the

Milner quote: page 956. notion of individual button in an elevator cabin, marked with a floor number — has an associated separate class, so that each corresponding object such as a button has its own virtual thread of control (processor). This is getting close to Milner's wish, quoted at the beginning of this chapter, of making all objects parallel. The benefit is that the system is entirely event-driven; it does not need to include any loop for examining repeatedly the status of objects, for example whether any button has been pressed.

The class texts below are only sketched, but provide a good idea of what a complete solution would be. In most cases the creation procedures have not been included.

> This implementation of the elevator example, adapted to control elevator displays on multiple screens and computers across the Internet (rather than actual elevators), has been used at several conferences to demonstrate concurrent and distributed O-O mechanisms.

Class *MOTOR* describes the motor associated with one elevator cabin, and the interface with the mechanical hardware:

separate class *MOTOR* **feature** {*ELEVATOR*}
    move (*floor*: *INTEGER*) **is**
        -- Go to *floor*; once there, report.
    do
        "Direct the physical device to move to *floor*"
        signal_stopped (*cabin*)
    end
    signal_stopped (*e*: *ELEVATOR*) **is**
        -- Report that elevator stopped on level *e*.
    do
        e•*record_stop* (*position*)
    end
feature {*NONE*}
    cabin: *ELEVATOR*
    position: *INTEGER* **is**
        -- Current floor level
    do
        Result := "The current floor level, read from physical sensors"
    end
end

The creation procedure of this class must associate an elevator, *cabin*, with every motor. Class *ELEVATOR* includes the reverse information through attribute *puller*, indicating the motor pulling the current elevator.

The reason for making an elevator and its motor separate objects is to reduce the grain of locking: once an elevator has sent a *move* request to its motor, it is free again, thanks to the wait by necessity policy, to accept requests from buttons either inside or outside the cabin. It will resynchronize with its motor upon receipt of a call to procedure *record_stop*, through *signal_stopped*. Only for a very short time will an instance of *ELEVATOR* be reserved by a call from either a *MOTOR* or *BUTTON* object

separate class *ELEVATOR* **creation**
    make

feature {*BUTTON*}

    accept (*floor*: *INTEGER*) **is**
          -- Record and process a request to go to *floor*.
      do
          record (*floor*)
          if not *moving* **then** *process_request* **end**
      end

feature {*MOTOR*}

    record_stop (*floor*: *INTEGER*) **is**
          -- Record information that elevator has stopped on *floor*.
      do
          moving := **false**; *position* := *floor*; *process_request*
      end

feature {*DISPATCHER*}

    position: *INTEGER*

    moving: *BOOLEAN*

feature {*NONE*}

    puller: *MOTOR*

    pending: *QUEUE* [*INTEGER*]
          -- The queue of pending requests
          -- (each identified by the number of the destination floor)

    record (*floor*: *INTEGER*) **is**
          -- Record request to go to *floor*.
      do
          "Algorithm to insert request for floor into pending"
      end

    process_request **is**
          -- Handle next pending request, if any.
      local
          floor: *INTEGER*
      do
          if not *pending*.*empty* **then**
              floor := *pending*.*item*
              actual_process (*puller*, *floor*)
              pending.*remove*
          end
      end

> *actual_process* (*m*: **separate** *MOTOR*; *floor*: *INTEGER*) **is**
>
> > -- Direct *m* to go to *floor*.
>
> **do**
>
> > *moving* := *True*; *m•move* (*floor*)
>
> **end**

end

Buttons are of two kinds: floor buttons, which passengers press to call the elevator to a certain floor, and cabin buttons, inside a cabin, which they press to make the cabin move to a certain floor. The two kinds send different requests: for a cabin button, the request is directed to a specific cabin; for a floor button, it can be handled by any elevator and so will be sent to a dispatcher object, which will poll the various elevators to select one that will handle the request. (The selection algorithm is left unimplemented below since it is irrelevant to this discussion; the same applies to the algorithm used by elevators to manage their *pending* queue of requests in class *ELEVATOR* above.)

Class *FLOOR_BUTTON* assumes that there is only one button on each floor. It is not difficult to update the design to support two buttons, one for up requests and the other for down requests.

It is convenient although not essential to have a common parent *BUTTON* for the classes representing the two kinds of button. Remember that the features exported by *ELEVATOR* to *BUTTON* are, through the standard rules of selective information hiding, also exported to the two descendants of this class.

separate class *BUTTON* **feature**

> *target*: *INTEGER*

end

separate class *CABIN_BUTTON* **inherit** *BUTTON* **feature**

> *cabin*: *ELEVATOR*
>
> *request* **is**
>
> > -- Send to associated elevator a request to stop on level *target*.
>
> **do**
>
> > *actual_request* (*cabin*)
>
> **end**
>
> *actual_request* (*e*: *ELEVATOR*) **is**
>
> > -- Get hold of *e* and send a request to stop on level *target*.
>
> **do**
>
> > *e•accept* (*target*)
>
> **end**

end

separate class *FLOOR_BUTTON* **inherit**

> *BUTTON*

feature

> *controller*: *DISPATCHER*
>
> *request* **is**
>
>> -- Send to dispatcher a request to stop on level *target*.
>>
>> **do**
>>
>>> *actual_request* (*controller*)
>>
>> **end**
>
> *actual_request* (*d*: *DISPATCHER*) **is**
>
>> -- Send to *d* a request to stop on level *target*.
>>
>> **do**
>>
>>> *d.accept* (*target*)
>>
>> **end**

end

The question of switching button lights on and off has been ignored. It is not hard to add calls to routines which will take care of this.

Here finally is class *DISPATCHER*. To develop the algorithm that selects an elevator in procedure *accept*, you would need to let it access the attributes *position* and *moving* of class *ELEVATOR*, which in the full system should be complemented by a boolean attribute *going_up*. Such accesses will not cause any problem as the design ensures that *ELEVATOR* objects never get reserved for a long time.

separate class *DISPATCHER* **creation**

> *make*

feature {*FLOOR_BUTTON*}

> *accept* (*floor*: *INTEGER*) **is**
>
>> -- Handle a request to send an elevator to *floor*.
>>
>> **local**
>>
>>> *index*: *INTEGER*; *chosen*: *ELEVATOR*
>>
>> **do**
>>
>>> "Algorithm to determine what elevator should handle the
>>>   request for *floor*"
>>>
>>> *index* := "The index of the chosen elevator"
>>>
>>> *chosen* := *elevators* @ *index*
>>>
>>> *send_request* (*chosen*, *floor*)
>>
>> **end**

feature {*NONE*}

> *send_request* (*e*: *ELEVATOR*; *floor*: *INTEGER*) **is**
> > -- Send to *e* a request to go to *floor*.
>
> **do**
> > *e*.*accept* (*floor*)
>
> **end**

> *elevators*: *ARRAY* [*ELEVATOR*]

feature {*NONE*} -- Creation

> *make* **is**
> > -- Set up the array of elevators.
>
> **do**
> > "Initialize array elevators"
>
> **end**

end

A watchdog mechanism

Along with the previous one, the following example shows the mechanism's applicability to real-time problems. It also provides a good illustration of the concept of duel.

We want to enable an object to perform a call to a certain procedure *action*, with the provision that the call will be interrupted, and a boolean attribute *failed* set to true, if the procedure has not completed its execution after *t* seconds. The only basic timing mechanism available is a procedure *wait* (*t*), which will execute for *t* seconds.

Here is the solution, using a duel. A class that needs the mechanism should inherit from the behavior class *TIMED* and provide an effective version of the procedure *action* which, in *TIMED*, is deferred. To let *action* execute for at most *t* seconds, it suffices to call *timed_action* (*t*). This procedure sets up a watchdog (an instance of class *WATCHDOG*), which executes *wait* (*t*) and then interrupts its client. If, however, *action* has been completed in the meantime, it is the client that interrupts the watchdog.

> **deferred class** *TIMED* **inherit**
> > *CONCURRENCY*
>
> feature {*NONE*}

> > *failed*: *BOOLEAN*; *alarm*: *WATCHDOG*

All routines with an argument t: REAL need the precondition t >= 0, omitted for brevity.

> > *timed_action* (*t*: *REAL*) **is**
> > > -- Execute action, but interrupt after *t* seconds if not complete.
> > > -- If interrupted before completion, set *failed* to true.
> >
> > **do**
> > > *set_alarm* (*t*); *unset_alarm* (*t*); *failed* := *False*
> >
> > **rescue**
> > > **if** *is_concurrency_interrupt* **then** *failed* := *True* **end**
> >
> > **end**

set_alarm (*t*: *REAL*) **is**
-- Set alarm to interrupt current object after *t* seconds.
do
-- Create alarm if necessary:
if *alarm* = *Void* **then** !! *alarm* **end**
yield; *actual_set* (*alarm*, *t*); *retain*
end

unset_alarm (*t*: *REAL*) **is**
-- Remove the last alarm set.
do
demand; *actual_unset* (*alarm*); *wait_turn*
end

action **is**
-- The action to be performed under watchdog control
deferred
end

feature {*NONE*} -- Actual access to watchdog

actual_set (*a*: *WATCHDOG*; *t*: *REAL*) **is**
-- Start up *a* to interrupt current object after *t* seconds.
do
a.*set* (*t*)
end

… Procedure *actual_unset* similar, left to the reader …

feature {*WATCHDOG*} -- The interrupting operation

stop **is**
-- Empty action to let watchdog interrupt a call to *timed_action*
do -- Nothing **end**

end -- class *TIMED*

separate class
    WATCHDOG
feature {*TIMED*}
    set (*caller*: **separate** *TIMED*; *t*: *REAL*) **is**
        -- After *t* seconds, interrupt *caller*;
        -- if interrupted before, terminate silently.
    require
        caller_exists: *caller* /= *Void*
    local
        interrupted: *BOOLEAN*
    do
        if not *interrupted* **then** *wait* (*t*); *demand*; *caller*. *stop*; *wait_turn* **end**
    rescue
        if *is_concurrency_interrupt* **then** *interrupted* := *True*; **retry end**
    end

See exercise E30.13, page 1036, about this procedure and the Business Card principle.

unset **is**

-- Remove alarm (empty action to let client interrupt *set*).

do -- Nothing **end**

feature {*NONE*}

early_termination: *BOOLEAN*

end -- class *WATCHDOG*

For clarity and to avoid mistakes every use of *retain* should, as here, include also the following *retain*, in the form *yield*; "Some call"; *retain*. Every use of *demand* (or *insist*) should similarly be of the form *demand*; "Some call"; *wait_turn*. You can use behavior classes to enforce this rule.

Accessing buffers

As a last example, let us wrap up the example of bounded buffers used several times in the presentation of the mechanism. We have seen that the class could be declared as just **separate class** *BOUNDED_BUFFER* [*G*] **inherit** *BOUNDED_QUEUE* [*G*] **end**, assuming the proper sequential *BOUNDED_QUEUE* class.

To use a call such as *q•remove* on an entity *q* of type *BOUNDED_BUFFER* [*T*], you must enclose it in a routine using *q* as formal argument. It may be useful for that purpose to provide a class *BUFFER_ACCESS* that fully encapsulates the notion of bounded buffer; application classes may inherit from *BUFFER_ACCESS*. There is nothing difficult about this behavior class, but it provides a good example of how we can encapsulate separate classes, directly derived from sequential ones such as *BOUNDED_QUEUE*, so as to facilitate their direct uses by concurrent applications.

indexing

description: *"Encapsulation of access to bounded buffers"*

class *BUFFER_ACCESS* [*G*] **is**

put (*q*: *BOUNDED_BUFFER* [*G*]; *x*: *G*) **is**

-- Insert *x* into *q*, waiting if necessary until there is room.

require

not *q•full*

do

q•put (*x*)

ensure

not *q•empty*

end

> *remove* (*q*: *BOUNDED_BUFFER* [*G*]) **is**
>> -- Remove an element from *q*, waiting if necessary
>> -- until there is such an element.
>
>> **require**
>>> **not** *q*.*empty*
>>
>> **do**
>>> *q*.*remove*
>>
>> **ensure**
>>> **not** *q*.*full*
>>
>> **end**
>
> *item* (*q*: *BOUNDED_BUFFER* [*G*]): *G* **is**
>> -- *Oldest element not yet consumed*
>
>> **require**
>>> **not** *q*.*empty*
>>
>> **do**
>>> *Result* := *q*.*item*
>>
>> **ensure**
>>> **not** *q*.*full*
>>
>> **end**

end

30.10 TOWARDS A PROOF RULE

(This section is for mathematically-inclined readers only. Although you may understand the basic ideas without having had a formal exposure to the theory of programming languages, full understanding requires that you be familiar with the basics of that theory, as given for example in [M 1990], whose notations will be used here.)

On first reading you may move to "DIS-CUSSION", 30.12, page 1028.

The basic mathematical property of sequential object-oriented computation was given semi-formally in the discussion of Design by Contract:

> {*INV* **and** *pre*} *body* {*INV* **and** *post*}

where *pre*, *post* and *body* are the precondition, postcondition and body of a routine, and *INV* is the class invariant. With suitable axiomatization of the basic instructions this could serve as the basis of a fully formal axiomatic semantics for object-oriented software.

Without going that far, let us express the property more rigorously in the form of a proof rule for calls. Such a rule is fundamental for a mathematical study of O-O software since the heart of object-oriented computation — whether sequential as before, or concurrent as we are now able to achieve — is operations of the form

> *t*.*f* (..., *a*, ...)

which call a feature *f*, possibly with arguments such as *a*, on a target *t* representing an object. The proof rule for the sequential case may be informally stated as follows:

The basic sequential proof technique

> If we can prove that the body of f, started in a state satisfying the precondition of f, terminates in a state satisfying the postcondition, then we can deduce the same property for the above call, with actual arguments such as a substituted for the corresponding formal arguments, and every non-qualified call in the assertions (of the form *some_boolean_property*) replaced by the corresponding property on t (of the form $t.some\_boolean\_property$).

For example, if we are able to prove that the actual implementation of *put* in class *BOUNDED_QUEUE*, assuming **not** *full* initially, produces a state satisfying **not** *empty*, then for any queue q and element a the rule allows us to deduce

$$\{\textbf{not } q.full\} \; q.put \, (x) \; \{\textbf{not } q.empty\}$$

More formally, we may express the basic proof rule as an adaptation to the object-oriented form of computation of Hoare's procedure proof rule:

$$\frac{\left\{INV \wedge \bigwedge_{p \,\in\, Pre \,(r)} p \right\} \; Body \,(r) \; \left\{INV \wedge \bigwedge_{q \,\in\, Post \,(r)} q \right\}}{\left\{ \bigwedge_{p \,\in\, Pre \,(r)} p' \right\} \; Call \,(r) \; \left\{ \bigwedge_{q \,\in\, Post \,(r)} q' \right\}}$$

Here *INV* is the class invariant, *Pre* (f) is the set of precondition clauses of f and *Post* (f) the set of its postcondition clauses. Recall that an assertion is the conjunction of a set of clauses, of the form

$$clause_1; \; \ldots; \; clause_n$$

The large "and" signs $\bigwedge$ indicate conjunction of all the clauses. The actual arguments of f have not been explicitly included in the call, but the primed expressions such as $t.q'$ indicate substitution of the call's actual arguments for the formal arguments of f.

> In the interest of conciseness, the rule is stated above in the form which does not support proofs of recursive routines. Adding such support, however, does not affect the present discussion. For details of how to handle recursion, see [M 1990].

The reason for considering the assertion clauses separately and then "anding" them is that this form prepares the rule's adaptation, described next, to separate calls in the concurrent case. Also of interest as preparation for the concurrent version is that you must take the invariant *INV* into account in the proof of the routine body (above the line), without any visible benefit for the proof of the call (below the line). More assertions with that property will appear in the concurrent rule.

What then changes with concurrency? Waiting on a precondition clause occurs only for a precondition of the form $t.cond$, where t is a formal argument of the enclosing routine, and is separate. In a routine of the form

$f(\ldots, a{:}\ T, \ldots)$ **is**

   require

      $clause1;\ clause2;\ \ldots$

   do

      $\ldots$

   end

any of the precondition clauses not involving any separate call on a separate formal argument is a correctness condition: any client must ensure that condition prior to any call, otherwise the call is in error. Any precondition clause involving a call of the form $a\bullet some\_$ $condition$, where a is a separate formal argument, is a wait condition which will cause calls to block if it is not satisfied.

These observations may be expressed as a proof rule which, for separate computation, replaces the preceding sequential rule:

$$\dfrac{\{INV \wedge \bigwedge_{p \in Pre\,(r)} p\ \}\ Body\,(r)\ \{INV \wedge \bigwedge_{q \in Post\,(r)} q\ \}}{\{\bigwedge_{p \in Nonsep\_Pre\,(r)} p'\ \}\ Call\,(r)\ \{\bigwedge_{q \in Nonsep\_Post\,(r)} q'\ \}}$$

where $Nonsep\_pre\ (f)$ is the set of clauses in f's precondition which do not involve any separate calls, and similarly for $Nonsep\_post\ (f)$.

This rule captures in part the essence of parallel computation. To prove a routine correct, we must still prove the same conditions (those above the line) as in the sequential rule. But the consequences on the properties of a call (below the line) are different: the client has fewer properties to ensure before the call, since, as discussed in detail earlier in this chapter, trying to ensure the separate part of the precondition would be futile anyway; but we also obtain fewer guarantees on output. The former difference may be considered good news for the client, the latter is bad news.

The separate clauses in preconditions and postconditions thus join the invariant as properties that must be included as part of the internal proof of the routine body, but are not directly usable as properties of the call.

The rule also serves to restore the symmetry between preconditions and postconditions, following a discussion that highlighted the role of the preconditions.

30.11 A SUMMARY OF THE MECHANISM

On first reading you may move to "DIS-CUSSION", 30.12, page 1028.

Here now is the precise description of the concurrency facilities presented in earlier sections. There is no new material in this section, which serves only as reference and may be skipped on first reading. The description consists of four parts: syntax; validity constraints; semantics; library mechanisms. It extends the sequential O-O mechanisms developed in the preceding chapters.

Syntax

The syntactic extension involves just one new keyword, separate.

A declaration of an entity or function, which normally appears as

   x: *TYPE*

may now also be of the form

   x: **separate** *TYPE*

In addition, a class declaration, which normally begins with one of class C, deferred class *C* and expanded class *C*, may now also be of a new form: separate class *C*. In this case *C* will be called a separate class. It follows from the syntax convention that a class may be at most one of: separated, expanded, deferred. As with expanded and deferred, the property of being separate is not inherited: a class is separate or not according to its own declaration, regardless of its parents' separateness status.

A type is said to be separate if it is either based on a separate class or of the form separate *T* for some *T* (in which case it is not an error, although redundant, for *T* to be separate — again the same convention as for expanded). An entity or function is separate if its type is separate. An expression is separate if it is either a separate entity or a call to a separate function. A call or creation instruction is separate if its target (an expression) is separate. A precondition clause is separate if it involves a separate call (whose target, because of rules that follow, can only be a formal argument).

Constraints

A Separateness Consistency rule in four parts governs the validity of separate calls:

- (1) If the source of an attachment (assignment instruction or assignment passing) is separate, its target entity must be separate too.

- (2) If an actual argument of a separate call is of a reference type, the corresponding formal argument must be declared as separate.

- (3) If the source of an attachment is the result of a separate call to a function returning a reference type, the target must be declared as separate.

- (4) If an actual argument of a separate call is of an expanded type, its base class may not include, directly or indirectly, any non-separate attribute of a reference type.

There is also a simple consistency rule on types (not given earlier): in a type of the form **separate** *TYPE*, the base class of *TYPE* must be neither deferred nor expanded.

For a separate call to be valid, the target of the call must be a formal argument of the enclosing routine.

If an assertion contains a function call, any actual argument of that call must, if separate, be a formal argument of the enclosing routine, if any (separate argument rule).

Semantics

Each object is handled by a processor, its handler. If the target t of a creation instruction is non-separate, the newly created object will be handled by the same processor as the creating object. If t is separate, the new object will be allocated to a new processor.

Once it has been created, an object will at any time be in either of two states: free and reserved. It is free if no feature is being executed on it, and no separate client is currently executing a routine that uses as actual argument a separate reference attached to it.

A processor will be in one of three states: idle, busy and suspended. It is busy if it is executing a routine whose target is an object that it handles. It becomes suspended if it attempts an unsuccessful call (defined below) whose target is an object that it handles.

The semantics of calls is affected only if one of more of the elements involved — target and actual arguments — are separate. The discussion assumes a call of the general form $t \cdot f\,(\ldots, s, \ldots)$ where f is a routine. (If f is an attribute, we will assume for simplicity that it is called through an implicit function returning its value.)

The call is executed as part of the execution of a routine on a certain object C_OBJ, which may only be in a busy state at that stage. The basic notion is the following:

Definition: satisfiable call

In the absence of *CONCURRENCY* features (described next), a call to a routine f, executed on behalf of an object C_OBJ, is satisfiable if and only if every separate actual argument having a non-void value, and hence attached to a separate object A_OBJ, satisfies the following two conditions if the routine uses the corresponding formal as target of at least one call:

S1 • A_OBJ is free or reserved by C_OBJ.

S2 • Every separate clause of the precondition of f has value true when evaluated for A_OBJ and the actual arguments given.

If a processor executes a satisfiable call, the call is said to be successful and proceeds immediately; C_OBJ remains reserved, its processor remains in the busy state, every A_OBJ becomes reserved, the target remains reserved, the target's handler becomes busy, and it starts executing the routine of the call. When the call terminates, the target's handler returns to its previous state (idle or suspended) and each A_OBJ object returns to its previous state (free or reserved by C_OBJ).

If the call is not satisfiable, it is said to be unsuccessful; C_OBJ enters the suspended state. The call attempt has no immediate effect on its target and actual arguments. If one or more earlier unsuccessful calls are now satisfiable, the processor selects one of them to become successful as just described. The default policy if more than one is satisfiable is to select the one that has been waiting longest.

The final semantic change is the definition of wait by necessity: if a client has started one of more calls on a certain separate object, and it executes on that object a call to a query, that call will only proceed after all the earlier ones have been completed, and any further client operations will wait for the query call to terminate. (We have seen that an optimizing implementation might apply this rule only to queries returning an *expanded result*.) When waiting for these calls to terminate, the client remains in the "reserved" state.

Library mechanisms

Features of class *CONCURRENCY* enable us in some cases to consider that condition S1 of the satisfiable call definition holds even if A_OBJ has been reserved by another object (the "holder"), assuming C_OBJ (the "challenger") has called *demand* or *insist*; if as a result the call is considered satisfiable, the holder will get an exception. This will only occur if the holder is in a "yielding" state, which it can achieve by calling *yield*.

To go back to the default non-yielding state, the holder can execute *retain*; the boolean query *yielding* indicates the current state. The challenger's state is given by the integer query *Challenging* which may have the value *Normal*, *Demanding* or *Insisting*.

To return to the default *Normal* state the challenger can execute *wait_turn*. The difference between *demand* and *insist* affects what happens if the holder is not *yielding*: with *demand* the challenger will get an exception; with *insist* it simply waits as with *wait_turn*.

When these mechanisms cause an exception in the holder or challenger, the boolean query *is_concurrency_exception* from class *EXCEPTIONS* has value true.

30.12 DISCUSSION

As a conclusion to this presentation, let us review the essential criteria that should guide the development of a concurrent O-O mechanism. These criteria served as a basis for the approach presented here; in a few cases, as will be seen, some more work remains to be done to achieve their full satisfaction. The goals include:

- Minimality of mechanism.
- Full use of inheritance and other object-oriented techniques.
- Compatibility with Design by Contract.
- Provability.
- Support for command-query distinction.
- Applicability to many forms of concurrency.
- Support for coroutine programming.
- Adaptability through libraries.
- Support for reuse of non-concurrent software.
- Support for deadlock avoidance.

We will also take a final look at the question of interleaving accesses to an object.

Minimality of mechanism

Object-oriented software construction is a rich and powerful paradigm, which, as noted at the beginning of this chapter, intuitively seems ready to support concurrency.

It is essential, then, to aim for the smallest possible extension. Minimalism here is not just a question of good language design. If the concurrent extension is not minimal, some concurrency constructs will be redundant with the object-oriented constructs, or will conflict with them, making the developer's task hard or impossible. To avoid such a situation, we must find the smallest syntactic and semantic *epsilon* that will give concurrent execution capabilities to our object-oriented programs.

The extension presented in the preceding sections is indeed minimal syntactically, since it is not possible to add less than one new keyword.

Full use of inheritance and other object-oriented techniques

It would be unacceptable to have a concurrent object-oriented mechanism that does not take advantage of all O-O techniques, in particular inheritance. We have noted that the "inheritance anomaly" and other potential conflicts are not inherent to concurrent O-O development but follow from specific choices of concurrency mechanisms, in particular active objects, state-based models and path-expression-like synchronization; the appropriate conclusion is to reject these choices and retain inheritance.

We have repeatedly seen how inheritance can be used to produce high-level behavior class (such as *PROCESS*) describing general patterns to be inherited by descendants. Most of the examples would be impossible without multiple inheritance.

Among other O-O techniques, information hiding also plays a central role.

Compatibility with Design by Contract

It is essential to retain the systematic, logic-based approach to software construction and documentation expressed by the principles of Design by Contract. The results of this chapter were indeed based on the study of assertions and how they fare in a concurrent context.

In that study we encountered a striking property, the concurrent precondition paradox, which forced us to provide a different semantics for assertions in the concurrent case. This gives an even more fundamental place to assertions in the resulting mechanism.

Support for command-query separation

"Objects as machines", page 751. A principle of object-oriented software construction was developed in preceding chapters: Command-Query Separation. The principle enjoins us not to mix commands (procedures), which change objects, and queries (functions and attributes), which return information about objects but do not change them. This precludes side-effect-producing functions.

It is commonly believed that the principle cannot hold in a concurrent context, as for example you cannot write

next_element := *buffer.item*

buffer.remove

and have the guarantee that the element removed by the second call is the same that the first instruction assigned to *next_item*. Between the two instructions, another client can mess up with the shared buffer. Such examples are often used to claim that one must have a side-effect-producing function *get*, which will both return an element and remove it.

This argument is plainly wrong. It is confusing two notions: exclusive access and routine specification. With the notation of this chapter, it is easy to obtain exclusive access without sacrificing the Command-Query Separation principle: simply enclose the two instructions above, with *buffer* replaced by *b*, in a procedure of formal argument *b*, and call that procedure with the attribute *buffer* as argument. Or, if you do *not* require the two operations to apply to the same element, and want to minimize the amount of time a shared resource is held, write *two* separate routines. This kind of flexibility is important for the developer. It can be provided, thanks to a simple exclusive access mechanism, whether or not functions may have side effects.

Applicability to many forms of concurrency

A general criterion for the design of a concurrent mechanism is that it should make it support many different forms of concurrency: shared memory, multitasking, network programming, client-server computing, distributed processing, real time.

With such a broad set of application areas, a language mechanism cannot be expected to provide all the answers. But it should lend itself to adaptation to all the intended forms of concurrency. This is achieved by using the abstract notion of processor, and relying on a distinct facility (Concurrency Control File, libraries...) to adapt the solution to any particular hardware architecture that you may have available.

Adaptability through libraries

Many concurrency mechanisms have been proposed over the years; some of the best known were reviewed at the beginning of this chapter. Each has its partisans, and each may provide the best approach for a certain problem area.

It is important, then, that the proposed mechanism should support at least some of these mechanisms. More precisely, the solution must be general enough to allow us to *program* various concurrency constructs in terms of that mechanism.

Here the facilities of the object-oriented method should again be put to good use. One of the most important aspects of the method is that it supports the construction of libraries for widely used schemes. The library construction facilities (classes, assertions, constrained and unconstrained genericity, multiple inheritance, deferred classes and others) should allow us to express many concurrency mechanisms in the form of library components. Examples of such encapsulating mechanisms (such as the *PROCESS* class and the behavior class for locks) have been presented in this chapter, and the exercises suggest a few more.

One may expect that a number of libraries will be produced, relying on the basic tools and complementing them, to support concurrency models catering to specific needs and tastes.

We have also seen the use of library classes such as *CONCURRENCY* to provide various refinements to the basic scheme defined by the language mechanism.

Support for coroutine programming

As a special case, coroutines provide a form of quasi-concurrency, interesting both in itself (in particular for simulation activities), and as a smoke test of the applicability of the mechanisms, since a general solution should adapt itself gracefully to boundary cases. We have seen how it is possible, once again using the library construction mechanisms of object technology, to express coroutines based on the general concurrent mechanism.

Support for reuse of non-concurrent software

It is necessary to support the reuse of existing, non-concurrent software, especially libraries of reusable software components.

Class BUFFER_ ACCESS was on page 1021.

We have seen how smooth the transition is between sequential classes such as *BOUNDED_QUEUE* and their concurrent counterparts such as *BOUNDED_BUFFER* (just write **separate class** *BOUNDED_BUFFER* [G] **inherit** *BOUNDED_QUEUE* [G] **end**). This result is somewhat tempered by the frequent desirability of encapsulation classes such as our *BUFFER_ACCESS*. Such encapsulation seems useful, however, and may be an inescapable consequence of the semantic differences between sequential and concurrent computation. Also note that such wrapper classes are easy to write.

Support for deadlock avoidance

One area in which more work remains necessary is how to guarantee deadlock avoidance.

Deadlock potential is a fact of concurrent life. For example any mechanism that can be used to program semaphores (and a mechanism that is *not* powerful enough to emulate semaphores would be viewed with suspicion) can cause deadlock, since semaphores are trivially open to that possibility.

"Locks", page 1009 and exercise E30.8, page 1036.

The solution lies partly in the use of high-level encapsulation mechanisms. For example a set of classes encapsulating semaphores, as was presented for locks, should come with behavior classes that automatically provide a *free* for every *reserve*, thereby guaranteeing deadlock avoidance for applications that follow the recommended practice by inheriting from the behavior class. This is, in my experience, the best recipe for deadlock avoidance.

This approach may not be sufficient, however, and it may be possible to devise simple non-deadlock rules, automatically checkable by a static tool. Such a rule (expressed as a methodological principle rather than a language validity rule, for fear it may be too restrictive) was given earlier: the *Business Card* principle. But more is needed.

Permitting concurrent access?

A final note on one of the principal properties of the approach: the requirement that at most one client may access any supplier object at any given time, preventing interleaving of routines and requiring any VIP treatment to use the duel mechanism.

"Concurrent accesses to an object", page 982.

The rationale was clear: if any challenger client can interrupt the execution of a routine at any time, we lose the ability to reason on our classes (through properties of the form {*INV* **and** *pre*} *body* {*INV* **and** *post*}) since the challenger can leave the object in an arbitrary state.

This objection would disappear if we only permitted challengers to execute a routine of a very special kind: an *applicative* routine (in the sense defined for functions in earlier chapters) which does not modify the object or, if it modifies it, cancels all its modifications before it leaves. This would assume a language mechanism to state that a routine is applicative, and compilers enforcing that property.

30.13 KEY CONCEPTS INTRODUCED IN THIS CHAPTER

- Concurrency and distribution are playing an increasing role in most application areas of computers.

- Concurrency has many variants, including multiprocessing and multiprogramming. The Internet, the Web and object request brokers bring even more possibilities.

- It is possible to use the fundamental schemes of object technology — classes, encapsulation, multiple inheritance, deferred classes, assertions and so on — for the greatest benefit of developers of concurrent and distributed applications.

- No active-passive object distinction is necessary or desirable. Objects are by nature able to perform many operations; making them active would restrict them to just one.

- A simple extension of the sequential object-oriented notation, using a single keywords (**separate**), covers all the major application areas of concurrency.

- Each object is handled by a processor. Processors are an abstract notion describing threads of control; a system can use as many processors as it wants regardless of the number of available computing devices (CPUs). It must be possible to define the mapping from processors to CPUs outside of the software proper.

- An object handled by a different processor is said to be separate.

- Calls on separate targets have a different semantics, asynchronous rather than synchronous. For that reason, any entity representing separate objects must be declared as such, using the keyword **separate**.

- Consistency rules, implying in particular that a separate entity may not be assigned to a non-separate one, ensure that there are no "traitors" — that no non-separate entity becomes attached to a separate object.

- To achieve exclusive access to a separate object, it suffices to use the corresponding reference as an argument to a separate call (a call with a separate target).

- The target of a separate call must itself be a separate formal argument of the enclosing routine.

- Preconditions on separate targets cannot keep their usual semantics as correctness conditions (this is the "concurrent precondition paradox"). They serve as wait conditions.

- The mechanism developed in this chapter covers multitasking, time-sharing, multi-threading, client-server computing, distributed processing on networks such as the Internet, coroutines and real-time applications.

30.14 BIBLIOGRAPHICAL NOTES

The approach to concurrency described in this chapter evolved from a presentation at TOOLS EUROPE [M 1990a] and was revised in [M 1993b], from which some of the material in this chapter (examples in particular) was derived. It is now known as SCOOP for "Simple Concurrent Object-Oriented Programming". John Potter and Ghinwa Jalloul have developed a variant that includes an explicit **hold** instruction [Jalloul 1991] [Jalloul 1994]. Wait by necessity was introduced by Denis Caromel [Caromel 1989] [Caromel 1993].

The first implementation of the model described here was developed by Terry Tang and Xavier Le Vourch. Both contributed new insights.

A good textbook on the traditional approaches to concurrency is [Ben Ari 1990]. Original references include: on semaphores, [Dijkstra 1968a], which also introduced the "dining philosophers" problem; on monitors, [Hoare 1974]; on path expressions, [Campbell 1974]. The original CSP model was described in [Hoare 1978]; the book [Hoare 1985] presents a revised model with special emphasis on its mathematical properties. Occam2 is described in [Inmos 1988]. A CSP and Occam archive is available at Oxford University: *http://www.comlab.ox.ac.uk/archive/csp.html* (I am grateful to Bill Roscoe from Oxford for help with details of CSP). CCS (Communicating Concurrent Systems) [Milner 1989] is another influential mathematically-based model. Although cited only in passing in this chapter, Carriero's and Gelernter's Linda method and tool [Carriero 1990] is a must know for anyone interested in concurrency.

A special issue of the *Communications of the ACM* [M 1993a] presents a number of important approaches to concurrent object-oriented programming, originally drawn from concurrency papers at various TOOLS conferences.

Another collection of papers that appeared at about the same time is [Agha 1993]. An earlier collective book edited by Yonezawa and Tokoro [Yonezawa 1987] served as catalyst for much of the work in the field and is still good reading. Other surveys include a thesis [Papathomas 1992] and an article [Wyatt 1992]. Yet another compilation of contributions by many authors [Wilson 1996] covers C++ concurrency extensions.

Hewitt's and Agha's *actors* model, which predates the object-oriented renaissance and comes from a somewhat different background, has influenced many concurrent O-O approaches; it is described in an article [Agha 1990] and a book [Agha 1986]. Actors are computational agents similar to active objects, each with a mail address and a behavior. An actor communicates with others through messages sent to their mail addresses; to achieve asynchronous communication, the messages are buffered. An actor processes messages through functions and by providing "replacement behaviors" to be used in lieu of the actor's earlier behavior after a certain message has been processed.

One of the earliest and most thoroughly explored parallel object-oriented languages is POOL [America 1989]; POOL uses a notion of active object, which was found to raise problems when combined with inheritance. For that reason inheritance was introduced into the language only after a detailed study which led to the separation of inheritance and subtyping mechanisms. The design of POOL is also notable for having shown, from the start, a strong concern for formal language specification.

Much of the important work in concurrent O-O languages has come from Japan. [Yonezawa 1987], already cited, contains the description of several influential Japanese developments, such as ABCL/1 [Yonezawa 1987a]. MUSE, an object-oriented operating system developed at the Sony Computer Science Laboratory, was presented by Tokoro and his colleagues at TOOLS EUROPE 1989 [Yokote 1989]. The term "inheritance anomaly" was introduced by Matsuoka and Yonezawa [Matsuoka 1993], and further papers by Matsuoka and collaborators which propose various remedies.

Work on distributed systems has been particularly active in France, with the CHORUS operating system, of which [Lea 1993] describes an object-oriented extension; the GUIDE language and system of Krakowiak *et al.* [Balter 1991]; and the SOS system of Shapiro *et al.* [Shapiro 1989]. In the area of programming massively parallel architectures, primarily for scientific applications, Jean-Marc Jézéquel has developed the ÉPÉE system [Jézéquel 1992], [Jézéquel 1996] (chapter 9)], [Guidec 1996].

Also influential has been the work done by Nierstrasz and his colleagues at the University of Genève around the Hybrid language [Nierstrasz 1992] [Papathomas 1992], which does not have two categories of objects (active and passive) but relies instead on the notion of thread of control, called *activity*. The basic communication mechanism is remote procedure call, either synchronous or asynchronous.

Other important projects include DRAGOON [Atkinson 1991], which, like the mechanism of this chapter, uses preconditions and postconditions to express synchronization, and pSather [Feldman 1993], based on the notion of thread and a predefined *MONITOR* class.

Many other developments would need to be added to this list. For more complete surveys, see the references cited at the beginning of this section. The proceedings of workshops regularly held at the ECOOP and OOPSLA conferences, such as [Agha 1988], [Agha 1991], [Tokoro 1992], describe a variety of ongoing research projects and are precious to anyone who wants to find out what problems researchers consider most pressing.

The work reported in this chapter has benefited at various stages from the comments and criticism of many people. In addition to colleagues cited in the first two paragraphs of this section they include Mordechai Ben-Ari, Richard Bielak, John Bruno, Paul Dubois, Carlo Ghezzi, Peter Löhr, Dino Mandrioli, Jean-Marc Nerson, Robert Switzer and Kim Waldén.

EXERCISES

E30.1 Printers

Page 962.

Complete the *PRINTER* class, implementing the job queue as a bounded buffer and making sure queue manipulation routines as well as *print* do not need to process the special "stop request" print job (*print* may have **not** *j.is_stop_request* as a precondition).

E30.2 Why import must be deep

Assume that a shallow import mechanism (rather than *deep_import*) were available. Construct an example that will produce an inconsistent structure — one in which a separate object is attached to a non-separate entity.

E30.3 The "inheritance anomaly"

"Synchronization for concurrent O-O computation", page 980.

In the *BUFFER* example used to illustrate the "inheritance anomaly", assume that each routine specifies the exit state in each case using a **yield** instruction, as in

> *put* (*x*: *G*) **is**
>> **do**
>>> "Add *x* to the data structure representing the buffer"
>>> **if** "All positions now occupied" **then**
>>>> **yield** *full*
>>> **else**
>>>> **yield** *partial*
>>> **end**
>> **end**

Write the corresponding scheme for *remove*. Then write the class *NEW_BUFFER* with the added procedure *remove_two* and show that the class must redefine both of the inherited features (along with the specification of which features are applicable in which states).

E30.4 Deadlock avoidance (research problem)

Page 990.

Starting from the Business Card principle, investigate whether it is feasible to eliminate some of the possible deadlocks by introducing a validity rule on the use of non-separate actual arguments to separate calls. The rule should be reasonable (that is to say, it should not preclude commonly useful schemes), enforceable by a compiler (in particular an incremental compiler), and easily explainable to developers.

E30.5 Priorities

"Duels and their semantics", page 999.

Examine how to add a priority scheme to the duel mechanism of class *CONCURRENCY*, retaining upward compatibility with the semantics defined in the presentation of procedures *yield*, *insist* and related ones.

E30.6 Files and the precondition paradox

Consider the following simple extract from a routine manipulating a file:

> *f*: *FILE*
>
> …
>
> **if** *f* /= *Void* **and then** *f*•*readable* **then**
> > *f*•*some_input_routine*
> > > -- *some_input_routine* is any routine that reads
> > > -- data from the file; its precondition is *readable*.
>
> **end**

Discuss how, in spite of the absence of obvious concurrency in this example, the precondition paradox can apply to it. (**Hint**: a file is a separate persistent structure, so an interactive user or some other software system can access the file in between the various operations performed by the extract.) Discuss what can happen as a consequence of this problem, and possible solutions.

E30.7 Locking

Rewrite the class *LOCKING_PROCESS* as an heir of class *PROCESS*.

Page 1010. Class PROCESS was on page 961.

E30.8 Binary semaphores

Write one or more classes implementing the notion of binary semaphore. (**Hint**: start from the classes implementing locks.) As suggested at the end of the discussion of locks, be sure to include high-level behavior classes, meant to be used through inheritance, which guarantee a correct pattern of *reserve* and *free* operations.

"Locks", page 1009.

E30.9 Integer semaphores

Write one or more classes implementing the notion of integer semaphore.

E30.10 Coroutine controller

Complete the implementation of coroutines by spelling out how the controller is created.

"Coroutines", page 1012.

E30.11 Coroutine examples

The discussion of Simula presents several examples of coroutines. Use the coroutine classes of the present chapter to implement these examples.

"Coroutine concepts", page 1118 (in the Simula chapter).

E30.12 Elevators

Complete the elevator example by adding all the creation procedures as well as the missing algorithms, in particular for selecting floor requests.

"An elevator control system", page 1014

E30.13 Watchods and the Business Card principle

Show that the procedure *set* of class *WATCHDOG* violates the Business Card principle. Explain why this is all right.

Page 1020.

E30.14 Once routines and concurrency

What is the appropriate semantics for once routines in a concurrent context: executed once per system execution, or once per processor?

31

Object persistence and databases

Executing an object-oriented application means creating and manipulating a certain number of objects. What happens to these objects when the current execution terminates? *Transient* objects will disappear with the current session; but many applications also need *persistent* objects, which will stay around from session to session. Persistent objects may need to be shared by several applications, raising the need for *databases*.

In this overview of persistence issues and solutions we will examine the three approaches that O-O developers have at their disposal for manipulating persistent objects. They can rely on **persistence mechanisms** from the programming language and development environment to get object structures to and from permanent storage. They can combine object technology with databases of the most commonly available kind (not O-O): **relational databases**. Or they can use one of the newer **object-oriented database systems**, which undertake to transpose to databases the basic ideas of object technology.

This chapter describes these techniques in turn, providing an overview of the technology of O-O databases with emphasis on two of the best-known products. It ends with a more futuristic discussion of the fate of database ideas in an O-O context.

31.1 PERSISTENCE FROM THE LANGUAGE

For many persistence needs it suffices to have, associated with the development environment, a set of mechanisms for storing objects in files and retrieving them from files. For simple objects such as integers and characters, we can use input-output facilities similar to those of traditional programming.

Storing and retrieving object structures

See "Deep storage: a first view of persistence", page 250.

As soon as composite objects enter the picture, it is not sufficient to store and retrieve individual objects since they may contain references to other objects, and an object deprived of its dependents would be inconsistent. This observation led us in an earlier chapter to the *Persistence Closure* principle, stating that any storage and retrieval mechanism must handle, together with an object, all its direct and indirect dependents. The following figure served to illustrate the issue:

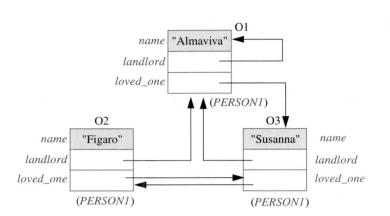

The Persistence Closure principle stated that any mechanism that stores O1 must also store all the objects to which it refers, directly or indirectly; otherwise when you retrieve the structure you would get a meaningless value (*"dangling reference"*) in the *loved_one* field for O1.

We saw the mechanisms of class *STORABLE* which provide the corresponding facilities: *store* to store an object structure and *retrieved* to access it back. This is a precious mechanism, whose presence in an O-O environment is by itself a major advantage over traditional environments. The earlier discussion gave a typical example of use: implementing the SAVE facility of an editor. Here is another, from ISE's own practice. Our compiler performs several passes on representations of the software text. The first pass creates an internal representation, known as an Abstract Syntax Tree (AST). Roughly speaking, the task of the subsequent passes is to add more and more semantic information to the AST (to "decorate the tree") until there is enough to generate the compiler's target code. Each pass finishes by a *store*; the next pass starts by retrieving the AST through *retrieved*.

The *STORABLE* mechanism works not only on files but also on network connections such as sockets; it indeed lies at the basis of the *Net* client-server library.

Storable format variants

Procedure *store* has several variants. One, *basic_store*, stores objects to be retrieved by the same system running on the same machine architecture, as part of the same execution or of a later one. These assumptions make it possible to use the most compact format possible for representing objects.

Another variant, *independent_store*, removes all these assumptions; the object representation is platform-independent and system-independent. It consequently takes a little more space, since it must use a portable data representation for floating-point and other numerical values, and must include some elementary information about the classes of the system. But it is precious for client-server systems, which must exchange potentially large and complex collections of objects among machines of widely different architectures, running entirely different systems. For example a workstation server and a PC client can run two different applications and communicate through the *Net* library, with the server application performing the fundamental computations and the client application taking care of the user interface thanks to a graphical library such as *Vision*.

Note that the storing part is the only one to require several procedures — *basic_store*, *independent_store*. Even though the implementation of retrieval is different for each format, you will always use a single feature *retrieved*, whose implementation will detect the format actually used by the file or network data being retrieved, and will automatically apply the appropriate retrieval algorithm.

31.2 BEYOND PERSISTENCE CLOSURE

The Persistence Closure principle is, in theory, applicable to all forms of persistence. It makes it possible, as we saw, to preserve the consistency of objects stored and retrieved.

In some practical cases, however, you may need to adapt the data structure before letting it be applied by mechanisms such as *STORABLE* or the O-O database tools reviewed later in this chapter. Otherwise you may end up storing more than you want.

The problem arises in particular because of shared structures, as in this setup:

Small structure with reference to big shared structure

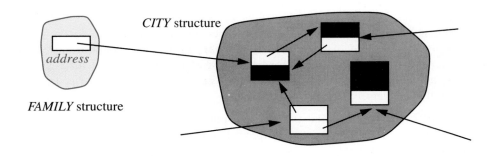

A relatively small data structure needs to be archived. Because it contains one or more references to a large shared structure, the Persistence Closure principle requires archiving that structure too. In some cases you may not want this. For example, as illustrated by the figure, you could be doing some genealogical research, or other processing on objects representing persons; a person object might, through an *address* field, reference a much bigger set of objects representing geographical information. A similar situation occurs in ISE's *ArchiText* product, which enables users to manipulate structured documents, such as programs or specifications. Each document, like the *FAMILY* structure in the figure, contains a reference to a structure representing the underlying grammar, playing the role of the *CITY* structure; we may want to store a document but not the grammar, which already exists elsewhere and may be shared by many documents.

In such cases you may want to "cut out" the references to the shared structure before storing the referring structure. This is, however, a delicate process. First, you must as always make sure that at retrieval time the objects will still be consistent — satisfy their invariants. But there is also a practical problem: to avoid complication and errors, you do not really want to modify the original structure; only in the stored version should references be cut out.

Once again the techniques of object-oriented software construction provide an elegant solution, based on the ideas of *behavior class* reviewed in the discussion of inheritance. One of the versions of the storing procedure, *custom_independent_store*, has the same effect as *independent_store* by default, but also lets any descendant of a library class *ACTIONABLE* redefine a number of procedures which do nothing by default, such as *pre_store* which will be executed just before an object is stored and *post_store* which will be executed after. So you can for example have *pre_store* perform

See "Deferred classes as partial implementations: the notion of behavior class", page 503.

> *preserve*; *address* := *Void*

where *preserve*, also a feature of *ACTIONABLE*, copies the object safely somewhere. Then *post_action* will perform a call to

> *restore*

which restores the object from the preserved copy.

For this common case it is in fact possible to obtain the same effect through a call of the form

> *store_ignore* ("*address*")

where *ignore* takes a field name as argument. Since the implementation of *store_ignore* may simply skip the field, avoiding the two-way copy of *preserve* and *restore*, it will be more efficient in this case, but the *pre_store-post_store* mechanism is more general, allowing any actions before and after storage. Again, you must make sure that these actions will not adversely affect the objects.

You may in fact use a similar mechanism to remove an inconsistency problem arising at retrieval time; it suffices to redefine the procedure *post_retrieve* which will be executed just before the retrieved object rejoins the community of approved objects. For example an application might redefine *post_retrieve*, in the appropriate class inheriting from *ACTIONABLE*, to execute something like

> *address* := *my_city_structure*•*address_value* (…)

hence making the object presentable again before it has had the opportunity to violate its class invariant or any informal consistency constraint.

There are clearly some rules associated with the *ACTIONABLE* mechanism; in particular, *pre_store* must not perform any change of the data structure unless *post_store* corrects it immediately thereafter. You must also make sure that *post_retrieve* will perform the necessary actions (often the same as those of *post_store*) to correct any inconsistency introduced into the stored structure by *pre_store*. Used under these rules, the mechanism lets you remain faithful to the spirit of the Persistent Closure principle while making its application more flexible.

31.3 SCHEMA EVOLUTION

A general issue arises in all approaches to O-O persistence. Classes can change. What if you change a class of which instances exist somewhere in a persistent store? This is known as the schema evolution problem.

> The word *schema* comes from the relational database world, where it describes the architecture of a database: its set of relations (as defined in the next section) with, for every relation, what we would call its type — number of fields and type of each. In an O-O context the schema will also be the set of types, given here by the classes.

Although some development environments and database systems have provided interesting tools for O-O schema evolution, none has yet provided a fully satisfactory solution. Let us define the components of a comprehensive approach.

*An object's **generating class** (or **generator**) is the class of which it is a direct instance. See "Basic form", page 219.*

Some precise terminology will be useful. **Schema evolution** occurs if at least one class used by a system that attempts to retrieve some objects (the **retrieving system**) differs from its counterpart in the system that stored these objects (the **storing system**). Object retrieval mismatch, or just **object mismatch** for short, occurs when the retrieving system actually retrieves a particular object whose own generating class was different in the storing system. Object mismatch is an individual consequence, for one particular object, of the general phenomenon of schema evolution for one or more classes.

> Remember that in spite of the terms "storing system" and "retrieving system" this whole discussion is applicable not only to storage and retrieval using files or databases, but also to object transmission over a network, as with the *Net* library. In such a case the more accurate terms would be "sending system" and "receiving system".

Exercise E31.1, page 1062, asks you to study the consequences of removing this assumption.

To keep the discussion simple, we will make the usual assumption that a software system does not change while it is being executed. This means in particular that all the instances of a class stored by a particular system execution refer to the same version of the class; so at retrieval time either all of them will produce an object mismatch, or none of them will. This assumption is not too restrictive; note in particular that it does not rule out the case of a database that contains instances of many different versions of the same class, produced by different system executions.

Naïve approaches

We can rule out two extreme approaches to schema evolution:

- You might be tempted to forsake previously stored objects (schema *revolution*!). The developers of the new application will like the idea, which makes their life so much easier. But the *users* of the application will not be amused.

- You may offer a migration path from old format to new, requiring a one-time, en masse conversion of old objects. Although this solution may be acceptable in some cases, it will not do for a large persistent store or one that must be available continuously.

What we really need is a way to convert old objects **on the fly** as they are retrieved or updated. This is the most general solution, and the only one considered in the rest of this discussion.

If you happen to need en-masse conversion, an on-the-fly mechanism will trivially let you do it: simply write a small system that retrieves all the existing objects using the new classes, applying on-the-fly conversion as needed, and stores everything.

On-the-fly object conversion

The mechanics of on-the-fly conversion can be tricky; we must be particularly careful to get the details right, lest we end up with corrupted objects and corrupted databases.

First, an application that retrieves an object and has a different version of its generating class may not have the rights to update the stored objects, which may be just as well since *other* applications may still use the old version. This is not, however, a new problem. What counts is that the objects manipulated by the application be consistent with their own class descriptions; an on-the-fly conversion mechanism will ensure this property. Whether to write back the converted object to the database is a separate question — a classical question of access privilege, which arises as soon as several applications, or even several sessions of the same application, can access the same persistent data. Database systems, object-oriented or not, have proposed various solutions

Regardless of write-back aspects, the newer and perhaps more challenging problem is how each application will deal with an obsolete object. Schema evolution involves three separate issues — detection, notification and correction:

- **Detection** is the task of catching object mismatches (cases in which a retrieved object is obsolete) at retrieval time.

- **Notification** is the task of making the retrieving system aware of the object mismatch, so that it will be able to react appropriately, rather than continuing with an inconsistent object (a likely cause of major trouble ahead!).

- **Correction** is the task, for the retrieving system, of bringing the mismatched object to a consistent state that will make it a correct instance of the new version of its class — a citizen, or at least a permanent resident, of its system of adoption.

All three problems are delicate. Fortunately, it is possible to address them separately.

Detection

We can define two general categories of detection policy: **nominal** and **structural**.

In both cases the problem is to detect a mismatch between two versions of an object's generating class: the version used by the system that stored the object, and the version used by the system which retrieves it.

In the nominal approach, each class version is identified by a version name. This assumes some kind of registration mechanism, which may have two variants:

- If you are using a configuration management system, you can register each new version of the class and get a version name in return (or specify the version name yourself).

- More automatic schemes are possible, similar to the automatic identification facility of Microsoft's OLE 2, or the techniques used to assign "dynamic IP addresses" to computers on the Internet (for example a laptop that you plug in temporarily into a new network). These techniques are based on random number assignments, with numbers so large as to make the likelihood of a clash infinitesimal.

Either solution requires some kind of central registry. If you want to avoid the resulting hassle, you will have to rely on the structural approach. The idea here is to associate with each class version a **class descriptor** deduced from the actual structure of the class, as defined by the class declaration, and to make sure that whenever a persistent mechanism stores objects it *also stores the associated class descriptors*. (Of course if you store many instances of a class you will only need to store one copy of the class descriptor.) Then the detection mechanism is simple: just compare the class descriptor of each retrieved object with the new class descriptor. If they are different, you have an object mismatch.

What goes into a class descriptor? There is some flexibility; the answer is a tradeoff between efficiency and reliability. For efficiency, you will not want to waste too much space for keeping class information in the stored structure, or too much time for comparing descriptors at retrieval time; but for reliability you will want to minimize the risk of missing an object mismatch — of treating a retrieved object as up-to-date if it is in fact obsolete. Here are various possible strategies:

C1 • At one extreme, the class descriptor could just be the class name. This is generally insufficient: if the generator of an object in the storing system has the same name as a class in the retrieving system, we will accept the object even though the two classes may be totally incompatible. Trouble will inevitably follow.

C2 • At the other extreme, we might use as class descriptor the entire class text — perhaps not as a string but in an appropriate internal form (abstract syntax tree). This is clearly the worst solution for efficiency, both in space occupation and in descriptor comparison time. But it may not even be right for reliability, since some class changes are harmless. Assume for example the new class text has added a routine, but has not changed any attribute or invariant clause. Then nothing bad can happen if we consider a retrieved object up-to-date; but if we detect an object mismatch we may cause some unwarranted trouble (such as an exception) in the retrieving system.

C3 • A more realistic approach is to make the class descriptor include the class name and the list of its attributes, each characterized by its name and its type. As compared to the nominal approach, there is still the risk that two completely different classes might have both the same name and the same attributes, but (unlike in case C1) such chance clashes are extremely unlikely to happen in practice.

C4 • A variation on C3 would include not just the attribute list but also the whole class invariant. With the invariant you should be assured that the addition or removal of a routine, which will not yield a detected object mismatch, is harmless, since if it changed the semantics of the class it would affect the invariant.

C3 is the minimum reasonable policy, and in usual cases seems a good tradeoff, at least to start.

Notification

What should happen when the detection mechanism, nominal or structural, has caught an object mismatch?

We want the retrieving system to know, so that it will be able to take the appropriate correction actions. A library mechanism will address the problem. Class *GENERAL* (ancestor of all classes) must include a procedure

> *correct_mismatch* **is**
>
> > **do**
> >
> > > ...See full version below ...
> >
> > **end**

correct in this procedure name is not an adjective but a verb, as in "Correct this mismatch, fast!". See "Grammatical categories", page 881.

with the rule that any detection of an object mismatch will cause a call to *correct_mismatch* on the temporarily retrieved version of the object. Any class can redefine the default version of *correct_mismatch*; like a creation procedure, and like any redefinition of the default exception handling procedure *default_rescue*, any redefinition of *correct_mismatch* must ensure the invariant of the class.

What should the default version of *correct_mismatch* do? It may be tempting, in the name of unobtrusiveness, to give it an empty body. But this is not appropriate, since it would mean that by default object retrieval mismatches will be ignored — leading to all kinds of possible abnormal behavior. The better global default is to raise an exception:

> *correct_mismatch* **is**
>
> > -- Handle object retrieval mismatch.
>
> > **do**
> >
> > > *raise_mismatch_exception*
> >
> > **end**

where the procedure called in the body does what its name suggests. It might cause some unexpected exceptions, but this is better than letting mismatches go through undetected. A project that wants to override this default behavior, for example to execute a null instruction rather than raise an exception, can always redefine *correct_mismatch*, at its own risk, in class *ANY*. (As you will remember, developer-defined classes inherit from *GENERAL* not directly but through *ANY*, which a project or installation can customize.)

"THE GLOBAL INHERITANCE STRUCTURE", page 580.

> For more flexibility, there is also a feature *mismatch_information* of type *ANY*, defined as a once function, and a procedure *set_mismatch_information* (*info*: *ANY*) which resets its value. This makes it possible to provide *correct_mismatch* with more information, for example about the various preceding versions of a class.

If you do expect object mismatches for a certain class, you will not want the default exception behavior for that class: instead you will redefine *correct_mismatch* so as to update the retrieved object. This is our last task: correction.

Correction

How do we correct a object that has been found, upon retrieval, to cause a mismatch? The answer requires a careful analysis, and a more sophisticated approach than has usually been implemented by existing systems or proposed in the literature.

The precise situation is this: the retrieval mechanism (through feature *retrieved* of class *STORABLE*, a database operation, or any other available primitive) has created a new object in the retrieving system, deduced from a stored object with the same generating class; but it has also detected a mismatch. The new object is in a temporary state and may be inconsistent; it may for example have lost a field which was present in the stored object, or gained a field not present in the original. Think of it as a foreigner without a visa.

Object mismatch

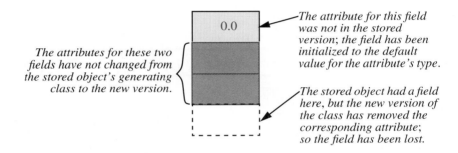

The attribute for this field was not in the stored version; the field has been initialized to the default value for the attribute's type.

The attributes for these two fields have not changed from the stored object's generating class to the new version.

The stored object had a field here, but the new version of the class has removed the corresponding attribute; so the field has been lost.

See "The role of creation procedures", page 371.

Such an object state is similar to the intermediate state of an object being created — outside of any persistence consideration — by a creation instruction !! *x.make* (...), just after the object's memory cell has been allocated and initialized to default values, but just before *make* has been called. At that stage the object has all the required components but is not yet ready for acceptance by the community since it may have inconsistent values in some of its fields; it is, as we saw, the official purpose of a creation procedure *make* to override default initializations as may be needed to ensure the invariant.

Let us assume for simplicity that the detection technique is structural and based on attributes (that is to say, policy C3 as defined earlier), although the discussion will transpose to the other solutions, nominal or structural. The mismatch is a consequence of a change in the attribute properties of the class. We may reduce it to a combination of any number of *attribute additions* and *attribute removals*. (If a class change is the replacement of the type of an attribute, we can consider it as a removal followed by an addition.) The figure above shows one addition and one removal.

Attribute removal does not raise any apparent difficulty: if the new class does not include a certain attribute present in the old class, the corresponding object fields are not needed any more and we may simply discard them. In fact procedure *correct_mismatch* does not need to do anything for such fields, since the retrieval mechanism, when creating a tentative instance of the new class, will have discarded them; the figure shows this for the bottom field — rather, non-field — of the illustrated object.

We might of course be a bit more concerned about the discarded fields; what if they were really needed, so that the object will not make sense without them? This is where having a more elaborate *detection* policy, such as structural policy C4 which takes the invariant into account, would be preferable.

The more delicate case is when the new class has **added** an attribute, which yields a new field in the retrieved objects, as illustrated by the top field of the object in the preceding figure. What do we do with such a field? We must initialize it somehow. In the systems I have seen offering some support for schema evolution and object conversion, the solution is to use a conventional default as initialization value (the usual choices: zero for numbers, empty for strings). But, as we know from earlier discussions of similar problems — arising for example in the context of inheritance — this may be *very* wrong!

See "Uniform Access", page 55, and "Definition and example", page 363.

Our standard example was a class *ACCOUNT* with attributes *deposits_list* and *withdrawals_list*; assume that a new version adds an attribute *balance* and a system using this new version attempts to retrieve an instance created from the previous version.

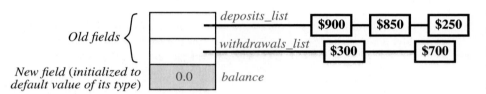

Old fields
deposits_list
$900 — $850 — $250
withdrawals_list
$300 — $700
New field (initialized to default value of its type)   0.0   *balance*

Retrieving an account object

(What is wrong with this picture?)

The purpose of adding the *balance* attribute is clear: instead of having to recompute an account's balance on demand we keep it in the object and update it whenever needed. The new class invariant reflects this through a clause of the form

     balance = deposits_list.total – withdrawals_list.total

But if we apply the default initialization to a retrieved object's *balance* field, we will get a badly inconsistent result, whose balance field does not agree with the record of deposits and withdrawals. On the above figure, *balance* is zero as a result of the default initialization; to agree with the deposits and withdrawals shown, it should be 1000 dollars.

Hence the importance of having the *correct_mismatch* mechanism. In such a case the class will simply redefine the procedure as

     correct_mismatch **is**
                -- Handle object retrieval mismatch by correctly setting up *balance*
       do
                balance := deposits_list.total – withdrawals_list.total
       end

If the author of the new class has not planned for this case, the default version of *correct_mismatch* will raise an exception, causing the application to terminate abnormally unless a **retry** (providing another recovery possibility) handles it. This is the right outcome, since continuing execution could destroy the integrity of the execution's object structure — and, worse yet, of the persistent object structure, for example a database. In the earlier metaphor, we will reject the object unless we can assign it a proper immigration status.

31.4 FROM PERSISTENCE TO DATABASES

Using *STORABLE* ceases to be sufficient for true database applications. Its limitations have been noted in the earlier discussion: there is only one entry object; there is no support for content-based queries; each call to *retrieved* re-creates the entire structure, with no sharing of objects between successive calls. In addition, there is no support in *STORABLE* for letting different client applications access the same persistent data simultaneously.

Although various extensions of the mechanism can alleviate or remove some of these problems, a full-fledged solution requires taking advantage of database technology.

O-O or not, a set of mechanisms for storing and retrieving data items ("objects" in a general sense) deserves being called a database management system if it supports the following features:

- Persistence: objects can outlive the termination of individual program sessions using them, as well as computer failures.

- Programmable structure: the system treats objects as structured data connected by clearly defined relations. Users of the system can group a set of objects into a collection, called a database, and define the structure of a particular database.

- Arbitrary size: there is no built-in limit (such as could result from a computer's main memory size or addressing capability) to the number of objects in a database.

- Access control: users can "own" objects and define access rights to them.

- Property-based querying: mechanisms enable users and programs to find database objects by specifying their abstract properties rather than their location.

- Integrity constraints: users can define some semantic constraints on objects and have the database system enforce these constraints.

- Administration: tools are available to monitor, audit, archive and reorganize the database, add users, remove users, print out reports.

- Sharing: several users or programs can access the database simultaneously.

- Locking: users or programs can obtain exclusive access (read only, read and write) to one or more objects.

- Transactions: it is possible to define a sequence of database operations, called a transaction, with the guarantee that either the whole transaction will be executed normally or, if it fails, it will not have visibly affected the state of the database.

  > The standard transaction example is a money transfer from a bank account to another, requiring two operations — debiting the first account and crediting the second — which must either succeed together or fail together. If they fail, any partial modification, such as debiting the first account, must be canceled; this is called *rolling back* the transaction.

The features listed are not exhaustive; they reflect what most current commercial systems offer, and what users have come to expect.

31.5 OBJECT-RELATIONAL INTEROPERABILITY

By far the most common form of database systems today is the **relational** kind, based on ideas developed by E. F. Codd in a 1970 article.

Definitions

A relational database is a set of *relations*, each containing a set of *tuples* (or *records*). A relation is also known as a *table* and a tuple as a *row* because it is convenient to present a relation in tabular form, as in

title	date	pages	author
"The Red and the Black"	1830	341	"STENDHAL"
"The Charterhouse of Parma"	1839	307	"STENDHAL"
"Madame Bovary"	1856	425	"FLAUBERT"
"Eugénie Grandet"	1833	346	"BALZAC"

The BOOKS relation

Each tuple is made of a number of *fields*. All the tuples in a relation have the same number and types of fields; in the example the first and last fields are strings, the other two are integers. Each field is identified by a name: *title*, *date* and so on in the above *BOOKS* example. The field names, or equivalently the columns, are known as *attributes*.

Some authors, notably Date, use "attribute name" for attribute and "attribute" for field.

Relational databases are usually *normalized*, meaning among other things that every field is a simple value (such as an integer, a real, a string, a date); it cannot be a reference to another tuple.

Operations

The relational model of databases comes with a *relational algebra* which defines a number of operations on relations. Three typical operations are selection, projection and join.

Selection yields a relation containing a subset of the rows of a given relation, based on some condition on the fields. Applying the selection condition "*pages* less than 400" to *BOOKS* yields a relation made of *BOOKS*'s first, second and last tuples.

The projection of a relation along one or more attributes is obtained by ignoring all the other fields, and removing any duplicate rows in the result. If we project the above relation along its last attribute we obtain a one-field relation with three tuples, "STENDHAL", "FLAUBERT" and "BALZAC"; if we project it along its first three attributes the result is a three-field relation, deduced from the above by removing the last column.

The join of two relations is a composite relation obtained by selecting type-compatible attributes in each of them and combining rows that match for these attributes. Assume that we also have a relation *AUTHORS*:

The* AUTHORS *relation

name	real_name	birth	death
"BALZAC"	"Honoré de Balzac"	1799	1850
"FLAUBERT"	"Gustave Flaubert"	1821	1880
"PROUST"	"Marcel Proust"	1871	1922
"STENDHAL"	"Henri Beyle"	1783	1842

Then the join of *BOOKS* and *AUTHORS* on the matching attributes *author* and *name* is the following relation:

Join of* BOOKS *and* AUTHORS *relations on* author *and* name *fields

title	date	pages	author/name	real_name	birth	death
"The Red and the Black"	1830	341	"STENDHAL"	"Henri Beyle"	1783	1842
"The Charterhouse of Parma"	1839	307	"STENDHAL"	"Henri Beyle"	1783	1842
"Madame Bovary"	1856	425	"FLAUBERT"	"Gustave Flaubert"	1821	1880
"Eugénie Grandet"	1833	346	"BALZAC"	"Honoré de Balzac"	1799	1850

Queries

The relational model permits queries — one of the principal database requirements of our earlier list — through a standardized language called SQL, with two forms: one to be used directly by humans, the other ("embedded SQL") to be used by programs. Using the first form, a typical SQL query is

> **select** *title*, *date*, *pages* **from** *BOOKS*

yielding the titles, dates and page numbers of all recorded books. As you will have noted, such a query is, in the relational algebra, a projection. Another example is

> **select** *title*, *date*, *pages*, *author* **where** *pages < 400*

corresponding in the relational algebra to a selection. The query

> **select**
>
> > *title*, *date*, *pages*, *author*, *real_name*, *birth*, *date*
>
> **from** *AUTHORS*, *BOOKS* **where**
>
> > *author* = *name*

is internally a join, yielding the same result as the join example given earlier.

Using relational databases with object-oriented software

The concepts of relational databases, as just sketched, bear a marked resemblance to the basic model of O-O computation. We can associate a relation with a class, and a tuple of that relation with an object — an instance of that class. We need a class library to provide us with the operations of relational algebra (corresponding to embedded SQL).

A number of object-oriented environments provide such a library for C++, Smalltalk or (with the *Store* library) the notation of this book. This approach, which we may call object-relational interoperability, has been used successfully by many developments. It is appropriate in either of the following circumstances:

- You are writing an object-oriented system which must use and possibly update existing corporate data, stored in relational databases. In such a case there is no other choice than using an object-relational interface.

- Your O-O software needs to store object structures simple enough to fit nicely in the relational view of things. (Reasons why it might *not* fit are explained next.)

If your persistence requirements fall outside of these cases, you will experience what the literature calls an *impedance mismatch* between the data model of your software development (object-oriented) and the data model of your database system (relational). You may then find it useful to take a look at the newest development in the database field: object-oriented database systems.

31.6 OBJECT-ORIENTED DATABASE FUNDAMENTALS

The rise of object-oriented databases has been fueled by three incentives:

D1 • The desire to provide object-oriented software developers with a persistence mechanism compatible with their development method — to remove the impedance mismatches.

D2 • The need to overcome conceptual limitations of relational databases.

D3 • The attempt to offer more advanced database facilities, not present in earlier systems (relational or not), but made possible and necessary by the general technological advance of the computer field.

The first incentive is the most obvious for someone whose background is O-O software development when he comes to the persistence question. But it is not necessarily the most important. The other two are pure database concerns, independent of the development method.

To study the concept of O-O database let us start by examining the limitations of relational systems (D2) and how they can fail to meet the expectations of an O-O developer (D1), then move on to innovative contributions of the O-O database movement.

Where relational databases stop

It would be absurd to deny the contribution of relational database systems. (In fact, whereas the first publications on O-O databases in the eighties tended to be critical of relational technology, the more recent trend is to describe the two approaches as complementary.) Relational systems have been one of the principal components in the growth of information technology since the seventies, and will be around for a long time. They are well adapted to situations involving data, possibly large amounts thereof, where

R1 • The structure of the data is regular: all objects of a given type have the same number and types of components.

R2 • The structure is simple: the component types all belong to a small set of predefined possibilities.

R3 • These types are drawn from a small group of predefined possibilities (integers, strings, dates…), each with fixed space requirements.

A typical example is a census or taxpayer database with many objects representing persons, each made of a fixed set of components for the name (string), date of birth (date), address (string), salary (integer) and a few more properties.

Property R3 rules out many multimedia, CAD-CAM and image processing applications, where some data elements, such as image bitmaps, are of highly variable sizes, and sometimes very large. It also precludes, as a result of the "normal form" requirements enforced by existing commercial tools, the possibility for an object to refer to another object. This is of course a dramatic limitation when compared to what we have come to taking for granted in the discussions of this book: whenever we had

An object with a reference to another object

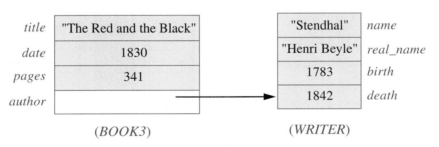

(*BOOK3*)   (*WRITER*)

the object-oriented model made it easy to access indirect properties of an object, such as *redblack.author.birth_year* (yielding *1783* if *redblack* is attached to the object on the left of the figure). A relational description will not be able to represent the reference field *author*, whose value is the denotation of another object.

There is a workaround in the relational model, but it is heavy and impractical. To represent the above situation, you will have two relations, *BOOKS* and *AUTHORS*, as introduced a few pages back. Then, to connect the two relations, you may perform a **join**, which was also shown in the first part of this discussion, using matching fields *author* for the first relation and *name* from the second.

To answer questions such as "What is the birth year of the author of *The Red and the* *The join example was*
Black?" the relational implementation will have to compute joins, projections etc.; here *on page 1049.*
we can use the join seen earlier and then project along the *date* attribute.

This technique works and is widely used, but it is only applicable for simple
schemes. The number of join operations would quickly become prohibitive in a system
that must regularly handle queries with many indirections, as "How many rooms are there
in the previous house of the manager of the department from which the lady who
graduated at the top of my wife's youngest maternal uncle's undergraduate class was
reassigned when the parent company went through its second round of venture funding?"
— no particular problem in an O-O system's run-time network of objects.

Object identity

The simplicity of the relational model follows in part from the identification of objects
with their values. A relation (table) is a subset of $A \times B \times \ldots$ for some sets $A, B, \ldots$, where
$\times$ represents cartesian product; in other words each one of the elements of the relation —
each object — is a tuple $<a1, b1, \ldots>$ where $a1$ is an element of A and so on. But such an
object has no existence other than its value; in particular, inserting an object into a relation
has no effect if the relation already has an identical tuple. For example inserting $<$"*The Red
and the Black*", *1830, 341,* "*STENDHAL*"$>$ into the above *BOOKS* relation does not
change the relation. This is very different from the dynamic model of O-O computation,
where we can have two identical objects:

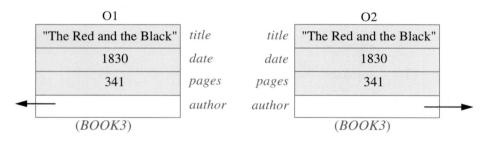

*Separate but
equal*

(*Both bottom refer-
ences are attached
to the same object.*)

As you will remember, *equal* (*obj1, obj2*) will have value true if *obj1* and *obj2* are
references attached to these objects, but *obj1* = *obj2* will yield false.

Being identical is not the same as being the same (ask any identical twins). This
ability to distinguish between the two notions is part of the modeling power of object
technology. It relies on the notion of **object identity**: any object has an existence
independent of its contents.

Visitors to the Imperial Palace in Kyoto are told both that the buildings are very ancient
and that each is rebuilt every hundred years or so. With the notion of object identity there
is no contradiction: the object is the same even if its contents have changed.

You are the same individual as ten years ago even if none of the molecules that made up
your body then remains in it now.

We can express object identity in the relational model, of course: just add to every object a special key field, guaranteed to be unique among objects of a given type. But we have to take care of it explicitly. With the O-O model, object identity is there by default.

In non-persistent O-O software construction, support for object identity is almost accidental: in the simplest implementation, each object resides at a certain address, and a reference to the object uses that address, which serves as immutable object identity. (This is not true any more in implementations, such as ISE's, which may move objects around for effective garbage collection; object identity is then a more abstract concept.) With persistence, object identify becomes a distinctive factor of the object-oriented model.

Maintaining object identity in a shared databases raises new problems: every client that needs to create objects must obtain a unique identity for them; this means that the module in charge of assigning identities must be a shared resource, creating a potential bottleneck in a highly concurrent setup.

The threshold model

After [Zdonik 1990]. From the preceding observations follows what has been called the threshold model of object-oriented databases: the minimum set of properties that a database system must satisfy if it deserves at all to be called O-O. (More advanced features, also desirable, will be discussed next.) There are four requirements for meeting the threshold model: **database, encapsulation, object identity** and **references**. The system must:

T1 • Provide database functionality, as defined earlier in this chapter.

T2 • Support encapsulation, that is to say allow hiding the internal properties of objects and make them accessible through an official interface.

T3 • Associate with each object an identification that is unique in the database.

T4 • Allow an object to contain references to other objects.

Notable in this list is the absence of some object-oriented mechanisms that we know are indispensable to the method, in particular inheritance. But this is not as strange as might appear at first. All depends on what you expect from a database system. A system at the threshold level might be a good **O-O database engine**, providing a set of mechanisms for storing, retrieving and traversing object structures, but leaving any higher knowledge about the semantics of these objects, such as the inheritance relations, to the design and programming language and the development environment.

The experience of early O-O database systems confirms that the database engine approach is reasonable. Some of the first systems went to the other extreme and had a complete "data model" with an associated O-O language supporting inheritance, genericity, polymorphism and so on. The vendors found that these languages were competing with O-O design and programming languages, and tended to *lose* such competitions (since a database language, will likely be less general and practical than one designed from the start as a universal programming language); they scurried in most cases to replace these proprietary offerings with interfaces to the main O-O languages.

Additional facilities

Beyond the threshold model a number of facilities are desirable. Most commercial systems offer at least some of them.

The first category includes direct support for more advanced properties of the O-O method: inheritance (single or multiple), typing, dynamic binding. This does not require more elaboration for the readers of this book. Other facilities, reviewed next, include: object versioning, schema evolution, long transactions, locking, object-oriented queries.

Object versioning

Object versioning is the ability to retain earlier states of an object after procedure calls have changed the state. This is particularly important as a result of concurrent accesses. Assume that an object O1 contains a reference to an object O2. A client changes some fields of O1, other than the reference. Another client changes O2. Then if the first client attempts to follow the reference, it may find a version of O2 that is inconsistent with O1.

Some O-O database systems address this problem by treating every object modification as the creation of a new object, thereby maintaining access to older versions.

Class versioning and schema evolution

Objects are not the only elements to require versioning: over time, their generating classes may change too. This is the problem of schema evolution, discussed at the beginning of this chapter. Only a few O-O database systems provide full support for schema evolution.

Long transactions

The concept of transaction has always been important in database systems, but classical transaction mechanisms have been directed towards *short* transactions: those which begin and end with a single operation performed by a single user during a single session of a computer system. The archetypal example, cited at the beginning of this chapter, is transferring a certain amount of money from one bank account to another; it is a transaction, since it requires an all-or-nothing outcome: either both operations (debiting one account and crediting the other) succeed, or both fail. The time it will take is on the order of seconds (less if we ignore user interaction).

Applications in the general idea of *design* of complex systems, such as CAD-CAM (computer-aided design and manufacturing of engineering products) and computer-aided software engineering, raise the need of *long* transactions, whose duration may be on the order of days or even months. During the design of a car, for example, one of the engineering teams may have to check out the carburetor part to perform some changes, and check it back in a week or two later. Such an operation has all the properties of a transaction, but the techniques developed for short transactions are not directly applicable.

The field of software development itself has obvious demand for long transactions, arising each time several people or teams work on a common set of modules. Interestingly, database technology has not been widely applied (in spite of many suggestions in the literature) to software development. The software field has instead developed for its own purposes a set of *configuration management* tools which address the specific issues of software component management, but also duplicate some standard database functions, most of the time without the benefit of database technology. This situation, surprising at first look, has a most likely explanation: the absence of support for long transactions in traditional database management systems.

Although long transactions may not conceptually require object technology, recent efforts to support them have come from O-O database systems, some of which offer a way to check any object in and out of a database.

Locking

Any database management system must provide some form of locking, to ensure safe concurrent access and updating. Early O-O database systems supported *page-level* locking, where the operating system determines the scope of a lock; this is inconvenient for large objects (which may extend over several pages) and small objects (which may fit several to a page, so that locking one will also lock the others). Newer systems provide *object-level* locking, letting a client application lock any object individually.

Recent efforts have tried hard to *minimize* the amount of locking that occurs in actual executions, since locking may cause contention and slow down the operation of the database. **Optimistic locking** is the general name for a class of policies which try to avoid placing a lock on an object a priori, but instead execute the possibly contentious operations on a copy, then wait as long as possible to update the master copy, locking it and reconciling conflicting updates at that time if necessary. We will see below an advanced form of optimistic locking in the Matisse case.

Queries

Database systems, it was recalled earlier, support queries. Here object-oriented systems can offer more flexibility than relational ones in the presence of schema evolution. Changing the schema of a relational database often means that you must change the query texts too and recompile them if appropriate. In an O-O database, the queries are relative to objects; you query the instances of a certain class with respect to some of their features. Here *instance* has, at least on option, its general sense covering both direct instances of a class and instances of its proper descendants; so if you add a descendant to a class the original queries on that class will be able to retrieve instances of the new descendant.

31.7 O-O DATABASE SYSTEMS: EXAMPLES

Since the mid-eighties a number of object-oriented database products have appeared. Some of the best-known product names are Gemstone, Itasca, Matisse, Objectivity, ObjectStore, Ontos, O_2, Poet, Versant. More recently a few companies such as UniSQL have introduced object-relational systems in an effort to reconcile the best of both approaches; the major relational database vendors are also proposing or announcing combined solutions, such as Informix's Illustra (based in part on UC Berkeley's POSTGRES project) and Oracle's announced Oracle 8 system.

To facilitate interoperability, a number of O-O database vendors have joined forces in the *Object Database Management Group*, which has proposed the ODMG standard to unify the general interface of O-O databases and their query language.

Let us take a look at two particularly interesting systems, Matisse and Versant.

Matisse

MATISSE, from ADB Inc., is an object-oriented database system with support for C, C++, Smalltalk and the notation of this book.

The official spelling is all upper case.

Matisse is a bold design with many non-conventional ideas. It is particularly geared towards large databases with a rich semantic structure and can manipulate very large objects such as images, films and sounds. Although it supports basic O-O concepts such as multiple inheritance, Matisse refrains from imposing too many constraints on the data model and instead serves as a powerful O-O database engine in the sense defined earlier in this chapter. Some of the strong points are:

- An original representation technique that makes it possible to split an object — especially a large object — over several disks, so as to optimize access time.

- Optimized object placement on disks.

- An automatic duplication mechanism providing a software solution to hardware fault tolerance: objects (rather than the disks themselves) can be mirrored across several disks, with automatic recovery in case of a disk failure.

- A built-in object versioning mechanism (see below).

- Support for transactions.

- Support for a client-server architecture in which a central server manages data for a possibly large number of clients, which keep a "cache" of recently accessed objects.

Matisse uses an original approach to the problem of minimizing locks. The mutual exclusion rule enforced by many systems is that several clients may read an object at once, but as soon as one client starts writing no other client may read or write. The reason, discussed in the concurrency chapter, is to preserve object integrity, as expressed by class invariants. Permitting two clients to write simultaneously could make the object inconsistent; and if a client is in the middle of writing, the object may be in an unstable state (one that does not satisfy the invariant), so that another client reading it may get an inconsistent result.

Writer-writer locks are clearly inevitable. Some systems, however, make it possible to breach the reader-writer exclusion by permitting read operations to occur even in the presence of a write lock. Such operations are appropriately called *dirty reads*.

Matisse, whose designers were clearly obsessed with the goal of minimizing locks, has a radical solution to this issue, based on object management: *no write operations*. Instead of modifying an existing object, a write operation (one, that is, which appears as such to the client software) will create a new object. As a result, it is possible to read objects without any locking: you will access a certain version of the database, unaffected by write operations that may occur after you start the read. You are also able to access a number of objects with the guarantee that they will all belong to the same version of the database, whereas with a more traditional approach you would have to use global locks or transactions, and incur the resulting performance penalties, to achieve the same result.

A consequence of this policy is the ability to go back to earlier versions of an object or of the database. By default, older versions are kept, but the system provides a "version collector" to get rid of unwanted versions.

Matisse provides interesting mechanisms for managing relations. If a class such as *EMPLOYEE* has an attribute *supervisor: MANAGER*, Matisse will on request maintain the inverse links automatically, so that you can access not only the supervisor of an employee but also all the employees managed by a supervisor. In addition, the query facilities can retrieve objects through associated keywords.

Versant

Versant, from Versant Object Technology, is an object-oriented database system with support for C++, Smalltalk and the notation of this book. Its data model and interface language support many of the principal concepts of O-O development, such as classes, multiple inheritance, feature redefinition, feature renaming, polymorphism and genericity.

Versant is one of the database systems conforming to the ODMG standard. It is meant for client-server architectures and, like Matisse, allows caching of the most recently accessed information, at the page level on the server side and at the object level for clients.

The design of Versant has devoted particular attention to locking and transactions. Locks can be placed on individual objects. An application can request a read lock, an update lock or a write lock. Update locks serve to avoid deadlock: if you have a read lock and want to write, you should first request an update lock, which will be granted only if no other client has done so; this still lets other clients read, until you request a write lock, which you are guaranteed to get. Going directly from read lock to write lock could cause deadlock: two clients each waiting indefinitely for the other to release its lock.

The transaction mechanism provides for both short and long transactions; an application may check out an object for any period. Object versioning is supported, as well as optimistic locking.

The query mechanism makes it possible to query all instances of a class, including instances of its proper descendants. As noted earlier, this makes it possible to add a class without having to redefine the queries applying to its previously existing ancestors.

Another interesting Versant capability is the event notification mechanism, which you can use to make sure that certain events, such as object update and deletion, will cause applications to receive a notification, enabling them to execute any associated actions that they may have defined for that purpose.

Versant provides a rich set of data types, including a set of predefined collection classes. It permits schema evolution, with the convention that new fields are initialized to default values. A set of indexing and query mechanism is available.

31.8 DISCUSSION: BEYOND O-O DATABASES

Let us conclude this review of persistence issues with a few musings on possible future evolutions. The observations that follow are tentative rather than final; they are meant to prompt further reflection rather than to provide concrete answers.

Is "O-O database" an oxymoron?

The notion of database proceeds from a view of the world in which the Data sit in the middle, and various programs are permitted to access and modify such Data:

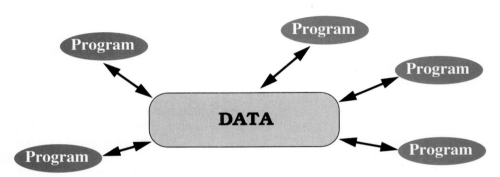

The database view

In object technology, however, we have learned to understand data as being entirely defined by the applicable operations:

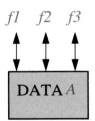 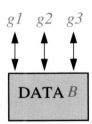 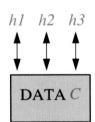

The O-O view

The two views seem incompatible! The notion of data existing independently of the programs that manipulate them ("data independence", a tenet reaffirmed in the first few pages of every database textbook) is anathema to the object-oriented developer. Should we then consider that "object-oriented database" is an oxymoron?

Perhaps not, but it may be worthwhile to explore how, in a dogmatic O-O context, we could obtain the effect of databases without really having databases. If we define (simplifying to the barest essentials the definition of databases given earlier in this chapter)

*"FROM PERSIS-
TENCE TO DATA-
BASES", 31.4, page
1047.*

DATABASE = PERSISTENCE + SHARING

the dogmatic view would consider the second component, data sharing, as incompatible with O-O ideas, and focus on persistence only. Then we would address the sharing needs through a different technique: concurrency! The picture becomes

Separating persistence from sharing

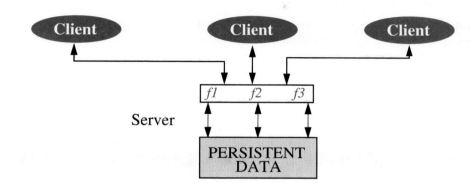

On concurrency and the **separate** *mechanism see chapter 30.*

Following O-O principles, the persistent data are implemented as a set of objects — instances of some abstract data types — and controlled by a certain server system. Client systems that need to manipulate the data will do so through the server; because the setup requires sharing and concurrent access, the clients will treat the server as **separate** in the sense defined by the discussion of concurrency. For example:

flights: **separate** *FLIGHT_DATABASE*; …

flight_details (*f*: **separate** *FLIGHT_DATABASE*;
        rf: *REQUESTED_FLIGHTS*): *FLIGHT* **is**

    do

        Result := *f•flight_details* (*rf*)

    end

reserve (*f*: **separate** *FLIGHT_DATABASE*; *r*: *RESERVATION*) **is**

    do

        f•reserve (*r*); *status* := *f•status*

    end

Then the server side requires no sharing mechanism, only a general persistence mechanism. We may also need tools and techniques to handle such matters as object versioning, which are indeed *persistence* rather than *database* issues.

The persistence mechanism could then become extremely simple, shedding much of the baggage of databases. We might even consider that *all objects are persistent by default*; transient objects become the exception, handled by a mechanism that generalizes garbage collection. Such an approach, inconceivable when database systems were invented, becomes less absurd with the constant decrease of storage costs and the growing availability of 64-bit virtual address spaces where, it has been noted, *"one could create a new 4-gigabyte object, the size of a full address space on a conventional 32-bit processor, once a second for 136 years and not exhaust the available namespace. This is sufficient to store all the data associated with almost any application during its entire lifetime."*

Quotation from [Sombrero-Web].

All this is speculative, and provides no proof that we should renounce the traditional notion of database. There is no need to rush and sell your shares of O-O database companies yet. Consider this discussion as an intellectual exercise: an invitation to probe further into the widely accepted notion of O-O database, examining whether the current approach truly succeeds in removing the dreaded *impedance mismatches* between the software development method and the supporting data storage mechanisms.

Unstructured information

A final note on databases. With the explosion of the World-Wide Web and the appearance of content-based search tools (of which some well-known examples, at the time of writing, are AltaVista, Web Crawler and Yahoo) it has become clear that we can access data successfully even in the absence of a database.

Database systems require that before you store any data for future retrieval you first convert it into a strictly defined format, the database schema. Recent studies, however, show that 80% of the electronic data in companies is unstructured (that is to say, resides outside of databases, typically in text files) even though database systems have been around for many years. This is where content-based tools intervene: from user-defined criteria involving characteristic words and phrases, they can retrieve data from unstructured or minimally structured documents. Almost anyone who has tried these tools has been bedazzled by the speed at which they can retrieve information: a second or two suffices to find a needle in a bytestack of thousands of gigabytes. This leads to the inevitable question: do we really need structured databases?

The answer is still yes. Unstructured and structured data will coexist. But databases are no longer the only game in town; more and more, sophisticated query tools will be able to retrieve information even if it is not in the exact format that a database would require. To write such tools, of course, object technology is our best bet.

31.9 KEY CONCEPTS STUDIED IN THIS CHAPTER

- An object-oriented environment should allow objects to be persistent — to remain in existence after the session creating them has terminated.

- A persistence mechanism should offer *schema evolution* to convert retrieved objects on the fly if their generating class has changed ("object mismatch"). This involves three tasks: detection, notification, correction. By default, a mismatch should cause an exception.

- Beyond persistence, many applications need database support, offering concurrent access to clients.

- Other properties of databases include querying, locking and transactions.

- It is possible to use O-O development in conjunction with relational databases, through a simple correspondence: classes to relations, objects to tuples.

- To gain full use of object technology and avoid impedance mismatches between the development and the data model, you may use object-oriented databases.

- Two interesting O-O database systems were studied: Matisse, providing original solutions for object versioning and redundancy, and Versant, providing advanced locking and transaction mechanisms.

- In a more tentative part of the discussion, some questions were raised as to the true compatibility of database principles with the O-O view, and the need for accessing unstructured as well as structured data.

31.10 BIBLIOGRAPHICAL NOTES

The original paper on the relational model is [Codd 1970]; there are many books on the topic. Probably the best-known database textbook, with particular emphasis on the relational model, is [Date 1995], the sixth edition of a book originally published in the mid-seventies. Another useful general-purpose text is [Elmasri 1989].

[Waldén 1995] contains a detailed practical discussion of how to make object-relational interoperability work. [Khoshafian 1986] brought the question of object identity to the forefront of O-O database discussions.

A good starting point for understanding the goals of object-oriented database systems and reading some of the original papers is [Zdonik 1990], a collection of contributions by some of the pioneers in the field, whose introductory chapter is the source of the "threshold model" concept used in the present chapter. The widely circulated "O-O Database System Manifesto" [Atkinson 1989], the result of the collaboration of a number of experts, has been influential in defining the goals of the O-O database movement. There are now a number of textbooks on the topic; some of the best known, in order of publication, are: [Kim 1990], [Bertino 1993], [Khoshafian 1993], [Kemper 1994], [Loomis 1995]. For further, regularly updated references, Michael Ley's on-line bibliography of database systems [Ley-Web] is precious. Klaus Dittrich's group at the University of Zürich maintains a "mini-FAQ" about O-O databases at *http:// www.ifi.unizh.ch/groups/dbtg/ObjectDB/ODBminiFAQ.html*. [Cattell 1993] describes the ODMG standard. For an appraisal, somewhat jaded, of the achievements and failures of O-O databases by one of the pioneers of the field, see [Stein 1995].

This chapter has benefited from important comments by Richard Bielak, particularly on schema evolution, Persistence Closure, queries in O-O databases, Versant and Sombrero. Its presentation of Versant is based on [Versant 1994], that of Matisse on [ADB 1995] (see also *http://www.adb.com/techovw/features.html*). I am indebted to Shel Finkelstein for helping me with the features of Matisse. O_2 is described in [Bancilhon 1992]. The Sombrero project [Sombrero-Web] has explored the implications of large address spaces on traditional approaches to persistence and databases.

A preview of some of this chapter's material on schema evolution appeared as [M 1996c]. The questioning of how well O-O and database concepts really match comes from two unpublished keynote lectures, presented in 1995 at TOOLS USA and the European Software Engineering Conference [M 1995d].

EXERCISES

E31.1 Dynamic schema evolution

Study how to extend the schema evolution techniques developed in this chapter to account for the case in which classes of a software system may change during the system's execution.

E31.2 Object-oriented queries

Discuss the form that queries may take in an object-oriented database management system.

32

Some O-O techniques for graphical interactive applications

Famous Designer has recently designed an automobile. It has neither a fuel gauge, nor a speedometer, nor any of the idiotic controls that plague other modern cars. Instead, if the driver makes a mistake, a large "?" lights up in the middle of the dashboard. "The experienced driver", says Famous, "will usually know what went wrong".

Unix folklore. (Instead of *"Famous Designer"*, the original names one of the principal contributors to Unix.)

$\mathcal{E}$legant user interfaces have become a required part of any successful software product. Advances in display hardware, ergonomics (the study of human factors) and software have taken advantage of interaction techniques first pioneered in the seventies: multiple windows so you can work on several jobs, mouse or other fast-moving device so you can show what you want, menus to speed up your choices, icons to represent important notions, figures to display information visually, buttons to request common operations.

The acronym GUI, for Graphical User Interface, has come to serve as a general slogan for this style of interaction. Related buzzwords include WYSIWYG (*What You See Is What You Get*), WIMP (*Windows, Icons, Menus, Pointing device*) and the phrase "direct manipulation", characterizing applications which give their users the impression that they work directly on the objects shown on the screen.

These impressive techniques, not long ago accessible only to users of a few advanced systems running on expensive hardware, have now become almost commonplace even on the most ordinary personal computers. So commonplace and popular, in fact, that a software developer can hardly expect any success from a product that uses just a line-oriented interface, or even one that is full-screen but not graphical.

Yet until recently the construction of interactive applications offering advanced graphical facilities remained so difficult as to justify what may be called the *Interface Conjecture*: the more convenient and easy an application appears to its users, the harder it will be for its developers to build.

One of the admirable advances of the software field over the past few years has been to start **disproving** the interface conjecture through the appearance of good tools such as interface builders.

More progress remains necessary in this fast-moving area. Object technology can help tremendously, and in fact the fields denoted by the two buzzwords, GUI and O-O, have had a closely linked history. Simply stated, the purpose of this chapter is to disprove the Interface Conjecture, by showing that to be user-friendly an application does not have to be developer-hostile. Object-oriented techniques will help us concentrate on the proper data abstractions, suggest some of these abstractions, and give us the ability to reuse everything that can be reused.

A complete exploration of O-O techniques for building graphical and interactive applications would take a book of its own. The aim of the present chapter is much more modest. It will simply select a few of the less obvious aspects of GUI building, and introduce a few fundamental techniques that you should find widely applicable if your work involves designing graphical systems.

32.1 NEEDED TOOLS

What tools do we need for building useful and pleasant interactive applications?

End users, application developers and tool developers

First, a point of terminology to avoid any confusion. The word "user" (one of the most abused terms in the computer field) is potentially misleading here. Certain people, called **application developers**, will produce interactive applications to be used by other people, to be called **end users**; a typical end user would be a dentist's assistant, using a system built by some application developer for recording and accessing patient history. The application developers themselves will rely, for their graphical needs, on tools built by the third group, **tool developers**. The presence of three categories is the reason why "user" without further qualification is ambiguous: the end users are the application developers' users; but the application developers themselves are the tool developers' users.

An **application** is an interactive system produced by a developer. An end user who uses an application will do so by starting a session, exercising the application's various facilities by providing the input of his choice. Sessions are to applications what objects are to classes: individual instances of a general pattern.

This chapter analyzes the requirements of developers who want to provide their end users with useful applications offering graphical interfaces.

Graphical systems, window systems, toolkits

Many computing platforms offer some tools for building graphical interactive applications. For the graphical part, libraries are available to implement designs such as GKS and PHIGS. For the user interface part, basic window systems (such as the Windows Application Programming Interface, the Xlib API under Unix and the Presentation Manager API under OS/2) are too low-level to make direct use convenient for application developers, but they are complemented by "toolkits", such as those based on the Motif user interface protocol.

All these systems fulfill useful needs, but they do not suffice to satisfy developers' requirements. Among their limitations:

- They remain hard to use. With Motif-based toolkits, developers must master a multi-volume documentation describing hundreds of predefined C functions and structures bearing such awe-inspiring names as *XmPushButtonCallbackStruct* — with the *B* of *Button* in upper case, but the *b* of *back* in lower case — or *XmNsubMenuId*. The difficulties and insecurities of C are compounded by the complexity of the toolkit. Using the basic Application Programming Interface of Windows is similarly tedious: to create an application, you must write the application's main loop to get and dispatch messages, a window procedure to catch user events, and other low-level elements.

- Although the toolkits cover user interface objects — buttons, menus and the like — some of them offer little on graphics (geometrical figures and transformations). To add true graphics to the interface is a significant effort.

- The toolkits are incompatible with each other. Motif, the Windows graphics and Presentation Manager, although based on essentially similar concepts, differ in many ways, some significant (in Windows and PM creating a user interface object displays it immediately, whereas under Motif you first build the corresponding structure and then call a "realize" operation to display it), some just a matter of convention (screen coordinates are measured from the top left in PM, from the bottom left in the others). Many user interface conventions also vary. Most of these differences are a nuisance to end users, who just want something that works and "looks nice", and do not care whether window corners are sharp or slightly rounded. The differences are an even worse nuisance to developers, who must choose between losing part of their potential market or wasting precious development time on porting efforts.

The library and the application builder

To answer the needs of developers and enable them to produce applications that will satisfy their end users, we must go beyond the toolkits and provide portable, high-level tools that relieve developers from the more tedious and repetitive parts of their job, allowing them to devote their creativity to the truly innovative aspects.

The toolkits provide a good basis, since they support many of the needed mechanisms. But we must hide their details and complement them with more usable tools.

The basis of the solution is a library of reusable classes, supporting the fundamental data abstractions identified in this chapter, in particular the notions of window, menu, context, event, command, state, application.

For some of the tasks encountered in building an application, developers will find it convenient to work not by writing software texts in the traditional fashion, but by relying on an interactive system, called an application builder, which will enable them to express their needs in a graphical, WYSIWIG form; in other words, to use for their own work the interface techniques that they offer to their users. An application builder is a tool whose end-users are themselves developers; they use the application builder to build the parts of their systems that may be specified visually and interactively. The term "application builder" indicates that this tool is far more ambitious than plain "interface builders", which only cover the user interface of an application. Our application builder must go further into expressing the structure and semantics of an application, stopping only where software text becomes the only reasonable solution.

In defining the library and the application builder, we should be guided, as always, by the criteria of reusability and extendibility. This means in particular that for every data abstraction identified below (such as context, command or state) the application builder should provide two tools:

- For reusability, a **catalog** (event catalog, context catalog, state catalog…) containing predefined representatives of the abstraction, which developers can include directly into their applications.

- For extendibility, an **editor** (context editor, command editor, state editor…) enabling developers to produce their own variants, either from scratch or more commonly by pulling an element from a catalog and then modifying it.

Using the object-oriented approach

In the object-oriented approach to software construction, the key step is to find the right data abstractions: the types of objects which characterize applications in the given area.

To advance our understanding of graphical user interfaces and devise good mechanisms for building applications, we must explore the corresponding abstractions. Some are obvious; others will prove more subtle.

Each of the abstractions encountered below will yield at least one class in the library. Some will yield a set of classes, all descending from a common ancestor describing the most general notion. For example, the library includes several classes describing variants of the notion of menu.

We will first examine the overall structure of a portable graphics library; then consider the main graphical abstractions covering the geometrical objects to be displayed, and the "interaction objects" supporting event-driven dialogues; finally we will study the more advanced abstractions describing applications: command, state, application itself.

32.2 PORTABILITY AND PLATFORM ADAPTATION

Some application developers want a portable library, which will enable them to write a single source text that will then adapt automatically to the look-and-feel of many platforms, at the price of a recompile but without any change. Others want the reverse: to gain full access to all the specific "controls" and "widgets" of a particular platform such as Microsoft Windows, but in a convenient fashion (rather than at the typically low level of the native libraries). Yet others want a bit of both: portability as the default, but the ability to go native when needed.

With a careful design, relying on a two-layer structure, we can try to satisfy all of them:

Graphical libraries architecture

Platform-independent library (*Vision*)

(See a similar archi tecture for concur- rency, page 970.)

WEL (Windows)	MEL (Motif)	PEL (Presentation Manager)	·············

To make things more concrete the figure shows the names of the corresponding components in ISE's environment, but the idea is applicable to any graphical library. At the top level (*Vision*) there is a portable graphical library; at the bottom level you find specialized libraries, such as *WEL* for Windows, adapted to one platform only.

See "AN APPLICA- TION: THE HANDLE TECHNIQUE", 24.3, page 817.

WEL and other bottom-level libraries can be used directly, but they also serve as the platform-dependent component of the top level: *Vision* mechanisms are implemented through WEL on Windows, MEL on Motif and so on. This technique has several advantages: for the application developers, it fosters compatibility of concepts and techniques; for the tool developers, it removes unneeded duplications, and facilitates the implementation of the top level (which relies on clean, abstract, assertion-equipped and inheritance-rich O-O libraries such as WEL, rather than interfacing directly with the C level, always a dangerous proposition). The connection between the two levels relies on the *handle* design pattern developed in an earlier chapter.

Application developers have a choice of level:

- If you want to ensure portability, use the higher layer. This is also of interest to developers who, even if they work for a single platform, want to benefit from the higher degree of abstraction provided by high-level libraries such as *Vision*.

- If you want to have direct access to all the specific mechanisms of a platform (for example the many "controls" provided by Windows NT), go to the corresponding lower-layer library.

The last comment touches on a delicate issue. How much platform-specific functionality do you lose by relying on a portable library? The answer is necessarily a tradeoff. Some early portable libraries used an *intersection* (or "lowest common denominator") approach, limiting the facilities offered to those that were present in native form in all the platforms supported. This is usually not enough. At the other extreme the library authors might use the *union* approach: provide every single mechanism of every supported platform, using explicit algorithms to simulate the mechanisms that are not natively available on a particular platform. This policy would produce an enormous and redundant library. The answer has to be somewhere in-between: the library authors must decide individually, for every mechanism present on some platforms only, whether it is important enough to warrant writing a simulation on the other platforms. The result must be a consistent library, simple enough to be used without knowledge of the individual platforms, but powerful enough to produce impressive visual applications.

For application developers, one more criterion in choosing between the two layers is performance. If your main reason for considering the top layer is abstraction rather than portability, you must be aware that including the extra classes will carry a space penalty (any time penalty should be negligible with a well-designed library), and decide whether it is worthwhile. Clearly, a one-platform library such as WEL will be more compact.

Finally, note that the two solutions are not completely exclusive. You can do the bulk of your work at the top level and provide some platform-specific goodies to users working on your top-selling platform. This has to be done carefully, of course; carelessly mixing portable and non-portable elements would soon cancel any expected benefits, even partial, of portable development. An elegant design pattern (which ISE has applied to some of its libraries) relies on assignment attempt. The idea is this. Consider a graphical object known through an entity *m* whose type is at the top level, say *MENU*. Any actual object to which it will become attached at run time will be, of course, platform-specific; so it will be an instance of a lower-layer class, say *WEL_MENU*. To apply platform-specific features you need an entity, say *wm*, of this type. You can use the following scheme:

> *wm* ?= *m*
>
> **if** *wm* = *Void* **then**
>
> > ... We are not on Windows! Do nothing, or something else ...
>
> **else**
>
> > ... Here we may apply any *WEL_MENU* (i.e. Windows-specific)
> >
> > feature to *wm* ...
>
> **end**

We can picture this scheme as a way to go into the Windows-only room. The room is locked, to prevent you from claiming, if someone finds you there, that you just wandered into it by accident. You are permitted to enter, but you must ask for the key, explicitly and politely. For such official and conditional requests to enter a special-purpose area, the key is assignment attempt.

32.3 GRAPHICAL ABSTRACTIONS

Many applications will use graphical figures, often representing objects from an external system. Let us see a simple set of abstractions that will cover this need.

Figures

First we need a proper set of abstractions for the graphical part of an interactive application. To keep things simple, this discussion will assume two-dimensional graphics.

Geographical maps provide an excellent model. A map (of a country, a region, a city) provides a visual representation of some reality. The design of a map uses several levels of abstraction:

- We must view the reality behind the model (in an already abstracted form) as a set of geometrical shape or **figures**. For a map the figures represent rivers, roads, towns and other geographical objects.

- The map will describe a certain set of figures, which may be called the **world**.

- The maps will show only a part of the world — one or more areas which we will call **windows**, and assume to be rectangular. For example a map can have one main window devoted to a country, and subsidiary windows devoted to large cities or outlying parts (as with Corsica in maps of France or Hawaii in maps of the USA).

- Physically the map appears on a physical display medium, the **device**. The device is usually a sheet of paper, but we may also use a computer screen. Various parts of the device will be devoted to the various windows.

The graphical abstractions

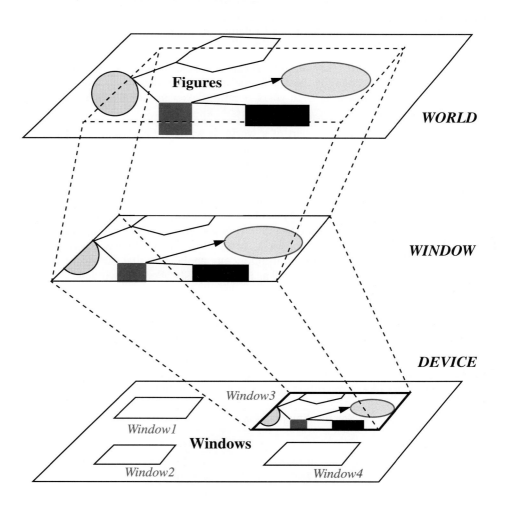

The four basic concepts — *WORLD*, *FIGURE*, *WINDOW*, *DEVICE* — transpose readily to general graphical applications, where the world may contain arbitrary figures of interest to a certain computer application, rather than just representations of geographical objects. Rectangular areas of the world (windows) will be displayed on rectangular areas of the device (the computer screen).

The figure on the previous page shows the three planes: world (bottom), window (middle) and device (top). The notion of window plays a central role, as each window is associated both with an area of the world and with an area of the device. Windows also cause the only significant extension to the basic map concepts: support for hierarchically nested windows. Our windows will be permitted to have subwindows, with no limit on the nesting level. (No nesting appears in the figure.)

Coordinates

We need two coordinate systems: device coordinates and world coordinates. Device coordinates measure the positions of displayed items on the device. On computer screens, they are often measured in pixels; a pixel (picture element) is the size of a small dot, usually the smallest displayable item.

There is no standard for the unit of world coordinates, and there should not be since the world coordinate system is best left for application developers to decide: an astronomer may wish to work in light years, a cartographer in kilometers, a biologist in millimeters or microns.

Because a window captures part of a world, it will have a certain world position (defined by the x and y world coordinates of its top-left corner) and a certain extent (horizontal and vertical lengths of the parts of the world covered). The world position and the extent are expressed in world coordinate units.

Because the window is displayed on part of a device, it has a certain device position (defined by the x and y device coordinates of its top-left corner) and a certain size on the device, all expressed in device coordinate units. For a window with no parent, the position is defined with respect to the device; for a subwindow, the position is always defined relative to the parent. Thanks to this convention, any application that uses windows may run with the whole screen to itself as well as in a previously allocated window.

Operations on windows

To take care of the hierarchical nature of windows we make class *WINDOW* an heir of class *TWO_WAY_TREE*, an implementation of trees. As a result, all hierarchical operations are readily available as tree operations: add a subwindow (child), reattach to a different enclosing window (parent) and so on. To set the world and device positions of a window, we will use one of the following procedures (all with two arguments):

	Set absolute position	Move, relative to current position
Position in world	*go*	*pan*
Position on device	*place_proportional* *place_pixel*	*move_proportional* *move_pixel*

The *_proportional* procedures interpret the values of their arguments as fractions of the parent window's height and width; arguments to the other procedures are absolute values (in world coordinates for *go* and *pan*, in device coordinates for the *_pixel* procedures). Procedures are similarly available to set the extent and size of a window.

Graphical classes and operations

All classes representing figures are descendants of a deferred class *FIGURE*; standard features include *display*, *hide*, *translate*, *rotate*, *scale*.

It is indispensable to keep the set of figure types extendible, allowing application developers (and, indirectly, end users of graphical tools) to define new types. We have seen how to do this: provide a class *COMPOSITE_FIGURE*, built by multiple inheritance from *FIGURE* and a container type such as *LIST* [*FIGURE*].

32.4 INTERACTION MECHANISMS

Let us now turn our attention to how our applications will interact with users.

Events

Modern interactive applications are **event-driven**: as the interactive user causes certain events to occur (for example by entering text at the keyboard, moving the mouse or pressing its buttons), certain operations get executed.

Innocuous as this description may seem, it represents a major departure from more traditional styles of interaction with users. In the old style (which is still by far the most common), a program that needed input from its user would get it by repeatedly executing scenarios of the form

... Perform some computation ...

print ("*Please type in the value for parameter xxx.*")

read_input

xxx := value_read

... Proceed with the computation, until it again needs a value from the user ...

In the event-driven style, roles are reversed: operations occur not because the software has reached a preset stage of its execution, but because a certain event, usually triggered by the interactive user, has caused execution of a certain component of the software. Input determines the software's execution rather than the reverse.

The object-oriented style of software development plays an important role in making such schemes possible. Dynamic binding, in particular, enables the software to call a feature on an object under the understanding that the form of the object will determine how it will handle the feature. The feature may be associated with an event and the object to a command; more on this below.

The notion of event is important enough in this discussion to yield a data abstraction. An event object (instance of the *EVENT* class) will represent a user action; examples are key press, mouse movement, mouse button down, mouse button up. These predefined events will be part of the event catalog.

In addition, it must be possible to define custom events, which a software component may send explicitly by a procedure call of the form *raise* (*e*).

Contexts and user interface objects

GUI toolkits offer a number of predefined "User Interface Objects": windows, menus, buttons, panels. Here is a simple example, an OK button.

A button

Superficially, a user interface object is just a figure. But unlike the figures seen above it usually has no relation with the underlying world: its role is limited to the handling of user input. More precisely, a user interface object provides a special case of **context**.

To understand the need for the notion of context, we must remember that an event generally does not suffice to determine the software's response. Pressing a mouse button, for example, will give different results depending on where the mouse cursor is. Contexts are precisely those conditions which determine the responses that an application associates with events.

In general, then, a context is simply a boolean value — a value which will be true or false at any instant of the software's execution.

The most common contexts are associated with user interface objects. A button such as the one above defines the boolean condition "is the mouse cursor inside the button?", a context. Contexts of this kind will be written *IN* (*uio*), where *uio* is the user interface object.

For every context *c* its negation *not c* is also a context; *not IN* (*uio*) is also called *OUT* (*uio*). The context *ANYWHERE* is always true; its negation *NOWHERE* is never true.

Our application builder should then have a context catalog, which will include *ANYWHERE* and contexts of the form *IN* (*uio*) for all commonly useful interface objects *uio*. In addition, we may wish to enable application developers to define their own contexts; the application builder will provide a context editor for this purpose. Among other facilities, the context editor makes it possible to obtain *not c* for any *c* (in particular a *c* from the catalog).

32.5 HANDLING THE EVENTS

We now have the list of events, and the list of contexts in which these events may be significant. We must describe what to do as a response to these events. The responses will involve *commands* and *transition labels*.

Commands

*"Command as a
class", page 699.*
Recognizing the notion of command as an important abstraction is a key step in producing good interactive applications.

This notion was studied as part of the Undoing case study. As you remember, a command object represents the information needed to execute a user-requested operation and, if undoing is supported, cancel it.

To the features defined in the earlier discussion, we will add the attribute *exit_label*, explained below.

Basic scheme

With contexts, events and commands we have the basic ingredients to define the basic operation of an interactive application, which our application builder should support: an application developer will select the valid context-event combinations (which events are recognized in which contexts) and, for every one of them, define the associated command.

This basic idea can provide the first version of an application builder. There should be catalogs of contexts and events (based on the underlying toolkit) as well as commands (provided by the development environment, and available for application developers to extend). A graphical metaphor should make it possible to select a context-event combination, for example left-click on a certain button, and select a command to be executed in response.

States

For a fully general scheme we should include an extra level of abstraction, giving the **Context-Event-Command-State** model of interactive graphical applications.

In an application a given context-event combination does not always have the same effect. For example, you might find yourself during a session in a situation where part of the screen looks like this:

*An exit
command*

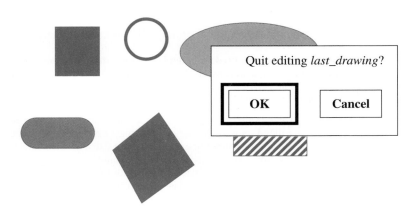

In this state the application recognizes various events in various contexts; for example you may click on a figure to move it, or request the Save command by clicking on the OK button shown. If you choose this latter possibility, a new panel appears:

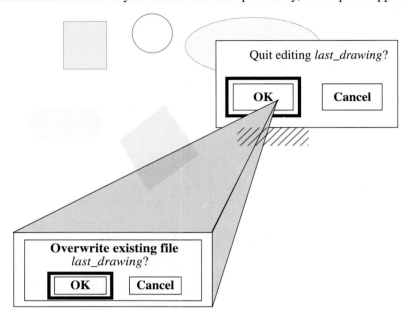

Confirming a command

At this stage only two context-event combinations will be accepted: clicking on the "OK" or on the "Cancel" button of the new panel. All others have been disabled (and the application has dimmed the rest of the figure as a reminder that everything but the two buttons is temporarily inactive). What happened is that the session has entered a new state of the application. States, also called *modes*, are a familiar notion in discussions of interactive systems, but are seldom defined precisely. Here we have the seeds for a formal definition: a state is characterized by a set of acceptable context-event combinations and a set of commands; for each context-event combination, the state defines the associated command. This will be restated as a mathematical definition below.

Many interactive applications, graphical or not, will have several states.

A typical example is the well-known *Vi* editor under Unix. Since this tool is not graphical, events are simply key presses (each keyboard key triggering a different event) and the contexts are various possible cursor positions (under a character, at beginning of line, at end of line etc.). A rough analysis of Vi indicates at least four states:

- In the basic state (which is also the initial one for an end user who calls the editor on a new or existing file), typing a letter key will, in most cases, directly execute a command associated with the letter. For example, typing x deletes the character at cursor position, if any. Some keys cause a transition to another state; for example typing a colon : leads to the command state, typing i leads to the insertion state, and typing R leads to the replacement state. Some letters cause unaccepted events; for example (unless it has been expressly defined as a macro) the letter z has no effect.

- In the command state, only one is available, at the bottom of the Vi window; it serves to enter commands such as "save" or "restart".

- In the insertion state, any key corresponding to a printable character is acceptable as an event; the corresponding character will be inserted into the text, causing displacement of any existing text to its right. The ESCAPE key gets the session back to the basic state.

- Replacement state is a variant of insertion state in which the characters that you type overwrite rather than displace the ones already in place.

*Partial state
diagram for Vi*

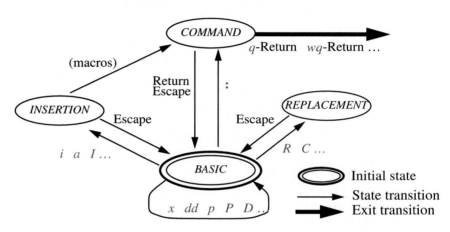

*The article was in
the special Smalltalk
issue of Byte
[Goldberg 1981].*

The literature on user interfaces is critical of states because they can be confusing to users. An early article on the Smalltalk user interface contained a picture of the article's author wearing a T-shirt that read "Don't mode me in!". It is indeed a general principle of sound user interface design to ensure that at every stage of a session end users should have as many commands as possible at their disposal (instead of having to change state before they can execute certain important commands).

In accordance with this principle, a good design will try to minimize the number of states. The principle does not mean, however, that this number should always be one. Such an extreme interpretation of the "don't mode me in" slogan could in fact decrease the quality of the user interface, as too many unrelated commands available at the same time may confuse end users. Furthermore, there may be good reasons to restrict the number of commands in a certain situation (for example when the application needs an urgent response from its end user).

States, in any case, should be explicit for the developers, and usually for the end users as well. This is the only way to enable developers to apply the user interface policy of their choice — whether of the strongly anti-modal persuasion or more tolerant.

So our application builder will provide developers with an explicit *STATE* abstraction; as for the other abstractions, there will be a state catalog, containing states that have proved to be of general use, and a state editor, enabling developers to define new states, often by modifying states extracted from the catalog.

Applications

The last major data abstraction is the notion of application.

All the previous abstractions were intermediate tools. What developers really want to build is applications. A text processing system, an investment banking system, a factory control system are examples of applications.

To describe an application, we need a set of states, transitions between these states, and the indication of which state is the initial one (in which all sessions will begin). We have seen that a state associates a certain response with every accepted context-event pair; the response, as noted, includes a command. To build complete applications, we may also need to include in a response some indication of the context-event pair which led to the response, so that different combinations may trigger transitions to different states. Such information will be called a transition label.

With states and transition labels we may build the transition diagram describing an entire application, such as the partial diagram for Vi shown on the preceding page.

Context-Event-Command-State: a summary

The abstractions just defined can serve as the basis for a powerful interactive application builder — not just an *interface* builder, but a tool that enables application developers to build entire applications graphically; they will explore visual catalogs of contexts, events and, most importantly, commands; selecting the desired elements graphically, they will build the desired context-event-command associations through a simple drag-and-drop mechanism until they have a complete application.

Because simple applications can often rely on just one state, the application builder should make the notion of state as unobtrusive as possible. More advanced applications, however, should be able to use as many states as they need, and (if only for interface consistency) to derive a new state incrementally from an existing one.

32.6 A MATHEMATICAL MODEL

Some of the concepts presented informally in this chapter, in particular the notion of state, have an elegant mathematical description based on the notion of *finite function* and the mathematical transformation known as *currying*.

Because these results are not used in the rest of the book, and mostly of interest to readers who like to explore the mathematical models of software concepts, the corresponding sections are not printed here but appear in electronic form in the CD-ROM accompanying this book, as a supplementary chapter entitled "mathematical background", an extract from [M 1995e].

32.7 BIBLIOGRAPHICAL NOTES

The ideas for an application builder sketched in this chapter derive largely from ISE's *Build* application builder, described in detail in [M 1995e], which also discusses in detail the underlying mathematical model. (This is the manual from which the extra chapter on the CD-ROM was extracted.)

Part F:

Applying the method in various languages and environments

*Previous chapters have developed hand in hand the object-oriented method and the supporting notation. Part F will study how to realize the ideas, or emulate them, in some of the most popular languages and environments. There are three broad categories. **Object-oriented languages** such as Smalltalk support many of the fundamental concepts. **Classical languages** such as Fortran are not O-O at all, but people who must still use them (for various reasons, often not technical) may want to apply as many O-O ideas as feasible within the limitations of these older approaches. Somewhere in-between, **encapsulation languages** such as Ada provide a first step to object orientation, essentially limited to modules based on abstract data types, but without classes or inheritance.*

Although the logical progression is from Classical to Encapsulation to O-O, it will be convenient to start with Encapsulation languages, focusing on Ada 83, as it provides a good reference to assess techniques applicable in classical languages, the category that will follow; we will end with a review of some of the principal O-O languages other than the notation of this book.

33

O-O programming and Ada

*I*n the nineteen-seventies, advances in programming methodology brought about a new generation of languages combining the control structures of Algol 60 and the data structuring constructs of Algol W and Pascal with better system structuring facilities and support for information hiding. Although their precise traits differ, these languages share a common spirit and may be collectively called the **encapsulation languages**. (They are also known in the literature as "object-based", a terminology that will be discussed in the next chapter.)

Although a complete list of encapsulation languages would be long, only a few have developed a sizable user community. Five deserve particular attention: **Modula-2**, a successor to Pascal designed at the Swiss Federal Institute of Technology by Niklaus Wirth, creator of Algol W, Pascal itself and (later) Oberon; **CLU**, developed at MIT under the direction of Barbara Liskov, which comes closest to realizing object-oriented concepts but lacks inheritance; **Mesa**, a Xerox effort with particular emphasis on describing inter-module relationships of large systems; **Alphard**, by Mary Shaw, William Wulf and Ralph London of Carnegie-Mellon University, which included an assertion mechanism; and **Ada**.

We will limit our study of how to approach O-O techniques in encapsulation languages to Ada, which, besides having attracted the most attention, is also the most complete (and complex) of these languages, embodying in some form most of the features found in the others. Modula-2, for example, does not offer genericity or overloading.

33.1 A BIT OF CONTEXT

Ada was a response to a crisis perceived in the mid-seventies by the software policy-makers of the US Department of Defense (DoD). They noted in particular that the various branches of the military were using more than 450 programming languages, many of them technically obsolete, gravely hampering contractor management, programmer training, technical progress, software quality and cost control.

Bearing in mind the successful precedent of COBOL (the result, in the late fifties, of a DoD call for a COmmon Business-Oriented Language), they put out successive versions of a Request For Proposals for a modern software engineering language capable of supporting embedded real-time applications. A first winnowing out of the several dozen initial responses led to four candidate designs, sealed and color-coded for fairness. The field was narrowed down to two, finally leading in 1979 to the selection of the Green language designed by Jean D. Ichbiah and his group at CII-Honeywell Bull in France (today's Bull). Following a few years' experience with the first industrial implementations, the language was revised and made into an ANSI standard in 1983.

Ada (as Green was renamed) began a new era in language design. Never before had a language be subjected to such intense examination before being released. Never before (in spite of some valiant efforts by the PL/I team) had a language been treated like a large-scale engineering project. Working groups comprising the best experts in many countries spent weeks reviewing the proposals and contributed — in those pre-Internet days — reams of comments. Like Algol 60 a generation earlier, Ada redefined not just the language landscape but the very notion of language design.

A recent revision of Ada has yielded a new language, now officially called Ada 95, which will be described at the end of this chapter. In the rest of the discussion, as elsewhere in this book, the name Ada without further qualification refers to the preceding version, Ada 83, by far the most widely used today.

Has Ada been successful? Yes and no. The DoD got what it had commissioned: thanks to a rigorous implementation of the "Ada mandate", Ada became in a few years the dominant technical language in the various branches of the US military, and of the military establishment of some other countries too. It has also achieved significant use in such non-military government agencies as NASA and the European Space Agency. But except for some inroads in computing science education — aided in part by DoD incentives — the language has only had limited success in the rest of the software world. It would probably have spread more widely were it not for the competition of the very ideas described in this book: object technology, which burst into the scene just as Ada and the industry were becoming ripe for each other.

The careful observer of language history can detect two ironies here. The first is that the designers of Ada were well aware of O-O ideas; although this is not widely known, Ichbiah had in fact written one of the first compilers for Simula 67, the original O-O language. As he has since explained when asked why he did not submit an O-O design to the DoD, he estimated that in the competitive bidding context of Ada's genesis such a design would be considered so far off the mainstream as to stand no chance of acceptance. No doubt he was right; indeed one can still marvel at the audacity of the design accepted by the DoD. It would have been reasonable to expect the process to lead to something like an improvement of JOVIAL (a sixties' language for military applications); instead, all four candidate languages were based on Pascal, a language with a distinct academic flavor, and Ada embodied bold new design ideas in many areas such as exceptions, genericity and concurrency. The second irony is that the Ada mandate, meant to force DoD software projects to catch up with progress in software engineering by retiring *older* approaches, has also had in the ensuing years the probably unintended effect of slowing down the adoption of *newer* (post-Ada) technology by the military-aerospace community.

> The lessons of Ada remain irreplaceable, and it is a pity that many of the O-O languages of the eighties and nineties did not pay more attention to its emphasis on software engineering quality. However obvious, this comment is all the more necessary because the occasion for discussing Ada in this book is often to contrast some of its solutions with those of O-O development — as will again happen several times in this chapter. The resulting critiques of Ada techniques should be viewed less as reproach than as homage to the precursor against which any new solution must naturally be assessed.

33.2 PACKAGES

See "Packages",
page 90.

Each of the encapsulation languages offers a modular construct for grouping logically related program elements. Ada calls it a package; corresponding notions are known as modules in Modula-2 and Mesa, and clusters in CLU.

"Modules and
types", page 170.

A class was defined as both a structural system component — a module — and a type. In contrast, a package is only a module. An earlier discussion described this difference by noting that packages are a purely *syntactic* notion, whereas classes also have a *semantic* value. Packages provide a way to distribute system elements (variables, routines …) into coherent subsystems; but they are only needed for readability and manageability of the software. The decomposition of a system into packages does not affect its semantics: one can transform a multi-package Ada system into a one-package system, producing exactly the same results, through a purely syntactical operation — removing all package boundaries, expanding generic derivations (as explained below) and resolving name clashes through renaming. Classes, for their part, are also a semantic construct: besides providing a unit of modular decomposition, a class describes the behavior of a set of run-time objects; this semantics is further enriched by polymorphism and dynamic binding.

An Ada package is a free association of program elements and may be used for various purposes. Sensible uses of this notion include writing a package to gather:

"Facility inherit-
ance", page 832.

- A set of related constants (as with facility inheritance).

- A library of routines, for example a mathematical library.

- A set of variables, constants and routines describing the implementation of one abstract object, or a fixed number of abstract objects, accessible only through designated operations (as we will do in Fortran in the next chapter).

- An abstract data type implementation.

The last use is the most interesting for this discussion. We will study it through the example of a stack package, adapted from an example in the Ada reference manual.

33.3 A STACK IMPLEMENTATION

Information hiding is supported in Ada by the two-tier declaration of packages. Every package comes in two parts, officially called "specification" and "body". The former term is too strong for a construct that does not support any formal description of package semantics (in the form of assertions or similar mechanisms), so we will use the more modest word "interface".

The standard Ada term
for "routine" is "sub-
program". We keep the
former for consistency
with other chapters.

The interface lists the public properties of the package: exported variables, constants, types and routines. For routines it only gives the headers, listing the formal arguments and their types, plus the result type for a function, as in:

function *item* (*s*: *STACK*) **return** *X*;

The body part of a package provides the routines' implementations, and adds any needed secret elements.

A simple interface

A first version of the interface part of a stack package may be expressed as follows. Note that the keyword **package** by itself introduces a package interface; the body, which will appear later, is introduced by **package body**.

> **package** *REAL_STACKS* **is**
>
> > **type** *STACK_CONTENTS* **is** *array* (*POSITIVE* **range** <>) **of** *FLOAT*;
> >
> > **type** *STACK* (*capacity*: *POSITIVE*) **is**
> > > **record**
> > > > *implementation*: *STACK_CONTENTS* (*1..capacity*);
> > > > *count*: *NATURAL* := 0;
> > > **end record**;
> >
> > **procedure** *put* (*x*: **in** *FLOAT*; *s*: **in out** *STACK*);
> >
> > **procedure** *remove* (*s*: **in out** *STACK*);
> >
> > **function** *item* (*s*: *STACK*) **return** *FLOAT*;
> >
> > **function** *empty* (*s*: *STACK*) **return** *BOOLEAN*;
> >
> > *Overflow, Underflow*: *EXCEPTION*;
>
> **end** *REAL_STACKS*;

This interface lists exported elements: the type *STACK* for declaring stacks, the auxiliary type *STACK_CONTENTS* used by *STACK*, the four basic routines on stacks, and two exceptions. Client packages will only rely on the interface (provided their programmers have some idea of the semantics associated with the routines).

This example suggests several general observations:

- It is surprising to see all the details of stack representation, as given by the declarations of types *STACK* and *STACK_CONTENTS*, appear in what should be a pure interface. We will see shortly the reason for this problem and how to correct it.

- Unlike the classes of object-oriented languages, a package does not by itself define a type. Here you must separately define a type *STACK*. One consequence of this separation, for the programmer who builds a package around an abstract data type implementation, is the need to invent two different names — one for the package and one for the type. Another consequence is that the routines have one more argument than their object-oriented counterparts: here they all act on a stack *s*, implicit in the stack classes given in earlier chapters.

- A declaration may define not only the type of an entity, but also its initial value. Here the declaration of *count* in type *STACK* prescribes an initial value of 0. It obviates the need for an explicit initialization operation corresponding to creation; this would not be the case, however, if a less straightforward initialization were required.

- A few details of Ada are needed to understand the type declarations: *POSITIVE* and *NATURAL* denote the subtypes of *INTEGER* covering positive and non-negative integers, respectively; a type specification of the form **array** (*TYPE* **range** <>), where <> is known as the Box symbol, describes a template for array types. To derive an actual type from such a template, you choose a finite subrange of *TYPE*; this is done here in *STACK*, which uses the subrange *1..capacity* of *POSITIVE*. *STACK* is an example of a parameterized type; any declaration of an entity of type *STACK* must specify an actual value for *capacity*, as in

  > *s*: *STACK* (*1000*)

- In Ada, every routine argument must be characterized by a mode: **in**, **out** or **in out**, defining the routine's rights on the corresponding actual arguments (read-only, write-only or update). In the absence of an explicit keyword, the default mode is **in**.

- Finally, the interface also specifies two exception names: *Overflow* and *Underflow*. An exception is an error condition that the programmer has decided to treat separately from the normal flow of control. The interface of the package should list any exceptions that may be raised by the package's routines and propagated to clients. More on the Ada exception mechanism below.

Using a package

Client code using the package is based on the interface. Here is an example from some package needing a stack of real numbers:

> *s*: *REAL_STACKS*.*STACK* (*1000*);
>
> *REAL_STACKS*.*put* (*3.5*, *s*); …;
>
> **if** *REAL_STACKS*.*empty* (*s*) **then** …;

An Ada environment must be able to compile such client code even if only the interface of *REAL_STACKS*, not its body, is available.

Syntactically, note how each use of an entity from this package (where "entities" here include type names such as *STACK* as well as routine names) must repeat the name of package *REAL_STACKS*, using dot notation. This could become tedious, hence the need for a more implicit form of qualification. If you include the directive

> **use** *REAL_STACKS*;

at the beginning of the client package, you may write the above extract more simply as

> *s*: *STACK* (*1000*);
>
> *put* (*3.5*, *s*); …;
>
> **if** *empty* (*s*) **then** …;

You still need the full form, however, for any entity whose name conflicts with the name of another accessible to the client package (that is to say, declared in that package itself or in another supplier listed in a **use** directive).

Some of the Ada literature advises programmers to stay away from the **use** directive altogether on the grounds that it hampers clarity: an unqualified reference such as *empty* (*s*) does not immediately tell the reader what supplier *empty* comes from (*REAL_STACKS* in the example). The equivalent in the object-oriented approach, *s.empty*, unambiguously indicates the supplier through the type of *s*.

A similar problem does arise in the O-O world because of inheritance: when you see a name in a class, it may refer to a feature declared in any ancestor. But we saw a technique that solves this problem at least in part: the notion of flat form.

"FLATTENING THE STRUCTURE", page 541.

Implementation

The body of the *REAL_STACKS* package might be declared along the following lines. Only one routine is shown in full.

```
package body REAL_STACKS is
        procedure put (x: in FLOAT; s: in out REAL_STACK) is
            begin
                if s.count = s.capacity then
                        raise Overflow
                end if;
                s.count := s.count + 1;
                s.implementation (count) := x;
            end put;
        procedure remove (s: in out STACK) is
                ... Implementation of remove ...
            end remove;
        function item (s: STACK) return X is
                ... Implementation of item ...
            end item;
        function empty (s: STACK) return BOOLEAN is
                ... Implementation of empty ...
            end empty;
end REAL_STACKS;
```

Two properties apparent in this example will be developed in more detail below: the use of exceptions to handle a run-time error by raising a special condition and treating it separately; and the need for the body to repeat most of the interface information (routine headers) that already appeared in the interface.

Genericity

The package as given is too specific; it should be made applicable to any type, not just *FLOAT*. To turn it into a generic package, use the following syntax:

> **generic**
> > **type** *G* **is private**;
> **package** *STACKS* **is**
> > ... As before, replacing all occurrences of *FLOAT* by *G* ...
> **end** *STACKS*;

See appendix B.

The **generic** clause is heavier syntax than our O-O notation for generic classes (**class** *C* [*G*]...) because it offers more options. In particular, the parameters declared in a **generic** clause may represent not just types but also routines. The appendix on genericity *vs.* inheritance will discuss these possibilities.

The **generic** clause is not repeated in the package body, which will be identical to the version given earlier, except for the substitution of *G* for *FLOAT* throughout.

The **is private** specification directs the rest of the package to treat *G* as a private type. This means that entities of the type may only be used in operations applicable to all Ada types: use as source or target of an assignment, as operand of an equality test, as actual argument in a routine, and a few other special operations. This is close to the convention used for unconstrained formal generic parameters in our notation. In Ada, other possibilities are also available. In particular, you can restrict the operations further by declaring the parameter as **limited private**, which essentially bars all uses other than as actual argument to a routine.

Although called a package, a generically parameterized module such as *STACKS* is really a package template, since clients cannot use it directly; they must derive an actual package from it by providing actual generic parameters. We may define a new version of our stack-of-reals package through such a generic derivation:

> **package** *REAL_STACKS_1* **is new** *STACKS* (*FLOAT*);

Generic derivation is the principal Ada mechanism for adapting modules. It is somewhat inflexible, since you can only choose between generic modules (parameterized, but not directly usable) or usable modules (not extendible any more). In contrast, inheritance allows arbitrary extensions to existing modules, according to the Open-Closed principle. Appendix B pursues the comparison further.

33.4 HIDING THE REPRESENTATION: THE PRIVATE STORY

Package *STACKS*, as given, fails to implement the principle of information hiding: the declarations of types *STACK* and *STACK_CONTENTS* are in the interface, allowing clients to access the representation of stacks directly. For example, a client might include code of the form

[1]

> **use** *REAL_STACKS_1*;...
> *s*: *STACK*; ...
> *s*•*implementation* (3) := 7.0; *s*•*last* := 51;

grossly violating the underlying abstract data type specification.

Conceptually, the type declarations belong in the body. Why did we not put them there in the first place? The explanation requires that we look, beyond the language, at programming environment issues.

One requirement on the Ada design, already mentioned, was that it should be possible to compile packages separately and, moreover, to compile a client of any package *A* as soon as you have access to the interface of *A*, but not necessarily to its body. This favors top-down design: to proceed with the work on a module, it suffices to know the specification of the facilities it needs; actual implementations may be provided only later.

So if you have access to the interface of *REAL_STACKS_1* (that is to say, the interface of *STACKS*, of which *REAL_STACKS_1* is just a generic derivation) you must be able to compile one of its clients. Such a client will contain declarations of the form

> **use** *REAL_STACKS_1*;...
>
> *s1*, *s2*: *STACK*; ...
>
> *s2* := *s1*;

which the poor compiler cannot properly handle unless it knows what size is taken up by an object of type *STACK*. But that can only be determined from the type declarations for *STACK* and the auxiliary type *STACK_CONTENTS*.

Hence the dilemma that faced the designers of Ada: conceptually, such declarations belong to the inferno — the body; but implementation concerns seem to require their inclusion in the paradise — the interface.

The solution retained was to create a purgatory: a special section of the package that is physically tied to the interface, and compiled with it, but marked in such a way that clients may not refer to its elements. The purgatory section is called the private part of the interface; it is introduced by the keyword **private** (also used, as we saw above, as a qualifier for protected types). Any declaration appearing in the private part is unavailable to clients. This scheme is illustrated by our final version of the stack package interface:

> **generic**
>
> > **type** *G* **is private**;
>
> **package** *STACKS* **is**
>
> > **type** *STACK* (*capacity*: *POSITIVE*) **is private**;
> >
> > **procedure** *put* (*x*: **in** *G*; *s*: **in out** *STACK*);
> >
> > **procedure** *remove* (*s*: **in out** *STACK*);
> >
> > **function** *item* (*s*: *STACK*) **return** *G*;
> >
> > **function** *empty* (*s*: *STACK*) **return** *BOOLEAN*;
> >
> > *Overflow, Underflow*: *EXCEPTION*;

private

    type *STACK_VALUES* **is array** (*POSITIVE* **range** <>) **of** *G*;

    type *STACK* (*capacity*: *POSITIVE*) **is**

        record

            implementation: *STACK_VALUES* (*1..capacity*);

            count: *NATURAL* := 0;

        end record

    end *STACKS*;

Note how type *STACK* must now be declared twice: first in the non-private part of the interface, where it is only specified as **private**; then again in the private part, where the full description is given. Without the first declaration, a line of the form *s*: *REAL_STACK* would not be legal in a client, since clients only have access to entities declared in the non-private part. This first declaration only specifies the type as **private**, barring clients from accessing any property of stack objects other than universal operations such as assignment, equality test and use as actual argument. This is consistent with the discussion of information hiding.

Type *STACK_VALUES* is purely internal, and irrelevant to clients: so it need only be declared in the package body.

[1] *was on page 1085.*
Make sure to understand that the information in the private part should really be in the package body, and only appears in the package specification for reasons of language implementation. With the new form of *STACKS* client code such as [1], which directly accessed the representation in a client, becomes invalid.

See "common mis-understanding" discussed on page 52.
Authors of clients modules can *see* the internal structure of *STACK* instances, but they cannot take advantage of it in their modules. This can be tantalizing (although one may imagine that a good Ada environment could hide this part from a client author requesting interface information about the class, in the manner of the **short** tool of earlier chapters). While surprising to newcomers, the policy does not contradict the rule of information hiding: as was pointed out during the discussion of that rule, the goal is not physically to prevent client authors from reading about the hidden details, but to prevent them from *using* these details.

Someone who would like to make things sound very complicated could summarize by the following two sentences (to be spoken very quickly to impress friend and foe): The private section of the public part of a package lists the implementation of those conceptually private types which must be declared in the public part although their implementation is not publicly available. In the non-private part, these types are declared private.

33.5 EXCEPTIONS

The *STACKS* generic package lists two exceptions in its interface: *Overflow* and *Underflow*. More generally, you may deal with error conditions by defining arbitrary exception names; Ada also includes predefined exceptions, triggered by the hardware or the operating system, for such cases as arithmetic overflow or exhaustion of memory.

Some elements of the Ada exception mechanism were introduced in the chapter on exceptions, so that we can limit ourselves to a brief examination of how exceptions fit in the Ada approach to software construction.

"How not to do it — an Ada example", page 415.

Simplifying the control structure

Exceptions as they exist in Ada are a technique for dealing with errors without impairing the control structure of normal processing. If a program performs a series of actions, each of which may turn out to be impossible because of some erroneous condition, the resulting control structure may end up looking like

```
action1;
if error1 then
      error_handling1;
else
      action2;
      if error2 then
            error_handling2;
      else
            action3;
            if error3 then
                  error_handling3;
            else
                  ...
```

Like others in this chapter, this example follows Ada's use of the semicolon as an instruction terminator.

The Ada exception mechanism is an effort to fight the complexity of such a scheme — where the elements that perform "useful" tasks sometimes look like a small archipelago in an ocean of error-handling code — by separating the handling of errors from their detection. There must still be tests to determine whether a certain erroneous condition has occurred; but the only action to take then is to raise a certain signal, the exception, which will be handled elsewhere.

Raising and handling an exception

To raise exceptions rather than handle errors in place, you may rewrite the extract as:

```
action1;
if error1 then raise exc1; end;
action2;
```

> if *error2* **then raise** *exc2*; **end**;
> *action3*;
> if *error3* **then raise** *exc3*; **end**;
>
> …

When an instruction **raise** *exc* is executed, control does not flow to the instructions that would normally follow, but is transferred to an **exception handler**. This disruption of the normal flow of control explains why the **else**… clauses are no longer necessary here. An exception handler is a special paragraph of a block or routine, of the form

> **exception**
>   **when** *exc1*, … => *treatment1*;
>   **when** *exc2* … => *treatment2*;
>
>   …

The handler that a **raise** *exc* will select is the first one that handles *exc* in the dynamic chain, that is to say the list of units beginning with the routine or block containing the **raise** and continuing with its caller, its caller's caller etc.

__The call chain__

(This figure origi-nally appeared on page 418.)

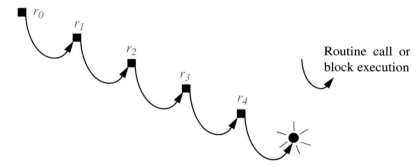

Routine call or block execution

A handler is said to handle *exc* if *exc* appears in one of its **when** clauses (or it has a clause of the form **when others**). If there is such a handler, the corresponding instructions (after the => symbol) are executed and the enclosing routine returns control to its caller, or terminates if it is the main program. (Ada does have a notion of main program.) If no handler in the dynamic chain handles *exc*, execution terminates and control goes back to the operating system, which presumably will print out an error message.

Discussion

See chapter 12.

It is interesting to compare the Ada exception mechanism with the one developed in the chapter on exceptions earlier in this book. There are technical differences and differences of methodology.

The technical differences, apart from the different ways of discriminating between exceptions (multiple **when** clauses *vs.* inheriting from class *EXCEPTIONS*), involve retrying, which the O-O design considered sufficiently important to warrant a special instruction, whereas Ada has no direct support for it and requires **goto** instructions or similar control structures.

The methodological difference follows from the strong policy that we adopted, *Page 417.* leading to the Disciplined Exception Handling principle that requires every exception handler, apart from the rare case of a "false alarm", to end in either **retrying** or official **failure** ("organized panic"). Ada is less strict in this respect, and we saw that as a consequence it is possible to misuse exceptions by executing a seemingly normal return without having handled the problem.

The need to avoid such dangerous situations led us to a basic rule, worth repeating:

> ### Ada exception rule
>
> The execution of any Ada exception handler should end by either executing a **raise** instruction or retrying the enclosing program unit.

Initially on page 416.

More generally, exceptions in the Ada spirit are control structures, helping to separate the handling of abnormal situations from their detection and hence to keep software structure simple. In practice, however, this hope is often disappointed.

When you write **raise** *some_exception*, you may have the impression of freeing yourself from the messy and boring task of taking care of strange cases, and instead concentrate on the core of the algorithm, handling normal cases. But raising an exception does not by itself solve the problem. Exceptions in the *STACKS* package are typical. An attempt to push an element into a full stack raises exception *Overflow*, and an attempt to access an element of an empty stack raises *Underflow*. How will you handle *Underflow*, the exception raised by a call to *remove* or *item* on an empty stack? As we saw in the discussion of Design by Contract, the routines themselves cannot reasonably contain a handler (*item* does not know what to do when applied to an empty stack); so the responsibility lies with the client, which should include code of the form

The **raise** *instructions appeared in REAL_STACKS, the initial variant of STACKS, page 1084.*

[2]
```
        use REAL_STACKS;
        procedure proc (…) is
            s: STACK; …
        begin
            … remove (s); …
        exception
            when Underflow => action1;
            …
        end proc;
```

So the client must specify exactly what happens in the erroneous case. Omitting the **when** *Underflow* clause would be a design error. Compare this with the usual, non-exception-based form of the call (written in the syntax of the rest of this book):

[3]
```
            if not s.empty then s.remove else action1 end
```

(or a variant which detects the error a posteriori). Form [2], using exceptions, differs from [3] in two aspects only:

"The a posteriori scheme", page 800.

- The code for handling the error, *action1*, is textually separate from the calls that may raise the error;

- Error handling is the same for all such calls if more than one.

See "Precondition design: tolerant or demanding?", page 354.

On the first point, although it is desirable to avoid the deeply nested **if**… **then**… **else**… error-handling structures cited at the beginning of this chapter, the place in the algorithm where an error is detected is often the one that has the best information to handle the error; and if you separate the two you may need to use complicated control structures for cases that require restarting or resuming processing.

On the second point, if a routine contains more than one call to *remove*, the way to deal with empty stacks will unlikely be the same in each case.

There are two general styles of exception usage: the **control structure style**, which views exceptions as a normal mechanism to handle all but the most common cases; and the **abnormal case style**, which reserves them for unpredictable situations, when all other mechanisms have failed. The **rescue/retry** approach described earlier in this book tends to favor the abnormal case style, although it can be used for the other style as well. Ada exception handling is more geared towards the control structure style.

You will decide for yourself which of the two styles you prefer; you should in any case remember, from this discussion and the earlier ones, not to place any naïve hope in the use of exceptions. With or without an exception mechanism, run-time errors are a fact of system life, which the software must handle explicitly. A good methodological approach, supported by an effective exception mechanism, can help; but some of the complexity is inherent to the problem of error handling, and no magical wand will make it go away.

33.6 TASKS

On CSP see "Communication-based mechanisms", page 979.

Besides packages, Ada offers another interesting modular construct: the task. Tasks are the basic Ada mechanism for handling concurrency; the underlying concurrency model is close to the CSP approach described in the concurrency chapter. But they also deserve a mention purely for their modular concepts, since they actually come closer than packages to supporting object-oriented concepts.

Syntactically, tasks share many aspects of packages. The main difference is that a task is not just a modular unit but the representation of a process, to be executed in parallel with other processes. So besides making up a syntactical unit it also describes a semantic component — unlike a package, and like a class.

Like a package, a task is declared in two parts, interface and body. Instead of routines, a task specification introduces a number of entries. To the client, entries look like procedures; for example, the interface of a buffer manager task may be

```
task BUFFER_MANAGER is
    entry read (x: out G);
    entry write (x: in G);
end BUFFER_MANAGER;
```

(Tasks may not be generic, so that type *G* has to be globally available, or a generic parameter of an enclosing package.) It is only the implementation of entries that distinguishes them from procedures: in the body, **accept** instructions will specify synchronization and other constraints on execution of the entries; here, for example, we might prescribe that only one *read* or *write* may proceed at any point in time, that *read* must wait until the buffer is not empty, and *write* until it is not full.

Besides individual tasks you may also specify a **task type**, and use it to create as many tasks — instances of the task type — as you need at run time. This makes tasks similar to classes, without inheritance. One can indeed conceive of an Ada realization of O-O concepts which would represent classes by task types and objects by their instances (perhaps even using **accept** instructions with different conditions to emulate dynamic binding). Because in sequential O-O computation we may expect classes to have many instances, this exercise is mostly of academic interest, given the overhead of creating a new process in current operating systems. Perhaps some day, in massively parallel hardware environments…

33.7 FROM ADA TO ADA 95

The Ada 95 version of the language is a major revision intended in particular to add O-O concepts. There is in fact no notion of class in the sense of this book (module *cum* type), but support for inheritance and dynamic binding for record types.

O-O mechanisms of Ada 95: an example

The package text at the top of the facing page illustrates some of the Ada 95 techniques; its meaning should be clear enough to a reader of this book. To derive a **new** type with more fields (the Ada 95 form of inheritance), you must have declared a type, such as *ACCOUNT*, as **tagged**; this of course contradicts the Open-Closed principle, since you must know in advance which types may have descendants and which may not. A **new** type may be derived from only one type; that is to say, there is no multiple inheritance. Note the syntax (**null record**, with, surprisingly, no **end**) for a derived type that adds no attribute.

Tagged types remain declared as records. The basic property of most O-O languages — that operations on a type become part of that type, and in fact, as we saw in the discussion of abstract data types, *define* the type — is not in force here: the routines that apply to a tagged type appear outside of its declaration, and take as argument a value of that type. (In languages generally recognized as object-oriented, *deposit* etc. would be part of the declaration of *ACCOUNT* and *compound* part of *SAVINGS_ACCOUNT*; they would not need their first arguments.) Here the only link between the routines and the type is that they must be declared as part of the same package; they do not even have to appear next to each other. Only the layout conventions, in the above example, indicate to the reader that certain routines are conceptually attached to certain tagged record types.

This is different from the usual view of O-O software construction. Although a tagged record type and the associated routines are, from a theoretical perspective, part of the same abstract data type, they do not form a syntactical unit — contradicting the Linguistic Modular Units principle, which suggested a close association between the modularizing concept and the syntactical structure.

"Linguistic Modular Units", page 53.

An Ada 95 package

The package may be better split off into three, with "child packages" for checking and savings accounts. See next page.

package *Accounts* **is**
  type *MONEY* **is digits** *12* **delta** *0.01*;

  type *ACCOUNT* **is tagged private**;
    procedure *deposit* (*a*: **in out** *ACCOUNT*; *amount*: **in** *MONEY*);
    procedure *withdraw* (*a*: **in out** *ACCOUNT*; *amount*: **in** *MONEY*);
    function *balance* (*a*: **in** *ACCOUNT*) **return** *MONEY*;

  type *CHECKING_ACCOUNT* **is new** *ACCOUNT* **with private**;
    function *balance* (*a*: **in** *CHECKING_ACCOUNT*) **return** *MONEY*;

  type *SAVINGS_ACCOUNT* **is new** *ACCOUNT* **with private**;
    procedure *compound* (*a*: **in out** *SAVINGS_ACCOUNT*; *period*: **in** *Positive*);

private
  type *ACCOUNT* **is tagged**
    record
        initial_balance: *MONEY* := *0.0*;
        owner: *String* (*1..30*);
    end record;

  type *CHECKING_ACCOUNT* **is new** *ACCOUNT* **with null record**;

  type *SAVINGS_ACCOUNT* **is new** *ACCOUNT* **with**
    record
        rate: *Float*;
    end record;
end *Accounts*;

"OVERLOADING AND GENERIC- ITY", 4.8, page 93.

The appearance of a new declaration for *balance* for *SAVINGS_ACCOUNT* signals a redefinition. Procedures *withdraw* and *deposit* are not redefined. As you will have recognized, this means that Ada 95 uses the *overloading* mechanism to obtain the O-O effect of *routine redefinition*. There is no syntactical mark (such as **redefine**) to signal a routine redefinition: to find out that function *balance* differs for *SAVINGS_ACCOUNT* from its base version in *ACCOUNT*, you must scan the text of the entire package. Here, of course, each routine version appears next to the corresponding type, with indentation to highlight the relationship, but this is a style convention, not a language rule.

A tagged type can be declared as **abstract**, corresponding to the notion of deferred class; you may make a routine **abstract** too instead of giving it a body.

A function returning a result of an abstract type must be abstract itself. This rule may seem strange at first, appearing to preclude writing an effective function returning, say, the top of a stack of figures, assuming *FIGURE* is abstract. In Ada, however, the result of such a function will typically be not of type *FIGURE* but of an "access type" describing references to instances of *FIGURE*. Then the function can be effective.

You can apply dynamic binding to entities of a tagged type, as in:

procedure *print_balance* (*a*: **in** *ACCOUNT'Class*) **is**

        -- Print current balance.

    begin

        Put (*balance* (*a*));

        New_Line;

    end *print_balance*;

You must request the dynamic binding explicitly by declaring the routine as a "classwide operation", as represented by the *'Class* qualification to the type of its argument; this is similar to the C++ obligation to declare any dynamically bound function as "virtual", except that here it is the client that must choose between static and dynamic binding.

"The C++ approach to binding", page 513.

Ada 95 allows you to define a "child package" *A.B* of an existing package *A*. This enables the new package to obtain features from *A* and add its own extensions and modifications. (This concept is of course close to inheritance — but distinct.) Instead of declaring the three account types in a single package as on the preceding page, it is indeed probably better to split the package into three, with *Accounts.Checking* introducing *CHECKING_ACCOUNT* and its routines, and *Accounts.Saving* doing the same for *SAVINGS_ACCOUNT*.

Ada 95 and object technology: an assessment

If you come to Ada 95 from a background in object technology, you will probably find the language befuddling at first. After a while, you should be able to master the various language mechanisms enabling you to obtain the effects of single inheritance, polymorphism and dynamic binding.

The price to pay, however, is complexity. To Ada 83, a sophisticated construction, Ada 95 has added a whole new set of constructs with many potential interactions both between themselves and with the old constructs. If you come from the O-O side and are used to the pristine simplicity of the notion of class, you will find that you have to learn the intricacies of at least five concepts, each covering some of the aspects of classes:

- Packages, which are modules but not types, can be generic, and offer something resembling inheritance: child packages (as well as a number of other options not detailed above, such as the possibility of declaring a child package as **private**).

- Tagged record types, which are types but not modules, and have a form of inheritance, although unlike classes they do not allow the syntactical inclusion of routines into a type declaration.

- Tasks, which are modules but not types and have no inheritance.

- Task types, which are modules and types, but cannot be generic (although they can be included in generic packages) and have no inheritance.

- "Protected types" (a notion we have not yet encountered), which are types and **may** include routines, as in

> **protected type** *ANOTHER_ACCOUNT_TYPE* **is**
>
> **procedure** *deposit* (*amount*: **in** *MONEY*);
>
> **function** *balance* **return** *MONEY*;
>
> **private**
>
> *deposit_list*: …; …
>
> **end** *ANOTHER_ACCOUNT_TYPE*;

making them at first similar to classes — but with no inheritance.

The combination of interacting possibilities is mind-boggling. Packages, for example, still have, in addition to the notion of child package, the Ada mechanisms of **use** and **with**, with explanations such as this one from a tutorial text:

From
[Wheeler-Web].

> *Private children are intended for "internal" packages that should only be "with'ed" by a restricted number of packages. A private child can only be "with'ed" by the body of its parent or by descendants of the private child's parent. In exchange for such a restrictive requirement, a private child gets a new authority: a private child's specification automatically sees both the public and private parts of all of its ancestors' specifications.*

No doubt it is possible to make sense of such explanations. But is the result worth the trouble?

> It is interesting to note that Jean Ichbiah, the creator of Ada, resigned publicly from the Ada 95 reviewing group after trying in vain for several years to keep the extensions simple. His long resignation letter includes comments such as: *A massive increase in complexity will result from 9X* [later renamed Ada 95] *adding one or more additional possibilities where Ada now offers two. For example, 9X adds*: […] *access parameters, to* **in**, **out**, *and* **in out**; *tagged types, to normal types; dispatched subprogram calls, to normal subprogram calls; use type clause, to use package clauses*; [Other examples skipped; overall 12 were included.] *With 9X, the number of interactions to consider is close to 60,000 since we have 3 or more possibilities in each case (that is, 3^{10}).*

The basic concepts of object technology, for all their power, are strikingly simple. Ada 95 may be the most ambitious effort so far to make them appear complicated.

Discussion: module and type inheritance

As a side observation following from this study of Ada 95, it is interesting to note that the Ada 95 design has found it necessary, along with the "inheritance" mechanism for tagged record types, to introduce the notion of child package. Ada, of course, has always kept module and type concepts separate, whereas classes are both. But then Ada 95 methodologists will suggest that when you introduce a descendant type such as *SAVINGS_ACCOUNT* you should declare it, for clarity and modularity, not in the original package (*Accounts*) but in a child package. If you generalize this advice, you will end up creating, along with the type hierarchy, a module hierarchy which follows it faithfully.

With the classes of object technology, such questions do not arise; classes being modules, there is by construction only one hierarchy.

The choices of Ada 95 show yet another example of the popular view that *"one should separate type inheritance from code reuse"*. Instead the insight of object technology since Simula has been to *unify* concepts: module and type, subtyping and module extension. Like any other bold unification of notions theretofore considered completely distinct, this idea can be scary at times, hence the attempts to reintroduce the distinction. But they would deprive us of the remarkable simplification that O-O ideas have brought to the understanding of software architecture.

"ONE MECHA-NISM, OR MORE?", 24.6, page 833; "The two styles", page 608.

Towards an O-O Ada

That Ada 95 seems hard to teach and to manage does not mean the idea of making Ada more O-O is doomed; one should simply set reasonable goals and keep a constant concern for simplicity and consistency. The Ada community might try again to develop an object-oriented extension, which should be accompanied by the removal of a few facilities to keep the language size palatable. Two general directions are possible:

- The first idea, close in spirit to what the design of Ada 95 has attempted to achieve, is to keep the package structure and introduce a notion of class that would generalize Ada's record types, with support for inheritance and dynamic binding. But these should be true classes, including the applicable routines. Such an extension would be similar in principle to that which led from C to C++. It should strive for minimalism, trying to reuse as much as possible of the existing mechanisms (such as with and use for packages), rather than introducing new facilities which would then cause the interaction problems mentioned by Ichbiah.

- The other approach would build on an observation made in the presentation of tasks earlier in this chapter. It was noted then that task types are close in spirit to classes, since they may have instances created at run time; but structurally they have most of the properties of packages (visibility and information hiding rules, separate compilation). This suggests adding a modular unit that, roughly, has the syntax of packages and the semantics of classes; think of it as a package-class, or as a task type that does not need to be concurrent. The notion of "protected type" may be a starting point; but of course, it should be integrated into the existing mechanism.

A thesis by Mats Weber explores the idea of package types. See the link in www.adahome.com/ Resources/Research/ Research.html.

Exercises at the end of this chapter ask you (if, like many software people, you like dabbling in language design experiments, if only to gain a better understanding of existing languages and, through them, of software issues) to explore these possibilities further.

Exercises 33.4 and E33.5, page 1098.

33.8 KEY CONCEPTS INTRODUCED IN THIS CHAPTER

- Ada, studied as a representative of the class of "encapsulation languages" which also includes Modula-2, offers modular decomposition constructs: packages (and tasks).

- The emphasis is on information hiding: interface and implementation are declared separately.

- Genericity increases the flexibility of packages.

- Conflicts between methodological requirements and language implementation concerns give rise to the "private" section, a conceptually secret element that is syntactically included in the interface..

- The package is a purely syntactic mechanism. Modules remain distinct from types. No inheritance mechanism is possible.

- Exceptions separate error detection from error handling, but provide no magic solution to the problem of run-time errors.

- The Ada exception mechanism should only be used in a disciplined fashion; any execution of an exception handler should terminate by either retrying the operation or signaling failure to the caller.

- Task types could in principle be used to implement classes without inheritance, but this solution is not practical in most current environments.

- Ada 95 enables the definition of a new record type as being derived from an existing type, with support for routine redefinition, polymorphism and dynamic binding.

33.9 BIBLIOGRAPHICAL NOTES

[Booch 1986a] discusses (under the label "object-oriented design", but not using classes, inheritance, polymorphism etc.) how to obtain some of the benefits of object orientation in Ada.

The official reference on Ada is [ANSI 1983], recommended neither as bedtime reading nor as introductory material. Numerous books are available to fulfill the latter need.

References on the other modular languages mentioned at the beginning of this chapter are [Mitchell 1979] for Mesa, [Wirth 1982] for Modula-2, and [Liskov 1981] for CLU. See also [Liskov 1986] on programming methodology, based on CLU. The reference on Alphard is [Shaw 1981].

The Ada 95 reference manual is available on-line at [Ada 95-Web]. [Wheeler-Web] is an on-line tutorial (prelude to an announced book). For a commented list of Ada 95 textbooks, see [Feldman-Web]. I am greatly indebted to Richard Riehle and Magnus Kempe for clarifying a number of points about Ada 95; the views expressed are as usual my own. Magnus Kempe is the source of the reference to Mats Weber's thesis.

EXERCISES

E33.1 Winning the battle without privates

The Ada compilation problem that gives rise to the **private** construct might appear to affect object-oriented languages as well if the underlying environment supports separate compilation of classes. In fact, the problem seems to be worse because of inheritance: a variable declared of type C may at run time refer to instances not only of C but of any descendant class; since any descendant may add its own attributes, the size of these instances is variable. If C is a deferred class, it is not even possible to assign a default size to its instances. Explain why, in spite of these remarks, the object-oriented notation of this book does not need a language construct similar to the **private** mechanism of Ada. (**Hint**: your discussion should consider in particular the following notions: expanded *vs.* reference types; deferred classes; and the techniques used in our O-O framework to produce abstract class specifications without requiring class authors to write two separate module separate parts.) Discuss the tradeoffs involved in both solutions. Can you suggest other approaches to the problem in the Ada framework?

"HIDING THE REP-RESENTATION: THE PRIVATE STORY", 33.4, page 1085.

E33.2 Generic routine parameters

Generic parameters to Ada packages may be not just types but also routines. Explain the relevance of this possibility to the implementation of object-oriented concepts, and its limitations. (See also appendix B.)

E33.3 Classes as tasks (for Ada programmers)

Rewrite class *COMPLEX* as an Ada task type. Show examples using the resulting type.

"Legitimate side effects: an example", page 759.

E33.4 Adding classes to Ada

(This language design exercise assumes a good knowledge of Ada 83.) Devise an adaptation of Ada (83) that keeps the notion of package but extends records to classes with polymorphism, dynamic binding and inheritance (single or multiple?), in line with general O-O principles.

E33.5 Package-classes

(This language design exercise assumes a good knowledge of Ada 83.) Using task types as inspiration, devise an adaptation of Ada (83) supporting packages that can be instantiated at run time and hence can play the role of classes, with polymorphism, dynamic binding and inheritance.

34

Emulating object technology in non-O-O environments

$\mathcal{F}$ortran, Cobol, Pascal, C, Basic, PL/I and even assembly language still account for a large part of the software being written or updated today. Clearly, a project using one of these languages will not be able to draw the full benefits of object technology, as this would require a notation such as the one we have studied in this book, and the supporting compiler, environment and libraries. But people who are required to use pre-O-O tools, often because of non-technical constraints, can still gain inspiration from object technology and use some of its concepts to improve the quality of their software development.

This chapter presents the techniques of *object emulation* that may enable you to approximate some of object technology. It will particularly examine the case of Fortran, Pascal and C. (Ada and other encapsulation languages were discussed in the preceding chapter; the following one covers O-O languages such as Simula, Smalltalk, Objective-C, C++ and Java.) This presentation will be directly applicable if you must use one of these languages. But it extends further:

- If you use another non-O-O language not on this list, such as Basic or Cobol, you should not have too much trouble transposing the concepts.

- Even if you are able to use an O-O language, the following discussion can give you a better grasp of the innovations of object technology and of the supporting implementation techniques (which often make use, internally, of older languages).

34.1 LEVELS OF LANGUAGE SUPPORT

In assessing how programming languages succeed in supporting object-oriented concepts, we may distinguish three broad categories (ignoring the lowest level, mostly containing assembly languages, which does not even support a routine construct):

- The **functional** level comprises languages whose unit of decomposition is the *routine*, a functional abstraction capturing a processing step. Data abstraction is handled, if at all, through definitions of data structures, either local to a routine or global.

- Languages at the **encapsulation** level provide a way to group a set of routines and data declarations in a syntactical unit, called a *module* or *package*; typically each unit can be compiled separately. This was discussed in some detail for Ada.

• Then we find **object-oriented** languages. This is not the place to be fussy about what exactly it takes to deserve this label — chapter 2 defined a set of criteria, and of course all of part C was devoted to analyzing O-O mechanisms in detail —, but we should at the very least expect some support for classes, inheritance, polymorphism and dynamic binding.

> For the second category, encapsulation languages, which supports a data abstraction mechanism but no classes, inheritance, polymorphism or dynamic binding, you will find that the literature commonly uses the term **object-based**, introduced in an article by Peter Wegner. Because the English words *based* and *oriented* do not readily evoke the conceptual difference between encapsulation techniques and O-O languages, "object-based" is a little hard to justify, especially to newcomers. Although either terminology is acceptable once you have defined the conventions, I have in the end decided to stick here to the phrases "encapsulation languages" and "object-oriented languages", which more clearly conjure up the conceptual difference.

See [Wegner 1987].

While we are on the subject of terminology: the term "functional language" is ambiguous since other parts of the literature apply it to a class of languages, based on mathematical principles and often deriving directly or indirectly from Lisp, which use side-effect-free functions instead of imperative constructs such as procedures and assignments. To avoid any confusion, the present book always uses the term *applicative* to denote this programming style. The word *function* in our use of "functional language" is to be contrasted with *object*, not (as when "functional" is a synonym for "applicative") with *procedure*. (To make a confusing situation worse, it is quite common to see "procedural" taken to mean "not object-oriented"! There is, however, no basis for such terminology; "procedural" normally means "imperative", as opposed to applicative; all the common O-O languages, including the notation of this book, are quite procedural.)

A general comment on O-O emulation. In its most basic form, object technology is "programming with abstract data types". You can apply a rudimentary form of the ideas, even at the functional level, by defining a set of strict methodological guidelines requiring every data access to go through routines. This assumes that you start from an object-oriented *design* that has defined ADTs and their features; then you will write a set of routines representing these features — *put, remove, item, empty* in our standard stack example — and require all client modules to go through these routines. This is a far cry from object technology proper, and can only work under the assumption that everyone in the team behaves; but, if you lack any kind of language support, it can be a start. We will call this technique the **disciplinary approach**.

34.2 OBJECT-ORIENTED PROGRAMMING IN PASCAL?

Pascal, introduced in 1970 by Niklaus Wirth, has been for many years the dominant language for teaching introductory programming in computing science departments, and has influenced many of the subsequent language designs. Pascal is definitely a functional language in the sense just defined.

Pascal proper

How much of the object-oriented approach can you implement in Pascal?

Not much. The Pascal program structure is based on a completely different paradigm. A Pascal program consists of a sequence of paragraphs, appearing in an immutable order: labels, constants, types, variables, routines (procedures and functions), and executable instructions. The routines themselves have the same structure, recursively.

This simple rule facilitates one-pass compilation. But it dooms any attempt at using O-O techniques. Consider what it takes to implement an ADT, such as the standard example of stacks represented by arrays: a few constants such as the array size, one or a few types such as the record type describing the stack implementation, a few variables such as the pointer to the stack top, and a few routines representing the operations on the abstract data type. In Pascal, these elements will be scattered all over the program: all the constants for various abstract data types together, all the types together and so on.

"Linguistic Modular Units", page 53. The resulting program structure is the opposite of O-O designs. Using Pascal would contradict the Linguistic Modular Units principle, which expresses that any modular policy you choose must be supported by the available language constructs, for fear of damaging composability, decomposability and other modularity requirements.

So if we take Pascal as defined by its official standard, there is little we can do to apply O-O techniques this language beyond what was called the disciplinary approach above: imposing a strict methodological rule for data accesses.

Modular extensions of Pascal

Beyond standard Pascal, many commercially available versions remove the restrictions on the order of declarations and include support for some form of module beyond the routine, including separate compilation. Such modules may contain more than one routine, together with associated constants, types and routines. The resulting languages and products, more flexible and powerful than Pascal, are Pascal only by name; they are not standardized, and in fact resemble more an encapsulation language such as Modula-2 or Ada, to which the applicable discussion is that of the preceding chapter.

Object-oriented extensions of Pascal

Over the years a number of companies have offered object-oriented extensions of Pascal, loosely known as "Object Pascal". Two are particularly significant:

- Apple's version, originating from a language originally called *Clascal* and used for some of the software in Apple's Macintosh and its Lisa predecessor.

- Borland's version of Pascal, most recently adapted as the programming language for Borland's *Delphi* environment.

The preceding discussion does not really apply to such languages since — even more than with the modular extensions — their connection to the original Pascal is essentially their name, syntactic style, and statically typed approach. Borland Pascal, in particular, is an O-O language with exception handling. It does not, however, support any of the mechanisms of genericity, assertions, garbage collection and multiple inheritance.

34.3 FORTRAN

FORTRAN should virtually eliminate coding and debugging

FORTRAN Preliminary Report, IBM, November 1954

Cited in [Wexelblat 1981].

The oldest surviving programming language, Fortran remains widely used for scientific computation. Shockingly perhaps for people who went on from it to such "structured" languages as Pascal, you can in fact get a little more O-O frills in Fortran, although this is partly thanks to facilities that may be considered low-level and were intended for other goals.

The official name is FORTRAN, although the less obtrusive form is commonly used too.

Some context

Fortran was initially designed, as a tool for programming the IBM 704, by an IBM team under John Backus (later also instrumental in the description of Algol), with a first general release in 1957. Fortran II followed, introducing subroutines. Fortran IV solidified the language in 1966 (Fortran III, 704-specific, was not widely distributed), and was standardized by ANSI. The next revision process led to Fortran 77, actually approved in 1978, with better control structures and some simplifications. An even longer revision yielded Fortran 90 and Fortran 95, which have been diversely met and have not quite replaced their predecessors.

For most people with a computing science degree earned after the First World War, Fortran is old hat, and they would rather be caught reading the Intel 4044 User's Manual than admit they know anything about *FORMAT* and arithmetic *IF* instructions. In reality, however, quite a few programmed in Fortran at some stage, and many other people who are programmers by any objective criterion, even if their business card reads "theoretical physicist", "applied mathematician", "mechanical engineer" or even, in a few cases, "securities analyst", use Fortran as their primary tool day in and day out. Fortran remains in common use not only for maintaining old software but even for starting new projects.

To the outsider it sometimes seems that scientific programming — the world of Fortran — has remained aloof from much of the evolution in software engineering. This is partly true, partly not. The low level of the language, and the peculiar nature of scientific computing (software produced by people who, although scientists by training, often lack formal software education), have resulted in some software of less than pristine quality. But some of the best and most robust software also comes from that field, including advanced simulations of extremely complex processes and staggering tools for scientific visualization. Such products are no longer limited to delicate but small numerical algorithms; like their counterparts in other application areas, they often manipulate complex data structures, rely on database technology, include extensive user interface components. And, surprising as it may seem, they are still often written in Fortran.

The *COMMON* technique

A Fortran system is made of a main program and a number of routines (subroutines or functions). How can we provide a semblance of data abstraction?

The usual technique is to represent the data through a so-called *COMMON* block, a Fortran mechanism for making data accessible to any routine that cares to want it, and to implement each of the associated exported features (such as *put* etc. for stacks) through a separate routine. Here for example is a sketch of a *put* routine for a stack of real numbers:

A C *at the first position on a line introduces a comment.*

```
      SUBROUTINE RPUT (X)
      REAL X
C
C     PUSH X ON TOP OF REAL STACK
C
      COMMON /STREP/ TOP, STACK (2000)
      INTEGER TOP
      REAL STACK
C
      TOP = TOP + 1
      STACK (TOP) = X
      RETURN
      END
```

This version does not have any overflow control; clearly it should be updated to test for *TOP* going over the array size. (The next version will correct this.) The function to return the top element is

```
      INTEGER FUNCTION RITEM
C
C      TOP ELEMENT OF REAL STACK
C
      COMMON /STREP/ TOP, STACK (2000)
      INTEGER TOP
      REAL STACK

      RITEM = STACK (TOP)
      RETURN
      END
```

which would similarly need to test for underflow (empty stack). *REMOVE* and other features will follow the same pattern. What unites the different routines, making sure that they access the same data, is simply the name of the common block, *STREP*. (It is in fact possible, in different routines, to pretend that the same common block contains data of different types and sizes if the total memory occupied somehow coincides, although in a family-oriented book like this one it is probably preferable to avoid going into details that might not be entirely suitable for the younger members of the audience).

The limitations are obvious: this implementation describes **one abstract object** (one particular stack of reals), not an abstract data type of which the software can create arbitrarily many instances at run time, as with a class. The Fortran world is very static: you must dimension all the arrays (here to 2000, a number picked arbitrarily). Because there is no genericity, you should in principle declare a new set of routines for each type of stack; hence the names *RPUT* and *RITEM*, where the *R* stands for Real. One can work around some of these problems, but not without considerable effort.

The multiple-entry subroutine technique

The *COMMON*-based technique, as you will have noted, violates the Linguistic Modular Units principle. In a system's modular structure, the routines are physically independent although conceptually related. You can all too easily update one and forget the others.

It is in fact possible to improve on this situation (without removing some of the other limitations just listed) through a language trait legalized by Fortran 77: multiple entry points to a single routine.

This extension — which was probably introduced for different purposes, but may be redeemed for the "good cause" — enables Fortran routines to have entry points other than the normal routine header. Client routines may call these entry points as if they were autonomous routines, and the various entries may indeed have different arguments. Calling an entry will start execution of the routine at the entry point. All entries of a routine share the persistent data of the routine; a persistent data item, which in Fortran 77 must appear in a *SAVE* directive, is one whose value is retained from one activation of a routine to the next. Well, you see where we are driving: we can use this technique to define a module that encapsulates an abstract object, almost as we would in one of the encapsulation languages. In Ada, for example, we could write a package with a data structure declaration, such as a stack representation, and a set of routines that manipulate these data. Here we will simulate the package with a subroutine, the data structure with a set of declarations that we make persistent through a *SAVE*, and each Ada routine (each feature of the corresponding class in an O-O language) with an entry. Each such entry must be followed by the corresponding instructions and a *RETURN*:

> *ENTRY (arguments)*
> … Instructions …
> *RETURN*

so that the various entry-delimited blocks are disjoint: control never flows from one block to the next. This is a restricted use of entry points, which in general are meant to allow entering a routine at any point and then continuing in sequence. Also note that clients will never call the enclosing subroutine under its own name; they will only call the entries.

The main difference with the preceding *COMMON*-based solution is that all the features of the underlying abstract data type now appear in the same syntactical unit. The second part of the facing page shows an example implementing an abstract object (stack of reals). The calls from a client will look like this:

> *LOGICAL OK*
> *REAL X*
> C
> *OK = MAKE ()*
> *OK = PUT (4.5)*
> *OK = PUT (–7.88)*
> *X = ITEM ()*
> *OK = REMOVE ()*
> *IF (EMPTY ()) A = B*

Look at this text for just a second, from a distance; you could almost believe that it is the use of a class, or at least of an object, through its abstract, officially defined interface!

A Fortran routine and its entry points must be either all subroutines, or all functions. Here since *EMPTY* and *ITEM* must be functions, all other entries are also declared as functions, including *MAKE* whose result is useless.

A stack module emulation in Fortran

```
C      -- IMPLEMENTATION OF ONE
C      -- ABSTRACT STACK OF REALS
C
       INTEGER FUNCTION RSTACK ()
       PARAMETER (SIZE=1000)
C
C      -- REPRESENTATION
C
       REAL IMPL (SIZE)
       INTEGER LAST
       SAVE IMPL, LAST
C
C      -- ENTRY POINT DECLARATIONS
C
       LOGICAL MAKE
       LOGICAL PUT
       LOGICAL REMOVE
       REAL ITEM
       LOGICAL EMPTY
C
       REAL X
C
C      -- STACK CREATION
C
       ENTRY MAKE ()
          MAKE = .TRUE.
          LAST = 0
       RETURN
C
C      -- PUSH AN ITEM
C
       ENTRY PUT (X)
          IF (LAST .LT. SIZE) THEN
             PUT = .TRUE.
             LAST = LAST + 1
             IMPL (LAST) = X
          ELSE
             PUT = .FALSE.
          END IF
       RETURN
```

```
C      -- REMOVE TOP ITEM
C
       ENTRY REMOVE (X)
          IF (LAST .NE. 0) THEN
             REMOVE = .TRUE.
             LAST = LAST – 1
          ELSE
             REMOVE = .FALSE.
          END IF
       RETURN
C
C      -- TOP ITEM
C
       ENTRY ITEM ()
          IF (LAST .NE. 0) THEN
             ITEM = IMPL (LAST)
          ELSE
             CALL ERROR
     *        ('ITEM: EMPTY STACK')
          END IF
       RETURN
C
C      -- IS STACK EMPTY?
C
       ENTRY EMPTY ()
          EMPTY = (LAST .EQ. 0)
       RETURN
C
       END
```

This style of programming can be applied successfully to emulate the encapsulation techniques of Ada or Modula-2 in contexts where you have no choice but to use Fortran. It suffers of course from stringent limitations:

- No internal calls are permitted: whereas routines in an object-oriented class usually rely on each other for their implementations, an entry call issued by another entry of the same subroutine would be understood as an instance of recursion — anathema to Fortran, and run-time disaster in many implementations.

- As noted, the mechanism is strictly static, supporting only one abstract object. It may be generalized to allow for a fixed number of objects (by transforming every variable into a one-dimensional array, and adding a dimension to every array). But there is no portable support for dynamic object creation.

- In practice, it seems that some Fortran environments (two decades after Fortran 77 was published!) do not deal too well with multiple-entry subroutines; in particular debuggers do not always know how to keep track of multiple entries. Before applying this technique to a production development, check with the local Fortran guru to find out whether it is wise to rely on this facility in your environment.

- Finally, the very idea of hijacking a language mechanism for purposes other than its probable design objective raises dangers of confusion and errors.

34.4 OBJECT-ORIENTED PROGRAMMING AND C

Born in a log cabinet, C quickly rose to prominence. Although most people interested in both C and object technology have focused on the O-O extensions of C discussed in the next chapter (C++, Objective-C, Java), it remains interesting to see how C itself can be made to emulate O-O concepts, if only to understand the techniques that have made C so useful as a stepping stone towards the implementation of more advanced languages.

Some context

C was designed at AT&T's Bell Laboratories as a portable language for writing operating systems. The first version of Unix had used assembly language, but a portable version soon appeared necessary, and C was designed around 1970 to make it possible. It was derived from ideas found in BCPL, a language of the sixties which, like C, can be mentioned in the same breath as "high-level", "machine-oriented" and "portable": high-level thanks to control structures comparable to those of Algol or Pascal; machine-oriented because you can manipulate data at the most elementary level, through addresses, pointers and bytes; portable because the machine-oriented concepts are so defined as to cover a wide variety of computer types.

C's timing could not have been better. In the late seventies Unix became the operating system of choice for many universities, and C spread with it. Then in the eighties the microcomputer revolution burst out, and C was ready to serve as its *lingua franca* — more scalable than Basic, more flexible than Pascal. At the same time Unix also enjoyed some commercial success, and along with Unix still came C. In a few years, a boutique product became the dominant language in large segments of the computing industry, including much of where the action really was.

Anyone interested in the progress of programming languages — even people who do not care too much for the language itself — has a political debt to C, and sometimes a technical one as well:

- Politically, C ended the fossilized situation that prevailed in the programming language world until around 1980. No one in industry wanted to hear (particularly after the commercial failure of Algol) about anything else than the sacred troika, Fortran for science, Cobol for business and PL/I for true blue shops. Outside of academic circles and a few R&D departments, any attempt at suggesting other solutions was met with as much enthusiasm as if it were a proposal to introduce a third brand of Cola drink. C broke that mindset, making it acceptable to think of the programming language as something you choose from a reasonably broad and evolving catalog. (A few years later, C itself became so entrenched that in some circles the choices seemed to have gone from three to one, but it is the fate of successful subversives that they become the new Establishment.)

- Technically, the portability and machine-closeness of C have made it an attractive solution as a target language of compilers for higher-level languages. The first C++ and Objective-C implementations used this approach, and compilers for many other languages, often having no visible connection to C, have followed their example. The advantages for the compiler writers and their users are: portability, since you can have a single C-generating compiler for your language and use C compilers (available nowadays for almost any computer architecture) to take care of platform dependencies; efficiency, since you can rely on the extensive optimization techniques that have been implemented in good C compilers; and ease of integration with ubiquitous C-based tools and components.

[Kernighan 1978], [Kernighan 1988].

With time, the contradiction between the two views of C — high-level programming language, and portable assembly language — has become more acute. Recent evolution of the ANSI standard for C (first published in 1990, following the earlier version known as *K&R* from the authors of the first C book, Kernighan and Ritchie) have made the language more typed — and hence less convenient for its use as a compiler's target code. It has even been announced that forthcoming versions will have a notion of class, obscuring the separation from C++ and Java.

Although an O-O extension of C simpler than C++ and Java may be desirable, one can wonder whether this evolution is the right one for C; a hybrid C-based O-O language will always remain a strange contraption, whereas the idea of a simple, portable, universally available, efficiently compilable machine-oriented language, serving both as a target language for high-level compilers and as a low-level tool for writing very short routines to access operating system and machine-dependent facilities (that is to say, for doing the same thing that assembly language used to do for C, only at the next level) remains as useful as it ever was.

Basics

As with any other language, you can apply to C the "disciplinary" technique of restricted data access, requiring all uses of data structures to go through functions. (All routines in C are functions; procedures are viewed as functions with a "void" result type.)

Beyond this, the notion of file may serve to implement higher-level modules. Files are a C notion on the borderline between the language and the operating system. A file is a compilation unit; it may contain a number of functions and some data. Some of the functions may be hidden from other files, and some made public. This achieves encapsulation: a file may contain all the elements pertaining to the implementation of one or more abstract objects, or an abstract data type. Thanks to this notion of file, you can essentially reach the *encapsulation language* level in C, as if you had Ada or Modula-2. As compared to Ada, however, you will be missing genericity and the distinction between specification and implementation parts.

In practice, a commonly used C technique is rather averse to O-O principles. Most C programs use "header files", which describe shared data structures. Any file needing the data structures will gain access to them through an "include" directive (handled by the built-in C preprocessor) of the form

   #include *<header.h>*

where *header.h* is the name of the header file (*.h* is the conventional suffix for such file names). This is conceptually equivalent to copying the whole header file at the point where the directive appears, and allows the including file to access directly the data structure definitions of the header file. As a result the C tradition, if not the language itself, encourages client modules to access data structures through their physical representations, which clearly contradicts the principles of information hiding and data abstraction. It is possible, however, to use header files in a more disciplined fashion, enforcing rather than violating data abstraction; they can even help you go some way towards defining interface modules in the style we studied for Ada in the preceding chapter.

Emulating objects

Beyond the encapsulation level, one of the more specialized and low-level features of C — the ability to manipulate pointers to functions — can be used to emulate fairly closely some of the more advanced properties of a true O-O approach. Although it is sufficiently delicate to suggest that its proper use is by compilers for higher-level languages rather than C programmers, it does deserve to be known.

In we take a superficial look at the notion of object as it exists in object technology, we might say that "every object has access to the operations applicable to it". This is a little naïve perhaps, but not altogether wrong conceptually. If, however, we take this view literally, we find that C directly supports the notion! It is possible for an instance of a "structure type" of C (the equivalent of record types in Pascal) to contain, among its fields, pointers to functions.

A C object with function references

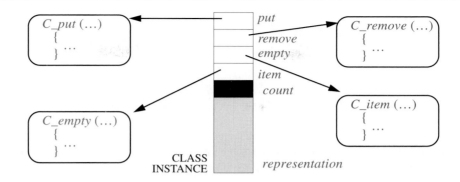

For example, a C structure type *REAL_STACK* may be declared by the type definition

typedef struct
    {
    /* Exported features */
        void (*remove) ();
        void (*put) ();
        float (*item) ();
        BOOL (*empty) ();
    /* Secret features (implementation) */
        int *count*;
        float *representation* [*MAXSIZE*];
    }
    REAL_STACK;

The braces { } delimit the components of the structure type; *float* introduces real numbers; procedures are declared as functions with a **void** result type; comments are delimited by /* and */. The other asterisks * serve to de-reference pointers; the idea in the practice of C programming is that you add enough of them until things seem to work, and if not you can always try a & or two. If this still does not succeed, you will usually find someone who knows what to do.

Here the last two components are an integer and an array; the others are references to functions. In the declaration as written, the comments about exported and secret features apply to the emulated class, but everything is in fact available to clients.

Each instance of the type must be initialized so that the reference fields will point to appropriate functions. For example, if *my_stack* is a variable of this type and *C_remove* is a stack popping function, you may assign to the *remove* field of the *my_stack* object a reference to this function, as follows:

my_stack•*remove* = *C_remove*

In the class being emulated, feature *remove* has no argument. To enable the *C_remove* function to access the appropriate stack object, you must declare it as

C_remove (*s*)

        REAL_STACK s;

    {

        … Implementation of *remove* operation …

    }

so that a client may apply *remove* to a stack *my_stack* under the form

    my_stack . *remove* (*my_stack*)

More generally, a routine *rout* which would have n arguments in the class will yield a C function *C_rout* with $n+1$ arguments. An object-oriented routine call of the form

    $x . rout\ (arg_1, arg_2, ..., arg_n)$

will be emulated as

    $x . C\_rout\ (x, arg_1, arg_2, ..., arg_n)$

Emulating classes

The preceding technique will work to a certain extent. It can even be extended to emulate inheritance.

Exercise E34.3, page 1112.

But it is inapplicable to any serious development: as illustrated in the figure of the preceding page, it implies that **every instance** of every class physically contains references to all the routines applicable to it. The space overhead would be prohibitive, especially with inheritance.

To bring this overhead down to an acceptable level, notice that the routines are the same for all instances of a class. So we may introduce for each class a run-time data structure, the **class descriptor**, containing references to the routines; we can implement it as a linked list or an array. The space requirements decrease dramatically: instead of one pointer per routine per object, we can use one pointer per routine *per class*, plus *one pointer per object* giving access to the class descriptor, as shown by the figure at the top of the following page.

Timewise we pay the price of an indirection: as shown in the figure, you have to go through the descriptor to find the function applicable to an object. The space economy and the simplification seem well worth this penalty.

There is no secret about it: the technique just sketched is what has made C useful as an implementation vehicle for object-oriented languages, starting with Objective-C and C++ in the early eighties. The ability to use function pointers, combined with the idea of grouping these pointers in a class descriptor shared by an arbitrary number of instances, yields the first step towards implementing O-O techniques.

This is only a first step, of course, and you must still find techniques for implementing inheritance (multiple inheritance in particular is not easy), genericity, exceptions, assertions and dynamic binding. To explain how this can be done would take another book. Let us, however, note one important property, deducible from what we have

***C objects
sharing a class
descriptor***

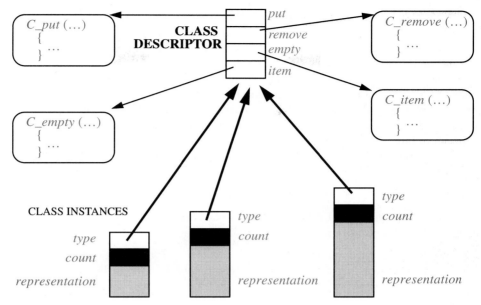

seen so far. Implementing dynamic binding, regardless of the details, will require run-time access to the type of each object, to find the proper variant of the feature f in a dynamically bound call $x \cdot f (\dots)$ (written here in O-O notation). In other words: in addition to its official fields, defined explicitly by the software developer through type declarations, each object will need to carry an extra internal field, generated by the compiler and accessible only to the run-time system, indicating the **type** of the object. Well, with the approach just defined, we already have a possible implementation of this type field — as a pointer to the class descriptor. This is the reason why the above figure uses the label *type* for such fields.

O-O C: an assessment

This discussion has shown that implementation techniques are available in C to emulate object-oriented ideas. But it does not mean that programmers should use these techniques. As with Fortran, the emulation does violence to the language. C's main strength is, as noted, its availability as a "structured assembly language" (a successor to BCPL and Wirth's PL/360), portable, reasonably simple and efficiently interpreted. Its basic concepts are very far from those of object-oriented design.

The danger in trying to force an object-oriented peg into a C hole is to get an inconsistent construction, impairing the software development process and the quality of the resulting products. Better use C for what it does well: small interfaces to low-level hardware or operating system facilities, and machine-generated target code; then when the time comes to apply object technology we should use a tool designed for that purpose.

34.5 BIBLIOGRAPHICAL NOTES

Techniques for writing Fortran packages based on the principles of data abstraction are described in [M 1982a]. They use routines sharing *COMMON* blocks, rather than multiple-entry routines. They go further in their implementation of object-oriented concepts than the techniques described in this chapter, thanks to the use of specific library mechanisms that provides the equivalent of dynamically allocated class instances. Such mechanisms, however, require a significant investment, and will have to be ported anew to each platform type.

I am indebted to Paul Dubois for pointing out that the multiple-entry Fortran technique, although definitely part of the standard, is not always supported well by current compilers.

[Cox 1990] (originally 1986) contains a discussion of C techniques for the implementation of object-oriented concepts.

The basic reference on the history of classical programming languages is a conference proceedings [Wexelblat 1981]; see [Knuth 1980] for the earliest efforts.

EXERCISES

E34.1 Graphics objects (for Fortran programmers)

Write a set of Fortran multiple-entry routines that implement basic graphics objects (points, circles, polygons). For a specification of the abstractions involved and the associated operations, you may rely on the GKS graphics standard.

E34.2 Genericity (for C programmers)

How would you transform the C emulation of a "real stack" class declaration into an emulated generic declaration, easy to adapt to stacks of any type G rather than just **float**?

E34.3 Object-oriented programming in C (term project)

Design and implement a simple object-oriented extension of C using the ideas of this chapter. You may write either a pre-processor, translating an extended version of the language into C, or a function package that does not change the language itself.

Approach the problem through three successive refinements:

- Implement first a mechanism allowing objects to carry their own references to available routines.

- Then see how to factor routine references at the class level.

- Finally, study how to add single inheritance to the mechanism.

Simula to Java and beyond: major O-O languages and environments

*E*ncouraged by the introduction of Simula in 1967, a number of object-oriented languages have appeared on the scene, highlighting various aspects of the approach. This chapter reviews some of the languages that have attracted the most attention: Simula; Smalltalk; C++ and other O-O extensions of C; Java.

The literature still lacks an in-depth comparative study of important O-O languages. The ambition of this chapter is of necessity more modest. In particular, the space allotted to each language is not an indication of the language's practical significance, and some of the most publicized will indeed get a fairly short treatment. Our goal is to learn about *issues* and *concepts*, finding them where we can, even if that means turning our attention for a while to one of the less hyped approaches. The risk of under-representing one of the principal players is not great, since one only has to look around to pick up articles and books describing it in generous detail. The real risk would be the reverse: to miss a promising idea just because the language supporting it (say Simula) does not currently enjoy top favor. In its coverage of notable languages, then, this survey is not equal-opportunity; it is instead, in its choice of notable language traits, a case of affirmative action.

Even when the concepts are the same or similar, the terms used to denote them in official language descriptions can vary. The discussion will use the native terms when they reflect language peculiarities; for simplicity and consistency, however, it uses the terminology of the rest of this book (designed as an attempt at unification) when differences are unimportant. For example you will read about Simula routines, procedures and functions, although the corresponding terms in official Simula usage are procedure, untyped procedure and typed procedure.

35.1 SIMULA

The undisputed founder of the House of Classes (Object Palace) is Simula, whose design was completed (if we ignore a few later updates, entirely minor) in 1967. This may seem hard to believe: a full-fledged object-oriented language was around, and implemented, *before* structured programming, before Parnas had published his articles on information hiding, many years before anyone had come up with the phrase "abstract data type". The Vietnam War was still a page-4 item; barricades had not yet sprung up in the streets of Paris; a mini-skirt could still cause a stir: away by the Northern shores of the Baltic a few fortunate software developers led by a handful of visionaries were already profiting from the power of classes, inheritance, polymorphism, dynamic binding and most of the other marvels of object orientation.

Background

Simula is actually a second design. In the early sixties, a language now known as Simula 1 was developed to support the programming of discrete-event simulations. Although not quite object-oriented in the full sense of the term, it already showed some of the key insights. "Simula" proper is Simula 67, designed in 1967 by Kristen Nygaard and Ole-Johan Dahl from the University of Oslo and the Norwegian Computing Center (Norsk Regnesentral). Nygaard has explained since how the decision to keep the name was meant to ensure continuity with the previous language and the link to its user community; but an unfortunate effect was that for a long time that name evoked for many people the image of a language meant only for discrete-event simulation — a relatively narrow application area — even though Simula 67 is definitely a general-purpose programming language, whose only simulation-specific features are a handful of instructions and a *SIMULATION* library class, used by a minority of Simula developers.

The name was shortened to just Simula in 1986; the current standard is from 1987.

Availability

Simula is often presented as a respectable but defunct ancestor. In fact it is still alive and enjoys the support of a small but enthusiastic community. The language definition is maintained by the "Simula Standards Group". Compilers are available for a variety of hardware and software environments from several companies, mostly Scandinavian.

Major language traits

We will take a general look at the basic properties of Simula. To some readers Simula will be passé, and the author of this book will not feel insulted if you skip to the next section, on Smalltalk. But if you do want to gain a full appreciation of object technology you will find Simula worth your time; the concepts are there in their original form, and a few of them show possibilities that may not yet, thirty years later, have been fully exploited.

Simula is an object-oriented extension of Algol 60. Most correct Algol programs are also correct Simula programs. In particular, the basic control structures are those of Algol: loop, conditional, switch (a multiple branch instruction, low-level precursor to Pascal's **case** instruction). The basic data types (integer, real etc.) are also drawn from Algol.

Like Algol, Simula uses at the highest level a traditional software structure based on the notion of main program. An executable program is a main program containing a number of program units (routines or classes). Simula environments do support, however, a form of separate class compilation.

Simula uses full block structure in the Algol 60 style: program units such as classes may be nested within one another.

All Simula implementations support automatic garbage collection. There is a small standard library, including in particular two-way linked lists used by the *SIMULATION* class studied later in this chapter.

See "References and simple values", page 272.

As in the notation of this book, the most common entities of non-basic types denote references to class instances, rather than the instances themselves. Instead of being implicit, however, this property is emphasized by the notation. You will declare the type of such an entity as **ref** (*C*), rather than just *C*, for some class *C*; and the corresponding operations will use special symbols: :− for an assignment where integer or real operands would use :=; == rather than = for equality; =/= rather than /= for inequality. An earlier chapter presented the rationale for and against this convention.

To create an instance, you will use, rather than a creation instruction, a **new** expression:

ref (*C*) *a*; …; *a* :− **new** *C*

Evaluation of the **new** expression creates an instance of *C* and returns a reference to it. A class may have arguments (playing the role of the arguments to creation procedures in our notation), as in

class *C* (*x*, *y*); **integer** *x*, *y*
    begin … **end**;

In this case, the **new** expression must provide corresponding actual arguments:

a :− **new** *C* (*3*, *98*)

The arguments may then be used in routines of the class; but unlike with creation instructions this gives only one initialization mechanism.

Besides routines and attributes, a class may contain a sequence of instructions, the **body** of the class; if so, the **new** call will execute these instructions. We will see how to use this possibility to make classes represents process-like computational elements rather than just passive objects as in most other O-O languages.

No assertion mechanism is provided. Simula supports single inheritance; to declare *B* as an heir of *A*, use

A **class** *B*;
    begin … **end**

To redefine a feature of a class in a descendant class, simply provide a new declaration; it will take precedence over the original one. (There is no equivalent to the **redefine** clause.)

The original version of Simula 67 did not have explicit information hiding constructs. In more recent versions, a feature declared as **protected** will be unavailable to clients; a protected feature which is further declared as **hidden** will also be unavailable to proper descendants. A non-protected feature may be protected by a proper descendant, but a protected feature may not be re-exported by proper descendants.

Deferred features are offered in the form of "virtual routines", appearing in a **virtual** paragraph at the beginning of the class. It is not necessary to declare the arguments of a virtual routine; this means that different effective definitions of a virtual routine may have different numbers and types of arguments. For example, a class *POLYGON* might begin

> **class** *POLYGON*;
>> **virtual**: **procedure** *set_vertices*
>
> **begin**
>> ...
>
> **end**

allowing descendants to provide a variable number of arguments of type *POINT* for *set_vertices*: three for *TRIANGLE*, four for *QUADRANGLE* etc. This flexibility implies that some of the type checking must be done at run time.

> C++ users should beware of a possible confusion: although inspired by Simula, C++ uses a different meaning for the word *virtual*. A C++ function is virtual if it is meant to be dynamically bound (it is, as we have seen, one of the most controversial aspects of C++ that you must specify this requirement explicitly). The C++ approximation to Simula's virtual procedures is called a "pure virtual function".

"The C++ approach to binding", page 513.

Simula supports polymorphism: if *B* is a descendant of *A*, the assignment *a1 :– b1* is correct for *a1* of type *A* and *b1* of type *B*. (Interestingly enough, assignment attempt is *almost* there: if the type of *b1* is an ancestor of the type of *a1*, the assignment will work if the run-time objects have the proper conformance relationship — source descendant of target; if not, however, the result will be a run-time error, rather than a special value which, as with assignment attempt, the software could detect and handle.) By default, binding is static rather than dynamic, except for virtual routines. So if *f* is a non-virtual feature declared at the *A* level, *a1*.*f* will denote the *A* version of *f* even if there is a different version in *B*. You can force dynamic binding by using the **qua** construct, as in

> (*a1* **qua** *B*).*f*

This, of course, loses the automatic adaptation of every operation to its target. You may however obtain the desired dynamic binding behavior (which may largely be considered a Simula invention) by declaring polymorphic routines as virtual. In many of the examples that we have studied, a polymorphic routine was not deferred but had a default implementation right from the start. To achieve the same effect, the Simula developer will add an intermediate class where the routine is virtual.

As an alternative to using **qua**, the **inspect** instruction makes it possible to perform a different operation on an entity *a1*, depending on the actual type of the corresponding object, which must be a descendant of the type *A* declared for *a1*:

> **inspect** *a1*
>> **when** *A* **do** ...;
>> **when** *B* **do** ...;
>> ...

This achieves the same effect but assumes that the set of descendants of a class is frozen, and runs into conflict with the Open-Closed principle

An example

Chapter 20. Compare with the final class texts in "AN OBJECT-ORIENTED ARCHITECTURE", 20.5, page 684.

The following class extracts illustrate the general flavor of Simula. They are drawn from the solution to the problem of full-screen entry systems.

The original STATE class appeared on page 686.

```
class STATE;
    virtual:
        procedure display;
        procedure read;
        boolean procedure correct;
    procedure message;
    procedure process;
begin
    ref (ANSWER) user_answer; integer choice;
    procedure execute; begin
            boolean ok;
        ok := false;
        while not ok do begin
            display; read; ok := correct;
            if not ok then message (a)
        end while;
        process;
    end execute
end STATE;
class APPLICATION (n, m);
        integer n, m;
begin
    ref (STATE) array transition (1:n, 0:m–1);
    ref (STATE) array associated_state (1:n);
    integer initial;

    procedure execute; begin
            integer st_number;
        st_number := initial;
        while st_number /= 0 do begin
                ref (STATE) st;
            st := associated_state (st_number); st.execute;
            st_number := transition (st_number, st.choice)
        end while
    end execute

    ...
end APPLICATION
```

The original APLICATION class appeared on page 690.

Coroutine concepts

Along with basic O-O mechanisms, Simula offers an interesting notion: coroutines.

The notion of coroutine was presented in the discussion of concurrency. Here is a brief reminder. Coroutines are modeled after parallel processes as they exist in operating systems or real-time software. A process has more conceptual autonomy than a routine; a printer driver, for example, is entirely responsible for what happens to the printer it manages. Besides being in charge of an abstract object, it has its own lifecycle algorithm, often conceptually infinite. The rough form of the printer process could be something like

"Coroutines", page 1012.

> **from** *some_initialization* **loop forever**
>
> > "Obtain a file to be printed"; "Print it"
>
> **end**

For a more complete description of a printer process see "Processes programmed", page 960.

In sequential programming, the relationship between program units is asymmetric: a program unit calls another, which will execute completely and return to the caller at the point of call. Communication between processes is more equal: each process pursues its own life, interrupting itself to provide information to, or get information from another.

Coroutines are similarly designed, but for execution on a single thread of control. (This sequential emulation of parallel execution is called *quasi-parallelism*.) A coroutine that "resumes" another interrupts its own execution and restarts its colleague at its last point of interruption; the interrupted coroutine may itself be later resumed.

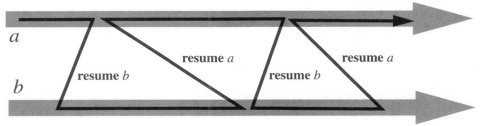

Coroutine sequencing

(This figure appeared originally on page 1012.)

Coroutines are particularly useful when each of several related activities has its own logic; each may be described as a sequential process, and the master-slave relationship implied by routines is not adequate. A frequent example is an input-to-output transformation in which different constraints are placed on the structure of the input and output files. Such a case will be discussed below.

Simula represents coroutines as instances of classes. This is appropriate since coroutines almost always need persistent data, and often have an associated abstract object. As we noted earlier, a Simula class has a **body**, made of one or more instructions. In a class representing a passive data abstraction, it will only serve as initialization of the class instances (the equivalent of our creation procedure); but in a coroutine it will be the description of a process. The body of a coroutine is usually a loop of the form

> **while** *continuation_condition* **do begin**
>   ... Actions...;
>   **resume** *other_coroutine*;
>   ...Actions ...
> **end**

For some of the coroutines in a system the *continuation_condition* is often *True* to yield the equivalent of an infinite process (although at least one coroutine should terminate).

A system based on coroutines generally has a main program that first creates a number of coroutine objects, and then resumes one of them:

> *corout1* :– **new** *C1*; *corout2* :– **new** *C2*; ...
> **resume** *corout$_i$*

On the parallel scheme see "A multi-launcher", page 988.

The evaluation of each **new** expression creates an object and starts executing its body. But the quasi-parallel nature of coroutines (as opposed to the true parallelism of processes) raises an initialization problem: with processes, each **new** would spawn off a new process and return control to the caller; but here only one coroutine may be active at any given time. If the **new** expression started the coroutine's main algorithm, the above main thread would never recapture control; for example it would never get a chance to create *C2* after spawning off *C1*.

Simula addresses this problem through the **detach** instruction. A coroutine may execute a **detach** to give control back to the unit that created it through a **new**. Coroutine bodies almost always begin (after initialization instructions if needed) with a **detach**, usually followed by a loop. After executing its **detach**, the coroutine will become suspended until the main program or another coroutine **resume**s it.

A coroutine example

Here is an illustration of the kind of situation in which coroutines may prove useful. You are requested to print a sequence of real numbers, given as input; but every eighth number (the eighth, the sixteenth, the twenty-fourth etc.) is to be omitted from the output. Furthermore, the output must appear as a sequence of lines, with six numbers per line (except for the last line if there are not enough numbers to fill it). So if i_n denotes the n-th input item, the output will start as

> $i1$ $i2$ $i3$ $i4$ $i5$ $i6$
> i_7 i_9 i_{10} i_{11} i_{12} i_{13}
> i_{14} i_{15} i_{17} etc.

Finally, the output should only include the first 1000 numbers thus determined.

This problem is representative of coroutine use because it conceptually involves three processes, each with its specific logic: the input, where the constraint is to skip every eighth item; the output, where the constraint is to go to the next line after every sixth item; and the main program, which is required to process 1000 items. Traditional control structures are not good at combining such processes with widely different constraints. A coroutine solution, on the other hand, will work smoothly.

Following the preceding analysis, we may use three coroutines: the **producer** (input), the **printer** (output) and the **controller**. The general structure is:

> **begin**
>> **class** *PRODUCER* **begin** … See next … **end** *PRODUCER*;
>> **class** *PRINTER* **begin** … See next … **end** *PRINTER*;
>> **class** *CONTROLLER* **begin** … See next … **end** *CONTROLLER*;
>> **ref** (*PRODUCER*) *producer*, **ref** (*PRINTER*) *printer*, **ref** (*CONTROLLER*) *controller*;
>> *producer* :– **new** *PRODUCER*; *printer* :– **new** *PRINTER*; *controller* :– **new** *CONTROLLER*;
>> **resume** *controller*
>
> **end**

This is a main program, in the usual sense; it creates an instance of each of the three coroutine classes and resumes one of them, the controller. Here are the classes:

> **class** *CONTROLLER*; **begin**
>> **integer** *i*;
>
> **detach**;
> **for** *i* := *1* **step** *1* **until** *1000* **do resume** *printer*
> **end** *CONTROLLER*;

> **class** *PRINTER*; **begin**
>> **integer** *i*;
>
> **detach**;
> **while true do**
>> **for** *i* := *1* **step** *1* **until** *8* **do begin**
>>> **resume** *producer*;
>>> *outreal* (*producer*.*last_input*);
>>> **resume** *controller*
>>
>> **end**;
>> *next_line*
>
> **end**
> **end** *PRINTER*;

> **class** *PRODUCER*; **begin**
>> **integer** *i*; **real** *last_input*, *discarded*;
>
> **detach**;
> **while true do begin**
>> **for** *i* := *1* **step** *1* **until** *6* **do begin**
>>> *last_input* := *inreal*; **resume** *printer*
>>
>> **end**;
>> *discarded* := *inreal*
>
> **end**
> **end** *PRODUCER*;

This scheme will not work if the program runs out of input before having printed 1000 output items. See exercise E35.1, page 1139.

Each class body begins with **detach** to allow the main program to proceed with the initialization of other coroutines. Procedure *outreal* prints a real number; function *inreal* reads and returns the next real on input; the extract assumes a procedure *next_line* that goes to the next line on input.

Coroutines fit well with the other concepts of object-oriented software construction. Note how decentralized the above scheme is: each process minds its own business, with limited interference from the others. The producer takes care of generating candidates from the input; the printer takes care of the output; the controller takes care of when to start and finish. As usual, a good check of the quality of the solution is the ease of extension and modification; it is indeed straightforward here to add a coroutine that will check for end of input (as requested by an exercise). Coroutines take decentralization, the hallmark of O-O architectures, one step further.

On the use of a concurrency mechanism to describe coroutines see "Coroutines", page 1012.

The architecture could be made even more decentralized. In particular, the processes in the above structure must still activate each other by name; ideally they should not have to know about each other except to communicate requested information (as when the printer obtains *last_input* from the producer). The simulation primitives studied below allow this; after that, the solution is to use a full concurrency mechanism, such as described in an earlier chapter. As you will remember, its platform-independence means that it will work for coroutines as well as true parallelism.

Sequencing and inheritance

"Synchronization for concurrent O-O computation", page 980.

Even if it does not use coroutine mechanisms (**detach**, **resume**), a Simula class may have a body (a sequence of instructions) in addition to its features, and so may take on the behavior of a process in addition to its usual role as an abstract data type implementation. When combined with inheritance, this property leads to a simpler version of what the discussion of concurrency called the *inheritance anomaly*, to which Simula, thanks to its limitation to single rather than multiple inheritance and coroutines rather than full parallelism, is able to provide a language solution.

For a class C let $body_C$ be the sequence of instructions declared as body of C and $actual\_body_C$ the sequence of instructions executed for every creation of an instance of C. If C has no parent, $actual\_body_C$ is just $body_C$. If C has a parent A (it can have at most one) then $actual\_body_C$ is by default the sequence of instructions

$actual\_body_A$; $body_C$

In other words, ancestors' bodies are executed in the order of inheritance. But this default may not be what you want. To supersede it, Simula offers the **inner** instruction which denotes the heir's body, so that the default policy is equivalent to having an **inner** at the end of the parent's body. If instead you write the body of A as

$instructions_1$; **inner**; $instructions_2$

then (assuming A itself has no parent) the execution of C will execute not its $body_C$ as written in the class but its $actual\_body_C$ defined as

$instructions_1$; $body_C$; $instructions_2$

Although the reasons for this facility are clear, the convention is rather awkward:

- In many cases descendants would need to create their instances differently from their ancestors. (Remember *POLYGON* and *RECTANGLE*.)

- Bodies of descendants, such as C here, become hard to understand: just reading $body_C$ does not really tell you what the execution will do.

- In addition, of course, the convention would not transpose easily to multiple inheritance, although this is not an immediate concern in Simula.

Such difficulties with **inner** are typical of the consequences of making objects active, as we found out when discussing concurrency.

"Active objects clash with inheritance", page 959.

Almost all object-oriented languages after Simula have departed from the **inner** convention and treated object initialization as a procedure.

Simulation

True to its origins, Simula includes a set of primitives for discrete-event simulation. It is no accident, of course, that the first O-O language was initially meant for simulation applications; more than in any other area, this is where the modeling power of the object-oriented method can illustrate itself.

A **simulation** software system analyzes and predicts the behavior of some external system — an assembly line, a chemical reaction, a computer operating system, a ship…

A **discrete-event simulation** software system simulates such an external system as having, at any time, a *state* that can change in response to *events* occurring at discrete instants. This differs from **continuous** simulation, which views the state as continuously evolving. Which of these two modeling techniques is best for a given external system depends not so much on whether the system is inherently continuous or discrete (often a meaningless question) as on what models we are able to devise for it.

Another competitor to discrete-event simulation is **analytical** modeling, whereby you simply build a mathematical model of the external system, then solve the equations. This is a very different approach. With discrete-event simulation, you run a software system whose behavior simulates the behavior of the external system: to get more significant results, you will increase the length of the period that you simulate in the external system's life, and so you will run the simulation longer. This is why analytical models are usually more efficient. But many physical systems are too complex to admit realistic yet tractable mathematical models; then simulation is the only possibility.

Many external systems lend themselves naturally to discrete event simulation. An example is an assembly line, where typical events may include a new part being entered into the line, a worker or machine performing a certain operation on one or more parts, a finished product being removed from the line, a failure causing the line to stop. You may use the simulation to answer questions about the modeled physical systems: how long does it take (average, minimum, maximum, standard deviation) to produce a finished product? How long will a given piece of machinery remain unused? What is the optimum inventory level? How long does it take to recover from a power failure?

The input to a simulation is a sequence of events with their occurrence times. It may come from measurements on the external systems (when the simulation is used to reconstruct and analyze past phenomena, for example a system failure); more commonly, it is produced by random number generators according to some chosen statistical laws.

A discrete-event model must keep track of external system time, also called **simulated time**, representing the time taken by external system operations such as performing a certain task on a certain part, or the instants at which certain events such as equipment failure will occur. Simulated time should not be confused with the **computing time** needed to execute the simulation system. For the simulation system, simulated time is simply a non-negative real variable, which the simulation program may only increase by discrete leaps. It is available in Simula through the query *time*, managed by the run-time system and modifiable through some of the procedures seen next.

Feature *time* and other simulation-specific features come from a library class *SIMULATION*, which may be used as parent by another class. Let us call "simulation class" any class that is a descendant of *SIMULATION*.

> In Simula, you may also apply inheritance to blocks: a block written under the form
> *C* **begin** ... **end** has access to all the features declared in class *C*. *SIMULATION* is often
> used in this way as parent of a complete program rather than just a class. So we can also
> talk of a "simulation program".

First, *SIMULATION* contains the declaration of a class *PROCESS*. (As noted earlier, Simula class declarations may be nested.) An instance of *PROCESS* represents a process of the external system. A simulation class can declare descendants of *PROCESS*, which we will call "process classes", and their instances just "processes". Among other properties, a process may be linked to other processes in a linked list (which means that *PROCESS* is a descendant of the Simula equivalent of class *LINKABLE*). A process may be in one of the following four states:

- **Active**, or currently executing.

- **Suspended**, or waiting to be resumed.

- **Idle**, or not part of the system.

- **Terminated**.

Any simulation (that is to say, any instance of a descendant of *SIMULATION*) maintains an **event list**, containing **event notices**. Each event notice is a pair <*process, activation_time*>, where *activation_time* indicates when the *process* must be activated. (Here and in the rest of this section any mention of time, as well as words such as "when" or "currently", refer to simulated time: the external system's time, as available through *time*.) The event list is sorted by increasing *activation_time*; the first process is active, all others are suspended. Non-terminated processes which are not in the list are idle.

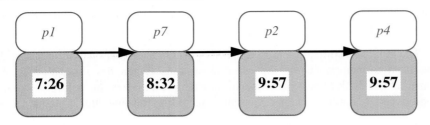

An event list

The basic operation on processes is activation, which schedules a process to become active at a certain time by inserting an event notice into the event list. Apparently for syntactical reasons, this operation is not a call to a procedure of class *SIMULATION*, but a specific instruction using the keyword **activate** or **reactivate**. (A procedure call would seem to be a more consistent approach; in fact the standard defines the semantics of *activate* through a fictitious procedure text.) The basic form of the instruction is

> **activate** *some_process scheduling_clause*

where *some_process* is a non-void entity of type conforming to *PROCESS*. The optional *scheduling_clause* is of one of

> **at** *some_time*
> **delay** *some_period*
> **before** *another_process*
> **after** *another_process*

The first two forms specify the position of the new event notice by its activation time (the sorting criterion for the event list); the new activation time is *max (time, some_time)* in the **at** form and *max (time, time + some_period)* in the **delay** form. The new event notice will be inserted after any other already present in the list with the same activation time, unless you specify **prior**. The last two forms specify the position with reference to another process in the list. A missing *scheduling_clause* is equivalent to **delay** *0*.

A process may activate itself at a later time by specifying itself as the target process *some_process*. In this case the keyword should be **reactivate**. This is useful to represent an external system task that takes some simulated time — but of course no computer time. So if you want to simulate a task that a worker takes three minutes (180 seconds) to perform, you can let the corresponding process *worker* execute the instruction

> **reactivate** *worker* **delay** *180*

This case is so common as to justify a special syntax, avoiding explicit self-reference:

> *hold* (*180*)

with exactly the same effect.

Procedure hold is part of the SIMU-LATION class.

As you may have guessed, processes are implemented as coroutines; the simulation primitives internally use the coroutine primitives that we have reviewed. The effect of *hold* (*some_period*), for example, may be approximately described (in syntax similar to the notation of this book but extended with **resume**) as

-- Insert new event notice into event list at position determined by its time:

my_new_time := max (time, time + some_period)

!! my_reactivation_notice.make (Current, my_new_time)

event_list.put (my_reactivation_notice)

-- Get first element of event list and remove it:

next := event_list.first; *event_list.remove_first*

-- Activate chosen process, advancing time if necessary:

time := time. max (next.when); **resume** *next.what*

assuming the following declarations:

my_new_time: *REAL*; *my_reactivation_notice, next*: *EVENT_NOTICE*

class *EVENT_NOTICE* **creation** *make* **feature**

    when: *REAL* -- i.e. time

    what: *PROCESS*

    make (t: REAL; p: PROCESS) **is**

        do *when := t*; *what := p* **end**

end

If a process becomes suspended by reactivating itself at a later time, execution will resume the first suspended process (the one with the earliest reactivation time) and, if its reactivation time is after the current time, correspondingly advance the current time.

*Exercise E35.2,
page 1139.*

As this example shows, the simulation primitives, although based on the coroutine primitives, belong to a higher level of abstraction; whenever possible it is preferable to use them rather than relying directly on coroutine mechanisms. In particular you may view *hold (0)* as a form of **resume** through which you let the underlying event list mechanism pick the process to be resumed, rather than specifying it explicitly.

A simulation example

Process classes and the simulation primitives provide an elegant mechanism for modeling external-world processes. Consider as an illustration a worker who may be asked to do either one of two tasks. Both may take a variable amount of time; the second requires switching on a machine *m*, which takes 5 minutes, and waiting for the machine to do its job.

*The Simula notation
this C, used within a
class C, is the equiv-
alent of Current as
used in the rest of
this book.*

```
PROCESS class WORKER begin
    while true do begin
        "Get next task type i and task duration d";
        if i = 1 then
            activate m delay 300; reactivate this WORKER after m;
        end;
        hold (d)
    end while
end WORKER
```

The operation "get next task type and task duration" will usually obtain the requested value from a pseudo-random number generator, using a specified statistical distribution. The Simula library includes a number of generators for common statistical laws. The type of m is assumed to be some process class *MACHINE* representing the behavior of machines. All actors of a simulation will be similarly represented by process classes.

Simula: an assessment

Like Algol 60 before it, Simula has made its contribution less by its commercial success than through its intellectual influence. The latter is everywhere; both in theory (abstract data types) and in practice, most of the developments of the past twenty years are children or grandchildren of the Simula ideas. As to the lack of widespread commercial success, a number of reasons can be invoked, but the most important one by far is as regrettable as it is obvious: like a few major inventions before it, Simula came too soon. Although a significant community immediately recognized the potential value of the ideas, the software field as a whole was not ready.

Thirty years later, as should be clear from the preceding overview, many of these ideas are as timely as ever.

35.2 SMALLTALK

The ideas for Smalltalk were laid out around 1970 at the University of Utah by Alan Kay, then a graduate student and part of a group that was particularly active in graphics, when he was asked to look at an Algol 60 compiler that had just been delivered to the department from Norway. Poring over it, he realized that the compiler actually went beyond Algol and implemented a set of notions that seemed directly relevant to Kay's other work. The supported Algol extension was, of course, Simula. When Kay later joined the Xerox Palo Alto Research Center (PARC), he used the same principles as the basis for his vision of an advanced personal computing environment. The other two principal contributors to the early development of Smalltalk at Xerox PARC were Adele Goldberg and Daniel Ingalls.

Smalltalk-72 evolved into Smalltalk-76, then Smalltalk-80, and versions were developed for a number of machines — initially Xerox hardware but later industry-standard platforms. Today Smalltalk implementations are available from several sources.

Language style

As a language, Smalltalk combines the influence of Simula with the free, typeless style of Lisp. The emphasis is on dynamic binding. No type checking is performed: in contrast with the approach emphasized in this book, the determination of whether a routine may be applied to an object only occurs at run time.

This, by the way, is not the standard Smalltalk terminology. A routine is called a "method" in Smalltalk; applying a routine to an object is called "sending a message" to the object (whose class must find the appropriate method to handle the message).

Another important feature that distinguishes the Smalltalk style from what we have studied in this book is the lack of a clear-cut distinction between classes and objects. Everything in the Smalltalk system is an object, including the classes themselves. A class is viewed as an instance of a higher-level class called a metaclass. This allows the class hierarchy to encompass all elements in the system; at the root of the hierarchy is the highest-level class, called *object*. The root of the subtree containing only classes is the metaclass *class*. The arguments for this approach include:

- Consistency: everything in Smalltalk follows from a single concept, object.

- Environment effectiveness: making classes part of the run-time context facilitates the development of symbolic debuggers, browsers and other tools that need run-time access to class texts

- Class methods: it is possible to define methods that apply to the class rather than to its instances. Class methods may be used to provide special implementations for standard operations like **new** which allocates instances of the class.

"Metaclasses",
page 168.
An earlier discussion considered the arguments for other, more static approaches, showing different ways to obtain the same results.

Messages

Smalltalk defines three main forms of messages (and associated methods): unary, keyword and binary. **Unary** messages express calls to routines without parameters, as in

> *acc1 balance*

which sends the message *balance* to the object associated with *acc1*. This is equivalent to the notation *acc1*.*balance* used in Simula and this book. Messages may, as here, return values. **Keyword** messages represent calls to routines with arguments, as in

> *point1 translateBy: vector1*
> *window1 moveHor: 5 Vert: –3*

The use of upper-case letters in the middle of a word, giving identifiers such as *translateBy*, is part of the established Smalltalk style. Note how the message name is collapsed with the keyword for the first argument. The corresponding syntax in Simula or our notation would have been *point1*.*translate* (*vector1*) and *window1*.*move* (5, –3).

Binary messages, similar to the infix functions of Ada and the notation of this book, serve to reconcile the "everything is an object" approach with more traditional arithmetic notations. Rather than

> *2 addMeTo: 3*

most people, at least from the older generations who learned arithmetic before object technology, still prefer to write *2+3*. Smalltalk's binary messages permits this latter form as essentially a synonym for the former. There is a snag, however: precedence. The expression $a + b * c$ means $(a + b) * c$. Smalltalk developers can use parentheses to re-establish standard precedence. Unary messages take precedence over binary messages, so that *window1 height + window2 height* has the expected meaning.

In contrast with Simula and the language of this book, Smalltalk classes may only export methods (routines). To export an attribute, you must write a function that gives access to its value. A typical example is

x | |
    ↑ *xx*

y | |
    ↑ *yy*

scale: *scaleFactor* | |
    xx <– *xx* * *scaleFactor*
    yy <– *yy* * *scaleFactor*

Methods *x* and *y* return the values of the instance variables (attributes) *xx* and *yy*. The up arrow ↑ means that the following expression is the value to be returned by the method to the sender of the corresponding message. Method *scale* takes an argument, *scaleFactor*. The vertical bars | | would delimit local variables if there were any.

Inheritance is an important part of the Smalltalk approach, but except for some experimental implementations it is limited to single inheritance. To enable a redefined method to call the original version, Smalltalk allows the developer to refer to the object viewed as an instance of the parent class through the name **super**, as in

aFunction: *anArgument* |...|
    ... **super** *aFunction*: *anArgument* ...

It is interesting to compare this approach with the techniques based on *Precursor* and repeated inheritance.

Exercise E35.5, page 1140. See "Keeping the original version of a redefined feature", page 555.

All binding is dynamic. In the absence of static typing, errors resulting from sending a message to an object that is not equipped with a proper method to handle it will cause run-time failure, rather than being caught by a compiler.

Dynamic typing also renders irrelevant some of the concepts developed earlier in this book: Smalltalk does not need language support for genericity since a generic structure such as a stack may contain elements of any type without any static coherence checks; neither are deferred routines meaningful, since if the software includes a call *x f* (the equivalent of $x.f$) there is no static rule requiring any particular class to provide a method *f*. Smalltalk provides, however, a run-time mechanism to raise an error if a class *C* receives a message corresponding to a method whose effective definitions only appear in proper descendants of *C*. (In the rest of this book, *C* would be a deferred class, and instances would only be created for non-deferred descendants of *C*.) For example, we could implement *rotate* in a class *FIGURE* by

rotate: *anAngle around*: *aPoint* | |
    self shouldNotImplement

The method *shouldNotImplement* is included in the general class *object* and returns an error message. The notation *self* denotes the current object.

Environment and performance

Much of Smalltalk's appeal has come from the supporting programming environments, among the first to include innovative interaction techniques (many of them devised by other Xerox PARC projects around the time of the original Smalltalk development) which have now become commonplace: multiple windows, icons, integration of text and graphics, pull-down menus and use of the mouse as a pointing and selecting device. Such staples of current O-O environment tools such as browsers, inspectors and O-O debuggers trace some of their roots to Smalltalk environments.

As with Simula, all commercial implementations support garbage collection. Smalltalk-80 and subsequent implementations are also renowned from their libraries of basic classes, covering important abstractions such as "collections" and "dictionaries", and a number of graphical concepts.

The lack of static typing has proved a formidable obstacle to the efficiency of software systems developed in Smalltalk. Although modern Smalltalk environments, no longer solely interpretative, provide some mechanisms for compiling methods, the unpredictability of run-time target types deprives most Smalltalk developers of a number of crucial optimizations that are readily available to compilers for statically typed languages (such as setting up arrays of functions references and hence ensuring constant-time resolution of dynamic binding, as discussed in the chapter on inheritance). Not surprisingly, many Smalltalk projects have reported efficiency problems. In fact, the common misconception that object technology carries a performance penalty can be attributed in part to experience with Smalltalk environments.

Smalltalk: an assessment

Smalltalk was instrumental in associating interactive techniques with the concepts of object technology, turning the abstract objects of Simula into visual objects that became suddenly comprehensible and appealing to a larger audience. Simula had impressed programming language and programming methodology experts; Smalltalk, through the famous August 1981 issue of *Byte*, dazzled the masses.

Considering how dated the concepts of Smalltalk appear today, the commercial success that it enjoyed in the early nineties is remarkable. It can be partly attributed to two independent *a contrario* phenomena:

- The "try the next one on the list" effect. Many people who were initially drawn to object technology by the elegance of the concepts were disappointed with hybrid approaches such as C++. When looking for a better embodiment of the concepts, they often went to the approach that the computer press has consistently presented as *the* pure O-O approach: Smalltalk. Many a Smalltalk developer is indeed someone who "just says no" to C or C-like development.

- The decline of Lisp. For a long time, many companies relied on Lisp variants (along with Prolog and a few other approaches grounded in Artificial Intelligence) for side projects involving quick development of prototypes and experiments. Starting in the mid-eighties, however, Lisp largely faded from the scene; Smalltalk naturally occupied the resulting vacuum.

The last observation provides a good idea of the scope of the Smalltalk approach. Smalltalk is an excellent tool for prototyping and experimentation, especially when visual interfaces are involved (it competes in this area with more recent tools such as Borland's Delphi or Microsoft's Visual Basic). But it has largely remained uninfluenced by later developments in software engineering methodology, as attested by the absence of static typing, assertion mechanisms, disciplined exception handling, deferred classes, all of which are important for mission-critical systems — or simply any system whose proper run-time behavior is important to the organization that has developed it. The performance problems noted above do not help.

The lesson is clear: it would not in my opinion be reasonable today for a company to entrust a significant production development to Smalltalk.

35.3 LISP EXTENSIONS

Like many other pre-O-O languages, Lisp has served as the basis for several object-oriented extensions; in fact many of the earliest O-O languages after Simula and Smalltalk were Lisp-based or Lisp-like. This is not surprising, since Lisp and its implementations have for many years offered mechanisms that directly help the implementation of object-oriented concepts, and have taken much longer to find their way into mainstream languages and their environments:

- A highly dynamic approach to the creation of objects.

- Automatic memory management with garbage collection.

- Ready implementation of tree-like data structures.

- Rich development environments, such as Interlisp in the seventies and its predecessors in the previous decade.

- Run-time selection of operations, facilitating the implementation of dynamic binding.

The conceptual distance to O-O concepts is, then, shorter if you start from Lisp than if you start from C, Pascal or Ada, so that the term "hybrid" commonly used for O-O extensions of these languages, such as the C-based hybrids which we will review in the next sections, is less appropriate for extensions of Lisp.

Artificial Intelligence applications, the prime application of Lisp and Lisp-like languages, have found in O-O concepts the benefits of flexibility and scalability. They have taken advantage of Lisp's uniform representation for programs and data to extend the object-oriented paradigm with notions such as "meta-object protocol" and "computational reflection" which apply some of the O-O principles not just to the description of run-time structures (objects) but also to the software structure itself (classes), generalizing the Smalltalk concept of metaclass and continuing the Lisp tradition of self-modifying software. For most developers, however, these concepts are a little far-off, and they do not blend too well with the software engineering emphasis on a strict separation between the static and dynamic pictures.

Three main contenders were vying for attention in the world of O-O Lisp in the eighties: *Loops*, developed at Xerox, initially for the Interlisp environment; *Flavors*, developed at MIT, available on several Lisp-oriented architectures; *Ceyx*, developed at INRIA. Loops introduced the interesting concept of "data-oriented programming", whereby you may attach a routine to a data item (such as an attribute). Execution of the routine will be triggered not only by an explicit call, but also whenever the item is accessed or modified. This opens the way to event-driven computation, a further step towards decentralizing software architectures.

The unification of the various approaches came with the Common Lisp Object System or CLOS (pronounced C-Los by most people), an extension of Common Lisp which was the first object-oriented language to have an ANSI standard.

35.4 C EXTENSIONS

Much of the late nineteen-eighties transformation of object technology from an attractive idea into an industrial practice can be attributed to the emergence and tremendous commercial success of languages that added object-oriented extensions to the stable stem of a widely available non-O-O language, C. The first such effort to attract widespread attention was Objective-C; the best known today is C++.

The language styles reflect two radically different approaches to the problem of "hybrid" language design, so called because it combines O-O mechanisms with those of a language based on entirely different principles. (Examples of hybrids based on languages other than C include Ada 95 and Borland Pascal.) Objective-C illustrates the *orthogonal* approach: add an O-O layer to the existing language, keeping the two parts as independent as possible. C++ illustrates the *merged* approach, intertwining concepts from both. The potential advantages of each style are clear: the orthogonal approach should make the transition easier, avoiding unexpected interferences; the merged approach should lead to a more consistent language.

Both efforts capitalized on the success of C, which had rapidly become one of the dominant languages in the industry. The appeal to managers was obvious, based on the prospect of turning C programmers into O-O developers without too much of a culture shock. The model (evoked by Brad Cox) was that of the C and Fortran preprocessors such as Ratfor which, in the seventies, enabled part of the software community to become familiar with concepts of "structured programming" while continuing to work in familiar language frameworks.

Objective-C

Designed at Stepstone Corporation (originally Productivity Products International) by Brad Cox, Objective-C is a largely orthogonal addition of Smalltalk concepts onto a C base. It was the base language for the NEXTSTEP workstation and operating system. Although obscured in part by the success of C++, Objective-C has retained an active user community.

As in Smalltalk, the emphasis is on polymorphism and dynamic binding, but current versions of Objective-C have departed from the Smalltalk model by offering static typing as an option (and for some of them, somewhat surprisingly, static *binding* as well). Here is an example of Objective-C syntax:

$=$ *Proceedings*: *Publication* {*id date*, *place*; *id articles*;}

    + *new* {*return* [[*super new*] *initialize*]}

    – *initialize* {*articles* = [*OrderedCollection new*]; *return self*;}

    – *add*: *anArticle* {*return* [*contents add*: *anArticle*];}

    – *remove*: *anArticle* {*return* [*contents remove*:*anArticle*];}

    – (*int*) *size* {*return* [*contents size*];}

=:

Class *Proceedings* is defined as heir to *Publication* (Objective-C supports single inheritance only). The braces introduce attributes ("instance variables"). The next lines describe routines; *self*, as in Smalltalk, denotes the current instance. The name *id* denotes, in the non-statically typed variant, a general class type for all non-C objects. Routines introduced by +, known as "class methods" as in Smalltalk, are meant for the class; this is the case here with the creation operation *new*. Others, introduced by –, are normal "object methods" that send messages to instances of the class.

Stepstone's Objective-C is equipped with a library of classes initially patterned after their Smalltalk counterparts. Many other classes are also available for NEXTSTEP.

C++

Originally designed by Bjarne Stroustrup at AT&T Bell Laboratories (an organization previously renowned, among other accomplishments, for its development of Unix and C), C++ quickly gained, starting around 1986, a leading position for industrial developments aiming to obtain some of the benefits of object technology while retaining compatibility with C. The language has remained almost fully *upward-compatible* with C (meaning that a valid C program is also, in normal circumstances, a valid C++ program).

Early C++ implementations were simple preprocessors that removed O-O constructs to yield plain C, based on techniques sketched in the preceding chapter. Today's compilers, however, are native C++ implementations; it has in fact become hard to find a C compiler that is not *also* a C++ compiler, requiring the user who just wants a basic C compiler to turn on a special "no C++ constructs" compilation option. This is a measure among many of the success of the approach. Compilers are available from many sources and for many platforms.

Originally, C++ was an attempt at providing a better version of C, improved in particular through a class construct and a stronger form of typing. Here is a class example:

```
class POINT {
    float xx, yy;
    public:
            void translate (float, float);
            void rotate (float);
            float x ();
            float y ();

            friend void p_translate (POINT ∗, float, float);
            friend void p_rotate (POINT ∗, float);
            friend float p_x (POINT ∗);
            friend float p_y (POINT ∗);
};
```

The first four routines are the normal, object-oriented interface of the class. As shown by this example, the class declaration only shows the headers of these routines, not their implementations (somewhat as in the output of the **short** command studied in earlier chapters). The routine implementations must be defined separately, which raises questions of scope for both compilers and human readers.

The other four routines are examples of "friend" routines. This notion is peculiar to C++ and makes it possible to call C++ routines from normal C code. Friend routines will need an extra argument representing the object to which an operation is applied; this argument is here of type *POINT* ∗, meaning pointer to *POINT*.

C++ offers a rich set of powerful mechanisms:

- Information hiding, including the ability to hide features from proper descendants.

- Support for inheritance. Original versions supported single inheritance only, but now the language has multiple inheritance. Repeated inheritance lacks the flexibility of sharing or replicating on a feature-by-feature basis, which from the discussion of these topics seemed quite important. Instead, you share or duplicate an entire feature set from the repeated ancestor.

"The C++ approach to binding", page 513.

- Static binding by default, but dynamic binding for functions specified as virtual; the C++ approach to this issue was discussed in depth in an earlier chapter.

- A notion of "pure virtual function", which resembles deferred features.

- Stricter typing than in traditional C, but still with the possibility of casting.

- Usually no garbage collection (because of the presence of casts and the use of pointers for arrays and similar structures), although some tools are available for suitably restrained programs.

- Because of the absence of automatic memory management by default, a notion of *destructor* for taking care of object disposal (complementing the *constructors* of a class, that is to say its creation procedures).

- Exception handling, again not part of the original definition but now supported by most compilers.

- A form of assignment attempt, "downcasting".

- A form of genericity, "templates", which suffers from two limitations: no constrained genericity; and, for reasons unclear to a non-implementer, a considerable burden on compile-time performance (known in the C++ literature as the *template instantiation problem*).

See "Efficiency considerations", page 327.

- Operator overloading.

- An *assert* instruction for debugging, but no assertions in the sense of support for Design by Contract (preconditions, postconditions, class invariants) tied to O-O constructs.

- Libraries available from various suppliers, such as the Microsoft Foundation Classes.

Complexity

The size of C++ has grown considerably since the language's first versions, and many people have complained about its complexity. That they have a point is illustrated, among many possible examples, by this little excerpt from a pedagogical article by a recognized C and C++ authority, chair of the C standards committee of the American National Standards Institute and author of several respected C++ books as well as the *Dictionary of Standard C*, from whom I was at some point hoping to learn the difference between the C++ notions of reference and pointer:

> *While a reference is somewhat like a pointer, a pointer is an object that occupies memory and has an address. Non-**const** pointers can also be made to point to different objects at run time. On the other hand, a reference is an alias to an object and does not, itself, occupy any memory. Its address and value are the address and value of the object to which it is aliased. And while you can have a reference to a pointer, you cannot have a pointer to a reference or an array of references, nor can you have an object of some reference type. References to the **void** type are also prohibited.*

From Rex Jaeschke's C++ column in DEC Professional, November 1991.

> *References and pointer are not interchangeable. A reference to an **int** cannot, for example, be assigned to a pointer to an **int** or vice versa. However, a reference to a pointer to an **int** can be assigned a pointer to an **int**.*

I swear I tried to understand. I was almost convinced I got the hang of it, although perhaps not being quite ready for the midterm exam yet. ("Give convincing examples of cases in which it is appropriate to use: (1) A pointer only. (2) A reference only. (3) Either. (4) Neither. No notes or Web browsers allowed".) Then I noticed I had missed the start of the next paragraph:

> *From what we have seen so far, it may not be obvious as to why references indeed exist.*

Oh well. Proponents of C++ would undoubtedly state that most users can ignore such subtleties. Another school holds that a programming language, the principal tool of software developers, should be based on a reasonable number of solid, powerful, perfectly understood concepts; in other words, that every serious user should know *all* of the language, and trust all of it. But it may be impossible to reconcile this view with the very notion of hybrid language — a notion which in the case of C++ irresistibly evokes Liszt's transcription of Schubert's admirable Wanderer Fantasy: add a full symphony orchestra, and *keep the piano*.

C++: an assessment

Booch interview:
http://www.
geekchic.com/repli-
que.htm. Knuth
interview: Dr.
Dobb's Journal, no.
246, April 1996,
pages 16-22.

C++ leaves few people indifferent. The eminent author Grady Booch lists it, in a "Geek Chic" interview, as his programming language of choice. Then, according to Donald Knuth, it would make Edsger Dijkstra *"physically ill to think of programming in C++"*.

C++ here could use the answer of Junia to Nero in Racine's *Britannicus*:

> *I have neither deserved, in all humility,*
> *Such excess of honor, nor such indignity.*

Disappointment with C++ indeed follows from exaggerated hopes. Earlier discussions in this book have carefully analyzed some of the language's more controversial design choices — especially in the areas of typing, memory management, inheritance conventions and dynamic binding — and shown that better solutions are available. But one cannot criticize C++ as if it were the be-all and end-all of object-oriented languages. What C++ has attempted, and achieved beyond anyone's dreams, was to catch a particular moment in the history of software: the time at which a large part of the profession and its managers were ready to try object technology, but *not* ready to shed their current practices. C++ was the almost magical answer: still C enough not to scare the managers; already O-O enough to attract the forward-looking members of the trade. In seizing the circumstance, C++ was only following the example of C itself, which, fifteen years earlier, was another product of coinciding opportunities — the need for a portable machine-oriented language, the development of Unix, the emergence of personal computers, and the availability of a few decommissioned machines at Bell Labs. The merits of C++ lie in the historic boost it gave to the development of object technology, making it presentable to a whole community that might not have accepted the ideas under a less conventional apparel.

That C++ is not the ideal object-oriented language, a comment regularly made by authors and lecturers in the field, and obvious enough to anyone who has studied the concepts, should not obscure this contribution. We must not indeed look at C++ as if it were destined to remain a major tool for the software engineering community well into the twenty-first century, as it would then be overstaying its welcome. In the meantime C++ has admirably played its role: that of a transition technology.

35.5 JAVA

Introduced by a Sun Microsystems team, Java gained considerable attention in the first few months of 1996, presented as the way to help tame the Internet. According to *ComputerWorld*, the number of press mentions of Java in the first six months of 1996 was 4325 (which we may multiply by 2 or 3 since this was presumably the US press only); as a point of comparison, Bill Gates was mentioned only 5096 times.

ComputerWorld, vol. 30, no. 29, 15 July 1996, page 122.

The principal contribution of Java is in implementation technology. Building on ideas already present in many other O-O environments but taken here to a new level, Java execution rests on a **bytecode** (a low-level, portable interpretable format) whose specification is in the public domain, and a widely available **virtual machine** to interpret bytecode programs. The virtual machine is simply a program, for which versions are available for many different platforms, and can be downloaded freely through the Internet; this enables almost anyone to execute bytecode programs produced by almost anyone else. Often you do not even have to download anything explicitly: the virtual machine is built in tools such as Web browsers; and such tools will be able to recognize references to a bytecode program, for example a reference embedded in a link on a Web page, so that they will then automatically download the program and execute it on the spot.

See "Remote execution", page 955.

The explosion of the Internet has given this technology a great momentum, and Sun has been able to convince many other major players to produce tools based on this technology. As the bytecode is largely separate from the language, it stands a good chance of becoming a medium of choice for compiler output, regardless of what the source language is. Compiler writers for such notations as O-O extensions of Pascal and Ada, as well as the notation of this book, have not been slow to recognize the opportunity for developing software that will run without any change, and without even the need to recompile, across all industry platforms.

Java is one of the most innovative developments in the software field, and there are many reasons to be excited about it. Java's language is not the main one. As an O-O extension of C, it has missed some of the lessons learned since 1985 by the C++ community; as in the very first version of C++, there is no genericity and only single inheritance is supported. Correcting these early oversights in C++ was a long and painful process, creating years of havoc as compilers never quite supported the same language, books never quite gave accurate information, trainers never quite taught the right stuff, and programmers never quite knew what to think.

Just as everyone in the C++ world has finally come up to speed, Java is starting along the same road. The language does have one significant benefit over C++: by removing the notion of arbitrary pointer, especially to describe arrays, it has finally made it possible to support garbage collection. For the rest, it seems to take no account of modern software engineering ideas: no assertion support (in fact, Java went so far as to remove the modest **assert** instruction of C and C++); partial reliance on run-time type checking; a confusing modular structure with three interacting concepts (classes, nested packages, source files); and ever the cryptic syntax bequeathed from C, with such lines as the following typical examples from the designers' book on the language:

From [Arnold 1996].

String [] *labels* = (*depth* == *0* ? *basic* : *extended*);

while ((*name* = *getNextPlayer*()) != *null*) {

exhibiting side-effect-producing functions as a way of life, use of = conflicting with the tradition of mathematics, semicolons sometimes required and sometimes illegal etc.

See "Formats for reusable component distribution", page 79.

That the language is uninspiring should not, however, detract from the contribution that Java technology has already made to portable software development. If it can eventually solve its current efficiency problems, Java could, through its bytecode, become the closest approximation (built from software rather than hardware, although "Java chips" have also been announced) to one of the oldest dreams of the computer industry: a truly universal machine.

35.6 OTHER O-O LANGUAGES

The languages reviewed so far are some of the best known, but by no means the only ones to have attracted significant attention. Here are a few other important contributions, which would each deserve a separate chapter in a book entirely devoted to object-oriented languages, and to which you can find references (books and Web pages) in the bibliographical section:

- *Oberon* is Niklaus Wirth's O-O successor to Modula-2, part of a more general project which also involves a programming environment and even hardware support.

- *Modula-3*, originally from Digital Equipment's research laboratory, is another modular language with class-like record types, also starting from Modula-2.

- *Trellis*, also from DEC Research, was among the first to offer both genericity and multiple inheritance.

- *Sather*, drawing in part from the concepts and notation of the first edition of this book, especially assertions, has the benefit of a public-domain implementation; its *pSather* version provides an interesting concurrency mechanism.

- *Beta* is a direct descendant of Simula, designed in Scandinavia with the collaboration of Kristen Nygaard (one of Simula's original authors). It introduces the *pattern* construct to unify the concepts of class, procedure, function, type and coroutine.

- *Self* is based not on classes but on "prototypes", supporting inheritance as a relation between objects rather than types.

"FROM ADA TO ADA 95", 33.7, page 1092; "Object-oriented extensions of Pascal", page 1101.

- *Ada 95* was discussed in the Ada chapter.

- *Borland Pascal* and other O-O extensions of Pascal were cited in the discussion of Pascal.

35.7 BIBLIOGRAPHICAL NOTES

Simula

[Dahl 1966] describes an initial version of Simula subsequently known as Simula 1. The current Simula, long known as Simula 67, was initially described by [Dahl 1970], which assumed Algol 60 as a basis and only described the Simula extensions. A chapter in the famous *Structured Programming* book of Dahl, Dijkstra and Hoare [Dahl 1972] brought the concepts to a wider audience. The language description was revised in 1984, incorporating the Algol 60 elements. The official reference is the Swedish national standard [SIS 1987]. For an account of Simula's history by its designers, see [Nygaard 1981].

The best known book on Simula is [Birtwistle 1973]. It remains an excellent introduction. A more recent text is [Pooley 1986].

Smalltalk

References on the earliest versions of Smalltalk (-72 and -76) are [Goldberg 1976] and [Ingalls 1978].

A special issue that *Byte* devoted to Smalltalk [Goldberg 1981] was the key event that brought Smalltalk to prominence long before supporting environments became widely available. The basic reference on the language is [Goldberg 1983], serving both as pedagogical description and reference; complementing it is [Goldberg 1985], which describes the programming environment.

For a good recent introduction to both the Smalltalk language and the VisualWorks environment see [Hopkins 1995]; for an in-depth treatment see Lalonde's and Pugh's two-volume set [Lalonde 1990-1991].

The story of Simula's original influence on Smalltalk (the "Algol compiler from Norway") comes from an interview of Alan Kay in *TWA Ambassador* (yes, an airline magazine), exact issue number forgotten — early or mid-eighties. I am indebted to Bob Marcus for pointing out the connection between Lisp's decline and Smalltalk's resurgence.

C extensions: Objective-C, C++

Objective-C is described by its designer in an article [Cox 1984] and a book [Cox 1990] (whose first edition dates back to 1986). Pinson and Wiener have written an introduction to O-O concepts based on Objective-C [Pinson 1991].

There are hundreds of books on C++. For a personal account of the language's history by its designer, see [Stroustrup 1994]. The original article was [Stroustrup 1984]; it was extended into a book [Stroustrup 1986], later revised as [Stroustrup 1991], which contains many tutorial examples and useful background. The reference manual is [Ellis 1990].

Ian Joyner has published several editions of an in-depth "C++ critique" [Joyner 1996] available on a number of Internet sites and containing detailed comparisons with other O-O languages.

Lisp extensions

Loops: [Bobrow 1982]; Flavors: [Cannon 1980], [Moon 1986]; Ceyx: [Hullot 1984]; CLOS: [Paepcke 1993].

Java

In the few months that followed the release of Java, many books have appeared on the topic. Those by the designing team include: [Arnold 1996] for a language tutorial, [Gosling 1996] as the language reference, and [Gosling 1996a] about the basic libraries.

The address shown is for the first message in the discussion; from there you can follow links to the rest of the thread.

A discussion about Java's lack of assertions in the style of this book (that is to say, supporting the principles of Design by Contract), conducted on Usenet in August 1995, appears at *http://java.sun.com/archives/java-interest/0992.html*.

Other languages

Oberon: [Wirth 1992], [Oberon-Web]. Modula-3: [Harbison 1992], [Modula-3-Web]. Sather: [Sather-Web]. Beta: [Madsen 1993], [Beta-Web]. Self: [Chambers 1991], [Ungar 1992].

EXERCISES

E35.1 Stopping on short files

"A coroutine example", page 1119.

Adapt the Simula coroutine example (printer-controller-producer) to make sure that it stops properly if the input does not have enough elements to produce 1000 output elements. (**Hint**: one possible technique is to add a fourth coroutine, the "reader".)

E35.2 Implicit resume

(This is a exercise on Simula concepts, but you may use the notation of the rest of this book extended with the simulation primitives described in this chapter.) Rewrite the producer-printer example in such a way that each coroutine does not need to resume one of its colleagues explicitly when it has finished its current job; declare instead the coroutine classes as descendants of *PROCESS*, and replace explicit **resume** instructions by *hold* (0) instructions. (**Hints**: recall that event notices with the same activation time appear in the event list in the order in which they are generated. Associate with each process a condition that needs to be satisfied for the process to be resumed.)

E35.3 Emulating coroutines

Devise a mechanism for emulating coroutines in an O-O language of your choice (such as the notation of the rest of this book) that does not provide coroutine support. (**Hint**: write a *resume* procedure, implemented as a loop containing a conditional instruction with a branch for every **resume**. Obviously, you may not for this exercise use the concurrency mechanism of chapter 30, which among other applications supports coroutines.) Apply your solution to the producer-printer-controller example of this chapter.

E35.4 Simulation

Using the notation of this book or another O-O language, write classes for discrete-event simulation, patterned after the Simula classes *SIMULATION*, *EVENT_NOTICE*, *PROCESS*. (**Hint**: you may use the techniques developed for the previous exercise.)

E35.5 Referring to a parent's version

Discuss the respective merits of Smalltalk's **super** technique against the techniques introduced earlier in this book to enable a redefined routine to use the original version: *Precursor* construct and, when appropriate, repeated inheritance.

"Keeping the original version of a redefined feature", page 555.

Part G:

Doing it right

Part G will briefly present an environment that seeks combines the most productive ideas developed in this book and makes them practically available.

36

An object-oriented environment

$\mathcal{L}$ate into Beethoven's Choral Symphony, a baritone breaks the stream of astounding but until then purely instrumental sounds to awake us to something even grander:

O my friends! No more of these tunes!
Let us strike up instead
Some more pleasant and friendly songs.

After reviewing in the preceding chapters some of the common approaches to O-O development, we should similarly end with a perhaps more modern and comprehensive approach (with no intended disparagement of the others; after all the Ninth's first three movements, before it goes vocal, already were pretty decent stuff.)

The diagram is on page 1149. This chapter presents an environment (ISE's) that relies on the principles developed in the rest of this book, and makes them available concretely to O-O software developers. A complete diagram of the environment appears later in this chapter; some of the principal components are included for trial purposes in the CD-ROM attached to this book.

The purpose of this presentation is to put the final touch to our study of object technology by showing how environment support can make the concepts convenient to use in practice. A caveat: nothing in this discussion suggests that the environment discussed below is perfect (in fact, it is still evolving). It is only one example of a modern O-O environment; others — such as Borland's Delphi to name just one — have met wide and deserved success. But we need to explore one environment in some depth to understand the connection between the method's principles and their day-to-day application by a developer sitting at a terminal. Many of the concepts will, I hope, be useful to readers using other tools.

36.1 COMPONENTS

The environment combines the following elements:

- An underlying *method*: the object-oriented method, as described in this book.
- A *language*, the notation presented in this book, for analysis, design and implementation.
- A set of *tools* for exploiting the method and the language: compiling, browsing, documenting, designing.
- *Libraries* of reusable software components.

The next sections sketch these various elements, except for the first which, of course, has been the subject of the rest of this book.

36.2 THE LANGUAGE

The language is the notation that we have devised in part C and applied throughout the book. We have essentially seen all of it; the only exceptions are a few technical details such as how to represent special characters.

Evolution

The first implementation of the language dates back to late 1986. Only one significant revision has occurred since then (in 1990); it did not change any fundamental concepts but simplified the expression of some of them. Since then there has been a continuous attempt at clarification, simplification and cleanup, affecting only details, and bringing two recent extensions: the concurrency mechanism of chapter 30 (concretely, the addition of a single keyword, **separate**) and the *Precursor* construct to facilitate redefinition. The stability of the language, a rare phenomenon in this field, has been a major benefit to users.

Openness

Although a full-fledged programming language, the notation is also designed to serve as a wrapping mechanism for components that may be written in other languages. The mechanism for including external elements — the **external** clause — was described in an earlier chapter. It is also possible, through the *Cecil* library, for external software to use the O-O mechanisms: create instances of classes, and call features on these objects, through dynamic binding (but of course with only limited static type checking).

Of particular interest are the C and C++ interfaces. For C++, a tool called *Legacy++* is available to produce, out of an existing C++ class, a "wrapper" class that will automatically include the encapsulation of all the exported features of the original. This is particularly useful to developers whose organizations may have used C++ as their first stop on the road to object orientation in the late eighties or early nineties, and now want to move on to a more complete and systematic form of the technology — without sacrificing their investment. Legacy++ smoothes the transition.

36.3 THE COMPILATION TECHNOLOGY

The first task of the environment is, of course, to let us execute our software.

Compilation challenges

Developed over many years and bootstrapped through several iterations, the compilation technology is an answer to a set of challenges:

C1 • The efficiency of the *generated code* must be excellent, comparable to what developers could obtain by using a classical language such as C. There is no reason to pay a significant performance price for O-O techniques.

C2 • The *recompilation time* after a change must be short. More precisely, it should be proportional to the size of the change, not to the size of the entire system. The crucial compilation concern, for developers working on a possibly large system, is the need to perform changes and see the results immediately.

C3 • A third requirement, which appeared more recently, is quickly becoming important: the need to support the fast delivery of applications through the Internet to users or potential users, for immediate execution.

The first two requirements, in particular, are hard to reconcile. C1 is usually addressed through extensive compiler optimizations that make the recompilation and linking process prohibitively long. C2 is well served by interpretive environments, which execute software on-the-fly with little or no processing, but to obtain this result they must sacrifice execution-time performance (C1) and static type checking.

The Melting Ice Technology

The compilation technology that deals with the preceding issues, known as the *Melting Ice Technology*, uses a mix of complementary techniques. Once you have compiled a system, it is said to be *frozen*, like a block of ice stored in the freezer. As you take out the system to start working on it (so the metaphor goes), you produce some heat; the melted elements represent the changes. Those elements will **not** cause a compile-link cycle, which would defeat the goal of fast recompilation (C2); the melted code is, instead, directly executable by the environment's execution engine.

*The Frozen
and the Melted*

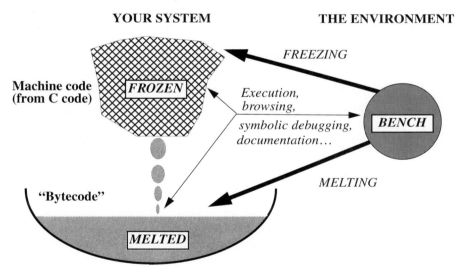

The tricky part (for the compiler implementers) is of course to make sure that the various components can work together, in particular that frozen code can call melted elements — even though it was not known, at freezing time, that they would later be melted! But the result is definitely worthwhile:

- Recompilation is fast. The waiting time is typically a few seconds.

- This is still a compilation approach: any recompilation will perform full type checking (without undue penalty on recompilation time because the checking, like the recompilation in general, is incremental: only the changed parts are rechecked).

- Run-time performance remains acceptable because for a non-trivial system a typical modification will only affect a small percentage of the code; everything else will be executed in its compiled form. (For maximum efficiency, you will use the *finalization* form of compilation, as explained below.)

As you perform more and more changes, the proportion of melted code will grow; after a while the effect on performance, time and space, may become perceptible. So it is wise to re-freeze every few days. Because freezing implies a C-compilation and linking, the time it takes is typically more on the order of minutes (or even an hour after several days of extensive changes). You can start this task in the background, or at night.

Dependency analysis

As should be the case in any modern development environment, the recompilation process is automatic; you will simply click on the Melt button of the Project Tool, in the interface described below, and the compiling mechanisms will silently determine the smallest set of elements that need to be recompiled; there is no need for "Make files" and the notation has no notion of "include file".

To compute what needs to be recompiled, the environment's tools first find out what you have changed, either from within the environment, using its own class editor, or through outside tools such as text editors (each class text being stored in a file, the time stamps provide the basic information). Then they use the two dependency relations, client and inheritance, to determine what else may have been affected and needs recompilation. In the client case, information hiding is an important help to minimize propagation: if a change to a class only affects secret features, its clients do not need recompilation.

To reduce melting time further, the grain of recompilation is not the class but the individual routine.

> Note that if you add an external element, for example a C function, a freeze will be required. Again this will be determined automatically.

Precompilation

In accordance with the method's emphasis on reusability, it is essential to allow software developers to put together carefully crafted sets of components — libraries —, compile them once and for all, and distribute them to other developers who will simply include them in their systems without having to know anything about their internal organization.

The precompilation mechanism achieves this goal. A special compilation option generates a compiled form of a set of classes; then it is possible (through the Ace file) to include a precompiled library in a new system.

On Ace files see "Assembling a system", page 198.

There is no limit to the number of precompiled libraries that you may include in a new system. The mechanism that combines precompiled libraries supports sharing: if two precompiled libraries B and C both rely on a third one A (as with the Vision graphical library and the Net client-server library, discussed later, which both rely on the Base libraries for data structures and fundamental algorithms), only one copy of A will be included provided both B and C use the same version of A.

"Formats for reusable component distribution", page 79.
The author of a precompiled library may want to prevent his customers from having access to the source code of the library (an early chapter discussed the pros and cons of this policy). It is indeed possible, when precompiling, to make the source code inaccessible. In that case users of the environment will be able, through the visual tools described later in this chapter, to browse the *short form* and the *flat-short form* of the library's classes, that is to say their interface (public) properties; but they will not be able to see their full text, let alone their flat form.

Remote execution

At the time of writing the plug-in mechanism has not yet been released.
The interpretive code generated by melting — conventionally known as *bytecode* and identified as such on the preceding figure — is platform-independent. To execute bytecode, it suffices to have a copy of the environment's Execution Engine, known as 3E and freely downloadable through the Internet.

By adding 3E as a **plug-in** to a Web browser, it will be possible to make code directly executable: if a browser's user clicks on a hyperlink corresponding to bytecode, 3E will automatically execute the corresponding code. This is the remote execution mechanism first popularized by Java.

3E actually comes in two flavors, distinguished by the accompanying precompiled libraries. The first, secure, is meant for Internet usage; to avoid security risks it only allows input and output to the terminal. The second, meant for Intranet (corporate network) usage, supports general I/O and other precompiled libraries.

An effort is also in progress to translate the bytecode into Java bytecode, to offer the supplementary possibility of executing the result of a development using a Java virtual machine.

Optimization

To generate the best possible code — goal C1 of the earlier discussion — frozen mode is not sufficient. Some crucial optimizations require having a complete, stable system:

- *Dead code removal* removes any routines that can never be called, directly or indirectly, from the system's root creation procedure. This is particularly important if you rely on many precompiled libraries, of which your system may only need a subset; a space gain of 50% is not uncommon.

"Static binding as an optimization", page 509 (also discusses inlining).
- *Static binding* which, as we studied in detail in the discussion of inheritance, should be applied by the compiler for features that are not redefined, or non-polymorphic entities.

- *Routine inlining*, also subject to compiler algorithms.

When you are still changing your system, these optimizations are not applicable, since your next editing move could invalidate the compiler's work. For example by adding just one call you may resuscitate a supposedly dead routine; by adding a routine redefinition, you cause a statically bound routine to require dynamic binding. Besides, such optimizations may require a complete pass through a system, for example to determine that no class redefines a certain routine; this makes them incompatible with incremental development.

As a result, these optimizations are part of a third form of compilation, **finalization**, complementing the other two (melting and freezing). For a large system finalization can take a few hours; but it leaves no stone unturned in removing anything that will not be needed and speeding up everything that is not optimal. The result is the most efficient executable form of the system.

The obvious opportunity for finalization is the delivery of a system, for a final or intermediate release. But many project leaders like to finalize once a week, at the time of the latest integration.

36.4 TOOLS

The figure on the facing page shows the general organization of the environment. The environment is of course used to bootstrap itself, and is written in the O-O notation (except for some elements of the runtime system, discussed next); this makes it an excellent testbed of the technology, and a living proof that it does scale up to large, ambitious systems (which, of course, we would not want to develop in any other way!).

Bench and the development process

The centerpiece is *Bench*, the graphical workbench for compilation, browsing (exploring classes and features), documentation, execution, debugging. When developing a system you will constantly interact with Bench. For example you can melt the latest version by clicking on the Melt button of the Bench's Project Tool, shown below.

As long as you are melting and freezing you can stay within Bench. When you finalize a system — also by clicking on a button, although for this operation and many others non-graphical commands are also available — the outcome will be a C program, which the environment will compile to machine code for your platform by calling the appropriate C compiler. Freezing too relies on C as intermediate code. The use of C has several benefits: C is available on just about every platform; the language is sufficiently low level to provide a good target format for a compiler; C compilers perform their own extensive optimizations. Two further advantages deserve emphasis:

- Thanks to C generation you can use the environment as a **cross-development** platform, by compiling the generated C on another platform. This is particularly useful for the production of embedded systems development, which typically uses a different platform for development and for final execution.

- The use of C as compilation technology helps implement the openness mechanisms discussed earlier, in particular the interfaces to and from existing software written in C and C++.

Finalized C code, once compiled, must be linked; at this stage it uses the **runtime system**, a set of routines providing the interface with the operating system: file access, signal handling, basic memory allocation.

> In the case of cross development of embedded systems, it is possible to provide a minimum form of the runtime, which, for example, does not include any I/O.

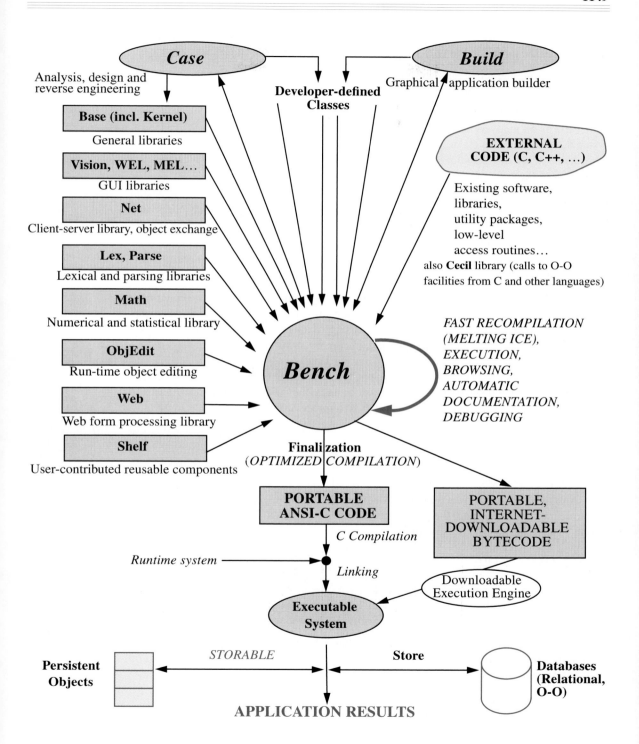

High-level tools

At the top of the figure on the preceding page, two high-level generation tools appear.

Build is an interactive application generator based on the Context-Event-Command-State model developed in an earlier chapter. You can use it to develop GUI (Graphical User Interface) applications graphically and interactively.

Chapter 32.

Case is an analysis and design workbench which provides the ability to reason on systems at a high level of abstraction, and through graphical representations. In accordance with the principles of **seamlessness** and **reversibility** introduced in the discussion of the software process, Case allows you both to:

Chapter 28.

- Devise system structures through graphical interaction — to produce visual representations of classes ("bubbles"), specify their relations through client and inheritance arrows, and group them into clusters —, relying on Case to generate the corresponding software texts in the end (**forward engineering**).

- Process existing class texts to produce the corresponding graphical representations, to facilitate exploring and restructuring (**reverse engineering**).

Particular attention has been devoted to making sure that developers can freely alternate between forward and reverse engineering. In particular, you can make changes on either the graphical or the textual form; Case provides a **reconciliation** mechanism which will merge the two sets of changes and, in case of conflicts, take you through a step-by-step decision process in which you will see the conflicting versions of a feature and choose, in each case, the version to be retained. This part of the tool is key to ensuring true reversibility, letting developers decide at each stage the level of abstraction and the notation, graphical or textual, that they find most appropriate.

The conventions of Case are drawn from the Business Object Notation described in an earlier chapter. BON supports in particular the tools' facilities for abstraction and **zooming**: it is essential, for large systems, to enable developers to work on an entire system, on a subsystem, on just a small cluster, choosing the exact level of abstraction they desire.

"THE BUSINESS OBJECT NOTA-TION", 27.7, page 919.

An example Case screen appears at the top of the facing page, showing a cluster from a chemical plant description, the properties of one of its classes (*VAT*), and the properties of one of the features of that class (*fill*).

36.5 LIBRARIES

A number of libraries appear on the general environment diagram of the preceding page. They play a considerable role in the software development process, providing developers with a rich set (several thousand classes) of reusable components. They include:

- The *Base* libraries, about 200 classes covering the fundamental data structures (lists, tables, trees, stacks, queues, files and so on). The most fundamental classes make up the *Kernel* library, governed by an international standard (ELKS).

- The graphical libraries: *Vision* for platform-independent GUI development; *WEL* for Windows, *MEL* for Motif, *PEL* for OS/2-Presentation Manager.

A cluster, class and feature under Case

(*Here on a Sparcstation with Motif, but versions exist for Windows and other look-and-feel variants.*)

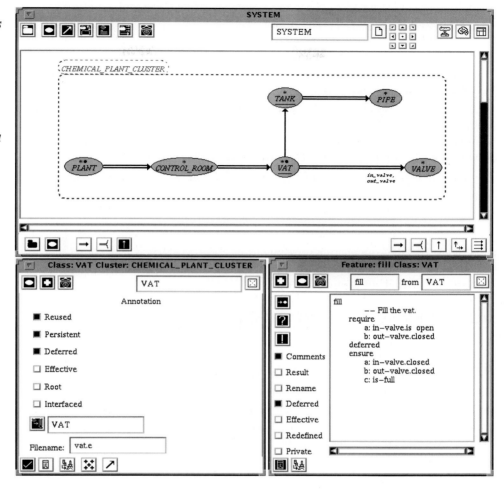

"Storable format variants", page 1038.

• *Net*, for client-server development, allowing the transferral of arbitrarily complex object structures over a network; the platforms may be the same or different (under *independent_store* the format is platform-independent).

• *Lex*, *Parse* for language analysis. Parse, in particular, provides an interesting approach to parsing, based on a systematic application of object-oriented concepts to parsing (each production modeled by a class; see the bibliographical notes). A supporting public-domain tool, YOOCC, serves as front-end for Parse.

"Object-oriented re-architecturing", page 441.

• *Math* is a numerical library providing an object-oriented view of the fundamental techniques of numerical computation. It is based internally on the NAG library and covers a large set of facilities. Some of its concepts were presented in an earlier chapter as an example of O-O re-architecturing of non-O-O mechanisms.

- *ObjEdit* provides facilities for editing objects interactively during execution.

- *Web* supports the processing of forms submitted by visitors to a Web site, advantageously replacing the Perl or C "CGI scripts" sometimes used for this purpose.

The bottom part of the environment diagram shows libraries used for taking care of persistence needs during execution: the *STORABLE* class and a few complementary tools, discussed in earlier chapters, support storage, retrieval and network transmission of object structures, self-contained through the application of the Persistence Closure principle; and the *Store* library is the database interface, providing mechanisms for accessing and storing data in relational databases (such as Oracle, Ingres, Sybase) and object-oriented databases.

This list is not exhaustive; other components are under development, and users of the environment have provided their own libraries, either free or commercial.

A particularly interesting combination is the use of *Net*, *Vision* and *Store* for building client-server systems: a server can take care of the database aspects through Store, and of the heaviest part the computation (possibly using Base, Math etc.); lean clients that only handle the user interface part can rely on Vision (or just one of the platform-specific libraries), and include little else.

36.6 INTERFACE MECHANISMS

To support the preceding concepts, the environment provides a visual interface, based on an analysis of the needs of developers and of the requirements of various platforms.

This brief presentation will only mention some of the most original aspects of the environment. Ample literature (see the bibliographic notes) is available on its other facilities; the reader familiar with other modern development environments will have no difficulty guessing some of the tools and possibilities not described here.

Platforms

The screenshots that follow were drawn from a session on a Sun Sparcstation, for no other reason than convenience. Other platforms supported at the time of writing include Windows 95 and Windows NT, Windows 3.1, OS/2, Digital's VMS (Alpha and Vax) and all major brands of Unix (SunOS, Solaris, Silicon Graphics, IBM RS/6000, Unixware, Linux, Hewlett-Packard 9000 Series etc.).

Although the general concepts are the same on every platform, and the environment supports source-code compatibility, the exact look-and-feel adapts to the conventions of each platform, especially for Windows which has its own distinctive culture.

The following screenshot shows a set of environment windows during a session. Although printed in black and white in this book, the display makes extensive use of colors, especially to distinguish the various parts of class texts (the default conventions, user-changeable, are keywords in blue, identifiers in black, comments in red).

Tools

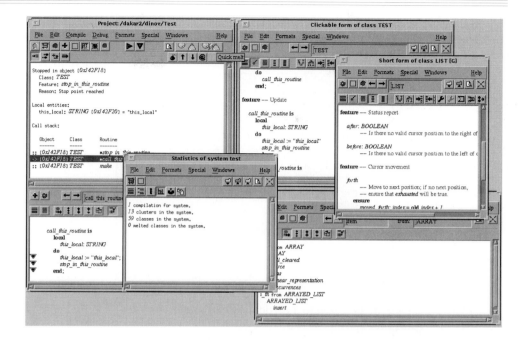

Tools

An environment consists of tools. In many cases those tools are *functional* tools, in the sense of being devoted to functions: a browser tool to browse, a debugger tool to debug, a pretty-printer tool to produce formated versions of software texts. A recent environment such as Sun's Java Workshop (as demonstrated in September of 1996) still conforms to this traditional pattern; to find the ancestors of a class (its parent, grandparent etc.) you start a special "browser" tool.

The disadvantage of this approach is that it is *modal*: it forces you to select first what you want to do, then what you want to do it to. The practice of software development is different. During the course of a debugging session, you may suddenly need a browsing facility: for example you discover that a routine causing trouble is a redefined version, and you want to see the original. If you see that original you may next want to see the enclosing class, its short form, and so on. Modal environments do not let you do this: you will have to go away from the "debugger tool" to a "browser tool" and restart from scratch to look for the item of interest (the routine) even though you had it in the other window.

Here too the object-oriented method provides a better approach. In the same way that we learned to trust object types rather than functions to define our software architectures, we can base our tools on the type of **development objects** that developers manipulate. So we will have no debugger or browser window, but instead a Class Tool, a Feature Tool, a System Tool, a Project Tool, an Object Tool, corresponding to the abstractions that O-O software developers deal with day in and day out: classes, features, systems (assemblies of classes), projects, and, at run-time, class instances ("objects" in the strict sense).

A Project Tool, for example, will keep track of your overall project. You use it among other applications to perform a Melt 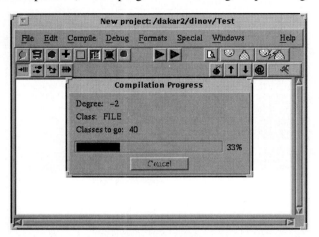, a Freeze or a Finalize; here is a Project Tool captured during a compilation, with a progress bar showing the percentage done:

Project Tool during a compilation

A Class Tool will be **targeted** to a particular class such as *LIST*:

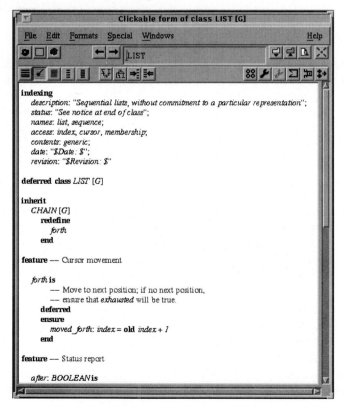

A Class Tool in default format

A Feature Tool, here attached to a Project Tool as part of a debugging session, shows both a feature and the progress of the execution, with mechanisms for step-by-step execution, displaying the call stacks (see the local entities' values in the Project Tool). The Feature Tool is targeted to feature *call_this_routine* of class *TEST*.

*Project and
Feature Tool
for debugging*

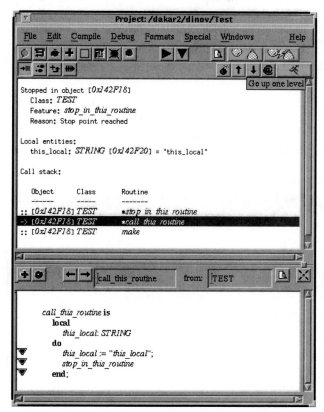

During an execution, you can also see an individual object through an Object Tool:

*An object and
its fields
captured
during
execution*

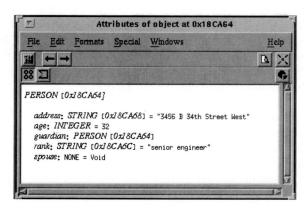

This shows the various fields of the objects. One of them, *guardian*, denotes a non-void reference; you can see the corresponding object by following the link, as we will shortly see.

You can of course have as many Class Tools, Feature Tools and Object Tools as you like, although there is only one System Tool and one Project Tool during a session.

Retargeting and browsing

Various techniques are available to change the target of a tool, for example to retarget the preceding Class Tool from *LIST* to *ARRAY*. One way is simply to type the new class name in the corresponding field (possibly with wild card characters as in *ARR**, to get a menu of matching names if you do not exactly remember).

But you can also used the **pick-and-throw** mechanism briefly introduced in an earlier chapter. If you right-click on a class name, such as *CHAIN* in the Class Tool targeted to *LIST*

See the figure entitled "Pick-and-throw", page 534

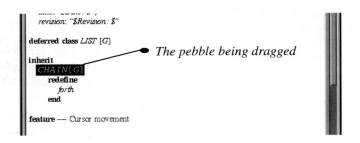

The pebble being dragged

Typed pick-and-throw

the cursor changes into a **pebble** of elliptical form, indicating that what you have picked is a class. The ellipse corresponds to the form of the class **hole** 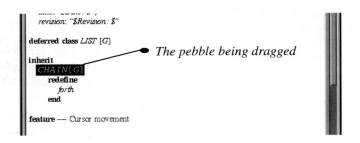; find the Class Tool that you want to retarget (the same or another), and drop the pebble into the hole, by right-clicking into it, to retarget the tool to the chosen class. For convenience you can actually drop it more or less anywhere into the tool, globally considered as a big hole. Rather than pick, drag and throw, you can control-right-click on an object — class, feature… — to start a new tool of the appropriate type, targeted to the object.

The pick-and-throw mechanism is a generalization of common drag-and-drop. Instead of having to maintain the button pressed, however, you work in three steps: the first right-click selects the object; you release the button immediately. Then you are in drag mode, where moving the mouse will cause the line attached to the original element (as on the above figure) to follow the pebble. Finally, you right-click again in the destination hole. This has three advantages over common drag-and-drop:

- Having to keep the mouse button pressed during the whole process, although acceptable for occasional drag-and-drop operations such as moving an element in an interface builder, can cause considerable muscle fatigue at the end of the day when you use it frequently.

- It is all too easy to slacken off the pressure for a split second and drop on the wrong place, often with unpleasant or even catastrophic consequences. (This has happened to me on Windows 95 while drag-and-dropping an icon representing a file; I involuntarily dropped it at a quite unintended place and had a hard time finding out what the operating system had done with the file.)

- Common drag-and-drop does not let you cancel the operation! Once you have picked an object, you *must* drop it somewhere; but there may not be such an acceptable somewhere if you have changed your mind. With the pick-and-throw mechanism, a left-click will cancel the entire operation at any time before throwing.

- Also note that the mechanism is **typed**: it will only let you drop a pebble into a matching hole. There is some tolerance: in the same way that polymorphism lets you attach a *RECTANGLE* object to a *POLYGON* entity, you can drop a feature pebble into a class hole (and see the enclosing class, with the feature highlighted). Again the environment's interaction mechanisms directly apply, for convenience and consistency, the concepts of the method. (Here the difference with common drag-and-drop mechanisms is not crucial, as some of them do have a limited form of typing.)

These, however, are just user interface issues. More important is the role of pick-and-throw, combined with other mechanisms of the environment, to provide an integrated set of mechanisms for all tasks of software development. If you look back at the Class Tool targeted to *LIST*, a deferred class from the Base libraries, you will note a row of format buttons (the second row of buttons from the top). They include:

- Class text ▤.

- Ancestors ▼.

- Short form ▤.

- Routines ✦.

- Deferred routines ✦.

and so on. Clicking on one of them will display the class text in the corresponding format. For example if you click on Ancestors the Class Tool will display the inheritance structure leading to *LIST* in the Base libraries:

In such a display, as in every other tool display, **everything of importance is clickable**. This means that if for example you notice class *CURSOR_STRUCTURE* and want to learn more about it, you can just right-click on it and use pick-and-throw to retarget this tool, or another, to the chosen class. Then you can choose another format, such as Short Form. If in that format you see the name of an interesting routine, you can again apply pick-and-throw to target a Feature Tool to it. In the Feature Tool, the available format buttons include **history** which shows all the adventures of a feature in the inheritance games: all the versions it has in various classes, after renaming, effecting, redefinition; and whenever it lists a class or a feature in showing this information, the environment will let you pick-and-throw the element.

Similarly, the debugging session shown earlier showed class and feature names in various places; to find out information on any of them, just use pick-and-throw. To see an object, such as *0X142F18* on the previous example (an internal identifier, by itself meaningless but clickable), control-right-click on it to start an Object Tool similar to the one we saw, displaying an instance of *PERSON*. In that tool, all fields are identified by their class names — clickable — and references are also clickable, so that you can easily explore the run-time data structures, however complex.

For each of the available formats, you can produce output in various forms such as HTML, TEX, Microsoft's Rich Text Format, FrameMaker MML, troff and so on (a small descriptive language enables you to define your own output forms or adapt an existing one). The output can be displayed, stored with the class files, or, if you want to produce on-line documentation for an entire project or cluster, stored in a separate directory.

These browsing mechanisms do not make any difference between built-in libraries and developer-defined classes. If an element of your software uses *INTEGER*, you can just control-right-click or use pick-and-throw to see that basic class in a Class Tool, in any available format. (As noted, the author of a precompiled library may elect to make the source unavailable, but you will still have access to the short and flat-short forms, with usual clickability properties.) This is of course in line with this book's general principle of uniformity and seamlessness, attempting as much as possible to use a single set of concepts throughout software development activities.

> In contrast, I tried in the aforementioned demo of Java Workshop to get some information about a redefined feature of a certain class, picked at random, but was told that there was no way the "browser tool" could handle that feature, since it turned out to come from a class of the predefined graphical library. The only way to get any information at all was to go to another tool and bring up the documentation — which had a one-line description of the feature. (*INTEGER* would probably also not be browsable since basic types are not classes in Java.)

The run-time mechanisms, in particular the debugging facilities (single-stepping, stop points and so on) all follow from these basic concepts. For example to put a stop point on an instruction or a routine you just drag-and-drop the chosen stop point location to a Stop Point hole ⬛.

Some holes, known as "buttonholes", double up as buttons. For example clicking on a Stop Point hole, treated as a button, will display in the Project Tool information about all the currently active stop points; such information being again clickable, you can easily remove existing stop points or add new ones to the list.

The systematic application of these techniques makes up a mechanism for proximity browsing where everything of interest is hyperlinked — far preferable, in my experience, to modal environments which force you to ask at each step "Am I browsing? Oh no, I am debugging, so I must start a browser tool. And what tool should I start to get the class documentation?".

You are neither debugging nor browsing nor documenting nor editing; you are using and building software, and the tools should let you do what you want on all the objects you want, at any time you want.

36.7 BIBLIOGRAPHICAL NOTES

For an up-to-date summary of the benefits of the environment see [M 1996b], also available on line [M-Web] along with many other technical documents and descriptions of actual projects.

A collective volume describing a set of industrial applications produced with the environment over the years, whose chapters are written by the project leaders in the companies involved, was published as [M 1993].

Among the publications that have described various aspects of the environments at successive stages of its evolutions are: [M 1985c], [M 1987b], [M 1987c], [M 1988], [M 1988a], [M 1988d], [M 1988f], [M 1989], [M 1993d], [M 1997].

The reference on the language is [M 1992]. The book *Reusable Software* [M 1994a] contains, along with a discussion of library design principles, a detailed description of the Base libraries.

Another book [M 1994] presents the environment as a whole. [M 1995c] describes the Case analysis and design workbench, and [M 1995e] the Build graphical application builder. The interface principles were presented in [M 1993d].

The YOOC compiler generator was developed by Christine Mingins, Jon Avotins, Heinz Schmidt and Glenn Maughan of Monash University [Avotins 1995] and is available from Monash's FTP site. The object-oriented parsing techniques of the underlying Parse library, initially presented in [M 1989d], are covered in [M 1994a].

The Math library was developed by Paul Dubois and is described in [Dubois 1997].

Many people have participated in the development of the environment. Some of the principal contributions are due to Éric Bezault (to whom I am also grateful for proofreading parts of this book), Reynald Bouy, Fred Deramat, Fred Dernbach (who built the original architecture of the current compiler), Sylvain Dufour, Fabrice Franceschi, Dewi Jonker, Patrice Khawam, Vince Kraemer, Philippe Lahire, Frédéric Lalanne, Guus Leeuw, Olivier Mallet, Raphaël Manfredi (who established the basis for the current runtime system), Mario Menger, Joost De Moel, David Morgan, Jean-Marc Nerson (especially for the initial versions), Robin van Ommeren, Jean-Pierre Sarkis, Glen Smith, Philippe Stephan (who originated many of the interface principles), Terry Tang, Dino Valente, Xavier Le Vourch, Deniz Yuksel. It is impossible to cite even a small part of the environment users who also helped through their feedback and suggestions

Epilogue, In Full Frankness Exposing the Language

*E*nthusiastically setting out to solve some of the most pressing problems of software engineering, this book has developed an ambitious method for developing quality systems. Since no method is possible without a supporting notation, we have had to devise, as we learned the various components of object-oriented software construction, what in the end turned out to be a complete lifecycle language for software analysis, specification, design, implementation, maintenance and documentation.

Instead of reading on page one, however, the name of the language that you would be using, you have been invited to participate with the author in developing the notation, chapter after chapter, notion after notion, construct after construct. And until now that language has remained nameless. Why? The reasons were sketched in the preface but may deserve some final elaboration.

First, I hope that even though you were warned that the notation already exists and is extensively documented in tens of published textbooks, hundreds of articles and thousands of Usenet messages, you earnestly accepted the pedagogical convention that you participated in its design as you were reading this book. Although this has made life a little harder for the author — imagine: having to *justify* every single construct, instead of bringing it to the people down from the top of Mount Sinai — the effort will have been worthwhile if it has succeeded in giving you a better understanding not only of what things are but of why they must be that way. Second, the convention has enabled us to concentrate on the method, not on notational details, making this book useful not just to people who will indeed have access to the language through one of the supporting commercial environments, but also to those readers who are required to use less complete O-O languages such as Smalltalk, C++, Ada 95, Java or Object Pascal, or even a non-O-O one such as C, Fortran, Pascal or Ada, to which one can apply the emulation techniques discussed in earlier chapters.

Fiction or not, the mystery is not very hard to penetrate. Even if you have not looked at the back cover of this book or read other works by the same author (including the complete language description [M 1992]), just a cursory glance at some of the bibliographical references will have revealed all there is to reveal. And books such as this one are meant to be not only read but re-read, so the surprise, if any, will not last long.

Even so, keeping the language name away from the discussion (except for a few hints that the alert reader may have noted) has enabled us to concentrate on the method. This is a little paradoxical, since one of the language's principal claims is that, alone among O-O languages, it is *also* a method, avoiding the gap between concept and expression, between analysis and design, between design and implementation, which plagues common O-O approaches and threatens to defeat some of the principal advantages of object technology. Not even the brightest-eyed Java or Smalltalk enthusiast will allege that his language of choice is a general-purpose tool for design, let alone analysis; and users of popular analysis notations such as OMT know that they must move to something else when it comes to producing the actual software. The ambition of the method-notation developed in this book is higher: to fulfill one of the main premises and promises of object technology, *seamlessness*, by serving as a faithful assistant that will accompany you throughout the software construction process.

Literary conventions have an end, so the time has now come, at the close of our extended tour of the beauties of object-oriented software construction, after thanking the reader for patiently going along, through all these pages, with the pedagogical pretense of an anonymous language, to lift the very thin veil that covered the name of our notation: welcome to the world of Eiffel.

Part H:

Appendices

Part H contains the appendices: an overview of some library classes; a discussion of genericity versus inheritance; a list of principles and definitions; a glossary; the bibliography; and the index.

A

Extracts from the Base libraries

Throughout the discussion, we have encountered references to a set of libraries collectively known as the "Base libraries", from which the most fundamental classes are grouped into the "Kernel library".

Reading such classes is a good way to learn more about the method by benefiting from the example of widely reused software components, which have been around for a long time and continue to evolve.

This page and the next are only the introduction to the appendix; the actual class texts, made available in electronic form so as to facilitate browsing, appear on the CD-ROM accompanying this book.

See "Criteria for view inheritance", page 856. A detailed presentation of the libraries has been published separately [M 1994a], which also describes the theoretical underpinnings — the general taxonomy principles used to classify the major data structures of computing science. A few of the basic ideas were summarized in the discussion of view inheritance.

Among the most important classes whose concepts were discussed in the previous chapters and whose text you will find on the CD-ROM are:

• *ARRAY*, describing one-dimensional arrays and relying on a flexible and general view of this notion (in particular, arrays can be freely resized to any dimension during the execution of a system).

• *LINKABLE*, describing cells of linked structures, chained one way to similar cells.

• *BI_LINKABLE*, the equivalent for two-way linked cells.

• *LIST*, a deferred class representing the general notion of list as "active data structure" with cursor, without commitment to a particular representation. (The next three classes provide specific implementations, using multiple inheritance through the "marriage of convenience" technique.)

• *ARRAYED_LIST*, giving an implementation by an array (whose resizability is particularly useful here).

• *LINKED_LIST*, a one-way linked list implementation, relying internally on class *LINKABLE*.

- *TWO_WAY_LIST*, a one-way linked list implementation, relying internally on class *BI_LINKABLE*.

- *TWO_WAY_TREE*, a widely used implementation of general trees, based on *TWO_WAY_LIST* for its representation and relying on the observation made in the chapter on multiple inheritance: if we merge the notion of tree and node, we can consider that a tree is both a list (as in *TWO_WAY_LIST*) and a list element (as in *BI_LINKABLE*).

All these classes, representing containers, are generic, with a single generic parameter representing the type of elements.

B

Genericity versus inheritance

The material that follows, and its appearance in an appendix, deserve some background explanation. Part of the original impetus for the work that eventually led to this book was a study that I performed in 1984; in preparation for a graduate course that I was to teach on "*advanced concepts in programming languages*", I compared the "horizontal" module extension mechanism of genericity, illustrated by Ada, Z, LPG and other generic languages, with the "vertical" mechanism of inheritance introduced by Simula: how these techniques differ, to what extent they compete, and to what extent they complement each other. This led to an article on "Genericity versus Inheritance" [M 1986], presented at the first OOPSLA conference, and to a chapter in the first edition of the present book.

When preparing this new edition I felt that both genericity and inheritance were now understood well enough, and their treatment detailed enough in the rest of the book, to make the chapter appear too specialized: useful mostly to readers interested in issues of language design or O-O theory. So I removed it. But then I found out that a regular flow of articles in the software press still showed must puzzlement over the issue, especially in the context of C++ for which many people seem to be searching for general guidelines on when to use "templates" and when to use inheritance. This means the discussion still has its place in a general presentation of object technology, although it is perhaps best severed from the main part of the text. Hence this appendix.

The topics reviewed are, in order: genericity; inheritance; how to emulate each of these mechanisms through the other; and, as a conclusion, how best to reconcile them.

If you have read carefully the remainder of this book, you will find the beginning of this discussion familiar since we must restart with the basics to get a full picture of each mechanism, of its contribution, and of its limitations. As we probe deeper and deeper, perhaps stepping briefly into a few dead ends along the way, the ideal combination of genericity and inheritance will progressively unfold before our eyes, imposing itself in the end as almost inevitable and letting us understand, in full detail, the fascinating relationship between the two principal methods for making software modules open to variation and adaptation.

B.1 GENERICITY

We begin our review by appraising the merits of genericity as it exists in a number of languages, object-oriented or not. Let us rely for convenience on the notations — semicolons and all — of the best known non-O-O generic language, Ada (meaning by default, as elsewhere in this book, Ada 83). So for the rest of this section we forget about O-O languages and techniques.

Only the most important form of Ada genericity will be considered: *type parameterization*, that is to say the ability to parameterize a software element (in Ada, a package or routine) by one or more types. Generic parameters have other, less momentous uses in Ada, such as parameterized dimensions for arrays. We may distinguish between *unconstrained* genericity, imposing no specific requirement on generic parameters, and *constrained* genericity, whereby a certain structure is required.

Unconstrained genericity

Unconstrained genericity removes some of the rigidity of static typing. A trivial example is a routine (in a language with Ada-like syntax but without explicit type declarations) to swap the values of two variables:

> **procedure** *swap* (x, y) **is**
>   **local** *t*;
> **begin**
> $t := x; x := y; y := t;$
> **end** *swap*;

This extract and the next few are in Ada or Ada-like syntax.

This form does not specify the types of the elements to be swapped and of the local variable t. This is too much freedom, since a call *swap* (a, b), where a is an integer and b a character string, will not be prohibited even though it is probably an error.

To address this issue, statically typed languages such as Pascal and Ada require developers to declare explicitly the types of all variables and formal arguments, and enforce a statically checkable type compatibility constraint between actual and formal arguments in calls and between source and target in assignments.The procedure to exchange the values of two variables of type G becomes:

> **procedure** G_swap $(x, y:$ **in out** $G)$ **is**
> $t: G;$
> **begin**
> $t := x; x := y; y := t;$
> **end** *swap*;

Demanding that G be specified as a single type averts type incompatibility errors, but in the constant haggling between safety and flexibility we have now erred too far away from flexibility: to correct the lack of safety of the first solution, we have made the solution inflexible. We will need a new procedure for every type of elements to be exchanged, for example *INTEGER_swap*, *STRING_swap* and so on. Such multiple declarations lengthen and obscure programs. The example chosen is particularly bad since all the declarations will be identical except for the two occurrences of G.

Static typing may be considered too restrictive here: the only real requirement is that the two actual arguments passed to any call of *swap* should be of the same type, and that their type should also be applied to the declaration of the local variable *t*. It does not matter what this type actually is as long as it satisfies these properties.

> In addition the arguments must be passed in **in out** mode, so that the procedure can change their values. This is permitted in Ada.

Genericity provides a tradeoff between too much freedom, as with untyped languages, and too much restraint, as with Pascal. In a generic language you may declare *G* as a generic parameter of *swap* or an enclosing unit. Ada indeed offers generic routines, along with the generic packages described in chapter 33. In quasi-Ada you can write:

> **generic**
>> **type** *G* **is private**;
>
> **procedure** *swap* (*x*, *y*: **in out** *G*) **is**
>> *t*: *G*;
>
> **begin**
>> *t* := *x*; *x* := *y*; *y* := *t*;
>
> **end** *swap*;

The only difference with real Ada is that you would have to separate interface from implementation, as explained in the chapter on Ada. Since information hiding is irrelevant for the discussion in this chapter, interfaces and implementations will be merged for ease of presentation.

The **generic**... clause introduces type parameters. By specifying *G* as "private", the writer of this procedure allows himself to apply to entities of type *G* (*x*, *y* and *t*) operations available on all types, such as assignment or comparison, and these only.

The above declaration does not quite introduce a routine but rather a routine pattern; to get a directly usable routine you will provide actual type parameters, as in

> **procedure** *int_swap* **is new** *swap* (*INTEGER*);
>
> **procedure** *str_swap* **is new** *swap* (*STRING*);

etc. Now assuming that *i* and *j* are variables of type *INTEGER*, *s* and *t* of type *STRING*, then of the following calls

> *int_swap* (*i*, *j*); *str_swap* (*s*, *t*); *int_swap* (*i*, *s*); *str_swap* (*s*, *j*); *str_swap* (*i*, *j*);

all but the first two are invalid, and will be rejected by the compiler.

More interesting than parameterized routines are parameterized packages. As a minor variation of our usual stack example, consider a queue package, where the operations on a queue (first-in, first out) are: add an element; remove the oldest element added and not yet removed; get its value; test for empty queue. The interface is:

```
generic
    type G is private;
package QUEUES is
    type QUEUE (capacity: POSITIVE) is private;
    function empty (s: in QUEUE) return BOOLEAN;
    procedure add (t: in G; s: in out QUEUE);
    procedure remove (s: in out QUEUE);
    function oldest (s: in QUEUE) return G;
private
    type QUEUE (capacity: POSITIVE) is
                -- The package uses an array representation for queues
        record
            implementation: array (0 .. capacity) of G;
            count: NATURAL;
        end record;
end QUEUES;
```

Again this does not define a package but a package pattern; to get a directly usable package you will use generic derivation, as in

```
package INT_QUEUES is new QUEUES (INTEGER);
package STR_QUEUES is new QUEUES (STRING);
```

Note again the tradeoff that generic declarations achieve between typed and untyped approaches. *QUEUES* is a pattern for modules implementing queues of elements of all possible types *G*, while retaining the possibility to enforce type checks for a specific *G*, so as to rule out such unholy combinations as the insertion of an integer into a queue of strings.

The form of genericity illustrated by both of the examples seen so far, swapping and queues, may be called *unconstrained* since there is no specific requirement on the types that may be used as actual generic parameters: you may swap the values of variables of any type and create queues of values of any type, as long as all the values in a given queue are of the same type.

Other generic definitions, however, only make sense if the actual generic parameters satisfy some conditions. This form may be called *constrained* genericity.

Constrained genericity

As in the unconstrained case, the examples of constrained genericity will include both a routine and a package.

Assume first you need a generic function to compute the minimum of two values. You can try the pattern of *swap*:

```
generic
    type G is private;
function minimum (x, y: G) return G is begin
        if x <= y then return x; else return y; end if;
end minimum;
```

From here on most routine declarations omit the in *mode specification for arguments, which is optional.*

Such a function declaration, however, does not always make sense; only for types G on which a comparison operator $<=$ is defined. In a language that enhances security through static typing, we want to enforce this requirement at compile time, not wait until run time. We need a way to specify that type G must be equipped with the right operation.

In Ada this will be written by treating the operator $<=$ as a generic parameter of its own. Syntactically it is a function; as a syntactic facility, it is possible to invoke such a function using the usual infix form if it is declared with a name in double quotes, here "$<=$". Again the following declaration becomes legal Ada if the interface and implementation are taken apart.

> **generic**
> > **type** G **is private**;
> > **with function** "$<=$" $(a, b: G)$ **return** *BOOLEAN* **is** $<>$;
> **function** $0(x, y: G)$ **return** G **is begin**
> > **if** $x <= y$ **then return** x; **else return** y **end if**;
> **end** *minimum*;

The keyword **with** introduces generic parameters representing routines, such as "$<=$".

You may perform a generic derivation *minimum* for any type, say *T1*, such that there exists a function, say *T1_le*, of signature **function** $(a, b: T1)$ **return** *BOOLEAN*:

> **function** *T1_minimum* **is new** *minimum* $(T1, T1\_le)$;

If function *T1_le* is in fact called "$<=$", more precisely if its name and type signature match those of the corresponding formal routine, then you do not need to include it in the list of actual parameters to the generic derivation. So because type *INTEGER* has a predefined "$<=$" function with the right signature, you can simply declare

> **function** *int_minimum* **is new** *minimum* $(INTEGER)$;

This use of default routines with matching names and types is made possible by the clause **is** $<>$ in the declaration of the formal routine, here "$<=$". Operator overloading, as permitted (and in fact encouraged) by Ada, plays an essential role: many different types will have a "$<=$" function.

This discussion of constrained genericity for routines readily transposes to packages. Assume you need a generic package for handling matrices of objects of any type G, with matrix sum and product as basic operations. Such a definition only makes sense if type G has a sum and a product of its own, and each of these operations has a zero element; these features of G will be needed in the implementation of matrix sum and product. The public part of the package may be written as follows:

> **generic**
> > **type** G **is private**;
> > *zero*: G;
> > *unity*: G;
> > **with function** "$+$" $(a, b: G)$ **return** G **is** $<>$;
> > **with function** "$*$" $(a, b: G)$ **return** G **is** $<>$;

```
package MATRICES is
      type MATRIX (lines, columns: POSITIVE) is private;
      function "+" (m1, m2: MATRIX) return MATRIX;
      function "*" (m1, m2: MATRIX) return MATRIX;
private
      type MATRIX (lines, columns: POSITIVE) is
            array (1 .. lines, 1 .. columns) of G;
end MATRICES;
```

Typical generic derivations are:

package *INTEGER_MATRICES* **is new** *MATRICES* (*INTEGER*, 0, 1);

package *BOOLEAN_MATRICES* **is**
   new *MATRICES* (*BOOLEAN*, **false**, **true**, "or", "and");

Again, you may omit actual parameters corresponding to formal generic routines (here "+" and "*") for type *INTEGER*, which has matching operations; but you will need them for *BOOLEAN*. (It is convenient to declare such parameters last in the formal list; otherwise keyword notation is required in derivations that omit the corresponding actuals.)

It is interesting here to take a look at the body (implementation) of such a package:

```
package body MATRICES is
      … Other declarations …
      function "*" (m1, m2: G) is
            result: MATRIX (m1'lines, m2'columns);
      begin
            if m1'columns /= m2'lines then
                  raise incompatible_sizes;
            end if;
            for i in m1'RANGE(1) loop
                  for j in m2'RANGE(2) loop
                        result (i, j) := zero;
                        for k in m1'RANGE(2) loop
                              result (i, j) := result (i, j) + m1 (i, k) * m2 (k, j)
                        end loop;
                  end loop;
            end loop;
            return result
      end "*";
end MATRICES;
```

This extract relies on some specific features of Ada:

- For a parameterized type such as *MATRIX* (*lines, columns*: *POSITIVE*), a variable declaration must provide actual parameters, e.g. *mm*: *MATRIX* (*100, 75*); you may then retrieve their values using apostrophe notation, as in *mm'lines* which in this case has value 100.

- If a is an array, $a'RANGE(i)$ denotes the range of values in its i-th dimension; for example $m1'RANGE(1)$ above is the same as $1 .. m1'lines$.

- If requested to multiply two dimension-wise incompatible matrices, the extract raises an exception, corresponding to the violation of an implicit precondition.

The minimum and matrix examples are representative of Ada techniques for constrained genericity. They also show a serious limitation of these techniques: only syntactic constraints can be expressed. All that a programmer may require is the presence of certain routines ("<=", "+", "∗" in the examples) with given types; but the declarations are meaningless unless the routines also satisfy some semantic constraints. Function *minimum* only makes sense if "<=" is a total order relation on G; and to produce a generic derivation of *MATRICES* for a type G, you should make sure that operations "+" and "∗" have not just the right signature, $G \times G \to G$, but also the appropriate properties: associativity, distributivity, *zero* a zero element for "+" and *unity* for "∗" etc. We may use the mathematical term **ring** for a structure equipped with operations enjoying these properties.

B.2 INHERITANCE

So much for pure genericity. The other term of the comparison is inheritance. To contrast it with genericity, consider the example of a general-purpose module library for files. First here is the outline of an implementation of "special files" in the Unix sense, that is to say, files associated with devices:

This extract and the next few are in the O-O notation of the rest of this book.

class *DEVICE* **feature**
     open (file_descriptor: INTEGER) **is do** … **end**
     close **is do** … **end**
     opened: *BOOLEAN*
end -- class *DEVICE*

An example use of this class is:

d1: *DEVICE*; *f1*: *INTEGER*; …
!! *d1*•*make*; *d1*•*open (f1)*;
if *d1*•*opened* **then** …

Consider next the notion of a tape device. For the purposes of this discussion, a tape unit has all the properties of devices, as represented by the three features of class *DEVICE*, plus the ability to rewind its tape. Rather than building a class from scratch, we may use inheritance to declare class *TAPE* as an extension-cum-modification of *DEVICE*. The new class extends *DEVICE* by adding a new procedure *rewind*, describing a mechanism applicable to tapes but not necessarily to other devices; and it modifies some of *DEVICE*'s properties by providing a new version of *open*, describing the specifics of opening a device that happens to be a tape drive.

Objects of type *TAPE* automatically possess all the features of *DEVICE* objects, plus their own (here *rewind*). Class *DEVICE* could have more heirs, for example *DISK* with its own specific features such as direct access read.

Objects of type *TAPE* will possess all the features of type *DEVICE*, possibly adapted (in the case of *open*), and complemented by the new feature *rewind*.

With inheritance comes polymorphism, permitting assignments of the form $x := y$, but only if the type of x is an ancestor of the type of y. The next associated property is dynamic binding: if x is a device, the call $x.open$ *(f1)* will be executed differently depending on the assignments performed on x before the call: after $x := y$, where y is a tape, the call will execute the tape version.

This is approximate terminology; "is an ancestor of" stands for "conforms to". Precise rules appear in earlier chapters.

We have seen the remarkable benefits of these inheritance techniques for reusability and extendibility. A key aspect was the Open-Closed principle: a software element such as *DEVICE* is both usable as it stands (it may be compiled as part of an executable system) and still amenable to extensions (if used as an ancestor of new classes).

Next come deferred features and classes. Here we note that Unix devices are a special kind of file; so you may make *DEVICE* an heir to class *FILE*, whose other heirs might include *TEXT_FILE* (itself with heirs *NORMAL* and *DIRECTORY*) and *BINARY_FILE*. The figure shows the inheritance graph, a tree in this case.

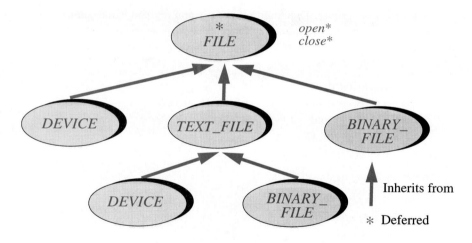

A simple inheritance hierarchy, with deferred and effective classes

Although it is possible to open or close any file, how these operations are performed depends on whether the file is a device, a directory etc. So *FILE* is a deferred class with deferred routines *open* or *close*, making descendants responsible for implementing them:

deferred class *FILE* **feature**
    open (*file_descriptor*: *INTEGER*) **is deferred end**
    close **is deferred end**;
end -- class *FILE*

Effective descendants of *FILE* will provide effective implementations of *open* and *close*.

B.3 EMULATING INHERITANCE WITH GENERICITY

To compare genericity with inheritance, we will study how, if in any way, the effect of each feature may be emulated in a language offering the other.

First consider a language such as Ada (again meaning Ada 83), offering genericity but not inheritance. Can it be made to achieve the effects of inheritance?

The easy part is name overloading. Ada, as we know, allows reusing the same routine name as many times as needed for operands of different types; so you can define types such as *TAPE*, *DISK* and others, each with its own version of the routines:

This extract and the next few are in Ada syntax.

procedure *open* (*p*: **in out** *TAPE*; *descriptor*: **in** *INTEGER*);
procedure *close* (*p*: **in out** *DISK*);

No ambiguity will arise if the routines are distinguished by the type of at least one operand. But this solution does not provide polymorphism and dynamic binding, whereby *d.close*, for example, would have a different effect after assignments *d := di* and *d := ta*, where *di* is a *DISK* and *ta* a *TAPE*.

To obtain the same effect, you have to use records with variant fields: define

type *DEVICE* (*unit*: *DEVICE_TYPE*) **is**
    record
        … Fields common to all device types …
        case *unit* **is**
            when *tape* => … *fields for tape devices* …;
            when *disk* => … *fields for disk devices* …;
            … Other cases …;
        end case
    end record

where *DEVICE_TYPE* is an enumerated type with elements *tape*, *disk* etc. Then there would be a single version of each the procedures on devices (*open*, *close* etc.), each containing a case discrimination of the form

case *d'unit* **is**
    when *tape* => … *action for tape devices* …;
    when *disk* => … *action for disk devices* …;
    … other cases …;
end case

See "Single Choice", page 61.

This uses explicit discrimination in each case, and closes off the list of choices, forcing every routine to know of all the possible variants; addition of new cases will cause changes to all such routines. The Single Choice principle expressly warned against such software architectures.

So the answer to the question of this section is essentially no:

> ### Emulating inheritance
> It appears impossible to emulate inheritance through genericity.

B.4 EMULATING GENERICITY WITH INHERITANCE

Let us see if we will have more luck with the reverse problem: can we achieve the effect of Ada-style genericity in an object-oriented language with inheritance?

The O-O notation introduced in earlier chapters does provide a generic parameter mechanism. But since we are comparing pure genericity versus pure inheritance, the rule of the game for some time, frustrating as it may be, is to pretend we have all but forgotten about that genericity mechanism. As a result the solutions presented in this section will be substantially more complex than those obtainable with the full notation, described in the rest of this book and in later sections. As you read this section, remember that the software extracts are not final forms, but for purposes of discussion only.

Surprisingly perhaps, the simulation turns out to be easier, or at least less artificial, for the more sophisticated form of genericity: constrained. So we begin with this case.

Emulating constrained genericity: overview

The idea is to associate a class with a constrained formal generic type parameter. This is a natural thing to do since a constrained generic type may be viewed, together with its constraining operations, as an abstract data type. Consider for example the Ada generic clauses in our two constrained examples, minimum and matrices:

> **generic**
> > **type** G **is private**;
> > **with function** "<=" $(a, b: G)$ **return** *BOOLEAN* **is** <>

This extract is in Ada syntax.

> **generic**
> > **type** G **is private**;
> > *zero*: G; *unity*: G;
> > **with function** "+" $(a, b: G)$ **return** G **is** <>;
> > **with function** "∗" $(a, b: G)$ **return** G **is** <>;

We may view these clauses as the definitions of two abstract data types, *COMPARABLE* and *RING_ELEMENT*; the first is characterized by a comparison operation "<=", and the second by features *zero*, *unity*, "+" and "∗".

In an object-oriented language, such types may be directly represented as classes. We cannot define these classes entirely, for there is no universal implementation of "<=", "+" etc.; rather, they are to be used as ancestors of other classes, corresponding to actual generic parameters. Deferred classes provide exactly what we need:

> **deferred class** *COMPARABLE* **feature**
> > **infix** "<=" (*other*: *COMPARABLE*): *BOOLEAN* **is deferred end**
> **end** -- class *COMPARABLE*

This extract and all remaining ones are in the O-O notation of this book.

deferred class *RING_ELEMENT* **feature**

 infix "+" (*other*: **like** *Current*): **like** *Current* **is**

  deferred

  ensure

   equal (*other*, *zero*) **implies** *equal* (*Result*, *Current*)

  end;

 infix "✳" (*other*: **like** *Current*): **like** *Current* **is deferred end**

 zero: **like** *Current* **is deferred end**

 unity: **like** *Current* **is deferred end**

end -- class *RING_ELEMENT*

Unlike Ada, the O-O notation allows us here to express abstract semantic properties, although only one of them has been included as an example (the property that $x + 0 = x$ for any x, appearing as a postcondition of **infix** "+").

"ANCHORED
DECLARATION",
16.7, page 598.

The use of anchored types (**like** *Current*) makes it possible to avoid some improper combinations, as explained for the *COMPARABLE* example next. At this stage replacing all such types by *RING_ELEMENT* would not affect the discussion.

Constrained genericity: routines

We can write a routine such as *minimum* by specifying its arguments to be of type *COMPARABLE*. Based on the Ada pattern, the function would be declared as

 minimum (*one*: *COMPARABLE*; *other*: **like** *one*): **like** *one* **is**

  -- Minimum of *one* and *other*

 do … **end**

In O-O development, however, every routine appears in a class and is relative to the current instance of that class; we may include *minimum* in class *COMPARABLE*, argument *one* becoming the implicit current instance. The class becomes:

COMPARABLE
becomes a "behav-
ior class", with an
effective feature rely-
ing on a deferred
one. See "Don't call
us, we'll call you",
page 504.

deferred class *COMPARABLE* **feature**

 infix "<=" (*other*: **like** *Current*): *BOOLEAN* **is**

  -- Is current object less than or equal to *other*?

  deferred

  end

 minimum (*other*: **like** *Current*): **like** *Current* **is**

  -- Minimum of current object and *other*

  do

   if *Current* <= *other* **then** *Result* := *Current* **else** *Result* := *other* **end**

  end

end -- class *COMPARABLE*

To compute the minimum of two elements, you must declare them of some effective descendant type of *COMPARABLE*, for which **infix** "<=" has been effected, such as

class *INTEGER_COMPARABLE* **inherit**
    COMPARABLE
creation
    put
feature -- Initialization
    put (*v*: *INTEGER*) **is**
              -- Initialize from *v*.
        do *item* := *new* **end**
feature -- Access
    item: *INTEGER*;
        -- Value associated with current object
feature -- Basic operations
    infix "<=" (*other*: **like** *Current*): *BOOLEAN* **is**
              -- Is current object less than or equal to *other*?
        do *Result* := (*item* <= *other*.*item*) **end**;
end -- class *INTEGER_COMPARABLE*

To find the minimum of two integers, you may now apply function *minimum* to entities *ic1* and *ic2*, whose type is not *INTEGER* but *INTEGER_COMPARABLE*:

    ic3 := *ic1*.*minimum* (*ic2*)

To use the generic **infix** "<=" and *minimum* functions, you must renounce direct references to integers, using *INTEGER_COMPARABLE* entities instead; hence the need for attribute *item* and routine *put* to access and modify the associated integer values. You will introduce a similar heirs of *COMPARABLE*, such as *STRING_COMPARABLE*, and *REAL_COMPARABLE*, for each type requiring a version of *minimum*.

Note that the mechanism of anchored declaration is essential to ensure type correctness. If the argument to *minimum* in *COMPARABLE* had been declared as a *COMPARABLE*, rather than **like** *Current*, then the following call would be valid:

    ic1.*minimum* (*c*)

even if *c* is a *COMPARABLE* but not an *INTEGER_COMPARABLE*. Clearly, such a call should be disallowed. This also applies to the previous example, *RING_ELEMENT*.

Having to declare features *item* and *put* for all descendants of *COMPARABLE*, and hence sacrificing the direct use of simple types, is unpleasant. There is also a performance cost: rather than manipulating integers or strings we must create and use **wrapper objects** of types such as *INTEGER_COMPARABLE*. But by paying this fixed price in both ease of use and efficiency we do achieve the full emulation of constrained genericity by inheritance. (In the final notation, of course, there will be no price at all to pay.)

Emulating constrained genericity (1)

It is possible to emulate constrained genericity through inheritance, by using wrapper classes and the corresponding wrapper objects.

Constrained genericity: packages

The previous discussion transposes to packages. To emulate the matrix abstraction which Ada implemented through the *MATRICES* package, we can use a class:

```
class MATRIX feature
        anchor: RING_ELEMENT is do end
        implementation: ARRAY2 [like anchor]
        item (i, j: INTEGER): like anchor is
                -- Value of (i, j) entry
            do Result := implementation.item (i, j) end
        put (i, j: INTEGER; v: like anchor) is
                -- Assign value v to entry (i, j).
            do implementation.put (i, j, v) end
    infix "+" (other: like Current): like Current is
                -- Matrix sum of current matrix and other
            local
                i, j: INTEGER
            do
                !! Result.make (…)
                from i := … until … loop
                    from j := … until … loop
                        Result. put ((item (i, j) + other.item (i, j)), i, j)
                        j := j + 1
                    end
                    i := i + 1
                end
            end
    infix "*" (other: like Current): like Current is
                -- Matrix product of current matrix by other
            local … do … end
end -- class MATRIX
```

The type of the argument to *put* and of the result of *item* raises an interesting problem: it should be *RING_ELEMENT*, but redefined properly in descendant classes. Anchored declaration is the solution; but here for the first time no attribute of the class seems to be available to serve as anchor. This should not stop us, however: we declare an **artificial anchor**, called *anchor*. Its only purpose is to be redefined to the proper descendant types of *RING_ELEMENT* in future descendants of *MATRIX* (that is to say, to *BOOLEAN_RING* in *BOOLEAN_MATRIX* etc.), so that all associated entities will follow. To avoid any space penalty in instances, *anchor* is declared as a function rather than an attribute. This technique of artificial anchors is useful to preserve type consistency when, as here, there is no "natural" anchor among the attributes of the class.

A few loop details have been left out, as well as the body of infix "*", but they are easy to fill in. Features *put* and *item* as applied to *implementation* will come from the library class *ARRAY2* describing two-dimensional arrays.

To define the equivalent of the Ada generic package derivation shown earlier

package *BOOLEAN_MATRICES* **is**
   new *MATRICES* (*BOOLEAN*, **false**, **true**, "or", "and");

we must first declare the "ring element" corresponding to booleans:

class *BOOLEAN_RING_ELEMENT* **inherit**
   RING_ELEMENT
         redefine *zero*, *unity* **end**
creation
   put
feature -- Initialization
   put (*v*: *BOOLEAN*) **is**
            -- Initialize from *v*.
      do *item* := *v* **end**
feature -- Access
   item: *BOOLEAN*
feature -- Basic operations
      infix "+" (*other*: **like** *Current*): **like** *Current* **is**
            -- Boolean addition: or
         do !! *Result*.*put* (*item* **or** *other*.*item*) **end**
      infix "*" (*other*: **like** *Current*): **like** *Current* **is**
            -- Boolean multiplication: and
         do !! *Result*.*put* (*item* **and** *other*.*item*) **end**
      zero: **like** *Current* **is**
            -- Zero element for boolean addition
         once !! *Result*.*put* (*False*) **end**
      unity: **like** *Current* **is**
            -- Zero element for boolean multiplication
         once !! *Result*.*put* (*True*) **end**
   end -- class *BOOLEAN_RING_ELEMENT*

Note how *zero* and *unity* are effected as once functions.

Then to obtain an equivalent to the Ada package derivation, just define an heir *BOOLEAN_MATRIX* of *MATRIX*, where you only need to redefine *anchor*, the artificial anchor; all the other affected types will follow automatically:

> class *BOOLEAN_MATRIX* **inherit**
>> *MATRIX*
>>> **redefine** *anchor* **end**
>
> **feature**
>> *anchor*: *BOOLEAN_RING_ELEMENT*
>
> **end** -- class *BOOLEAN_MATRIX*

See the box on page 1178.

This construction achieves the effect of constrained genericity using inheritance, confirming for packages the emulation result initially illustrated for routines.

Unconstrained genericity

The mechanism for simulating unconstrained genericity is the same; we can simply treat this case as a special form of constrained genericity, with an empty set of constraints. As above, formal type parameters will be interpreted as abstract data types, but here with no relevant operations. The technique works, but becomes rather heavy to apply since the dummy types do not correspond to any obviously relevant data abstraction.

Let us apply the previous technique to both our unconstrained examples, swap and queue, beginning with the latter. We need a class, say *QUEUABLE*, describing objects that may be added to and retrieved from a queue. Since this is true of any object, the class has no other property than its name:

> class *QUEUABLE* **end**

We may now declare a class *QUEUE*, whose operations apply to *QUEUABLE* objects. (Remember that this class is not offered as a paragon of good O-O design: we are still voluntarily playing with an impoverished version of the O-O notation, devoid of genericity.) Routine postconditions have been left out for brevity. Although in principle function *item* could serve as an anchor, its body will not change in descendants, so it is better to use an artificial anchor *item_anchor* to avoid having to redefine *item*.

> **indexing**
>> *description*: *"First-in-first out queues, implemented through arrays"*
>
> **class** *QUEUE* **creation**
>> *make*
>
> **feature** -- Initialization
>
>> *make* (*m*: *INTEGER*) **is**
>>> -- Create queue with space for *m* items.
>>
>>> **require**
>>>> $m >= 0$
>>
>>> **do**
>>>> !! *implementation*•*make* (*1*, *m*); *capacity* := *m*
>>>>
>>>> *first* := *1*; *next* := *1*
>>
>>> **end**

feature -- Access

    capacity, first, next, count: INTEGER

    item: **like** *item_anchor* **is**

          -- Oldest element in queue

      require

        not *empty*

      do

        Result := implementation∙item (first)

      end

feature -- Status report

    empty: *BOOLEAN* **is**

        -- Is queue empty?

    do *Result := (count = 0)* **end**

    full: *BOOLEAN* **is**

        -- Is representation full?

    do *Result := (count = capacity)* **end**

feature -- Element change

    put (*x*: **like** *item_anchor*) **is**

        -- Add *x* at end of queue

      require

        not *full*

      do

        implementation∙put (x, next); count := count + 1; next := successor (next)

      end

    remove **is**

        -- Remove oldest element

      require

        not *empty*

      do

        first := successor (first); count := count – 1

      end

    feature {*NONE*} -- Implementation
       item_anchor: *QUEUABLE* **is do end**
       implementation: *ARRAY* [**like** *item_anchor*]

       successor (*n*: *INTEGER*): *INTEGER* **is**
           -- Next value after *n*, cyclically in the interval *1 .. capacity*
         require
           n >= *1*; *n* <= *capacity*
         do
           Result := (*n* \\ *capacity*) + *1*
         end

    invariant
       0 <= *count*; *count* <= *capacity*; *first* >= *1*; *next* >= *1*
       (**not** *full*) **implies** ((*first* <= *capacity*) **and** (*next* <= *capacity*))
       (*capacity* = *0*) **implies** *full*
       -- Items, if any, appear in array positions *first*, … *next* – *1* (cyclically)
    end -- class *QUEUE*

For an alternative technique see e.g. "A buffer is a separate queue", page 990.

Bounded queue implementations elsewhere in this book rely on the technique of keeping one position open. Here, we allocate *capacity* elements and keep track of *count*. There is no particular reason, other than to illustrate alternative implementation techniques.

To get the equivalent of generic derivation (so as to obtain queues of a specific type) you must, as with the *COMPARABLE* example, define descendants of *QUEUABLE*:

    class *INTEGER_QUEUABLE* **inherit**
       QUEUABLE
    creation
       put
    feature -- Initialization
       put (*n*: *INTEGER*) **is**
           -- Initialize from *n*.
         do *item* := *n* **end**
    feature -- Access
       item: *INTEGER*

    feature {*NONE*} -- Implementation
       item_anchor: *INTEGER* **is do end**
    end -- class *INTEGER_QUEUABLE*

and similarly *STRING_QUEUABLE* etc.; then declare the corresponding descendants of *QUEUE*, redefining *item_anchor* appropriately in each.

Emulating unconstrained genericity

It is possible to emulate unconstrained genericity through inheritance, by using wrapper classes and the corresponding wrapper objects.

B.5 COMBINING GENERICITY AND INHERITANCE

It appears from the previous discussion that inheritance is the more powerful mechanism since we have not found a reasonable way to simulate it with genericity. In addition:

- You can express the equivalent of generic routines or packages in a language with inheritance, but this requires some duplication and complication. The verbosity is particularly hard to justify for unconstrained genericity, which requires just as much emulation effort even though it is theoretically simpler.

- Type checking introduces difficulties in the use of inheritance to emulate genericity.

Anchored declaration solves the second problem. (The reader familiar with the *Chapter 17.* detailed discussion of typing in an earlier chapter will, however, have noted the potential for system validity problems, which we do not need to explore further since they will disappear in the solutions finally retained below.)

Let us see how we can solve the first problem by introducing (reintroducing, that is) the appropriate form of genericity.

Unconstrained genericity

Since the major complication arises for unconstrained genericity even though it should be the simpler case, it seems adequate to provide a specific genericity mechanism for this case, avoiding the need to rely on inheritance. Consequently, we allow our classes to have unconstrained generic parameters: as we are now (at last) allowed to remember from earlier chapters, a class may be defined as

> **class** C [G, H, ...] ...

where the parameters represent arbitrary types. To obtain a directly usable type you use a generic derivation, using types as actual generic parameters:

> x: C [*DEVICE*, *RING_ELEMENT*, ...]

This immediately applies to the queue class, which we can simply declare as

> **indexing**
>   *description*: "*First-in-first out queues, implemented through arrays*"
> **class** *QUEUE* [G] **creation**
>   ... The rest as before, but removing the declaration of *item_anchor*
>   and replacing all occurrences of type **like** *item_anchor* by G ...
> **end** -- class *QUEUE*

We get rid of class *QUEUABLE* as well as *INTEGER_QUEUABLE* and other such descendants; to have a queue of integers, we simply use type *QUEUE* [*INTEGER*], manipulating integers directly rather than through intermediate wrapper objects.

This is a remarkable simplification, suggesting that in spite of the theoretical possibility of emulating unconstrained genericity through inheritance, it is desirable in practice to introduce a generic mechanism into the object-oriented framework.

> ### Providing unconstrained genericity
>
> Along with inheritance, it is desirable to provide a specific notation for declaring classes as generic (unconstrained).

Constrained genericity

For constrained genericity we can explore the same general scheme. In the matrix example:

class *MATRIX* [*G*] **feature**

    anchor: *RING_ELEMENT* [*G*]

    …Other features as before …

end -- class *MATRIX*

with ring elements now declared as

deferred class *RING_ELEMENT* [*G*] **feature**

    item: *G*

    put (*new*: *G*) **is do** *item* := *new* **end**

    …Other features as before …

end -- class *RING_ELEMENT*

Using the same a generic parameter in two related classes, *RING_ELEMENT* and *MATRIX*, ensures type consistency: all the elements of a given matrix will be of type *RING_ELEMENT* [*G*] for the same *G*.

We can similarly make class *COMPARABLE* generic:

deferred class *COMPARABLE* [*G*] **feature**

    item: *G*

    put (*new*: *G*) **is do** *item* := *new* **end**

    …Other features (**infix** "<=", *minimum*) as before …

end -- class *COMPARABLE*

The features of the class (**infix** "<=", *minimum*) represent the constraints (the **with** routines of the Ada form). The earlier descendants become extremely simple:

class *INTEGER_COMPARABLE* **inherit**

    COMPARABLE [*INTEGER*]

creation

    put

end

(Note that this is the whole class, not a sketch with features to be added!) The same scheme immediately applies to all other variants such as *STRING_COMPARABLE*.

The technique is indeed fairly simple to apply, leading to one more emulation principle:

> ### Emulating constrained genericity (2)
>
> It is possible to emulate constrained genericity through inheritance and unconstrained genericity, by using wrapper classes and the corresponding wrapper objects.

But we are again paying a price: we need to reintroduce wrapper classes such as *INTEGER_COMPARABLE*. This is less shocking than in the earlier solution, because then we had to pay that price for the unconstrained case as well, even though it is conceptually very simple. Here it seems easier to justify the need for wrapper classes and objects since constrained genericity is a relatively sophisticated idea.

Based on these observations, the notation of this book and compilers for it did not initially — for a little over two years, late 1985 to early 1988 — have special support for constrained genericity. The first edition of this book mentioned the possibility of such support, proposing as an exercise the exact design of an appropriate language construct. But it did not take very long afterwards to realize that most applications were not ready to pay the price of wrapper classes and objects, and to integrate the exercise's solution into the notation; the compilers soon followed.

Exercise 19.5, page 422 of [M 1988]. *Later printings mentioned that the extension had been integrated into the language.*

The notation in question is, of course, the one earlier chapters have used to specify constrained genericity, as in

    class *MATRIX* [*G –> RING_ELEMENT*] …

and

    class *SORTABLE_LIST* [*G –> COMPARABLE*] …

where *RING_ELEMENT* and *COMPARABLE* are the original versions, deferred and non-generic. As noted in the first presentation of this notation in an earlier chapter, it is a remarkable combination of genericity and inheritance, avoiding all the extra baggage of earlier solutions:

- We do not need, like Ada, to use routines as generic parameters (**with** clauses). Only types can be generic parameters; this is simple, consistent and easy to learn.

- We do not need any special wrapper classes and objects. If you want a matrix of integers, you declare it as *MATRIX* [*INTEGER*] and use plain integers to set and retrieve its elements; if you want a sortable list of strings, you declare it as *SORTABLE_LIST* [*STRING*] and use plain strings.

The semantics, as you will remember, is that G represents not an arbitrary type any more, but a type that must conform to the constraint (be based on a descendant class). A generic derivation such as *MATRIX* [*T*] is valid if and only if T is such a type; this is true of *INTEGER* but not, for example, of *STRING*. Similarly, *STRING* will inherit from *COMPARABLE* and hence will be acceptable as an actual generic parameter for the class *SORTABLE_LIST*; but this is not true of a class *COMPLEX* (for complex numbers) which has no associated order relation. The symbol *–>* was chosen, as you will also remember, to evoke the arrow of inheritance diagrams.

> ### Providing constrained genericity
>
> Along with unconstrained genericity, it is desirable to provide constrained genericity by relying on inheritance rules (through the notion of type conformance) to define constraints on permissible actual generic parameters.

As a last detail, you will remember that in this scheme constrained genericity becomes the more basic facility: the unconstrained case, as in *QUEUE* [*G*], is understood as an abbreviation for *QUEUE* [*G* –> *ANY*] where *ANY* denotes the class that serves as ancestor to all developer-defined classes. This has the consequence of defining precisely the operations applicable to *G*: those, coming from *ANY*, which are applicable to all classes, including general-purpose features such as *clone*, *print* and *equal*.

The introduction of constrained genericity provides the final touch to the delicate combination of inheritance and genericity detailed in this chapter. I hope that you will find the result consistent, elegant, and *minimal* in the sense that although no component of the edifice is redundant (as it should indeed always be immediately clear, for any particular circumstance, which of the various possibilities is the appropriate one), removing any one of them would lead us to one of the situations that we found unacceptable or unpleasant in the earlier sections of this appendix: unacceptable because we cannot do what we want, as when we were trying to emulate inheritance with genericity; unpleasant when we could do what we want but at the price of such complications as the use of artificial wrapper classes and inefficient wrapper objects. The proper combination of inheritance and genericity should help make our choices not only acceptable but pleasant too.

B.6 KEY CONCEPTS INTRODUCED IN THIS APPENDIX

- Both genericity and inheritance aim to increase the flexibility of software modules.
- Genericity is a static technique, applicable in O-O and non-O-O contexts, permitting the definition of modules parameterized by types.
- There are two forms of genericity: unconstrained, imposing no requirements on the parameters; constrained, requiring parameters to be equipped with specific operations.
- Inheritance permits incremental module construction, by extension and specialization. It opens the way to polymorphism and dynamic binding.
- It does not seem possible to obtain the power of inheritance through genericity.
- Pure inheritance can be used to emulate genericity, but at the expense of heaviness in expression, performance penalties (mostly space) and type difficulties.
- A good compromise is to combine the full power of inheritance and redefinition with genericity, at least in its unconstrained form. This is achieved by permitting classes to have generic parameters.
- It is also desirable to provide constrained genericity, which relies on the notion of type conformance, itself following from inheritance. Unconstrained genericity can then be viewed as a special case, using the universal class *ANY* as the constraint.
- The resulting construction seems elegant and minimal.

B.7 BIBLIOGRAPHICAL NOTES

The material for this chapter originated with an article at the first OOPSLA conference [M 1986]. The Trellis language [Schaffert 1986] also offered the combination of multiple inheritance with constrained and unconstrained genericity.

EXERCISES

E-B.1 Artificial anchors

The artificial anchor *anchor* is declared as an attribute of class *MATRIX* and thus entails a small run-time space overhead in instances of the class. Is it possible to avoid this overhead by declaring *anchor* as a "once function", whose body may be empty since it will never need to be evaluated? (**Hint**: consider type rules.)

E-B.2 Binary trees and binary search trees

Write a generic "binary tree" class *BINARY_TREE*; a binary tree (or binary node) has some root information and two optional subtrees, left and right. Then consider the notion of "binary search tree" where a new element is inserted on the left of a given node if its information field is less than or equal to the information of that node, and to the right otherwise; this assumes that there is a total order relation on "informations". Write a class *BINARY_SEARCH_TREE* implementing this notion, as a descendant of *BINARY_TREE*. Make the class as general as possible, and its use by a client, for an arbitrary type of "informations" with their specific order relation, as easy as possible.

E-B.3 More usable matrices

Add to the last version obtained for class *MATRIX* two functions, one for access and one for modification, which in contrast to *item* and *put* will allow clients to manipulate a matrix of type *MATRIX* [*G*] in terms of elements of type *G* rather than *RING_ELEMENT* [*G*].

E-B.4 Full queue implementations

Expand the queue example by defining a deferred class *QUEUE*, completing the class of this chapter (now called *ARRAYED_QUEUE*, inheriting from *QUEUE* and *ARRAY*, and with proper postconditions), and adding a class *LINKED_QUEUE* for the linked list implementation (based on inheritance from *LINKED_LIST* and *QUEUE*).

C

Principles, rules, precepts and definitions

D

A glossary of object technology

This glossary provides brief definitions of the principal terms of object technology, discussed in detail in the rest of this book. *Italics font* in a definition marks a term or phrase, other than the ubiquitous "class" and "object", that is itself the subject of another definition.

Abstract class

See *deferred class*.

Abstract data type (ADT)

A set of mathematical elements specified by listing the functions applicable to all these elements and the formal properties of these functions.

Abstract object

An element of an *ADT*.

Ancestor (of a class)

The class itself, or one of its direct or indirect parents.

Assertion

A formal condition describing the semantic properties of software elements, especially routines and loops. Used in expressing *contracts*. Assertions include in particular *preconditions*, *postconditions*, *class invariants* and *loop invariants*.

Assignment attempt

An operation that conditionally attaches an object to a reference, only if the object's type *conforms* to the type declared for the corresponding *entity*.

Asynchronous call

A call which lets its caller proceed before it completes. Antonym: *synchronous call*.

Attribute

The description of a *field* present in all the instances of a class. Along with the *routine*, one of the two forms of *feature*.

Behavior class

A class, usually *deferred*, describing a set of adaptable behaviors through *effective routines* relying on some components (usually *deferred features*) that may be *redeclared* to capture specific variants of the general behaviors.

Class
A partially or totally implemented abstract data type. Serves both as a *module* and as a *type* (or type pattern if the class is *generic*.)

Class invariant
An *assertion* which must be satisfied on creation of every instance of a class, and preserved by every exported routine of the class, so that it will be satisfied by all instances of the class whenever they are externally observable.

Client
A class that uses the features of another, its *supplier*, on the basis of the supplier's interface specification (*contract*).

Cluster
A group of related classes or, recursively, of related clusters.

Component
See *reusable software component*.

Concurrent
Able to use two or more *processors*. Antonym: *sequential*.

Conformance
A relation between types. A type conforms to another if it is derived from it by inheritance.

Constrained genericity
A form of *genericity* where a formal generic parameter represents not an arbitrary type, but one that is required to *conform* to a certain type, known as the constraint. See *constrained genericity*.

Container data structure
An *object* whose primary use is to provide access to a number of other objects. Examples include lists, queues, stacks, arrays.

Contract
The set of precise conditions that govern the relations between a *supplier* class and its *clients*. The contract for a class includes individual contracts for the exported routines of the class, represented by preconditions and postconditions, and the global class properties, represented by the class invariant. See also *Design by Contract*.

Contravariance
The policy allowing a feature *redeclaration* to change the *signature* so that a new result type will *conform* to the original but the original argument types conform to the new. See also: *covariance*, *novariance*.

Covariance
The policy allowing a feature *redeclaration* to change the *signature* so that the new types of both arguments and result *conform* to the originals. See also: *contravariance*, *novariance*.

Current object (or: current instance)
During the execution of an object-oriented software system, the target of the most recently started routine call.

Defensive programming

A technique of fighting potential errors by making every module check for many possible consistency conditions, even if this causes redundancy of checks performed by *clients* and *suppliers*. Contradicts *Design by Contract*.

Deferred class

A class which has at least one *deferred feature*. Antonym: *effective class*.

Deferred feature

A feature which, in a certain class, has a specification but no implementation. May be declared as deferred in the class itself, or inherited as deferred and not *effected* in the class. Antonym: *effective feature*.

Descendant (of a class)

The class itself, or one of its direct or indirect heirs.

Design by Contract

A method of software construction that designs the components of a *system* so that they will cooperate on the basis of precisely defined *contracts*. See also: *defensive programming*.

Direct instance (of a class)

An object built according to the mold defined by the class.

Dynamic

Occurring during the execution of a *system*. See also *run time*. Antonym: *static*.

Dynamic binding

The guarantee that every execution of an operation will select the correct version of the operation, based on the type of the operation's target.

Dynamic typing

The policy whereby applicability of operations to their target objects is only checked at run time, prior to executing each operation.

Effect

A class effects a feature if it inherits it in *deferred* form and provides an *effecting* for that feature.

Effecting

A *redeclaration* which provides an implementation (as *attribute* or *routine*) of a feature inherited in *deferred* form.

Effective class

A class which only has *effective features* (that is to say, does not introduce any *deferred feature*, and, if it inherits any deferred feature, effects it). Antonym: *deferred class*.

Effective feature

A feature declared with an implementation — either as a routine which is not *deferred*, or as an *attribute*. Antonym: *deferred feature*.

Encapsulation

See *information hiding*.

Entity

A name in the software text that denotes a run-time value (*object* or *reference*).

Event-driven computation

A style of software construction where developers define the control structure by listing possible external events and the system's response to each of them, rather than by specifying a pre-ordained sequence of steps.

Exception

The inability of a routine to achieve its *contract* through one of its possible strategies. May result in particular from a *failure* of a routine called by the original routine. Will be treated as *resumption*, *organized panic* or *false alarm*.

Exporting a feature

Making the feature available to *clients*. Exports may be selective (to specified classes only) or general.

Extendibility

The ability of a software system to be changed easily in response to different choices of requirements, architecture, algorithms or data structures.

Failure

The inability of a routine's execution to fulfill the routine's *contract*. Must trigger an *exception*.

False alarm

Along with *resumption* and *organized panic*, one of the three possible responses to an *exception*; resumes the execution of the current strategy, possibly after taking some corrective action.

Feature renaming

The attribution, by a class, of a new name to an inherited feature, not changing any other property. See also *redeclaration*.

Field

One of the values making up an *object*.

Function

A routine which returns a result. (The other form of routine is the *procedure*.)

Garbage collection

A facility provided by the *runtime* to recycle the memory space used by objects that have become useless. Garbage collection is automatic, that is to say does not require any change to the text of the *systems* whose objects are being recycled.

Generalization

The process of turning specialized program elements into general-purpose, reusable software components.

Generating class

Same as *generator*.

Generator (of an object)

The class of which the object is a *direct instance*.

Generic class

A class having formal parameters representing types. Such a class will yield a type only through *generic derivation*.

Generic derivation

The process of providing a type for each formal generic parameter of a *generic class*, yielding a type as a result.

Genericity

The support, by a software notation, for type-parameterized modules; specifically, in an O-O notation, for *generic classes*. Can be *unconstrained* or *constrained*.

Heir (of a class)

A class that inherits from the given class. Antonym: *parent*.

Identity

See *object identity*.

Information hiding

The ability to prevent certain aspects of a class from being accessible to its clients, through an explicit *exporting* policy and through reliance on the *short form* as the primary vehicle for class documentation.

Inheritance

A mechanism whereby a class is defined in reference to others, adding all their features to its own.

Instance (of a class)

An object built according to the mold defined by the class or any one of its proper descendants. See also *direct instance, proper descendant, generator*.

Instance variable

Smalltalk term for attribute.

Interface (of a class)

See *contract, abstract data type*.

Invariant

See *class invariant, loop invariant*.

Iterator

A control structure describing preordained sequencing of some actions but not defining the actions themselves. Iterators often apply to data structures, such as an iterator describing the traversal of a list or a tree.

Loop invariant

An *assertion* which must be satisfied prior to the first execution of a loop, and preserved by every iteration, so that it will hold on loop termination.

Loop variant

An integer expression which must be non-negative prior to the first execution of a loop, and decreased by every iteration, so that it will garantee loop termination.

Message

Routine call.

Metaclass

A class whose instances are classes themselves.

Method

Smalltalk term for routine.

Module

A unit of software decomposition. In the object-oriented approach, classes provide the basic form of module.

Multiple inheritance

The unrestricted form of inheritance, whereby a class may have any number of parents. Antonym: *single inheritance*.

Non-separate

Antonym of *separate*.

Novariance

The policy allowing prohibiting any feature *redeclaration* from changing the *signature*. See also: *contravariance*, *covariance*.

Object

A run-time data structure made of zero or more values, called *fields*, and serving as the computer representation of an *abstract object*. Every object is an instance of some class.

Object identity

A property that uniquely identifies an object independently of its current contents (*fields*).

Object-oriented

Built from *classes*, *assertions*, *genericity*, *inheritance*, *polymorphism* and *dynamic binding*.

Object-oriented analysis

The application of *object-oriented* concepts to the modeling of problems and systems from both software and non-software domains.

Object-oriented database

A repository of *persistent objects*, permitting their storage and retrieval on the basis of *object-oriented* concepts, and supporting database properties such as concurrent access, locking and transactions.

Object-oriented design

The process of building the architecture of *systems* through *object-oriented* concepts.

Object-oriented implementation

The process of building executable software systems through *object-oriented* concepts. Differs from *object-oriented design* primarily by the level of abstraction.

Organized panic

Along with *resumption* and *false alarm*, one of the three possible responses to an *exception*; abandons the execution of the current strategy, triggering an exception in the caller, after restoring the *class invariant* for the *current object*.

Overloading

The ability to let a feature name denote two or more operations.

Package

A module of non-object-oriented languages such as Ada, providing encapsulation of a set of variables and routines.

Parallel

See *concurrent*.

Parameterized class

See *generic class*.

Parent (of a class)

A class from which the given class inherits. Antonym: *heir*.

Persistence

The ability of a software development environment or language to make objects *persistent* and support the retrieval of persistent objects for use by systems.

Persistent object

An object that (through storage in a file or database or transmission across a network) survives executions of systems that create or manipulate it. Antonym: *transient object*.

Polymorphic data structure

A *container data structure* hosting objects of two or more possible types.

Polymorphism

The ability for an element of the software text to denote, at run time, objects of two or more possible types.

Postcondition

An *assertion* attached to a routine, which must be guaranteed by the routine's body on return from any call to the routine if the *precondition* was satisfied on entry. Part of the *contract* governing the routine.

Precondition

An *assertion* attached to a routine, which must be guaranteed by every client prior to any call to the routine. Part of the *contract* governing the routine.

Predicate

See *assertion*.

Procedure

A routine which does not return a result. (The other form of routine is the *function*.)

Processor

A mechanism providing a single thread of computation. May be a physical device, such as the CPU of a computer, or a software device, such as a task or thread of an operating system.

Program

See *system*.

Proper ancestor (of a class)
> A direct or indirect parent of the class.

Proper descendant (of a class)
> A direct or indirect heir of the class.

Redeclaration
> A feature declaration which, instead of introducing a new feature, adapts some properties (such as the *signature*, *precondition*, *postcondition*, implementation, *deferred/effective* status, but not the name) of a feature inherited from a *parent*. A redeclaration may be a *redefinition* or an *effecting*. See also *feature renaming*.

Redefinition
> A *redeclaration* which is not an *effecting*, that is to say, changes some properties of a feature inherited as effective, or changes the specification of a feature inherited as *deferred* while leaving it deferred.

Reference
> A run-time value that uniquely identifies an object.

Renaming
> See *feature renaming*.

Retrying
> Along with *organized panic* and *false alarm*, one of the three possible responses to an *exception*; tries a new strategy for achieving the routine's *contract*.

Reusability
> The ability of a software development method to yield software elements that can be used in many different applications, and to support a software development process relying on pre-existing *reusable software components*.

Reusable software component
> An element of software that can be used by many different applications.

Reversible development
> A software development process that lets insights gained in later phases affect the results obtained in earlier phases. Normally part of a *seamless development* process.

Root class
> The *generator* of a system's *root object*. Executing the system means creating an instance of the root class (the root object), and calling a creation procedure on that instance.

Root object
> The first object created in the execution of a system.

Routine
> A computation defined in a class, and applicable to the instances of that class. Along with the *attribute*, one of the two forms of *feature*.

Runtime (noun, one word)
> Any set of facilities supporting the execution of systems. See also next entry.

Run time (noun, two words)

The time when a *system* is being executed. Also used as an adjective, with a hyphen, as in "the run-time value of an *entity*". See also *dynamic* and previous entry.

Schema evolution

Change to one or more classes of which some *persistent* instances exist.

Seamless development

A software development process which uses a uniform method and notation throughout all activities, such as problem modeling and analysis, design, implementation and maintenance. See also *reversible development*.

Selective export

See *exporting a feature*.

Separate

Handled by a different *processor*. Antonym: non-separate.

Sequential

Running on only one *processor*. Antonym: *concurrent*.

Short form (of a class)

A form of class documentation generated from the class text, showing only interface properties of the class. The short form documents the *contract* attached to the class and the underlying *abstract data type*.

Signature (of a feature)

The type part of the feature's specification. For an attribute or a function, includes the result type; for a routine, includes the number of arguments and the type of each.

Single inheritance

A restricted form of inheritance whereby each class may have at most one parent. Antonym: *multiple inheritance*.

Software component

See *reusable software component*.

Specification (of a class)

The *short form* of the class.

Specification (of a feature)

The properties of a feature that are relevant to a client. Includes the name, *signature*, header comment and *contract* of the feature.

Subcontract

The ability of a class to let some proper *descendant* handle some of its feature calls, thanks to *redeclaration* and *dynamic binding*.

Supplier

A class that provides another, its *client*, with features to be used through an interface specification (*contract*).

Static

Applying to the text of a *system*, not to a particular execution. Antonym: *dynamic*.

Static binding

The premature choice of operation variant, resulting in possibly wrong results and (in favorable cases) run-time system crash.

Static typing

The ability to check, on the basis of the software text alone, that no execution of a system will ever try to apply to an object an operation that is not applicable to that object.

Synchronous call

A call which forces the caller to wait until it completes. Antonym: *asynchronous call*.

System

A set of classes that can be assembled to produce an executable result.

Template

C++ term for *generic class* (for *unconstrained genericity* only).

Traitor

A reference to a *separate* object, associated in the software text with an *entity* that is declared as non-separate.

Transient object

An object that exists only during the execution of the system that creates it. Antonym: *persistent object*.

Type

The description of a set of objects equipped with certain operations. In the object-oriented approach every type is based on a class.

Type checking, typing

See *static typing*, *dynamic typing*.

Unconstrained genericity

A form of *genericity* where a formal generic parameter represents an arbitrary type. See *constrained genericity*.

Variant

See *loop variant*.

E

Bibliography

This bibliography has two parts: works by other authors; works by the author of the present book. See also, in the chapter on inheritance methodology (page 868), a list of references on classification in the biological sciences.

E.1 WORKS BY OTHER AUTHORS

[Abrial 1980]
Jean-Raymond Abrial: *The Specification Language Z: Syntax and "Semantics"*, Oxford University Computing Laboratory, Programming Research Group Technical Report, Oxford, April 1980.

[Abrial 1980a]
Jean-Raymond Abrial, Stephen A.Schuman and Bertrand Meyer: *A Specification Language*, in *On the Construction of Programs*, eds. R. McNaughten and R.C. McKeag, Cambridge University Press, 1980.

[Ada 95-Web]
Ada 95 Reference Manual: Language and Standard Library, on-line at *http://lglwww.epfl.ch/Ada/LRM/9X/rm9x/rm9x-toc.html*.

[ADB 1995]
Matisse 2.3 Tutorial, Report DE/95/03/0022-M2DOC-TUA, ADB S.A., Paris, January 1995.

[Agha 1986]
Gul Agha: *ACTORS: A Model of Concurrent Computation in Distributed Systems*; MIT Press, Cambridge (Mass.), 1986.

[Agha 1988]
Gul Agha, Peter Wegner and Akinori Yonezawa (eds.): *Proceeding of the ACM SIGPLAN Workshop on Object-Based Concurrent Programming*, San Diego, 26-27 September, 1988; in *ACM SIGPLAN Notices*, vol. 24, no. 4, 1988.

[Agha 1990]
Gul Agha: *Concurrent Object-Oriented Programming*, in *Communications of the ACM*, vol. 33, no. 9, September 1990, pages 125-141.

[Agha 1991]
Gul Agha, Carl Hewitt, Peter Wegner and Akinori Yonezawa (eds.): *Proceedings of the ECOOP-OOPSLA Workshop on Object-Based Concurrent Programming*, Ottawa, 21-22 October 1990; in *OOPS Messenger (ACM)*, vol. 2, no. 2, April 1991.

[Agha 1993]
Gul Agha, Peter Wegner and Akinori Yonezawa (eds.): *Research Directions in Concurrent Object-Oriented Programming*, MIT Press, Cambridge (Mass.), 1993.

[Aho 1974]
Alfred V. Aho , John E. Hopcroft and Jeffrey D. Ullman: *The Design and Analysis of Computer Algorithms*, Addison-Wesley, Reading (Mass.), 1974.

[Aho 1983]
   Alfred V. Aho , John E. Hopcroft and Jeffrey D. Ullman: *Data Structures and Algorithms*, Addison-Wesley, Reading (Mass.), 1983.

[Alagar 1995]
   Vangalur S. Alagar and Rokia Missaoui (eds.): *Object-Oriented Technology for Database and Software Systems*, World Scientific Publishers, Singapore, 1995.

[America 1989]
   Pierre America and Marcel Beemster: *A portable implementation of the language POOL*; in *TOOLS 1* (*Proceedings of TOOLS EUROPE 1989*), ed. Jean Bézivin, SOL, Paris, 1989, pages 347-353.

[America 1989a]
   Pierre America: *Book Review*: *"Object-Oriented Software Construction"* (a review of the first edition of the present book, [M 1988]), *Science of Computer Programming*, vol. 12, 1989, pages 83-92.

[ANSI 1983]
   ANSI (American National Standards Institute) and US Government Department of Defense, Ada Joint Program Office: *Military Standard*: *Ada Programming Language*, ANSI/MIL-STD-1815A-1983, February 17, 1983.

[Arnold 1996]
   Ken Arnold and James Gosling: *The Java Programming Language*, Addison-Wesley, Reading (Mass.), 1996.

[Atkinson 1989]
   M. Atkinson, F. Bancilhon, D. DeWitt, K. Dittrich, D. Maier, and S. Zdonik: *The Object-Oriented Database System Manifesto*, in *Proc. First Intl. Conf. on Deductive and Object-Oriented Databases*, Kyoto, Japan, December 1989, pages 223-40. On-line: *http://www.cs.cmu.edu/Web/People/clamen/OODBMS/Manifesto.html*. Also in [Bancilhon 1992].

[Atkinson 1991]
   Colin Atkinson: *Object-Oriented Reuse, Concurrency and Distribution*, ACM Press (Addison Wesley), New York, 1991.

[Avotins 1995]
   Jon Avotins, Christine Mingins and Heinz Schmidt: *Yes! An Object-Oriented Compiler Compiler*, in *TOOLS 17* (*Technology of Object-Oriented Languages and Systems*), eds. Raimund Ege, Madhu Singh, and Bertrand Meyer, Prentice Hall, Englewood Cliffs (N.J.) 1995, pages 191-205.

[Bachelard 1960]
   Gaston Bachelard: *La Formation de l'Esprit scientifique*: *Contribution à une Psychanalyse de la Connaissance objective*, Lib. Phil. J. Vrin, Paris, 1960.

[Baker 1972]
   F. Terry Baker: *Chief Programmer Team Management of Production Programming*, in *IBM Systems Journal*, vol. 11, no. 1, 1972, pages 56-73.

[Balter 1991]
   R. Balter et al.: *Architecture and Implementation of Guide, an Object-Oriented Distributed System*, in *Computing Systems*, vol. 4, 1991.

[Bancilhon 1992]
   François Bancilhon, Claude Delobel and P. Kanellakis (eds.): *Building an Object-Oriented Database System*: *The Story of O2*, Morgan Kaufmann Publishers, Menlo Park (Calif.), 1992.

[Baudoin 1996]
   Claude Baudoin and Glenn Hollowell: *Realizing the Object-Oriented Lifecycle*, Prentice Hall Object-Oriented Series, Upper Saddle River (N.J.), 1996.

[Ben Ari 1990]
   Mordechai Ben Ari: *Principles of Concurrent and Distributed Programming*, Prentice Hall, Hemel Hempstead (U.K.), 1990.

[Bert 1983]

Didier Bert: *Manuel de Référence du Langage LPG, Version 1.2*, Rapport R-408, IFIAG, IMAG Institute, Grenoble University, December 1983.

[Bertino 1993]

Elisa Bertino and Lorenzo Martino: *Object-Oriented Database Systems, Concepts and Architecture*, Addison-Wesley, Reading (Mass.), 1993.

[Beta-Web]

Mjølner BETA System Home page at *http://www.mjolner.dk/*.

[Bielak 1993]

Richard Bielak and James McKim: *The Many Faces of a Class*, in *TOOLS 11* (*Technology of Object-Oriented Languages and Systems*), eds. Raimund Ege, Madhu Singh and Bertrand Meyer, Prentice Hall, Englewood Cliffs (N.J.), 1993, pages 153-161.

[Bielak 1994]

Richard Bielak and James McKim: *Let There be … Objects*, in *Journal of Object-Oriented Programming*, vol. 7, no. 6, October 1994, pages 71-74.

[Biggerstaff 1984]

Ted J. Biggerstaff and Alan J. Perlis (Eds): *Special Issue on Software Reusability*, in *IEEE Transactions on Software Engineering*, vol. SE-10, no. 5, September 1984, pages 474-609.

[Biggerstaff 1989]

Ted J. Biggerstaff and Alan J. Perlis (eds): *Software Reusability*, ACM Press (Addison-Wesley), New York, 1989. (Two volumes.)

[Birtwistle 1973]

Graham M. Birtwistle, Ole-Johan Dahl, Bjorn Myhrhaug and Kristen Nygaard: *Simula Begin*, Studentliteratur (Lund, Sweden) and Petrocelli/Charter (New York) 1973. (This is the imprint on my copy, although every bibliography I have seen lists the publisher as "Auerbach publishers".)

[Bobrow 1982]

Daniel G. Bobrow and Mark J. Stefik: *LOOPS: an Object-Oriented Programming System for Interlisp*, Xerox PARC, 1982.

[Boehm 1978]

Barry W. Boehm, J.R. Brown, G. McLeod, Myron Lipow and M. Merrit: *Characteristics of Software Quality*, TRW Series of Software Technology, North-Holland Publishing Co., Amsterdam, 1978.

[Boehm 1979]

Barry W. Boehm: *Software Engineering — As It Is*, in *Proceedings of the 4th International Conference on Software Engineering*, Munich, IEEE, September 1979, pages 11-21.

[Boehm 1981]

Barry W. Boehm: *Software Engineering Economics*, Prentice Hall, Englewood Cliffs (N.J.), 1981.

[Boehm 1988]

Barry W. Boehm: *A Spiral Model of Software Development and Enhancement*, in *IEEE Computer*, no. 5, vol. 21, May 1988, pages 61-72.

[Booch 1986]

Grady Booch: *Object-Oriented Development*, in *IEEE Transactions on Software Engineering*, vol. SE-12, no. 2, pages 211-221, February 1986.

[Booch 1986a]

Grady Booch: *Software Engineering with Ada*, Benjamin/Cummings Publishing Co., Menlo Park (Calif.), 1983 (new edition, 1986).

[Booch 1994]

Grady Booch: *Object-Oriented Analysis and Design With Applications, Second Edition*, Benjamin/Cummings, Menlo Park (Calif.), 1994.

[Brachman 1983]
Ronald J. Brachman: *What IS-A and isn't: An Analysis of Taxonomic Links in Semantic Networks*, in *Computer (IEEE)*, vol. 16, no. 10, pages 67-73, October 1983.

[Breu 1995]
Ruth Breu and Michael Breu: *A Methodology of Inheritance*, in *Software — Concepts and Tools* (Springer-Verlag), vol. 16, no. 3, 1995, pages 113-123.

[Bright 1995]
Walter Bright: *Optimizing C++ Code*, in *Dr. Dobb's Journal*, no. 233, August 1995, pages 88-89.

[Brooks 1974]
Fred P. Brooks: *The Mythical Man-Month*, Addison-Wesley, Reading (Mass.), 1974.

[Bruce 1997]
Kim B. Bruce: *Typing in Object-Oriented languages: Achieving Expressiveness and Safety*, in *ACM Computing Surveys*, to appear.

[Burstall 1977]
Rod M. Burstall and Joseph A. Goguen: *Putting Theories Together to Make Specifications*, in *Proceedings of 5th International Joint Conference on Artificial Intelligence*, Cambridge (Mass.), 1977, pages 1045-1058.

[Burstall 1981]
Rod M. Burstall and Joseph A. Goguen: *An Informal Introduction to Specifications using Clear*, in *The Correctness Problem in Computer Science*, eds. R. S. Boyer and J. S. Moore, Academic Press, London, 1981, pages 185-213.

[Buxton 1976]
John M. Buxton, Peter Naur and Brian Randell (eds.) *Software Engineering Concepts and Techniques* (Proceedings of 1968 NATO Conference on Software Engineering), Van Nostrand Reinhold, New York, 1976.

[Campbell 1974]
Roy H. Campbell and A. Nico Habermann: *The Specification of Process Synchronization by Path Expressions*, Lecture Notes in Computer Science 16, Springer-Verlag, Berlin-New York, 1974, pp. 89-102.

[Cannon 1980]
H. I. Cannon: *Flavors*, Technical Report, MIT Artificial Intelligence Laboratory, Cambridge (Mass.), 1980.

[Cardelli 1984]
Luca Cardelli: *A Semantics of Multiple Inheritance*, in *Semantics of Data Types*, eds. Gilles Kahn, David B. McQueen and Gordon Plotkin, Lecture Notes in Computer Science 173, Springer-Verlag, Berlin-New York, 1984, pages 51-67. Revised version in *Information and Computation*, no. 76, 1988, pages 138-164. Also in [Zdonik 1990], pages 59-83.

[Cardelli 1984a]
Luca Cardelli: *Basic Polymorphic Typechecking*, AT&T Bell Laboratories Computing Science Technical Report, 1984. Revised version in *Science of Computer Programming*, vol. 8, no. 2, 1987.

[Cardelli 1985]
Luca Cardelli and Peter Wegner: *On understanding Types, Data Abstraction and Polymorphism*, in *ACM Computing Surveys*, vol. 17, no. 4, 1985, pages 471-522.

[Caromel 1989]
Denis Caromel: *Service, Asynchrony, and Wait-by-Necessity*, in *Journal of Object-Oriented Programming*, vol. 2, no. 4, Nov.-Dec. 1989, pp. 12-18.

[Caromel 1993]
Denis Caromel: *Toward a Method of Object-Oriented Concurrent Programming*, in [M 1993a], pages 90-102.

[Carriero 1990]
Nicholas Carriero and David Gelernter: *How to Write Parallel Programs: A First Course*, MIT Press, Cambridge (Mass.), 1990.

[Castagna 1995]
Giuseppe Castagna: *Covariance and Contravariance*: *Conflict without a Cause*, in *ACM Transactions on Programming Languages and Systems*, vol. 17, no. 3, 1995, pages 431-447.

[Castagna 1996]
Giuseppe Castagna: *Le Modèle fondé sur la Surcharge* : *Une Visite Guidée* (The Overloading-Based Model: A Guided Tour), in *TSI (Technique et Sciences Informatiques)*, vol. 15, no. 6, 1996.

[Cattell 1993]
R. G. G. Cattell (ed.): *The Object Database Standard*: *ODMG-93*, Morgan Kaufmann, Menlo Park (Calif.), 1993.

[Chambers 1991]
Craig Chambers, David Ungar, Bay-Wei Change and Urs Hölzle: *Parents are Shared Parts of Objects*: *Inheritance and Encapsulation in SELF*, in *Lisp and Symbolic Computation*: *An International Journal*, vol. 4, no. 3, 1991.

[Chen 1976]
Peter P.S. Chen: *The Entity-Relationship model — Towards a Unified View of Data*, in *ACM Transactions on Database Systems*, vol. 1, no. 1, March 1976, pages 9-36.

[Coad 1990]
Peter Coad and Edward Nash Yourdon: *Object-Oriented Analysis*, Prentice Hall, Englewood Cliffs (N.J.), 1990.

[Codd 1970]
E.F. Codd: *A Relational Model of Data for Large Shared Data Banks*, in *Communications of the ACM*, vol. 13, no. 6, June 1970, pages 377- 387.

[Cohen 1984]
Jacques Cohen and Tim Hickey: *Performance Analysis of On-the-Fly Garbage Collection*, in *Communications of the ACM*, vol. 27, no. 11, November 198, pages 1143-1154.

[Cohen 1991]
Bernard Cohen: *The Inverted Curriculum*, Report, National Economic Development Council, London, 1991.

[Coleman 1994]
Derek Coleman et al.: *Object-Oriented Development*: *The Fusion Method*, Prentice Hall Object-Oriented Series, Englewood Cliffs (N.J.), 1994.

[Computer 1996]
Gurus Share Insights on Objects (interview with Grady Booch, Ivar Jacobson and James Rumbaugh), in *Computer* (IEEE), Object Technology department, vol. 29, no. 6, June 1996, pages 95-98.

[Cook 1989]
William R. Cook: *A Proposal for Making Eiffel Type-Safe*, in *ECOOP 89* (Proceedings of 1989 European Conference on Object-Oriented Programming, Nottingham, U.K., 10-14 July 1989), ed. Stephen Cook, Cambridge University Press, 1989, pages 57-70.

[Cook 1994]
Steve Cook and John Daniels: *Designing Object Systems*, Prentice Hall Object-Oriented Series, Hemel Hempstead (U.K.), 1994.

[Cox 1984]
Brad J. Cox: *Message/Object Programming*: *An Evolutionary Change in Programming Technology*, in *IEEE Software*, vol. 1, no. 1, January 1984, pages 50-69.

[Cox 1986]
Brad Cox et al.: *User Interface Frameworks* (position papers for a panel), in *OOPSLA '86 Conference Proceedings*, Portland (Oreg.), Sept. 29-Oct. 2, 1986, published as *SIGPLAN Notices*, vol. 21, no. 11, Nov. 1986, pages 497-501.

[Cox 1990]
Brad J. Cox and Andrew J. Novobilski: *Object-Oriented Programming*: *An Evolutionary Approach*, *2nd edition.*, Addison-Wesley, Reading (Mass.), 1990. (Original edition, first author only: 1986.)

[Cox 1992]
Brad J. Cox: *Superdistribution and Electronic Objects*, in *Dr. Dobb's Journal*, no. 193, October 1992, pages 44-48.

[Cristian 1985]
Flaviu Cristian: *On Exceptions, Failures and Errors*, in *Technology and Science of Informatics*, vol. 4, no. 4, July-August 1985.

[Curry 1984]
Gael A. Curry and Robert M. Ayers: *Experience with Traits in the Xerox Star Workstation*, in *IEEE Transactions on Software Engineering*, vol. SE-10, no. 5, September 1984, pages 519-527.

[Dahl 1966]
Ole-Johan Dahl and Kristen Nygaard: *SIMULA — An Algol-based Simulation Language*, in *Communications of the ACM*, vol. 9, no. 9, September 1966, pages 671-678

[Dahl 1970]
Ole-Johan Dahl, Bjorn Myrhaug and Kristen Nygaard: (Simula 67) *Common Base Language*, Norsk Regnesentral (Norwegian Computing Center), Publication N. S-22, Oslo, October 1970. (Revised version, February 1984.)

[Dahl 1972]
Ole-Johan Dahl and C.A.R. Hoare: *Hierarchical Program Structures*, in Dahl, Dijkstra, Hoare, *Structured Programming*, Academic Press, 1972, pages 175-220

[Dami-Web]
Web page at *http://cuiwww.unige.ch/OSG/Hop/types.html*, from 1996 on (list of links to articles and researchers on O-O type theory.)

[Date 1995]
Chris J. Date: *An Introduction to Database Systems*, sixth edition, Addison-Wesley, Reading (Mass.), 1995.

[Dekleva 1992]
Sasa M. Dekleva: *Software Maintenance: 1990 Status*, in *Software Maintenance: Research and Practice*, John Wiley and Sons, New York, vol. 4, 1992.

[DeMarco 1978]
Tom DeMarco: *Structured Analysis and System Specification*, Yourdon Press, New York, 1978.

[DeMarco 1988]
Tom DeMarco and Tim Lister: *Peopleware*, Dorset Publishing, New York, 1988.

[DeRemer 1976]
Frank DeRemer and Hans H. Kron: *Programming-in-the-Large Versus Programming-in-the-Small*, in *IEEE Transactions on Software Engineering*, vol. SE-2, no. 2, June 1976, pages 80-86.

[Dijkstra 1968]
Edsger W. Dijkstra: *Go To Statement Considered Harmful*, in *Communications of the ACM*, vol. 15, no. 10, October 1972, pages 859-866.

[Dijkstra 1968a]
Edsger W. Dijkstra: *Co-operating Sequential Processes*, in *Programming Languages*, ed. F. Genuys, Academic Press, New York, 1968. pp. 43-112.

[Dijkstra 1976]
Edsger W. Dijkstra: *A Discipline of Programming*, Prentice Hall, Englewood Cliffs (N.J.), 1976.

[Dijkstra 1978]
E. W. Dijkstra, L. Lamport, A.J. Martin, C.S. Scholten and E.F.M. Steffens: *On-the-Fly Garbage Collection: An Exercise in Cooperation*, in *Communications of the ACM*, vol. 21, no. 11, November 1978 , pages 966-975.

[Dubois 1997]
Paul Dubois: *Object Technology for Scientific Computing*, Prentice Hall, Englewood Cliffs (N.J.) 1997.

[Duke 1991]
Roger Duke, Paul King, Gordon Rose and Graeme Smith: *The Object-Z Specification Language*, in *TOOLS 5 (Technology of Object-Oriented Languages and Systems)*, Santa Barbara, (Calif.), 1991, eds. Tim Korson, Vijay Vaishnavi and Bertrand Meyer, Prentice Hall, Englewood Cliffs (N.J.), 1991, pages 465-483.

[Eliëns 1995]
Anton Eliëns: *Principles of Object-Oriented Software Development*, Addison-Wesley, Reading (Mass.), 1995.

[Ellis 1990]

Margaret Ellis and Bjarne Stroustrup: *The Annotated C++ Reference Manual*, Addison-Wesley, Reading (Mass.), 1990.

[Elmasri 1989]

Ramez Elmasri and Shamkant B. Navathe: *Fundamentals of Database Systems*, Benjamin Cummings, Redwood City (Calif.), 1989.

[Embley 1992]

D.W. Embley, B.D. Kurtz, and S.N. Woodfield: *Object-oriented Systems Analysis: A Model-driven Approach*, Prentice-Hall, Englewood Cliffs (N.J.), 1992.

[Feldman 1979]

Stuart I. Feldman: *Make — A Program for Maintaining Computer Programs*, in *Software, Practice and Experience*, vol. 9, 1979, pages 255-265.

[Feldman 1993]

Jerome A. Feldman, Chu-Cheow Lim and Thomas Rauber: *The Shared-Memory Language pSather on a Distributed-Memory Multiprocessor*; in *Proc. Workshop on Languages, Compilers and Run-Time Environments for Distributed Memory Multiprocessors, SIGPLAN Notices*, vol. 28, no. 1, January 1993, pages 17-20.

[Feldman-Web]

Michael B. Feldman and Magnus Kempe (eds.): *Ada 95 Textbooks: Brief Reviews*, on-line at *http://www.adahome.com/Resources/Books/ada95reviews.html*, 1996 on.

[Firesmith 1995]

Donald G. Firesmith and Edward M. Eyckholt: *Dictionary of Object Technology, the Definitive Desk Reference*, SIGS Books, New York, 1995.

[Floyd 1967]

Robert W. Floyd: *Assigning Meanings to Programs*, in *Proc. American Mathematical Society Symp. in Applied Mathematics*, vol. 19, 1967, pages 19-31.

[Futatsugi 1985]

Kokichi Futatsugi, Joseph A. Goguen, Jean-Pierre Jouannaud and José Meseguer: *Principles of OBJ2*, in *Proceedings of the 1985 ACM Symposium on Principles of Programming Languages*, vol. 12, 1985, pages 52-66.

[Gamma 1995]

Erich Gamma, Richard Helm, Ralph Johnson, and John Vlissides: *Design Patterns: Elements of Reusable Object-Oriented Software*, Addison-Wesley, Reading (Mass.), 1995.

[Gannon 1975]

John D. Gannon and Jim J. Horning: *Language Design for Programming Reliability*, in *IEEE Transactions on Software Engineering*, vol. SE-1, no. 2, June 1975.

[Geschke 1975]

C.M. Geschke and J.G. Mitchell: *On the Problem of Uniform References to Data Structures*, in *SIGPLAN Notices*, vol. 10, no. 6, June 1975, pages 31-42.

[Ghezzi 1991]

Carlo Ghezzi, Mehdi Jazayeri, and Dino Mandrioli: *Fundamentals of Software Engineering*, Prentice Hall, Englewood Cliffs (N.J.), 1991.

[Ghezzi 1997]

Carlo Ghezzi and Mehdi Jazayeri: *Programming Language Structures, second edition*, John Wiley and Sons, New York, 1987; third edition announced for 1997.

[Gil 1994]

Joseph Gil and Ricardo Szmit: *Software Boards via Configurable Objects*, in *TOOLS 14 (Technology of Object-Oriented Languages and Systems)*, Santa Barbara (California), 1994, eds Raimund Ege, Madhu Singh and Bertrand Meyer, Prentice Hall, Englewood Cliffs (N.J.), 1994, pages 303-317.

[Gindre 1989]
Cyrille Gindre and Frédérique Sada: *A Development in Eiffel: Design and Implementation of a Network Simulator*, in *Journal of Object-Oriented Programming*, vol. 2, no. 2, May 1989, pages 27-33, Revised version in [M 1992a], pages 199-214.

[Girod 1991]
Xavier Girod: *Conception par Objets — MECANO: Une Méthode et un Environnement de Construction d'Appplications par Objets*, PhD Thesis, Université Joseph Fourier (Grenoble), 21 June 1991.

[Goguen 1978]
Joseph A. Goguen, J. W. Thatcher and E. G. Wagner: *An Initial Algebra Approach to the Specification, Correctness and Implementation of Abstract Data Types*, in Raymond T. Yeh (ed.), *Current Trends in Programming Methodology*, vol. 4, Prentice Hall, Englewood Cliffs (N.J.), 1978, pages 80-149.

[Goguen 1984]
Joseph A. Goguen: *Parameterized Programming*, in *IEEE Transactions on Software Engineering*, vol. SE-10, no. 5, September 1984, pages 528-543.

[Goldberg 1976]
Adele Goldberg and Alan Kay (Eds): *Smalltalk-72 Instruction Manual*, Technical Report SSL-76-6, Xerox Palo Alto Research Center, March 1976.

[Goldberg 1981]
Adele Goldberg and others: *Special issue on Smalltalk-80*, in *Byte Magazine*, August 1981.

[Goldberg 1983]
Adele Goldberg and David Robson: *Smalltalk-80: The Language and its Implementation*, Addison-Wesley, Reading (Mass.), 1983.

[Goldberg 1985]
Adele Goldberg: *Smalltalk-80: The Interactive Programming Environment*, Addison-Wesley, Reading (Mass.), 1985.

[Goldberg 1995]
Adele Goldberg and Kenneth S. Rubin: *Succeeding with Objects: Decision Frameworks for Project Management*, Addison-Wesley, Reading (Mass.), 1995.

[Gore 1996]
Jacob Gore: *Object Structures: Building Object-Oriented Software Components with Eiffel*, Addison-Wesley, Reading (Mass.), 1996.

[Gosling 1996]
James Gosling, Bill Joy and Guy Steel, *The Java Language Specification*, Addison-Wesley, Reading (Mass.), 1996.

[Gosling 1996a]
James Gosling, Frank Yellin and the Java Team: *The Java Application Programming Interface*, vol.1 (*Core Packages*) and vol. 2 (*Window Toolkit and Applets*), Addison-Wesley, Reading (Mass.), 1996.

[Graham 1995]
Ian Graham: *Migrating to Object Technology*, Addison-Wesley, Wokingham (U.K.), 1995.

[Gries 1981]
David Gries: *The Science of Programming*, Springer-Verlag, Berlin-New York, 1981.

[Guidec 1996]
Frédéric Guidec, Jean-Marc Jézéquel and Jean-Louis Pacherie: *An Object-Oriented Framework for Supercomputing*, in special issue on Software Engineering for Distributed Computing of the *Journal of Systems and Software*, June 1996.

[Guttag 1977]
John V. Guttag: *Abstract Data Types and the Development of Data Structures*, in *Communications of the ACM*, vol. 20, no. 6, June 1977, pages 396-404.

[Guttag 1978]
John V. Guttag and Jim J. Horning: *The Algebraic Specification of Abstract Data Types*, in *Acta Informatica*, vol. 10, 1978, pages 27-52.

[Guttag 1985]
John V. Guttag, Jim J. Horning and Jeannette M. Wing: *Larch in Five Easy Pieces*, Report 5, Digital Systems Research Center, Palo Alto (Calif.), 24 July 1985.

[Hadamard 1945]
Jacques Hadamard: *La Psychologie de l'Invention dans le Domaine mathématique*, Albert Blanchard, Paris, 1948. Extension of earlier English edition: *The Psychology of Invention in the Mathematical Field*, Princeton University Press, Princeton (N.J.), 1945; more recent reprint available from Dover Publications, New York.

[Halbert 1987]
Daniel C. Halbert and Patrick D. O'Brien: *Using Types and Inheritance in Object-Oriented Languages*, in *ECOOP 87: European Conference on Object-Oriented Programming*, Paris, June 1987, pages 23-34. Revised version in *IEEE Software*, vol. 4, no. 5, September 1987, pages 71-79.

[Harbison 1992]
Samuel P. Harbison: *Modula-3*, Prentice Hall, Englewood Cliffs (N.J.), 1992.

[Hayes 1988]
Ian J. Hayes (Ed.): *Specification Case Studies*, Prentice Hall International, Hemel Hempstead (U.K.), 1988.

[Heliotis 1996]
James Heliotis: *Eiffel in Computer Science Education*, in *Journal of Object-Oriented Programming*, vol. 9, no. 2, May 1996, pages 64-66, 82.

[Henderson-Sellers 1990]
Brian Henderson-Sellers and Julian M. Edwards: *The Object-Oriented Systems Life Cycle*, in *Communications of the ACM*, vol. 33, no. 9, September 1990, pages 142-159.

[Henderson-Sellers 1991]
Brian Henderson-Sellers: *A BOOK of Object-Oriented Knowledge*, Prentice Hall Object-Oriented Series, Sydney (Australia), 1991.

[Henderson-Sellers 1994]
Brian Henderson-Sellers and Julian M. Edwards: *BOOKTWO of Object-Oriented Knowledge*: *The Working Object*, Prentice Hall Object-Oriented Series, Sydney (Australia), 1991.

[Henderson-Sellers 1994a]
Brian Henderson-Sellers and James McKim: *Contracting*: *What's in it for the Supplier?*, in *TOOLS 14* (*Technology of Object-Oriented Languages and Systems*), Santa Barbara (California), 1994, eds Raimund Ege, Madhu Singh and Bertrand Meyer, Prentice Hall, Englewood Cliffs (N.J.), 1994, pages 179-186.

[Henderson-Sellers 1996]
Brian Henderson-Sellers and Ian Graham: *OPEN*: *Towards Method Convergence?*, in *Computer* (IEEE), Object Technology department, vol. 29, no. 4, April 1996, pages 86-89.

[Henderson-Sellers 1996a]
Brian Henderson-Sellers: *Object-Oriented Metrics*: *Measures of Complexity*, Prentice Hall Object-Oriented Series, Upper Saddle River (N.J.), 1996.

[Hoare 1966]
C.A.R. Hoare and Niklaus Wirth: *A Contribution to the Development of ALGOL*, in *Communications of the ACM*, vol. 9, no. 6, June 1966, pages 413-431. Reprinted in C.A.R. Hoare and C. B. Jones (ed.), *Essays in Computing Science*, Prentice Hall International, Hemel Hempstead (U.K.), 1989, pages 31-43.

[Hoare 1969]
C.A.R. Hoare: *An Axiomatic Basis for Computer Programming*, in *Communications of the ACM*, vol. 12, no. 10, October 1969, pages 576-580, 583. Reprinted in [Hoare 1989], pages 45-58.

[Hoare 1972]
C.A.R. Hoare: *Editorial: The Quality of Software*, in *Software, Practice and Experience*, vol. 2, no. 2, 1972, pages 103-105.

[Hoare 1972a]
C.A.R. Hoare: *Proof of Correctness of Data Representations*, in *Acta Informatica*, vol. 1, 1972, pages 271-281. Reprinted in [Hoare 1989], pages 103-115.

[Hoare 1973]
C.A.R. Hoare: *Hints on Programming Language Design*, Stanford University Artificial Intelligence memo AIM-224/STAN-CS-73-403. Reprinted in [Hoare 1989], pages 193-216.

[Hoare 1974]
C.A.R. Hoare: *Monitors: An Operating System Structuring Concept*, in *Communications of the ACM*, vol. 17, no. 10, October 1974, pages 549-557. Reprinted in [Hoare 1989], pages 171-191.

[Hoare 1978]
C.A.R. Hoare: *Communication Sequential Processes*, in *Communications of the ACM*, vol. 21, no. 8, August 1978, pages 666-677. Reprinted in [Hoare 1989], pages 259-288.

[Hoare 1981]
C.A.R. Hoare: *The Emperor's Old Clothes* (1980 Turing Award lecture), in *Communications of the ACM*, vol. 24, no. 2, February 1981, pages 75-83. Reprinted in [Hoare 1989], pages 1-18.

[Hoare 1985]
C.A.R. Hoare: *Communicating Sequential Processes*; Prentice Hall International, Hemel Hempstead (U.K.), 1985.

[Hoare 1989]
C.A.R. Hoare and C. B. Jones (ed.): *Essays in Computing Science* (reprints of Hoare's papers), Prentice Hall International, Hemel Hempstead (U.K.), 1989.

[Hopkins 1995]
Trevor Hopkins and Bernard Horan: *Smalltalk — An Introduction to Application Development Using VisualWorks*, Prentice Hall Object-Oriented Series, Hemel Hempstead (U.K.), 1995.

[Horowitz 1984]
Ellis Horowitz and John B. Munson: *An Expansive View of Reusable Software*, in *IEEE Transactions on Software Engineering*, vol. SE-10, no. 5, September 1984, pages 477-487.

[Hullot 1984]
Jean-Marie Hullot: *Ceyx, Version 15: I — une Initiation*, Rapport Technique no. 44, INRIA, Rocquencourt, 1984.

[IEEE 1990]
IEEE Computer Society: *Glossary of Software Engineering Terminology*, ed. Jane Radatz, standard 1990-610.12 (revision of 1983-729). Also ANSI standard, 2/91.

[IEEE 1993]
IEEE Computer Society: *Classification of Software Errors/Faults/Failures*, ed. Richard Evans, standard 1993-1044.

[Ingalls 1978]
Daniel H. H. Ingalls: *The Smalltalk-76 Programming System: Design and Implementation*, in *Proceedings of the ACM Principles of Programming Languages Symposium*, January 1978.

[Inmos 1988]
Inmos Ltd.: *Occam 2 Programming Manual*, Prentice Hall International, Hemel Hempstead (U.K.), 1988.

[ISE 1996]
Interactive Software Engineering Inc.: *ArchiText User's Manual*, Technical Report TR-EI-33.AT, 1996.

[Jackson 1975]
Michael A. Jackson: *Principles of Program Design*, Academic Press, London, 1975.

[Jackson 1983]
Michael A. Jackson: *System Development*, Prentice Hall International, Hemel Hempstead (U.K.), 1983.

[Jacobson 1992]
Ivar Jacobson, Magnus Christerson, Patrik Jonsson and Gunnar Övergaard: *Object-Oriented Software Engineering: A Use Case Driven Approach*, Addison-Wesley, Wokingham (England), 1992.

[Jalloul 1991]

Ghinwa Jalloul and John Potter: *Models for Concurrent Eiffel*, in *TOOLS 6* (*Technology of Object-Oriented Languages and Systems*), eds. J. Potter, M. Tokoro and B. Meyer, Prentice Hall, Sydney (Australia), 1991, pp. 183-191.

[Jalloul 1994]

Ghinwa Jalloul: *Concurrent Object-Oriented Systems*: *A Disciplined Approach.*, PhD Dissertation, University of Technology, Sydney (Australia), June 1994.

[Jézéquel 1992]

Jean-Marc Jézéquel: *ÉPÉE: an Eiffel Environment to Program Distributed Parallel Computers*; in *ECOOP'92 proceedings, Lecture Notes in Computer Science 611*, Springer-Verlag, Berlin, July 1992. Revised version in *Journal of Object-Oriented Programming*, vol. 6, no. 2, May 1993, pp. 48-54.

[Jézéquel 1996]

Jean-Marc Jézéquel: *Object-Oriented Software Engineering with Eiffel*, Addison-Wesley, Reading (Mass.), 1996.

[Johnson 1995]

Paul Johnson: *"Marconi" Proposal for the Eiffel Library Kernel Standard*, archives of the NICE library committee discussions, Nonprofit International Consortium for Eiffel, 1995.

[Johnston 1971]

J.B. Johnston: *The Contour Model of Block Structured Processes*, in *SIGPLAN Notices*, vol. 6, no. 2, February 1971, pages 55-82.

[Jones 1980]

Cliff B. Jones: *Software Development: A Rigorous Approach*, Prentice Hall International, Hemel Hempstead (U.K.), 1980.

[Jones 1984]

T. Capers Jones: *Reusability in Programming*: *A Survey of the State of the Art*, in *IEEE Transactions on Software Engineering*, vol. SE-10, no. 5, September 1984, pages 488-494.

[Jones 1986]

Cliff B. Jones: *Systematic Software Development Using VDM*, Prentice Hall International, Hemel Hempstead (U.K.), 1986.

[Joyner 1996]

Ian Joyner: *C++ Critique, third edition*, available on several Internet sites including *http:// www.progsoc.uts.edu.au/~geldridg/cpp/cppcv3.html* and *ftp://ftp.inria.fr/doc/lang/cpp.crit.ps.gz*. (For others, perform a search on the keywords "Joyner" and "C++ critique".)

[Kemper 1994]

Alfons Kemper and Guido Moerkotte: *Object-Oriented Database Management*: *Applications in Engineering and Computer Science*, Prentice Hall, Englewood Cliffs (N.J.), 1994.

[Kernighan 1978]

Brian W. Kernighan and Dennis M. Ritchie: *The C Programming Language*, Prentice Hall, Englewood Cliffs (N.J.), 1978.

[Kernighan 1988]

Brian W. Kernighan and Dennis M. Ritchie: *The C Programming Language, second edition*, Prentice Hall, Englewood Cliffs (N.J.), 1988 (covers the ANSI standard version of the languages).

[Kilov 1994]

Haim Kilov and James Ross: *Information Modeling*: *An Object-Oriented Approach*, Prentice Hall Object-Oriented Series, Englewood Cliffs (N.J.), 1994.

[Khoshafian 1986]

Setrag Khoshafian and George P. Copeland: *Object Identity*, in *OOPSLA '86 Conference Proceedings*, Portland (Oreg.), Sept. 29-Oct. 2, 1986, published as *SIGPLAN Notices*, vol. 21, no. 11, Nov. 1986, pages 406-416. Also in [Zdonik 1990], pages 37-46.

[Khoshafian 1993]

Setrag Khoshafian: *Object-Oriented Databases*, John Wiley and Sons, New York, 1993.

[Kim 1990]

Won Kim: *Introduction to Object-Oriented Databases*, MIT Press, Cambridge (Mass.), 1990.

[Knudsen 1993]
   Jørge Lindskov Knudsen, Mats Löfgren, Ole Lehrmann Madsen, Boris Magnusson: *Object-Oriented Environments*: *The Mjølner Approach*, Prentice Hall Object-Oriented Series, Hemel Hempstead (U.K.), 1993.

[Knuth 1968]
   Donald E. Knuth: *The Art of Computer Programming*, *Vol. 1*: *Fundamental Algorithms*, Addison-Wesley, Menlo Park (Calif.), 1968.

[Knuth 1973]
   Donald E. Knuth: *The Art of Computer Programming*, *Vol. 3*: *Sorting and Searching*, Addison-Wesley, Menlo Park (Calif.), 1973.

[Knuth 1980]
   Donald E. Knuth and Luis Trabb Pardo: *The early development of Programming Languages*, in *A History of Computing in the Twentieth Century*, N. Metropolis, J. Howlett and Gian-Carlo Cota (eds.), Academic Press, New York, 1980, pages 197-273.

[Knuth 1981]
   Donald E. Knuth: *The Art of Computer Programming*, *Vol. 2*: *Seminumerical Algorithms*, Addison-Wesley, Menlo Park (Calif.), 1969. Second edition, 1981.

[Knuth 1984]
   Donald E. Knuth: *Literate Programming*, in *The Computer Journal*, vol. 27, no. 2, May 1984, pages 97-111.

[Krief 1996]
   Philippe Krief: *Prototyping with Objects*, Prentice Hall Object-Oriented Series, Hemel Hempstead (U.K.), 1996.

[Lalonde 1990-1991]
   Wilf R. Lalonde and John R. Pugh: *Inside Smalltalk*, Prentice Hall, Englewood Cliffs (N.J.), 1990 (volume 1) and 1991 (volume 2).

[Lampson 1977]
   Butler W. Lampson, Jim J. Horning, Ralph L. London, J. G. Mitchell and Gerard L. Popek: *Report on the Programming Language Euclid*, in *SIGPLAN Notices*, vol. 12, no. 2, February 1977, pages 1-79.

[Language-Web]
   Eiffel Home Page, at *http://www.eiffel.com*.

[Lano 1994]
   Kevin Lano and Howard Haughton (eds.): *Object-Oriented Specification Case Studies*, Prentice Hall Object-Oriented Series, Hemel Hempstead (U.K.), 1994.

[Lea 1993]
   Rodger Lea, Christian Jacquemot and Eric Pillevesse: *COOL: System Support for Distributed Programming*, in [M 1993a], pp. 37-46.

[Ley-Web]
   Michael Ley: *Bibliography WWW Server on Database Systems and Logic Programming*, on-line Web archive at *http://www.informatik.uni-trier.de/~ley/db/index.html*.

[Lieberherr 1989]
   Karl J. Lieberherr and Ian M. Holland: *Assuring Good Style for Object-Oriented Programs*, in *IEEE Software*, vol. 6, no. 5, September 1989, pages 38-48.

[Lieberman 1987]
   Henry Lieberman: *Concurrent Object-Oriented Programming in Act 1*; in [Yonezawa 1987], pages 9-36.

[Lientz 1980]
   Bennet P. Lientz and E. Burton Swanson: *Software Maintenance Management*: *a Study of the Maintenance of Computer Application Software in 487 Data Processing Organizations*, Addison-Wesley, Reading (Mass.), 1980.

[Liskov 1974]
   Barbara H. Liskov and Stephen N. Zilles: *Programming with Abstract Data Types*, Computation Structures Group, Memo no. 99, MIT, Project MAC, Cambridge (Mass.) 1974. (See also *SIGPLAN Notices*, 9, 4, April 1974, pages 50-59.)

[Liskov 1979]
Barbara H. Liskov and Alan Snyder: *Exception Handling in CLU*, in *IEEE Transactions on Software Engineering*, vol. SE-5, no. 6, November 1979, pages 546-558.

[Liskov 1981]
Barbara H. Liskov, Russel Atkinson, T. Bloom, E. Moss, J. Craig Schaffert, R. Scheifler and Alan Snyder: *CLU Reference Manual*, Springer-Verlag, Berlin-New York, 1981.

[Liskov 1986]
Barbara H. Liskov and John Guttag: *Abstraction and Specification in Program Development*, MIT Press, Cambridge (Mass.), 1986.

[Loomis 1995]
Mary E. S. Loomis: *Object Databases*: *The Essentials*, Addison-Wesley, Reading (Mass.), 1995.

[M 19*XX*]
Bibliographic references of this form indicate works by the author of the present book, listed separately in the second part of this bibliography (E.2, page 1221).

[Madsen 1993]
Ole Lehrmann Madsen, Birger Møller-Pedersen, Kristen Nygaard: *Object-Oriented Programming in the BETA Programming Language*, Addison-Wesley, Wokingham (U.K.), 1993.

[Martin 1992]
James Martin and James J. Odell: *Object-Oriented Analysis and Design*, Prentice Hall, Englewood Cliffs (N.J.), 1992.

[Matsuoka 1993]
Satoshi Matsuoka and Akinori Yonezawa: *Analysis of Inheritance Anomaly in Object-Oriented Concurrent Programming Languages*, in [Agha 1993], pp 107-150.

[McCall 1977]
James McCall (ed.): *Factors in Software Quality*, Technical Report, General Electric, 1977.

[McGregor 1992]
John D. McGregor and David A. Sykes: *Object-Oriented Software Development*: *Engineering Software for Reuse*, Van Nostrand Reinhold, New York, 1992.

[McIlroy 1976]
M.D. McIlroy: *Mass-produced Software Components*, in [Buxton 1976], pages 88-98.

[McKim 1992]
James McKim: *Teaching Object-Oriented Programming and Design*, in *Eiffel Outlook*, vol. 2, no. 3, September-October 1992, pages 8-19.

[McKim 1992a]
James McKim and David Mondou: *Class Interface Design*, in *TOOLS 8* (*Technology of Object-Oriented Languages and Systems*), eds. Raimund Ege, Madhu Singh, and Bertrand Meyer, Prentice Hall, Englewood Cliffs (N.J.) 1992, pages 151-161.

[McKim 1995]
James McKim: *Class Interface Design and Programming by Contract*, tutorial summary in *TOOLS 18* (*Technology of Object-Oriented Languages and Systems*), eds. Christine Mingins, Roger Duke and Bertrand Meyer, Prentice Hall, Englewood Cliffs (N.J.), 1995, pages 433-470.

[McKim 1996]
James McKim: *Programming by Contract*, in *Computer* (IEEE), Object Technology department, vol. 29, no. 3, March 1996, pages 109-111.

[McKim 1996a]
James McKim: *Programming by Contract*: *Designing for Correctness*, in *Journal of Object-Oriented Programming*, vol. 9, no. 2, May 1996, pages 70-74.

[McMenamin 1984]
Stephen M. McMenamin and John F. Palmer: *Essential Systems Analysis*, Yourdon Press, New York, 1984.

[Mills 1973]
Harlan D. Mills and F. Terry Baker: *Chief Programmer Teams*, in *Datamation*, vol. 19, no. 2, December 1973, pages 58-61.

[Mills 1975]
Harlan D. Mills: *How to Write Correct Programs and Know It*, in *Proceedings International Conference on Reliable Software*, Los Angeles (Calif.), April 1975, published as *ACM SIGPLAN Notices*, 10, June 1975, pages 363-370. Also in Mills's book *Software Productivity*, Little, Brown and Company, Boston, 1983, pages 193-214.

[Milner 1978]
Robin Milner: *A Theory of Type Polymorphism in Programming*, in *Journal of Computer and System Sciences*, vol. 17, 1978, pages 348-375.

[Milner 1989]
Robin Milner: *Communication and Concurrency*; Prentice Hall International, Hemel Hempstead (U.K.), 1989.

[Mingins 1993]
Christine Mingins, Bogdan Durnota and Glen Smith: *Collecting Software Metrics Data for the Eiffel Class Hierarchy*, in *TOOLS 15* (*Technology of Object-Oriented Languages and Systems*), eds. Christine Mingins and Bertrand Meyer, Prentice Hall, Englewood Cliffs (N.J.), 1993, pages 427-435.

[Mingins 1995]
Christine Mingins: *Designing Software Metrics* (Tutorial notes), TOOLS Pacific (Technology of Object-Oriented Languages and Systems), Melbourne, 1995.

[Mitchell 1979]
John G. Mitchell, W. Maybury and R. Sweet: *Mesa Language Manual* (*Version 5.0*), Xerox Research Center, Palo Alto (Calif.), Report CSL-79-3, April 1979.

[Modula-3-Web]
Modula-3 Home Page at *http://www.research.digital.com/SRC/modula-3/html/*.

[Moffat 1981]
David V. Moffat: *Enumerations in Pascal, Ada and Beyond*, in *SIGPLAN Notices*, vol. 16, no. 2, February 1981, pages 77-82.

[Moon 1986]
David A. Moon: *Object-Oriented Programming with Flavors*, in *OOPSLA '86 Conference Proceedings*, Portland (Oreg.), Sept. 29-Oct. 2, 1986, published as *SIGPLAN Notices*, vol. 21, no. 11, Nov. 1986, pages 1-8.

[Mössenböck 1993]
Hans Mössenböck: *Object-Oriented Programming in Oberon-2*, Springer-Verlag, Berlin, 1992.

[Nerson 1992]
Jean-Marc Nerson: *Applying Object-Oriented Analysis and Design*, in *Communications of the ACM*, vol. 35, no. 9, September 1992, pages 63-74.

[Nierstrasz 1992]
Oscar Nierstrasz: *A Tour of Hybrid: A Language for Programming with Active Objects*; in [M 1992a], pages 167-182.

[NSIA 1985]
NSIA: (National Security Industry Association): *Proceedings of the first Joint DoD-Industry Symposium on the STARS program*, San Diego (Calif.), 30 April – 2 May 1985.

[Nygaard 1981]
Kristen Nygaard and Ole-Johan Dahl: *The Development of the SIMULA languages*, in *History of Programming Languages*, ed. Richard L. Wexelblat, Academic Press, New York, 1981, pages 439-493.

[Oberon-Web]
Oberon Home Page, at *http://ics.inf.ethz.ch/Oberon.html*.

[Ong 1993]
C.L. Ong and W.T. Tsai: *Class and Object Extraction from Imperative Code*, in *Journal of Object-Oriented Programming*, vol. 6, no. 1, March-April 1993, pages 58-68.

[Orr 1977]
Ken T. Orr: *Structured Systems Development*, Yourdon Press, New York, 1977.

[Osmond 1995]
Roger F. Osmond: *Essential of Successful O-O Project Management: Designing High Performance Projects*, tutorial notes, TOOLS USA 95 (Technology of Object-Oriented Languages and Systems), Santa Barbara (Calif.), July 1995.

[Paepcke 1993]
Andreas Paepcke (ed.): *Object-Oriented Programming: The CLOS Perspective*, MIT Press, Cambridge (Mass.), 1993.

[Page-Jones 1980]
Meilir Page-Jones: *The Practical Guide to Structured Systems Design*, Yourdon Press, New York, 1980.

[Page-Jones 1995]
Meilir Page-Jones: *What Every Programmer Should Know about Object-Oriented Design*, Dorset House, New York, 1995.

[Papathomas 1992]
Michael Papathomas: *Language Design Rationale and Semantic Framework for Concurrent Object-Oriented Programming*; PhD Thesis, Université de Genève, 1992.

[Parnas 1972]
David Lorge Parnas: *A Technique for Software Module Specification with Examples*, in *Communications of the ACM*, vol. 15, no. 5, May 1972, pages 330-336.

[Parnas 1972a]
David Lorge Parnas: *On the Criteria to Be Used in Decomposing Systems into Modules*, in *Communications of the ACM*, vol. 15, no. 12, December 1972, pages 1053-1058.

[Parnas 1986]
David Lorge Parnas and Paul C. Clemens: *A Rational Design Process: How and Why to Fake It*, in *IEEE Transatctions on Software Engineering*, vol. SE-12, no. 2, February 1986, pages 251-257.

[Petroski 1994]
Henry Petroski: *The Evolution of Useful Things*, Vintage Books, New York, 1994. (Original hardcover: Alfred A. Knopf, New York, 1992.)

[Pinson 1991]
Lewis J. Pinson and Richard S. Wiener: *Objective C: Object-Oriented Programming Techniques*, Addison-Wesley, Reading (Mass.), 1991.

[Pooley 1986]
Robert J. Pooley: *An Introduction to Programming in SIMULA*, Blackwell Scientific, Oxford, 1986.

[Pree 1994]
Wolfgang Pree: *Design Patterns for Object-Oriented Software Development*, ACM Press (Addison-Wesley), New York, 1994.

[Randell 1975]
Brian Randell: *System Structure for Software Fault Tolerance*, in *IEEE Transactions on Software Engineering*, vol. SE-1, no. 2, June 1975, pages 220-232.

[Rich 1989]
Charles Rich and Richard C. Waters: *Formalizing Reusable Software Components in the Programmer's Apprentice*, in [Biggerstaff 1989].

[Rist 1995]
Robert Rist and Robert Terwilliger: *Object-Oriented Programming in Eiffel*, Prentice Hall Object-Oriented Series, Sydney (Australia), 1995.

[Rumbaugh 1991]
James Rumbaugh, Michael Blaha, William Premerlani, Frederick Eddy and William Lorensen: *Object-Oriented Modeling and Design*, Prentice Hall, Englewood Cliffs (N.J), 1991.

[Sather-Web]
Sather Home Page at *http://http.icsi.berkeley.edu/Sather/sather.html*.

[Schaffert 1986]
    Craig Schaffert, Topher Cooper, Bruce Bullis, Mike Kilian and Carrie Wilpolt: *An Introduction to Trellis-Owl*, in *OOPSLA '86 Conference Proceedings*, Portland (Oreg.), Sept. 29-Oct. 2, 1986, published as *SIGPLAN Notices*, vol. 21, no. 11, Nov. 1986, pages 9-16.

[Schweitzer 1991]
    Michael Schweitzer and Lambert Strether: *Eiffel/S Compiler and Runtime*, User's manual, SiG Computer GmbH, Braunfels-Altenkirchen (Germany), 1991.

[Shang 1996]
    David Shang: *Is a Cow an Animal?* and *Subtypes and Convertible Types*, in *Object Currents* (on-line publication), SIGS, New York, January and June 1996, at *http://www.sigs.com/publications/docs/oc/9601/oc9601.c.shang.html* (second article: *9606/oc9606.c.shang.html*).

[Shapiro 1989]
    Marc Shapiro, Philippe Gautron and Laurence Mosseri: *Persistence and Migration for C++ Objects*; in *ECOOP 1989* (*European Conference on Object-Oriented Programming*), ed. Steve Cook, Cambridge University Press, Cambridge (England), pages 191-204.

[Shaw 1981]
    Mary Shaw et al.: *Alphard: Form and Content*, Springer-Verlag, Berlin-New York, 1981.

[Shlaer 1992]
    Sally Shlaer and Steve Mellor: *Object Lifecycles: Modeling the World in States*, Prentice Hall, Englewood Cliffs (N.J.), 1992.

[Shneiderman 1980]
    Ben Shneiderman: *Software Psychology*, Little, Brown and Company, Boston (Mass.), 1980.

[Shneiderman 1987]
    Ben Shneiderman: *Designing the User Interface: Strategies for Effective Human-Computer Interaction, Second Edition*, Addison-Wesley, Reading (Mass.), 1992. (First edition: 1987.)

[Simons 1995]
    Anthony J.H. Simons: *Rationalising Eiffel's Type System*, in *TOOLS 18* (*Technology of Object-Oriented Languages and Systems*), eds. Christine Mingins, Roger Duke and Bertrand Meyer, Prentice Hall, Englewood Cliffs (N.J.) 1995, pages 365-377.

[SIS 1987]
    SIS: *Data Processing- Programming Languages — SIMULA*, Standardiseringskommissionen i Sverige (Swedish Standards Institute), Svensk Standard SS 63 61 14, 20 May 1987.

[Snyder 1986]
    Alan Snyder: *Encapsulation and Inheritance in Object-Oriented Programming Languages*, in *OOPSLA '86 Conference Proceedings*, Portland (Oreg.), Sept. 29-Oct. 2, 1986, published as *SIGPLAN Notices*, 21, 11, November 1986, pages 38-45.

[Sombrero-Web]
    Sombrero Project at the Arizona State University: *http://www.eas.asu.edu/~sasos*.

[Spivey 1988]
    J. Michael. Spivey: *Understanding Z: A Specification Language and its Formal Semantics*, Cambridge University Press, Cambridge, 1988.

[Spivey 1992]
    J. Michael Spivey: *The Z Notation: A Reference Manual*, second edition, Prentice Hall International, Hemel Hempstead (U.K.), 1992.

[Stallman 1992]
    Richard Stallman: *Why Software Should be Free*, Free Software Fundation, Boston (Mass.), 24 April 1992.

[Standish 1984]
    Thomas A. Standish: *An Essay on Software Reuse*, in *IEEE Transactions on Software Engineering*, vol. SE-10, no. 5, September 1984, pages 494-497

[Stein 1995]
  Jacob Stein: *Les SGBD Objets n'ont pas tenu leurs Promesses* (Object-Oriented Databases Have Not Fulfilled their Promises), interview by B. Meyer, in *L'OBJET*, vol. 1, no. 3, September 1995, pages 25-27.

[Stroustrup 1984]
  Bjarne Stroustrup: *Data Abstraction in C*, in *AT&T Bell Laboratories Technical Journal*, vol. 63, no. 8, Part 2, October 1984, pages 1701-1732.

[Stroustrup 1986]
  Bjarne Stroustrup: *The C++ Programming Language*, Addison-Wesley, Menlo Park (Calif.), 1986. (Superseded by [Stroustrup 1991].)

[Stroustrup 1991]
  Bjarne Stroustrup: *The C++ Programming Language, Second Edition*, Addison-Wesley, Menlo Park (Calif.), 1991. (Revised edition of [Stroustrup 1986].)

[Stroustrup 1994]
  Bjarne Stroustrup: *The Design and Evolution of C++*, Addison-Wesley, Reading (Mass.), 1994.

[Suzuki 1982]
  Norihisa Suzuki: *Analysis of Pointer "Rotation"*, in *Communications of the ACM*, vol. 25, no. 5, May 1982, pages 330-335.

[Szypersky 1993]
  Clemens Szypersky, Stephen Omohundro and Stephan Murer: *Engineering a Programming Language: The Type and Class System of Sather*, International Computer Science Institute TechReport Tr-93-064, Berkeley (Calif.), 1993. Available on-line from *http://www.icsi.berkeley.edu/~sather/Publications/tr-93-064.html*.

[Tabourier 1986]
  Yves Tabourier: *De l'autre côté de Merise – Systèmes d'Information et Modèles d'Entreprise*, Les Editions d'Organisation, Paris, 1986.

[Tardieu 1984]
  Hubert Tardieu, Arnold Rochfeld and René Colletti: *La Méthode Merise, Principes et Outils* (2nd Edition), Les Editions d'Organisation, Paris, 1984.

[Tokoro 1992]
  Mario Tokoro, Oscar Nierstrasz and Peter Wegner (eds.): *Proceedings of ECOOP 1991 Workshop on Object-Based Concurrent Computing*; Lecture Notes in Computer Science 612, Springer-Verlag, Berlin-New York, 1992.

[Tracz 1988]
  Will Tracz: *Software Reuse: Emerging Technology (Tutorial)*, IEEE, Catalog number EH0278-2, 1988.

[Tracz 1995]
  Will Tracz: *Confessions of a Used Program Salesman: Institutionalizing Software Reuse*, Addison-Wesley, Reading (Mass.), 1995.

[Ungar 1984]
  David Ungar: *Generation Scavenging: A Non-disruptive High Performance Storage Reclamation Algorithm*, in *Proceedings of ACM SIGSOFT/SIGPLAN Software Engineering Symposium on Practical Software Development Environments*, Pittsburgh, Penn., April 23-25, 1984, *ACM Software Engineering Notes*, 9, 3, and *SIGPLAN Notices*, 19, 5, May 1984, pages 157-167. (See also *The Design and Evaluation of a High Performance Smalltalk System*, PhD Thesis, Report UCB/CSD 86/287, EECS, Computer Science Division, University of California, Berkeley, February 1986.)

[Ungar 1992]
  David Ungar, Randall B. Smith, Craig Chambers and Urs Hölzle: *Object, Message and Performance: How they Coexist in Self*, in *Computer (IEEE)*, vol. 25, no. 10, October 1992, pages 53-64.

[van Wijngaarden 1975]
  Aad van Wijngaarden, B. J. Mailloux, J.E.L Peck, C.H.A. Koster, Michel Sintzoff, Charles H. Lindsey, Lambert G.L.T. Meertens and R.G. Fisker: *Revised Report on the Algorithmic Language Algol 68*, in *Acta Informatica*, vol. 5, 1975, pages 1-236.

[Versant 1994]
   C++/Versant Usage Guide, *VERSANT Release 3.0*, Versant Object Technology, Menlo Park (Calif.), 1994.

[Waldén 1995]
   Kim Waldén and Jean-Marc Nerson: *Seamless Object-Oriented Software Architecture*: *Analysis and Design of Reliable Systems*, Prentice Hall, Hemel Hempstead (U.K.), 1995.

[Waters 1984]
   Richard C. Waters: *The Programmer's Apprentice*: *Knowledge Based Program Editing*, in *Interactive Programming Environments*, eds. David R. Barstow, Howard E. Shrobe and Erik Sandewall, McGraw-Hill, New York, 1984, pages 464-486.

[Weber 1992]
   Franz Weber: *Getting Class Correctness and System Correctness Equivalent — How to Get Covariance Right*, in *TOOLS 8* (*Technology of Object-Oriented Languages and Systems*), eds. Raimund Ege, Madhu Singh, and Bertrand Meyer, Prentice Hall, Englewood Cliffs (N.J.) 1992, pages 199-213.

[Wegner 1987]
   Peter Wegner: *Dimensions of Object-Based Language Design*, in *OOPSLA '87 Conference Proceedings*, Orlando (Fla.), 4-8 October 1987, published as *SIGPLAN Notices*, vol. 22, no. 12, Dec. 1987, pages 168-182.

[Weiser 1987]
   Mark Weiser: *Source Code*, in *Computer* (IEEE), vol. 20, no. 11, November 1987, pages 66-73.

[Wexelblat 1981]
   Richard L. Wexelblat (ed.): *History of Programming Languages* (Proceedings of a 1978 ACM SIGPLAN conference), Academic Press, New York, 1981.

[Welsh 1977]
   Jim Welsh, W. Sneeringer and C.A.R. Hoare: *Ambiguities and Insecurities in Pascal*, in *Software, Practice and Experience*, vol. 7, 1977, pages 685-696.

[Wheeler-Web]
   Scott Wheeler, *Lovelace*, on-line Ada 95 tutorial at *http://lglsun.epfl.ch/Ada/Tutorials/Lovelace/lovelace.html*.

[Wiener 1988]
   Richard Wiener and Lewis Pinson: *Introduction to Object-Oriented Programming and C++*, Addison-Wesley, 1988.

[Wiener 1995]
   Richard Wiener: *Software Development Using Eiffel*: *There can be Life Other than C++*, Prentice Hall Object-Oriented Series, Englewood Cliffs (N.J.), 1995.

[Wiener 1996]
   Richard Wiener, *An Object-Oriented Introduction to Computer Science Using Eiffel*, Prentice Hall Object-Oriented Series, Englewood Cliffs (N.J.), 1996.

[Wiener 1997]
   Richard Wiener, *An Object-Oriented Introduction to Data Structures Using Eiffel*, Prentice Hall Object-Oriented Series, Englewood Cliffs (N.J.), 1997.

[Wilson 1996]
   Gregory V. Wilson and Paul Liu (eds.): *Parallel Programming Using C++*, MIT Press, Cambridge (Mass.), 1996.

[Wirfs-Brock 1990]
   Rebecca Wirfs-Brock, Brian Wilkerson and Laura Wiener: *Designing Object-Oriented Software*, Prentice Hall, Englewood Cliffs (N.J), 1990.

[Wirth 1971]
   Niklaus Wirth: *Program Development by Stepwise Refinement*, in *Communications of the ACM*, vol. 14, no. 4, 1971, pages 221-227.

[Wirth 1982]
   Niklaus Wirth: *Programming in Modula-2*, Springer-Verlag, Berlin-New York, 1982.

[Wirth 1992]

Niklaus Wirth and Martin Reiser: *Programming in Oberon — Steps Beyond Pascal and Modula*, Addison-Wesley, Reading (Mass.), 1992

[Wyatt 1992]

Barbara B. Wyatt, Krishna Kavi and Steve Hufnagel: *Parallelism in Object-Oriented Languages: A Survey*, in *IEEE Software* November 1992. vol. 9, no. 6, pp. 56-66.

[Yokote 1989]

Yasuhiko Yokote, Fumio Teraoka, Masaki Yamada, Hiroshi Tezuka and Mario Tokoro: *The Design and Implementation of the MUSE Object-Oriented Distributed Operating System*, in *TOOLS 1* (*Technology of Object-Oriented Languages and Systems*), ed. Jean Bézivin, SOL, Paris, 1989, pages 363-370.

[Yonezawa 1987]

Akinori Yonezawa and Mario Tokoro (eds): *Object-Oriented Concurrent Programming*; MIT Press, Cambridge (Mass.), 1987.

[Yonezawa 1987a]

Akinori Yonezawa et al.: *Modelling and Programming in an Object-Oriented Concurrent Language ABCL/1*; in [Yonezawa 1987], pages 55-89.

[Yourdon 1979]

Edward Nash Yourdon and Larry L. Constantine: *Structured Design: Fundamentals of a Discipline of Computer Program and Systems Design*, Prentice Hall, Englewood Cliffs (N.J.), 1979.

[Yourdon 1989]

Edward Nash Yourdon: *Modern Structured Analysis*, Yourdon Press (Prentice Hall), Englewood Cliffs (N.J.), 1989.

[Zdonik 1990]

Stanley B. Zdonik and David Maier: *Readings in Object-Oriented Database Systems*, Morgan Kaufmann, Menlo Park (Calif.), 1990.

E.2 WORKS BY THE AUTHOR OF THE PRESENT BOOK

[M 1976]

La Description des Structures de Données (The Description of Data Structures) in *Bulletin de la Direction des Etudes et Recherches d'Electricité de France*, Série C (Informatique) Clamart, no. 2, 1976.

[M 1978]

(with Claude Baudoin) *Méthodes de Programmation* (Methods for Programming), Eyrolles, Paris, 1978. Revised third edition, 1984.

[M 1979]

Quelques Concepts importants des Langages de Programmation modernes et leur Expression en Simula 67 (Some Important Concepts of Modern Programming Languages and their Expression in Simula 67), in *Bulletin de la Direction des Etudes et Recherches d'Electricité de France*, Série C (Informatique), Clamart, no. 1, 1979, pages 89-150. Also in GROPLAN 9, AFCET (French Computer Society), 1979.

[M 1982]

A Three-Level Approach to Data Structure Description, and Notational, Framework in *ACM-NBS Workshop on Data Abstraction, Databases and Conceptual Modelling*, Pingree Park, Colorado, 25-26 June 1981 (published as January 1982 issues of ACM *SIGPLAN, SIGMOD, SIGART* newsletters), eds. Michael Brodie and Steven Zilles, pages 164-166.

[M 1982a]

Principles of Package Design, in *Communications of the ACM*, vol. 25, no. 7, pages 419-428, July 1982.

[M 1983]

Towards a Two-Dimensional Programming Environment, in *Proceedings of the European Conference on Integrated Computing Systems* (ECICS 82), Stresa (Italy), 1-3 September 1982, eds. Pierpaolo Degano and Erik

Sandewall, North-Holland, Amsterdam, 1983, pages 167-179. Reprinted in *Readings in Artificial Intelligence*, Tioga Press, Palo Alto (Calif.), 1983.

[M 1984]
  (with Jean-Marc Nerson) *CEPAGE, a Full-Screen Structured Editor*, in *Software Engineering: Practice and Experience*, ed. Emmanuel Girard, North Oxford Academic, Oxford, 1984, pp. 60-65.

[M 1985a]
  On Formalism in Specifications, in *IEEE Software*, vol. 3, no. 1, January 1985, pages 6-25, Reprinted in T. Colburn, J. Fetzer, and T. Rankin (eds.), *Program Verification: Fundamental Problems in Computer Science*, Kluwer Academic Publishers, Dordrecht (The Netherlands), 1993, and in Dutch, French and other translations.

[M 1985b]
  M: A System Description Method, Technical Report TRCS85-15, University of California, Santa Barbara, Computer Science Department, 1985.

[M 1985c]
  Eiffel: A Language for Software Engineering, Technical Report TRCS85-19, University of California, Santa Barbara, Computer Science Department, December 1985.

[M 1986]
  Genericity versus inheritance, in *OOPSLA '86 Conference Proceedings*, Portland (Oreg.), Sept. 29-Oct. 2, 1986, published as *SIGPLAN Notices*, vol. 21, no. 11, Nov. 1986, pages 391-405. Revised version in *The Journal of Pascal, Ada and Modula-2*, 1988.

[M 1987]
  Reusability: the Case for Object-Oriented Design, in *IEEE Software*, March 1987 vol. 4, no. 2 , March 1987, pages 50-64.

[M 1987a]
  Design by Contract, Technical Report TR-EI-12/CO, ISE Inc., 1987.

[M 1987b]
  Eiffel: Programming for Reusability and Extendibility, in *SIGPLAN Notices*, vol. 22, no. 2, February 1987, pages 85-94.

[M 1987c]
  (with Jean-Marc Nerson and Masanobu Matsuo) *Eiffel: Object-Oriented Design for Software Engineering*, in *Proceedings of ESEC 87 (First European Software Engineering Conference)*, Strasbourg, 8-11 September 1987, eds. H.K. Nichols and D. Simpson, Springer-Verlag, Berlin, 1987, pages 221-229.

[M 1988]
  Object-Oriented Software Construction, Prentice Hall, Hemel Hempstead (U.K.), 1988 (the first edition of the present book).

[M 1988a]
  Eiffel: Basic Reference, Technical Report TR-EI-2/BR, ISE Inc., 1988. (Obsolete; see [M 1992].)

[M 1988b]
  Bidding Farewell to Globals, in *Journal of Object-Oriented Programming*, vol. 1, no. 3, September 1988, pages 73-76.

[M 1988c]
  Harnessing Multiple Inheritance, in *Journal of Object-Oriented Programming*, vol. 1, no. 4, November 1988, pages 48-51.

[M 1988d]
  The Eiffel Environment, in *Unix Review*, vol. 6, no. 8, August 1988, pages 44-55.

[M 1988e]
  Disciplined Exceptions, Technical Report TR-EI-13/EX, ISE Inc., 1988.

[M 1988f]
  Eiffel: A Language and Environment for Software Engineering, in *Journal of Systems and Software*, 1988.

[M 1989]
  From Structured Programming to Object-Oriented Design: The Road to Eiffel, in *Structured Programming*, vol. 10, no. 1, 1989, pages 19-39.

[M 1989a]
The New Culture of Software Development: Reflections on the Practice of Object-Oriented Design, in TOOLS 89 (Technology of Object-Oriented Languages and Systems), Angkor/SOL, Paris, November 1989, pages 13-23, Revised version in Journal of Object-Oriented Programming, vol. 3, no. 4, November-December 1990, pages 76-81; reprinted in [M 1992a], pp. 51-81.

[M 1989b]
Static Typing for Eiffel, Technical Report TR-EI-18/ST, ISE Inc., 1989.

[M 1989c]
Writing Correct Software, in Dr. Dobbs' Journal, December 1989, pages 48-63.

[M 1989d]
(with Philip Hucklesby) The Eiffel Object-Oriented Parsing Library, in TOOLS 89 (Technology of Object-Oriented Languages and Systems), Paris, November 1989, published by SOL, Paris, 1989, pp. 501-507.

[M 1989e]
You Can Write, But Can You Type?, in Journal of Object-Oriented Programming, vol. 1, no. 6, March-April 1989, pages 58-67.

[M 1990]
Introduction to the Theory of Programming Languages, Prentice Hall, Hemel Hempstead (U.K.), 1990. Second printing, 1991.

[M 1990a]
Sequential and Concurrent Object-Oriented Programming, in TOOLS '90 (Technology of Object-Oriented Languages and Systems), Paris, June 1990, published by Angkor/SOL, Paris, 1990, pp. 17-28.

[M 1990b]
Tools for the New Culture: Lessons from the Design of the Eiffel Libraries, in Communications of the ACM, vol. 33, no. 9, September 1990, pages 40-60.

[M 1992]
Eiffel: The Language, Prentice Hall Object-Oriented Series, 1991; second revised printing, 1992.

[M 1992a]
(editor, with Dino Mandrioli) Advances in Object-Oriented Software Engineering, Prentice-Hall, 1992.

[M 1992b]
Design by Contract, in [M 1992a], pages 1-50.

[M 1992c]
Applying "Design by Contract", in Computer (IEEE), vol. 25, no. 10, October 1992, pages 40-51 (slightly revised version of [M 1987a]).

[M 1993]
(editor, with Jean-Marc Nerson) Object-Oriented Applications, Prentice Hall Object-Oriented Series, 1993.

[M 1993a]
(editor): Special issue on Concurrent Object-Oriented Programming, in Communications of the ACM, vol. 36, no. 9, September 1993.

[M 1993b]
Systematic Concurrent Object-Oriented Programming, in [M 1993a], pp. 56-80.

[M 1993c]
Towards an Object-Oriented Curriculum, in Journal of Object-Oriented Programming, vol. 6, no. 2, May 1993, pages 76-81. Revised version in TOOLS 11 (Technology of Object-Oriented Languages and Systems), eds. Raimund Ege, Madhu Singh and Bertrand Meyer, Prentice Hall, Englewood Cliffs (N.J.), 1993, pages 585-594.

[M 1993d]
What is an Object-Oriented Environment? Five Principles and their Application, in Journal of Object-Oriented Programming, vol. 6, no. 4, July 1993, pages 75-81.

[M 1993e]
Eiffel vs. C++, Technical Report TR-EI-59/CE, ISE Inc., 1993 (also available at http://www.eiffel.com).

[M 1994]
   An Object-Oriented Environment: *Principles and Applications*, Prentice Hall Object-Oriented Series, 1994.

[M 1994a]
   Reusable Software: *The Base Object-Oriented Libraries*, Prentice Hall Object-Oriented Series, 1994.

[M 1995]
   Object Success: *A Manager's Guide to Object Technology, its Impact on the Corporation, and its Use for Reengineering the Software Process*, Prentice Hall Object-Oriented Series, 1995.

[M 1995a]
   Beyond Design by Contract: *Putting More Formality into Object-Oriented Development*, keynote presentation at TOOLS EUROPE conference, Versailles (France), 1995. (Transparencies only.)

[M 1995b]
   On the Role of Methodology: *Advice to the Advisors*, in [Alagar 1995], pages 1-5.

[M 1995c]
   EiffelCase: *Engineering Object-Oriented Software, Forward and Backward* (manual), TR-EI-53/EA, ISE Inc., January 1995.

[M 1995d]
   An Alternative to Object-Oriented Databases?, keynote presentations at TOOLS USA, Santa Barbara (Calif.) and ESEC (European Conference on Software Engineering), Sitges (Spain), 1995. (Transparencies only.)

[M 1995e]
   Building Graphical Applications with EiffelBuild (manual), TR-EI-43/UI, ISE Inc., April 1995.

[M 1996]
   The Reusability Challenge, in *Computer* (*IEEE*), Object Technology department, vol. 29, no. 2, February 1996, pages 76-78.

[M 1996a]
   Static Typing, in *Object Technologies for Advanced Software*, eds. Kokichi Futatsugi and Satoshi Matsuoka, Springer Lecture Notes in Computer Science 1049, Springer Verlag, Berlin, 1996, pages 57-75.

[M 1996b]
   Why Your Next Project Should Use Eiffel, in *Journal of Object-Oriented Programming*, vol. 9, no. 2, May 1996, pages 59-63, 82.

[M 1996c]
   Schema Evolution: *Concepts, Terminology and Solutions*, in *Computer* (*IEEE*), Object Technology department, vol. 29, no. 10, October 1996, pages 119-121.

[M 1997]
   ISE Eiffel: *The Environment* (manual), TR-EI-39/IE, ISE Inc., 1997, regularly updated (first edition 1993).

[M 1997a]
   (with Jean-Marc Jézéquel) *Design by Contract*: *The Lessons of Ariane*, in *Computer* (*IEEE*), Object Technology Department, vol. 30, no. 1, January 1997.

[M 199?]
   (with Christine Mingins) *Touch of Class*: *Learning to Program Well — A Modern Introduction to Software Using Object Technology*, in preparation.

[M-video]
   Object Technology Course, set of five video lectures, originally for Europace (1992), available from ISE.

[M-Web]
   On-line technology papers at *http://www.eiffel.com/doc/manuals/technology*, from 1995 on.

Index

CD-ROM AND ENVIRONMENT INSTRUCTIONS

CD-ROM contents

The CD-ROM accompanying this book contains readme files and the following directories:

- **OOSC_2**: The complete hyperlinked version of the book, plus supplementary material, in Adobe Acrobat format.
- **Envir**: A time-limited version of some of the principal components of the object-oriented environment described in Chapter 36 of the book, for Windows NT and Windows 95. (Contact ISE, at the address given on the next page, for versions on other major industry platforms.)
- **Acrobat**: the Acrobat Reader installation for many platforms, from Adobe Systems Incorporated.

Depending on the platform there may be differences in letter case for file and directory names. For example **OOSC_2** may appear as **oosc_2**.

Platform Compatibility

Reading the CD-ROM has been successfully tested on several platforms including **Windows 3.1, Windows 95, Windows NT, OS/2, Unix** (Solaris, SunOS, Linux), and **Macintosh** (System 7). CD-ROM compatibility is, however, a tricky business; neither the author nor the publisher can guarantee that your specific computer, CD-ROM drive and operating system version will be able to read the CD.

Note in particular that the CD-ROM uses the ISO format, which may not be supported by some older Macintoshes. On a Unix platform, you need support for the "Rock Ridge" CD format; if, when listing the files you see names of the form *README.TXT;1* and *README.PDF;1* (instead of **readme.txt** and **readme.pdf**), then your operating system does not recognize the Rock Ridge format and you should ask your OS vendor for the corresponding patch. (We have encountered this problem with some versions of HP and DEC Unix.) You will still be able to read the files, but their names will be wrong; among other consequences, cross-file hyperlinks in Acrobat documents will not work.

Using the CD-ROM version of the book

To work with the hyperlinked version of the book you may start from any of the following Adobe Acrobat files, all in the directory **OOSC_2**:

- The short table of contents (chapters only): file **OOSC_SHO.pdf**.
- The full table of contents (chapters only): file **OOSC_TAB.pdf**.
- The index: file **OOSC_IND.pdf**.

(From the file **README.PDF,** click the chosen file name above to open it under Acrobat Reader.)

Installing the Adobe Acrobat Reader *(for PC and Unix users):*

To read the files you will need to have the Adobe Acrobat Reader. If you do not already have the Reader on your computer, you may install it from the CD-ROM:

- Go to the directory **Acrobat**, which contains the versions for different platforms (from Adobe).
- Read the file **Platform.txt** to find the instructions and files for your platform.
- Perform the installation instructions as indicated.
- Make sure to read the file **License.pdf** which states the Adobe license terms.

Installing the Adobe Acrobat Reader *(for Mac users):*

- Copy the file "Install Acrobat Reader 3.0" from the CD to your hard drive.
- Double-click the file "Install Acrobat Reader 3.0" (this will cause all of your current Mac applications to quit).
- Follow the instructions on your screen.

Installing and using the object-oriented development environment

To install the object-oriented development environment for Windows NT or Windows 95:
- Go to the directory **Envir**.
- Double-click on **setup.exe** (from the Windows Explorer) to start the installation process.

Memory and system requirements

- For Adobe Acrobat: see the Adobe Acrobat documentation. On Windows 95, the executable takes up about **3 MB**, but more may be needed during installation.
- For the hyperlinked version of the book: about **25 MB**; Adobe Acrobat Reader installed.
- For the object-oriented environment: the recommended installation, including the WEL graphical library and the Base libraries of fundamental data structures and algorithms, takes up about **70 MB**. A minimal default installation with no precompiled libraries (you can precompile libraries later yourself) takes about **20 MB**. You need a 386 or higher Intel-compatible model, **16 MB** memory (**32 MB** recommended).

Purchasing the environment

To remove the time limitation on the use of the environment, contact ISE as indicated on the first screen that comes up when you start the environment (click "Purchase" for details). The address is:

ISE Inc., 270 Storke Road, Suite 7
Santa Barbara, CA 93117 USA
Phone 805-685-1006, Fax 805-685-6869, E-mail <sales@tools.com>

Special discount: if you discovered the environment through this book, you are entitled to a special "OOSC-2 reader" discount. Be sure to mention it when contacting ISE.

Versions for other platforms

Besides Windows NT and Windows 95, the environment is available for a wide variety of industry platforms, such as Unix (Sun, HP, DEC, IBM, SGI...), OS/2, Linux, VMS. Please contact ISE for details.

Video course

A 6-tape video course *Object-Oriented Software Construction* by Bertrand Meyer, on the topics of this book, is available in both NTSC (US) and PAL formats. Please contact ISE for ordering information.

LICENSE AGREEMENT AND LIMITED WARRANTY

READ THE FOLLOWING TERMS AND CONDITIONS CAREFULLY BEFORE OPENING THIS CD PACKAGE, *OBJECT-ORIENTED SOFTWARE CONSTRUCTION, 2/E*. THIS LEGAL DOCUMENT IS AN AGREEMENT BETWEEN YOU AND PRENTICE-HALL, INC. (THE "COMPANY"). BY OPENING THIS SEALED CD PACKAGE, YOU ARE AGREEING TO BE BOUND BY THESE TERMS AND CONDITIONS. IF YOU DO NOT AGREE WITH THESE TERMS AND CONDITIONS, DO NOT OPEN THE CD PACKAGE. PROMPTLY RETURN THE UNOPENED CD PACKAGE AND ALL ACCOMPANYING ITEMS TO THE PLACE YOU OBTAINED THEM FOR A FULL REFUND OF ANY SUMS YOU HAVE PAID.

1. **GRANT OF LICENSE:** In consideration of your purchase of this book, and your agreement to abide by the terms and conditions of this Agreement, the Company grants to you a nonexclusive right to use and display the copy of the enclosed software program (hereinafter the "SOFTWARE") on a single computer (i.e., with a single CPU) at a single location so long as you comply with the terms of this Agreement. The Company reserves all rights not expressly granted to you under this Agreement.

2. **OWNERSHIP OF SOFTWARE:** You own only the magnetic or physical media (the enclosed CD) on which the SOFTWARE is recorded or fixed, but the Company and the software developers retain all the rights, title, and ownership to the SOFTWARE recorded on the original CD copy(ies) and all subsequent copies of the SOFT-WARE, regardless of the form or media on which the original or other copies may exist. This license is not a sale of the original SOFTWARE or any copy to you.

3. **COPY RESTRICTIONS:** This SOFTWARE and the accompanying printed materials and user manual (the "Documentation") are the subject of copyright. The individual programs on the CD are copyrighted by the authors of each program. Some of the programs on the CD include separate licensing agreements. If you intend to use one of these programs, you must read and follow its accompanying license agreement. You may not copy the Documen-tation or the SOFTWARE, except that you may make a single copy of the SOFTWARE for backup or archival pur-poses only. You may be held legally responsible for any copying or copyright infringement which is caused or encouraged by your failure to abide by the terms of this restriction.

4. **USE RESTRICTIONS:** You may not network the SOFTWARE or otherwise use it on more than one com-puter or computer terminal at the same time. You may physically transfer the SOFTWARE from one computer to another provided that the SOFTWARE is used on only one computer at a time. You may not distribute copies of the SOFTWARE or Documentation to others. You may not reverse engineer, disassemble, decompile, modify, adapt, translate, or create derivative works based on the SOFTWARE or the Documentation without the prior written con-sent of the Company.

5. **TRANSFER RESTRICTIONS:** The enclosed SOFTWARE is licensed only to you and may not be trans-ferred to any one else without the prior written consent of the Company. Any unauthorized transfer of the SOFT-WARE shall result in the immediate termination of this Agreement.

6. **TERMINATION:** This license is effective until terminated. This license will terminate automatically without notice from the Company and become null and void if you fail to comply with any provisions or limitations of this license. Upon termination, you shall destroy the Documentation and all copies of the SOFTWARE. All provisions of this Agreement as to warranties, limitation of liability, remedies or damages, and our ownership rights shall sur-vive termination.

7. **MISCELLANEOUS:** This Agreement shall be construed in accordance with the laws of the United States of America and the State of New York and shall benefit the Company, its affiliates, and assignees.

8. **LIMITED WARRANTY AND DISCLAIMER OF WARRANTY:** The Company warrants that the SOFT-WARE, when properly used in accordance with the Documentation, will operate in substantial conformity with the description of the SOFTWARE set forth in the Documentation. The Company does not warrant that the SOFT-WARE will meet your requirements or that the operation of the SOFTWARE will be uninterrupted or error-free. The Company warrants that the media on which the SOFTWARE is delivered shall be free from defects in materi-als and workmanship under normal use for a period of thirty (30) days from the date of your purchase. Your only remedy and the Company's only obligation under these limited warranties is, at the Company's option, return of

the warranted item for a refund of any amounts paid by you or replacement of the item. Any replacement of SOFTWARE or media under the warranties shall not extend the original warranty period. The limited warranty set forth above shall not apply to any SOFTWARE which the Company determines in good faith has been subject to misuse, neglect, improper installation, repair, alteration, or damage by you. EXCEPT FOR THE EXPRESSED WARRANTIES SET FORTH ABOVE, THE COMPANY DISCLAIMS ALL WARRANTIES, EXPRESS OR IMPLIED, INCLUDING WITHOUT LIMITATION, THE IMPLIED WARRANTIES OF MERCHANTABILITY AND FITNESS FOR A PARTICULAR PURPOSE. EXCEPT FOR THE EXPRESS WARRANTY SET FORTH ABOVE, THE COMPANY DOES NOT WARRANT, GUARANTEE, OR MAKE ANY REPRESENTATION REGARDING THE USE OR THE RESULTS OF THE USE OF THE SOFTWARE IN TERMS OF ITS CORRECTNESS, ACCURACY, RELIABILITY, CURRENTNESS, OR OTHERWISE.

IN NO EVENT, SHALL THE COMPANY OR ITS EMPLOYEES, AGENTS, SUPPLIERS, OR CONTRACTORS BE LIABLE FOR ANY INCIDENTAL, INDIRECT, SPECIAL, OR CONSEQUENTIAL DAMAGES ARISING OUT OF OR IN CONNECTION WITH THE LICENSE GRANTED UNDER THIS AGREEMENT, OR FOR LOSS OF USE, LOSS OF DATA, LOSS OF INCOME OR PROFIT, OR OTHER LOSSES, SUSTAINED AS A RESULT OF INJURY TO ANY PERSON, OR LOSS OF OR DAMAGE TO PROPERTY, OR CLAIMS OF THIRD PARTIES, EVEN IF THE COMPANY OR AN AUTHORIZED REPRESENTATIVE OF THE COMPANY HAS BEEN ADVISED OF THE POSSIBILITY OF SUCH DAMAGES. IN NO EVENT SHALL LIABILITY OF THE COMPANY FOR DAMAGES WITH RESPECT TO THE SOFTWARE EXCEED THE AMOUNTS ACTUALLY PAID BY YOU, IF ANY, FOR THE SOFTWARE.

SOME JURISDICTIONS DO NOT ALLOW THE LIMITATION OF IMPLIED WARRANTIES OR LIABILITY FOR INCIDENTAL, INDIRECT, SPECIAL, OR CONSEQUENTIAL DAMAGES, SO THE ABOVE LIMITATIONS MAY NOT ALWAYS APPLY. THE WARRANTIES IN THIS AGREEMENT GIVE YOU SPECIFIC LEGAL RIGHTS AND YOU MAY ALSO HAVE OTHER RIGHTS WHICH VARY IN ACCORDANCE WITH LOCAL LAW.

ACKNOWLEDGMENT

YOU ACKNOWLEDGE THAT YOU HAVE READ THIS AGREEMENT, UNDERSTAND IT, AND AGREE TO BE BOUND BY ITS TERMS AND CONDITIONS. YOU ALSO AGREE THAT THIS AGREEMENT IS THE COMPLETE AND EXCLUSIVE STATEMENT OF THE AGREEMENT BETWEEN YOU AND THE COMPANY AND SUPERSEDES ALL PROPOSALS OR PRIOR AGREEMENTS, ORAL, OR WRITTEN, AND ANY OTHER COMMUNICATIONS BETWEEN YOU AND THE COMPANY OR ANY REPRESENTATIVE OF THE COMPANY RELATING TO THE SUBJECT MATTER OF THIS AGREEMENT.

Should you have any questions concerning this Agreement or if you wish to contact the Company for any reason, please contact in writing at the address below.

Robin Short

Prentice Hall PTR

One Lake Street

Upper Saddle River, New Jersey 07458

About the Author

Bertrand Meyer is equally at ease in the software industry and in the world of academic computing science.

As founder of ISE Inc., located in Santa Barbara (California), one of the first companies in the world to devote its activity entirely to object technology, he has played a major role in establishing the industrial viability of the approach. He has directed the design of systems totalling hundreds of thousands of object-oriented lines, and thousands of library classes reused in diverse projects throughout the world.

He also frequently consults for Fortune 500 companies and has advised several governments on their computing initiatives. He has been a keynote speaker at many conferences such as OOPSLA, TOOLS, the European Software Engineering Conference, the Australian Software Engineering Conference, Object Expo, Object World, etc., and has presented hundreds of seminars worldwide on a variety of technical and management topics. Aside from his industrial role he has taught at universities in the U.S., Europe and Australia.

As a best-selling author with 10 books to his credit, he has published books with Prentice Hall on theoretical topics (*Introduction to the Theory of Programming Languages*) as well as industrial applications of object technology (*Object-Oriented Applications*) and management issues (*Object Success: A Manager's Guide to Object Technology*). He is also the author of the definitive reference on the Eiffel language (*Eiffel: The Language*). His book *Reusable Software* is both an extensive discussion of the methodological principles of reusable software construction and a detailed description of practical reusable components, based on a "Linnaean taxonomy" of the fundamental objects in computing. He is also the editor of the Object-Oriented Series, with more than 25 titles in print by various authors on many topics of object technology.